Alberta Elders' Cree Dictionary

alperta ohci kehtehayak nehiyaw otwestamâkewasinahikan

alperta ohci kehtehayak nehiyaw otwestamâkewasinahikan

Edited by Earle Waugh

Alberta Elders' Cree Dictionary

Nancy LeClaire & George Cardinal

Cree Consultants
Emily Hunter
Rose Hilbach
Billy Joe Laboucan
Julia Cardinal
Harold Cardinal
Emilia Noskiye
Cheryl Sheldon
Verna Sorenson
William Yellowknee
Dehlia Gray
Albert Lightening
Walter Lightening
Ray G. Cardinal
Sage Cardinal
Nicole M. Martell
Lorna B. L'Hirondelle
Nancy E. Modeste

DUVAL HOUSE
PUBLISHING

The University
of Alberta Press

Published jointly by
    The University of Alberta Press
    Ring House 2
    Edmonton, Alberta, Canada T6G 2E1
        and
    Duval House Publishing/Les Editions Duval, Inc.
    18120 – 102 Avenue
    Edmonton, Alberta T5S 1S7

ISBN 0–88864–284–9 (pbk.)
ISBN 0–88864–309–8 (bound)
Printed in Canada 5 4 3

Canadian Cataloguing in Publication Data

LeClaire, Nancy, 1911–1986.
    Alberta elders' Cree dictionary =
    Alperta ohci kehtehayak nehiyaw otwestamâkewasinahikan

    Copublished by: Duval House Pub.
    ISBN 0–88864–309–8 (bound) — ISBN 0–88864–284–9 (pbk.)

    1. Cree language—Dictionaries—English. 2. English language—Dictionaries—Cree.
I. Cardinal, George, 1921– II. Waugh, Earle H., 1936– III. Hunter, Emily– IV. Title.
V. Title: Alperta ohci kehtehayak nehiyaw otwestamâkewasinahikan.
PM988.L42 1998   497'.3   C98–910382–X

∞ Printed on acid-free paper.
Printed and bound by Quality Color Press, Edmonton, Alberta.

The University of Alberta Press and Duval House Publishing gratefully acknowledge the
support received for our publishing programmes from the Canada Council for the Arts. In
addition, we also gratefully acknowledge the financial support of the Government of
Canada through the Book Publishing Industry Development Program for our publishing
activities.

Contents

kakisteyimiht nehiyaw

Honoring the Cree people

Foreword

"When a Language Dies, a Nation Dies"

IN ORDER TO RETAIN YOUR OWN IDENTITY you must live in your own cultural environment, and language is a major component of a person's identity.

Today there is a greater recognition and knowledge of the Cree language. There is a growing demand for Cree cultural history, language and traditions of the Cree Nation.

Many years ago the Cree people were not allowed to speak their own language. This created a lost generation of Aboriginal people who really did not understand their identity and their culture.

If you look at Canadian names you will see the influence that the Cree language has had on Canadian culture and identity.

There have been many Cree/English dictionaries written. As in any dictionary there needs to be continual revisions. *The Alberta Elders' Cree Dictionary/alperta ohci kehtehayak nehiyaw otwestamâkewasinahikan* is the latest and most concise dictionary of Alberta's Cree language.

The Cree consultants must be commended for the excellent work that they have put into this most worthwhile project.

THELMA J. CHALIFOUX
The Senate of Canada

nakayaskamohtahiwewin
Introduction

NEHIYAWEWIN METONI MIYOHTÂKWAN PEKISKWEWIN namoya wehkac. Takeh nipemakahk eyokoh ohci kakeh tepiyimoyan kita ni sohkamakiyan kita masinahaman kihte *alperta ohci kehtehayak nehiyaw otwestamâkewasinahikan.* Aniskac ni mosômpanak opekiskwaweniwaw macikah nesta ni pekiskwewin. Namoya ni nitaweyihten kita nipîmakahk mina enitaweyihtaman anohc nehiyaw kiskinwahamakewak kita âpacitatwaw mistahi kita nesoh kamakwak.

Ayisk oma nehiyawewin pahpîcoses esa esi pikiskwanowew pahpîtos etîh kohtaskanesihk macikah pîtoses esi masinahikatew. Taspwa, sakaw nehiyawewin osam pokoh nikîh apacihtan.

Maka namoya masinahikan ohci awîyak takeh maci nehiyawew poko kita kocet pekiskwewin. Tapiskoc awasis ka maci pekiskwet onekihikwah ohci. Oma masinahikan ka osehtayan nehiyaw awasisak kita âpacitatwaw ekâ onehiyaweweniwaw kita wanikiskisitotahkwaw.

Alberta Elders' Cree Dictionary/alperta ohci kehtehayak nehiyaw otwestamâkewasinahikan piskoc okihtawihiwiwewin ni mosômpanak ohcih.

THE CREE LANGUAGE IS A BEAUTIFUL LANGUAGE, therefore it should never die off. I guess this is one of the main reasons that I decided to participate in the writing of the *Alberta Elders' Cree Dictionary/ alperta ohci kehtehayak nehiyaw otwestamâkewasinahikan.* It is the language of my ancestors, so it is also my native language; I would like to keep it ongoing as long as possible, even forever. Also, I hope this book could help some of our present Cree language teachers.

As the Cree language is such a complex language, the grammar seems to change a little bit from one district to another. So I would say that my language is from the northeastern corner of Alberta. It is a mixture of Northern or Woods Cree and Plains Cree. For example, Northern Cree has some different word endings than the Plains Cree.

Now this book will not help you to speak because no book can, but it is intended to help you along if you are learning the Cree language. In order to speak you have to practice speaking, like a little child learning to speak from her or his parents.

Alberta Elders' Cree Dictionary/alperta ohci kehtehayak nehiyaw otwestamâkewasinahikan is an honoring gift to all my great Cree ancestors.

GEORGE CARDINAL

Preface

THIS DICTIONARY IS A GIFT FROM THE ELDERS to the Cree people of Alberta. The Alberta Elders' Dictionary Project began in the mid 1970s through the initiative of Sister Nancy LeClaire, a Samson Cree from Hobbema who had a great personal love for the Cree language. Sister Nancy, as she was known to everyone, believed that an authoritative dictionary of the language spoken by many Alberta Cree would not only aid Cree youth in becoming more fluent in her beloved language, but would provide a bridge for the rest of Albertans to appreciate its beauty. She therefore called upon those elders whose wisdom and understanding of the Cree language were known and respected throughout the province.

The Cree people of northern Alberta constitute the largest Aboriginal language group in the province, and Alberta Cree also have fellow Cree-speakers across Canada. Cree speakers are part of the Algonquian language group, which is the most widespread of all Canadian Aboriginal language groups. There are three major dialects found among the people in Alberta, and Sister Nancy insisted that the dictionary be based upon both the Northern Cree ("TH" dialect) and the Plains Cree ("Y" dialect). As well, she originally wanted to include variant words from the "R" dialect of Saskatchewan and Manitoba, but as she progressed, she found this impossible to complete. She sought and received financial assistance from the Samson Cree Nation to undertake a dictionary project, and asked me to work with her in bringing together a team that would complete the task.

Technically our project began with Fr. Albert Lacombe's *Dictionnaire de la Langue Crise*; we edited it to eliminate words that were not recognized by local Cree, and proceeded with the arduous process of providing translations of the Cree words into contemporary English. Clearly the dictionary we devised could not be a reference dictionary, which Fr. Lacombe seemed to have hoped he could create; rather, we merely wanted a serviceable record of local Cree words with their translations. A tool for students of the language up to senior high school seemed a reasonable goal. Sister Nancy utilized the insights of many elders and Cree consultants in this process, including those so disparate in age (at that time) as Albert Lightening of Hobbema (80) and Harold Cardinal of Sucker Creek (30), along with many others noted below. Thus it should be emphasized that this dictionary is based upon the language as it is used by Alberta's Cree speakers as we have been able to collect it. This means that there may well be many words that we have missed, or that are used in other ways by some people. We hope that you will inform us of these, so that subsequent editions can include them. The same, of course, holds true for spelling mistakes and inconsistencies.

The work had progressed to the Cree letter "n" when Sister Nancy died. This left us with the task of completing the Cree-English section, and formulating the entire English-Cree portion. We were fortunate to be able to find a number of elders to help us continue this worthwhile project, especially George Cardinal, originally from Wabasca. We also had the financial support of a number of agencies, without which carrying on would have been most difficult. We especially appreciated the help of the Native Education Project of Alberta Education during the many years it took to complete the project.

During the early period of the dictionary, the work of Father Rogier Vandersteene became known to me; he had laboured among the Cree in several settlements in northern Alberta before his untimely death. A superb Cree speaker, he had developed a 500-page manuscript on learning Cree. Many words, not listed in Lacombe's text, were incorporated from Vandersteene's work. Other sources were also checked, including Anne Anderson's writings, the curriculum of the School of Native Studies at the University of Alberta, prepared by Emily Hunter and Betty Karpinski, and the word list of the Cree Curriculum of Northland School Division, prepared under Mary Cardinal-Collins. We sought Cree plant lore from various published sources, especially Bro. Frederick Leach's publication *60 Years with Indians and Letters on Lake Winnipeg*. We referred to *A Dictionary of the Cree Language*, an Anglican publication of Reverend E.A. Watkins, edited by Ven. R. Faries. Finally, it will be clear that we were much assisted by the publications of David Pentland, H. Christoph Wolfart, C.D. Ellis and Freda Ahenakew. Our sincere appreciation for the assistance we have received from these sources.

A dictionary of this sort is not just a collection of words and their meanings, but represents something of what the community it serves requires. Hence, we have incorporated suggestions from a wide variety of Alberta bands for making the dictionary more usable for their members. Sister Nancy had originally hoped to include all new words in a supplementary section. We have had to abandon this idea. Instead, what words we thought helpful, though not yet accepted widely by Cree speakers, or words that reflect recent English influence, or idiomatic Cree that did not appear connected directly to traditional Cree usage are now found in the supplemental section—New Terms—of the English-Cree dictionary.

We have paid special attention throughout to terms that are commonly used in government, court and social institutions, and because Cree has no concept of swearing an oath have included a Cree statement of commitment before the court in the Appendices. We have also provided appendices on kinship terms, months and numbers.

Word and meaning contributions have been made by many people, including Harold Cardinal of Sucker Creek, Julia Cardinal of Saddle Lake, Ray Cardinal of Saddle Lake, Sage Cardinal of Edmonton, Dehlia Gray of Edmonton, Rose Hilbach of Hobbema, Emily Hunter of Goodfish Lake, Billy Joe Laboucan of Peace River, Albert Lightening of Hobbema, Walter Lightening of Hobbema, Nicole Martell of Waterhen Lake, Emilia

Noskiye of Peace River, Verna Sorenson of Lake Eden, Cheryl Sheldon of Kinuso and William Yellowknee of Slave Lake. Many of them talked to other Cree speakers during the many years of this project, so quite likely over 100 Cree people have had input into this process.

Cree students at the University of Alberta in Edmonton worked diligently on the final stages of the English-Cree section of the dictionary, juggling academic schedules with the demands of the project. Nicole Martell worked for many months, adding parts of speech, clarifying meanings and extensively cross-checking against the Cree-English dictionary as well as other countless tasks. Sage Cardinal contributed her extensive knowledge of the Cree language by clearing up inconsistencies in family relationships, word meanings, numbers, alphabetization, and adding parts of speech. Lorna L'Hirondelle's deep knowledge of Cree grammar and eye for detail, always invaluable skills for working on a dictionary, were much appreciated. Nancy Modeste expanded her knowledge of Cree as she worked on adding parts of speech. Ray Cardinal's historical knowledge and expertise in Plains Cree added greatly to balancing the mix of dialects and clarifying many word meanings. Also, Ray's understanding of Cree grammar made it possible to add parts of speech to many phrases, to aid the user in understanding how a phrase should be used. Finally, we hope that the youngest participants in the project, two-year-old, Gabriella Cardinal, and newborn, Corey Cardinal Jr., follow their grandfather's (Harold Cardinal) and mother's (Nicole Martell) deep commitment to their language and become part of the next generation of Cree scholars.

The project has also undergone many changes in format, from words written in scribblers during Sister Nancy's time, to typed recipe cards, to several computer software systems. Over the years many students at the University of Alberta, including my children—Richard, Jane and Kimberly, worked at inputting data. In addition, the people who have worked on inputting material numbers in the teens, including many students hired during summers on the effective STEP program. During the last two years, Mary Mahoney-Robson, editor, worked with the Cree students and Karen Chow at the University of Alberta Press, and with Shauna Babiuk, Tracy Menzies, Jeffrey Miles and Michael Poulin at Duval House Publishing, on the final stages of the project. These people have almost performed miracles in bringing the text into publishable shape. Further back in time, Judith Sprigings worked in a permanent part-time manner on the inputting as well as funding development; she provided us with skills beyond the call of duty. If the text is relatively consistent and free of typos, we happily ascribe accolades to this wonderful group of people.

We were pleased when Jane Ash Poitras agreed to allow us to use one of her paintings for the cover. Alan Brownoff at the University of Alberta Press designed the text and the cover.

We express our deepest appreciation for all those who have assisted us, even if your name does not appear here. We have received much from all these enthusiastic participants.

xv

Throughout the many years of this undertaking, we have had the support and goodwill of Religious Studies of the University of Alberta, and its administrative assistant, Lois Larson, without whose assistance the project would have faltered. During this prolonged period, a number of organizations have supported this venture, including various government agencies, institutions and organizations; we have placed their names on a separate page as a special recognition for their contributions. Our deepest gratitude to them.

Like many Aboriginal languages in Canada, Cree is losing ground rapidly. This is tragic, since Cree was probably the first *lingua franca* of Canada, and most likely much early communication between explorers, fur traders, settlers and missionaries was carried on in Cree. Thus the Cree people have contributed significantly to our common life together, much of it unheralded and unrecognized. It is not easy to translate one's religious, cultural and social realities into another idiom; the existence of this book is testimony to the abilities of the Cree people to transform their intellectual world and to incorporate into it a wholly different scheme of understanding. In a small way, then, *Alberta Elders' Cree Dictionary/alperta ohci kehtehayak nehiyaw otwestamâkewasinahikan* demonstrates the amazing achievement of Alberta's Cree people in the last hundred plus years. Thus, apart from the very ordinary value of providing the right word for the right idea, we hope this dictionary will contribute to stemming the tide of the loss of Cree, providing another resource for the preservation and expansion of a rich part of our Alberta cultural heritage, and demonstrating the impressive intellectual resources of the Cree people. If some of these are accomplished, it will indeed be like a Hudson's Bay blanket used for many years as a measurement of quality and pride—it will benefit everyone who has the joy of using it. When eventually a better version is produced, it will be because Cree has moved towards its rightful place as a valuable language for all Canadians.

OKISTATOWÂN
(DR. EARLE H. WAUGH)
Project Director & Editor

Acknowledgements

SISTER NANCY LeCLAIRE'S ORIGINAL VISION of an Alberta Cree dictionary was generously funded by the *Samson Cree Nation*, beginning in 1975. Without their support the project would not have been started.

Additional funding in 1989 for the middle stages of the project came from the *Alberta Multicultural Commission*.

The continued support of *Alberta Education's Native Education Project* has been crucial as the project grew. Beginning in 1991, the branch has been instrumental in providing funding for Cree consultants, research, text inputting, and publication costs. The efforts of the staff at the Native Education Project have made it possible to complete the project.

Northlands School Division No. 61 provided funding for the later stages of the project.

Over the years, the *Alberta Career Development and Employment Summer Temporary Employment Program (STEP)* assisted in paying wages of several research assistants from the late 1980s to the early 1990s. *Alberta Family and Social Services* granted funds from its Employment Skills Program Project: Extended Sponsor Group to pay a Cree Translation typist.

In 1994, Mike Cardinal, Minister of Family and Social Services, contributed a grant from the *Native Services Unit* toward publishing of the manuscript.

Private funding came from *The McLean Foundation* of Toronto, and *Stampeder Explorations Ltd.* of Calgary. We are especially grateful for the interest both these corporations have shown in this project.

Through a joint application with the *Aboriginal Multi-Media Society of Alberta (AMMSA)*, the *Department of the Secretary of State of Canada* awarded a grant from its Multiculturalism and Citizenship program for the dictionary.

Additional funding has come from the *University of Alberta—the Endowment Fund for the Future* from the *Faculty of Arts*; the Self-Funded Grants Program of the *Research Grants Office*, and the *Central Research Fund*, administered by the Vice-President Research.

Without the generous financial support of these many different groups, the *Alberta Elders' Cree Dictionary/alperta ohci kehtehayak nehiyaw otwestamâkewasinahikan* would not have been possible. We acknowledge their support and honor them for their contribution.

Helping You Use the Dictionary

THE ALBERTA ELDERS' CREE DICTIONARY/ALPERTA OHCI KEHTEHAYAK NEHIYAW OTWESTAMÂKEWASINAHIKAN is an amalgam of many different sources. The Cree-English section was constructed quite differently than the English-Cree section and different people had input to each section. The Cree-English section is the most authoritative and is based on the 3rd person singular form. Often the words appearing in the English-Cree section are descriptive and phrasal, so they do not appear exactly as used in the Cree-English section. In most cases, you will have to check both the Cree-English section and the English-Cree section to find just the right word.

We have tried to include the commonly used words and have indicated when there are alternative words or spellings (indicated as *Alt.*) between Northern Cree and Plains Cree as well as other variant terms (indicated as *Var.*). If there is no indication that a word is *(Northern)* or *(Plains)*, the word is commonly used by Alberta Cree, although many lengthy discussions have ensued on specific words. In addition to Northern Cree and Plains Cree, there are several types of Cree words that have been indicated —*(Archaic Cree)*, *(French Cree)*, and even *(Modern Cree)* to note a word that has recently come into usage. Words from other native languages have appeared in other Cree dictionaries and we assume that some of these words may have been included but not distinguished. While we have made every effort to incorporate as much diversity as possible, we have not been able to provide all the variations available, either because they were not at our command, or we realized that the task was so immense the dictionary would never be published. In that sense, this dictionary is only a provisional document to this point in time, and cannot claim to exhaust the Cree language in Alberta, let alone in other provinces.

Although Sister Nancy's background was Plains Cree, the resources we had most available to us in the later stages of the dictionary were Northern. Thus the dictionary gives a dominant position to Northern Cree, especially in the way the English-Cree section was formulated. This is first and foremost because the translator was George Cardinal, and his Cree was the Northern Cree he learned in the Wabasca/Demerais region of Northern Alberta. Subsequent changes built upon his fundamental word list. When no exact Cree word existed for translating an English word, George Cardinal gave an approximate translation.

All Plains Cree words appearing on the Cree-English side were incorporated into the English-Cree side but many definitions are Northern based and the Plains Cree meanings were not available to us. There does not seem to be any way of reducing the confusion caused by having these two major linguistic families together in one volume. Nevertheless, because of the way Cree people interact, it was deemed necessary to give words from both if they were available. Unfortunately we probably have not provided all the words of each dialect, but we have tried to be as complete as our sources allowed. Future editions of this dictionary will address this inconsistency.

There are also variant spellings here because Cree words are spelled differently depending upon local custom and elder usage. In addition, local variation in pronunciation leads to different transliteration customs. These are reflected here as fully as possible. Where the custom is widely recognized, we have tried to be as consistent as possible with it

In the supplemental section of the English-Cree dictionary, an extensive list of New Terms has been developed. These are words that loosely define the English concept, but have not been accepted into mainstream Cree usage. This explains why there are long phrases in the English-Cree section and in the supplemental New Terms that are really more descriptions than translations.

Our team of Cree students at the University of Alberta added the parts of speech in the English-Cree section, including the closest approximation for the descriptive phrases, i.e.: a phrase that is referring to an action that is inanimate and intransitive would be marked (VII)—

daylight *kâ kîsiwâpahk* (VII).

and a phase describing a thing that is animate would be marked (NA)—

ice-fisherman *miskwamîhk kâ paktahwât awîyak* (NA).

Please remember that for phrases the part of speech is a generalization to aid a speaker in using the phrase and the parts of speech for individual words are not indicated. Linguists would break the phrases into individual words:

ice-fisherman *miskwamîhk* (LN) *kâ paktahwât* (VTI) *awîyak* (PR).

But for the purposes of this dictionary, it was decided to categorize the phrases with a single part of speech.

Since Cree recognizes no gender-based biological distinctions in its basic structure, we have signalled this by using "s/he" as the fundamental pronominal indicator in the English definitions. The use of "s/he", "her/him", "her/his", and "herself/himself" often made very complex sentences in the English definitions, for example:

kiskinohtahew (VTA) S/he guides her/him or shows her/him where to go.

but we hope this unbiased gender style will increase the awareness of the essentially gender-neutral manner at the heart of Cree speech.

Some Points to Remember About Cree

- Words in this dictionary follow the patterns identified as **stem-class codes** by Cree scholars; these give valuable information about the word. They are enclosed in a bracket immediately after the word. The list below is based upon the work of Freda Ahenakew:

(NA)	animate noun
(NI)	inanimate noun
(NDA)	animate noun, dependent
(NDI)	inanimate noun, dependent
(LN)	location noun
(VAI)	verb of type AI (animate actor, usually intransitive)
(VII)	verb of type II (inanimate actor, intransitive)
(VTA)	verb of type TA (animate goal, transitive)
(VTI)	verb of type TI (inanimate goal, usually transitive)
(PR)	pronoun
(PP)	personal pronoun
(IP)	independent pronoun
(IPC)	indeclinable particle
(IPV)	indeclinable pre-verb particle
(IPN)	indeclinable pre-noun particle
(INM)	indeclinable nominal
(DPR)	dependent particle

- Cree divides everything according to a life principle. If it has an inner life-force, it is said to be animate. If it is sedentary and has no evident life principle in it, it is inanimate. However, this generalization sometimes breaks down. It is not always possible to predict whether a word is animate or inanimate. For example, "**asinîy** (NA) A rock" is animate whereas "**asiskîy** (NI) A piece of soil" is inanimate, quite the opposite to what we would expect. The stem-class codes after the noun will provide this information for you.

- Verbal parts of a sentence state that something always is the case (i.e.: "it is green") or that something was impacted upon (i.e.: "he hit the ball"). We call the first *intransitive* and the second *transitive*. The intransitive verb is quite capable of existing without any description: "It is" could be complete in itself, without the description, "green". Moreover, the intransitive is closer to expressing a continuous state of affairs or a permanent character.

However, you can see how the transitive word needs "the ball" in order to make sense of the "he hit". The stem-class codes after these verbs will provide the information about how they are understood by Cree speakers.

- In general, all verbs are indicated by using the 3rd person singular form. Thus, in the Cree-English section, **pimiskohtew** *pl.* **pimiskohtewak** (VAI) is translated as "S/he walks on top of the ice"; the plural form would logically read "They walk on top of the ice" but has not been included. Verbal forms that have more complex meanings, which require varying indicators, are broken down in the text as:

miyimawinew (VTA) S/he dampens it (animate).
miyimawinam (VTI) S/he dampens it.
miyimawiniwew (VTA) S/he dampens someone.
miyimawinikew (VTI) S/he dampens something.

 Cree speakers will immediately recognize the difference between the animate and inanimate form, but it has been indicated here for those not so familiar with Cree discourse. Sometimes Cree verbal forms do not follow a consistent pattern. We have tried to indicate these words by including the variant forms and their meanings. If there are no variant forms, the verb is considered standard in its verbal endings, in which case, you will find only the singular and plural forms.

- We have utilized some recent protocols in this dictionary, although not as many as every linguist would like. In general, we have followed the system utilized by Freda Ahenakew. For example, the 'tch' sound, as in **Saskatchewan** is written here only as a 'c'. Hence, using our transliteration system, we should write the word as **Saskacewan**. Our transliteration system does not use 'u' but instead has short and long 'o' sounds. Therefore, you will find short and long 'a' , 'i', and 'o' in this dictionary. Generally speaking, the short 'a' sounds like the vowel in the English word **but**, the short 'i' sounds like the vowel in the word **tin**, the short 'o' sounds like **hood**; similarly the long 'â' sounds like **land**, the long 'î' sounds like **been**, the long 'ô' sounds like **host**. Typically, the long 'e' sound does not appear with a circumflex, which, according to our system, would have indicated its long character. Rather, when we write 'e', it sounds long, that is, it sounds something like **beat**. Note that the use of 'e' is normally a signal of Plains Cree. In this dictionary, we use ' for a glottal stop or the aspirated 'h' only sparingly.

 Inconsistently, however, we have retained '-sêw' sometimes where our system would have required '-sîw', because the sound of local speakers required a different 'ê' sound, and the elders insisted that it be indicated. Northern 'ê' would be pronounced as an English 'i' but Plains 'ê' has a different sound, 'eh' as in 'eha'. Inevitably all transliteration systems leave out details which some insist should be included, and as a result we have usually left out marks indicating glottal stops or aspirations. We have recognized that it is impossible to reflect all the nuances of spoken Cree in print. We believe that sound patterns for this language can really only be learned from native speakers of Cree, and that any transliteration system is a compromise.

• Writing the sounds of Cree has always caused great problems for dictionary writers. Many elders grew up using a form of syllabic writing. Syllabic writing had the advantage of reflecting Cree letters for Cree sounds, and scholars like Ellis prefer to use Cree words as the basis for a keyword system based on Cree words. Not all the elders we worked with liked that system, for the simple reason that they were not sure all Cree speakers would pronounce the sound the same way. Some thought all Cree speakers were more familiar with English as a kind of common language and that it was better to relate Cree to English. Obviously, this dictionary has not solved all the problems in translating Cree sounds into a written text.

• For those who wish to read further about Cree, we have provided a select bibliography at the back of the dictionary. In our view, the writings of Ellis, Wolfart, Pentland and Ahenakew provide the most advanced work on the Cree language today.

Using the Dictionary If You Know Cree

Alberta Elders' Cree Dictionary/alperta ohci kehtehayak nehiyaw otwestamâkewasinahikan has been designed with the intention of the Cree-English being the most authoritative. If you know Cree and wish to look up a word, proceed to the Cree-English section for your word. Once you have found the word, you will not find there variations of definition, but the most adequate translation of that particular word. If you wish to locate different definitions of the Cree word, please turn to the English-Cree section and look up words related to the English word provided as a translation for your original Cree word. This will give you access to variations and diverse related notions. Hence you will need to **refer to both sections** of the dictionary to exhaust the sources of information available to you in this book. Moreover, you will notice that the definitions are usually provided in the Cree-English section only in the 3rd person singular form, while the English-Cree section will have a more full range of necessary pronominal indicators.

Remember that Cree has some long and short vowels, which, in this dictionary, constitute separate letters of the Cree alphabet. You will find short vowel words first and long vowel words second, e.g.: "**acimosis** *pl.* **acimosisak** (NA) A puppy" is under a separate letter section than "**âmômey** (NI) Honey." All long vowels are indicated here with a circumflex (ˆ) above the vowel. We have used the circumflex because we found the macron (the straight line (ˉ) above the letter) to be printed so close to the letter that it was not clear. Long vowel letter sections appear **after** short vowels letter sections in this dictionary.

Cree speakers will notice that we have generally not been able to accommodate the grammatical category of obviation. The obviative rests on the Cree characteristic of reference, where, for example, a conversation may focus on someone nearby (usually designated as proximate) while also referring to someone much further away. Here and there throughout the text, obviate forms, indicated as (ob.) may appear, but we have not systematically included these.

Because of the dialect differences which Alberta Cree use, if there are variant spellings available, you will see the different words or even the different spellings for the same word, for example:

yiwahwew (VTA) S/he pounds her/him. *Var.* **iyiwahwew**.

If we have been able to indicate the linguistic family, we have cross-referenced the alternative spellings and indicated the linguistic family where we have evidence for this kind of difference in two separate entries.

yâwehakwan *pl.* **yâwehakwanwa** (VII) The sound can be heard at a distance. *(Northern). Alt.* **yâwehtâkwan** *(Plains)*.

and

yâwehtâkwan *pl.* **yâwehtâkwanwa** (VII) The sound can be heard at a distance. *(Plains). Alt.* **yâwehakwan** *(Northern)*.

Where there is no indication, this means that both families use the same word, or we have not been able to determine an alternative usage.

Hence you should be able to find the word's spelling other than the one with which you are familiar, as long as we have been able to determine it from our consultants or sources. If the word is a noun, and has more than a singular form, both singular and plural endings will be indicated. If there is no plural form, only one ending will appear.

When you find the word, you will note that there is a part of the word that seems to express a basic meaning. This has traditionally been called the "root", although there are problems doing so. In reality, there are some words in Cree with a constellation of related meanings. If there is more than one meaning, we have tried to include the secondary meaning at the end of each entry. Thus, the best way to find related meanings and words that embody these meanings is to turn to the English-Cree section, where you will find a cluster of meanings that relate to the original definition you encountered in the Cree-English section. We have not expanded the pages in the dictionary in order to include all meanings in the English-Cree section by their own entry in the Cree-English.

One of the most significant aspects of Cree is the way in which endings and pre-fixed particles can give other nuances to the meaning. Not all of these appear on the Cree-English side of the dictionary. Also because of lack of space, we have placed many of these under the English word on the English-Cree side. To find these variations, you should turn to the English-Cree section and look up under the principal word of the translation. If they have been available to us, we have placed these words there along with their various English meanings.

Using the Dictionary If You Know English

If you do not know the word in Cree, turn first to the English-Cree section and find the English word. The Cree translation of the English word will appear there. Very seldom can you translate from one language into another by a single word. This is because no two languages have the same concepts. Many times an English word cannot be translated by one Cree word, since there is no Cree word that means exactly the same as the English word. When this happens, we have not given a translation but a short Cree explanation. This might involve two or three words and sometimes almost a sentence. The "translation" will give a Cree explanation for the idea which the English word is trying to express. We have also attempted to use the closest Cree root in this translation/explanation so that you can then go to the Cree side and find how Cree speakers have expressed this notion. It is not always easy to spot the root of the word in this process, but a little experience will help you master it.

With this word, you can then go to the Cree-English side to see what different words are constructed from the Cree root. By and large these are all clustered together in proximity to each other in the text. Here, too you can see if the verbal form has standard endings and, if not, what the endings and their meanings are.

Some English words are new, even for English speakers. If the word is recent or modern, or no Cree translation has gained universal acceptance, we have still included it (unless it is controversial) in the supplemental section, "New Terms" in the English-Cree Dictionary section. Many of these are local or regional interpretations of English terms, like television, but since the dictionary will be used by Cree broadcasters, whatever information we were able to find, we have included.

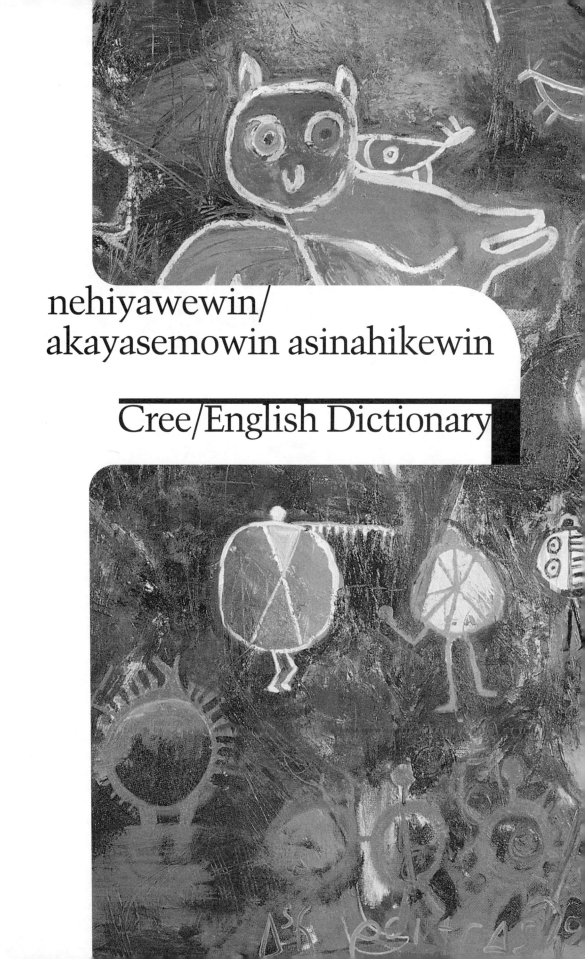

nehiyawewin/ akayasemowin asinahikewin

Cree/English Dictionary

a

acahkos *pl.* **acahkosak** (NA) A star.

acimosis *pl.* **acimosisak** (NA) A pup or a puppy; a newborn dog.

acosis *pl.* **acosisak** (NA) An arrow.

acoskewinis *pl.* **acoskewinisa** (NI) A small chore.

acowihisiw *pl.* **acowihisiwak** (VTA) S/he depreciates her/his own ability; s/he puts herself/himself down.

acowihkotew *pl.* **acowihkotewa** (VII) It has been whittled down; it has been reduced.

acowinikewin *pl.* **acowinikewina** (NI) The act of condensing or making smaller; condensation.

acowisihcikewin *pl.* **acowisihcikewina** (NI) Being condensed or reduced.

acônikewin *pl.* **acônikewina** (NI) An abbreviation.

acôpecikewin *pl.* **acôpecikewina** (NI) The act of abating; abatement.

acôpekiskwewin *pl.* **acôpekiswewina** (NI) The act of abbreviating; shortening of words.

acôwihew *pl.* **acôwihewak** (VTA) S/he reduced her/him in size; s/he cut her/him down.

ahcanis *pl.* **ahcanisak** (NA) A ring for the finger.

ahcâhk *pl.* **ahcâhkwak** (NA) A spirit; a star.

ahcikatew *pl.* **ahcikatewak** (VTA) S/he advises her/him to hide it elsewhere; s/he hides it somewhere else. *(Plains)*. *Alt.* **tahcikatew** *(Northern)*.

ahcikâpawiw *pl.* **ahcikâpawiwak** (VAI) S/he shifts her/his standing position; s/he stands in another place.

ahcimâmitoneyihtam *pl.* **ahcimâmitoneyihtamwa** (VTI) S/he reconsiders it.

ahcipicîhew (VTA) S/he makes her/him relocate.

  ahcipicîtâw (VTI) S/he moves the camp some place else.

  ahcipicîhiwew (VTA) S/he relocates the people.

  ahcipicîcikew (VTI) S/he relocates things.

ahkostimew (VTI) S/he gets them all wet. *(Northern)*. *Alt.* **akohcimew** *(Plains)*.

  ahkostitâw (VTI) S/he gets it all wet.

  ahkostimiwew (VTA) S/he gets people all wet.

  ahkosticikew (VTI) S/he get things all wet.

ahkwacipimîy *pl.* **ahkwacipimîya** (NI) Rendered grease, i.e.: tallow.

ahpô (IPC) Or; maybe; assume.

ahpô cî (IPC) Or is it?

ahpô etikwe (IPC) Maybe; more possibly.

ahpô kiya (IPC) As you like; it is up to you.

ahpô niya (IPC) Even me; despite that.

ahpônâni (IPC) If only it was like that; if only.

ahtisihcikewin *pl.* **ahtisihcikewina** (NI) The act of innovation.

akahkway *pl.* **akahkwayak** (NA) A blood sucker, i.e.: a leech; a snail.

akask *pl.* **akaskwak** (NA) A spear or long, sharp stick.

akaskocepihk *pl.* **akaskocepihka** (NI) An arrowroot that is used for medicine.

akayasemowin (NI) English.

akâwâcikew *pl.* **akâwâcikewak** (VAI) S/he is allusive; (VTA) s/he is attracted to someone.

akâwâcikewin *pl.* **akâwâcikewina** (NI) The act of coveting.

akâwâsowewin (NI) The act of allurement; penchant toward.

akâwâtamowin *pl.* **akâwâtamowina** (NI) The act of enticement; being enticed.

akâwâteyihtamowin *pl.* **akâwâteyihtamowina** (NI) Being envious.

akâwâtihtowin *pl.* **akâwâtihtowina** (NI) Being carnal.

akâwâtohcikewin *pl.* **akâwâtohcikewina** (NI) Having a hankering.

akihcikewin *pl.* **akihcikewina** (NI) The act of performing calculations; numeration.

akihtâson *pl.* **akihtâsona** (NI) A number; a figure.

akihtâsowepinikewin *pl.* **akihtâsowepinikewina** (NI) Being arithmetical.

akohcimew *pl.* **akohcimewak** (VTA) S/he soaks them; s/he puts them in water. *(Plains)*. *Alt.* **ahkostimew** *(Northern)*.

akohkahtew *pl.* **akohkahtewa** (VII) It is burnt onto the pot.

akohkasam (VTI) S/he burns it onto the pot; s/he welds it.

  akohkaswew (VTI) S/he welds them.

akohkasikeskiw *pl.* **akohkasikewkiwa** (VTI) S/he habitually burns everything to the pot.

akohpisiw *pl.* **akohpisiwak** (VAI) S/he has a bandage on.

akohpisiwâkan *pl.* **akohpisiwâkana** (NI) A dressing.

akohpisowin *pl.* **akohpisowina** (NI) A bandage.

akokâpawiw *pl.* **akokâpawiwak** (VTA) S/he stands against her/him or it.

akokwâcikan *pl.* **akokwâcikana** (NI) A patch; decal.

akopayihiw *pl.* **akopayihiwak** (VAI) S/he moves against something or someone; s/he bumps against something or someone.

akopitew (VTA) S/he places a bandage on her/him.

  akopitam (VTI) S/he puts a bandage on it.

  akopisiwew (VTA) S/he bandages everyone.

  akopicikew (VTI) S/he bandages everything.

akosicikewin *pl.* **akosicikewina** (NI) Annexation; addition.

akosimowin *pl.* **akosimowina** (NI) The act of nestling.

akotaw *pl.* **akotawa** (VTI) S/he hangs it.

3

akotew *pl.* **akotewa** (VII) It is hanging.

akotew (VTA) S/he hangs her/him up, i.e., with a rope. *(Plains). Alt.* **kosâwehpitew** *(Northern).*

　akotam (VTI) S/he hangs it downward.

　akosiwew (VTA) S/he hangs someone downward.

　akocikew (VTI) S/he hangs things downward.

akotitowin *pl.* **akotitowina** (NI) Suspended in air; death by hanging. *(Plains). Alt.* **kosâwehpisiwewin** *(Northern).*

akôhkasikew *pl.* **akôhkasikewak** (VAI) S/he welds.

akwahpisiw *pl.* **akwahpisiwak** (VAI) S/he is tied onto something; s/he is laced up.

akwahpitew (VTI) It is tied on.

　akwahpitam (VTI) S/he tied it on something.

　akwahpisiwew (VTA) S/he tied somebody to something.

　akwahpicikew (VTI) S/he tied something onto something.

akwamohcikan *pl.* **akwamohcikana** (NI) An attachment; a tool used to hold something, e.g.: a clamp. *(Plains and Northern variant). Alt.* **takwamohcikan** *(Northern).*

akwamohcikewin *pl.* **akwamohcikewina** (NI) The act of appending; the act of applying (something).

akwanahikan *pl.* **akwanahikana** (NI) A cover for something, i.e.: a canopy.

akwanahikewin *pl.* **akwanahikewina** (NI) The act of covering.

akwanâpowehikan *pl.* **akwanâpowehikana** (NI) A cover; a lid.

akwascikewin *pl.* **akwascikewina** (NI) The act of placing things against each other.

akwastew *pl.* **akwastewa** (VII) It is sitting against something.

akwâhotew *pl.* **akwâhotewa** (VII) It is blown to shore.

akwâpinam *pl.* **akwâpinamwa** (VTI) S/he drags it from the water.

akwâpinew *pl.* **akwâpinewak** (VTA) S/he grabs her/him from the water.

akwâpitew (VTA) S/he pulls her/him ashore.

　akwâpitam (VTI) S/he pull it ashore.

　akwâpisiwew (VTA) S/he pulls everybody ashore.

　akwâpicikew (VTI) S/he pulls things ashore.

akwâwahonihtak *pl.* **akwâwahonihtakwa** (NI) A piece of driftwood.

akwâwew *pl.* **akwâwewak** (VAI) S/he dries moose meat.

akwâyapâyew (VTA) S/he is drifting ashore.

　akwâyapâyew (VTI) It is drifting ashore.

akwâyapotew *pl.* **akwâyapotewa** (VII) It has floated ashore.

akwâyâpakiw *pl.* **akwâyapâkiwak** (VAI) S/he has floated ashore.

akweyimew *pl.* **akweyimewak** (VTA) S/he identifies it with her/him.

akweyitamawew *pl.* **akweyitamawewak** (VTA) S/he identifies it as belonging to her/him; s/he thinks it belongs to someone else.

amacowewin *pl.* **amacowewina** (NI) The act of ascending.

amacowinekanewin *pl.* **amacowinekanewina** (NI) The act of leading the way up.

amâhamawew *pl.* **amâhamawewak** (VTA) S/he scares it away so that it will not come close to others; s/he has disturbed the place so that nothing will come to it.

amâhew (VTA) S/he scares it away, i.e.: wild game.

　amâtaw (VTI) S/he frightens everything away.

　amâhiwew (VTA) S/he frightens them away.

　amâcikew (VTI) S/he frightens something away.

amâmew (VTA) Her/his talking scares her/him away.

　amâwihtâw (VTA) S/he frightens things away with loud noise.

　amâwehcikew (VTA) S/he frightens everyone away with loud music.

amâwekahikew *pl.* **amâwekahikewak** (VTA) Her/his chopping has scared everything away.

amâweswew (VTA) S/he scares things away with her/his shots.

　amâwesâwew (VTA) Her/his shootings frighten things intentionally.

　amâwesikew (VTA) Her/his shooting frightens them away.

amisk *pl.* **amiskwak** (NA) Beaver.

amiskosâkahikan (NI) The Cree name for the settlement of Beaver Lake.

amiskowestih *pl.* **amiskowestiha** (NI) A beaver house.

amiskosîs *pl.* **amiskosîsak** (NA) A beetle, i.e.: a water beetle or weevil.

amiskowesinâw *pl.* **amiskowesinâwa** (NI) Beaver glands or castors.

amiskwaciwâskahikan (NA) The Cree word for the city of Edmonton, literally "beaver mountain house."

amiskwayan *pl.* **amiskwayana** (NI) A beaver pelt.

amiskwâyiw *pl.* **amiskwâyiwa** (NI) A beaver tail.

ana (DPR) That one (animate).

anihi (DPR) Those things over there (inanimate).

aniki (DPR) Those (animate).

anikwacâs *pl.* **anikwacâsak** (NA) A squirrel.

anikwacâsimîciwin (NI) Peanut butter; squirrel food; squirrel grease. *(Plains). Alt.* **pakânipimiy** *(Northern).*

anima (DPR) That one (inanimate).

aniskamatisiw *pl.* **aniskamatisiwak** (VTA) S/he buttons herself/himself.

4

aniskamân *pl.* **aniskamânak** (NA) A button.

aniskamâtew (VTA) S/he buttons her/him.

    aniskamâtaw (VTA) S/he is buttoned up.

    aniskamâsiwew (VTA) S/he buttons people up.

    aniskamâcikew (VTI) S/he buttons things up.

anohc (IPC) Today.

anohc poko (IPC) Newly; just now. *(Plains). Var.* **anohc piko**.

anohc takwâkin (IPC) This fall.

anohcîke (IPC) Lately.

apacihcikan *pl.* **âpacihcikana** (NI) Something useful or being useful.

apahkwânekin *pl.* **apahkwânekinwa** (NI) A waterproof covering for shelter, i.e.: a tarpaulin. *(Northern). Alt.* **apahkwâsonekin** *(Plains).*

apahkwâsonekin *pl.* **apahkwâsonekinwa** (NI) A waterproof covering for shelter, i.e.: a tarpaulin. *(Plains). Alt.* **apahkwânekin** *(Northern).*

apasoy *pl.* **apasoyak** (NA) A teepee pole. *(Plains). Alt.* **apasoyâhtik** *(Northern).*

apasoyâhtik *pl.* **apasoyâhtikwa** *or* **apasoyâhtikwak** (NI) *or* (NA) A teepee pole. *(Northern). Alt.* **apasoy** *(Plains).*

apihkâcikewin *pl.* **apihkâcikewina** (NI) Being interwoven; braiding; knitting.

apihkâtew (VAI) S/he makes braids or it is braided.

    apihkâtam (VTI) S/he braided it.

apihkewin *pl.* **apihkewina** (NI) The act of tatting; the act of weaving; the act of braiding.

apisâsin *pl.* **apisâsinwa** (VII) It is small; it is wee.

apiscacihkos *pl.* **apiscacihkosak** (NA) A pronghorn; an antelope.

apiscawâsisiwiwin *pl.* **apiscawâsisiwiwina** (NI) Being a baby; babyhood.

apiscimososowayânis *pl.* **apiscimososowayânisa** (NI) A deerskin.

apiscisehcikanis *pl.* **apiscisehcikanisa** (NI) A miniaturized item.

apisicisip *pl.* **apisicisipsak** (NA) A teal.

apisis (IPC) A little; a dab.

apisisîsiw *pl.* **apisisîsiwak** (VAI) S/he is small or little.

apiwin *pl.* **apiwina** (NI) A seat or place to sit.

apiwineyâw *pl.* **apiwineyâwa** (VII) It is made like a place to sit.

apiwinihkewin *pl.* **apiwinihkewina** (NI) The act of making places to sit, i.e.: seating.

apotascikewin *pl.* **apotascikewina** (NI) The act of ransacking.

apoy *pl.* **apoyak** (NA) A paddle for rowing; shovel.

apwesiwin *pl.* **apwesiwina** (NI) Being sweaty; perspiration.

asahpicekewin *pl.* **asahpicekewina** (NI) The act of binding; the act of making a bundle.

asaimîna (IPC) All over again. *(Northern). Alt.* **âsay mîna** *(Plains).*

asamew *pl.* **asamewak** (VTA) S/he feeds her/him; s/he serves her/him food.

asascikewin *pl.* **asascikewina** (NI) The act of piling.

asawâkâmepicikan *pl.* **asawâkâmepicikana** (NI) Something you pull across the water with something on it, i.e.: a ferry.

asawâpotew *pl.* **asawâpotewa** (VTI) It is floating across by the current.

asawâsow *pl.* **asawâsowak** (VAI) S/he is blown across. *(Northern). Alt.* **asawepâsow** *(Plains).*

asawâstan *pl.* **asawâstanwa** (VII) It is blown across. *(Northern). Alt.* **asawepâstan** *(Plains).*

asawepâsow *pl.* **asawepâsowak** (VAI) S/he is blown across. *(Plains). Alt.* **asawâsow** *(Northern).*

asawepâstan *pl.* **asawepâstanwa** (VII) It is blown across. *(Plains). Alt.* **asawâstan** *(Northern).*

asâhtin *pl.* **asâhtinwa** (VII) It is dull; not sharp.

asâm *pl.* **asâmak** (NA) A snowshoe.

asâmyâpiy *pl.* **asâmyâpiya** (NI) Strings of a snowshoes, i.e.: the thong.

asâwesis *pl.* **asâwesisak** (NA) A type of fish, i.e.: a perch.

asâwi *pl.* **asâwa** (NI) A rotten egg. *(Northern). Alt.* **piskac wâwi** *(Plains).*

ascikakan *pl.* **ascikakana** (NI) A canister.

ascikewikamik *pl.* **ascikewikamikwa** (NI) A storage shed.

ascimew *pl.* **ascimewak** (VTA) S/he says that s/he or it belongs to her/him.

ascipitew *pl.* **ascipitewak** (VTA) S/he pulls them together.

ascotinis *pl.* **ascotinisa** (NI) A bonnet.

aseciwan *pl.* **aseciwana** (VII) The water is flowing backwards.

asehâw *pl.* **asehâwak** (VAI) S/he is demoted. *(Plains). Alt.* **astamapiw** *(Northern).*

asehtamew *pl.* **asehtamewak** (VAI) S/he backtracks on the trail. *Alt.* **asehtew** *(Plains).*

asemamitoneyimew (VTA) S/he thinks of her/him from the past. *Alt.* **pemamitoneyimew** *(Plains).*

    asemamitoneyitam (VTI) S/he thinks in the past; s/he is reminiscing.

    asemamitoneyimiwew (VTA) S/he thinks of people from the past.

    asemamitoneyicikew (VTI) S/he thinks only of the past.

asenamâkewin *pl.* **asenamâkewina** (NI) The act of refusing.

5

asenikewin *pl.* **asenikewina** (NI) A rejected item, i.e.: a cull; repulsion.

asepakamahikewin *pl.* **asepakamahikewina** (NI) The act of backhanding.

asepicikewin *pl.* **asepicikewina** (NI) Abase.

asesin *pl.* **asesina** (NI) The front, upper part of a moccasin, i.e.: a vamp or tongue.

aseyâpoyowin *pl.* **aseyâpoyowina** (NI) The act of backsliding.

asikan *pl.* **asikanak** (NA) A sock; stocking.

asikanihkawew (VTA) S/he makes her/him socks.
  asikanihkâkew (VTA) S/he makes socks for everybody.

asikanihkâkan *pl.* **asikanihkâkana** (NI) A knitting needle.

asikanihkew *pl.* **asikanihkewak** (VAI) S/he makes some socks.

asinis *pl.* **asinisak** (NA) A pebble.

asiniwaciy *pl.* **asiniwaciya** (NA) A mountain.

asiniwaciwacihkos *pl.* **asiniwaciwacihkosak** (NA) A mountain goat. *(Northern). Alt.* **pikiwayastak** *(Plains).*

asiniwipayihcikewin *pl.* **asiniwipayihcikewina** (NI) Concrete; pavement. *(Plains). Alt.* **asinîhkahcikewin** *(Northern).*

asinîhkahcikewin *pl.* **asinîhkahcikewina** (NI) Concrete; pavement. *(Northern). Alt.* **asiniwipayihcikewin** *(Plains).*

asinîwepinikewin (NI) The game of curling.

asinîwipayihcikan (NI) Cement.

asinîy *pl.* **asinîyak** (NA) A rock.

asipayowin *pl.* **asipayowina** (NI) The act of reversing.

asisewekinowat *pl.* **asisewekinowata** (NI) A gunny sack. *(Plains). Alt.* **kâsecihcâkaniwat** *(Northern).*

asisîy *pl.* **asisîya** (NI) Seaweed.

asiskîwan *pl.* **asiskîwiwa** (VII) It is muddy.

asiskîwiw *pl.* **asiskîwanwa** (VII) It is full of dirt; it is dusty.

asiskîwîyâkan *pl.* **asiskîwîyâkana** (NI) A piece of earthenware or crockery.

asiskîy *pl.* **asiskîya** (NI) A piece of soil; a piece of dirt.

asiskonâtisowin *pl.* **asiskonâtisowina** (NI) The act of rapaciousness; rapacity. *(Northern). Alt.* **asponâtisowin** *(Plains).*

asiwahew (VTA) S/he puts her/him inside a bag.
  asiwahtâw (VTI) S/he puts it inside a bag.
  asiwahiwew (VTA) S/he puts them inside a bag.
  asiwacikew (VTI) S/he puts things inside a bag.

asiwasiw *pl.* **asiwasiwak** (VAI) S/he is inside; s/he is inside the bag or container.

asiwatâsiw *pl.* **asiwatâsiwak** (VTA) S/he is loading the container. *(Northern). Alt.* **asowacikew** *(Plains).*

asiwatew *pl.* **asiwatewa** (VII) It is contained in a bag; it is inside, i.e.: bag, container, house, etc.

askawew *pl.* **askawewa** (NI) Open water in spring break-up, i.e.: during spring ice break, the open water in a frozen lake.

askâhtik *pl.* **askâhtikwak** (NA) A green tree.

askâskosiy *pl.* **askâskosiya** (NI) A stem of green hay.

askâw *pl.* **askâwa** (VTI) It is raw.

askâwew *pl.* **askâwewak** (VAI) S/he eats raw eggs.

askâwi *pl.* **askâwa** (NI) A raw egg.

askekin *pl.* **askekinwa** (NI) A piece of raw hide.

askihk *pl.* **askihkwak** (NA) A pail; a bucket.

askihkohkânis *pl.* **askihkohkânisak** (NA) A motor.

askihtakonâkwan *pl.* **askihtakonâkwanwa** (VII) It looks green. *(Northern).*

askihtakonâkwan *pl.* **askihtakonâkwanwa** (VII) It looks blue. *(Plains). Alt.* **sepihkonakwan** *(Northern).*

askihtakosiw *pl.* **askihtakosiwak** (VAI) S/he or it is green. *(Northern).*

askihtakosiw *pl.* **askihtakosiwak** (VAI) S/he or it is blue. *(Plains). Alt.* **sepihkosiw** *(Northern).*

askihtakwâw *pl.* **askihtakwâwa** (VII) It is green.

askihtakwâw *pl.* **askihtakwâwak** (VAI) S/he or it is blue. *(Plains). Alt.* **sîpihkosiw** *(Northern).*

askimâtamawew *pl.* **askimâtamawewak** (VTA) S/he laces snowshoes for her/him.

askimâtew (VTI) S/he laces it or them.
  askimâcikêw (VTA) S/he is lacing, i.e.: the baby into the backpack.

askimew *pl.* **askimewak** (VAI) S/he is lacing snowshoes.

askipahkwesikan (NA) Flour.

askipekihtak *pl.* **askipekihtakwa** (NI) A piece of wet wood, i.e.: green wood.

askipiw *pl.* **askipiwak** (VAI) S/he eats something raw.

askipohew (VTA) S/he makes her/him eat something raw.
  askipohwew (VTA) S/he makes somebody else eat something raw.

askipwâw *pl.* **askipwâwa** (NI) A potato.

askitin *pl.* **askitinwa** (VII) It is raw, i.e.: meat.

askitiw *pl.* **askitiwak** (VAI) It is raw, i.e.: bread or bannock.

askiwiyâs *pl.* **askiwiyâsa** (NI) A piece of raw meat.

askiya (NA) Muskeg moss, i.e.: used in diapers.

askîhk pehtakosiw *pl.* **askîhk pehtakosiwak** (VAI) Her/his voice is heard in the ground or earth.

askîwatâmiw *pl.* **askîwatâmiwak** (VAI) Her/his voice is amplified by the ground.

askîy *pl.* **askîya** (NI) A year; earth; world; land; country.

askôkewin *pl.* **askôkewina** (NI) The act of following, i.e.: discipleship; subsequent.

asocikew *pl.* **asocikewak** (VAI) S/he made a promise.

asomew (VTA) S/he puts a curse on her/him.

asomiwew (VTA) S/he warns everyone to be on guard for her/him.

asotam (VAI) S/he promises.

asocikew (VTA) S/he promises something or makes a promise.

asotamakew *pl.* **asotamakewak** (VAI) S/he has promised something to someone.

asotamawew *pl.* **asotamawewak** (VTA) S/he promises her/him.

asotamowin *pl.* **asotamowina** (NI) A promise; a vow.

asowacikan *pl.* **asowacikana** (NI) A container; a pocket; a bin.

asowacikew *pl.* **asowacikewak** (VTA) S/he is loading the container. *(Plains). Alt.* **asiwatâsiw** *(Northern).*

asowacikewin *pl.* **asowacikewina** (NI) The act of bagging.

asoweyihtamowin *pl.* **asoweyihtamowina** (NI) To be wary.

aspapowin *pl.* **aspapowina** (NI) A riding saddle.

aspapowiniwat *pl.* **aspapowiniwata** (NI) A saddlebag.

aspâwikanehikan *pl.* **aspâwikanehikana** (NI) A saddlecloth; a saddleblanket.

aspihiwewin *pl.* **aspihiwewina** (NI) Being one-sided.

aspisâwâcikan *pl.* **aspisâwâcikana** (NI) A pattern; a blue print model. *(Plains). Alt.* **ayîsihcikan** *(Northern).*

aspitahkoskewin *pl.* **aspitahkoskewina** (NI) A footrest; a mat; carpet.

aspîkinâkan *pl.* **aspîkinâkana** (NI) A holster; a sheathe.

asponâtisowin *pl.* **asponâtisowina** (NI) The act of rapaciousness; rapacity. *(Plains). Alt.* **asiskonâtisowin** *(Northern).*

astahcikon *pl.* **astahcikona** (NI) Cache.

astamapiw *pl.* **astamapiwak** (VAI) S/he is demoted. *(Northern). Alt.* **asehâw** *(Plains).*

astâhiwewin *pl.* **astâhiwewina** (NI) The act of making people conscious.

astâskamik (IPC) Right on the ground.

astâskamikwa (NA) Savannah moss; treeless ground moss.

astâskwapitam (VTI) S/he ties it to a tree or pole.

astâskwapisiwew (VTA) S/he ties someone to a tree or pole.

astâskwapicikew (VTI) S/he ties things to a tree or pole.

astewawew *pl.* **astewawewak** (VTA) S/he bet her/him. *(Plains). Var.* **astowew**.

astis *pl.* **astisak** (NA) A mitten or glove.

astotin *pl.* **astotina** (NI) A hat.

astowew *pl.* **astowewak** (VTA) S/he bet her/him. *Alt.* **astewawew** *(Plains).*

asweyihcikewin *pl.* **asweyihcikewina** (NI) The act of war iness.

asweyihtam *pl.* **asweyihtamwak** (VTA) S/he looks out for it; s/he is aware of it.

asweyihtamowew (VTI) S/he takes precautions for her/him.

asweyihtamiwew (VTA) S/he takes precautions for her/him.

asweyihtamâkew (VTA) S/he takes precautions for everybody.

asweyimew (VTA) S/he takes precaution against her/him; s/he is on guard against her/him; s/he prepares or gets ready for her/him.

asweyitam (VTI) S/he takes precautions against it.

asweyimiwew (VTA) S/he takes precautions against her/him.

asweyicikew (VTI) S/he takes precautions against everything; s/he is prepared for everyone/everything.

atameyihcikewin *pl.* **atameyihcikewina** (NI) The act of accusing; accusation; quibble.

atamihikowin *pl.* **atamihikowina** (NI) Being appreciative.

atamihiwewin *pl.* **atamihiwewina** (NI) The act of gratification; satisfaction.

atamikâpawiw *pl.* **atamikâpawiwak** (VTA) S/he stands with her/his back towards her/him. *Alt.* **atimikâpawiw** *(Plains).*

ataminâwin *pl.* **ataminâwina** (NI) The act of appreciation.

atamiskâkew *pl.* **atamiskâkewak** (VAI) S/he shakes hands.

atamiskâkewin *pl.* **atamiskâkewina** (NI) The act of greeting someone by shaking hands, i.e.: salutations.

atâmaskamik (IPC) In the underworld.

atâmayiwinis *pl.* **atâmayiwinisa** (NI) An undergarment. *Var.* **atâmiyôwayiwinis**.

atâmeyihtam *pl.* **atâmeyihtamwa** (VTI) S/he suspects it.

atâmeyimew *pl.* **atâmeyimewak** (VTA) S/he suspects her/him; s/he blames another person for her/his misfortune. *(Plains). Alt.* **pakamimew** *(Northern).*

atâwakewin *pl.* **atâwakewina** (NI) The act of speculating or selling.

atâwewikamik *pl.* **atâwewikamikwa** (NI) A store.

atâwewin *pl.* **atâwewina** (NI) The act of buying.

ati tipiskâw (VII) It is getting dark.

atihk *pl.* **atihkwak** (NA) A caribou.

atihkamek *pl.* **atihkamekwak** (NA) A whitefish.

atihkomin *pl.* **atihkomina** (NI) A deerberry.

atihkwayân *pl.* **atihkwayâna** (NI) A caribou hide.

atihtenihkwew *pl.* **atihtenihkwewak** (VAI) Her/his face is stained.

atihtew *pl.* **atihtewa** (VII) It is ripe, as in berries.

7

atihtewayi *pl.* **atihtewayiya** (NI) Something that is blotchy or stained.

atihtewsisiw *pl.* **atihtewisiwak** (VAI) S/he is stained.

atim *pl.* **atimwak** (NA) A dog.

atimahpinatowin *pl.* **atimahpinatowina** (NI) The act of fighting like dogs, i.e.: a dog fight.

atimikâpawin *pl.* **atimikâpwinak** (VTA) S/he stands with her/his back towards her/him. *(Plains).* *Var.* **atamikapawiw.**

atimikâpawîstawew *pl.* **atimikâpawîstawewak** (VTA) S/he stands with her/his back to someone else's back.

atimotâpânâsk *pl.* **atimotâpânâskwak** (NA) A dogsled.

atipis *pl.* **atipisak** (NA) A string of a racquet or snowshoes; rawhide string.

atisamân *pl.* **atisamâna** (NI) A smudge. *(Plains).* *Alt.* **tasamân** *(Northern).*

atisamânihkawew (VTA) S/he makes a smudge for them. *(Plains).* *Alt.* **tasamânihkawew** *(Northern).*

atisamânihkew (VTI) S/he makes a smudge.

atisamânihkâkew (VTI) S/he makes a smudge with it.

atisamânihkwewin *pl.* **atisamânihkwewina** (NI) The act of making a smudge for horses or cattle. *(Plains).* *Alt.* **tasamanihkewin** *(Northern).*

atisikan *pl.* **atisikana** (NI) A dye.

atoskewin *pl.* **atoskewina** (NI) An industry; a job.

awa (DPR) This one (animate).

awa nâway pîsim (IPC) Last month. *(Plains).* *Alt.* **awa otâhk pîsim** *(Northern).*

awa otâhk pîsim (IPC) Last month. *(Northern).* *Alt.* **awa nâway pîsim** *(Plains).*

awa pîsim (IPC) This month.

awahkanihkewin *pl.* **awahkanihkewina** (NI) The act of exploitation or slavery.

awahkâsowewin *pl.* **awahkâsowewina** (NI) Being servile; servility.

awahkewin *pl.* **awahkewina** (NI) The act of servitude.

awasiw *pl.* **awasiwak** (VAI) S/he warms up.

awasokocawânâpiskos *pl.* **awasokocawânâpiskosak** (NA) A warming stove or heater. *(Plains).* *Alt.* **awaswâkan** *(Northern).*

awaswâkan *pl.* **awaswâkanak** (NA) A heater or a warmer. *(Northern).* *Alt.* **awasokocawânâpiskos** *(Plains).*

awâsis *pl.* **awâsisak** (NA) A child; a tot.

awâsisicâpânâskos *pl.* **awâsisicâpânâskosak** (NA) A stroller; a little wagon.

awâsisihkân *pl.* **awâsisihkânak** (NA) A doll.

awâsisîwiwin *pl.* **awâsisîwiwina** (NI) Being a child; childhood.

awicicestawew (VTA) S/he extends her/his hand to her/him. *(Northern).* *Alt.* **isiniskestawew** *(Plains).*

awicicestam (VTA) S/he extends her/his hand to it.

awicicestâkew (VTA) S/he extends her/his hand to everybody.

awicicestâk (VTA) S/he extends her/his hand to anybody.

awicicew *pl.* **awicicewak** (VAI) S/he extends her/his hands. *(Northern).* *Alt.* **isiniskestakew** *(Plains).*

awiniskestawew (VTA) S/he extends her/his arm towards her/him. *(Northern).*

awiniskestam (VTI) S/he extends her/his arm to it.

awiniskestâkew (VTA) S/he extends her/his arm to everybody.

awiniskestâk (VTA) S/he extends her/his arm to anybody.

awiniskew *pl.* **awiniskewak** (VAI) S/he extends her/his arms. *(Northern).*

awîna (IPC) Who.

awînipan (IPC) An expression meaning "it's a long time coming."

awîyak (PR) Someone.

ayahcatim *pl.* **ayahcatimwak** (NA) A strange dog.

ayahcinam *pl.* **ayahcinamwa** (VTI) S/he hides it in the ground.

ayahcinawew (VTA) S/he sees her/him as foreign.

ayahcinam (VTI) S/he sees it as foreign.

ayahcinâkew (VTA) S/he sees everybody as foreign.

ayahcinew (VTA) S/he covers her/him with earth; s/he buries her/him.

ayahcinam (VTI) S/he covers it with earth.

ayahciniwew (VTA) S/he covers somebody with earth.

ayahcinikew (VTI) S/he covers something with earth.

ayahciyiniw *pl.* **ayahciyiniwak** (NA) A stranger or outsider, i.e.: historically Plains Crees used it to describe the Blackfoot peoples; Northern Crees use the word to indicate the Slavey-speaking people.

ayahkotonâmowin *pl.* **ayahkotonâmowina** (NI) The act of speaking gibberish.

ayahteyimew (VTA) S/he does not like her/him and treats her/him like an outcast; s/he thinks s/he or it is out of place; s/he is uncomfortable with her/him or it; s/he is unfriendly or anti-social; s/he treats her/him as a stranger; s/he treats her/him or it as odd.

ayahteyitam (VTI) S/he does not like it and treats it like an outcast.

ayahteyimiwew (VTA) S/he does not like them and treats them like an outcast.

ayahteyicikew (VTI) S/he does not like anything.

ayahtokamik (NI) Someone else's place.

ayahwew (VTI) S/he buries her/him in the ground.

ayaham (VTI) S/he buries it.

ayahowew (VTA) S/he buries someone.

ayahikew (VTI) S/he buries something.

ayakaskisihtâw *pl.* **ayakaskisihtâwak** (NA) The act of widening.

ayamihâw *pl.* **ayamihâwak** (VTA) S/he prays to God; a layman or religious member.

ayamihâwin *pl.* **ayamihâwina** (NI) Christian praying; Christian prayer; Christian religion; a group of Christian prayers, i.e.: a litany.

ayamihcikew *pl.* **ayamihcikewak** (VAI) S/he reads.

ayamihcikewin *pl.* **ayamihcikewina** (NI) Reading material.

ayamihestamakewin *pl.* **ayamihestamakewina** (NI) The act of exorcism.

ayamihewâhtik *pl.* **ayamihewâhtikwak** (NA) A cross; a crucifix; a rood.

ayamihewâtisowin *pl.* **ayamihewâtisowina** (NI) Being spiritual; spirituality.

ayamihewâyi (VII) Liturgical.

ayamihewikamik (NI) A church.

ayamihewikîsikâw (VII) It is Sunday; the Sabbath.

ayamihewiskwew *pl.* **ayamihewiskwewak** (NA) A priestess.

ayamihewiskwewinâhk (IPC) At the convent.

ayamihewitapiskâkan *pl.* **ayamihewitapiskâkana** (NI) A stole. *(Plains). Alt.* **kîsokwayawehon** *(Northern).*

ayamihewiyasiwiwin *pl.* **ayamihewiyasiwiwina** (NI) A canon.

ayamihewiyiniw *pl.* **ayamihewiyiniwak** (NA) A member of the clergy, i.e.: a chaplain, a pastor, or a minister; a Catholic priest. *(Northern). Alt.* **pahkwâyamihewiyiniwiwin** *(Plains).*

ayamihewiyiniwiwin *pl.* **ayamihewiyiniwiwinak** (NA) Being a minister or Catholic priest; deaconry.

ayamihtâw *pl.* **ayamihtâwak** (VAI) S/he reads.

ayapahkamikan (IPC) Things are very busy.

ayapakinew (VTI) S/he bends her/him many different ways.

  ayapakinam (VTI) S/he bends it many different ways.

  ayapakiniwew (VTA) S/he bends someone many different ways.

  ayapakinikew (VTI) S/he bends something many different ways.

ayapasinâstewekin *pl.* **ayapasinâstewekinwa** (NI) Calico, i.e.: cloth.

ayapaskâw (NI) The Cree name for the settlement of Fort Chipewyan.

ayapatinâw *pl.* **ayapatinâwa** (VII) The terrain is hilly.

ayapâhtakâw *pl.* **ayapâhtakâwa** (VII) There are plenty of trees. *(Northern). Alt.* **ayapâhtikoskâw** *(Plains).*

ayapâhtik *pl.* **ayapâhtikwa** (NI) A float for a gill net.

ayapâhtikoskâw *pl.* **ayapâhtikoskâwa** (VII) There are plenty of trees. *(Plains). Alt.* **ayapâhtakâw** *(Northern).*

ayapâskweyâw *pl.* **ayapâskweyâwak** (VAI) There are clumps of shrubs or trees in succession.

ayapihkew *pl.* **ayapihkewak** (VTA) S/he makes nets.

ayapihkewin *pl.* **ayapihkewina** (VTI) The act of making nets; netting.

ayapikamâw *pl.* **ayapikamâwa** (VII) There are plenty of inlets on the lake.

ayapiministikweyâw *pl.* **ayapiministikweyâwa** (VII) There are a chain of islands; there are many, many islands.

ayapinikesk (VTA) One who is obsessively inquisitive or curious.

ayapinikewin *pl.* **ayapinikewina** (NI) The act of rummaging; rummage.

ayapiy *pl.* **ayapiyak** (NA) A gill net.

ayasâwâc (IPC) Altogether different. *(Plains).*

ayasihtakinew (VTA) S/he covers her/him with evergreen branches.

  ayasihtakinam (VTI) S/he covers it with evergreen branches.

  ayasihtakiniwew (VTA) S/he covers them with evergreen branches.

  ayasihtakinikew (VTI) S/he covers everything with evergreen branches.

ayaskosiwepinew (VTA) S/he covers her/him with hay.

  ayaskosiwepinam (VTI) S/he covers it with hay.

  ayaskosiwepiniwew (VTA) S/he covers them with hay.

  ayaskosiwepinikew (VTI) S/he covers everything with hay.

ayâhkwemâw *pl.* **ayâhkwemâwak** (VTA) The words spoken to her/him are very strong; the words spoken give her/him a tough time, i.e.: it is a reprimand.

ayâhkweyihtamowin *pl.* **ayâhkweyihtamowina** (NI) Being diligent; dilgence.

ayâhpayiw *pl.* **ayâhpayiwak** (VAI) S/he staggers.

ayâkonehwew (VTI) S/he buries her/him with snow.

  ayâkoneham (VTI) S/he buries it with snow.

  ayâkonehowew (VTI) S/he buries someone with snow.

  ayâkonehikew (VTI) S/he buries something with snow.

ayâsawi (IPC) From one to another. *(Northern).*

ayâspîs (IPC) Once in a while; sparse; very seldom.

ayâtan *pl.* **ayâtanwa** (VII) It is tight.

ayâtapow *pl.* **ayâtapowak** (VAI) S/he sits firmly. *(Northern). Alt.* **ayitapow** *(Plains).*

ayâtaskisiw *pl.* **ayâtaskisiwak** (VAI) It has been planted firmly or solidly rooted.

ayâtâhew (VTI) S/he places it firmly. *(Northern).*

  ayâtâstaw (VTI) S/he places things very firmly.

  ayâtâwew (VTI) S/he tightens it up.

  ayâtâscikew (VTI) S/he places things very tightly.

9

ayâtisiw *pl.* **ayâtisiwak** (VAI) S/he is a well balanced person.

ayâtisowin *pl.* **ayâtisowina** (NI) A well balanced personality.

ayâw *pl.* **ayâwak** (VTA) S/he has it on; s/he is at a certain place.

ayâwâwasowin *pl.* **ayâwâwasowina** (NI) The act of childbearing; gestation; impregnated; pregnancy.

ayâwew *pl.* **ayâwewak** (VTA) S/he has them; s/he owns them.

ayâwin *pl.* **ayâwina** (NI) Having a possession or place where one stays.

ayeskosiw *pl.* **ayeskosiwak** (VAI) S/he is tired; s/he is dog tired, i.e.: her/his muscles are sore.

ayeyimow *pl.* **ayeyimowak** (VAI) S/he sneezes.

ayeyimowin *pl.* **ayeyimowina** (NI) The act of sneezing. *(Northern). Alt.* **câhcâmowin** *(Plains).*

ayihkwew *pl.* **ayihkwewak** (NA) A steer.

ayihkwew mostos *pl.* **ayihkewak mostosak** (NA) An ox.

ayihkwewimostos *pl.* **ayihkwewimostoswak** (NA) A castrated steer.

ayikinônâcikan *pl.* **ayikinônâcikanak** (NA) A mushroom.

ayikîpîsim (NI) April; the frog moon or month *(Plains). Var.* **ayîkiwipîsim.**

ayikos *pl.* **ayikosak** (NA) An ant. *Var.* **eyik; ikos; eyikos; iyikos.**

ayikowisti *pl.* **ayikowista** (NI) An ant hill. *(Northern). Alt.* **iyikowîsti** *(Plains).*

ayinânemitanaw (IPC) Eighty.

ayinânemitanawâw (IPC) Eighty times, eightieth time.

ayinânew (IPC) Eight.

ayinânewâw (IPC) Eight times, eighth time.

ayinânewâw mitâtahtomitanaw (IPC) Eight hundred.

ayînânewosâp (IPC) Eighteen.

ayînânewosâpwâw (IPC) Eighteen times, eighteenth time.

ayipayiw *pl.* **ayipayiwa** *or* **ayipayiwak** (VII) *or* (VAI) It or s/he is covered over by some material.

ayisihew (VTA) It is the way in which s/he shapes her/him.

ayisitaw (VTI) It is the way s/he shapes it.

ayisihiwew (VTA) It is the way s/he shapes people.

ayisicikew (VTI) It is the way s/he shapes everything.

ayisinawew (VTA) S/he mimicks her/him; s/he follows someone else's ideas. *(Plains).*

ayisinam (VTI) S/he mimicks it.

ayisitohtawew (VTA) S/he mimicks people.

ayisinâkew (VTA) S/he mimicks everything.

ayisinâkes *pl.* **ayisinâkesak** (NA) A monkey. *(Northern). Alt.* **ocayisinâkes** *(Plains).*

ayisinâkew *pl.* **ayisinâkewak** (VAI) S/he imitates and mocks others.

ayisinâkewin *pl.* **ayisinâkewina** (NI) The act of imitation; impersonality; mimicry; mockery.

ayisipiwakan (VII) It tastes like stagnant water.

ayisipiy *pl.* **ayisipiya** (NI) Stagnant water.

ayisitohtawew (VAI) S/he mimicks her/his words.

ayisitohtam (VTI) S/he mimicks it.

ayisitohtatâkew (VTA) S/he mimicks everyone.

ayisiyinihkân *pl.* **ayisiyinihkânak** (NA) A mannequin; a scarecrow.

ayisiyiniw *pl.* **ayisiyiniwak** (NA) A person; a human being.

ayisiyiniwan *pl.* **ayisiyiniwanwa** (VII) It is like a human being.

ayisiyiniwiw *pl.* **ayisiyiniwiwak** (VAI) S/he is a human being.

ayisiyiniwiwin *pl.* **ayisiyiniwiwina** (NI) Humanity.

ayitapow *pl.* **ayitapowak** (VAI) S/he sits firmly. *(Plains). Alt.* **ayâtapow** *(Northern).*

ayiwâk (IPC) More; more than; greater; for more; much more; some more. *(Plains). Alt.* **ayiwâk ohci** *(Northern).*

ayiwâk ohci (IPC) More; more than; greater; for more; much more; some more. *(Northern). Alt.* **ayiwâk** *(Plains).*

ayiwâkahew (VTA) S/he chops it or her/him longer than necessary, e.g.: a tree.

ayiwâkaham (VTI) S/he chops it too long.

ayiwâkahikew (VTI) S/he chops everything too long.

ayiwâkakihcikew *pl.* **ayiwâkakihcikewak** (VAI) S/he charges more.

ayiwâkakimew (VTI) S/he overcharges her/him.

ayiwâkakihtam (VTI) S/he overcharges for it.

ayiwâkakimiwew (VTA) S/he overcharges everybody.

ayiwâkakicikew (VTI) S/he overcharges for everything.

ayiwâkan *pl.* **ayiwâkanwa** (NI) Having quality.

ayiwâkâtisiw *pl.* **ayiwâkâtisiwak** (VAI) S/he has an excessive character. *Alt.* **ayiwâkâyîhtiw** *(Plains).*

ayiwâkâyîhtiw *pl.* **ayiwâkâyîhtiwak** (VAI) S/he has an excessive character. *(Plains). Var.* **ayiwâkatisiw.**

ayiwâkehkin (IPC) Exclamation of big surprise, e.g.: "Oh my God, you're not kidding? That is terrible."

ayiwâkemiywihtam *pl.* **ayiwâkimiywihtamwak** (VAI) S/he is overjoyed.

ayiwâkes (IPC) A little more; additional; extra; amply.

ayiwâkesîs (IPC) A tiny bit more; a touch more.

ayiwâkeyâtowin *pl.* **ayiwâkeyâtowina** (NI) The act of being abundant to excess; outnumber.

ayiwâkeyimew (VTA) S/he favors her/him more; s/he thinks highly of her/him.

ayiwâkeyitam (VTI) S/he favors it.

ayiwâkeyimiwew (VTA) S/he favors everybody.

ayiwâkeyicikew (VTI) S/he favors everything.

ayiwâkeyimisowin *pl.* **ayiwâkeyimisowina** (NI) An arrogance that respects no one.

ayiwâkeyimototawew (VTA) S/he is very arrogant towards her/him; s/he thinks herself/himself superior; s/he challenges her/him or it or others.

ayiwâkeyimototam (VTI) S/he is very arrogant towards it.

ayiwâkeyimototâkew (VTA) S/he is very arrogant toward everyone.

ayiwâkeyimototâcikew (VTI) S/he is very arrogant toward everything.

ayiwâkeyimow *pl.* **ayiwâkeyimowak** (VAI) S/he is arrogant.

ayiwâkeyimowin *pl.* **ayiwâkeyimowina** (NI) Being arrogant; being odious; the act of being militant; militancy.

ayiwâkimew (VTA) S/he amplifies her/his false accusations.

ayiwâkimiwew (VTA) S/he accuses people falsely.

ayiwâkimiyew *pl.* **ayiwâkimiyewak** (VTA) S/he gives her/him more than is needed.

ayiwâkipayihew (VAI) S/he has some left over.

ayiwâkipayitâw (VAI) S/he has some of it left over.

ayiwâkipayihiwew (VAI) S/he has some people left over.

ayiwâkipayiw *pl.* **ayiwâkipayiwa** *or* **ayiwâkipayiwak** (VII) *or* (VAI) It *or* s/he has more than it *or* s/he needs.

ayiwâkipew *pl.* **ayiwâkipewak** (VAI) S/he drinks more than s/he needs.

ayiwâkisâwâtew *pl.* **ayiwâkisâwâtewak** (VTA) S/he cuts her/him more than necessary, e.g.: while butchering moose.

ayiwâkisâwâtam (VTI) S/he cuts it more than necessary.

ayiwâkisâwâsiwew (VTA) S/he cuts people more than necessary.

ayiwâkisâwâcikew (VTI) S/he cuts things more than necessary.

ayiwâkiskam (VAI) S/he is over it; s/he makes herself/himself bigger than the other person.

ayiwâkiskâkew (VAI) S/he is over everybody.

ayiwâkiskâcikew (VAI) S/he is over everything.

ayiwâkiskawew *pl.* **ayiwâkiskawewak** (VTA) S/he is taller than her/him. *(Northern).* Alt. **cayôskawew** *(Plains).*

ayiwâkispihtisiw *pl.* **ayiwâkispihtisiwak** (NA) A superior worker or a harder worker. *(Northern).* Alt. **kakâyawisiw** *(Plains).*

ayiwepihew (VTA) S/he makes her/him rest.

ayiwepitâw (VTI) S/he gives it rest.

ayiwepihiwew (VTA) S/he gives everybody rest.

ayiwepicikew (VTI) S/he gives everything rest.

ayiwepiw *pl.* **ayiwepiwak** (VAI) S/he is resting.

ayiwepiwin *pl.* **ayiwepiwina** (NI) A rest or nap; a place to rest.

ayiwinis *pl.* **ayiwinisa** (NI) A piece of cloth; a piece of material; apparel; a suit of clothing; garb.

ayiwinisekin *pl.* **ayiwinisekinwa** (NI) Cloth; cloth bag; cloth for making clothes. *(Plains).* Alt. **ayiwinisihkakanekin** *(Northern).*

ayiwinisihkakanekin (NI) Cloth for making a suit. *(Northern).* Alt. **ayiwinisekin** *(Plains).*

ayîkis *pl.* **ayîkisak** (NA) A frog or toad.

ayîkisis *pl.* **ayîkisisak** (NA) A tadpole.

ayîkiwipîsim (NI) April; the frog moon or month. *Alt.* **ayikîpîsim** *(Plains).*

ayîsihcikan *pl.* **ayîsihcikana** (NI) A pattern. *(Northern).* Alt. **aspisâwâcikan** *(Plains).*

ayîtahpisiw *pl.* **ayîtahpisiwak** (VAI) S/he is tied securely. *(Plains).* Alt. **âyâtâhpisiw** *(Northern).*

ayîtahpitew (VTI) S/he fastens it firmly. *(Plains).* Alt. **ayâtâhpitew** *(Northern).*

ayâtahpitam (VTI) S/he ties it firmly.

ayâtahpisiwew (VTI) S/he fasten them in a secure manner.

ayâtahpicikew (VTI) S/he has tied it well.

ayopayowin *pl.* **ayopayowina** (NI) The act of being immersed; immersion. *Var.* **kohtâpayowin**.

ayoskan *pl.* **ayoskanak** (NA) A raspberry. *(Northern).*

ayoskanahtik (NA) A rasberry bush. *Alt.* **miskaminatik** *(Plains).*

aywâstin (VII) The wind ceases; it is calm.

11

â

âcimisowin *pl.* âcimisowina (NI) The act of confessing.

âcimostakewin *pl.* âcimostakewina (NI) The act of providing information; storytelling; being informational.

âcimsostâkewin *pl.* âcimsostâkewina (NI) A confession to a priest.

âhâcinâcikew *pl.* âhâcinâcikewak (VAI) S/he makes double trips to get her/his possessions; s/he portages.

âhâpihtaw (IPC) Half and half.

âhâsiw *pl.* âhâsiwak (NA) A crow.

âhâsiw okitowin *pl.* âhâsiw okitowina (NI) The act of a crow calling out; the calling of a crow.

âhâspîhtaw (IPC) Once in a while; sporadical. *Var.* âhâspis, âskaw.

âhkameyihtam *pl.* âhkameyihtamwa (VTI) S/he never stops trying it, i.e.: diligently works; s/he does not give up on it.

âhkameyihtamowin *pl.* âhkameyihtamowina (NI) The act of diligence; consistency; insistence; persistance; determination.

âhkiskiw *pl.* âhkiskiwak (NA) A prairie chicken.

âhkosepewin *pl.* âhkosepewina (NI) Being hungover from alcohol or over indulgence.

âhkosiw *pl.* âhkosiwak (VAI) S/he is sick, i.e.: an invalid.

âhkosiwâyâwin *pl.* âhkosiwâyâwina (NI) The act of feeling unwholesome or sickly.

âhkosiwin *pl.* âhkosiwina (NI) Being diseased; having an illness.

âhkospakwan *pl.* âhkospakwanwa (VII) It is bitter; it tastes sour.

âhkwan *pl.* âhkwanwa (VII) It is painful.

âhkwatihtâw *pl.* âhkwatihtâwa (VTI) S/he freezes it.

âhkwatin *pl.* âhkwatinwa (VII) It is frozen.

âhkwatisowin *pl.* âhkwatisowina (NI) Being difficult.

âhkwetawesâkew *pl.* âhkwetawesâkewak (VAI) S/he wears a coat over another coat.

âhtahew (VTA) S/he puts her/him aside; s/he places her/him differently or in a different place.
  âhtastâw (VTI) S/he puts it aside.
  âhtascikew (VTI) S/he puts things aside.

âhtahpitam (VTI) S/he has retied it.
  âhtahpisiwew (VTI) S/he has retied them.
  âhtahpicikew (VTI) S/he has retied things.

âhtapiw *pl.* âhtapiwak (VTA) S/he changes her/his sitting position; s/he moves to sit in a different location.

âhtapiwin *pl.* âhtapiwina (NI) The act of changing a sitting position or moving to sit in another location.

âhtascikan *pl.* âhtascikana (NI) Something used to move other items; movable.

âhtascikewin *pl.* âhtascikewina (NI) The act of removal.

âhtaskihâw *pl.* âhtaskihâwak (NA) It has been removed and planted elsewhere.

âhtasowewin *pl.* âhtasowewina (NI) The act of abrogating.

âhtastew *pl.* âhtastewa (VII) The thing is moved to another place.

âkawâsiw *pl.* âkawâsiwak (VAI) S/he is in the shade.

âkawâskweyâhk (IPC) In the shelter of a dense forest or wood.

âkawâstehikan *pl.* âkawâstehikana (NI) Built for shade, i.e.: an umbrella.

âkawâstehikewin *pl.* âkawâstehikewina (NI) The act of making shade.

âkawâstehon *pl.* âkawâstehona (NI) A sunshade.

âkawâyâhk (IPC) Out of sight; on the far side; away from, i.e.: lee (of an island).

âkawâyihk (IPC) Isolated and hidden from view.

âkayâsimow *pl.* âkayâsimowak (VAI) S/he speaks English.

âkayâsimowin (NI) The English language.

âkâm askîhk (NI) Across the land, i.e.: overseas.

âkâmâyihk (NI) Across the way.

âkâmihk (NI) Across the water or across the lake.

âkohkwepicikana (NI) Blinders.

âkokâpawiw *pl.* âkokâpawiwak (VTA) S/he blocks my view; s/he is blocked from my view.

âkwaskitinew (VTA) S/he is hugging her/him.
  âkwaskitinam (VTI) S/he is hugging something.
  âkwaskitiniwew (VTA) S/he is hugging everybody.
  âkwaskitinikew (VTI) S/he is hugging.

âkwaskitinitowin *pl.* âkwaskitinitowina (NI) The act of embracing.

âkwaskitinkewin *pl.* âkwaskitinkewina (NI) The act of hugging.

âmaciwetahew (VTA) S/he takes her/him up a ladder or stairs. *(Plains). Alt.* kihcekositahew *(Northern).*
  âmaciwetataw (VTI) S/he takes it up.
  âmaciwetahiwew (VTA) S/he takes people up.
  âmaciwetahcikew (VTI) S/he takes things up.

âmopewayisîs *pl.* âmopewayisîsak (NA) A hummingbird. *(Northern). Alt.* âmopiyesîs *(Plains).*

âmopiyesîs *pl.* âmopiyesîsak (NA) A hummingbird. *(Plains). Alt.* âmopewayisîs *(Northern).*

âmowaciston *pl.* âmowacistonwa (NI) A beehive.

âmô *pl.* âmôwak (NA) Bee.

âmôme aspahcikewin (NI) Honey spread.

13

âmômey (NI) Honey.

ânaskohpicikâkan *pl.* **ânaskohpicikâkana** (NI) An attachment.

âniskômohcikewin *pl.* **âniskômohcikewina** (NI) The act of connecting; connection.

ânweciyihikewin *pl.* **ânweciyihikewina** (NI) Being incredulous; denial.

ânwehtam *pl.* **ânwehtamwak** (VAI) S/he denies.

ânwehtamowin *pl.* **ânwehtamowina** (NI) Denying; repudiation; scepticism or skepticism; unbelieving.

ânwehtawew *pl.* **ânwehtawewak** (VAI) S/he denies what the other says.

ânweyihtamowin *pl.* **ânweyihtamowina** (NI) Conscious refusal.

âpacihâw *pl.* **âpacihâwak** (VTA) S/he has been cured; s/he has been utilised effectively.

âpacihcikan *pl.* **âpacihcikana** (NI) Equipment; a tool.

âpacihew *pl.* **âpacihewak** (VTA) S/he cures her/him; s/he helps her/him or utilises her/him effectively.

âpacihisiw *pl.* **âpacihisiwak** (VTA) S/he cures herself/himself.

âpacihiw *pl.* **âpacihiwak** (VAI) A threat: "lucky for her/him (that s/he got away)" or "s/he is lucky or else."

âpacihiwewin *pl.* **âpacihiwewina** (NI) The act of curing.

âpacihowin *pl.* **âpacihowina** (NI) The act of doing something for one's own good.

âpahastimwew *pl.* **âpahastimwewak** (VTA) S/he unhooks a team of horses; s/he takes the harness off. (*Plains and Northern variant*). *Alt.* **tasinastimwew** *(Northern)*.

âpahikan *pl.* **âpahikana** (NI) A wrench.

âpahikewin *pl.* **âpahikewina** (NI) The act of unravelling. *(Plains). Alt.* **âpahonikewin** *(Northern)*.

âpahonikewin *pl.* **âpahonikewina** (NI) The act of unravelling. *(Northern). Alt.* **âpahikewin** *(Plains)*.

âpahopicikewin *pl.* **âpahopicikewina** (NI) Act of quickly untying.

âpakosîs *pl.* **âpakosîsak** (NA) A mouse.

âpakosîsimîcowin *pl.* **âpakosîsimîcowina** (NI) Mouse food, i.e.: Cree slang for cheese.

âpatan *pl.* **âpatanwa** (VII) It is useful.

âpateyihtamowin *pl.* **âpateyihtamowina** (NI) Hope; creed or articles of faith.

âpateyimew (VTA) S/he has faith in her/him; s/he feels s/he has use for her/him or it.

âpateyitam (VTI) S/he has faith in it.

âpateyimiwew (VTA) S/he has faith in them.

âpateyicikew (VTI) S/he has faith in things.

âpateyitâkosiw *pl.* **âpateyitâkosiwak** (NA) One who is given a sense of usefulness or confidence.

âpatisiw *pl.* **âpatisiwak** (VAI) S/he is useful.

âpehowin *pl.* **âpehowina** (NI) The act of revenge.

âpihtaw (IPC) Half.

âpihtawakâm (IPC) In midstream.

âpihtawisiyaw *pl.* **âpihtawisiyawa** (NI) A midrift; belt area of the stomach.

âpihtawkosisan *pl.* **âpihtawkosisanak** (NA) A Métis person.

âpihtâkîsikanohk (IPC) South; towards the south or in a southerly direction. (*Plains and Northern variant*). *Alt.* **sâwanohk** *(Northern)*; **kîsopwenohk** *(Northern)*.

âpihtâkîsikan mîcisowin *pl.* **âpihtâkîsikan mîcisowina** (NI) Lunch.

âpihtâkîsikâw (VII) It is noon.

âpihtâtipiskâw (NI) It is midnight.

âpihtâwâyihk (NI) In the middle; mid.

âpiscimôsis *pl.* **âpiscimôsisak** (NA) A deer. (*Plains). Alt.* **âpisimôsos** *(Northern)*.

âpisimôsos *pl.* **âpisimôsosak** (NA) A deer. (*Northern). Alt.* **âpiscimôsis** *(Plains)*.

âpisimôsôwiyâs *pl.* **âpisimôsôwiyâsa** (NI) One piece of venison.

âpisisinokîsikâw *pl.* **âpisisinokîsikâwa** (NI) Easter.

âpisisinowin *pl.* **âpisisinowina** (NI) The act of resurrection.

âpoceyâw *pl.* **âpoceyâwa** (VII) It is inside out.

âsawahotâsiw (VAI) S/he ferries things across the current in a canoe.

âsawahocikew (VAI) S/he takes things across the current in a canoe.

âsawahotew *pl.* **âsawahotewa** (VII) It floats across the current.

âsawahôkiw *pl.* **âsawahôkiwak** (VTA) S/he floats across from shore to shore.

âsawapakiw *pl.* **âsawapakiwak** (VTA) S/he is floating across by the current.

âsawâkâmemow *pl.* **âsawâkâmemowa** (NI) A road that leads across.

âsawâkâmeyâtakâw *pl.* **âsawâkâmeyâtakâwak** (VTA) S/he wades across.

âsawiwskohtew *pl.* **âsawiskohtewak** (VAI) S/he is walking across the ice.

âsawohtâw *pl.* **âsawohtâwa** (VTI) S/he takes it across.

âsawohtew *pl.* **âsawohtewak** (VAI) S/he walks across.

âsay (IPC) Already. (*Plains). Alt.* **sâsay** *(Northern)*.

âsay mîna (IPC) All over again. (*Plains). Alt.* **asaimîna** *(Northern)*.

âsiwahonâna *pl.* **âsiwahonâna** (NI) A crossing.

âsiwahoyew (VTA) S/he ferries her/him across the water.

âsiwahotâw (VTI) S/he ferries it across the water.

âsiwahoyiwew (VTA) S/he ferries people across the water.

âsiwahocikew (VTI) S/he ferries things across the water; s/he brings everyone or everything across the water.

âsiwahôcikan *pl.* **âsiwahôcikana** (NI) A ferry.

âsîyân *pl.* **âsîyânak** (NA) A diaper. *(Northern).*

âskaw (IPC) It happens once in a while; now and then; sometimes.

âsohtin *pl.* **âsohtinwa** (VTA) It leans on something.

âsohtitâw (VTI) S/he leans it against something.
　âsôsimew (VTA) S/he leans them against something.
　âsôcikew (VTI) S/he leans something onto something.

âsokan *pl.* **âsokana** (NI) A bridge.

âsokanihkew *pl.* **âsokanihkewak** (VAI) S/he makes a bridge.

âsokanihkewin *pl.* **âsokanihkewina** (NI) The act of bridging.

âsokapawiw *pl.* **âsokapawiwak** (VTA) S/he leans against something while standing.

âsokâpawîstawew (VTA) S/he leans on her/him while standing.
　âsokâpawîstam (VTI) S/he leans on something while standing.
　âsokâpawîstâkew (VTA) S/he is leaning on others while standing.

âsokew *pl.* **âsokewak** (VTA) S/he walks on the bridge.

âsokewin *pl.* **âsokewina** (NI) The act of walking on a bridge.

âsosimiw *pl.* **âsosimiwak** (VTA) S/he leans her/him against something.

âsosimow *pl.* **âsosimowak** (VTA) S/he leans on something.

âsosin *pl.* **âsosinwak** (VTA) S/he is leaning on something.

âsostisimow (VTI) S/he places her/his feet on something for support.
　âsostisimiwew (VTA) S/he places other people's feet on something for support.

âsowaham *pl.* **âsowahamwak** (VTA) S/he is gone across.

âsowahamawew (VTA) S/he goes across for her/him.
　âsowahamakew (VTA) S/he goes across for someone else.

âsowahamwestamawew *pl.* **âsowahamwestamawewak** (VTA) S/he goes across the water for her/him.

âsowakamehtew *pl.* **âsowakamehtewak** (VAI) S/he crosses the road. *(Plains). Alt.* **pîmiskanawew** *(Northern).*

âsowakâmetisahwew (VTA) S/he makes her/him cross the road. *(Plains). Alt.* **pîmiskanawehew** *(Northern).*
　âsowakâmetisataw (VTI) S/he makes it cross the road.
　âsowakâmetisahiwew (VTA) S/he makes people cross the road.
　âsowakâmetisacikew (VTI) S/he makes things cross the road.

âspamohcikan *pl.* **âspamohcikana** (NI) A steel bearing, i.e.: for a car wheel; a rubber ring.

âspihtaw (IPC) Periodic; once in a while.

âspihtawiyikohk (IPC) In a sporadic manner; sporadically.

âspîs (IPC) Not often; very seldom.

âstamahisow *pl.* **âstamahisowak** (VTA) S/he demotes herself/himself; s/he humbles herself/himself.

âstameyemowin *pl.* **âstameyemowina** (NI) The act of being inferior; inferiority.

âstaweyâpâwacikewin *pl.* **âstaweyâpâwacikewina** (NI) The act of dousing; putting out a fire with water.

âstâskwapitew *pl.* **âstâskwapitewa** (VII) It is tied to a tree or pole.

âstehowew (NA) A healer. *Alt.* **otiyinikahiwew** *(Plains).*

âstehtin *pl.* **âstehtinwa** (VII) It is continuous and then has a sudden break.

âstehwew (VTA) S/he makes her/him feel better. *Var.* **âstewepawew**.

âstepayiw *pl.* **âstepayiwak** (VAI) S/he is healed.

âstepayowin *pl.* **âstepayowina** (NI) The act of recuperation.

âsteskam *pl.* **âsteskamwa** (VTI) S/he bypasses something.

âsteskawew (VTA) S/he missed her/him on the trail.
　âsteskâkew (VTA) S/he missed them on the trail.
　âsteskâcikew (VTA) S/he missed everyone on the trail.

âsteyihcikew *pl.* **âsteyihcikewak** (VAI) S/he accuses someone.

âsteyimiwew *pl.* **âsteyimiwewak** (VTA) S/he lays blame on her/him.

âswastâw *pl.* **âswastâwa** (VTI) S/he leans it up against something.

âsyâstehtew *pl.* **âyâstehtewak** (VTA) S/he walks by the place where s/he should have been.

âtaweyihtamowin *pl.* **âtaweyihtamowina** (NI) The act of rejecting; rejection.

âtaweyimiw *pl.* **âtaweyimiwak** (VTA) S/he rejects her/him.

âtayohkan *pl.* **âtayohkanak** (NA) A legendary figure.

âtayohkewin *pl.* **âtayohkewina** (NI) A fairy tale or myth.

âtâ (IPC) Although.

âw (IPC) Okay or all right.

âw mâka (IPC) Okay then.

âwacimihtew *pl.* **âwacimihtewak** (VTA) S/he gathers firewood.

âwatâswâkan *pl.* **âwatâswâkanak** (NA) A truck.

âwenâkosiw *pl.* **âwenâkosiwak** (VAI) S/he sort of resembles someone; s/he looks something like her/him. *(Plains). Alt.* **yâwinâkosiw** *(Northern).*

âwenâkwan *pl.* **âwenâkwanwa** (VII) It sort of resembles something; it looks something like it. *(Plains). Alt.* **yâwenâkwan** *(Northern).*

15

âyakaskisiw *pl.* **âyakaskisiwak** (VAI) S/he is wide, i.e.:
fat. *(Plains). Alt.* **taswekisiw** *(Northern).*

âyâspîhtaw (IPC) Once in a while.

âyâtamow (VAI) It is stuck on tightly. *(Northern). Alt.*
âyîtamow *(Plains).*

âyâtataw (VTI) S/he puts it on firmly.

âyâtahiwew (VTA) S/he places people very firmly.

âyâtacikew (VTI) S/he attaches something firmly.

âyâtâhpisiw *pl.* **âyâtâhpisiwak** (VAI) S/he is tied
securely. *(Northern). Alt.* **ayîtahpisiw** *(Plains).*

âyâtâhpitew (VTI) S/he fastens it firmly. *(Northern). Alt.*
ayîtahpitew *(Plains).*

âyâtâhpitam (VTI) S/he ties it firmly.

âyâtâhpisiwew (VTI) S/he fasten them in a secure
manner.

âyâtâhpicikew (VTI) S/he has tied it well.

âyimahkamikan (IPC) A difficult time period.

âyimahkamikisowin *pl.* **âyimahkamikisowina** (NI)
Being problematic.

âyiman (VII) It is difficult.

âyimanohk (IPC) In a difficult place; hard times.

âyimeyimew (VTA) S/he finds her/him difficult.

âyimeyitam (VTI) S/he finds it difficult.

âyimeyicikew (VTI) S/he finds things difficult.

âyimihew (VTA) S/he gives her/him a rough time; s/he is
very tough on her/him.

âyimitâw (VTI) S/he gives it problems.

âyimihiwew (VTA) S/he gives everyone problems.

âyimihisiw *pl.* **âyimihisiwak** (VTA) S/he needlessly gives
herself/himself a hard time.

âyimihisowin *pl.* **âyimihisowina** (NI) The act of giving
oneself a hard time.

âyimihiwew *pl.* **âyimihiwewak** (VAI) S/he is difficult to
handle.

âyimihowin *pl.* **âyimihowina** (NI) Having a
disadvantage.

âyimipayiwin *pl.* **âyimipayiwina** (NI) The act of being in
a commotion.

âyimomew (VTA) S/he gossips about her/him.

âyimotam (VTI) S/he gossips about it.

âyimomiwew (VTA) S/he gossips about everyone.

âyimomiwewin *pl.* **âyimomiwewina** (NI) Being
impertinent; impertinence.

âyimwew *pl.* **âyimwewak** (VAI) S/he gossips.

âyimwewin *pl.* **âyimwewina** (NI) The act of gossiping;
declamation.

âyitaw (IPC) Both sides; each side of something.

âyitawahew (VTA) S/he places her/him on both sides.

âyitawastâw (VTI) S/he places it on both sides.

âyitawacikew (VTI) S/he places things on each side.

âyitawakâm (IPC) On each side of the water; on both
sides of the river or lake.

âyitawapîw *pl.* **âyitawapiwak** (VAI) S/he pulls from
either side.

âyitawatinâw *pl.* **âyitawatinâwa** (IPC) On each side there
are mountains.

âyitawihtin *pl.* **âyitawihtinwa** (VII) It fits on both sides.

âyitawinew (VTA) S/he holds her/him with both hands.

âyitawinam (VTI) S/he holds something with both
hands.

âyitawiniwew (VTA) S/he holds someone with both
hands.

âyitawinikew (VTI) S/he holds everything with both
hands.

âyitawiniskew *pl.* **âyitawiniskewak** (VAI) S/he uses
either of her/his arms; s/he is ambidextrous.

âyitawiniskewin *pl.* **âyitawiniskewina** (NI) The act of
being ambidextrous; having ambidexterity.

âyitawisin *pl.* **âyitawisinwak** (VAI) S/he is firmly in
place on both sides.

âyîtamow (VAI) It is stuck on tightly. *(Plains). Alt.*
âyâtamow *(Northern).*

âyîtastaw (VTI) S/he puts it on firmly.

âyîtahiwew (VTA) S/he places people very firmly.

âyîtascikew (VTI) S/he attaches something firmly.

C

cacâstapiwin *pl.* cacâstapiwina (NI) The act of being swift or moving quickly; swiftness. *(Plains)*. Alt. tastapayâwin *(Northern)*.

cacihkokanewin *pl.* cacihkokanewina (NI) Being angular in shape; angularity.

cacikwewin *pl.* cacikwewina (NI) The act of screeching. *(Northern)*

cacowihiwewin *pl.* cacowihiwewina (NI) The act of pre-emption.

cahcahkasinâsowin *pl.* cahcahkasinâsowina (NI) Being speckled.

cahcahkayo (NA) A black bird. *(Northern)*. Alt. cahcahkayowak *(Plains)*.

cahcahkayowak (NA) A black bird. *(Plains)*. Var. cahcahkaro. Alt. cahcahkayo *(Northern)*.

cahcahkinosew *pl.* cahcahkinosewak (NA) A grayling, i.e.: a speckled brook trout. *(Northern)*

cahcakiw *pl.* cahcakiwak (NA) A pelican.

cahkasinahwew (VTA) S/he makes a dot on her/him.
   cahkasinaham (VTI) S/he makes a dot on it.
   cahkasinahowew (VTA) S/he makes dots on people.
   cahkasinahikew (VTI) S/he makes dots.

cahkaskiswew (VTA) S/he is burning her/him with a flame.
   cahkaskisam (VTI) S/he burns it with a flame.
   cahkaskisowew (VTI) S/he burns things with a flame.

cahkatahikew *pl.* cahkatahikewak (VAI) S/he trips and falls.

cahkatawew (VTA) S/he pecks at her/him with her/his beak.
   cahkataham (VTI) S/he pecks at it with her/his beak.
   cahkatahowew (VTA) S/he pecks at someone with her/his beak.
   cahkatahikew (VTI) S/he pecks at things with her/his beak.

cahkatayeskawew (VTA) S/he dug her/his spur on the horse's side.
   cahkatayeskam (VTI) S/he spurs something.
   cahkatayeskâkew (VTA) S/he spurs someone.
   cahkatayeskâcikew (VTI) S/he spurs everything.

cahkatayeskâcikan *pl.* cahkatayeskâcikana (NI) A spur.

cahkâpawew (VTA) S/he poked her/his eye.
   cahkâpaham (VTI) S/he pokes its eye.
   cahkâpahowew (VTA) S/he pokes someone's eye.
   cahkâpahikew (VTI) S/he pokes peoples' eyes.

cahkâpicin *pl.* cahkâpicinwak (VTA) A branch poked her/his eye.

cahkâs (NI) Ice cream *(slang)*. Var. miskwamew manahikan *(literal)*.

cahkâskopayihew (VTA) S/he suspends her/him in the air on a see-saw.
   cahkâskopayitâw (VTI) S/he suspends it up in the air.
   cahkâskopayihowew (VTA) S/he suspends people.
   cahkâskopayihikew (VTI) S/he suspends things.

cahkâskopayiw *pl.* cahkâskopayiwa *or* cahkâskopayiwak (VII) *or* (VAI) It *or* s/he is suspended on air on a see-saw; it *or* s/he is suspended in the air.

cahkâstenikâkan *pl.* cahkâstenikâkana (NI) A spotlight.

cahkâstenikew *pl.* cahkâstenikewakak (VAI) Her/his lights are brightly shining.

cahkâstew *pl.* cahkâstewa (VII) There is sun shining or the light is shining brightly.

cahkâsteyâw *pl.* cahkâsteyâwa (VII) It is shimmery.

cahkâyowew *pl.* cahkâyowewak (VAI) Her/his tail is up in the air.

cahkicin *pl.* cahkicinwak (VAI) S/he got poked with a sharp object.

cahkipases *pl.* cahkipasesak (NA) A grey goose.

cahkipehikan *pl.* cahkipehikana (NI) A dot or Cree syllablic consonant.

cahkipehikew (VTA) S/he writes or makes signs, marks, dots or diagrams; s/he writes syllabics.
   cahkipeham (VTI) S/he makes marks on it.
   cahkipehowew (VTA) S/he makes marks on people.
   cahkipehikew (VTI) S/he makes marks on things.

cahkipehikewin *pl.* cahkipehikewina (NI) The act of making dots.

cahkisehikanasiniy *pl.* cahkisehikanasiniya (NI) A type of lighter used to spark a fire, i.e.: a flintstone. *(Plains)*. Alt. saskihcikan *(Northern)*.

cakâsiw *pl.* cakâsiwak (VAI) The sun is shining in her/his eyes. *(Northern)*. Alt. sîwâsiw *(Plains)*.

cakek *pl.* cakekak (NA) A coot; a mudhen.

camohkaham *pl.* camohkahamwak (VAI) S/he makes a loud splash, i.e.: a beaver with its tail.

camohkahikew *pl.* camohkahikewak (VAI) S/he is making a loud splashing sound.

canawiw *pl.* canawiwak (VAI) S/he is rushed for time; busy.

capasis (IPC) A little bit lower or below.

cayoskawew (VTA) S/he is taller than her/him. *(Plains)*. Alt. pasciskawew *(Northern)*.
   cayoskam (VTI) S/he is taller than it.
   cayoskâkew (VTA) S/he is taller than someone.
   cayoskâcikew (VTI) S/he is taller than everything.

câhcâhmew *pl.* câhcâhmewak (VAI) S/he sneezes because of sneezing powder or pepper.

câhcâhmohew (VTA) S/he makes her/him sneeze with something, i.e.: sneezing powder or pepper.

17

câhcâhmohsam (VTI) S/he fills the place with sneezing powder or pepper.

câhcâhmohiwew (VTA) S/he makes people sneeze with something.

câhcâhmohsikew (VTI) S/he burns sneezing powder or pepper.

câhcâhmohik *pl.* **câhcâhmohikak** (VTA) It makes her/him sneeze.

câhcâhmosikan *pl.* **câhcâhmosikana** (NI) A sneezing powder.

câhcâhmowin *pl.* **cahcahmowina** (NI) The act of sneezing because of sneezing powder or pepper.

câhkâmatinaw *pl.* **câhkâmatinawa** (VII) It is a steep, rugged mountain.

câhcâmowin *pl.* **câhcâmowina** (NI) The act of being made to sneeze. *(Plains). Alt.* **ayeyimowin** *(Northern).*

câhkipayiw *pl.* **câhkipayiwa** *or* **câhkipayiwak** (VII) *or* (VAI) It *or* s/he protrudes upwards, i.e.: a boil.

câstapiw *pl.* **câstapiwak** (VAI) S/he is very quick.

câstapiwaskawîwin *pl.* **câstapiwaskawîwina** (NI) The act of being nimble or very fast. *(Plains). Alt.* **tâstapwaskawewin** *(Northern).*

câstapiwin *pl.* **câstapiwina** (NI) The act of being quick; being sleight or having dexterity. *(Plains). Alt.* **tâstapiwin** *(Northern).*

câstapowew *pl.* **câstapowewak** (VAI) S/he talks quickly; s/he has fast speech.

cestahaskosiwâkan *pl.* **cestahaskosiwâkana** (NI) A pitch fork.

cestahaskwasiwewin *pl.* **cestahaskwasiwewina** (NI) The act of crucifying; crucification.

cestahaskwâsiw *pl.* **cestahaskwâsiwak** (VAI) S/he is nailed onto something.

cestahaskwâtew (VTA) S/he speared her/him onto something.

  cestahaskwâtam (VTI) S/he spears it on.

  cestahaskwâsiwew (VTA) S/he spears someone.

  cestahaskwâcikew (VTI) S/he spears things on.

cestekaham (VTI) S/he pegs it into the ground. *(Plains). Alt.* **cistikaham** *(Northern).*

cestekahikew (VTI) S/he pegs it all around.

cestekahamwa (VTI) They peg it into the ground.

cikahkwewepahwew (VTA) S/he knocked her/him unconscious.

  cikahkwewepahowew (VTA) S/he knocks someone out.

  cikahkwewepahikew (VTA) S/he knocks people unconscious.

cikawâsisihew (VAI) S/he takes a few off.

  cikawâsisitâw (VAI) S/he makes it smaller in numbers.

cikawâsisihiwew (VAI) S/he makes people smaller in numbers.

cikawâsisicikew (VAI) S/he makes things smaller in numbers.

cikawâsisiwan *pl.* **cikawâsisiwanwa** (VII) It is only a few in number.

cikawâsisiwiw *pl.* **cikawâsisiwiwak** (VAI) S/he is of a smaller number, i.e.: few in number.

cikawâsiwâw (IPC) A few times.

cikâstehtin *pl.* **cikâstehtinwa** (VII) Its shadow can be seen; reflected (by rays of light).

cikâstenew (VTA) S/he casts her/his shadow across her/him.

  cikâstenam (VTI) S/he casts her/his shadow across something.

  cikâsteniwew (VTA) S/he casts her/his shadow across people.

  cikâstenikew (VAI) S/he casts shadows.

cikâstepayihcikewin *pl.* **cikâstepayihcikewina** (NI) The act of showing a panorama.

cikâstepayihiwewin *pl.* **cikâstepayihiwewina** (NI) The act of screening.

cikâstepekihtin *pl.* **cikâstepekihtinwa** (VII) Its reflection can be seen in the water.

cikâstepekisin *pl.* **cikâstepekisinwak** (VAI) Her/his reflection can be seen in the water.

cikâstesimew (VTA) S/he casts a shadow of her/him.

  cikâstetitâw (VTI) S/he casts a shadow of it.

  cikâstesimiwew (VTA) S/he casts shadows of someone.

  cikâstecikew (VTI) S/he casts shadows of things.

cikâstesimowin *pl.* **cikâstesimowina** (NI) The act of casting a shadow.

cikâstesin *pl.* **cikâstesinwak** (VAI) Her/his shadow can be seen.

cikâstesinowin *pl.* **cikâstesinowina** (NI) A shadow.

cikâsteskawew (VTA) S/he casts her/his shadow on her/him.

  cikâsteskam (VTI) S/he casts her/his shadow on it.

  cikâsteskakew (VTA) S/he casts her/his shadow on people.

  cikâsteskacikew (VTI) S/he casts shadows on things.

cikemâ (IPC) And so it happened.

cimahew (VTA) S/he plants it in the ground like a tree.

  cimatâw (VTI) S/he puts up a fence post or telephone pole.

  cimacikew (VTI) S/he plants things in the ground.

cimanaskwatohtak *pl.* **cimanaskwatohtakwa** (NI) A dried out tree with the top broken off.

cimasiw *pl.* **cimasiwak** (VAI) It is standing, i.e.: tree.

cimatew *pl.* **cimatewa** (VII) It is standing, i.e.: teepee.

cimâsin *pl.* **cimâsinwa** (VII) It is short.

cimâyos âpiscimôsos *pl.* **cimâyosak âpiscimôsosmak** (NA) A mule deer.

cimâyowew *pl.* **cimâyowewak** (VAI) S/he has a short tail.

cimicihcew *pl.* **cimicihcewak** (VAI) S/he has a short hand.

cimihkwew *pl.* **cimihkwewak** (VAI) S/he has a short face.

cimikâtew *pl.* **cimikâtewak** (VAI) S/he has short legs.

cimikwayawew *pl.* **cimikwayawewak** (VAI) Her/his neck is short.

cimipitew (VTA) S/he shortens it by pulling.
　cimipitam (VTI) S/he pulls it shorter.
　cimipicikew (VTI) S/he pulls things shorter.

cimisâwâtew (VTA) S/he makes it (animate) short by cutting.
　cimisâwâtam (VTI) S/he cuts it short.
　cimisâwâsowew (VTA) S/he cuts people short.
　cimisâwâcikew (VTI) S/he cuts things short.

cimisicesiw *pl.* **cimisicesiwak** (VAI) S/he has a little, short foot.

cimisihew (VTA) S/he makes them too short.
　cimisitâw (VTI) S/he makes it too short.
　cimisicikew (VTI) S/he makes things too short.

cimisisow *pl.* **cimisisowak** (VAI) S/he is of short stature.

cimisitew *pl.* **cimisitewak** (VAI) S/he has a large, short foot.

cimiyawesiw *pl.* **cimiyawesiwak** (VAI) S/he has a little, short body.

cimiyawew *pl.* **cimiyawewak** (VAI) S/he has a large, short body.

cipahikanis *pl.* **cipahikanisa** (NI) One minute.

ciscemâs *pl.* **ciscemâsak** (NA) A little pouch of tobacco.

cistahisîpwâkanis *pl.* **cistahisîpwâkanisa** (NI) A little table fork. *(Northern). Alt.* **cîscayisîpwâkanis** *(Plains).*

cistanihkwânân *pl.* **cistanihkwânâna** (NI) A lace for mocassins made from moosehide. *Alt.* **cîstanihkwanâniyâpiy** *(Plains),* **cîstanihkwânaniyapi** *(Northern).*

cistawesimew (VTA) S/he makes an echo when s/he dropped her/him.
　cistawetitâw (VTI) S/he makes an echo when s/he dropped it.
　cistawesimew (VTA) S/he makes an echo when s/he dropped her/him.
　cistawecikew (VTI) S/he makes an echo when s/he drops things.

cistâwehtin *pl.* **cistâwehtinwa** (VII) It is creating echoes.

cistâwepayiw *pl.* **cistâwepayiwak** (VAI) The place is full of echoes. *(Northern). Alt.* **cistâwew** *(Plains).*

cistâwesin *pl.* **cistâwesinwak** (VAI) S/he is creating echoes.

cistâwew *pl.* **cistâwewak** (VAI) It echoes; the place is full of echoes. *(Plains). Alt.* **cistâwepayiw** *(Northern).*

cistâweyâw (VII) The place is full of echoes.

cistemâw *pl.* **cistemâwak** (NA) A large amount of tobacco.

cistikaham (VTI) S/he pegs it into the ground. *(Northern). Alt.* **cestekaham** *(Plains).*
　cistikahikew (VTI) S/he pegs it all around.

cistipitew (VTA) S/he scratched her/him with her/his nails.
　cistipitam (VTI) S/he scratches it with her/his nails.
　cistipisiwew (VTA) S/he scratches someone with her/his nails.
　cistipicikew (VTI) S/he scratches some things with her/his nails.

ciwepayiw *pl.* **ciwepayiwak** (VAI) S/he or it makes an echoing sound.

ciwew (NI) State of echoing.

cî (IPC) Question marker.

cîcikwâyiwew *pl.* **cîcikwâyiwewak** (VAI) It has a hairless tail.

cîcîkîniw (VTA) S/he scratched her/him when s/he was itchy.
　cîcîkînam (VTI) S/he scratches it.
　cîcîkîniwew (VTA) S/he scratches someone.
　cîcîkînikew (VTI) S/he scratches something.

cîcîkîwin *pl.* **cîcîkîwina** (NI) The act of scratching an itch.

cîhcîkipitew (VTA) S/he scratched her/him briefly.
　cîhcîkipitam (VTI) S/he scratches it briefly.
　cîhcîkipisiwew (VTA) S/he scratches someone.
　cîhcîkipicikew (VTI) S/he scratches others.

cîhcîkîw *pl.* **cîhcîkîwak** (VTA) S/he scratches her/his itch.

cîhcîpipayiw *pl.* **cîhcîpipayiwak** (VAI) S/he twitches.

cîhcîpitehewin *pl.* **cîhcîpitehewina** (NI) The act of palpitation.

cîhkeyihtam *pl.* **cîhkeyihtamwak** (VAI) S/he is happy with it.

cîhkeyihtamowin *pl.* **cîhkeyihtamowina** (NI) Enjoyment or happiness.

cîhkeyihtâkosiw *pl.* **cîhkeyihtâkosiwak** (VTA) People are happy with her/him.

cîhkeyihtâkosiwin *pl.* **cîhkeyihtâkosiwina** (NI) Being in the good books of everyone.

cîhkeyihtâkwan *pl.* **cîhkeyihtâkwanwa** (VTI) People are happy with it.

cîhkeyimew (VTA) S/he is happy with her/him.
　cîhkeyitam (VAI) S/he is happy.
　cîhkeyimiwew (VTA) S/he is happy with someone.
　cîhkeyicikew (VTI) S/he is happy about something.

cîkahikan *pl.* **cîkahikana** (NI) An axe.

19

cîkahikanâhtik *pl.* **cîkahikanâhtikwa** (NI) An axe handle.

cîkahtawâyâhk (IPC) Adjacency.

cîkahwew (VTA) S/he chopped her/him with an axe.
  cîkaham (VTI) S/he chops it.
  cîkahowew (VTA) S/he chops someone.
  cîkahikew (VTI) S/he chops something.

cîkakâm (IPC) Close to shore.

cîkaskamik (IPC) Close to the ground.

cîkaskowew (VTA) S/he follows her/him closely. *(Plains). Alt.* **kanoskawew** *(Northern).*
  cîkaskam (VTI) S/he follows it closely.
  cîkaskew (VTA) S/he follows someone closely.
  cîkascikew (VTI) S/he follows something.

cîkayihk (IPC) Closer to the edge.

cîkâhtaw (IPC) Pretty close to; adjacent; approximate.

cîkâyâw *pl.* **cîkâyâwak** (VAI) S/he is thought to be nearby. *(Plains). Alt.* **pesweyihtakosiw** *(Northern).*

cîki (IPC) Near.

cîkinâhk *pl.* **cîkinâhkwak** (NA) A nit.

cîkinikân (IPC) Anterior; real close to the front. *(Northern)*

cîkipek (IPC) Close to water.

cîkistikwân (IPC) Close to the head.

cîpacistahwew (VTA) S/he pierces her/him through with a spear.
  cîpacistaham (VTI) S/he pierces it through with a spear.
  cîpacistahowew (VTA) S/he pierces someone through with a spear.
  cîpacistahikew (VTI) S/he pierces things through with a spear.

cîpatâskwahikan *pl.* **cîpatâskwahikana** (NI) Something sharp used to skewer meat to cook over a campfire.

cîpay *pl.* **cîpayak** (NA) A ghost.

cîpay kîsikâw *or* **cîpay tipiskâw** (NI) Halloween.

cîpayah ka nimihitotwâw (NA) The ghosts dancing in the skies, i.e.: Aurora Borealis. *(Northern). Alt.* **kânîmihitocik** *(Plains).*

cîpayikamik *pl.* **cîpayikamikwa** (NI) A ghost house or a haunted house.

cîpayiwat *pl.* **cîpayiwata** (NI) A ghost bag.

cîposiw *pl.* **cîposiwak** (VAI) S/he is pointed.

cîpwaskisiw *pl.* **cîpwaskisiwak** (VAI) It has grown pointed.

cîpwaskitew *pl.* **cîpwaskitewa** (VII) It is standing pointed, i.e.: teepee.

cîpwâw *pl.* **cîpwâwa** (VII) It has a point.

cîsawatew (VTI) S/he slices them to pieces.
  cîsawatam (VTA) S/he slices it to pieces.
  cîsawacikew (VTI) S/he slices things to pieces.

cîscayisîpwâkanis (NI) A small table fork; a salad fork. *(Plains). Alt.* **cîstahitîpwâkanis** *(Northern).*

cîscayisîpwâkanis *pl.* **cîscayisîpwâkanisa** (NI) A large table fork. *(Plains). Alt.* **cîstahitîpwâkan** *(Northern).*

cîsihew (VTA) S/he deceives her/him by pretending to be someone else; s/he fooled her/him; s/he misleads her/him.
  cîsitâw (VTI) S/he deceives it by pretending to be someone else.
  cîsihiwew (VTA) S/he deceives someone by pretending to be someone else.
  cîsicikew (VTA) S/he deceives everyone by pretending to be someone else.

cîsihiw *pl.* **cîsihiwak** (VAI) S/he is mistaken; mistaking one for someone else.

cîsihiwewin *pl.* **cîsihiwewina** (NI) A thing that deceives people.

cîsihkemiw *pl.* **cîsihkemiwak** (NA) One who lies to fool people.

cîsihowin *pl.* **cîsihowina** (NI) Being mistaken.

cîsimew (VTA) S/he deceived her/him or told a fib to her/him.
  cîsimiwew (VTA) S/he deceived someone by her/his talking.
  cîsicikew (VTA) S/he deceived people by her/his doing.

cîsimiwew *pl.* **cîsimiwewak** (NA) A teller of fibs.

cîsimiwewin *pl.* **cîsimiwewina** (NI) Delusion; error; deceptive talk; falsehood.

cîstahicîpwâkan *pl.* **cîstahicîpwâkana** (NI) A large table fork. *(Northern). Alt.* **cîscayisîpwâkanis** *(Plains).*

cîstahikan *pl.* **cîstahikana** (NI) An innoculation needle.

cîstahikâsiwin *pl.* **cîstahikâsiwina** (NI) The act of being injected.

cîstahitîpwâkan (NI) A large table fork. *(Northern). Alt.* **cîscayisîpwâkanis** *(Plains).*

cîstahitîpwâkanis (NI) A small table fork; a salad fork. *(Northern). Alt.* **cîscayisîpwâkanis** *(Plains).*

cîstahwew (VTA) S/he poked her/him with something sharp, i.e.: a needle.
  cîstaham (VTI) S/he pokes it with something sharp.
  cîstahowew (VTA) S/he pokes someone with something sharp.
  cîstahikew (VTI) S/he pokes things with something sharp.

cîstanihkwanâniyâpiy *pl.* **cîstanihkwanâniyâpiya** (NI) A lace for moccasins made from moosehide. *(Plains). Var.* **cistanihkwânân.** *Alt.* **cîstanihkwânaniyapi** *(Northern).*

cîstanihkwânaniyapi *pl.* **cistanihkwânaniyapa** (NI) A lace for moccasins made from moosehide. *(Northern). Var.* **cistanihkwânân.** *Alt.* **cîstanihkwanâniyâpiy** *(Plains).*

cîstanikwanâtew (VTA) S/he puts laces on her/his moccasins for her/him.

20

cîstanikwanâtam (VTI) S/he puts laces on moccasins.

cîstanikwanâsiwew (VTI) S/he puts laces on things.

cîstanikwanâcikew (VTA) S/he laces mocassins.

cîstaskwan *pl.* **cîstaskwana** (NI) A spear. *(Northern). Alt.* **tahkahcikan** *(Plains).*

cîstâpâniyâpey *pl.* **cîstâpâniyâpeya** (NI) A form of rope to lace up a toboggan. *(Northern)*

cîstâskwânostikwân *pl.* **cîstâskwânostikwâna** (NI) A spearhead. *(Northern). Alt.* **tahkahcikakanistikwân** *(Plains).*

cîstekahikan *pl.* **cîstekahikana** (NI) A teepee peg. *(Plains). Alt.* **cîstîkahikan** *(Northern).*

cîstiniwewin *pl.* **cîstiniwewina** (NI) Being mauled; being lacerated or scratched.

cîstîkahikan *pl.* **cîstîkahikana** (NI) A teepee peg. *(Northern). Alt.* **cîstekahikan** *(Plains).*

cîstnew (VTA) S/he pinched her/him with her/his nail.

cîstnam (VTI) S/he pinches it with her/his nails.

cîstniwew (VTA) S/he pinches people with her/his nails.

cîstnikew (VTI) S/he pinches things with her/his nails.

cohkanâpisîs *pl.* **cohkanâpisîsak** (NA) An insect called the dragonfly; a Cree slang word for "helicopter." *(Northern). Alt.* **cowikanâpisîs** *(Plains).*

cowehkahtew *pl.* **cowehkahtewa** (VII) It sizzles while cooking.

cowehkocin *pl.* **cowehkocinwak** (VAI) It makes a sizzling or whistling sound like a spinning top.

coweskihtew *pl.* **coweskihtewak** (VAI) Her/his ears are ringing.

cowikanâpisîs *pl.* **cowikanâpisîsak** (NA) An insect called the dragonfly; a Cree slang word for "helicopter". *(Plains). Alt.* **cohkanâpisîs** *(Northern).*

ehâ (IPC) Yes. *(Plains). Alt.* **îhi** *(Northern).*

ehâpihtawakimiht pîsim (IPC) The middle of the month.

ehispayik *pl.* **ehispayikwa** (IPC) Used as a indication of time: "in a week's time." *(Plains). Alt.* **ihispayik** *(Northern).*

ekosesa (IPC) A story telling expression: "and so it was, once upon a time". *(Plains). Alt.* **ekwahîsa** *(Northern).*

ekosi (IPC) So, that's it.

ekosi mâka (IPC) Well, that's it.

ekosi pita (IPC) That's it for now.

ekosiyisi (IPC) Like that.

ekospi (IPC) In the past; or at that time.

ekwa (IPC) And; now; let's go now.

ekwa kiya (short question) In the sense of what are you going to do? "And what about you?"

ekwahîsa (IPC) A story telling expression: "and so it was, once upon a time". *(Northern). Alt.* **ekosesa** *(Plains).*

ekwayâc (IPC) For the first time; only then. *(Plains). Alt.* **ekwayâk** *(Northern).*

ekwayâk (IPC) For the first time; only then. *(Northern). Alt.* **ekwayâc** *(Plains).*

emâtakimiht pîsim (IPC) The start of the month or the beginning of the month.

emekwâpimatisit (IPC) While s/he was alive; when she was living.

emestakimiht pîsim (IPC) The end of the month.

emihkwân *pl.* **emihkwânak** (NA) A big spoon.

emihkwânis *pl.* **emihkwânisak** (NA) A small spoon; a teaspoon.

esa (IPC) An expression used when someone is starting to tell a story.

esâwa (IPC) And so it went.

esis *pl.* **esisak** (NA) A clam; an oyster.

espayik (IPC) That is how it was.

etikwe (IPC) Supposingly; probably; perhaps; maybe.

eyik *pl.* **eyikosak** (NA) An ant. *Var.* **eyikos; ayikos; iyikos.**

23

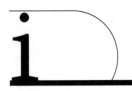

ihispayik *pl.* **ihispayikwa** (IPC) Used as a indication of time: "in a week's time." *(Northern). Alt.* **ehispayik** *(Plains).*

ihkahipewin *pl.* **ihkahipewina** (NI) The act of bailing water.

ihkapaswa (NI) A fireweed plant.

ihkwa *pl.* **ihkwak** (NA) A louse.

ihtateyihcikewin *pl.* **ihtateyihcikewina** (NI) The act of expecting something.

isâstâw *pl.* **isâstâwa** (VTI) That is how s/he puts or organizes it.

isâyâhiwewin *pl.* **isâyâhiwewina** (NI) The act of characterising.

isâyâwin *pl.* **isâyâwina** (NI) Character.

isi (IPC) An expression used when giving a direction and then pointing the way.

isicikâtowin *pl.* **isicikâtowina** (NI) The act of business affairs.

isihcikew *pl.* **isihcikewak** (VAI) S/he makes a big feast or banquet; s/he throws a big party.

isihcikewin *pl.* **isihcikewina** (NI) A large banquet; a resource.

isihew (VTA) S/he makes her/him that way.
> **isitâw** (VTI) S/he makes it that way.
> **isihiwew** (VTA) That is how s/he makes them.
> **isicikew** (VTI) That is how s/he makes things.

isikisikâw (IPC) An expression indicating the weather: "the weather is like…". *(Northern). Alt.* **isiwepan** *(Plains)*

isiniskestakew *pl.* **isiniskestakewak** (VAI) S/he extends her/his hands. *(Plains). Alt.* **awicicew** *(Northern).*

isiniskestawew (VTA) S/he extends her/his hand to her/him. *(Plains). Alt.* **awicicestawew** *(Northern).*
> **isiniskestatam** (VTA) S/he extends her/his hand to it.
> **isiniskestatâkew** (VTA) S/he extends her/his hand to everybody or anybody.

isiswehtin *pl.* **isiswehtinwa** (VII) It scatters about into pieces. *(Plains). Var.* **siswehtin** *(Northern). Alt.* **saswetin** *(Plains).*

isiswesin *pl.* **isiswesinwak** (VAI) It scatters about into pieces. *(Plains). Alt.* **saswesin** *(Northern).*

isiwepan (IPC) An expression indicating the weather: "the weather is like….". *(Plains). Alt.* **isikisikâw** *(Northern).*

isiyihkâsiw *pl.* **isiyihkâsiwak** (VAI) S/he is called or named.

isiyikâtew *pl.* **isiyikâtewa** (VII) It is called.

iskew *pl.* **iskewa** (VTI) S/he breaks up the beaver lodges.

iskipew *pl.* **iskipewa** (NI) High water; a flood.

iskoces *pl.* **iskocesa** (NI) A piece of red hot charcoal, i.e.: an ember.

iskonikan *pl.* **iskonikana** (NI) Something that is held for another day; a reservation.

iskopayihcikan *pl.* **iskopayihcikana** (NI) The remainder; leftovers.

iskopayiwin *pl.* **iskopayiwina** (NI) Being limited.

iskosihcikewin *pl.* **iskosihcikewina** (NI) The act of etching or outlining.

iskotew *pl.* **iskotewa** (NI) A fire.

iskotewâpoy *pl.* **iskotewâpoya** (NI) One type of liquor or "fire water", i.e.: whiskey.

iskotewitâpân *pl.* **iskotewitâpânak** (NA) A train or locomotive. *(Plains). Alt.* **pîwâpiskomeskanaw** *(Northern).*

iskotewôsih *pl.* **iskotewôsiha** (NI) A steamer or "fire boat."

iskoyikomiewâyâwin *pl.* **iskoyikomiewâyâwina** (NI) Having sniffles. *(Northern). Alt.* **sîskawakomewewin** *(Plains).*

iskwahtakâhk (IPC) At the treeline.

iskwanakwepson *pl.* **iskwanakwepsona** (NI) An armband.

iskwâhtem *pl.* **iskwâhtema** (NI) A door.

iskwâpohkahcikan *pl.* **iskwâpohkahcikana** (NI) A dreg. *(Northern). Alt.* **sîkawâcowasikan** *(Plains).*

iskwâskisew *pl.* **iskwâskisewa** (NI) A piece of charcoal.

iskwesis *pl.* **iskwesisak** (NA) A girl.

iskwesisihkân (NA) Barley.

iskwew *pl.* **iskwewak** (NA) A woman.

iskwewowin (NA) Being a woman; womanhood.

iskweyânihk (IPC) At the end; or worse.

ispahâkeyimowin *pl.* **ispahâkeyimowina** (NI) The act of emphasising; emphasis; the act of relying on an authority or someone's help; quotation.

ispakehamowin *pl.* **ispakehamowina** (NI) The act of soaring.

ispatinâw *pl.* **ispatinâwa** (NI) A high hill.

ispâw *pl.* **ispâwa** (VII) It is high.

ispimeskamik (IPC) Aloft.

ispimihk (IPC) Up.

ispimihkitakoh (IPC) Upstairs.

ispimihkitapowin (NI) Looking upwards.

ispî (IPC) When (not used as an interrogative).

ispîhci (IPC) Than.

ispîhcipîsâkwahk (IPC) At capacity.

itahtopiponew *pl.* **itahtopiponewak** (VAI) S/he is so many winters old.

itahtwayak (IPC) At each place; a number of places.

25

itahtwâw (IPC) Each time; every time.

itakihtew *pl.* **itakihtewa** (VII) It costs [i.e.: $10.00].

itakisiw *pl.* **itakisiwak** (VAI) S/he costs [i.e.: $10.00].

itamahcihiw *pl.* **itamahcihiwak** (VAI) S/he feels.

itamahcihiwin *pl.* **itamahcihiwina** (NI) How someone is feeling; health.

itâhkômiw *pl.* **itâhkômiwak** (VAI) S/he is kin with or related to.

itâkamascikan *pl.* **itâkamascikana** (NI) A distilled liquid.

itâmiyaw *pl.* **itâmiyawa** (NI) One internal organ.

itâmpek (IPC) In an abyss.

itâtisiwin *pl.* **itâtisiwina** (NI) Having a certain behaviour, i.e.: demeanour.

itehikewin *pl.* **itehikewina** (NI) The act of stirring.

iteyihtamiwin *pl.* **iteyihtamiwina** (NI) The way someone thinks; whim.

itohtahew *pl.* **itohtahewak** (VTA) S/he takes him some place.

itohtâw *pl.* **itohtâwa** (VTI) S/he takes it over there.

itôcikasiw *pl.* **itôcikasiwak** (VAI) It was done to her/him. *(Northern). Alt.* **itôtawâw** *(Plains).*

itôtam *pl.* **itôtamwak** (VAI) S/he does it; s/he makes it.

itôtam (VTI) S/he does it.

itôtâkew (VTI) S/he does it to everybody.

itôtamakewin *pl.* **itôtamakewina** (NI) The act of doing it for others.

itôtamâkew (VTA) S/he does it for others.

itôtamâmawew (VTA) S/he does it for her/him.

itôtawâw *pl.* **itôtawâwak** (VAI) It was done to her/him. *(Plains). Alt.* **itôcikasiw** *(Northern).*

itôtawew *pl.* **itôtawewak** (VTA) S/he does it to her/him.

itwahikâkan *pl.* **itwahikâkana** (NI) A pointer.

itwahwew (VTA) S/he points to her/him.

itwaham (VTI) S/he points at it.

itwahowew (VTA) S/he points at someone.

itwahikew (VTI) S/he points somewhere.

iyâpewimôswa *pl.* **iyâpewimôswak** (NA) A bull moose. *Alt.* yapew *(Northern).*

iyikawiskâw *pl.* **iyikawiskâwa** (NI) A sandy prairie. *(Plains). Alt.* **yekâwimaskotew** *(Northern).*

iyikopiwan (NI) A mist. *(Plains). Alt.* **kaskawahkamin** *(Northern).*

iyikopiwipîsim (NI) November; the frosty moon or month.

iyikos *pl.* **iyikosak** (NA) An ant. *Var.* **ayikos; eyik; ikos; eyikos; iyikos.**

iyikowîsti (NI) An ant hill. *(Plains). Alt.* **ayikowisti** *(Northern).*

iyikwatin *pl.* **iyikwatinwa** (VII) It is full of frost.

iyinikinosew *pl.* **iyinikinosewak** (NA) A pike or jackfish.

iyinimin *pl.* **iyinimina** (NI) A high blueberry. *(Plains). Alt.* **niskimin** *(Northern).*

iyinisihew (VTA) S/he makes her/him in a smart manner.

iyinisitâw (VTI) S/he makes it cleverly.

iyinisihiwew (VTA) S/he makes them smartly.

iyinisihcikew (VTI) S/he makes everything smartly.

iyinisikahtew (VTA) S/he imparts wisdom to her/him.

iyinisikatam (VTI) S/he imparts wisdom to it.

iyinisikasiwew (VTA) S/he imparts wisdom to them.

iyinisikacikew (VTI) S/he imparts wisdom to everything.

iyinisip *pl.* **iyinisipak** (NA) A type of mallard; a drake. *(Plains and Northern variant). Alt.* **wihpitwânsip** *(Northern).*

iyinisiw *pl.* **iyinisiwak** (VAI) S/he is wise; s/he is intelligent.

iyinisiwâyâwin *pl.* **iyinisiwâyâwina** (NI) Being brilliant; brilliancy.

iyinisowin *pl.* **iyinisowina** (NI) Wisdom; knowledge; astute; brilliance; intelligence or knowledgeable.

iyinitoyisihcikewin *pl.* **iyinitoyisihcikewina** (NI) Being handmade. *(Plains). Alt.* **moscôsehcikewin** *(Northern).*

iyipâcihew (VTA) S/he dirties her/him.

iyipâcitâw (VTI) S/he dirties it.

iyipâcihiwew (VTA) S/he dirties everyone.

iyipâcicikew (VTI) S/he dirties everything.

iyipâtan *pl.* **iyipâtanwa** (VII) It is dirty.

iyipâteyimew (VTA) S/he finds her/him dirty.

iyipâteyihtam (VTI) S/he finds it dirty.

iyipâteyimiwew (VTA) S/he finds them dirty.

iyipâteyicikew (VTI) S/he makes things dirty.

iyipâtinew (VTI) S/he gets her/him dirty with her/his hands.

iyipâtinam (VTI) S/he gets it dirty with her/his hands.

iyipâtiniwew (VTA) S/he gets everyone dirty with her/his hands.

iyipâtinikew (VTI) S/he gets everything dirty with her/his hands.

iyipâtiskawew (VTA) S/he tramps mud or dirt on her/him and makes her/him dirty or unclean.

iyipâtiskam (VTI) S/he makes it muddy with her/his feet.

iyipâtiskâkew (VTA) S/he makes everyone muddy.

iyipâtiskâcikew (VTI) S/he makes mud marks everywhere.

iyisâc (IPC) Reluctant.

iyitomeskanaw *pl.* **iyitomeskanawa** (NI) A road that forks off the main road, i.e.: a secondary road. *(Plains). Alt.* **naskweskanaw** *(Northern).*

iyiwahikan *pl.* **iyiwahikanak** (NA) A piece of dried meat (pounded).

iyiwahikew *pl.* **iyiwahikewa** (VTI) S/he is pounding the meat.

26

iyiwahwew (VTA) S/he pounds her/him.
  iyiwaham (VTI) S/he pounds it.
  iyiwahowew (VTA) S/he pounds everyone.
  iyiwahikew (VTI) S/he pounds dry meat.
iyiwanisihisiw *pl.* **iyiwanisihisiwak** (VAI) S/he fasts.

iyiwanisihisohew (VTA) S/he makes her/him fast.
  iyiwanisihisohiwew (VTA) S/he makes people fast.
iyiwanisihisowin *pl.* **iyiwanisihisowina** (NI) The act of fasting.
iyiwatew *pl.* **iyiwatewak** (VAI) Her/his stomach is empty.

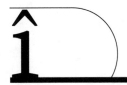

î

îhi (IPC) Yes. *(Northern). Alt.* **ehâ** *(Plains).*

înîwiw *pl.* înîwiwak (VAI) Her/his sore is healed.
(Plains). Alt. **kîkîw** *(Northern).*

îwahikanihkew *pl.* îwahikanihkewak (VAI) S/he mashes
dry meat.

îyâyaw (VAI) S/he would rather do something else.

îyehitowin *pl.* îyehitowina (NI) The act of creating
enthusiasm among people.

îyihkos *pl.* îyihkosak (NA) A tonsil.

îyihkwa *pl.* îyihkwak (NA) A gland.

îyikatehtew *pl.* îyikatehtewak (VAI) S/he walks away.

îyinisiwâyâwin *pl.* îyinisiwâyâwina (NI) Being spiffy.

îyinisiwin *pl.* îyinisiwina (NI) Intelligence; wisdom;
knowledgeable; brilliance.

îyintopihew *pl.* îyintopihewak (NA) A grouse.

îyipâtan (VII) It is dirty.

îyipisihcikewin *pl.* îyipisihcikewina (NI) The act of
setting something slantwise.

îyipiyâmatin (IPC) On a hillside.

k

kahcipitew (VTA) S/he grabs her/him.
  kahcipitam (VTI) S/he grabs it.
  kahcipisiwew (VTA) S/he grabs people.
  kahcipicikew (VTI) S/he grabs things.
kahcitinamawew *pl.* **kahcitinamawewak** (VTA) S/he enabled her/him.
kahkakow *pl.* **kahkakowak** (NA) A crow. *(Northern).*
kahkakow *pl.* **kahkakowak** (NA) A raven. *(Plains).*
kahkan *pl.* **kahkanwa** (NI) Something in good condition; not broken.
kahkapepayiw *pl.* **kahkapepayiwak** (VAI) S/he falls with legs splayed.
kahkekwask (IPC) Back and forth.
kahkewak *pl.* **kahkewakwak** (NA) A piece of dried meat.
  kahkewakwa (ob.).
kahkihtwam (IPC) Over again.
kahkisiw *pl.* **kahkisiwak** (VAI) S/he is whole; complete.
kahkiyaw (IPC) All; entire; the whole thing, i.e.: integral.
kahkiyaw kîkwây (IPC) All of everything.
kahkiyipa nawac (IPC) Frequently.
kahkominakâk (NI) Pepper. *(Northern).* Alt.
  papeskomina *(Plains).*
kahkweyihtam *pl.* **kahkweyihtamwak** (VAI) S/he is jealous.
kahkweyihtamowin *pl.* **kahkweyihtamowina** (NI) Jealousy.
kahkweyihtowak (VTA) They are jealous of each other.
kahkweyimew (VTA) S/he is jealous of her/him.
  kahkweyitam (VTA) S/he is a jealous type.
  kahkweyimiwew (VTA) S/he is jealous of people.
  kahkweyicikew (VTI) S/he is jealous of everything.
kahtapahew (VTI) S/he places things here and there, i.e.: staggered.
  kahtapastâw (VTI) S/he places things here and there, i.e.: staggered.
  kahtapahiwew (VTA) S/he places everyone here and there, i.e.: staggered.
  kahtapascikew (VTI) S/he places everything here and there, i.e.: staggered.
kahtapipayiw *pl.* **kahtapipayiwa** (VII) It moves out of place; it spreads apart.
kahtinikewin *pl.* **kahtinikewina** (NI) The act of attainment; derive; procurement; acquire. *(Northern).* Alt. **kahtitinikewin** *(Plains).*
kahtiskawew (VTA) S/he succeeds in kicking her/him.
  kahtiskam (VTI) S/he succeeds in kicking it.
  kahtiskâkew (VTA) S/he succeeds in kicking someone.

kahtiskâcikew (VTI) S/he succeeds in kicking something.
kahtitinikewin *pl.* **kahtitinikewina** (NI) The act of attainment; derive; procurement; acquire. *(Plains).* Alt. **kahtinikewin** *(Northern).*
kakasisiwat *pl.* **kakasisiwatawa** (NI) A Canada thistle. *(Northern).* Var. **kokaminakasiwit**.
kakayesâyamihâw *pl.* **kakayesâyamihâwak** (VAI) S/he pretends to pray.
kakayesihew (VTA) S/he cheats her/him; s/he deceives her/him.
  kakayesitam (VTI) S/he thinks it is dishonest.
  kakayesihiwew (VTA) S/he is deceptive; s/he is a cheater.
  kakayesicikew (VTI) S/he makes deception; s/he fools people; s/he believes in cheating; s/he is cheating.
kakayesihtwâw *pl.* **kakayesihtwâwak** (VAI) S/he is deceitful.
kakayesihtwâwin *pl.* **kakayesihtwâwina** (NI) The act of deceitful conduct.
kakayesipikiskwew *pl.* **kakayesipikiskwewak** (VAI) S/he speaks with a forked tongue; s/he speaks deceitfully.
kakayesitipahikan *pl.* **kakayesitipahikana** (NI) False measurement or false time.
kakayesitôtawew (VTA) S/he acts improperly by cheating her/him.
  kakayesitôtam (VTA) S/he cheats.
  kakayesitôtâkew (VTA) S/he cheats everyone.
kakayesiwin *pl.* **kakayesiwina** (NI) The act of cheating; deceit.
kakayesiwinâkosiw *pl.* **kakayesiwinâkosiwak** (NA) S/he appears or looks sneaky. *(Plains).* Alt. **kîmôcinâkosiw** *(Northern).*
kakayesiyihtâkosiw *pl.* **kakayesiyihtâkosiwak** (VAI) S/he is considered deceitful, misleading or dishonest.
kakayesiyimew (VTA) S/he suspects her/him to be a cheater; s/he deceives with her/his words.
  kakayesiyitam (VTI) S/he suspects it to be a cheater.
  kakayesiyimiwew (VTA) S/he suspects everyone to be cheaters.
  kakayesiyicikew (VTI) S/he suspects everything to be cheaters.
kakayesiyitâkwan *pl.* **kakayesiyitâkwanwa** (VII) A misleading thought, i.e.: "it sounds suspicious and may not be true."
kakâyawâtan *pl.* **kakâyawâtanwa** (VII) It is good because it is tough, durable or solid.
kakâyawâteyimew (VTA) S/he finds her/him a very good worker.
  kakâyawâteyitam (VTI) S/he thinks it is working well.
  kakâyawâteyimiwew (VTA) S/he finds everyone hard working.

31

kakâyawâteyicikew (VTI) S/he thinks everything is working well.

kakâyawâtisiw *pl.* **kakâyawâtisiwak** (VAI) S/he is an energetic person.

kakâyawâtoskew *pl.* **kakâyawâtoskewak** (VAI) S/he works well; s/he is a hard worker.

kakâyawicimew *pl.* **kakâyawicimewak** (VAI) S/he is a good rower.

kakâyawisiw *pl.* **kakâyawisiwak** (NA) An industrious worker *Var.* **okâyawisiw** (VAI); s/he consistently works hard. *(Plains). Alt.* **ayiwâkispihtisiw** *(Northern).*

kakâyawiyiniw *pl.* **kakâyawiyiniwak** (NA) An adventurous person who is always prepared to go.

kakâyawohtew *pl.* **kakâyawohtewak** (VAI) S/he is a good walker.

kakecisayawin *pl.* **kakecisayawina** (NI) Being vulnerable; vulnerability. *(Northern). Alt.* **wahkepinewin** *(Plains).*

kakepatisihkasostawew *pl.* **kakepatisihkasostawewak** (VTA) S/he behaves foolishly towards her/him.

kakepatisihkâsow *pl.* **kakepatisihkâsowak** (VAI) S/he acts crazily. *(Northern). Alt.* **mohcohkâsow** *(Plains).*

kakepatisihkewin *pl.* **kakepatisihkewina** (NI) The act of being foolish or acting like a clown.

kakepâcâyihtiw *pl.* **kakepâcâyihtiwak** (VAI) S/he acts foolishly; s/he does crazy things. *(Plains). Alt.* **kakepatisihkew** *(Northern).*

kakepâcihtwâwin *pl.* **kakepâcihtwâwina** (NI) Foolish conduct or behavior. *(Northern). Alt.* **kakepâtinikewin** *(Plains).*

kakepâteyimew (VTA) S/he finds her/him crazy.

kakepâteyitam (VTI) S/he thinks that it is foolish.

kakepâteyimiwew (VTA) S/he thinks that others are fools.

kakepâteyicikew (VTA) S/he thinks that everyone is a fool.

kakepâtinikewin *pl.* **kakepâtinikewina** (NI) Foolish conduct or behavior. *(Plains). Alt.* **kakepâcihtwâwin** *(Northern).*

kakepâtis *pl.* **kakepâtisak** (NA) A stupid person; a moron.

kakepâtisihkew *pl.* **kakepâtisihkewak** (VAI) S/he acts foolishly. *(Northern). Alt.* **kakepâcâyihtiw** *(Plains).*

kakepâtisiw *pl.* **kakepâtisiwak** (VAI) S/he is foolish.

kakeskimâwasiw *pl.* **kakeskimâwasiwak** (VTA) S/he counsels or advises children.

kakeskimew (VTA) S/he gives her/him advice.

kakeskimiwew (VTA) S/he gives advice; s/he preaches.

kakeskwew *pl.* **kakeskwewak** (VAI) S/he is hyperactive.

kakeskwewin *pl.* **kakeskwewina** (NI) Hyperactive.

kakeskwiwiyiniw *pl.* **kakeskwiwiyiniwak** (NA) A person acting in a hyperactive manner. *(Northern).*

kaketâwâtisiw *pl.* **kaketâwâtisiwak** (VAI) S/he is showing maturity.

kaketôkawew (VTA) S/he acts in deference to her/him; s/he is syncophantic; s/he asks for forgiveness.

kaketôkam (VTI) S/he acts in deference of it.

kaketôkâkew (VTA) S/he acts in deference of everyone.

kaketôkâcikew (VTI) S/he acts in deference of everything.

kakihcimow *pl.* **kakihcimowak** (VAI) S/he praises herself/himself; s/he is talkative, i.e.: a phrase usually used when referring to small children.

kakihcimowin *pl.* **kakihcimowina** (NI) The act of praising or adulating oneself.

kakihtâweyimew (VTA) S/he takes her/him as an adult because of her/his maturity.

kakihtâweyitam (VAI) S/he thinks like an adult.

kakihtâweyimiwew (VTA) S/he thinks of them as adults.

kakihtâweyihcikew (VTA) S/he thinks of others as adults.

kakwayakeyimew (VTA) S/he deeply hates her/him.

kakwayakeyitam (VTI) S/he deeply hates it.

kakwayakeyimiwew (VTA) S/he deeply hates everyone.

kakwayakeyicikew (VTI) S/he deeply hates everything.

kakwayakinawew (VTA) S/he sees her/him and finds her/him hideous.

kakwayakinam (VTI) S/he sees and finds it hideous.

kakwayakinakew (VTA) S/he sees and finds people hideous.

kakwâtakihisiw *pl.* **kakwâtakihisiwak** (VTA) S/he makes herself/himself suffer.

kakwâtakihtâwin *pl.* **kakwâtakihtâwina** (NI) The act of being distressed or suffering.

kakwâyakan *pl.* **kakwâyakanwa** (NI) Something that is abhorrent or loathsome.

kakwâyakâpamew (VTA) S/he sees her/him in a loathsome way, i.e.: in a dream or visually.

kakwâyakâpatam (VTI) S/he sees it in a loathsome way, i.e.: in a dream or visually.

kakwâyakâpamiwew (VTA) S/he sees everyone in a loathsome way, i.e.: a dream or visually.

kakwâyakâpacikew (VTI) S/he sees everything in a loathsome way or sight, i.e.: a dream or visually.

kakwâyakeyihtâkosowin *pl.* **kakwâyakeyihtâkosowina** (NI) Being hated greatly. *(Northern). Alt.* **pakwâtikosiwin** *(Plains).*

kakwâyakeyihtâkwan *pl.* **kakwâyakeyihtâkwanwa** (VII) It is greatly hated.

kakwâyakihtâkosiw *pl.* **kakwâyakihtâkosiwak** (VAI) Her/his singing sounds really terrible.

kakwâyakinew (VTA) S/he tickles her/him.
  kakwâyakinam (VTI) S/he tickles it.
  kakwâyakiniwew (VTA) S/he tickles someone.
  kakwâyakinikew (VTA) S/he tickles everyone.

kakwecihkemow *pl.* **kakwecihkemowak** (VAI) S/he asks; s/he inquires.

kakwecihkemowin *pl.* **kakwecihkemowina** (NI) The act of asking or inquiring.

kakwecikemiw *pl.* **kakwecikewmiwak** (VAI) S/he asks.

kakwecimew (VTA) S/he asks her/him.
  kakwecimiwew (VTA) S/he asks people.

kakwecisimew (VTA) S/he lies to her/him.
  kakwecisimiwew (VTA) S/he lies to everyone.
  kakwecisicihkemow (VAI) S/he lies all the time.

kakwespanâc (IPC) An expression meaning, "it is dangerous and must be handled carefully."

kakwespaneyihtâkosiw *pl.* **kakwespaneyihtâkosiwak** (VAI) S/he is considered dangerous by everyone.

kakwespaneyihtâkosiwin *pl.* **kakwespaneyihtâkosiwina** (NI) Being thought of as dangerous.

kakwespaneyihtâkwan *pl.* **kakwespaneyihtâkwanwa** (VII) It is thought of as dangerous.

kakwespaneyihtâkwanohk (IPC) In a dangerous place.

kakwespaneyimew (VTA) S/he is afraid of her/him and thinks of her/him as dangerous.
  kakwespaneyitam (VTI) S/he is afraid of it and thinks of it as dangerous.
  kakwespaneyimiwew (VTA) S/he is afraid of everyone and thinks of everyone as dangerous.
  kakwespaneyihcikew (VTI) S/he is afraid of things and thinks of everything as dangerous.

kakweyâhiwin *pl.* **kakweyâhiwina** (NI) The act of hurrying.

kakweyâhomakan *pl.* **kakweyâhomakanwa** (VII) It operates quickly.

kakweyâhow *pl.* **kakweyâhowak** (VAI) S/he hurries; s/he rushes.

kanawapokewin *pl.* **kanawapokewina** (NI) The act of keeping and guarding the house.

kanawastimwân *pl.* **kanawastimwânak** (NA) A fenced in place for keeping horses; a corral or paddock. **kanawastimwâna** (ob.).

kanawastimwew *pl.* **kanawastimwewak** (VTA) S/he keeps or guards horses.

kanawastimwewin *pl.* **kanawastimwewina** (NI) The act of keeping horses.

kanawâpahcikâkan *pl.* **kanawâpahcikâkana** (NI) An object that magnifies sight; magnifying glass.

kanawâpamew (VTA) S/he looks at her/him. *(Northern)*. *Alt.* **kitâpamew** *(Plains)*.
  kanawâpatam (VTI) S/he looks at it.
  kanawâpamiwew (VTA) S/he looks at people.
  kanawâpahcikew (VTI) S/he looks at things.

kanawâpâkan *pl.* **kanawâpâkana** (NI) A device for looking at far away things; a telescope.

kanawâpokew *pl.* **kanawâpokewak** (VAI) S/he keeps and guards the house.

kanaweyihtamawew (VTA) S/he retains it for safekeeping for her/him or for others.
  kanaweyihtam (VTI) S/he keeps it.
  kanaweyihtamâkew (VTA) S/he keeps it for someone.

kanaweyihtamâkewin *pl.* **kanaweyihtamâkewina** (NI) The act of safekeeping something for someone else.

kanaweyihtamâsiw *pl.* **kanaweyihtamâsiwak** (VTA) S/he keeps it for herself/himself.

kanaweyihtamâsowin *pl.* **kanaweyihtamâsowina** (NI) The act of keeping something for oneself.

kanaweyihtâkosowin *pl.* **kanaweyihtâkosowinak** (NA) The act of receiving divine care from God, i.e.: providence. **kanaweyihtâkosowina** (ob.).

kanaweyimâwasowin *pl.* **kanaweyimâwasowina** (NI) The act of babysitting.

kanaweyimew (VTA) S/he keeps or guards her/him; s/he takes care of her/him.
  kanaweyitam (VTI) S/he keeps or guards it; s/he looks after or tends it.
  kanaweyimiwew (VAI) S/he is a guard or keeper.
  kanaweyicikew (VTI) S/he keeps or guards things.

kanaweyimostoswew *pl.* **kanaweyimostoswewak** (VTA) S/he keeps or guards her/his cows.

kanaweyimowewin *pl.* **kanaweyimowewinak** (NI) The act of protecting someone. **kanaweyimowewina** (ob.).

kanaweyitamohew (VTA) S/he confides it to her/him for safekeeping.
  kanaweyitamotâw (VTI) S/he makes a safety device to keep it for her/him.
  kanaweyitamohiwew (VTA) S/he makes someone keep it for her/him.

kanawipisiskiwew *pl.* **kanawipisiskiwewak** (VTA) S/he keeps or tends the animals.

kanawipisiskiwikamik *pl.* **kanawipisiskiwikamikwa** (NI) An animal-keeping house; a barn.

kanawisimow *pl.* **kanawisimowak** (VAI) S/he has protection from a charm.

kanawisimowin *pl.* **kanawisimowina** (NI) Something that offers protection, i.e.: a bear claw or amulet.

kanawisimowiniwin *pl.* **kanawisimowiniwina** (NI) Protective charm.

33

kanawiskotawew *pl.* **kanawiskotawewak** (VTA) S/he is guarding against it, i.e.: fire warden in a forest.

kanawiwaskahikanew *pl.* **kanawiwaskahikanewak** (NA) A security guard or house guardian.

kanâcihcikan *pl.* **kanâcihcikana** (NI) A purgative, a laxative. *(Northern). Alt.* **sâposikan** *(Plains).*

kanâcihew (VTA) S/he cleans her/him.

　kanâcitâw (VTI) S/he cleans it.

　kanâcihiwew (VTA) S/he cleans someone.

　kanâcihcikew (VTI) S/he cleans something.

kanâcihiwin *pl.* **kanâcihiwina** (NI) The act of preening; spruce up.

kanâcihow *pl.* **kanâcihowak** (VAI) S/he is neat and tidy; s/he is neatly dressed, tidy. *(Plains). Alt.* **nahâwisiw** *(Northern).*

kanâcipimâtisiw *pl.* **kanâcipimâtisiwak** (VAI) S/he lives a clean life, i.e.: morally; virginal.

kanâcipimâtisiwin *pl.* **kanâcipimâtisiwina** (NI) The act of having purity of life.

kanâtahcâkwew *pl.* **kanâtahcâkwewak** (VAI) S/he has a clean or pure soul.

kanâtahcâkwewin *pl.* **kanâtahcâkwewinak** (NI) A pure soul or sinless.

kanâtan *pl.* **kanâtanwa** (VII) It is neat and clean.

kanâteyihtâkosiw *pl.* **kanâteyihtâkosiwak** (VAI) S/he is considered faultless.

kanâteyihtâkosiwin *pl.* **kanâteyihtâkosiwina** (NI) Considered faultless.

kanâteyihtâkwan *pl.* **kanâteyihtâkwanwa** (VII) It is considered faultless.

kanâteyimew (VTA) S/he considers her/him of faultless, pure, unblemished character.

　kanâteyitam (VTI) S/he considers it of faultless, pure character.

　kanâteyimiwew (VTA) S/he considers people of faultless, pure character.

　kanâteyicikew (VTI) S/he considers things of faultless, pure character.

kanâtisiwin *pl.* **kanâtisiwina** (NI) The act of being neat and clean; neatness.

kanâwâpamew (VTA) S/he is looking at her/him.

　kanâwâpatam (VTI) S/he is looking at something.

　kanâwâpacikew (VTI) S/he is looking at lots of things.

kanesihk (IPC) Each other; one another.

kani (IPC) In effect; indeed; wait a second; I just thought of it; that's right; also an expression of agreement.

kanoskawew (VTA) S/he follows her/him closely. *(Northern). Alt.* **cîkaskowew** *(Plains).*

　kanoskam (VTI) S/he follows it closely.

　kanoskew (VTA) S/he follows someone closely.

　kanoscikew (VTI) S/he follows something.

kapatehwew (VTI) S/he ladles fish from the pot.

kapateham (VTI) S/he ladles meat from the pot.

kapatehikew (VTI) S/he ladles food from the pot.

kapatenew (VTA) S/he pulls her/him ashore.

　kapatenam (VTI) S/he pulls it ashore; s/he takes it from water.

　kapateniwew (VTA) S/he brings people ashore.

　kapatenikew (VTI) S/he brings things ashore; s/he reels it in; s/he removes it from water.

kapatepitew (VTA) S/he pulls her/him into shore. *(Plains). Alt.* **seskipitew** *(Northern).*

　kapatepam (VTI) S/he pulls it to shore.

　kapatepewak (VTA) S/he pulls people to shore.

kapateskwew *pl.* **kapateskwewak** (VTA) S/he serves herself/himself from the cooking pot.

kapatetisahwew (VTA) S/he chases her/him out of the water.

　kapatetisahikew (VTA) S/he chases everyone out of the water.

kapatewepaham *pl.* **kapatewepaham** (VTI) S/he paddles her/his canoe into shore. *(Plains). Alt.* **seskaham** *(Northern).*

kapateyâskwahikan *pl.* **kapateyâskwahikana** (NI) A fishing gaff.

kapateyâskwahwew (VTA) S/he draws her/him out of the water with a gaft; s/he draws her/him out of the pot with a fork.

　kapateyâskwaham (VTI) S/he draws it out of the water or pot.

　kapateyâskwahikew (VTI) S/he draws something out of the water or pot.

kapâhotew *pl.* **kapâhotewa** (VII) It is on the shore, i.e.: driftwood.

kapâw *pl.* **kapâwak** (VAI) S/he arrives by boat or canoe; s/he disembarks. *(Plains). Alt.* **misakâw** *(Northern).*

kapâwin *pl.* **kapâwina** (NI) The act of disembarking; a landing, a dock; a portage.

kapâwin *pl.* **kapâwinak** (NA) A boat dock. *(Plains). Alt.* **onikewin** *(Northern).*

kapekîsik (IPC) All day.

kapesihiwewin *pl.* **kapesihiwewina** (NI) The act of providing accommodation.

kapesiw *pl.* **kapesiwak** (VAI) S/he camps for the night; s/he stays at a hotel.

kapesiwin *pl.* **kapesiwina** (NI) A camp; a resting spot; a campground.

kapesowinihkew *pl.* **kapesowinihkewak** (VAI) S/he prepares a place to camp.

kapesowinihkewin *pl.* **kapesowinihkewina** (NI) The act of preparing a campground.

kapetipisk (IPC) All night.

kasikanew *pl.* **kasikanewak** (VAI) S/he has stockings on.

34

kasispowihew (VTI) S/he keeps it in memory of the past.
kasispowitâw (VTI) S/he keeps stuff from the past for the future.
kasispowicikew (VTI) S/he brings us through the past to the future.
kaskacihtin *pl.* **kaskacihtinwa** (VII) It broke right off, i.e.: a hammer or axe handle. *(Northern). Alt.* **nâtwâtin** *(Plains).*
kaskahpicikan *pl.* **kaskahpicikana** (NI) A medicine bundle.
kaskahpitew (VTI) S/he bundles it up.
kaskahpicikew (VTI) S/he bundles things securely.
kaskahpitam (VTI) S/he bundles it up securely; s/he ties it securely.
kaskamocâyâwin *pl.* **kaskamocâyâwina** (NI) The state of personal inertia.
kaskamotâpahtew (VII) It is very smokey; poor visibility.
kaskamôtan (VII) It is airless.
kaskapowehikew *pl.* **kaskapowehikewa** (VTI) S/he seals up something or cans it. *(Northern). Alt.* **kaskâpiskahikew** *(Plains).*
kaskapowehsimew (VTA) S/he stored them in sealers. *(Northern). Alt.* **kaskâpiskawew** *(Plains).*
kaskapowehsitataw (VTI) S/he stored it in sealers.
kaskapowehsicikew (VTI) S/he stored everything in sealers.
kaskapowicikewin *pl.* **kaskapowicikewina** (NI) The act of sealing up something. *(Northern). Alt.* **kaskâpiskahikewin** *(Plains).*
kaskatin *pl.* **kaskatinwa** (VII) It freezes up.
kaskatinâw *pl.* **kaskatinâwa** (NI) A butte.
kaskatinowipîsim (NI) October; the freeze-up moon or month.
kaskawahkamin (NI) A mist. *(Northern). Alt.* **iyikopiwan** *(Plains).*
kaskawahkamin (VII) It is foggy. *(Plains). Alt.* **kaskawahkamiw** *(Northern)*
kaskawahkamiw (VII) It is foggy. *(Northern). Alt.* **kaskawahkamin** *(Plains).*
kaskawan (VII) There is a fog.
kaskawanipcotâw (VII) It is a misty rain.
kaskâpahtenikewin *pl.* **kaskâpahtenikewina** (NI) Making smoke, i.e.: a smudge.
kaskâpahtew *pl.* **kaskâpahtewa** (VII) It is smokey; (NI) smoke.
kaskâpasiw *pl.* **kaskâpasiwak** (VAI) S/he is engulfed in smoke.
kaskâpaswew (VTI) S/he smokes them, i.e.: fish.
kaskâpasam (VTI) S/he smokes it, i.e.: meat.
kaskâpasikew (VTI) S/he makes a smudge.

kaskâpiskahikan *pl.* **kaskâpiskahikana** (NI) Something stored in sealers.
kaskâpiskahikew *pl.* **kaskâpiskahikewa** (VTI) S/he seals up something or cans it. *(Plains). Alt.* **kaskapowehikew** *(Northern).*
kaskâpiskahikewin *pl.* **kaskâpiskahikewina** (NI) The act of sealing up something. *(Plains). Alt.* **kaskapowicikewin** *(Northern).*
kaskâpiskawâw *pl.* **kaskâpiskawâwak** (NA) Someone is sealed in. *(Plains). Alt.* **kaskâpowesin** *(Northern).*
kaskâpiskawew (VTA) S/he stored them in sealers. *(Plains). Alt.* **kaskapowehsimew** *(Northern).*
kaskâpiskatataw (VTI) S/he stored it in sealers.
kaskâpiskacikew (VTI) S/he stored everything in sealers.
kaskâpiskaham (VAI) S/he is canning.
kaskâpitesin *pl.* **kaskâpitesinwak** (VTA) S/he breaks her/his teeth in a fall.
kaskâpowesin *pl.* **kaskâpowesinwak** (NA) Someone is sealed in. *(Northern). Alt.* **kaskâpiskawâw** *(Plains).*
kaskewew *pl.* **kaskewewak** (VAI) S/he portages.
kaskewewin *pl.* **kaskewewinak** (NA) A portage trail. **kaskewewina** (ob.).
kaskeyihtamâyâwin *pl.* **kaskeyihtamâyâwina** (NI) Being lonesome; depression; languishing.
kaskeyihtamowin *pl.* **kaskeyihtamowina** (NI) Being filled with longing; yearn; bereavement; homesick.
kaskeyihtâkwan *pl.* **kaskeyihtâkwanwa** (VII) It feels lonely.
kaskeyimew (VTA) S/he is lonesome for her/him.
kaskeyitam (VTA) S/he is lonesome for it.
kaskeyimiwew (VTA) S/he is lonesome for someone.
kaskeyicikew (VTI) S/he is lonesome for everything.
kaskihcikewin *pl.* **kaskihcikewina** (NI) Being capable; capability. *(Northern). Alt.* **nakacihtâwin** *(Plains).*
kaskihew (VTA) S/he wins her/him over.
kaskitâw (VTI) S/he can do it.
kaskihiwew (VTA) S/he can win people over.
kaskicikew (VTI) S/he can get things done her/his way.
kaskihkahtew (VTI) It is cooked until tender.
kaskihkahsam (VTI) S/he cooks it until tender.
kaskihkahsikew (VTI) S/he cooks everything until tender.
kaskihkasiw *pl.* **kaskihkasiwak** (VAI) It is cooked until tender.
kaskihkocikan *pl.* **kaskihkocikana** (NI) A machine that cuts up tobacco plugs for use in a pipe.
kaskihkotew (VTI) S/he minces it up.
kaskihkotam (VTI) S/he minces it right up.
kaskihkocikew (VTI) S/he minces things up.

35

kaskihtakahikew (VTI) S/he locks everything up with a key.

kaskihtakaham (VTI) S/he locks it up with a key.

kaskihtakahwew *pl.* **kaskihtakahwewak** (VTA) S/he locks her/him up.

kaskihtamawew *pl.* **kaskihtamawewak** (VTA) S/he does a good deed for her/him.

kaskihtâwin *pl.* **kaskihtâwina** (NI) Having ability; authority; rights.

kaskikwâsiw (VAI) S/he sews or stitches.

kaskikwâtam (VTI) S/he sews it up.

kaskikwâsohiwew (VTA) S/he makes people sew.

kaskikwâcikew (VTI) S/he sews things up.

kaskikwâsonâpisk *pl.* **kaskikwasonâpiskwak** (NA) A thimble.

kaskikwâsowin *pl.* **kaskikwâsowina** (NI) The act of sewing.

kaskikwâsowiyiniw *pl.* **kaskikwâsowiyiniwak** (NA) A person who sews.

kaskikwâtam (VTA) S/he sews it.

kaskikwâmowew (VTA) S/he sews it for her/him.

kaskikwâtew *pl.* **kaskikwâtewa** (VII) It is sewn.

kaskikwepitew (VTA) S/he breaks her/his neck by wrestling.

kaskikwepitam (VTI) S/he breaks the neck of something.

kaskikwepitamowew (VTA) S/he breaks the neck for someone else.

kaskikwepicikew (VTA) S/he breaks necks.

kaskikwesin *pl.* **kaskikwesinwak** (VTA) S/he breaks her/his neck in a fall or by accident.

kaskinew (VTI) S/he breaks a little tree off.

kaskinam (VTI) S/he breaks off a twig or a branch.

kaskinikew (VTI) S/he breaks a bunch of twigs.

kaskipitonesin *pl.* **kaskipitonesinwak** (VTA) S/he breaks her/his arm in a fall.

kaskisâkâsihk (IPC) In heavy brush; brushy.

kaskitesiw *pl.* **kaskitesiwak** (VAI) S/he is black.

kaskitesowin *pl.* **kaskitesowina** (NI) Being black; blackness.

kaskitew (NI) Gunpowder.

kaskitewahikewin *pl.* **kaskitewahikewina** (NI) The act of making something black; blacking.

kaskitewastim *pl.* **kaskitewastimwak** (NA) A black dog or horse.

kaskitewaw *pl.* **kaskitewawa** (VII) It is black.

kaskitewihkwenew (VTA) S/he blackens her/his face.

kaskitewihkwenikew (VTA) S/he blackens peoples' faces.

kaskitewihkwew *pl.* **kaskitewihkwewak** (VAI) S/he is black faced.

kaskitewimihkwâw (IPC) It is dark purple in color, i.e.: mauve.

kaskitewistikwân *pl.* **kaskitewistikwânak** (NA) A black-haired person. **kaskitewistikwâna** (ob.).

kaskitewiyâs *pl.* **kaskitewiyâsak** (NA) A black-skinned person.

kaskitipiskâw (VII) It is a pitch dark night.

kaspakatotew *pl.* **kaspakatotewa** (VII) It is bone dry, i.e.: ground or soil.

kaspinew *pl.* **kaspinewa** (VTI) S/he breaks it with a crunchy noise.

katawasisin *pl.* **katawasisinwa** (VII) It looks beautiful, gorgeous.

katawasisiw *pl.* **katawasisiwak** (VAI) S/he is handsome or beautiful.

katikoniw *pl.* **katikoniwak** (VAI) S/he stays overnight, i.e.: a sojourn.

katohpinew *pl.* **katohpinewak** (VAI) S/he has a chronic sickness i.e.: tuberculosis. *(Northern)*

kawacihcewaciw *pl.* **kawacihcewaciwak** (VAI) S/he has cold hands.

kawacisitewaciw *pl.* **kawacisitewaciwak** (VAI) S/he has cold feet.

kawaciw *pl.* **kawaciwak** (VAI) S/he is cold.

kawahkatosiw *pl.* **kawahkatosiwak** (VAI) S/he can't stand up because s/he didn't eat enough.

kawahkatosohew (VTA) S/he starves her/him so much s/he can't stand up.

kawahkatosohiwew (VTA) S/he starves others till they can't stand up.

kawatimew *pl.* **kawatimewak** (VTA) S/he makes her/him cold.

kawatin *pl.* **kawatinwa** (VII) An expression indicating "it is cold."

kawawew *pl.* **kawawewak** (VTA) S/he knocks the tree or her/him or it down.

kawâsiw *pl.* **kawâsiwak** (VAI) S/he or it is blown down by the wind, i.e.: a tree blown down.

kawâstan *pl.* **kawâstanwa** (VII) It is blown down by the wind, i.e.: a house blown down.

kawepahwew (VTA) S/he punches her/him and knocks her/him down.

kawepaham (VTI) S/he punches it and knocks it down, as with a hammer.

kawepahikew (VTI) S/he punches things and knocks them down.

kawepahowew (VTA) S/he punches people and knocks them down, i.e.: with a fist.

kawihkwasiw *pl.* **kawihkwasiwak** (VAI) S/he falls asleep.

kawipayiw *pl.* **kawipayiwa** or **kawipayiwak** (VII) *or* (VAI) It *or* s/he falls down.

kawipitew (VTA) S/he pulls her/him and s/he falls down.

kawipitam (VTI) S/he pulls it and it falls down.

kawipisiwew (VTA) S/he pulls someone and they fall down.

kawipicikew (VTI) S/he pulls things and they fall down.

kawisimiw *pl.* **kawisimiwak** (VAI) S/he retires or goes to bed.

kawisimonahew (VTA) S/he puts her/him to bed.
kawisimonahiwew (VTA) S/he puts her/him to bed.
kawisimonahiwew *pl.* **kawisimonahiwewak** (VTA) S/he puts someone to bed.

kawisimowin *pl.* **kawisimowinak** (NA) The act of retiring or going to bed. **kawisimowina** (ob.).

kawisimôhew (VTA) S/he makes her/him go to bed or fall into bed.
kawisimôhiwew (VTA) S/he makes someone go to bed or fall into bed.

kawisiw *pl.* **kawisiwak** (VAI) It is rough to the touch.

kawiskosiw *pl.* **kawiskosiwak** (VAI) S/he collapses from the weight.

kawiskotew *pl.* **kawiskotewa** (VII) It collapses from the load.

kawôtinikewin *pl.* **kawôtinikewina** (NI) The act of retaking; subtract.

kayahte (IPC) Before, ere.

kayâs (IPC) Long time ago, once upon a time; it's been a long time.

kayâsâyiwan *pl.* **kayâsâyiwanwa** (VII) It is old, ancient.

kayâsâyiwiw (VII) It is aged, old, ancient.

kayâseskamik (IPC) A very, very long time ago; anciently.

kayesowin *pl.* **kayesowina** (NI) The act of doing something crooked; deceitful.

kâcikatew *pl.* **kâcikatewa** (VII) It is hidden.

kâcikâsiw *pl.* **kâcikâsiwak** (VAI) S/he is hidden; s/he is very well concealed.

kâcikewin *pl.* **kâcikewina** (NI) A hideaway; something hidden.

kâcitawew (VTI) S/he succeeds in hitting her/him.
kâcitaham (VTI) S/he succeeds in hitting it.
kâcitahikew (VTI) S/he succeeds in hitting everything.

kâcitinew (VTA) S/he catches her/him; s/he apprehends her/him; s/he arrests her/him.
kâcitiniwew (VTA) S/he catches someone.
kâcitinikew (VTI) S/he catches something.

kâkecihiwewin *pl.* **kâkecihiwewina** (NI) The act of consoling; the act of placating.

kâkecimew (VTA) S/he speaks consolingly to her/him.
kâkecitotam (VTI) S/he speaks consolingly of it.
kâkecimiwew (VTA) S/he speaks consolingly to people.

kâkecisiw *pl.* **kâkecisiwak** (VAI) S/he is sore or stiff.

kâkecisowin *pl.* **kâkecisowina** (NI) Being sensitive to pain.

kâkesimototawew (VTA) S/he communicates with the spirit world; s/he prays to God; s/he communicates with God; s/he supplicates Him.
kâkesimototam (VTA) S/he communicates with it.
kâkesimototâkew (VTA) S/he communicates with the spirit world for help.

kâkesimow *pl.* **kâkesimowak** (VAI) S/he supplicates the spirits with humility; s/he prays to God with humility.

kâkesimowin *pl.* **kakesimowina** (NI) Communion with the spirits; a Christian prayer.

kâkeskihkemowin *pl.* **kâkeskihkemowina** (NI) A sermon or instruction; the act of preaching a sermon.

kâkecihew (VTA) S/he consoles her/him.
kâkecitâw (VTI) S/he treats it with respect.
kâkecihiwew (VTA) S/he consoles people.

kâketôkâsiw *pl.* **kâketôkâsiwak** (VTA) S/he acts in great deference to herself/himself; s/he treats herself/himself with respect.

kâketôkâsiwin *pl.* **kâketôkâsiwina** (NI) An act of deference out of respect, submission.

kâkihcimew (VTA) S/he praises her/him; s/he speaks approvingly to her/him. *(Northern). Alt.* **mamihcîmew** *(Plains).*
kâkihcimiwew (VTA) S/he praises other people.

kâkikehani (IPC) It will always be so; consequently.

kâkitaw (IPC) Carefully; with caution. *(Northern). Alt.* **peyahtik** *(Plains).*

kâkwa *pl.* **kâkwak** (NA) A porcupine.

kâkwayaskwesâyâhk (IPC) An expression meaning being perfect; perfectible. *(Northern). Alt.* **kwayaskwâtisiwin** *(Plains).*

kâkwayâtascikehk (IPC) An expression meaning prearranging.

kâkwayiwat *pl.* **kâkwayiwata** (NI) A vase made of birch bark.

kâmâmak *pl.* **kâmâmakwak** (NA) A large butterfly.

kâmâyâpitehk (VAI) Having buckteeth.

kâmiyosicik kinosewak *or* **kâmiyostwaw kinosewak** (NA) The Cree name for the Reserve of Goodfish Lake means "where the fish are good."

kâmwacinâkosiw *pl.* **kâmwacinâkosiwak** (VAI) S/he looks sad or depressed.

kâmwacinâkwan *pl.* **kâmwacinâkwanwa** (VII) It looks depressing.

kâmwatapiw *pl.* **kâmwatapiwak** (VAI) S/he is sitting silently and not talking.

kâmwâcihiwewin *pl.* **kâmwâcihiwewinak** (NA) The act of making someone quiet; quiet. **kâmwâcihiwewina** (ob.).

37

kâmwâcihtâkosiw *pl.* **kâmwâcihtâkosiwak** (VAI) S/he sounds sad.

kâmwâcihtâkwan *pl.* **kâmwâcihtâkwanwa** (VII) It is a sad sound.

kâmwâcipikiskwewin *pl.* **kâmwâcipikiskwewinak** (NA) Soothingly quiet speech. **kâmwâcipikiskwewina** (ob.).

kâmwâcisiw *pl.* **kâmwâcisiwak** (VAI) S/he is calm, quiet.

kâmwâtan *pl.* **kâmwâtanwa** (VII) It is melancholy, i.e.: depressing; it is a quiet isolated place; sad, quiet surroundings, i.e.: serene.

kâmwâtapiwin *pl.* **kâmwâtapiwina** (NI) The act of sitting quietly and not moving.

kâmwâteyihtâkosiw *pl.* **kâmwâteyihtâkosiwak** (VAI) S/he is thought of as sad and depressed.

kâmwâteyihtâkosiwin *pl.* **kâmwâteyihtâkosiwinak** (NA) Being thought of as very quiet. **kâmwâteyihtâkosiwina** (ob.).

kâmwâteyihtâkwan *pl.* **kâmwâteyihtâkwanwa** (VII) It is thought of as being depressing.

kâmwâteyimew (VTA) S/he finds her/him very quiet. *(Plains). Alt.* **koskwâwâteyemew** *(Northern).* S/he finds her/him depressed or sad. *(Northern)*

   kâmwâteyitam (VTI) S/he finds things melancholic or sad.

   kâmwâteyimiwew (VTA) S/he finds people very quiet.

   kâmwâteyicikew (VTI) S/he finds things very quiet.

kâmwâtisiw *pl.* **kâmwâtisiwak** (VAI) S/he is melancholic, depressed, sad.

kâmwâtisiwin *pl.* **kâmwâtisiwina** (NI) Melancholic, depressed, sad; quietude.

kânîmihitocik (NA) The Aurora Borealis. *(Plains). Alt.* **cîpayah ka nimihitotwâw** *(Northern).*

kâsakew *pl.* **kâsakewak** (VAI) S/he is greedy and s/he eats a lot; s/he is gluttonous.

kâsakewin *pl.* **kâsakewina** (NI) Overeating or gluttony; greedy; voracious.

kâsecihcâkaniwat *pl.* **kâsecihcâkaniwata** (NI) A gunny sack. *(Northern). Alt.* **asewekinowat** *(Plains).*

kâsehkwehon *pl.* **kâsehkwehona** (NI) A cloth used for drying.

kâsenamâkewin *pl.* **kâsenamâkewina** (NI) Forgiveness.

kâsenamâtowin *pl.* **kâsenamâtowinak** (NA) The act of forgiving; pardonable. **kâsenamâtowina** (ob.).

kâsepayiw *pl.* **kâsepayiwak** *or* **kâsepayiwa** (VTA) *or* (VTI) It erases by itself.

kâsisin *pl.* **kâsisinwa** (VII) It is sharp.

kâsispowepinam *pl.* **kâsispowepinamwa** (VTI) S/he throws something away by accident.

kâsîcihcâkan *pl.* **kâsîcihcâkana** (NI) A hand towel.

kâsîcihcenew *pl.* **kâsîcihcenewak** (VTA) S/he wipes someone else's hands clean.

kâsîcihcewin *pl.* **kâsîcihcewina** (NI) The act of wiping one's own hands clean.

kâsîhamawew *pl.* **kâsîhamawewak** (VTA) S/he erases it for her/him.

kâsîhkwâkan *pl.* **kâsîhkwâkana** (NI) Something to wash the face with.

kâsîhkwehew (VTA) S/he makes her/him wash her/his face.

   kâsîhkweniwew (VTA) S/he washes faces.

kâsîhkwenew (VTA) S/he washes another's face.

   kâsîhkweniwew (VTA) S/he washes faces.

kâsîhkwew *pl.* **kâsîhkwewak** (VTA) S/he washes her/his own face.

kâsînamawew (VTA) S/he forgives her/him. *(Northern). Alt.* **poneyihtamawew** *(Plains).*

kâsînamakew (VTA) S/he forgives them; s/he pardons her/his sins.

kâsînamâsiw *pl.* **kâsînamâsiwak** (VAI) S/he forgives herself/himself, i.e.: erases her/his sin.

kâsînamâsowin *pl.* **kâsînamâsowina** (NI) Self-forgiveness, i.e.: erasing sins; a pardon for oneself.

kâsinew (VTI) S/he erases them.

   kâsinam (VTI) S/he erases it.

   kâsiniwew (VTA) S/he erases others or everyone.

kâsipacikewin *pl.* **kâsipacikewina** (NI) The act of shaving something.

kâsispomew (VTA) S/he speaks deceptively to her/him.

   kâsispomiwew (VTA) S/he speaks deceptively to people.

kâsispomow *pl.* **kâsispomowak** *or* **kâsispomowa** (VAI) *or* (VII) It *or* s/he sticks out too long.

kâsiw *pl.* **kâsiwak** (VAI) S/he hides.

kâskahikewin *pl.* **kâskahikewina** (NI) The act of scraping.

kâskipâsiw *pl.* **kâskipâsiwak** (VAI) S/he shaves.

kâskipâson *pl.* **kâskipâsonak** (NA) A razor. **kâskipâsona** (ob.).

kâskipâsowin *pl.* **kâskipâsowina** (NI) The act of shaving.

kâskipâtew (VTA) S/he shaves her/him.

   kâskipâtam (VTI) S/he shaves it.

   kâskipâsiwew (VTA) S/he shaves people.

   kâskipâcikew (VTI) S/he shaves anything and everything.

kâskiskinew (VTI) S/he rips the seams apart with care.

   kâskiskinam (VTI) S/he rips out a seam.

   kâskiskinikew (VTI) S/he detaches everything, i.e.: sewing.

kâskiskipitew (VTI) S/he tears the seams apart with force.

   kâskiskipitam (VTI) S/he tears it off.

   kâskiskipicikew (VTI) S/he tears things off.

kâskostawew (VTA) S/he hides from her/him or others.

38

kâskostatam (VTI) S/he hides from it.

kâskostatâkew (VTA) S/he hides from everyone.

kâspahtam (VTI) S/he eats it with a crunching noise

kâspamew (VTI) S/he eats them with a crunching noise.

kâspahcikew (VTI) S/he makes a crunching noise as s/he eats.

kâspâkatosiw *pl.* **kâspâkatosiwak** (VAI) It is bone dry, i.e.: a loaf of bread.

kâspâw *pl.* **kâspâwa** (VII) It is brittle, i.e.: cast iron.

kâspihkasikanis *pl.* **kâspihkasikanisak** (NA) Something that is dry and brittle; toast. *(Plains). Alt.* **kâspisiw** *(Northern).*

kâspihkaswew (VTI) S/he cooks the toast crispy.

kâspihkasam (VTI) S/he cooks the bacon brittle.

kâspihkasikew (VTI) S/he cooks it until it is brittle.

kâspisiw *pl.* **kâspisiwak** (NA) Something that is dry and brittle; toast. *(Northern). Alt.* **kâspihkasikanis** *(Plains).*

kâspohtin *pl.* **kâspohtinwa** (VII) It is too long; it sticks out.

kâspopayiw *pl.* **kâspopayiwa** *or* **kâspopayiwak** (NI) *or* (NA) Something *or* someone that goes beyond (the mark).

kâtahkohtastâhk (VTI) *(Conj. mode)* Onto, something placed on top.

kâtamawew *pl.* **kâtamawewak** (VTA) S/he hides it from her/him; secrets it away; conceals it.

kâtew (VTA) S/he hides her/him; s/he conceals her/him.

kâtaw (VTI) S/he hides it.

kâsiwew (VTA) S/he hides people.

kâcikew (VTI) S/he hides things.

kâwayinohtehk (IPC) An expression meaning "in retreat".

kâwâw *pl.* **kâwâwa** (VII) It is rough to the touch.

kâwâwâyipeyâk (IPC) An expression meaning "there are puddles everywhere", i.e.: "it is puddly"

kâwepinamihk (NI) Something thrown away.

kâya (IPC) Don't.

kehcinahetowin *pl.* **kehcinahetowina** (NI) Being assured.

kehcinahiwewin *pl.* **kehcinahiwewina** (NI) The act of ensuring.

kehcinâ (IPC) An expression meaning "for sure" or "I assure you."

kehcinâhowin *pl.* **kehcinâhowina** (NI) Being imminent; proven; substantial; surely; actual.

kehcinâhowinihk (IPC) In the affirmative.

kehkâhtoskiwin *pl.* **kehkâhtoskiwina** (NI) Being quarrelsome.

kehkâhtowak (VAI) They are arguing.

kehkâhtowin *pl.* **kehkâhtowina** (NI) The act of arguing; altercation.

kehkâmew *pl.* **kehkâmewak** (VTA) S/he scolds her/him.

kehkâwitam *pl.* **kehkâwitamwak** (VAI) S/he is scolding.

kehkâwitaskiw *pl.* **kehkâwitaskiwak** (VAI) S/he is known for arguing; s/he likes to argue.

kekâc (IPC) Almost; nearly; just about.

kekâymitâht (IPC) Nine. *(Plains). Alt.* **kîkâmitâtaht** *(Northern).*

keko (IPC) What is it?

kekoc (IPC) If only.

kekwahâkes *pl.* **kekwahâkesak** (NA) A small wolverine. *Var.* **kihkwahâkes.**

kekwanohk (IPC) What kind of place?

kenikîhkohtew (VTI) S/he sharpens it to a point with a knife.

kenikîhkohtam (VTI) S/he sharpens it to a point with a knife.

kenikîhkohcikew (VTI) S/he sharpens everything to a point with a knife.

kepâcâyâwin *pl.* **kepâcâyâwina** (NI) Being guileless.

kepâcâyihtiw *pl.* **kepâcâyihtiwak** (VAI) S/he does things in a stupid way.

kepâtan *pl.* **kepâtanwa** (VII) It is foolish and stupid.

kepâteyimew (VTA) S/he thinks s/he is dumbfounded.

kepâteyitam (VTI) S/he thinks it is dumbfounding.

kepâteyimiwew (VTA) S/he thinks others are dumbfounded.

kepâteyihcikew (VTA) S/he thinks everybody is dumbfounded.

kepâtisiw *pl.* **kepâtisiwak** (VAI) S/he is stupid or "not all there."

kepâtisiwin *pl.* **kepâtisiwina** (NI) Being foolish or absurd.

kesahkamikan *pl.* **kesahkamikanwa** (VII) An expression indicating the happening or event is all over or finished up, i.e.: a party or dance: "everything is over with" or "it is over."

kesahkamikisiw *pl.* **kesahkamikisiwak** (VAI) S/he is finished with it or s/he is finished with what s/he is doing.

kesahkamikisiwin *pl.* **kesahkamikisiwina** (NI) The act of finishing the occasion or event.

kesawew *pl.* **kesawewak** (VAI) Used when referring to a prime fur bearing animal: "her/his fur is full grown."

kesawewin *pl.* **kesawewina** (NI) Being prime; having full grown prime fur.

kesâc (IPC) An expression meaning "better now than later" or "might as well do it now."

kesâpewiw *pl.* **kesâpewiwak** (VAI) He is a full grown man.

kesâpewiwin *pl.* **kesâpewiwina** (NI) Being a full grown man.

39

kesihcikewin *pl.* **kesihcikewina** (NI) Something finished or the final, completed product.

kesihew (VTA) S/he finished her/him.
  kesitâw (VTI) S/he finished it.
  kesihiwew (VTA) S/he is finished with everybody.
  kesihcikew (VTI) S/he finished everything.

kesihow *pl.* **kesihowak** (VAI) S/he overdid it and played herself/himself out.

kesihowin *pl.* **kesihowina** (NI) The act of overdoing oneself or playing oneself out.

kesihtamawew (VTA) S/he finished it for her/him.
  kesehtamakew (VTA) S/he finished it for someone.
  kesehtamakesihcikew (VTI) S/he finished things.

kesikos *pl.* **kesikosak** (NA) Your aunt. *Var.* **kimamasis**.

kesiskotâtowak (VAI) They arrive at the same time.

kesiskotâtowin *pl.* **kesiskotâtowina** (NI) The act of arriving at the same time.

keskihkwepitew (VTA) S/he rips the face off someone's picture.
  keskihkwepitam (VTI) S/he rips the face off its picture.
  keskihkwepisiwew (VTA) S/he rips the face off someone's picture.
  keskihkwepicikew (VTI) S/he rips the faces off things in a picture.

keskwemew *pl.* **keskwemewak** (VTA) Her/his talking makes her/him act wild or crazy.

kespâkihtâsowin (NI) The end count, i.e.: one million.

keswân (IPC) An expression meaning "it happened unintentionally"; coincidence.

ketahtawe (IPC) One of these times.

ketayiwinisewin *pl.* **ketayiwinisewina** (NI) The act of disrobing; unclad.

ketisk (IPC) Just.

ketowatenowewin *pl.* **ketowatenowewina** (NI) The act of relieving a heavy burden, i.e.: disburden.

kewahiskweyiw *pl.* **kewahiskweyiwak** (VTA) Her/his head shakes unintentionally.

kewâcawâsis *pl.* **kewâcawâsisak** (NA) A child orphan.

kewâcihew (VTA) S/he made an orphan out of her/him.
  kewâcitâw (VTA) S/he goes around like an orphan.
  kewâcihiwew (VTA) S/he makes orphans out of people.

kewâcihikowisiw *pl.* **kewâcihikowisiwak** (VAI) God makes her/him an orphan.

kewâcihowin *pl.* **kewâcihowina** (NI) The act of being alone or reclusive.

kewâcipimatisiw *pl.* **kewâcipimatisiwak** (VAI) S/he lives like a recluse.

kewâciyinis *pl.* **kewâciyinisak** (NA) An adult orphan.

kewâtan *pl.* **kewâtanwak** (NA) A lonely and abandoned feeling; desolate.

kewâteyihtâkosiw *pl.* **kewâteyihtâkosiwak** (VAI) S/he is thought of as being forsaken.

kewâteyihtâkosiwin *pl.* **kewâteyihtâkosiwina** (NI) The act of being thought of as forsaken.

kewâteyihtâkwan *pl.* **kewâteyihtâkwanwa** (VII) It is sentimental or nostalgic.

kewâteyimew (VTA) S/he thinks of her/him as an orphan.
  kewâteyitam (VTA) S/he has a feeling of abandonment.
  kewâteyimiwew (VTA) S/he has a feeling of abandonment for someone.
  kewâteyihcikew (VTA) S/he has a feeling of abandonment for everyone.

kewâteyimow *pl.* **kewâteyimowak** (VAI) S/he finds herself/himself forsaken.

kewâteyimowin *pl.* **kewâteyimowina** (NI) The act of feeling lonely and abandoned.

kewâtisiw *pl.* **kewâtisiwak** (VAI) S/he is orphaned.

kewâtîsiw *pl.* **kewâtîsiwak** (VAI) S/he is an orphan.

kewâtisowin *pl.* **kewâtisowina** (NI) Being fatherless.

ketisk (IPC) Just.

keyâpic (IPC) Furthermore; once again; still; more; some more; again.

kicâspinatew (VTA) S/he makes a kill of great value, i.e., a moose. *(Northern)*
  kicâspinatam (VTI) S/he kills something of great value.
  kicâspinasiwew (VTA) S/he kills someone of great value.
  kicâspinacikew (VTI) S/he kills lots of things of great value.

kicikamiw *pl.* **kicikamiwak** (NA) A very large body of water, i.e.: ocean or sea. *(Northern). Alt.* **kihcikamiy** *(Plains)*.

kicikatahikewin *pl.* **kicikatahikewina** (NI) An indentation.

kicikâw *pl.* **kicikâwa** (VII) It has a notch.

kicikihkotew (VII) It has a notch made with a knife.
  kicikihkotam (VAI) S/he makes a notch with a knife.
  kicikihkocikew (VAI) S/he makes a notch on things.

kicikikawew (VAI) S/he makes notches with an axe.
  kicikikaham (VII) S/he makes a notch on it.
  kicikikahikew (VAI) S/he makes notches on trees.

kicikisiw *pl.* **kicikisiwak** (VAI) S/he has a notch.

kicikisiwin *pl.* **kicikisiwina** (NI) Having a notch.

kiciskâpitew *pl.* **kiciskâpitewak** (VTA) S/he gnashes or grinds her/his teeth.

kiciskihtâkosiwin *pl.* **kiciskihtâkosiwina** (NI) Having a loud and harsh voice; stridence.

kicistâpiskahikan *pl.* **kicistâpiskahikana** (NI) A stick or vine used for cleaning a gun.

40

kicistinahokiw *pl.* **kicistinahokiwak** (VAI) S/he is delayed by the wind or bad weather.

kicistinahokowin *pl.* **kicistinahokowina** (NI) A delay caused by a big wind.

kiciwam *pl.* **kiciwamak** (NA) Your cousin.

kihcâspinasiw *pl.* **kihcâspinasiwak** (VAI) S/he made a great kill.

kihceyihtam (VTI) S/he respects it. *(Plains). Alt.* **kihkâteyihtam** *(Northern).*

kihceyihmiwew (VTA) S/he respects others.

kihceyihcikew (VTI) S/he respects anything.

kihceyihtâkosiw *pl.* **kihceyihtâkosiwak** (VAI) S/he is venerable; in high esteem.

kihceyihtâkosowin *pl.* **kihceyihtâkosowina** (NI) The act of showing reverence; reverential; esteem, great consideration; respected; revered. *(Plains). Alt.* **kihceyimikosowin** *(Northern).*

kihceyihtâkwan *pl.* **kihceyihtâkwanwa** (VII) Venerable, esteemable; it is well respected; it is respected. *(Plains). Alt.* **kihkâteyihtâkwan** *(Northern).*

kihceyihtâsosiw *pl.* **kihceyihtâsosiwak** (VAI) S/he is well respected. *(Plains). Alt.* **kihkâteyihtâkosiw** *(Northern).*

kihceyimew (VTA) S/he has great esteem for her/him; s/he has great consideration; s/he thinks a lot of her/him.

kihceyitam (VTI) S/he has great esteem for it; s/he thinks a lot of it.

kihceyimiwew (VTA) S/he has great esteem for people; s/he thinks a lot of people.

kihceyihcikew (VTI) S/he has great esteem for things; s/he thinks a lot about things.

kihceyimikosowin *pl.* **kihceyimikosowina** (NI) Respected; revered. *(Northern). Alt.* **kihceyihtâkosowin** *(Plains).*

kihceyimow *pl.* **kihceyimowak** (VTA) S/he thinks highly of herself/himself.

kihceyimowin *pl.* **kihceyimowinak** (NA) The act of thinking highly of oneself; snooty.

kihci ayamihewiyiniw *pl.* **kihci ayamihewitiniwak** (NA) A bishop or the great holy father.

kihcihkawan *pl.* **kihcihkawanwa** (VII) It is of a great value.

kihcihkawisiw *pl.* **kihcihkawisiwak**, **kihcihkawisiwa** (VAI) *or* (VII) S/he or it is of a great value.

kihcihkawisiwin *pl.* **kihcihkawisiwina** (NI) Being of great value or esteem.

kihcihtwâwan *pl.* **kihcihtwâwanwa** (VII) It is holy.

kihcihtwâweyihtâkwan *pl.* **kihcihtwâweyihtâkwanwa** (VII) It is thought of as holy.

kihcihtwâweyimew (VTA) S/he thinks of her/him as holy, saintly; s/he thinks of her/him as venerable.

kihcihtwâweyitam (VTI) S/he thinks of it as holy.

kihcihtwâweyimiwew (VTA) S/he thinks of people as holy.

kihcihtwâweyicikew (VTI) S/he thinks of things as holy.

kihcihtwâwihkâsowin *pl.* **kihcihtwâwihkâsowina** (NI) The act of making a show of sanctity or piety; sanctimony.

kihcihtwâwihkewin *pl.* **kihcihtwâwihkewina** (NI) The act of consecrating; santification.

kihcihtwâwisâyâwin *pl.* **kihcihtwâwisâyâwina** (NI) Being blessed; beatitude; being divine; divinity.

kihcihtwâwisihew (VTA) S/he makes her/him sacred, holy or saintly.

kihcihtwâwisitâw (VTI) S/he makes it sacred or holy.

kihcihtwâwisihiwew (VTA) S/he makes people sacred or holy.

kihcihtwâwisicikew (VTI) S/he makes things sacred or holy.

kihcihtwâwisihow *pl.* **kihcihtwâwisihowak** (VAI) S/he is dressed holy or venerably.

kihcihtwâwisihowin *pl.* **kihcihtwâwisihowina** (NI) The act of wearing a sacred garment.

kihcihtwâwisiw *pl.* **kihcihtwâwisiwak** (VAI) S/he is holy.

kihcihtwâwisiwin *pl.* **kihcihtwâwisiwina** (NI) Being sacred or holy.

kihcikamiy *pl.* **kihcikamiyak** (NA) A very large body of water, i.e.: ocean or sea. *(Plains). Alt.* **kicikamiw** *(Northern).*

kihcikîsikohk (IPC) In heaven; heavenly.

kihcikîsik (NA) Heaven.

kihcinahowakeyimew *pl.* **kihcinahowakeyimewak** (VTA) S/he looks at her/him with great admiration. *(Plains). Alt.* **kihcinawew** *(Northern).*

kihcinawew *pl.* **kihcinawewak** (VTA) S/he looks at her/him with great admiration. *(Northern). Alt.* **kihcinahowakeyimew** *(Plains).*

kihciniskehk (IPC) On the right hand side.

kihcipayihew (VTA) S/he makes a great start for her/him. *(Northern). Alt.* **miyopayihew** *(Plains).*

kihcipayitâw (VTA) Somebody starts well.

kihcipayihiwew (VTA) S/he makes a great start for somebody.

kihcipayihcikew (VTI) S/he makes a great start for things.

kihcipikiskwew *pl.* **kihcipikiskwewak** (VAI) S/he makes an oath.

kihcipikiskwewin *pl.* **kihcipikiskwewina** (NI) An oath; an aver; authenticate.

kihcitwâwasowewina (NI) Holy orders.

kihcitwâwmare (NA) The Blessed Virgin.

41

kihcitwewin *pl.* **kihcitwewina** (NI) The act of speaking the truth by swearing on the Bible.

kihciwikihtowin *pl.* **kihciwikihtowina** (NI) A church sanctioned marriage; the act of being married in a church.

kihciwikowin *pl.* **kihciwikowina** (NI) Abode.

kihciwiyasowewin *pl.* **kihciwiyasowewina** (NI) The highest court; the Supreme Court of Canada; Assize court.

kihcôkimâskwew *pl.* **kihcôkimâskwewak** (NA) A queen.

kihcôkimâw *pl.* **kihcôkimâwak** (NA) The king or grand chief.

kihew *pl.* **kihewak** (NA) An eagle.

kihewataniy *pl.* **kihewataniyak** (NA) An eagle feather.

kihicitwâweyimowewin *pl.* **kihicitwâweyimowewina** (NI) The act of thinking someone is hallowed.

kihitwew *pl.* **kihcitwewak** (VAI) S/he speaks the truth by swearing on the Bible.

kihkahtowak (VAI) They have a heated discussion.

kihkaspitew (VTA) S/he can clearly taste the fish.

kihkaspitam (VTI) S/he can clearly taste the meat.

kihkaspisiwew (VTA) S/he has a very clear taste of them.

kihkaspihcikew (VTI) S/he can really taste anything.

kihkâhtow *pl.* **kihkâhtowak** (VTA) S/he is having a vehement argument.

kihkâmahtew (VII) It has a cooking odor.

kihkâmahtam (VTI) S/he detects a strong smell.

kihkâmahsawew (VTI) S/he makes a strong smell.

kihkâmâkosiw *pl.* **kihkâmâkosiwak** (VAI) S/he has a strong odor.

kihkâmâkwan *pl.* **kihkâmâkwanwa** (VII) It has a strong odor.

kihkâmâsiw *pl.* **kihkâmâsiwak** (VAI) It has a strong odor, i.e.: a peace pipe.

kihkâmâstew *pl.* **kihkâmâstewa** (VII) It has a strong smokey odor.

kihkânawew (VTA) S/he sees her/him clearly or s/he recognizes her/him.

kihkânam (VTI) S/he sees it clearly or recognizes it.

kihkânakew (VTA) S/he sees her/him clearly or recognizes her/him.

kihkânakosiw (VTA) S/he is seen clearly or recognized.

kihkânâkosiw *pl.* **kihkânâkosiwak** (VAI) S/he can be seen plainly or clearly.

kihkânâkwan *pl.* **kihkânâkwanwa** (VII) It is seen plainly or clearly.

kihkâspakosiw *pl.* **kihkâspakosiwak** (VAI) The fish has distinctive taste.

kihkâspakwan *pl.* **kihkâspakwanwa** (VII) The meat has distinctive taste.

kihkâteyihtam (VTI) S/he respects it. *(Northern)*. *Alt.* **kihceyihtam** *(Plains)*.

kihkâteyihmiwew (VTA) S/he respects others.

kihkâteyihhcikew (VTI) S/he respects anything.

kihkâteyihtâkosiw *pl.* **kihkâteyihtâkosiwak** (VAI) S/he is well respected. *(Northern)*. *Alt.* **kihceyihtâsosiw** *(Plains)*.

kihkâteyihtâkwan *pl.* **kihkâteyihtâkwanwa** (VII) It is well respected; it is respected. *(Northern)*. *Alt.* **kihceyihtâkwan** *(Plains)*.

kihkâteyimew *pl.* **kihkâteyimewak** (VTA) S/he has a respectful feeling for her/him; s/he respects her/him.

kihkâwihtawew (VTA) S/he hears her/him plainly or clearly.

kihkâwihtam (VTI) S/he hears it plainly or clearly.

kihkâwihtakew (VTA) S/he hears people plainly or clearly; s/he hears others clearly.

kihkâwihtâkosiw *pl.* **kihkâwihtâkosiwak** (VAI) S/he can be heard plainly or clearly.

kihkâwihtâkosiwin *pl.* **kihkâwihtâkosiwina** (NI) The act of being heard plainly or clearly.

kihkâwihtâkwan *pl.* **kihkâwihtâkwanwa** (VII) It can be heard plainly or clearly.

kihkâyapamohiwewin *pl.* **kihkâyapamohiwewina** (NI) The act of making something evident; evince.

kihkâyâsawew *pl.* **kihkâyâsawewak** (VAI) The light is bright or clear; a gleam.

kihkâyâstew *pl.* **kihkâyâstewa** (VII) There is bright moonlight; a glow.

kihkihtowin *pl.* **kihkihtowina** (NI) The state of having a real heated discussion.

kihkimew (VTA) S/he gives her/him a good talking to.

kihkitam (VTI) S/he gives it a good talking to.

kihkimiwew (VTA) S/he gives them a good talking to.

kihkihcikew (VTI) S/he gives things a good talking to.

kihkwahaskân *pl.* **kihkwahaskâna** (NI) A grave.

kihkwahâkes *pl.* **kihkwahâkesak** (NA) A small wolverine. *Var.* **kekwahâkes**.

kihkwahâkew *pl.* **kihkwahâkewak** (NA) A large wolverine.

kihtaskowew (VTA) S/he follows her/him at a distance.

kihtaskotam (VTI) S/he follows it at a distance.

kihtaskokew (VTA) S/he follows at a distance.

kihtawew (VTA) S/he sinks her/him with a pole or stick.

kihtaham (VTI) S/he sinks it with a pole or stick.

kihtahowew (VTA) S/he sinks others with a pole or stick.

kihtahikew (VTI) S/he sinks things with a pole or stick.

kihtânew (VTA) S/he dips her/him or it under water, i.e.: during a baptism.

kihtânam (VTI) S/he dips it underwater, i.e.: pants.

kihtâniwew (VTA) S/he dips others underwater.

kihtânikew (VTI) S/he dips things underwater.

kihtehaya (NA) Elder.

kihtehayiwiw *pl.* **kihtehayiwiwak** (VAI) S/he is old, aged, ancient.

kihtehayowin *pl.* **kihtehayowina** (NI) The act of being old; old age.

kihtehyâtisiw *pl.* **kihtehyâtisiwak** (VAI) S/he acts old.

kihtehyâtisiwin *pl.* **kihtehyâtisiwina** (NI) Acting old.

kihtewewin *pl.* **kihtewewina** (NI) The act of sounding deep-throated.

kihtimeyihcikewin *pl.* **kihtimeyihcikewina** (NI) The act of feeling monotony.

kihtimeyihtam *pl.* **kihtimeyihtamwak** (VTI) S/he is tired of it.

kihtimeyimew (VTA) S/he is tired of her/him.

kihtimeyitam (VTI) S/he is tired of it.

kihtimeyimiwew (VTA) S/he is tired of people.

kihtimeyihcikew (VTI) S/he is tired of things.

kihtimikan *pl.* **kihtimikanak** (NA) A lazy bones.

kihtimikanew *pl.* **kihtimikanewak** (VAI) S/he is a lazy bones.

kihtimikanewin *pl.* **kihtimikanewina** (NI) Being a lazy bones.

kihtimiw *pl.* **kihtimiwak** (VAI) S/he is lazy.

kihtimiwin *pl.* **kihtimiwina** (NI) Being lazy.

kihtimpehew (VAI) S/he is tired of waiting for her/him.

kihtimpetâw (VII) S/he is tired of waiting for it.

kihtimpehiwew (VAI) S/he is tired of waiting for people.

kikakohtin *pl.* **kikakohtinwa** (NI) Something mixed in the water with something else.

kikakotew *pl.* **kikakotewa** (NI) Something that hangs with something else, i.e.: hat and coat.

kikamohew (VTI) S/he attached it to something.

kikamocikew (VTI) S/he attached things.

kikamow *pl.* **kikamowak** (VAI) It is attached to something.

kikapowehtin *pl.* **kikapowehtinwa** (VII) It is loaded, i.e.: a gun.

kikasâkew *pl.* **kikasâkewak** (VAI) S/he has a coat or dress on.

kikasâmew *pl.* **kikasâmewak** (VAI) S/he wears snowshoes.

kikasikanew *pl.* **kikasikanewak** (VAI) S/he wears socks.

kikaskisinew *pl.* **kikaskisinewak** (VAI) S/he has shoes on.

kikastisew *pl.* **kikastisewak** (VAI) S/he has gloves or mitts on.

kikastotinew *pl.* **kikastotinewak** (VAI) S/he has a hat on.

kikawes *pl.* **kikawesak** (NA) Your godmother. *Var.* **kikawe**.

kikayiwinsahew (VTA) S/he put clothes on her/him. *(Northern). Alt.* **postayiwinisahew** *(Plains)*.

kikayiwinsatâw (VTI) S/he puts clothes on the body.

kikayiwinsahiwew (VTA) S/he puts clothes on the people.

kikayiwinsew *pl.* **kikayiwinsewak** (VAI) S/he has clothes on. *(Northern). Alt.* **postayiwinisew** *(Plains)*.

kiki (IPC) With.

kikihtin *pl.* **kikihtinwa** (VII) It fits into; it mixes well. *(Northern)*

kikinew (VTI) S/he mixes them with something else.

kikinam (VTI) S/he mixes it with something else.

kikiniwew (VTI) S/he mixes others with something else.

kikinikew (VTI) S/he mixes other things with something else.

kikiskam *pl.* **kikiskamwak** (VTI) S/he wears it.

kikitâsew *pl.* **kikitâsewak** (VAI) S/he had pants on. *(Northern). Alt.* **postitâsew** *(Plains)*.

kikosew *pl.* **kikosewak** (VAI) S/he is with her/his own family.

kikosewin *pl.* **kikosewina** (NI) A family setting; the act of being with family.

kikosisihkawin *pl.* **kikosisihkawinak** (NA) Your godson.

kimanitominaw (NA) Our God; Jesus Christ.

kimamasis *pl.* **kimamasisak** (NA) Your aunt. *Var.* **kesikos**.

kiminicâkanihkew *pl.* **kiminicâkanihkewak** (VAI) S/he gives birth to an illegitimate child. *(Plains) Alt.* **pikwatôsew** *(Northern)*.

kimisâhiw *pl.* **kimisâhiwak** (VTA) S/he wipes herself/himself clean after a bowel movement.

kimisâhon *pl.* **kimisâhona** (NI) A piece of toilet paper.

kimisâhowin *pl.* **kimisâhowina** (NI) The act of wiping oneself clean after a bowel movement.

kimosôm *pl.* **kimosômak** (NA) Your grandfather. *Var.* **kimosômiwaw**.

kimosômiwaw *pl.* **kimosômiwawak** (NA) Your grandfather. *Var.* **kimosôm**.

kimotamakewin *pl.* **kimotamakewina** (NI) The act of stealing from someone else.

kimotamawew *pl.* **kimotamawewak** (VTA) S/he steals from her/him.

kimotastimwew *pl.* **kimotastimwewak** (VTA) S/he steals a horse.

kimotastinwâtew *pl.* **kimotastinwâtewak** (VTA) S/he steals horses from her/him.

kimotastinwewin *pl.* **kimotastimwewina** (NI) The act of stealing a horse.

kimotayowinisew *pl.* **kimotayowinisewak** (VTI) S/he steals clothes.

kimotiw *pl.* **kimotiwak** (VAI) S/he steals.

kimotiwin *pl.* **kimotiwina** (NI) The act of stealing; robbery; stolen; swag; theft.

43

kimowan (VII) It is raining.

kimowanahasîs *pl.* **kimowanahasîswak** (NA) A bird that announces the rain, i.e.: a type of snipe such as a killdeer. *(Plains). Alt.* **pacaskahask** *(Northern).*

kimowanâpiy (NA) Rainwater.

kimowanihtâw *pl.* **kimowanihtâwak** (VAI) S/he makes it rain.

kinepik *pl.* **kinepikwak** (NA) A snake.

kinepikocepihk *pl.* **kinepikocepihkwak** (NA) A piece of snakeroot. **kinepikocepihka** (ob.). *(Northern). Alt.* **namepin** *(Plains).*

kinepikos *pl.* **kinepikosak** (NA) A small snake.

kinepikwasakay *pl.* **kinepikwasakayak** (NA) A snakeskin.

kinîkihikonawak (NA) Our parents.

kinohew (VTI) S/he made it too long.

    kinotâw (VTI) S/he made them too long.

    kinocikew (VTI) S/he makes things too long.

kinohtakâw *pl.* **kinohtakâwa** (VII) The house has a long floor.

kinohtakisiw *pl.* **kinohtakisiwak** (VAI) It has a long floor, i.e.: a trailer. *(Northern)*

kinokamâw *pl.* **kinokamâwa** (VII) It is a long lake.

kinokâtew *pl.* **kinokâtewak** (VAI) S/he has long legs.

kinosehew (VTI) S/he makes it too long.

    kinosetâw (VTI) S/he makes them too long.

    kinosecikew (VTI) S/he makes things too long.

kinosew *pl.* **kinosewak** (NA) A fish.

kinosewayakay *pl.* **kinosewayakaya** (NI) A fish's scales. *(Plains). Alt.* **wayakay** *(Northern).*

kinosewpimiy *pl.* **kinosewpimiya** (NI) Fish oil; cod liver oil.

kinosiw *pl.* **kinosiwak** (VAI) S/he is tall.

kinwaskisiw *pl.* **kinwaskisiwak** (VAI) It stands tall, i.e.: a tree.

kinwaskosiw *pl.* **kinwaskosiwak** (NA) S/he is tall and slim, i.e.: a long tree or a tall person.

kinwâpekisiw *pl.* **kinwâpekisiwak** (VAI) S/he is long and skinny.

kinwâpekiyawew *pl.* **kinwâpekiyawewak** (VAI) S/he has a long body.

kinwâpicikanân *pl.* **kinwâpicikanâna** (NI) An eyetooth.

kinwâpiskâw *pl.* **kinwâpiskâwa** (VTI) It is a long piece of steel or a gun barrel.

kinwâskitew *pl.* **kinwâskitewa** (VII) It stands tall, i.e.: a pole. *(Northern).*

kinwâskweyiniw *pl.* **kinwâskweyiniwak** (NA) A long, tall person, i.e.: lanky or a beanpole.

kinwâw *pl.* **kinwâwa** (VII) It is long.

kinwekan *pl.* **kinwekanwa** (VII) It is long, i.e.: bolt of cloth.

kinwekisiw *pl.* **kinwekisiwak** (VAI) It is long, i.e.: a deerhide.

kinwes (IPC) A long time.

kipahamawew (VTA) S/he closes it for her/him; s/he shuts it for her/him.

    kipahamakew (VTI) S/he closes things for others.

kipahikan *pl.* **kipahikana** (NI) A cork.

kipahikâsiw *pl.* **kipahikâsiwak** (VAI) S/he is closed in or locked up; in jail.

kipahikâsiwin *pl.* **kipahikâsiwina** (NI) The act of being confined or locked up, as in jail.

kipahikâsowikamik *pl.* **kipahikâsowikamikwa** (NI) A jail cell. *(Northern). Alt.* **kipahitowikamik** *(Plains).*

kipahikâtew *pl.* **kipahikâtewa** (VII) It is closed or shutdown, i.e.: store.

kipahikewin *pl.* **kipahikewina** (NI) The act of confining.

kipahitowikamik *pl.* **kipahitowikamikwa** (NI) A jail cell. *(Plains). Alt.* **kipahikâsowikamik** *(Northern).*

kipahon *pl.* **kipahonak** (NA) A midriff; a ribcage. **kipahona** (ob.).

kipahotowikamik *pl.* **kipahotowikamikwa** (NI) A jail.

kipapiw *pl.* **kipapiwak** (VAI) S/he sits blocking others.

kipascikewin *pl.* **kipascikewina** (NI) The act of obstructing; obstruction.

kipaskapowinan *pl.* **kipaskapowinana** (NI) An eyelid. *(Northern). Alt.* **pasakwâpiwinân** *(Plains).*

kipaskwahikan *pl.* **kipaskwahikana** (NI) A bung; a stopper.

kipastew *pl.* **kipastewa** (VII) It sits blocking others or it is in the way.

kipatâhtam *pl.* **kipatâhtamwak** (VAI) S/he fainted.

kipawew (VTA) S/he closes her/him in.

    kipaham (VTI) S/he closes it in.

    kipahowew (VTA) S/he closes people in.

    kipahikew (VTI) S/he closes things in.

kipâpowehikan *pl.* **kipâpowehikana** (NI) A cork for a bottle.

kipihcimew (VTA) S/he coaxes her/him to stop.

    kipihcitâw (VTI) S/he coaxes it to stop.

    kipihcihiwew (VTA) S/he coaxes them to stop.

    kipihcicikew (VTI) S/he makes things stop.

kipihcipayiw *pl.* **kipihcipayiwa** or **kipihcipayiwak** (VII) *or* (VAI) It *or* s/he stops suddenly.

kipihcipayowin *pl.* **kipihcipayowina** (NI) A sudden stop.

kipihciw *pl.* **kipihciwak** (VAI) S/he stops. *(Northern). Alt.* **nakiw** *(Plains).*

kipihciwak (VAI) S/he stops. *(Northern). Alt.* **nakiw** *(Plains).*

kipihciwin *pl.* **kipihciwina** (NI) The act of stopping. *(Northern). Alt.* **nakiwin** *(Plains).*

kipihtakahikâsiw *pl.* **kipihtakahikâsiwak** (VAI) S/he is nailed shut.

kipihtakahikâtew *pl.* **kipihtakahikâtewa** (VII) It is nailed shut.

kipihtakahwew (VTA) S/he nails her/him shut.

44

kipihtakaham (VTI) S/he nails it shut.

kipihtakahowew (VTA) S/he nails them shut.

kipihtakahikew (VTI) S/he nails things shut.

kipihtamiskawew (VTA) S/he is kicking the breathe out of her/him; s/he winds her/him.

kipihtamiskakew (VTA) S/he is kicking the breathe out of someone.

kipihtamiskacikew (VTA) S/he is kicking the breathe out of everyone.

kipihtew *pl.* **kipihtewak** (VAI) S/he is deaf.

kipihtowew *pl.* **kipihtowewak** (VAI) S/he shuts up or stops talking.

kipihtowewin *pl.* **kipihtowewina** (NI) The act of shutting up or stopping talk.

kipinew (VTA) S/he keeps her/him inside.

kipinam (VTI) S/he holds it in.

kipiniwew (VTA) S/he keeps people inside.

kipinikew (VTI) S/he keeps things inside.

kipiskawew (VTA) S/he is standing in her/his way or blocking her/him; s/he is blocking her/his way; s/he blocks her/him with her/his body; s/he is hindering her/him or blocking her/him.

kipiskam (VTA) S/he is standing in the way.

kipiskâkew (VTA) S/he is standing in everyone's way.

kipiskâcikew (VTA) S/he stands in the way.

kipiskâkewin *pl.* **kipiskâkewina** (NI) The act of standing in the way or blocking others.

kipistanehew (VTA) S/he gives her/him a nosebleed with her/his hand.

kipistanehowew (VTA) S/he gives others a nosebleed with her/his hand.

kipistanehikew (VTI) S/he gives nosebleeds.

kipistanewin *pl.* **kipistanewina** (NI) Having a nosebleed.

kipistaniw *pl.* **kipistaniwak** (VAI) S/he has a nosebleed.

kipitonewin *pl.* **kipitonewina** (NI) The act of remaining silent; being mum.

kipiw *pl.* **kipiwak** (VAI) S/he is in the process of lying down.

kipoc (IPC) A slang word for someone who is unable to talk; a mute. *Var.* **kipocihkân.**

kipocihkân (IPC) A slang word for someone who is unable to talk; a mute. *Var.* **kipoc.**

kipohtenew (VTA) S/he holds the door shut on her/him.

kipohtenam (VTI) S/he holds the door shut.

kipohteniwew (VTA) S/he holds the door shut on people.

kipohtenikew (VTI) S/he holds the door shut on things.

kipokwâcikan *pl.* **kipowâcikana** (NI) Something that is sewed up.

kipokwâtamawew (VTA) S/he sews things up for them.

kipokwâtamatam (VTI) S/he sews it up.

kipokwâtamakew (VTI) S/he sews things up.

kipokwâtamawewak (VTA) They sew things up for them.

kiposiw *pl.* **kiposiwak** (NA) It is plugged or clogged, i.e.: a smoking pipe.

kiposkatowin *pl.* **kiposkatowina** (NI) Being congested.

kiposkawew (VTA) S/he is standing in her/his way or blocking her/him; s/he is blocking her/his way; s/he blocks her/him with her/his body; s/he is hindering her/him or blocking her/him.

kiposkam (VTA) S/he is standing in the way.

kiposkâkew (VTA) S/he is standing in everyone's way.

kiposkâcikew (VTA) S/he stands in the way.

kipotisahikewin *pl.* **kipotisahikewina** (NI) The act of forbidding entrance; forbidding others from going.

kipotisawew (VTA) S/he forbids her/him from coming.

kipotisaham (VTI) S/he forbids it from coming.

kipotisahowew (VTA) S/he forbids others from coming.

kipotisahikew (VTA) S/he forbids everyone from coming.

kipotonehikewnihk (IP) An expression indicating a person who becomes speechless.

kipotonehwew (VTA) Her/his words shut her/him up.

kipotonehmiwew (VTA) Her/his words shut others up.

kipotonehhikew (VTA) Her/his words shut everyone up.

kipotonenew (VTA) S/he holds her/his mouth shut.

kipotoneniwew (VTA) S/he holds other mouths shut.

kipotonenikew (VTA) S/he holds everyone's mouth shut.

kipwatamâpahtew *pl.* **kipwatamâpahtewa** (VII) The smoke is suffocating.

kipwatamâpasikewin *pl.* **kipwatamâpasikewina** (NI) The act of making suffocating smoke.

kipwatâmâpasiw *pl.* **kipwatâmâpasiwak** (VAI) S/he is choking from the smoke.

kipwatâmâpasiwin *pl.* **kipwatâmâpasiwina** (NI) The act of choking from smoke.

kipwatâmâpaswew (VTA) S/he chokes her/him with smoke; s/he suffocates her/him with smoke.

kipwatâmâpasam (VTI) S/he chokes it with smoke.

kipwatâmâpasawew (VTA) S/he chokes everyone with smoke.

kipwatâmâpasikew (VTI) S/he fills the place with smoke.

kipwatâmopayiw *pl.* **kipwatâmopayiwak** (VAI) S/he chokes up and is unable to breathe.

kipwatâmopayowin *pl.* **kipwatâmopayowina** (NI) The act of choking up and not being able to breathe.

kipwâpahtew *pl.* **kipwâpahtewa** (VII) Unable to see because of the smoke.

45

kipwâpasikewin *pl.* **kipwâpasikewina** (NI) The act of not being able to see for the smoke.

kipwâskwahon *pl.* **kipwâskwahona** (NI) Safety pin.

kipwâskwahonis *pl.* **kipwâskwahonisa** (NI) A clip.

kipwâw *pl.* **kipwâwa** (NI) Something plugged or clogged up.

kisacihew *pl.* **kisacihewak** (VTA) S/he makes her/him stay.

kisakamisiw *pl.* **kisakamisiwak** (VAI) The kettle is heated up. *(Northern)*

kisakamiswew (VTA) S/he heats up the tea kettle.

kisakamisam (VTA) S/he heats up the water.

kisakamisikew (VTA) S/he makes hot water.

kisâcimew (VTA) S/he talks her/him into staying longer.

kisâcimiwew (VTA) S/he talks someone into staying longer.

kisâciw *pl.* **kisâciwak** (VAI) S/he decides to stay for good.

kisâkamisamawew (VTA) S/he heats up the water for someone.

kisâkamisamasam (VTI) S/he heats it up.

kisâkamitehkwew *pl.* **kisâkamitehkwewak** (VAI) S/he drinks a hot broth; soup.

kisâkamitehkwewin *pl.* **kisâkamitehkwewina** (NI) The act of drinking a hot broth.

kisâkamitew *pl.* **kisâkamitewa** (VII) It is hot, i.e.: soup or water.

kisânesiw *pl.* **kisânesiwak** (VAI) The drum is warmed up.

kisâneswew *pl.* **kisâneswewak** (VTI) S/he is warming up, i.e.: a drum.

kisâpiskisiw *pl.* **kisâpiskisiwak** (VAI) It is hot, as in iron, or pot, i.e.: a frying pan or drum.

kisâpiskiswew (VTI) S/he heats up the frying pan.

kisâpiskisam (VTI) S/he heats up the iron.

kisâpiskisamowew (VTI) S/he heats it up for her/him.

kisâpiskisikew (VTI) S/he heats it up.

kisâpiskitew *pl.* **kisâpiskitewa** (VII) It is a hot piece of iron.

kisâstaw (IPC) Sort of; it might be.

kisâtam (VTA) S/he is hanging around her/him; s/he stays with her/him.

kisâtew (VTA) S/he is lingering around her/him.

kisâcimiwew (VTA) S/he makes others stay.

kisâteyimew (VTA) S/he won't leave people.

kisâteyihcikew (VTA) S/he won't leave people.

kisâteyimew (VTA) S/he does not want to leave her/him and s/he lingers; s/he doesn't like the idea of leaving her/him; s/he sort of takes to her/him.

kisâteyitam (VTA) S/he made up her/his mind to stay.

kisâteyimiwew (VTA) S/he made up her/his mind to stay with people.

kisâteyihcikew (VTI) S/he keeps them in her/his mind.

kiscâyâw *pl.* **kiscâyâwak** (VAI) S/he stays there forever; s/he stays there permanently.

kiscâyâwin *pl.* **kiscâyâwina** (NI) The act of being permanent, i.e.: permanancy or belonging somewhere.

kiscikânis *pl.* **kiscikânisa** (NI) A vegetable; a vegetable seed for planting in the ground. *(Plains). Alt.* **pîwi kistikân** *(Northern)*.

kisehtowak (VTA) They make each other angry.

kisehtwowin *pl.* **kisehtwowina** (NI) The act of making someone angry by talking too much.

kisekotew *pl.* **kisekotewa** (VII) It is moving fast, like a bullet.

kisemanito (NA) The great positive force or quality in the universe; God.

kisemanitokâsowin *pl.* **kisemanitokâsowinak** (NA) The act of pretending to be a high spirit power. **kisemanitokâsowina** (ob.).

kisemanitokâtew (VTA) S/he believes her/him to reflect the good quality, power or mystery in the universe.

kisemanitokâtam (VTA) S/he sees the great good mystery present in her/him.

kisemanitokâsiwew (VTA) S/he attributes to people the good quality of the universe.

kisemanitokâhcikew (VTI) S/he attributes to things the good spirit of the universe.

kisemanitonâhk (IPC) In the spirit world; in heaven.

kisemanitowakeyimow *pl.* **kisemanitowakeyimowak** (VTA) S/he thinks of herself/himself as the great postive mystery in the universe; s/he thinks of herself/himself as God.

kisemanitowakeyimowin *pl.* **kisemanitowakeyimowina** (NI) Thinking of oneself as the great spirit or God.

kisemanitoweyimew (VTA) S/he thinks of her/him as embodying the great positive power or good spirit; s/he takes her/him as being God.

kisemanitoweyitam (VTA) S/he takes it as God.

kisemanitoweyimiwew (VTA) S/he takes people as God.

kisemanitoweyihcikew (VTA) S/he takes things as an expression of the great mystery.

kisemanitowiw *pl.* **kisemanitowiwak** (VAI) S/he is the great quality, power or mystery; s/he is God.

kisemanitowiwin *pl.* **kisemanitowiwina** (NI) The quality of having the great mystery or God.

kisemanitowokosisâniwiw *pl.* **kisemanitowokosisâniwiwak** (NA) He is the son of God.

kisepayowin *pl.* **kisipayowina** (NI) The act of going fast.

46

kisepekinikewin *pl.* **kisepekinikewina** (NI) The act of doing laundry or washing clothes.

kisepîsim (NI) January; the elder moon or month *(Northern)*; the cold moon or month *(Plains)*.

kisestawew (VTA) S/he is upset with her/him.

kisestam (VTI) S/he is mad at it.

kisestâkew (VTA) S/he is mad at someone.

kisestâkewin *pl.* **kisestâkewina** (NI) The act of being upset with someone.

kisestâtowin *pl.* **kisestâtowina** (NI) Being upset with each other.

kisew *pl.* **kisewak** (VAI) Used in reference to a bird or animal showing protective instincts: "s/he is protective."

kisewateyimew (VTA) S/he thinks of her/him in a kindly way.

kisewateyitam (VTI) S/he thinks of it in a kindly way.

kisewateyimiwew (VTA) S/he thinks of people in a kindly way.

kisewateyihcikew (VTI) S/he thinks of everything in a kindly way.

kisewâtisiw *pl.* **kisewâtisiwak** (VAI) S/he is kind; s/he is very kind and charitable.

kisewâtisiwokeyimew (VTA) S/he thinks of her/him as being very kind.

kisewâtisiwokeyitam (VTI) S/he thinks it is kindly.

kisewâtisiwokeyimiwew (VTA) S/he thinks people are kindly.

kisewâtisiwokeyihcikew (VTI) S/he thinks everything is kindly.

kisewâtisiwokeyimow *pl.* **kisewâtisiwokeyimowak** (VTA) S/he thinks herself/himself as being kindly.

kisewâtisiwokeyimowin *pl.* **kisewâtisiwokeyimowina** (NI) The act of thinking that oneself is very kind.

kisewâtisowin *pl.* **kisewâtisowina** (NI) The act of being kind; kind-hearted.

kisewâtotawew (VTA) S/he is kind to her/him and giving her/him tender loving care; s/he acts kindly to her/him.

kisewâtotam (VTI) S/he is kind to it and giving it loving care.

kisewâtotâkew (VTA) S/he is kind to someone and giving someone loving care.

kisewehcikewin *pl.* **kisewehcikewina** (NI) The act of throwing something down with a thump.

kisewehtâwin *pl.* **kisewehtâwina** (NI) The act of making a ruckus; a rumpus.

kisewemohcikâkan *pl.* **kisewemohcikâkana** (NI) Something used to make sound louder, i.e.: an amplifier.

kisewesimowewin *pl.* **kisewesimowewina** (NI) The act of throwing someone down with a thump.

kisewewin *pl.* **kisewewina** (NI) Loudness or being loud; vocal.

kiseweyâhpowin *pl.* **kiseweyâhpowina** (NI) The act of laughing loudly; guffaw.

kisewin *pl.* **kisewina** (NI) This word is used with birds or animals and means "the act of showing a mother's protective instinct."

kiseyinewakeyimew (VTA) S/he thinks of her/him as being an old man.

kiseyinewakeyitam (VTI) S/he thinks like an old man.

kiseyinewakeyimiwew (VTA) S/he regards other people as old men.

kiseyinewakeyihcikew (VTA) S/he finds everybody old.

kiseyinewakeyimow *pl.* **kiseyinewakeyimowak** (VTA) S/he thinks herself/himself as an old man.

kiseyinewiwin *pl.* **kiseyinewiwina** (NI) The act of being an old man.

kiseyiniw *pl.* **kiseyiniwak** (NA) An old man.

kisihcikewin *pl.* **kisihcikewina** (NI) Something all finished; fulfilment.

kisik (IPC) At the same time.

kisikâpayiw *pl.* **kisikâpayiwa** (VII) It is moving fast.

kiskeyihtamohiwewin *pl.* **kiskeyihtamohiwewina** (NI) The act of indicating.

47

kisimew (VTA) S/he upsets her/him with her/his talking.

kisimiwew (VTA) S/he makes people mad with her/his speech.

kisihcikew (VTA) Everyone is mad at her/his speech.

kisimow *pl.* **kisimowak** (VTA) S/he upsets herself/himself by her/his talk.

kisin (VII) It is cold.

kisinâw (VII) It feels cold.

kisipan *pl.* **kisipanwa** (VII) It is the end; completed.

kisipaskamik *pl.* **kisipaskamikwa** (NI) The end of a piece of land.

kisipaskamikâw *pl.* **kisipaskamikâwa** (NI) Where the muskeg ends.

kisipatinâw *pl.* **kisipatinâwa** (NI) Where the hills ends.

kisipayihew (VTA) S/he finishes with them or her/him.

kisipayitaw (VTI) S/he finishes with it.

kisipayihiwew (VTA) S/he finishes with everyone.

kisipayihcikew (VTI) S/he finishes everything off.

kisipayiw *pl.* **kisipayiwak** *or* **kisipayiwa** (VAI) *or* (VII) An expression used when referring to the end of a meeting or business, i.e.: "it is finished."

kisipayowin *pl.* **kisipayowina** (NI) The act of coming to an end; consquence; the end.

kisipâskweyaw *pl.* **kisipâskweyawa** (NI) The end of the timber line.

kisipâw *pl.* **kisipâwa** (VII) It has an end.

kisipâyihk (LN) At the very end, i.e.: hallway.

kisipekihtakinikew *pl.* **kisipekihtakinikewak** (VTI) S/he is washing the floor.

kisipekihtakinikewin *pl.* **kisipekihtakinikewina** (NI) The act of washing the floor.

kisipekikonewew *pl.* **kisipekikonewewak** (VAI) S/he had a mouthwash.

kisipekinamawew (VTA) S/he is washing something for her/him.

kisipekinamanikew (VTA) S/he washes for other people.

kisipekinew (VTA) S/he is washing her/him.

kisipekinam (VTI) S/he washes it.

kisipekiniwew (VTA) S/he washes someone.

kisipekinikew (VTI) S/he washes something.

kisipekinicihcenew *pl.* **kisipekinicihcenewak** (VTA) S/he is washing her/his hands.

kisipekinikan *pl.* **kisipekinikana** (NI) Soap.

kisipikamâw *pl.* **kisipikamâwa** (NI) The end of a lake.

kisipisiw *pl.* **kisipisiwak** (VAI) It has an end.

kisipistikweyâw *pl.* **kisipistikweyâwa** (NI) The end of a river flow.

kisis *pl.* **kisisak** (NA) Your uncle. *Var.* **kocawîs**.

kisisamawew (VTA) S/he heats it up for her/him.

kisisamakew (VTA) S/he heats up the place.

kisisaweyimew *pl.* **kisisaweyimewak** (VAI) S/he is finished blessing her/him.

kisisikakan *pl.* **kisisikakana** (NI) A burner.

kisisimew (VTA) S/he made her/him puncture herself/himself, i.e.: stepping on a nail.

kisisimiwew (VTA) S/he makes people puncture themselves.

kisisin *pl.* **kisisinwak** (VTA) S/he stepped on a needle and punctured her/his foot.

kisisiw *pl.* **kisisiwak** (VAI) S/he is hot or has a fever.

kisiskapayihcikewin *pl.* **kisiskapayihcikewina** (NI) An increase in speed; accleration.

kisiskâpayonihk (IPC) An expression used to indicate speed; speedily.

kisiskâpayowin *pl.* **kisiskâpayowina** (NI) The act of going faster; accelerating.

kisiskâtôtamowin *pl.* **kisiskâtôtamowina** (NI) The act of rapidity.

kisiskâyâmowin *pl.* **kisiskâyâmowina** (NI) The act of leaving in a hurry.

kisiskotewahkan *pl.* **kisiskotewahkanwa** (VII) The fire is hot.

kisiskotewahkisiw *pl.* **kisiskotewahkisiwak** (VAI) It has lots of heat, i.e.: a hot stove.

kisisohiwewin *pl.* **kisisohiwewina** (NI) The act of making someone feverish.

kisisowayâwin *pl.* **kisisowayâwina** (NI) The act of feeling feverish.

kisisowin *pl.* **kisisowina** (NI) The act of having a fever.

kisisôcîpihk *pl.* **kisisôcîpihkak** (NA) A fever-root.

kisisôcîpihka (ob.).

kisitew *pl.* **kisitewa** (VII) It is hot.

kisiwaskatew *pl.* **kisiwaskatewak** (VAI) S/he has an upset stomach.

kisiwaskatewin *pl.* **kisiwaskatewina** (NI) Having an upset stomach.

kisiwâhitowak (VTA) They are upset with each other.

kisiwâhiwewin *pl.* **kisiwâhiwewina** (NI) The act of making someone upset; making someone mad.

kisiwâk (VII) It is near.

kisiwâsowin *pl.* **kisiwâsowina** (NI) The act of being enraged or angry.

kisiwew *pl.* **kisiwewak** (VAI) S/he or it is loud.

kiskahamawew (VTA) S/he gives her/him a haircut; s/he cuts her/his hair. *(Plains). Alt.* **paskwahamawew** *(Northern).*

kiskahamakew (VTA) S/he gives haircuts.

kiskatikan *pl.* **kiskatikana** (NI) A shinbone.

kiskawew (VTI) S/he wears it.

kiskamohiwew (VTI) S/he makes others wear it.

kiskânak *pl.* **kiskânakwak** (NA) A female dog or slang for a prostitute; a bitch.

kiskânakos *pl.* **kiskânakosak** (NA) A small female dog, i.e.: a small bitch.

kiskeyihcikan *pl.* **kiskeyihcikana** (NI) Something everyone knows.

kiskeyihtâkosiwin *pl.* **kiskeyihtâkosiwina** (NI) Being known; famed.

kiskeyihtâkwan *pl.* **kiskeyihtâkwana** (NI) Something known by everyone.

kiskeyimâw *pl.* **kiskeyimâwak** (VAI) S/he is known. *(Northern). Alt.* **nistaweyimâw** *(Plains).*

kiskeyimew (VTA) S/he knows her/him. *(Northern). Alt.* **nistaweyimew** *(Plains).*

kiskeyitam (VTI) S/he knows.

kiskeyimiwew (VTA) S/he knows people.

kiskeyihcikew (VTI) S/he knows things.

kiskeyitamohew *pl.* **kiskeyitamohewak** (VTA) S/he lets her/him know.

kiskeyitamowin *pl.* **kiskeyitamowina** (NI) Knowledge.

kiskiman *pl.* **kiskimana** (NI) A file.

kiskimanihkewin *pl.* **kiskimanihkewina** (NI) The act of making a file.

kiskimew (VTA) S/he makes an appointment with her/him.

kiskitam (VTI) S/he makes an appointment with something.

kiskimiwew (VTA) S/he makes an appointment with someone.

kiskihcikew (VTA) S/he makes an appointment with everyone.

kiskimowin *pl.* **kiskimowina** (NI) The act of making an appointment.

kiskinawâc (NI) An identification mark.

kiskinawâcihokispison *pl.* **kiskinawâcihokispisona** (NI) A very fancy or ornate bracelet.

kiskinawâteyihcikan *pl.* **kiskinawâteyihcikana** (NI) The act of belonging to; attribution; having a characteristic.

kiskinohamawâkan *pl.* **kiskinohamwâkanak** (NA) A learner. *(Plains)*. *Alt.* **kiskinohamâkan** *(Northern)*.

kiskinohamawew *pl.* **kiskinohamawewak** (VTA) S/he taught her/him.

kiskinohamâkan *pl.* **kiskinohamâkanak** (NA) A learner. *(Northern)*. *Alt.* **kiskinohamawâkan** *(Plains)*.

kiskinohamâkewin *pl.* **kiskinohamâkewina** (NI) The act of teaching.

kiskinohamâkewyiniw *pl.* **kiskinohamâkewyiniwak** (NA) A teaching person, i.e.: a male teacher.

kiskinohamâkosiwin *pl.* **kiskinohamâkosiwina** (NI) The act of going to school and learning.

kiskinohamâsiwin *pl.* **kiskinohamâsiwina** (NI) The act of teaching oneself, i.e.: self-discipline.

kiskinohamâtowikamik *pl.* **kiskinohamâtowikamikwa** (NI) A school house.

kiskinohamâtôtâpânâsk *pl.* **kiskinohamâtôtâpânâskwak** (NA) A school bus.

kiskinohtahew (VTA) S/he guides her/him or shows her/him where to go.

kiskinohtataw (VTI) S/he guides it to the right place.

kiskinohtahiwew (VTA) S/he guides people to the right place.

kiskinohtahiwewin *pl.* **kiskinohtahiwewina** (NI) The act of guiding; guidance.

kiskinowâcihcikan *pl.* **kiskinowâcihcikanak** (NA) A decoration.

kiskinowâcihew (VTA) S/he decorates her/him.

kiskinowâcitâw (VTI) S/he decorates it.

kiskinowâcihiwew (VTA) S/he decorates people.

kiskinowâcihcikew (VTI) S/he decorates things.

kiskinowâpahikewin *pl.* **kiskinowâpahikewina** (NI) The act of imitating in order to learn.

kiskinowâpamew (VTA) S/he imitates her/him in order to learn.

kiskinowâpatam (VTI) S/he copies it.

kiskinowâpamiwew (VTA) S/he copies people.

kiskinowâpahcikew (VTI) S/he copies things.

kiskinowâsohtawew (VTA) S/he listens to her/his teaching.

kiskinowâsohtam (VTI) S/he listens to its teaching.

kiskinowâsohtâkew (VTA) S/he listens to peoples' teaching.

kiskinowâtâpâwahew (VAI) S/he performs a quick baptism.

kiskinowâtâpâwatâw (VAI) S/he performs a quick blessing over it.

kiskinowâteyimew (VAI) S/he makes a mental note of her/him.

kiskinowâteyitam (VTI) S/he makes a mental note of it.

kiskinowâteyimiwew (VTA) S/he makes a mental note of people.

kiskinowâteyihcikew (VTI) S/he makes a mental note of everything.

kiskinwawew (VTA) S/he is describing someone.

kiskinwaham (VTI) S/he describes it.

kiskinwahikew (VTI) S/he describes something.

kiskisisiwiw *pl.* **kiskisisiwiwak** (VAI) She is a mare.

kiskisiw *pl.* **kiskisiwak** (VAI) S/he remembers.

kiskisiwin *pl.* **kiskisiwina** (NI) The act of remembering.

kiskisohew (VTA) S/he reminds her/him of someone.

kiskisohiwew (VTA) S/he makes people remember.

kiskisohcikew (VTI) S/he makes things to make people remember.

kiskisohiwewin *pl.* **kiskisohiwewina** (NI) The act of reminding someone; enlighten; monument.

kiskisomew (VTA) S/he reminds her/him by telling her/him.

kiskisomik (VTI) It reminds her/him of something when s/he hears about it.

kiskisomiwew (VTA) S/he talks to people to remind them of something.

kiskisopayowin *pl.* **kiskisopayowina** (NI) Being reminded; bethought.

kiskisototawew (VTA) S/he remembers her/him.

kiskisototam (VTI) S/he remembers it.

kiskisototâkew (VTA) S/he remembers people.

kiskisototâkewin *pl.* **kiskisototâkewina** (NI) In memoriam.

kiskiwehikan *pl.* **kiskiwehikana** (NI) Something used as a reminder, i.e.: a datebook.

kiskiwehow *pl.* **kiskiwehowak** (VAI) S/he wears an emblem.

kiskiwehowin *pl.* **kiskiwehowina** (NI) The act of wearing something to be recognized by, i.e.: an emblem.

kiskiwewew (VTA) S/he prophetically designates her/his spirit identity or signature; s/he puts an identity mark on her/him.

kiskiweham (VTI) S/he prophetically designates its spirit identity.

49

kiskiwehowew (VTA) S/he prophetically designates peoples' spirit identity.

kiskiwehikew (VTI) S/he prophetically designates things' spirit identity.

kisopwemyocisin (NI) A warm breeze. *(Plains). Alt.* **sâwaniyowew** *(Northern).*

kisowapowin *pl.* **kisowapowina** (NI) The act of sitting and sulking.

kisowinâkosiwin *pl.* **kisowinâkosiwina** (NI) The act of looking angry.

kisôtôtâkewin *pl.* **kisôtôtâkewina** (NI) The act of agitating someone; agitation; pique.

kisôwahiwewin *pl.* **kisôwahiwewina** (NI) Offend.

kisôwahpinew *pl.* **kisôwahpinewak** (VTA) Her/his illness makes her/him upset and bitter.

kisôwahpinewin *pl.* **kisôwahpinewina** (NI) The act of being upset and bitter because of illness.

kisôwaskatewin *pl.* **kisôwaskatewina** (NI) Colic; having a bellyache.

kisôwâhew (VTA) S/he made her/him angry or upset.

kisôwâhiwew (VTA) S/he made others angry.

kisôwâhitowin *pl.* **kisôwâhitowina** (NI) The act of making each other angry; offence or offense; aggravation.

kisôwâhtwâw *pl.* **kisôwâhtwâwak** (VTA) S/he gets others mad at her/him.

kisôwâhtwâwin *pl.* **kisôwâhtwâwinak** (NA) The act of making others mad at someone.

kisôwâsiw *pl.* **kisôwâsiwak** (VAI) S/he is angry.

kisôwâsiwin *pl.* **kisôwâsiwina** (NI) Being angry; ire.

kisôwâyawin *pl.* **kisôwâyawina** (NI) The act of being fretful or edgy; being hostile.

kisôweyihtam *pl.* **kisôweyihtamwak** (VAI) Her/his thoughts are full of bitterness; cranky.

kisôweyihtamowin *pl.* **kisôweyihtamowina** (NI) Having bitter thoughts; indignation; irritation; anguished; the act of being anguished.

kisôweyimew (VTA) S/he thinks of her/him with bitterness.

kisôweyitam (VTI) S/he is bitter.

kisôweyimiwew (VTA) S/he is bitter to others.

kisôweyihcikew (VTI) S/he is bitter to everything.

kisôwinâkosiw *pl.* **kisôwinâkosiwak** (VAI) S/he looks angry.

kisôwinâkwan *pl.* **kisôwinâkwanwa** (VII) It looks upset.

kisôwisâyâwin *pl.* **kisôwisâyâwina** (NI) The act of feeling disgruntled.

kispakaciw *pl.* **kispakaciwak** (VAI) It is frozen thick, i.e.: ice.

kispakamow *pl.* **kispakamowak** (VAI) It is on thick.

kispakastâw (VTI) S/he piles it thick like hay.

kispakahew (VTI) S/he piles them thick like spruce boughs.

kispakahcikew (VTI) S/he piles things thick.

kispakatin *pl.* **kispakatinwa** (VII) It is frozen thick, i.e.: a whole lake or river.

kispakâw *pl.* **kispakâwa** (VII) It is thick, i.e.: wood.

kispakekan *pl.* **kispakekanwa** (VII) The hide or blanket is thick.

kispakekihtin *pl.* **kispakekihtinwa** (VII) The book is thick.

kispakekin *pl.* **kispakekinwa** (NI) A thick hide.

kispakekinwekisiw *pl.* **kispakekinwekisiwak** (VAI) It has a thick hide, i.e.: cariboo hide.

kispakekinwew *pl.* **kispakekinwewak** (VAI) S/he has a thick hide.

kispakekisiw *pl.* **kispakekisiwak** (VAI) It is thick like a beaver hide.

kispakikihcikewin *pl.* **kispakikihcikewina** (NI) The act of thickening. *(Plains). Alt.* **kispakikihcikiwin** *(Northern).*

kispakikihcikiwin *pl.* **kispakikihcikiwina** (NI) The act of thickening. *(Northern). Alt.* **kispakikihcikewin** *(Plains).*

kispakinew (VAI) S/he has a thick roll of bills.

kispakinam (VTI) S/he folds it thickly.

kispakinikew (VTI) S/he folds everything thickly.

kispakisiw *pl.* **kispakisiwak** (VAI) S/he is thick.

kispakisîhew (VTA) S/he makes it thick, i.e.: bannock.

kispakisîtâw (VTI) S/he makes it thick.

kispakisîhiwew (VTA) S/he makes people thick.

kispakisîhcikew (VTI) S/he makes things thick.

kispakisowin *pl.* **kispakisowina** (NI) Being thick.

kispakiswew (VTA) S/he cuts it thickly.

kispakisam (VTI) S/he cuts it thickly.

kispakisowew (VTA) S/he cuts someone thickly.

kispakisikew (VTI) S/he cuts things thickly.

kispewâtew (VTA) S/he defends her/him. *Var.* **kispewew.**

kispewâtam (VTI) S/he defends it.

kispewâsowew (VTA) S/he defends someone.

kispewâcikew (VTA) S/he defends others.

kispewew (VTA) S/he defends her/him. *Var.* **kispewâtew**

kispetam (VTI) S/he defends it.

kispesowew (VTA) S/he defends someone.

kispecikew (VTA) S/he defends others.

kispewewin *pl.* **kispewewina** (NI) The act of defending someone.

kispison *pl.* **kispisona** (NI) A cuff; a wristlet.

kistahcâw *pl.* **kistahcâwa** (NI) Solid ground.

kistahew (VTA) S/he founds or establishes her/him solidly.

kistastâw (VTI) S/he places it solidly.

kistahiwew (VTA) S/he places someone solidly.

kistacikew (VTI) S/he places things solidly.

kistahwew (VTA) S/he shoots her/him point blank.

kistaham (VTI) S/he shoots it point blank.

kistahowew (VTA) S/he hits someone point blank.

kistahikew (VTA) S/he hits others point blank.

kistapiw *pl.* **kistapiwak** (VAI) S/he is paraplegic.

kistapiwin *pl.* **kistapiwina** (NI) The act of being paraplegic.

kistaskisiw *pl.* **kistaskisiwak** (VAI) The tree stands solid.

kistastew *pl.* **kistastewa** (VII) It is solidly placed or established.

kistatamohtâw *pl.* **kistatamohtâwak** (VAI) S/he makes a well beaten path.

kistatamow *pl.* **kistatamowa** (VII) A path or road that is well travelled.

kistâpâwahew (VTA) S/he soaks it, i.e.: the laundry.

kistâpâwahtâw (VTI) S/he soaks it by hand.

kistâpâwahiwew (VTA) S/he soaks someone personally.

kistâpâwahcikew (VTI) S/he soaks things by hand.

kistâpiskâw *pl.* **kistâpiskâwa** (NI) The rock is solid.

kisteyihcikâsiw *pl.* **kisteyihcikâsiwak** (VAI) S/he is thought of as honorable.

kisteyihcikâtew *pl.* **kisteyihcikâtewa** (VII) It is honored.

kisteyihtâkosiw *pl.* **kisteyihtâkosiwak** (VAI) S/he is honorable.

kisteyihtâkosiwin *pl.* **kisteyihtâkosiwina** (NI) The act of being honored.

kisteyihtâkwan *pl.* **kisteyihtâkwanwa** (VII) It is honorable.

kistikân *pl.* **kistikâna** (NI) Grain.

kiscikânis *pl.* **kiscikânisak** (NA) A vegetable plant something like a pea or bean; vegetable garden. **kiscikânisa** (ob.).

kistikew *pl.* **kistikewak** (VAI) S/he grows things, i.e.: vegetables or grain.

kistohkan *pl.* **kistohkana** (NI) The door of a teepee.

kistokew *pl.* **kistokewak** (VTI) S/he resides permanently.

kistôtew *pl.* **kistôtewak** (VAI) S/he is together with the entire family.

kistôtewewin *pl.* **kistôtewewinak** (NA) Being together with the entire family. **kistôtewewina** (ob.).

kiswahewin *pl.* **kiswahewina** (NI) The act of provoking.

kitahamakewin *pl.* **kitahamakewina** (NI) The act of telling people to stop doing something wrong; counselling; admonition.

kitahamawew (VTA) S/he tells her/him to stop.

kitahamakew (VTA) S/he tells people to stop.

kitansihkawin *pl.* **kitansihkawinak** (NA) Your goddaughter.

kitasew *pl.* **kitasewak** (VAI) S/he is wearing pants. *(Northern). Alt.* **postitâsew** *(Plains).*

kitâmawew *pl.* **kitâmawewak** (VAI) S/he consumed all of the other person's food.

kitânawew *pl.* **kitânawewak** (VAI) S/he consumed everything.

kitânawewin *pl.* **kitânawewina** (NI) The act of consuming everything.

kitâpamew (VTA) S/he looks at her/him. *(Plains). Alt.* **kanawâpamew** *(Northern).*

kitâpatam (VTI) S/he looks at it.

kitâpamiwew (VTA) S/he looks at people.

kitâpahcikew (VTI) S/he looks at things.

kitâw *pl.* **kitâwak** (VTI) S/he ate it.

kitihkawew (VTA) S/he sideswipes her/him.

kitihkaham (VTI) S/he sideswipes it.

kitihkahikew (VTI) S/he sideswipes things.

kitihkimew (VTA) S/he says something that insults her/him indirectly.

kitihkihtam (VTI) S/he is affronted by her/his speech.

kitihkimiwew (VTA) S/he affronts people.

kitihkihcikew (VTI) S/he affronts things by her/his speech.

kitimahâw *pl.* **kitimahâwak** (VAI) S/he is being treated poorly.

kitimahew (VTA) S/he treats her/him poorly.

kitimatâw (VTI) S/he treat it poorly.

kitimahiwew (VTA) S/he treats people poorly.

kitimahisiw *pl.* **kitimahisiwak** (VTA) S/he treats herself/himself poorly.

kitimahisowin *pl.* **kitimahisowina** (NI) The act of treating oneself poorly.

kitimahiwewin *pl.* **kitimahiwewina** (NI) The act of abusing someone.

kitimahtâsiw *pl.* **kitimahtâsiwak** (VTA) S/he is cruel to someone.

kitimahtâsowin *pl.* **kitimahtâsowina** (NI) Being cruel.

kitimakinâwew (VTA) S/he felt sorry for her/him.

kitimakinânam (VTI) S/he feels sorry for it.

kitimakinâkew (VTA) S/he feels sorry for people.

kitimakinânâkew (VTA) S/he feels sorry for others.

kitimakiyihtam *pl.* **kitimakiyihtamwak** (VTI) Her/his thoughts are full of sorrow about it.

kitimâkahkamikan (NI) A sorry state of events.

kitimâkan *pl.* **kitimâkanwa** (NI) A sorry or unfortunate situation.

kitimâkâcimisow *pl.* **kitimâkâcimisowak** (VAI) S/he tells a hard luck story about her/his life. *(Plains). Alt.* **kwâtakimow** *(Northern).*

kitimâkeyihcikew *pl.* **kitimâkeyhihcikewak** (VTI) S/he feels sorry for everything.

kitimâkeyihtamawew *pl.* **kitimâkeyihtamawewak** (VTA) Her/his thoughts of her/him are mournful.

kitimâkeyimew (VTA) S/he pities her/him.

kitimâkeyitam (VTI) S/he pities it.

kitimâkeyimiwew (VTA) S/he pities people.

kitimâkeyihcikew (VTI) S/he pities things.

kitimâkeyimowin *pl.* **kitimâkeyimowina** (NI) The act of feeling passionate about a subject.

kitimâkihkahtew *pl.* **kitimâkihkahtewa** (NI) Something poorly burned. *Var.* **kwâtakihkahtew**.

kitimâkihtawew (VTA) S/he sounded sorrowful to her/him.

kitimâkitam (VTI) S/he feels sorry for what s/he heard.

kitimâkitâkew (VTA) S/he feels sorry for people when s/he hears them.

kitimâkihtâkewin *pl.* **kitimâkihtâkewina** (NI) The act of being responsive towards someone; amenable.

kitimâkimamitoneyîhcikan *pl.* **kitimâkimamitoneyîhcikana** (NI) The act of feeling sad; a mental state of mind.

kitimâkimew (VTA) S/he slanders her/him.

kitimâkitam (VTI) S/he slanders with what s/he heard.

kitimâkimiwew (VTA) S/he slanders people.

kitimâkisihcikew (VTA) S/he slanders grievously.

kitimâkinâkewin *pl.* **kitimâkinâkewina** (NI) Having or displaying empathy.

kitimâkinâtowin *pl.* **kitimâkinâtowina** (NI) The act of feeling sorry for someone.

kitimâkisiw *pl.* **kitimâkisiwak** (VAI) S/he is poor or lacking possessions; the way a person lives in their behavior and bad attitude; an impoverished attitude and lifestyle.

kitimâkiskwewewin *pl.* **kitimâkiskwewewina** (NI) Being dowdy.

kitimâkisowin *pl.* **kitimâkisowina** (NI) The act of being poor; an unhappy person.

kitinew (VTA) S/he detains her/him; s/he stops her/him from going somewhere; s/he prevents her/him from leaving.

kitinam (VTI) S/he detains it.

kitiniwew (VTA) S/he detains people.

kitinikew (VTI) S/he holds things back.

kitinikewin *pl.* **kitinikewina** (NI) The act of being prevented; preventable; prevention.

kitisimow *pl.* **kitisimowak** (VAI) S/he does not want to leave.

kitisimowâtisiw *pl.* **kitisimowâtisiwak** (VAI) S/he likes staying in one place.

kitisimowâtisowin *pl.* **kitisimowâtisowina** (NI) The act of not wanting to leave.

kitisimowin *pl.* **kitisimowina** (NI) The act of wanting to stay.

kitisimôtotawew *pl.* **kitisimôtotawewak** (VTA) S/he will not leave her/him.

kitiskinew (VTA) S/he dropped her/him.

kitiskinam (VTI) S/he dropped it.

kitiskiniwew (VTA) S/he dropped someone.

kitiskinikew (VTI) S/he dropped something.

kitiskinikeskowin *pl.* **kitiskinikeskowina** (NI) The act of continually dropping things, being butterfingered.

kitiskipayihew (VTA) S/he dropped her/him accidently.

kitiskipayitâw (VTI) S/he dropped it accidently.

kitiskipayihiwew (VTA) S/he drops people accidently.

kitiskipayihcikew (VTI) S/he drops things accidently.

kitiskipayiw *pl.* **kitiskipayiwa** *or* **kitiskipayiwak** (VII) *or* (VAI) It *or* s/he falls off accidently.

kitiskipitew (VTI) S/he pulls it off accidently.

kitiskipitam (VTI) S/he pulls it off accidently.

kitiskipihcikew (VTI) S/he pulls things off accidently.

kitiwehkwâmiw *pl.* **kitiwehkwâmiwak** (VAI) S/he is snoring. *(Plains). Alt.* **matwehkwâmiw** *(Northern).*

kitohâcikew (VAI) S/he makes an animal call.

kitohcikan *pl.* **kitohcikana** (NI) A musical instrument.

kitohcikew *pl.* **kitohcikewak** (VTI) S/he makes music; s/he plays an instrument.

kitohcikewin *pl.* **kitohcikewina** (NI) Making music with an instrument.

kitohew (VAI) S/he calls, i.e.: to animals; s/he makes a call imitating a certain animal; s/he imitates an animal or a duck.

kitohtâw (VAI) S/he makes it sound or turns it on.

kitotew (VTA) S/he rebukes her/him; s/he reprimands; s/he bawls her/him out.

kitowew (VTA) S/he rebukes someone.

kitow *pl.* **kitowak** (VAI) S/he or it called, i.e.: moose or other animals call out.

kitowepayihew (VTI) S/he rattles it; s/he makes it sound, i.e.: like a bell.

kitowepayitâw (VTI) S/he makes a rattle noise with it.

kitowepayihcikew (VTI) S/he makes a rattle noise with things.

kitowepayiw *pl.* **kitowepayiwa** *or* **kitowepayiwak** (VII) *or* (VAI) It *or* s/he rattles.

kitowin *pl.* **kitowina** (NI) The act of animals calling out.

kitow sâkahikan (NI) The Cree name for the settlement of Calling Lake.

kiyâskiwin *pl.* **kiyâskiwina** (NI) The act of being untruthful.

kiyikawahew (VAI) S/he mixes them or blends them together; s/he puts them together.

kiyikawastâw (VII) S/he mixes it with something; s/he places it mixed up.

kiyikawahiwew (VII) S/he mixes it with people.

kiyikawascikew (VII) S/he mixes it with things.

kiyokawew *pl.* **kiyokawewak** (VTA) S/he visits with her/him. *(Plains). Alt.* **kîhokawew** *(Northern).*

kiyomâskawew (VTA) S/he bothers her/him unceasingly; s/he bothers her/him by staying.

kiyomâskam (VAI) S/he is bothersome.

kiyomâskâkew (VTA) S/he bothers people.

kiyomâskâcikew (VTI) S/he bothers everything.

kiyomâyeyimew (VTA) S/he finds her/him bothersome; s/he is bothered by her/him.

kiyomâyeyitam (VTI) S/he is bothered by it.

kiyomâyeyimiwew (VTA) S/he is worried about her/him.

kiyomâyeyicikew (VTI) S/he is bothered by things happening.

kîcimos pl. **kîcimosak** (NA) One's "beau."

kîhcekositahew (VTA) S/he takes her/him up a ladder or stairs. *(Northern). Alt.* **âmaciwetahew** *(Plains).*

kîhcekositataw (VTI) S/he takes it up.

kîhcekositahiwew (VTA) S/he takes people up.

kîhcekositahcikew (VTI) S/he takes things up.

kîhcekosiw pl. **kîhcekosiwak** (VAI) S/he climbs up stairs or a ladder; clamber.

kîhcekosiwin pl. **kîhcekosiwina** (NI) The act of climbing or going up stairs or a ladder.

kîhcekosiwinâhtik pl. **kîhcekosiwinâhtikwa** (NI) A ladder or stairway.

kîhcekosîtisahwew (VTA) S/he chases her/him up something.

kîhcekosîtisaham (VTI) S/he sends it upstairs.

kîhcekosîtisahowew (VTA) S/he sends people upstairs.

kîhcekosîtisahikew (VTA) S/he sends everyone upstairs.

kîhkihew (VTA) S/he nags her/him and makes her/him nervous.

kîhkitâw (VTA) S/he provokes nervousness.

kîhkihiwew (VTA) S/he makes others nervous.

kîhkihcikew (VTA) S/he makes everyone nervous.

kîhokawew pl. **kîhokawewak** (VTA) S/he visits with her/him. *(Northern). Alt.* **kiyokawew** *(Plains).*

kîhokew pl. **kîhokewak** (VAI) S/he visits.

kîhokewin pl. **kîhokewina** (NI) The act of visiting.

kîhtwam (IPC) Next time.

kîhtwamiyimew (VTA) S/he thinks of her/him over and over again; s/he remembers her/him.

kîhtwamiyitam (VTI) S/he thinks of it over and over again.

kîhtwamiyimiwew (VTA) S/he thinks of people over and over again.

kîhtwamiyihcikew (VTI) S/he thinks of things over and over again.

kîhwîhtamakawin pl. **kîhwîhtamakawina** (NI) The act of having been advised.

kîkawenamowin pl. **kîkawenamowina** (NI) The art of mixing.

kîkawinew (VTA) S/he mixes them or blends them with something else. *(Plains)*

kîkawititâw (VTI) S/he mixes them or blends them with something else.

kîkawimiwew (VTI) S/he mixes them or blends them with something else.

kîkahcikew (VTI) S/he mixes them or blends them with something else.

kîkâmitâtaht (IPC) Nine. *(Northern). Alt.* **kekâymitâht** *(Plains).*

kîkâmitâtahtomitanaw (IPC) Ninety.

kîkâmitâtahtomitanawâw (IPC) Ninety times, ninetieth time.

kîkâmitâtahtosâp (IPC) Nineteen.

kîkâmitâtahtosâpâw (IPC) Nineteen times, nineteenth time.

kîkâmitâtahtwâw (IPC) Nine times, ninth time.

kîkâmitâtahtwâw mitâtahtomitanaw (IPC) Nine hundred.

kîkihk (IPC) In your own home.

kîkisep (IPC) This past morning.

kîkisepâmiciwin pl. **kîkisepâmiciwina** (NI) Breakfast food. *(Northern)*

kîkisepâ mîcisowin pl. **kîkisepâ mîcisowina** (NI) Breakfast or eating breakfast.

kîkisepâ mîcowin (NI) Cereal, porridge; buckwheat; morning food.

kîkisepâyâw (VII) It is kind of early in the morning; it feels like early morning.

kîkiwâw (NA) Used when speaking about a group of homes: "Your home; your house."

kîkîw pl. **kîkîwak** (VAI) Her/his sore is healed. *(Northern). Alt.* **inîwiw** *(Plains).*

kîkîwin pl. **kîkîwina** (NI) The act of healing a sore. *(Northern)*

kîkway pl. **kîkwaya** (NI) Something or a thing.

kîkwây (IPC) Indicates a question is being asked, i.e.: "what or what do you want?"

kîkwâya pl. **kîkwâyak** (IPC) What kind of things?

kîmahpinatew pl. **kîmahpinatewa** (NI) A dirty fight; an unfair scrap; an illegal fight or illegal kill.

kîmâhew (VTA) S/he sneaks up and surprises it or her/him.

kîmâhkawew (VTA) S/he sneaks up and surprises them.

kîmâkâkew (VTA) S/he sneaks up and surprises people.

kîmâkâcikew (VTA) S/he sneaks up and surprises them.

kîmâpamew (VTA) S/he peeks at her/him, i.e.: Peeping Tom; s/he spies on her/him.

kîmâpatam (VTI) S/he peeks at it.

kîmâpamiwew (VTA) S/he peeks at people.

kîmâpahcikew (VTI) S/he peeks at them.

kîmihtam pl. **kîmihtamak** (VTA) S/he listens in a furtive manner.

53

kîmihtaw *pl.* **kîmihtawak** (VAI) S/he eavesdrops.

kîmihtawew (VAI) S/he is eavesdropping on them or her/him.

kîmihtam (VAI) S/he is eavesdropping.

kîmihtakew (VAI) S/he eavesdrops on everybody.

kîminew (VTA) S/he caressed her/his private parts.

kîminam (VTI) S/he caressed its private parts.

kîminiwew (VTA) S/he caressed someone's private parts.

kîminikew (VTA) S/he is caressing someone's private parts.

kîminikewin *pl.* **kîminikewinak** (NA) The act of touching someone intimately. **kîminikewina** (ob.).

kîminisiw *pl.* **kîminisiwak** (VTA) S/he is fondling or caressing herself/himself.

kîminisiwin *pl.* **kîminisiwinak** (NA) The act of fondling or caressing oneself. **kîminisiwina** (ob.).

kîminitowak (VTA) They are fondling or caressing each other.

kîminitowin *pl.* **kîminitowina** (NI) The act of fondling or caressing each other.

kîminîcâkan *pl.* **kîminîcâkanak** (NA) An illegitimate child; a bastard.

kîminîcâkanihkawew (VTA) He made her pregnant with an illegitimate child.

kîminîcâkanihkakew (VTA) He caused someone to have a child.

kîminîcâkanihkew *pl.* **kîminîcâkanihkewak** (VTA) He has fathered a child out of wedlock.

kîminîcâkanihkewin *pl.* **kîminîcâkanihkewinak** (NA) The act of fathering a child out of wedlock. **kîminîcâkanihkewina** (ob.)

kîmisiw *pl.* **kîmisiwak** (VAI) S/he is devious or sneaky.

kîmisiwin *pl.* **kîmisiwina** (VTI) The act of being devious or sneaky.

kîmîw *pl.* **kîmîwak** (VAI) S/he snuck away.

kîmîwin *pl.* **kîmîwina** (NI) The act of sneaking away.

kîmôc (IPC) Quietly, on the sly; sneaky or devious silence.

kîmôcinâkosiw *pl.* **kîmôcinâkosiwak** (NA) S/he appears or looks sneaky. *(Northern). Alt.* **kakayesiwinâkosiw** *(Plains).*

kîmôcipîkiskwew *pl.* **kîmôcipîkiskwewak** (VAI) S/he whispers. *(Northern). Alt.* **kimwew** *(Plains).*

kîmôcipîkiskwewin *pl.* **kîmôcipîkiskwewina** (NI) The act of whispering. *(Northern). Alt.* **kimwewin** *(Plains).*

kîmôcisâkihitowin *pl.* **kîmôcisâkihitowina** (NI) The act of loving on the sly; secret love.

kîmôciyawehew (VTA) S/he makes her/him secretly angry.

kîmôciyawehtwâw (VTA) S/he makes others upset.

kîmôciyawehiwew (VTA) S/he makes everyone upset.

kîmôciyawesiw *pl.* **kîmôciyawesiwak** (VAI) S/he is secretly angry; s/he is hiding her/his anger; s/he keeps her/his temper to herself/himself.

kîmôciyawesiwin *pl.* **kîmôciyawesiwina** (NI) Being secretly angry or seething mad but not showing it; silent rage.

kîmôtahkamikan (VII) It is done in a sneaky or underhanded way.

kîmotowin *pl.* **kîmotowina** (NI) The act of absconding.

kîmôtâpiwin *pl.* **kîmôtâpiwina** (NI) The act of peeking.

kîmôtâtisiwin *pl.* **kîmôtâtisiwina** (NI) The act of being artificial; artificiality; disloyal; fallacy; guileful; insincerity; implausibility; a sham.

kîmôtisiw *pl.* **kîmôtisiwak** (VAI) S/he acts sneaky or underhandedly.

kîmôtisiwin *pl.* **kîmôtisiwina** (NI) The act of being sneaky or underhanded; the act of secrecy.

kimwew *pl.* **kimwewak** (VAI) S/he whispers. *(Plains). Alt.* **kîmôcipîkiskwew** *(Northern).*

kimwewin *pl.* **kimwewina** (NI) The act of whispering. *(Plains). Alt.* **kîmôcipîkiskwewin** *(Northern).*

kînikatahikew (VTI) S/he is hacking it to a point.

kînikataham (VTI) S/he is hacking it to a point.

kînikatahikewak (VTA) S/he is hacking it to a point.

kînikâw *pl.* **kînikâwa** (VII) It is pointed and sharp, i.e.: a knife.

kînikikahwew (VTI) S/he chops it to a point with an axe; s/he chops it to a sharp point, i.e.: a fence post.

kînikikaham (VTA) S/he sharpens one stick.

kînikikahikew (VTA) S/he sharpens a whole bunch of sticks.

kînikikotew *pl.* **kînikikotewak** (VAI) S/he has a pointed nose.

kînikisiw *pl.* **kînikisiwak** (VAI) It is pointed, i.e.: a rock.

kînipocikan *pl.* **kînipocikana** (NI) A sharpener. *Var.* **tâsahikan**.

kînipotamawew (VTA) S/he sharpens it for her/him.

kînipotamakew (VTI) S/he sharpens tools.

kînipotâw (VTI) S/he sharpens it, i.e.: an axe.

kînipoyew (VTI) S/he sharpens them (posts).

kînipocikew (VTI) S/he sharpens things.

kînweseskamik (IPC) A very, very long time.

kîpîw *pl.* **kîpîwak** (VAI) S/he lays down from a sitting position; s/he stretches out fully.

kîsaweyimew (VTA) S/he has blessed her/him.

kîsaweyitam (VTI) S/he has blessed it.

kîsaweyimiwew (VTA) S/he has blessed people.

kîsaweyihcikew (VTI) S/he has blessed things.

kîsâspine (IPC) An expression meaning "might as well."

kîsihcikâsiw *pl.* **kîsihcikâsiwak** (VAI) Used when referring to a completed product: "it is all finished."

54

kîsihcikâtew *pl.* **kîsihcikâtewa** (VII) Used when referring to a completed project: "it is all finished."

kîsik (NI) Sky.

kîsikanisiw *pl.* **kîsikanisiwak** (VAI) S/he spends the whole day.

kîsikanisowin *pl.* **kîsikanisowina** (NI) The act of spending the whole day.

kîsikayastew (VII) On a moonlight night when the moon shines like the daylight.

kîsikâw (VII) It is day or daytime or daylight.

kîsinam (VTA) S/he tans deerhide or cariboo hide.

kîsinam (VTI) S/he is tanning moosehide.

kîsinikew (VTI) S/he is finishing off the moosehide.

kîsinateyimew (VAI) S/he regrets her/his behavior.

kîsinateyimiwew (VAI) S/he has regrets and grieves over everyone.

kîsinateyicikew (VAI) S/he has regrets and grieves over everything.

kîsinateyimisiw *pl.* **kîsinateyimisiwak** (VAI) S/he regrets or repents her/his sins and feels humble about herself/himself; s/he does not think much of herself/himself.

kîsinâc (VII) It is unfortunate, regretable, too bad.

kîsinâcihew (VTA) S/he brings her/him misfortune; s/he "finished" her/him; s/he makes it bad for her/him.

kîsinâcitâw (VTA) S/he brings grief or sorrow.

kîsinâcihiw *pl.* **kîsinâcihiwak** (VTA) S/he brings misfortune upon herself/himself; s/he brings grief, sorrow upon herself/himself; s/he depresses herself/himself; s/he wasted herself/himself unnecessarily; s/he makes it bad for herself/himself.

kîsinâcihowin *pl.* **kîsinâcihowina** (NI) The act of bringing misfortune upon oneself.

kîsinâtahkamikan *pl.* **kîsinâtahkamikanwa** (VII) It is an extreme misfortune that is happening.

kîsinâtahkamikisiw *pl.* **kîsinâtahkamikisiwak** (VAI) S/he is causing extreme misfortune; s/he did something awful.

kîsinâtahkamikisiwin *pl.* **kîsinâtahkamikisiwina** (NI) The act of causing extreme misfortune.

kîsinâteyihtam *pl.* **kîsinâteyihtamwak** (VTI) S/he thinks it is remorseful or awful.

kîsinâteyihtamowin *pl.* **kîsinâteyihtamowina** (NI) The act of thinking something is remorseful or awful.

kîsinâteyimisiwin *pl.* **kîsinâteyimisiwina** (NI) The act of repentence.

kîsinikiw *pl.* **kîsinikiwak** (VAI) S/he is tanning hide.

kîsinikowin *pl.* **kîsinikowina** (NI) The act of tanning hide.

kîsipakâw *pl.* **kîsipakâwa** (VII) The leaves are full grown.

kîsiskâw (IPC) An expression meaning "without delay; just for a little while; just for a minute."

kîsiskwehtin *pl.* **kîsiskwehtinwa** (VII) The neck broke off in the fall, i.e.: bottle.

kîsistohtawew (VAI) S/he is reacting to a moose call; s/he is answering a moose call. *(Northern) Alt.* **naskwewasihtawew** *(Plains).*

kîsistohtam (VAI) S/he reacts to the moose call.

kîsistohtakew (VAI) S/he reacts to someone's moose call.

kîsiswew (VTA) S/he cooks it, i.e.: fish.

kîsisam, (VTI) S/he cooks it, i.e.: meat or berries.

kîsisowew (VTA) S/he burns someone.

kîsisikew (VTI) S/he burns things.

kîsitew *pl.* **kîsitewa** (VII) It is cooked.

kîsiyihtew *pl.* **kîsiyihtewak** (VAI) The snow has melted for good.

kîsiyiw *pl.* **kîsiyiwak** (VTI) S/he destroyed it completely.

kîsiyiwin *pl.* **kîsiyiwina** (NI) The act of destroying something completely.

kîskahamâw *pl.* **kîskahamâwak** (VAI) S/he has a haircut. *(Plains). Alt.* **paskwahamâw** *(Northern).*

kîskahcâw *pl.* **kîskahcâwa** (NI) The edge of a dirt cliff.

kîskanakowayân *pl.* **kîskanakowayâna** (NI) A vest.

kîskatahikan *pl.* **kîskatahikana** (NI) A stump.

kîskatahikâsiw *pl.* **kîskatahikâsiwak** (VAI) It is chopped off, i.e.: tree.

kîskatahikâtew *pl.* **kîskatahikâtewa** (VII) It is chopped off, i.e.: fence post.

kîskatahikew *pl.* **kîskatahikewak** (VAI) S/he chops things off.

kîskatahikewin *pl.* **kîskatahikewina** (NI) The act of chopping things off.

kîskatahosiwin *pl.* **kîskatahosiwina** (NI) The act of chopping oneself off.

kîskatahwew (VTI) S/he chops it off.

kîskataham (VTI) S/he chops it off.

kîskatahowew (VTA) S/he chops someone off.

kîskatahikew (VTI) S/he chops something off.

kîskatawahkâw *pl.* **kîskatawahkâwa** (NI) A cut bank.

kîskatinâw *pl.* **kîskatinâwa** (NI) A cliff.

kîskâpiskâw *pl.* **kîskâpiskâwa** (NI) A rocky cliff or a broken off piece of metal.

kîskâw *pl.* **kîskâwa** (VII) It is broken off or part of it is gone.

kîskâyôs *pl.* **kîskâyôsak** (NA) A bobtail.

kîskâyoweswew (VTA) S/he cuts the tail off.

kîskâyowesam (VTI) S/he cuts the tail off it.

kîskâyowesowew (VTA) S/he cuts the tail off someone.

kîskâyowesikew (VTI) S/he cuts the tail off things.

kîskâyowetahwew (VTA) S/he chops the tail off.

kîskâyowetaham (VTI) S/he chops the tail off it.

kîskâyowetahowew (VTA) S/he chops the tail off someone.

55

kîskâyowetahikew (VTI) S/he chops the tail off something.

kîskâyowew *pl.* **kîskâyowewak** (VAI) It has no tail.

kîskâyowewin *pl.* **kîskâyowewina** (NI) Having no tail.

kîskicâsis *pl.* **kîskicâsisak** (NA) A pair of shorts. *Var.* **kîskitâs.**

kîskihkahtew *pl.* **kîskihkahtewa** (VII) It burnt off.

kîskihkasiw *pl.* **kîskihkasiwak** (VAI) It burns off.

kîskihkasowin *pl.* **kîskihkasowina** (NI) The act of burning off.

kîskihkaswew (VTA) S/he burns her/him off.

kîskihkasam (VTI) S/he burns it off.

kîskihkasamowew (VTI) S/he burns it off for her/him.

kîskihkasikew (VTI) S/he burns something off.

kîskihkemowinâhtik *pl.* **kîskihkemowinâhtikwa** (NI) Pulpit; a lecturn.

kîskihkotew (VTI) S/he cuts them off with a knife.

kîskihkotam (VTI) S/he cuts it off with a knife.

kîskihkocikew (VTI) S/he cuts things off with a knife.

kîskihkwenew (VTA) S/he tears the face off someone from a picture.

kîskihkwenam (VTA) S/he tears the face off it.

kîskihkweniwew (VTA) S/he tears the face off people in the picture.

kîskihkwenikew (VTI) S/he tears the face off things.

kîskihkwesin *pl.* **kîskihkwesinwak** (VAI) Her/his face is scraped in a fall.

kîskihkweswew (VTA) S/he cuts or severs the face from her/his picture.

kîskihkwesam (VTI) S/he cuts or severs its face in the picture.

kîskihkwesiwew (VTA) S/he cuts or severs faces in the picture.

kîskihkwesikew (VTI) S/he cuts or severs the face off things in the picture.

kîskimâskaciw *pl.* **kîskimâskaciwak** (VAI) S/he is numb with cold.

kîskimâskaciwin *pl.* **kîskimâskaciwina** (NI) Being numb with cold.

kîskimicihcew *pl.* **kîskimicihcewak** (VAI) Her/his hands are numb or have gone to sleep.

kîskimipayiw *pl.* **kîskimipayiwak** (VAI) S/he is feeling numb.

kîskimipayiwin *pl.* **kîskimipayiwina** (NI) Numbness.

kîskimisitew *pl.* **kîskimisitewak** (VAI) Her/his feet are numb or have gone to sleep.

kîskimisiw *pl.* **kîskimisiwak** (VAI) S/he is numb.

kîskimisiwin *pl.* **kîskimisiwina** (NI) Feeling numb.

kîskimistewaciw *pl.* **kîskimistewaciwak** (VAI) Her/his feet are numb with cold.

kîskinew (VTA) S/he broke it (animate) off with her/his hands.

kîskinam (VTI) S/he broke it off with her/his hands.

kîskiniwew (VTA) S/he cuts people off.

kîskinikew (VTI) S/he broke something off.

kîskipayihew (VTA) S/he makes her/him break off or detach by shaking.

kîskipayitâw (VTI) S/he makes it break off or detach by shaking.

kîskipayihiwew (VTA) S/he breaks off or detaches people from something.

kîskipayihcikew (VTI) S/he breaks off or detaches those things from something.

kîskipayiw *pl.* **kîskipayiwa** *or* **kîskipayiwak** (VII) *or* (VAI) It *or* s/he broke off by itself.

kîskipitew (VAI) S/he snaps it off with her/his hands.

kîskipitam (VTI) S/he snaps it off.

kîskipisiwew (VTA) S/he pulls people off something.

kîskipicikew (VTI) S/he pulls things off something.

kîskipocikan *pl.* **kîskipocikana** (NI) A saw.

kîskipocikewin *pl.* **kîskipocikewina** (NI) The act of sawing.

kîskipocikewiyînow *pl.* **kîskipocikewiyînowak** (NA) A man who uses a saw.

kîskipocimihtâkan *pl.* **kîskipocimihtâkana** (NI) A bucksaw.

kîskipohew (VTA) S/he saws them off, i.e.: logs.

kîskipotâw (VTI) S/he saws it off.

kîskipohiwew (VTA) S/he saws someone.

kîskipocikew (VTI) S/he saws something.

kîskipotâkan *pl.* **kîskipotâkana** (NI) Something sawed off.

kîskisikan *pl.* **kîskisikana** (NI) A detaching instrument.

kîskisikâkan *pl.* **kîskisikâkana** (NI) A cutting tool.

kîskisikâsiw *pl.* **kîskisikâsiwak** (VTA) It is cut off, i.e.: pants.

kîskisikâtew *pl.* **kîskisikâtewa** (VII) It is cut off, i.e.: rope, wire.

kîskisosiw *pl.* **kîskisosiwak** (VTA) S/he cuts herself/himself off from people or on the phone.

kîskisosiwin *pl.* **kîskisosiwina** (NI) The act of cutting oneself off from people or hanging up the phone.

kîskiswew (VTI) S/he cuts it off.

kîskisam (VTI) S/he cuts it off.

kîskisowew (VTA) S/he cuts others off.

kîskisawacikew (VTI) S/he cuts things off.

kîskitâs *pl.* **kîskitâsa** (NI) A pair of pants with legs cut off, i.e.: cutoffs; shorts. *Var.* **kîskicâsis.**

kîskowehon *pl.* **kîskowehona** (NI) A flag.

kîskwehayâwin *pl.* **kîskwehayâwina** (NI) Being frantic.

kîskwehew (VTA) S/he makes her/him go wild or crazy.

kîskwetâw (VTA) Creates wildness.

kîskwehiwew (VTA) S/he drives people crazy.

kîskwehiwewin *pl.* **kîskwehiwewina** (NI) The act of witchery.

kîskwehkamikisiw pl. **kîskwehkamikisiwak** (VAI) S/he gets into everything.

kîskwehkamikisiwin pl. **kîskwehkamikisiwina** (NI) The act of being wild, crazy, uncontrolled.

kîskwehkwasiwin pl. **kîskwehkwasiwina** (NI) A nightmare.

kîskwepâhew (VTA) S/he got her/him drunk, intoxicated.

   kîskwephiwew (VTA) S/he makes people drunk.

kîskwepew pl. **kîskwepewak** (VAI) S/he is drunk, intoxicated.

kîskwepewâkan pl. **kîskwepewâkana** (NI) Something used to become intoxicated; an intoxicant.

kîskwepewin pl. **kîskwepewina** (NI) Drunkenness; inebriation; intoxication.

kîskwesimew pl. **kîskwesimewak** (VTA) S/he dazed her/him by pounding her/his head on something.

kîskwesin pl. **kîskwesinwak** (VAI) S/he is stunned, dazed; s/he broke her/his own neck in a fall.

kîskwesiw pl. **kîskwesiwak** (VAI) S/he is made dizzy by smoke.

kîskwew pl. **kîskwewak** (VAI) S/he is crazy; s/he is insane.

kîskwewin pl. **kîskwewina** (NI) The act of going crazy or mad; lunacy.

kîskweyawesiw pl. **kîskweyawesiwak** (VAI) S/he is screaming angry. *(Plains and Northern variant)*; *Alt.* **sohkeyawesiw** *(Northern)*.

kîskweyâpamow pl. **kîskweyâpamowak** (VAI) S/he is dizzy.

kîskweyâtisiw pl. **kîskweyâtisiwak** (VAI) S/he has a wild character or personality.

kîskweyâtisiwin pl. **kîskweyâtisiwinak** (NA) A crazy character. **kîskweyâtisiwina** (ob.).

kîskweyeyihtam pl. **kîskweyeyihtamwak** (VAI) S/he is going crazy over something.

kîskweyihtâkosiw pl. **kîskweyihtâkosiwak** (VAI) S/he is seen as wild or crazy.

kîskweyihtâkwan pl. **kîskweyihtâkwanwa** (VII) It is thought of as crazy.

kîsohpikewatisiw pl. **kîsohpikewatisiwak** (VAI) S/he acts mature or full grown.

kîsohpikiw pl. **kîsohpikiwak** (VAI) S/he is all grown up.

kîsohpikiweyimew (VTA) S/he thinks s/he is mature.

   kîsohpikiweyitam (VTI) S/he thinks it is mature.

   kîsohpikiweyimiwew (VTA) S/he thinks others are mature.

   kîsohpikiweyihcikew (VTA) S/he thinks everyone is mature enough.

kîsohpikiwin pl. **kîsohpikiwina** (NI) Being all grown up; maturation.

kîsokew pl. **kîsokewak** (VAI) S/he finished her/his house, or putting up her/his teepee.

kîsokwayawehon pl. **kîsokwayawehona** (NI) A stole. *(Northern)*. *Alt.* **ayamihewitapiskâkan** *(Plains)*.

kîsopwehkahtew pl. **kîsopwehkahtewa** (VII) It is heated, i.e.: a house. *(Northern)*. *Alt.* **kîsowihkahtew** *(Plains)*.

kîsopweniyotin pl. **kîsopweniyotina** (NI) A chinook wind. *(Northern)*. *Alt.* **saskan** *(Plains)*.

kîsopwenohk (IPC) South. *(Northern)*. *Alt.* **âpihtâkîsikanohk** *(Plains)*.

kîsopwew (VII) Used when referring to the weather: "it is warm out".

kîsowahpison pl. **kîsowahpisonak** (NA) A scarf.

kîsowâsin (IPC) An expression meaning "it is slightly warm; it is lukewarm."

kîsowâw pl. **kîsowâwa** (VII) It is warm, i.e.: house.

kîsowâyaw (IPC) It is temperate.

kîsowâyâwin pl. **kîsowâyâwina** (NI) Being tepid.

kîsowihkahtew pl. **kîsowihkahtewa** (VII) It is heated, i.e.: a house. *(Plains)*. *Alt.* **kîsopwehkahtew** *(Northern)*.

kîsowihkasam (VTI) S/he heats the place up.

   kîsowihkasiwew (VTA) S/he heats someone up.

   kîsowihkasikew (VTI) S/he has heated the place up.

kîsowihkwâmiw pl. **kîsowihkwâmiwak** (VAI) S/he sleeps warmly.

kîsônew (VTA) S/he holds her/him to get her/him warm.

   kîsônam (VTI) S/he holds it to keep it warm.

   kîsôniwew (VTA) S/he holds someone to keep her/him warm.

   kîsônikew (VTI) S/he holds something to keep it warm.

kîsôsiw pl. **kîsôsiwak** (VAI) S/he is warm.

kîsôskawew (VTA) S/he keeps her/him warm with her/his body.

   kîsôskam (VTI) S/he keeps it warm with her/his body.

   kîsôskâkew (VTA) S/he keeps her/him warm with her/his body.

   kîsôskâcikew (VTI) S/he keeps things warm with her/his body.

kîsôsowin pl. **kîsôsowina** (NI) Being warm.

kîspahkepayik (IPC) Upwards.

kîspin (IPC) If.

kîspinatam (VTI) S/he earns it.

   kîspinatew (VTI) S/he earns it.

   kîspinacikew (VTI) S/he earns it for herself/himself.

kîspinatamawew (VTA) S/he earns it for her/him.

   kîspinatamakew (VTI) S/he earns it for others.

kîspinatamâkewin pl. **kîspinatamâkewina** (NI) The act of earning for someone.

57

kîspinatamâsiw *pl.* **kîspinatamâsiwak** (VTA) S/he earns it for herself/himself; s/he brings it on herself/himself.

kîspinatamâsowin *pl.* **kîspinatamâsowina** (NI) The act of earning or deserving just rewards.

kîspinesa (IPC) If only.

kîspisiw *pl.* **kîspisiwak** (VAI) Her/his skin is chapped.

kîspiw *pl.* **kîspiwak** (VAI) S/he has had enough to eat; s/he is satiated.

kîspohew (VTA) S/he has given her/him enough to eat.

  kîspoyiwew (VTA) S/he has given people enough to eat.

kîsposkoyiw *pl.* **kîsposkoyiwak** (VAI) S/he is satisfied after eating.

kîspowin *pl.* **kîspowina** (NI) Having enough to eat.

kîsta (IPC) You too (singular).

  kîstanaw (IPC) We or us too.

  kîstawaw (IPC) You too (plural).

kîstepiw *pl.* **kîstepiwak** (VAI) S/he cooks. *(Northern).* *Alt.* **piminawasiw** *(Plains).*

kîstepohew (VTA) S/he makes someone cook for her/him. *(Northern).* *Alt.* **piminawatew** *(Plains).*

  kîstepohiwew (VTA) S/he makes someone cook.

kîstepowâpisk *pl.* **kîstepowâpiskwa** (NI) A griddle.

kîstepowin *pl.* **kîstepowina** (NI) The act of cooking.

kîstepwatâw *pl.* **kîstepwatâwak** (VAI) S/he is being cooked for.

kîwahohtew *pl.* **kîwahohtewak** (VTA) A bullmoose searching for a mate.

kîweham *pl.* **kîwehamwak** (NA) A bird flying south.

kîwehâw *pl.* **kîwehâwak** (VTA) S/he flies home, i.e.: ducks fly south.

kîwehoyew (VTA) S/he takes her/him home in a boat; s/he sails her/him home.

  kîwehotâw (VTI) S/he takes it home by boat.

  kîwehoyiwew (VTA) S/he takes her/him home by boat.

  kîwehocikew (VTI) S/he takes things home by boat.

kîwehtahew (VTA) S/he takes her/him to her/his home.

  kîwehtatâw (VTI) S/he takes it home.

  kîwehtahiwew (VTA) S/he takes someone home.

  kîwehtawehcikew (VTI) S/he takes things home.

kîwetin (NA) A north wind; a blizzard.

kîwetinohk (IPC) Up north or in the north.

kiwetinotâhk (IPC) North or towards north; up the northern way.

kîwetisaham *pl.* **kîwetisahamwak** (VAI) S/he sends back what is sent.

kîwew *pl.* **kîwewak** (VAI) S/he went home; s/he returned home.

kîwewin *pl.* **kîwewina** (NI) The act of going home.

kîya (PP) You (singular).

kîyawaw (PP) You (plural).

kîyakasewin *pl.* **kîyakasewina** (NI) Itchy skin sickness.

kîyakihtâw *pl.* **kîyakihtâwak** (VAI) S/he makes noises to attract attention.

kîyakihtâwin *pl.* **kîyakihtâwina** (NI) The act of making a muffled noise.

kîyakinam *pl.* **kîyakinamwak** (VTI) S/he makes a muffled noise.

kîyakinew (VTA) S/he tickles her/him; s/he makes her/him itchy.

  kîyakinam (VTI) S/he tickles it.

  kîyakiniwew (VTA) S/he tickles others.

  kîyakinikew (VTA) S/he likes to tickle.

kîyakinowewin *pl.* **kîyakinowewina** (NI) The act of tickling.

kîyakisimow *pl.* **kîyakisimowak** (VTA) S/he rubs herself/himself against something because s/he is itchy.

kîyakisiw *pl.* **kîyakisiwak** (VAI) S/he is itchy.

kîyakisiwin *pl.* **kîyakisiwina** (NI) The act of being itchy.

kîyakistahikewin *pl.* **kîyakistahikewina** (NI) The act of prickling someone.

kîya mâka (IPC) An expression meaning "and how about you?"

kîyamâtisiw *pl.* **kîyamâtisiwak** (VAI) S/he is a quiet person.

kîyasiw *pl.* **kîyasiwak** (VAI) S/he runs swiftly.

kîyasowin *pl.* **kîyasowina** (NI) The act of running swiftly.

kîyawema (IPC) It might be; it might have been; a sudden change in the way you think.

kîyâm (IP) An expression of approval or acceptance; it's okay.

kîyâmapiw *pl.* **kîyâmapiwak** (VAI) S/he sits still.

kîyâmastew *pl.* **kîyâmastewa** (VII) It sits still.

kîyâmâtisiwin *pl.* **kîyâmâtisiwina** (NI) The act of being quiet.

kîyâmikâpawiw *pl.* **kîyâmikâpawiwak** (VAI) S/he stands very still.

kîyâmikâpawostawew (VTA) S/he stands still for her/him.

  kîyâmikâpawostam (VTI) S/he stands still for it.

  kîyâmikâpawostâkew (VTA) S/he stands still for people.

kîyânaw (PR) We, us (inclusive).

kîyâskiw *pl.* **kîyâskiwak** (VAI) S/he lies.

kîyâskiwâcimow *pl.* **kîyâskiwâcimowak** (VAI) S/he tells a false story; s/he tells untrue stories.

kîyâskiwin *pl.* **kîyâskiwina** (NI) A lie; something not true; a fib.

kîyâskîhew (VTA) S/he makes her/him tell a lie.

  kîyâskîtâw (VTI) S/he tells false stories about something.

kîyâskîhiwew (VTA) S/he tells false stories about people.

kîyâskîmew (VTA) S/he tells her/him a lie.

kîyâskîmiwew (VTA) S/he lies to people.

kîyâsoskwac (IPC) "You go by yourself."

kîyikawepayiwin *pl.* **kîyikawepayiwina** (NI) Being involved; involvement.

kîyikawi (NI) Something mixed with something else; mixed together.

kîyikawinew (VTI) S/he mixes or blends it together; s/he mixes or blends them up with her/his hands.

kîyikawinam (VTI) S/he mixes or blends it with something.

kîyikawiniwew (VTA) S/he mixes people with others.

kîyikawinikew (VTI) S/he mixes or blends things with other things.

kîyikawisimew (VTA) S/he mixes them or blends them with something else. *(Northern)*

kîyikawititâw (VTI) S/he mixes it with something else.

kîyikawimiwew (VTA) S/he mixes people with others.

kîyikawihcikew (VTI) She mixes things together with something else.

kîyipa (IPC) Soon. *(Northern). Alt.* **wîpac** *(Plains).*

kîyipahpinewin *pl.* **kîyipahpinewina** (NI) A sudden death from illness.

kîyipan *pl.* **kîyipanwa** (VII) It happens fast or quickly, i.e.: as in time elasped.

kîyipinew (VTA) S/he uses her/him up quickly or fast.

kîyipinam (VTI) S/he uses it up quickly or fast.

kîyipiniwew (VTA) S/he uses them up quickly or fast.

kîyipinikew (VTI) S/he uses everything up quickly or fast.

kîyipiw *pl.* **kîyipiwak** (VAI) S/he acts quickly, promptly; s/he does something with speed; s/he is fast or adept.

kîyipiwin *pl.* **kîyipiwina** (NI) The act of being fast or quick.

kîyiposewin *pl.* **kîyiposewina** (NI) The act of multiplying offspring.

kîyomâhew (VTA) S/he bothers her/him; s/he worries or bothers her/him.

kîyomâtâw (VTI) S/he bothers it.

kîyomâhiwew (VTA) S/he bothers people.

kîyomâhcikew (VTI) S/he bothers things.

kocawâkanis *pl.* **kocawâkanisa** (NI) A match.

kocawîs *pl.* **kocawîsak** (NA) Your uncle. *Var.* **kisis**.

kocihcikwanipayihohk (IPC) An expression indicating "when one is bending down on one knee in worship or respect"; genuflect.

kocihew (VTA) S/he tries or tests her/him or it.

kocitâw (VTI) S/he tries it.

kocihiwew (VTA) S/he tries someone.

kocicikew (VTI) S/he tries things.

kocinikamiw *pl.* **kocinikamiwak** (VAI) S/he tries or attempts to sing.

kocipitikoskihk (IPC) An expression referring to muscle spasms; fitful.

kocipîkiskwew *pl.* **kocipîkiskwewak** (VAI) S/he tries or attempts to speak.

kocipîkiskwewin *pl.* **kocipîkiskwewina** (NI) An attempt to talk.

kociskawew (VAI) S/he tries it on, i.e.: a stocking, pants, or gloves.

kociskakam (VAI) S/he tries it on, i.e.: a jacket.

kociskâwew *pl.* **kociskâwewak** (VAI) S/he gallops.

kociskâwewin *pl.* **kociskâwewina** (NI) A galloping horse race.

kocispitew (VTA) S/he tastes it.

kocispitam (VTI) S/he tastes it.

kocispicikew (VTI) S/he tastes other foods.

kociw *pl.* **kociwak** (VTI) S/he tries or attempts to do something.

kociwin *pl.* **kociwina** (NI) An attempt or an act of trying; objectivity.

kohcawes *pl.* **kohcawesak** (NA) Your godfather. *Var.* **kikohtawe**.

kohcipastewew *pl.* **kohcipastewewak** (VTI) *(Archaic Cree)* S/he inhales the smoke.

kohcipayihcikewin *pl.* **kohcipayihcikewina** (NI) The act of swallowing; a gulp.

kohcipayihew (VTA) S/he swallows her/him.

kohcipayitâw (VTI) S/he swallows it.

kohcipayihcikew (VTI) S/he swallows things.

kohkom *pl.* **kohkomak** (NA) Your grandmother. *Var.* **kohkomwâw**.

kohkomin *pl.* **kohkominak** (NA) A cucumber; "our late grandmother". **kohkomina** (ob.). *(Northern). Alt.* **kohkompaninaw** *(Plains).*

kohkominaw *pl.* **kohkominawak** (NA) A spider (*slang*).

kohkomwâw *pl.* **kohkomwâwak** (NA) Your grandmother. *Var.* **kohkom**.

kohkompaninaw *pl.* **kohkompaninawak** (NA) A cucumber; "our late grandmother". **kohkompanina** (ob.). *(Plains). Alt.* **kohkomin** *(Plains).*

kohkôs *pl.* **kohkôsak** (NA) A pig.

kohkôsimicowin *pl.* **kohkôsimicowina** (NI) Bran. *(Northern)*

kohkôsiminihkwewin *pl.* **kohkôsiminihkwewina** (NI) Swill.

kohkôsis *pl.* **kohkôsisak** (NA) A piglet.

kohkôsiwiyin *pl.* **kohkôsiwiyinwa** (NI) Pig fat.

kohkôsowayân *pl.* **kohkôsowayâna** (NI) A pigskin.

kohkôsowiyâs *pl.* **kohkôsowiyâsa** (NI) Pork.

59

kohkwâwâteyimew (VTA) S/he finds her/him to have a good character.

kohkwâwâteyitam (VTI) S/he thinks it is all right.

kohkwâwâteyimiwew (VTA) S/he thinks people are okay.

kohkwâwâteyicikew (VTI) S/he thinks things are okay.

kohkwâwâtisiw *pl.* **kohkwâwâtisiwak** (VAI) S/he has a good character.

kohkwâwâtisiwin *pl.* **kohkwâwâtisiwina** (NI) Act of having a good character.

kohtâpayowin *pl.* **kohtâpayowina** (NI) The act of being immersed; immersion. *Var.* **ayopayowin**.

kohpâskwahamihk (IPC) An expression meaning prying something up by force.

kohpâteyihtâkosiwin *pl.* **kohpâteyihtâkosiwina** (NI) The act of being thought of as contemptible.

kohpâteyimew *pl.* **kohpâteyimewak** (VTA) S/he finds her/him contemptible.

kohpâteyitakosiw *pl.* **kohpâteyitakosiwak** (VAI) S/he is thought of as being contemptible.

kohpâteyitâkwan *pl.* **kohpâteyitâkwanwa** (VII) It is considered contemptible.

kohtâpayowin *pl.* **kohtâpayowina** (NI) The act of being immersed; immersion. *Var.* **ayopayowin**.

kokaminakasiwit *pl.* **kokaminakasiwitawa** (NI) A Canada thistle. *(Northern). Var.* **kakasisiwat**. *Alt.* **okâminakasiy** *(Plains)*.

kokâwîhk (IPC) A respectful term for having a mother.

kokihtâwihtowin *pl.* **kokihtâwihtowina** (NI) An exchange of presents.

kokinew (VTA) S/he holds her/him under water with her/his hands; s/he dunks her/him under water.

kokinam (VTI) S/he holds it under water.

kokiniwew (VTA) S/he holds someone under water.

kokinikew (VTI) S/he holds things under water.

kokipitew (VTA) S/he pulls her/him quickly under water with her/his hands; s/he pulls her/him under water.

kokipitam (VTI) S/he pulls it under water.

kokipisiwew (VTA) S/he pulls someone under water.

kokipinikew (VTI) S/he pulls things under water.

kokisikohayâhwin *pl.* **kokisikohayâhwina** (NI) The state of feeling angelic.

kokiw *pl.* **kokiwak** (VAI) S/he dives.

kokîhew (VTA) S/he makes her/him dive.

kokîtaw (VTI) S/he makes it go under water.

kokîhiwew (VTA) S/he makes people go under water.

kokîsip *pl.* **kokîsipak** (NA) A goldeye duck.

kokîwin *pl.* **kokîwina** (NI) The act of diving.

kokosiwiw *pl.* **kokosiwiwak** (VAI) S/he is dirty or untidy.

kokosiwiwin *pl.* **kokosiwiwina** (NI) Being dirty or untidy.

komâmâhk (IPC) Having a mother.

komiyastowânit *pl.* **komiyastowânitwak** (NA) A person who has a long beard.

konowiw (VII) There is snow.

konôwan *pl.* **konôwanwa** (VII) It is full of snow.

konôwâpoy (NI) Snow water.

konta (IPC) Without reason. *(Plains). Alt.* **kwanta** *(Northern)*.

kopiwawayâk *pl.* **kopiwawayâkwa** (NI) Something fuzzy.

kosawinakwahk (IPC) Something that is yellowish; amber.

kosâmiyatihk (NI) An expression indicating that "it is too crowded."

kosâpahcikan *pl.* **kosâpahcikana** (NI) A tent used in the shaking tent ceremony.

kosâpahtam *pl.* **kosâpahtamwak** (VAI) S/he is a practitioner of spirit rites.

kosâpahtamowin *pl.* **kosâpahtamowina** (NI) The act of practicing spirit rites.

kosâpepayiw *pl.* **kosâpepayiwak** *or* **kosâpepayiwa** (VAI) *or* (VII) S/he *or* it has sunk into the water.

kosâpepityew (VTA) S/he submerges her/him in the water.

kosâpepitam (VTI) S/he pulls it under water.

kosâpepisiwew (VTA) S/he pulls someone under water.

kosâpepicikew (VTI) S/he pulls things under water.

kosâpeskawew (VTA) S/he sinks her/him into the water with her/his weight.

kosâpeskam (VTA) S/he sinks it under water with her/his weight.

kosâpeskacikew (VTA) S/he sinks things under water with her/his weight.

kosâpew *pl.* **kosâpewak** (VAI) S/he sinks into the water.

kosâpewin *pl.* **kosâpewina** (NI) The act of sinking or submerging.

kosâwehpisiwewin *pl.* **kosâwehpisiwewina** (NI) Suspended in air; death by hanging. *(Northern). Alt.* **akotitowin** *(Plains)*.

kosâwehpitew (VTA) S/he hangs her/him up with a rope. *(Northern). Alt.* **akotew** *(Plains)*.

kosâwehpitam (VTI) S/he hangs it upside down.

kosâwehpisiwew (VTA) S/he hangs someone upside down.

kosâwehpicikew (VTI) S/he hangs things upside down.

kosâwekocin *pl.* **kosâwekocinwak** (NA) Suspended in the air.

kosâwekotew *pl.* **kosâwekotewwa** (VII) It is hanging.

kosâwenew (VTA) S/he packs her/him hanging down.

kosâwenam (VTI) S/he packs it hanging down.

kosâweniwew (VTA) S/he packs someone hanging down.

kosâwenikew (VTI) S/he packs things hanging down.

kosikohew (VTA) S/he makes her/him heavy with a load.

kosikotâw (VTI) S/he makes it heavy with a load.

kosikohiwew (VTA) S/he makes someone heavy with a load.

kosikocikew (VTI) S/he makes things heavy with a load.

kosikoskohew (VTA) S/he makes her/him heavy with a pack.

kosikoskotâw (VTI) S/he makes a heavy load.

kosikoskoyiwew (VTA) S/he makes someone heavy with a load.

kosikoskocikew (VTI) S/he makes something heavy with a load.

kosikwan *pl.* **kosikwanwa** (VII) It is heavy.

kosikwateyihtâkosiw *pl.* **kosikwateyihtâkosiwak** (VAI) S/he is regarded as being heavy; s/he is judged or considered heavy.

kosikwateyihtâkwan *pl.* **kosikwateyihtâkwanwa** (VII) It is regarded as being heavy.

kosikwateyimew (VTA) S/he figures her/him to be heavy.

kosikwateyitam (VTI) S/he figures things are too heavy.

kosikwateyimiwew (VTA) S/he figures people are too heavy.

kosikwateyicikew (VTI) S/he figures things are too heavy.

kosikwatiw *pl.* **kosikwatiwak** (VAI) S/he is heavy.

kosikwatiwin *pl.* **kosikwatiwina** (NI) Being heavy; hefty.

kosiwewin *pl.* **kosiwewina** (NI) Being fearful of someone.

koskohew (VTA) S/he wakes her/him up by making noise.

koskohiwew (VTA) S/he wakes people up by making noise.

koskomew (VTA) S/he wakes her/him up with her/his talking.

koskomiwew (VTA) They wake people up with their talking.

koskonâkwan *pl.* **koskonâkwanwa** (VII) An expression used when looking at something and saying "it looks scary."

koskonew (VTA) S/he wakes her/him up.

koskoniwew (VTA) S/he wakes someone up.

koskonikew (VTA) S/he wakes people up.

koskonowewin *pl.* **koskonowewina** (NI) The act of awakening.

koskopitew (VTA) S/he shakes her/him awake.

koskopitam (VTI) S/he shakes it up briskly.

koskopisiwew (VTA) S/he wakes people up briskly.

koskopicikew (VTI) S/he shakes things up briskly.

koskoskopayihew (VTA) S/he is rocking it, i.e.: a boat.

koskoskopayitâw (VTA) S/he is rocking it off.

koskoskopayihiwew (VTA) S/he is rocking someone off.

koskoskopayicikew (VTI) S/he is rocking things off.

koskoskopayiw *pl.* **koskoskopayiwak** *or* **koskoskopayiwa** (VAI) *or* (VII) S/he *or* it is wavering. *(Northern). Alt.* **nanamipayiw** *(Plains).*

koskoskopayowin *pl.* **koskoskopayowina** (NI) The act of shaking. *(Northern). Alt.* **nanamipayowin** *(Plains).*

koskoskwâw *pl.* **koskoskwâwa** (VII) It shakes or rocks; it is not steady, i.e.: a boat or canoe.

koskowepinew (VTA) S/he shakes her/him.

koskowepihiwew (VTA) S/he shakes someone off.

koskowepicikew (VTI) S/he shakes things off.

koskwâwâtahkamikan *pl.* **koskwâwâtahkamikanwa** (NI) The state of pensiveness.

koskwâwâtapiw *pl.* **koskwâwâtapiwak** (VAI) S/he is sitting quietly.

koskwâwâtapiwin *pl.* **koskwâwâtapiwina** (NI) The act of sitting quietly.

koskwâwâteyemew (VTA) S/he finds her/him very quiet. *(Northern). Alt.* **kâmwâteyimew** *(Plains).*

koskwâwâteyetam (VTI) S/he finds things melancholic or sad.

koskwâwâteyemiwew (VTA) S/he finds people very quiet.

koskwâwâteyecikew (VTI) S/he finds things very quiet.

koskweyihtamowina (NI) Hysteria; hysterics. *(Plains)*

koskweyihtâkwan *pl.* **koskweyihtâkwanwa** (VII) It is amazing or astonishing.

koskweyimew (VTA) S/he is amazed with her/him.

koskweyitam (VTI) S/he is amazed with it.

koskweyimiwew (VTA) S/he is amazed with someone.

koskweyicikew (VTI) S/he is amazed with things.

kosokonayahcikewin *pl.* **kosokonayahcikewina** (NI) The act of creating a burden.

kospamow *pl.* **kospamowa** (NI) A road leading into the woods or a road going up a hill.

kospaneyihtâkosiw *pl.* **kospaneyihtâkosiwak** (VAI) S/he is to be dreaded or feared.

kospaneyihtâkwan *pl.* **kospaneyihtâkwanwa** (VII) It is to be dreaded or feared.

kospaneyimew (VTA) S/he dreads her/him.

kospaneyitam (VTI) S/he fears it.

kospaneyimiwew (VTA) S/he fears people.

kospaneyicikew (VTI) S/he fears things.

61

kospipahtâw *pl.* **kospipahtâwak** (VAI) S/he runs into the woods.

kospitisahwew (VTA) S/he runs or chases her/him into the woods.

kospitisaham (VTI) S/he chases something into the woods.

kospitisahowew (VTA) S/he chases someone into the woods.

kospitisahikew (VTA) S/he chases everybody into the woods.

kospow *pl.* **kospowak** (VAI) S/he walks into the woods.

kospowin *pl.* **kospowina** (NI) The act of running headlong into the woods.

kostaciwâyâwin *pl.* **kostaciwâyâwina** (NI) The act of sensing danger or peril. *(Northern). Alt.* **kostâciwin** *(Plains).*

kostamowin *pl.* **kostamowina** (NI) Fear.

kostanakeyimowin *pl.* **kostanakeyimowina** (NI) Being fearsome; having audacity; being a show-off; being stuck-up.

kostateyihtâkwan *pl.* **kostateyihtâkwanwa** (VII) It is to be feared or dreaded.

kostateyimew (VTA) S/he finds her/him fearful.

kostateyitam (VTI) S/he finds it fearful.

kostateyimiwew (VTA) S/he finds people fearful.

kostateyicikew (VTA) S/he finds everyone fearful.

kostâciw *pl.* **kostâciwak** (VAI) S/he is fearful.

kostâciwin *pl.* **kostâciwina** (NI) Being fearful; the act of sensing danger or peril. *(Plains). Alt.* **kostaciwâyâwin** *(Northern).*

kostâsinâkwan *pl.* **kostâsinâkwanwa** (VII) It looks tremendous in size; fearsome.

kostâteyihtâkosiw *pl.* **kostâteyihtâkosiwak** (VAI) S/he is regarded as being fearful or dreadful.

kostâtikosiw *pl.* **kostâtikosiwak** (VAI) S/he is to be feared or dreaded.

kostâtikwan *pl.* **kostâtikwanwa** (VII) It is fearful or dreadful.

kostew (VTA) S/he fears her/him.

kostam (VTI) S/he is scared of it.

kosiwew (VTA) S/he is scared of people.

kostonâmew *pl.* **kostonânewak** (VTA) S/he is afraid to talk to her/him.

kostonâmiw *pl.* **kostonâmiwak** (VAI) S/he is afraid to speak.

kostonâmowin *pl.* **kostonâmowina** (NI) The act of being fearful to speak.

kotahaskwâtew (VTA) S/he takes a random shot at her/him; s/he fires a shot at her/him and misses.

kotahaskwâtam (VTI) S/he shoots at it.

kotahaskwâsiwew (VTA) S/he shoots at someone.

kotahaskwew *pl.* **kotahaskwewak** (VAI) S/he fires a random shot; s/he shoots and misses.

kotahaskwewin *pl.* **kotahaskwewina** (NI) The act of shooting at targets or target practice.

kotak *pl.* **kotaka** (VII) Another or another one.

kotamew *pl.* **kotamewak** (VTI) S/he tastes it, i.e.: fish.

kotapastew *pl.* **kotapastewa** (VII) Upside down; reversed. *(Northern). Alt.* **kwatapastew** *(Plains).*

kotapâhoyew (VTA) S/he capsizes the canoe when someone is paddling with her/him. *(Northern). Alt.* **kwatapâhohew** *(Plains).*

kotapâhotâw (VTI) S/he capsizes the canoe; s/he tips it over.

kotapâhoyiwew (VTA) S/he capsizes someone in a canoe.

kotapâhocikew (VTI) S/he capsizes things in the canoe.

kotapinew (VTA) S/he turns her/him over while s/he is in a boat. *(Northern). Alt.* **kwatapinew** *(Plains).*

kotapinam (VTA) S/he turns the boat over.

kotapiniwew (VTA) S/he turns someone over in a boat; s/he turns over.

kotapiwepiskawew (VTI) S/he kicks it and tips it over. *(Northern). Alt.* **kwatapiwipiskawew** *(Plains).*

kotapiwepiskam (VTI) S/he kicks it and tips it over.

kotapiwepiskâkew (VTA) S/he kicks and tips someone over.

kotapiwepiskâcikew (VTI) S/he kicks things and tips things over.

kotapîhew (VTA) S/he makes her/him capsize; s/he rolls her/him over; s/he capsizes her/him; s/he turns her/him over. *(Northern). Alt.* **kwatapîhew** *(Plains).*

kotapîtâw (VTI) S/he makes it capsize.

kotapîhiwew (VTA) S/he makes others capsize.

kotapîcikew (VTI) S/he empties things all over.

kotapîhk (IPC) Tugging on something.

kotapîw *pl.* **kotapîwak** (VAI) S/he capsizes. *(Northern). Alt.* **kwatapîw** *(Plains).*

kotaskeham *pl.* **kotaskehamwak** (VAI) S/he measures the depth of the water.

kotatâmowin *pl.* **kotatâmowina** (NI) A singing rehearsal.

kotawahkân (NI) A mustard plaster.

kotawân *pl.* **kotawânwa** (NI) A campfire pit.

kotawânâpisk *pl.* **kotawânâpiskwa** (NI) A stove.

kotâwinew (VTA) S/he pushes her/him under.

kotâwinam (VTI) S/he pushes it under.

kotâwipayiw *pl.* **kotâwipayiwa** or **kotâwipayiwak** (VII) or (VAI) It or s/he sinks under.

koteskanit *pl.* **koteskanitwâw** (NA) An antlered animal. *(Plains). Alt.* **kôtîskanit** *(Northern).*

koteyimew (VTA) S/he examines or tests her/him mentally.

koteyitam (VTI) S/he examines or tries it.

koteyimiwew (VTA) S/he examines or tests someone.

koteyihcikew (VTA) S/he examines or tests everyone.

kotikonew (VTA) S/he sprains someone's joints.

kotikonam (VTI) S/he sprains it.

kotikoniwew (VTA) S/he sprains everyone's joints.

kotikonikew (VTI) S/he sprains everything.

kotokohtin *pl.* **kotokohtinwa** (VII) A sprained joint.

kotokopayiw *pl.* **kotokopayiwak** (VAI) It is out of joint, i.e.: disjointed.

kotokosimew (VTA) S/he sprains an ankle by throwing someone.

kotokotitâw (VTA) S/he sprains a finger.

kotokosimiwew (VTA) S/he sprains someone's ankle.

kotokosin *pl.* **kotokosinwak** (VTA) S/he sprains an ankle or foot by falling.

kotokoswew *pl.* **kotokoswewak** (VTA) S/he cuts the joints of an animal.

kowicewâkanihk (IPC) An expression indicating partnership or agreement; conformity.

koyakihcikehk (IPC) An expression indicating something is being analysed.

kôcawâsimsihk (IPC) An expression used to refer to birth; natality.

kôciwamihtohk (NI) Being cousins.

kôna (NA) Snow.

kôsâmiyawesihk (IPC) An expression indicating frustration.

kôtamihtâsohwin *pl.* **kôtamihtâsohwina** (NI) The state of interfering.

kôtîskanit *pl.* **kôtîskanitwâw** (NA) An antlered animal. *(Northern)*. *Alt.* **koteskanit** *(Plains)*.

kwahkosiw *pl.* **kwahkosiwak** (NA) S/he is on fire.

kwahkoswew (VTA) S/he sets fire to her/him.

kwahkosam (VTI) S/he sets fire to it.

kwahkosiwew (VTA) S/he sets fire to someone.

kwahkosikew (VTI) S/he sets things on fire.

kwahkotew *pl.* **kwahkotewa** (VII) It is on fire; it is in flames *(Plains and Northern variant)*. *Alt.* **wayatew** *(Northern)*.

kwahosonâhtik *pl.* **kwahosonâhtikwa** (NI) A raft pole.

kwahtâpekisiw (IPC) S/he is tall and thin, i.e.: stalky.

kwanta (IPC) Without reason. *(Northern)*. *Alt.* **konta** *(Plains)*.

kwantapikiskwewin *pl.* **kwantapikiskwewina** (NI) The act of pointless talking; gabbing away.

kwantatôtamôwin *pl.* **kwantatôtamôwina** (NI) The act of reacting without reason; purposeless.

kwapahamawew (VTA) S/he dips water out for her/him.

kwapahikew (VTA) S/he dips water out for people.

kwapawew (VTA) S/he dips it out, i.e.: fish.

kwapaham (VTI) S/he dips something out, i.e.: meat.

kwapahikew (VTI) S/he dips it out.

kwapikawew (VTA) S/he hauls water for her/him.

kwapikâkew (VTI) S/he hauls water with it.

kwaskwenitowew *pl.* **kwaskwenitowewak** (VAI) S/he plays with a bouncing ball, i.e.: basketball or football.

kwaskweyâskwahowin *pl.* **kwaskweyâskwahowina** (NI) The act of hurdling.

kwatakihew (VTA) S/he makes her/him suffer.

kwatakitâw (VAI) S/he suffers.

kwatakihiwew (VTA) S/he makes people suffer.

kwatapastew *pl.* **kwatapastewa** (VII) Upside down; reversed. *(Plains)*. *Alt.* **kotapastew** *(Northern)*.

kwatapâhohew (VTA) S/he capsizes the canoe when someone is paddling with her/him. *(Plains)*. *Alt.* **kotapâhoyew** *(Northern)*.

kwatapâhotâw (VTI) S/he capsizes the canoe.

kwatapâhoyiwew (VTA) S/he capsizes someone in a canoe.

kwatapâhocikew (VTI) S/he capsizes things in the canoe.

kwatapinew (VTA) S/he turns her/him over while s/he is in a boat. *(Plains)*. *Alt.* **kotapinew** *(Northern)*.

kwatapinam (VTA) S/he turns the boat over.

kwatapiniwew (VTA) S/he turns someone over in a boat; s/he turns over.

kwatapiwipiskawew (VTI) S/he kicks it and tips it over. *(Plains)*. *Alt.* **kotapiwepiskawew** *(Northern)*.

kwatapiwipiskam (VTI) S/he kicks it and tips it over.

kwatapiwipiskâkew (VTA) S/he kicks and tips someone over.

kwatapiwipiskâcikew (VTI) S/he kicks things and tips things over.

kwatapîhew (VTA) S/he makes her/him capsize;. s/he rolls her/him over; s/he capsizes her/him; s/he turns her/him over. *(Plains)*. *Alt.* **kotapîhew** *(Northern)*.

kwatapîtâw (VTI) S/he makes it capsize.

kwatapîhiwew (VTA) S/he makes others capsize.

kwatapîcikew (VTI) S/he empties things all over.

kwatapîw *pl.* **kwatapîwak** (VAI) S/he capsizes. *(Plains)*. *Alt.* **kotapîw** *(Northern)*.

kwayakihew (VTA) S/he betrays her/him; s/he schemes against her/him

kwayakitâw (VTA) S/he betrays it. **kwayakihiwew** (VTA) S/he betrays others.

kwayakonam (VTI) S/he takes it out.

kwayakonew (VTA) S/he takes them out.

kwayakoniwew (VTA) S/he takes someone out.

kwayakonikew (VTI) S/he takes things out.

kwayakwamohcikewin *pl.* **kwayakwamohcikewina** (NI) The act of protruding.

kwayas kawihtamihk (IPC) Telling the truth.

63

kwayas kâtotamihk (IDP) A correct statement; to tell the truth.

kwayask (IPC) It is straight right or correct; it is straight or honest.

kwayaskascikewin *pl.* **kwayaskascikewina** (NI) Being in alignment; adjustment.

kwayaskâtisiw *pl.* **kwayaskâtisiwak** (VAI) S/he has an honest character.

kwayaskâtisiwin *pl.* **kwayaskâtisiwina** (NI) Having an honest character.

kwayaskohtawew (VTA) S/he understands her/him correctly or perfectly.

kwayaskohtam (VTI) S/he understands correctly.

kwayaskohtakew (VTA) S/he understands people.

kwayaskohsecikew (VTI) S/he does things right.

kwayaskohtowin *pl.* **kwayaskohtowina** (NI) A mutual understanding; define; forthright.

kwayaskomew (VTA) S/he correctly informs her/him.

kwayaskotam (VTA) S/he understands correctly.

kwayaskomiwew (VTA) S/he informs people correctly.

kwayaskocikew (VTI) S/he straightens things up.

kwayaskomowewin *pl.* **kwayaskomowewina** (NI) Correct information; true data.

kwayaskonikewin *pl.* **kwayaskonikewina** (NI) The act of reacting correctly; expressly; unbending; the act of performing formally; formality.

kwayaskopayihcikewin *pl.* **kwayaskopayihcikewina** (NI) The act of being fair; fairly.

kwayaskopayihew (VTA) S/he makes it go right for her/him; s/he makes her/him go in the right direction.

kwayaskopayitâw (VTI) S/he makes it right.

kwayaskopayihiwew (VTA) S/he makes it right for people.

kwayaskopayicikew (VTI) S/he makes things go right.

kwayaskopayiw *pl.* **kwayaskopayiwak** (VAI) It goes right or well.

kwayaskosâwâcikan *pl.* **kwayaskosâwâcikana** (NI) Something that cuts straight, i.e.: a trimmer.

kwayaskosihcikewin *pl.* **kwayaskosihcikewina** (NI) The act of doing things on condition; a right deal; the act of formalizing something; properly.

kwayaskosihowin *pl.* **kwayaskosihowina** (NI) The act of dressing formally.

kwayaskowewin *pl.* **kwayaskowewina** (NI) The act of expressing oneself in the proper way; a plan.

kwayaskwahew (VTI) S/he places it correctly; s/he emends.

kwayaskwastâw (VTI) S/he straightens it.

kwayaskwayiwew (VTA) S/he straightens someone.

kwayaskwacikew (VTI) S/he straightens things.

kwayaskwahitowin *pl.* **kwayaskwahitowina** (NI) The act of being specific with words; categorically.

64

kwayaskwascikewin *pl.* **kwayaskwascikewina** (NI) Correction; formation; regulate.

kwayaskwaskitew (VII) It stands straight up, i.e.: vertical.

kwayaskwâtisiw *pl.* **kwayaskwâtisiwak** (VAI) S/he is of a pure, moralistic character.

kwayaskwâtisiwin (IPC) An expression meaning being perfect; perfectible. *(Plains)*. *Alt.* **kâkwayaskwesâyâhk** *(Northern)*.

kwayaskwâtisiwin *pl.* **kwayaskwâtisiwina** (NI) The act of being decent; decency; perfectibility; righteousness; having discipline. *(Plains)*. *Alt.* **kwayaskwesâyawin** *(Northern)*.

kwayaskwesâyawin *pl.* **kwayaskwesâyawina** (NI) The act of being decent; decency; perfectibility; righteousness. *(Northern)*. *Alt.* **kwayaskwâtisiwin** *(Plains)*.

kwayaskweyihcikâsiw *pl.* **kwayaskweyihcikâsiwak** (VAI) S/he is thought to be comprehensible.

kwayaskweyihcikâtew *pl.* **kwayaskweyihcikâtewa** (VII) It is thought to be comprehensible.

kwayaskweyihcikewin *pl.* **kwayaskweyihcikewina** (NI) The act of thinking in a truthful or realistic way; relevance; solve.

kwayaskweyihtam *pl.* **kwayaskweyihtamwak** (VAI) S/he has a correct opinion; s/he has a legitimate viewpoint.

kwayaskweyihtamohew (VTA) S/he makes her/him understand correctly or perfectly; s/he makes her/him comprehend.

kwayaskweyihtamohtâw (VTI) S/he makes something understandable correctly or perfectly.

kwayaskweyihtamohiwew (VTA) S/he makes someone understood correctly or perfectly.

kwayaskweyihtamocikew (VTA) S/he makes people understand correctly or perfectly.

kwayaskweyihtamowin *pl.* **kwayaskweyihtamowinak** (NA) Conceptually correct, thinking properly.

kwayaskweyihtamoyicikâsiw *pl.* **kwayaskweyihtamoyicikâsiwak** (VAI) S/he is comprehensible.

kwayaskweyihtamoyicikâtew *pl.* **kwayaskweyihtamoyicikâtewa** (VII) It is comprehensible.

kwayaskweyimew (VTA) S/he has a correct opinion of her/him.

kwayaskweyitam (VTI) S/he has a correct opinion of it.

kwayaskweyimiwew (VTA) S/he has a correct opinion of people.

kwayaskweyicikew (VTI) S/he has a correct opinion of things.

kwayastew *pl.* **kwayastewak** (VAI) S/he enters into a hole.

kwayasteyâmiw *pl.* **kwayasteyâmiwak** (VAI) S/he escapes into a hole.

kwâpahikan *pl.* **kwâpahikana** (NI) A dipper. *Var.* **kwâpahopâkan.**

kwâpahopâkan *pl.* **kwâpahopâkana** (NI) A dipper. *Var.* **kwâpahikan.**

kwâpikew *pl.* **kwâpikewak** (VAI) S/he hauls water.

kwâpikewin *pl.* **kwâpikewina** (NI) The act of getting water by the bucket.

kwâsihew (VTA) S/he elopes with her/him.
　kwâsitâw (VTI) S/he takes it away.
　kwâsicikew (VTI) S/he takes things away.

kwâsihiskwewewew *pl.* **kwâsihiskwewewak** (VTA) He elopes with a woman.

kwâsihiskwewewin *pl.* **kwâsihiskwewewina** (NI) Elopement; taking off with a woman.

kwâsihiwewin *pl.* **kwâsihiwewina** (NI) The act of eloping.

kwâskocisîs *pl.* **kwâskocisîsak** (NA) A grasshopper; a cricket.

kwâskohtâpewin *pl.* **kwâskohtâpewina** (NI) The act of skipping.

kwâskwehtin *pl.* **kwâskwehtinwa** (VII) It bounces up and down; it ricochets *(Plains). Alt.* **wâskwetin** *(Northern).*

kwâskwenitowân *pl.* **kwâskwenitowâna** (NI) A bouncing ball, i.e.: for basketball or football.

kwâskwepayiw *pl.* **kwâskwepayiwa** *or* **kwâskwepayiwak** (VII) *or* (VAI) It *or* s/he rebounds; it *or* s/he boomerangs.

kwâskwepicikewin *pl.* **kwâskwepicikewina** (NI) The act of fishing with a rod.

kwâskwesin (IPC) It is jarred.

kwâskweyâskwaham (VTI) S/he pitches it, i.e.: like hay.
　kwâskweyâskwahwew (VTA) S/he pitches them upwards.
　kwâskweyâskwahowew (VTA) S/he pitches someone upward.
　kwâskweyâskwahikew (VTI) S/he pitches something upward.

kwâskweyâskwahosiw *pl.* **kwâskweyâskwahosiwak** (VAI) S/he walks with crutches.

kwâskweyâskwahoswâkan *pl.* **kwâskweyâskwahoswâkana** (NI) A crutch.

kwâtakatâmowin *pl.* **kwâtakatâmowina** (NI) The act of bewailing, i.e.: lamentation.

kwâtakeyihtamowin *pl.* **kwâtakeyihtamowina** (NI) The act of mental suffering.

kwâtakeyimew (VTA) S/he has a poor opinion of her/him.
　kwâtakeyitam (VTI) S/he has a poor opinion of it.

kwâtakeyimiwew (VTA) S/he has a poor opinion of people.

kwâtakeyicikew (VTI) S/he has a poor opinion of things.

kwâtakeyimowin *pl.* **kwâtakeyimowina** (NI) The act of feeling passive; passivity.

kwâtakihesôstamawew (VTA) S/he suffers for her/him.
　kwâtakihesôstam (VTI) S/he suffers for it.
　kwâtakihesôstamâkew (VTA) S/he suffers for others.

kwâtakihisiw *pl.* **kwâtakihisiwak** (VTA) S/he makes herself/himself suffer.

kwâtakihisowin *pl.* **kwâtakihisowina** (NI) Personal suffering.

kwâtakihiwewin *pl.* **kwâtakihiwewina** (NI) The act of oppressing; oppression.

kwâtakihkahtew *pl.* **kwâtakihkahtewa** (NI) Something poorly burned. *Var.* **kitimâkihkahtew.**

kwâtakihkasiw *pl.* **kwâtakihkasiwak** (VAI) S/he suffers from a burn.

kwâtakihkaswew (VTA) S/he makes her/him suffer from a burn.
　kwâtakihkasam (VTA) S/he makes a poor job of burning.
　kwâtakihkasiwew (VTA) S/he makes a poor job of burning others.
　kwâtakihkasikew (VTI) S/he makes a poor job of burning something.

kwâtakihtâw *pl.* **kwâtakihtâwak** (VAI) S/he suffers.

kwâtakihtâwin *pl.* **kwâtakihtâwina** (NI) The act of suffering.

kwâtakimew (VTA) S/he speaks poorly of her/him.
　kwâtakimiwew (VTA) S/he speaks poorly of people.

kwâtakimow *pl.* **kwâtakimowak** (VAI) S/he tells a hard luck story about her/his life. *(Northern). Alt.* **kitimâkâcimisow** *(Plains).*

kwâyakeyihcikewin *pl.* **kwâyakeyihcikewina** (NI) The act of abhorring something.

kwâyakinikâkan *pl.* **kwâyakinikâkanak** (NA) A tickler. **kwâyakinikâkana** (ob.).

kweskasowewin *pl.* **kweskasowewina** (NI) The act of making a legal amendment. *(Plains). Alt.* **kwesketasowewin** *(Northern).*

kweskâpohkewin *pl.* **kweskâpohkewina** (NI) The act of making an antidote; antidotal.

kweskâyamihâw *pl.* **kwekâyamihâwak** (NA) A convert. **kwekâyamihâwa** (ob.).

kwesketasowewin *pl.* **kwesketasowewina** (NI) The act of making a legal amendment. *(Northern). Alt.* **kweskasowewin** *(Plains).*

kweskiwepinikewin *pl.* **kwekiwepinikewina** (NI) The act of doing something that can be reversed; averse; reversible.

65

kweskîwin *pl.* **kwekîwina** (NI) The act of going back to a former position, i.e.: revert; changing direction, i.e.: veer.

kwespanâtisiw *pl.* **kwespanâtisiwak** (VAI) S/he is rough, harsh, and rude. *(Northern)*

kwespanâtisiw *pl.* **kwespanâtisiwak** (VAI) S/he is very cautious. *(Plains)*

kwetamâw *pl.* **kwetamâwak** (VAI) S/he is in need; s/he is short on provisions.

kwetamâwin *pl.* **kwetamâwina** (NI) The act of being needy.

kwetaweyecikewin *pl.* **kwetaweyecikewina** (NI) The act of expressing regret or grief; deplore.

kwetaweyimew (VTA) S/he misses her/him or longs for her/him; s/he misses her/him being there.

kwetaweyitam (VTI) S/he misses it or longs for it.

kwetaweyimiwew (VTA) S/he misses or longs for people.

kwetaweyihcikew (VTA) S/he misses someone.

kweyahowin *pl.* **kweyahowina** (NI) The act of reacting fast or quickly; fastness.

macacowayas (NI) The Cree name for the settlement of Gift Lake.

macayiwiw *pl.* **macayiwiwak** (VAI) S/he does evil.

macâcimew (VTA) S/he tells evil stories about her/him.

  macâtotam (VTI) S/he tells evil stories about it.

  macâcimiwew (VTA) S/he tells evil stories about someone.

  macâtocikew (VTI) S/he tells evil stories about things.

macâcimow *pl.* **macâcimowak** (VAI) S/he tells an evil story; s/he slanders.

macâcimowin *pl.* **macâcimowina** (NI) An evil story; a slander.

macâhcâhk *pl.* **macâhcâhkwak** (NA) An evil soul; an evil spirit.

macâspinew *pl.* **macâspinewak** (VAI) S/he has a bad disease (generally used to refer to venereal disease).

macâspinewin *pl.* **macâspinewina** (NI) A bad disease; a sexually transmitted disease.

macâtisiw *pl.* **macâtisiwak** (VAI) S/he is an evil person; s/he is evil.

macâtisiwin *pl.* **macâtisiwina** (NI) Being an evil person; acrimony; cruelty; guilt; villianous.

macâyimomew (VTA) S/he gossips maliciously about her/him; s/he maligns her/him.

  macâyimotam (VTI) S/he gossips maliciously of it.

  macâyimomiwew (VTA) S/he speaks maliciously of others.

  macâyimocikew (VTI) S/he speaks maliciously of things.

macâyimwew *pl.* **macâyimwewak** (VTA) S/he maligns other people.

macâyimwewin *pl.* **macâyimwewina** (NI) The act of making false or misleading statements about someone with the intent to injure; malicious talk or false gossip.

macâyiwiwin *pl.* **macâyiwiwina** (NI) The act of doing evil.

maceyihtamowin *pl.* **maceyihtamowina** (NI) The act of being contemptible.

maceyihtâkisiw *pl.* **maceyihtâkisiwak** (VAI) S/he is considered contemptible.

maceyimew (VTA) S/he despises her/him; s/he thinks s/he is bad.

  maceyitam (VTI) S/he despises it.

  maceyimiwew (VTA) S/he despises someone.

  maceyicikew (VTI) S/he despises things.

macihkwew *pl.* **macihkwewak** (VAI) S/he has an evil face.

macihtwâwâyâwin *pl.* **macihtwâwâyâwina** (NI) The act of being snide.

macihtwâwin *pl.* **macihtwâwina** (NI) Being grouchy; vehemence; wickedness.

macihtwâwisâyâwin *pl.* **macihtwâwisâyâwina** (NI) Being austere; austerity.

macikastewin *pl.* **macikastewina** (NI) The act of being full of pep, i.e.: a wild horse.

macikosisaniwiw *pl.* **macikosisaniwiwak** (VAI) He is an evil son.

macikosisân *pl.* **macikosisânak** (NA) An evil son (not commonly used).

macikwanasa (NA) Ragweed; house refuge; weeds; dusty.

macimanito *pl.* **macimanitowak** (NA) The great negative mystery or quality in the universe (translated by Christians as Satan or the devil).

macimanitowiw *pl.* **macimanitowiwak** (VAI) S/he is the great negative spirit.

macimâkosiw *pl.* **macimâkosiwak** (VAI) S/he smells badly.

macimâkwan *pl.* **macimâkwanwa** (VII) It smells badly.

macimâmitoneyihcikan *pl.* **macimâmitoneyihcikana** (NI) An evil mind.

macimâmitoneyimew (VTA) S/he has evil thoughts about her/him or about them.

  macimâmitoneyitam (VTI) S/he has an evil mind.

  macimâmitoneyimiwêw (VTA) S/he has evil thoughts about someone.

  macimâmitoneyicikêw (VTI) S/he has evil thoughts about things.

macinâkwan *pl.* **macinâkwanwa** (VII) It appears evil; bad.

macipayihcikewin *pl.* **macipayihcikewina** (NI) The act of being enterprising.

macipayihiwewin *pl.* **macipayihiwewina** (NI) The act of causing a happening, i.e.: instigate.

macipayiwin *pl.* **macipayiwina** (NI) Unfortunate circumstances.

macipikiskwew *pl.* **macipikiskwewak** (VAI) S/he speaks in an evil manner.

macistikwânewin *pl.* **macistikwânewina** (NI) The act of being obstinate; obstinacy; the act of being hard-headed; balky; ornery.

macitôtamowin *pl.* **macitôtamowina** (NI) Evildoing.

macitôtâtowin *pl.* **macitôtâtowina** (NI) The act of brutalizing someone.

maciyimiwewin *pl.* **maciyimiwewina** (NI) The act of despising someone.

macîsâyawin *pl.* **macîsâyawina** (NI) Being depraved; devious.

67

macîteyihcikewin *pl.* **macîteyihcikewina** (NI) The act of continually blaming other people; baleful.

macîteyihtam *pl.* **macîteyihtamwak** (VAI) S/he thinks incorrectly. *(Plains)*. *Alt.* **naspâciteyitam** *(Northern)*.

mah (IPC) An exclamation: "Attention!"

mahâpohew (VTA) S/he takes her/him downstream in a canoe.

mahâpotaw (VTI) S/he takes it downstream in a canoe.

mahâpoyiwew (VTA) S/he takes people downstream.

mahâpocikew (VTI) S/he takes things downstream.

mahâpokow *pl.* **mahâpokowak** (VAI) S/he drifts downstream.

mahâpotew *pl.* **mahâpotewa** (VII) It drifts downstream.

mahâpoyiw *pl.* **mahâpoyiwak** (VAI) S/he drifts downstream in a canoe.

mahâpoyiwin *pl.* **mahâpoyiwina** (NI) The act of drifting downstream in a canoe.

mahihkan *pl.* **mahihkanak** (NA) A wolf.

mahihkanâhtik *pl.* **mahihkanâhtikwak** (NA) A white willow or wolf shrub.

mahihkaniwayân *pl.* **mahihkaniwayânak** (NA) A wolfskin.

mahihkaniwiw *pl.* **mahihkaniwiwak** (VAI) S/he is a wolf.

mahkahk *pl.* **mahkahkwa** (NI) A wash tub.

mahkaskwâw *pl.* **mahkaskwâwa** (NI) A huge cloud.

mahkastimowiw *pl.* **mahkastimowiwak** (NA) A huge animal, i.e.: a dog or horse.

mahkâpit *pl.* **mahkâpita** (NI) A large size tooth, i.e.: a tusk.

mahkâskâw *pl.* **mahkâskâwa** (VII) There are big waves on a lake, i.e.: surf.

mahkesîs *pl.* **mahkesîsak** (NA) A fox.

mahkesîsimin *pl.* **mahkesîsîminah** (NA) A foxberry.

mahkisihcikewin *pl.* **mahkisihcikewina** (NI) The act of expanding something.

mahkisîhcikewin *pl.* **mahkisîhcikewina** (NI) The act of enlarging; the act of dilating; amplitude.

mahkisîhew (VTA) S/he makes it bigger; s/he makes it larger.

mahkisîtâw (VTI) S/he makes something bigger.

mahkisîhiwew (VTA) S/he makes someone bigger.

mahkisîhcikew (VTI) S/he makes things bigger.

mahkiskamowin *pl.* **mahkiskamowina** (NI) Making a large footprint.

mahkwan *pl.* **mahkwana** (NI) A heel.

mahmahkâkonepayiw *pl.* **mahmahkâkonepayiwa** (NI) A sudden and heavy snowfall; a blizzard. *(Plains)*. *Alt.* **pahkihtakonakâw** *(Northern)*.

mahmâyahcâw *pl.* **mahmâyahcâwa** (NI) A large area of rough ground.

mahmeskwaciwepinikewin *pl.* **mahmeskwaciwepinikewina** (NI) The act of alternating; alternation.

mahohtahew (VTA) S/he takes her/him downstream.

mahohtatâw (VTI) S/he takes it downstream.

mahohtahiwew (VTA) S/he takes people downstream.

mahohtacikew (VTI) S/he takes things downstream.

mahohteskanaw *pl.* **mahohteskanawa** (NI) A road leading downstream.

mahohtew *pl.* **mahohtewak** (VAI) S/he walks downstream.

mahohtewin *pl.* **mahohtewina** (NI) A walk with the stream or current.

mahpinew *pl.* **mahpinewak** (VAI) S/he moans with pain; s/he is constantly complaining.

mahpinewin *pl.* **mahpinewina** (NI) The act of moaning with pain.

mahtakoskawew (VTA) S/he settles or lays on top of her/him.

mahtakoskakew (VTA) S/he settles or lays on top of someone.

mahtakoskam (VTI) S/he settles or lays on top of something.

mahtakoskacikew (VTI) S/he settle or lays on top of everything.

mahtâmin *pl.* **mahtâminak** (NA) One ear of corn; cob of corn.

mahti (IPC) Let us; would you [please].

makîkway (IPC) Nil; nothing.

makotowepayowin *pl.* **makotowepayowina** (NI) Being curly; the act of being curly.

makwahcikanâpisk *pl.* **makwahcikanâpiskwa** (NI) One set of pliers or metal pinchers.

mamahkâskâw *pl.* **mamahkâskâwa** (VII) There is a big wave.

mamahtawisihcikew *pl.* **mamahtawisihcikewak** (VAI) S/he performs spiritually powerful acts.

mamahtawiyiniw *pl.* **mamahtawitiniwak** (NA) A person who performs spiritually powerful acts or magic, i.e.: a wizard.

mamahtâwisiw *pl.* **mamahtâwisiwak** (VAI) S/he is gifted with spiritual power; s/he is spiritually powerful.

mamahtâwisiwin *pl.* **mamahtâwisiwina** (NI) A spirit power; magical; mystical; shamanic.

mamahtâwitotam *pl.* **mamahtâwitôtamwak** (VAI) S/he does miraculous acts.

mamahtâwpayiw *pl.* **mamahtâwipayiwa** *or* **mamahtâwpayiwak** (VII) *or* (VAI) It *or* s/he happens in a miraculous way or manner.

mamawapowin *pl.* **mamawapowina** (NI) An organized gathering, meeting or assembly, i.e.: a business meeting.

mamawisipwehtewin *pl.* **mamawisipwehtewina** (NI) The act of a concerted departure; exodus.

mamawîsihcikewin *pl.* **mamawîsihcikewina** (NI) The act of doing business in a joint manner; incorporate.

mamâhtâkomew (VTA) S/he glorifies her/him.

mamâhtâkotam (VTI) S/he glorifies it.

mamâhtâkomiwew (VTA) S/he glorifies people.

mamâhtâkonâkohcikew (VTI) S/he shows glory and exaltation.

mamâhtâkosiw *pl.* **mamâhtâkosiwak** (VAI) S/he is glorified or exalted.

mamâhtâkosiwin *pl.* **mamâhtâkosiwina** (NI) Exaltation; glorification.

mamâhtâkweyimew (VTA) S/he considers her/him spiritually powerful.

mamâhtâkweyitam (VTI) S/he finds it powerful or extraordinary.

mamâhtâkweyimiwew (VTA) S/he finds them powerful.

mamâhtâkweyicikew (VTA) S/he finds others powerful.

mamâhtâwan *pl.* **mamâhtâwanwa** (VII) It is spiritually effective, i.e.: a prayer.

mamâhtâweyimew (VTA) S/he thinks her/him to be supernaturally gifted.

mamâhtâweyitam (VTI) S/he thinks it is a supernatural gift.

mamâhtâweyimiwew (VTA) S/he thinks someone is supernaturally gifted.

mamâhtâweyicikew (VTI) S/he thinks everything is spiritually charged.

mamâhtâwihew (VTA) S/he empowers her/him to do extraordinary things.

mamâhtâwitâw (VTI) S/he empowers it.

mamâhtâwihiwew (VTA) S/he empowers people with spiritual gifts.

mamâhtâwicikew (VTI) S/he empowers that in a spiritual way.

mamâhtâwihikowin *pl.* **mamâhtâwihikowina** (NI) The spiritual power given.

mamâhtâwihikowinisiw *pl.* **mamâhtâwihikowinisiwak** (VAI) S/he is given special spiritual gifts for accomplishing extraordinary things.

mamâhtâwihikowisiwin *pl.* **mamâhtâwihikowisiwina** (NI) A gift of bestowing spiritual power.

mamâhtâwihiwewin *pl.* **mamâhtâwihiwewina** (NI) The spiritual power is transferred to others.

mamâpinewin *pl.* **mamâpinewina** (NI) Being in chronic pain.

mamâtâkwan *pl.* **mamâtâkwanwa** (VII) It is glorious.

mamâyipimohtewin *pl.* **mamâyipimohtewina** (NI) The act of twaddling; the act of not being able to walk in a straight line.

mameskawipayiw (IPC) An expression meaning "that happens by chance."

mamihcâyâwin *pl.* **mamihcâyâwina** (NI) The act of behaving in a highly dignified manner; dignity.

mamihcihiwew *pl.* **mamihcihiwewak** (VAI) S/he makes people proud of her/him.

mamihcimâw *pl.* **mamihcimâwak** (IPC) S/he is praised; compliment.

mamihcimew (VTA) S/he praises her/him; s/he flaunts her/him or adulates her/him.

mamihcimiwew (VTA) S/he praises others.

mamihcimikosiw *pl.* **mamihcimikosiwak** (VAI) S/he is highly praised.

mamihcimisiw *pl.* **mamihcimisiwak** (VTA) S/he boasts about herself/himself.

mamihcimisowin *pl.* **mamihcimisowina** (NI) Boastfulness; self-promoting.

mamihcimitowin *pl.* **mamihcimitowina** (NI) The act of talking proudly of someone else; cajole.

mamihcimow *pl.* **mamihcimowak** (VAI) S/he flaunts herself/himself or sings herself/himself praises; s/he brags about herself/himself.

mamihcimowewin *pl.* **mamihcimowewina** (NI) Congratulation; dignify; eulogy; flattery; laud.

mamihcimowin *pl.* **mamihcimowina** (NI) The act of bragging.

mamihcitotamowin *pl.* **mamihcitotamowina** (NI) The act of doing something to be proud of; acknowledgement.

mamihcîmew (VTA) S/he praises her/him; s/he speaks approvingly to her/him. *(Plains). Alt.* **kâkihcimew** *(Northern).*

mamihcîmiwew (VTA) S/he praises other people.

mamihtâkiyawiwin *pl.* **mamihtâkiyawiwina** (NI) Being graceful. *(Plains). Alt.* **nahâkeyawewin** *(Northern).*

mamihteyihtâkosiw *pl.* **mamihteyihtâkosiwak** (VAI) S/he is praiseworthy.

mamihteyihtâkosiwin *pl.* **mamihteyihtâkosiwina** (NI) The act of being praiseworthy.

mamihteyimew (VTA) S/he is proud of her/him.

mamihteyitam (VTI) S/he is proud of it.

mamihteyimiwew (VTA) S/he is proud of people.

mamihteyicikew (VTI) S/he is proud of things.

mamihtisiw *pl.* **mamihtisiwak** (VAI) S/he is proud.

mamihtisowin *pl.* **mamihtisowina** (NI) Being proud.

mamihtôtam (VTI) S/he boasts about it.

mamihtômiwew (VTA) S/he praises people.

mamisitotâkew *pl.* **mamisitotâkewak** (VTA) S/he has confidence in people; s/he trusts people.

69

mamisîtotam *pl.* **mamisîtotama** (VTI) S/he has confidence in it.

mamisîtotawew (VTA) S/he trusts her/him.
  mamisîtotam (VTI) S/he trusts it.
  mamisîtotakew (VTA) S/he trusts people.

mamisîtotâkewin *pl.* **mamisîtotâkewina** (NI) The act of trusting someone; dependability; reliability.

mamisîw *pl.* **mamisîwak** (VTA) S/he trusts someone.

mamisîwakeyimew (VTA) S/he considers her/him to be trustworthy or s/he has utmost confidence in her/him.
  mamisîwakeyitam (VTI) S/he trusts it.
  mamisîwakeyimiwew (VTA) S/he trusts people.
  mamisîwakeyicikew (VTI) S/he trusts things.

mamisîwâtisiw *pl.* **mamisîwâtisiwak** (VAI) S/he believes herself/himself to be reliable. *(Plains). Alt.* **yâkwâmeyimow** *(Northern).*

mamisîwin (NI) Trust.

mamiywasinâstew (VII) It is colorful.

manacihew (VTA) S/he respects her/him or them; s/he saves her/him or it.
  manacitâw (VTI) S/he respects it.
  manacihiwew (VTA) S/he respects people.
  manacicikew (VTI) S/he respects things.

manahikan *pl.* **manahikana** (NI) Cream; butterfat.

manahipimâtew (VTI) S/he skims the cream off; s/he removes the cream.
  manahipimâtam (VTI) S/he skims it off the top.

manahipimew *pl.* **manahipimewak** (VAI) S/he skims off the grease or the lard.

manahipimewin *pl.* **manahipimewina** (NI) The act of skimming off grease.

manahiskiwew *pl.* **manahiskiwewak** (VAI) S/he gathers or picks pitch from spruce, i.e.: spruce gum.

manahiskiwewin *pl.* **manahiskiwewina** (NI) The act of gathering or picking pitch from spruce trees.

manasahkew *pl.* **manasahkewak** (VAI) S/he feeds people; s/he shares her/his food.

manasihciwin *pl.* **manasihciwina** (NI) The act of being lazy and not wishing to work too hard; indolence.

manaskosiwew *pl.* **manaskosiwewak** (VTA) S/he cuts hay with a scythe.

manaskosiwewin *pl.* **manaskosiwewina** (NI) The action of cutting hay with a scythe.

manaskosîwâkan *pl.* **manaskosîwâkana** (NI) An instrument for cutting hay, or scythe.

manatisiwâyâwin *pl.* **manatisiwâyâwina** (NI) The act of being gentle; gentleness.

manawatew (VTA) S/he plunders her/him or them.
  manawatam (VTI) S/he plunders it.
  manawasiwew (VTA) S/he plunders someone.
  manawacikew (VTI) S/he plunders everything.

manaway (NI) A cheek.

manâcihcikew *pl.* **manâcihcikewak** (VAI) S/he saves; s/he does not spend.

manâcihcikewin *pl.* **manâcihcikewina** (NI) The act of preserving; preservation.

manâcihitowin *pl.* **manâcihitowina** (NI) The act of venerating or respecting something; veneration.

manâcihiwewin *pl.* **manâcihiwewina** (NI) The act of venerating someone.

manâcihtamawew *pl.* **manâcihtamawewak** (VTA) S/he saves it for her/him or them.

manâcimâkan *pl.* **manâcimâkanak** (NA) A respected in-law.

manâcimew (VTA) S/he speaks respectfully of her/him or them.
  manâcimiwew (VTA) S/he speaks respectfully of people.

manâhow *pl.* **manâhowak** (VAI) S/he helps herself/himself to things, i.e.: after a death.

manâhowin *pl.* **manâhowina** (NI) Appropriation, to take exclusive possession of things.

manâtisiw *pl.* **manâtisiwak** (VAI) S/he is respectful or polite.

manâtisiwin *pl.* **manâtisiwina** (NI) The act of respect or politeness; considerate; gentle; mannerly; respectability; tact; venerable.

manâtôtawew (VTA) S/he treats her/him or them with respect or esteem.
  manâtôtam (VTI) S/he treats it with respect.
  manâtôtakew (VTA) S/he treats people with respect.

manâwânis (NI) A place where eggs are gathered, i.e.: a slough.

manâwew *pl.* **manâwewak** (VAI) S/he gathers or picks eggs.

manâwewin *pl.* **manâwewina** (NI) The act of hunting and gathering eggs.

manihkomânew *pl.* **manihkomânewak** (VTA) S/he defends herself/himself with a knife.

manikawew (VTI) S/he chops them off with an axe.
  manikaham (VTI) S/he chops it off with an axe.
  manikahikew (VTI) S/he chops things off with an axe.

manikwayaweswew (NA) S/he cuts his/her neck or its neck with a knife.
  manikwayawesam (NI) S/he cuts its neck with a knife.
  manikwayawesikew (VTA) S/he cuts the neck with a knife.

maninew (VTA) S/he removes them off with her/his hand.
  maninam (VTI) S/he removes it.
  maninikew (VTI) S/he removes things.
  maninewak (VTA) They remove them with their hands.

manipayiw *pl.* **manipayiwa** *or* **manipayiwak** (VII) *or* (VAI) It *or* s/he comes off on its own.

manipitew (VTA) S/he pulled them off.

manipitam (VTI) S/he pulled it off.

manipicikew (VTI) S/he pulls things off.

manisawâtew (VTA) S/he cuts her/him or them off.

manisawâtam (VTI) S/he cuts it off.

manisawâsiwew (VTA) S/he cuts someone off.

manisawâcikew (VTI) S/he cuts things off.

manisikâkan *pl.* **manisikâkana** (NI) An instrument for cutting, i.e.: a sickle; a slicer.

manisikewin *pl.* **manisikewina** (NI) The act of harvesting crops or grain.

manistikwâneswew (VTA) S/he cuts off her/his head or their heads.

manistikwânesam (VTI) S/he cuts the head off it.

manistikwânesowew (VTA) S/he cuts the head off someone.

manistikwânesikew (VTI) S/he cuts heads off.

maniswew (VTA) S/he cuts her/him or them with scissors or a knife.

manisowew (VTA) S/he cuts someone with scissors or a knife.

manisikew (VTI) S/he cuts something with scissors or a knife.

manito (NA) Sacred power or God; the basic mysterious quality in the universe. *(Northern). Alt.* **manitow** *(Plains).*

manitohâyawin (NI) The act of attempting to be sacred or holy.

manitohkân *pl.* **manitohkânak** (NA) The objects embodying sacred power or spirit power; totem.

manitohkâsiw *pl.* **manitohkâsiwak** (VAI) S/he performs religious rites.

manitohkâsiwin *pl.* **manitohkâsiwina** (NI) Rites or religious ceremonies.

manitohkâtew (VTA) S/he worships the sacred.

manitohkâtam (VTI) S/he worships it as sacred.

manitohkâsiwew (VTA) S/he worships someone as sacred.

manitohkâcikew (VTI) S/he worships things as sacred.

manitohkew *pl.* **manitohkewak** (VTA) S/he makes her/him a spirit power.

manitohkewin *pl.* **manitohkewina** (NI) Sacred power in a concrete form.

manito kîsikan pîsim (NI) December; God's moon. *Alt.* **pawacakinasîs** *(Northern);* **pawahcakinasîs** *(Plains).*

manitomekiwin (NI) Something given by the great spirit; God-given.

manitominâhtik *pl.* **manitominâhtikwak** (NA) A black currant tree or bush.

manitopahkwesikan *pl.* **manitopahkwesikanak** (NA) God's bread; Eucharist.

manitopiwâpisk *pl.* **manitopiwâpiskwa** (NI) A powerful steel, i.e.: a magnet.

manitoskâtâsk *pl.* **manitoskâtâskwak** (NA) A medicine root or a musquash root or a ginger root. *(Northern). Alt.* **wehkesk** *(Plains).*

manitow (NA) Sacred power or God; the basic mysterious quality in the universe. *(Plains). Alt.* **manito** *(Northern).*

manitowakeyimow *pl.* **manitowakeyimowak** (VTA) S/he thinks that the divine resides in her/him.

manitowakeyimowin *pl.* **manitowakeyimowina** (NI) The act of holding oneself to be divine.

manitowan *pl.* **manitowanwa** (VII) It is the expression of spirit power.

manitowatâmiw *pl.* **manitowatâmiwak** (VAI) S/he speaks inspired by the spirit power.

manitowatâmowin *pl.* **manitowatâmowina** (NI) Inspiration of the spirit power.

manitowayân *pl.* **manitowayânak** (NA) A spirit power wrap or sacred cloth; an alter cloth.

manitowâtan *pl.* **manitowâtanwa** (VII) It has spirit power or it is religious.

manitowâtisiw *pl.* **manitowâtisiwak** (VAI) S/he is spiritually powerful; s/he is religious or devout.

manitowâtisiwin *pl.* **manitowâtisiwina** (NI) The act of being spiritually powerful or devout.

manitowekin *pl.* **manitowekinwa** (NI) A special cloth used in sacred ceremonies, i.e.: in a priest's vestments; a fine quality fabric, i.e.: velvet.

manitoweyihcikewin *pl.* **manitoweyihcikewina** (NI) Being a devoted admirer; idolatrous.

manitoweyimew (VTA) S/he believes her/him to express sacred power; s/he believes her/him to be divine.

manitoweyitam (VTI) S/he believes it to embody the sacred power.

manitoweyimiwew (VTA) S/he holds or believes others to embody sacred power, i.e.: ancestoral divinity.

manitoweyicikew (VTI) S/he believes things to be spiritually charged.

manitoweyimowewin *pl.* **manitoweyimowewina** (NI) The act of worshipping someone; deification.

manitoweyitamowin *pl.* **manitoweyitamowina** (NI) Thinking about sacred notions.

manitowikosisân *pl.* **manitowikosisânak** (NA) The Son of God.

manitowimasinahikan *pl.* **manitowimasinahikana** (NI) The Holy Bible or God's writing.

manitowiw *pl.* **manitowiwak** (VAI) S/he has medicine power or sacred power.

manitowiwin *pl.* **manitowiwina** (NI) The act of expressing sacred power; divinity.

71

manitowokeyimew (VTA) S/he thinks of her/him as embodying sacred power; s/he believes her/him to be God.

manitowokeyitam (VTA) S/he believes in God.

manitowokeyimiwew (VTA) S/he believes in someone as God.

manitowokeyicikew (VTI) S/he believes in things as God.

manitômin *pl.* **manitôminak** (NA) A black currant.

manîcos *pl.* **manîcosak** (NA) An insect; a roach.

manokatew (VTA) S/he sets up a tent for someone else; s/he pitches a tent for someone else.

manokatam (VTI) S/he sets up a tent over it.

manokasiwew (VTA) S/he sets up tents for people.

manokacikew (VTI) S/he sets up tents to cover things.

mansikâsowin *pl.* **mansikâsowina** (NI) The act of being cut open during an operation, i.e.: an incision.

masakay *pl.* **masakayak** (NA) A piece of skin; human skin. *(Plains). Alt.* **wasakay** *(Northern).*

masaskocihcenew (VTI) S/he takes it from her/his hand.

masaskocihceniwew (VTI) S/he takes things from her/his hand.

masaskocihcenikew (VTA) S/he takes everyone's hand.

masaskohkahtew *pl.* **masaskohkahtewa** (VII) It is completely burned off, i.e.: grass.

masaskohkasiw *pl.* **masaskohkasiwak** (VAI) S/he is all burned off.

masaskohkaswew (VTA) S/he burns her/him or them completely.

masaskohkasam (VTI) S/he burns it all off.

masaskohkasowew (VTA) S/he burns someone off.

masaskohkasikew (VTI) S/he burns everything off.

masaskohtin *pl.* **masaskohtinwa** (VII) It is completely broken off.

masaskonamawew (VTA) S/he deprives her/him of everything completely.

masaskonamakew (VTI) S/he deprives everything from everyone.

masaskonew (VTA) S/he takes it away from her/him.

masaskonam (VTI) S/he grabs everything.

masaskoniwew (VTA) S/he grabs it before everyone.

masaskonikew (VTI) S/he grabs everything from somewhere.

masaskoniwewin *pl.* **masaskoniwewina** (NI) The act of seizing possessions from a person; the act of divesting property from someone; wrest.

masaskopayiw *pl.* **masaskopayiwak** (VAI) It all broke off.

masaskopitew (VTA) S/he pulled them all off.

masaskopitam (VTI) S/he pulled it all off.

masaskopisiwew (VTA) S/he pulled everyone off from somewhere.

masaskopicikew (VTI) S/he pulled everything off.

masaskosinwak (NA) They are completely, totally broken off.

masaskoyawew (VTA) S/he deprives her/him of everything in a game.

masaskoyatam (VTI) S/he deprives it of everything in a game.

masaskoyakew (VTA) S/he deprives everyone of everything in a game.

masân *pl.* **masânak** (NA) A nettle.

masânâhtik *pl.* **masânâhtikwak** (NA) A fern.

masihkewin *pl.* **masihkewina** (NI) The act of wrestling.

masinahamawew (VTA) S/he writes for her/him or s/he owes her/him or is in debt to her/him.

masinahamakew (VTA) S/he writes for someone or s/he owes someone.

masinahamâkewin *pl.* **masinahamâkewina** (NI) The act of owing a debt; the act of writing a letter.

masinahamâtowin *pl.* **masinahamâtowina** (NI) The act of corresponding with someone; the act of owing a debt to someone.

masinahikan *pl.* **masinahikana** (NI) A letter to someone; a book.

masinahikanâhtik *pl.* **masinahikanâhtikwak** (NA) A pencil.

masinahikanâpiskos (NA) A pen.

masinahikanâpoy *pl.* **masinahikanâpoya** (NI) Ink.

masinahikanekin *pl.* **masinahikanekinwa** (NI) Paper.

masinahikanis *pl.* **masinahikanisa** (NI) A leaflet; a small book.

masinahikâkew *pl.* **masinahikâkewa** (VTI) S/he writes with it.

masinahikâsiw *pl.* **masinahikâsiwak** (VAI) S/he is historically recorded.

masinahikâtew *pl.* **masinahikâtewa** (VII) It is written.

masinahikehew (VTA) S/he is hired.

masinahikehiwew (VTA) S/he hires someone.

masinahikehisiw *pl.* **masinahikehisiwak** (VTA) S/he hires herself/himself.

masinahikesîs *pl.* **masinahikesîsak** (NA) A secretary. *Var.* **omasinahikesis**.

masinahikew *pl.* **masinahikewak** (VAI) S/he writes; s/he contracts a debt.

masinahikewapiskos *pl.* **masinahikewapiskosa** (NI) A pen nib.

masinahikewin *pl.* **masinahikewina** (NI) The act of writing; a writing of credit note (I.O.U.).

masinahikewinâhtik *pl.* **masinahikewinâhtikwa** (NI) A blackboard.

masinahikewiyiniw *pl.* **masinahikewiyiniwak** (NA) A mailman or letter carrier.

masinahwew (VTA) S/he draws her/him.

masinaham (VTI) S/he draws it.

masinahowew (VTA) S/he draws someone.

masinahikew (VTA) S/he depicts her/him.

masinasiw *pl.* **masinasiwak** (VAI) S/he is stained with different colors; s/he is coloured or marked.

masinatahikewin *pl.* **masinatahikewina** (NI) The act of stamping something; personalize; tooling; typing.

masinâsiwin *pl.* **masinâsiwina** (NI) A beauty spot or mark.

masinâskisikan *pl.* **masinâskisikana** (NI) A branding iron.

masinâskisikewin *pl.* **masinâskisikewina** (NI) The act of branding animals.

masinâskiswew (VTA) S/he brands the animal.

masinâskisam (VTI) S/he puts a brand on it.

masinâskisowew (VTA) S/he puts a brand on someone.

masinâskisikew (VTI) S/he puts a brand on something.

masinâsowatim *pl.* **masinâsowatimwak** (NA) A spotted horse, i.e.: a pinto.

masinâsowin *pl.* **masinâsowina** (NI) A spot on the body, i.e.: a birthmark.

masinâstehikâsowin *pl.* **masinâstehikâsowina** (NI) Being striped.

masinâstew *pl.* **masinâstewa** (VII) It is stained with many different colors; it is coloured.

masinâstewihkwew *pl.* **masinâstewihkwewak** (VAI) Her/his face is stained in different colors, i.e.: a clown.

masinihcikewin *pl.* **masinihcikewina** (NI) The act of making a mark on something.

masinihkotew (VTI) S/he carves it.

masinihkotam (VTI) S/he carves it.

masinihkosiwew (VTI) S/he carves people images.

masinihkocikew (VTI) S/he carves things.

masinihkwehosiw *pl.* **masinihkwehosiwak** (VAI) S/he paints or colours her/his face.

masinihkwewew (VTA) S/he paints her/his face.

masinihkweham (VTI) S/he paints its face.

masinihkwehowew (VTA) S/he paints someone's face.

masinihkwehikew (VTI) S/he paints faces.

masinikwâcikaneyâpiy *pl.* **masinikwâcikaneyâpiya** (NI) A sewing tape.

masinipayiwin *pl.* **masinipayiwina** (NI) A picture.

masinipehikan *pl.* **masinipehikana** (NI) A painting.

masinipehikanâhtik *pl.* **masinipehikanâhtikwa** (NI) A paint brush for picture painting.

masinipewew (VTA) S/he paints or draws her/him.

masinipeham (VTI) S/he paints it.

masinipehowew (VTA) S/he paints someone.

masinipehikew (VTI) S/he paints things.

masinistahamâkew *pl.* **masinistahamâkewnak** (VAI) S/he embroiders for others.

masinistawew (VTA) S/he embroiders it.

masinistaham (VTI) S/he embroiders it.

masinistahowew (VTA) S/he embroiders something.

masinistahikew (VTI) S/he embroiders something.

maskahcihiwewin *pl.* **maskahcihiwewina** (NI) The act of pillaging; the act of taking goods away by force; impoverishment.

maskahtwew *pl.* **maskahtwewak** (VAI) S/he pillages.

maskahtwewin *pl.* **maskahtwewina** (NI) Taking somebody's possessions.

maskamew (VTA) S/he plunders her/him.

maskamiwew (VTI) S/he takes things from people or someone.

maskasiy *pl.* **maskasiyak** (NA) A fingernail.

maskawahew (VTA) S/he places her/him solidly.

maskawastâw (VTI) S/he places it solidly.

maskawahiwew (VTA) S/he places people solidly.

maskawahtik *pl.* **maskawahtikwak** (NA) Oak tree. *Var.* **mistikominâhtik, wemistikosiwâhtik.**

maskawascikew *pl.* **maskawascikewa** (VTI) S/he places things solidly.

maskawatin *pl.* **maskawatinwa** (VII) It is hardened by the cold, i.e.: a creek or lake.

maskawâhtik *pl.* **maskawâhtikwak** (NA) A hard wood, i.e.: oak.

maskawâkamow *pl.* **maskawâkamowa** (VII) It is a strong liquid, i.e.: alcohol.

maskawâkonakâw (VII) There is crusty snow.

maskawâpekan *pl.* **maskawâpekanwa** (NI) Strong cord or rope.

maskawâpiskâw *pl.* **maskawâpiskâwa** (VII) It is a strong bar of iron.

maskawâpiskisiw *pl.* **maskawâpiskisiwak** (VTA) It is a strong, resistable piece of iron, i.e.: a cast iron frying pan.

maskawâskaciw *pl.* **maskawâskaciwak** (VAI) S/he is hardened by the cold; s/he is frozen stiff.

maskawâskatimew (VTA) S/he freezes it.

maskawâskatihtâw (VTI) S/he freezes it solid.

maskawâskatimiwew (VTA) S/he freezes others.

maskawâskatihcikew (VTI) S/he freezes everything solid.

maskawâskosiw *pl.* **maskawâskosiwak** (VAI) It is hard, strong tree.

maskawâskwan *pl.* **maskawâskwanwa** (NI) Hard piece of wood or pole.

maskawâtisiw *pl.* **maskawâtisiwak** (VAI) S/he has a strong character; s/he is durable.

maskawâtisiwin *pl.* **maskawâtisiwina** (NI) Strength of character.

maskawâw *pl.* **maskawâwa** (VTI) It is hard or strong.

maskawâyâwin *pl.* **maskawâyâwina** (NI) Being hardy; hardiness.

73

maskawekin *pl.* **maskawekinwa** (NI) A strong piece of fabric or cloth. *(Plains and Northern variant); Alt.* **sohkekin** *(Northern).*

maskawekiniwiw *pl.* **maskawekiniwiwa** (VII) It is a strong fabric or cloth, i.e.: heavy canvas. *(Plains and Northern variant); Alt.* **sohkekan** *(Plains).*

maskawekisiw *pl.* **maskawekisiwak** (VAI) It is a durable pair of pants. *(Plains and Northern variant); Alt.* **sohkekisiw** *(Northern).*

maskaweyihtam *pl.* **maskaweyihtamwak** (VAI) S/he is resolute, firmly decided.

maskaweyihtamowin *pl.* **maskaweyihtamowina** (NI) A decided, or strong resolution.

maskawihkahtew *pl.* **maskawihkahtewa** (VII) It is cooked hard; hardened by fire.

maskawihkasikan (NI) Cheese; something cooked hard; something pressed together. *(Northern). Alt.* **mâkwahikan** *(Plains).*

maskawihkasiw *pl.* **maskawihkasiwak** (VTA) It is cooked hard by fire.

maskawihkaswew (VTA) S/he cooks it hard, i.e.: bannock.

maskawihkasam (VTI) S/he cooks it too hard, i.e.: like meat.

maskawihkasikew (VTI) S/he cooks something real hard.

maskawipîwâpisk *pl.* **maskawipîwâpiskwa** (NI) A strong piece of steel or iron.

maskawisihew (VTA) S/he makes it or her/him or them strong.

maskawisitâw (VTI) S/he makes it strong or solid.

maskawisihiwew (VTA) S/he makes others strong or solid.

maskawisicikew (VTI) S/he makes things strong or solid.

maskawisiw *pl.* **maskawisiwak** (VAI) S/he is strong or physically powerful.

maskawisiwakeyimew (VTA) S/he finds her/him strong or physically powerful.

maskawisiwakeyitam (VTI) S/he finds it strong or physically powerful.

maskawisiwakeyimiwew (VTA) S/he finds people strong or physically powerful.

maskawisiwakeyicikew (VTI) S/he finds things strong.

maskawisiwin *pl.* **maskawisiwina** (NI) Strength.

maskawisiwiyiniwiw *pl.* **maskawisiwiyiniwiwak** (VAI) He is a muscular man. *(Plains). Alt.* **sohkapewiw** *(Northern).*

maskawisîweyimew (VTA) S/he thinks her/him or them to be strong.

maskawisîweyitam (VTI) S/he thinks it is strong.

maskawisîweyimiwew (VTA) S/he thinks people are strong.

maskawisîweyicikew (VTI) S/he thinks everything is strong.

maskawiskowakâw (NI) Hardened mud.

maskawitehew (VTA) S/he makes her/him strong of heart.

maskawitehesehtâw (VTI) S/he makes something strong of heart.

maskawiteheniwew (VTA) S/he makes people strong of heart.

maskawitehesihcikew (VTI) S/he does things with a strong heart.

maskawitehew *pl.* **maskawitehewak** (VAI) S/he has a strong heart.

maskawitehewin *pl.* **maskawitehewina** (NI) The act of being adamant; hardness of heart.

maskek *pl.* **maskekwa** (NI) Muskeg.

maskekopak *pl.* **maskekopakwa** (NI) A white flower or leaf that grows in the muskeg; an herbal tea called Labrador tea.

maskekosihta *pl.* **maskekosihtak** (NA) A muskeg spruce. *Var.* **maskekwâsihta.**

maskekowan *pl.* **maskekowana** (VII) It is a muskeg.

maskekowiyiniw *pl.* **maskekowiyiniwak** (NA) A Swampy Cree person. *Var.* **omaskekiw.**

maskihkiwapiy (NI) Tea. *(Plains). Var.* **maskihkiwaypoy.** *Alt.* **lite** *(Northern, French Cree).*

maskihkiwâpoy *pl.* **maskihkiwâpoya** (NI) Medicine water or spirit power liquid.

maskihkiwiskwew *pl.* **maskihkiwiskwewak** (NA) A medicine woman or nurse.

maskihkiwîyiniwiw *pl.* **maskihkiwîyiniwiwak** (VAI) S/he has many spirit power gifts; s/he is a shaman.

maskihkîs *pl.* **maskihkîsa** (NI) A candy or chocolate.

maskihkîwahcikos *pl.* **maskihkîwahcikosa** (NI) Any medicine root, i.e.: such as aloe.

maskihkîwakan *pl.* **maskihkîwakanwa** (NI) Medicine vapour, aroma, odor.

maskihkîwan *pl.* **maskihkîwana** (NI) That characteristic that all great medicine possesses.

maskihkîwikamik *pl.* **maskihkîwikamikwa** (NI) A clinic; a pharmacy.

maskihkîwiyiniw *pl.* **maskihkîwiyiniwak** (NA) Someone who treats illness, i.e.: medicine man, shaman, doctor.

maskihkîwopakwa (NI) Medicine leaves or herbs with spirit power benefit.

maskihkîy *pl.* **maskihkîya** (NI) A healing potion or a medicine gift that has spirit power benefits.

maskihkîya (NI) Herbs. *Var.* **maskihkîwâhtikwa.**

maskikan *pl.* **maskikana** (NI) A human chest.

maskimot *pl.* **maskimota** (NI) A bag.

maskimotihkew *pl.* **maskimotihkewak** (VAI) S/he makes a bag.

74

maskisin *pl.* **maskisina** (NI) A low-cut footwear, i.e.: a moccasin.

maskisinihkanisa (NI) Imitation shoes, i.e.: sandals; thongs.

maskisinihkawew *pl.* **maskisinihkawewak** (VTA) S/he makes footwear for her/him, i.e.: shoes or moccasins.

maskisinihkew *pl.* **maskisinihkewa** (VTI) S/he makes footwear, i.e.: shoes or moccasins.

maskomin *pl.* **maskomina** (NI) A bearberry.

maskominânâhtik *pl.* **maskominânâhtikwak** (NA) A mountain ash tree. Also used by Northern Cree for Red Willow from which kinnikinik is made. *(Plains). Alt.* **waciwahtik** *(Northern).*

maskosihikew *pl.* **maskosihikewak** (VTA) S/he makes hay.

maskosiskâw (VII) It is grassy; there is plenty of grass or hay.

maskosiwastotin *pl.* **maskosiwastotina** (NI) A straw hat.

maskosiwikamik *pl.* **maskosiwikamikwa** (NI) A shelter made of grass or hay, i.e.: a straw house.

maskosiwistikwân (NI) Grasshead.

maskosiy *pl.* **maskosiya** (NI) One blade of grass or hay.

maskosiya (NI) Hay.

maskotehk (NA) The Cree name for the settlement of High Prairie. *(Plains). Alt.* **maskotewisipiy** *(Northern).*

maskotew *pl.* **maskotewa** (NI) Prairie; bald prairie.

maskotewan *pl.* **maskotewanwa** (VII) It is a prairie.

maskotewimostos *pl.* **maskotewimostoswak** (NA) A prairie cow.

maskotewisipiy (NA) The Cree name for the settlement of High Prairie. *(Northern). Alt.* **maskotehk** *(Plains).*

maskotewiw *pl.* **maskotewiwa** (VII) There is prairie around that lake or those lakes.

maskotewiyiniw *pl.* **maskotewiyiniwak** (NA) A prairie man.

maskwa *pl.* **maskwak** (NA) A bear; bruin.

maskwacîs (NI) The Cree name for the settlement of Hobbema means "Bear mountain"; Bear Hills.

maskwayân *pl.* **maskwayânak** (NA) A bear hide.

maskwemotâs *pl.* **maskwemotâsa** (NI) A seamless sack made from bear skin; a pemmican bag.

masowewin *pl.* **masowewina** (NI) The act of seduction.

mastahtew *pl.* **mastahtewak** (VAI) S/he sees that her/his tracks are on top of hers/his.

mastamew *pl.* **mastamewak** (VAI) S/he tracks over her/his footprints.

mastaw (IPC) Just recently.

matay *pl.* **mataya** (NI) A stomach; a belly.

matâwisiw *pl.* **matâwisiwak** (VAI) S/he appears out of the bush or wood.

matotisân *pl.* **matotisâna** (NI) A sweat lodge.

matotisânihkew *pl.* **matotisânihkewa** (VTI) S/he makes or prepares a sweat bath.

matotisiw *pl.* **matotisiwak** (VAI) S/he is having a sweat bath.

matwehkwâmiw *pl.* **matwehkwâmiwak** (VAI) S/he is snoring. *(Northern). Alt.* **kitiwehkwâmiw** *(Plains).*

matwemâtiw *pl.* **matwemâtiwak** (VAI) S/he can be heard crying from a distance.

matwesimew (VTI) S/he throws it on the floor.

matwetitâw (VTI) S/he lets it fall noisily.

matwetahikewin *pl.* **matwetahikewina** (NI) The act of striking blows or rapping audibly.

matwetawew (VTA) S/he strikes something noisily.

matwetaham (VTI) S/he strikes it noisily.

matwetahikew (VTA) S/he strikes something noisily.

matwewew (VAI) The gun shot can be heard.

matweyaskatin *pl.* **matweyaskatinwa** (VII) It is so cold you can hear it crackle.

mawasakokwâcikewstamâkew (VTA) S/he sews things together for others.

mawasakokwâcikew (VTI) S/he sews things together.

mawasakopitew (VTA) S/he gathers them together in a hurry.

mawasakopitam (VTI) S/he gathers it all together in a hurry.

mawasakopisiwew (VTA) S/he gathers people in a hurry.

mawasakopicikew (VTI) S/he gathers things in a hurry.

mawasakotisawew (VTA) S/he chases them together.

mawasakotisaham (VTI) S/he sends it all together.

mawasakotisahowew (VTA) S/he sends people all together.

mawasakotisahikew (VTA) S/he sends everybody together.

mawasakowepawew (VTA) S/he stacks them in a pile.

mawasakowepaham (VTI) S/he stacks or piles the hay.

mawasakowepahikew (VTI) S/he stacks the hay in a pile.

mawasakwahew (VTA) S/he piles them together.

mawasakwastâw (VTI) S/he piles it together.

mawasakwahiwew (VTA) S/he piles people together.

mawikan *pl.* **mawikana** (NI) The back.

mawinehikew *pl.* **mawinehikewak** (VAI) S/he competes.

mawinehikewin *pl.* **mawinehikewina** (NI) A competition or challenge.

mawinehotowin *pl.* **mawinehotowina** (NI) The act of competing; a bout; vying for first place.

mawineskawew (VTA) S/he challenges her/him or them.

mawineskakam (VTI) S/he challenges it.

mawineskakâkew (VTA) S/he challenges people.

75

mawineskâkewin *pl.* **mawineskâkewina** (NI) The act of challenging someone; defy; rivalry.

mawineskâtowin *pl.* **mawineskâtowina** (NI) The act of having a duel.

mawinewew (VTA) S/he competes against her/him or them.

mawineham (VTI) S/he is competing against it.

mawinehowew (VTA) S/he competes against someone.

mawinehikew (VTA) S/he competes against anyone.

mawisiw *pl.* **mawisiwak** (VTA) S/he picks berries.

mawisowin *pl.* **mawisowina** (NI) The act of picking of berries.

mawiswatew (VTA) S/he picks a certain kind of berry from the trees, i.e.: ripe berries.

mawiswatam (VTA) S/he picks certain berries.

mayakosiw *pl.* **mayakosiwak** (VAI) S/he is unlucky.

mayakosiwin *pl.* **mayakosiwina** (NI) Having bad luck; hapless.

mayakoskawew (VTA) S/he brings her/him bad luck; s/he causes her/him bad or ill luck.

mayakoskam (VTI) S/he brings bad luck.

mayakoskâkew (VTA) S/he brings bad luck to people.

mayakoskâcikew (VTI) S/he brings bad luck to everything.

mayakwamew *pl.* **mayakwamewak** (VTA) S/he puts a bad curse on her/him or brings her/him bad luck.

mayakwamitowin *pl.* **mayakwamitowina** (NI) The act of placing a curse on someone.

mayakwan *pl.* **mayakwanwa** (VII) It is unlucky.

mayaw (IPC) As soon as.

mayes (IPC) Before or ere. *(Plains). Var.* **pâmayes**. *Alt.* **namic** *(Northern).*

mayinikewin *pl.* **mayinikewina** (NI) The act of awkwardness or clumsiness; the act of perpetrating a downfall; the act of having a downfall.

mayipayihew (VTA) S/he makes her/him have bad luck.

mayipayitâw (VTI) S/he causes bad luck.

mayipayihiwew (VTA) S/he causes people bad luck.

mayipayicikew (VTI) S/he causes everything bad luck.

mayitôtawew (VTA) S/he treats her/him badly.

mayitôtawaw (VAI) S/he is being treated badly.

mayitôtam (VAI) S/he does bad things.

mayitôtâkew (VTA) S/he does bad things to others.

mâcâpacihew (VTA) S/he starts to use her/him.

mâcâpacitâw (VTI) S/he starts to use it.

mâcâpacihiwew (VTA) S/he starts to use people.

mâcâpacicikew (VTI) S/he starts to use things.

mâcâtoskew *pl.* **mâcâtoskewak** (VAI) S/he starts to work.

mâcihtawin *pl.* **mâcihtawina** (NI) The starting point.

mâci ka (IPC) So.

mâcimîcisiw *pl.* **mâcimîcisiwak** (VAI) S/he starts to eat.

mâcipayihew (VTA) S/he starts her/him or it, i.e.: a motor.

mâcipayitâw (VTI) S/he starts it.

mâcipayihiwew (VTA) S/he starts others.

mâcipayihcikew (VTI) S/he starts things up.

mâcipayiw *pl.* **mâcipayiwa** (VII) It starts, i.e.: a meeting.

mâcipîkiskwew *pl.* **mâcipîkiskwewak** (VAI) S/he is starting to talk.

mâcisekwan (IPC) An expression meaning "Spring is starting."

mâcisimow *pl.* **mâcisimowak** (VAI) S/he starts dancing.

mâcisimowin *pl.* **mâcisimowina** (NI) The opening dance.

mâcisimowinihkew *pl.* **mâcisimowinihkewak** (VAI) S/he organizes an opening dance.

mâcistan *pl.* **mâcistanwa** (NI) Ice starting to move down the river.

mâcîpayiwin *pl.* **mâcîpayiwina** (NI) Hunting on horse back.

mâcîpiciw *pl.* **mâcîpiciwak** (VAI) S/he goes on a moose hunting trip.

mâcîstawew (VTA) S/he hunts her/him up.

mâcîstam (VTI) S/he hunts it up.

mâcîstâkew (VTA) S/he hunts people up.

mâcîw *pl.* **mâciwak** (VAI) S/he hunts.

mâcîwanehikew (VAI) S/he started trapping or setting traps.

mâham *pl.* **mâhamwak** (VAI) S/he is paddling downstream in a canoe or boat.

mâhamowin *pl.* **mâhamowina** (NI) The act of paddling downstream.

mâhiskam *pl.* **mâhiskamwak** (VAI) S/he goes shopping.

mâhiskamohtahew (VTA) S/he takes her/him shopping.

mâhiskamohtatâw (VTI) S/he takes something to the shopping centre.

mâhiskamohtahiwew (VTA) S/he takes people shopping.

mâhiskamôskanaw *pl.* **mâhiskamôskanawa** (NI) The road to the store.

mâhmeskwatascikewinihk (IPC) An expression indicating items are being rotated; rotational.

mâhmiywâpahkewin *pl.* **mâhmiywâpahkewina** (NI) The act of admiring.

mâka (IPC) But.

mâka mena (IPC) An expression of annoyance meaning "it happened again."

mâka-ôma (IPC) An expression of annoyance meaning "here it is again."

mâkohew (VTA) S/he irritates her/him in a threatening way.

mâkotâw (VTI) S/he irritates it in a threatening way.

mâkohiwew (VTA) S/he irritates someone in a threatening way.

mâkotâsow (VTA) S/he irritates everyone in a threatening way.

mâkwa *pl.* **mâkwak** (NA) A loon.

mâkwahikan (NI) Cheese; something cooked hard; something pressed together. *(Plains). Alt.* **maskawihkasikan** *(Northern).*

mâmahkâskâw (VII) The lake is full of whitecaps. *(Plains). Alt.* **wâpimahkâskâw** *(Northern).*

mâmaskacinâkosiw *pl.* **mâmaskacinâkosiwak** (VAI) S/he looks dazzling.

mâmaskâc (IPC) An exclamation of surprise, "it is astonishing or surprising" or "amazing."

mâmaskâcâyihtiw *pl.* **mâmaskâcâyihtiwak** (VAI) S/he acts pompously.

mâmaskâcâyihtowin *pl.* **mâmaskâcâyihtowina** (NI) The act of showing off.

mâmaskâcihcikew *pl.* **mâmaskâcihcikewak** (VAI) S/he achieves awe-inspiring wonders.

mâmaskâcihcikewin *pl.* **mâmaskâcihcikewina** (NI) The act of achieving awe-inspiring wonders or marvels.

mâmaskâcihkin (VII) It is an extraordinary happening.

mâmaskâcihtawew (VTA) S/he listens to her/him with wonderment.

mâmaskâcihtam (VTI) S/he finds that it sounds wonderful.

mâmaskâcihtâkew (VTA) S/he finds people sound wonderful.

mâmaskâcihtâkwan (VTI) It sounds wonderful.

mâmaskâcihtâkosiw *pl.* **mâmaskâcihtâkosiwak** (VAI) S/he sounds wonderful.

mâmaskâcihtâkosiwin *pl.* **mâmaskâcihtâkosiwina** (NI) A voice with extraordinary tone.

mâmaskâcinawew (VTA) S/he looks at her/him with amazement.

mâmaskâcinam (VTI) S/he looks at it with amazement.

mâmaskâcinâkew (VTA) S/he looks at people with amazement.

mâmaskâcinâkwan *pl.* **mâmaskâcinâkwanwa** (VII) It looks dazzling; it looks admirable.

mâmaskâsâpahcikewin *pl.* **mâmaskâsâpahcikewina** (NI) Being phenomenal.

mâmaskâtamowin *pl.* **mâmaskâtamowina** (NI) Being surprised; amazed; amazement; wonderment; taken aback.

mâmaskâtapamew (VTA) S/he regards her/him with awe.

mâmaskâtapatam (VTI) S/he regards it with awe.

mâmaskâtapakew (VTA) S/he regards others with awe.

mâmaskâtapacikew (VTI) S/he regards things with awe.

mâmaskâtâpisin *pl.* **mâmaskâtâpisinwak** (VAI) S/he is surprised by what s/he sees.

mâmaskâtew (VTA) S/he is surprised at the way s/he is now.

mâmaskâtam (VTI) S/he finds it strange.

mâmaskâsiwew (VTA) S/he finds people strange.

mâmaskâcikew (VTI) S/he finds things strange.

mâmaskâteyihcikewin *pl.* **mâmaskâteyihcikewina** (NI) The act of feeling awe.

mâmaskâteyihtâkosiw *pl.* **mâmaskâteyihtâkosiwak** (VAI) S/he is wonderful or amazing.

mâmaskâteyihtâkwan *pl.* **mâmaskâteyihtâkwanwa** (VII) It is wonderful or amazing.

mâmaskâteyimew (VTA) S/he thinks s/he has changed.

mâmaskâteyitam (VTI) S/he thinks it has changed.

mâmaskâteyimiwew (VTA) S/he thinks people have changed.

mâmaskâteyicikew (VTI) S/he thinks things have changed.

mâmaskâtikohkâsiw *pl.* **mâmaskâtikohkâsiwak** (VAI) S/he is cocky; s/he makes you feel indebted.

mâmaskâtikohkâsowin *pl.* **mâmaskâtikohkâsowina** (NI) The act of being cocky.

mâmaskâtikonikewin *pl.* **mâmaskâtikonikewina** (NI) Being cocky; obtrusion; stagy.

mâmaskâtikosiw *pl.* **mâmaskâtikosiwak** (VAI) S/he is fascinated by it.

mâmaskâtikosiwin *pl.* **mâmaskâtikosiwina** (NI) Being fascinated.

mâmaskâtikwan *pl.* **mâmaskâtikwanwa** (VII) It is fascinating.

mâmawahew (VTA) S/he gets them together.

mâmawastâw (VTI) S/he gets it together.

mâmawahiwew (VTA) S/he gets everyone together.

mâmawascikew (VTI) S/he gets everything together.

mâmawastew (VTI) It is put all together.

mâmawâyâwin *pl.* **mâmawâyâwina** (NI) A gathering or meeting place, i.e.: a hangout.

mâmawihisicikewin *pl.* **mâmawihisicikewina** (NI) The act of working together in a concerted effort, i.e.: a barn raising.

mâmawihitowin *pl.* **mâmawihitowina** (NI) A gathering of people. *Var.* **mâmawopayowin**.

mâmawinâtisaham *pl.* **mâmawinâtisahamwak** (VAI) S/he orders for it all at once.

mâmawinâtomew (VTA) S/he calls them together for the assembly, gathering, meeting.

mâmawinâtotam (VTI) S/he calls for things all together.

mâmawinâtomiwew (VTA) S/he calls everybody together.

mâmawinâtocikew (VTI) S/he calls for everything together.

mâmawinew (VTA) S/he assembles them.

mâmawinam (VTI) S/he assembles it.

77

mâmawiniwew (VTA) S/he assembles everybody.

mâmawinikew (VTI) S/he assembles everything.

mâmawinikewin *pl.* **mâmawinikewina** (NI) The act of assembling or gathering items together; an assemblage; ensemble.

mâmawinitowin *pl.* **mâmawinitowinak** (NA) An affilation; confederation; a grouping; a horde; society.

mâmawipayiw *pl.* **mâmawipayiwa** *or* **mâmawipayiwak** (VII) *or* (VAI) It *or* s/he comes together all by itself or assembles itself.

mâmawipayowin *pl.* **mâmawipayowina** (NI) An informal gathering of people.

mâmawipicikewin *pl.* **mâmawipicikewina** (NI) An amalgamation.

mâmawitisawew (VTA) S/he drives them together, i.e.: horses or cattle.

mâmawitisaham (VTI) S/he drives or compels aspects of the situation to cohere.

mâmawitisahowew (VTA) S/he drives people together.

mâmawitisahikew (VTA) S/he drives everyone together.

mâmawiwikowin *pl.* **mâmawiwikowina** (NI) The act of living together, i.e.: communal.

mâmawiyask (IPC) The most or above all.

mâmawokamâtowak (VTA) They assemble themselves to help one another.

mâmâkwahcikewin *pl.* **mâmâkwahcikewina** (NI) The act of gnawing; chewing something; ruminate.

mâmâmitoneyihtowak (VTA) They constantly think of each other. *(Plains). Alt.* **tâpitaweyihtowak** *(Northern).*

mâmâsihkewin *pl.* **mâmâsihkewina** (NI) The act of behaving rashly.

mâmâsimâciwin *pl.* **mâmâsimâciwina** (NI) The act of being sloppy. *(Plains). Alt.* **wîyipapawewin** *(Northern).*

mâmâsisihkewin *pl.* **mâmâsisihkewina** (NI) The act of being careless when making things.

mâmeskoc (IPC) Alternately, each in turn.

mâmihk (NI) Downstream.

mâmiskomew (VTA) S/he talks about her/him or them.

mâmiskotam (VTI) S/he talks about it.

mâmiskomiwew (VTA) S/he talks about people.

mâmiskocikew (VTI) S/he talks about things.

mâmiskôtamawew (VTA) S/he mentions it to her/him or them.

mâmiskôtamakew (VTA) S/he talks to others about it.

mâmiskôtamâkewin *pl.* **mâmiskôtamâkewina** (NI) The act of mentioning something to someone.

mâmitoneyihcikan *pl.* **mâmitoneyihcikana** (NI) The mind; conscience.

mâmitoneyihcikanihk (LN) In the mind; mentally.

mâmitoneyihcikewin *pl.* **mamitoneyihcikewina** (NI) Concentration.

mâmitoneyihtam *pl.* **mâmitoneyihtamwak** (VAI) S/he thinks about it.

mâmitoneyihtamowin *pl.* **mâmitoneyihtamowina** (NI) The act of thinking; emotive; imagination.

mâmitoneyimew (VTA) S/he thinks about her/him.

mâmitoneyitam (VTI) S/he thinks about it.

mâmitoneyimiwew (VTA) S/he thinks about someone.

mâmitoneyicikew (VTI) S/he thinks about things.

mâmitoneyimisiw *pl.* **mâmitoneyimisiwak** (VTA) S/he thinks about herself/himself.

mâmitoneyimisiwin *pl.* **mâmitoneyimisiwina** (NI) The act of thinking of oneself; self-interest.

mâmiwakâcimew (VTA) S/he uses provoking speech with her/him.

mâmiwakâcitam (VTI) S/he takes her/his speech as offensive.

mâmiwakâcimiwew (VTA) S/he uses provoking speech to people.

mâmiwakâcicikew (VTI) S/he does things in a provoking manner.

mâmiwâkâcimow *pl.* **mâmiwâkâcimowak** (VAI) S/he uses provocative language.

mâmiwâkâcimowin *pl.* **mâmiwâkâcimowina** (NI) The act of using provocative language.

mâna (IPC) Usually. *(Plains). Alt.* **mânah** *(Northern).*

mânah (IPC) Usually. *(Northern). Alt.* **mâna** *(Plains).*

mânipoko (IPC) It seems like.

mânokew *pl.* **mânokewak** (VAI) S/he sets up or pitches a tent.

mânokewin *pl.* **mânokewina** (NI) The act of setting up or pitching a tent.

mâsihew (VTA) S/he wrestles with her/him.

mâsitâw (VTI) S/he wrestles with it.

mâsihiwew (VTA) S/he wrestles with someone.

mâsicikew (VTI) S/he wrestles around things.

mâsihitowak (VAI) They wrestle.

mâsihitowin *pl.* **mâsihitowina** (NI) The sport of wrestling.

mâsihkew *pl.* **mâsihkewak** (VAI) S/he wrestles.

mâsihtâw *pl.* **mâsihtâwa** (VTI) S/he wrestles with it; s/he works at it.

mâsikes *pl.* **mâsikesak** (NA) Cedar. *Var.* **minisihkes**.

mâsikeskopiyesîs *pl.* **mâsikeskopiyesîsak** (NA) A cedar bird (i.e.: a Cedar wax wing). *(Plains). Alt.* **sihtipiwâyisis** *(Northern).*

mâskakân *pl.* **mâskakâna** (NI) Something that is used up or worn out.

mâskâw *pl.* **mâskâwa** (VII) It is imperfect, not reliable, faulty.

mâskicihciw *pl.* **mâskicihciwak** (VAI) S/he has a deformed hand.

mâskihiwewin *pl.* **mâskihiwewina** (NI) The act of deforming or crippling someone; deformation.

mâskikan *pl.* **mâskikana** (NI) A deformed bone.

mâskikanew *pl.* **mâskikanewak** (VAI) Her/his bone is deformed.

mâskikâtew *pl.* **mâskikâtewak** (VAI) S/he has a lame or deformed leg.

mâskikin *pl.* **mâskikinwa** (VII) It grows crippled or deformed, i.e.: a bone.

mâskikiw *pl.* **mâskikiwak** (VAI) S/he grows crippled or deformed.

mâskinihtâwikiwin *pl.* **mâskinihtâwikiwina** (NI) Being born with a deformity.

mâskipayiw *pl.* **mâskipayiwak** (VAI) S/he walks with a limp.

mâskipitonew *pl.* **mâskipitonewak** (VAI) S/he has a deformed arm.

mâskisimowin (NI) The round dance or lame dance.

mâskisitew *pl.* **mâskisitewak** (VTA) S/he has a deformed foot.

mâskisiw *pl.* **mâskisiwak** (VAI) S/he is crippled.

mâskisiwin *pl.* **mâskisiwina** (NI) The act of being crippled.

mâskôc (IPC) Perhaps, maybe.

mâskôcâyiman (IPC) It must be difficult.

mâtaham (VTA) S/he scrapes it, i.e.: a moosehide.
mâtahikew (VTI) S/he is removing the hair from the hide.

mâtahikan *pl.* **mâtahikana** (NI) A scraping instrument or a piece of steel for scraping the fur off the skin or hide.

mâtahikew *pl.* **mâtahikewak** (VTA) S/he scrapes the hair off.

mâtahikewin *pl.* **mâtahikewina** (NI) The act of scraping the hair off moosehide.

mâtahpinew *pl.* **mâtahpinewak** (VAI) S/he starts to be sick; s/he becomes ill.

mâtahpinewin *pl.* **mâtahpinewina** (NI) The start of a sickness; the onset of illness.

mâtakamikisowin *pl.* **mâtakamikisowina** (NI) Procedures.

mâtakimihci pîsim (IPC) The start or beginning of next month.

mâtamahcihow *pl.* **mâtamahcihowak** (VAI) S/he starts feeling pain.

mâtayak (IPC) Early.

mâtâhaw (VTA) S/he is tracked.
mâtâtâw (VTI) It is tracked.
mâtâhiwew (VTA) S/he is tracking someone.
mâtâcikew (VTI) S/he sees lots of tracks.

mâtâhew *pl.* **mâtâhewak** (VTA) S/he finds the footprints, tracks, trace, trail; s/he arrives on a track of someone.

mâtinamawew (VTA) S/he offers her/him something.
mâtinamakew (VTA) S/he shares with everyone.

mâtinamâkewin *pl.* **mâtinamâkewina** (NI) The act of offering or giving.

mâtinawew *pl.* **mâtinawewak** (VAI) S/he offers or gives.

mâtinawewin *pl.* **mâtinawewina** (NI) The act of offering something.

mâtisâwâtew (VTA) S/he starts cutting it.
mâtisâwâtam (VTI) S/he starts cutting it.
mâtisâwâsiwew (VTA) S/he starts cutting people.
mâtisâwâcikew (VTI) S/he starts cutting things.

mâtow (VAI) S/he cries.

mâtoweham *pl.* **mâtowehamwak** (VAI) S/he starts drumming for the celebration.

mâtowehikan *pl.* **mâstowehikanak** (NA) A starting drum for celebration.

mâtowehikew *pl.* **mâtowehikewak** (VTA) S/he beats the starting drum in a celebration song.

mâtowin *pl.* **mâtowina** (NI) The act of crying.

mâtowinâpoy *pl.* **mâtowinâpoya** (NI) A tear.

mâtowitam *pl.* **mâtowitamak** (VAI) S/he starts to speak.

mâwacihcikew *pl.* **mâwacihcikewak** (VAI) S/he collects and s/he saves.

mâwacihcikewin *pl.* **mâwacihcikewina** (NI) A collection.

mâwacihew (VTA) S/he collects them; s/he saves them.
mâwacitâw (VTI) S/he collects it.
mâwacihiwew (VTA) S/he gathers people.
mâwacicikew (VTI) S/he gathers things.

mâwacihitowak (VTA) They gather together.

mâwacihitowin *pl.* **mâwacihitowina** (NI) A gathering.

mâwacinikân (IPC) An expression meaning "way in front; foremost."

mâwasakokwâtew (VTA) S/he sews them together, i.e.: a pair of pants.
mâwasakokwâtam (VTI) S/he sews them all altogether, i.e.: patches for a quilt.

mâwasakonam *pl.* **mâwasakonamwa** (VTI) S/he bunches it together.

mâwasakonew (VTA) S/he gathers them up.
mâwasakonam (VTI) S/he gathers it up.
mâwasakoniwew (VTA) S/he gathers people up.
mâwasakonikew (VTI) S/he gathers things up.

mâwasakonikewin *pl.* **mâwasakonikewina** (NI) The act of accumulating by gathering; accumulation.

mâwasakopayihew (VTA) S/he bunches them all together; s/he makes them come together.
mâwasakopayitâw (VTI) S/he bunches it together.
mâwasakopayihiwew (VTA) S/he bunches people together.
mâwasakopayicikew (VTI) S/he bunches things together.

mâwasakopayiw *pl.* **mâwasakopayiwa** *or*
mâwasakopayiwak (VII) *or* (VAI) Everything *or*
everyone comes together by itself or themselves;
everything *or* everyone mixes together.

mâwasakwahpitew (VTA) S/he ties them in bunches.
mâwasakwahpitam (VTI) S/he ties it together.
mâwasakwahpisiwew (VTA) S/he ties up everybody.
mâwasakwahpicikew (VTI) S/he ties up everything.

mâwasakwahwew *pl.* **mâwasakwahwewak** (VTA) S/he
mixes them up.

mâwasakwascikew *pl.* **mâwasakwascikewa** (VTI) S/he
piles things together.

mâwatahew *pl.* **mâwatahewak** (VTA) S/he gathers furs.

mâwatascikewina (NI) Contents; gatherings for future
use.

mâwikan *pl.* **mâwikana** (NI) An entire spine.

mâyacihkosis *pl.* **mâyacihkosisak** (NA) A lamb; a small
lamb; lambkin.

mâyahcâw *pl.* **mâyahcâwa** (NI) Rough and uneven
ground. *(Plains). Alt.* **pîkwahcâw** *(Northern).*

mâyahiwewin *pl.* **mâyahiwewina** (NI) The act of
discrediting someone; discredit.

mâyakopayowin *pl.* **mâyakopayowina** (NI) Having very
bad luck; misadventure.

mâyapiw *pl.* **mâyapiwak** (VAI) S/he sits improperly.

mâyascikewin *pl.* **mâyascikewina** (NI) The act of
creating disorder or disarranging.

mâyaskamikâw *pl.* **mâyaskamikâwa** (NI) Spongy
ground; dry muskeg.

mâyaskâpôwin *pl.* **mâyaskâpôwina** (NI) Being bug-eyed.

mâyaskisiw *pl.* **mâyaskisiwak** (NA) A crooked plant.

mâyasowâsowewin *pl.* **mâyasowâsowewina** (NI)
Malediction or the act of putting a curse or hex on
someone.

mâyasowâtew *pl.* **mâyasowâtewak** (VTA) S/he puts a hex
on her/him.

mâyastew *pl.* **mâyastewa** (VII) It is placed improperly.

mâyatihk *pl.* **mâyatihkwak** (NA) A sheep; a bighorn
sheep.

mâyatihkowayân *pl.* **mâyatihkowayânak** (NA) A
sheepskin.

mâyatihkowiyâs *pl.* **mâyatihkowiyâsa** (NI) Sheep meat;
mutton.

mâyatihkwayân *pl.* **mâyatihkwayânak** (NA) A goatskin.

mâyatinâw *pl.* **mâyatinâwa** (NI) A rough, rugged hill.

mâyatiskos *pl.* **mâyatiskosak** (NA) A small sheep.

mâyâcimowin (NI) Bad news.

mâyâhtik *pl.* **mâyâhtikwa** (NI) A poorly formed tree.

mâyâpiskaw *pl.* **mâyâpiskawwa** (NI) The iron is full of
dents.

mâyâpiskinikan *pl.* **mâyâpiskinikana** (NI) A poorly
made iron.

mâyâpiskisiw *pl.* **mâyâpiskisiwak** (NA) Iron or steel that
is bent out of shape.

mâyâpitewin *pl.* **mâyâpitewina** (NI) Being bucktoothed.

mâyâtan *pl.* **mâyâtanwa** (VII) It is ugly.

mâyâtisiw *pl.* **mâyâtisiwak** (VAI) S/he is ugly.

mâyâtisiwin *pl.* **mâyâtisiwina** (NI) Being ugly.

mâyâyâw *pl.* **mâyâyâwak** (VAI) S/he is not feeling well.

mâyâyâwin *pl.* **mâyâyâwina** (NI) The act of not feeling
well; distress.

mâyesihcikewin *pl.* **mâyesihcikewina** (NI) The act of
being biased; flaw.

mâyeyihcikew *pl.* **mâyeyihcikewak** (VTA) S/he rebels
against someone.

mâyeyihcikewin *pl.* **mâyeyihcikewina** (NI) Rebellion.

mâyeyihtamowin *pl.* **mâyeyihtamowina** (NI) Thinking
in a disdainful manner.

mâyeyihtâkosiw *pl.* **mâyeyihtâkosiwak** (VAI) S/he is
despised.

mâyeyihtâkwan *pl.* **mâyeyihtâkwanwa** (VII) It is
contemptible.

mâyeyimew (VTA) S/he is not intimidated by her/him;
s/he is not scared of her/him.
mâyeyitam (VTI) S/he is not intimidated by it.
mâyeyimiwew (VTA) S/he is not intimidated by
anyone.
mâyeyihcikew (VTI) S/he is not intimidated by
anything.

mâyihkwew *pl.* **mâyihkwewak** (VAI) S/he has a
disfigured face.

mâyihkweyiw *pl.* **mâyihkweyiwak** (VAI) S/he makes
faces.

mâyihkweyowin *pl.* **mâyihkweyowina** (NI) The act of
contorting one's face.

mâyihtâkosiw *pl.* **mâyihtâkosiwak** (VAI) S/he does not
sound good; s/he has a gruff voice.

mâyikisikâw *pl.* **mâyikisikâwa** (NI) A bad weather, bad
day.

mâyimahcihow (VTA) S/he feels badly; unhealthy.

mâyimahcihowin *pl.* **mâyimahcihowina** (NI) The act of
discomfort.

mâyimâmiskomowewin *pl.* **mâyimâmiskomowewina**
(NI) Being defamatory.

mâyimitos *pl.* **mâyimitosak** (NA) A black poplar tree;
balsam poplar; cottonwood.

mâyinawew (VTA) S/he looks at her/him and thinks s/he
is ugly.
mâyinam (VTI) S/he looks at it and thinks it is ugly.
mâyinakew (VTA) S/he looks at everyone and thinks
everyone is ugly.
mâyinakohcikew (VTI) Her/his actions don't look
good.

mâyinâkosiw *pl.* **mâyinâkosiwak** (VAI) S/he looks poorly; s/he has an ugly appearance; s/he doesn't look good.

mâyinâkwan *pl.* **mâyinâkwanwa** (NI) It looks bad.

mâyinew (VTA) S/he holds her/him awkwardly.

mâyinam (VTI) S/he holds it awkwardly.

mâyiniwew (VTA) S/he holds someone awkwardly.

mâyinikew (VTI) S/he holds something quite improperly.

mâyinikeskiw *pl.* **mâyinikeskiwak** (VAI) S/he has a habit of doing things carelessly.

mâyinikeskiwin *pl.* **mâyinikeskiwina** (NI) The act of carelessness or negligence.

mâyinikew *pl.* **mâyinikewak** (VAI) S/he does something awkwardly or clumsily.

mâyipayihiwewin *pl.* **mâyipayihiwewina** (NI) The act of causing trouble for someone; troublemaking.

mâyipayiw *pl.* **mâyipayiwak** *or* **mâyipayiwa** (VAI) *or* (VII) S/he has a death or misfortune in the family; it does not run right, i.e.: a motor; s/he has bad or evil luck.

mâyipayiwin *pl.* **mâyipayiwina** (NI) The act of having a death or misfortune in a family; the act of having poor success or bad luck.

mâyipicikewin *pl.* **mâyipicikewina** (NI) The act of behaving in a disconcerning manner; disconcert.

mâyisihcikewin *pl.* **mâyisihcikewina** (NI) Being blotchy.

mâyiskawew (VTA) S/he does not fit in with her/him; s/he is not suited for her/him.

mâyiskam (VTI) S/he doesn't fit in with it.

mâyiskâkew (VTA) S/he doesn't fit in with others.

mâyitôtam *pl.* **mâyitôtamwak** (VAI) S/he does it all wrong; s/he is wrong. *(Plains). Alt.* **naspâtisiw** *(Northern).*

mâyitôtamowewin *pl.* **mâyitôtamowewina** (NI) The act of causing someone to do a detrimental act.

mâyitôtamowin *pl.* **mâyitôtamowina** (NI) The act of doing things wrong; improper conduct or misconduct; villainy; the act of being wrong. *(Plains). Alt.* **naspâtisiwin** *(Northern).*

mâyitôtâkewin *pl.* **mâyitôtâkewina** (NI) The act of being malevolent towards someone.

mâyitôtâtowin *pl.* **mâyitôtâtowina** (NI) The act of betrayal.

mâyiwecehtowin *pl.* **mâyiwecehtowina** (NI) The act of being in conflict with someone; being discordant; discord; disaffected.

mecimwâtasinahikewin *pl.* **mecimwâtasinahikewina** (NI) The act of avoiding payment; bilk.

mecimwâtisinowin *pl.* **mecimwâtisinowina** (NI) Being bedridden; being immobile.

mehmew *pl.* **mehmewak** (NA) A dove.

mekastimwâtew (VTA) S/he gives her/him a horse.

mekastimwâwew (VTA) S/he gives others horses.

mekastimwâmwew (VTI) S/he gives horses away.

mekinawewin *pl.* **mekinawewina** (NI) The act of giving a gift, present.

mekiskwewewin *pl.* **mekiskwewewina** (NI) The act of giving a daughter away for marriage; betrothal.

mekiw *pl.* **mekiwak** (VAI) S/he gives.

mekiwin *pl.* **mekiwina** (NI) A thing that you give away; a present or gift; betroth; contribution; emit.

mekoskâcihiwewin *pl.* **mekoskâcihiwewina** (NI) The act of harassing; harassment.

mekowin *pl.* **mekowina** (NI) The act of donating; donation. *(Plains). Alt.* **mikowin** *(Northern).*

mekwan *pl.* **mekwanak** (NA) A feather.

mekwaskawew (VAI) S/he meets her/him by chance.

mekwaskam (VTI) S/he arrives just in time.

mekwâ ayamihâw *pl.* **mekwâ ayamihâwak** (VAI) S/he is at prayer or doing spiritual devotions at the moment.

mekwâ ayisiyininâhk (IPC) Among a crowd of people. *Var.* **mekwânohk**.

mekwâc (IPC) Right now, at this time, as of now; meanwhile; in the interval.

mekwâcoma (IPC) Currently.

mekwâcowanohk (IPC) In the middle of the current.

mekwâkimowan (VII) It is raining right now.

mekwâkîsikâw (VII) It is daytime right now.

mekwâmîcisiw *pl.* **mekwâmîcisiwak** (VAI) S/he is eating right now.

mekwânesohkamâkewin *pl.* **mekwânesohkamâkewina** (NI) The act of being in the midst of helping someone; helping right now.

mekwânohk (IPC) In the middle of or among people; amid.

mekwâsakâhk (IPC) In the middle of the forest.

mekwâtipiskâw (VII) It is time right now.

memohc (IPC) Clearly, in the open; exactly.

mesaponan *pl.* **mesaponana** (NI) An eyelash. *Var.* **mîsapowinân, mesapowinan, mîsaponan.**

mesapowinan *pl.* **mesapowinana** (NI) An eyelash. *Var.* **mîsapowinân, mesaponan, mîsaponan.**

mescacâkanis *pl.* **mescacâkanisak** (NA) A little coyote. *(Plains). Alt.* **miscacâkanis** *(Northern).*

mescacesis *pl.* **mescacesisak** (NA) A little brat; an orphan.

mescakas *pl.* **mescakasa** (NI) A strand of hair. *(Plains). Alt.* **mestakay** *(Northern).*

mescakasa (NI) A mane of hair. *(Plains). Alt.* **mestakaya** *(Northern).*

mescihew (VTA) S/he eradicates them or kills them off.

mescitâw (VTI) S/he destroys everything.

mescihiwew (VTA) S/he destroys everyone.

81

mescicikew (VTA) S/he destroys everything and everyone.

mescihkwekawiw *pl.* **mescihkwekawiwak** (VAI) S/he hemorrhages or loses all her/his blood.

mescihtâsiw *pl.* **mescihtâsiwak** (VTA) S/he eradicates everyone.

mescihtâsiwin *pl.* **mescihtâsiwina** (NI) Eradication or total destruction.

mescikawew (VTA) S/he chops them all up.

mescikaham (VTI) S/he chops it all up.

mescikahowew (VTA) S/he chops them all up.

mescikahikew (VTI) S/he chops everything all up.

mescikawiw *pl.* **mescikawiwak** *or* **mescikawiwa** (VAI) *or* (VII) It all leaked out.

mescinew *pl.* **mescinewak** (VAI) S/he loses her/his whole family from illness.

mescinewak *pl.* **mescinewakak** (VAI) They all died from illness.

mescinewin *pl.* **mescinewina** (NI) The act of one person losing her/his whole family from illness.

mescipayiw *pl.* **mescipayiwak** (VAI) S/he is exhausted or totally used up.

mescipayowin *pl.* **mescipayowina** (NI) The act of deteriorating.

mescipicikewin *pl.* **mescipicikewina** (NI) The act of absorbing liquid; or picking up all the berries.

mescisôpahcikewin *pl.* **mescisôpahcikewina** (NI) The act of total absorption; absorbed.

meskanaw *pl.* **meskanawa** (NI) A road.

meskocipakowayânew *pl.* **meskocipakowayânewak** (VAI) S/he changes her/his shirt.

meskocipayiw *pl.* **meskocipayiwa** *or* **meskocipayiwak** (VII) *or* (VAI) It *or* s/he changed on its *or* her/his own.

meskocipayiwin *pl.* **meskocipayiwina** (NI) The act of changing.

meskotahew (VTA) S/he exchanges her/his or its place.

meskotastâw (VTI) S/he changes it around.

meskotahiwew (VTA) S/he changes people.

meskotascikâkewin *pl.* **meskotascikâkewina** (NI) Something that acts as a replacement; substitutive.

meskotascikewin *pl.* **meskotascikewina** (NI) Something replaced; replacement; rotation; substitution.

meskotaskisinew *pl.* **meskotaskisinewak** (VAI) S/he changes shoes.

meskotonamawew *pl.* **meskotonamawewak** (VTA) S/he exchanges it with her/him.

meskotonamâkewin *pl.* **meskotonamâkewina** (NI) The act of exchanging things. *Var.* **meskotonikewin**.

meskotonikew *pl.* **meskotonamâtowak** (VAI) S/he trades.

meskotônew (VTA) S/he changes her/him.

meskotônam (VTI) S/he exchanges it.

meskotôniwew (VTA) S/he exchanges others.

meskotônikew (VTI) S/he exchanges things.

mestahpinasiwewin *pl.* **mestahpinasiwewina** (NI) The act of annihilating; annihilation. *(Northern)*. *Alt.* **mestapinatihiwin** *(Plains)*.

mestakay *pl.* **mestakaya** (NI) A strand of hair. *(Northern)*. *Alt.* **mescakas** *(Plains)*.

mestakaya (NI) A mane of hair. *(Northern)*. *Alt.* **mescakasa** *(Plains)*.

mestakâhkâna (NA) Artificial hair; a wig.

mestan (NA) Tree sap.

mestaniwiw *pl.* **mestaniwiwak** (VAI) It is full of sap.

mestapinatihiwin *pl.* **mestapinatihiwina** (NI) The act of annihilating; annihilation. *(Plains)*. *Alt.* **mestahpinasiwewin** *(Northern)*.

mestasiw *pl.* **mestasiwak** (VAI) S/he eats the sap of the trees.

mestatew *pl.* **mestatewak** (NA) A big brat; a teenage orphan.

mestâmohkew (VTA) S/he chases them all away. *(Plains)*. *Alt.* **pawitisahwew** *(Northern)*.

mestâmoham (VTA) S/he chases game out of the whole area.

mestâmohikew (VTA) S/he chases everything away.

mestâpahtepayowin *pl.* **mestâpahtepayowina** (NI) The act of evaporating; evaporation.

mestâpitewin *pl.* **mestâpitewina** (NI) Being toothless.

mestâsiw *pl.* **mestâsiwak** (VAI) It is all blown out like snow.

mestâskisiw *pl.* **mestâskisiwak** (VAI) S/he is all burned.

mestâskiswew (VTA) S/he burns her/him or them or it all, i.e.: tobacco in a pipe.

mestâskisam (VTI) S/he burned something all up.

mestâskisowew (VTA) S/he burns someone all up.

mestâskisikew (VTI) S/he burns things all up.

mestâskitew *pl.* **mestâskitewa** (VII) It is all burned off, i.e.: from a forest fire.

mestihkaswew (VTA) S/he burns them up.

mestihkasam (VTI) S/he burns it entirely; s/he burns it all.

mestihkasowew (VTA) S/he burns someone all up.

mestihkasikew (VTI) S/he burns things up.

mestihtin *pl.* **mestihtinwa** (VTI) It is all used up or worn out, i.e.: a moccasin; it is entirely worn out.

mestinew (VTI) S/he uses it all up or spends it.

mestinam (VTI) S/he used something all up or spends it.

mestiniwew (VTI) S/he used something all up on someone else.

mestinikew (VTI) S/he used up all her/his money.

mestinikewin *pl.* **mestinikewina** (NI) The act of reducing costs; retrenchment. *(Plains)*. *Alt.* **nîkimestinkewin** *(Northern)*.

mestinisiw *pl.* **mestinisiwak** (VTA) S/he ruined herself/ himself financially.

mestisin *pl.* **mestisinwak** (VAI) It is used up, worn out.

metawâkan *pl.* **metawâkana** (NI) A toy.

metawâkâtew (VTA) S/he plays or sports with her/him; s/he caresses her/him; s/he ridicules her/him.

metawâkâtâw (VTA) S/he plays or sports with her/ him.

metawâkâhiwew (VTA) S/he plays or sports with someone.

metawâkâcikew (VTI) S/he plays or sports with things.

metawâkâtisowin *pl.* **metawâkâtisowina** (NI) The act of ejaculating; ejaculation. *(Plains). Alt.* **sîsîkocipicikewin** *(Northern).*

metawâkew *pl.* **metawâkewak** (VAI) S/he plays or sports with it.

metawew *pl.* **metawewak** (VAI) S/he plays or amuses herself/himself.

metawewin *pl.* **metawewina** (NI) A game or sport such as lacrosse.

metoni (IPC) An expression meaning "yes; indeed; very true; quite."

metoninahiwin *pl.* **metoninahiwina** (NI) Being ingenious or skilled; ingenuity.

metoniwâhyaw (IPC) Farthermost.

meweyihtamohiwewin *pl.* **neweyihtamohiwewina** (NI) The act of causing someone to be enraptured; enrapture.

meyakan *pl.* **meyakanwa** (VII) It smells like excrement. *(Plains). Alt.* **miyakan** *(Northern).*

meyakisiw *pl.* **meyakisiwak** (VAI) S/he smells like excrement. *(Plains). Alt.* **miyakisiw** *(Northern).*

meyastowâna (NI) Whiskers; a moustache.

meyawayamowin (NI) Delight; happiness; elation. *(Northern). Alt.* **miywâtamowin** *(Plains).*

meyawâtamohiwewin *pl.* **meyawâtamohiwewina** (NI) The act of causing someone elation.

meyâniskam *pl.* **meyâniskamwak** (VAI) There is her/his new or fresh track. *Var.* **miyânam**.

meyih (NI) Excrement.

mcyomâmiokomiwcwin *pl.* **mcyomâmiokomiwcwina** (NI) The act of giving someone a good reputation by saying kind or good words about them; reputed.

meywâtisowin *pl.* **meywâtisowina** (NI) Being amiable.

meywâyisinâkewin *pl.* **meywâyisinâkewina** (NI) The act of being exemplary; exemplification.

micicâskâhk (NI) A crotch.

micihcikepayîs *pl.* **micihcikepayîsak** (NA) A Volkswagon; sniffing machine (slang).

micihcikom *pl.* **micihcikomak** (NA) A wart.

micihcinaskasiy *pl.* **micihcinaskasiyak** (NA) A thumbnail.

micihciy *pl.* **micihciya** (NI) A hand.

micihcîkom *pl.* **micihcîkoma** (NI) A wart. *(Plains). Alt.* **ocehcekom** *(Northern).*

micimahpisiw *pl.* **micimahpisiwak** (VAI) S/he is tied down.

micimahpitew (VTA) S/he ties her/him down. *Var.* **nicimahpitew**.

micimahpitam (VTI) S/he ties it down.

micimahpisiwew (VTA) S/he ties someone down.

micimahpicikew (VTI) S/he ties things down.

micimaskwahwew (VTA) S/he pins her/him or it down.

micimaskwaham (VTI) S/he has pinned something down.

micimaskwahowew (VTA) S/he has pinned someone down.

micimaskwahikew (VTI) S/he has things pinned down.

micimâpay *pl.* **micimâpaya** (NI) Homemade broth or soup.

micimâpohkakew *pl.* **micimâpohkakewak** (VAI) S/he makes soup with it.

micimâpohkân *pl.* **micimâpohkâna** (NI) Canned soup.

micimâpohkew *pl.* **micimâpohkewak** (VAI) S/he makes soup.

micimew *pl.* **micimewak** (VAI) S/he holds onto something.

micimeyimew (VTA) S/he has a fixed idea about her/him or them.

micimeyitam (VTI) S/he has a fixed idea about it.

micimeyimiwew (VTA) S/he has a fixed idea about others.

micimeyicikew (VTI) S/he has a fixed idea about things.

miciminew (VTA) S/he holds on for support.

miciminam (VTI) S/he holds onto it.

miciminiwew (VTA) S/he holds onto others.

miciminikew (VTI) S/he holds onto things.

miciminikan *pl.* **miciminikana** (NI) A handle.

miciminkewin *pl.* **miciminkewina** (NI) The act of holding.

miciminowewin *pl.* **miciminowewina** (NI) The act of ostracizing someone; shunning.

micimohiw *pl.* **micimohiwak** (VAI) S/he is stuck.

micimohtin *pl.* **micimohtinwa** (VII) It is stuck; run aground, or hung-up.

micimopicikewin *pl.* **micimopicikewina** (NI) Being helpless; helplessness.

micimosin *pl.* **micimosinwak** (VTA) S/he is stuck, run aground, or hung-up.

micimoskowakâw *pl.* **micimoskowakâwa** (VII) It is muddy and sticky, i.e.: on a mucky clay road.

micimoskowew *pl.* **micimoskowewak** (VAI) S/he is stuck in the mud.

83

micisiw *pl.* **micisiwak** (VAI) S/he eats.

micisohew (VTA) S/he makes her/him eat.

　micisohiwew (VTA) S/he makes others eat.

micisohkawew *pl.* **micisohkawewak** (VTA) S/he makes her/him something to eat. *(Northern). Alt.* **piminawatew** *(Plains).*

micisowikamik *pl.* **micisowikamikwa** (NI) A restaurant, cafe, cafeteria.

micisowin *pl.* **micisowina** (NI) The act of eating; a meal.

micistatayâpiy *pl.* **micistatayâpiyak** (NA) A muscle. *(Northern). Alt.* **omakohkew** *(Plains).*

micitew (VTA) S/he defecates on her/him.

　micitam (VTI) S/he defecates on it.

miciw *pl.* **miciwak** (VAI) S/he eats it or consumes it; s/he munches it.

micohcôsimihkânis *pl.* **micohcôsimihkânisak** (NA) A nipple on a breast.

mihcâpiskâw *pl.* **mihcâpiskâwa** (VII) It is a huge piece of iron, i.e.: a railroad rail or steel pole.

mihcâskosiw *pl.* **mihcâskosiwak** (VAI) It is large, like a tree.

mihcâskoyawew *pl.* **mihcâskoyawewak** (VAI) S/he has a huge body.

mihcâskwan *pl.* **mihcâskwanwa** (VII) It is a large, round pole.

mihcecis (IPC) Several.

mihcet (IPC) Numerous; many, in great quantity. *(Plains). Alt.* **okistakewi** *(Northern).*

mihcetin *pl.* **mihcetinwa** (VII) There are many of them.

mihcetiw *pl.* **mihcetiwak** (VAI) S/he has a large family.

mihcetiwak (VAI) They are numerous. *(Plains). Alt.* **okistakeweyatowak** *(Northern).*

mihcetohkamâtowak (VAI) They are helping one another; numerous people are helping one another.

mihcetohkamwak (VAI) Numerous people are helping each other.

mihcetohkwâmiwak (VAI) Numerous people help each other.

mihcetokâtew *pl.* **mihcetokâtewak** (VAI) S/he or it has several legs.

mihcetomacwewes *pl.* **mihcetomacwewesa** (NI) A gun that shoots many shots, double barrelled.

mihcetominakâw *pl.* **mihcetominakâwa** (NI) A cluster of berries. *(Northern). Alt.* **mînisiskâw** *(Plains).*

mihcetomitanaw (IPC) Several hundred.

mihcetopikiskwew *pl.* **mihcetopikiskwewak** (VAI) S/he speaks many languages.

mihcetosew *pl.* **mihcetosewak** (VAI) S/he gave birth to a large family.

mihcetowin *pl.* **mihcetowina** (NI) Having an extensive family.

mihcetôskanawa (VII) There are many roads.

mihcetwâpitew *pl.* **mihcetwâpitewak** (VAI) S/he has several teeth.

mihcetwâw (IPC) Many times.

mihcetweyak (IPC) Many different directions or manners.

mihcetweyakan *pl.* **mihcetweyaskanwa** (VII) It is divided into numerous parts.

mihcetweyakihew (VAI) S/he divides them into numerous parts or classes.

　mihcetweyakitâw (VAI) S/he divides it in various ways.

　mihcetweyakihiwew (VTA) S/he divides people into various ways.

　mihcetweyakicikew (VTI) S/he divides things into numerous parts.

mihcetweyakisiwak (VAI) They are divided in numerous or many different ways.

mihcetweyihkâtew (VTA) S/he calls her/him by numerous or several names.

　mihcetweyihkâtam (VTI) S/he gives it numerous or several names.

　mihcetweyihkâsiwew (VTA) S/he gives people numerous or several names.

　mihcetweyihkâcikew (VTI) S/he gives things numerous or several names.

mihcikwan *pl.* **mihcikwana** (NI) A knee.

mihcitwâw (IPC) Oftentimes.

mihcowihkwew *pl.* **mihcowihkwewak** (VAI) S/he has a bloody face.

mihkawikiw *pl.* **mihkawikiwak** (VAI) S/he runs fast.

mihkihkwan *pl.* **mihkihkwana** (NI) A scraper that removes the flesh from a hide; a sharp bone or stone for fleshing hide.

mihkitew (VTA) S/he fleshes it with a bone, i.e.: a beaver hide.

　mihkitam (VTA) S/he fleshes the hide.

　mihkicikew (VTA) S/he fleshes something.

mihko sihkwâtam *pl.* **mihko sihkwâtamak** (VAI) S/he spits blood.

mihkocihcew *pl.* **mihkocihcewak** (VAI) S/he has a red hand.

mihkohew (VTA) S/he makes her/him red.

　mihkotâw (VTI) S/he makes it red.

　mihkohiwew (VTA) S/he makes someone red.

mihkohkwepayiw *pl.* **mihkohkwepayiwak** (VAI) S/he blushes; her/his face reddens.

mihkohkwew *pl.* **mihkohkwewak** (VAI) S/he has a red face.

mihkomin *pl.* **mihkomina** (NI) A red berry.

mihkonâkwan (VII) It is reddish in color, i.e.: maroon.

mihkopayiw *pl.* **mihkopayiwa** *or* **mihkopayiwak** (VII) *or* (VAI) It *or* s/he becomes red.

84

mihkosiw *pl.* **mihkosiwak** (VAI) S/he is red.

mihkosiwin *pl.* **mihkosiwina** (NI) Being red.

mihkoskahtak *pl.* **mihkoskahtakwak** (NA) A red Jack pine.

mihkostikwân *pl.* **mihkostikwânak** (NA) A red haired person, that is, a red head; a strawberry blonde person.

mihkostitew *pl.* **mihkostitewak** (VAI) S/he has red feet.

mihkowan *pl.* **mihkowana** (VII) There is blood on it.

mihkowatâmow *pl.* **mihkowatâmowak** (VAI) Her/his breath smells like blood.

mihkowâpoy *pl.* **mihkowâpoya** (NI) A blood soup or broth.

mihkowâspinew *pl.* **mihkowâspinewak** (VAI) She is menstruating; s/he has a blood discharge.

mihkowicihcew *pl.* **mihkowicihcewak** (VAI) S/he has bloody hands.

mihkowihew *pl.* **mihkowihewak** (VAI) S/he makes her/him bloody.

mihkowisitew *pl.* **mihkowisitewak** (VAI) S/he has bloody feet.

mihkowiw *pl.* **mihkowiwak** (VAI) S/he is bloody.

mihkoyapiy *pl.* **mihkoyapiya** (NI) A blood vessel, or a vein.

mihkwasew *pl.* **mihkwasewak** (VAI) S/he has red skin, i.e.: a sunburn; s/he has measles.

mihkwasewin *pl.* **mihkwasewina** (NI) Measles.

mihkwaskwan (VII) The sky is red.

mihkwatow *pl.* **mihkwatowak** (NA) A red fungus.

mihkwâhtik *pl.* **mihkwâhtikwak** (NA) A redwood.

mihkwâkamiw *pl.* **mihkwâkamiwa** (VII) It is red liquid.

mihkwâkamiwisipiy (NA) A red river.

mihkwâkan *pl.* **mihkwâkana** (NI) Countenance; visage; face.

mihkwâkanihkân *pl.* **mihkwâkanihkâna** (NI) An imitation face or mask.

mihkwânikwacâs *pl.* **mihkwânikwacâsak** (NA) A red squirrel.

mihkwâpemak *pl.* **mihkwâpemakwa** (NI) A red willow.

mihkwâpisimosos (NA) The Cree word for the settlement of Red Deer. *(Northern)*

mihkwâpoy *pl.* **mihkwâpoya** (NI) Red water.

mihkwâsiht *pl.* **mihkwâsihtak** (NA) A red cedar.

mihkwâstew *pl.* **mihkwâstewa** (VII) The light is red.

mihkwâw *pl.* **mihkwâwa** (VII) It is red.

mihkwekin *pl.* **mihkwekinwa** (NI) A red cloth, material.

mihpan *pl.* **mihpana** (NI) A lung.

mihtawakay *pl.* **mihtawakaya** (NI) An ear.

mihtawakayâspinewin *pl.* **mihtawakayâspinewina** (NI) Having an earache. *(Plains)*. *Alt.* **teyehtawakayewin** *(Northern)*.

mihtawew *pl.* **mihtawewak** (VAI) S/he pouts because s/he does not have enough.

mihtawewin *pl.* **mihtawewina** (NI) The act of pouting.

mihtaweyimew (VTA) S/he pouts at her/him.

mihtaweyitam (VTI) S/he pouts over it.

mihtaweyimiwew (VTA) S/he pouts over others.

mihtâcikewin *pl.* **mihtâcikewina** (NI) The act of grieving for someone or something; regrettable.

mihtâtamawew *pl.* **mihtâtamawewak** (VTA) S/he feels sorry for her/him or them for losing it.

mihtâtamowin *pl.* **mihtâtamowina** (NI) The act of repentance; penitence; repentance; rue; bemoan.

mihtâtew (VAI) S/he regrets losing her/him; s/he is sorry to lose her/him.

mihtâtam (VTI) S/he regrets losing it.

mihtâsiwew (VTA) S/he regrets losing someone; is regretful over losing someone.

mihtâcikew (VTI) S/he regrets losing things.

mihtih *pl.* **mihtiha** (NI) One piece of firewood.

mihtot *pl.* **mihtota** (NI) A flood raft.

mihyawimohtiw *pl.* **mihyawimohtiwak** (NA) A caterpillar. *(Northern)*. *Alt.* **mohtew** *(Plains)*.

mikisimow *pl.* **mikisimowak** (VAI) It barks.

mikisimowin *pl.* **mikisimowina** (NI) The act of barking.

mikosow *pl.* **mikosowak** (NA) A bald eagle.

mikisowipîsim (NI) February; the eagle moon or month; the bald eagle moon or month *(Plains)*.

mikitew (VAI) It barks at her/him.

mikitam (VTI) S/he barks at it.

mikisiwew (VTA) S/he barks at someone.

mikitik *pl.* **mikitikwak** (NA) A kneecap. *Var.* **okitik**.

mikohtaskway *pl.* **mikohtaskwaya** (NI) A person's windpipe, i.e.: trachea.

mikohtâkan *pl.* **mikohtâkana** (NI) A throat; a gullet.

mikosisimâw *pl.* **mikosisimâwak** (NA) Someone looked upon as a son.

mikoskâcihew (VTA) S/he annoys her/him or them.

mikoskâcitâw (VTI) S/he bothers it.

mikoskâcihiwew (VTA) S/he bothers others.

mikoskâcicikew (VTI) S/he bothers things.

mikoskâcihitowak (VTA) They annoy one another.

mikoskâcihiwewin *pl.* **mikoskâcihiwewina** (NI) The act of annoying someone; perturbation; pester; scathing.

mikoskâcimew (VTA) S/he annoys her/him with her/his speech.

mikoskâcitâw (VTI) S/he gives it a bad time.

mikoskâcimiwew (VTA) S/he gives someone a bad time with her/his talk.

mikoskâsihtâkosiw *pl.* **mikoskâsihtâkosiwak** (VAI) S/he makes an annoying or bothersome noise.

mikoskâsihtâkwan *pl.* **mikoskâsihtâkwana** (VII) It makes an annoying or bothersome noise.

mikoskâteyihtamihew (VTA) S/he causes her/him worries.

85

mikoskâteyihtamitâw (VAI) S/he causes worries.

mikoskâteyihtamihowew (VTA) S/he causes worries for others.

mikoskâteyihtamihiwew (VTA) S/he cause worries for everyone.

mikoskâteyimew (VTA) S/he finds her/him annoying.

mikoskâteyitam (VTI) S/he finds it annoying.

mikoskâteyimiwew (VTA) S/he finds others annoying.

mikoskâteyicikew (VTI) S/he finds everything annoying.

mikoskâtisiw *pl.* **mikoskâtisiwak** (VAI) S/he is annoying or a pest; s/he complains; s/he whines.

mikoskâtisiwin *pl.* **mikoskâtisiwina** (NI) The act of being annoying or a pest.

mikot *pl.* **mikota** (NI) A nose; a human nose. *(Plains). Alt.* **paswâkan** *(Northern).*

mikowin *pl.* **mikowina** (NI) The act of donating; donation. *(Northern). Alt.* **mekowin** *(Plains).*

mikwayaw *pl.* **mikwayawa** (NI) A neck.

mikwâskonew *pl.* **mikwâskonewa** (NI) A chin.

mimikonew (VTA) S/he rubs it during cleaning, i.e.: pants or a diaper.

mimikonam (VTI) S/he rubs it together to make it soft.

mimikoniwew (VTA) S/he rubs on someone.

mimikonikew (VTI) S/he rubs things together.

mimikopâtinew (VTI) S/he rinses it.

mimikopâtinam (VTI) S/he rinses something.

mimikopâtinowew (VTA) S/he rinses someone.

mimikopâtinikew (VTI) S/he rinses things.

mimikopitew (VTA) S/he shakes her/him or them briskly.

mimikopitam (VTI) S/he shakes it briskly.

mimikopisiwew (VTA) S/he shakes someone briskly.

mimikopicikew (VTI) S/he shakes things briskly.

mimikwapiw *pl.* **mimikwapiwak** (VTA) S/he rubs her/his own eyes.

mina (IPC) Again, also.

minahew (VTA) S/he gives her/him a drink.

minahiwew (VAI) S/he gives drinks.

minahikoskâw *pl.* **minahikoskâwa** (VII) There are numbers of spruce.

minahow *pl.* **minahowak** (VAI) S/he kills wild game.

minahowin *pl.* **minahowina** (NI) The act of killing wild game.

minihkwâcikan *pl.* **minihkwâcikana** (NI) A mug.

minihkwâcikanis *pl.* **minihkwâcikanisa** (NI) A cup. *(Northern). Alt.* **minihkwewîyâkanis** *(Plains).*

minihkwâtew (VTI) S/he sells it to buy drinks.

minihkwâtam (VTI) S/he sells things for drinks.

minihkwâsiwew (VTA) S/he sells people for drinks.

minihkwâcikew (VTI) S/he sells everything for drinks.

minihkwew *pl.* **minihkwewak** (VAI) S/he drinks.

minihkwewikamik *pl.* **minihkwewikamikwa** (NI) A bar; a tavern.

minihkwewin *pl.* **minihkwewina** (NI) The act of drinking.

minihkwewîyâkanis *pl.* **minihkwewîyâkanisa** (NI) A cup. *(Plains). Alt.* **minihkwâcikanis** *(Northern).*

minikwahastimwew *pl.* **minikwahastimwewak** (VTA) S/he waters the horses.

minikwahew *pl.* **minikwahewak** (VTA) S/he makes her/him drink.

minikwewâspinewin *pl.* **minikwewâspinewina** (NI) The act of being addicted to alcohol; alcoholism.

miniscikos *pl.* **miniscikosa** (NI) An isle; an islet or small island.

minisiwan *pl.* **minisiwanwa** (VII) It bears fruit.

minisiwiw *pl.* **minisiwiwa** *or* **minisiwiwak** (VII) *or* (VAI) It bears fruit, i.e.: a fruit tree.

ministik *pl.* **ministikwa** (NI) An island.

ministikosihtiskâw *pl.* **ministikosihtiskâwa** (NI) A clump of spruce trees; an island covered by spruce trees. *Var.* **ministikominâhikoskâw.**

ministikowiw *pl.* **ministikowiwa** (VII) There is an island.

ministikwâpiskâw *pl.* **ministikwâpiskâwa** (NI) It is a rocky island.

ministikwâskweyâw *pl.* **ministikwâskweyâwa** (VII) There is a clump of bushes; there is a wooded island.

miniwatimiwiw *pl.* **miniwatimiwiwa** (VII) There is a point or a cape. *(Northern). Alt.* **neyâw** *(Plains).*

minôs *pl.* **minôsak** (NA) A cat.

minôsis *pl.* **minôsisak** (NA) A kitten.

mipwâm *pl.* **mipwâmwak** (NA) A thigh or hind quarter.

mipwâmikan *pl.* **mipwâmikanwa** (NI) A thigh bone.

misakamehwew (VTA) S/he goes right through them all; s/he goes all the way from one side to the other, i.e.: through the waves.

misakameham (VTI) S/he goes right through to the end of it.

misakamehikew (VTI) S/he goes right through things.

misakamepayiw *pl.* **misakamepayiwa** *or* **misakamepayiwak** (VII) *or* (VAI) It or s/he goes all the way to the end of the road.

misakâme (IPC) Goes all the way.

misakâmepitam *pl.* **misakâmepitamwak** (VAI) S/he pulls it all the way.

misakâmeskawew *pl.* **misakâmeskawewak** (VTA) S/he bypasses them.

misakâw *pl.* **misakâwak** (VAI) S/he arrives by boat or canoe. *(Northern). Alt.* **kapâw** *(Plains).*

misamew *pl.* **misamewak** (VAI) S/he labors.

misamewin *pl.* **misamewina** (NI) The act of laboring.

misamihew *pl.* **misamihewak** (VTA) S/he makes it or her/him labor.

misaskenam *pl.* **misaskenamwak** (VAI) S/he touches the ground or bottom in the water with her/his feet.

misaskwatwâhtik *pl.* **misaskwatwâhtikwa** (NI) The wood of a saskatoon shrub; saskatoon berry *(Northern).* *Alt.* **misâskwatominaht** *(Plains).*

misawâc (IPC) Despite, in spite of.

misawewin *pl.* **misawewina** (NI) The act of having been disappointed; the act of having learned a lesson.

misawihew *pl.* **misawihewak** (VTA) S/he disappoints her/him by her/his actions.

misawihiwewin *pl.* **misawihiwewina** (NI) The act of disappointing someone.

misawiw *pl.* **misawiwak** (VAI) S/he has been disappointed; s/he learned her/his lesson.

misayekitonewin *pl.* **misayekitonewina** (NI) The act of blabbering; a blabber-mouth.

misâskwat *pl.* **misâskwatwa** (NI) A saskatoon shrub or bush.

misâskwatominaht *pl.* **misâskwatominahtwak** (NA) The wood of a saskatoon shrub. *(Plains).* *Alt.* **misaskwatwâhtik** *(Northern).*

misâskwatômin *pl.* **misâskwatômina** (NI) A saskatoon berry.

misâw *pl.* **misâwa** (VII) It is big or large.

miscacâkanis *pl.* **miscacâkanisak** (NA) A little coyote. *(Northern).* *Alt.* **mescacâkanis** *(Plains).*

miscacimosis *pl.* **miscacimosisak** (NA) A colt.

miscanaskos *pl.* **miscanaskosak** (NA) A marmot.

miscihtâpiskâkan *pl.* **miscihtâpiskâkana** (NI) A bandana or bandanna.

miscikokamikos *pl.* **miscikokamikosa** (NI) A shack.

misicihcân *pl.* **misicihcâna** (NI) The thumb.

misihew (VTA) S/he gets her/him into trouble.

  misimew (VTA) S/he tells on her/him.

misihkemow *pl.* **misihkemowak** (VTA) S/he reports others, accuses others, i.e.: a stool pigeon.

misihkemowin *pl.* **misihkemowina** (NI) The act of informing against someone.

misihkwaniyâpiy *pl.* **misihkwaniyâpiya** (NI) The jugular vein. *(Northern).* *Alt.* **misihkwân** *(Plains).*

misihkwân *pl.* **misihkwânya** (NI) The jugular vein. *(Plains).* *Alt.* **misihkwaniyâpiy** *(Northern).*

misihtakâw *pl.* **misihtakâwa** (NI) A large room; or a large piece of wood; log.

misikamâw *pl.* **misikamâwa** (VII) The lake is large.

misikeskipocikan *pl.* **misikeskipocikana** (NI) A large saw.

misikihew *pl.* **misikihewak** (NA) A large eagle.

misikitiw *pl.* **misikitiwak** (VAI) S/he is corpulant.

misikitiwin *pl.* **misikitiwina** (NI) Being a large size; bulky.

misikwâhkotew *pl.* **misikwâhkotewa** (NI) A raging fire; a huge flame.

misimacîtôtamowin *pl.* **misimacîtôtamowina** (NI) The act of doing a drastic action; atrocity; terrorist activity.

misimew *pl.* **misimewak** (NA) S/he chews it.

misiminôs *pl.* **misiminôsak** (NA) A cougar; lynx. *(Plains).* *Alt.* **misipisiw** *(Northern),* **pakwaciminôs** *(Plains).*

misimisihew *pl.* **misimisihewak** (NA) A chicken.

misimiskowew *pl.* **misimiskowewak** (VAI) S/he chews gum.

misimisowin *pl.* **misimisowina** (NI) The act of admitting or confessing.

misinâpeminôs *pl.* **misinâpeminôsak** (NA) A large male cat.

misinocihew *pl.* **misinocihewak** (VTA) S/he defeats her/him decisively; s/he trounces her/him.

misipahkahahkwân *pl.* **misipahkahahkwânak** (NA) A large chicken. *(Northern).* *Alt.* **misipahpahahkwân** *(Plains).*

misipahpahahkwân *pl.* **misipahpahahkwânak** (NA) A large chicken. *(Plains).* *Alt.* **misipahkahahkwân** *(Northern).*

misipahpahscîs *pl.* **misipahpahscîsak** (NA) A large woodpecker. *(Northern).* *Alt.* **opâhpâhkwecakahikesîs** *(Plains).*

misipisiw *pl.* **misipisiwak** (NA) A cougar; lynx. *(Northern).* *Alt.* **pakwaciminôs**, **misiminôs** *(Plains).*

misipocikan *pl.* **misipocikana** (NI) A rubbing tool used to soften a hide. *(Plains).* *Alt.* **sinikopocikan** *(Northern).*

misipohew (VAI) S/he uses a rubbing tool to soften a hide, i.e.: a beaver skin. *(Plains).* *Alt.* **sinikopohew** *(Northern).*

  misipohtâw (VTI) S/he uses a rubbing tool to soften a moose hide.

  misipohcikew (VTI) S/he uses a rubbing tool to soften a hide.

misisâhk *pl.* **misisâhkwak** (NA) A horsefly.

misisâhkoskâw (NI) A place with abundant horseflies or bullflies.

misisâkahikan *pl.* **misisâkahikana** (NI) A large lake.

misisitân *pl.* **misisitâna** (NI) A big toe.

misit *pl.* **misita** (NI) A foot.

misitaksiyapiy *pl.* **misitaksiyapiya** (NI) The large intestine, i.e.: colon.

misitawâw *pl.* **misitawâwa** (NI) A big space; a spacious area.

misiw *pl.* **misiwak** (VAI) S/he defecates; s/he has a bowel movement.

87

misiwanâcihcikew *pl.* **misiwanâcihcikewak** (VAI) S/he spoils things.

misiwanâcihcikewin *pl.* **misiwanâcihcikewina** (NI) The act of spoiling things; contamination; debauch.

misiwanâcihew (VTA) S/he spoils it or her/him; s/he damages it or her/him.

misiwanâcitâw (VTI) S/he spoils it.

misiwanâcihiwew (VTA) S/he spoils someone.

misiwanâcicikew (VTI) S/he spoils things.

misiwanâcihikewin *pl.* **misiwanâcihikewina** (NI) The act of being destructive; destructible; vandalism.

misiwanâcimew (VTA) S/he speaks to ruin her/his reputation.

misiwanâcihtâw (VTI) S/he spoils something.

misiwanâcimiwew (VTA) S/he speaks badly about people.

misiwanâcipayowin *pl.* **misiwanâcipayowina** (NI) The act of devastation.

misiwanâtan *pl.* **misiwanâtanwa** (VII) It is spoiled; it is rotten.

misiwanâtisiw *pl.* **misiwanâtisiwak** (VAI) S/he is spoiled; s/he is rotten.

misiwanâtisiwin *pl.* **misiwanâtisiwina** (NI) Spoilage; waste; deterioration.

misiwâpamek *pl.* **misiwâpamekwak** (NA) A whale. *(Plains). Alt.* **mistamek** *(Northern).*

misiwâpos *pl.* **misiwâposwak** (NA) A hare.

misiwâti *pl.* **misiwâta** (NI) A chasm.

misiwepaskwaskaw *pl.* **misiwepaskwaskawa** (NI) A whole area of grassland. *(Northern). Alt.* **misiwepaskwâw** *(Plains).*

misiwepaskwâw *pl.* **misiwepaskwâwa** (NI) A whole area of grassland. *(Plains). Alt.* **misiwepaskwaskaw** *(Northern).*

misiwepayihcikan *pl.* **misiwepayihcikana** (NI) A pill.

misiwepayihew (VTA) S/he swallows it in one gulp.

misiwepayitâw (VTI) S/he swallows something in one gulp.

misiwepayicikew (VTI) S/he swallows everything in one gulp.

misiwepayiw *pl.* **misiwepayiwa** (VII) It congeals or coagulates.

misiwesiw *pl.* **misiwesiwak** (VAI) S/he is completely whole; s/he is all in one piece.

misiwesiwin *pl.* **misiwesiwina** (NI) Being whole or in one piece.

misiweskamik (IPC) All over the world.

misiwetâpânâsk *pl.* **misiwetâpânâskwak** (NA) A van.

misiwetehiskamik (IPC) In the whole universe.

misiweyâhtik *pl.* **misiweyâhtikwa** (NI) A whole piece of wood, i.e.: a plank or log.

misiweyâw *pl.* **misiweyâwa** (VII) It is whole; it is all in one piece.

misiweyispayiw *pl.* **misiweyispayiwak** *or* **misiweyispayiwa** (VAI) *or* (VII) It goes everywhere.

misiweyita (IPC) Everywhere.

misiwiyâpiy *pl.* **misiwiyâpiya** (NI) A piece of bowel.

misiyâpiskâw *pl.* **misiyâpiskâwa** (VII) It is rusty.

miskahtik *pl.* **miskahtikwa** (NI) A brow; a forehead.

miskam *pl.* **miskamwa** (VTI) S/he found it; s/he discovered it.

miskaminatik *pl.* **miskaminatikwak** (NA) A rasberry bush. *(Plains). Alt.* **ayoskanahtik** *(Northern).*

miskamowin *pl.* **miskamowina** (NI) The act of discovering; discovery.

miskawâsihiwewin *pl.* **miskawâsihiwewina** (NI) The act of inciting; incitement.

miskawastimwew *pl.* **miskawastimwewak** (VTA) S/he finds a horse.

miskawâhew (VTA) S/he initiates her/him into something.

miskawâhtâw (VTA) S/he initiates herself/himself into something.

miskawâhiwew (VTA) S/he initiates someone into something.

miskawâhtâwin *pl.* **miskawâhtâwina** (NI) The act of detecting; detectable.

miskawâwew *pl.* **miskawâwewak** (VAI) S/he finds an egg.

miskawew (VTA) S/he finds her/him or them or it.

miskam (VTI) S/he finds something.

miskâkew (VTA) S/he finds someone.

miskâcikewin *pl.* **miskâcikewina** (NI) The act of locating. *(Northern). Alt.* **miskâkewin** *(Plains).*

miskâkewin *pl.* **miskâkewina** (NI) The act of locating. *(Plains). Alt.* **miskâcikewin** *(Northern).*

miskât *pl.* **miskâta** (NI) A leg.

miskihtekom *pl.* **miskihtekomak** (NA) Earwax.

miskinâhk *pl.* **miskinâhkwak** (NA) A tortoise; a turtle.

miskîsik *pl.* **miskîsikwa** (NI) An eye.

miskîsikomin *pl.* **miskîsikomina** (NI) A red current berry.

miskonew (VTA) S/he feels for her/him with her/his hands.

miskonam (VTI) S/he feels for it with her/his hands.

miskoniwew (VTA) S/he feels people with her/his hand.

miskonikew (VTI) S/he feels for things.

miskosihcikew *pl.* **miskosihcikewak** (VAI) S/he finds ways to do something.

miskotâkay *pl.* **miskotâkaya** (NI) A dress; a jacket; a coat.

miskotâkekin *pl.* **miskotâkekinwa** (NI) A piece of gingham material.

88

miskowan *pl.* **miskowana** (NI) An animal nose.

miskwamew manahikan (NI) Ice cream. *Var.* **cahkâs** (slang).

miskwamiy *pl.* **miskwamiyak** (NA) Ice; a huge hail stone.

miskwamiy pahkisin *pl.* **miskwamiyak pahkisinak** (VAI) It is hailing. *(Plains). Alt.* **sîsîkanihtaw** *(Northern).*

miskwamîs (NA) A small hail stone.

miskwan *pl.* **miskwana** (NI) A liver.

miskweyimew (VTA) S/he finds a way to deal with her/him; s/he figures her/him out.

miskweyitam (VTI) S/he finds a way to deal with it.

miskweyimiwew (VTA) S/he finds a way to deal with people.

miskweyihcikew (VTI) S/he finds a way to deal with things.

misôkan *pl.* **misôkana** (NI) The backside of the body; the rear.

mispayaw *pl.* **mispayawa** (NI) A woman's womb.

mispikekan *pl.* **mispikekana** (NI) A rib bone.

mispiskwan *pl.* **mispiskwana** (NI) A back.

mispiton *pl.* **mispitona** (NI) An arm.

mispon (VII) It snows; or it is snowing.

misponihtâw *pl.* **misponihtâwak** (VAI) S/he makes it snow.

misponipayiw (VII) There is a snow flurry.

mistahaya *pl.* **mistahayak** (NA) A grizzly bear. *Var.* **okistatowân.**

mistahi (IPC) Much; lots of it.

mistahisôminis *pl.* **mistahisôminisak** (NA) A grape. *Var.* **minisihkân.**

mistahiyinimin *pl.* **mistahiyinimina** (NI) A huckleberry.

mistahkesiw *pl.* **mistahkesiwak** (NA) A lion; a mountain lion.

mistahôsih *pl.* **mistahôsiha** (NI) A big canoe.

mistakeyimisowin *pl.* **mistakeyimisowina** (NI) Being audacious; conceited.

mistakihtew (VTI) It is costly.

mistakwanakotew *pl.* **mistakwanakotewak** (NA) A six-year-old and older bull moose.

mistamek *pl.* **mistamekwak** (NA) A big fish; a salmon; a whale. *(Northern). Alt.* **misiwâpamek** *(Plains).*

mistanask *pl.* **mistanaskwak** (NA) A badger.

mistasiniy *pl.* **mistasiniyak** (NA) A boulder.

mistaskihk *pl.* **mistaskihkwa** (NI) A large pail or a caldron.

mistatayepinew *pl.* **mistatayepinewak** (VTA) S/he has an enlarged stomach from a disease.

mistatayepinewin *pl.* **mistatayepinewina** (NI) Enlarged stomach disease.

mistatayew *pl.* **mistatayewak** (VAI) S/he has a large stomach, i.e.: a potbelly.

mistatayewin *pl.* **mistatayewina** (NI) Having a large stomach, i.e.: potbelly.

mistatim *pl.* **mistatimwak** (NA) An aged horse; an old nag.

mistatimokamik *pl.* **mistatimokamikwa** (NI) A big dog house.

mistatimowiyâs (NI) Horseflesh.

mistatimwâyo *pl.* **mistatimwâyowa** (NI) A horsetail.

mistayek *pl.* **mistayekwak** (NA) A large frog.

mistâpakosîs *pl.* **mistâpakosîsak** (NA) A door mouse.

mistâpew *pl.* **mistâpewak** (NA) A large man or a giant.

mistâpewiwin *pl.* **mistâpewiwina** (NI) Being a husky man.

mistâpiskihkomân *pl.* **mistâpiskihkomâna** (NI) A machete or a large bladed knife.

mistâpos *pl.* **mistâposwak** (NA) A jack rabbit.

misteyihcikewin *pl.* **misteyihcikewina** (NI) The act of exultation; exult.

misteyimisowin *pl.* **misteyimisowina** (NI) Being haughty about oneself.

mistihkomân *pl.* **mistihkomâna** (NI) A large knife.

mistik *pl.* **mistikwa** (NI) A stick; a club.

mistikokamik *pl.* **mistikokamikwa** (NI) A wooden cabin or log house.

mistikomahkahkos *pl.* **mistikomahkahkosa** (NI) A wooden barrel; a stave.

mistikominâhtik *pl.* **mistikominâhtikwak** (NA) Oak tree. *Var.* **maskawahtik, wemistikosiwâhtik.**

mistikonâpew *pl.* **mistikonâpewak** (NA) A carpenter; one who builds houses. *Var.* **owâskahikanihkew.**

mistikonâpewiwin *pl.* **mistikonâpewiwina** (NI) The act of being a carpenter; carpentry.

mistikopakân *pl.* **mistikopakânak** (NA) An acorn.

mistikowan *pl.* **mistikowanwa** (VII) It is wooden.

mistikowanehikan *pl.* **mistikowanehikana** (NI) A wooden trap.

mistikowat *pl.* **mistikowata** (NI) A wooden box.

mistikowatihkawew (VTA) S/he makes her/him a wooden box.

mistikowatihkâkew (VTI) S/he makes a wooden box with it.

mistikowatihkân *pl.* **mistikowatihkâna** (NI) A wooden box, i.e.: a crate.

mistikowatihkew *pl.* **mistikowatihkewak** (VAI) S/he makes a wooden box.

mistikowemihkwân *pl.* **mistikowemihkwânak** (NA) A wooden spoon.

mistikowiw *pl.* **mistikowiwak** (VAI) It is wooden.

mistikôsih *pl.* **mistikôsiha** (NI) A wooden boat.

mistikwaskihk *pl.* **mistikwaskihkwak** (NA) A drum; a tom-tom.

mistikwaskisin *pl.* **mistikwaskisina** (NI) A shoe or boot; a wooden shoe.

89

mistikwân *pl.* **mistikwâna** (NI) A head.

mistikwânikan *pl.* **mistikwânikana** (NI) A skull bone.

mistiyâpew *pl.* **mistiyâpewak** (NA) A big bull moose.

miswakaniwiw *pl.* **miswakaniwiwak** (VAI) S/he is wounded; s/he is injured.

miswâkan *pl.* **miswâkanak** (NA) A wounded animal or person.

mitahtahkwan *pl.* **mitahtahkwana** (NI) A wing.

mitakisiy *pl.* **mitakisiya** (NI) A penis.
> *Alt.* **nâpewsikewakan** *(Northern)*; **nâpewâpacihcikan** *(Plains)*.

mitakisiyâpiy *pl.* **mitakisiyâpiya** (NI) An intestine or entrail.

mitakom (NI) Mucus. *(Northern).* *Alt.* **akik** *(Plains)*.

mitânisimâw *pl.* **mitânisimâwak** (NA) Someone looked upon as a daughter.

mitâpiskan *pl.* **mitâspiskana** (NI) A jaw.

mitâs *pl.* **mitâsak** (NA) A pair of pants or breeches; trousers. *Var.* **wihkwepân** *(Archaic Cree)*.

mitâsihkawew (VTA) S/he makes her/him a pair of pants.
> **mitâsihkâkew** (VTI) S/he makes a pair of pants with it.
> **mitâsihkâcikew** (VTI) S/he makes pairs of pants with it for people.

mitâsihkew *pl.* **mitâsihkewak** (VAI) S/he makes a pair of pants.

mitâtaht (IPC) Ten.

mitâtahtomitanaw (IPC) One hundred.

mitâtahtomitanawâw (IPC) A hundred times, hundredth time.

mitâtahtomitanawâw kihci mitâtahtomitanaw (IPC) One-hundred thousand.

mitâtahtomitanawiw (VII) It is one hundredth.

mitâtahtowan *pl.* **mitâtahtowana** (VII) There is ten of it; it is tenth place.

mitâtahtowiw *pl.* **mitâtahtowiwak** (VAI) S/he is the tenth.

mitâtahtwâw (NI) Ten times; tenth time.

mitâtahtwâw kihci mitâtahtomitanaw (IPC) Ten thousand.

miteh *pl.* **miteha** (NI) A heart.

miteskan *pl.* **miteskanak** (NA) Antler; a sharp horn, i.e.: a prong. *(Plains).* *Alt.* **oteskan** *(Northern)*.

miteyaniy *pl.* **miteyaniya** (NI) A tongue.

miteyikom *pl.* **miteyikomak** (NA) A nostril.

mitihkôkan *pl.* **mitihkôkana** (NI) An armpit.

mitihtikosiw *pl.* **mitihtikosiwak** (NA) A kidney.

mitihkôkanihk (LN) Under the arm.

mitihtew (VTA) S/he follows her/his tracks or trail.
> **mitihtam** (VTI) S/he follows its tracks.
> **mitihcikew** (VTI) S/he follows tracks.

mitihtiman *pl.* **mitihtimana** (NI) A shoulder.

mitimew *pl.* **mitimewak** (VAI) S/he follows the road or path.

mitisiy *pl.* **mitisiya** (NI) A belly button; navel; umbilicus; a gizzard.

mitohtôsim *pl.* **mitohtôsimak** (NA) A breast; a teat; an udder.

mitokan *pl.* **mitokana** (NI) A pelvis.

mitokanikan *pl.* **mitokanikana** (NI) A hipbone.

mitoni (IPC) Very; fully.

mitonikeswân (VII) It is timely.

mitôn *pl.* **mitôna** (NI) A mouth.

mitôsimiskwemimâw *pl.* **mitôsimiskwemimâwak** (NA) A step daughter. (generic term)

mitôskwan *pl.* **mitôskwana** (NI) An elbow.

mitsoway *pl.* **mitsowayak** (NA) A scrotum.

miwasin *pl.* **miwasinwa** (VII) It is attractive; it looks very fine. *(Northern).* *Alt.* **mîywâsin** *(Plains)*.

miweyihcikewin *pl.* **miweyihcikewina** (NI) Something pleasing.

miweyihtamohiwewin *pl.* **miweyihtamohiwewina** (NI) Being charming towards someone.

miweyihtamowin *pl.* **miweyihtamowina** (NI) The act of contentment; contented.

miweyihtâkosiwin *pl.* **miweyihtâkosiwina** (NI) Being charming.

miweyimew (VTA) S/he likes her/him or them.
> **miweyitam** (VTI) S/he likes it or s/he is glad.
> **miweyimiwew** (VTA) S/he likes others.
> **miweyicikew** (VTI) S/he likes things.

miyacowân *pl.* **miyacowâna** (NI) Pubic hair. *(Plains).* *Alt.* **opîwâwin** *(Northern)*.

miyakan *pl.* **miyakanwa** (VII) It smells like excrement. *(Northern).* *Alt.* **meyakan** *(Plains)*.

miyakisiw *pl.* **miyakisiwak** (VAI) S/he smells like excrement. *(Northern).* *Alt.* **meyakisiw** *(Plains)*.

miyamawâw *pl.* **miyamawâwa** (VII) It is damp, humid. *(Northern).* *Alt.* **miyimawâw** *(Plains)*.

miyamawinew (VTA) S/he dampens it (animate). *(Northern).* *Var.* **miyamapawataw**. *Alt.* **miyimawinew** *(Plains)*.
> **miyamawinam** (VTI) S/he dampens it.
> **miyamawiniwew** (VTA) S/he dampens someone.
> **miyamawinikew** (VTI) S/he dampens something.

miyamawisiw *pl.* **miyamawisiwak** (VAI) S/he or it is damp; s/he or it is moist. *(Northern).* *Alt.* **miyimawisiw** *(Plains)*.

miyamawisowin *pl.* **miyamawisowina** (NI) Dampness; being moist. *(Northern).* *Alt.* **miyimawisiwin** *(Plains)*.

miyamâpawew *pl.* **miyamâpawewa** (VII) It is dampened by water.

miyaskawew (VTA) S/he passes her/him on the road, path or trail.

miyaskam (VTI) S/he passes it.

miyaskâkew (VTA) S/he passes everyone.

miyastowân *pl.* **miyastowâna** (NI) A beard.

miyastowew *pl.* **miyastowewak** (VAI) He has a beard; he is bearded.

miyaw *pl.* **miyawa** (NI) A body.

miyawatam *pl.* **miyawatamwak** (VAI) S/he is joyous.

miyawâtamowin *pl.* **miyawâtamowina** (NI) Having pleasure; pleasurable; the act of celebrating joyfully.

miyawâtew (VTA) S/he is delighted with her/him.

miyawâtam (VTI) S/he is delighted by it.

miyawâtikosiw *pl.* **miyawâtikosiwak** (VAI) S/he is joyful.

miyawâtikosiwin *pl.* **miyawâtikosiwina** (NI) The act of being joyful.

miyawâtikwan *pl.* **miyawâtikwana** (VII) It is pleasant.

miyâmew (VTA) S/he smells her/him or them.

miyâtam (VTI) S/he smells it.

miyâmiwew (VTA) S/he smells others.

miyâcikew (VTI) S/he smells things.

miyânikwan *pl.* **miyânikwanwa** (VII) It is a fresh trail, track.

miyâskatew (VTA) S/he passes her/him over the top. *(Plains). Alt.* **pâstinew** *(Northern).*

miyâskanam (VTI) S/he passes it over the top.

miyâskaniwew (VTA) S/he passes someone over the top.

miyâskanikew (VTI) S/he passes things over the top.

miyâw *pl.* **miyâwa** (NI) Something given.

miyew *pl.* **miyewak** (VTA) S/he gives it to her/him.

miyi *pl.* **miya** (NI) An abcess or a collection of pus.

miyicimin *pl.* **miyiciminak** (NA) A bean.

miyimawâw *pl.* **miyimawâwa** (VII) It is damp, humid. *(Plains). Alt.* **miyamawâw** *(Northern).*

miyimawinew (VTA) S/he dampens it (animate). *(Plains). Alt.* **miyamawinew** *(Northern).*

miyimawinam (VTI) S/he dampens it.

miyimawiniwew (VTA) S/he dampens someone.

miyimawinikew (VTI) S/he dampens something.

miyimawisiw *pl.* **miyimawisiwak** (VAI) S/he or it is damp, o/he or it is moist. *(Plains). Alt.* **miyamawisiw** *(Northern).*

miyimawisiwin *pl.* **miyimawisiwina** (NI) Dampness; being moist. *(Plains). Alt.* **miyamawisowin** *(Northern).*

miyiwin *pl.* **miyiwina** (NI) Being abscessed.

miyiwiw *pl.* **miyiwiwak** (VAI) S/he has an abcess.

miyîciminahtik *pl.* **miyîciminahtikwak** (NA) A bean stalk.

miyîcîmin *pl.* **miyîcîminak** (NA) A bean. *(Plains). Alt.* **peswîmin** *(Northern).*

miyîkwak *pl.* **miyîkwakwa** (NI) A gland. *(Plains). Alt.* **oyihk** *(Northern).*

miyohkwâmiwin *pl.* **miyohkwâmiwina** (NI) A good sleep.

miyohkwenâkosiw *pl.* **miyohkwenâkosiwak** (VAI) S/he has a pleasant face.

miyohkwew *pl.* **miyohkwewak** (VAI) Her/his face reflects a moral purity.

miyohtâkosiw *pl.* **miyohtâkosiwak** (VAI) S/he has an attractive voice.

miyohtâkosiwin *pl.* **miyohtâkosiwina** (NI) The act of singing with an inspiring voice.

miyohtwâw *pl.* **miyohtwâwak** (VAI) S/he is morally upright; s/he is kind.

miyohtwâwin *pl.* **miyohtwâwina** (NI) Being a soft-hearted person; being amicable; being good natured; being morally upright; being kind. *(Plains). Alt.* **yoskâtisiwin** *(Northern).*

miyohtwâwisâyâwin *pl.* **miyohtwâwisâyâwina** (NI) The act of being gentle in manner; blandish.

miyokanawâpamew (VTA) S/he looks at her/him with benevolence.

miyokanawâpatam (VTI) S/he looks at it with benevolence.

miyokanawâpacikew (VTI) S/he looks at things with benevolence.

miyokaskihcikewin *pl.* **miyokaskihcikewina** (NI) The act of being able to attain an end; a goal; attainability.

miyokihcikewin *pl.* **miyokihcikewina** (NI) Being fertile or plentiful; fertility.

miyokiskinwahikewin *pl.* **miyokiskinwahikewina** (NI) The act of attribution; attributable.

miyokîsikâw *pl.* **miyokîsikâwa** (VII) It is a nice day, i.e.: good weather.

miyomahcihow *pl.* **miyomahcihowak** (VAI) S/he feels well.

miyomahcihowewin *pl.* **miyomahcihowewina** (NI) The act of feeling stimulated; stimulation.

miyomahcihowin *pl.* **miyomahcihowina** (NI) The act of feeling euphoria; luxuriate.

miyomâkosiw *pl.* **miyomâkosiwak** (VAI) S/he smells pleasant.

miyomâkosiwin *pl.* **miyomâkosiwina** (NI) The act of smelling pleasant.

miyomâkwan *pl.* **miyomâkwanwa** (VII) It has a pleasant scent.

miyometawestamâkewin *pl.* **miyometawestamâkewina** (NI) The act of making music for someone; entertaining.

miyomohew (VTI) S/he adjusts it perfectly. *(Northern). Alt.* **miywamohew** *(Plains).*

miyomotâw (VTI) S/he adjusts it perfectly.

91

miyomocikew (VTI) S/he adjusts things perfectly.

miyonawew (VTA) S/he finds her/him attractive, i.e.: beautiful or handsome.

miyonam (VTI) S/he finds it pretty.

miyonâkew (VTA) S/he finds others beautiful.

miyonâkohew (VTA) S/he beautifies her/him.

miyonâkotâw (VTI) S/he makes it look attractive.

miyonâkocikew (VTI) S/he makes things look beautiful.

miyonâkosiwin *pl.* **miyonâkosiwina** (NI) Being glamorous; loveliness; sumptuous.

miyonâkwan *pl.* **miyonâkwanwa** (VII) It looks dandy; good, nice.

miyonew (VTA) S/he has total control over her/him or them.

miyonam (VTI) S/he has total control over it.

miyoniwew (VTA) S/he has total control over people.

miyonikew (VTI) S/he has total control over things.

miyopayihcikewin *pl.* **miyopayihcikewina** (NI) The act of causing a good occurrence; efficiency; manipulation; resolved.

miyopayihew (VTA) S/he makes a great start for her/him. *(Plains). Alt.* **kihcipayihew** *(Northern).*

miyopayitâw (VTA) Somebody starts well.

miyopayihiwew (VTA) S/he makes a great start for somebody.

miyopayihcikew (VTI) S/he makes a great start for things.

miyopayiw *pl.* **miyopayiwak** (VAI) S/he is fortunate or lucky; it runs well, i.e.: a motor.

miyopayowin *pl.* **miyopayowina** (NI) Being prosperous; prosperity.

miyopayowinihk (LN) In a lucky place; luckily. (not commonly used)

miyopimatisiwin *pl.* **miyopimatisiwina** (NI) The act of leading an exemplary life.

miyopimâtisiw *pl.* **miyopimâtisiwak** (VAI) S/he leads an exemplary life; a good life.

miyopîkiskwâtew (VTA) S/he speaks kindly to her/him.

miyopîkiskwâtam (VTI) S/he speaks kindly about it.

miyopîkiskwâsiwew (VTA) S/he speaks kindly to people.

miyopîkiskwâcikew (VTI) S/he speaks kindly about things.

miyosihow *pl.* **miyosihowak** (VAI) S/he is well groomed; s/he is well dressed.

miyosihowin *pl.* **miyosihowina** (NI) The act of being well groomed or well dressed; the act of dressing in finery.

miyosiwin *pl.* **miyosiwina** (NI) Being beautiful; beauty; refinement.

miyoskamikâw *pl.* **miyoskamikâwa** (VII) A good piece of land; better ground.

miyoskamiki (VII) When spring comes or when it is spring.

miyoskamin (NI) It is springtime; it is spring, the season. *(Plains). Alt.* **sekwan** *(Northern).*

miyoskamiw (VII) It is spring. *Var.* **sekwan**.

miyoskamîhk (NI) Last spring.

miyoskâkowin *pl.* **miyoskâkowina** (NI) The act of taking medicine that is conducive to health.

miyoskwewiw *pl.* **miyoskwewiwak** (VAI) She has a beautiful personality.

miyotawâw (IPC) An expression meaning "all clear".

miyotehew *pl.* **miyotehewak** (VAI) S/he has a kind, good heart.

miyotehewin *pl.* **miyotehewina** (NI) Kind heartedness; good heartedness; benignity; heartiness.

miyotinikewin *pl.* **miyotinikewina** (NI) The act of taking something in good faith; approval; acceptance.

miyotipiskâw *pl.* **miyotipiskâwa** (VII) It is a pleasant night.

miyotôtamowin *pl.* **miyotôtamowina** (NI) A benevolent action.

miyotôtawew (VTA) S/he treats her/him kindly; s/he does her/him a good turn.

miyotôtam (VTI) S/he does kind deeds.

miyotôtâkew (VTA) S/he does kind deeds for someone.

miyotôtâkewin *pl.* **miyotôtâkewina** (NI) The act of paying tribute to someone by performing an act of kindness; a tribute.

miyow *pl.* **miyowak** (VAI) S/he performs perfectly.

miyow isâyâwin *pl.* **miyow isâyâwina** (NI) Being in good health.

miyowakamiw *pl.* **miyowakamiwa** (NI) A pure or good liquid.

miyowâcimow *pl.* **miyowâcimowak** (VAI) S/he tells a good story; s/he brings good news.

miyowâcimowin *pl.* **miyowâcimowina** (NI) A good story, or good news. *(Northern). Alt.* **miywâcimowin** *(Plains).*

miyowâhtik *pl.* **miyowâhtikwak** (NA) A good tree.

miyowâpewiw *pl.* **miyowâpewiwak** (VAI) He is a handsome man.

miyowâpiskâw *pl.* **miyowâpiskâwa** (NI) A smooth metal.

miyowâpiskis *pl.* **miyowâpiskisak** (NA) A piece of fine metal with a smooth surface, i.e.: a clothes iron.

miyowâskosiw *pl.* **miyowâskosiwak** (VAI) The tree is a fine one.

miyowâskwan *pl.* **miyowâskwanwa** (VII) It is a good pole. *(Northern). Alt.* **miywâskwan** *(Plains).*

miyowâtisiwin *pl.* **miyowâtisiwina** (NI) Being of good character; a good personality.

miyowâyâw *pl.* **miyowâyâwak** (VAI) S/he is well.

miyowâyâwin *pl.* **miyowâyâwina** (NI) Being well or in good health.

miyowâyihtiw *pl.* **miyowâyihtiwak** (VAI) S/he acts with good behavior; s/he behaves well.

miyowâyihtowin *pl.* **miyowâyihtowina** (NI) A morally good act.

miyowicehtowin *pl.* **miyowicehtowina** (NI) An alliance, amity, co-operative.

miyowicewâkanihtowin *pl.* **miyowicewâkanihtowina** (NI) Being cordial towards someone.

miyowicihiwewin *pl.* **miyowicihiwewina** (NI) The act of relating well with other people; sociality.

miyowihowin *pl.* **miyowihowina** (NI) The act of having a good name or prestige.

miyowin *pl.* **miyowina** (NI) Being skilled. *(Northern).* *Alt.* **takahkîwin** *(Plains).*

miywamohew (VTI) S/he adjusts it perfectly. *(Plains).* *Alt.* **miyomohew** *(Northern).*

miywamotâw (VTI) S/he adjusts it perfectly.

miywamocikew (VTI) S/he adjusts things perfectly.

miywanohk (IPC) In a good place, inviting.

miywâcimowin *pl.* **miywâcimowina** (NI) A good story, or good news. *(Plains).* *Alt.* **miyowâcimowin** *(Northern).*

miywâskwan *pl.* **miywâskwanwa** (VII) It is a good pole. *(Plains).* *Alt.* **miyowâskwan** *(Northern).*

miywâtamowin (NI) Delight; happiness; elation. *(Plains).* *Alt.* **meyawayamowin** *(Northern).*

mîcimihkahcikan *pl.* **mîcimihkahcikana** (NI) A scent used for trapping.

mîcisowinâhtik *pl.* **mîcisowinâhtikwa** (NI) A table.

mîciwin *pl.* **mîciwina** (NI) Food.

mîcimin *pl.* **mîciminak** (NA) A green pea. *(Plains).* *Alt.* **lepwa** *(French Cree slang).*

mîhyawesiw *pl.* **mîhyawesiwak** (VAI) S/he is furry.

mîhyaweyâw *pl.* **mîhyaweyâwa** (VII) It is furry.

mîkis *pl.* **mîkisak** (NA) A bead.

mîkisihkahcikewin *pl.* **mîkisihkahcikewina** (NI) The act of doing beadwork; beading.

mîkisiyâkan *pl.* **mîkisiyâkana** (NI) A porcelain or glass plate; a crock.

mîkowâhp *pl.* **mîkowâhpa** (NI) A teepee.

mîna (IPC) Also; and.

mînâpihtaw (IPC) And a half.

mînis (NI) A wild berry or fruit.

mînisâhtik *pl.* **mînisâhtikwak** (NA) A wild fruit tree.

mînisâpowiw (IPC) An expression meaning "it is juicy, i.e.: succulent."

mînisihkân (NI) A domestic berry, i.e.: a grape.

mînisihkeskâw *pl.* **mînisihkeskâwa** (NI) A place where there are many berries.

mînisiskâw *pl.* **mînisiskâwa** (NI) A berry patch; a cluster of berries. *(Plains).* *Alt.* **mihcetominakâw** *(Northern).*

mînowin *pl.* **mînowina** (NI) The act of recovering or rebounding; rebound; recovery.

mîpit (NI) A tooth.

mîsahamawew *pl.* **mîsahamawewak** (VTA) S/he mends it for her/him.

mîsahaskisinewin *pl.* **mîsahaskisinewina** (NI) The act of mending shoes; resole.

mîsahayapiw *pl.* **mîsahayapiwak** (VAI) S/he mends the net.

mîsaponan *pl.* **mîsaponana** (NI) An eyelash. *Var.* **mîsapowinân, mesapowinan, mesaponan.**

mîsapowinân *pl.* **mîsapowinâna** (NI) An eyelash. *Var.* **mesapowinan, mesaponan, mîsaponan.**

mîsawew (VTA) S/he mends it or them; s/he repairs it. **mîsaham** (VTI) S/he mends it.

mîsahowew (VTA) S/he mends for someone.

mîsahikew (VTI) S/he mends something or anything.

mîcacâkanis (NA) A little coyote. *(Northern).* *Alt.* **mescacakanis** *(Plains).*

mîscakâs *pl.* **mîscakâsa** (NI) A hair on the head.

mîsikohkâna (NI) His/her goggles; eye glasses.

mîsikokanân *pl.* **mîsikokanâna** (NI) An eye socket.

mîskisikohkâna (NI) His/her goggles; eye glasses.

mîskisikokanân *pl.* **mîskisikokanâna** (NI) His/her eye socket.

mîstacakan *pl.* **mîstacakana** (NA) A big coyote.

mîtisohkâsiw *pl.* **mîtisohkâsiwak** (VAI) S/he pretends to eat.

mîtos *pl.* **mîtosak** (NA) A poplar tree.

mîwat *pl.* **mîwata** (NI) A medicine bag; a bundle that contains sacred power objects.

mîwatihkew *pl.* **mîwatihkewak** (VAI) S/he makes a medicine bag; s/he makes a bundle that contains sacred power objects.

mîwihew (VTA) S/he scares her/him away. **miwitâw** (VTA) S/he scares all of them (animate).

mîwihiwew (VTA) S/he scares everyone away.

mîyopayowin *pl.* **mîyopayowina** (NI) Having good luck; a success.

mîyosiw *pl.* **mîyosiwak** (VAI) S/he is beautiful; s/he looks lovely.

mîywâsin *pl.* **mîywâsina** (VII) It is attractive; it looks very fine. *(Plains).* *Alt.* **miwasin** *(Northern).*

mohcihk (IPC) On the ground; on the floor.

mohcohkâsow *pl.* **mohcohkâsowak** (VAI) S/he acts crazily. *(Plains).* *Alt.* **kakepatisihkâsow** *(Northern).*

mohew (VTA) S/he makes her/him cry. **mohiwew** (VTA) S/he makes others cry.

momew (VTA) S/he makes her/him cry with her/his speech or singing.

93

mohtew *pl.* **mohtewak** (NA) A caterpillar. *(Plains). Alt.* **mihyawimohtiw** *(Northern).*

monahikewin *pl.* **monahikewina** (NI) The act of digging in the ground; performing ground work.

moscimiweyihtowin *pl.* **moscimiweyihtowina** (NI) Having an affinity with someone else.

moscimiyew *pl.* **moscimiyewak** (VTA) S/he simply gives it to her/him.

moscosis *pl.* **moscosisak** (NA) A calf.

moscôsehcikewin *pl.* **moscôsehcikewina** (NI) Being handmade. *(Northern). Alt.* **iyinitoyisihcikewin** *(Plains).*

mosesitew *pl.* **mosesitewak** (VAI) Her/his feet are bare. *(Northern). Alt.* **sâsâkihtiw** *(Plains).*

moseskatenew (VTA) S/he makes her/him naked.
  moseskatenam (VTI) S/he makes it naked.
  moseskateniwew (VTA) S/he makes people naked.
  moseskatenikew (VTA) S/he makes someone naked.

moseskatepitew (VTA) S/he pulls off all her/his clothes.
  moseskatepitam (VTI) S/he pulls the covering off it.
  moseskatepisiwew (VTA) S/he pulls clothes off someone.
  moseskatepicikew (VTA) S/he pulls clothes off everyone.

moseskatepitisowin *pl.* **moseskatepitisowina** (NI) The act pulling off all clothing; undressing.

moseskatew *pl.* **moseskatewak** (VAI) S/he is naked.

moseskatewin *pl.* **moseskatewina** (NI) Nakedness.

mosestikwânew *pl.* **mosestikwânewak** (VAI) Her/his head is bare.

mosihew (VTA) S/he senses her/his presence.
  mositâw (VTI) S/he senses something.
  mosihiwew (VTA) S/he senses people.
  mosicikew (VTI) S/he senses things.

mosihowin *pl.* **mosihowina** (NI) Intuition; a sign prophesying the future; an omen; a sense of feeling.

mosihtâwin *pl.* **mosihtâwina** (NI) A physical sensation or feeling.

mosisepitonew *pl.* **mosisepitonewak** (VAI) Her/his arms are bare.

mosopiyesîs *pl.* **mosopiyesîsak** (NA) A moose bird. *(Plains). Alt.* **môsopiwayisîs** *(Northern).*

mostaskamikâw (VII) As the snow melts in the spring time, the ground or earth begins to appear. *(Plains). Alt.* **pânâkohtew** *(Northern).*

mostâsihtakosiw *pl.* **mostâsihtakosiwak** (VAI) S/he has an annoying voice.

mostos *pl.* **mostoswak** (NA) A cow.

mostosokamik *pl.* **mostosokamikwa** (NI) A cow barn.

mostosomiy *pl.* **mostosomiya** (NI) Dung.

mostosowayân *pl.* **mostosowayânak** (NA) A cow or buffalo robe.

mostosowîyâs *pl.* **mostosowîyâsa** (NI) Beef.

mostoswekin *pl.* **mostoswekinwa** (NI) A cow hide.

moswekin *pl.* **moswekinwa** (NI) A moosehide.

mowâkonew *pl.* **mowâkonewak** (VAI) S/he eats snow.

mowew *pl.* **mowewak** (VTA) S/he eats them.

moyehcikewin *pl.* **moyehcikewina** (NI) Having an instinct about something; apprehend; percipience.

moyesowin *pl.* **moyesowina** (NI) The act of being skeptical.

moyetamowin *pl.* **moyetamowina** (NI) The act of being apprehensive.

moyeyihtamowin *pl.* **moyeyihtamowina** (NI) Skeptical.

moyeyimew (VTA) S/he is skeptical of her/him; s/he suspects her/him.
  moyeyitam (VTI) S/he is skeptical of it.
  moyeyimiwew (VTA) S/he is skeptical of someone.
  moyeyicikew (VTI) S/he is skeptical of things.

moywihkac (IPC) Never. *(Northern). Alt.* **namawihkâc, namoyawihkâc** *(Plains).*

môcikâyâwin *pl.* **môcikâyâwina** (NI) Being cheerful; high spirits; scrumptious.

môcikesâyâwin *pl.* **môcikesâyâwina** (NI) Being airy; airly; amenity.

môcikeyihtam (VII) S/he is in a cheery mood.

môcikeyihtamowin *pl.* **môcikeyihtamowina** (NI) Being exuberant; exuberance.

môcikihitowin *pl.* **môcikihitowina** (NI) The act of enchanting each other.

môcikihiwewin *pl.* **môcikihiwewina** (NI) The act of enlivening someone's life; the act of enchanting; excitation; enliven; regale.

môcikihtâwin *pl.* **môcikihtâwina** (NI) The act of amusement; frolic; merriment; rollick.

môcikihtâwinihkewin *pl.* **môcikihtâwinihkewina** (NI) The act of merry making; revelry.

môcikihtâwipewin *pl.* **môcikihtâwipewina** (NI) The act of carousing; a binge.

môcikimisowin *pl.* **môcikimisowina** (NI) The act of creating self-happiness through speech.

môcikisowin *pl.* **môcikisowina** (NI) Being amused; frivolity; jollity; joviality; jubilant.

môcohkâsowewin *pl.* **môcohkâsowewina** (NI) The act of making a spoof or hoax.

môcohkâsowin *pl.* **môcohkâsowina** (NI) Being full of antics; clowning around.

môcowâtisiw *pl.* **môcowâtisiwak** (VAI) S/he is a crazy type or character.

môcowâtisiwin *pl.* **môcowâtisiwina** (NI) Craziness; foolishness.

môcoweyimew (VTA) S/he thinks s/he or they are crazy or foolish.
  môcoweyitam (VTI) S/he thinks it is crazy or foolish.

môcoweyimiwew (VTA) S/he thinks people are crazy or foolish.

môcoweyicikew (VTI) S/he thinks everyone is crazy or foolish.

môcowiw *pl.* **môcowiwak** (VAI) S/he is crazy; funny.

môcowiwin *pl.* **môcowiwina** (NI) The act of craziness; the act of foolishness.

môhcohiwewin *pl.* **môhcohiwewina** (NI) The act of stupefying.

môhcohkân *pl.* **môhcohkânak** (NA) A clown; a dummy; a lout.

môhcohkâsoskiwin *pl.* **môhcohkâsoskiwina** (NI) The act of being a buffoon.

môhcohkâsowewin *pl.* **môhcohkâsowewina** (NI) Acting crazy; bedazzle; the act of tricking or trying to fool others.

môhcopayowin *pl.* **môhcopayowina** (NI) The act of going berserk.

môhcowisâyâwin *pl.* **môhcowisâyâwina** (NI) Being nonsensical; being goofy; ineptitude; silliness.

môhkâhasiw *pl.* **môhkâhasiwak** (NA) A bittern.

môhkicowanipek *pl.* **môhkicowanipekwa** (NI) An undercurrent in a stream; spring.

môhkocikan *pl.* **môhkocikana** (NI) A hand tool to smooth wood surfaces or a machine to smooth lumber in a mill.

môhkocikewikamik *pl.* **môhkocikewikamikwa** (NI) A woodworking workshop; a planer mill.

môhkocikewiyiniw *pl.* **môhkocikewiyiniwak** (NA) A planer craftsman.

môhkomanihkan *pl.* **môhkomanihkana** (NI) A blade.

môhkomân *pl.* **môhkomâna** (NI) A knife.

môhkomânis *pl.* **môhkomânisa** (NI) A small knife.

môhkotâkan *pl.* **môhkotâkana** (NI) A carving knife.

môhkotew (VTA) S/he carves it or planes it.

môhkotam (VTI) S/he planes it.

môhkocikew (VTI) S/he planes lumber.

môhtew *pl.* **môhtewak** (NA) A pimple; a worm.

môminew *pl.* **môminewak** (VAI) S/he eats berries from the fruit tree.

mônahatihkâtew (VTA) S/he unearths her/him or it; s/he digs her/him out.

mônahatihkâtam (VTI) S/he unearths something.

mônahatihkâsiwew (VTA) S/he unearths someone.

mônahatihkâcikew (VTI) S/he unearths things.

mônahicepihkwewin *pl.* **mônahicepihkwewina** (NI) The act of uprooting.

mônahikakew *pl.* **mônahikakewak** (VAI) S/he digs the ground with it.

mônahikâkan *pl.* **mônahikâkana** (NI) A grub hoe, used for removing tree roots.

mônahipân *pl.* **mônahipâna** (NI) A well.

mônahipânihkân *pl.* **mônahipânihkâna** (NI) A cistern.

mônahipew *pl.* **mônahipewak** (VAI) S/he digs a well.

mônahwew (VTA) S/he digs them out.

mônaham (VTI) S/he digs something.

mônahowew (VTA) S/he digs someone.

mônahikew (VTI) S/he digs something.

môniyaskwew *pl.* **môniyaskwewak** (NA) A white woman.

môniyâwiw *pl.* **môniyâwiwak** (VAI) S/he is a white person.

mônîyâw *pl.* **mônîyâwak** (NA) A white person.

môsahkinew (VTA) S/he picks them up.

môsahkinam (VTI) S/he picks it up.

môsahkiniwew (VTA) S/he picks up people.

môsahkinikew (VTI) S/he picks things up.

môsahkinikewina (NA) Pickings.

môsâpew *pl.* **môsâpewak** (NA) A bachelor; an unmarried, single man; a widower.

môsâpewiwin *pl.* **môsâpewiwina** (NI) The act of being unattached or being a bachelor.

môsihtestamawew (VTA) S/he feels her/his pain; s/he empathizes with her/him. *(Plains).* Alt. **wîsakeyitamostamawew** *(Northern).*

môsihtestamatâw (VTA) S/he feels its pain.

môsihtestamakew (VTA) S/he feel people's pain.

môsisinîy *pl.* **môsisinîya** (NI) A bullet; a shell.

môsiskwew *pl.* **môsiskwewak** (NA) An unmarried or single woman; a widow.

môskestawew (VTA) S/he charges at her/him.

môskestam (VTI) S/he charges at it.

môskestâkew (VTA) S/he charges at someone.

môskescikew (VTI) S/he charges at things.

môskicowanipek *pl.* **môskicowanipekwa** (NI) A ground spring; a fountain.

môskinew (VTA) S/he uncovers and reveals her/him.

môskinam (VTI) S/he uncovers and reveals it.

môskiniwew (VTA) S/he uncovers and reveals people.

môskinikew (VTI) S/he uncovers and reveals something.

môskipew *pl.* **môskipewak** (VAI) S/he floats to the surface and reveals herself/himself.

môskipitew (VTA) S/he pulls her/him or it into view.

môskipitam (VTI) S/he pulls it into view.

môskipisiwew (VTA) S/he pulls someone into view.

môskipicikew (VTI) S/he pulls things into view.

môskîw *pl.* **môskîwak** (VAI) S/he reveals herself/himself; s/he shows herself/himself; s/he emerges.

môskohew (VTA) S/he makes her/him cry.

môskomew (VTA) S/he makes her/him cry with her/his speech or singing.

môskweyihtam *pl.* **môskweyihtamwak** (VAI) S/he cries over something sad.

môsopiwayisîs *pl.* **môsopiwayisîsak** (NA) A moose bird. *(Northern).* Alt. **mosopiyesîs** *(Plains).*

95

môsoskowan *pl.* **môsoskowanwa** (NI) A moose nose. *(Plains).*

môsômin *pl.* **môsômina** (NI) A mooseberry or a high bush cranberry.

môstasenew (VTA) S/he holds her/him while s/he is nude.

môstasenam (VTI) S/he holds it while it is nude.

môstaseniwew (VTA) S/he holds someone who is nude.

môstasenikew (VTA) S/he holds nude people.

môstasewin *pl.* **môstasewina** (NI) Being nude or stark naked.

môstawikanehowewin *pl.* **môstawikanehowewina** (NI) The act of disproving something.

môstawinawew (VTA) S/he desires her/him on seeing her/him; s/he is sexually attracted to her/him.

môstawinam (VTI) S/he desires it.

môstawinâkew (VTA) S/he desires people.

môstâpekasenisiw *pl.* **môstâpekasenisiwak** (VTA) S/he strips off all her/his clothes.

môstâpekasew *pl.* **môstâpekasewak** (VAI) S/he is nude; s/he has no clothes on.

môstâpekasewin *pl.* **môstâpekasewina** (NI) The act of being nude; the act of being without clothes; bareness; nudity.

môstâpekasewisimowin *pl.* **môstâpekasewisimowina** (NI) The act of dancing in the nude; erotic.

môstâskopitonew *pl.* **môstâskopitonewak** (VAI) Her/his arms are nude or bare.

môstâskosâwew *pl.* **môstâskosâwewak** (VAI) S/he smokes pure pipe tobacco.

môstohtew *pl.* **môstohtewak** (VAI) S/he goes on foot.

môswa *pl.* **môswak** (NA) A moose.

môteyâpisk *pl.* **môteyâpiskwa** (NI) A bottle.

mwesiskawew (VTA) S/he misses her/him by arriving too late.

mwesiskam (VTI) S/he misses it by arriving too late.

mwesiskâkew (VTA) S/he misses people by arriving too late.

mwestamew (VAI) S/he arrives too late to eat.

mwestatam (VAI) S/he arrives too late to have a bite of it.

mwestacikew (VAI) S/he arrives too late and misses everything.

mwestas (IPC) After; another time; later; afterward; by and by.

mwestawew (VAI) S/he misses her/him by firing too late.

mwestaham (VTI) S/he misses it by firing too late.

mwestahowew (VTA) S/he misses someone.

mwestahikew (VTI) S/he misses everything.

mwestâsihtâkosiwak (VAI) They are annoying to listen to continously.

mwestâsihtâkwan *pl.* **mwestâsihtâkwanwa** (VII) It is annoying to listen to continously.

mwestâteyimew (VTA) S/he is annoyed to see her/him.

mwestâteyitam (VTI) S/he is annoyed with it.

mwestâteyimiwew (VTA) S/he is annoyed with people.

mwestâteyicikew (VTI) S/he is annoyed with everything.

mwestinew (VTA) S/he misses her/him when trying to catch her/him.

mwestinam (VTI) S/he misses it when trying to catch it.

mwestiniwew (VTA) S/he misses someone when trying to catch someone.

mwestinikew (VTI) S/he misses everything when trying to catch everything.

n

na (IPC) A statement used when handing something over to someone, "here".

nahahew (VTA) S/he puts them away.

nahastâw (VTI) S/he puts it away.

nahayhiwew (VTA) S/he puts someone away.

nahascikew (VTI) S/he puts things away.

nahapiw pl. nahapiwak (VAI) S/he sits down.

nahapiwikamik pl. nahapiwikamikwa (NI) A toilet. (Plains). Alt. sikiwkamik (Northern).

nahapîstawew (VTA) S/he sits down beside her/him.

nahapîstam (VTI) S/he sits down beside it.

nahapîstâkew (VTA) S/he sits down beside someone.

nahascikewin pl. nahascikewina (NI) The act of ordering items; the act of processing fruit or meat; conserve; contain; hoarding.

nahastâsiw pl. nahastâsiwak (VAI) S/he arranges the bedding; s/he makes up a bed.

nahastâsiwin pl. nahastâsiwina (NI) The act of arranging bedding.

nahastew pl. nahastewa (VII) It is put away.

nahawâw pl. nahawâwa (VII) It is neat or orderly. (Northern). Alt. nahâwastew (Plains).

nahawekinew (VTA) S/he folds them.

nahawekinam (VTI) S/he folds clothing.

nahawekinikew (VTI) S/he folds things.

nahâhkis pl. nahâhkisak (NDA) A son-in-law.

nahâkaniskwem pl. nahâkaniskwemak (NDA) A daughter-in-law.

nahâkeyawewin pl. nahâkeyawewina (NI) Being graceful. (Northern). Alt. mamihtâkiyawiwin (Plains).

nahâpahcikewin pl. nahâpahcikewina (NI) Having an ability to focus well; sharp-eye focus.

nahâpamew (VTA) S/he makes a positive identification of her/him.

nahâpahtam (VTI) S/he makes a positive identification of it.

nahâpamiwew (VTA) S/he makes a positive identification of people.

nahâpahcikew (VTI) S/he makes a positive identifcation of things.

nahâpaminâkosiw pl. nahâpaminâkosiwak (VAI) S/he has a distinctive identity.

nahâpaminâkwan pl. nahâpaminâkwanwa (VII) It has a distinctive identity.

nahâpiw pl. nahâpiwak (VAI) S/he has good eyesight.

nahâpiwin pl. nahâpiwina (NI) Having good eyesight.

nahâsiwewin pl. nahâsiwewina (NI) The act of having a good shot.

nahâskiwewin pl. nahâskiwewina (NI) The act of being a good shot (with a gun).

nahâskwew pl. nahâskwewak (VAI) S/he is a good shot (with a gun).

nahâstwew pl. nahâstwewak (VAI) S/he has a good shot (with a bow and arrow).

nahâwascikewin pl. nahâwascikewina (NI) The act of arranging, or tidying.

nahâwastew pl. nahâwastewa (VII) It is neat or orderly. (Plains). Alt. nahawâw (Northern).

nahâwisiw pl. nahâwisiwak (VAI) S/he is neat and tidy. (Northern). Alt. kanâcihow (Plains).

nahetikitiw pl. nahetikitiwak (VAI) S/he is just the right size.

naheyeyihtamowin pl. naheyeyihtamowina (NI) The act of being appeased.

naheyihmew (VTA) S/he warmly accepts her/him; s/he feels good about her/him.

naheyihtam (VTI) S/he warmly accepts it.

naheyihmiwew (VTA) S/he warmly accepts people.

naheyihhcikew (VTI) S/he warmly accepts things.

naheyihtamowin pl. naheyihtamowina (NI) The act of warmly accepting something; the act of embracing something; the act of feeling good about something.

naheyihtowak (VTA) They warmly accept each other; they feel good about each other.

naheyihtowin pl. naheyihtowina (NI) The act of feeling acceptance with one another.

nahihtam pl. nahihtamwak (VAI) S/he is an effective listener; s/he listens well.

nahihtamowin pl. nahihtamowina (NI) The act of being an effective listener or listening well.

nahihtawew pl. nahihtawewak (VTA) S/he obeys his directions without complaint; s/he accepts his directions.

nahihtin pl. nahihtinwa (VII) It fits well.

nahinakosiwin pl. nahinakosiwina (NI) The act of appearing the same; uniformity.

nahinew (VTA) S/he buries her/him.

nahinam (VTI) S/he buries it.

nahiniwew (VTA) S/he buries people.

nahinikew (VTI) S/he buries something.

nahinowewikamik pl. nahinowewikamikwak (NA) A building where burials take place, i.e.: a funeral home.

nahinowewin pl. nahinowewina (NI) A burial; entomb.

nahipayiw pl. nahipayiwa (VTI) It fits well; it suits well.

nahipayowin pl. nahipayowina (NI) The act of being suitable; suitability.

nahisimew (VTA) S/he makes it fit into something.

97

nahisitaw (VTI) S/he makes it suitable.

nahisimiwew (VTA) S/he fits people into something.

nahisihcikew (VTI) S/he makes things suitable.

nahisin *pl.* **nahisinwak** (VAI) S/he fits into something.

nahiskamowin *pl.* **nahiskamowina** (NI) The act of being adaptable; befitting.

nahiskawew (VTA) S/he is compatible with her/him.

nahiskam (VTI) S/he is compatible for it.

nahiskâkew (VTA) S/he is compatible for people.

nahiskâcikew (VTI) S/he makes things compatible.

nahiw *pl.* **nahiwak** (VAI) S/he is skillful or adept at sports. *Var.* **nakaciw**.

nahiwepinikewin *pl.* **nahiwepinikewina** (NI) Being apt; aptitude.

nahiwin *pl.* **nahiwina** (NI) Being skilled or adept at something, i.e.: sports; adroit; keenness.

nahiyawemototâkew (VTA) S/he speaks to people in Cree.

nahiyawemototawew (VTA) S/he speaks to her/him in Cree.

nahiyehew *pl.* **nahiyehewak** (VAI) S/he breathes easily.

nahiyikohk (IPC) Just the right amount; adequate.

nahîspihcâw *pl.* **nahîspihcâwa** (VII) It is just the right size.

nahkawiyiniw *pl.* **nahkawiyiniwak** (VAI) A person of the Saulteaux tribe, i.e.: s/he is Saulteaux.

nakacihew (VTA) S/he is familiar with him/her.

nakacihiwew (VTA) S/he is used to people.

nakacihtamohiwewin *pl.* **nakacihtamohiwewina** (NI) The act of being someone familiar.

nakacihtâwin *pl.* **nakacihtâwina** (NI) The act of being accustomed; acuity; mastery; being capable; capability. *(Plains). Alt.* **kaskihcikewin** *(Northern).*

nakacipahew (VTA) S/he outran her/him or them; s/he leaves him behind.

nakacipatwâw (VTI) S/he runs away without it.

nakacipahiwew (VTA) S/he outruns people.

nakacitâw (VTI) S/he is familiar with it.

nakahaskwân *pl.* **nakahaskwânak** (NA) An arrow stopper, i.e.: a shield.

nakamiw *pl.* **nakamiwa** (VII) It ends or doesn't go any further.

nakamohtâw *pl.* **nakamohtâwak** (VAI) S/he ends it, i.e.: the road.

nakatahwew (VTA) S/he leaves her/him behind in the canoe race.

nakatahhowew (VTA) S/he leaves others behind in a canoe race.

nakataskew *pl.* **nakataskewak** (VAI) S/he leaves this world; s/he died.

nakatâmotocikewin *pl.* **nakatâmotocikewina** (NI) The act of evacuating; evacuation.

nakatâmototawew (VTA) S/he leaves others and runs away by herself/himself.

nakatâmototam (VTI) S/he leaves it and runs away by herself/himself.

nakatâmototâkew (VTA) S/he leaves everybody and runs away by herself/himself.

nakatew (VTA) S/he leaves her/him.

nakatam (VTI) S/he leaves it.

nakasiwew (VTA) S/he leaves everyone.

nakacikew (VTI) S/he leaves something.

nakayaskamohtahiwewin *pl.* **nakayaskamohtahiwewina** (NI) The act of a person introducing other people to each other; introduction.

nakayâhtawew (VTA) S/he is familiar with hearing her/his voice.

nakayâhtam (VTI) S/he is familiar with hearing it.

nakayâhtâkew (VTA) S/he is familiar with hearing people.

nakayânawew (VTA) S/he is used to seeing her/him. *(Northern). Alt.* **nakayâpamew** *(Plains).*

nakayânam (VTI) S/he is used to it.

nakayânakêw (VTA) S/he is used to seeing one person.

nakayânamewak (VTA) S/he is used to seeing people.

nakayâpamew (VTA) S/he is used to seeing him. *(Plains). Alt.* **nakayânawew** *(Northern).*

nakayâpahtam (VTI) S/he is used to it.

nakayâpahkew (VTA) S/he is used to seeing one person.

nakayâpamewak (VTA) S/he is used to seeing people.

nakayâpahtamwak (VTI) S/he is used to seeing things.

nakayâsiw *pl.* **nakayâsiwak** (VAI) S/he has been tamed.

nakayâskamohtahew (VTA) S/he introduces her/him to someone.

nakayâskamohtahiwew (VTA) S/he introduces other people.

nakayâskamohtahitowin *pl.* **nakayâskamohtahitowina** (NI) The act of introducing yourself to someone else; introductory.

nakayâtotamowinihk (IP) In a customary manner; customarily.

nakâham (VTI) S/he puts a barrier up to prevent it from proceeding.

nakâhowew (VTA) S/he puts a barrier up to prevent people from proceeding.

nakâhikew (VTI) S/he puts a barrier up to prevent things from proceeding.

nakâhtin *pl.* **nakâhtinwa** (VII) It is inhibited or prevented from going any further.

nakânew (VTA) S/he inhibits her/him; s/he stops her/him.

nakânam (VTI) S/he inhibits it.

98

nakâniwew (VTA) S/he inhibits people.

nakânikew (VTI) S/he inhibits things.

nakâsin *pl.* **nakâsinwak** (VAI) S/he is inhibited: s/he prevented from going further.

nakâwew (VTA) S/he puts a barrier up to prevent her/him from proceeding; s/he blocks or inhibits her/him with something.

nakâyâhew *pl.* **nakâyâhewak** (VTA) S/he breaks it in, i.e.: a horse for riding.

nakâyâhotew *pl.* **nakâyâhotewa** (VII) It is snagged on something, i.e.: something floating down the river.

nakâyâsiw *pl.* **nakâyâsiwak** (VTA) The wind impedes his progress.

nakâyâsowin *pl.* **nakâyâsowina** (NI) The act of being impeded.

nakihew (VTA) S/he makes her/him stop.

nakinam (VTI) S/he makes it stop.

nakihiwew (VTA) S/he makes people stop.

nakinikew (VTI) S/he makes things stop.

nakinamâkewin *pl.* **nakinamâkewina** (NI) The act of prohibiting; prohibition; revocation.

nakinamôwewin *pl.* **nakinamôwewina** (NI) The act of cancelling something.

nakinew (VTA) S/he stops her/him.

nakinam (VTI) S/he stops it.

nakiniwew (VTA) S/he stops someone.

nakinikew (VTI) S/he stops things.

nakinikewin *pl.* **nakinikewina** (NI) The act of intervening; forbidding; intervention; preclusion; supression; termination.

nakinowewin *pl.* **nakinowewina** (NI) The act of impeding; impediment; inhibition.

nakipayiw *pl.* **nakipayiwak** (VAI) It (animate) stopped by itself.

nakipitew (VTA) S/he pulls it or her/him to a stop.

nakipitam (VTI) S/he pulls it to a stop.

nakipisiwew (VTA) S/he pulls people to a stop.

nakipicikew (VTI) S/he pulls things to a stop.

nakiskawew (VTA) S/he meets her/him.

nakiskakam (VTI) S/he meets it.

nakiskakâkew (VTA) S/he meets someone.

nakiskâtowak (VAI) They meet.

nakiskâtowin *pl.* **nakiskâtowina** (NI) The act of meeting or contacting someone.

nakiw *pl.* **nakiwak** (VAI) S/he stops. *(Plains). Alt.* **kipihciw** *(Northern).*

nakiwin *pl.* **nakiwina** (NI) The act of stopping. *(Plains). Alt.* **kipihciwin** *(Northern).*

nakîstawew (VTA) S/he discontinues because s/he is apprehensive of her/him.

nakîstam (VTI) S/he discontinues because s/he is apprehensive of it.

nakîstâkew (VTA) S/he discontinues because s/he is apprehensive of someone.

nakîw *pl.* **nakîwak** (VAI) S/he stopped.

nakîwin *pl.* **nakîwina** (NI) A stop or a place where people embark or disembark, i.e.: a bus stop.

nakwatisiw *pl.* **nakwatisiwak** (VAI) S/he hauls her/his moose meat.

nakwâcikewin *pl.* **nakwâcikewina** (NI) The act of snaring; ensnare.

nakwâsiw *pl.* **nakwâsiwak** (VAI) S/he is snared, i.e.: by a rope or net; s/he is caught in a snare or rope; s/he is caught on a hook.

nakwâtew (VTA) S/he hooks or snares her/him or it; s/he catches it in the net; it is caught.

nakwâtam (VTI) S/he hooks or snares it.

nakwâsiwew (VTA) S/he hooks or snares someone.

nakwâcikew (VTI) S/he hooks or snares things.

namahcîw *pl.* **namahcîwak** (VAI) S/he is left-handed.

namahcîwin *pl.* **namahcîwina** (NI) Being left-handed.

namahtin *pl.* **namahtinwa** (NI) The left hand.

namahtinihk (LN) Left, the direction or location.

namahtinisk (IPC) With the left hand.

namakîkway (IPC) Nothing or none. *(Plains). Alt.* **namoya kîkway** *(Northern).*   99

namatakon *pl.* **namatakonwa** (VII) It is all gone.

namatew *pl.* **namatewak** (VAI) S/he is not there anymore.

namawihkâc (IPC) Never. *(Plains). Var.* **namoyawihkâc.** *(Plains). Alt.* **moywihkac** *(Northern).*

namâwîyak (PR) No one or nobody.

namehew (VTA) S/he sees tracks.

namehiwew (VTA) S/he sees someone's tracks.

namehtâw *pl.* **namehtâwak** (VAI) S/he makes fresh and visible tracks.

namehtâwin *pl.* **namehtâwina** (NI) The act of making tracks.

namekos *pl.* **namekosak** (NA) A lake trout.

namepin *pl.* **namepinwak** (NA) A piece of snakeroot. *(Plains). Alt.* **kinepikocepihk** *(Northern).*

namepiy *pl.* **namepiyak** (NA) A sucker, the fish.

nameskanawew *pl.* **nameskanawewak** (VAI) S/he leaves visible tracks.

namestek *pl.* **namestekwak** (NA) A dried, smoked fish.

namew *pl.* **namewak** (NA) A sturgeon.

namic (IPC) Before or ere. *(Northern). Alt.* **mayes,** **pâmayes** *(Plains).*

namohac (IPC) It is okay; there is nothing wrong; no place. *Var.* **namananitaw.**

namoya (IPC) No. Also a negative mark for not.

namoya kîkway (IPC) Nothing or none. *(Northern). Alt.* **namakîkway** *(Plains).*

namoya nânitaw (IPC) I'm fine; or nowhere.

namoya nîya kâtôtamân (IPC) There is no legal
equivalent in Cree for the terms of "not guilty" or
"guilty". For a plea of "not guilty", a speaker
would use the above expression to indicate "I am
not responsible or I did not do it".

namoyaceskwa (IPC) Not yet.

namoyakîspiw *pl.* **namoyakîspiwak** (VAI) S/he has not
appeased her/his hunger; s/he is still hungry.

namoyakwayask (VII) It is disorderly; disordered;
improper, incorrect.

namoyamamisîwin *pl.* **namoyamamisîwina** (NI) The act
of being incompetent; incompetence; not
trustworthy.

namoyawihkâc (IPC) Never. *(Plains). Var.* **namawihkâc.**
(Plains). Alt. **moywihkac** *(Northern).*

namoyâhpô (IPC) Not even; not at all; "no way".

namoyâyiwâk (IPC) All over; not greater or more than.

nanahtew *pl.* **nanahtewa** (VII) There are heat waves.
(Northern). Alt. **nânâtehtew** *(Plains).*

nanakataweyimowin *pl.* **nanakataweyimowina** (NI) The
act of positive thinking.

nanamahcipayiw (IPC) An expression used to indicate an
earthquake or tremor and means "the ground
trembles." *(Northern). Alt.* **nanamaskipiyiw**
(Plains).

nanamaskipiyiw (IPC) An expression used to indicate an
earthquake or tremor and means "the ground
trembles." *(Plains). Alt.* **nanamahcipayiw**
(Northern).

nanamâskaciw *pl.* **nanamâskaciwak** (VAI) S/he shivers
with coldness.

nanamâskaciwin *pl.* **nanamâskaciwina** (NI) The act of
shivering with coldness.

nanamipayiw *pl.* **nanamipayiwa** *or* **nanamipayiwak** (VII)
or (VAI) It shakes *or* s/he is shivering; s/he is
vibrating; s/he is wavering. *(Plains). Alt.*
koskoskopayiw *(Northern).*

nanamipayowaspinewin (NI) Parkinson's disease.

nanamipayowin *pl.* **nanamipayowina** (NI) The act of
shaking; the act of shivering; trembling or
unsteady; tremulous; vibrating. *(Plains). Alt.*
koskoskopayowin *(Northern).*

nanamipiteyâskaciw *pl.* **nanamipiteyâskaciwak** (VAI)
S/he is so cold her/his teeth chatter.

nanaskomôkîsikâw (NI) Thanksgiving Day.

nanatohkokwâsiw *pl.* **nanatohkokwâsiwak** (VAI) S/he
sews various materials together; s/he quilts.

nanânisk (IPC) All in pieces; in all directions.

nanânistahew (VTA) S/he scatters the pieces all over.

nanânistastâw (VTI) S/he scatters things all over.

nanânistayiwew (VTA) S/he scatters people all over.

nanânistinam (VTI) S/he takes it apart.

nanânistinew (VTA) S/he takes them apart.

nanânistiniwew (VTA) S/he takes someone apart.

nanânistinikew (VTI) S/he takes things apart.

nanânistipitam (VTI) S/he shreds it into pieces.

nanânistipitew (VTI) S/he shreds them into pieces.

nanânistipisiwew (VTA) S/he spreads the group of
people all over.

nanânistipicikew (VTI) S/he shreds things into pieces.

nanânistipitew (VTA) S/he tears them into pieces.

nanânistipitam (VTI) S/he tears it into pieces.

nanânistipisiwew (VTA) S/he tears people into pieces.

nanânistipicikew (VTI) S/he tears things into pieces.

nanânistohtewak (VAI) They fan out to different places.

nanânistohtewin *pl.* **nanânistohtewina** (NI) The act of
fanning out to different places.

nanâskomew (VTA) S/he thanks her/him.

nanâskomiwew (VTA) S/he thanks people.

nanâskomow *pl.* **nanâskomowak** (VAI) S/he is thankful.

nanâskomowakeyimow *pl.* **nanâskomowakeyimowak**
(VAI) S/he is feeling thankful.

nanâskomowin *pl.* **nanâskomowina** (NI) Being thankful.

nanâskomowinihk (IPC) In a thankful manner;
thankfully.

nanâtaweyimow *pl.* **nanâtaweyimowak** (VAI) S/he is
grateful to be cured.

nanâtawihiwewiyiniw *pl.* **nanâtawihiwewiyiniwak** (NA)
A medicine person who uses the good spirit to
offset evil spirits.

nanâtohk (IP) All kinds of things or a variety; different
kinds.

nanâtohkîkway *pl.* **nanâtohkîwaya** (VII) It is composed
of many kinds of things.

nanâtohkokwâtam (VAI) S/he makes a quilt.

nanâtohkokwâsôwew (VTI) S/he sews everything
together for someone.

nanâtohkokwâcikew (VAI) S/he makes quilts.

nanâtohkokwâtew *pl.* **nanâtohkokwâtewa** (NI)
Something sewn using colored materials, i.e.: a
quilt.

nanâtohkomew (VTA) S/he exposes all kinds of things
about her/him.

nanâtohkotam (VTI) S/he exposes everything about it.

nanâtohkomiwew (VTA) S/he exposes everything
about people.

nanâtohkonakosiw *pl.* **nanâtohkonakosiwak** (VAI) S/he
has no visually distinguishing features.

nanâtohkonâkwan *pl.* **nanâtohkonâkwanwa** (VII) It is
multicolored.

nanâtohkonikewin *pl.* **nanâtohkonikewina** (NI) The act
of being erratic; acrobatic.

nanâtohkosihew (VTA) S/he configures all kinds of
shapes; s/he makes a variety of things out of them.

nanâtohkositâw (VTI) S/he configures all kinds of shapes with it.

nanâtohkosihiwew (VTA) S/he organizes diverse groups among the people.

nanâtohkosisihcikew (VTI) S/he configures all kinds of things.

nanâtohkôskânesiw *pl.* **nanâtohkôskânesiwak** (VAI) Her/his heritage is composed of various ethnic groups.

nanâtohkwahpinew *pl.* **nanâtohkwahpinewak** (VAI) S/he has various ailments.

nanâtohkwahpinewin *pl.* **nanâtohkwahpinewina** (NI) All kinds of ailments.

nanâtohkwascikewin *pl.* **nanâtohkwascikewina** (NI) The act of jumbling things.

nanâtohkwâkomew (VAI) Her/his relatives are very diverse.

nanâtohkwâkotam (VAI) Her/his lineage is diverse.

nanâtohkwâkomiwew (VAI) S/he has many different relatives.

nanâtohkwisâyâw *pl.* **nanâtohkwisâyâwak** (VAI) S/he has multiple personalities; schizophrenia; different diseases.

nanihkâcacimow *pl.* **nanihkâcacimowak** (VAI) S/he is telling a story.

nanihkâcacimôwin *pl.* **nanihkâcacimôwina** (NI) The act of telling a story.

nanihkâcihew (VTA) S/he treats her/him with kid gloves.

nanihkâcitâw (VTI) S/he treats it with great care.

nanihkâcihiwew (VTA) S/he treats people with kid gloves.

nanihkâcihcikew (VTI) S/he treats them with great reserve.

nanihkâcimew (VTA) S/he reluctantly speaks about her/him.

nanihkâciâtotam (VTI) S/he speaks reluctantly about it.

nanihkâcimiwew (VTA) S/he speaks reluctantly about people.

nanihkâcimiw *pl.* **nanihkâcimiwak** (VAI) S/he is telling a story hurriedly.

nanihkâcimowin *pl.* **nanihkâcimowina** (NI) The act of telling a story in a hurry.

nanihkâcipayiw *pl.* **nanihkâscipayiwa** *or* **nanihkâscipayiwakak** (VII) *or* (VAI) It *or* s/he is involved in a long, drawn out, slow process.

nanihkâtan *pl.* **nanihkâtanwa** (VII) It is a weak situation; slow process.

nanihkâtâspinew *pl.* **nanihkâtâspinewa** (VTI) S/he is weak and sickly for a long time.

nanihkâteyimew (VTA) S/he has reservations about her/him.

nanihkâteyitam (VTI) S/he has reservations about it.

nanihkâteyimiwew (VTA) S/he has reservations about someone.

nanihkâteyihcikew (VTI) S/he has reservations about things.

nanihkâtisiwin *pl.* **nanihkâtisiwina** (NI) Being run down; chronically stressed out. *(Northern). Alt.* **nanihkisiwin** *(Plains).*

nanihkâtowew *pl.* **nanihkâtowewak** (VAI) S/he sounds reluctant.

nanihkâtowewin *pl.* **nanihkâtowewina** (NI) The act of sounding reluctant.

nanihkeyimowin *pl.* **nanihkeyimowina** (NI) The act of requiring immediate attention; urgently.

nanihkihew (VTA) S/he hurries her/him up.

nanihkitâw (VTI) S/he hurries it up.

nanihkihiwew (VTA) S/he hurries people up.

nanihkihcikew (VTI) S/he hurries things up.

nanihkimew (VTA) S/he tells her/him to hurry.

nanihkikowitam (VTA) S/he tells others to hurry.

nanihkimiwew (VTA) S/he tells people to hurry.

nanihkipayiw *pl.* **nanihkipayiwa** *or* **nanihkipayiwak** (VII) *or* (VAI) It *or* s/he is always in a rush (i.e.: a moose).

nanihkipayowin *pl.* **nanihkipayowina** (NI) The act of always being in a rush; terse; untimely.

nanihkisiw *pl.* **nanihkisiwak** (VAI) S/he is in a hurry.

nanihkisiwin *pl.* **nanihkisiwina** (NI) The act of being in a hurry; the act of being rushed for time; making haste; immediacy; racy; impatience. *(Plains). Alt.* **nanihkâtisiwin** *(Northern).*

nanihkitisawew (VTA) S/he commands or orders her/him to hurry.

nanihkitisaham (VTI) S/he commands or orders it to hurry up.

nanihkitisahowew (VTA) S/he commands or orders someone to hurry up.

nanihkitisahikew (VTA) S/he commands or orders everyone to hurry up.

nanihkowitam (VTA) S/he commands or orders everyone to hurry up.

nanihkowimiwew (VTA) S/he commands or orders people to hurry.

nanmiyawepayiw *pl.* **nanamiyawepayiwak** (VAI) Her/his body shakes.

nanoyacihew (VTA) S/he is teasing her/him.

nanoyacitâw (VTI) S/he is teasing it.

nanoyacihiwew (VTA) S/he is teasing people.

nanoyacihcikew (VTI) S/he is teasing things.

nanoyacihitowak (VTA) They are teasing each other.

nanoyacihiwesk *pl.* **nanoyacihiweskak** (NA) A prankster.

nanoyacihiwewin *pl.* **nanoyacihiwewina** (NI) The act of playing a prank; a tease.

nanoyacihtowin *pl.* **nanoyacihtowina** (NI) The act of joking with each other; quip; ribbing.

nanoyacimew (VTA) S/he is joking with her/him.

nanoyacimiwew (VTA) S/he jokes with people.

nanoyacihcikew (VTI) S/he does things jokingly.

nanoyacimowewin *pl.* **nanoyacimowewina** (NI) The act of being jocular.

nanoyatisiskowin *pl.* **nanoyatisiskowina** (NI) Being a rascal; rascality.

nanoyatisiskowinihk (IPN) In a rascally manner; rascally.

nanoyatisiw *pl.* **nanoyatisiwak** (VAI) S/he is teasing.

nanoyatisiwin *pl.* **nanoyatisiwina** (NI) The act of teasing.

nanoyatwew *pl.* **nanoyatwewak** (VAI) S/he is telling jokes.

nanoyatwewin *pl.* **nanoyatwewina** (NI) The act of telling jokes; banter.

napakahcikowâyis *pl.* **napakahcikowâyisak** (NA) A toboggan drawn by horses or dogs (Plains). Alt. **ocâpâsôwâyis** (Northern).

napakasihta *pl.* **napakasihtak** (NA) A Canada balsam spruce.

napakaskihk *pl.* **napakaskihkwak** (NA) A flat pail or pot.

napakâhtik *pl.* **napakâhtikwak** (NA) A toboggan. (Plains). Alt. **napakitâpânâsk** (Northern).

napakâpiskâw *pl.* **napakâpiskâwa** (VII) It is a flat metal or flat rock.

napakâpiskisiw *pl.* **napakâpiskisiwak** (VAI) The iron or rock has a flat surface.

napakâsihtipikiw *pl.* **napakâsihtipikiwak** (NA) Balsam gum or pitch.

napakâskisiw *pl.* **napakâskisiwak** (VAI) The tree stands flat against an outcropping.

napakâskwan *pl.* **napakâskwanwa** (VII) It is flat, i.e.: a pole.

napakâw *pl.* **napakâwa** (VII) It is flat.

napakicîkahikan *pl.* **napakicîkahikana** (NI) A broad axe; a pickaxe.

napakihew (VTA) S/he makes her/him flat.

napakitâw (VTI) S/he makes it flat.

napakihiwew (VTA) S/he makes people flat.

napakihcikew (VTI) S/he makes things flat.

napakihkotew (VTI) S/he cuts it flat.

napakihkotam (VTA) S/he cuts it flat.

napakihkohcikew (VTI) S/he cuts things flat.

napakihtak *pl.* **napakihtakwa** (NI) A plank or a wooden board.

napakihtakâw *pl.* **napakihtakâwa** (VII) It is flat, i.e.: a wooden floor.

napakihtakisiw *pl.* **napakihtakisiwak** (VAI) It has a flat, wooden surface.

napakikaham (VTI) S/he chops it flat.

napakikahwew (VTA) S/he chops them flat.

napakikahikew (VTI) S/he chops things flat.

napakikinosew *pl.* **napakikinosewak** (NA) A fish called a goldeye; a flat fish.

napakinam (VTI) S/he flattens it with her/his hands.

napakinew (VTA) S/he flattens them with her/his hands.

napakinikew (VTI) S/he flattens things with her/his hands.

napakinew (VTA) S/he flattens her/him by holding her/him down by the head.

napakinam (VTI) S/he flattens it.

napakiniwew (VTA) S/he flattens someone by holding them down by the head.

napakinikew (VTI) S/he flattens things.

napakisiw *pl.* **napakisiwak** (VAI) It is flat; s/he is flattened. (Plains). Alt. **samakisiw** (Northern).

napakitâpânâsk *pl.* **napakitâpânâskwak** (NA) A toboggan. (Northern). Alt. **napakâhtik** (Plains).

napakiyâkan *pl.* **napakiyâkana** (NI) A flat plate; a salver.

napatehkapiw *pl.* **napatehkapiwak** (VAI) S/he sees with only one eye; s/he has only one eye.

napatehkasikan *pl.* **napatehkasikanak** (NA) A single crusted pie.

napatekâm (IPC) On one side of.

napatekâpawiwak (VAI) They are standing off to one side.

napatekâtew *pl.* **napatekâtewak** (VAI) S/he is one-legged.

napatekwâskohtiw *pl.* **napatekwâskohtiwak** (NA) A hopper; s/he hops from one foot to the other. (Plains).

napatemiw *pl.* **napatemiwa** or **napatemiwak** (VII) or (VAI) It or s/he hangs from one side.

napateniskew *pl.* **napateniskewak** (IPC) With one-handedness.

napatepitew *pl.* **napatepitewak** (VAI) S/he pulls it from one side.

napatepitonew *pl.* **napatepitonewak** (VAI) S/he has only one arm.

napatepiw *pl.* **napatepiwak** (VAI) S/he sits on one side.

napatesiw *pl.* **napatesiwak** (VAI) S/he is one-sided.

napateskisinew *pl.* **napatekisinewak** (VAI) S/he wears only one shoe.

napatestew *pl.* **napatestewa** (VII) It sits on one side.

napateyâw *pl.* **napateyâwa** (VII) It is one-sided.

napâwis itokwe (IPC) An expression meaning "why now after all the damage done?"

napihkâsiwin *pl.* **napihkâsiwina** (NI) The act of being brave or courageous; bravery; dauntless; gallantry; heroism; intrepid.

napistim *pl.* **napistimak** (NA) A male dog.

naponew (VTA) S/he holds them together.
  naponam (VTI) S/he holds two things together.
  naponiwew (VTA) S/he holds two people together.
  naponikew (VTI) S/he holds something with both hands.
napopayiw *pl.* **napopayiwa** or **napopayiwak** (VII) *or* (VAI) It *or* s/he comes together.
napwahew (VTA) S/he puts them together.
  napwastâw (VTI) S/he puts two things together.
napwahpicikan *pl.* **napwahpicikana** (NI) Something used to tie things together; a lash.
napwahpitew (VTA) S/he ties it or them together.
  napwahpitam (VTI) S/he ties two things together.
  napwahpisiwew (VTA) S/he ties two people together.
  napwahpicikew (VTI) S/he ties two things together.
napwekinew (VTA) S/he folds it or them.
  napwekinam (VTI) S/he folds it.
  napwekinikew (VTI) S/he folds things.
napwen *pl.* **napwenak** (NA) A frying pan. *(Plains). Alt.* **lapewel** *(Northern);* **seseskihkwân** *(Archaic Cree).*
nasipetisawew (VTA) S/he sends her/him or them down the hill to the water's edge.
  nasipetisaham (VTI) S/he sends it down the hill to the water's edge.
  nasipetisahowew (VTA) S/he sends people down the hill to the water's edge.
  nasipetisahikew (VTA) S/he sends everyone down the hill to the water's edge.
naskohtowak (VTA) They respond to or answer each other.
naskohtowin *pl.* **naskohtowina** (NI) The act of responding to or answering one another.
naskomohtowin *pl.* **naskomohtowina** (NI) An answering service.
naskwaham *pl.* **naskwahamwak** (VAI) S/he joins in the song.
naskwahamawew (VAI) S/he sings with her/him.
  naskwahamawâtam (VTI) S/he sings along with the song.
  naskwahamakew (VTI) S/he sings with other people.
naskwahamâtowin *pl.* **naskwahamâtowina** (NI) The act of joining in the song.
naskwâkan *pl.* **naskwâkana** (NI) A defensive weapon.
naskwâstamâsowin *pl.* **naskwâstamâsowina** (NI) The act of retaliating; retaliation; self-defence.
naskwâw *pl.* **naskwâwak** (VAI) S/he defends herself/himself.
naskwâwin *pl.* **naskwâwina** (NI) The act of defending oneself.
naskwenam (VTI) S/he picks it up along the way.
  naskwenew (VTA) S/he picks them up along the way.
  naskweniwew (VTA) S/he picks up people along the way.

naskwenikew (VTI) S/he picks up things along the way.
naskweskanaw *pl.* **naskweskanawa** (NI) A road that forks off the main road, i.e.: a secondary road. *(Northern). Alt.* **iyitomeskanaw** *(Plains).*
naskwewasimow *pl.* **naskwewasimowak** (VAI) S/he responds or answers.
naskwewasimowin *pl.* **naskwewasimowina** (NI) The act of responding to or answering someone.
naskwewosihew (VAI) S/he made repairs along the way.
  naskwewositâw (VTI) S/he made repairs to it along the way.
  naskwewosihcikew (VTI) S/he made repairs to things along the way.
naskweyasimew (VTA) S/he responds to or answers her/him or them.
  naskweyasihtam (VTI) S/he responds to or answers to it.
  naskweyasimiwew (VTA) S/he responds to or answers to people.
naspacinawew (VTA) S/he sees her/him in the wrong way or manner.
  naspacinakew (VTA) S/he sees people in the wrong way or manner.
naspacinâkosiw *pl.* **naspacinâkosiwak** (VAI) S/he does not look right. *(Northern)*
naspacinâkwan *pl.* **naspacinâkwanwa** (VII) It does not look right. *(Northern)*
naspapamew (VTA) S/he reproduces her/him in her/his mind, i.e.: an artist's subject.
  naspapatam (VTI) S/he reproduces it in her/his mind.
  naspapamiwew (VTA) S/he reproduces people in her/his mind.
  naspapahcikew (VTI) S/he reproduces things in her/his mind.
naspasinahikan *pl.* **naspasinahikana** or **naspasinahikanak** (NA) *or* (NI) A replication.
naspasinahikew *pl.* **naspasinahikewak** (VAI) S/he summarizes the description in writing; s/he reproduces the scene through painting.
naspasinahikewin *pl.* **naspasinahikewina** (NI) The act of summarizing the description in writing; the act of reproducing a scene through painting; art; portray.
naspasinahwew (VTA) S/he draws her/him.
  naspasinaham (VTI) S/he draws it.
  naspasinahowew (VTA) S/he draws someone.
  naspasinahikew (VTI) S/he draws anything.
naspatowewin *pl.* **naspatowewina** (NI) The act of saying the wrong things.
naspâc (IPC) Wrong; or opposite.
naspâcayamihâw *pl.* **naspâcayamihâwak** (VAI) S/he follows the wrong religion; a cult.

naspâcâyamihawin *pl.* **naspâcâyamihawina** (NI) An incorrect religious path.

naspâcipayowin *pl.* **naspâcipayowina** (NI) The act of adversity.

naspâciteyimew (VTA) S/he thinks wrongly of her/him.

naspâciteyitam (VTI) S/he thinks wrongly of it.

naspâciteyimiwew (VTA) S/he thinks wrongly of people.

naspâciteyihcikew (VTI) S/he thinks wrongly of things.

naspâciteyitam *pl.* **naspâciteyitamwak** (VAI) S/he thinks incorrectly. *(Northern). Alt.* **macîteyihtam** *(Plains).*

naspâciteyitamowin *pl.* **naspâciteyitamowina** (NI) The act of thinking incorrectly.

naspâcitotamowin *pl.* **naspâcitotamowina** (NI) The act of doing the wrong thing.

naspâciwepinikewin *pl.* **naspâciwepinikewina** (NI) The act of having a negative attitude; contradictory.

naspâcîteyihcikan *pl.* **naspâcîteyihcikana** (NI) An incorrect thought.

naspâtahew (VTA) S/he puts her/him in the wrong place.

naspâtastâw (VTI) S/he puts it in the wrong place.

naspâtahiwew (VTA) S/he puts people in the wrong place.

naspâtacikew (VTI) S/he puts things in the wrong place.

naspâtapiw *pl.* **naspâtapiwak** (VAI) S/he sat facing the wrong way.

naspâtastew *pl.* **naspâtastewa** (VII) It sits facing the wrong way.

naspâtâpamew (VTA) S/he looks at her/him from the wrong side.

naspâtâpatam (VTI) S/he sees it the wrong way.

naspâtâpamiwew (VTA) S/he sees people the wrong way.

naspâtâpahcikew (VTI) S/he sees things the wrong way.

naspâteyihcikeskiwin *pl.* **naspâteyihcikeskiwina** (NI) Being pessimistic.

naspâtisiw *pl.* **naspâtisiwak** (VAI) S/he is wrong. *(Northern). Alt.* **mâyitôtam** *(Plains).*

naspâtisiwin *pl.* **naspâtisiwina** (NI) The act of being wrong. *(Northern). Alt.* **mâyitôtamowin** *(Plains).*

naspâtowew *pl.* **naspâtowewak** (VAI) S/he is saying the wrong things.

naspicinipiw *pl.* **naspicinipiwak** (VAI) S/he is dead. *(Northern). Alt.* **nipiw; pônipimâtisiw** *(Plains).*

naspisâwâtew (VTA) S/he cuts the model out.

naspisâwâtam (VTI) S/he cuts it out.

naspisâwâsiwew (VTA) S/he cuts everyone's model out.

naspisâwâcikew (VTI) S/he cuts everything's image out.

naspisihcikan *pl.* **naspisihcikana** (NI) An image or representation.

naspisihcikewin *pl.* **naspisihcikewina** (NI) The act of duplicating; duplication.

naspisihew (VTA) S/he made an image or likeness of someone.

naspisitâw (VTI) S/he made an image of it.

naspisihiwew (VTA) S/he makes images of people.

naspisihcikew (VTI) S/he makes images of things.

naspisihisiw *pl.* **naspisihisiwak** (VTA) S/he made an image or likeness of herself/himself.

naspisihisowin *pl.* **naspisihisowina** (NI) The act of making an image or likeness of oneself.

naspitawew (VTA) S/he resembles her/him; s/he looks like her/him.

naspitam (VTI) S/he resembles it.

naspitâkew (VTA) S/he resembles others.

naspitâtowak (VAI) They resemble one another.

naspitâtômakan *pl.* **naspitâtômakanwa** (VII) It resembles something else.

natahohtew *pl.* **natahohtewak** (VAI) S/he walks up stream.

natimihk (IPC) Up stream.

natohtam (VTI) S/he listens to it.

natohwew (VTA) S/he listens to them.

natohtâkew (VTA) S/he listens to people.

natomahcihowin *pl.* **natomahcihowina** (NI) The act of touching; tactility.

natomeskonikewin *pl.* **natomeskonikewina** (NI) Being tactile.

natonam (VTI) S/he searches for it; s/he looks for it.

natowew (VTA) S/he searches for them.

natonâkew (VTA) S/he looks for someone.

natonikewin *pl.* **natonikewina** (NI) The act of searching for something; investigate; the act of prowling around.

natopayistawew (VAI) S/he searches for her/him on horseback or in a car.

natopayistam (VII) S/he searches for it on horseback or in a car.

natopayistâkew (VAI) S/he searches for someone on horseback or in a car.

natotam *pl.* **natotamwak** (VTA) S/he orders or sends for it.

natotamawew (VTA) S/he beseeches them for something.

natotamakew (VTA) S/he beseeches people for something.

natotamâwin *pl.* **natotamâwina** (NI) The act of beseeching or imploring; beggary; importunity.

nawaciw *pl.* **nawaciwa** (VTI) S/he roasts it.

nawacîwin *pl.* **nawacîwina** (NI) The act of roasting something.

nawakikâpawiw *pl.* **nawakikâpawiwak** (VAI) S/he stands bent over.

nawakinew (VTA) S/he bends her/him or them over.
  nawakinam (VTI) S/he bends it over.
  nawakiniwew (VTA) S/he bends people over.

nawakipayiw *pl.* **nawakipayiwa** or **nawakipayiwak** (VII) or (VAI) It or s/he is something soft that doubles over.

nawakiskweyistawew (VTA) S/he bows her/his head at her/him.
  nawakiskweyistam (VTA) S/he bows her/his head.
  nawakiskweyistâkew (VTA) S/he bows her/his head at people.

nawakiskweyiw *pl.* **nawakiskweyiwak** (VAI) Her/his head is bowed.

nawakiskweyiwin *pl.* **nawakiskweyiwina** (NI) The act of bowing the head.

nawakîstawew (VTA) S/he bends over for her/him.
  nawakîstam (VTI) S/he bends over for it.
  nawakîstâkew (VTA) S/he bends over for people.

nawakîw *pl.* **nawakîwak** (VAI) S/he bends over.

nawakîwin *pl.* **nawakîwina** (NI) The act of bending over.

nawasonew (VTA) S/he chooses her/him.
  nawasonam (VTI) S/he chooses it.
  nawasoniwew (VTA) S/he chooses people.
  nawasonikew (VTI) S/he chooses things.

nawasonikewin *pl.* **nawasonikewina** (NI) Having an option.

nawasowâpamew (VTA) S/he chooses her/him by looking at her/him.
  nawasowâpatam (VTI) S/he chooses it by looking at it.
  nawasowâpamiwew (VTA) S/he chooses someone by looking at them.
  nawasowâpahcikew (VTI) S/he chooses things by looking at them.

nawasoyâpamiw *pl.* **nawasoyâpamiwak** (VAI) S/he selects one from a large group.

nawasoyâpamowin *pl.* **nawasoyâpamowina** (NI) The act of selecting one from a large group.

nawasôh (IPC) A choice.

nawaswâtew (VTA) S/he chases after her/him or them.
  nawaswâtam (VTI) S/he chases after It.
  nawaswâsiwew (VTA) S/he chases after people.
  nawaswâhcikew (VTI) S/he chases after things.

nawaswâtitowak (VTA) They chase after each other.

nawaswew *pl.* **nawaswewak** (VTA) S/he chases her/him or them.

nawaswewin *pl.* **nawaswewina** (NI) The act of chasing someone.

nawatahikew *pl.* **nawatahikewa** (VTI) S/he is knocking or shooting at something while it is in mid-flight, i.e.: duck hunting or hitting a baseball.

nawatahikewin *pl.* **nawatahikewina** (NI) The act of knocking or shooting something while it is in mid-flight.

nawatahwew (VTA) S/he knocks or shoots it or them while they were in mid-flight, i.e.: ducks.
  nawataham (VTI) S/he shot it in flight.
  nawatahowew (VTA) S/he shot someone on the go.
  nawatahikew (VTA) S/he shot ducks in flight.

nawatamew (VTA) S/he grabs her/him with her/his teeth when s/he passed by.
  nawatatam (VTI) S/he grabs it with her/his teeth while in mid-air.
  nawatamiwew (VTA) S/he grabs someone with her/his teeth when s/he passed by.
  nawatahcikew (VTI) S/he grabs things with her/his teeth while in mid-air.

nawatinew (VTA) S/he catches it in mid-air, i.e.: a ball; s/he catches a bus.
  nawatinam (VTI) S/he catches it in midair.
  nawatiniwew (VTA) S/he catches someone on the go.
  nawatinikew (VTI) S/he catches something in midair.

nawawew (VTA) S/he chases after her/him in a canoe.
  nawaham (VTI) S/he chases after something by canoe.
  nawahowew (VTA) S/he chases after others by canoe.
  nawahikew (VTA) S/he chases after everyone by canoe.

nawayapiw *pl.* **nawayapiwak** (VAI) S/he sits in the back.

nawayimew (VTA) S/he follows her/him afterwards. *(Plains). Alt.* **nâwayimâtew** *(Northern).*
  nawayitam (VTI) S/he follows the trail afterwards.
  nawayisiwew (VTA) S/he follows others afterward.
  nawayihcikew (VTA) S/he follows everyone afterwards.

nawehpitam (VTI) S/he ties it on a slant.
  nawehpihcikew (VTI) S/he ties everything on a slant.

nawehpitew *pl.* **nawehpitewa** (VII) It is tied on a slant.

nawekapawiw *pl.* **nawekapawiwak** (VAI) S/he stands slumped to one side.

nawemow *pl.* **nawemowak** (VAI) It hangs at an angle.

nawenew (VTA) S/he holds her/him at an angle.
  nawenam (VTI) S/he holds it at an angle.
  nawenikew (VTI) S/he holds things at an angle.

nawepiw *pl.* **nawepiwak** (VAI) S/he sits slumped to one side.

nawesiw *pl.* **nawesiwak** (VAI) It stands at an angle.

naweskisiw *pl.* **naweskisiwak** (VAI) The tree grows at an angle.

naweskitâw *pl.* **naweskitâwa** (VTI) S/he makes it stands off to one side.

naweskitew *pl.* **naweskitewa** (VII) It leans to one side, i.e.: a teepee.

105

naweskweyistawew (VTA) S/he tilts her/his head to one side for her/him.

naweskweyistam (VTA) S/he tilts her/his head to one side for it.

naweskweyistâkew (VTA) S/he tilts her/his head to one side for people.

naweskweyiw *pl.* **naweskweyiwak** (VAI) S/he tilts her/his head to one side.

naweskweyiwin *pl.* **naweskweyiwina** (NI) The act of tilting one's head to one side.

nawestâw (VTI) S/he places it on a slant.

nawehew (VTA) S/he places them on a slant.

nawehcikew (VTI) S/he places things on a slant.

naweyâskohtin *pl.* **naweyâskohtinwa** (VII) It leans to the side.

naweyâskosin *pl.* **naweyâskosinwak** (NI) Leaning sideways.

naweyâskwamiw *pl.* **naweyâskwamiwa** *or* **naweyâskwamiwak** (VII) *or* (VAI) It *or* s/he leans to the side.

naweyâw *pl.* **naweyâwa** (VII) It is built on an angle.

nayahcikan *pl.* **nayahcikana** (NI) A pack sack or back pack.

nayahcikaniwat *pl.* **nayahcikaniwata** (NI) A rucksack.

nayahcikâkan *pl.* **nayahcikâkana** (NI) A packboard.

nayahcikewiyiniw *pl.* **nayahcikewiyiniwak** (NA) A person who packs things on her/his back.

nayahtahâw *pl.* **nayahtahâwak** (VTA) It is loaded on her/him; s/he is accused.

nayahtahew (VTA) S/he makes her/him pack something on her/his back; s/he is blamed for something.

nayahtahâw (VTI) S/he is made to pack something.

nayahtahiwew (VTA) S/he makes people pack something.

nayawiw *pl.* **nayawiwak** (VAI) S/he is out of breath.

nayâwasiw *pl.* **nayâwasiwak** (VTA) S/he carries a baby on her/his back.

nayâwasiwin *pl.* **nayâwasiwina** (NI) The act of carrying a baby on one's back; piggyback.

nayestawihew (VAI) S/he only gets her/him or one.

nayestawitaw (VAI) S/he only gets it.

nayestawihiwew (VAI) S/he only gets one person.

nayestawipayiw *pl.* **nayestawipayiwa** *or* **nayestawipayiwak** (VII) *or* (VAI) It *or* s/he happens just exclusively to her/him; it *or* s/he only happens to her/him.

nayew (VTA) S/he packs her/him on her/his back.

nayahtam (VTI) S/he packs it on her/his back.

nayiwew (VTA) S/he packs someone on her/his back.

nayahcikew (VTI) S/he packs something on her/his back.

nayewac (IPC) Somewhere along the way.

nayewac kîsikâw (IPC) Sometime during the day.

nayihtawiw *pl.* **nayihtawiwak** (VAI) S/he has a difficult or hard time.

nayihtâwan *pl.* **nayihtâwanwa** (VII) It is difficult or hard to do.

nayihtâwewin *pl.* **nayihtâwewina** (NI) The act of having a hard time; difficulty.

ayimisiwin *pl.* **ayimisiwina** (NI) The act of having a hard time; difficulty.

nayihtâweyihtam *pl.* **nayihtâweyihtamwak** (VAI) S/he thinks it is too difficult or it is hard to do.

nayihtâweyihtamihew (VAI) S/he makes her/him think long and hard about someone or something.

nayihtâweyihtamihiwew (VAI) S/he makes people think long and hard about something.

nayihtâweyihtamowin *pl.* **nayihtâweyihtamowina** (NI) The act of thinking of something as being too difficult or hard to do.

nayihtâweyihtâkosiw *pl.* **nayihtâweyihtâkosiwak** (VTA) People think of her/him as being difficult or hard to get along with.

nayihtâweyihtâkwan *pl.* **nayihtâweyihtâkwanwa** (VII) It is thought of as being difficult or hard to understand.

nayihtâweyimew (VTA) S/he thinks of her/him as difficult or hard to get along with; s/he is doubtful of her/him or them; s/he is uncertain of her/him or them.

nayihtâweyitam (VTA) S/he thinks of her/him as difficult or hard to deal with.

nayihtâweyimiwew (VTA) S/he thinks of people as difficult or hard to get along with.

nayihtâweyihcikew (VTI) S/he thinks of things as difficult or hard to get along with.

nayihtâwihew (VTA) S/he makes it difficult or hard for her/him.

nayihtâwitâw (VTI) S/he makes it hard for it to get along.

nayihtâwihiwew (VTA) S/he makes it hard for people to get along.

nayihtâwisihcikew (VTI) S/he makes things hard to take.

nayihtâwihtawew (VTA) S/he finds it difficult or hard to listen to her/him.

nayihtâwihtam (VTI) S/he finds it difficult or hard to listen to something.

nayihtâwihtâkew (VTA) S/he finds it difficult or hard to listen to someone.

nayihtâwinâkosiw *pl.* **nayihtâwinâkosiwak** (VAI) S/he looks difficult, hard, rough.

nayihtâwinâkwan *pl.* **nayihtâwinâkwanwa** (VII) It looks difficult, hard, rough.

nayihtâwipîkiskwew *pl.* **nayihtâwipîkiskwewak** (VAI) S/he speaks with difficulty.

nayihtâwisiw *pl.* **nayihtâwisiwak** (VAI) S/he is difficult to get along with.

nayihtâwisiwin *pl.* **nayihtâwisiwina** (NI) To be difficult or hard to get along with others.

nayimaham (VAI) S/he paddles against the wind.

nayiman (VII) The direction is against the wind.

nayimiskam *pl.* **nayimiskamwak** (VAI) S/he goes against the wind.

nayimohtew *pl.* **nayimohtewak** (VAI) S/he walks against the wind.

nayistaw (IPC) Always; exclusively; continuously; only. *(Northern). Alt.* **neyistaw** *(Plains).*

nâ (IPC) Question marker; is it so?

nâcikewin *pl.* **nâcikewina** (NI) The act of retrieving; retrieval.

nâcimihtew *pl.* **nâcimihtewak** (VAI) S/he gets some wood.

nâcinehamawew (VTA) S/he requests medicine from her/him.

nâcinehamakew (VTA) S/he requests medicine from others.

nâcinehikew *pl.* **nâcinewhikewak** (VAI) S/he makes a request for medicine.

nâciyôscikewin *pl.* **nâciyôscikewina** (NI) The act of sneaking up on someone.

nâciyôstawew (VTA) S/he sneaks up on her/him.

nâciyôstam (VTI) S/he sneaks up on it.

nâciyôstâkew (VTA) S/he sneaks up on someone.

nâha (PR) That one over there.

nâhnakowew *pl.* **nâhnakowewak** (VAI) S/he stutters.

nâhnâway (IPC) An expression indicating "being lined up or being lined up in a row".

nâkasohtamowin *pl.* **nâkasohtamowina** (NI) The act of listening well or carefully; harken.

nâkasohtawew (VTA) S/he listens to her/him very carefully.

nâkasohtam (VTI) S/he listens to it very carefully.

nâkasohtâkew (VTA) S/he listens to people very carefully.

nâkatâpahkcwin *pl.* **nâkatâpahkcwina** (NI) The act of observing an example to follow; observance.

nâkatâpamew (VTA) S/he examines what s/he does with great care; s/he oversees her/him carefully.

nâkatâpatam (VTI) S/he examines what it does with great care.

nâkatâpamiwew (VTA) S/he examines what someone does with great care.

nâkatâpahcikew (VTI) S/he examines what things do with great care.

nâkateyihcikewin *pl.* **nâkateyihcikewina** (NI) The act of scrutinizing; scrutiny; heedful.

nâkateyimew (VTA) S/he takes care of her/him.

nâkateyitam (VTI) S/he takes care of it.

nâkateyimiwew (VTA) S/he takes care of others.

nâkateyihcikew (VTI) S/he takes care of things.

nâkateyimisiw *pl.* **nâkateyimisiwak** (VTA) S/he looks after herself/himself; s/he nurtures herself/himself.

nâkateyimisowin *pl.* **nâkateyimisowina** (NI) The act of looking after oneself; the act of nurturing oneself; self-control.

nâkateyimiwewinihk (IP) In a protecting manner; protectingly.

nâkatohkew *pl.* **nâkatohkewak** (VAI) S/he is respectful; s/he is courteous.

nânapâcihcikewin *pl.* **nânapâcihcikewina** (NI) The act of repairing or cleaning something.

nânapâcihtamawew *pl.* **nânapâcihtamawewak** (VTA) S/he repairs it for her/him.

nânapâcihtâw (VTI) S/he repairs it.

nânapâcihew (VTA) S/he repairs them.

nânapâcihiwew (VTA) S/he repairs people.

nânapâcihcikew (VTI) S/he repairs things.

nânapo (IPC) Both of them.

nânapwahpicikan *pl.* **nânapwahpicikana** (NI) A hobble (for a horse).

nânapwahpitew (VTA) S/he ties her/his legs together.

nânapwahpitam (VTI) S/he ties it or them together.

nânapwahpisiwew (VTA) S/he ties someone's legs together.

nânapwahpihcikew (VTI) S/he hobbles horses.

nânapwekinew (VTA) S/he folds it/them up. *(Plains). Alt.* **oyeyimew.**

nânapwekinam (VTI) S/he folds blankets up.

nânapwekinikew (VTI) S/he folds things up.

nânâmiskwestâkewin *pl.* **nânâmiskwestâkewina** (NI) The act of nodding.

nânâmiskweyiw *pl.* **nânâmiskweyiwak** (VAI) S/he nods her/his head.

nânâmiskweyowin *pl.* **nânâmiskweyowina** (NI) The act of nodding the head.

nânôtchtcw *pl.* **nânôtchtcwa** (VII) There are heat waves. *(Plains). Alt.* **nanahtew** *(Northern).*

nânekâminew (VTA) S/he promotes her/him ahead of everybody.

nânekâminam (VTI) S/he promotes it ahead of everything.

nânekâminiwew (VTA) S/he promotes others ahead of everybody.

nânekâmisiw *pl.* **mânekâmisiwak** (VAI) S/he promotes herself/himself over everyone else.

107

nânekâmisowin *pl.* **nânekâmisowina** (NI) The act of promoting oneself over everyone else.

nânitâw (IPC) About that much; about.

nânôsamâcipayiw *pl.* **nânôsamâcipayiwa** or **nânôsamâcipayiwak** (VII) or (VAI) It or s/he goes to extreme (i.e.: a dog).

nânôsamâciwihew (VTA) S/he makes them go to extremes.

nânôsamâciwitâw (VTI) S/he makes it go to extremes.

nânôsamâciwihiwew (VTA) S/he makes people go to extremes.

nânôsamâciwihcikew (VTI) S/he makes things go to extremes.

nânôsawi (VAI) Following or trailing something.

nâpehkâsowiyiniw *pl.* **nâpihkâsowiyiniwak** (NA) A brave, a warrior.

nâpekohkôs *pl.* **nâpikohkôsak** (NA) A hog; a boar.

nâpemaskwa *pl.* **nâpemaskwak** (NA) A male bear.

nâpemayacikos *pl.* **nâpemayacikosak** (NA) A goat.

nâpemayokwatay *pl.* **nâpemayokwatayak** (NA) A bullfrog.

nâpemek *pl.* **nâpemekwak** (NA) A male fish.

nâpemostos *pl.* **nâpemostoswak** (NA) A bull. *Var.* **îyâpew.**

nâpemow *pl.* **nâpemowak** (VAI) S/he talks like s/he is a man; s/he talks bravely.

nâpeniska *pl.* **nâpeniskak** (NA) A male goose or gander.

nâpepâkahahkwân *pl.* **nâpepâkahahkwânak** (NA) A rooster or male chicken. *Var.* **napemisihew.**

nâpesip *pl.* **nâpesipak** (NA) A male duck or a drake.

nâpesis *pl.* **nâpesisak** (NA) A little boy.

nâpestim *pl.* **nâpestimwak** (NA) A male horse or a stud; stallion.

nâpew (NA) A man. *(Plains). Alt.* **nâpiw** *(Northern).*

nâpewakeyimew (VAI) S/he thinks him to be a good man.

nâpewakeyitam (VAI) S/he thinks like a man.

nâpewakeyimiwew (VAI) S/he thinks of people to be like men.

nâpewakeyimow *pl.* **nâpewakeyimowak** (VTA) S/he thinks of herself/himself as a man.

nâpewâyâw *pl.* **nâpewâyâwak** (NA) S/he feels like a man. (not commonly used)

nâpewewin *pl.* **nâpewewina** (NI) Being male; maleness.

nâpewinâkosiwin *pl.* **nâpewinâkosiwina** (NI) Being manly; manlike.

nâpewiw *pl.* **nâpewiwak** (VAI) He is a man.

nâpew owîtisânimew (VAI) S/he has him as a brother.

nâpihkâsiw *pl.* **nâpihkâsiwak** (VAI) S/he is brave.

nâpihkwân (NI) A ship.

nâpiw (NA) A man. *(Northern). Alt.* **nâpew** *(Plains).*

nâsipehtahew (VTA) S/he takes her/him or them down the hill to the water.

nâsipehtahâw (VTA) S/he is taken down the hill to the water.

nâsipehtahiwew (VTA) S/he takes people down the hill to the water.

nâsipehtacikew (VTA) S/he takes things down the hill to the water.

nâsipemiw *pl.* **nâsipemiwa** (VII) It leads downwards.

nâsipepahtâw *pl.* **nâsipepahtâwak** (VAI) S/he runs towards the water.

nâsipeskanaw *pl.* **nâsipeskanawa** (NI) The road that leads towards the river or water.

nâsipetimihk (LN) On the water's edge.

nâsipew *pl.* **nâsipewak** (VAI) S/he goes down the hill to the water's edge.

nâsipewin *pl.* **nâsipewina** (NI) The act of going down the hill to the water's edge.

nâsiwew *pl.* **nâsiwewak** (VAI) S/he fetches or gets people.

nâspicipikopayiw *pl.* **nâspicipikopayiwak** (VAI) It broke once and for all.

nâspiciteyihcikan *pl.* **nâspiciteyihcikana** (NI) A one-track mind.

nâspiciteyihtam *pl.* **nâspiciteyihtamwak** (VAI) S/he has a one-track mind.

nâspiciteyihtamowin *pl.* **nâspiciteyihtamowina** (NI) The act of having a one-track mind.

nâspiciwiyasowewin *pl.* **nâspiciwiyasowewina** (NI) A ruling from the highest court.

nâspitamiw *pl.* **nâspitamiwak** (VAI) S/he has run away for good or forever.

nâspitawew (VTA) S/he knocks her/him dead.

nâspitaham (VTI) S/he kills it.

nâspitahowew (VTA) S/he kills people.

nâspitahikew (VTA) S/he kills everyone.

nâspitâmowin *pl.* **nâspitâmowina** (NI) The act of running away for good.

nâspitisimew (VTA) S/he kills her/him by throwing her/him.

nâspitititâw (VTI) S/he kills it by throwing.

nâspitisin *pl.* **nâspitisinwak** (VAI) S/he kills herself/himself on impact.

nâspitohtawew (VAI) S/he asks or requests in a ritual manner for a spiritual ceremonial.

nâspitohtam (VAI) S/he asks for help in a native ceremonial.

nâspitohtâkew (VAI) S/he asks for help through a spiritual ceremony.

nâspitôtamowin *pl.* **nâspitôtamowina** (NI) The act of following an example.

nâtaham *pl.* **nâtahamwak** (VAI) S/he paddles up stream.

nâtahohew (VTA) S/he fetches or gets her/him with a canoe.

nâtahotâw (VTI) S/he fetches or gets it with a canoe.

nâtahohiwew (VTA) S/he fetches or gets people with a canoe.

nâtahohcikew (VTI) S/he fetches or gets things with a canoe.

nâtakameyâstan *pl.* **nâtakameyâstanwa** (VII) It is blown towards shore.

nâtakasiw *pl.* **nâtakasiwak** (VAI) S/he wades towards shore.

nâtakâmeham *pl.* **nâtakâmehamwak** (VAI) S/he goes towards shore by swimming or paddling a canoe.

nâtakâmepitew (VTA) S/he pulls her/him toward shore.

nâtakâmepitam (VTI) S/he pulls it towards shore.

nâtakâmepisiwew (VTA) S/he pulls people towards shore.

nâtakâmepihcikew (VTI) S/he pulls things to shore.

nâtakâmeyâsiw *pl.* **nâtakâmeyâsiwak** (VTA) S/he is blown by the wind towards shore.

nâtakwew *pl.* **nâtakwewak** (VAI) S/he goes to get, see or check her/his snares.

nâtamawew (VTA) S/he sides with her/him in a fight.

nâtamakew (VTA) S/he sides with others.

nâtamawew *pl.* **nâtamawewak** *or* **nâtamawewa** (VTA) *or* (VTI) S/he obtains it for her/him; s/he went to get it for her/him; s/he fetches it for her/him.

nâtamâkewin *pl.* **nâtamâkewina** (NI) The act of avenging.

nâtasinahikanewin *pl.* **nâtasinahikanewina** (NI) The act of asking for payment on a bill.

nâtaskew *pl.* **nâtaskewak** (VAI) S/he fetches or goes to get some moss.

nâtaskosiwew *pl.* **nâtaskosiwewak** (VAI) S/he fetches or goes to get some hay.

nâtawihew (VTA) S/he provides the healing medicine for her/him.

nâtawitâw (VTI) S/he provides the healing medicine for it.

nâtawihiwew (VTA) S/he provides the healing medicine for people.

nâtawihcikew (VTA) S/he provides the healing medicine for them.

nâtawihisiw *pl.* **nâtawihisiwak** (VAI) S/he provides healing medicine for herself/himself, i.e.: boil roots.

nâtawihiwewin *pl.* **nâtawihiwewina** (NI) The act of providing healing medicine.

nâtawihow *pl.* **nâtawihowak** (VAI) S/he is taking healing medicine.

nâtawihowin *pl.* **nâtawihowina** (NI) A healing medicine; medicate; remedy.

nâtawihwâkan *pl.* **nâtawihwâkana** (NI) A curative.

nâtawiskâkewin *pl.* **nâtawiskâkewina** (NI) Having an ailment.

nâtayapiw *pl.* **nâtayapiwa** (VTI) S/he visits her/his net; s/he checks her/his net.

nâtayapiwin *pl.* **nâtayapiwina** (NI) The act of visiting or checking nets.

nâtâhwew (VTA) S/he goes towards her/him by swimming or paddling a canoe.

nâtâham (VTI) S/he goes towards it by swimming or paddling a canoe.

nâtâhowew (VTA) S/he goes towards people by swimming or paddling a canoe.

nâtâmototamowin *pl.* **nâtâmototamowina** (NI) The act of looking to someone else for assistance or recourse.

nâtâmototawew (VTA) S/he runs to her/him for assistance; s/he runs to her/him for help; s/he runs to her/him for protection.

nâtâmototam (VTI) S/he goes to it for assistance.

nâtâmototâkew (VTA) S/he goes to people for assistance.

nâtew (VTA) S/he goes and gets her/him.

nâtam (VTI) S/he goes for it.

nâsiwew (VTA) S/he goes for someone.

nâcikew (VTI) S/he goes for things.

nâtiskotawew *pl.* **nâtiskotawewak** (VAI) S/he goes to get some red hot coals for a fire.

nâtitowak (VTA) They walk towards each other.

nâtowatâmew *pl.* **nâtowatâmewak** (VTA) S/he goes for her/him and packs her/him on her/his back.

nâtowatew *pl.* **nâtowatewak** (VAI) S/he goes for it and packs it on her/his back.

nâtôpew *pl.* **nâtôpewak** (VAI) S/he goes to get refreshments, i.e.: pop, etc.

nâtwâham (VTI) S/he breaks it apart with something heavy, i.e.: an axe.

nâtwâhwew (VTA) S/he breaks them apart with something heavy.

nâtwâhikew (VTI) S/he breaks things apart with something heavy.

nâtwâhtin *pl.* **nâtwâhtinwa** (VII) It broke when it fell.

nâtwâpayiw *pl.* **nâtwâpayiwak** (VAI) It broke in half, i.e.: a pencil, a tree.

nâtwâsimew *pl.* **nâtwâsimewak** (VTA) S/he breaks them, i.e.: snowshoes.

nâtwâsin *pl.* **nâtwâsinwak** (VAI) It broke when it fell.

nâtwâskawew (VTA) S/he breaks it with her/his weight, i.e.: a tree.

nâtwâskam (VTI) S/he breaks the stick or pole with her/his weight.

nâtwâtin *pl.* **nâtwâtinwa** (VII) It broke right off, i.e.: a hammer or axe handle. *(Plains). Alt.* **kaskacihtin** *(Northern).*

nâtwâyâsiw *pl.* nâtwâyâsiwak (VAI) It was broken by the
wind, i.e.: a tree.

nâtwâyâskohtin *pl.* nâtwâyâskohtinwa (VII) It lays
broken on the ground, i.e.: a dead tree or pole.

nâtwâyâskosin *pl.* nâtwâyâskosinwak (VAI) It lays
broken on the ground.

nâtwâyâstan *pl.* nâtwâyâstanwa (VII) It breaks from the
wind.

nâway (IPC) Behind; in the back. *(Plains). Alt.* otâhk
(Northern).

nâway pîsim (IPC) Last month. *(Plains). Alt.* otâhk
pîsim *(Northern).*

nâwayikâpawiw *pl.* nâwayikâpawiwak (VAI) S/he stands
in the back of the line.

nâwayimâtam (VTI) S/he follows in the tracks.

nâwayimâsiwew (VTA) S/he follows behind in the
tracks of someone.

nâwayimâhcikew (VTA) S/he follows other people's
tracks.

nâwayimâtew (VTA) S/he follows her/him afterwards.
(Northern). Alt. nawayimew *(Plains).*

nâwayimâtam (VTI) S/he follows the trail afterwards.

nâwayimâsiwew (VTA) S/he follows others afterward.

nâwayimâhcikew (VTA) S/he follows everyone
afterwards.

nâwayimew *pl.* nâwayimewak (VAI) S/he follows
afterwards.

nehcipitew (VTA) S/he pulls her/him down off
something, i.e.: from a shelf.

nehcipitam (VTI) S/he pulls it down.

nehcipisiwew (VTA) S/he pulls someone down.

nehcipihcikew (VTI) S/he pulls things down.

nehcîcâyihk (IPC) Below or going downwards;
downstairs.

nehiyaw *pl.* nehiyawak (NA) An aboriginal person; a
Cree.

nehiyaw cahkipewasinahikewin *pl.* nehiyaw
cahkipewasinahikewina (NI) Syllabic writing.
(Plains). Alt. nehiyawasinahikewin *(Northern).*

nehiyawasinahikâtew *pl.* nehiyawasinahikâtewa (VII) It
is written (in syllabics or Roman orthography).

nehiyawasinahikewin *pl.* nehiyawasinahikewina (NI)
Syllabic writing. *(Northern). Alt.* nehiyaw
cahkipewasinahikewin *(Plains).*

nehiyawaskiy *pl.* nehiyawaskiya (NI) Aboriginal land or
territory; reservation.

nehiyawemow *pl.* nehiyawemowak (VAI) S/he speaks
Cree.

nehiyawemowin *pl.* nehiyawemowina (NI) The act of
speaking Cree. *Var.* nehiyawewin.

nehiyawew *pl.* nehiyawewak (VAI) S/he speaks an
aboriginal language, i.e.: Cree.

nehiyawewin *pl.* nehiyawewina (NI) A Cree language.

nehiyawimasinahikan *pl.* nehiyawimasinahikana (NI) A
Cree book.

nehiyawiskwesis *pl.* nehiyawiskwesisak (NA) A Cree
girl.

nehiyawitôtawew (VTA) S/he treats her/him like an
aboriginal person.

nehiyawitôtam (VTA) S/he acts like an aboriginal
person.

nehiyawitôtâkew (VTA) S/he treats people like
aboriginals.

nehiyâwiw *pl.* nehiyâwiwak (NA) S/he is Cree.

nehîcipayiw *pl.* nehîcipayiwa *or* nehîcipayiwak (VII) *or*
(VAI) It *or* s/he fell off.

nehpemapiw *pl.* nehpemapiwak (VAI) S/he sits
impatient to go.

nehpemascikewin *pl.* nehpemascikewina (NI) The act of
having a predisposition.

nehpemastew *pl.* nehpemastewa (VII) It sits close at
hand.

nehpemew *pl.* nehpemewak (VAI) S/he is ready; s/he is
set to go.

nehpemewin *pl.* nehpemewina (NI) The act of being
ready; the act of being set to go.

neki (PR) Those.

nemah (NA) A gesture of defiance.

nemahpitew *pl.* nemahpitewak (VTA) S/he ties him
loosely; s/he or it is tied loosely; they tie her/him
loosely.

nemakohpew *pl.* nemakohpewak (VAI) S/he takes
blankets or a sleeping bag with her/him.

nemaskisinew *pl.* nemaskisinewak (VAI) S/he takes
footwear with her/him.

nemawin *pl.* nemawina (NI) A lunch or food taken along
for the trip.

nemawinihkew (VAI) S/he makes lunches; s/he makes
provisions; s/he prepares lunches.

nemawinihkawew (VTA) S/he makes lunches for
people.

nemâskohtin *pl.* nemâskohtinwa (VII) It is leaning over
just above the ground; s/he is suspended in mid-air.

nemâskosin *pl.* nemâskosinwak (VAI) S/he is leaning
over just above the ground; it is suspended in mid-
air.

nemâskwawew (VTA) S/he suspends her/him in mid-air
with a pole.

nemâskwaham (VTI) S/he suspends it in midair with a
pole.

nemâskwahikew (VTI) S/he suspends things in midair
with a pole.

nemâskwehew (VTA) S/he gives her/him a weapon to
take along.

nemâskwehiwew (VTA) S/he gives people weapons.

nemâskwew *pl.* **nemâskwewak** (VAI) S/he takes a weapon with her/him.

nemâskwewin *pl.* **nemâskwewina** (NI) Taking a weapon along on a trip.

nemâw *pl.* **nemâwak** (VAI) S/he takes a lunch with her/him.

nemitanaw (IPC) Forty.

nemitanaw ihtasowak (VAI) There are forty of them.

nemitanawâw (IPC) Forty times, fortieth time.

nemow *pl.* **nemowak** (VAI) S/he growls, i.e.: dog.

nemowin *pl.* **nemowina** (NI) The act of growling.

nepepiw *pl.* **nepepiwak** (VAI) S/he stays up late at a wake.

nepewakeyihtâkwan *pl.* **nepewakeyihtâkwanwa** (VII) It is thought of as embarrassing. *Var.* **nîpewakeyihtâkwan.**

nepewakeyimew (VTA) S/he is embarrassed by her/him. *Var.* **nîpewakeyimew.**

nepewakeyitam (VTI) S/he is embarrassed by it.

nepewakeyimiwew (VTA) S/he is embarrassed by people.

nepewakeyihcikew (VTA) S/he is embarrassed by things.

nepewisîstawew (VTA) S/he is embarrassed by her/him.

nepewakeyimiw *pl.* **nepewakeyimiwak** (VAI) S/he is ashamed of herself/himself; embarrassed. *Var.* **nîpewakeyimiw.**

nepewakeyimowin *pl.* **nepewakeyimowina** (NI) The act of being ashamed of oneself. *Var.* **nîpewakeyimowin.**

nepewâkâc (VAI) It is embarrassing. *Var.* **nîpewâkâc.**

nepewâspinew *pl.* **nepewâspinewak** (VAI) S/he has a sickness.

nepewâspinewin *pl.* **nepewâspinewina** (NI) The act of having a sickness.

nepewihew (VTA) S/he makes her/him embarrassed.

nepewihiwew (VTA) S/he makes people embarrassed.

nepewihcikew (VTI) S/he makes it embarrassing for others.

nepewihiwewin *pl.* **nepewihiwewina** (NI) The act of embarrassing someone; the act of making someone ashamed, i.e.: humilation. *Var.* **nîpewihiwewin.**

nepewimew (VTA) S/he embarrasses her/him with her/his words. *Var.* **nîpewimew.**

nepewinakosiw *pl.* **nepewinakosiwak** (VAI) S/he looks shameful in appearance; bashful. *Var.* **nîpewinakosiw.**

nepewinâhtik *pl.* **nepewinâhtikwa** (NI) A bedstead.

nepewinâkwan *pl.* **nepewinâkwanwa** (VII) It is embarrassing. *Var.* **nîpewinâkwan.**

nepewisiw *pl.* **nepewisiwak** (VAI) S/he is shy. *Var.* **nîpewisiw.**

nepewisîstawew (VTA) S/he is ashamed to look at her/him. *Var.* **nîpewisîstawew.**

nepewisîstam (VTI) S/he is ashamed to look at it.

nepewisîstâkew (VTA) S/he is ashamed to look at people.

nepewisowin *pl.* **nepewisowina** (NI) Being shy. *Var.* **nîpewisowin.**

nepewisowinihk (IPC) In a shy manner; shyly. *Var.* **nîpewisowinihk.**

nepewotam (VAI) Her/his description of it is embarrassing. *Var.* **nîpewotam.**

nepewomiwew (VTA) S/he embarrasses people.

nepewosihcikew (VTI) S/he does embarrassing things.

nepihkân *pl.* **nepihkâna** (NI) A flower. *(Plains). Var.* **wâpikwaniy** *(Plains); Alt.* **wapikwanew** *(Northern).*

nepitehew (VTA) S/he places them up all in a row; s/he sets them up all in a row.

nepitestâw (VTI) S/he places something all in a row.

nepitehiwew (VTA) S/he places people in a row.

nepitescikew (VTI) S/he places things all in a row.

nepitesimew (VTA) S/he lays them all in a row.

nepitesitaw (VTI) S/he puts them in a row.

nepitesimiwew (VTA) S/he lays people all in a row.

nepitescikew (VTI) S/he puts things all in a row.

nepitesin *pl.* **nepitesinwak** (VAI) S/he lays in the same row as the group.

nepitetin *pl.* **nepitetinwa** (VII) It fits in the groove.

nepiwahcâw *pl.* **nepiwahcâwa** (VII) The ground is wet. *Var.* **nîpiwahcâw.**

nesowan *pl.* **nesowanwa** (VII) It is fragile.

nesowâtisiw *pl.* **nesowâtisiwak** (VAI) S/he has a fragile constitution; infirmity.

nesowâtisiwin *pl.* **nesowâtisiwina** (NI) Having a fragile constitution; being weak after an illness.

nesowâyâwin *pl.* **nesowâyâwina** (NI) The act of being frail in one's health.

nesoweyimew (VTA) S/he thinks s/he is weak.

nesoweyitam (VTI) S/he thinks it is weak.

nesoweyimiwew (VTA) S/he thinks others or people are weak.

nesoweyihcikew (VTA) S/he thinks everybody is weak.

nesoweyimisiw *pl.* **nesoweyimisiwak** (VAI) S/he finds herself/himself too weak to perform.

nesowihew (VTA) S/he makes her/him weak.

nesowitâw (VTI) S/he makes it weak.

nesowihiwew (VTA) S/he makes someone weak.

nesowicikew (VTI) S/he makes things weak.

nesowinâkohcikew *pl.* **nesowinâkohcikewak** (VAI) Everything s/he does looks frail.

nesowipayiw *pl.* **nesowipayiwak** (VAI) S/he becomes weak.

nesowisiw *pl.* **nesowisiwak** (VAI) Her/his condition is frail.

nesowisiwin *pl.* **nesowisiwina** (NI) Being in a frail condition; debility.

nesowitehew *pl.* **nesowitehewak** (VAI) S/he has a weak heart.

nesowitehewin *pl.* **nesowitehewina** (NI) Having a weak heart.

nestohkwekawiw *pl.* **nestohkwekawiwak** (VAI) S/he is weak from a blood loss.

nestohtew *pl.* **nestohtewak** (VAI) S/he is tired from walking.

nestohtewin *pl.* **nestohtewina** (NI) The act of being tired from walking; scuffed.

nestokayâsâyi *pl.* **nestokayâsâya** (VII) It is antiquated.

nestokâtew *pl.* **nestokâtewak** (VAI) Her/his legs are tired.

nestomahcihow *pl.* **nestomahcihowak** (VAI) S/he feels tired.

nestomahcihowin *pl.* **nestomahcihowina** (NI) The act of feeling weary or tired.

nestopitonew *pl.* **nestopitonewak** (VAI) Her/his arms are tired.

nestosiw *pl.* **nestosiwak** (VAI) S/he is tired.

nestosiwin *pl.* **nestosiwina** (NI) The act of being tired.

nestoyawew *pl.* **nestoyawewak** (VAI) Her/his body is tired.

nestwapinew *pl.* **nestwapinewak** (VTA) S/he is tired of being in pain.

nestwatâmowin *pl.* **nestwatâmowina** (NI) The act of breathing hard, i.e.: puffing.

nestwâkonâmiw *pl.* **nestwâkonâmiwak** (VAI) S/he is tired from running in deep snow.

nestwâsiw *pl.* **nestwâsiwak** (VAI) S/he is tired from being in the sun.

nestwâtakâw *pl.* **nestwâtakâwak** (VAI) S/he is tired from walking in water.

nete (IPC) Over there.

newapiwak (VAI) There are four of them sitting together.

newayak (IPC) Four places or four directions.

newayakisiw *pl.* **newayakisiwak** (VAI) S/he has four personalities.

newâw (IPC) Four times, fourth time.

newâw mitâtahtomitanaw (IPC) Four hundred.

newihew (VTA) S/he makes four of them.

　newitâw (VTI) S/he makes four of it.

　newihiwew (VTA) S/he makes four groups.

　newihcikew (VTI) S/he makes four groups of things.

newo (IPC) Four.

newohsâp (IPC) Fourteen.

newohsoneyas *pl.* **newohsoneyasak** (NA) Four quarters or a dollar.

newokâtew *pl.* **newokâtewak** (NA) A wagon. *(Plains).* *Alt.* **tihtipitapânâsk** *(Plains)*, **tihtipitâpânâsk** *(Northern).*

newo kîsikâw (VII) It is Thursday.

newopehikan *pl.* **newopehikanak** (NA) Four dollars.

newosâpwâw (IPC) Fourteen times, fourteenth time.

newoyâkan *pl.* **newoyâkanwa** (NI) Four servings or platefuls of food.

neyâhtakâw *pl.* **neyâhtakâwa** (NI) Jackpine ridge; a promontory covered with jackpines.

neyâk (IPC) Ahead of time.

neyâpiskâw *pl.* **neyâpiskâwa** (NI) A rocky promontory.

neyâskweyâw *pl.* **neyâskweyâwa** (NI) A wooded promontory.

neyâw *pl.* **neyâwa** (VII) There is a point or a cape. *(Plains).* *Alt.* **miniwatimiwiw** *(Northern).*

neyistaw (IPC) Always; exclusively; continuously; only. *(Plains).* *Alt.* **nayistaw** *(Northern).*

neyometawewak (IPC) A game for four.

nicahkos (NA) Women say "my brother's wife".

nicicim *pl.* **nicicimak** (NA) My grandson or my granddaughter (diminutive). *Var.* **nôsisim.**

niciwam *pl.* **niciwamak** (NA) Brothers say "my brother"; my first cousin, *Var.* **nistes, nimis, nîtim.**

niciwamihkawin *pl.* **niciwamihkawinak** (NA) My stepbrother; my adopted brother.

nicosim *pl.* **nicosimak** (NA) My nephew; my stepson.

nihcikâw *pl.* **nihcikâwa** (NI) A dark outline in the distance.

nihcikisiw *pl.* **nihcikisiwak** (VAI) Her/his outline is in the distance.

nihciwepawew (VTA) S/he knocks her/him down off something.

　nihciwepaham (VTI) S/he knocks it down.

　nihciwepahowew (VTA) S/he knocks someone down.

　nihciwepahikew (VTI) S/he knocks things down.

nihciwepinew (VTA) S/he throws her/him down off something.

　nihciwepinam (VTI) S/he throws it down.

　nihciwepiniwew (VTA) S/he throws people down.

　nihciwepinikew (VTI) S/he throws things down.

nihtaciwepayiw *pl.* **nihtaciwepayiwa** *or* **nihtaciwepayiwak** (VII) *or* (VAI) It *or* s/he falls down the hill or drives down the hill.

nihtaciwew *pl.* **nihtaciwewak** (VAI) S/he goes down, i.e.: a hill or stairway.

nihtaciwewin *pl.* **nihtaciwewina** (NI) The act of going down a hill or stairway.

nihtakosiw *pl.* **nihtakosiwak** (VAI) S/he steps down, i.e.: off something.

nihtakosîwin *pl.* **nihtakosîwina** (NI) The act of dismounting.

nihtâmatin (IPC) Down the hill.

nihtâmâmawâyâwin *pl.* **nihtâmâmawâyâwina** (NI) The act of being together; togetherness.

nihtânikamow *pl.* **nihtânikamowak** (VAI) S/he is a excellent singer.

nihtâpekinew (VTA) S/he lets her/him down with a rope.
　nihtâpekinam (VTI) S/he lets it down with a rope.
　nihtâpekiniwew (VTA) S/he lets people down with a rope.
　nihtâpekinikew (VTI) S/he lets things down with a rope.

nihtâsiw *pl.* **nihtâsiwak** (VAI) It blew off or down, i.e.: diaper off a clothesline.

nihtâstan *pl.* **nihtâstanwa** (VII) It blew off or down, i.e.: a facecloth off a clothesline.

nihtâwasinahikew *pl.* **nihtâwasinahikewak** (VAI) S/he is an excellent writer.

nihtâwew *pl.* **nihtâwewak** (VAI) S/he is an excellent speaker.

nihtâwewekinâwasiw *pl.* **nihtâwewekinâwasiwak** (VAI) S/he is good at wrapping up the baby.

nihtâwewekinâwasiwin *pl.* **nihtâwewekinâwasiwina** (NI) Being good at wrapping up a baby.

nihtâweyihtamowin *pl.* **nihtâweyihtamowina** (NI) The act of having keen insight; acumen; the act of thinking in a rational manner; rationality.

nihtâwihcikewin *pl.* **nihtâwihcikewina** (NI) The act of making crafts; crafty; creation.

nihtâwikihcikan *pl.* **nihtâwikihcikana** (NI) Produce from a good garden.

nihtâwikihcikew *pl.* **nihtâwikihcikewak** (VAI) S/he is planting the garden.

nihtâwikihcikewin *pl.* **nihtâwikihcikewina** (NI) The act of planting a good garden.

nihtâwikihew (VAI) She gives birth.
　nihtâwikitâw (VTI) S/he grows it well.
　nihtâwikihiwew (VTA) S/he grows something.
　nihtâwikihcikew (VTI) S/he grows things well.

nihtâwikiw *pl.* **nihtâwikiwak** (VAI) S/he is born.

nihtâwikiwin *pl.* **nihtâwikiwina** (NI) The act of being born; a birth.

nihtâwisimow *pl.* **nihtâwisimowak** (VAI) S/he is an excellent dancer.

nihtâwosihcikewin *pl.* **nihtâwosihcikewina** (NI) The act of being an expert at making crafts; craftsmanship.

nikamiw *pl.* **nikamiwak** (VAI) S/he sings.

nikamohew *pl.* **nikamohewak** (VTA) S/he makes her/him sing.

nikamon *pl.* **nikamona** (NI) A song. *(Northern). Alt.* **nikamowin** *(Plains).*

nikamostawew (VTA) S/he sings for her/him.
　nikamostam (VTI) S/he sings about it.
　nikamostâkew (VTA) S/he sings for people.

nikamowin *pl.* **nikamowina** (NI) A song; the act of singing. *(Plains). Alt.* **nikamon** *(Northern).*

nikawihkawin *pl.* **nikawihkawinak** (NA) My godmother.

nikâwîs *pl.* **nikâwîsak** (NA) My stepmother.

nikâwiy *pl.* **nikâwiyak** (NA) My mother. *Var.* **nimâmâ.**

nikik *pl.* **nikikwak** (NA) An otter.

nikikowayân *pl.* **nikikowayânak** (NA) An otter skin.

nikomin *pl.* **nikomina** (NI) A wild blueberry.

nikosihsikawin *pl.* **nikosihsikawinak** (NA) My godson.

nikosis *pl.* **nikosisak** (NA) My son; men say "my brother's son". *Var.* **nitôsim.**

nikotwâsikwâw (IPC) Six times, sixth time.

nikotwâsikwâw mitâtahtomitanaw (IPC) Six hundred.

nikotwâsik (IPC) Six.

nikotwâsik kîsikâw (VII) It is Saturday.

nikotwâsomitanaw (IPC) Sixty.

nikotwâsomitanawâw (IPC) Sixty times, sixtieth time.

nikotwâsosâp (IPC) Sixteen.

nikotwâsosâpwaw (IPC) Sixteen times, sixteenth time.

nimâmâ *pl.* **nimâmâsak** (NA) My mother. *Var.* **nikâwiy.**

nimâmâsis *pl.* **nimâmâsisak** (NA) My mother's sister or my maternal aunt.

nimis *pl.* **nimisak** (NA) My older sister; my first cousin, *Var.* **nistes, niciwam, nîtim.**

nimisihkawin *pl.* **nimisihkawinak** (NA) My stepsister.

nimitaham *pl.* **nimitahamwak** (VAI) The bullmoose removes the velvet off its horns by scrapping.

nimitâsipahtâw *pl.* **nimitâsipahtâwak** (VAI) S/he runs out onto the road.

nimitâsipayiw *pl.* **nimitâsipayiwa** *or* **nimitâsipayiwak** (VII) *or* (VAI) It *or* s/he runs out from somewhere into the open, i.e.: horse.

nimitâsiw *pl.* **nimitâsiwak** (VAI) S/he goes out into the open, i.e.: onto a lake or into town.

nimitâw (IPC) Being far out in the water.

nimitâwahamwak (VAI) They are going far out in the water, i.e.: a lake.

nimitâweyâskweyâw *pl.* **nimitâweyâskweyâwa** (VII) A wooded point, i.e.: on a lake.

nimosôm *pl.* **nimosômak** (NA) My grandfather; my grandpa; my grand uncle.

nimosôm nitanskotapan *pl.* **nimosômak nitanskotapanak** (NA) My great-grandfather.

nimosôminan *pl.* **nimosôminanak** (NA) Our grandfather.

ninahâhkisîm *pl.* **ninahâhkisîmak** (NA) My daughter-in-law. *(Plains). Var.* **ninahâkaniskwem.**

ninahâkaniskwem *pl.* **ninahâkaniskwemak** (NA) My daughter-in-law. *Alt.* **ninahâhkisîm** *(Plains).*

ninâpem *pl.* **ninâpemak** (NA) My husband.

113

ninipâsiwin *pl.* **ninipâsiwina** (NI) The act of dozing. *(Northern). Alt.* **nipepayisiwin** *(Plains).*

ninîkihikwak (NA) My parents.

nipahâpakwewin *pl.* **nipahâpakwewina** (NI) The act of dying of thirst.

nipahâpâkwahew (VTA) S/he did not give her/him a drink and s/he is dying of thirst.

nipahâpâkwahiwew (VTA) S/he makes people die of thirst.

nipahâpâkwew *pl.* **nipahâpâkwewak** (VAI) S/he is dying of thirst.

nipahâyâwin *pl.* **nipahâyâwina** (NI) The act of feeling dead tired; lifeless.

nipahew (VTA) S/he killed her/him.

nipatâw (VTI) S/he killed it.

nipahiwew (VTA) S/he kills someone.

nipahcikew (VTI) S/he kills lots of animals.

nipaheyihtam *pl.* **nipaheyihtamwak** (VAI) S/he died of loneliness; s/he pines for someone.

nipaheyihtamowin *pl.* **nipaheyihtamowina** (NI) The act of dying of loneliness.

nipahihkwasiw *pl.* **nipahihkwasiwak** (VAI) S/he is extremely drowsy.

nipahikisâstew (VII) It is sweltering hot.

nipahimiw *pl.* **nipahimiwak** (VAI) S/he cried herself/himself to death.

nipahisimew (VTA) S/he killed him on impact or in a collision.

nipahisimiwew (VTA) S/he killed people on impact or in a collision.

nipahisin *pl.* **nipahisinwak** (VAI) S/he was killed in an accident.

nipahisiw *pl.* **nipahisiwak** (VTA) S/he killed herself/himself.

nipahisiwin *pl.* **nipahisiwina** (NI) The act of killing oneself.

nipahiskawew (VTA) S/he kills her/him by falling on her/him.

nipahiskam (VTI) S/he killed it by falling on it.

nipahiskâkew (VTA) S/he killed people by falling on them.

nipahiskohew (VTA) S/he kills her/him by feeding her/him too much; s/he fed her/him too much and s/he died.

nipahiskohiwew (VTA) S/he kills people by feeding them too much.

nipahiskoyiw *pl.* **nipahiskoyiwak** (VTA) S/he kills herself by overeating; s/he ate herself/himself to death.

nipahitehewin *pl.* **nipahitehewina** (NI) The act of being afraid to act; cowardly.

nipahiwew *pl.* **nipahiwewak** (VTA) S/he murders people.

nipahôsew *pl.* **nipahôsewak** (VTA) She dies while giving birth.

nipahtâkew *pl.* **nipahtâkewak** (VTA) S/he murdered someone.

nipahtâkewin *pl.* **nipahtâkewina** (NI) The act of murdering someone.

nipawiscikewin *pl.* **nipawiscikewina** (NI) The act of enduring or challenging; endurance.

nipâhkwesimowin *pl.* **nipâhkwesimowina** (NI) A trance-inducing ceremonial dance.

nipâpâ *pl.* **nipâpâsak** (NA) My father. *Var.* **nohtâwiy**.

nipâpâsis *pl.* **nipâpâsisak** (NA) My father's brother or my paternal uncle. *Var.* **nôhkomis, nôhcâwîs**.

nipâskiw *pl.* **nipâskiwak** (VAI) S/he likes to sleep.

nipâw *pl.* **nipâwak** (VAI) S/he is sleeping.

nipâwayiwinisa (NI) Bedclothes.

nipâwikamik *pl.* **nipâwikamikwa** (NI) A bedroom.

nipâwin *pl.* **nipâwina** (NI) The act of sleeping.

nipehâw *pl.* **nipehâwak** (VAI) S/he is anaesthetized.

nipehew (VTA) S/he anaesthetizes her/him; s/he makes her/him go to sleep.

nipehiwew (VTA) S/he anaesthetizes people.

nipepayisiwin *pl.* **nipepayisiwina** (NI) The act of dozing. *(Plains). Alt.* **ninipâsiwin** *(Northern).*

nipewâpiy *pl.* **nipewâpiya** (NI) A watery liquid.

nipewâspinew *pl.* **nipewâspinewak** (VAI) S/he has a sleeping sickness.

nipewâspinewin *pl.* **nipewâspinewina** (NI) The act of having sleeping sickness.

nipewin *pl.* **nipewina** (NI) A bed.

nipewinâhtik *pl.* **nipewinâhtikwa** (NI) A bed frame or headboard.

nipewinihkew *pl.* **nipewinihkewak** (VAI) S/he makes a bed.

nipiw *pl.* **nipiwak** (VAI) S/he died or s/he is dead. *(Plains). Alt.* **naspicinipiw** *(Northern),* **pônipimâtisiw** *(Plains).*

nipîhkahtew (VTI) S/he dilutes it.

nipîhkahtam (VTI) S/he dilutes it.

nipîhkahtâkew (VTI) S/he dilutes liquid for people.

nipîhkahcikew (VTI) S/he water things down.

nipîskâw *pl.* **nipîskâwa** (VII) There are water puddles everywhere.

nipîwan *pl.* **nipîwanwa** (VII) It is wetland.

nipîwiw *pl.* **nipîwiwak** (VAI) It is watery.

nipîy (NI) Water; aqua.

nipohkâsototawew (VAI) S/he feints death to people; s/he plays dead to people.

nipohkâsototam (VTA) S/he plays dead to it.

nipohkâsototâkew (VTA) S/he plays dead to someone.

nipowatisiw *pl.* **nipowatisiwak** (VAI) Her/his spirit life is dead.

nipowâyâwin *pl.* **nipowâyâwina** (NI) The act of being inactive or dormant.

nipowin *pl.* **nipowina** (NI) The act of dying.

nipowipayowin *pl.* **nipowipayowina** (NI) The act of being partially paralyzed; paralysis.

nipowisiw *pl.* **nipowisiwak** (VAI) S/he is totally paralyzed. *(Northern). Alt.* **nipômakisiw** *(Plains).*

nipowisiwin *pl.* **nipowisiwina** (NI) The act of being totally paralyzed. *(Northern). Alt.* **nipomakisiwin** *(Plains).*

nipômakisiw *pl.* **nipômakisiwak** (VAI) S/he is totally paralyzed. *(Plains). Alt.* **nipowisiw** *(Northern).*

nipômakisiwin *pl.* **nipômakisiwina** (NI) The act of being totally paralyzed. *(Plains). Alt.* **nipowisiwin** *(Northern).*

nipôstamakewin *pl.* **nipôstamakewina** (NI) The act of willingly dying for a cause; martyrdom.

nisihkâc (IPC) Gradually.

nisihkâcâtisiw *pl.* **nisihkâcâtisiwak** (VAI) S/he acts in a slow and steady manner. *(Northern). Alt.* **peyahtikowisiw** *(Plains).*

nisihkepayiw *pl.* **nisihkepayiwak** (VAI) S/he is cantering, i.e.: a horse.

nisihkepayowin *pl.* **nisihkepayowina** (NI) The act of cantering.

nisikos *pl.* **nisikosak** (NA) My father's sister or my paternal aunt; my mother-in-law.

nisis *pl.* **nisisak** (NA) My mother's brother or my maternal uncle; my father-in-law.

nisîmis *pl.* **nisîmisak** (NA) My younger brother or my sister.

nisitihtamowin *pl.* **nisitihtamowina** (NI) The act of perceiving through the senses; understanding.

nisitohtamohiwewin *pl.* **nisitohtamohiwewina** (NI) The act of clarifying; clarification.

nisitohtâkosiwin *pl.* **nisitohtâkosiwina** (NI) The act of emphasising one's speech to be understood; accent.

niska *pl.* **niskak** (NA) A goose; a Canada goose.

niskasiniy *pl.* **niskasiniya** (NI) A buckshot.

niskimin *pl.* **niskimina** (NI) A high blueberry. *(Northern). Alt.* **iyinimin** *(Plains).*

niskipîsim (NA) March; the goose moon or month.

nistam (IPC) The first time; initially; originally.

nistamahew (VTA) S/he puts her/him first.

nistamastâw (VTI) S/he puts it first.

nistamahiwew (VTA) S/he puts people first.

nistamascikew (VTI) S/he puts things first.

nistaman *pl.* **nistamanwa** (VII) It is first.

nistamapiw *pl.* **nistamapiwak** (VAI) S/he sits first in line.

nistamapiwin *pl.* **nistamapiwina** (NI) The act of sitting first in line.

nistamastew *pl.* **nistamastewa** (VII) It is sitting first in line.

nistamayisiyiniw *pl.* **nistamayisiyiniwak** (IPC) The first person.

nistamohtew *pl.* **nistamohtewak** (VAI) S/he walks first; s/he leads the way.

nistamôkosisan *pl.* **nistamokosisânak** (NA) My first-born son.

nistamôsân *pl.* **nistamôsânak** (NA) My first-born child.

nistamôsâniwiw *pl.* **nistamôsâniwiwak** (VAI) S/he is the first-born child.

nistawâyâw (NA) The Cree name for Fort McMurray meaning "the merging of three rivers."

nistaweyihtâkosiw *pl.* **nistaweyihtâkosiwak** (VAI) S/he is well known.

nistaweyihtâkosiwin *pl.* **nistaweyihtâkosiwina** (NI) The act of making prominent; accentuate.

nistaweyihtâkwan *pl.* **nistaweyihtâkwanwa** (VII) It is well known.

nistaweyimâw *pl.* **nistaweyimâwak** (VAI) S/he is known. *(Plains). Alt.* **kiskeyimâw** *(Northern).*

nistaweyimew (VTA) S/he knows her/him; s/he knows about her/him. *(Plains). Alt.* **kiskeyimew** *(Northern).*

nistaweyitam (VTI) S/he knows; s/he knows about it.

nistaweyimiwew (VTA) S/he knows people; s/he knows about people.

nistaweyihcikew (VTI) S/he knows things; s/he knows about things.

nistawinawew (VTA) S/he recognizes her/him.

nistawinâkew (VTA) S/he recognizes her/him.

nistawinam (VTI) S/he recognizes it.

nistawinâkewin *pl.* **nistawinâkewina** (NI) The act of recognizing; recognition.

nistâpawayisiw *pl.* **nistâpawayisiwak** (VTA) S/he drowned herself/himself.

nistâpawew *pl.* **nistâpawewak** (VAI) S/he drowned.

nistâpawewin *pl.* **nistâpawewina** (NI) The act of drowning.

nistâpâwahew (VTA) S/he drowned her/him.

nistâpâwatâw (VTI) S/he drowned it with water, i.e.: fire.

nistâpâwahiwew (VTA) S/he drowns someone.

nistâseyimew (VAI) S/he senses her/his total personal support.

nistâseyitam (VAI) S/he senses support from it.

nistâseyimiwew (VAI) S/he continously supports people.

nistâseyihcikew (VAI) S/he is aware of continuous strong support.

nistâseyimow *pl.* **nistâseyimowak** (VAI) S/he is aware of being supported.

nistâseyimowin *pl.* **nistâseyimowina** (NI) The act of being aware of being supported.

nistâsiskawew (VTA) S/he gives her/him a supporting feeling.

115

nistâsiskam (VTA) S/he provides others with a sense of support.

nistâsiskâkew (VTA) S/he provides people with a sense of support.

nistes pl. **nistesak** (NA) My older brother; my first cousin, *Var.* **nimis, niciwam, nîtim.**

nistim pl. **nistimak** (NA) My daughter-in-law or my sister's daughter; men say "my sister's daughter"; women say "my brother's daughter".

nistinwaw (VII) There are three of them.

nisto (IPC) Three.

nisto kîsikâw (VII) It is Wednesday.

nistohkamwak (VAI) Three of them are doing it, or working on it.

nistohkawewak (VAI) There are three against her/him.

nistohtam pl. **nistohtamwak** (VAI) S/he understands it.

nistohtamohiwewin pl. **nistohtamohiwewina** (NI) The act of interpreting to gain understanding; interpretation.

nistohtamowin pl. **nistohtamowina** (NI) The act of understanding.

nistohtawew (VTA) S/he understands her/him.
  nistohtam (VTI) S/he understands.
  nistohtâkew (VTA) S/he understands people.

nistohtâkosiw pl. **nistohtâkosiwak** (VAI) S/he is understandable.

nistohtâkwan pl. **nistohtâkwanwa** (VII) It is understandable.

nistokâtew pl. **nistokâtewak** (VAI) S/he is three legged.

nistomitanaw (IPC) Thirty.

nistomitanawâw (IPC) Thirty times, thirtieth time.

nistosâp (IPC) Thirteen.

nistosâpwâw (IPC) Thirteen times, thirteenth time.

nistospitew (VTA) S/he recognises the taste of them.
  nistospitam (VTI) S/he recognises the taste of it.

nistotamohew (VTA) S/he makes her/him understand.
  nistotamotâw (VTI) S/he makes it understandable.
  nistotamohiwew (VTA) S/he makes people understand.

nistoyâkan pl. **nistoyâkanwa** (NI) Three servings or three platefuls of food.

nistôtewak (NA) Three babies; triplets.

nistwahew (VAI) S/he puts them in threes.
  nistwastâw (VTA) S/he puts them in three places.
  nistwahiwew (VTA) S/he puts people by threes.
  nistwasecikew (VTI) S/he puts things by threes.

nistwayak (IPC) In three places.

nistwayakihiw pl. **nistwayakihiwak** (VAI) S/he has three elements to her/his existence.

nistwayakihowin pl. **nistwayakihowina** (NI) The act of being in threes; triples.

nistwayakisi (IPC) In three different ways.

nistwâw (IPC) Three times, third time.

nistwâw kihci mitâtahtomitanaw (IPC) Three thousand.

nistwâw mitâtahtomitanaw (IPC) Three hundred.

nitahtâmowin pl. **nitahtâmowina** (NI) The act of borrowing.

nitanisihkawin pl. **nitanisihkawinak** (NA) My niece; my stepdaughter; my goddaughter.

nitanskotapân pl. **nitanskotapânak** (NA) My great-grandchild, *Var.* **nôsisim**; my great-grandparent.

nitânis pl. **nitânisak** (NA) My daughter.

nitawamiskwew pl. **nitawamiskwewak** (VTA) S/he searches for beaver.

nitawaskewin pl. **nitawaskewina** (NI) The act of exploring for a piece of land; exploration.

nitawaskwew pl. **nitawaskwewak** (VTA) S/he searches for bear.

nitawastimwew pl. **nitawastimwewak** (VTA) S/he searches for horses.

nitawâc (IPC) An expression indicating resentfulness; an expression indicating a total reversal of plans.

nitawâhtâw pl. **nitawâhtâwak** (VTA) S/he searches for something in an optimistic way.

nitawâpamew (VTA) S/he goes to see her/him.
  nitawâpatam (VTI) S/he goes to look at it.
  nitawâpamiwew (VTA) S/he goes to see people.
  nitawâpahcikew (VTI) S/he goes to see things.

nitawâyamihâw pl. **nitawâyamihâwak** (VAI) S/he went to church.

nitawemâw pl. **nitawemâwak** (NA) Brothers say "my sister".

nitaweyihcikewin pl. **nitaweyihcikewina** (NI) The act of needing something; needful.

nitaweyihtamawew (VTA) S/he wants it for her/him.
  nitaweyihtamakew (VTA) S/he wants things for people.
  nitaweyihtamawewak (VTA) They want it for her/him.

nitaweyihtamowin pl. **nitaweyihtamowina** (NI) The act of wanting something.

nitaweyihtestamawew (VTA) S/he wants something for someone else.
  nitaweyihtestamakew (VTA) S/he wants something for other people.

nitaweyimew (VTA) S/he wants her/him.
  nitaweyitam (VTI) S/he wants it.
  nitaweyimiwew (VTA) S/he wants people.
  nitaweyihcikew (VTI) S/he wants things.

nitawikiskeyimew (VTA) S/he studies her/him.
  nitawikiskeyitam (VTI) S/he studies it.
  nitawikiskeyimiwew (VTA) S/he studies people.
  nitawikiskeyihcikew (VTI) S/he studies things.

nitawiminahew (VTA) S/he goes and gives her/him a drink.

116

nitawiminahiwew (VTA) S/he goes and gives people a drink.

nitawiminahiw *pl.* **nitawiminahiwak** (VTA) S/he goes and kills an animal for food, i.e.: moose.

nitawiminahowin *pl.* **nitawiminahowina** (NI) The act of going to kill something, i.e.: a moose.

nitawimîcisiw *pl.* **nitawimîcisiwak** (VAI) S/he went to eat.

nitawimostoswew *pl.* **nitawimostoswewak** (VTA) S/he searches for cattle.

nitawîtew *pl.* **nitawîtewak** (VTA) S/he goes and tells her/him.

nitikwatim *pl.* **nitikwatimak** (NA) Men say "my sister's son"; women say "my brother's son".

nitisaniskwew *pl.* **nitisaniskwewak** (NA) Sisters say "my sister".

nitomiskwewewin *pl.* **nitomiskwewewina** (NI) The act of proposing marriage to someone; a proposal.

nitosis *pl.* **nitosisak** (NA) My aunt; my mother-in-law.

nitôsim *pl.* **nitôsimak** (NA) My nephew; men say "my brother's son", *Var.* **nikosis**; women say "my sister's son"; my stepson.

nitôsimiskwem *pl.* **nitôsimiskwemak** (NA) My stepdaughter; my adopted daughter; men say "my brother's daughter" women say "my sister's daughter".

nitôtem *pl.* **nitôtemak** (NA) My close friend; crony.

nitwahâhcikew *pl.* **nitwahâhcikewa** (VTI) S/he searches for signs or tracks of animals.

nitwakonewew (VAI) S/he makes a hole in the snow for someone. *(Plains). Alt.* **twâkonehwew** *(Northern).*

nitwakoneham (VAI) S/he makes an opening or pathway in the snow.

nitwakonehowew (VAI) S/he makes an opening in the snow for people.

nitwakonehikew (VTI) S/he makes an opening in the snow for things.

niwîkimâkan *pl.* **niwîkimâkanak** (NA) My marriage partner; someone you live with, i.e.: my spouse.

niya (PR) Me; I; mine.

niya wiya (IPC) Just me.

niyakâtôtamân (IPC) There is no legal equivalent in Cree for the terms of "guilty" or "not guilty". For a plea of "guilty", a speaker would use the above expression to indicate "I am responsible for doing it."

niyaman *pl.* **niyamanwa** (VII) It is slight.

niyamâsin *pl.* **niyamâsinwa** (VII) "It is built meagerly." Used when referring to small items, i.e.: a table.

niyamâtan *pl.* **niyamâtanwa** (VII) Used when referring to large items, i.e.: a house, "it is poorly constructed."

niyamâtisiw *pl.* **niyamâtisiwak** (VAI) S/he is a weakling.

niyamâw *pl.* **niyamâwa** (VII) It is tiny and frail, i.e.: a canoe.

niyamisiw *pl.* **niyamisiwak** (VAI) It is poorly built.

nîcakos *pl.* **nîcakosak** (NA) Second cousin, what a woman calls a woman.

nîcimos *pl.* **nîcimosak** (NA) Second cousin, what a man calls a woman or what a woman calls a man. *Var.* **nîtim.**

nîcisân *pl.* **nîcisânak** (NA) My sibling; my sister or brother. *Var.* **nîtisân.**

nîhtinew (VTA) S/he takes her/him down.

nîhtinam (VTI) S/he takes it down.

nîhtiniwew (VTA) S/he takes someone down.

nîhtinikew (VTI) S/he takes things down.

nîkakocin *pl.* **nîkakocinwak** (VAI) S/he is slackening her/his speed, i.e.: a car; s/he is reducing her/his speed.

nîkakotew *pl.* **nîkakotewa** (VII) It its slackening it speed; it is reducing its speed.

nîkamostamakewin *pl.* **nîkamostamakewina** (NI) The act of singing a song for someone, i.e.: a dedication.

nîkanapîhew (VTA) S/he makes her/him sit in front of others; s/he makes her/him boss.

nîkanapîhiwew (VTA) S/he makes someone sit in front of others.

nîkân (IPC) First; ahead; before.

nîkânahâw *pl.* **nîkânahâwak** (VAI) S/he is put ahead or in front.

nîkânamohtâw *pl.* **nîkânamohtâwak** (VAI) S/he places it ahead of others.

nîkânapiw *pl.* **nîkânapiwak** (VAI) S/he sits in the front.

nîkânapiwin *pl.* **nîkânapiwina** (NI) The act of sitting ahead of others; the act of being made a boss; assignment.

nîkânapîhiwewin *pl.* **nîkânapîhiwewina** (NI) The act of giving someone an assignment; assign; constitute.

nîkânapîstawew (VTA) S/he is seated in front of her/him.

nîkânapîstam (VTA) S/he is the head of a certain group.

nîkânapîstâkew (VTA) S/he is ahead of everybody else.

nîkâneyihtâkosiw *pl.* **nîkâneyihtâkosiwak** (VAI) S/he is considered to be more important.

nîkâneyihtâkosiwin *pl.* **nîkâneyihtâkosiwina** (NI) To be considered as being more important.

nîkâneyihtâkwan *pl.* **nîkâneyihtâkwanwa** (VII) It is considered as being more important.

nîkâneyimew (VTA) S/he thinks of her/him ahead or before others.

nîkâneyitam (VTI) S/he thinks of it as being first.

nîkâneyimiwew (VTA) S/he thinks of people first.

nîkâneyihcikew (VTI) S/he thinks of things first.

117

nîkâneyimisiw *pl.* **nîkâneyimisiwak** (VTA) S/he thinks of herself/himself first.

nîkâneyimiw *pl.* **nîkâneyimiwak** (VAI) S/he thinks ahead.

nîkânihew (VTA) S/he puts her/him ahead or in front.

nîkânitâw (VTI) S/he puts it ahead or in front.

nîkânihiwew (VTA) S/he puts someone ahead or in front.

nîkâniascikew (VTI) S/he puts things ahead or in front.

nîkânikât *pl.* **nîkânikâta** (NI) A front leg; a foreleg.

nîkânikiskeyimew (VTA) S/he knows her/him before everyone else.

nîkânikiskeyitam (VTI) S/he knows it before everyone else.

nîkânikiskeyimiwew (VTA) S/he knows people before everyone else.

nîkânikiskeyihcikew (VTI) S/he knows things before everyone else.

nîkânikiskowehikewin *pl.* **nîkânikiskowehikewina** (NI) The act of foretelling the future, i.e.: prophesying.

nîkânipayiw *pl.* **nîkânipayiwa** *or* **nîkânipayiwak** (VII) *or* (VAI) It *or* s/he goes ahead.

nîkânipayîstawew (VTA) S/he rides her/his horse ahead of her/him.

nîkânipayîstakew (VTA) S/he rides ahead of people.

nîkânitisawew (VTA) S/he sends her/him ahead.

nîkânitisaham (VTI) S/he sends it ahead.

nîkânitisahowew (VTA) S/he sends people ahead.

nîkânitisahikew (VTA) S/he sends everyone ahead.

nîkânîsiw *pl.* **nîkânîsiwak** (VAI) S/he is leading by a slim margin.

nîkânîsiwin *pl.* **nîkânîsiwina** (NI) Leading or being ahead by a slim margin.

nîkânîw *pl.* **nîkânîwak** (VAI) S/he is leading.

nîkânîwin *pl.* **nîkânîwina** (NI) Being ahead or being in the lead; excel; leadership; progression; superiority.

nîkânohtew *pl.* **nîkânohtewak** (VAI) S/he walks ahead or in front.

nîkimestinkewin *pl.* **nîkimestinkewina** (NI) The act of reducing costs; retrenchment. *(Northern)*. *Alt.* **mestinikewin** *(Plains)*.

nîkimôsihtâwin *pl.* **nîkimôsihtâwina** (NI) The act of relieving pain; assuage.

nîkinikan *pl.* **nîkinikana** (NI) A unit of construction; a modular piece.

nîkinikewin *pl.* **nîkinkewina** (NI) The act of regulating; modulation.

nîkipayowin *pl.* **nîkipayowina** (NI) The act of becoming less.

nîmâhew (VTA) S/he makes her/him a lunch to take with her/him.

nîmâhiwew (VTI) S/he provided lunch for people.

nîmicîkahikanew *pl.* **nîmicîkahikanewak** (VAI) S/he takes an axe with her/him.

nîmihitow *pl.* **nîmihitowak** (VAI) S/he dances.

nîmihitowikamik *pl.* **nîmihitowikamikwa** (NI) A dance hall.

nîmihitowin *pl.* **nîmihitowina** (NI) A dance.

nîmihitowinihkew *pl.* **nîmihitowinihkewak** (VAI) S/he sponsors a dance; s/he organizes a dance.

nîmihkomânew *pl.* **nîmihkomânewak** (VAI) S/he takes a knife with her/him.

nîpawascikew *pl.* **nîpawascikewak** (VAI) S/he makes things stand up.

nîpawihew (VTA) S/he makes her/him stand.

nîpawihtâw (VTI) S/he makes it stand.

nîpawihiwew (VTA) S/he makes someone stand.

nîpawistawew (VTA) S/he challenges her/him; s/he stands up to her/him.

nîpawistam (VTI) S/he challenges it.

nîpawistâkew (VTA) S/he challenges people.

nîpawiw *pl.* **nîpawiwak** (VAI) S/he stands.

nîpawiwin *pl.* **nîpawiwina** (NI) The act of standing.

nîpâhtew *pl.* **nîpâhtewak** (VAI) S/he walks or travels late into the night.

nîpâhtewin *pl.* **nîpâhtewina** (NI) The act of walking or travelling late into the night.

nîpâtipisk (IPC) During the night.

nîpâwâsakotenikewin *pl.* **nîpâwâsakotenikewina** (NI) Nightlighting.

nîpâyamihâwin *pl.* **nîpâyamihâwina** (NI) Christmas time or Noel; the time of singing yuletide hymns; Midnight mass.

nîpâyamihewisihta *pl.* **nîpâyamihewisihtak** (NA) A Christmas tree.

nîpâyâstew (TII) There is moonlight.

nîpewihew (VTA) S/he embarrasses her/him.

nîpewihiwew (VTA) S/he embarrasses everyone.

nîpihki (IPC) Next summer. *(Plains)*. *Alt.* **nîpihkih** *(Northern)*.

nîpihkih (IPC) Next summer. *(Northern)*. *Alt.* **nîpihki** *(Plains)*.

nîpin *pl.* **nîpinwa** (NI) Summertime.

nîpinapiw *pl.* **nîpinapiwak** (VAI) S/he sits throughout the summer.

nîpinaskamikâw (VAI) The ground is just like it is in summer.

nîpinâyâw (VII) It feels like summer.

nîpiniminân *pl.* **nîpiniminâna** (NI) A cranberry.

nîpinisiw *pl.* **nîpinisiwak** (VTA) S/he stayed all summer.

nîpinohk (IPC) Last summer.

nîpisihkopâw *pl.* **nîpisihkopâwa** (NI) A clump of willows.

nîpisîskâw (NI) A willowy area.

nîpisîy *pl.* **nîpisîya** (NI) A willow.

nîpisîyâhtik *pl.* **nîpisîyâhtikwak** (NA) A willow stick.

nîpîskâw (IPC) The tree is fully leafed out.

nîpîy *pl.* **nîpîya** (NI) A leaf.

nîscas *pl.* **nîscasak** (NA) Second cousin, a man calls a man.

nîso (IPC) Two.

nîso kîskikâw (VII) It is Tuesday.

nîsohew (VTI) S/he makes two out of them.

nîsotâw (VTI) S/he makes two out of something.

nîsohiwew (VTA) S/he makes two out of people.

nîsosihcikew (VTI) S/he makes two out of things.

nîsohkamawew (VTA) S/he helps her/him with something. *(Plains). Var.* **wîcohkamawew.** *Alt.* **ohcikamawew** *(Northern).*

nîsohkamatam (VTI) S/he helps it up.

nîsohkamakew (VTA) S/he helps someone; s/he helps people.

nîsohkamâkewin *pl.* **nîsohkamâkewina** (NI) Being of help to someone; aiding someone; backing; coordination.

nîsohkamâtowak (VTA) They help each other.

nîsohkamâtowin *pl.* **nîsohkamâtowina** (NI) The act of helping one another; succour.

nîsohkamwak (VAI) Two people in a canoe.

nîsohkawew (VAI) S/he takes on two people.

nîsohkam (VTI) S/he takes on two things.

nîsohkâkew (VTA) S/he helps someone else.

nîsohkwâmiwak (VAI) Two of them sleep together.

nîsohtakaw *pl.* **nîsohtakawa** (VII) It has double flooring, i.e.: in a trailer.

nîsokâpawiwak (VAI) Two of them stand together.

nîsopayihcikewin *pl.* **nîsopayihcikewina** (NI) The act of making two things come together; concurrence.

nîsosâp (IPC) Twelve. *Var.* **mitâtaht mîna nîso.**

nîsosâpwâw (IPC) Twelve times, twelfth time.

nîsositew *pl.* **nîsositewak** (VAI) S/he is two footed.

nîsostahwew *pl.* **nîsostahwewak** (VTA) S/he hits both in one shot.

nîsotipiskwew *pl.* **nîsotipiskwewak** (VAI) S/he is gone for two nights.

nîsowak (VAI) There are two of them; the two of them went together.

nîsôskân (NI) Two of a kind.

nîsôskisin *pl.* **nîsôskisinak** (NA) Material for two pairs of moccasins or shoes.

nîsôskwewew *pl.* **nîsôskwewewak** (VAI) He has two wives.

nîsôteskawew *pl.* **nîsôteskawewak** (VAI) S/he is a twin to her/him.

nîsôtew *pl.* **nîsôtewak** (NA) A twin.

nîsôtewiwak (VAI) They are twins.

nîsta (PR) Me too.

nîstanaw (IPC) Twenty.

nîstanowâw (IPC) Twenty times, twentieth time.

nîstâw *pl.* **nîstâwak** (NA) My brother-in-law; men say "my sister's husband".

nîstohew (VTA) S/he makes her/him tired.

nîstohiwew (VTA) S/he tires people out.

nîswahew (VTA) S/he puts the people together in pairs.

nîswastâw (VTI) S/he puts two things together in pairs.

nîswayiwew (VTA) S/he is putting people together in pairs.

nîswascikew (VTI) S/he puts two things together.

nîswamiw *pl.* **nîswamiwa** (VII) It runs parallel, i.e.: trails; doubled.

nîswayak (IPC) In two places or two directions.

nîswayakan *pl.* **nîswayakanwa** (VII) It is divided, a split road.

nîswayakemow *pl.* **nîswayakemowa** (NI) A forked road.

nîswayakisiw *pl.* **nîswayakisiwak** (VAI) S/he has a double personality.

nîswâpiskâw *pl.* **nîswâpiskâwa** (VII) It consists of two pieces of metal, i.e.: a double barreled shotgun.

nîswâw (IPC) Twice, two times, second time.

nîswâw kihci mitâtahtomitanaw (IPC) Two thousand.

nîswâw kisipakihtasowin (IPC) Two million.

nîswâw mitâtahtomitanaw (IPC) Two hundred.

nîswesihcikewin *pl.* **nîswesihcikewina** (NI) The act of agreeing or making a deal, i.e.: by two parties.

nîtawâpamiskwewewin *pl.* **nîtawâpamiskwewewina** (NI) The act of two lovers visiting each other, i.e.: a courtship.

nîtim *pl.* **nîtimak** (NA) My sister-in-law; women say "my sister's husband"; men say "my brother's wife"; my first cousin, *Var.* **nistes, nimis, niciwam;** second cousin, what a man calls a woman or what a woman calls a man, *Var.* **nîcimos.**

nîtisân *pl.* **nîtisânak** (NA) My brother or my sister; sisters say "my brother". *Var.* for my brother, **nîcisân.**

nîwa (NA) My wife. *Var.* **nîwah.**

nîwah (NA) My wife. *Var.* **nîwa.**

nîyanân (PR) We, us.

nîyânan (IPC) Five.

nîyânano kîsikâw (VII) It is Friday.

nîyânanomitanaw (IPC) Fifty.

nîyânanomitanawâw (IPC) Fifty times, fiftieth time.

nîyânanosâp (IPC) Fifteen.

nîyânanosâpwâw (IPC) Fifteen times, fifteenth time.

nîyânanwâw (IPC) Five times, fifth time.

nîyânanwâw mitâtahtomitanâw (IPC) Five hundred.

119

nocihastimwew *pl.* **nocihastimwewak** (VTA) S/he whips her/his dog team or team of horses.

nocihew (VTA) S/he whips her/him; s/he traps for it.

nocitâw (VTI) S/he traps for something.

nocihiwew (VTA) S/he whips people.

nocihcikew (VTI) S/he traps for fur.

nocihiskwewâtew (VTA) He pursues her; he tries to get her for a girlfriend.

nocihiskwewâsiwew (VTA) He tries to make girlfriends.

nocihkawew (VTA) S/he is flirting with her/him, i.e.: someone else's spouse.

nocihkâkew (VTA) S/he flirts with women/men.

nohkôm *pl.* **nohkômak** (NA) My grandmother; my grandma; my granny or my grannie; my great-aunt.

nohkômnan *pl.* **nohkômnanak** (NA) Our grandmother.

nohkôm nitanskotapan *pl.* **nohkômak nitanskotapanak** (NA) My great-grandmother.

nohkwacikew *pl.* **nohkwacikewak** (VAI) S/he licks it, i.e.: a plate.

nohkwâtew (VTA) S/he licks her/him; s/he fawns over her/him.

nohkwâtam (VTI) S/he licks it.

nohkwâsiwew (VTA) S/he licks people.

nohkwâcikew (VTI) S/he licks.

nohtaskoyiw *pl.* **nohtaskoyiwak** (VAI) Her/his appetite is not fulfilled.

nohtâskohew (VTA) S/he underfeeds her/him.

nohtâskohiwew (VTA) S/he underfeeds someone.

nohtâskohewak (VTA) They underfeed her/him or them.

nohtawehkawin *pl.* **nohtawehkawinak** (NA) My godfather

nohtâwew (VTA) Her/his throw or shot falls short of her/him. *(Plains). Alt.* **nohtehwew** *(Northern).*

nohtâham (VTI) Her/his throw or shot falls short of it.

nohtâhowew (VTA) Her/his throw falls short of someone.

nohtâhikew (VTI) Her/his shot or throw falls short of something.

nohtâwiy *pl.* **nohtâwiyak** (NA) My father. *Var.* **nipâpâ**.

nohtehkatehew (VTA) S/he makes her/him go hungry.

nohtehkatehiwew (VTA) S/he can't feed people enough.

nohtehkatew *pl.* **nohtehkatewak** (VAI) S/he is hungry.

nohtehkatewin *pl.* **nohtehkatewina** (NI) The act of being hungry; appetite; starvation.

nohtehkwamiw *pl.* **nohtehkwamiwak** (VAI) S/he had to spend the night short of her/his destination. *(Northern)*

nohtehkwasiw *pl.* **nohtehkwasiwak** (VAI) S/he is sleepy.

nohtehkwasiwin *pl.* **nohtehkwasiwina** (NI) The act of being sleepy.

nohtehkwastimew (VTA) S/he reduces her/his sleeping time.

nohtehkwastimiwew (VTA) S/he reduces their sleeping time.

nohtehwew (VTA) Her/his throw or shot falls short of her/him. *(Northern). Alt.* **nohtâwew** *(Plains).*

nohteham (VTI) Her/his throw or shot falls short of it.

nohtehowew (VTA) Her/his throw falls short of someone.

nohtehikew (VTI) Her/his shot or throw falls short of something.

nohtekweskisâyâwin *pl.* **nohtekweskisâyâwina** (NI) The act of trying to improve someone's manners, ways, lifestyle; ameliorative.

nohtepayiw *pl.* **nohtepayiwa** *or* **nohtepayiwak** (VII) *or* (VAI) It *or* s/he runs short of something, i.e.: money or sugar.

nohtepayiwin *pl.* **nohtepayiwina** (NI) The act of running short of something; lacking; shortage.

nohtesimew (VTA) S/he exhausts her/him; s/he tires her/him out; s/he plays her/him out.

nohtesimiwew (VTA) S/he exhausts people.

nohtesin *pl.* **nohtesinwak** (VAI) S/he is exhausted.

nohteyapâkwewin *pl.* **nohteyapâkwewina** (NI) Dehydration.

nohteyâpakwew *pl.* **nohteyâpakwewak** (VAI) S/he is dehydrated.

nokohtâwin *pl.* **nokohtâwina** (NI) The act of exposing; disclosure or to show something.

nokosestawew (VTA) S/he reveals herself/himself to them.

nokosestam (VTI) S/he reveals herself/himself to it.

nokosestâkew (VTA) S/he reveals herself/himself to people.

nokosistamawew (VII) S/he is representing them. *(Northern). Alt.* **tapapistamawew** *(Plains).*

nokosistamakew (VAI) S/he is representing people.

nokosiw *pl.* **nokosiwak** (VAI) S/he is revealed.

nokosiwin *pl.* **nokosiwina** (NI) The act of being revealed or to make an appearance.

nomehkam (VTI) S/he commences working on it for a while.

nomehiwew (VTA) S/he commences working on people.

nomehkawew *pl.* **nomehkawewak** (VTA) S/he commences working on her/him for a while.

nomih (IPC) A while. *Var.* **nomes**.

nomihew (VTA) S/he commences work on her/him for a while.

nomitâw (VTI) S/he commences working on it for a while.

nomihiwew (VTA) S/he commences working on someone for a while.

nomihcikew (VTI) S/he commences work on things for a while.

nomihkahtawew (VTA) S/he commences whittling on them for a while. *(Plains). Alt.* **nomihkotew** *(Northern).*

nomihkahtatam (VTI) S/he commences whittling on it for a while.

nomihkotew (VTA) S/he commences whittling on them for a while. *(Northern). Alt.* **nomihkahtawew** *(Plains).*

nomihkotam (VTI) S/he commences whittling on it for a while.

nomisîhew (VTA) S/he commences making them for a while and then stops.

nomisîtâw (VTI) S/he commences making it for a while and then stops.

nomisîhcikew (VTI) S/he commences making things for a while and then stops.

nososkawew (VTA) S/he scouts her/him from a safe distance.

nososkam (VTI) S/he scouts it from a safe distance.

nososkâkew (VTA) S/he scouts someone from a safe distance.

nososkâcikew (VTI) S/he scouts things from a safe distance.

notacaskwew *pl.* **notacaskwewak** (VTA) S/he traps muskrat.

notaskinahew (VTA) S/he is full and s/he cannot fit her/him in; s/he has run out of room and cannot fit her/him or them in.

notaskinatâw (VTI) S/he is full and s/he cannot fit it in.

notaskinahiwew (VTA) S/he is full and cannot fit people in.

notaskinahcikew (VTI) S/he is full and cannot fit everything in.

notaskinew *pl.* **notaskinewak** (VAI) There is no room for her/him.

notimâhtik *pl.* **notimâhtikwa** or **notimâhtikwak** (NI) *or* (NA) A round log. *(Northern). Alt.* **wâweyiyahtik** *(Plains).*

notimâpiskisiw *pl.* **notimâpiskisiwak** (VAI) It is rounded, i.e.: a heating stove.

notimâskosiw *pl.* **notimâskosiwak** (VAI) It is round and tall, i.e.: a telephone pole or tree.

notimâskwan *pl.* **notimâskwanwa** (VII) It is round in shape.

notimâw *pl.* **notimâwa** (VII) It is round. *(Northern). Alt.* **wâweyiyâw** *(Plains).*

notimisiw *pl.* **notimisiwak** (VAI) S/he is round in shape.

notokew *pl.* **notokewak** (NA) An old woman. *Var.* **nôtikwew.**

notsipew *pl.* **notspewak** (VAI) S/he hunts for ducks.

nôcihâwasowin *pl.* **nôcihâwasowina** (NI) The act of spanking children.

nôcihcikeskanâw *pl.* **nôcihcikeskanâwa** (NI) A trapline.

nôcihcikew *pl.* **nôcihcikewak** (VAI) S/he is trapping.

nôcihcikewin *pl.* **nôcihcikewina** (NI) Trapping.

nôcihiskwewew *pl.* **nôcihiskwewewak** (VAI) He is sexually involved with a woman.

nôcihiskwewewin *pl.* **nôcihiskwewewina** (NI) The act of being sexually involved with women.

nôcihitowak (VAI) They are mating, i.e.: animals.

nôcikinosewew *pl.* **nôcikinosewewak** (VAI) S/he is fishing; s/he is an angler.

nôcikinosewewin *pl.* **nôcikinosewewina** (NI) The act of fishing.

nôcikwesiw *pl.* **nôcikwesiwak** (NA) An elderly woman or used when referring to one's wife. *(Plains). Alt.* **nôcokwîsiw** *(Northern).*

nôcokwîsiw *pl.* **nôcokwîsiwak** (NA) An elderly woman or used when referring to one's wife. *(Northern). Alt.* **nôcikwesiw** *(Plains).*

nôhawasiw *pl.* **nôhawasiwak** (VAI) She breastfeeds; she nurses.

nôhawasowin *pl.* **nôhawasowina** (NI) The act of breastfeeding.

nôhcâwîs *pl.* **nôhcâwîsak** (NA) My father's brother or my paternal uncle. *Var.* **nôhkomis, nipâpâsis.**

nôhew *pl.* **nôhewak** (VTA) She breastfeeds her/him; she nurses her/him.

nôhkômis *pl.* **nôhkômisak** (NA) My father's brother or my paternal uncle, *Var.* **nipâpâsis, nôhcâwîs;** my stepfather *(Northern).*

nôkohosôstawew (VTA) S/he exposes herself/himself to them.

nôkohosôstam (VTI) S/he exposes herself/himself to it.

nôkohosôstâkew (VTA) S/he exposes herself/himself to someone.

nôkohow *pl.* **nôkohowak** (VAI) S/he is exposed.

nôkotâw (VTI) S/he exposes it.

nôkohew (VTA) S/he exposes them.

nôkohiwew (VTA) S/he exposes someone.

nôkohcikew (VTI) S/he exposes things.

nôkwan (VII) It is revealed.

nôkwanâhtikosiw *pl.* **nôkwanâhtikosiwak** (VAI) Her/his tracks are visible.

nôkwanâtikwan *pl.* **nôkwanâtikwanwa** (VII) It is easy tracking.

nômanak (IPC) A few minutes; in a little while. *Var.* **nomanakes**.

nônâtew (VTA) S/he sucks them.

  nônâtam (VTI) S/he sucks it.

  nônâsiwew (VTA) S/he sucks people.

  nônâhcikew (VTI) S/he sucks something.

nônehew *pl.* **nônehewak** (VTA) She suckles him.

nôniw *pl.* **nôniwak** (VTA) S/he suckles.

nôsamâc (IPC) Overdoing.

nôsamâcihisowin *pl.* **nôsamâcihisowina** (NI) The act of overdoing things.

nôsawih (IPC) Following after.

nôsehaya *pl.* **nôsehayak** (NA) A female of any animal.

nôsekohkôs *pl.* **nôsekohkôsak** (NA) A female pig; a sow.

nôsemahkesîs *pl.* **nôsemahkesîsak** (NA) A female fox; a vixen.

nôsemaskwa *pl.* **nôsemaskwak** (NA) A female bear.

nôsemayatihk *pl.* **nôsemayatihkak** (NA) A female sheep; ewe.

nôsemek *pl.* **nôsemekwak** (NA) A female fish.

nôsemostos *pl.* **nôsemostoswak** (NA) A cow. *(Northern).* *Alt.* **onîcâniw** *(Plains).*

nôseniska *pl.* **nôseniskak** (NA) A female goose.

nôsepahpahahkwân *pl.* **nôsepahpahahkwânak** (NA) A female chicken; a hen.

nôses *pl.* **nôsesak** (NA) A mother moose with offspring; a mother moose with one calf.

nôsesip *pl.* **nôsesipak** (NA) A female duck.

nôsisim *pl.* **nôsisimak** (NA) My grandchild; my granddaughter or my grandson, *Var.* **nicicim** (diminutive); my grandnephew or my grandniece; my great-granddaughter; my great-grandchild, *Var.* **nitanskotapân**.

nôsisim iskwesis *pl.* **nôsisimak iskwesisak** (NA) My granddaughter.

nôsisim nitanskotapan *pl.* **nôsisimak nitanskotapanak** (NA) My great-grandson.

nôsism napesis *pl.* **nôsismak napesisak** (NA) My grandson.

nôtaskwew *pl.* **nôtaskwewak** (VTA) S/he traps bear.

nôtikwewiw *pl.* **nôtikwewak** (VAI) S/he has become an old woman. *(Plains).* *Alt.* **nôtokwewiw** *(Northern).*

nôtimâkan *pl.* **nôtimâkanak** (NA) An opponent.

nôtimew *pl.* **nôtimewak** (VAI) S/he walks on deep snow without snowshoes.

nôtinastimwew *pl.* **nôtimastimwewak** (VAI) S/he fights with her/his horse.

nôtinew (VTA) S/he fights her/him; s/he spars with her/him or them.

  nôtinam (VTI) S/he fights it.

  nôtiniwew (VTA) S/he fights someone.

nôtinicowinis *pl.* **nôtinicowinisa** (NI) A small fight or scuffle; a tustle.

nôtinikakanahtik *pl.* **nôtinikakanahtikwa** (NI) A club with a heavy end; a bludgeon.

nôtinikew *pl.* **nôtinikewak** (VAI) S/he fights.

nôtinikewin *pl.* **nôtinikewina** (NI) A fight; a war; an assault.

nôtinitomâkan *pl.* **nôtinitomâkanak** (NA) Fighting partner; someone to fight with.

nôtinitomew *pl.* **nôtinitomewak** (VTA) S/he fights her/him. *(Northern).* *Alt.* **wîcinôtinitômew** *(Plains).*

nôtinitowak (VAI) They fight each other.

nôtinitowin *pl.* **nôtinitowina** (NI) A fight.

nôtokwewiw *pl.* **nôtokwewiwak** (VAI) S/he has become an old woman. *(Northern).* *Alt.* **nôtikwewiw** *(Plains).*

122

O

ocakosimâw *pl.* **ocakosimâwak** (NA) Sister-in-law. **ocakosiwâwa** (ob.).

ocayapihkes *pl.* **ocayapihkesak** (NA) The bug that makes nets; a spider.

ocayisinâkes *pl.* **ocayisinâkesak** (NA) A monkey. *(Plains). Alt.* **ayisinâkes** *(Northern).*

ocâpâsôwâyis *pl.* **ocâpâsôwâyisak** (NA) A buckboard. *(Northern).*

ocehcekom *pl.* **ocehcekoma** (NI) A wart. *(Northern). Alt.* **micihcîkom** *(Plains).*

ocehcîkomiw *pl.* **ocehcîkomiwak** (VAI) S/he has a wart.

ocehtokîsikâw *pl.* **ocehtokîsikâwa** (NI) The kissing day; New Year's Day.

ocehtowak (VTA) They are kissing.

ocehtowin *pl.* **ocehtowina** (NI) The act of kissing; a kiss.

ocek *pl.* **ocekwak** (NA) A fisher, a carnivorous mammal of the weasel family.

ocemew (VTA) S/he kisses her/him.
　ocetam (VTI) S/he kisses it.
　ocemiwew (VTA) S/he kisses others.
　ocehcikew (VTI) S/he kisses things, i.e.: the Bible, the Cross.

ocemiwew *pl.* **ocemiwewak** (VAI) S/he kisses.

ocepihk *pl.* **ocepihkwa** (NI) A root.

ocepihkiw *pl.* **ocepihkiwak** (VAI) It has a root.

ocepihkowan *pl.* **ocepihkowanwa** (VII) It has roots.

ocesihiwew *pl.* **ocesihiwewak** (NA) A deceiver.

ocesihkwîwin *pl.* **ocesihkwîwina** (NI) The act of having many scars on the face; a scarface. *(Northern). Alt.* **ocikihkwewin** *(Plains).*

ocesisiw *pl.* **ocesisiwak** (VAI) S/he has a scar. *(Northern). Alt.* **ocikisiw** *(Plains).*

ocesisiwin *pl.* **ocesisiwina** (NI) A scar; a pockmark. *(Northern). Alt.* **ocikisiwin** *(Plains).*

ocestatay *pl.* **ocestataya** (NI) A tendon.

ocestatayâply *pl.* **ocestatayâplya** (NI) A ligament. *Var.* **micestatay.**

ocestiw *pl.* **ocestiwak** (VAI) S/he takes one step.

ocicâhk *pl.* **ocicâhkwak** (NA) A crane or a long legged bird.

ocihcikwanipayihowin *pl.* **ocihcikwanipayihowina** (NI) The act of bending down on one knee; genuflection.

ocihcipayiw *pl.* **ocihcipayiwak** (NA) Time commences or starting time.

ocihcipayiwin *pl.* **ocihcipayiwina** (NI) Expired time; event.

ocikihkwew *pl.* **ocikihkwewak** (VAI) S/he has a scar on her/his face.

ocikihkwewin *pl.* **ocikihkwewina** (NI) The act of having many scars; a scarface. *(Plains). Alt.* **ocesihkwîwin** *(Northern).*

ocikisiw *pl.* **ocikisiwak** (VAI) S/he has a scar. *(Plains). Alt.* **ocesisiw** *(Northern).*

ocikisiwin *pl.* **ocikisiwina** (NI) A scar; a pockmark. *(Plains). Alt.* **ocesisiwin** *(Northern).*

ocikwâcikan *pl.* **ocikwâcikana** (NI) A gaff hook.

ocipicikan *pl.* **ocipicikana** (NI) A long pole with a hook to pull something out of the water, i.e.: a dead beaver.

ocipihkwew *pl.* **ocipihkwewak** (VAI) S/he inhales the pipe smoke.
　otamew *pl.* **otamewak** (VAI) S/he inhales the pipe smoke.

ocipitew (VTA) S/he pulls her/him.
　ocipitam (VTI) S/he pulls it.
　ocipisiswew (VTA) S/he pulls people.
　ocipicikew (VTI) S/he pulls things.

ocipitikiw *pl.* **ocipitikiwak** (VAI) S/he has cramps; convulsions.

ocipitikowin *pl.* **ocipitikowina** (NI) The act of cramping; a spasm; convulsion.

ocipwasakayehkasiw *pl.* **ocipwasakayehkasiwak** (VAI) Her/his skin is burned and shrivelled.

ociwama *pl.* **ociwamiwâwa** (ob.) (NA) His stepbrother or his adopted brother.

ociwâmihtowak (VAI) They are cousins.

ociwâmihtowin *pl.* **ociwâmihtowina** (NI) Being cousins; a cousin relationship.

ociwâmihtowinihk (IPC) In a cousinly manner.

ociwâmimâw *pl.* **ociwâmimâwak** (VAI) He is a cousin.

ociwâmiskwemâw *pl.* **ociwâmiskwemâwak** (VAI) She is a cousin.

ocîsihiwew *pl.* **ocîsihiwewak** (NA) One who deceives people by her/his actions.

ocônipes *pl.* **ocônipesak** (NA) A lake herring. *(Plains). Alt.* **otônipiy.** *(Northern).*

ohcekwanapiw *pl.* **ohcekwanapiwak** (VAI) S/he kneels.

ohcekwanapiwin *pl.* **ohcekwanapiwina** (NI) The act of kneeling.

ohcestamawew *pl.* **ohcestamawewak** (VTA) S/he procures it for her/him.

ohcestamâkew *pl.* **ohcestamâkewak** (VTA) S/he procures it for others.

ohcestamâkewin *pl.* **ohcestamâkewina** (NI) The act of procuring something for someone.

123

ohcikamawew (VTA) S/he helps her/him with
  something. *(Northern). Alt.* **wîcohkamawew,
  nîsohkamawew** *(Plains).*
  ohcikamatam (VTI) S/he helps it up.
  ohcikamakew (VTA) S/he helps someone up.
ohcikawâpiw *pl.* ohcikawâpiwak (VAI) S/he sheds tears.
ohcikawiw *pl.* ohcikawiwa (VII) It leaks, i.e.: a roof.
ohcikwanapîstawew (VTA) S/he kneels before or in front
  of her/him.
  ohcikwanapîstawewtam (VTI) S/he kneels in front of
    it.
  ohcikwanapîstawewtâkew (VTA) S/he kneels in front
    of people.
ohcinatew (VTA) S/he contends against her/him for it.
  ohcinataw (VTA) Someone contends her/him for it.
  ohcinasiwew (VTA) S/he contends against someone
    else for it.
ohcinew *pl.* ohcinewak (VAI) S/he suffers from her/his
  ridicule; s/he affects her/him negatively.
ohcinewin *pl.* ohcinewina (NI) A suffering caused by
  ridicule.
ohcipayihew (VTA) S/he makes her/him come from a
  different direction. *(Northern)*
  ohcipayitâw (VTI) S/he makes it come from a different
    direction.
  ohcipayihiwew (VTA) S/he makes someone come
    from a different direction.
  ohcipayihcikew (VTI) S/he makes things come from a
    different direction.
ohcipayiw *pl.* ohcipayiwak (VAI) S/he comes from that
  direction.
ohciskâw *pl.* ohciskâwa (VII) It shoots accurately over
  long distances, i.e.: a gun.
ohcistikosiw *pl.* ohcistikosiwak (VAI) The spruce tree
  provides shelter from rain.
ohcistikwan *pl.* ohcistikwanwah (VAI) There is shelter
  out of the elements, i.e.: a bus shelter.
ohcistin *pl.* ohcistinwa (VII) It leaks, i.e.: a canoe.
ohcitaw (IPC) On purpose; planned or according to plan;
  consequently.
ohciyawesiw *pl.* ohciyawesiwak (VAI) S/he is angry over
  something.
ohcîwin *pl.* ohcîwina (NI) The origin.
ohkoma (ob.) (NA) Her or his grandmother.
ohkomimâw *pl.* ohkomimâwak (NA) A grandmother.
ohkomisimâw *pl.* ohkomisimâwak (NA) A stepfather.
  (Northern). Alt. **ohtâwihkawin** *(Plains).*
ohkomiwâwa (ob.) (NA) Their grandmother.
ohpahikew *pl.* ohpahikewak (VAI) S/he jacks it up.
ohpahopîsim (NA) August; the flying moon or month
  (Plains). Alt. **ohpahowipîsim** *(Northern).*

ohpahow *pl.* ohpahowak (VAI) S/he flies away, i.e.: like a
  bird.
ohpahowipîsim (NA) August; the flying moon or month
  (Northern). Alt. **ohpahopîsim** *(Plains).*
ohpahpekipicikan *pl.* ohpahpekipicikana (NI) A crane or
  a machine for lifting.
ohpahpekipitew (VTA) S/he lifts her/him up with rope or
  cable.
  ohpahpekipitam (VTI) S/he lifts it up with a rope or
    cable.
  ohpahpekipisiwew (VTA) S/he lifts people up with a
    rope or cable.
  ohpahpekipihcikew (VTI) S/he lifts things up with a
    rope or cable.
ohpahpitew (VTA) S/he ties them up in an upright
  position.
  ohpahpitam (VTI) S/he ties it up in an upright
    postition.
  ohpahpisiwew (VTA) S/he ties someone up in an
    upright position.
  ohpahpihcikew (VTI) S/he ties things up in an upright
    position.
ohpanahpinew *pl.* ohpanahpinewak (VAI) S/he has
  tuberculosis.
ohpanahpinewin (NI) The lung disease tuberculosis;
  bilious.
ohpawew (VTA) S/he jacks them up.
  ohpaham (VTI) S/he jacks it up.
  ohpahowew (VTA) S/he jacks people up.
  ohpahikew (VTI) S/he jacks things up.
ohpâsiw *pl.* ohpâsiwak (VAI) S/he is blown up in the air.
ohpâsiwin *pl.* ohpâsiwina (NI) The act of elevating.
ohpâskwahikewin *pl.* ohpâskwahikewina (NI) The act of
  lifting something up by force; hoisting.
ohpâskwawew (VTA) S/he lifts her/him up with a stick
  or pole.
  ohpâskwaham (VTI) S/he lifts it up with a pole.
  ohpâskwahowew (VTA) S/he lifts people up with a
    pole.
  ohpâskwahikew (VTI) S/he lifts things up with a pole.
ohpâskweyâw *pl.* ohpâskweyâwak (VAI) The trees stand
  upright on the face of the mountain.
ohpâstan *pl.* ohpâstanwa (VII) It is blown upwards.
ohpihkasikan *pl.* ohpihkasikana (NI) Baking powder.
ohpikihâwasiw *pl.* ohpikihâwasiwak (VAI) S/he raises
  children.
ohpikihâwasiwin *pl.* ohpikihâwasiwina (NI) The raising
  of children; procreation.
ohpikihew (VTA) S/he raises her/him.
  ohpikitâw (VTI) S/he raises it; he grows it.
  ohpikihiwew (VTA) S/he raises someone.

ohpikihcikew (VTI) S/he raises things; s/he grows things.

ohpikow *pl.* **ohpikowak** (VAI) S/he grows up. (NA) It grows, i.e.: carrot

ohpikowin *pl.* **ohpikowina** (NI) The act of growing up.

ohpime (IPC) Some other place; away; out of here.

ohpimepayiw *pl.* **ohpimepayiwa** *or* **ohpimepayiwak** (VII) *or* (VAI) It *or* s/he moves to another place.

ohpinamawew (VTA) S/he lifts it up for her/him.
　ohpinamâkew (VTI) S/he lifts it for someone.

ohpinew (VTA) S/he lifts her/him up.
　ohpinam (VTI) S/he lifts it up.
　ohpiniwew (VTA) S/he lifts people up.
　ohpinikew (VTI) S/he lifts things up.

ohpiniskeyiw *pl.* **ohpiniskeyiwak** (VTA) S/he lifts her/his arm up.

ohpipayiw *pl.* **ohpipayiwa** *or* **ohpipayiwak** (VII) *or* (VAI) It *or* s/he rises up.

ohpiskâw *pl.* **ohpiskâwak** (VAI) S/he rises up in the air.

ohpiskâwikîsikâw *pl.* **ohpiskâwikîsikâwa** (NI) Ascension Day, the Christian celebration of Christ's resurrection and ascension to heaven.

ohpiskweyiw *pl.* **ohpiskweyiwak** (VTA) S/he lifts her/his head.

ohpiw *pl.* **ohpiwak** (VAI) S/he jumps up.

ohpwepitew *pl.* **ohpwepitewak** (VTA) S/he stirs up a hornet nest.

ohtacihew (VTA) S/he provides sustenance for her/him.
　ohtacitâw (VTI) S/he provides something for it.
　ohtacihiwew (VTA) S/he supports sustenance for people.

ohtacihow *pl.* **ohtacihowak** (VAI) S/he sustains herself/himself by that means.

ohtahipew *pl.* **ohtahipewak** (VAI) S/he draws water from here.

ohtâsiw *pl.* **ohtâsiwak** (VAI) S/he is blown from that side.

ohtâstan *pl.* **ohtâstanwa** (VII) It is blown from that side.

ohtâwihkawew *pl.* **ohtâwihkawewak** (VTA) He becomes her/his father.

ohtâwihkawin *pl.* **ohtâwihkawinak** (NA) A godfather (*Northern*); a stepfather (*Plains*). *Alt.* **ohkomisimâw** (*Northern*).

ohtâwiskâkew *pl.* **ohtâwiskâkewak** (VAI) He is a father of people.

ohtâwiskakam *pl.* **ohtâwiskakamak** (VAI) He is a father to it.

ohtâwiskawew *pl.* **ohtâwiskawewak** (VAI) He is her/his surrogate father.

ohtâwîmâw *pl.* **ohtâwîmâwak** (NA) A father. *Var.* **opâpâmâw**.

ohtew *pl.* **ohtewa** (VII) It is boiling.

ohteyimew (VTA) S/he is at enmity with her/him.
　ohteyitam (VTI) S/he is at enmity because of it.
　ohteyimiwew (VTA) S/he is at enmity with someone else.
　ohteyihcikew (VTI) S/he is at enmity because of things.

ohtinamakewin *pl.* **ohtinamakewina** (NI) The act of providing; provided.

ohtiskawikapawistawew (VTA) S/he stands facing her/him; s/he stands face to face with her/him; s/he stands face to face with her/him.
　ohtiskawikapawistam (VTI) S/he stands facing it.
　ohtiskawikapawistakew (VTA) S/he stands facing people.

okahtam *pl.* **okahtamwak** (VTA) S/he sucks it out, i.e.: smoke from a pipe.

okakeskimiwew *pl.* **okakeskimiwewak** (NA) A preacher. *Var.* **okakeskihkemow**.

okakwâtakihiwew *pl.* **okakwâtakihiwewak** (NA) A tormenter; one who torments others.

okanawastimwew *pl.* **okanawastimwewak** (NA) A horse guard; one who looks after horses.

okanawâpahkew *pl.* **okanawâpahkewak** (NA) A bystander; onlooker; one who is an onlooker; a fan.

okanawepisiskiwew *pl.* **okanawepisiskiwewak** (NA) An animal sentry; one who looks after animals.

okanaweyihcikew *pl.* **okanaweyihcikewak** (NA) A keeper or game warden; one who looks after game; a security.

okanaweyimâwasiw *pl.* **okanaweyimâwasiwak** (NA) A babysitter; one who looks after children.

okanawiskwahtawin *pl.* **okanawiskwahtawinak** (NA) A guard or doorkeeper. (*Plains*)

okanawitipiskew *pl.* **okanawitipiskewak** (VAI) S/he guards at night; s/he is a night watchman.

okanâcihcikew *pl.* **okanâcihcikewak** (NA) A cleaner or janitor; one who cleans up.

okanowiskwahtawiw *pl.* **okanowiskwahtawiwak** (NA) A porter; one who looks after the door.

okaskâpasikew *pl.* **okaskâpasikewak** (NA) A smoker; one who makes a smudge.

okawisa *pl.* **okawisiwâwa** (ob.) (NA) Their stepmother.

okâminakasiy *pl.* **okâminakasiyak** (NA) A Canada thistle; a thorn, i.e., from a rose bush. *Var.* **kakasisiwat**.

okâminakasiyaw (VII) It is thorny.

okâminakasiyiwit (VAI) It is a thorny plant. *Alt.* **kokaminakasiwit** (*Northern*).

okâminakasîwâhtik *pl.* **okâminakasîwâhtikwak** (NA) The Alberta rose bush; buckthorn.

okâsakiwiyiniw *pl.* **okâsakiwiyiniwak** (NA) A greedy person.

125

okâskipâsiwew *pl.* **okâskipâsiwewak** (NA) A barber; one who shaves people.

okâw *pl.* **okâwak** (NA) A pickerel.

okâwiyak *pl.* **okâwiyakak** (NA) A porcupine quill. *(Plains)*

okâwîmâw *pl.* **okâwîmâwak** (NA) A mother (generic).

okâwîmew *pl.* **okâwîmewak** (VTA) S/he has her as a mother. *Var.* **omâmâmew.**

okâwîmiwew *pl.* **okâwîmiwewak** (VAI) S/he has someone as a mother.

okâwiw *pl.* **okâwiwak** (VAI) S/he has a mother. *(Plains).* *Alt.* **omâmâw** *(Northern).*

okâyawisiw *pl.* **okâyawisiwak** (NA) An industrious worker. *(Plains).*

okihcinisk *pl.* **okihciniskiwâwa** (NI) Her/his right hand; their right hands.

okihcitâwihiwewin *pl.* **okihcitâwihiwewina** (NI) The act of bestowing.

okikacimewak (NA) A family of 10-15 beaver.

okimahkaniwiwin *pl.* **okimahkaniwiwina** (NI) The act of being a chief; a chieftainship.

okimahkân *pl.* **okimahkânak** (NA) A leader of a clan or tribe, i.e.: a chief.

okimahkânihkew *pl.* **okimahkânihkewak** (VTA) S/he makes her/him chief.

okimaweyihtâkosiw *pl.* **okimaweyihtâkosiwak** (VAI) S/he is thought to be worthy of being boss.

okimâskwiw *pl.* **okimâskwiwak** (NA) The boss's wife; she is the boss's wife; a queen.

okimâw *pl.* **okimâwak** (NA) A leader on a job site, i.e.: a boss; government leader, manager.

okimâwahiwewin *pl.* **okimâwahiwewina** (NI) The act of giving someone authority to act or lead.

okimâwakeyimisowin *pl.* **okimâwakeyimisowina** (NI) The act of thinking of oneself as being an authoritative figure or a chief.

okimâwapiwin *pl.* **okimâwapiwina** (NI) Being in authority.

okimâwastotin *pl.* **okimâwastotina** (NI) A boss's hat; a crown; chief's war bonnet.

okimâweyimew (VTA) S/he thinks of her/him as the boss.

  okimâweyitam (VTI) S/he thinks of it as a king.

  okimâweyimiwew (VTA) S/he thinks of people as kings.

okimâwikamik *pl.* **okimâwikamikwa** (NI) The boss's house; government building.

okimâwikosisan *pl.* **okimâwikosisanak** (NA) The boss's son.

okimâwiw *pl.* **okimâwiwak** (VAI) S/he is boss.

okimâwiwin *pl.* **okimâwiwina** (NI) The act of being boss; government worker.

okimotiw *pl.* **okimotiwak** (NA) A robber; swagger.

okiniwâhtik *pl.* **okiniwâhtikwak** (NA) A rosehip bush.

okiniy *pl.* **okiniyak** (NA) A rosehip; a tomato.

okinomwacayeses *pl.* **okinomwacayesesak** (NA) A three-year-old bull moose.

okipahowew *pl.* **okipahowewak** (NA) A prison guard; one who is on guard.

okisewâtisiw *pl.* **okisewâtisiwak** (NA) A kind-hearted person; one who is kind-hearted.

okisikow *pl.* **okisikowak** (NA) An angel.

okiskinohamâkew *pl.* **okiskinohamâkewak** (NA) A teacher; an educator; one who teaches. *Var.* **okiskinwahamakew.**

okiskinohtahiwew *pl.* **okiskinohtahiwewak** (NA) A guide; one who guides.

okiskinwahamakew *pl.* **okiskinwahamakewak** (NA) A teacher; an educator; one who teaches. *Var.* **okiskinohamâkew.**

okiskinwahamâkosiw *pl.* **okiskinwahamâkosiwak** (NA) One who goes to school.

okiskinwâhamawâkan *pl.* **okiskinwâhamawâkanak** (VAI) S/he is his/her student.

  okiskinwâkanimawew (VAI) One who teaches someone.

okiskinwâhamâwâkan *pl.* **okiskinwâhamâwâkanak** (NA) One who studies.

okiskowehikew *pl.* **okiskowehikewak** (NA) A seer; one who foretells.

okisowâhiwew *pl.* **okisowâhiwewak** (NA) An antagonist; an offender; one who causes other people to become angry.

okisôtotâkew *pl.* **okisôtotâkewak** (NA) An agitator; one who instigates action.

okistakew ayisiyiniwak (NA) Numerous people in a group.

okistakeweyatowak (VAI) They are numerous. *(Northern).* *Alt.* **mihcetiwak** *(Plains).*

okistakewi (IPC) Numerous. *(Northern).* *Alt.* **mihcet** *(Plains).*

okistatowân *pl.* **okistatowânak** (NA) A very large, old bear; a grizzly bear. *Var.* **mistahaya.**

okitimâkinâkew *pl.* **okitimâkinâkewak** (NA) A sympathizer; one who feels sorry for others.

okitimâkisiw *pl.* **okitimâkisiwak** (NA) A poor person; one who is poor.

okitohcikew *pl.* **okitohcikewak** (NA) A person who plays music, i.e.: on a stereo or an instrument; one who plays music.

okîsikosis *pl.* **okîsikosisak** (NA) A cherub.

okîskwepew *pl.* **okîskwepewak** (NA) A drunk person; a person who is continually drunk.

okîskwow *pl.* **okîskwowak** (NA) A crazy, wild, insane person.

okocihtâwiyiniw *pl.* **okocihtâwiyiniwak** (NA) An adventurer.

okosâpahcikew *pl.* **okosâpahcikewak** (NA) A conjurer; a shaman.

okosimâw *pl.* **okosimâwak** (NA) A son.

okosisihkâw (VTA) S/he adopts him as a son. *(Plains).* *Alt.* **okosisimew** *(Northern);* s/he sponsors him as godson.

okosisimew (VTA) S/he adopt him as a son. *(Northern).* *Alt.* **okosisihkâw** *(Plains).*

okosisimiwew (VTA) S/he adopts others as sons.

okôkiw *pl.* **okôkiwak** (NA) An diver; one who dives.

okômâw *pl.* **okômâwak** (NA) A great-grandmother. *Var.* **otanskotapew.**

okwaskwepayihos *pl.* **okwaskwepayihosak** (NA) A flea.

okwayaskwahiwew *pl.* **okwayaskwahiwewak** (NA) A disciplinarian; one who keeps people in order.

okwayaskwascikew *pl.* **okwayaskwascikewak** (NA) An adjuster or adjustor; one who puts things in order.

okwâtakihiwew *pl.* **okwâtakihiwewak** (NA) An oppressor; one who abuses other people.

omacipayihcikew *pl.* **omacipayihcikewak** (NA) An instigator; one who starts things.

omacipayihtâw *pl.* **omacipayihtâwak** (NA) An instigator.

omakohkew *pl.* **omakohkewak** (NA) A muscle. *(Plains).* *Alt.* **micistatayâpiy** *(Northern).*

omamâhtâwisiw *pl.* **omamâhtâwisiwak** (NA) A mystic; one who is able to perform mysterious acts.

omanisikew *pl.* **omanisikewak** (NA) A carver; one who cuts things up.

omanitomow *pl.* **omanitomowak** (VTA) S/he idolizes her/him.

omanitoweyihcikew *pl.* **omanitoweyihcikewak** (NA) An idolator; one who worships gods.

omasinahikesîs *pl.* **omasinahikesîsak** (NA) A secretary.

omasinahikesîsiwiw *pl.* **omasinahikesîsiwiwak** (VAI) S/he is a secretary.

omasinahikew *pl.* **omasinahikewak** (NA) A writer.

omaskahtwew *pl.* **omaskahtwewak** (NA) An ouster; one who takes things away from others.

omaskawisiwiyiniw *pl.* **omaskawisiwiyiniwak** (NA) A muscular or strong man. *(Plains).* *Alt.* **sohkâpew** *(Northern).*

omawinehikew *pl.* **omawinehikewak** (NA) A contestant; one who challenges.

omawineskâkew *pl.* **omawineskâkewak** (NA) An aggressor; one who is aggressive.

omâciw *pl.* **omâciwak** (NA) A hunter; a big game hunter.

omâmaskâsiwew *pl.* **omâmaskâsiwewak** (NA) An alarmist; one who becomes over-excited unnecessarily.

omâmâmew *pl.* **omâmâmewak** (VTA) S/he has her as a mother. *Var.* **okâwîmew.**

omâmâw *pl.* **omâmâwak** (VAI) S/he has a mother. *(Northern).* *Alt.* **okâwiw** *(Plains).*

omâmâwaw *pl.* **omâmâwawak** (NA) A mother. *Var.* **okâwîmâw.**

omâmihkwew *pl.* **omâmihkwewak** (NA) A woman from down the river, i.e.: a Stoney woman.

omâtiw *pl.* **omâtiwak** (NA) A weeper; one who cries.

omâw *pl.* **omâwak** (NA) The stomach of a cow or moose; tripe.

omâwasakonikew *pl.* **omâwasakonikewak** (NA) An accumulator; one who gather things.

omâyipayihcikew *pl.* **omâyipayihcikewak** (NA) A controversialist; one who provokes an argument.

omekinawew *pl.* **omekinawewak** (VAI) One who shares food.

omekiw *pl.* **omekiwak** (NA) An almsgiver; a contributor; one who gives or donates.

ometawestamâkew *pl.* **ometawestamâkewak** (NA) An entertainer; one who entertains others.

ometawew *pl.* **ometawewak** (NA) A bowler; a juggler; a player; one who plays.

omikiy *pl.* **omikiya** (NI) A crusted sore; a scab.

omikîw *pl.* **omikîwak** (VAI) S/he has scabs.

omikîwâspinewin *pl.* **omikîwâspinewina** (NI) Leprosy; impetigo.

omikîwin *pl.* **omikîwina** (NI) Having sores.

ominahiwew *pl.* **ominahiwewak** (NA) A bartender; one who serves drinks.

ominihkwewâspinew *pl.* **ominihkwewâspinewak** (NA) An alcoholic; one who drinks to excess.

omisahkomew *pl.* **omisahkomewak** (VAI) S/he has her as an older sister. *(Plains).* *Alt.* **omisimiw** *(Northern).*

omisihkemow *pl.* **omisihkemowak** (NA) A stool pigeon. *Var.* **omisimiwew.**

omisimâw *pl.* **omisimâwak** (NA) The eldest sister.

omisimâwiw *pl.* **omisimâwiwak** (VAI) She is the eldest sister.

omisimiw *pl.* **omisimiwak** (VAI) S/he has her as an older sister. *(Northern).* *Alt.* **omisahkomew** *(Plains).*

omisiwanâcicikew *pl.* **omisiwanâcicikewak** (NA) A spoiler; one who spoils everything.

omiweyihtamohiwew *pl.* **omiweyihtamohiwewak** (NA) A charmer; one who makes another person like her/him.

omiyawâtamôhiwew *pl.* **omiyawâtamôhiwewak** (NA) A pleaser or delighter; one who delights others.

omiyotinikew *pl.* **omiyotinikewak** (NA) An acceptor; one who tolerates things.

omiyowâpahkew *pl.* **omiyowâpahkewak** (NA) An admirer; one who admires. *(Northern). Alt.* **otakâwâcikew** *(Plains).*

omîcaskosîs *pl.* **omîcaskosîsak** (NA) A barn swallow.

omîcowiniw *pl.* **omîcowiniwak** (VAI) S/he has food.

omohtewihkwewin *pl.* **omohtewihkwewina** (NI) Having pimples on the face.

omoscikwâsôw *pl.* **omoscikwâsôwak** (NA) A sewer; a tailor; one who sews by hand.

omôsahkinikew *pl.* **omôsahkinikewak** (NA) A picker; one who picks things up by rummaging.

omôsihtawin *pl.* **omôsihtawina** (NI) A state indicating that something feels sensual.

omosôma (ob.) (NA) Her or his grandfather.

omosômâw *pl.* **omosômâwak** (NA) A great-grandfather; a great-uncle. *Var.* **otanskotapew.**

omosômimâw *pl.* **omosômimâwak** (NA) A grandfather; a grandpa.

omosômiwâwa (ob.) (NA) Their grandfather.

onahascikew *pl.* **onahascikewak** (NA) A preserver; one who perserves food.

onahâhkisîmâw *pl.* **onahâhkisîmâwak** (NA) A son-in-law.

onakiniwew *pl.* **onakiniwewak** (NA) An inhibitor; one who impedes action.

onanatohkonikew *pl.* **onanatahkonikewak** (NA) A performer of feats; one who performs numerous feats.

onanâtohkonikew *pl.* **onanâtohkonikewak** (NA) A clumsy person. *(Plains). Alt.* **yikicik** *(Northern).*

onanihkihiwew *pl.* **onanihkihiwewak** (NA) A hastener; one who is always hurrying others.

onanweyacimiwew *pl.* **onanweyacimiwewak** (NA) A twit; one who makes annoying jokes.

onapatehkâpipayihiw *pl.* **onapatehkâpipayihiwak** (NA) A winker; one who winks.

onaspasinahikew *pl.* **onaspasinahikewak** (NA) An artist. *(Northern). Alt.* **otâpasinahikew** *(Plains).*

onatahisipewatim *pl.* **onatahisipewatimwak** (NA) A retriever.

onatonikew *pl.* **onatonikewak** (NA) A tracer; one who tracks down game and people.

onatowew *pl.* **onatowewak** (NA) An Iroquois; one who is Iroquois.

onawasônikew *pl.* **onawasônikewak** (NA) A selector; one who makes the choice.

onawaswew *pl.* **onawaswewak** (NA) A chaser; one who chases.

onayahcikew *pl.* **onayahcikewak** (NA) A carrier; one who carries packs; one who packs or carries her/him or it on his/her shoulders; the name for the Carrier people. *(Plains). Alt.* **onîkâtew** *(Northern).*

onâcikew *pl.* **onâcikewak** (NA) A delivery person; one who delivers items; a fetcher.

onâkateyihcikew *pl.* **onâkateyihcikewak** (NA) An overseer; one who oversees activities.

onâkateyimiwew *pl.* **onâkateyimiwewak** (NA) A protector; one who is a guard.

onâpehkâsowiyinîs *pl.* **onâpehkâsowiyinîsak** (NA) A young brave or warrior, i.e.: used when referring to a younger person.

onâpemiw *pl.* **onâpemiwak** (VAI) She has a husband.

onâtamâkew *pl.* **onâtamâkewak** (NA) A defender; an errand boy.

onekihikiw *pl.* **onekihikiwak** (VAI) S/he has parents.

onekihikomâw *pl.* **onekihikomâwak** (NA) A parent. *(Northern). Alt.* **onîkihikomâw** *(Plains)*; a great-grandparent. *Var.* **otanskotapew.**

onekihikomâwiwin *pl.* **onekihikomâwiwina** (NI) Being a parent; parenthood.

onekihikow *pl.* **onekihikowak** (VAI) S/he has parents.

onîkihikomâw *pl.* **onîkihikomâwak** (NA) A parent. *(Plains). Alt.* **onekihikomâw** (NA) *(Northern).*

onihcikiskwapiwin (NI) The Cree name for the Reserve of Saddle Lake, meaning "a mirage".

onihtâwasinahikew *pl.* **onihtâwasinahikewak** (NA) An artist; one who draws well.

onikewin *pl.* **onikewina** (NI) A portage; (NA) a boat dock. *(Northern). Alt.* **kapâwin** *(Plains).*

onikohtew *pl.* **onikohtewak** (NA) A woodcutter; one who chops wood.

onipahtâkew *pl.* **onipahtâkewak** (NA) A murderer; a killer.

onitawaskiwiyiniw *pl.* **onitawaskiwiyiniwak** (NA) An explorer of land; one who explores.

onitawâpenikew *pl.* **onitawâpenikewak** (NA) An inspector; a viewer; one who inspects. *(Plains). Alt.* **owâpahcikew** *(Northern).*

onîcaniw *pl.* **onîcaniwak** (NA) A dry cow, i.e.: used when referring to a female moose.

onîcaniwmôswa *pl.* **onîcaniwmôswak** (NA) A female moose.

onîcâniw *pl.* **onîcâniwak** (NA) A cow. *(Plains). Alt.* **nôsemostos** *(Northern).*

onîkânapîhiwew *pl.* **onîkânapîhiwewak** (NA) An assigner; one who provides tasks to be completed.

onîkânîw *pl.* **onîkânîwak** (NA) A chieftain; a headman; one who leads; a leader.

onîkânohtâkew *pl.* **onîkânohtâkewak** (NA) A pathfinder; one who leads others.

onîkâtew *pl.* **onîkâtewak** (VTA) S/he packs or carries her/him or it on his/her shoulders; (NA) the name for the Carrier people. *(Northern). Alt.* **onayahcikew** *(Plains).*

onîkew *pl.* **onîkewak** (VTA) S/he packs or carries on her/his shoulders. *(Northern)*

onîsohkamâkew *pl.* **onîsohkamâkewak** (NA) A helper; a supporter; one who provides aid.

onîswaskomew onîswaskomewak (NA) A mother moose with two calves.

onocayikowiw *pl.* **onocayikowiwak** (NA) A bird of prey, i.e.: a falcon. *(Northern)*. *Alt.* **onôtayikowew** *(Plains)*.

onocipewayisisowew *pl.* **onocipewayisisowewak** (NA) A sparrow hawk. *(Northern)*. *Alt.* **onocipiyesiwew** *(Plains)*.

onocipiyesiwew *pl.* **onocipiyesiwewak** (NA) A sparrow hawk. *(Plains)*. *Alt.* **onocipewayisisowew** *(Northern)*.

onôcâpakosîsiwew *pl.* **onôcâpakosîsiwewak** (NA) A mouser; one who hunts mice.

onôcihcikew *pl.* **onôcihcikewak** (NA) A trapper; one who works a trapline.

onôcihitowipîsim (NA) September; the mating moon or month.

onôtayikowew *pl.* **onôtayikowewak** (NA) A bird of prey, i.e.: a falcon. *(Plains)*. *Alt.* **onocayikowiw** *(Northern)*.

opacawanisîs *pl.* **opacawanisîsak** (NA) A one-year old bear.

opahkonikew *pl.* **opahkonikewak** (NA) A skinner; one who skins animals.

opakahamâw *pl.* **opakahamâwak** (NA) A drummer; one who beats the drum.

opakitawâw *pl.* **opakitawâwak** (NA) A fisherman. *Var.* **pakitawâwiyiniw**.

opakiteyihcikew *pl.* **opakiteyihcikewak** (NA) An abstainer; one who abstains.

opaminikew *pl.* **opaminikewak** (NA) A controller; one who directs a plan.

opapâmohcicikew *pl.* **opapâmohcicikewak** (NA) A carter; one who peddles goods.

opapâmohtew *pl.* **opapâmohtewak** (NA) A traveller.

opapâmpiciw *pl.* **opapâmpiciwak** (NA) A voyager; a transient, a nomad.

opasihkwetahikew *pl.* **opasihkwetahikewak** (NA) A smacker; one who slaps faces.

opaskîyâkew *pl.* **opaskîyâkewak** (NA) A winner; one who wins.

opaskowipîsim (NA) July; the moulting moon or month.

opaspiw *pl.* **opaspiwak** (NA) A survivor; one who survives an accident.

opâhpâhkwecakahikesîs *pl.* **opâhpâhkwecakahikesîsak** (NA) A large woodpecker. *(Plains)*. *Alt.* **misipahpahscîs** *(Northern)*.

opâpâmâw *pl.* **opâpâmâwak** (NA) A father. *Var.* **ohtâwîmâw**.

opâskahopîsim (NA) June; the egg-hatching moon or month *(Plains)*. *Alt.* **opâskâwewowipîsim** *(Northern)*; **opâskâwehopîsim** *(Northern)*.

opâskâwehopîsim (NA) June; the egg hatching moon or month *(Northern)*. *Var.* **opâskâwewowipîsim** *(Northern)*. *Alt.* **opâskahopîsim** *(Plains)*.

opâskâwewowipîsim (NA) June; the egg hatching moon or month *(Northern)*. *Var.* **opâskâwehopîsim** *(Northern)*. *Alt.* **opâskahopîsim** *(Plains)*.

opâskisikew *pl.* **opâskisikewak** (NA) A gunman; one who fires guns.

opâspaskow *pl.* **opâspaskowak** (NA) A quail.

opâstâhow *pl.* **opâstâhowak** (NA) A transgressor; one who commits sin.

opeyakôskânesiw *pl.* **opeyakôskânesiwak** (NA) A tribesman.

opeyakweyimisiw *pl.* **opeyakweyimisiwak** (NA) An individualist; one who thinks of herself/himself as being unique.

opikihitowin *pl.* **opikihitowina** (NI) Being generative.

opimâcihiwew *pl.* **opimâcihiwewak** (NA) A lifesaver; one who saves lives; a saviour; a provider; Christ.

opimihâw *pl.* **opimihâwak** (NA) A pilot. *(Plains)*. *Alt.* **opimiyaw** *(Northern)*.

opimipayihcikew *pl.* **opimipayihcikewak** (NA) A dominator; one who runs people or things.

opimitisahikew *pl.* **opimitisahikewak** (NA) An adherent; one who likes to follow others.

opimiyaw *pl.* **opimiyawak** (NA) A pilot. *(Northern)*. *Alt.* **opimihâw** *(Plains)*.

opimohtahiwew *pl.* **opimohtahiwewak** (NA) A driver, conductor, or chauffeur; one who drives.

opimotahkwew *pl.* **opimotahkwewak** (NA) An archer; one who shoots arrows.

opiniyâwewipîsim (NA) May; the egg laying moon or month. *(Plains)*. *Alt.* **sâkipakâwipîsim** *(Northern)*. *Var.* **apiniyâwepîsim**.

opiwayâyi *pl.* **opiwayâyiya** (NI) Something that is feathery or fuzzy.

opîkiskwestamâkew (NA) Someone who speaks for others, i.e.: a spokesperson or lawyer; counsel; orator; one who speaks on the behalf of others.

opîscîwâcikwasow *pl.* **opîscîwâcikwasowak** (NA) A meadowlark. *(Plains)*. *Alt.* **wasepescan** *(Northern)*.

opîtatowemow *pl.* **opîtatowemowak** (VAI) S/he speaks in Ukrainian.

opîtatowew *pl.* **opîtatowewak** (NA) A Ukrainian person.

opîtatowewiwin *pl.* **opîtatowewiwina** (NI) Being a Ukrainian.

opîway *pl.* **opîwaya** (NI) A piece of body hair.

opîwâwin *pl.* **opîwâwina** (NI) Pubic hair. *(Northern). Alt.* **miyacowân** *(Plains)*.

oposiw *pl.* **oposiwak** (NA) A passenger.

opwâmowiyâs *pl.* **opwâmowiyâsa** (NI) Thigh meat; loin.

osahikew *pl.* **osahikewak** (VTA) S/he scares the game away.

osahwew (VTI) S/he scares it.

osahikew (VTI) S/he scares everything away.

osakihiwew *pl.* **osakihiwewak** (NA) An adorer; one who loves others.

osameyimew (VTA) S/he is exasperated by her/him.

osameyitam (VTI) S/he is exasperated by it.

osameyimiwew (VTA) S/he is exasperated by people.

osameyihcikew (VTI) S/he is exasperated by things.

osamipew *pl.* **osamipewak** (VAI) S/he drinks to excess.

osâkaskinahtamohiwew *pl.* **osâkaskinahtamohiwewak** (NA) An applicant; one who fills out applications.

osâkocihiwew *pl.* **osâkocihiwewak** (NA) A conqueror; one who conquers.

osâkoteyimowew *pl.* **osâkoteyimowewak** (NA) A bewitcher; one who hexes other people.

osâm apisis (IPC) Too little.

osâm mihcet (IPC) Too many.

osâm mistahi (IPC) Too much.

osâmahkamik (IPC) Too many or an excessive amount.

osâmahkamikan *pl.* **osâmahkamikanwa** (VII) There is a lot of trouble.

osâmahkamikisiw *pl.* **osâmahkamikisiwak** (VAI) S/he makes too much fuss; s/he acts too much.

osâmeweyihtamohiwewin *pl.* **osâmeweyihtamohiwewina** (NI) The act of being overwhelmed; overwhelming.

osâmeyatin *pl.* **osâmeyatinwa** (VII) It is abundant.

osâmeyatiw *pl.* **osâmeyatiwak** (VAI) S/he is one too many.

osâmeyihtam *pl.* **osâmeyihtamwak** (VAI) S/he thinks in desperation.

osâmeyihtamowin *pl.* **osâmeyihtamowina** (NI) The act of thinking in desperation.

osâmeyihtâkwan *pl.* **osâmeyihtâkwanwa** (VII) It is despairing.

osâmihew (VTA) S/he overworks her/him.

osâmitâw (VTI) S/he overworks it.

osâmihiwew (VTA) S/he overworks people.

osâmihcikew (VTI) S/he overworks things.

osâmihisiw *pl.* **osâmihisiwak** (VTA) S/he overworks herself/himself.

osâmihisiwin *pl.* **osâmihisiwina** (NI) Excessiveness; the act of overworking oneself.

osâmihowin *pl.* **osâmihowina** (NI) The act of overworking herself/himself.

osâmimew (VTA) S/he exaggerates her/his speech about her/him.

osâmimiwew (VTA) S/he exaggerates her/his talk about people.

osâmihcikew (VTI) S/he exaggerates about everything.

osâmipayiw *pl.* **osâmipayiwa** *or* **osâmipayiwakak** (VII) *or* (VAI) It *or* s/he goes too far; it *or* s/he is extreme.

osâmiskoyiw *pl.* **osâmiskoyiwak** (VAI) S/he overeats and is sick.

osâmitonew *pl.* **osâmitonewak** (VAI) S/he is a chatterer.

osâmitonewin *pl.* **osâmitonewina** (NI) The act of being a chatterer.

osâmitôn *pl.* **osâmitônak** (NA) A chatter-box.

osâmpoko (IPC) Mainly; principally; chiefly; generally.

osâpohtew *pl.* **osâpnohtewak** (NA) A passerby; s/he walks right by.

osâwahkesîs *pl.* **osâwahkesîsak** (NA) A red fox.

osâwask *pl.* **osâwaskwak** (NA) A brown bear.

osâwaskopiyesîs *pl.* **osâwaskopiyesîsak** (NA) A yellow warbler. *(Plains). Alt.* **osâwaskopîwâyisis** *(Northern)*.

osâwaskopîwâyisis *pl.* **osâwaskopîwâyisisak** (NA) A yellow warbler. *(Northern). Alt.* **osâwaskopiyesîs** *(Plains)*.

osâwaskwan *pl.* **osâwaskwanwa** (VII) The pole has a yellow color.

osâwaskwâw (VII) The sky is yellow.

osâwâpân (NI) S/he is phlegmatic.

osâwâpew *pl.* **osâwâpewak** (VAI) S/he has phlegm.

osâwâpisk *pl.* **osâwâpiskwak** (NA) A penny.

osâwâpiskâw *pl.* **osâwâpiskâwa** (VII) It is yellow iron.

osâwâpiskisiw *pl.* **osâwâpiskisiwak** (VAI) The iron is yellow.

osâwâpîwâyisis *pl.* **osâwâpîwâyisisak** (NA) A goldfinch.

osâwâpoy *pl.* **osâwâpo ya** (NI) A yellow liquid, i.e.: lemonade.

osâwâs *pl.* **osâwâsak** (NA) An orange fruit.

osâwâsa *pl.* **osâwâsak** (NA) An orange.

osâwâskotew *pl.* **osâwâskotewak** (VAI) It shines a yellow color.

osâwâw *pl.* **osâwâwa** (VII) It is yellow or orange.

osâwekan *pl.* **osâwekanwa** (VII) The cloth is yellow.

osâwekin *pl.* **osâwekinwa** (NI) Yellow cloth.

osâwipahkwesikan *pl.* **osâwipahkwesikanak** (NA) A loaf of brown bread.

osâwisiw *pl.* **osâwisiwak** (VAI) It is orange in color.

osâwisoniyawiw *pl.* **osâwisoniyawiwa** (VII) It has the color of gold; it is golden.

osâwisowin *pl.* **osâwisowina** (NI) Being yellow in color.

osâwisôniyâw *pl.* **osâwisôniyâwak** (NA) Gold or gold nugget.

oseskamikâw *pl.* **oseskamikâwa** (VII) It is elevated ground, i.e.: foothills.

osetinâw *pl.* **osetinâwa** (VII) It is an elevated hillside, i.e.: a knoll.

oseyâpiskâw *pl.* **oseyâpiskâwa** (NI) A rocky outcrop in the hillside.

oseyâw *pl.* **oseyâwa** (VII) It is raised ground.

osihcâw *pl.* **osihcâwa** (NI) A long ridge of ground.

osihcikan *pl.* **osihcikana** *or* **osihcikanak** (NI) *or* (NA) A homemade item.

osihcikew *pl.* **osihcikewak** (VAI) S/he makes or constructs something.

osihcikewin *pl.* **osihcikewina** (NI) The act of making something; build; construction; contrive; development; production.

osihew (VTA) S/he makes them.

  ositâw (VTI) S/he makes it.

  osihiwew (VTA) S/he makes people.

  osihcikew (VTI) S/he makes things.

osihkihpimiw *pl.* **osihkihpimiwak** (VAI) S/he has a boil.

osihkiskâkew *pl.* **osihkiskâkewak** (NA) A tempter; s/he tempts people.

osihomakan *pl.* **osihomakanwa** (VII) It builds up by itself, a storm; self developing.

osihtamawew (VTI) S/he makes it for her/him.

  osihtamakew (VTI) S/he makes it for people.

osikiyâs *pl.* **osikiyâsak** (NA) A lizard.

osikohew (VTA) S/he causes her to have a still born baby.

  osikohiwew (VTA) S/he causes people to have still born babies.

osikohow *pl.* **osikohowak** (VTA) She has a still born baby.

osikohowin *pl.* **osikohowina** (NI) The act of having a still born baby.

osikosimâw *pl.* **osikosimâwak** (NA) A mother-in-law; a paternal aunt.

osikosimew (VTA) S/he makes her miscarry by means of a car crash.

  osikosimiwew (VTA) S/he made people miscarry by means of car crashes.

osikosin *pl.* **osikosinwak** (VAI) She miscarries after falling.

osikosiw *pl.* **osikosiwak** (VAI) S/he has a mother-in-law.

osikotatahikew *pl.* **osikotatahikewak** (NA) An assailant; s/he assaults unsuspecting victims.

osikow *pl.* **osikowak** (VTA) She causes her own miscarriage.

osikowin *pl.* **osikowina** (NI) The act of miscarrying.

osikwanay *pl.* **osikwanaya** (NI) A fish tail. *(Plains). Alt.* **osikwanâs** *(Northern).*

osikwanâs *pl.* **osikwanâsa** (NI) A fish tail. *(Northern). Alt.* **osikwanay** *(Plains).*

osimisk *pl.* **osimiskwa** (NI) A leaf bud.

osipwepayihcikew *pl.* **osipwepayihcikewak** (NA) An activator; s/he initiates things.

osisimâw *pl.* **osisimâwak** (NA) A father-in-law.

osisimâwiw *pl.* **osisimâwiwak** (VAI) He is a father-in-law.

osisiw *pl.* **osisiwak** (VAI) S/he has a father-in-law.

osiskawew (VTA) S/he scares her/him away.

  osiskahcikew (VTA) S/he scares something away.

osisopekahikew *pl.* **osisopekahikewak** (NA) A painter; one who paints. *(Plains). Alt.* **osopîkahikiw** *(Northern).*

osîkinikew *pl.* **osîkinikewak** (NA) A barkeeper; s/he fills glasses.

osîmimâw *pl.* **osîmimâwak** (NA) A younger sibling; younger brother or younger sister.

osîmimâwiw *pl.* **osîmimâwiwak** (VAI) S/he is the youngest sibling of the family.

osîsâwew *pl.* **osîsâwewak** (NA) An acrobat; one who practices and builds up her/his muscles.

oskac (IPC) At first; firstly; first.

oskakocin *pl.* **oskakocinwak** (VAI) It is a new moon.

oskakotew *pl.* **oskakotewa** (VII) It is newly hung.

oskan *pl.* **oskana** (NI) A bone.

oskanaskosiy *pl.* **oskanaskosiya** (NI) Brome grass or bone grass.

oskanipimiy *pl.* **oskanipimiya** (NI) Bone marrow or grease.

oskaniwiw *pl.* **oskaniwiwak** (VAI) S/he is bony.

oskasâkay *pl.* **oskasâkaya** (NI) A new coat or dress.

oskaskosiwinakwan *pl.* **oskaskosiwinakwanwa** (NI) Having appearance of fresh grass; green. *(Plains).*

oskaskosiy *pl.* **oskaskosiya** (NI) New spring grass; fresh grass.

oskastim *pl.* **oskastimwak** (NA) A young horse, i.e.: usually refers to a yearling.

oskayiwihew (VTA) S/he makes her/him young.

  oskayiwitâw (VTI) S/he makes it new.

  oskayiwihiwew (VTA) S/he makes someone young.

  oskayiwihcikew (VTI) S/he makes things new.

oskâcihk *pl.* **oskâcihkwa** (NI) A tool for punching holes in leather or moosehide, i.e.: an awl.

oskâcihkow *pl.* **oskâcihkowak** (VAI) S/he has an awl.

oskâhcakos *pl.* **oskâhcakosak** (NA) A lodgepole pine.

oskâhtak *pl.* **oskâhtakwak** (NA) A jack pine.

oskâhtakâw *pl.* **oskâhtakâwa** (VII) It is a jack pine ridge.

oskâhtakopikîs *pl.* **oskâhtakopikîsak** (NA) Pine pitch.

oskâkonakâw (NI) Freshly fallen snow which is easy for tracking. *(Plains). Alt.* **paskakonakâw** *(Northern).*

oskâpew *pl.* **oskâpewak** (NA) A young man.

131

oskâpôskitew *pl.* **oskâpôskitewa** (VII) A newly burned off area.

oskâtâsk *pl.* **oskâtâskwak** (NA) A carrot.

oskâyi *pl.* **oskayiya** (VII) It is new.

oskâyis *pl.* **oskâyisak** (NA) A young moose or baby moose.

oskâyiwan *pl.* **oskâyiwanwa** (VII) It is new.

oskâyiwiw *pl.* **oskâyiwiwak** (VAI) S/he is young.

oskâyiwiwin *pl.* **oskâyiwiwina** (NI) Being youthful.

oskiciyahtik *pl.* **oskiciyahtikwa** (NI) A homemade pipestem.

oskicîy *pl.* **oskicîya** (NI) A pipestem.

oskihcikewin *pl.* **oskihcikewina** (NI) The act of making something fresh; freshen.

oskihtak *pl.* **oskihtakwak** (NA) A young or new tree.

oskimekwanis *pl.* **oskimekwanisa** (NI) A pinfeather.

oskimispon (VII) There is new or fresh snow.

oskimoscosis *pl.* **oskimoscosisak** (NA) A newborn calf.

oskinâkohcikewin *pl.* **oskinâkohcikewina** (NI) The act of rejuvenating.

oskinîkiskwew *pl.* **oskinîkiskwewak** (NA) A young woman.

oskinîkiskwewiw *pl.* **oskinîkiskwewiwak** (VAI) She is a young woman.

oskinîkiw *pl.* **oskinîkiwak** (NA) A youth.

oskisîhow *pl.* **oskisîhowak** (VAI) S/he wears new clothes.

oskisîhowin *pl.* **oskisîhowina** (NI) The act of wearing new clothes.

oskiskwewiw *pl.* **oskiskwewiwak** (NA) A new wife.

oskitakosin *pl.* **oskitakosinwak** (NA) A newcomer; one who has just arrived.

oskitâkosin (VII) It is early in the evening.

oskiwîyâs *pl.* **oskiwîyâsa** (NI) Fresh meat.

oskîsikomin *pl.* **oskîsikomina** (NI) A logan berry.

oskotâkâw *pl.* **oskotâkâwak** (VAI) S/he has a coat or jacket.

oskoweskwamotayew *pl.* **oskoweskwamotayewak** (NA) A four-year-old bull moose.

oskwatim *pl.* **oskwatima** (NI) A beaver dam.

oskwatimihkewin *pl.* **oskwatimihkewina** (NI) The act of building a rock dam, i.e.: a dike.

osohkayamihâw *pl.* **osohkayamihâwak** (NA) An evangel; one who prays hard.

osopew *pl.* **osopewak** (VAI) The fat on top of the tenderloin of a moose.

osopîkahikiw *pl.* **osopîkahikiwak** (NA) A painter; one who paints. *(Northern). Alt.* **osisopekahikew** *(Plains).*

osow *pl.* **osowak** (VAI) It boils.

osowaskwa (NA) The foxtail plant.

osowew *pl.* **osowewa** (VII) S/he boiled it.

osôhew *pl.* **osôhewak** (VTA) S/he makes it boil.

ospasew *pl.* **ospasewa** (NI) A wishbone of a bird.

ospwâkan *pl.* **ospwâkanak** (NA) A pipe.

ospwâkanasiniy *pl.* **ospwâkanasiniyak** (NA) A stone shaped into a pipe.

ostesimâw *pl.* **ostesimâwak** (NA) The eldest brother.

ostesimâwiw *pl.* **ostesimâwiwak** (VAI) He is the eldest brother.

ostikwânahikewin *pl.* **ostikwânahikewina** (NI) The act of butting someone with your head.

ostikwânisâponikan *pl.* **ostikwânisâponikana** (NI) A straight or head pin.

ostimâw *pl.* **ostimâwak** (NA) A daughter-in-law.

ostimimâw *pl.* **ostimimâwak** (NA) A niece or a daughter-in-law.

ostostotam *pl.* **ostostotamwak** (VAI) S/he coughs.

ostostotamowin *pl.* **ostostotamowina** (NI) A cough.

ostostotamômaskihkîy *pl.* **ostostotamômaskihkîya** (NI) A cough syrup; a cough remedy.

oswâw *pl.* **oswâwak** (VAI) It is boiled.

osweyakâmahikew *pl.* **osweyakâmahikewak** (NA) A splasher; one who splashes.

otahcikan *pl.* **otahcikana** (NI) Something that is absorbent.

otahcikewimaskihkiy *pl.* **otahcikewimaskihkiya** (NI) A medicine man's technique for sucking out poison; a poultice.

otahcipiw *pl.* **otahcipiwak** (NA) A porker; one who is being fattened up.

otahkahew (VTA) S/he places them behind.

   otahkastâw (VTI) S/he places it behind.

   otahkahiwew (VTA) S/he places people behind.

   otahkahcikew (VTI) S/he places things behind.

otahkiskacikew *pl.* **otahkiskacikewak** (NA) A kicker; one who kicks; one who complains.

otahkowiw *pl.* **otahkowiwak** (VAI) S/he is behind or running late. *(Northern). Alt.* **otâhkesin** *(Plains).*

otahowewina (NI) A group or collection of winnings.

otahwew (VTA) S/he wins from her/him; s/he beats her/him at a game.

   otahowew (VTA) S/he wins from everyone.

otakâwâcikew *pl.* **otakâwâcikewak** (NA) An admirer; one who admires. *(Plains). Alt.* **omiyowâpahkew** *(Northern).*

otamew (VTA) S/he gives her/him mouth-to-mouth resuscitation.

   otamiwew (VTA) S/he gives people mouth-to-mouth resuscitation.

otameyihtamowin *pl.* **otameyihtamowina** (NI) A preoccupation.

otameyihtâkwan *pl.* **otameyihtâkwanwa** (VII) It is preoccupying.

otameyimew (VAI) S/he is preoccupied with her/him.

otameyitam (VII) S/he is preoccupied with it.

otameyimiwew (VII) S/he is preoccupied with people.

otamihew (VTA) S/he makes her/him waste his time.

otamihiwew (VTA) S/he makes people waste their time.

otamihiwewin *pl.* **otamihiwewina** (NI) The act of hindering someone; hindrance.

otamihtâsowin *pl.* **otamihtâsowina** (NI) The act of interferring; interference.

otamimew (VTA) S/he delays her/him with her/his talking.

otamiwew (VTA) S/he delays people by talking.

otamisipwehtew *pl.* **otamisipwehtewak** (VAI) S/he is absent without a good reason.

otamiyiw *pl.* **otamiyiwak** (VAI) S/he is busy or occupied.

otamiyowin *pl.* **otamiyowina** (NI) The act of being busy.

otanisihkawin *pl.* **otanisihkawinak** (NA) A stepdaughter or adopted daughter. *Var.* **otôsimiskwew**.

otanskotapan *pl.* **otanskotapanak** (NA) Great-grandchild; great-granddaughter; great-grandson; great-nephew; great-niece; great-grandfather, *Var.* **omosômâw**; great-grandmother, *Var.* **okômâw**; great-grandparent, *Var.* **onekihikomâw**; great-uncle, *Var.* **omosômâw**; great-aunt.

otapewatim *pl.* **otapewatimak** (NA) A sled dog.

otapewin *pl.* **otapewina** (NI) The act of pulling, dragging something behind oneself.

otapihkew *pl.* **otapihkewak** (NA) A weaver; one who weaves things.

otasahkew *pl.* **otasahkewak** (NA) A welfare worker, a literal Cree term meaning "s/he is a feeder of people."

otasahpicikew *pl.* **otasahpicikewak** (NA) A binder; one who binds items together.

otascikew *pl.* **otascikewak** (NA) A gambler; one who likes betting.

otaskiw *pl.* **otaskiwak** (VAI) S/he has land.

otaskôkew *pl.* **otaskôkewak** (NA) A disciple; a follower; one who follows.

otastisiwak *pl.* **otastisiwakwa** (NI) The softest, tenderest meat which is found along the spine of an animal, i.o.: tenderloin.

otatâhcikewin *pl.* **otatâhcikewina** (NI) The act of inhaling; inhalation.

otatâwew *pl.* **otatâwewak** (NA) A buyer; one who trades.

otatâwewiyiniw *pl.* **otatâwewiyiniwak** (NA) A merchant or salesman. *Var.* **ocacâwes**.

otatoskew *pl.* **otatoskewak** (NA) A handyman; menial laborer; a worker; one who does odd jobs.

otayahcikiw *pl.* **otayahcikiwak** (NA) A hopper; one who hops from one foot to the other. *(Northern)*

otayamihâw *pl.* **otayamihâwak** (NA) Someone who prays; a Christian; religious person.

otayamihcikew *pl.* **otayamihcikewak** (NA) A reader.

otayamihestamâkew *pl.* **otayamihestamâkewak** (NA) One who prays for people; an intercessor.

otayâhkonikew *pl.* **otayâhkonikewak** (NA) A busybody; one who is very active.

otayisinâkew *pl.* **otayisinâkewak** (NA) An imitator; impersonator; one who imitates.

otâcimisohiwew *pl.* **otâcimisohiwewak** (NA) A confessor.

otâcimostâkew *pl.* **otâcimostâkewak** (NA) An informer; one who gives information.

otâcimow *pl.* **otâcimowak** (NA) A storyteller; one who tells legends.

otâhk (IPC) Behind; in the back. *(Northern)*. *Alt.* **nâway** *(Plains)*.

otâhk pîsim (IPC) Last month. *(Northern)*. *Alt.* **nâway pîsim** *(Plains)*.

otâhkekât *pl.* **otâhkekâta** (NI) A hind leg.

otâhkepayowin *pl.* **otâhkepayowina** (NI) The act of being tardy; tardily.

otâhkesin *pl.* **otâhkesinak** (VAI) S/he is behind or running late. *(Plains)*. *Alt.* **otahkowiw** *(Northern)*.

otâhkipicikewin *pl.* **otâhkipicikewina** (NI) The act of delaying; backset; retardation.

otâhkipitew (VTA) S/he delays them.

otâhkipitam (VTI) S/he delays it.

otâhkipisiwew (VTA) S/he delays someone.

otâhkipihcikew (VTI) S/he delays things.

otâhkwaham *pl.* **otâhkwahamwak** (NA) The person who holds the helm or rudder in a boat, i.e.: a pilot.

otâkamascikew *pl.* **otâkamascikewak** (NA) A distiller; one who makes home brew.

otâkosin (VII) It is evening.

otâkosîhk (IPC) Yesterday.

otâkwan mîcisowin *pl.* **otâkwan mîcisowina** (NI) Suppertime.

otâkwanimitsiw *pl.* **otâkwanimitsiwak** (VAI) S/he has supper. (Literally: S/he has an evening meal.)

otâkwanisiw *pl.* **otâkwanisiwak** (VAI) S/he has run out of time, the sun is going down; s/he arrives in the evening.

otâkwanohtew *pl.* **otâkwanohtewak** (VAI) S/he walks till late evening.

otâkwanohtewin *pl.* **otâkwanohtewina** (NI) The act of walking in the late evening; a walk in the late evening.

otâmaciwew *pl.* **otâmaciwewak** (NA) A climber.

otâmapistawew (VTA) S/he detains her/him with her/his visit.

otâmapistatam (VTA) It detains her/him.

otâmapistatâkew (VTA) Someone detains her/him.

otâmâkatisiw *pl.* **otâmâkatisiwak** (VAI) S/he is detained by her/his hunger.

otânisihkâw *pl.* **otânisihkâwak** (VTA) S/he has her as a god daughter. *(Northern)*

otânisihkâwew *pl.* **otânisihkâwewak** (VTA) S/he has her for a daughter. *(Plains). Alt.* **otânisimew** *(Northern).*

otânisimâw *pl.* **otânisimâwak** (NA) A daughter.

otânisimew *pl.* **otânisimewak** (VTA) S/he has her as a daughter. *(Northern). Alt.* **otânisihkâw** *(Plains).*

otânisiw *pl.* **otânisiwak** (VAI) S/he has a daughter.

otâpahâkan *pl.* **otâpahâkanak** (NA) A harness horse or a work horse.

otâpapestamâkew *pl.* **otâpapestamâkewak** (NA) A priest who takes the place of another; one who replaces someone.

otâpasinahikew *pl.* **otâpasinahikewak** (NA) An artist. *(Plains). Alt.* **onaspasinahikew** *(Northern).*

otâpânâsk *pl.* **otâpânâskwak** (NA) A vehicle; wagon.

otâpânihkâtew (VTA) S/he loads her/his toboggan.

    otâpânihkâtam (VTI) S/he loads it on her/his toboggan.

otâpânihkew *pl.* **otâpânihkewak** (VAI) S/he prepares a proper load for her/his toboggan.

otâpâniyâpiy *pl.* **otâpâniyâpiya** (NI) A harness.

otâpâsiw *pl.* **otâpâsiwak** (VAI) S/he goes for a ride.

otâpâtew (VTA) S/he gives her/him a ride.

    otâpâtam (VTI) S/he gives it a ride.

    otâpâsiwew (VTA) S/he gives people a ride.

otâpew *pl.* **otâpewak** (VTA) S/he drags or pulls a sleigh behind her/him.

otâpiskanikan *pl.* **otâpiskanikana** (NI) A jawbone; a jowel.

otâpwehtam *pl.* **otâpwehtamak** (NA) A believer; one who believes.

otâsiyânahpisowin *pl.* **otâsiyânahpisowinak** (NA) The Cree traditional meaning was "a loincloth" now used for a diaper. *(Archaic Cree).*

otâskanaw *pl.* **otâskanawa** (NI) The road behind.

otâskwawew (VTA) S/he draws them out of the water with a stick or pole.

    otâskwaham (VTI) S/he draws it out of the water with a pole.

    otâskwahowew (VTA) S/he draws people out of the water with a pole.

    otâskwahikew (VTI) S/he draws things out of the water with a pole.

otehimin *pl.* **otehimina** (NI) A strawberry.

otehiminâhtik *pl.* **otehiminâhtikwak** (NA) A strawberry plant.

otehipak *pl.* **otehipakwa** (NI) A cabbage.

134

otehiw *pl.* **otehiwak** (VAI) S/he has a heart or compassion.

otehiwin *pl.* **otehiwina** (NI) Compassion, goodness of heart.

otehye *pl.* **otehya** (NI) A shoulder blade.

otemiw *pl.* **otemiwak** (VAI) S/he has horses or dogs.

otepwew *pl.* **otepwewak** (NA) A caller; one who calls, i.e.: at a square dance.

oteskan *pl.* **oteskanak** (NA) A sharp horn, i.e.: a prong. *(Northern). Alt.* **miteskan** *(Plains).*

oteskaniw *pl.* **oteskaniwak** (VAI) It (animate) has horns.

oteyisih (IPC) Used to specify direction, "this way."

otihtapascikewin *pl.* **otihtapascikewina** (NI) The act of being upturned.

otihtapihtin *pl.* **otihtapihtinwa** (VII) S/he falls upside down.

otihtapisin *pl.* **otihtapisinwak** (VAI) S/he lies face down.

otihtapiskwepiw *pl.* **otihtapiskwepiwak** (VAI) S/he sits with her/his head down.

otihtew (VTA) S/he overtakes her/him.

    otihtam (VTI) S/he overtakes it.

    otihsiwew (VTA) S/he overtakes people.

otihtinew (VTA) S/he seizes or grabs her/him; s/he rapes her/him.

    otihtinam (VTI) S/he seizes it.

    otihtiniwew (VTA) S/he seizes someone.

    otihtinikew (VTI) S/he seizes things.

otihtinitowak (VAI) They seize or grasp each other.

otihtinitowin *pl.* **otihtinitowina** (NI) The act of seizing or grasping one another.

otihtinkewin *pl.* **otihtinkewina** (NI) A rape.

otihtipipayiw *pl.* **otihtipipayiwak** (NA) A wheel.

otikinehikew *pl.* **otikinehikewak** (NA) A stunner; one who likes to knock-out other people.

otikwatimâw *pl.* **otikwatimâwak** (NA) A nephew. *Alt.* **tehkwatim** (slang).

otinamawew (VTA) S/he obtains or purchases it for her/him.

    otinamakew (VTA) S/he obtains for someone.

otinamâsiw *pl.* **otinamâsiwak** (VTA) S/he unjustly appropriates it for herself/himself.

otinamâsiwin *pl.* **otinamâsiwina** (NI) The act of unjust appropriation; the act of taking something without consent.

otinaskew *pl.* **otinaskewak** (VAI) S/he homesteads.

otinew (VTA) S/he takes him/her.

    otinam (VTI) S/he takes it.

    otiniwew (VTA) S/he takes someone.

otinikâsiwin *pl.* **otinikâsiwina** (NI) The act of being arrested.

otinikew *pl.* **otinikewak** (VAI) S/he buys.

otinikewinihk (IPC) In captivity.

otiniwewin *pl.* **otiniwewina** (NI) The act of being captivated or captive.

otiyinihiwew (NA) A healer. *(Plains). Var.* **âstehowew.**

otipeyihcikiw *pl.* **otipeyihcikiwak** (NA) A possessor; one owns something.

otipeyimisiw *pl.* **otipeyimisiwak** (NA) A spoiled brat.

otisâpamew (VTA) S/he lives long enough to see her/him, i.e.: an antiquarian.

otisâpatam (VTI) S/he lives long enough to see it.

otisâpamiwew (VTA) S/he lives long enough to see people.

otisâpahcikew (VTI) S/he lives long enough to see things.

otisihkân *pl.* **otisihkâna** (NI) A turnip.

otiskawapiw *pl.* **otiskawapiwak** (VAI) S/he is sitting facing someone.

otiskawastew *pl.* **otiskawastewa** (VII) It is sitting facing someone.

otiskawikâpawiw *pl.* **otiskawikâpawiwak** (VAI) S/he stands facing this way.

otiskawiskawew (VTA) S/he faces her/him.

otiskawiskakam (VTI) S/he faces it.

otiskawiskakâkew (VTA) S/he faces people.

otiskawiskakâcikew (VTI) S/he faces things.

otiyiwanisihisiw *pl.* **otiyiwanisihisiwak** (NA) A fasting person; one who fasts.

otîhkipayihcikewin *pl.* **otîhkipayihcikewina** (NI) The act of shrinking; the act of making less.

otohpikihcikew *pl.* **otohpikihcikewak** (NA) A grower; one who works with plants.

otohpikihiwew *pl.* **otohpikihiwewak** (NA) A breeder; one who breeds animals.

otoyascikew *pl.* **otoyascikewak** (NA) A spotter; one who acts as a lookout.

otoyiskowakinikew *pl.* **otoyiskowakinikewak** (NA) A moulder; one who shapes clay or mud; a potter. *(Northern). Alt.* **owîceskoyakinikew** *(Plains).*

owîceskoyakinikew *pl.* **owîceskoyakinikewak** (NA) A moulder; s/he shapes clay or mud; a potter. *(Plains). Alt.* **otoyiskowakinikew** *(Northern).*

otoywâscikew *pl.* **otoywâscikewak** (NA) A psychic.

otônipiy *pl.* **otônipiyak** (NA) A lake herring, Tulipee. *(Northern). Alt.* **ocônipes.** *(Plains).*

otôsihcikew *pl.* **otôsihcikewak** (NA) A creator of things; a builder.

otôsihiwew *pl.* **otôsihiwewak** (NA) A creator or maker of people. (Not commonly used.)

otôsimiskwew *pl.* **otôsimiskwewak** (NA) A stepdaughter or adopted daughter. *Var.* **otanisihkawin.**

otôskwanihk (LN) The Cree name for the city of Calgary means "at the elbow."

otôtâpânâskiw *pl.* **otôtâpânâskiwak** (VAI) S/he has a vehicle.

otôtemihkâtew (VTA) S/he is friendly to her/him. *(Northern). Alt.* **otôtemiw** *(Plains).*

otôtemiskam (VTA) S/he is friendly.

otôtemiskâkew (VTA) S/he is friendly to people.

otôtemihtowin *pl.* **otôtemihtowina** (NI) The act of being friendly; being friendly; a friendship; sociability; a social acquaintance. *(Plains). Alt.* **otôtemiwewin** *(Northern).*

otôtemimew (VTA) S/he regards her/him as a friend.

otôtemiwew (VTA) S/he regards others as a relative or friend.

otôtemimiwew (VTA) S/he is friendly to people.

otôtemimow *pl.* **otôtemimowak** (VAI) S/he is sociable.

otôtemiw (VTA) S/he is friendly to her/him. *(Plains). Alt.* **otôtemihkâtew** *(Northern).*

otôtemiskam (VTI) S/he is friendly.

otôtemiskawew (VTA) S/he is friendly to people.

otôtemiw *pl.* **otôtemiwak** (VAI) S/he makes friends.

otôtemiwewin *pl.* **otôtemiwewina** (NI) The act of being friendly. *(Northern). Alt.* **otôtemihtowin** *(Plains).*

otôyakihcikew *pl.* **otôyakihcikewak** (NA) An assessor; one who assesses goods.

owaninewiyiniw *pl.* **owaninewiyiniwak** (NA) A good-humored person.

owaniskâw *pl.* **owaniskâwak** (NA) A riser; one who rises.

owaskahikanihkew *pl.* **owaskahikanihkewak** (NA) A carpenter; one who builds houses.

owayesihiwew *pl.* **owayesihiwewak** (NA) An artificer; one who creates debts; a con artist.

owayesihtâw *pl.* **owayesihtâwak** (NA) A pretender; one who pretends to be what s/he is not.

owâpahcikew *pl.* **owâpahcikewak** (NA) An inspector; viewer; one who inspects. *(Northern). Alt.* **onitawâpenikew** *(Plains).*

owâpâspinew *pl.* **owâpâspinewak** (NA) A leper.

owâtihkew *pl.* **owâtihkewak** (NA) A burrower; one who digs holes.

owihcikew *pl.* **owihcikewak** (NA) An announcer; one who announces things.

owikiw *pl.* **owikiwak** (NA) A resident; one who resides in a certain place.

owîcewâkanimew (VTA) S/he makes her/him her/his companion.

owîcewâkanimiwew (VTA) S/he has people as her/his friends.

owîcewâkaniw *pl.* **owîcewâkaniwak** (VAI) S/he has companions.

owîcihtâsiw *pl.* **owîcihtâsiwak** (NA) A welfare or social worker; one who is a helper of people.

owîhcekihcikew *pl.* **owîhcekihcikewak** (NA) One who causes unpleasant smells.

owîhtamakew *pl.* **owîhtamakewak** (NA) An adviser or advisor; one who advises.

135

owîkimâkan *pl.* **owîkimâkanak** (NA) Someone you live with; a life partner; a married spouse.

owîkimâkanimew (VTA) S/he has her/him as a spouse.

owîkimâkanimiwew (VTA) S/he is a married person.

owîkimâkaniw *pl.* **owîkimâkaniwak** (VAI) S/he has a spouse.

owîkitiw *pl.* **owîkitiwak** (NA) A spouse; a married partner. *Var.* **wikimâkan**.

oyahew (VTA) S/he sets her/him up; s/he starts her/him out; s/he places her/him correctly, well, right.

oyahiwew (VTA) S/he sets others up.

oyascikew (VTI) S/he sets things up.

oyahisiw *pl.* **oyahisiwak** (NA) A shaper of metal, i.e.: a blacksmith.

oyahisiwikamik *pl.* **oyahisiwikamikwa** (NI) A blacksmith shop.

oyahiwewin *pl.* **oyahiwewina** (NI) The act of placing things in a certain mannner; designate; placement.

oyahowewin *pl.* **oyahowewina** (NI) The act of placing things in categories; categorization.

oyahpitew (VTA) S/he harnesses a horse or sets a net; s/he ties properly; s/he ties her/him up well.

oyahpitam (VTI) S/he harnesses it.

oyahpisiwew (VTA) S/he harnesses someone.

oyahpicikew (VTI) S/he harnesses horses.

oyahwew (VAI) S/he shapes or repairs them, i.e.: a blacksmith repairing implements. *(Northern)*

oyaham (VTI) S/he shapes or repairs it.

oyahowew (VTA) S/he shapes or repairs others.

oyahikew (VII) S/he shapes or repairs things.

oyakan *pl.* **oyakana** (NI) A plate.

oyakihcikewin *pl.* **oyakihcikewina** (NI) The act of analysing; analysis; analytic; assessment; estimation; evaluation; valued.

oyakihtamawew (VTA) S/he estimates its value for her/him.

oyakihtamakew (VTA) S/he estimates its value for people.

oyakimew (VTA) S/he estimates her/his value.

oyakitam (VTI) S/he estimates its value.

oyakimiwew (VTA) S/he estimates people's value.

oyakihcikew (VTI) S/he estimates the value of things.

oyapamew (VTA) S/he aims at her/him; s/he sets or adjusts her/his sights on her/him.

oyapatam (VTI) S/he aims at it.

oyapakew (VTA) S/he aims at someone.

oyapahcikew (VTI) S/he aims at things.

oyasiwewin *pl.* **oyasiwewina** (NI) The law or affairs.

oyaskinahew *pl.* **oyaskinahewak** (VAI) S/he prepares her/his pipe.

oyaskinahtawew *pl.* **oyaskinahtawewak** (VAI) S/he prepares a pipe for her/him.

oyaskinahtâw (VII) S/he organizes or arranges things in a box.

oyaskinahiwew (VTA) S/he arranges people in special houses.

oyasowâtew (VTA) S/he takes her/him to court.

oyasowâtam (VTI) S/he takes it to court.

oyasowâsiwew (VTA) S/he takes someone to court.

oyasowâcikew (VTI) S/he takes things to court.

oyasowew *pl.* **oyasowewak** (NA) A judge, i.e.: at a contest.

oyasowewikamik *pl.* **oyasowewikamikwa** (NI) A courthouse.

oyasowewin *pl.* **oyasowewina** (NI) A legal judgement; a court case.

oyasowewiyiniw *pl.* **oyasowewiyiniwak** (NA) A court judge.

oyâkanihkew *pl.* **oyâkanihkewak** (VAI) S/he makes plates.

oyâkanikamik *pl.* **oyâkanikamikwa** (NI) A place for dishes; a cupboard. *Var.* **akocikan**.

oyâkanikamikohkewin *pl.* **oyâkanikamikohkewina** (NI) The act of doing cabinetwork.

oyâpahcikan *pl.* **oyâpahcikana** (NI) The sight on a gun.

oyâpahcikew *pl.* **oyâpahcikewak** (VAI) S/he aims a gun.

oyecikewin *pl.* **oyecikewina** (NI) The act of thinking in a discerning manner; discernment.

oyehcikewin *pl.* **oyehcikewina** (NI) The act of envisioning.

oyekinew (VTA) S/he folds them up, i.e.: pants. *(Northern)*

oyekinam (VTI) S/he folds blankets up.

oyekinikew (VTI) S/he folds things up.

oyesehcikewin *pl.* **oyesehcikewina** (NI) The act of having a motive; incentive; inflection.

oyeyihtam *pl.* **oyeyihtamwak** (VAI) S/he makes her/his mind up about it.

oyeyihtamâsiw *pl.* **oyeyihtamâsiwak** (VAI) S/he thinks about what s/he is going to do.

oyeyimew (VTA) S/he thinks about what s/he is going to have her/him do. *Alt.* **nânapwekinew** *(Plains)*.

oyeyitam (VTI) S/he puts her/his mind to it.

oyeyimiwew (VTA) S/he puts her/his mind to people.

oyeyihcikew (VTA) S/he puts her/his mind about people.

oyeyitamowin *pl.* **oyeyitamowina** (NI) A reflection, premeditation.

oyihk *pl.* **oyihkwa** (NI) A gland. *(Northern)*. *Alt.* **miyîkwak** *(Plains)*.

oyihkotew (VTA) S/he carves them with a knife.

oyihkotam (VTI) S/he carves it with a knife.

oyihkohcikew (VTI) S/he carves things.

oyikahwew (VTA) S/he chops it into shape; s/he carves it into shape, i.e.: with an axe.

oyikaham (VTI) S/he chops it into shape.

oyikahowew (VTA) S/he chops out someone's image.

oyikahikew (VTI) S/he chops things accordingly.

oyikâpawiwin *pl.* **oyikâpawiwina** (NI) A stance.

oyimew (VTA) S/he tells her/him what to do; s/he incites her/him. *(Northern). Alt.* **wiyomew** *(Plains).*

oyitam (VTI) S/he incites it.

oyimiwew (VTA) S/he tells people what to do.

oyihcikew (VTI) S/he incites things.

oyinew (VTA) S/he organizes her/him with care; s/he arranges her/him with care.

oyinam (VTI) S/he organizes it with care.

oyiniwew (VTA) S/he organizes people with care.

oyinikew (VTI) S/he organizes things with care.

oyinikewin *pl.* **oyinikewina** (NI) The act of predominating.

oyiniwewin *pl.* **oyiniwewina** (NI) The act of assimulating or organizing; assimilative.

oyiskowakinew (VTA) S/he molds her/him the way s/he wants.

oyiskowakinam (VTI) S/he molds it the way s/he wants.

oyiskowakiniwew (VTA) S/he molds someone the way s/he wants.

oyiskowakinikew (VTI) S/he molds things the way s/he wants.

oyotam (VTA) S/he tells it what to do; s/he gives orders.

oyotimiwew (VTA) S/he tells people what to do.

oyotascikew (VTI) S/he places things.

oywastawew (VTA) S/he has a premonition about her/him.

oywastatam (VTI) S/he has a premonition about it.

oywastatakew (VTA) S/he has a premonition about someone.

oywastacikew (VTA) S/he has premonitions.

oywâscikewin *pl.* **oywâscikewina** (NI) A premonition.

137

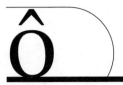

Ô

ôcenas *pl.* ôcenasa (NI) A town.

ôcew *pl.* ôcewak (NA) A fly.

ôhi (PR) These ones here.

ôhô *pl.* ôhôwak (NA) An owl.

ôhôhisâyâwin *pl.* ôhôhisâyâwina (NI) Being owl-like.

ôhôsis *pl.* ôhôsisak (NA) An owlet.

ôkwâsihiwew *pl.* ôkwâsihiwewak (NA) An abductor; s/he steals away with a person or thing.

ôsi *pl.* ôsa (NI) A canoe or boat, i.e.: a vessel.

ôsihmawikanihkân *pl.* ôsihmawikanihkâna (NI) The central main frame in a boat, i.e.: a keel.

ôta (IPC) Here.

ôtahmâcipayiw *pl.* ôtahmâcipayiwak *or* ôtahmâcipayiwaka (VII) *or* (VAI) It *or* s/he starts from here.

ôtenaw *pl.* ôtenawa (NI) A city.

ôtenâwihtâw *pl.* ôtenâwihtâwak (VAI) S/he makes it a town.

ôtenâwiwin *pl.* ôtenâwiwina (NI) The act of living in town; a town is growing like a city.

ôtitwestamâkew *pl.* ôtitwestamâkewak (NA) An interpreter.

ôye (IPC) Then; at that time.

ôyow *pl.* ôyowak (VAI) S/he howls. *(Northern). Alt.* wiyoyow *(Plains).*

ôyowin *pl.* ôyowina (NI) The act of howling. *(Northern). Alt.* wiyoyowin *(Plains).*

139

p

pacaskahask *pl.* **pacaskahaskwak** (NA) A bird that announces the rain, i.e.: a type of snipe such as a killdeer. *(Northern). Alt.* **kimowanahasîs** *(Plains).*

pacimew (VTA) S/he says annoying words to her/him. *(Northern). Alt.* **wîspâcimew** *(Plains).*

 pacimiwew (VTA) S/he says annoying words to others.

pacipayiw *pl.* **pacipayiwak** (VAI) It derailed, i.e.: a train; s/he or it slid off, i.e.: a car; s/he misses her/his chance.

pahkahahkwan *pl.* **pahkahahkwanak** (NA) A chicken. *(Northern). Alt.* **pahpahahkwân** *(Plains).*

pahkaham *pl.* **pahkahamwak** (VAI) S/he has a pulse. *(Northern). Alt.* **pâhkahokow** *(Plains).*

pahkekin *pl.* **pahkekinwa** (NI) A hide.

pahkekinohkew *pl.* **pahkekinohkewak** (VAI) S/he tans hides.

pahkekinohkewikamik *pl.* **pahkekinohkewikamikwa** (NI) A tannery; a smoke house.

pahkekinohkewin *pl.* **pahkekinohkewina** (NI) The act of tanning hides.

pahki (IPC) A part: a portion of.

pahkihtakonakâw *pl.* **pahkihtakonakâwa** (NI) A cloudburst. *(Northern). Alt.* **mahmahkâkonepayiw** *(Plains).*

pahkihtapekipitew (VTA) S/he pulls her/him down with a rope.

 pahkihtapekipitam (VTI) S/he pulls it down with a rope.

 pahkihtapekipisiwew (VTA) S/he pulls people down with a rope.

 pakihtapekipicikew (VTI) S/he pulls things down with a rope.

pahkihtâpekinew *pl.* **pahkihtâpekinewak** (VAI) S/he loosens the rope on her/him.

pahkihtin *pl.* **pahkihtinwa** (VII) It falls down.

pahkihtitâw *pl.* **pahkihtitâwak** (VTA) It fell when o/he dropped it.

pahkikawihew (VTI) S/he makes it drip.

 pahkikawitâw (VTI) S/he makes it drip.

 pahkikawihiwew (VTA) S/he makes people drip.

 pahkikawicikew (VTI) S/he makes things drip.

pahkikawinew (VTA) S/he makes her/him or it drip by squeezing.

 pahkikawinam (VTI) S/he makes it drip by squeezing.

 pahkikawiniwew (VTA) S/he makes someone drip by squeezing.

pahkikawinikew (VTI) S/he makes things drip by squeezing.

pahkikawiw *pl.* **pahkikawiwa** *or* **pahkikawiwak** (VII) *or* (VAI) It *or* s/he drips.

pahkikawiwin *pl.* **pahkikawiwina** (NI) The act of dripping.

pahkipestâw (NA) A slight, gentle rain at the start of a storm.

pahkisimew (VTA) S/he drops her/him.

 pahkisihtitâw (VTI) S/he drops it.

 pahkisihcikew (VTI) S/he drops things.

pahkisimow (VAI) The sun sets.

pahkisimôtâhk (NI) West or towards where the sun sets.

pahkisin *pl.* **pahkisinwak** (VAI) S/he falls down.

pahkisinowin *pl.* **pahkisinowina** (NI) The act of falling.

pahkisiw *pl.* **pahkisiwak** (VAI) It explodes; the car blew up.

pahkisiwin *pl.* **pahkisiwina** (NI) Being exploded.

pahkiswâw *pl.* **pahkiswâwak** (VAI) S/he is struck by an explosion set off by someone else.

pahkiswew (VTA) S/he blows her/him up, i.e.: with an explosive.

 pahkisam (VTI) S/he blows it up.

 pahkisiwew (VTA) S/he blows up people.

 pahkisikew (VTI) S/he blows something up.

pahkitew *pl.* **pahkitewa** (VII) It explodes.

pahkitewaciy *pl.* **pahkitewaciya** (NI) Exploding mountains; volcano.

pahkitewipimiy *pl.* **pahkitewipimiya** (NI) A chemical used to ignite material; combustable chemicals such as gas or propane. *(Plains). Alt.* **pahkwehkasikan** *(Northern).*

pahkocihcewew *pl.* **pahkocihcewewak** (VTA) S/he drys her/his hands for her/him. *(Plains). Alt.* **pâhkocihcenew** *(Northern).*

pahkohkwehon *pl.* **pahkohkwehona** (NI) A face towel.

pahkohkwehonis *pl.* **pahkohkwehonisa** (NI) A face cloth.

pahkohkwehow *pl.* **pahkohkwehowak** (VAI) Her/his face is dry. *(Plains). Alt.* **pâhkohkwakanew** *(Northern).*

pahkonew (VTA) S/he skins them, i.e.: usually used to refer to large animals such as a moose or a cow.

 pahkonam (VTI) S/he skins it.

 pahkoniwew (VTA) S/he skins someone.

 pahkonikew (VTI) S/he skins animals.

pahkopepahtâw *pl.* **pahkopepahtâwak** (VAI) S/he runs into the water.

pahkopew *pl.* **pahkopewak** (VAI) S/he goes into the water; s/he walks into the water.

pahkopewaskisin *pl.* **pahkopewaskisina** (NI) A pair of stretchy footwear, i.e.: rubber boots. *(Plains). Alt.* **sîpekaskisin** *(Northern).*

141

pahkopewin *pl.* **pahkopewina** (NI) The act of going or walking into the water.

pahkwacipitew (VTI) S/he pulls it off the wall.

pahkwacipitam (VTI) S/he pulls something off.

pahkwacipisiwew (VTA) S/he pulls someone out of a mudhole.

pahkwacipicikew (VTI) S/he pulls things off.

pahkwahtew *pl.* **pahkwahtewa** (NI) A ground fire. *(Northern). Alt.* **pâhkwahcitew** *(Plains).*

pahkwatiteskâw *pl.* **pahkwatiteskâwa** (NI) A burned out piece of land, i.e.: an old burn. *(Plains). Alt.* **weposkâw** *(Northern).*

pahkwâyamihewiyiniwiwin (NA) Catholic Priest; priesthood. *(Plains). Alt.* **ayamihewiyiniw** *(Northern).*

pahkwehkasikan *pl.* **pahkwehkasikana** (NI) A chemical used to ignite material; combustable chemicals such as gas or propane. *(Northern). Alt.* **pahkitewipimiy** *(Plains).*

pahkwehtin *pl.* **pahkwehtinwa** (VII) When it falls, a piece breaks off.

pahkwehtitâw (VAI) S/he breaks a piece off it by throwing it down.

pahkwehtisimewak (VAI) S/he breaks a piece off them by throwing them down.

pahkwekawew (VTA) S/he chops off a piece of them.

pahkwekaham (VTI) S/he chops off a piece of it.

pahkwekahikew (VTI) S/he chops off a piece of things.

pahkwenew (VTA) S/he breaks off a piece from them with her/his hands.

pahkwenam (VTI) S/he breaks off a piece of it.

pahkweniwew (VTA) S/he breaks up a group of people.

pahkwenikew (VTI) S/he breaks up a bunch of things.

pahkwenikan *pl.* **pahkwenikana** (NI) A broken off piece; a chunk.

pahkwenikewin *pl.* **pahkwenikewina** (NI) The act of subtracting; subtraction.

pahkwepayiw *pl.* **pahkwepayiwa** *or* **pahkwepayiwak** (VII) *or* (VAI) It *or* s/he breaks off in pieces.

pahkwepicikan *pl.* **pahkwepicikana** (NI) A torn off piece.

pahkwepitew (VTI) S/he tears a piece off.

pahkwepitam (VTI) S/he tears off a piece.

pahkwepisiwew (VTA) S/he tears apart a group of people.

pahkwepicikew (VTI) S/he tears off a bunch of things.

pahkwesawatew (VTI) S/he slices a piece of bread.

pahkwesawatam (VTI) S/he slices a piece of meat.

pahkwesawacikew (VTI) S/he slices things.

pahkwesâwâcikan *pl.* **pahkwesâwâcikana** (NI) A slice.

pahkwesikan *pl.* **pahkwesikanak** (NA) Bannock. *Var.* **napakinikan.**

pahkwesikanâhtik *pl.* **pahkwesikanâhtikwa** (NI) A stick used to cook bannock over an open fire.

pahkwesikanâhtikwaskosîs *pl.* **pahkwesikanâhtikwaskosîsa** (NI) Wheat straw.

pahkwesikanâpoy *pl.* **pahkwesikanâpoya** (NI) A gravy.

pahkwesikanihkew *pl.* **pahkwesikanihkewak** (VAI) S/he makes bannock or bread.

pahkwesikanimin *pl.* **pahkwesikaniminak** (NA) A wheat seed.

pahkwesin *pl.* **pahkwesinwak** (VAI) A piece breaks off.

pahkwesiw *pl.* **pahkwesiwak** (VAI) A thing is broken off.

pahkweskawew (VTI) S/he kicks a part of it off.

pahkweskam (VTI) S/he kicks a part of it off.

pahkweskâcikew (VTI) S/he kicks part of the things off.

pahkweswew (VTI) S/he slices a piece off, i.e.: bread.

pahkwesam (VTI) S/he slices a piece off, i.e.: meat.

pahkwesikew (VTI) S/he slices a piece off, i.e.: something.

pahkwewew (VTI) S/he breaks off a piece by striking it, i.e.: with a hammer.

pahkweham (VTI) S/he breaks a piece off by hitting.

pahkwehikew (VTI) S/he breaks pieces off things by striking them.

pahkweyâw *pl.* **pahkweyâwa** (VII) It breaks and now it has a piece missing.

pahpahahkwân *pl.* **pahpahahkwânak** (NA) A chicken. *(Plains). Alt.* **pahkahahkwan** *(Northern).*

pahpahkwecakahikesîs *pl.* **pahpahkwecakahikesîsak** (NA) A woodpecker. *(Plains). Alt.* **pahpahscîs** *(Northern).*

pahpahscîs *pl.* **pahpahscîsak** (NA) A woodpecker. *(Northern). Alt.* **pahpahkwecakahikesîs** *(Plains).*

pahpakwac (VII) It is entertaining, i.e.: a distraction.

pahpakwacihew (VTA) S/he entertains her/him; s/he amuses her/him or them.

pahpakwacitâw (VTI) S/he entertains it.

pahpakwacihiwew (VTA) S/he entertains people.

pahpakwacicikew (VTI) S/he entertains things.

pahpapamapiw *pl.* **pahpapamapiwak** (VAI) S/he sits and holds meetings here and there. *(Northern). Alt.* **papâmimâmawopiw** *(Plains).*

pahpawahkew *pl.* **pahpawahkewak** (VAI) It shakes its wings.

pahpawihew (VTA) S/he makes her/him shake herself/himself.

pahpawitaw (VAI) S/he shakes, i.e.: to get rid of dust or crumbs.

pahpawicikew (VTI) S/he shakes things, i.e.: to get rid of dust or crumbs.

pahpawinew (VTA) S/he dusts her/him off with a shake.

pahpawinam (VTI) S/he dusts it off with a shake.

pahpawiniwew (vta) S/he dusts people off with a shake.

pahpawihcikew (vti) S/he dusts things off with a shake.

pahpawipayihew *pl.* **pahpawipayihewak** (vta) S/he shakes the dust off her/him. *Var.* **pahpawipayihtâw.**

pahpawisimew (vta) S/he dusts them off her/him by banging them on something.

pahpawisititâw (vti) S/he dusts it off by banging it on something.

pahpawisisimiwew (vta) S/he dusts people off with force.

pahpawisicikew (vti) S/he dusts things off by banging them on something.

pahpawistesimiw *pl.* **pahpawistesimiwa** (vti) S/he stamps her/his boots to remove snow or dirt.

pahpawiw *pl.* **pahpawiwak** (vta) S/he shakes herself/himself, i.e.: a dog.

pahpawiwepinew (vta) S/he dusts it off by shaking it.

pahpawiwepinikew (vta) S/he dusts them off by shaking.

pahpawîwin *pl.* **pahpawîwina** (ni) The act of shaking oneself.

pahpayakitonewin *pl.* **pahpayakitonewina** (ni) The act of prattling; loquacity; prattle.

pahpâmâhokow *pl.* **pahpâmâhokowak** (vai) S/he floats around from here to there.

pahpâmâhotew *pl.* **pahpâmâhotewa** (vii) It floats around from here to there.

pahpâmâstew *pl.* **pahpâmâstewa** (vii) It sits here, there and everywhere.

pahpâmohtew *pl.* **pahpâmohtewak** (vai) S/he walks or travels everywhere.

pahpemamon (vti) It is on crooked.

pahpihiwewin *pl.* **pahpihiwewina** (ni) The act of deriding someone.

pahpihkâsiwin *pl.* **pahpihkâsiwina** (ni) The act of simpering.

pahpiskihtahew (vti) S/he divides them into small pieces.

pahpiskihtatâw (vti) S/he divides it into small pieces.

pahpiskihtahiwew (vta) S/he divides people into small pieces.

pahpiskihtascikew (vti) S/he divides things into small bundles.

pahpiskihtascikewin *pl.* **pahpiskihtascikewina** (ni) The act of segmenting; segmentation.

pahpiskihtinikewin *pl.* **pahpiskihtinikewina** (ni) The act of dismembering.

pahpiskokanân *pl.* **pahpiskokanâna** (ni) A knucklebone. *(Northern). Alt.* **piskokanân** *(Plains).*

pahpiskosiw *pl.* **pahpiskosiwak** (vai) S/he is lumpy.

pahpiskwâw *pl.* **pahpiskwâwa** (vii) It is lumpy.

pahpitosipayowin *pl.* **pahpitosipayowina** (ni) The act of having variation.

pahtehikan *pl.* **pahtehikana** (ni) A wood chip used by beavers in their houses for bedding.

pakahatowan *pl.* **pakahatowanak** (na) A ball for games, i.e.: a baseball. *(Northern). Alt.* **pâkahtowân** *(Plains).*

pakahcikan *pl.* **pakahcikana** (ni) Something used to boil in, i.e.: a kettle.

pakahkam (ipc) It is apparent; it could be; I think so; perhaps, probably.

pakahkamâyâw *pl.* **pakahkamâyâwak** (vai) S/he is conscious.

pakahkameyihtam *pl.* **pakahkameyihtamwak** (vai) S/he regains consciousness.

pakahkâpamew (vta) S/he looks at her/him distinctly.
  pakahkâpatam (vti) S/he looks at it distinctly.
  pakahkâpamiwew (vta) S/he looks at people distinctly.
  pakahkâpacikew (vti) S/he looks at things distinctly.

pakahkeyimew (vta) S/he finds her/him sensible.
  pakahkeyitam (vti) S/he finds it sensible.
  pakahkeyimiwew (vta) S/he finds people sensible.
  pakahkeyicikew (vti) S/he finds things sensible.

pakahkinam (vti) S/he sees it very distinctly.
  pakahkinawew (vta) S/he sees someone very distinctly.
  pakahkinakew (vta) S/he sees people very distinctly.

pakahkinâkosiw *pl.* **pakahkinâkosiwak** (vai) S/he appears very distinctly.

pakahkinâkwan *pl.* **pakahkinâkwanwa** (vii) It appears very distinctly.

pakamahâwasiw *pl.* **pakamahâwasiwak** (vta) S/he hits her/his children.

pakamahikâsiw *pl.* **pakamahikâsiwak** (vai) S/he is hit or beaten.

pakamahikâtew *pl.* **pakamahikâtewa** (vii) It is hit or beaten.

pakamahikew *pl.* **pakamahikewak** (vai) S/he boxes for sport.

pakamahikewin *pl.* **pakamahikewina** (ni) The act of boxing for sport; striking.

pakamahotowin *pl.* **pakamahotowina** (ni) The act of giving a blow, i.e.: to the head.

pakamahwew (vta) S/he hits her/him; s/he beats her/him up.
  pakamaham (vti) S/he hits it.
  pakamahowew (vta) S/he hits someone.

pakamâcâpawew (vta) S/he hits her/him in the eye.
  pakamâcâpahowew (vta) S/he hits people in the eye.

143

pakamâcâpahikew (VTA) S/he hits everyone in the eye.

pakamâkanis *pl.* **pakamâkanisa** (NI) A hammer.

pakamâtihpehikewin *pl.* **pakamâtihpehikewina** (NI) The act of wielding something for hitting someone on the head.

pakamihkwehwew (VTA) S/he strikes her/his face.

pakamihkweham (VTI) S/he strikes its face.

pakamihkwehowew (VTA) S/he strikes someone's face.

pakamihkwehikew (VTA) S/he strikes peoples' faces.

pakamihkwesin *pl.* **pakamihkwesinwak** (VAI) S/he scrapes her/his face in a fall.

pakamihtin *pl.* **pakamihtinwa** (VII) It bangs against something.

pakamimew *pl.* **pakamimewak** (VTA) S/he blames another person for her/his misfortune. *(Northern).* *Alt.* **atâmeyimew** *(Plains).*

pakamipayiw *pl.* **pakamipayiwa** *or* **pakamipayiwak** (VII) *or* (VAI) It *or* s/he rebounds automatically.

pakamisimew (VTA) S/he throws her/him down roughly.

pakamihtitâw (VTI) S/he throws it down roughly.

pakamisimiwew (VTA) S/he throws people down roughly.

pakamicicikew (VTI) S/he throws things down roughly.

pakamisimisiw *pl.* **pakamisimisiwak** (VTA) S/he bumps herself/himself on something roughly.

pakamisin *pl.* **pakamisinwak** (VTA) S/he bumps herself/himself roughly, i.e.: falling down.

pakamiskawew (VTA) S/he bumps against her/him roughly.

pakamiskam (VTI) S/he bumps against it roughly.

pakamiskâkew (VTA) S/he bumps against someone roughly.

pakamiskâcikew (VTI) S/he bumps against things roughly.

pakamiskohtin *pl.* **pakamiskohtinwa** (VII) It falls on the ice roughly.

pakamiskosimew (VTA) S/he throws her/him down on the ice roughly.

pakamiskotitâw (VTI) S/he throws it on the ice roughly.

pakamiskosimiwew (VTA) S/he throws someone on the ice roughly.

pakamiskocicikew (VTI) S/he throws things on the ice roughly.

pakamiskosin *pl.* **pakamiskosinwak** (VAI) S/he falls on the ice roughly.

pakamitonehwew (VTA) S/he strikes her/him on the mouth.

pakamitoneham (VTI) S/he strikes it on the mouth.

pakamitonehowew (VTA) S/he strikes people on the mouth.

pakamitonehikew (VTA) S/he strikes everybody on the mouth.

pakaskamiw *pl.* **pakaskamiwa** (VII) It is a well used way.

pakaskasinâstew *pl.* **pakaskasinâstewa** (VII) It has distinctive colours.

pakaskâpamew (VTA) S/he sees her/him clearly.

pakaskâpatam (VTI) S/he sees it clearly.

pakaskâpamiwew (VTA) S/he sees people clearly.

pakaskâpacikew (VTA) S/he sees things clearly.

pakaskeyimew (VTA) S/he thinks s/he is intelligible.

pakaskeyitam (VTI) S/he thinks it is intelligible.

pakaskeyimiwew (VTA) S/he thinks people are intelligible.

pakaskeyicikew (VTI) S/he thinks things are intelligible.

pakaskeyitamowin *pl.* **pakaskeyitamowina** (NI) The act of thinking something is intelligible.

pakaskihtawew (VTA) S/he hears her/him well; s/he understands her/him well.

pakaskihtam (VTI) S/he hears it clearly.

pakaskihtâkew (VTA) S/he hears people clearly.

pakaskihtâkosiw *pl.* **pakaskihtâkosiwak** (VAI) Her/his voice is intelligible.

pakaskihtâkwan *pl.* **pakaskihtâkwanwa** (VII) It is very intelligible.

pakaskinawew (VTA) S/he recognises her/his type of character.

pakaskinam (VTI) S/he recognises it clearly.

pakaskinâkosiw *pl.* **pakaskinâkosiwak** (VAI) S/he is clearly visible; s/he is in the open.

pakaskinâkosiwin *pl.* **pakaskinâkosiwina** (NI) Clear visibility or clear appearance.

pakaskinâkwan *pl.* **pakaskinâkwanwa** (VII) It is clearly visible; it is in the open.

pakaskisowin *pl.* **pakaskisowina** (NI) Having a distinctive character.

pakaskowehikewin *pl.* **pakaskowehikewina** (NI) The act of speaking with distinction.

pakaskowew *pl.* **pakaskowewak** (VAI) S/he speaks distinctively.

pakaskowewin *pl.* **pakaskowewina** (NI) The act of speaking distinctively.

pakastawepayiw *pl.* **pakastawepayiwa** *or* **pakastawepayiwak** (VII) *or* (VAI) It *or* s/he falls in the water.

pakastawewepinew (VTA) S/he throws her/him into the water.

pakastawewepinam (VTI) S/he throws it into the water.

pakastawewepiniwew (VTA) S/he throws people in the water.

pakastawewepinikew (VTI) S/he throws things in the water.

pakastawewew (VTA) S/he makes her/him fall into the water.

pakastaweham (VTI) S/he makes it fall into the water.

pakastawehowew (VTA) S/he makes people fall into the water.

pakastawehikew (VTI) S/he makes things fall into the water.

pakâhcikewaskihk *pl.* **pakâhcikewaskihkwak** (NA) A cooking pot.

pakâhcikewin *pl.* **pakâhcikewina** (NI) Something boiled in water, i.e.: a dumpling.

pakâhtâkohkew *pl.* **pakâhtâkohkewak** (VAI) S/he cooks something in water; s/he boils, i.e.: stew or soup.

pakâhtâkohkewin *pl.* **pakâhtâkohkewina** (NI) The act of cooking in water or boiling food, i.e.: soup or stew.

pakâhtâw *pl.* **pakâhtâwa** (VTI) S/he boils it.

pakâhtew *pl.* **pakâhtewa** (VII) It is boiled, i.e.: meat of an animal.

pakânâhtik *pl.* **pakânâhtikwak** (NA) A nut tree or shrub.

pakânipimiy (NI) Peanut butter; squirrel food; squirrel grease. *(Northern). Alt.* **anikwacâsimîciwin** *(Plains).*

pakâsimew *pl.* **pakâsimewak** (VTA) S/he boils them in water.

pakâsimow *pl.* **pakâsimowak** (VAI) S/he is swimming.

pakâsimowin *pl.* **pakâsimowina** (NI) The act of swimming.

pakâsiw *pl.* **pakâsiwak** (VAI) It is boiled, i.e.: a fish.

pakesiw *pl.* **pakesiwak** (VAI) S/he plays the Cree hand game.

pakesîwin *pl.* **pakesîwina** (NI) The act of playing the Cree hand game.

pakicipayowin *pl.* **pakicipayowina** (NI) The act of secreting; secretion.

pakicipihkoweyâkanis *pl.* **pakicipihkoweyâkanisa** (NI) Ashcan. *(Plains). Alt.* **pihkoyakanis** *(Northern).*

pakiciwepinew (VTA) S/he releases her/him quickly.

pakiciwepinam (VTI) S/he releases it quickly.

pakiciwepiniwew (VTA) S/he releases people.

pakiciwepinikew (VTI) S/he releases things.

pakiciwepiskâcikan *pl.* **pakiciwepiskâcikana** (NI) A tripper, i.e.: something that causes someone to trip and fall.

pakicîw *pl.* **pakicîwak** (VAI) S/he releases herself/himself.

pakicîwin *pl.* **pakicîwina** (NI) The act of releasing.

pakihkotew (VII) It is whittled until thin. *(Northern). Alt.* **papakisâwâtew** *(Plains).*

pakihkotam (VTI) S/he carves it until thin.

pakihkosiwew (VTA) S/he carves someone until thin.

pakihkocikew (VTI) S/he carves things until thin.

pakitahwâw *pl.* **pakitahwâwak** (VAI) S/he sets fishing nets.

pakitahwâwin *pl.* **pakitahwâwina** (NI) The act of fishing by setting nets.

pakitahwâwiyiniw *pl.* **pakitahwâwiyiniwak** (NA) A fisherman. *Var.* **opakitahwâw.**

pakitahwestamawew (VTA) S/he sets fishing nets for him/her.

pakitahwestamakew (VTA) S/he sets fishing nets for people.

pakitapihkenew (VTA) S/he lowers her/him down with a rope.

pakitapihkenam (VTI) S/he lowers it down with a rope.

pakitapihkeniwew (VTA) S/he lowers people down with a rope.

pakitapihkenikew (VTI) S/he lowers things down with a rope.

pakitasinâpân *pl.* **pakitasinâpâna** (NI) An anchor made with a rock.

pakitatamiw *pl.* **pakitatamiwak** (VAI) S/he gasps her/his final breath.

pakitatâhtam *pl.* **pakitatâhtamwak** (VTA) S/he exhales; s/he lets her/his breath out.

pakitatâhtamowin *pl.* **pakitatâhtamowina** (NI) The act of exhaling.

pakiteyihcikewin *pl.* **pakiteyihcikewina** (NI) The act of submitting.

pakiteyihtamawew (VTA) S/he grants remission for her/him.

pakiteyihtamâkew (VTA) S/he grants remission for someone.

pakiteyihtamâkewin *pl.* **pakiteyihtamâkewina** (NI) Remission or abatement, i.e.: of sins.

pakiteyihtamowin *pl.* **pakiteyihtamowina** (NI) The act of forsaking; the act of letting go.

pakiteyimew (VTA) S/he forsakes her/him; s/he disowns him/her.

pakiteyihtam (VTI) S/he forsakes it.

pakiteyimiwew (VTA) S/he forsakes someone.

pakiteyihcikew (VTI) S/he forsakes things.

pakiteyimisiw *pl.* **pakiteyimisiwak** (VTA) S/he abandons or gives up on herself/himself.

pakiteyimisowin *pl.* **pakiteyimisowina** (NI) Self-abandonment.

pakiteyimisôstawew (VTA) S/he abandons herself/himself to her/him.

pakiteyimisôstam (VTI) S/he abandons herself/himself to it.

pakiteyimisôstakêw (VTA) S/he abandons herself/himself to people.

pakiteyimow *pl.* **pakiteyimowak** (VAI) S/he surrenders.

pakiteyimowin *pl.* **pakiteyimowina** (NI) The act of surrendering; renunciation; the act of consenting; submission.

pakitinamwak (VAI) S/he let go.

pakitinamawew (VTA) S/he permits or allows her/him.
  pakitinamakew (VTA) S/he permits or allows everyone.

pakitinamâkew *pl.* **pakitinamâkewak** (VAI) S/he permits; s/he allows.

pakitinamâkewin *pl.* **pakitinamâkewina** (NI) The act of permitting.

pakitinasôstawew (VTA) S/he offers a sacrifice to her/him.
  pakitinasôstam (VTI) S/he offers a sacrifice to it.
  pakitinasôstâkew (VTA) S/he offers a sacrifice to someone.
  pakitinasôstawew (VTA) They offer a sacrifice to her/him.

pakitinâsiw *pl.* **pakitinâsiwak** (VAI) S/he offers a sacrifice.

pakitinâsiwin *pl.* **pakitinâsiwina** (NI) The act of offering.

pakitinâsowinâhtik *pl.* **pakitinâsowinâhtikwa** (NI) A sacrificial altar.

pakitinâsôstamawew (VTA) S/he offers a sacrifice for her/him.
  pakitinâsôstamakew (VTA) S/he offers a sacrifice for others.

pakitinâw (VAI) S/he is discharged.

pakitinew (VTA) S/he lets her/him go.
  pakitinam (VTI) S/he lets it go.
  pakitiniwew (VTA) S/he lets people go.
  pakitinikew (VTI) S/he lets things go.

pakitinikan *pl.* **pakitinikana** (NI) A seed.

pakitinikew *pl.* **pakitinikewak** (VAI) S/he seeds; s/he plants; s/he sows.

pakitinikewin *pl.* **pakitinikewina** (NI) The act of sowing or seeding.

pakitinisiw *pl.* **pakitinisiwak** (VAI) S/he resigns.

pakitinisowin *pl.* **pakitinisowina** (NI) The act of resigning oneself.

pakitinowewin *pl.* **pakitinowewina** (NI) The act of being discharged; liberated; granting permission.

pakiwayân *pl.* **pakiwayâna** (NI) A shirt. *(Plains). Alt.* **pakowayan** *(Northern).*

pakohcenew *pl.* **pakohcenewak** (VTA) S/he guts it; s/he removes its intestines. *(Northern). Alt.* **pikohcenew** *(Plains).*

pakonehtin *pl.* **pakonehtinwa** (VII) It is pierced.

pakonehwew (VTA) S/he pierces it.
  pakoneham (VII) S/he pierces a hole in it; s/he makes a hole in it.
  pakonehikew (VTI) S/he pierces things.

pakonenew (VTI) S/he pierces a hole with her/his hand; s/he makes a hole with her/his hands.
  pakonenam (VTI) S/he pierces it with his/her hands.
  pakoneniwew (VTA) S/he pierces people with her/his hands.
  pakonenikew (VTI) S/he pierces things with her/his hands.

pakonesimew (VTI) S/he makes a hole or pierces it against something, i.e.: the ground.
  pakonetitâw (VTI) S/he makes a hole or pierces it by banging it on something.
  pakonesimiwew (VTA) S/he makes a hole or pierces people by banging them with something.
  pakonehcikew (VTI) S/he makes a hole or pierces things by banging them on something.

pakonesin *pl.* **pakonesinwak** (VAI) It is pierced.

pakoneyâw *pl.* **pakoneyâwa** (VII) It has a hole, i.e.: in a shirt or tent.

pakonisiw *pl.* **pakonisiwak** (VAI) S/he has a hole, i.e.: in a water pail.

pakoseyihtamowin *pl.* **pakoseyihtamowina** (NI) Hoping for something.

pakoseyihtâkosiw *pl.* **pakoseyihtâkosiwak** (VAI) S/he brings or provides hope.

pakoseyihtâkwan *pl.* **pakoseyihtâkwanwa** (NI) Something that brings or provides hope.

pakoseyimew (VTA) S/he hopes to get something from her/him.
  pakoseyitam (VTI) S/he hopes to get something from it.
  pakoseyimiwew (VTA) S/he hopes to get something from people.
  pakoseyicikew (VTI) S/he hopes to get something for things.

pakoseyimiw *pl.* **pakoseyimiwak** (VAI) S/he has hope.

pakoseyimowin *pl.* **pakoseyimowina** (NI) The act of hoping; prospective.

pakosihew (VTA) S/he begs her/him.
  pakositâw (VAI) S/he begs.
  pakosihiwew (VTA) S/he begs people.
  pakosicikew (VTI) S/he begs for things.

pakosihtâwiyiniw *pl.* **pakosihtâwiyiniwak** (NA) A beggar.

pakowayan *pl.* **pakowayana** (NI) A shirt. *(Northern). Alt.* **pakiwayân** *(Plains).*

pakowayanekin *pl.* **pakowayanekinwa** (NI) A cotton cloth; broadcloth; shirting.

pakwaciminôs *pl.* **pakwaciminôsak** (NA) A cougar; lynx. *(Plains). Alt.* **misipisiw** *(Northern),* **misiminôs** *(Plains).*

pakwahtehiw *pl.* **pakwahtehiwak** (VAI) S/he wears a belt.

pakwahtehon *pl.* **pakwahtehona** (NI) A belt; waistband.

pakwahtehonihkew *pl.* **pakwahtehonihkewak** (VAI) S/he makes belts.

pakwahtehwew (VTA) S/he puts a belt on her/him.

pakwahtehowew (VTA) S/he puts a belt on someone.

pakwanaw (NI) Guesswork.

pakwanawayimomew (VAI) Her/his gossip about her/him is unsubstantiated.

pakwanawayimotam (VTI) Her/his gossip about it is unsubstantiated.

pakwanawayimomiwew (VTA) Her/his gossip about people is unsubstantiated.

pakwanawayimocikew (VTI) Her/his gossip about things is unsubstantiated.

pakwanawâhtaw *pl.* **pakwanawâhtawak** (VAI) S/he does it without believing it will succeed; s/he is dubious.

pakwanaweyihtamowin *pl.* **pakwanaweyihtamowina** (NI) The act of guessing.

pakwanaweyimew (VTA) S/he takes a guess about her/him; s/he knows nothing about her/him.

pakwanaweyihtam (VTI) S/he takes a guess at it.

pakwanaweyimiwew (VTA) S/he takes a guess at people.

pakwanaweyicikew (VTI) S/he takes a guess at things.

pakwanawihtam *pl.* **pakwanawihtamwak** (VAI) It is foretold.

pakwanawimew *pl.* **pakwanawimewak** (VTA) S/he speaks to her/him in a dubious manner.

pakwanawisiw *pl.* **pakwanawisiwak** (VAI) S/he acts in a dubious manner.

pakwanawisiwin *pl.* **pakwanawisiwina** (NI) Being dubious; an uncertain action.

pakwataskamik *pl.* **pakwataskamikwa** (NI) Barren land.

pakwataskiy *pl.* **pakwataskiya** (NI) Uninhabited land.

pakwatastim *pl.* **pakwatastimwak** (NA) An untamed horse; a mustang. *(Plains). Alt.* **pikwatastim** *(Northern)*.

pakwâcikan *pl.* **pakwâcikanak** (NA) A hated item.

pakwâcikewin *pl.* **pakwâcikewina** (NI) The act of detesting something.

pakwâcipisiskiw *pl.* **pakwâcipisiskiwak** (NA) A wild or untamed animal.

pakwâsowewin *pl.* **pakwâsowewina** (NI) The act of hatred; loathing.

pakwâtamowin *pl.* **pakwâtamowina** (NI) The act of abhorring something.

pakwâtew (VTA) S/he hates her/him.

pakwâtam (VTI) S/he hates it.

pakwâsiwew (VTA) S/he hates others.

pakwâcikew (VTI) S/he hates things.

pakwâteyihcikewin *pl.* **pakwâteyihcikewina** (NI) The act of feeling antipathy.

pakwâteyihtâkosiw *pl.* **pakwâteyihtâkosiwak** (VAI) S/he is hated.

pakwâteyihtâkosiwin *pl.* **pakwâteyihtâkosiwina** (NI) The act of being thought of as being detestible or hateful.

pakwâteyimew (VTA) S/he finds her/him distasteful.

pakwâteyitam (VTI) S/he finds it distasteful.

pakwâteyimiwew (VTA) S/he finds people distasteful.

pakwâteyicikew (VTI) S/he find things distasteful.

pakwâteyitâkwan *pl.* **pakwâteyitâkwanwa** (VII) It is hated.

pakwâtikosiw *pl.* **pakwâtikosiwak** (VAI) S/he is hateful, detestible, distasteful.

pakwâtikosiwin *pl.* **pakwâtikosiwina** (NI) The act of being hated or detested; being hated greatly. *(Plains). Alt.* **kakwâyakeyihtâkosowin** *(Northern)*.

pakwâtikwan *pl.* **pakwâtikwanwa** (VII) It is hateful.

pakwâtitowak (VTA) They hate each other.

pakwâtitowin *pl.* **pakwâtitowina** (NI) The act of having a mutual hatred for one another.

pamihew (VTA) S/he attends to her/him; s/he serves her/him; s/he ministers to her/him or them.

pamitaw (VTI) S/he attends to it.

pamihiwew (VTA) S/he attends to people.

pamicikew (VTI) S/he attends to things.

pamihisiw *pl.* **pamihisiwak** (VTA) S/he attends to herself/himself.

pamihisiwin *pl.* **pamihisiwina** (NI) The act of attending to oneself; the act of personal care.

pamihiwewin *pl.* **pamihiwewina** (NI) The act of attending to someone; the act of taking care of someone.

pamihow *pl.* **pamihowak** (VAI) S/he owns things. *(Plains and Northern variant). Alt.* **tipiyicikîw** *(Northern)*.

pamihowina (NI) Assets; the act of owning something; domain. *(Plains and Northern variant). Alt.* **tipeyicikîwina** *(Northern)*.

paminew (VTA) S/he looks after her/him.

paminam (VTI) S/he looks after it.

paminiwew (VTA) S/he looks after people.

paminikew (VTI) S/he looks after things.

paminowewin *pl.* **paminowewina** (NI) The act of being dependant.

papahew *pl.* **papahewak** (VTA) S/he quickly brings her/him over, i.e.: by car; s/he transports her/him.

papakapiskisiw *pl.* **papakapiskisiwak** (VAI) It is a thin piece of iron.

papakatin *pl.* **papakatinwa** (VII) It is thinly frozen, i.e.: ice.

papakâsin *pl.* **papakâsinwa** (VII) It is thin.

papakekan *pl.* **papakekanwa** (VII) The cloth is thin.

papakekin *pl.* **papakekinwa** (NI) A thin cloth. *(Northern). Alt.* **papakekinos** *(Plains)*.

147

papakekinos *pl.* **papakekinoswa** (NI) A thin cloth. *(Plains). Alt.* **papakekin** *(Northern).*

papakihtak *pl.* **papakihtakwa** (NI) A thin board.

papakisâwâtam *pl.* **papakisâwâtamwa** (VTI) S/he sliced it thinly.

papakisâwâtew (VII) It is whittled until thin. *(Plains). Alt.* **pakihkotew** *(Northern).*

papakisâwâtam (VTI) S/he carves it until thin.

papakisâwâsiwew (VTA) S/he carves someone until thin.

papakisâwâcikew (VTI) S/he carves things until thin.

papakisâwâtew *pl.* **papakisâwâtewa** (VII) It is sliced thinly.

papakisihew (VTA) S/he makes them thin.

papakisitâw (VTI) S/he makes it thin.

papakisihiwew (VTA) S/he makes people thin.

papakisicikew (VTI) S/he makes things thin.

papakisiw *pl.* **papakisiwak** (VAI) S/he is thin.

papakiswew (VTI) S/he slices them thinly.

papakisam (VTI) S/he slices it thinly.

papakisikew (VTA) S/he slices things thinly.

papamîhkawew *pl.* **papamîhkawewak** (VTA) S/he follows her/him everywhere.

papaseyihtam *pl.* **papaseyihtamwak** (VAI) S/he is in a hurry.

papasihew (VTA) S/he makes her/him hurry.

papasitâw (VTI) S/he hurries it.

papasihiwew (VTA) S/he hurries someone.

papayihew (VTI) S/he regurgitates it.

papayitâw (VTI) S/he regurgitates something.

papayicikew (VTI) S/he regurgitates things.

papayihtâw (VTI) S/he regurgitates it.

papayiw *pl.* **papayiwak** (VAI) S/he comes riding all over the place.

papasîw *pl.* **papasîwak** (VAI) S/he does things in a hurry.

papasîwin *pl.* **papasîwina** (NI) The act of doing things in a hurry.

papâmamiw *pl.* **papâmamiwak** (VAI) S/he flees or runs here and there.

papâmatwemow *pl.* **papâmatwemowak** (VAI) S/he goes crying here and there.

papâmâpahokow *pl.* **papâmâpahokowak** (VAI) S/he drifts around in the water.

papâmâpotew *pl.* **papâmâpotewa** (VII) It drifts around in the water.

papâmâsiw *pl.* **papâmâsiwak** (VAI) S/he is blown here and there by the wind.

papâmâstan *pl.* **papâmâstanwa** (VII) It is blown here and there by the wind.

papâmâstew *pl.* **papâmâstewa** (VII) It sits indescriminately.

papâmeyihtamowin *pl.* **papâmeyihtamowina** (NI) The act of being footloose.

papâmeyimow (VAI) S/he is footloose; s/he can't settle down.

papâmeyitam (VAI) S/he is always on the go.

papâmi (IPC) All over the place, everywhere.

papâmihâw *pl.* **papâmihâwak** (VAI) S/he flies all over the place. *(Plains). Alt.* **papâmiyâw** *(Northern).*

papâmimâmawopiw *pl.* **papâmimâmawopiwak** (VAI) S/he sits and holds meetings here and there. *(Plains). Alt.* **pahpapamapiw** *(Northern).*

papâmipahtâw *pl.* **papâmipahtâwak** (VAI) S/he runs everywhere.

papâmipahtâwin *pl.* **papâmipahtâwina** (NI) The action of running everywhere.

papâmipayiw *pl.* **papâmipayiwa** *or* **papâmipayiwak** (VII) *or* (VAI) It *or* s/he travels all over the place, i.e.: on horseback.

papâmipiciw *pl.* **papâmipiciwak** (VAI) S/he moves all over the place.

papâmipiciwin *pl.* **papâmipiciwina** (NI) The act of moving all over the place.

papâmiskanawew *pl.* **papâmiskanawewak** (VAI) S/he leaves her/his tracks everywhere.

papâmitâcimow *pl.* **papâmitâcimowak** (VAI) S/he crawls around everywhere.

papâmiyâw *pl.* **papâmiyâwak** (VAI) S/he flies all over the place. *(Northern). Alt.* **papâmihâw** *(Plains).*

papâmohtahew (VTA) S/he carries her/him everywhere.

papâmohtatâw (VTI) S/he carries it everywhere.

papâmohtahiwew (VTA) S/he carries people everywhere.

papâmohtacikew (VTI) S/he carries things everywhere.

papâmohtewin *pl.* **papâmohtewina** (NI) The act of walking everywhere.

papâseyihtamowin *pl.* **papâseyihtamowina** (NI) The act of being in a hurry or making haste; the act of being eager; being avid.

papâsimew (VTA) S/he tells her/him to hurry, to make haste.

papâsitam (VTA) What s/he hears makes her/him hurry.

papâsimiwew (VTA) S/he tells someone to hurry.

papehtâkopayiw *pl.* **papehtâkopayiwak** (VAI) S/he is making mumbling sounds.

papeskomina (NI) Pepper. *(Plains). Alt.* **kahkominakâk** *(Northern).*

papestin *pl.* **papestinwa** (NI) A snow drift.

papestinowan *pl.* **papestinowana** (NI) Having snow drifting over, i.e.: on a road.

papetan *pl.* **papetanwa** (VII) It is a slow process.

papetohtew *pl.* **papetohtewak** (VAI) S/he is a slow walker.

papewew *pl.* **papewewak** (VAI) S/he is a lucky person.

papewewin *pl.* **papewewina** (NI) The act of having luck; gainful.

papihkâsohâyâwin *pl.* **papihkâsohâyâwina** (NI) The act of being giggly.

papiwemew (VTA) S/he makes her/him lucky with her/his words.

papiwetam (VTI) S/he makes it lucky with her/his words.

papiwemiwew (VTA) S/he makes someone lucky with her/his words.

papiwecikew (VTI) S/he makes things lucky with her/his words.

papiweskawew (VTA) S/he brings her/him luck; s/he is her/his lucky charm.

papiweskam (VTI) S/he is a lucky charm to it.

papiweskakew (VTA) S/he is a lucky charm to people.

papiweskacikew (VTI) S/he is a lucky charm to things.

papiwihew (VTA) S/he makes her/him lucky.

papiwitâw (VTI) S/he makes it lucky.

papiwihiwew (VTA) S/he makes someone lucky.

papiwicikew (VTI) S/he makes things lucky.

papîcew *pl.* **papîcewak** (VAI) S/he is really slow going; s/he does things slowly.

papîcîyimew (VTA) S/he finds her/him slow going.

papîcîyitam (VTI) S/he finds it slow going.

papîcîyimiwew (VTA) S/he finds someone slow going.

papîcîyicikew (VTI) S/he finds things slow going.

papwâstahohtew *pl.* **papwâstahohtewak** (VAI) S/he walks slowly. *(Plains). Alt.* **pekihkâtohtew** *(Northern),* **yîkicikâtohtew** *(Plains).*

papwâstawiw *pl.* **papwâstawiwak** (VAI) S/he goes slowly. *(Plains). Alt.* **pekihkâciw** *(Northern).*

pasahcâw *pl.* **pasahcâwa** (VII) It is a ravine.

pasahcipayiw *pl.* **pasahcipayiwa** (VII) It is a crack, fissure, crevice in the ground, i.e.: in a field.

pasahcisikew *pl.* **pasahcisikewak** (VAI) S/he makes a furrow in the ground, i.e.: a fireguard.

pasahikew *pl.* **pasahikewak** (VAI) S/he hews timber with a broad axe.

pasahikewicîkahikan *pl.* **pasahikewicîkahikana** (NI) An axe for squaring timber, i.e.: a broad axe.

pasahikewiyiniw *pl.* **pasahikewiyiniwak** (NA) One who squares timber, i.e.: a hewer.

pasahkapehew (VTA) S/he makes her/him blink when s/he pretends to hit her/him.

pasahkapehowew (VTA) S/he makes others blink when s/he pretends to hit them.

pasahkapehikew (VTA) S/he makes people blink when s/he pretends to hit them.

pasahkapiw *pl.* **pasahkapiwak** (VAI) S/he blinks her/his eyes.

pasahwew (VTI) S/he hews logs.

pasaham (VTI) S/he hews it.

pasahikew (VTI) S/he hews things.

pasakoceskowakâw *pl.* **pasakoceskowakâwa** (VII) It is gummy, gluey mud, i.e.: on a road.

pasakohtin *pl.* **pasakohtinwa** (VII) It is glued on something; it is stuck to something.

pasakosimew (VAI) S/he rubs them on something sticky.

pasakohtitâw (VTI) S/he rubs it on something sticky.

pasakosimiwew (VTA) S/he rubs someone on something sticky.

pasakohcikew (VTI) S/he rubs things on something sticky.

pasakosin *pl.* **pasakosinwak** (VAI) It fell on something sticky; s/he is stuck to something.

pasakosiw *pl.* **pasakosiwak** (VAI) It is sticky, i.e.: spruce gum.

pasakoskiwahew (VTA) S/he sticks them together with spruce gum; s/he glues them together.

pasakoskiwataw (VTI) S/he sticks it together with spruce gum.

pasakoskiwacikew (VTA) S/he sticks things together with spruce gum.

pasakoskiwâcikan *pl.* **pasakoskiwâcikana** (NI) A glue or paste. *Var.* **pasakwahikan.**

pasakoskow *pl.* **pasakoskowak** (NA) Sticky spruce gum.

pasakoskowakâw *pl.* **pasakoskowakâwa** (VII) It is muddy, i.e.: a field.

pasakoskowew *pl.* **pasakoskowewak** (VAI) It is sticky with spruce gum.

pasakwahwew (VTA) S/he makes them sticky.

pasakwaham (VTI) S/he makes it sticky.

pasakwahowew (VTA) S/he makes people sticky.

pasakwahikew (VTI) S/he makes things sticky.

pasakwamohew (VTA) S/he sticks them together.

pasakwamotâw (VTI) S/he sticks it on.

pasakwamocikew (VTI) S/he sticks things together.

pasakwapipayiw *pl.* **pasakwapipayiwak** (VAI) Her/his eyes close.

pasakwapiwin *pl.* **pasakwapiwina** (NI) The act of closing the eyes.

pasakwaskicân *pl.* **pasakwaskicâna** (NI) Tobacco juice that congeals around a pipestem; nicotine juice.

pasakwâpiw *pl.* **pasakwâpiwak** (VAI) S/he closes her/his eyes.

pasakwâpiwinân *pl.* **pasakwâpiwinâna** (NI) An eyelid. *(Plains). Alt.* **kipaskapowinan** *(Northern).*

pasakwâpoy *pl.* **pasakwâpoya** (NI) A sticky liquid, like honey.

pasakwâw *pl.* **pasakwâwa** (VII) It is sticky, i.e.: molasses.

pasastehâwasiw *pl.* **pasastehâwasiwak** (VTA) S/he whips her/his children.

pasastehâwasiwin *pl.* **pasastehâwasiwina** (NI) The act of whipping children.

pasastehikan *pl.* **pasastehikana** (NI) A whip; a bullwhip.

pasastehikanihkawew *pl.* **pasastehikanihkawewak** (VTA) S/he makes a whip for her/him.

pasastehikanihkâkew *pl.* **pasastehikanihkâkewak** (VAI) S/he makes a whip with it.

pasastehikanihkew *pl.* **pasastehikanihkewak** (VAI) S/he makes a whip.

pasastehowewin *pl.* **pasastehowewina** (NI) The act of whipping someone; lash; scourge.

pasastehwew (VTA) S/he whips her/him.
   pasasteham (VTI) S/he whips it.
   pasastehowew (VTA) S/he whips someone.
   pasastehikew (VTI) S/he whips things.

pasâpiskâw *pl.* **pasâpiskâwa** (VII) It is a rocky ravine in the mountains.

pascicehosiw *pl.* **pascicehosiwak** (VTA) S/he slaps her/his own hands.

pascihcehwew (VTA) S/he slaps her/his hands.
   pascihcehowew (VTA) S/he slaps someone on the hands.
   pascihcehikew (VTA) S/he slaps everybody on the hands.

pascikwâskohtiw *pl.* **pascikwâskohtiwak** (VAI) S/he jumps over.

pascipayiw *pl.* **pascipayiwak** or **pascipayiwa** (VAI) *or* (VII) S/he *or* it goes over.

pasciskawew (VTA) S/he is taller than her/him. *(Northern). Alt.* **cayoskawew** *(Plains).*
   pasciskam (VTI) S/he is taller than it.
   pasciskâkew (VTA) S/he is taller than someone.
   pasciskâcikew (VTI) S/he is taller than everything.

pascitahkoskew *pl.* **pascitahkoskewak** (VAI) S/he stepped over. *(Plains). Alt.* **pastahkoskew** *(Northern).*

pasciwepinew (VTA) S/he throws her/him or it over.
   pasciwepinam (VTI) S/he threw something over.
   pasciwepiniwew (VTA) S/he throws people over.
   pasciwepinikew (VTI) S/he throws things over.

pasciwepinikewin *pl.* **pasciwepinikewia** (NI) The act of being excessive.

pasihkocikan *pl.* **pasihkocikana** (NI) An instrument for carving a wood groove; a gouging chisel.

pasihkocikew *pl.* **pasihkocikewak** (VAI) S/he chisels a groove on a piece of wood.

pasihkocikewin *pl.* **pasihkocikewina** (NI) The act of chiseling a groove on a piece of wood.

pasihkotew (VTA) S/he chisels a groove on them.
   pasihkotam (VTI) S/he chisels a groove on it.
   pasihkocikew (VTI) S/he chisels a groove on things.

pasihkwehwew (VTA) S/he slaps her/him in the face.
   pasihkwehowew (VTA) S/he slaps someone in the face.
   pasihkwehikew (VTA) S/he slaps people in the face.

pasihkwenew (VTA) S/he shoves her/his face aside.

pasihkweniwew (VTA) S/he shoves someone's face aside.

pasihkwenikew (VTA) S/he shoves peoples' faces aside.

pasihkwepitew (VTA) S/he scratches her/his face with her/his nails.

pasihkwepitam (VTI) S/he scratches its face with her/his nails.

pasihkwepisiwew (VTA) S/he scratches someone's face with her/his nails.

pasihkwepicikew (VTA) S/he scratches peoples' faces with her/his nails.

pasikohew (VTA) S/he makes her/him stand up.
   pasikotâw (VTI) S/he makes it stand up.
   pasikohiwew (VTA) S/he makes someone stand up.
   pasikocikew (VTI) S/he makes things stand up.

pasikonew (VTA) S/he helps her/him to stand up.
   pasikonam (VTI) S/he stands it up.
   pasikoniwew (VTA) S/he stands people up.
   pasikonikew (VTI) S/he stands things up.

pasikopahtâw *pl.* **pasikopahtâwak** (VAI) S/he stands up very quickly; s/he jumps to her/his feet.

pasikotisaham (VTI) S/he sets it up; s/he institutes it.
   pasikotisahowew (VTA) S/he sets people up.
   pasikotisahikew (VTI) S/he sets things up.

pasikotisahwew *pl.* **pasikotisahwewak** (VTA) S/he makes her/him stand up quickly.

pasikow *pl.* **pasikowak** (VAI) S/he stands up.

pasikowin *pl.* **pasikowina** (NI) The act of standing up.

pasikôstawew (VTA) S/he affirms it in her/his presence.
   pasikôstam (VTI) S/he affirms it.
   pasikôstâkew (VTA) S/he gives people moral support.
   pasikôstâcikew (VTI) S/he affirms things.

pasisâwew *pl.* **pasisâwewak** (VTA) S/he burns the prairie grass.

pasisiw *pl.* **pasisiwak** (VAI) S/he is burned out by a bush fire.

pasiskwehpison *pl.* **pasiskwehpisona** (NI) A head band.

pasistikwanepitew (VTA) S/he ties a band around her/his head.
   pasistikwanepisiwew (VTA) S/he ties a band around someone's head.
   pasistikwanepicikew (VTA) S/he ties a band around others' heads.

pasiswew (VTA) S/he burns her/him out with a bush fire.
   pasisam (VTI) S/he burns the country.
   pasisowew (VTA) S/he burns the people out with a bush fire.
   pasisikew (VTI) S/he burns the grass or hay.

pasitahew (VTA) S/he puts her/him over the top.
   pasitastâw (VTI) S/he puts it over the top.
   pasitahiwew (VTA) S/he puts people over the top.
   pasitascikew (VTI) S/he puts things over the top.

pasitâhtawiw *pl.* **pasitâhtawiwa** (VTI) S/he climbs over, i.e.: a fence.

pasitâmacowew *pl.* **pasitâmacowewak** (VAI) S/he climbed over, i.e.: a hill or mountain.

pasitew *pl.* **pasitewa** (NI) A fire caused by lightning.

pasiw *pl.* **pasiwak** (VAI) S/he can smell it.

pasiwin *pl.* **pasiwina** (NI) The act of smelling.

paskakonakâw (VII) Freshly fallen snow which is easy for tracking. *(Northern)*. *Alt.* **oskâkonakâw** *(Plains)*.

paskakonakewin *pl.* **paskakonakewina** (NI) The act of making fresh tracks in the snow.

paskamew (VAI) S/he gnaws on it for her/him, i.e.: a dog on a rope; s/he chews off the rope for her/him.
  paskatam (VTI) S/he gnaws it off.
  paskamiwew (VTA) S/he gnaws someone off.
  paskacikew (VTI) S/he gnaws things off.

paskâkonakew *pl.* **paskâkonakewak** (VAI) S/he makes fresh tracks in the snow.

paskâkonakiyâw (VII) It is freshly fallen snow which makes for good tracking.

paskâpew *pl.* **paskâpewak** (VAI) S/he breaks it, i.e.: a rope.

paskehtahew (VTA) S/he takes her/him off to the side of the road.
  paskehtatâw (VTI) S/he takes it off to the side of the road.
  paskehtahiwew (VTA) S/he takes people off to the side of the road.
  paskehtacikew (VTI) S/he takes things off to the side of the road.

paskehtin *pl.* **paskehtinwa** (NI) A branch or fork off a river, i.e.: a tributary.

paskemow *pl.* **paskemowa** (NI) A minor road that branches off the main road.

paskepayihowin *pl.* **paskepayihowina** (NI) The act of being alienated; alienation.

paskesiwin *pl.* **paskesiwina** (NI) An animal quarter.

paskestikweyaw *pl.* **paskestikweyawa** (NI) A fork on a river.

pasketisahwew (VTA) S/he chases her/him in a different direction.
  pasketisaham (VTI) S/he chases it in a different direction.
  pasketisahowew (VTA) S/he chases people in a different direction.
  pasketisahikew (VTI) S/he chases everyone in a different direction.

pasketisinew (VTA) S/he shifts them over to one side.
  pasketisinam (VTI) S/he shifts it over to the one side.
  pasketisiniwew (VTI) S/he shifts someone over to one side.
  pasketisinikew (VTI) S/he shifts things over to one side.

paskew *pl.* **paskewak** (VAI) S/he changes another direction.

paskewihew (VTA) S/he leaves her/him and goes in another direction.
  paskewitâw (VTI) S/he leaves it and goes in another direction.
  paskewiyiwew (VTA) S/he leaves someone and goes in another direction.
  paskewicikew (VTI) S/he leaves things and goes in another direction.

paskewin *pl.* **paskewina** (NI) The act of changing direction; separation.

paskeyâkepayowin *pl.* **paskeyâkepayowina** (NI) The act of being predominant; prevalence.

paskeyâkew *pl.* **paskeyâkewak** (VAI) S/he won.

paskeyâkewin *pl.* **paskeyâkewina** (NI) The act of being superior; preponderance.

paskeyâw *pl.* **paskeyâwa** (VII) It branches off in another direction.

paskipayiw *pl.* **paskipayiwa** or **paskipayiwak** (VII) *or* (VAI) It broke apart, i.e.: rope.

paskipitew (VTA) S/he breaks it off by pulling, i.e.: a thread.
  paskipitam (VTI) S/he breaks it off by pulling, i.e.: a rope.

paskisiw *pl.* **paskisiwak** (VAI) S/he was burned by a spark.

paskiswew (VTI) S/he cuts them off.
  paskisam (VTI) S/he cuts it off.
  paskisowew (VTA) S/he cuts someone off.
  paskisikew (VTI) S/he cuts things off.

paskitahpicikan *pl.* **paskitahpicikana** (NI) A leather strap.

paskitahpisiw *pl.* **paskitahpisiwak** (VAI) S/he is strapped or bound.

paskitahpitew (VTA) S/he ties a rope around her/him.
  paskitahpitam (VTI) S/he ties a rope around it.
  paskitahpisiwew (VTA) S/he ties a rope around someone.
  paskitahpicikew (VTI) S/he ties a rope around things.

paskitatayehpitew (VTA) S/he ties her/him around the stomach.
  paskitatayehpisiwew (VTA) S/he ties people around the belly.
  paskitatayehpicikew (VTI) S/he ties horses around the belly.

paskitatayepicikan *pl.* **paskitatayepicikana** (NI) The strap of a saddle, i.e.: the girth.

paskitepayiw *pl.* **paskitepayiwa** or **paskitepayiwak** (VII) *or* (VAI) It *or* s/he sparks, i.e.: a fire cracker or a flint.

paskitew *pl.* **paskitewa** (VII) A spark from the fire.

151

paskitewasiniy *pl.* **paskitewasiniya** (NI) A stone that sparks fire, i.e.: flint. *(Northern). Alt.* **sikisehikan** *(Plains).*

paskiyakewin *pl.* **paskiyakewina** (NI) The act of defeating someone; trounce.

paskiyawew (VTA) S/he defeats her/him.
　paskiyâkew (VTA) S/he is the winner.

paskohkasiw *pl.* **paskohkasiwak** (VAI) It is singed.

paskonew *pl.* **paskonewak** (VAI) S/he is fat, i.e.: used to refer to animals that are ready to be slaughtered or hunted.

paskopitew (VTI) S/he plucks it, i.e.: removes the feathers.
　paskopitam (VTI) S/he plucks it, i.e.: weeds from a garden.
　paskopicikwew (VTI) S/he plucks them, i.e.: ducks or weeds in a garden.

paskosikâkan *pl.* **paskosikâkana** (NI) A hair clipper.

paskosiw *pl.* **paskosiwak** (VAI) It is hairless; it has no fur.

paskostikwânew *pl.* **paskostikwânewak** (VAI) S/he has a bald head.

paskostikwânewkihew *pl.* **paskostikwânewkihewak** (NA) A bald eagle.

paskoswew (VTA) S/he cuts off her/his hair, i.e.: a haircut.
　paskosam (VTI) S/he cuts the hair off it.
　paskosowew (VTA) S/he cuts hair off people.
　paskosikew (VTI) S/he is cutting hair off.

paskow *pl.* **paskowak** (VAI) S/he is molting, i.e.: a duck.

paskowin *pl.* **paskowina** (NI) The act of molting plumage or feathers.

paskwaciy *pl.* **paskwaciya** (NI) A bare mountain.

paskwahamâw *pl.* **paskwahamâwak** (VAI) S/he has a haircut. *(Northern). Alt.* **kîskahamâw** *(Plains).*

paskwahamâwew (VTA) S/he gives her/him a haircut; s/he cuts her/his hair. *(Northern). Alt.* **kiskahamawew** *(Plains).*
　paskwahamâkew (VTA) S/he gives haircuts.

paskwahwew (VTA) S/he scrapes the fur from the skin.
　paskwaham (VTA) S/he scrapes the hair off the hide.
　paskwahikew (VTA) S/he scrapes the hair.

paskwatahikan *pl.* **paskwatahikana** (NI) A machine for clearing land of trees.

paskwatahikew (VAI) S/he clears land, i.e.: for a homestead.
　paskwatawew (VAI) S/he cut them all off, i.e.: trees.
　paskwataham (VAI) S/he clears a piece of land.

paskwatahikewin *pl.* **paskwatahikewina** (NI) The act of clear-cutting a piece of land.

paskwatihpehtew (VTA) S/he scalps her/him.
　paskwatihpehowew (VTA) S/he scalps everyone.
　paskwatihpehikew (VTA) S/he scalps people.

paskwatihpenew (VTA) S/he skins her/his head.
　paskwatihpeniwew (VTA) S/he skins someone's head.
　paskwatihpenikew (VTA) S/he skins peoples' heads.

paskwatinâw *pl.* **paskwatinâwa** (NI) A hill.

paskwâskisiw *pl.* **paskwâskisiwak** (VAI) It shoots out red-hot spark, i.e.: a fire.

paskwâskitew *pl.* **paskwâskitewa** (VII) The fire throws sparks.

paskwâtihpeswew (VTA) S/he shaves her/his head; s/he removes all her/his hair.
　paskwâtihpeskew (VTA) S/he shaves someone's head.

paskwâtihpewin *pl.* **paskwâtihpewina** (NI) Being bald-headed.

paskwâw *pl.* **paskwâwa** (NI) A clearing; a treeless piece of land; a prairie.

paskwâwatimosis *pl.* **paskwâwatimosisak** (NA) A praire dog. *Var.* **pasowahkesîs**.

paskwâw'mostos *pl.* **paskwâw'mostoswak** (NA) A buffalo *(Northern). Alt.* **paskwâwimostos** *(Plains).*

paskwâwimostos *pl.* **paskwâwimostoswak** (NA) A buffalo *(Plains). Alt.* **paskwâw'mostos** *(Northern).*

paskwâwiyiniw *pl.* **paskwâwiyiniwak** (NA) A Plains Cree person.

pasôhew *pl.* **pasôhewak** (VTA) S/he makes her/him smell it.

pasowahkesîs *pl.* **pasowahkesîsak** (NA) A prairie dog. *Var.* **paskwâwatimosis**.

paspaham *pl.* **paspahamwak** (VAI) S/he passes through any opening.

paspâpiw *pl.* **paspâpiwak** (VAI) S/he peers at the window, i.e.: looking out or in.

paspinasiw *pl.* **paspinasiwak** (VTA) S/he just barely missed killing them.

paspinatew (VTA) S/he just about killed them.
　paspinatam (VTI) S/he just about got it.
　paspinasiwew (VTA) S/he just about gets someone.
　paspinacikew (VTI) S/he just about gets everything.

paspinew *pl.* **paspinewak** (VAI) S/he pushes her/him through an opening.

paspitisinew (VTA) S/he hands or passes her/him through an opening.
　paspitisinam (VTI) S/he hands it through an opening.
　paspitisiniwew (VTA) S/he hands someone through an opening.
　paspitisinikew (VTI) S/he hands things through an opening.

paspîhiwewin *pl.* **paspîhiwewina** (NI) The act of saving someone; deliverance; vindication.

paspîw *pl.* **paspîwak** (VAI) S/he has successfully escaped or eluded the danger.

paspîwin *pl.* **paspîwina** (NI) The act of successfully escaping or eluding danger; clearance; survival.

152

pastahkoskew *pl.* **pastahkoskewak** (VAI) S/he stepped over. *(Northern). Alt.* **pascitahkoskew** *(Plains).*

pastâciwahtew *pl.* **pastâciwahtewa** (VII) It boils over, i.e.: water.

pastâciwasiw *pl.* **pastâciwasiwak** (VAI) It boils over, i.e.: a pot.

pastipew *pl.* **pastipewa** (VII) The water floods or overflows.

pastohtew *pl.* **pastohtewak** (VAI) S/he walks over.

pastonehwew (VAI) S/he slaps her/his mouth.

pastoneham (VTI) S/he slaps it on the mouth.

pastonehowêw (VTA) S/he slaps someone on the mouth.

pastonehikêw (VTI) S/he slaps people on the mouth.

pastosiwan *pl.* **pastosiwanwa** (NI) A whirlwind or tornado.

pastosiwiw *pl.* **pastosiwiwa** (VII) There is a whirlwind or a tornado.

paswâkan *pl.* **paswâkana** (NI) A nose. *(Northern). Alt.* **mikot** *(Plains).*

pasweskoyiw *pl.* **pasweskoyiwak** (VAI) S/he is sick after eating too much fat.

pasweyâw *pl.* **pasweyâwa** (VII) It is greasy.

pataham *pl.* **patahamwa** (VTI) S/he misses her/his road or trail.

patahikehew (VTA) S/he makes her/him miss her/his target.

patahiketâw (VTI) S/he makes it miss its target.

patahikew *pl.* **patahikewa** (VTI) S/he misses her/his target.

patahwew (VTA) S/he misses her/him, i.e.: with an arrow or gun.

pataham (VTI) S/he misses it, i.e.: a target or road.

patahowew (VTA) S/he misses people.

patahikew (VTI) S/he misses things.

patakimew (VAI) S/he miscounted them.

patakihtam (VTI) S/he miscounted it.

patakimiwew (VTA) S/he miscounted people.

patakihcikew (VTI) S/he miscounted things.

patakonew (VTA) S/he holds her/him down with her/his hands.

patakonam (VTI) S/he holds it down with her/his hands.

patakoniwew (VTA) S/he holds people down with her/his hands.

patakonikew (VTI) S/he holds things down with her/his hands.

patakonkewin *pl.* **patakonkewina** (NI) The act of repressing; repression.

patakoskawew (VTA) S/he settles on top of her/him and holds her/him down.

patakoskam (VTI) S/he settles on it and holds it down.

patakoskâkew (VTA) S/he settles on people and holds them down.

patakoskâcikew (VTI) S/he settles on things and holds them down.

patakwahwew (VTA) S/he holds her/him down with something heavy.

patakwaham (VTI) S/he holds it down with something heavy.

patakwahowew (VTA) S/he holds someone down with something heavy.

patakwahikew (VTI) S/he holds things down with something heavy.

patamew (VTA) S/he misses grabbing it with her/his teeth.

patahtam (VTI) S/he misses grabbing it with her/his teeth.

patacikew (VTI) S/he misses grabbing things with her/his teeth.

patamisk *pl.* **patamiskwak** (NA) A two-year-old beaver.

patapehew (VTA) S/he makes her/him miss her/his chair.

patapetaw (VTI) S/he makes it miss its chair.

patapehiwew (VTA) S/he makes someone miss their chair.

patapiskweyiw *pl.* **patapiskweyiwak** (VAI) S/he bows her/his head; s/he bends her/his neck down.

patapitisahwew (VTA) S/he makes her/him lose her/his place, i.e.: a chair.

patapitisaham (VTI) S/he makes it lose its place.

patapitisahowew (VTA) S/he makes people lose their place.

patapitisahikew (VTI) S/he makes things lose their place.

patapiw *pl.* **patapiwak** (VAI) S/he misses her/his chair.

patapiwin *pl.* **patapiwina** (NI) The act of missing one's chair.

patasinahwew (VTA) S/he has written or marked her/him down wrong.

patasinaham (VTI) S/he has written it the wrong way.

patasinahowew (VTA) S/he has written or marked someone down the wrong way.

patasinahikew (VTI) S/he has written or marked everything down the wrong way.

pataskenam *pl.* **pataskenamwak** (VAI) S/he misses touching the ground or bottom in the water with her/his feet.

patasowâtew (VTA) S/he judges her/him wrongly.

patasowâtam (VTI) S/he judges it wrongly.

patasowâsiwew (VTA) S/he judges people wrongly.

patasowâcikew (VTI) S/he judges things wrongly.

patatâmiw *pl.* **patatâmiwak** (VAI) S/he misses singing the right pitch.

153

patawpayowin *pl.* **patawpayowina** (NI) The act of being bulgy and moving slowly; lumbering.

patâpahtamohew (VTA) S/he makes her/him lose sight of it.

  patâpahtamotaw (VTI) S/he makes it lose sight.

patâpamew (VTA) S/he misses sighting her/him.

  patâpahtam (VTI) S/he misses sighting of it.

  patâpamiwew (VTA) S/he misses sighting people.

  patâpahcikew (VTI) S/he misses sighting things.

pateyihcikewin *pl.* **pateyihcikewina** (NI) The act of having delusions.

patinew (VTA) S/he misses catching it, i.e.: a ball.

  patinam (VTI) S/he misses catching it, i.e.: a train.

  patiniwew (VTA) S/he misses catching people.

patiskawew (VTA) S/he misses her/him, i.e.: either a planned or unplanned encounter.

  patiskam (VTI) S/he misses it.

  patiskâkew (VTA) S/he misses people.

patote (IPC) Out of place.

patoteciwan *pl.* **patoteciwanwa** (VII) It flows off in another direction.

patotepayiw *pl.* **patotepayiwak** (VAI) It fell off or slid off to one side.

patoteskanaw (IPC) Off to the side of the road, i.e.: wayside.

patowew *pl.* **patowewak** (VAI) S/he speaks and says the wrong things.

pawacakinasîs (NA) December; the tree cleaning moon or month *(Northern)*. *Alt.* **pawahcakinasîs** *(Plains)*. *Var.* **manito kîsikan pîsim**.

pawahamoyâw (VII) It is tree cleaning time, i.e.: the wind blows and the snow falls from the trees.

pawahcakinasîs (NA) December; drift clearing moon or month *(Plains)*. *Alt.* **pawacakinasîs** *(Northern)*. *Var.* **manito kîsikan pîsim**.

pawahtakinew (VTA) S/he cleans the snow off the trees.

  pawahtakinam (VTA) S/he cleans the snow off the trees.

  pawahtakinikew (VTA) S/he is cleaning the snow off the trees.

pawahtakipayiw *pl.* **pawahtakipayiwak** (VAI) The tree becomes clean of snow.

pawakan *pl.* **pawakanak** (NA) A tribal totem figure encountered in the dream world and which subsequently represents spiritual power. *(Plains)*. *Alt.* **powâkan** *(Northern)*.

pawaskwew (VAI) The sun filtrates through the clouds. *(Northern)*. *Alt.* **pesâkâstew** *(Plains)*.

pawatew (VAI) S/he has a spirit dream. *(Plains)*. *Alt.* **powatew** *(Northern)*.

  pawasowew (VTA) S/he dreams of someone.

  pawacikew (VTI) S/he dreams of things.

pawawew (VTA) S/he dusts or brushes them off.

  pawaham (VTI) S/he dusts or brushes it off.

  pawahowew (VTA) S/he dusts or brushes off someone.

  pawahikew (VTI) S/he dusts or brushes off things.

pawâhtâw *pl.* **pawâhtâwak** (VAI) S/he lives in accord with her/his spirit helper.

pawâmiw *pl.* **pawâmiwak** (VAI) S/he has a secret spirit helper; s/he has an animal identity or guardian spirit.

pawâmowin *pl.* **pawâmowina** (NI) Having a secret spirit helper.

pawâsiw *pl.* **pawâsiwak** (VAI) It is all cleaned off by the wind, i.e.: a spruce tree.

pawâstan *pl.* **pawâstanwa** (VII) It is cleaned off by the wind, i.e.: a road blown free of snow.

pawâtahikana (NA) Something that is cleaned off or filtered out, i.e.: chaff. *(Northern)*. *Alt.* **piwihtakahikana** *(Plains)*.

pawâtamowin *pl.* **pawâtamowina** (NI) The act of dreaming. *(Plains)*. *Alt.* **pawatamowin** *(Northern)*.

pawâyihk (IPC) Only partially visible; clarity is hampered by an obstacle.

paweyaw *pl.* **paweyawa** (VII) It is too fatty. *Var.* **wiyiniwiw**.

pawihkaswew (VTA) S/he burns them off something else.

  pawihkasam (VTI) S/he burns it off.

  pawihkasikew (VTI) S/he burns something off.

pawinawew (VTA) S/he does not see her/him fully; is not clearly visible.

  pawinam (VTA) S/he can scarcely see.

  pawinâkew (VTA) S/he scarcely sees anybody.

pawinehkwâmiw *pl.* **pawinehkwâmiwak** (VAI) S/he has a fitful sleep.

pawinekwasiw *pl.* **pawinekwasiwak** (VAI) S/he is drowsy.

pawinew (VTA) S/he rubs it or them off.

  pawinam (VTI) S/he rubs it off.

  pawinikew (VTI) S/he rubs things off.

pawipayiw *pl.* **pawipayiwa** *or* **pawipayiwak** (VII) *or* (VAI) It *or* s/he rubs right off.

pawisimew (VTA) S/he rubs them off.

  pawihtitâw (VTI) S/he rubs it off.

  pawihcikew (VTI) S/he rubs things off.

pawistikowiw *pl.* **pawistikowiwa** (VII) It has rapids.

pawitisahamawew (VTA) S/he scares them away, i.e.: wild game, and does not leave any for the next person. *(Northern)*. *Alt.* **sekihtamawew** *(Plains)*.

  pawitisahamakew (VTA) S/he scares all the game away for other people.

pawitisahikâtew *pl.* **pawitisahikâtewa** (VII) In that area, all the game has been scared away.

pawitisahwew (VTA) S/he chases them all away. *(Northern). Alt.* **mestâmohkew** *(Plains).*

pawitisaham (VTA) S/he chases game out of the whole area.

pawitisahikew (VTA) S/he chases everything away.

pawosimew (VTA) S/he scarcely sees her/him, i.e.: through fog or thick bush.

pawotitâw (VTI) S/he scarcely sees it.

pawosimiwew (VTA) S/he scarcely sees people.

payipahikan *pl.* **payipahikana** (NI) A machine for boring holes, i.e.: a drill; a borer.

payipahwew (VTA) S/he bores a hole in them.

payipaham (VTI) S/he drills a hole in it.

payipahikew (VTI) S/he drills a hole in things.

payipâw *pl.* **payipâwa** (VII) It has a hole through it, i.e.: like a straw.

payipihkocikanâhtik *pl.* **payipihkocikanâhtikwa** (NI) A brace for use in drilling wood.

payipihtakahikan *pl.* **payipihtakahikana** (NI) A drill bit for wood.

payipisiw *pl.* **payipisiwak** (VAI) It has a hole in it, i.e.: a pipe.

payipiswew (VTI) S/he cuts a hole in them.

payipisam (VTI) S/he cuts a hole in it.

payipisikew (VTI) S/he cuts a hole in things.

pâhkahokohew (VTA) S/he feels her/his pulse.

pâhkahokohiwew (VTA) S/he feels peoples' pulses.

pâhkahokow *pl.* **pâhkahokowak** (VAI) S/he has a pulse. *(Plains). Alt.* **pahkaham** *(Northern).*

pâhkawihokowin *pl.* **pâhkawihokowina** (NI) The act of having a pulse; a heartbeat.

pâhkocicehosiw *pl.* **pâhkocicehosiwak** (VTA) S/he wipes her/his own hands dry.

pâhkocicehwew (VTA) S/he wipes her/his hands dry for her/him.

pâhkociceham (VTA) S/he wipes its hands dry.

pâhkocicehowew (VTA) S/he wipes peoples' hands dry.

pâhkocicehikew (VTA) S/he wipes hands dry.

pâhkocicew *pl.* **pâhkocicewak** (VAI) Her/his hands are dry.

pâhkocihcenew *pl.* **pâhkocihcenewak** (VTA) S/he drys her/his hands for her/him. *(Northern). Alt.* **pahkocihcewew** *(Plains).*

pâhkohkwakanew *pl.* **pâhkohkwakanewak** (VAI) Her/his face is dry. *(Northern). Alt.* **pahkohkwehow** *(Plains).*

pâhkohkwehon *pl.* **pâhkohkwehona** (NI) A towel or material used for drying or wiping something.

pâhkohkwehow *pl.* **pâhkohkwehowak** (VTA) S/he dries her/his own face.

pâhkopayiw *pl.* **pâhkopayiwa** *or* **pâhkopayiwak** (VII) *or* (VAI) It *or* s/he becomes dry.

pâhkositehosiw *pl.* **pâhkositehosiwak** (VAI) S/he wipes her/his own feet dry.

pâhkositehwew (VTA) S/he wipes her/his feet dry for her/him.

pâhkositehowew (VTA) S/he wipes someone's feet dry.

pâhkositehikew (VTA) S/he wipes other peoples' feet dry.

pâhkosiw *pl.* **pâhkosiwak** (VAI) S/he or it is dried, i.e.: by the sun. *(Northern). Alt.* **pâsow** *(Plains).*

pâhkwacask *pl.* **pâhkwacaskwak** (NA) A migrating muskrat; a muskrat on dry ground.

pâhkwacaskos *pl.* **pâhkwacaskosak** (NA) A vole.

pâhkwahcâw *pl.* **pâhkwahcâwa** (VII) The ground is dry.

pâhkwahcitew *pl.* **pâhkwahcitewa** (NI) A ground fire. *(Plains). Alt.* **pahkwahtew** *(Northern).*

pâhkwahwew (VTI) S/he dries them.

pâhkwaham (VTI) S/he dries it up.

pâhkwahowew (VTA) S/he dries people up.

pâhkwahikew (VTI) S/he dries something up.

pâhkwastew *pl.* **pâhkwastewa** (VII) It is dried up or parched.

pâhkwatahtam *pl.* **pâhkwatahtamwak** (VAI) Her/his breathing is dry.

pâhkwataskamikâw (NI) Dried ground, i.e.: a desert.

pâhkwatâmiw *pl.* **pâhkwatâmiwak** (VAI) Her/his breath is dry.

pâhkwatâmowin *pl.* **pâhkwatâmowina** (NI) Feverish, heated, or dry breath.

pâhkwayamihâwin (NI) The Catholic religion.

pâhkwayâkanâkan *pl.* **pâhkwayâkanâkana** (NI) A dish towel.

pâhkwayâw (VAI) There is little humidity; it is kind of dry.

pâhkwâw *pl.* **pâhkwâwa** (VII) The water is shallow.

pâhkwestehikew *pl.* **pâhkwestehikewak** (VAI) S/he cracks or snaps the whip.

pâhkwestehikewin *pl.* **pâhkwestehikewina** (NI) The act of cracking or snapping a whip.

pâhkwestewew (VTA) S/he whips her/him loudly, noisily.

pâhkwesteham (VTI) S/he whips it with a loud noise.

pâhkwestehowew (VTA) S/he whips someone with a loud noise.

pâhkwestehikew (VTI) S/he snaps the whip with a loud noise.

pâhpahkawinam *pl.* **pâhpahkawinamwa** (VII) S/he is dripping it.

pâhpeyakwan iteyihtamwak (VAI) They constantly have the same ideas or thinking. *(Plains). Alt.* **tâpitaweyihtamwak** *(Northern).*

pâhpihew (VTA) S/he laughs at her/him; s/he makes fun of her/him.

155

pâhpitâw (vti) S/he laughs at it.

pâhpihiwew (vta) S/he laughs at someone.

pâhpicikew (vti) S/he laughs at things.

pâhpiw *pl.* **pâhpiwak** (vai) S/he laughs.

pâhpowin *pl.* **pâhpowina** (ni) A laugh; laughter.

pâkacapiw *pl.* **pâkacapiwak** (vai) S/he has swollen eyes.

pâkahamawew (vta) S/he strikes the drum for her/him.

pâkahamakew (vta) S/he strikes the drum for someone.

pâkahamâw *pl.* **pâkahamâwa** (vti) S/he strikes the drum.

pâkahamâwin *pl.* **pâkahamâwina** (ni) The act of striking the drum.

pâkahatowân *pl.* **pâkahatowânak** (na) A baseball. *(Northern)*

pâkahokiw *pl.* **pâkahokiwak** (vai) S/he feels a pulse.

pâkahokowin *pl.* **pâkahokowina** (ni) A pulsation or pulse.

pâkahtowân *pl.* **pâkahtowânak** (na) A ball for games, i.e.: a baseball or soccer ball. *(Plains)*. *Alt.* **tihtipinatowân** *(Northern)*.

pâkahtowew *pl.* **pâkahtowewak** (vai) S/he plays ball, i.e.: football. *(Plains)*. *Alt.* **tihtipinatowew** *(Northern)*.

pâkân *pl.* **pâkânak** (na) A nut.

pâkâtâham *pl.* **pâkâtâhamwak** (vai) Her/his scraping makes it swell up.

pâkicihcew *pl.* **pâkicihcewak** (vai) S/he has a swollen hand or hands.

pâkihkwepayiw *pl.* **pâkihkwepayiwa** *or* **pâkihkwepayiwak** (vii) *or* (vai) It *or* s/he has a swollen face.

pâkikâtew *pl.* **pâkikâtewak** (vai) S/he has a swollen leg or legs.

pâkinew (vta) S/he causes her/him to swell by her/his grip.

pâkinam (vti) S/he causes it to swell by her/his grip.

pâkiniwew (vta) S/he causes people to swell by her/his grip.

pâkinikew (vti) S/he causes things to swell by her/his grip.

pâkipayihew (vta) S/he makes her/him swell.

pâkipayitaw (vti) S/he makes it swell.

pâkipayihiwew (vta) S/he makes someone swell.

pâkipayicikew (vti) S/he makes things swell.

pâkipayiw *pl.* **pâkipayiwak** (vai) S/he or it is swollen.

pâkipayowin *pl.* **pâkipayowina** (ni) A swelling.

pâkisitew *pl.* **pâkisitewak** (vai) S/he has a swollen foot or feet.

pâkitonew *pl.* **pâkitonewak** (vai) S/he has a swollen mouth.

pâkiyawew *pl.* **pâkiyawewak** (vai) S/he has a swollen body.

pâmayes (ipc) Before; prior.

pâmayes, mayes (ipc) Before or ere. *(Plains)*. *Alt.* **namic** *(Northern)*.

pânahikew *pl.* **pânahikewak** (vta) S/he cleans the snow off something.

pânahwew (vta) S/he cleans or clears the snow off her/him.

panaham (vti) S/he cleans or clears the snow off it.

panahowew (vta) S/he cleans or clears the snow off someone.

panahikew (vti) S/he cleans or clears the snow off things.

pânâkohtew (vii) As the snow melts in the spring time, the ground or earth begins to appear. *(Northern)*. *Alt.* **mostaskamikâw** *(Plains)*.

pâpahahkwan *pl.* **pâpahahkwanak** (na) A pullet.

pâpahtâw *pl.* **pâpahtâwak** (vai) S/he comes running.

pâpakopayiw *pl.* **pâpakopayiwak** (vai) It is lacerated.

pâpakosiniwin *pl.* **pâpakosiniwina** (ni) The act of being lacerated; laceration.

pâpakositesin *pl.* **pâpakositesinwak** (vai) S/he has lacerated feet.

pâpakwasakayesiniwin *pl.* **pâpakwasakayesiniwina** (ni) The act of having an abrasion.

pâpihaw *pl.* **pâpihawak** (vai) S/he flies this way; s/he comes flying; s/he arrives by plane.

pâpitikonew (vta) S/he rolls them continuously.

pâpitikonam (vti) S/he rolls it.

pâpitikoniwew (vta) S/he rolls someone.

pâpitikonikew (vti) S/he rolls something.

pâpitikoniskew *pl.* **pâpitikoniskewak** (vai) S/he makes a fist continuously.

pâsekinwew *pl.* **pâsekinwewak** (vta) S/he dries a moose hide.

pâsimihtân *pl.* **pâsimihtâna** (ni) A cord of firewood.

pâsiminân *pl.* **pâsiminâna** (ni) A dried berry.

pâsiminew *pl.* **pâsiminewa** (vti) S/he dries berries.

pâsinâsikew (vta) S/he dries her/his clothes for her/him.

pâsinâsiwew (vta) S/he dries clothes for someone.

pâsinâsiw *pl.* **pâsinâsiwak** (vta) S/he dries her/his own clothes.

pâsipakwew *pl.* **pâsipakwew** (vti) S/he dries leaves.

pâsiw *pl.* **pâsiwak** (vai) S/he is dry.

pâskamew (vta) S/he cracks it with her/his teeth.

pâskatam (vti) S/he cracks it open with her/his teeth, i.e.: nut.

pâskacikew (vti) S/he cracks something with her/his teeth.

pâskapowenew (vta) S/he opens it, i.e.: a jar.

156

pâskapowenam (VTI) S/he opens it, i.e.: a bottle.

pâskapowenikew (VTI) S/he opens things in boxes.

pâskâpahwew (VTA) S/he hits her/him and makes her/him blind.

pâskâpahowew (VTA) S/he hits someone and blinds her/him.

pâskâpahikew (VTA) S/he hits people and blinds them.

pâskâpiw *pl.* **pâskâpiwak** (VAI) S/he is blind.

pâskâpiwin *pl.* **pâskâpiwina** (NI) Being blind.

pâskâwehocikewin *pl.* **pâskâwehocikewina** (NI) The act of incubating eggs for hatching; incubation.

pâskâwehow *pl.* **pâskâwehowak** (VAI) It hatches, i.e.: an egg.

pâskekinew (VTA) S/he removes the wrapping.

pâskekinam (VTI) S/he removes the wrapping off it.

pâskekinikew (VTI) S/he removes the wrapping off things.

pâskekinikan *pl.* **pâskekinikana** (NI) A page of a book.

pâskekinikâsiw *pl.* **pâskekinikâsiwak** (VAI) The wrapping or covering is removed off of her/him.

pâskekinikâtew *pl.* **pâskekinikâtewa** (VII) The wrapping is removed off it.

pâskeskanaweyâw *pl.* **pâskeskanaweyâwa** (NI) A road that branches, forks, or divides.

pâskinamawew (VTA) S/he opens or uncovers it for her/him.

pâskinamakew (VTA) S/he opens or uncovers them for people.

pâskinamawewak (VTA) They open or uncover it for her/him.

pâskinew (VTA) S/he opens or uncovers them.

pâskinam (VTI) S/he opens or uncovers it.

pâskiniwew (VTA) S/he opens or uncovers people.

pâskinikew (VTI) S/he opens or uncovers things.

pâskinokew *pl.* **pâskinokewa** (VTI) S/he is dismantling her/his teepee; s/he takes apart her/his teepee.

pâskinokewin *pl.* **pâskinokewina** (NI) The act of uncovering or unwrapping a teepee and leaving just the poles standing.

pâskipayiw *pl.* **pâskipayiwa** or **pâskipayiwak** (VII) *or* (VAI) It *or* s/he broke open on its own.

pâskipitew (VTA) S/he pulls the covers off her/him.

pâskipitam (VTI) S/he pulls the covers off it.

pâskipisiwew (VTA) S/he pulls the covers off people.

pâskipiscikew (VTI) S/he pulls the covers off things.

pâskisikan *pl.* **pâskisikana** (NI) A gun.

pâskisikanâhtik *pl.* **pâskisikanâhtikwa** (NI) A gun stalk.

pâskisikanâpisk *pl.* **pâskisikanâpiskwa** (NI) A gun barrel.

pâskisikanis *pl.* **pâskisikanisa** (NI) A small gun; a small calibre firearm; pistol; revolver.

pâskisikew *pl.* **pâskisikewak** (VAI) S/he fires a shot.

pâskisikewin *pl.* **pâskisikewina** (NI) The act of firing a shot.

pâskisosiw *pl.* **pâskisosiwak** (VTA) S/he shot herself/himself.

pâskisosiwin *pl.* **pâskisosiwina** (NI) The act of shooting oneself.

pâskiswew (VTA) S/he shoots her/him.

pâskisam (VTI) S/he shoots it.

pâskisowew (VTA) S/he shoots someone.

pâskisikew (VAI) S/he shoots.

pâskitonew *pl.* **pâskitonewak** (VTA) S/he opens her/his mouth.

pâskîw *pl.* **pâskîwak** (VAI) S/he uncovers herself/himself, i.e.: throws off the blankets.

pâskîwin *pl.* **pâskîwina** (NI) The act of uncovering.

pâsohew *pl.* **pâsohewak** (VTA) S/he made her/him dry off.

pâsow *pl.* **pâsowak** (VAI) S/he or it is dried, i.e.: by the sun. *(Plains).* Alt. **pâhkosiw** *(Northern).*

pâstahwew (VTA) S/he shoots over her/him; s/he overthrew her/him.

pâstaham (VTI) S/he shoots over it.

pâstahowew (VTA) S/he shoots over people.

pâstahikew (VTI) S/he shoots over everything.

pâstakiw *pl.* **pâstakiwak** (VAI) S/he is licking her/his lips.

pâstakiwin *pl.* **pâstakiwina** (NI) The act of licking the lips.

pâstamew (VTA) S/he cracks them with her/his teeth, i.e.: a nut.

pâstatam (VTI) S/he cracks it with her/his teeth.

pâstasiw *pl.* **pâstasiwak** (VAI) S/he eats marrow from a bone.

pâstasiwin *pl.* **pâstasiwina** (NI) The act of eating marrow from a bone.

pâstâhew (VTA) S/he causes or influences her/him to commit sinful acts.

pâstâhiwew (VTA) S/he causes or influences others to commit sinful acts.

pâstâham (VTI) S/he invokes sin or evil on it.

pâstâhowew (VTA) S/he makes people commit sin.

pâstâhow *pl.* **pâstâhowak** (VAI) S/he sins.

pâstâhowin *pl.* **pâstâhowina** (NI) A sin; the act of committing sins; transgression.

pâstâmâw *pl.* **pâstâmâwa** or **pâstâmâwak** (VII) *or* (VAI) It *or* s/he is being cursed by someone.

pâstâmew (VTA) S/he invokes a curse on her/him or them; s/he talks badly about her/him.

pâstâmiwew (VTA) S/he invokes a curse on people.

pâstâmiw *pl.* **pâstâmiwak** (VTA) S/he curses herself/himself; s/he plagues herself/himself with bad luck.

157

pâstâmowin *pl.***pâstamowina** (NI) The act of cursing oneself; the act of plaguing oneself with bad luck.

pâstâskow *pl.* **pâstâskowa** (VTI) S/he is stepping over.

pâstew *pl.* **pâstewa** (VII) It is dry.

pâstewacâpiw *pl.* **pâstewacâpiwak** (VAI) Her/his eyes are dry. *(Plains). Alt.* **pâstewiskisikwew** *(Northern).*

pâstewahkatosiw *pl.* **pâstewahkatosiwak** (VAI) It is dried out, i.e.: a tree.

pâstewapiw *pl.* **pâstewapiwak** (VAI) S/he is sitting in a dry spot, i.e.: during a rainstorm.

pâstewâhkatotew *pl.* **pâstewâhkatotewa** (VII) It is dried out or parched, i.e.: the ground.

pâstewâhtik *pl.* **pâstewâhtikwa** *or* **pâstewâhtikwak** (NI) *or* (NA) A dried piece of wood or trees.

pâstewimiht *pl.* **pâstewimihti** (NI) One piece of dried firewood; a stack of dried firewood.

pâstewipak *pl.* **pâstewipakwa** (VII) It is dried out, i.e.: a leaf.

pâstewiskisikwew *pl.* **pâstewiskisikwewak** (VAI) Her/his eyes are dry. *(Northern). Alt.* **pâstewacâpiw** *(Plains).*

pâstewitonew *pl.* **pâstewitonewak** (VAI) S/he has a dry mouth or lips.

pâstihtin *pl.* **pâstihtinwa** (VII) It cracks when it falls, i.e.: a globe from a lamp or an egg.

pâstinew (VTA) S/he cracks them with her/his fingers.

> **pâstinam** (VTI) S/he cracks it with her/his fingers.

> **pâstinikew** (VTI) S/he cracks things with her/his fingers.

pâstinew (VTA) S/he passes her/him over the top. *(Northern). Alt.* **miyâskatew** *(Plains).*

> **pâstinam** (VTI) S/he passes it over the top.

> **pâstiniwew** (VTA) S/he passes someone over the top.

> **pâstinikew** (VTI) S/he passes things over the top.

pâstipayiw *pl.* **pâstipayiwa** *or* **pâstipayiwak** (VII) *or* (VAI) It *or* s/he cracks on its her/his own.

pâstisin *pl.* **pâstisinwak** (VAI) It blew out or it cracked open, i.e.: a car tire.

pâswew (VTA) S/he dries her/him.

> **pâsam** (VTI) S/he dries it.

> **pâsowew** (VTA) S/he dries someone.

> **pâsikew** (VTI) S/he dries things.

pâswewokwew *pl.* **pâswewokwewa** (VTI) S/he dries meat.

pâtosâhk (IPC) In the virgin land.

pâwistik *pl.* **pâwistikwa** (NI) A rapid.

pecastamiskâw *pl.* **pecastamiskâwak** (VAI) S/he is paddling towards us, i.e.: a person in a canoe or a muskrat in the water. *(Northern). Alt.* **peciskâw** *(Plains).*

pecastamohtew *pl.* **pecastamohtewak** (VAI) S/he is walking towards us.

pecicimew *pl.* **pecicimewak** (VAI) S/he swims or paddles in this direction.

peciciwan *pl.* **peciciwanwa** (VII) It is flowing this way, i.e.: a river.

pecikâtew *pl.* **pecikâtewa** (VII) It is delivered.

pecikewin *pl.* **pecikewina** (NI) The act of fetching.

pecimew *pl.* **pecimewak** (VTA) S/he calls out and makes it come towards her/him, as in calling a moose.

pecinâkosiw *pl.* **pecinâkosiwak** (VAI) S/he appears in the distance and is headed this way.

pecinâkwan *pl.* **pecinâkwanwa** (VII) It appears in the distance and is headed this way.

pecipayiw *pl.* **pecipayiwak** *or* **pecipayiwa** (VAI) *or* (VII) S/he *or* it edges this way.

pecipitew (VTA) S/he pulls them towards herself/himself.

> **pecipitam** (VTI) S/he pulls it towards herself/himself.

> **pecipicikew** (VTI) S/he pulls things towards herself/himself.

peciskâw *pl.* **peciskâwak** (VAI) S/he is paddling towards us, i.e.: a person in a canoe or a muskrat in the water. *(Plains). Alt.* **pecastamiskâw** *(Northern).*

peciwâpan (VAI) Daylight is incoming, i.e.: daybreak. *(Northern). Alt.* **petâpan** *(Plains).*

peciwiyew *pl.* **peciwiyewak** (VTA) S/he used her/his spiritual power to make them come to her/him.

pehciyaweskawew (VTA) It possesses or enters her/his body.

> **pehciyaweskâkew** (VTA) S/he possesses or enters peoples' bodies.

pehew (VTA) S/he waits for her/him.

> **pehtâw** (VTI) S/he waits for it.

> **pehhiwew** (VTA) S/he waits for people.

pehiw *pl.* **pehiwak** (VAI) S/he waits.

pehkokawân *pl.* **pehkokawânak** (NA) A winter vehicle; a sleigh. *(Plains). Alt.* **pipon'tâpânâsk** *(Northern).*

pehowin *pl.* **pehowina** (NI) The act of waiting; a waiting place.

pehtam *pl.* **pehtamwak** (VAI) S/he hears.

pehtamowin *pl.* **pehtamowina** (NI) The act of hearing.

pehtawew (VTA) S/he hears her/him.

> **pehtâkew** (VTA) S/he hears people.

pehtâkopicikan *pl.* **pehtâkopicikana** (NI) Something used to make noise; a noisemaker.

pehtâkopicikewin *pl.* **pehtâkopicikewina** (NI) The act of making sounds.

pehteyihtam *pl.* **pehteyihtamwak** (VAI) S/he thinks the distance is too great; s/he thinks it is a long way.

pehteyimew (VTA) S/he thinks s/he is a long ways away.

> **pehteyimiwew** (VTA) S/he thinks someone is a long ways away.

> **pehteyicikew** (VTI) S/he thinks things are a long ways away.

pehteyitamowin *pl.* **pehteyitamowina** (NI) The act of thinking that the distance is too far.

pehtikamâw (VAI) It is quite a distance across, i.e.: a lake.

pehtohkasiw *pl.* **pehtohkasiwak** (VAI) It is cooked on the inside and its outside peels off, i.e.: a baked potato.

pehtohkaswew (VTA) S/he cooks them on the inside.
  pehtohkasam (VTI) S/he cooks it on the inside.
  pehtohkasikew (VTI) S/he cooks things on the inside.

pehtwatew (VTI) S/he smokes it, i.e.: a pipe.
  pehtwatam (VTI) S/he smokes grass.

pekakamow (VII) It is a clouded or muddy liquid, i.e.: turbid.

pekatew *pl.* **pekatewak** (VAI) S/he burps.

pekatewin *pl.* **pekatewina** (NI) The act of burping.

pekâkamihtaw *pl.* **pekâkamihtawa** (VTI) S/he makes the water murky by swimming in it.

pekâkaminam *pl.* **pekâkaminamwa** (VTI) S/he makes the water murky by walking in it.

pekihkâcipayiw *pl.* **pekihkâcipayiwa** (VII) It goes slowly.

pekihkâcitâw *pl.* **pekihkâcitâwak** (VAI) S/he goes there slowly.

pekihkâciw *pl.* **pekihkâciwak** (VAI) S/he goes slowly. *(Northern). Alt.* **papwâstawiw** *(Plains).*

pekihkâtan *pl.* **pekihkâtanwa** (VII) It is slow coming.

pekihkâteyihtam *pl.* **pekihkâteyihtamwak** (VAI) S/he is a slow thinker.

pekihkâteyihtamowin *pl.* **pekihkâteyihtamowina** (NI) The act of thinking slowly; a slow decision.

pekihkâteyimew (VTA) S/he finds her/him a slow thinker.
  pekihkâteyitam (VTI) S/he finds it slow.
  pekihkâteyimiwew (VTA) S/he finds people slow or dense.

pekihkâtisiw *pl.* **pekihkâtisiwak** (VAI) S/he is slow or sluggish; s/he takes a long time to do things.

pekihkâtisiwin *pl.* **pekihkâtisiwina** (NI) The act of being slow or sluggish.

pekihkâtohtew *pl.* **pekihkâtohtewak** (VAI) S/he walks slowly. *(Northern). Alt.* **yîkicikâwohtew**, **papwâstahohtew** *(Plains).*

pekiwewin *pl.* **pekiwewina** (NI) The act of coming home or arriving.

pekîwehcikew *pl.* **pekîwehcikewak** (VAI) S/he brings things home.

pekîwehtahew (VTA) S/he brings her/him home.
  pekîwehtatâw (VTI) S/he brings it home.
  pekîwehtahiwew (VTA) S/he brings people home.

pekopepayowin *pl.* **pekopepayowina** (NI) The act of breaking the surface of the water; the act of appearing out of the water.

pekopew *pl.* **pekopewak** (VAI) S/he surfaces from underwater.

pekopewin *pl.* **pekopewina** (NI) The act of surfacing or rising to the top.

pemahopak *pl.* **pemahopakwak** (NA) A wild bean bush.

pemahwew (VTI) S/he winds or screws them.
  pemaham (VTI) S/he winds or screws it.
  pemahikew (VTI) S/he winds or screws things.

pemâmitâwew *pl.* **pemâmitâwewak** (VTA) S/he is dawdling on the way.

pemetawew *pl.* **pemetawewak** (VAI) S/he came to play.

pemihtakawew (VTI) S/he screws it into the wood.
  pemihtakaham (VTI) S/he screws it into the wood.
  pemihtakahikew (VTI) S/he screws things into the wood.

penâsipeciwan *pl.* **penâsipeciwanwa** (NI) Water that is flowing down the hill or mountain, as from a spring.

penâsipehtahew (VTA) S/he brings her/him down the hill.
  penâsipehtâw (VTI) S/he brings it down the hill.
  penâsipehtahiwew (VTA) S/he brings people down the hill.
  penâsipehcikew (VTI) S/he brings things down the hill.

penâsipemon *pl.* **penâsipemona** (NI) It leads down, i.e.: a road down a hill.

penâsipepayiw *pl.* **penâsipepayiwa** *or* **penâsipepayiwak** (VII) *or* (VAI) It *or* s/he comes down the hill.

penâsipew *pl.* **penâsipewak** (VAI) S/he goes down the hill.

penâsopepahtâw *pl.* **penâsopepahtâwak** (VAI) S/he comes running down the hill.

penâtew (VTA) S/he comes and gets her/him.
  penâtam (VTI) S/he comes and gets it.
  penâsiwew (VTA) S/he comes and gets someone.
  penâcikew (VTI) S/he comes and gets things.

penihtaciwew *pl.* **penihtaciwewak** (VAI) S/he is coming down, i.e.: stairs or a hill.

penihtâskow *pl.* **penihtâskowak** (VAI) S/he climbs down, i.e.: a pole or tree.

penôkosiw *pl.* **penôkosiwak** (VAI) S/he can be seen approaching; s/he is in sight.

penôkwan *pl.* **penôkwanwa** (VII) It can be seen approaching; it is in sight.

pesâkâstew (VAI) The sun filtrates through the clouds. *(Plains). Alt.* **pawaskwew** *(Northern).*

pesicin *pl.* **pesicinwak** (VAI) S/he accidently scratched herself/himself.

pesihkotew (VTA) S/he scratches or carves grooves on them with a knife.

159

pesihkotam (VTA) S/he scratches or carves grooves on it with a knife.

pesihkocikew (VTA) S/he scratches or carves grooves on things with a knife.

pesimohkanitipahikan *pl.* **pesimohkanitipahikana** (NI) One hour measured by a clock. *(Northern). Alt.* **peyaktipahikan** *(Plains).*

pesîsiw *pl.* **pesîsiwak** (VAI) S/he brings herself/himself.

pesohamew *pl.* **pesohamewak** (VAI) S/he takes small steps.

pesohtawew (VTA) S/he hears her/him nearby.

pesohtam (VTI) S/he hears it nearby.

pesohtâkew (VTA) S/he hears people nearby.

pesohcikew (VTI) S/he hears things nearby.

pesonâkosiw *pl.* **pesonâkosiwak** (VAI) S/he appears to be nearby.

pesonâkwan *pl.* **pesonâkwanwa** (VII) It appears to be nearby.

pesowew *pl.* **pesowewak** (VTA) S/he brings someone or her/him here.

pesweyekin *pl.* **pesweyekinwa** (NI) A piece of soft, fluffy material; flannelette.

pesweyihtakosiw *pl.* **pesweyihtakosiwak** (VAI) S/he is thought to be nearby. *(Northern). Alt.* **cîkâyâw** *(Plains).*

pesweyihtâkwan *pl.* **pesweyihtâkwanwa** (VII) It is thought to be nearby.

peswîmin *pl.* **peswîminak** (NA) A bean. *(Northern). Alt.* **miyîcîmin** *(Plains).*

petamawew *pl.* **petamawewak** (VTA) S/he brings it for her/him.

petamew (VTA) S/he sucks them up.

petahtam (VTI) S/he sucks it up.

petahcikew (VTI) S/he sucks things up.

petâmiw *pl.* **petâmiwak** (VAI) S/he flees in this direction.

petâpan (VAI) Daylight is incoming, i.e.: daybreak. *(Plains). Alt.* **peciwâpan** *(Northern).*

petâpoyiw *pl.* **petâpoyiwak** (VAI) S/he comes here by train.

petâsiw *pl.* **petâsiwak** (VAI) S/he comes in this direction because s/he is being blown by the wind.

petâstan *pl.* **petâstanwa** (VII) It comes in this direction because it is being blown by the wind.

petâstew (VII) The moon is coming up.

petâw *pl.* **petâwak** (IPC) S/he brought it.

petâwahew (VTI) S/he hauls them here, i.e.: cattle.

petâwatâw (VTI) S/he hauls it here, i.e.: manure.

petâwayiwew (VTA) S/he hauls people here.

petâwacikew (VTI) S/he hauls things here.

peteyimew (VTA) S/he makes her/him come to her/him by her/his thoughts.

peteyitam (VTI) S/he makes it come by thought.

peteyimiwew (VTA) S/he makes people come by thought.

petisawew (VTA) S/he sends her/him here; s/he sends them by mail.

petisaham (VTI) S/he sends it here.

petisahowew (VTA) S/he sends someone here.

petisahikew (VTI) S/he sends things here.

petosâyâwin *pl.* **petosâyâwina** (NI) The act of diverging from the normal standard; aberrance; abnormality; repugnancy.

petowatam *pl.* **petowatamwak** (VAI) S/he can be heard coming in this direction by her/his talking.

petoweham *pl.* **petowehamwak** (VAI) S/he can be heard coming in this direction by her/his drumming. *Var.* **petweweham**.

petowehtam *pl.* **petowehtamwak** (VAI) S/he hears it coming.

petowehtin *pl.* **petowehtinwa** (VII) It can be heard coming in this direction, i.e.: hail.

petowenam *pl.* **petowenamwak** (VAI) S/he is heard walking in this direction.

petowesin *pl.* **petowesinwak** (VAI) S/he is heard coming in this direction.

pewihkotew (VTA) S/he cuts them all up.

pewihkotam (VTI) S/he cuts it all up.

pewihkocikew (VTI) S/he cuts things all up.

peyahtik (IPC) Carefully; with caution; very gently; very slowly; to be cautious. *(Plains). Alt.* **kâkitaw** *(Northern).*

peyahtikesâyâwin *pl.* **peyahtikesâyâwina** (NI) The act of being boorish.

peyahtikowatisiw *pl.* **peyahtikowatisiwak** (VAI) S/he is a cautious person.

peyahtikowisiw *pl.* **peyahtikowisiwak** (VAI) S/he acts in a slow and steady manner; s/he is slow. *(Plains). Alt.* **nisihkâcâtisiw** *(Northern).*

peyahtikowisowin *pl.* **peyahtikowisowina** (NI) Slow operation; slow or measured. *(Plains). Alt.* **peyahtikoyisâyâwin** *(Northern).*

peyahtikoyisâyâwin *pl.* **peyahtikoyisâyâwina** (NI) Having prudence. *(Northern). Alt.* **peyahtikowisowin** *(Plains).*

peyahtikwesayâwin *pl.* **peyahtikwesayâwina** (NI) The act of being lax or slow; laxity; simplicity.

peyahtikweyihtam *pl.* **peyahtikweyihtamwak** (VAI) S/he is cautious.

peyahtikweyihtamowin *pl.* **peyahtikweyihtamowina** (NI) Being cautious.

peyahtikweyimew (VTA) S/he considers her/him to be a cautious person.

peyahtikweyitam (VTI) S/he considers it cautiously.

peyahtikweyimiwew (VTA) S/he considers someone cautiously.

peyahtikweyicikew (VTI) S/he considers things cautiously.

peyahwew (VTA) S/he or it scales them, i.e.: a fish.
   peyahikew (VAI) S/he is scaling.

peyak (IPC) One.

peyak ayamihewikîsikâw (NI) One week.

peyak tipahikan (NI) One yard; one o'clock.

peyakiw *pl.* **peyakiwak** (VAI) S/he is alone; s/he travels alone.

peyakocihcew *pl.* **peyakocihcewak** (VAI) S/he has only one hand.

peyakohew (VAI) S/he depends on only one person.
   peyakohtâw (VII) S/he depends on only one thing.
   peyakohiwew (VAI) S/he depends only on someone.
   peyakohcikew (VII) S/he depends on only one thing.

peyakohkam *pl.* **peyakohkamwak** (VAI) S/he is alone in her/his canoe.

peyakohkawew (VTA) S/he handles her/him alone or by herself/himself.
   peyakohkam (VTI) S/he handles it alone or by herself/himself.
   peyakohkâkew (VTA) S/he handles people alone or by herself/himself.

peyakohkwamiw *pl.* **peyakohkwamiwak** (VAI) S/he sleeps alone.

peyakohtâwin *pl.* **peyakohtâwina** (NI) The act of doing things in the same manner; operating in one manner; particularity.

peyakohtew *pl.* **peyakohtewak** (VAI) S/he walks alone.

peyakokamikwew *pl.* **peyakokamikwewak** (VAI) S/he has only one dwelling or home.

peyakokew *pl.* **peyakokewak** (VAI) S/he lives or dwells alone.

peyakokonew *pl.* **peyakokonewna** (NI) A mouthful.

peyakomin *pl.* **peyakomina** (NI) One berry.

peyakonisk *pl.* **peyakoniskewina** (NI) A unit of measurement indicating one armful or approximately six feet from finger tip to finger tip.

peyakoniskeyâw *pl.* **peyakoniskeyâwa** (VII) Referring to a Cree unit of measurement equivalent to six feet. It is about six feet long, i.e.: a canoe.

peyakoniskisiw *pl.* **peyakoniskisiwak** (VAI) Referring to a Cree unit of measurement equivalent to six feet. It is about six feet long, i.e.: a toboggan.

peyakopehikan *pl.* **peyakopehikanak** (NA) An ace or number one in a deck of playing cards.

peyakopehikew *pl.* **peyakopehikewak** (VAI) S/he plays one ace or s/he has all four aces.

peyakosâp (IPC) Eleven.

peyakosâpowiwa (VII) There are eleven of them. *(Northern). Alt.* **peyakosâyihtasiwak** *(Plains).*

peyakosâpwâw (IPC) Eleven times, eleventh time.

peyakosâpwâw mitâtahtomitanaw (IPC) Eleven hundred.

peyakosâyihtasiwa (VII) There are eleven of them. *(Plains). Alt.* **peyakosâpowiwak** *(Northern).*

peyakosihcikew *pl.* **peyakosihcikewak** (VAI) S/he does it all alone.

peyakoskânesowak (VAI) They are one family, one tribe, or one nation.

peyakoskâniwin *pl.* **peyakoskâniwina** (NI) The act of being one of the family or tribe.

peyakowin *pl.* **peyakowina** (NI) Being alone; privacy; unaccompanied.

peyakowîcihiwewin *pl.* **peyakowîcihiwewina** (NI) The act of being alone or friendless.

peyakôskân (NA) One family; one bond; one tribe; one nation.

peyaktipahikan *pl.* **peyaktipahikana** (NI) One hour measured by a clock. *(Plains). Alt.* **pesimohkanitipahikan** *(Northern).*

peyakwahtayiyâw *pl.* **peyakwahtayiyâwa** (VII) It is worth just one pelt.

peyakwan (IPC) An expression meaning "it is the same one" or "it is the same to me."

peyakwanohk (IPC) In only one place.

peyakwapiw *pl.* **peyakwapiwak** (VAI) S/he sits alone there.

peyakwaskasowewin *pl.* **peyakwaskasowewina** (NI) The act of leaving someone unattended or alone.

peyakwaskatew (VTA) S/he leaves her/him alone or by herself/himself.
   peyakwaskatam (VTI) S/he leaves it alone or by itself.
   peyakwaskasiwew (VTA) S/he leaves people alone or by themselves.
   peyakwaskacikew (VTI) S/he leaves things alone or by themselves.

peyakwaskatitowin *pl.* **peyakwaskatitowina** (NI) The act of being deprived or left alone by a death; bereft.

peyakwaskinahiwewin *pl.* **peyakwaskinahiwewina** (NI) The act of being secluded or alone; seclusive.

peyakwaskinewin *pl.* **peyakwaskinewina** (NI) The act of seclusion.

peyakwayihk (NI) One of a kind; one pair.

peyakwayiwinis *pl.* **peyakwayiwinisa** (NI) A suit.

peyakwâpisk *pl.* **peyakwâpiskwak** (NA) One pintful; one dollar.

peyakwâw (IPC) Once, one time, first time.

peyakwâw kihci mitâtahtomitanaw (IPC) Thousand; one thousand.

peyakwâw kisipakihtasowin (IPC) Million; one million.

peyakwekan (NI) A single layer of cloth.

peyakweyihtam *pl.* **peyakweyihtamwak** (VAI) S/he is obsessed with one thought.

peyakweyihtamowin *pl.* **peyakweyihtamowina** (NI) An obsessive thought.

peyakweyimew (VTA) S/he is obsessed with her/him; s/he thinks only of her/him.

peyakweyitam (VTI) S/he thinks only of it.

peyakweyimiwew (VTA) S/he thinks only of one person.

peyakweyihcikew (VTI) S/he thinks only of one thing.

peyakweyimisiw *pl.* **peyakweyimisiwak** (VAI) S/he is self-centered; s/he thinks only of herself/himself.

peyakweyimisowin *pl.* **peyakweyimisowina** (NI) The act of being self-centered or thinking only of oneself.

peyakweyimow *pl.* **peyakweyimowak** (VAI) S/he thinks s/he is all alone or isolated.

peyakweyimowin *pl.* **peyakweyimowina** (NI) The act of thinking that oneself is isolated.

peyaseyihtam *pl.* **peyaseyihtamwak** (VAI) S/he feels relieved about it.

peyaseyihtamowin *pl.* **peyaseyihtamowina** (NI) The act of feeling relieved.

peyaseyimow *pl.* **peyaseyimowak** (VAI) S/he is relieved that it happened as it did.

peyaseyimowin *pl.* **peyaseyimowina** (NI) The act of being relieved after an occurence.

peyasipayiw *pl.* **peyasipayiwa** *or* **peyasipayiwak** (VII) *or* (VAI) It *or* s/he comes sliding down a chute.

peyasipitew (VTA) S/he came and pulled her/him or them down.

peyasipitam (VTI) S/he came and pulled it down.

peyasipicikew (VTI) S/he came and pulled things down.

peyasiwepahwew (VTA) S/he came up and knocked her/him backwards.

peyasiwepaham (VTI) S/he came up and knocked it backwards.

peyasiwepahowew (VTA) S/he came up knocked someone backwards.

peyasiwepahikew (VTI) S/he came up and knocked things backwards.

peyâsaskew *pl.* **peyâsaskewak** (VAI) S/he descends from heaven to the earth, i.e.: Christ.

peyâsew *pl.* **peyâsewak** (VAI) S/he descends from the air to the ground, i.e.: a bird.

peyâsipayihew *pl.* **peyâsipayihewak** (VTA) S/he slides her/him down a chute.

peyohchipayiw (VAI) S/he comes from there.

peyohpinew (VTI) S/he comes to lift them.

peyohpinam (VTI) S/he comes to lift it.

peyohpiniwew (VTA) S/he comes to lift people.

peyohpinikew (VTI) S/he comes to lift things.

peyohtohtew *pl.* **peyohtohtewak** (VAI) S/he walks from there.

picikîskisîs *pl.* **picikîskisîsak** (NA) A chickadee.

picikwâs *pl.* **picikwâsak** (NA) An apple.

picitwâw *pl.* **picitwâwak** (VAI) S/he moves her/his belongings a little bit at a time. *(Northern).* *Alt.* **piciwak** *(Plains).*

picitwâwin *pl.* **picitwâwina** (NI) The act of moving ones belongings a little bit at a time. *(Northern).* *Alt.* **picîwin** *(Plains).*

piciw *pl.* **piciwak** (VAI) S/he moves and makes her/his home elsewhere; s/he relocates.

piciwak *pl.* **piciwakak** (VAI) S/he moves her/his belongings a little bit at a time. *(Plains).* *Alt.* **picitwâw** *(Northern).*

picîwin *pl.* **picîwina** (NI) The act of moving one's home to a new area; the act of relocating; the act of moving one's belongings a little bit at a time. *(Plains).* *Alt.* **picitwâwin** *(Northern).*

pihcâpekos *pl.* **pihcâpekosa** (NI) An inlet. *(Plains).* *Alt.* **wasas** *(Northern).*

pihcâw *pl.* **pihcâwa** (VII) It is far; it is a long way.

pihcihkomân *pl.* **pihcihkomâna** (NI) A case for a knife; a sheath or scabbard.

pihcikonew *pl.* **pihcikonewa** (NI) Interior or inside of the mouth.

pihcipacikan *pl.* **pihcipacikana** (NI) A funnel.

pihcipihkwân *pl.* **pihcipihkwâna** (NI) A pouch for carrying gun powder.

pihcipihkwew *pl.* **pihcipihkwewak** (VTA) S/he loads her/his muzzle-loader gun.

pihcipimew *pl.* **pihcipimewak** (VAI) S/he gases up her/his vehicle.

pihcipoyâkan *pl.* **pihcipoyâkana** (NI) A type of basket used as a collection plate.

pihcisin *pl.* **pihcisinwak** (VAI) S/he lays inside.

pihciskanawâtew (VAI) S/he surrounds someone else's trail.

pihciskanawâtam (VTI) S/he surrounds it.

pihciskanawâcikew (VTI) S/he surrounds things.

pihciskanawew *pl.* **pihciskanawewak** (VAI) S/he surrounds the trail.

pihciskawew (VTA) S/he circles or surrounds her/him.

pihciskam (VTI) S/he circles or surrounds it.

pihciskâkew (VTA) S/he circles or surrounds people.

pihcitahcâhkoweskawew *pl.* **pihcitahcâhkoweskawewak** (VAI) S/he becomes part of her/his psyche; the spirit helper becomes part of her/his identity. *(Northern).* *Alt.* **pihtâkoyaweskawew** *(Plains).*

pihciteheskawew (VAI) S/he enters or fills her/his heart, i.e.: Christ.

pihciteheskâkew (VAI) S/he enters peoples' hearts.

pihcitonewkawew *pl.* **pihcitoneskawewak** (VTA) It enters her/his mouth.

pihciwepinew (VTA) S/he throws her/him in.
　pihciwepinam (VTI) S/he throws it in.
　pihciwepiniwew (VTA) S/he throws someone in.
　pihciwepinikew (VTI) S/he throws things in.

pihcones *pl.* **pihconesa** (NI) A blouse.

pihekwâw *pl.* **pihekwâwa** (VII) It is rough and hard to swallow. *(Plains). Alt.* **piyekwan** *(Northern).*

pihesiw *pl.* **pihesiwak** (NA) A thunderbird. *(Plains). Alt.* **piyisiw** *(Northern).*

pihesîs *pl.* **pihesîsak** (NA) A quail.

pihew *pl.* **pihewak** (NA) A wood partridge; a grouse.

pihiciskanaw (NI) Encircling a specific area, e.g.: the territory of a moose.

pihiktewatâmowin *pl.* **pihiktewatâmowina** (NI) The result of exhaling in cold temperature; steam vapor.

pihkahcewâpos (NI) Coffee. *(Plains). Alt.* **pihkahtewâpoy** *(Northern),* **wespâkamicewâpôs** *(Plains).*

pihkahtew *pl.* **pihkahtewa** (VII) It is charred; it is distorted by fire. *(Plains). Alt.* **pihkihkahtew** *(Northern).*

pihkahtewâpoy (NI) Coffee. *(Northern). Alt.* **pihkahcewâpos,** **wespâkamicewâpôs** *(Plains).*

pihkasiw *pl.* **pihkasiwak** (VAI) S/he is tanned or darkened by the sun; s/he is distorted by fire. *(Plains). Alt.* **pihkihkasiw** *(Northern).*

pihkaswew (VTA) S/he charred them; s/he burns it black, i.e.: pan on a stove.
　pihkasam (VTI) S/he chars it.
　pihkasikew (VTA) S/he chars food.

pihkaswew (VTI) S/he makes it bend by applying heat. *(Plains). Alt.* **pihkihkaswew** *(Northern).*
　pihkasam (VTI) S/he makes it bend by applying heat, i.e.: a blacksmith.
　pihkasowew (VTA) S/he makes someone bend by applying heat.
　pihkasikew (VTI) S/he makes things bend by applying heat.

pihkâw *pl.* **pihkâwa** (VII) It is bent over.

pihkekinew (VTI) S/he folds them in two.
　pihkekinam (VTI) S/he folds it in two.
　pihkekinikew (VTI) S/he folds things in two.

pihkicihceyiw *pl.* **pihkicihceyiwak** (VTA) S/he folds her/his own hands.

pihkihkahtew *pl.* **pihkihkahtewa** (VII) It is distorted by fire. *(Northern). Alt.* **pihkahtew** *(Plains).*

pihkihkasiw *pl.* **pihkihkasiwak** (VAI) S/he is distorted by fire. *(Northern). Alt.* **pihkasiw** *(Plains).*

pihkihkaswew (VTI) S/he makes it bend by applying heat. *(Northern). Alt.* **pihkaswew** *(Plains).*

pihkihkasam (VTI) S/he makes it bend by applying heat, i.e.: a blacksmith.
　pihkihkasowew (VTA) S/he makes someone bend by applying heat.
　pihkihkasikew (VTI) S/he makes things bend by applying heat.

pihkihkomânis *pl.* **pihkihkomânisa** (NI) A pocket knife.

pihkikestawew (VTA) S/he bends her/his knee for her/him.
　pihkikestam (VTI) S/he bends her/his knee for it.
　pihkikestâkew (VTA) S/he bends her/his knee for someone.

pihkikeyiw *pl.* **pihkikeyiwak** (VAI) S/he bends her/his own knee.

pihkikin *pl.* **pihkikinwa** (VII) It grows crooked or bent out of shape.

pihkikow *pl.* **pihkikowak** (VAI) S/he grows crooked or bent out of shape.

pihkinew (VTA) S/he bends her/him or them.
　pihkinam (VTI) S/he bends it.
　pihkiniwew (VTA) S/he bends people.
　pihkinikew (VTI) S/he bends things.

pihkipitew (VTA) S/he bends them by pulling.
　pihkipitam (VTI) S/he bends it by pulling.
　pihkipicikew (VTI) S/he bends things by pulling.

pihkipitonepitew *pl.* **pihkipitonepitewak** (VTA) S/he bends her/his arm by pulling.

pihkipitonew *pl.* **pihkipitonewak** (VAI) Her/his arm is bent.

pihkisiw *pl.* **pihkisiwak** (VAI) S/he is bent over. *(Northern). Alt.* **pihkiw** *(Plains).*

pihkiskawew (VTA) S/he bends it with a kick.
　pihkiskam (VTI) S/he bends it by kicking it, i.e.: a car fender.

pihkiw *pl.* **pihkiwak** (VAI) S/he is bent over. *(Plains). Alt.* **pihkisiw** *(Northern).*

pihkoh (NI) Ashes.

pihkohew (VTA) S/he saves her/him; s/he helps her/him get through.
　pihkotâw (VTI) S/he saves it.
　pihkohiwew (VTA) S/he saves people.
　pihkocikew (VTI) S/he saves things.

pihkohiwewin *pl.* **pihkohiwewina** (NI) The act of saving people; the act of helping people get through.

pihkohow *pl.* **pihkohowak** (VAI) S/he frees herself/himself by breaking away or breaking loose.

pihkohowin *pl.* **pihkohowina** (NI) The act of becoming free.

pihkohtawin *pl.* **pihkohtawina** (NI) Achievement.

pihkohtâw *pl.* **pihkohtâwa** (VTI) S/he achieves it.

pihkonâkosiw *pl.* **pihkonâkosiwak** (VAI) S/he is gray.

pihkonâkwan *pl.* **pihkonâkwanwa** (VII) It is gray.

pihkowan *pl.* **pihkowanwa** (VII) It is covered in ashes.

163

pihkowiw *pl.* **pihkowiwak** (VAI) S/he is covered with ashes.

pihkoyakanis *pl.* **pihkoyakanisa** (NI) Ashcan. *(Northern).* *Alt.* **pakicipihkoweyâkanis** *(Plains).*

pihkwâkew *pl.* **pihkwâkewak** (VAI) S/he is dripping blood.

pihkwâpoy *pl.* **pihkwâpoya** (NI) Lye.

pihpihciw *pl.* **pihpihciwak** (NA) A robin.

pihtahcâpân *pl.* **pihtahcâpâna** (NI) A case for holding arrows, i.e.: a quiver. *(Northern).* *Alt.* **pihtatwan** *(Plains).*

pihtapek *pl.* **pihtapekwa** (NI) Dead water, i.e.: a slough or lagoon.

pihtascikewin *pl.* **pihtascikewina** (NI) The act of inserting; insertion.

pihtasinân *pl.* **pihtasinâna** (NI) A pouch for carrying gunpowder pellets.

pihtatwan *pl.* **pihtatwana** (NI) A case for holding arrows, i.e.: a quiver. *(Plains).* *Alt.* **pihtahcâpân** *(Northern).*

pihtawawayiwinisa (NI) An undergarment.

pihtawesâkân *pl.* **pihtawesâkâna** (NI) A slip or petticoat.

pihtawesâkew *pl.* **pihtawesâkewak** (VAI) She wears a slip or petticoat.

pihtawetasew *pl.* **pihtawetasewak** (VAI) S/he wears underpants; s/he wears long johns or underwear.

pihtawetâsân *pl.* **pihtawetâsânak** (NA) A man's underpants; long johns or underwear.

pihtawinikan *pl.* **pihtawinikana** (NI) The inside lining for clothes.

pihtâkiyaw *pl.* **pihtâkiyawa** (NI) Inside the body; inwardly.

pihtâkoyaweskawew *pl.* **pihtâkoyaweskawewak** (VAI) S/he becomes part of her/his psyche; the spirit helper becomes part of her/his identity. *(Plains).* *Alt.* **pihcitahcâhkoweskawew** *(Northern).*

pihtâpawahew (VTA) S/he infuses liquid into her/him, i.e.: an enema.

   pihtâpawatâw (VTI) S/he infuses liquid into it.

   pihtâpawahiwew (VTA) S/he infuses liquid into people.

   pihtâpawacikew (VTI) S/he infuses liquid into things.

pihtâsiw *pl.* **pihtâsiwa** (VTI) S/he loaded her/his gun, i.e.: a rifle.

pihtâsiwin *pl.* **pihtâsiwina** (NI) The act of loading a gun.

pihtâskoteweyâw *pl.* **pihtâskoteweyâwa** (NI) An endless prairie vista.

pihtikweciwan *pl.* **pihtikweciwanwa** (VII) It is seeping.

pihtohkasikan *pl.* **pihtohkasikana** (NI) Something cooked from the inside, i.e.: a meat pie.

pihtokahâkan *pl.* **pihtokahâkanak** (NA) Someone who is let in; someone admitted.

pihtokahew (VTA) S/he takes her/him in.

pihtokatâw (VTI) S/he takes it in.

pihtokahiwew (VTA) S/he takes people in.

pihtokacikew (VTI) S/he takes things in.

pihtokahiwewin *pl.* **pihtokahiwewina** (NI) The act of initiating; inauguration; integration.

pihtokamik (IPC) The interior of a building.

pihtokwawew (VTA) S/he enters into someone's house.

   pihtokakew (VTA) S/he enters peoples' rooms or homes.

pihtokwemow *pl.* **pihtokwemowa** (VII) It enters or leads into it, i.e.: a railroad track going into a tunnel.

pihtokwepahtâw *pl.* **pihtokwepahtâwak** (VAI) S/he runs inside.

pihtokwepayihcikewin *pl.* **pihtokwepayihcikewina** (NI) The act of allowing something to begin or enter; inception.

pihtokwepayihiwewin *pl.* **pihtokwepayihiwewina** (NI) The act of penetration; penetrative.

pihtokwepayiw *pl.* **pihtokwepayiwak** (VAI) It enters into something.

pihtokwepayowin *pl.* **pihtokwepayowina** (NI) Way of approach; access; the act of being penetrating.

pihtokwew *pl.* **pihtokwewak** (VAI) S/he enters; s/he went inside.

pihtokwewin *pl.* **pihtokwewina** (NI) The act of entering; an entrance.

pihtokwewinihk (IPC) In the entrance; entry.

pihtonew (VTA) S/he peels it off by pulling, i.e.: the skin off a banana; s/he skins it, i.e.: usually used to refer to small fur bearing animals such as muskrat or beaver. *(Plains).* *Alt.* **pihtôpitew** *(Northern).*

   pihtotam (VTI) S/he peels it by pulling, i.e.: moosehide.

   pihtocikew (VTI) S/he peels things by pulling.

   pihtonam (VTI) S/he skins it off.

   pihtoniwew (VTA) S/he skins someone off.

   pihtonikew (VTA) S/he skins something off.

pihtonikewin *pl.* **pihtonikewina** (NI) The act of skinning and fleshing a pelt.

pihtopekipayowin *pl.* **pihtopekipayowina** (NI) Having a blister; a blister.

pihtosakepayiw *pl.* **pihtosakepayiwak** (VAI) Her/his skin peels off.

pihtosikan *pl.* **pihtosikana** (NI) Something skinned and fleshed.

pihtoskawew (VTI) S/he puts on or wears an undergarment. *(Northern).* *Alt.* **postiskawew** *(Plains).*

   pihtoskam (VTI) S/he puts on or wears an undershirt.

pihtoswew (VTA) S/he fleshes them with a knife.

   pihtosam (VTI) S/he fleshes it with a knife.

pihtôpekinew (VTA) S/he gave it a blister.

pihtôpekinam (VTA) S/he gives her/his hands a blister.

pihtôpekipayiw *pl.* **pihtôpekipayiwa** *or* **pihtôpekipayiwak** (VII) *or* (VAI) It or s/he is blistered.

pihtôpitew (VTA) S/he peels it off by pulling, i.e.: the skin off a banana. *(Northern). Alt.* **pihtonew** *(Plains).*

pihtôpitam (VTI) S/he peels it by pulling, i.e.: moosehide.

pihtôpicikew (VTI) S/he peels things by pulling.

pihtwâhew (VTA) S/he gave her/him a smoke.

pihtwâhiwew (VTA) S/he gives someone a smoke.

pihtwâw *pl.* **pihtwâwak** (VAI) S/he smokes.

pihtwâwin *pl.* **pihtwâwina** (NI) The act of smoking.

pikihkâtam (VTI) S/he patched it with tar or spruce pitch.

pikihkâcikew (VTI) S/he patches things with tar or spruce pitch.

pikihkâtew *pl.* **pikihkâtewa** (VII) It is patched with tar or spruce gum.

pikihtew (VAI) There is smoke rising in the distance.

pikihtewatâmiw *pl.* **pikihtewatâmiwak** (VAI) Her/his breath is visible, like a vapour, in the cold air.

pikinatahwew (VTI) S/he breaks or smashes them into small pieces.

pikinataham (VTI) S/he breaks or smashes it all up.

pikinatahikew (VTI) S/he breaks or smashes things up.

pikiskaciwâwi *pl.* **pikiskaciwâwiha** (NI) Rotten egg.

pikiskatihtâw *pl.* **pikiskatihtâwak** (VAI) S/he makes it rot or spoil.

pikiskatin *pl.* **pikiskatinwa** (VII) It is rotten or spoiled.

pikiskâcihcikew *pl.* **pikiskâcihcikewak** (VTA) S/he makes things go rotten.

pikiw *pl.* **pikiwak** (NA) A piece of chewing substance, i.e.: gum.

pikiwan *pl.* **pikiwanwa** (VII) It is gummy, i.e.: full of spruce pitch.

pikiwayastak *pl.* **pikiwayastakwak** (NA) A mountain goat. *(Plains). Alt.* **asiniwaciwacihkos** *(Northern).*

pikiwekin *pl.* **pikiwekinwa** (NI) A starched linen. *(Northern). Alt.* **sîtawekin** *(Plains).*

pikiwiw *pl.* **pikiwiwak** (VAI) It is gummy.

pikohcenew *pl.* **pikohcenewak** (VTA) S/he guts it; s/he removes its intestines. *(Plains). Alt.* **pakohcenew** *(Northern).*

pikwaciminôs *pl.* **pikwaciminôsak** (NA) A wildcat.

pikwaciwâpayômin *pl.* **pikwaciwâpayôminak** (NA) A grain of wild rice.

pikwaciyiniw *pl.* **pikwaciyiniwak** (NA) A solitary person; a recluse; a savage person; a brute.

pikwan *pl.* **pikwana** (NI) A flute. *(Northern). Alt.* **pipikwanis** *(Plains).*

pikwanâhtik *pl.* **pikwanâhtikwak** (NA) A part of a bullrush, i.e.: a cattail. *Var.* **otâwask**.

pikwataskamik (NI) An area where nothing grows, i.e.: a desert.

pikwataskamikâw *pl.* **pikwataskamikâwa** (VII) It is a desert-like.

pikwataskiy *pl.* **pikwataskiya** (NI) Wild or untamed country where nothing grows, i.e.: desert land.

pikwatastim *pl.* **pikwatastimwak** (NA) An untamed horse; a mustang. *(Northern). Alt.* **pakwatastim** *(Plains).*

pikwatehtew *pl.* **pikwatehtewak** (NA) A large bullfrog. *Var.* **mayokowatay**.

pikwatôsân *pl.* **pikwatôsânak** (NA) An adopted child or person.

pikwatôsew *pl.* **pikwatôsewak** (VAI) S/he gives birth to an illegitimate child. *(Northern). Alt.* **kiminicâkanihkew** *(Plains).*

pimacihew (VTA) S/he saved her/him; s/he supports her/him.

pimacitâw (VTI) S/he saved it.

pimacihiwew (VTA) S/he saves someone.

pimacicikew (VTI) S/he saves things.

pimâcihiwewin *pl.* **pimâcihiwewina** (NI) The act of saving a life; nourishment; salvation; the act of redemption.

pimâcihow *pl.* **pimâcihowak** (VAI) S/he makes a good living.

pimâcihowin *pl.* **pimâcihowina** (NI) The act of making a good living.

pimâhokow *pl.* **pimâhokowak** (VAI) S/he drifts along in the water.

pimâmeyihtam *pl.* **pimâmeyihtamwak** (VAI) S/he objects to it.

pimâmeyimew (VTA) S/he is antagonistic towards her/him; s/he holds a grudge against her/him.

pimâmeyitam (VTA) S/he is hostile towards someone.

pimâmeyimiwew (VTA) S/he holds a grudge against someone.

pimâmeyicikew (VTI) S/he holds a grudge against things.

pimâmeyimow *pl.* **pimâmeyimowak** (VAI) S/he holds a grudge.

pimâmeyimowin *pl.* **pimâmeyimowina** (NI) The act of holding a grudge.

pimâmeyitamowin *pl.* **pimâmeyitamowina** (NI) Having antagonism.

pimâminawew (VTA) S/he looks at her/him with antagonism.

pimâminam (VTI) S/he looks at it with antagonism.

pimâminâkew (VTA) S/he looks at people with antagonism.

165

pimâpekastesimowewin *pl.* **pimâpekastesimowewina**
(NI) The act of laying in a prostrate position;
prostration.

pimâpohew (VTA) S/he makes her/him drift along with
the current.

pimâpotâw (VTI) S/he makes it drift with the current.

pimâpohiwew (VTA) S/he makes people drift with the
current.

pimâpocikew (VTI) S/he makes things drift with the
current.

pimâpotew *pl.* **pimâpotewa** (VII) It drifts along in the
water.

pimâsiw *pl.* **pimâsiwak** (VAI) S/he sails by.

pimâsiwin *pl.* **pimâsiwina** (NI) The action of sailing.

pimâskohtin *pl.* **pimâskohtinwa** (VII) It is lying on the
ground, i.e.: a pole.

pimâskosin *pl.* **pimâskosinwak** (VAI) It is lying on the
ground, i.e.: a tree.

pimâstan *pl.* **pimâstanwa** (VII) It is wafted by or carried
by the wind.

pimâtakâw *pl.* **pimâtakâwak** (VAI) S/he waded in the
water.

pimâtakâwin *pl.* **pimâtakâwina** (NI) The act of wading
in the water.

pimâtan *pl.* **pimâtanwa** (VII) It is alive.

pimâtisimakihtâwin *pl.* **pimâtisimakihtâwina** (NI) The
act of animating something; animation.

pimâtisiw *pl.* **pimâtisiwak** (VAI) S/he is alive.

pimâtisiwin *pl.* **pimâtisiwina** (NI) A life.

pimâtisîskawew (VTA) S/he makes her/him live.

pimâtisîskam (VTI) S/he makes it live.

pimâtisîskâkew (VTA) S/he makes people live.

pimâtisîstawew (VTA) S/he lives for her/him.

pimâtisîstam (VTI) S/he lives for it.

pimâtisîstâkew (VTA) S/he lives for people.

pimâtisîwâhtik *pl.* **pimâtisîwâhtikwak** (NA) A tree of
life.

pimic (IPC) From the side or sideways.

pimicikâpawiw *pl.* **pimicikâpawiwak** (VAI) S/he stands
sideways.

pimicistinoweskam *pl.* **pimicistinoweskamwak** (VAI)
S/he is travelling crosswind or sideways.

pimiciwan *pl.* **pimiciwana** (VII) It flows, i.e.: a
watercourse.

pimihâw *pl.* **pimihâwak** (VAI) S/he flies past.

pimihkân *pl.* **pimihkâna** (NI) Moose tallow; a bag of
pemmican; a native delicacy from dry moosemeat
and moose fat.

pimihkânâpohkew *pl.* **pimihkânâpohkewak** (VAI) S/he
makes a stew from pemmican.
Var. **cîsâwânâpohkew.**

pimihkânâpoy *pl.* **pimihkânâpoya** (NI) Pemmican soup;
stew made from pemmican. *Var.* **cîsâwânâpoy.**

pimihkâniwat *pl.* **pimihkâniwata** (NI) A bag or container
for pemmican made from a moose bladder.

pimihkewin *pl.* **pimihkewina** (NI) The act of rendering
fat to grease; the act of pounding dry moose meat
and mixing it with moose fat.

pimihkiw *pl.* **pimihkiwak** (VAI) S/he renders fat to
grease; s/he makes a native delicacy of dry meat
mixed with moose fat.

pimihtin *pl.* **pimihtinwa** (VII) It is flowing, i.e.: a river.

pimikwâskohtow *pl.* **pimikwâskohtowak** (VAI) S/he
jumps by.

piminawasiw *pl.* **piminawasiwak** (VAI) S/he cooks.
(Plains). Alt. **kîstepiw** *(Northern).*

piminawasowikamik *pl.* **piminawasowikamikwa** (NI) A
kitchen. *Var.* **kestepowikamik.**

piminawatew *pl.* **piminawatewak** (VTA) S/he makes
someone cook for her/him; s/he makes her/him
something to eat. *(Plains). Alt.* **kîstepohew;**
micisohkawew *(Northern).*

piminawatiwew (VTA) S/he makes someone cook.

pimipahtâw *pl.* **pimipahtâwak** (VAI) S/he runs, i.e.: in a
race or an election.

pimipahtâwin *pl.* **pimipahtâwina** (NI) The act of
running, i.e.: in a race or an election.

pimipahtwâw *pl.* **pimipahtwâwak** (VAI) S/he runs along
with it.

pimipayihew (VTA) S/he runs her/him, i.e.: a vehicle.

pimipayitâw (VTI) S/he runs it.

pimipayihikew (VTI) S/he runs things.

pimipayihiwewin *pl.* **pimipayihiwewina** (NI) The act of
dominating someone; domination.

pimipayiw *pl.* **pimipayiwak** (VAI) S/he travels or passes
by.

pimipayowin *pl.* **pimipayowina** (NI) The act of passing
by.

pimipiciw *pl.* **pimipiciwak** (VAI) S/he is in the process of
moving.

pimipiciwin *pl.* **pimipiciwina** (NI) The act of being in
the process of moving camp; the act of setting out
on a long journey.

pimisâkâmepicikew *pl.* **pimisâkâmepicikewak** (VAI)
S/he pulls from one end to the other.

pimisâposkawew (VTA) S/he goes right by them; s/he
passes her/him by.

pimisâposkam (VTI) S/he goes right by it.

pimisâposkâkew (VTA) S/he goes right by people.

pimisimew (VTA) S/he lays her/him down.

pimisimiwew (VTA) S/he lays people down.

pimisin *pl.* **pimisinak** (VAI) S/he is laying down.

pimiskâw *pl.* **pimiskâwak** (VAI) S/he is paddling a canoe;
s/he is rowing a boat; s/he is steering the canoe or
boat. *Alt.* **tahkwahikew** *(Northern).*

166

pimiskâwin *pl.* **pimiskâwina** (NI) The act paddling a canoe; the act of rowing a boat; the act of navigating a boat or canoe.

pimiskohtew *pl.* **pimiskohtewak** (VAI) S/he walks on top of the ice; s/he is walking on ice. *(Plains and Northern variant). Alt.* **wâskitskohtew** *(Northern).*

pimitahew (VTA) S/he places her/him crossways.

pimitastâw (VTI) S/he places it crossways.

pimitascikew (VTI) S/he places things crossways.

pimitahkonew (VTA) S/he passes by while holding her/ him or it in her/his arms; s/he carries her/him in her/his arms.

pimitahkonam (VTI) S/he passes by while holding it in her/his arms.

pimitahkoniwew (VTA) S/he passes by while holding someone in her/his arms.

pimitahkonikew (VTI) S/he passes by while holding things in her/his arms.

pimitamiw *pl.* **pimitamiwa** (VII) It is extended crossways.

pimitamohew (VAI) S/he sticks them on crossways.

pimitamotâw (VTI) S/he sticks it on crossways.

pimitamocikew (VTI) S/he sticks things on crossways.

pimitapiw *pl.* **pimitapiwak** (VAI) S/he is seated crossways.

pimitaskamik (IPC) Crossways across the earth.

pimitaskamikweskam *pl.* **pimitaskamikweskamwa** (VTI) S/he goes crossways over the land, i.e.: from one side to the other.

pimitaskwahew (VTI) S/he hangs them crossways, i.e.: on a pole.

pimitaskwastâw (VTI) S/he places the pole crossways.

pimitaskwascikew (VTI) S/he places poles crossways.

pimitaskwamiw *pl.* **pimitaskwamiwa** (VII) It extends crossways onto the road.

pimitaskwamohew (VTI) S/he extends them crossways, i.e.: on the road.

pimitaskwamohtâw (VTI) S/he places it crossways.

pimitaskwamohcikew (VTI) S/he places things crossways.

pimitastew *pl.* **pimitastewa** (VII) It is placed crossways.

pimitâcimow *pl.* **pimitâcimowak** (VAI) S/he crawls, i.e.: on her/his knees.

pimitâcimowin *pl.* **pimitâcimowina** (NI) The act of crawling on one's knees.

pimitehtapiw *pl.* **pimitehtapiwak** (VAI) S/he passes by on horseback.

pimitew *pl.* **pimitewa** (VII) It is an oily liquid.

pimitisahikewin *pl.* **pimitisahikewina** (NI) The act of following behind someone; adherence.

pimitisawew (VTA) S/he follows behind her/him.

pimitisaham (VTI) S/he follows behind it.

pimitisahowew (VTA) S/he follows behind people.

pimitisahikew (VTA) S/he follows behind everybody.

pimiwakan *pl.* **pimiwakanwa** (VII) It tastes like grease.

pimiwan *pl.* **pimiwanwa** (VII) It is full of grease.

pimiwâhtik *pl.* **pimiwâhtikwak** (NA) An olive tree.

pimiwiw *pl.* **pimiwiwak** (VAI) It is greasy.

pimiy (NI) Grease, oil, lard.

pimîwakan *pl.* **pimîwakanwa** (VII) It smells greasy or oily.

pimohceskanas *pl.* **pimohceskanasa** (NI) A minor walking path.

pimohtahew *pl.* **pimohtahewak** (VAI) S/he makes her/ him walk.

pimohtahiwew *pl.* **pimohtahiwewak** (VTA) S/he is a travel guide.

pimohtatâw (VTI) S/he takes it with her/him; s/he carries it with her/him.

pimohtahiwew (VTA) S/he takes people with her/him.

pimohcikew (VTI) S/he takes things with her/him.

pimohtâtam *pl.* **pimohtâtamwak** (VAI) S/he walks through the country or on the road.

pimohteskanaw *pl.* **pimohteskanawa** (NI) A major walking path.

pimohteskanawew *pl.* **pimohteskanawewak** (VAI) S/he continually walks or treads on the same road.

pimohtew *pl.* **pimohtewak** (VAI) S/he walks.

pimohtewin *pl.* **pimohtewina** (NI) The act of walking.

pimosinâtew (VTA) S/he throws something at her/him, i.e.: a stone.

pimosinâtam (VTI) S/he throws something at it.

pimosinâsiwew (VTA) S/he throws something at someone.

pimosinâcikew (VTI) S/he throws something at something.

pimotahkwakan *pl.* **pimotahkwakana** (NI) An instrument for launching an arrow, i.e.: a bow. *Var.* ahcapiy.

pimotahkwew *pl.* **pimotahkwewa** (VTI) S/he shoots or launches the arrow.

pimowehtawew (VTA) S/he hears her/him pass by.

pimowehtam (VTI) S/he hears it pass by.

pimowehtâkew (VTA) S/he hears people pass by.

pimowestin (NI) A wind that is heard passing by.

pimowihew (VTA) S/he carries her/him along.

pimowitâw (VTI) S/he carries it along.

pimowihiwew (VTA) S/he carries someone along.

pimowicikew (VTI) S/he carries things along.

pimpatawatim *pl.* **pimpatawatimwak** (NA) A trotter, i.e.: a horse.

pimpayihcikewin *pl.* **pimpayihcikewina** (NI) The act of operating a machine.

pimwew (VTA) S/he shoots an arrow at her/him.

167

pimôtam (VTI) S/he shoots an arrow at it.

pimôcikew (VTI) S/he shoots an arrow at things.

pinahihkwâkan *pl.* **pinahihkwâkana** (NI) A fine comb for combing off lice.

pinahihkwân *pl.* **pinahihkwâna** (NI) A fine comb.

pinawehikan *pl.* **pinawehikana** (NI) A hair brush.

pinawew *pl.* **pinawewak** (VAI) She lays her eggs.

pinâskiw (NI) Autumn, the season of falling leaves. *Var.* **takwâkin.**

pinâstan *pl.* **pinâstanwa** (VII) It is blown off.

pinâwewin *pl.* **pinâwewina** (NI) The act of laying eggs.

pinikanew *pl.* **pinikanewak** (VAI) Her/his bones turn to jelly from fright.

pinipayiw *pl.* **pinipayiwa** (VII) It falls off the shelf.

pinipayiw *pl.* **pinipayiwak** (VAI) It falls off to pieces.

pinipocikan *pl.* **pinipocikana** (NI) A grinder; a grinding mill.

pinipocikâsiw *pl.* **pinipocikâsiwak** (VAI) It is milled or ground, e.g.: wheat. *Alt.* **piniposiw.**

pinipocikâtew *pl.* **pinipocikâtewa** (VII) It is milled or ground.

pinipocikew *pl.* **pinipocikewak** (VAI) S/he grinds.

pinipocikewin *pl.* **pinipocikewina** (NI) The act of grinding or being chafed.

pinipocikewiyiniw *pl.* **pinipocikewiyiniwak** (NA) A miller.

pinipohew (VTI) S/he grinds it, i.e.: wheat.

pinipotâw (VTI) S/he grinds it, i.e.: wood.

pinipocikew (VTI) S/he grinds things.

piniposiw *pl.* **piniposiwak** (VAI) It is ground or milled, e.g.: wheat. *Alt.* **pinipocikâsiw.**

pinipotew *pl.* **pinipotewa** (VII) It is ground or milled.

pipikosiw *pl.* **pipikosiwak** (VAI) It has an uneven or rough surface.

pipikwahcâw *pl.* **pipikwahcâwa** (VII) It is uneven; it is uneven ground.

pipikwanis *pl.* **pipikwanisa** (NI) A flute. *(Plains). Alt.* **pikwan** *(Northern).*

pipikwatinâw *pl.* **pipikwatinâwa** (VII) There is an uneven or rough hill.

pipikwâw *pl.* **pipikwâwa** (VII) It has uneven or rough surface.

pipon *pl.* **piponwa** (VII) It is winter.

pipon'tâpânâsk *pl.* **pipon'tâpânâskwak** (NA) A winter vehicle; a sleigh. *(Northern). Alt.* **pehkokawân** *(Plains).*

piponasâkay *pl.* **piponasâkaya** (NI) A winter jacket.

piponaskisin *pl.* **piponaskisina** (NI) A winter boot.

piponâskos *pl.* **piponâskosak** (NA) A one-year old animal, i.e.: a yearling.

piponâskosowiw *pl.* **piponâskosowiwak** (VAI) S/he is a one-year-old animal.

piponâyâw (IPC) It is just like winter.

piponisiw *pl.* **piponisiwak** (VAI) S/he spends the winter here.

piponisiwin *pl.* **piponisiwina** (NI) The act of spending the winter someplace.

piscipiw *pl.* **piscipiwak** (VAI) S/he took poison.

piscipowin *pl.* **piscipowina** (NI) A poison.

piscipowiniwiw *pl.* **piscipowiniwiwa** (VII) It is poisonous.

piscipowoces *pl.* **piscipowocesak** (NA) A poisonous fly, e.g.: a malaria mosquito.

piscipoyew (VTA) S/he poisons her/him on purpose.

piscipotâw (VTI) S/he poisons it on purpose.

piscipoyiwew (VTA) S/he poisons people on purpose.

piscipocikew (VTI) S/he poisons things on purpose.

piscipoyisiw *pl.* **piscipoyisiwak** (VTA) S/he poisons herself/himself.

piscipoyiwiwiyiniw *pl.* **piscipoyiwiwiyiniwak** (NA) A poisoner.

pisikwatisiw *pl.* **pisikwatisiwak** (VAI) S/he fornicates; s/he acts immorally or unchastely; s/he commits adultery. *(Plains). Alt.* **pisikwâcitôtam** *(Northern).*

pisikwâcâyihtiw *pl.* **pisikwâcâyihtiwak** (VAI) S/he acts in a lewd, unchaste manner.

pisikwâcâyihtowin *pl.* **pisikwâcâyihtowina** (NI) The act of being lewd.

pisikwâcimâmitoneyicikan *pl.* **pisikwâcimâmitoneyicikana** (NI) An impure or unchaste mind.

pisikwâcinâkosiwin *pl.* **pisikwâcinâkosiwina** (NI) Being impure, i.e.: oversexed; sexy.

pisikwâcîsâyâwin *pl.* **pisikwâcîsâyâwina** (NI) The act of being adulterous; the act of being flirtatious.

pisikwâciteyihcikan *pl.* **pisikwâciteyihcikana** (NI) An impure or unchaste thought.

pisikwâciteyimew (VAI) S/he has erotic thoughts about him/her.

pisikwâciteyitam (VTI) S/he has a unchaste mind.

pisikwâciteyimimew (VTA) S/he has a unchaste mind about someone.

pisikwâciteyihcikew (VTA) S/he has a unchaste mind about everybody.

pisikwâcitôtam *pl.* **pisikwâcitôtamwak** (VAI) S/he commits adultery. *(Northern). Alt.* **pisikwatisiw** *(Plains).*

pisikwâcitôtamowin *pl.* **pisikwâcitôtamowina** (NI) The act of committing adultery.

pisikwâciyiniw *pl.* **pisikwâciyiniwak** (NA) An unchaste person; a "rake".

pisikwâtâpamew (VTA) S/he looks at her/him suggestively.

pisikwâtâpatam (VTI) S/he has an erotic dream.

168

pisikwâtâpamiwew (VTA) S/he has a sexy look about her/him.

pisikwâtâpacikew (VTI) S/he looks at pornography.

pisikwâteyimew (VTA) S/he thinks s/he is immoral.

pisikwâteyitam (VAI) S/he thinks immoral thoughts.

pisikwâteyimiwew (VTA) S/he thinks immoral thoughts of people.

pisikwâteyicikew (VTI) S/he thinks immoral thoughts of things.

pisikwâtiskwew *pl.* **pisikwâtiskwewak** (NA) An immoral, unchaste woman; a prostitute.

pisikwâtisowin *pl.* **pisikwâtisowina** (NI) Fornication; immorality; seduction; the act of being lustful; intimacy; perversity.

pisikwâtonâmiw *pl.* **pisikwâtonâmiwak** (VAI) S/he speaks immorally, unchastely.

pisikwâtonâmowin *pl.* **pisikwâtonâmowina** (NI) The act of speaking immorally or unchastely.

pisimaneyapey *pl.* **pisimaneyapeya** (NI) A string for a racquet. *Alt.* **pîsâkanâpiy** *(Plains).*

pisimâtew *pl.* **pisimâtewak** (VAI) S/he laces the racquet.

pisimew *pl.* **pisimewak** (VAI) S/he is lacing, i.e.: a racquet.

pisin *pl.* **pisinwak** (VAI) S/he has something in her/his eye.

pisinihew *pl.* **pisinihewak** (VAI) S/he sticks something in her/his eye.

pisinowin *pl.* **pisinowina** (NI) Having something in the eye.

pisisikwâpisk *pl.* **pisisikwâpiskwa** (NI) Nothing but iron.

pisisikwâstew *pl.* **pisisikwâstewa** (VII) It sits empty.

pisisikwâw *pl.* **pisisikwâwa** (VII) It is empty.

pisiskâpamew (VTA) S/he just happens to see her/him.

  pisiskâpahtam (VTI) S/he sees it right away.

  pisiskâpahkew (VTA) S/he sees people right away.

  pisiskâpahcikew (VTI) S/he sees things right away.

pisiskeyihtamowin *pl.* **pisiskeyihtamowina** (NI) Care and attention.

pisiskeyihtâkosiw *pl.* **piskeyihtâkosiwak** (VAI) S/he is worthy of care.

pisiskeyihtâkosiwin *pl.* **pisiskeyihtâkosiwina** (NI) Someone worthy of being cared for.

pisiskeyihtâkwan *pl.* **pisiskeyihtâkwanwa** (VII) It is worthy of care.

pisiskeyimew (VTA) S/he cares for him; s/he takes care of her/him.

  pisiskeyitam (VTI) S/he cares for it.

  pisiskeyimiwew (VTA) S/he cares for people.

  pisiskeyicikew (VTI) S/he cares for things.

pisiskeyimiwewin *pl.* **pisiskeyimiwewina** (NI) The act of caring for someone.

pisisikihtawew (VAI) S/he is repulsed by what others say.

pisiskihtam (VAI) S/he is repulsed by her/his speech.

pisiskihtâkew (VAI) S/he is repulsed by people's speech.

pisiskiw *pl.* **pisiskiwak** (NA) An animal or beast; livestock; stock.

pisiskîs *pl.* **pisiskîsak** (NA) A small animal, i.e.: a possum or raccoon.

pisiskîwâyis *pl.* **pisiskîwâyisak** (NA) A creature.

pisiskowicepihk *pl.* **pisiskowicepihkwa** (NI) Mitrewort.

pisiskowisihtwâw *pl.* **pisiskowisihtwâwak** (VAI) S/he acts like an animal. *Var.* **pisiskowihkâsiw.**

pisiskowiw *pl.* **pisiskowiwak** (VAI) S/he is an animal.

pisiskowiwin *pl.* **pisiskowiwina** (NI) The act of acting like an animal.

pisiw *pl.* **pisiwak** (NA) A lynx.

piskac wâwi *pl.* **piskac wâwa** (NI) A rotten egg. *(Plains).* *Alt.* **asâwi** *(Northern).*

piskihcasin *pl.* **piskihcasinwa** (VII) It is separated or divided.

piskihcâyâw *pl.* **piskihcâyâwa** (VII) It is separated or divided into compartments.

piskihcihew (VTA) S/he separates her/him.

  piskihcitâw (VTI) S/he separates it.

  piskihcihiwew (VTA) S/he separates people.

  piskihcicikew (VTI) S/he separates things.

piskihcihow *pl.* **piskihcihowak** (VAI) S/he separates herself/himself.

piskihcikipaham *pl.* **piskihcikipahamwa** (VTI) S/he separates or divides it into compartments or rooms.

piskihcikipahikâtew *pl.* **piskihcikipahikâtewa** (VII) It is separated or divided into compartments or rooms; it is divided or separated into rooms.

piskihtakihcikewin *pl.* **piskihtakihcikewina** (NI) The act of being exceptional.

piskihtascikewin *pl.* **piskihtascikewina** (NI) The act of separating; an exception.

piskihtaskinewin *pl.* **piskihtaskinewina** (NI) The act of being isolated or alone; isolation.

piskihtinam *pl.* **piskihtinamwa** (VTI) S/he separates it or pulls it apart.

piskihtinamawew *pl.* **piskihtinamawewak** (VTA) S/he separates it or pulls it apart for someone.

piskihtisiw *pl.* **piskihtisiwak** (NA) Separated into pieces.

piskihtowew *pl.* **piskihtowewak** (VAI) S/he speaks a separate or different language.

piskihtowewin *pl.* **piskihtowewina** (NI) A separate or different language.

piskis (IPC) Apart from; separate.

piskohkopâw *pl.* **piskohkopâwa** (VII) There is a thicket, or a clump of bushes.

piskokanân *pl.* **piskokanâna** (NI) A knucklebone; a knuckle. *(Plains). Alt.* **pahpiskokanân** *(Northern).*

169

piskopayiw *pl.* **piskopayiwak** (VAI) S/he has lumps all over.

piskosikwâw *pl.* **piskosikwâwa** (VII) It is lumpy ice.

piskosiw *pl.* **piskosiwak** (VAI) S/he has a lump, i.e.: in one place.

piskosiwin *pl.* **piskosiwina** (NI) A lump.

piskwahcâw *pl.* **piskwahcâwa** (NI) A lump or hump in the ground.

piskwahew (VTI) S/he piles them in a lump; s/he piles them up.

 piskwastâw (VTI) S/he piles it up in a lump.

 piskwascikew (VTI) S/he piles things up in a lump.

piskwapiskaw *pl.* **piskwapiskawa** (NI) A low rocky or sandy ridge near the water line, i.e.: a reef.

piskwatanaskahikan *pl.* **piskwatanaskahikanak** (NA) A tall tree that is topped off.

piskwatanaskahwew (VTA) S/he tops off the tall tree; s/he removes the tree top.

 piskwatanaskaham (VTA) S/he chops the top off the pole.

 piskwatanaskahikew (VTA) S/he chops the top off something.

piskwatastew *pl.* **piskwatastewa** (NI) A mound.

piskwatinâw *pl.* **piskwatinâwa** (NI) A knoll.

piskwâkonakâw *pl.* **piskwâkonakâwa** (VII) There is a lump in the snow.

piskwâw *pl.* **piskwâwa** (VII) There is a lump on it.

piskwâwikanew *pl.* **piskwâwikanewak** (VAI) S/he has a lump on her/his back, i.e.: a hunchback person.

piskwâwikanewatim *pl.* **piskwâwikanewatimak** (NA) A hump back animal, i.e.: camel. *(Plains). Alt.* **piskwâwikanewipisiskiw** *(Northern).*

piskwâwikanewipisiskiw *pl.* **piskwâwikanewipisiskiwak** (NA) A hump back animal, i.e.: camel. *(Northern). Alt.* **piskwâwikanewatim** *(Plains).*

pisohtaw (VTI) S/he wedges it between two objects.

 pisohcikew (VTI) S/he wedges things between two objects.

pisoskawew (VTA) S/he brushes against him.

 pisoskam (VTI) S/he brushes against it.

 pisoskakew (VTA) S/he brushes against people.

 pisoskacikew (VTI) S/he brushes against things.

pispiskocewayik *pl.* **pispiskocewayikwak** (NA) A long legged spider, i.e.: daddy longlegs. *(Plains). Var.* **ocayapihkes.**

pistahwew (VTA) S/he strikes her/him accidently.

 pistaham (VTI) S/he strikes it accidently.

 pistahowew (VTA) S/he strikes someone accidently.

 pistahikew (VTI) S/he hits things accidently.

pistamew (VTA) S/he bites her/him accidently.

 pistahtam (VTI) S/he bites it accidently.

pistamiwew (VTA) S/he bites someone accidently.

pistacikew (VTI) S/he bites things accidently.

pistinew (VTA) S/he takes her/him by mistake.

 pistinam (VTI) S/he takes it by mistake.

 pistiniwew (VTA) S/he takes someone by mistake.

 pistinikew (VTI) S/he takes things by mistake.

pistiskawew (VTA) S/he kicks her/him accidently.

 pistiskam (VTI) S/he kicks it accidently.

 pistiskâkew (VTA) S/he kicks someone accidently.

pistisosiw *pl.* **pistisosiwak** (VTA) S/he cuts herself/himself accidently.

pistiswew (VTA) S/he cuts her/him accidently.

 pistisam (VTI) S/he cuts it accidently.

 pistisowew (VTA) S/he cuts someone accidently.

 pistisikew (VTI) S/he cuts things accidently.

piswahcahikewin *pl.* **piswahcahikewina** (NI) The act of faltering or tripping over something.

piswahwew (VTA) S/he trips over her/him.

 piswaham (VTI) S/he trips over it.

 piswahowew (VTA) S/he trips over someone.

 piswahikew (VTI) S/he trips over something.

pitihkohtâw *pl.* **pitihkohtâwak** (VAI) S/he is noisy.

pitikonam *pl.* **pitikonamwak** (VAI) S/he rolls it up.

pitikonew (VTA) S/he rolls her/him into a ball.

 pitikonam (VTI) S/he rolls it like a ball.

 pitikoniwew (VTA) S/he rolls people into a ball.

 pitikonikew (VTI) S/he rolls things into a ball.

pitikonikan *pl.* **pitikonikana** (NI) Something rolled into a ball.

pitikoniskew *pl.* **pitikoniskewak** (VTA) S/he makes her/his hand into a fist.

pitikosiw *pl.* **pitikosiwak** (VAI) S/he has a stubby figure.

pitikwahpicikewin *pl.* **pitikwahpicikewina** (NI) The act of entwining, i.e.: lacing up a bundle.

pitikwâw *pl.* **pitikwâwa** (VII) It is stubby, i.e.: ball-shaped.

pitoteyihtowak (VAI) They have a difference of opinion of each other.

piwahtakinew (VTA) S/he is picking up old spruce boughs from a teepee.

 piwahtakinam (VTA) S/he cleans out the old spruce boughs from a teepee.

 piwahtakinikew (VTA) S/he cleans out the old spruce boughs.

piwâyi *pl.* **piwâyiha** (NI) Something of worthless value.

piwihtakahikana (NI) Something that is cleaned off or filtered out; wood kindling. *(Plains). Alt.* **pawâtahikana** *(Northern).*

piyaseyimew (VAI) S/he is thankful to have her/him around.

 piyaseyitam (VTI) S/he is thankful with it.

 piyaseyimiwew (VAI) S/he is thankful with people.

piyaseyicikew (VII) S/he is thankful with things.

piyekosiw *pl.* **piyekosiwak** (VAI) It is rough and hard to swallow.

piyekoskohew (VAI) S/he feeds them food too dry to swallow.

piyekoskohewew (VAI) S/he feeds people food too dry to swallow.

piyekosowin *pl.* **piyekosowina** (NI) Being rough and hard to swallow.

piyekwan *pl.* **piyekwana** (VII) It is rough and hard to swallow. *(Northern). Alt.* **pihekwâw** *(Plains).*

piyesisikot *pl.* **piyesisikota** (NI) A beak of a bird. *(Plains). Alt.* **pîwâyisisokot** *(Northern).*

piyesîsikitowin *pl.* **piyesîsikitowina** (NI) A bird call. *(Plains). Alt.* **pîwâyiskitohâcikan** *(Northern).*

piyesîsimîciwin *pl.* **piyesîsimîciwina** (NI) Birdseed. *(Plains). Alt.* **pîwâyisisomîciwin** *(Northern).*

piyesîsis *pl.* **piyesîsisak** (NA) A nestling. *(Plains). Alt.* **pîwâyisisis** *(Northern).*

piyisiw *pl.* **piyisiwak** (NA) A thunderbird. *(Northern). Alt.* **pihesiw** *(Plains).*

pîkâkamiw *pl.* **pîkâkamiwa** (VII) It is dirty water.

pîkinâw *pl.* **pîkinâwak** (VAI) It is all in pieces.

pîkinew (VTA) S/he dismantles them with her/his hands.

pîkinam (VTI) S/he dismantles it with her/his hands.

pîkinikew (VTI) S/he dismantles things with her/his hands.

pîkinihkahtew *pl.* **pîkinihkahtewa** (VII) It is cremated; it is reduced to ashes.

pîkinihkasiw *pl.* **pîkinihkasiwak** (VAI) S/he is cremated; s/he is reduced to ashes.

pîkinihkaswew (VII) It is burned to ashes.

pîkinihkaswew (VTI) *or* (VTA) S/he cremates them; s/he reduces her/him or them to ashes.

pîkinihkasam (VTI) S/he cremates it.

pîkinihkasikew (VTI) S/he cremates everything.

pîkinipayihew (VTI) S/he scatters them in tiny pieces.

pîkinipayihtâw (VTI) S/he scatters it in small pieces.

pîkinipayihcikew (VTI) S/he scatters things in small pieces.

pîkinipayiw *pl.* **pîkinipayiwak** *or* **pîkinipayiwa** (VII) *or* (VAI) It or s/he breaks into many pieces.

pîkinipitew (VTI) S/he breaks them into small pieces.

pîkinipitam (VTI) S/he breaks it into small pieces.

pîkinipicikew (VTA) S/he breaks things into small pieces.

pîkinipohew (VTI) S/he grinds or crushes them up, i.e.: wheat into flour.

pîkinipohtâw (VTI) S/he grinds or crushes it all up.

pîkinipohcikew (VTI) S/he grinds or crushes things all up.

pîkinisinwa (VTI) They break into pieces, i.e.: wood.

pîkinisinwak (VTA) They break into pieces, i.e.: pebbles, rocks.

pîkinisiw *pl.* **pîkinisiwak** (VAI) It is broken into small pieces.

pîkiniwepawew (VTI) S/he breaks them into small pieces by hitting them.

pîkiniwepaham (VTI) S/he breaks it into small pieces by hitting it.

pîkiniwepahikew (VTI) S/he breaks things into small pieces by hitting it.

pîkinsâwâtew (VTI) S/he cuts them into small pieces.

pîkinsâwâtam (VTI) S/he cuts it into small pieces.

pîkinsâwâcikew (VTI) S/he cuts things into small pieces.

pîkinsimew (VTI) S/he breaks them into pieces with force.

pîkinihtitâw (VTI) S/he breaks it into pieces with force.

pîkinihcikew (VTI) S/he breaks things into pieces with force.

pîkiseyâpahtew (VII) There is a thick, dense, misty fog.

pîkiseyâw *pl.* **pîkiseyâwa** (VII) It is a misty, foggy day.

pîkiskacinâkwan *pl.* **pîkiskacinâkwanwa** (VII) It looks lonely.

pîkiskacinâskosiw *pl.* **pîkiskacinâskosiwak** (VAI) S/he looks sad and lonely.

pîkiskasihtâkosiw *pl.* **pîkiskasihtâkosiwak** (VAI) S/he sounds sad and lonely.

pîkiskâcihew *pl.* **pîkiskâcihewak** (VTA) S/he makes her/him sad and lonely.

pîkiskâcimew (VTA) S/he saddens her/him with her/his words.

pîkiskâcitam (VTI) S/he is sad when s/he hears it.

pîkiskâcimiwew (VTA) S/he saddens people when they hear her/him.

pîkiskâcicikew (VTI) S/he makes things sad.

pîkiskâsihtawew (VTA) S/he becomes sad and lonely when s/he hears her/him.

pîkiskâsihtam (VTI) It makes her/him sad and lonely when s/he hears it.

pîkiskâsihtâkew (VTA) It makes her/him sad and lonely when s/he hears people.

pîkiskâsihtâkwan *pl.* **pîkiskâsihtâkwanwa** (VII) It sounds sad and lonely.

pîkiskâtahpinew *pl.* **pîkiskâtahpinewak** (VAI) Her/his illness makes her/him depressed; s/he is tired of being sick.

pîkiskâtamacihow *pl.* **pîkiskâtamacihowak** (VAI) S/he feels isolated.

pîkiskâtan *pl.* **pîkiskâtanwa** (VII) It is isolated; it is depressingly alone.

pîkiskâteyihtam *pl.* **pîkiskâteyihtamwak** (VAI) S/he feels sad and lonely.

pîkiskâteyihtamowin *pl.* **pîkiskâteyihtamowina** (NI)
Loneliness; feeling alone.

pîkiskâteyihtâkosiw *pl.* **pîkiskâteyihtâkosiwak** (VAI)
People think of her/him as sad and depressed.

pîkiskâteyihtâkosiwin *pl.* **pîkiskâteyihtâkosiwina** (NI)
The act of being thought of as being sad and
depressed.

pîkiskâteyihtâkwan *pl.* **pîkiskâteyihtâkwanwa** (VII) It is
sad; it is lamentable; it is depressing.

pîkiskâteyimew (VTA) S/he finds her/him melancholic.
pîkiskâteyitam (VTI) S/he finds it melancholic.
pîkiskâteyimiwew (VTA) S/he finds people
melancholic.
pîkiskâteyicikew (VTI) S/he finds things melancholic.

pîkiskâtikosiw *pl.* **pîkiskâtikosiwak** (VAI) S/he is sad
and depressed.

pîkiskâtikosiwin *pl.* **pîkiskâtikosiwina** (NI) The act of
sadness and depression, or dejection.

pîkiskâtikwan *pl.* **pîkiskâtikwanwa** (VII) It is
lamentable.

pîkiskâtisiw *pl.* **pîkiskâtisiwak** (VAI) S/he is a
melancholic person or character.

pîkiskâtisiwin *pl.* **pîkiskâtisiwina** (NI) The act of being
melancholic.

pîkiskewew *pl.* **pîkiskewewak** (VAI) Her/his flesh tastes
tough.

pîkiskewinihk (IP) In verbal form; orally; utterance.

pîkiskwâsowewin *pl.* **pîkiskwâsowewina** (NI) The act of
consulting with someone; consultation.

pîkiskwâtew (VTA) S/he talks to her/him.
pîkiskwâtam (VTI) S/he talks about it.
pîkiskwâsiwew (VTA) S/he talks to people.
pîkiskwâcikew (VTI) S/he talks about things.

pîkiskwatitowin *pl.* **pîkiskwatitowina** (NI) The act of
talking to one another; dialogue.

pîkiskweskiw *pl.* **pîkiskweskiwak** (VAI) S/he is too
talkative.

pîkiskweskiwin *pl.* **pîkiskweskiwina** (NI) The act of
being petulant.

pîkiskwestamâkewin *pl.* **pîkiskwestamâkewina** (NI) The
act of talking for someone; attest; oration.

pîkiskwew *pl.* **pîkiskwewak** (VAI) S/he talks.

pîkiskwewin *pl.* **pîkiskwewina** (NI) The act of talking;
discourse.

pîkohtin *pl.* **pîkohtinwa** (VII) It breaks after a fall, i.e.: a
person's leg or an axe handle.

pîkokahwew (VTI) S/he chopped them up.
pîkokaham (VTI) S/he chopped it up.
pîkokahikew (VTI) S/he chopped things up.

pîkonew (VTA) S/he breaks her/him financially.
pîkonam (VTI) S/he breaks it.
pîkoniwew (VTA) S/he breaks people.
pîkonikew (VTI) S/he breaks things.

pîkonikew *pl.* **pîkonikewak** (VAI) S/he breaks or destroys
things.

pîkonikewin *pl.* **pîkonikewina** (NI) The action of
breaking or destroying things; damage.

pîkonisiw *pl.* **pîkonisiwak** (VTA) S/he destroys or ruins
herself/himself.

pîkonisiwin *pl.* **pîkonisiwina** (NI) The act of self-
destruction; suicide.

pîkopayiw *pl.* **pîkopayiwa** *or* **pîkopayiwak** (VII) *or* (VAI) It
or s/he broke; it *or* s/he is broken.

pîkopayowin *pl.* **pîkopayowina** (NI) Being broke.

pîkopepayiw *pl.* **pîkopepayiwa** *or* **pîkopepayiwak** (VII) *or*
(VAI) It *or* s/he breaks the surface of the water.

pîkopicikan *pl.* **pîkopicikana** (NI) Something used to
break ground, i.e.: a plow.

pîkopicikew *pl.* **pîkopicikewa** (VTI) S/he plows the
ground; s/he is ripping things up.

pîkopicikewin *pl.* **pîkopicikewina** (NI) The act of
plowing the land; the act of ripping things up.

pîkopitew (VTI) S/he tears them apart.
pîkopitam (VTI) S/he tears it apart.
pîkopisiwew (VTA) S/he breaks people.
pîkopicikew (VTI) S/he tears things.

pîkosimew (VTA) S/he breaks it when s/he drops it.
pîkotitaw (VTI) S/he breaks it when s/he drops it.
pîkohcikew (VTI) S/he breaks things when s/he drops
them.

pîkosin *pl.* **pîkosinwak** (VAI) It breaks when it falls, i.e.:
a clock.

pîkoskawew (VTI) S/he steps on them or kicks them and
breaks them.
pîkoskam (VTI) S/he steps on it or kicks it and breaks
it.
pîkoskâcikew (VTI) S/he steps on things or kicks
things and breaks them.

pîkostikwânesin *pl.* **pîkostikwânesinwak** (VTA) S/he
falls and cracks her/his head.

pîkostikwânewew (VTA) S/he cracks open someone's
head and gives them a scar.
pîkostikwâneham (VTI) S/he cracks open its head and
gives it a scar.

pîkoswew (VTI) S/he cuts them into pieces or bits.
pîkosam (VTI) S/he cuts it into pieces.
pîkosikew (VTI) S/he cuts things into pieces.

pîkotehewin *pl.* **pîkotehewina** (NI) The act of being
heart broken.

pîkwacipayiw *pl.* **pîkwacipayiwa** (VII) Honeycombed
ice, i.e.: rough ice which is usually formed during
the spring break up.

pîkwahcâw *pl.* **pîkwahcâwa** (NI) Rough ground.
(Northern). Alt. **mâyahcâw** *(Plains).*

pîkwamew (VTI) S/he tears them with her/his teeth.
pîkwahtam (VTI) S/he tears it with her/his teeth.

pîkwamiwew (VTA) S/he tears people with her/his
　　teeth.
pîkwacikew (VTI) S/he tears things with her/his teeth.
pîkwaskisinew *pl.* **pîkwaskisinewak** (VAI) S/he has torn
　　shoes.
pîkwastehwew (VTA) S/he winds it too tight and it
　　broke, i.e.: a clock's spring.
　　pîkwasteham (VTA) S/he winds it too tight and it
　　　broke.
　　pîkwastehikew (VTA) S/he winds them too tight and
　　　they broke.
pîkwatahikan *pl.* **pîkwatahikana** (NI) Something that
　　became broken when it was hit.
pîkwatahwew (VTA) S/he breaks them by striking them.
　　pîkwataham (VTI) S/he breaks it by striking it.
　　pîkwatahowew (VTA) S/he disfigures someone by
　　　striking her/him.
　　pîkwatahikew (VTI) S/he breaks things by striking
　　　them.
pîkwatamiw *pl.* **pîkwatamiwak** (VAI) S/he or it gnaws a
　　hole in the ice, i.e.: a beaver who breaks through
　　the ice and creates a breathing hole.
pîkwatamowin *pl.* **pîkwatamowina** (NI) The act of
　　gnawing a hole in the ice.
pîkwataskawiw *pl.* **pîkwataskawiwa** (VII) There are
　　holes that formed in the ice in the spring.
pîkwawew (VTA) S/he wrecked or ruined it with
　　something heavy, i.e.: a hammer or axe.
　　pîkwaham (VTI) S/he wrecked it with something
　　　heavy.
　　pîkwahikew (VTI) S/he wrecked things with
　　　something heavy.
pîkwâsiw *pl.* **pîkwâsiwak** (VAI) It is torn by the wind.
pîkwâstan *pl.* **pîkwâstanwa** (VII) It is torn by the wind.
pîkweyihtamowin *pl.* **pîkweyihtamowina** (NI) Anxiety;
　　suspense.
pîkweyimew (VTA) S/he worries about her/him; s/he is
　　concerned about her/him or them.
　　pîkweyitam (VTI) S/he is worried about it.
　　pîkweyimiwew (VTA) S/he is worried about people.
　　pîkweyicikew (VTI) S/he is worried about things.
pîmahpitew *pl.* **pîmahpitewa** (VII) It is tied crooked.
pîmakamehpisiw *pl.* **pîmakamehpisiwak** (VAI) S/he
　　wears suspenders.
pîmakâm (IPC) Going across on an angle, i.e.: crossways.
pîmakâmeham *pl.* **pîmakâmehamwak** (VAI) S/he goes
　　crossways over the water to the other shore.
pîmakâmehpison *pl.* **pîmakâmehpisonah** (NI) A
　　suspender.
pîmamiw *pl.* **pîmamiwa** (VII) The road is crooked;
　　something is off kilter.
pîmapiskahwân *pl.* **pîmapiskahwâna** (VII) It is screwed
　　into place. *Var.* **pîmaspiskahikâtew.**

pîmascehikanis *pl.* **pîmascehikanisa** (NI) A small burr.
pîmâhtik *pl.* **pîmâhtikwak** (NA) A twisted tree.
pîmâpiskahikan *pl.* **pîmâpiskahikana** (NI) A screwdriver
　　used on steel objects.
pîmâpiskawew (VTI) S/he screws them into the metal.
　　pîmâpiskham (VTI) S/he screws it into the metal.
　　pîmâpiskhowew (VTA) S/he screws someone into the
　　　metal.
　　pîmâpiskhikew (VTI) S/he screws something into the
　　　metal.
pîmâpiskihtin *pl.* **pîmâpiskihtinwa** (VII) It is crooked
　　and twisted or warped, i.e.: something metallic
　　such as a car door.
pîmâpiskisin *pl.* **pîmâpiskisinwak** (VAI) It is crooked
　　and twisted or warped, i.e.: something metallic
　　such as a frying pan.
pîmâpiskisiw *pl.* **pîmâpiskisiwak** (VAI) It is twisted out
　　of shape.
pîmâsiw *pl.* **pîmâsiwak** (VAI) It is blown crooked by the
　　wind.
pîmâsiwin *pl.* **pîmâsiwina** (NI) Being blown crooked by
　　the wind.
pîmâskisiw *pl.* **pîmâskisiwak** (VAI) It stands crooked or
　　twisted.
pîmâskwan *pl.* **pîmâskwanwa** (VII) It is crooked and
　　twisted, i.e.: a pole.
pîmâskweyâw *pl.* **pîmâskweyâwa** (NI) A growth of trees
　　angling across the prairie to provide a wind break.
pîmâw *pl.* **pîmâwa** (VII) It is crooked or slanted;
　　misshapen.
pîmihcakahikanis *pl.* **pîmihcakahikanisa** (NI) A small
　　screwdriver used on wooden objects.
pîmihtakahikan *pl.* **pîmihtakahikana** (NI) A screwdriver
　　used on wooden objects.
pîmihtakinew (VTI) S/he screws them on by hand.
　　pîmihtakinam (VTI) S/he screws it on by hand.
　　pîmihtakinikew (VTI) S/he screws things on by hand.
pîmikwâtew (VTI) S/he sews them on crooked.
　　pîmikwâtam (VTI) S/he sews it on crooked.
　　pîmikwâcikew (VTI) S/he sews things on crooked.
pîmikwenew (VTA) S/he twists her/his neck off.
　　pîmikwenam (VTI) S/he twists the neck off
　　　something.
　　pîmikweniwew (VTA) S/he twists the neck off people.
　　pîmikwenikew (VTI) S/he twists the neck off things.
pîminahkwân *pl.* **pîminahkwâna** (NI) A rope.
pîminahkwânis *pl.* **pîminahkwânisa** (NI) A piece of
　　small twine or string.
pîminew (VTA) S/he twists her/him.
　　pîminam (VTI) S/he twists it.
　　pîminiwew (VTA) S/he twists someone.
　　pîminikew (VTI) S/he twist something.

173

pîminikan *pl.* **pîminikana** (NI) A piece of tobacco twisted in a roll. *(Northern). Alt.* **wiyetinihan** *(Plains).*

pîminikanis *pl.* **pîminikanisa** (NI) A small twisting tool for making holes, i.e.: an awl.

pîminikâsiw *pl.* **pîminikâsiwak** (VAI) It is wound or turned, i.e.: like a clock.

pîminikâtew *pl.* **pîminikâtewa** (VII) It is wound or turned.

pîminikepayiw *pl.* **pîminikepayiwa** (VII) It winds automatically.

pîmisiw *pl.* **pîmisiwak** (VAI) S/he is crooked or slanted.

pîmisîhew (VTI) S/he makes them crooked.

  pîmisîtaw (VTI) S/he makes it crooked.

  pîmisîhiwew (VTA) S/he makes people crooked.

  pîmisîcikew (VTI) S/he makes things crooked.

pîmiskam *pl.* **pîmiskamwa** (VII) S/he wears it crooked or cockeyed, i.e.: a hat; s/he found it on her/his way up.

pîmiskanawehew (VTA) S/he makes her/him cross the road. *(Northern). Alt.* **âsowakâmetisahwew** *(Plains).*

  pîmiskanawetaw (VTI) S/he makes it cross the road.

  pîmiskanawehiwew (VTA) S/he makes people cross the road.

  pîmiskanawecikew (VTI) S/he makes things cross the road.

pîmiskanawew *pl.* **pîmiskanawewak** (VAI) S/he crosses the road. *(Northern). Alt.* **âsowakamehtew** *(Plains).*

pîmiskawew *pl.* **pîmiskawewak** (VAI) S/he wears crooked or cockeyed, i.e.: shirt; s/he found her/him or them on her/his way up.

pîmiskweyiw *pl.* **pîmiskweyiwak** (VTA) S/he twists her/his own neck.

pîmoyiw *pl.* **pîmoyiwak** (VTA) S/he packs or carries it under her/his arms.

pîmoyowin *pl.* **pîmoyowina** (NI) The act of packing or carrying something under the arm.

pîsâkanâpiy *pl.* **pîsâkanâpiya** (NI) A rope or cord made of moose or deer hide; a string for a racquet *(Plains).*

pîsâkopayihew (VTI) S/he makes them plentiful; s/he makes them last.

  pîsâkopaytâw (VTI) S/he makes it plentiful.

  pîsâkopayhiwew (VTA) S/he can find plenty of people for a job.

  pîsâkopaycikew (VTI) S/he can make things plentiful.

pîsâkopayiw *pl.* **pîsâkopayiwa** *or* **pîsâkopayiwak** (VII) *or* (VAI) It *or* s/he is plentiful or in abundance.

pîsâkopayowin *pl.* **pîsâkopayowina** (NI) The act of being plentiful or in abundance.

pîsâkosiw *pl.* **pîsâkosiwak** (VAI) It contains a great deal of space or room; it is of great dimensions.

pîsâkosiwin *pl.* **pîsâkosiwina** (NI) Having plenty of space or room.

pîsâkwan *pl.* **pîsâkwanwa** (VII) It contains a great deal of space or room; it is large or of great dimensions.

pîsâkweyimew (VTI) S/he finds them plentiful.

  pîsâkweyitam (VTI) S/he finds it plentiful.

  pîsâkweyimiwew (VTA) S/he finds there are plenty of people.

  pîsâkweyicikew (VTI) S/he finds there are plenty of things.

pîsim *pl.* **pîsimwak** (NA) The sun; a month.

pîsimohkân *pl.* **pîsimohkânak** (NA) A clock.

pîsimohkânis *pl.* **pîsimohkânisak** (NA) A wristwatch or pocket watch.

pîsimowiw *pl.* **pîsimowiwan** (VII) The sun is shining.

pîsimoyâpiy *pl.* **pîsimoyâpiya** (NI) A rainbow; a halo.

pîsimwâspinew *pl.* **pîsimwâspinewak** (VAI) She has her monthly menstruation.

pîsimwâspinewin *pl.* **pîsimwâspinewina** (NI) The act of menstruating.

pîskwa *pl.* **pîskwak** (NA) A nighthawk.

pîstew *pl.* **pîstewa** (NI) Foam; froth; soapsuds.

pîstewatâmiw *pl.* **pîstewatâmiwak** (VAI) S/he is foaming at the mouth.

pîstewatâmowin *pl.* **pîstewatâmowina** (NI) The act of foaming at the mouth.

pîstewâciwahtew *pl.* **pîstewâciwahtewa** (VII) It boiled until it was foaming.

pîstewâciwasiw *pl.* **pîstewâciwasiwak** (VAI) It boiled until it was foaming.

pîstewâciwaswew (VTA) S/he boils them until they were foaming.

  pîstewâciwasam (VTI) S/he boils it until it is foamy.

  pîstewâciwasikew (VTI) S/he boils something until it is foamy.

pîswasin *pl.* **pîswasinwa** (VII) An ancient Cree way of saying "it is nearby" or "it is not that far".

pîswâpamew (VTA) S/he sees her/him nearby; s/he saw her/him close-up.

  pîswâpahtam (VTI) S/he sees it nearby.

  pîswâpahkew (VTA) S/he sees someone nearby.

  pîswâpahcikew (VTI) S/he sees things nearby.

pîswehcâw *pl.* **pîswehcâwa** (NI) A soft spongy piece of ground.

pîswepahkwesikan *pl.* **pîswepahkwesikanak** (NA) A soft, spongy loaf of bread.

pîswepayiw *pl.* **pîswepayiwa** *or* **pîswepayiwak** (VII) *or* (VAI) It *or* s/he is bloated or swollen.

pîswepicikan *pl.* **pîswepicikana** (NI) A tool or machine used for carding or fluffing wool, i.e.: a steel comb.

pîswepiway *pl.* **pîswepiwaya** (NI) A soft, fluffy feather, i.e.: down.

pîswesiw *pl.* **pîsweswiwak** (VAI) It is fluffy.

pîswewayân *pl.* **pîswewayâna** (NI) A piece of soft, fluffy cloth, i.e.: flannel.

pîsweyâkonakâw (VII) It is soft, fluffy snow that is falling.

pîsweyâw *pl.* **pîsweyâwa** (VII) It is woolly.

pîtosâya *pl.* **pîtosâyak** (VAI) It is a different kind.

pîtosâyamihâwin *pl.* **pîtosâyamihâwina** (NI) A different religion.

pîtosâyihtiw *pl.* **pîtosâyihtiwak** (VAI) S/he acts different.

pîtoseyimew (VTA) S/he finds her/him different.

   pîtoseyitam (VTI) S/he finds it different.

   pîtoseyimiwew (VTA) S/he finds people different.

   pîtoseyicikew (VTI) S/he finds things different.

pîtosihtawew (VTA) S/he understands her/him in a different manner.

   pîtosihtam (VTI) S/he understands it in a different manner.

   pîtosihtâkew (VTA) S/he understands people in a different manner.

pîtosihtâkosiw *pl.* **pîtosihtâkosiwak** (VAI) S/he sounds different; s/he has an accent.

pîtosinawew (VTA) S/he sees her/him in a different way.

   pîtosinam (VTI) S/he sees it in a different way.

   pîtosinâkew (VTA) S/he sees people in a different way.

pîtosinâkohcikewin *pl.* **pîtosinâkohcikewina** (NI) The act of differentiation.

pîtosinâkosiw *pl.* **pîtosinâkosiwak** (VAI) S/he looks different.

pîtosinâkosiwin *pl.* **pîtosinâkosiwina** (NI) The act of looking or appearing to be different.

pîtosinâkwan *pl.* **pîtosinâkwanwa** (VII) It looks different; differentiate.

pîtosipayiw *pl.* **pîtosipayiwa** (VII) It becomes different.

pîtosisâyâw *pl.* **pîtosisâyâwak** (VAI) S/he is different.

pîtosisihiwewin *pl.* **pîtosisihiwewina** (NI) The act of disfiguring; disfigurement.

pîtosisiwepinikewin *pl.* **pîtosisiwepinikewina** (NI) The act of going the other way; abberation.

pîtoteyihcikewin *pl.* **pîtoteyihcikewina** (NI) The act of thinking differently; remonstrant; opposition.

pîtoteyihtam *pl.* **pîtoteyihtamwa** (VTI) S/he thinks it differently.

pîtoteyihtamowin *pl.* **pîtoteyihtamowina** (NI) A different kind of thought.

pîtoteyimew (VTA) S/he finds her/him to be different or changed.

   pîtoteyitam (VTI) S/he finds it to be different or changed.

   pîtoteyimiwew (VTA) S/he finds people to be different or changed.

   pîtoteyicikew (VTI) S/he finds things to be different or changed.

pîwahcikan *pl.* **pîwahcikana** (NI) A crumb.

pîwamew (VAI) S/he drops crumbs while eating, i.e.: bread; s/he drops bits and pieces while eating.

   pîwahtam (VAI) S/he drops bits and pieces while eating.

   pîwacikew (VAI) S/he drops bits and pieces all over.

pîwan *pl.* **pîwanwa** (VII) It is drifting, i.e.: snow.

pîwastew *pl.* **pîwastewa** (VII) It is scattered about; it is thinly spread, i.e.: sparce.

pîwayâna (NI) Something showy but of little value, i.e.: trumpery.

pîwâcihiw *pl.* **pîwâcihiwak** (VAI) S/he has a degrading or demoralizing lifestyle.

pîwâcihowin *pl.* **pîwâcihowina** (NI) The act of having a degrading or demoralizing lifestyle.

pîwâpisk *pl.* **pîwâpiskwa** (NI) Metal, i.e.: iron or steel; ore.

pîwâpiskokîskipocikan *pl.* **pîwâpiskokîskipocikana** (NI) A hacksaw.

pîwâpiskokotawânâpisk *pl.* **pîwâpiskokotawânânpiskwa** (NI) A steel or iron stove.

pîwâpiskomeskanaw *pl.* **pîwâpiskomeskanawa** (NI) A railroad. *(Northern).* *Alt.* **iskotewitâpân** *(Plains).*

pîwâpiskopîminahkwân *pl.* **pîwâpiskopîminahkwâna** (NI) A steel rope or cable.

pîwâpiskos *pl.* **pîwâpiskosa** (NI) A piece of metal; a telephone; a piece of wire; one penny; a can.

pîwâpiskowan *pl.* **pîwâpiskowanwa** (VII) It has steel in it. *Var.* **pîwâpiskowiw.**

pîwâpiskoyâkan *pl.* **pîwâpiskoyâkana** (NI) An iron or metal plate.

pîwâpiskwahcanis *pl.* **pîwâpiskwahcanisa** (NI) A steel ring.

pîwâpiskwapoy *pl.* **pîwâpiskwapoyak** (NA) A shovel.

pîwâpiskwaskihk *pl.* **pîwâpiskwaskihkwak** (NA) A metal pail.

pîwâpiskwemihkwân *pl.* **pîwâpiskwemihkwânak** (NA) A metal spoon.

pîwâstan *pl.* **pîwâstanwa** (VII) It is blown and scattered about by the wind.

pîwâyisis *pl.* **pîwâyisisak** (NA) A small bird. *(Northern).* *Alt.* **pîyesîs** *(Plains).*

pîwâyisisis *pl.* **pîwâyisisisak** (NA) A nestling. *(Northern).* *Alt.* **piyesîsis** *(Plains).*

pîwâyisisokot *pl.* **pîwâyisisokota** (NI) A beak of a bird. *(Northern).* *Alt.* **piyesisikot** *(Plains).*

pîwâyisisomîciwin *pl.* **pîwâyisisomîciwina** (NI) Birdseed. *(Northern).* *Alt.* **piyesîsimîciwin** *(Plains).*

pîwâyiskitohâcikan *pl.* **pîwâyiskitohâcikana** (NI) A bird call. *(Northern).* *Alt.* **piyesîsikitowin** *(Plains).*

pîweyihcikewin *pl.* **pîweyihcikewina** (NI) The act of showing insolence.

175

pîweyihtamowin *pl.* **pîweyihtamowina** (NI) The act of thinking of something as being worthless.

pîweyihtâkosiw *pl.* **pîweyihtâkosiwak** (VAI) S/he is thought of as being worthless.

pîweyihtâkwan *pl.* **pîweyihtâkwanwa** (VII) It is thought of as being worthless.

pîweyimew *pl.* **pîweyimewak** (VTA) S/he thinks s/he is worthless; s/he has a low opinion of her/him; s/he thinks of her/him scornfully.

> **pîweyitam** (VTI) S/he thinks of it as worthless.
>
> **pîweyimiwew** (VTA) S/he thinks of people as worthless.
>
> **pîweyicikew** (VTI) S/he thinks of things as worthless.

pîweyimisiw *pl.* **pîweyimisiwak** (VTA) S/he believes herself/himself to be worthless; s/he has a low opinion of herself/himself.

pîweyimisiwin *pl.* **pîweyimisiwina** (NI) The act of believing oneself to be worthless; having a low opinion of oneself.

pîweyimiwewin *pl.* **pîweyimiwewina** (NI) The act of believing someone is worthless.

pîweyimowin *pl.* **pîweyimowina** (NI) Humility.

pîwi kistikân *pl.* **pîwi kistikâna** (NI) A vegetable; a vegetable seed for planting in the ground. *(Northern). Alt.* **kiscikânis** *(Plains).*

pîwihew (VTA) S/he treats her/him with disrespect; s/he abuses her/him or them.

> **pîwitâw** (VTI) S/he treats it with disrespect.
>
> **pîwihiwew** (VTA) S/he treats people with disrespect.
>
> **pîwicikew** (VTI) S/he treats things with disrespect.

pîwihiw *pl.* **pîwihiwak** (VAI) S/he treats herself/himself disrespectfully.

pîwihiwewin *pl.* **pîwihiwewina** (NI) Being abusive by showing no respect.

pîwihkocikan *pl.* **pîwihkocikana** (NI) A knife used for cutting kindling for a fire.

pîwihkotâkan *pl.* **pîwihkotâkana** (NI) A piece of kindling.

pîwihtakahikan *pl.* **pîwihtakahikana** (NI) A piece of kindling made by an axe, i.e.: a wood chip.

pîwihtakahwew (VTA) S/he chops them into small pieces, i.e.: wood chips; s/he cuts the log in pieces for firewood.

> **pîwihtakaham** (VTI) S/he chops it into chips.
>
> **pîwihtakahikew** (VTA) S/he makes wood chips.

pîwikahikan *pl.* **pîwikahikana** (NI) A chip of wood; a splinter of wood.

pîwikahwew (VTA) S/he chops them into chips; s/he scatters chips from her/his chopping.

> **pîwikaham** (VTI) S/he chops it into chips.
>
> **pîwikahikew** (VTA) S/he makes chips by chopping.

pîwimew *pl.* **pîwimewak** (VTA) S/he voices to her/him her/his scorn or disapproval of him.

pîwinawew (VTA) S/he looks at her/him with scorn; s/he sees her/him or them as low-down or shameful.

> **pîwinam** (VTI) S/he looks at it with scorn.
>
> **pîwinâkew** (VTA) S/he looks at people with scorn.

pîwinâkohow *pl.* **pîwinâkohowak** (VAI) S/he feels scornful of herself/himself.

pîwinâkohowin *pl.* **pîwinâkohowina** (NI) The act of being self-scorning.

pîwinâkosiw *pl.* **pîwinâkosiwak** (VAI) S/he looks scornful.

pîwinâkwan *pl.* **pîwinâkwanwa** (VII) It looks scornful.

pîwipayiw *pl.* **pîwipayiwa** *or* **pîwipayiwak** (VII) *or* (VAI) It *or* s/he scatters; it *or* s/he falls in bits.

pîwipitew (VTA) S/he disperses it; s/he carefully drops bits of something, e.g.: seeds.

> **pîwipitam** (VTI) S/he disperse it all over.
>
> **pîwipicikew** (VTI) S/he disperses things all over.

pîwisikan *pl.* **pîwisikana** (NI) A remnant or a leftover piece of cloth.

pîwiswew (VTI) S/he leaves remnants of them cut up; s/he leaves bits and pieces of it cut up.

> **pîwisam** (VTI) S/he leaves remnants of it cut up.
>
> **pîwisikew** (VTI) S/he leaves remnants of things cut up.

pîwitôhtâkewin *pl.* **pîwitôhtâkewina** (NI) The act of being discourteous; discourtesy.

pîwiwepinew (VTI) S/he scatters or flings it about or around like powder.

> **pîwiwepinam** (VTI) S/he scatters or flings it about or around like powder.
>
> **pîwiwepinikew** (VTI) S/he scatters or flings things about or around like powder.

pîwomew (VAI) S/he voices to other people her/his scorn or disrespect of her/him; s/he is outspoken and critical.

> **pîwotam** (VII) S/he voices to other people her/his scorn or disapproval of it.
>
> **pîwomiwew** (VAI) S/he voices to other people her/his scorn or disapproval of others.
>
> **pîwohcikew** (VII) S/he voices to other people her/his scorn or disapproval of things.

pîyesîs *pl.* **pîyesîsak** (NA) A small bird. *(Plains). Alt.* **pîwâyisis** *(Northern).*

pohtâtakinam *pl.* **pohtâtakinamwak** (VAI) S/he placed her/his finger inside the hole.

pohtinew (VTA) S/he holds her/him in.

> **pohtinam** (VTI) S/he holds it in.
>
> **pohtinikew** (VTI) S/he holds things in.

pomehiwewin *pl.* **pomehiwewina** (NI) The act of being dejected; dejection; discouragement; disillusionment; the act of being inexpedient.

pomemetowin *pl.* **pomemetowina** (NI) The act of denouncing something; denouncement; discouraging one another.

pomew *pl.* **pomewak** (VAI) S/he is discouraged; s/he gave up.

pomewin *pl.* **pomewina** (NI) The act of being discouraged or giving up.

pomewisâyâwin *pl.* **pomewisâyâwina** (NI) Being mopish.

pomeyihtamohiwewin *pl.* **pomeyihtamohiwewina** (NI) The act of making someone feel dispirited or lose hope; discouragement.

pomeyimew (VTA) S/he is discouraged with her/him; s/he has no faith in her/him; s/he gave up on her/him.

　pomeyitam (VTI) S/he is discouraged with it.

　pomeyimiwew (VTA) S/he is discouraged with people.

　pomeyicikew (VTI) S/he is discouraged with things.

ponâhkosiw *pl.* **ponâhkosiwak** (VAI) Her menstruation is finished; she is well again.

poneyihtamawew (VTA) S/he forgives her/him. *(Plains).* *Alt.* **kâsînamawew** *(Northern).*

　poneyihtamakew (VTA) S/he forgives them; s/he pardons her/his sins.

poneyihtamawew (VTA) S/he pardons or forgives her/him.

　poneyihtamakew (VTA) S/he pardons people.

poneyihtamâkewin *pl.* **poneyihtamâkewina** (NI) A pardon; forgiveness.

poneyihtamâtowak (VTA) They pardon each other or forgive each other.

poneyimew (VAI) S/he ceases to think about her/him.

　poneyitam (VTI) S/he ceases to think about it.

　poneyimiwew (VTA) S/he ceases to think about people.

　poneyicikew (VTI) S/he ceases to think about things.

poni ayâw *pl.* **poni ayâwak** (VAI) S/he ceases to be here; s/he ceased having it.

poni pimâtisiw *pl.* **poni pimâtisiwak** (VAI) S/he ceases to live; s/he is deceased.

ponihew (VTA) S/he ceases to bother her/him; s/he leaves her/him alone.

　ponitâw (VTI) S/he leaves it alone.

　ponihiwew (VTA) S/he leaves people alone.

ponihkahtew *pl.* **ponihkahtewa** (VII) S/he is stoking up the fire for them; a fire was made.

ponihtâwin *pl.* **ponihtâwina** (NI) The act of relinquishing; relinquishment.

poninohew *pl.* **poninohewak** (VTA) She ceases breastfeeding her/him.

poninokosiw *pl.* **poninokosiwak** (VAI) S/he disappears out of sight.

poninôkwan *pl.* **poninôkwanwa** (VII) It disappears out of sight.

ponipayihcikewin *pl.* **ponipayihcikewina** (NI) The act of eliminating.

ponipayiw *pl.* **ponipayiwa** (VII) It ceases, i.e.: a meeting.

poniwâhkohtowin *pl.* **poniwâhkohtowina** (NI) Stopping a relationship; desisting.

poniwicewew *pl.* **poniwicewewak** (VTA) S/he ceases to live with her/him; s/he separates from her/him.

poniyayomihâw *pl.* **poniyayomihâwak** (VAI) S/he finishes praying.

posihtasôs (VTA) S/he loads the toboggan for her/him. *(Plains).* *Alt.* **postâpanihkawew** *(Northern).*

　posihtatâw (VTA) Her/his toboggan is loaded with her/him on.

　posihtahiwew (VTI) S/he makes people load the toboggan.

posihtâsiw *pl.* **posihtâsiwa** (VTI) S/he is loading things into a vehicle.

posihtâsiwin *pl.* **posihtâsiwina** (NI) The act of loading something, i.e.: a vehicle or wagon.

posihtâsohwiniw *pl.* **posihtâsohwiniwak** (NA) A boatman; a loader; a stevedore.

posikawiw *pl.* **posikawiwa** or **posikawiwak** (VII) *or* (VAI) It *or* s/he leaks into something.

posiskihew (VTA) S/he makes them hollow.

　posiskitâw (VTI) S/he makes it hollow.

　posiskicikew (VTI) S/he makes things hollow.

posiwepawew (VTA) S/he knocks her/him into something.

　posiwepaham (VTI) S/he knocks it into something.

　posiwepahikew (VTI) S/he knocks things into something.

posiwepinew (VTA) S/he throws her/him or it into the vehicle.

　posiwepinam (VTI) S/he throws it into the vehicle.

　posiwepiniwew (VTA) S/he throws people into the vehicle.

　posiwepinikew (VTI) S/he throws things into the vehicle.

poskisiw *pl.* **poskisiwak** (VAI) It is hollow or concave.

poskohtin *pl.* **poskohtinwa** (VII) Refers to a hole that develops after hitting something solid, i.e.: canoe against a rock, "it has a hole in it."

poskopayiw *pl.* **poskopayiwa** (VII) There is a hole in it.

poskopitew (VTI) S/he tore a hole in them.

　poskopitam (VTI) S/he tore a hole in it.

　poskopicikew (VTI) S/he tore a hole in things.

poskosawâtew (VTA) S/he makes a hole or an incision on her/him.

　poskosawâtâw (VTA) S/he has an incision on her/him.

　poskosawâcikew (VTI) S/he makes holes or incisions on things.

postamohew (VTA) S/he puts them in their place.

　postamotâw (VTI) S/he puts it in its place.

177

postamohiwew (VTA) S/he puts people in their places.

postamohcikew (VTI) S/he puts things in their places.

postasakahew (VTA) S/he put a coat on her/him.

postasakahtaw (VTI) S/he puts a coat on it.

postasakahiwew (VTA) S/he puts coats on people.

postasâkew *pl.* **postasâkewak** (VAI) S/he puts on her/his own coat.

postasâmew *pl.* **postasâmewak** (VAI) S/he puts on her/his own snowshoes.

postaskisinahew *pl.* **postaskisinahewak** (VTA) S/he puts shoes on her/him.

postaskisinew *pl.* **postaskisinewak** (VAI) S/he puts on her/his own shoes; s/he puts on her/his own footwear.

postaspastâkanew *pl.* **postaspastâkanewak** (VAI) S/he puts on her/his own apron.

postastisahew *pl.* **postastisahewak** (VAI) S/he puts gloves on her/him.

postastotinahew *pl.* **postastotinahewak** (VTA) S/he puts a hat on her/him.

postastotinew *pl.* **postastotinewak** (VAI) S/he puts on her/his own cap or hat.

postayiwinisahew *pl.* **postayiwinisahewak** (VTA) S/he puts clothes on her/him; s/he dresses her/him. *(Plains). Alt.* **kikayiwinsahew** *(Northern)*.

postayiwinisatâw (VTI) S/he puts clothes on the body.

postayiwinisahiwew (VTA) S/he puts clothes on the people.

postayiwinisew *pl.* **postayiwinisewak** (VAI) S/he puts on her/his own clothes; s/he has clothes on. *(Plains). Alt.* **kikayiwinsew** *(Northern)*.

postâpanihkawew (VTA) S/he loads the toboggan for her/him. *(Northern). Alt.* **posihtasôs** *(Plains)*.

postâpanihkatâw (VTA) Her/his toboggan is loaded with her/him on.

postâpanihkahiwew (VTI) S/he makes people load the toboggan.

postiskawew (VTI) S/he puts on or wears an undergarment. *(Plains). Alt.* **pihtoskawew** *(Northern)*.

postiskam (VTI) S/he puts on or wears an undershirt.

postitâsahew *pl.* **postitâsahewak** (VTA) S/he puts a pair of pants on her/him.

postitâsew *pl.* **postitâsewak** (VAI) S/he puts pants on; s/he puts on her/his own pants. *(Plains). Alt.* **kikitâsew** *(Northern)*.

powatam *pl.* **powatamwak** (VAI) S/he dreams about it. *(Northern). Alt.* **powâtam** *(Plains)*.

powatamowin *pl.* **powatamowina** (NI) The act of dreaming. *(Northern). Alt.* **pawâtamowin** *(Plains)*.

powatew (VAI) S/he has a spirit dream. *(Northern). Alt.* **pawatew** *(Plains)*.

powasowew (VTA) S/he dreams of someone.

powacikew (VTI) S/he dreams of things.

powâcikewaskih *pl.* **powâcikewaskihka** (NI) Dreamland. *Var.* **pawatamowaskîhk**, **powâtamowaskîhk**.

powâkan *pl.* **powâkanak** (NA) A tribal totem figure encountered in the dream world and which subsequently represents spiritual power. *(Northern). Alt.* **pawakan** *(Plains)*.

powâtam *pl.* **powâtamwak** (VAI) S/he dreams about it. *(Plains). Alt.* **powatam** *(Northern)*.

poyakamew (VTA) S/he peels them with her/his teeth.

poyakatam (VTI) S/he peels it with her/his teeth.

poyakacikew (VTI) S/he peels things with her/his teeth.

poyakawew (VTA) S/he peels them with an axe.

poyakaham (VTI) S/he peels it with an axe.

poyakahikew (VTI) S/he peels things with an axe.

poyakeskin'kewihkomân *pl.* **poyakeskin'kewihkomâna** (NI) A drawknife.

poyakeskin'kewin *pl.* **poyakeskin'kewina** (NI) The act of flaying, i.e.: removing bark.

poyakin'kewin *pl.* **poyakin'kewina** (NI) The act of peeling something.

poyakinew (VTA) S/he peels them.

poyakinam (VTI) S/he peels it.

poyakinikew (VTI) S/he peels somethings.

poyakipitew (VTA) S/he peels them by pulling, i.e.: the skin off a banana.

poyakipitam (VTI) S/he peels it by pulling it.

poyakipicikew (VTI) S/he peels something by pulling it.

poyakiswew (VTA) S/he peels them with a knife.

poyakisam (VTI) S/he peels it with a knife.

poyakisikew (VTI) S/he peels things with a knife.

poyawesis *pl.* **poyawesisak** (NA) A one-year-old beaver.

poyiw *pl.* **poyiwak** (VAI) S/he quit; s/he ceases work.

poyiwin *pl.* **poyiwina** (NI) The act of quitting.

poyonikamowin *pl.* **poyonikamowina** (NI) A hymn sung when ending a church service, i.e.: a recessional.

pômemew (VTA) S/he discourages her/him.

pômemiwew (VTA) S/he discourages people.

pômecikew (VTI) S/he discourages situations.

pônam *pl.* **pônamwak** (VAI) S/he makes a fire.

pônamowew *pl.* **pônamowewak** (VTA) S/he makes a fire for her/him.

pônamowin *pl.* **pônamowina** (NI) An old campfire site; making fire.

pônâpamew (VTA) S/he lost sight of her/him.

pônâpahtam (VTI) S/he lost sight of it.

pônâpacikew (VTI) S/he lost sight of things.

pônâyamihewikîsikâw (VII) It is Monday.

pônew (VTA) S/he makes a fire with it, i.e.: a tree.
  pônam (VTI) S/he makes a fire.
  pônikew (VTI) S/he makes a fire all over.
pônipimâtisiw *pl.* **pônipimâtisiwak** (VAI) S/he is dead. *(Plains). Alt.* **naspicinipiw** *(Northern)*; *Var.* **nipiw** *(Plains).*
pôniyawesiw *pl.* **pôniyawesiwak** (VAI) S/he ceases being angry.
pôniyotin (VII) The wind has ceased.
pônosew *pl.* **pônosewak** (VAI) S/he is sterile; she cannot give birth to children.
pônosewin *pl.* **pônosewina** (NI) Sterility; the act of not being able to give birth to children.
pônowemew *pl.* **pônowemewak** (VTA) S/he ceases arguing with her/him.
pônowihtam *pl.* **pônowihtamak** (VAI) S/he ceases talking.
pôsahkwâmiw *pl.* **pôsahkwâmiwa** *or* **pôsahkwâmiwak** (VII) *or* (VAI) It *or* s/he sleeps soundly.
pôsihew (VTA) S/he loads her/him into a vehicle.
  pôsitâw (VTI) S/he loads it into the vehicle.
  pôsihiwew (VTA) S/he loads people into the vehicle.
  pôsicikew (VTI) S/he loads things into the vehicle.
pôsipayiw *pl.* **pôsipayiwa** *or* **pôsipayiwak** (VII) *or* (VAI) It *or* s/he falls in.
pôsiskâw *pl.* **pôsiskâwa** (VII) It is deeply hollowed out.
pôsiw *pl.* **pôsiwak** (VAI) S/he embarks in a conveyance; s/he gets into a vehicle.
pôsiwin *pl.* **pôsiwina** (NI) The act of embarking on or getting into a conveyance or vehicle.
pôskonew (VTA) S/he makes a hole in them with her/his hands.
  pôskonam (VTI) S/he makes a hole in it with her/his hands.
  pôskonikew (VTI) S/he makes a hole in things with her/his hands.
pôskosâwâcikew *pl.* **pôskosâwâcikewak** (VAI) S/he cuts holes in it or them.
pôskosimew (VTA) S/he makes a hole in them when s/he throws or drops them down.
  pôskohtâw (VTA) S/he makes a hole in it when s/he throws or drops it down.
  pôskocikew (VTI) S/he makes a hole in things when s/he throws or drops things down.
pôskosin *pl.* **pôskosinwak** (VAI) Refers to a hole that develops after hitting something solid, i.e.: a tire, "it has a hole in it."
pôskoskawew (VTA) S/he made a hole in them by kicking them.
  pôskoskam (VTI) S/he makes a hole in it by kicking it.
  pôskoskâcikew (VTI) S/he makes a hole in things by kicking things.

pôskoswew (VTA) S/he cuts an opening or hole into them with scissors.
  pôskosam (VTA) S/he cuts an opening into it with scissors.
  pôskosikew (VTA) S/he cuts an opening into things with scissors.
pôskwahwew (VTA) S/he pierces a hole into them with something sharp.
  pôskwaham (VTI) S/he pierces a hole into it with something sharp.
  pôskwahikew (VTA) S/he pierces a hole in peoples' heads.
pôskwaskisinew *pl.* **pôskwaskisinewak** (VAI) S/he has a hole in her/his shoe.
pôskwatawew (VTA) S/he pierces them by hitting them.
  pôskwataham (VTI) S/he pierces a hole in it by hitting it.
  pôskwatacikew (VTI) S/he pierces a hole in things by hitting them.
pôskwatihpew *pl.* **pôskwatihpewak** (VAI) S/he has a hole in her/his head.
pôskwâtihpehwew (VTA) S/he made a hole in her/his head by hitting her/him.
  pôskwâtihpeham (VTA) S/he made a hole in its head by hitting it.
  pôskwâtihpehikew (VTA) S/he made a hole in peoples' heads by hitting them.
pôskwâw *pl.* **pôskwâwa** (NI) A hole in something, e.g.: a garment.
pôtacikew *pl.* **pôtacikewak** (VAI) S/he blew on something; someone who blows.
pôtatew (VTA) S/he blew on her/him.
  pôtatam (VTI) S/he blew on it.
  pôtasiwew (VTA) S/he blew on people.
  pôtacikew (VTI) S/he blew on something.
pôtawipayiw *pl.* **pôtawipayiwak** (VAI) S/he is puffy or swollen.
pôtawipayowin *pl.* **pôtawipayowina** (NI) The act of being bloated; protuberance.
pôtawisiw *pl.* **pôtawisiwak** (VAI) S/he is rotund.
pôtâcikan *pl.* **pôtâcikana** (NI) A whistling instrument; something you blow on. *(Plains). Alt.* **tepwepicikan** *(Northern).*
pôtâcikesîs *pl.* **pôtâcikesîsak** (NA) A male; someone who blows.
pôtôma (IPC) And so it was; and here it was.
pwakomohew *pl.* **pwakomohewak** (VTA) S/he makes her/him vomit.
pwakomowin *pl.* **pwakomowina** (NI) The act of becoming sick to the stomach; nauseated; vomit.
pwasitisahikewin *pl.* **pwasitisahikewina** (NI) The act of bluffing someone. *Var.* **pihtokwepayihiwewin**.

pwatawiyiniwiwin *pl.* **pwatawiyiniwiwina** (NI) Being spiritless.

pwawiw *pl.* **pwawiwak** (VAI) She is pregnant, i.e.: refers to pregnant animals.

pwâkomohkwewin *pl.* **pwâkomohkwewina** (NI) Vomiting blood.

pwâkomosikan *pl.* **pwâkomosikana** (NI) A medicine that induces vomiting, i.e.: an emetic.

pwâkomotôtam *pl.* **pwâkomotôtamwak** (VAI) S/he vomits on it.

pwâkomow *pl.* **pwâkomowak** (VAI) S/he vomits.

pwâstaweyimew (VTA) S/he thinks s/he is slow moving.

  pwâstaweyitam (VTI) S/he thinks it is slow moving.

  pwâstaweyimiwew (VTA) S/he thinks people are slow moving.

  pwâstaweyicikew (VTI) S/he thinks things are slow moving.

pwâstawimatwewew *pl.* **pwâstawimatwewewa** (VII) The gun is slow firing, i.e.: a muscle loader.

pwâstawipayiw *pl.* **pwâstawipayiwak** (VAI) It comes real slow.

pwâstawitakosin *pl.* **pwâstawitakosinwak** (VAI) S/he is slow arriving.

pwâstawiw *pl.* **pwâstawiwak** (VAI) S/he is slow moving.

pwâstawîwin *pl.* **pwâstawîwina** (NI) The act of being slow moving.

pwâtawihew (VTA) S/he is unable to get through to her/him and abandons the attempt; s/he can't handle her/him or them.

  pwâtawitâw (VTI) S/he can't handle it.

  pwâtawihiwew (VTA) S/he can't handle people.

  pwâtawicikew (VTI) S/he can't handle things.

pwâtimow *pl.* **pwâtimowak** (VAI) S/he speaks Sioux.

pwâtiyiniw *pl.* **pwâtiyiniwak** (NA) A Sioux person.

pwâtowew *pl.* **pwâtowewak** (VAI) S/he is Sioux.

pwâtômowin (NI) The Sioux language.

pwâwatahtâw *pl.* **pwâwatahtâwa** (VTI) S/he places a heavy load on it.

pwâwatew *pl.* **pwâwatewak** (VAI) S/he has a heavy load.

pwâwatewin *pl.* **pwâwatewina** (NI) Having a heavy load.

pwâwâtahew *pl.* **pwâwâtahewak** (VTA) S/he loads her/him heavily.

pwekitiw *pl.* **pwekitiwak** (VAI) S/he is flatulent.

pwekitowin *pl.* **pwekitowina** (NI) The act of being flatulent; the act of passing intestinal gas.

S

sakahikan *pl.* **sakahikana** (NI) A nail.

sakâpihkan *pl.* **sakâpihkana** (NI) A chain.

sakâskwahikewin *pl.* **sakâskwahikewina** (NI) The act of fastening.

sakâskwahon *pl.* **sakâskwahona** (NI) A pin; badge; a fastener.

sakâskwahonis *pl.* **sakâskwahonisa** (NI) A safety pin for diapers.

sakâskwawew (VTI) S/he pins them securely. *(Plains).* *Alt.* **sanâskwahwew** *(Northern).*

sakâskwaham (VTI) S/he pins it securely.

sakâskwahowew (VTA) S/he pins people securely.

sakâskwahikew (VTI) S/he pins things securely.

sakâw *pl.* **sakâwa** (NI) A forest, bush.

sakâwimehmew *pl.* **sakâwimehmewak** (NA) A wood pigeon.

sakâwmostos *pl.* **sakâwmostosak** (NA) A woods bison.

sakâyiyiniw *pl.* **sakâyiyiniwak** (NA) A backwoods person; a woods person; a bush person.

sakicihcikan *pl.* **sakicihcikana** (NI) A clamp.

sakikwenew (VTA) S/he grabs her/his neck.

sakikwenam (VTI) S/he grabs it by the neck.

sakikweniwew (VTA) S/he grabs people by the neck.

sakikwenikew (VTI) S/he grabs something by the neck.

samakâw *pl.* **samakâwa** (VII) It is flattened. *(Northern).* *Alt.* **wapakâw** *(Plains).*

samakinew (VTA) S/he flattens her/him by holding her/him down by the head.

samakinam (VTI) S/he flattens it.

samakiniwew (VTA) S/he flattens someone by holding them down by the head.

samakinikew (VTI) S/he flattens things.

samakipayihow *pl.* **samakipayihowak** (VAI) S/he crouches down suddenly.

samakipayiw *pl.* **samakipayiwa** *or* **samakipayiwak** (VII) *or* (VAI) It *or* s/he goes down/flat, ie: a tire or a muskrat.

samakipitew (VTA) S/he pulls her/him down flat.

samakipitam (VTI) S/he flattens it with a pull.

samakipisiwew (VTA) S/he flattens someone with a pull.

samakipicikew (VTI) S/he flattens things with a pull.

samakisiw *pl.* **samakisiwak** (VAI) S/he is flattened. *(Northern).* *Alt.* **napakisiw** *(Plains).*

samakiskawew (VTA) S/he flattens her/him by settling on top of her/him.

samakiskam (VTI) S/he flattened it by settling on top of it.

samakiskâkew (VTA) S/he flattens people by settling on top of them.

samakiskâcikew (VTI) S/he flattens things by settling on top of them.

sanaskamohew (VAI) S/he attaches them securely together. (Refers primarily to a marriage.)

sanaskamotâw (VTI) S/he attaches it securely together.

sanaskamohiwew (VTA) S/he attaches people securely together.

sanaskamocikew (VTI) S/he attaches things securely together.

sanaskamow *pl.* **sanaskamowa** *or* **sanaskamowak** (VII) *or* (VAI) It *or* s/he is securely attached.

sanaskatowew *pl.* **sanaskatowewak** (VAI) The fur is thick and prime.

sanaskâw *pl.* **sanaskâwa** (VII) It is securely built.

sanaskekan *pl.* **sanaskekanwa** (VII) It has a fine texture, e.g.: material.

sanaskekin *pl.* **sanaskekina** (NI) A fine textured cloth.

sanaskihew (VTI) S/he joins them firmly together; s/he glues them together firmly.

sanaskihtâw (VTI) S/he joins it firmly together.

sanaskihiwew (VTA) S/he joins people firmly together.

sanaskihcikew (VTI) S/he joins things firmly together.

sanaskinew (VTA) S/he fastens them firmly together.

sanaskinam (VTI) S/he fastens it firmly together.

sanaskiniwew (VTA) S/he fastens people firmly together.

sanaskinikew (VTI) S/he fastens things firmly together.

sanaskipayiw *pl.* **sanaskipayiwa** (VII) It is fused, i.e.: two boards.

sanaskipitew (VTI) S/he pulls them together securely; s/he fastens it well or joins it.

sanaskipitam (VTI) S/he pulls it together securely.

sanaskipisiwew (VTA) S/he pulls people together securely.

sanaskipicikew (VTI) S/he pulls things together securely.

sanaskisiw *pl.* **sanaskisiwak** (VAI) It is firmly joined.

sanâskwahwew (VTI) S/he pins them securely. *(Northern).* *Alt.* **sakâskwawew** *(Plains).*

sanâskwaham (VTI) S/he pins it securely.

sanâskwahowew (VTA) S/he pins people securely.

sanâskwahikew (VTI) S/he pins things securely.

saposikan *pl.* **saposikana** (NI) A laxative of any kind, i.e.: castor oil.

181

sapowepinew (VTA) S/he throws her/him right through.
　sapowepinam (VTI) S/he throws it right through.
　sapowepiniwew (VTA) S/he throws people right through.
　sapowepinikew (VTI) S/he throws things right through.
sasâkisiwin *pl.* **sasâkisiwina** (NI) The act of scrimping; being stingy.
sascoyawehew *pl.* **sascoyawehewak** (VTA) S/he infuriated her/him very quickly. *(Plains). Alt.* **sasoyawehew** *(Northern).*
sascoyawesiw *pl.* **sascoyawesiwak** (VAI) S/he became infuriated very quickly. *(Plains). Alt.* **sasoyawesiw** *(Northern).*
sascoyawesiwin *pl.* **sascoyawesiwina** (NI) The act of becoming infuriated very quickly. *(Plains). Alt.* **sasoyawesowin** *(Northern).*
sasepihtam *pl.* **sasepihtamwak** (VAI) S/he is disobedient.
sasepihtamowin *pl.* **sasepihtamowina** (NI) Disobedience.
sasepihtawew (VTA) S/he disobeys her/him.
　sasepihtam (VTA) S/he disobeys anyone.
　sasepihtakew (VTA) S/he disobeys all people.
saseskihkwan *pl.* **saseskihkwanak** (NA) A frying pan. *(Northern). Var.* **lapwel**; *Alt.* **seseskihkwân** *(Plains).*
saskahcâw (VII) The ground is thawing.
saskahikâkan *pl.* **saskahikâkana** (NI) Something to light a fire with, i.e.: a lighter. *(Northern). Alt.* **saskicepicikanis** *(Plains).*
saskahiw *pl.* **saskahiwak** (VAI) S/he uses a cane.
saskahon *pl.* **saskahona** (NI) A cane.
saskahotew *pl.* **saskahotewak** (VAI) S/he walks with a cane.
saskamiw *pl.* **saskamiwak** (VAI) S/he receives communion; s/he puts food in her/his mouth.
saskamohew *pl.* **saskamohewak** (VTA) S/he puts something in the other person's mouth.
saskamowin *pl.* **saskamowina** (NI) The act of receiving communion or putting something in the mouth.
saskan (VII) It is thawing.
saskan *pl.* **saskana** (NI) A chinook wind. *(Plains). Alt.* **kîsopweniyotin** *(Northern).*
saskaniyotin (NI) A south wind. *(Plains and Northern variant). Alt.* **sâwaniyôtin** *(Northern).*
saskatahtam *pl.* **saskatahtamwak** (VAI) S/he is bored of that food.
saskâkonakâw (VAI) The snow becomes slushy.
saskicepicikanis *pl.* **saskicepicikanisa** (NI) Something to light a fire with, i.e.: a lighter. *(Plains). Alt.* **saskahikâkan** *(Northern).*
saskihcikan *pl.* **saskihcikana** (NI) A type of lighter used to spark a fire, i.e.: a flintstone. *(Northern). Alt.* **cahkisehikanasiniy** *(Plains).*

saskisimew (VTI) S/he lights a fire with a flintstone.
　saskititâw (VTI) S/he lights a match.
　saskisikew (VTI) S/he lights a fire.
saskisiw *pl.* **saskisiwak** (VAI) S/he is lighted on fire; s/he is in flames.
saskiswew (VTA) S/he lights or sets fire to her/him.
　saskisam (VTI) S/he lights or sets fire to it.
　saskisikew (VTI) S/he light or sets fire to things.
saskitew *pl.* **saskitewa** (VII) It is lighted on fire; it is in flames.
saskwatwemowin *pl.* **saskwatwemowina** (NI) The act of giving a screeching war whoop.
sasoyawehew *pl.* **sasoyawehewak** (VTA) S/he infuriated her/him very quickly. *(Northern). Alt.* **sascoyawehew** *(Plains).*
sasoyawesiw *pl.* **sasoyawesiwak** (VAI) S/he became infuriated very quickly. *(Northern). Alt.* **sascoyawesiw** *(Plains).*
sasoyawesowin *pl.* **sasoyawesowina** (NI) The act of becoming infuriated very quickly. *(Northern). Alt.* **sascoyawesiwin** *(Plains).*
saswepayihew *pl.* **saswepayihewak** (VAI) S/he scatters it about. *(Northern). Alt.* **siswepayihew** *(Plains).*
saswepayiw *pl.* **saswepayiwa** (VII) It scatters about. *(Northern). Alt.* **siswepayiw** *(Plains).*
saswesin *pl.* **saswesinwak** (VAI) It scatters about into pieces. *(Northern). Var.* **siswesin**; *Alt.* **isiswesin** *(Plains).*
saswetin *pl.* **saswetinwa** (VII) It scatters about into pieces. *(Northern). Var.* **siswehtin**; *Alt.* **isiswehtin** *(Plains).*
saswetisahwew (VTA) S/he sends them scattering in every direction, i.e.: cattle. *(Northern)*
　saswetisaham (VTI) S/he sends them scattering all over, i.e.: letters.
　saswetisahowew (VTA) S/he sends people scattering in every direction.
　saswetisahikew (VTI) S/he sends things scattering in every direction.
saswewepinew (VTI) S/he scatters it by tossing it, i.e.: grain.
　saswewepinam (VTI) S/he scatters it all over by tossing it.
　saswewepiniwew (VTA) S/he scatters people all over by tossing them.
　saswewepinikew (VTI) S/he scatters things all over by tossing them.
sawahkew *pl.* **sawahkewak** (VAI) S/he glides to a landing, i.e.: a bird.
sawahtiw *pl.* **sawahtiwak** (VAI) S/he straightens her/his legs out.
sawânakeyimew (VAI) S/he is envious of her/him.
　sawânakeyimow (VAI) S/he is an envious person.

sawânakeyimowew (VAI) S/he is envious of people.

sawânakeyicikew (VII) S/he is envious about things.

sawânakeyimotatawew (VTA) S/he acts envious towards her/him.

sawânakeyimotatam (VTI) S/he is envious about it.

sawânakeyimotatâkew (VTA) S/he is envious about people.

sawânakeyimow *pl.* **sawânakeyimowak** (VAI) S/he is envious.

sawânakeyimowin *pl.* **sawanakeyimowina** (NI) Being envious; envy; jealousy.

saweyihcikâsiw *pl.* **saweyihcikâsiwak** (VAI) S/he is blessed.

saweyihcikâtew *pl.* **saweyihcikâtewa** (VII) It is blessed.

saweyihcikew *pl.* **saweyihcikewak** (VAI) S/he blesses.

saweyihcikewin *pl.* **saweyihcikewina** (NI) An act of blessing; consecration; the act of being blessed; beatification.

saweyihtakwan *pl.* **saweyihtakwanwa** (VII) It has been blessed.

saweyihtamowin *pl.* **saweyihtamowina** (NI) A blessing of something.

saweyihtâkosiw *pl.* **saweyihtâkosiwak** (VAI) S/he has been blessed.

saweyihtâkosiwin *pl.* **saweyihtâkosiwina** (NI) The state of being blessed.

saweyimew (VTA) S/he blesses her/him.

saweyimiwew (VTA) S/he bless people.

saweyicikew (VTI) S/he blesses things.

saweyimikosiw *pl.* **saweyimikosiwak** (VAI) S/he is favored by the spirits; s/he is blessed by God.

saweyimikowisiwin *pl.* **saweyimikowisiwina** (NI) The act of being favored by the spirits.

sâkahikanis *pl.* **sâkahikanisa** (NI) A small lake.

sâkaskinepahew (VTA) S/he fills them up with liquid.

sâkaskinepatâw (VTI) S/he fills it up with water.

sâkaskinepahiwew (VTA) S/he fills people up with liquid.

sâkaskinepacikew (VTI) S/he fills things with liquid.

sâkaskineposihtâsowin *pl.* **sâkaskineposihtâsowina** (NI) Having a boatload.

sâkawâpiskisiw *pl.* **sâkawâpiskisiwak** (VAI) It is a narrow or slender piece of metal.

sâkawâskwan *pl.* **sâkawâskwanwa** (VII) It is a narrow or slender piece of wood.

sâkawâw *pl.* **sâkawâwa** (VII) It is narrow or slender.

sâkâhikan *pl.* **sâkâhikana** (NI) A lake.

sâkâstenohk (LN) East, towards the sunrise.

sâkihew *pl.* **sâkihewak** (VAI) S/he loves him/her.

sâkihitowin *pl.* **sâkihitowina** (NI) The act of being in love, i.e.: a mutual love.

sâkihiwew *pl.* **sâkihiwewak** (VAI) S/he is affectionate.

sâkipakâw (VAI) It is dense and leafy; a bloom.

sâkipakâwipîsim (NA) May; the leaf budding moon or month. *(Northern). Alt.* **opiniyâwewipîsim** *(Northern). Var.* **apiniyâwepîsim**.

sâkitawâhk (NI) The Cree name for the settlement of Peace River.

sâkocihikowin *pl.* **sâkocihikowina** (NI) The act of being besotted.

sâkocihiwewin *pl.* **sâkocihiwewina** (NI) The act of convincing another person; subjugation.

sâkohikowin *pl.* **sâkohikowina** (NI) The act of failing.

sâkoteyimowewin *pl.* **sâkoteyimowewina** (NI) The act of bewitching someone; mesmerism.

sâkowew *pl.* **sâkowewak** (VAI) S/he shouts out a war whoop.

sâkowewin *pl.* **sâkowewina** (NI) The act of shouting out a war whoop.

sâkwes *pl.* **sâkwesak** (NA) A mink.

sâkweyimow *pl.* **sâkweyimowak** (VAI) S/he gives up or is disheartened.

sâmawew (VTA) S/he touches her/him with something, i.e.: a stick.

sâmaham (VTI) S/he touches it with something.

sâmahowew (VTA) S/he touches people with something.

sâmahikew (VTI) S/he touches something with something.

sâmiskawew (VTA) S/he touches her/him with her/his body.

sâmiskam (VTI) S/he touches it with her/his body.

sâmiskâkew (VTA) S/he touches people with her/his body.

sâpikanew *pl.* **sâpikanewak** (VAI) S/he has vitality.

sâpociwan *pl.* **sâpociwana** (VII) It flows right through.

sâpohâw *pl.* **sâpohâwak** (VAI) S/he flies right through. *(Plains). Alt.* **sâpoyaw** *(Northern)*.

sâpohkwamiw *pl.* **sâpohkwamiwak** (VAI) S/he slept right through.

sâpohtahew *pl.* **sâpohtahewak** (VTA) S/he takes him right through.

sâpohtewin *pl.* **sâpohtewina** (NI) A passageway.

sâpomin *pl.* **sâpominak** (NA) A gooseberry.

sâpominâhtik *pl.* **sâpominâhtikwak** (NA) A gooseberry bush.

sâponawew (VTA) S/he sees her/him right through something. *(Northern). Alt.* **isâpwâpamew** *(Plains)*.

sâponâkew (VTA) S/he sees right through people.

sâponew (VTA) S/he gets through them, i.e.: a crowd.

sâponam (VTI) S/he goes through it.

sâponiwew (VTA) S/he goes through people.

sâponikew (VTI) S/he goes through things.

sâponikan *pl.* **sâponikana** (NI) A sewing needle.

sâponikanis *pl.* **sâponikanisa** (NI) A small needle.

183

sâponôkosiw *pl.* **sâponôkosiwak** (VAI) S/he can be seen through it.

sâponôkosiwin *pl.* **sâponôkosiwina** (NI) Being transparent; transparence.

sâponôkwan *pl.* **sâponôkwanwa** (VII) It can be seen through it.

sâpopacikewin *pl.* **sâpopacikewina** (NI) The act of sprinkling.

sâpopahew (VAI) S/he wets them; s/he puts water on them.

sâpopatâw (VTI) S/he wets it.

sâpopahiwew (VTA) S/he wets people.

sâpopacikew (VTI) S/he wets things.

sâpopayihew (VTI) S/he makes them go right through.

sâpopayitâw (VTI) S/he makes it go right through.

sâpopayihiwew (VTA) S/he makes people go right through.

sâpopayicikew (VTI) S/he makes things go right through.

sâpopayiw *pl.* **sâpopayiwa** *or* **sâpopayiwak** (VII) *or* (VAI) It *or* s/he passes right through.

sâpopew *pl.* **sâpopewa** *or* **sâpopewak** (VII) *or* (VAI) It *or* s/he is wet.

sâpopeyâw (VII) It is kind of wet, i.e.: dewy.

sâposcahikewinis *pl.* **sâposcahikewinisa** (NI) A pinhole.

sâposikan *pl.* **sâposikana** (NI) A purgative, a laxative. *(Plains). Alt.* **kanâcihcikan** *(Northern).*

sâposiw *pl.* **sâposiwak** (VAI) S/he has diarrhea.

sâposkawew (VAI) S/he passes right through them.

sâposkam (VTI) S/he passes right through it.

sâposkâkew (VTA) S/he passes right through people.

sâposowin *pl.* **sâposowina** (NI) Diarrhea.

sâpostahikewin *pl.* **sâpostahikewina** (NI) The act of piercing with a needle.

sâpostahwew (VTA) S/he puts the needle right through her/him; s/he pierces her/him right through.

sâpostaham (VTI) S/he puts a needle right through.

sâpostahowew (VTA) S/he puts a needle right through someone.

sâpostahikew (VTI) S/he puts a needle right through things.

sâpostawâw *pl.* **sâpostawâwa** (VII) There is an opening that leads right through, i.e.: a passage.

sâpostaweskawew (VTI) S/he steps right through them.

sâpostaweskam (VTI) S/he steps right through it.

sâpostaweskâkew (VTA) S/he steps right through people.

sâpostawisiw *pl.* **sâpostawisiwak** (VAI) There is a passage, i.e.: an opening right through.

sâpostawisowin *pl.* **sâpostawisowina** (NI) Having a passageway.

sâpostawiyâw *pl.* **sâpostawiyâwa** (VII) It has a passage or an opening.

sâposwew (VTA) S/he cuts right through her/him.

sâposam (VTI) S/he cuts right through it.

sâposowew (VTA) S/he cuts right through people.

sâposikew (VTI) S/he cuts right through things.

sâpoyahkiw *pl.* **sâpoyahkiwak** (VAI) S/he crawls right through, i.e.: an opening.

sâpoyaw *pl.* **sâpoyawak** (VAI) S/he flies right through. *(Northern). Alt.* **sâpohâw** *(Plains).*

sâpoyawesiw *pl.* **sâpoyawesiwak** (VAI) Her/his anger rages on or right through the week(s).

sâpoyowehtawin *pl.* **sâpoyowehtawina** (NI) The act of letting fresh air in, i.e.: ventilate.

sâpoyowew *pl.* **sâpoyowewak** (VAI) S/he feels the air or draught right through.

sâpwamew (VTA) S/he bites her/him right through.

sâpwahtam (VTI) S/he bites right through it.

sâpwamiwew (VTA) S/he bites right through people.

sâpwahcikew (VTI) S/he bites right through things.

sâpwamiw *pl.* **sâpwamiwa** (VII) It passes right through, i.e.: a road.

sâpwasiw *pl.* **sâpwasiwak** (VAI) S/he is translucent.

sâpwaskopayihtâw *pl.* **sâpwaskopayihtâwak** (VAI) S/he throws it right through on a pole.

sâpwâpamew (VTA) S/he x-rays her/him; s/he sees her/him right through something *(Plains).*

sâpwâpahtam (VTI) S/he x-rays it.

sâpwâpamiwew (VTA) S/he x-rays people.

sâpwâpahcikew (VTI) S/he x-rays things.

sâpwâsiwin *pl.* **sâpwâsiwina** (NI) Translucency.

sâpwâstan *pl.* **sâpwâstanwa** (VII) The wind blows right through it.

sâpwâstew *pl.* **sâpwâstewa** (VII) It is translucent.

sâpweyihtamowin *pl.* **sâpweyihtamowina** (NI) Being earnest; intended; intention.

sâsakicipayiw *pl.* **sâsakicipayiwak** (VAI) S/he fell and landed on her/his back.

sâsakicisin *pl.* **sâsakicisinwak** (VAI) S/he lies on her/his back.

sâsakiciwepawew (VTA) S/he knocks her/him flat onto her/his back.

sâsakiciwepaham (VTI) S/he knocks it flat onto its back.

sâsakiciwepahowew (VTA) S/he knocks someone flat onto their back.

sâsakiciwepahikew (VTA) S/he knocks people flat onto their backs.

sâsakiciwepinew (VTA) S/he throws her/him down on her/his back.

sâsakiciwepinam (VTI) S/he throws it on its backs.

sâsakiciwepiniwew (VTA) S/he throws someone on their back.

sâsakiciwepinikew (VTI) S/he throws things backwards.

sâsakitisimew (VTA) S/he makes her/him lie on her/his back.

sâsakitisimiwew (VTA) S/he lies people on their backs.

sâsay (IPC) Already. *(Northern). Var.* **âsay** *(Northern); Alt.* **âsay** *(Plains).*

sâsâkawaskosiw *pl.* **sâsâkawaskosiwak** (VAI) S/he is skinny and tall.

sâsâkawâpiskâw *pl.* **sâsâkawâpiskâwa** (VII) It is slender, i.e.: steel or metal.

sâsâkawâpiskos *pl.* **sâsâkawâpiskosak** (NA) A chipmunk.

sâsâkihtiw *pl.* **sâsâkihtiwak** (VAI) S/he is barefoot; her/his feet are bare. *(Plains). Alt.* **mosesitew** *(Northern).*

sâsâkihtiwin (NI) Being barefoot.

sâsâkinikâtew *pl.* **sâsâkinikâtewak** (VAI) S/he is bare-legged.

sâsâkinistikwân *pl.* **sâsâkinistikwâna** (NI) A bare, uncovered head.

sâsâkominan *pl.* **sâsâkominanak** (NA) An elderberry.

sâsâkosiw *pl.* **sâsâkosiwak** (VAI) S/he is gangly.

sâsâkoyawew *pl.* **sâsâkoyawewak** (VAI) S/he has a slender build.

sâsepatawapiw *pl.* **sâsepatawapiwak** (VAI) S/he is able to keep her/his eyes open for a long time.

sâsipimâtew (VTI) S/he fries the fat to make grease, i.e.: sirloin fat.

sâsipimâtam (VTA) S/he fries the fat to make grease, fat.

sâsipimâcikew (VTA) S/he is frying the fat to make grease.

sâsipimew *pl.* **sâsipimewak** (VAI) S/he fries fat to make grease; s/he melts fat to make grease.

sâsîpeyihtam *pl.* **sâsîpeyihtamak** (VAI) S/he is patient; s/he puts up with a lot. *(Plains). Alt.* **sîpeyihcikew** *(Northern).*

sâsîpihkeyimew (VAI) S/he is patient with him. *(Plains). Alt.* **sipeyimew** *(Northern).*

sâsîpihkeyitam (VAI) *or* (VII) S/he is patient with it.

sâsîpihkeyiniwew (VAI) S/he is patient with people.

sâsîpihkeyicikew (VAI) *or* (VII) S/he is patient with things.

sâskwatwemiw *pl.* **sâskwatwemiwak** (VAI) S/he gives a screeching war whoop.

sâstehtin *pl.* **sâstehtinwa** (VII) It is rancid, i.e.: grease or something with fat. *(Northern). Var.* **sâsteyâw** *(Northern); Alt.* **sâsteyâw** *(Plains).*

sâstesin *pl.* **sâstesinwak** (VAI) It is rancid, i.e.: grease or something with fat.

sâsteyâw *pl.* **sâsteyâwa** (VII) It is rancid, i.e.: grease or something with fat. *(Plains and Northern variant). Alt.* **sâstehtin.**

sâsteyâw *pl.* **sâsteyâwa** (VII) It went rancid.

sâwahtôhew *pl.* **sâwahtôhewak** (VTA) S/he straightens their legs out.

sâwahtôpitew *pl.* **sâwahtôpitewak** (VTA) S/he pulls her/his legs and straightens them out.

sâwahtôsin *pl.* **sâwahtôsinwak** (VAI) S/he lies with her/his legs straightened or stretched out.

sâwaniyowew (NI) A warm breeze. *(Northern). Alt.* **kisopwemyocisin** *(Plains).*

sâwaniyôtin (NI) A south wind. *(Northern). Var.* **saskaniyotin** *(Northern); Alt.* **saskaniyotin** *(Plains).*

sâwanohk (IPC) Towards the south or in a southerly direction. *(Northern). Var.* **âpihtâkisikanohk** *(Northern); Alt.* **âpihtâkisikanohk** *(Plains).*

sehkatimew (VTA) S/he makes her/him skinny or thin.

sehkatimiwew (VTA) S/he makes people skinny or thin.

sehke (VAI) It is voluntary; it runs by itself.

sehkepimipayîs *pl.* **sehkepimipayîswak** (NA) A vehicle that runs by itself, i.e.: a car. *(Plains). Var.* **sehkes** *(Plains); Alt.* **wihcekitâpânâsk** *(Northern).*

sehkes *pl.* **sehkeswak** (NA) A stinking vehicle; a vehicle that runs by itself, i.e.: a car. *(Plains). Var.* **sehkepimipayîs** *(Plains); Alt.* **wihcekitâpânâsk** *(Northern).*

sekâpamiw *pl.* **sekâpamiwak** *or* **sekâpamiwa** (VAI) *or* (VII) S/he *or* it is terrified by the sight of her/him.

sekâtisiw *pl.* **sekâtisiwak** (VAI) Her/his behavior is terrifying or scary.

sekihew (VTA) S/he scares her/him.

sekihiwew (VTA) S/he scares people.

sekihcikew (VTA) S/he scares everyone.

sekihiwew (VTA) Her/his talking scares her/him. *(Plains). Alt.* **sekimew** *(Northern).*

sekihimiwew (VTA) Her/his talking scares people.

sekihicikew (VTA) S/he scares everybody.

sekihkwew *pl.* **sekihkwewak** (VAI) S/he has a scared or horrified expression on her/his face. *(Northern). Alt.* **seseskinâkosiw** *(Plains).*

sekihtamawew (VTA) S/he scares them away, i.e.: wild game, and does not leave any for the next person. *(Plains). Alt.* **pawitisahamawew** *(Northern).*

sekihtamakew (VTA) S/he scares all the game away for other people.

sekimew (VTA) Her/his talking scares her/him. *(Northern). Alt.* **sekihiwew** *(Plains).*

sekimiwew (VTA) Her/his talking scares people.

sekicikew (VTA) S/he scares everybody.

185

sekinâkosiw *pl.* **sekinâkosiwak** (VAI) S/he looks scared. *(Northern). Alt.* **seseskinâkosiw** *(Plains).*

sekipatowew *pl.* **sekipatowewak** (VAI) S/he braids her/ his own hair.

sekipatwân *pl.* **sekipatwâna** (NI) A braid of hair.

sekipatwâw *pl.* **sekipatwâwak** (VAI) S/he has braids (often used to identify a person of Chinese descent.)

sekipayiw *pl.* **sekipayiwa** *or* **sekipayiwak** (VII) *or* (VAI) It *or* s/he spills.

sekipestâw (VII) It is pouring rain.

sekipitew (VTA) S/he spills them by pulling or pushing it.

  sekipitam (VTI) S/he spills it.

  sekipicikew (VTI) S/he spills everything.

sekiseweyimew (VAI) S/he thinks s/he is scared or frightened.

  sekiseweyitam (VTI) S/he thinks it is scarey.

  sekiseweyimiwew (VTA) S/he thinks people are scarey.

  sekiseweyicikew (VTI) S/he thinks things are scarey.

sekisimew (VTI) S/he stumbles and spills them out.

  sekihtitâw (VTI) S/he stumbles and spills it.

  sekihcikew (VTI) S/he stumbles and spills everything.

sekisiw *pl.* **sekisiwak** (VAI) S/he is scared or frightened or horrified.

sekisiwin *pl.* **sekisiwina** (NI) Being scared or frightened.

sekohciwanihew (VTI) S/he drains it or them.

  sekohciwanitâw (VTI) S/he drains it.

  sekohciwanicikew (VTI) S/he drains things.

sekohkahtew *pl.* **sekohkahtewa** (VII) It is burned to ashes.

sekohkasiw *pl.* **sekohkasiwak** (VAI) S/he or it burned to ashes.

sekohkaswew (VTA) S/he burns or reduces them to ashes.

  sekohkasam (VTI) S/he burns or reduces it to ashes.

  sekohkasikew (VTI) S/he burns or reduces things to ashes.

sekohkinam *pl.* **sekohkinamwak** (VTA) S/he strains it.

sekohtin *pl.* **sekohtinwa** (VII) It is stuck or wedged between.

sekonew (VTI) S/he empties or cleans out the buckets; s/he slips her/him underneath to hide her/him; s/he slips it underneath to hide it; s/he slips things underneath to hide them; they slip her/him underneath to hide her/him.

  sekonam (VTI) S/he takes everything out it, i.e.: a box.

  sekonikew (VTI) S/he takes things out of boxes.

sekopayiw *pl.* **sekopayiwak** *or* **sekopayiwa** (VII) *or* (VAI) It *or* s/he slid or rolled underneath something.

sekopâtinew (VTI) S/he puts it through a strainer.

  sekopâtinam (VTI) S/he puts it through a strainer.

sekopâtinikew (VTI) S/he puts everything through a strainer.

sekopâtinikan *pl.* **sekopâtinikana** (NI) A strainer. *Var.* **sapokawihcikan.**

sekosimew (VTA) S/he slips her/him between the walls.

  sekotitâw (VTI) S/he slips it between two trees.

  sekocikew (VTI) S/he slips things between two tree.

sekosin *pl.* **sekosinwak** (VAI) S/he or it is stuck or wedged between.

sekow *pl.* **sekowak** (VAI) S/he crawls or creeps underneath something.

sekoyahkinew (VTA) S/he pushes her/him or it underneath or in between.

  sekoyahkinam (VTI) S/he pushes it underneath or in between.

  sekoyahkiniwew (VTA) S/he pushes people between or underneath.

  sekoyahkinikew (VTI) S/he pushes things between or underneath.

sekoyahkiw *pl.* **sekoyahkiwak** (VAI) S/he crawls under, i.e.: blankets.

sekoyahkîhew (VTA) S/he makes her/him crawl underneath. *(Northern). Alt.* **sikoyahkinew** *(Plains).*

  sekoyahkîhiwew (VTA) S/he makes someone crawl underneath.

sekwahew (VTI) S/he puts them underneath.

  sekwastâw (VTI) S/he puts it underneath.

  sekwacikew (VTI) S/he puts things underneath.

sekwahkatosiw *pl.* **sekwahkatosiwak** (VAI) It shrinks when drying; dried up.

sekwamohew (VTI) S/he sticks them in underneath.

  sekwamohtâw (VTI) S/he sticks it in underneath.

  sekwamohcikew (VTI) S/he sticks things in underneath.

sekwamow *pl.* **sekwamowak** (VAI) It is attached underneath.

sekwan (VII) It is springtime. *(Northern). Alt.* **miyoskamin** *(Plains).*

sekwasiw *pl.* **sekwasiwak** (VAI) S/he sticks an object underneath her/his own belt or inside his/her jacket.

sekwâhkatotew *pl.* **sekwâhkatotewa** (VII) It shrinks when drying.

sekwâpitehiw *pl.* **sekwâpitehiwak** (VAI) S/he uses a toothpick.

sekwâpitehon (NI) A toothpick.

semak (IPC) Right now; right away; immediately. *(Plains). Alt.* **sîmâk** *(Northern).*

semakohtew *pl.* **semakohtewak** (VAI) S/he walks right through without stopping.

senipân *pl.* **senipânak** (NA) A piece of ribbon. *(Plains). Alt.* **sînipân** *(Northern).*

senipânasapâp *pl.* **senipânasapâpak** (NA) A silk thread.

senipânitâpiskâkan *pl.* **senipânitâpiskâkana** (NI) A silk handkerchief or a silk neck scarf.

sepâskopitew (VTA) S/he pulled her/his net under the ice.

   sepâskopitam (VTI) S/he pulls it under the ice.

   sepâskopicikew (VTI) S/he pulls things under the ice.

sepekipitew (VTI) S/he stretched them by pulling them.

   sepekipitam (VTI) S/he stretches it by pulling.

   sepekipicikew (VTI) S/he stretches things.

sepihkonakwan *pl.* **sepihkonakwanwa** (VII) It looks blue. *(Northern). Alt.* **askihtakonâkwan** *(Plains).*

sepihkosiw *pl.* **sepihkosiwak** (VAI) S/he or it is blue. *(Northern). Alt.* **askihtakosiw** *(Plains).*

sesesiw *pl.* **sesesiwak** (NA) A shore bird, i.e.: a snipe.

seseskeyimew (VAI) S/he is wary and leery of her/him.

   seseskeyitam (VAI) *or* (VII) S/he is wary and leery.

   seseskeyimiwew (VAI) S/he is wary and leery of people.

   seseskeyicikew (VAI) *or* (VII) S/he is wary and leery of things.

seseskihkwân *pl.* **seseskihkwânak** (NA) A frying pan. *(Archaic Cree). Alt.* **lapewel** *(Northern),* **napwen** *(Plains).*

seseskihkwân *pl.* **seseskihkwânak** (NA) A frying pan. *(Plains). Var.* **lapwel** *(Northern);* *Alt.* **saseskihkwan** *(Northern).*

seseskinâkosiw *pl.* **seseskinâkosiwak** (VAI) S/he looks scared; s/he has a scared or horrified expression on her/his face. *(Plains). Alt.* **sekihkwew;** **sekinâkosiw** *(Northern).*

sesipaskwatahtikoskâw (VII) There are many maple trees; there are many sugar canes.

sesipâskwat *pl.* **sesipâskwata** (NI) Sugar. *(Northern). Alt.* **sîwinikan** *(Plains).*

sesipâskwatâhtik *pl.* **sesipâskwatâhtikwak** (NA) A maple tree; sugar cane.

sesipâskwatâhtikonîpîy *pl.* **sesipâskwatâhtikonîpîya** (NI) A maple leaf.

sesipâskwatihkahtew (VTI) S/he sweetens them with sugar.

   sesipaskwatihkahtam (VTI) S/he sweetens it with sugar.

   sesipâskwatihkahcikew (VTI) S/he sweetens things with sugar.

sesipâskwatihkawew *pl.* **sesipâskwatihkawewak** (VTA) S/he made sugar for her/him.

sesipâskwatihkâkew *pl.* **sesipâskwatihkâkewak** (VAI) S/he made sugar with it.

sesipâskwatômahkahk *pl.* **sesipâskwatômahkahkwa** (NI) A sugar barrel.

sesipâskwatwâhtikwâpoy *pl.* **sesipâskwatwâhtikwâpoya** (NI) Maple sugar liquid; maple syrup.

seskaham *pl.* **seskahamwa** (VTI) S/he paddles her/his canoe into shore. *(Northern). Alt.* **kapatewepaham** *(Plains).*

seskepison *pl.* **seskepisona** (NI) A garter.

seskepitew (VTA) S/he puts garters on her/him.

   seskepitam (VTI) S/he puts garters on it.

   seskepicikew (VTI) S/he puts garters on things.

seskipitew (VTA) S/he pulls her/him into shore. *(Northern). Alt.* **kapatepitew** *(Plains).*

   seskipitam (VTI) S/he pulls it to shore.

   seskipisiwew (VTA) S/he pulls people to shore.

   seskipicikew (VTA) *or* (VTI) S/he pulls things to shore.

seskisiw *pl.* **seskisiwak** (VAI) S/he goes into the woods or bush.

seskitisahwew (VTA) S/he chases her/him or them into the woods.

   seskitisaham (VTI) S/he chases it into the woods.

   seskitisahowew (VTA) S/he chases people into the woods.

   seskitisahikew (VTI) S/he chases things into the woods.

sestak *pl.* **sestakak** (NA) A skein of yarn for knitting.

sestakwasâkay *pl.* **sestakwasâkaya** (NI) A woolen coat, i.e.: a sweater. *(Northern). Alt.* **sîpihkiskawasâkay** *(Plains).*

sestakwây *pl.* **sestakwâya** (VII) A woolen article.

sewepayihew (VTI) S/he rings it by shaking it, i.e.: a bell. *(Plains). Alt.* **sîwepayihew** *(Northern).*

   sewepayitaw (VTI) S/he makes it ring by shaking it.

   sewepayicikew (VTI) S/he makes things ring by shaking them.

sewepayiw *pl.* **sewepayiwa** *or* **sewepayiwak** (VII) *or* (VAI) It *or* s/he is ringing, i.e.: a bell rings.

sewepicikanis *pl.* **sewepicikanisak** (NA) A buzzer.

sewepitew (VTI) S/he rings it, i.e.: a bell.

   sewepitam (VTI) S/he rings it, i.e.: the phone.

   sewepicikew (VTI) S/he rings for things.

sewihew (VTI) S/he sweetens them. *(Northern). Alt.* **siwinew** *(Plains).*

   sewitâw (VTI) S/he sweetens it.

   sewicikew (VTI) S/he sweetens things.

sewiyâkan *pl.* **sewiyâkanak** (NA) A bell. *(Plains). Alt.* **soweyakan** *(Northern).*

seyâpitestawew (VTA) S/he snarls and bares her/his teeth to her/him. *(Northern). Alt.* **sîyâpitestawew** *(Plains).*

   seyâpitestam (VTA) S/he snarls and bares her/his teeth at it.

   seyâpitestakew (VTA) S/he snarls and bares her/his teeth at people.

187

seyâpitew *pl.* **seyâpitewak** (VAI) S/he snarls and bares her/his teeth. *(Northern)*. *Alt.* **sîyâpitew** *(Plains)*.

seyâpitewin *pl.* **seyapitewina** (NI) The act of snarling and baring one's teeth. *(Northern)*. *Alt.* **sîyâpitewin** *(Plains)*.

sihcihew (VTA) S/he puts pressure on her/him; s/he forces her/him or pushes her/him to it. *(Plains)*
  sihcitâw (VTI) S/he puts pressure on it.
  sihcihiwew (VTA) S/he puts pressure on people.
  sihcicikew (VTI) S/he puts pressure on things.

sihcihisiw *pl.* **sihcihisiwak** (VAI) S/he puts pressure on herself/himself; s/he forces herself/himself. *(Plains)*. *Alt.* **sihciw** *(Northern)*.

sihcihtin *pl.* **sihcihtinwa** (VII) It is a tight fit.

sihcipayihcikan *pl.* **sihcipayihcikana** (NI) An instrument for cinching a load of wood, i.e.: a cinch.

sihcipayihew (VTA) S/he makes them tight.
  sihcipayitâw (VTI) S/he makes it tight.
  sihcipayihiwew (VTA) S/he makes someone tight.
  sihcipayicikew (VTI) S/he makes things tighten.

sihcipayiw *pl.* **sihcipayiwa** or **sihcipayiwak** (VII) or (VAI) It or s/he tightens up.

sihcisimew (VTA) S/he wedges them in; s/he puts her/him or them in snuggly or firmly.
  sihcihtitâw (VTI) S/he wedges it in.
  sihcihcikew (VTI) S/he wedges things in.

sihcisin *pl.* **sihcisinwak** (VTA) S/he is wedged in.

sihcisis (NA) A dwarf spruce. *(Plains)*

sihciw *pl.* **sihciwak** (VAI) S/he puts pressure on herself/himself; s/he forces herself/himself. *(Northern)*. *Alt.* **sihcihisiw** *(Plains)*.

sihciwin *pl.* **sihciwina** (NI) The act of putting pressure on oneself; the act of forcing onself.

sihcîsâyâwin *pl.* **sihcîsâyâwina** (NI) The act of being tense or feeling pressure. *(Northern)*. *Alt.* **sihtamahcihowin** *(Plains)*.

sihcowihew (VTA) S/he forces or pushes her/him to it.
  sihcowitaw (VTI) S/he forces or pushes it to it.
  sihcowiyiwew (VTA) S/he forces or pushes people to it.

sihkaceyimew (VTA) S/he finds her/him skinny. *(Northern)*
  sihkaceyimiwew (VTA) S/he finds people skinny.

sihkaciw *pl.* **sihkaciwak** (VAI) S/he is skinny; s/he is lank.

sihkaciwin *pl.* **sihkaciwina** (NI) Being skinny.

sihkacîhiwewin *pl.* **sihkacîhiwewina** (NI) The act of making someone skinny; emaciation.

sihkateyimew (VTA) S/he finds him/her skinny. *(Plains)*
  sihkateyimiwew (VTA) S/he finds people skinny.

sihkihew (VTA) S/he persuades her/him. *(Northern)*. *Alt.* **sihkiskawew** *(Plains)*.
  sihkihiwew (VTA) S/he persuades people.

sihkihkemow *pl.* **sihkihkemowak** (VAI) S/he is persuasive.

sihkihkemowin *pl.* **sihkihkemowina** (NI) Persuasion. *(Northern)*. *Alt.* **sihkiskâkewin** *(Plains)*.

sihkihp *pl.* **sihkihpak** (NA) A diving bird, i.e.: a grebe.

sihkihp *pl.* **sihkihpak** (NA) A boil; an infected boil, i.e.: a carbuncle.

sihkihtasowin *pl.* **sihkihtasowina** (NI) The act of spooking or scaring someone.

sihkimew (VTA) S/he encourages her/him verbally.
  sihkimiwew (VTA) S/he encourages people verbally.
  sihkicikew (VTI) S/he encourages things verbally.

sihkimowew *pl.* **sihkimowewak** (VAI) S/he is a persuasive type; s/he is always encouraging.

sihkimowewin *pl.* **sihkimowewina** (NI) The act of being a persuasive type.

sihkiskakewin *pl.* **sihkiskakewina** (NI) An inspirational discourse; infusion.

sihkiskawew (VTA) S/he inspires her/him to act. *Alt.* **sihkihew** *(Northern)*.
  sihkiskam (VTI) S/he inspires it to act.
  sihkiskâkew (VTA) S/he inspires people to act.
  sihkiskâcikew (VTI) S/he inspires everything to act.

sihkiskâkew *pl.* **sihkiskâkewak** (VAI) S/he is constantly providing inspiration; s/he aids in initiating; s/he gives inspiration.

sihkiskâkewin *pl.* **sihkiskâkewina** (NI) Persuasion. *(Plains)*. *Alt.* **sihkihkemowin** *(Northern)*.

sihkiw *pl.* **sihkiwak** (VAI) S/he spits or expectorates.

sihkos *pl.* **sihkosak** (NA) A weasel.

sihkosowayân *pl.* **sihkosowayânak** (NA) A weasel pelt.

sihkowin (NI) Spittle; saliva.

sihkwatew (VTA) S/he spits on her/him.
  sihkwatam (VTI) S/he spits on it.
  sihkwasiwew (VTA) S/he spits on someone.
  sihkwacikew (VTI) S/he spits on things.

sihpostahwew (VAI) S/he sews them and they are puckered.
  sihpostaham (VII) S/he sews it and it is puckered.
  sihpostahikew (VII) S/he sews things and they are puckered.

sihta *pl.* **sihtak** (NA) A spruce tree; a common spruce; an evergreen. *Var.* **minahik**.

sihtahcâpew *pl.* **sihtahcâpewak** (VTA) S/he tightens up her/his long bow; s/he bands her/his long bow firmly.

sihtahpison *pl.* **sihtahpisona** (NI) A girdle.

sihtahpitew (VTA) S/he ties her/him tightly.
  sihtahpitam (VTI) S/he ties it firmly.
  sihtahpisiwew (VTA) S/he ties people firmly.
  sihtahpicikew (VTI) S/he ties things firmly.

sihtahwew (VTA) S/he tightens it.
  sihtaham (VTI) S/he tightens it.

sihtahowew (VTA) S/he tightens people.

sihtahikew (VTI) S/he tightens things.

sihtamahcihowin *pl.* **sihtamahcihowina** (NI) The act of being tense or feeling pressure. *(Plains). Alt.* **sihcîsâyâwin** *(Northern).*

sihtamohew (VTA) S/he fits them tightly together; s/he puts them firmly together.

sihtamohtaw (VTI) S/he fits it tightly together.

sihtamohiwew (VTA) S/he fits people tightly together.

sihtamocikew (VTI) S/he fits things tightly together.

sihtatoskewin *pl.* **sihtatoskewina** (NI) The act of doing hard labor.

sihtawahikewin *pl.* **sihtawahikewina** (NI) The act of chinking a loghouse.

sihtâpihkwân *pl.* **sihtâpihkwâna** (NI) A spruce needle.

sihtipikiw *pl.* **sihtipikiwak** (NA) Spruce gum or pitch.

sihtipiwâyisis *pl.* **sihtipiwâyisisak** (NA) A cedar bird (i.e.: a Cedar wax wing). *(Northern). Alt.* **mâsikeskopiyesîs** *(Plains).*

sihtiskawew (VII) They are tight fitting, i.e.: gloves.

sihtiskam (VII) It fits too tightly on her/him.

sihtiskakew (VAI) S/he fits tightly in a crowd.

sihtiskosowin *pl.* **sihtiskosowina** (NI) The act of being burdened or loaded.

sihtiskotatowak (VAI) They are fitted tightly together; they are crowded together.

sihtiskotatowin *pl.* **sihtiskotatowina** (NI) The act of being fitted tightly together.

sihtwaspitew (VTA) S/he laces her/him in firmly, i.e.: in a toboggan.

sihtwaspitam (VTI) S/he laces it in firmly.

sihtwaspisiwew (VTA) S/he laces people in firmly.

sihtwaspicikew (VTI) S/he laces things in firmly.

sikak *pl.* **sikakwak** (NA) A skunk. *(Northern). Alt.* **wîncoyesis** *(Plains).*

sikâkomin *pl.* **sikâkominak** (NA) A skunk berry.

sikâkwan *pl.* **sikâkwana** (NI) The ham string on a leg; Achilles tendon.

sikâkwayân *pl.* **sikâkwayânak** (NA) A skunk pelt.

sikihkwamiw *pl.* **sikihkwamiwak** (VAI) S/he wets the bed.

sikisehikan *pl.* **sikisehikana** (NI) A stone that sparks fire, i.e.: flint. *(Plains). Alt.* **paskitewasiniy** *(Northern).*

sikitew *pl.* **sikitewak** (VTA) S/he urinates on her/him.

sikiwkamik *pl.* **sikiwkamikwa** (NI) A toilet. *(Northern). Alt.* **nahapiwikamik** *(Plains).*

sikocâyâwin *pl.* **sikocâyâwina** (NI) The act of being curt or snappish.

sikocihew (VTA) S/he startles her/him; s/he catches her/him unawares or surprises her/him.

sikocitâw (VTI) S/he catches it by surprise.

sikocihiwew (VTA) S/he catches people by surprise.

sikocicikew (VTI) S/he catches things by surprise.

sikohkotew (VTI) S/he cuts them up into small pieces.

sikohkotam (VTI) S/he cuts it up into small pieces.

sikohkocikew (VTI) S/he cuts things up into small pieces.

sikokahtâw *pl.* **sikokahtâwak** (VAI) S/he has the hiccups.

sikonew (VTI) S/he crushes them with her/his hands.

sikonam (VTI) S/he crushes it with her/his hands.

sikonikew (VTI) S/he crushes things with her/his hands.

sikopocikan *pl.* **sikopocikana** (NI) A machine for cutting things up; a slicer.

sikopocikâsow *pl.* **sikopocikâsowak** (VAI) It is cut up, i.e.: tobacco. *(Northern). Alt.* **sokopocikâsow** *(Plains).*

sikoskawew (VTA) S/he crushes her/him with her/his foot.

sikoskam (VTI) S/he crushes it with her/his foot.

sikoskâcikew (VTI) S/he crushes things up by stomping.

sikow *pl.* **sikowak** (VAI) S/he urinates.

sikowepawew (VTI) S/he crushes them to pieces by striking them.

sikowepaham (VTI) S/he crushes it to pieces.

sikowepahikew (VTI) S/he crushes things to pieces.

sikowin *pl.* **sikowina** (NI) Urine; the act of urinating.

sikoyahkinew (VTA) S/he makes her/him crawl underneath. *(Plains). Alt.* **sekoyahkîhew** *(Northern).*

sikoyahkihiwew (VTA) S/he makes someone crawl underneath.

sikwahcahikewin *pl.* **sikwahcahikewina** (NI) The act of cultivating land; cultivation; tillage.

sikwahwew (VTI) S/he crushes them.

sikwaham (VTI) S/he crushes it.

sikwahikew (VTI) S/he crushes things.

sikwatahikâsiw *pl.* **sikwatahikâsiwak** (VAI) S/he is crushed or smashed to pieces.

sikwatahikâtew *pl.* **sikwatahikâtewa** (VII) It is crushed or smashed to pieces.

sikwatahkewin *pl.* **sikwatahkewina** (NI) The act of smashing something to pieces.

sikwatahwew (VTA) S/he crushes or grinds them to pieces.

sikwataham (VTI) S/he crushes or grinds it to pieces.

sikwatahikew (VTI) S/he crushes or grinds things to pieces.

simacikâpawiw *pl.* **simacikâpawiwak** (VAI) S/he stands upright on her/his hind legs, i.e.: horse.

simaciw *pl.* **simaciwak** (VAI) S/he rears up, i.e.: a horse about to mate; s/he stands on her/his hind legs.

simatapiw *pl.* **simatapiwak** (VAI) S/he is sitting upright.

simatinew (VTA) S/he holds her/him upright.
　simatinam (VTI) S/he holds it upright.
　simatiniwew (VTA) S/he holds someone upright.
　simatinikew (VTI) S/he holds things upright.
simâkanihkomân *pl.* **simâkanihkomâna** (NI) A soldier's knife.
simâkanis (NA) A police or law officer.
sinikohtakahikan *pl.* **sinikohtakahikana** (NI) A floor brush.
sinikohtakahwew (VAI) S/he scrubs it with a brush, i.e.: a floor in a trailer.
　sinikohtakaham (VAI) S/he scrubs the floor in a house.
　sinikohtakahikew (VAI) S/he scrubs the floor with a brush.
sinikonew (VTA) S/he rubs her/him.
　sinikonam (VTI) S/he rubs it.
　sinikoniwew (VTA) S/he rubs someone.
　sinikonikew (VTI) S/he rubs things.
sinikopocikan *pl.* **sinikopocikana** (NI) A rubbing tool used to soften a hide. *(Northern)*. *Alt.* **misipocikan** *(Plains)*.
sinikopohew (VAI) S/he uses a rubbing tool to soften a hide, i.e.: a beaver skin. *(Northern)*. *Alt.* **misipohew** *(Plains)*.
　sinikopohtâw (VTI) S/he uses a rubbing tool to soften a moose hide.
　sinikopohcikew (VTI) S/he uses a rubbing or softening tool.
sinikosimew (VTA) S/he rubs her/him against something.
　sinikohtitâw (VTI) S/he rubs it against something.
　sinikohcicikew (VTI) S/he rubs things against something.
sinikosimiw *pl.* **sinikosimiwak** (VTA) S/he rubs herself/himself on something.
sinikosimowin *pl.* **sinikosimowina** (NI) A place where horses rub themselves, i.e.: a post or tree.
sinikoskawew (VTA) S/he rubs her/his body against him.
　sinikoskam (VTI) S/he rubs his/her body against it.
　sinikoskâkew (VTA) S/he rubs her/his body against someone.
　sinikoskâcikew (VTI) S/he rubs her/his body against things.
sinikwacapinisiw *pl.* **sinikwacapinisiwak** (VAI) S/he rubs or wipes her/his own eyes.
sinikwacâpinew *pl.* **sinikwacâpinewak** (VTA) S/he rubs or wipes her/his eyes for her/him.
sinikwahikan *pl.* **sinikwahikana** (NI) A rubbing brush or cloth used for shining or polishing.
sinikwahikewin *pl.* **sinikwahikewina** (NI) The act of smearing.
sinikwahwew (VTI) S/he rubs it or them.

sinikwahikew (VTI) S/he rubs something.
sinikwastowehikan *pl.* **sinikwastowehikana** (NI) A shaving brush used to brush on foam.
sinikwastowehosiw *pl.* **sinikwastowehosiwak** (VTA) S/he brushes her/his own face with a soap brush.
sinikwastowehwew (VTA) S/he brushes her/his beard with a soap brush.
　sinikwastoweham (VTA) S/he brushes her/his own beard with a brush.
　sinikwastowehowew (VTA) S/he brushes people with a soap brush.
　sinikwastowehikew (VTA) S/he brushes everyone with a soap brush.
sinikwastowenew (VTA) S/he strokes his beard for him.
　sinikwastoweniwew (VTA) S/he strokes people's beards.
　sinikwastowenikew (VTA) S/he strokes everyone's beard.
sinikwastowenisiw *pl.* **sinikwastowenisiwak** (VTA) He strokes his own beard.
sipekipayiw *pl.* **sipekipayiwak** (VAI) It is stretchy, i.e.: a wool sock. *(Plains)*. *Alt.* **sipihkisiw** *(Northern)*.
sipekipayiwitâs *pl.* **sipekipayiwitâsak** (NA) A pair of stretch pants, i.e.: resilient. *(Plains)*. *Alt.* **sîpihkitâs** *(Northern)*.
sipeyimew (VAI) S/he is patient with her/him. *(Northern)*. *Alt.* **sâsîpihkeyimew** *(Plains)*.
　sipeyitam (VAI) *or* (VII) S/he is patient with it.
　sipeyiniwew (VAI) S/he is patient with people.
　sipeyicikew (VAI) *or* (VII) S/he is patient with things.
sipihkisiw *pl.* **sipihkisiwak** (VAI) It is stretchy, i.e.: a wool sock. *(Northern)*. *Alt.* **sipekipayiw** *(Plains)*.
sipihkopiwâyisîs *pl.* **sipihkopiwâyisîsak** (NA) A bluebird. *(Northern)*. *Alt.* **sipihkopiyesîs** *(Plains)*.
sipihkopiyesîs *pl.* **sipihkopiyesîsak** (NA) A bluebird. *(Plains)*. *Alt.* **sipihkopiwâyisîs** *(Northern)*.
sipihkosiw *pl.* **sipihkosiwak** (VAI) It is blue in color. *(Plains)*. *Alt.* **sîpihkwekisiw** *(Northern)*.
sipihkwâw *pl.* **sipihkwâwa** (VII) It is blue in color. *(Plains)*. *Alt.* **sîpihkwekan** *(Northern)*.
sipikihkâw *pl.* **sipikihkâwak** (VAI) S/he resists the ravages of age; s/he is old but strong. *(Plains)*. *Alt.* **sîpikihkâw** *(Northern)*.
sipiyawesiw *pl.* **sipiyawesiwak** (VAI) S/he remains angry for a long time.
sipweham *pl.* **sipwehamwak** (VAI) S/he lead in singing a song.
sipwehtahew (VTA) S/he takes her/him away with her/him.
　sipwehtatâw (VTI) S/he takes it away with her/him.
　sipwehtahiwew (VTA) S/he takes people away with her/him.

sipwehcikew (VTI) S/he takes things away with her/him.

sipwehtew *pl.* **sipwehtewak** (VAI) S/he departs; s/he leaves.

sipwehtewin *pl.* **sipdwehtewina** (NI) The act of departure.

sipwepayihcikewin *pl.* **sipwepayihcikewina** (NI) The act of driving forward by force, i.e.: propel; to start an organization.

sipwepayihew (VTI) S/he starts them.

sipwepayitâw (VTI) S/he starts it.

sipwepayihiwew (VTA) S/he starts people.

sipwepayicikew (VTI) S/he starts things.

sipwepayiw *pl.* **sipwepayiwa** *or* **sipwepayiwak** (VII) *or* (VAI) It *or* s/he departed riding in a vehicle or riding a horse.

sipwetisahwew (VTA) S/he sends her/him away.

sipwetisaham (VTI) S/he sends it away.

sipwetisahowew (VTA) S/he sends people away.

sipwetisahikew (VTI) S/he sends things away.

sipweyahcahkwew *pl.* **sipweyahcahkwewak** (VAI) Her/his soul has departed; s/he dies.

sipweyâsiw *pl.* **sipweyâsiwak** (VAI) S/he is blown away by the wind.

sipweyâstan *pl.* **sipweyâstanwa** (VII) It has blown away by the wind.

sisikoc (IPC) Suddenly; instantly.

sisikocihew (VTA) S/he startles her/him; s/he catches her/him unawares or surprises her/him.

sisikocitâw (VTI) S/he catches it by surprise.

sisikocihiwew (VTA) S/he catches people by surprise.

sisikocicikew (VTI) S/he catches things by surprise.

sisikocimew (VAI) S/he startles her/him with her/his speech.

sisikocimiwew (VAI) S/he startles people with her/his speech.

sisikociwihew (VTA) S/he startle her/him by catching her/him unaware.

sisikociwihtâw (VTI) S/he startles it by catching it unaware.

sisikociwihiwew (VTA) S/he startles people by catching them unaware.

sisikotahpinew *pl.* **sisikotahpinewak** (VAI) S/he has a sudden fatal illness.

sisikoteyihtam *pl.* **sisikoteyihtamwak** (VAI) S/he is shocked or astounded

sisikoteyihtamowin *pl.* **sisikoteyihtamowina** (NI) The act of being shocked or astounded.

sisikoteyimew (VTA) S/he is shocked or astounded by her/him.

sisikoteyitam (VTI) S/he is shocked or astounded by it.

sisikoteyimiwew (VTA) S/he is shocked or astounded by someone.

sisikoteyicikew (VTI) S/he is shocked or astounded by things.

sisone (IPC) Along the side, i.e.: lake shore; on the edge.

sisonecimew *pl.* **sisonecimewa** (VTI) S/he paddles the canoe along the shore line.

sisonehtew *pl.* **sisonehtewak** (VAI) S/he walks along the side.

sisonepayiw *pl.* **sisonepayiwa** *or* **sisonepayiwak** (VII) *or* (VAI) It *or* s/he rides along side.

sisonesâkahikanihk (LN) Along the lake shore; along the shore. *(Plains). Alt.* **sonesâkahikanihk** *(Northern).*

sisonesîpihk (LN) Along the riverside. *(Plains). Alt.* **sonîsîpîhk** *(Northern).*

sisoneskanâhk (LN) It is on the roadside. *(Plains). Alt.* **soneskanâhk** *(Northern).*

sisoneskawew (VAI) S/he walks along beside her/him.

sisoneskam (VAI) S/he walks along side of it.

sisoneskâkew (VAI) S/he walks along side of people.

sisopâtew (VTA) S/he splashes water on her/him. *Var.* **siswepekahwew.**

sisopâtam (VTI) S/he splashes water on it.

sisopatihowew (VTA) S/he splashes water on people.

sisopâcikew (VTI) S/he splashes water on things.

sisopeham (VTA) S/he paints it. *(Plains). Alt.* **sopeham** *(Northern).*

sisopehowew (VTA) S/he paints people.

sisopehikew (VTI) S/he paints things.

sisopekahikâkan *pl.* **sisopekahikâkanwa** (NI) A large paint brush, i.e.: for painting a house. *(Plains). Alt.* **sopekahikâkan** *(Northern).*

sisopekahoswâkan *pl.* **sisopekahoswâkana** (NI) A rub or liniment. *Var.* **sisopekahotowin.**

sisopekahwew (VTA) S/he paints her/him; s/he rubs her/him with ointment.

sisopekaham (VTI) S/he paints it.

sisopekahowew (VTA) S/he paints people.

sisopekinew (VTA) S/he rubs ointment on her/him.

sisopekinam (VTI) S/he rubs medicine on it.

sisopekiniwew (VTA) S/he rubs medicine on people.

sisopekinikew (VTA) S/he rubs medicine on everyone.

sisoskowakinew (VTA) S/he rubs her/him with mud or with whitewash.

sisoskowakinam (VTI) S/he rubs mud on it.

sisoskowakiniwew (VTA) S/he rubs mud on people.

sisoskowakinikew (VTI) S/he rubs mud on things.

siswepayihew *pl.* **siswepayihewak** (VTA) S/he spreads them all over. *(Plains). Alt.* **saswepayihew** *(Northern).*

siswepayihtâw (VTI) S/he spreads it all over.

siswepayihiwew (VTA) S/he spreads people all over.

191

siswepayihcikew (VTI) S/he spreads things all over.

siswepayiw *pl.* **siswepayiwak** (VAI) It scatters about. *(Plains). Alt.* **saswepayiw** *(Northern).*

siswepekahwew (VTA) S/he splashes water on her/him. *Var.* **sisopâtew.**

siswepekaham (VTI) S/he splashes water on it.

siswepekahowew (VTA) S/he splashes water on people.

siswepekahikew (VTI) S/he splashes water on things.

siwihtâkanâpoy *pl.* **siwihtâkanâpoya** (NI) Salty water, i.e.: ocean brine.

siwihtâkanihkew *pl.* **siwihtâkanihkewak** (VAI) S/he makes salt.

siwinew (VTI) S/he sweetens them. *(Plains). Alt.* **sewihew** *(Northern).*

siwinam (VTI) S/he sweetens it.

siwinikew (VTI) S/he sweetens things.

siwpahkwesikan *pl.* **siwpahkwesikanak** (NA) A cake. *(Northern). Alt.* **wâwipahkwesikan** *(Plains).*

sîkaciwahtew *pl.* **sîkaciwahtewa** (VII) It boils and spills over, i.e.: water.

sîkaciwasiw *pl.* **sîkaciwasiwak** (VAI) It boils and spills over, i.e.: a pail.

sîkahahcikasiwin *pl.* **sîkahahcikasiwina** (NI) A ritual bath, i.e.: a baptism.

sîkahahcikâsiw *pl.* **sîkahahcikâsiwak** (VAI) S/he is baptised.

sîkahahtakew *pl.* **sîkahahtakewak** (VAI) S/he pours water over someone; s/he performs a baptism.

sîkahahtakewin *pl.* **sîkahahtakewina** (NI) The act of pouring water over someone; the act of performing a baptism; christening.

sîkahahtawew (VTA) S/he pours water over her/him; s/he baptised her/him.

sîkahahtam (VTI) S/he pours water on it.

sîkahahtakew (VTA) S/he pours water over people.

sîkaham (VAI) S/he combs the hair on it.

sîkahowew (VTA) S/he combs people's hair.

sîkahwew (VTA) S/he combs her/him.

sîkahon *pl.* **sîkahona** (NI) A comb.

sîkahow *pl.* **sîkahowak** (VTA) S/he combs her/his own hair.

sîkahwakan *pl.* **sîkahwakana** (NI) A hairbrush.

sîkahwew (VTA) S/he combs her/his hair for her/him.

sîkaham (VTI) S/he combs the hair on it.

sîkahowew (VTA) S/he combs the hair on people.

sîkanâpâwew *pl.* **sîkanâpâwewak** *or* **sîkanâpâwewa** (VII) *or* (VAI) It *or* s/he is soaking wet, i.e.: saturated.

sîkastan *pl.* **sîkastanwa** (VII) It is spilled or upset by the wind; it is blown down.

sîkawâcowasikan *pl.* **sîkawâcowasikana** (NI) A dreg. *(Plains). Alt.* **iskwâpohkahcikan** *(Northern).*

sîkawicowanihcikewin *pl.* **sîkawicowanihcikewina** (NI) The act of draining water.

sîkawihew (VTA) S/he empties him/her. *(Northern). Alt.* **sîkonew** *(Plains).*

sîkawitâw (VTI) S/he empties it, i.e.: a pail.

sîkawihiwew (VTA) S/he empties everybody.

sîkawicikew (VTI) S/he empties everything.

sîkawihow *pl.* **sîkawihowak** (VAI) S/he evacuates everything; s/he empties everything out. *(Northern). Alt.* **sîkonikew** *(Plains).*

sîkawihowin *pl.* **sîkawihowina** (NI) The act of evacuating everything or emptying everything out. *(Northern). Alt.* **sîkonikewin** *(Plains).*

sîkawipayihcikan *pl.* **sîkawipayihcikana** (NI) A sifter.

sîkawipayihew (VTI) S/he sifts them.

sîkawipayihtaw (VTI) S/he sifts it.

sîkawipayihiwew (VTA) S/he sifts people.

sîkawipayicikew (VTI) S/he sifts something.

sîkawiw *pl.* **sîkawiwak** (VTA) S/he empties or evacuates the place.

sîkâsiw *pl.* **sîkâsiwak** (VAI) It is spilled or upset by the wind, i.e.: a pail of grain.

sîkinamawew *pl.* **sîkinamawewak** (VTA) S/he pours her/him a cup of something.

sîkinew (VTI) S/he pours them out, i.e.: a pail of strawberries; s/he empties them.

sîkinam (VTI) S/he pours it out.

sîkinikew (VTI) S/he pours something, i.e.: a bartender pours a drink.

sîkiskawew (VTI) S/he kicked them and they spilled.

sîkiskam (VTI) S/he kicked it and spilled it.

sîkiskâcikew (VTI) S/he kicks everything over.

sîkiwepinew (VTA) S/he empties or drains it, i.e.: a pail.

sîkiwepinam (VTI) S/he empties or drains it.

sîkiwepinikew (VTI) S/he empties or drains everything.

sîkonew (VTA) S/he empties him/her. *(Plains). Alt.* **sîkawihew** *(Northern).*

sîkotâw (VTI) S/he empties it, i.e.: a pail.

sîkohiwew (VTA) S/he empties everybody.

sîkocikew (VTI) S/he empties everything.

sîkonikew *pl.* **sîkonikewak** (VAI) S/he evacuates everything; s/he empties everything out. *(Plains). Alt.* **sîkawihow** *(Northern).*

sîkonikewin *pl.* **sîkonikewina** (NI) The act of evacuating everything or emptying everything out. *(Plains). Alt.* **sîkawihowin** *(Northern).*

sîmâk (IPC) Right now; right away; immediately. *(Northern). Alt.* **semak** *(Plains).*

sînew (VTI) S/he rinses them and wrings them out by hand.

sînam (VTI) S/he rinses it and wrings it out by hand.

192

sînikew (VTI) S/he rinses things and wrings things out by hand.

sînipân *pl.* **sînipânak** (NA) A piece of ribbon. *(Northern). Alt.* **senipân** *(Plains).*

sînipitew (VTI) S/he puts them through the automated wringer.

sînipitam (VTI) S/he puts it through the automated wringer.

sînipicikew (VTI) S/he puts things through the automated wringer.

sîpahikan *pl.* **sîpahikana** (NI) A stretcher for pelts.

sîpahwew (VTI) S/he stretches them on a stretcher.

sîpaham (VTI) S/he stretches it on a stretcher.

sîpahikew (VTI) S/he stretches pelts.

sîpan *pl.* **sîpanwa** (VII) It is interminable.

sîpapiw *pl.* **sîpapiwak** (VAI) S/he patiently sits for long periods of time.

sîpaskisiw *pl.* **sîpaskisiwak** (VAI) It is ageless, i.e.: a tree.

sîpaskitew *pl.* **sîpaskitewa** (VII) It is ageless, i.e.: an old log house.

sîpaskwâtew (VTI) S/he stuffs or packs them with something.

sîpaskwâtam (VTI) S/he stuffs it up.

sîpaskwâsiwew (VTA) S/he stuffs people up.

sîpaskwâcikew (VTI) S/he stuffs things up.

sîpâhtewin *pl.* **sîpâhtewina** (NI) A place that can be walked under, i.e.: an archway.

sîpâpicikan *pl.* **sîpâpicikana** (NI) A jigger used to pull fish nets underneath ice. *(Northern). Alt.* **sîpâwepahikan** *(Plains).*

sîpâpitew (VTI) S/he pulls them underneath.

sîpâpitam (VTI) S/he pulls it underneath.

sîpâpicikew (VTI) S/he pulls things underneath.

sîpâsiw *pl.* **sîpâsiwak** (VAI) S/he goes under something, i.e.: a fence.

sîpâskopicikaneyâpiy *pl.* **sîpâskopicikaneyâpiya** (NI) A rope for passing the fish net under the ice; a draw line.

sîpâwepahikan *pl.* **sîpâwepahikana** (NI) A jigger used to pull fish nets underneath ice. *(Plains). Alt.* **sîpâpicikan** *(Northern).*

sîpâyâw *pl.* **sîpâyâwa** (VII) It is durable or long lasting.

sîpâyâwin *pl.* **sîpâyâwina** (NI) The act of being durable; durability.

sîpekaskisin *pl.* **sîpekaskisina** (NI) A pair of stretchy footwear, i.e.: rubber boots. *(Northern). Alt.* **pahkopewaskisin** *(Plains).*

sîpekipayiw *pl.* **sîpekipayiwak** *or* **sîpekipayiwa** (VII) *or* (VAI) It *or* s/he is stretched.

sîpekiwayân *pl.* **sîpekiwayâna** (NI) A piece of stretchy material.

sîpewisiw *pl.* **sîpewisiwak** (VAI) S/he has stamina or lasting strength.

sîpewisowin *pl.* **sîpewisowina** (NI) Having stamina or lasting strength.

sîpeyihcikew *pl.* **sîpeyihcikewak** (VAI) S/he is patient; s/he puts up with a lot. *(Northern). Alt.* **sâsîpeyihtam** *(Plains).*

sîpeyihtamowin *pl.* **sîpeyihtamowina** (NI) The act of being patient.

sîpihkâw *pl.* **sîpihkâwa** (VII) It is resilient.

sîpihkisiw *pl.* **sîpihkisiwak** (VAI) S/he is resilient.

sîpihkiskawasâkay *pl.* **sîpihkiskawasâkaya** (NI) A woolen coat, i.e.: a sweater. *(Plains). Alt.* **sestakwasâkay** *(Northern).*

sîpihkiskawitâs *pl.* **sîpihkiskawitâsa** (NI) A pair of stretchy, woolen pants.

sîpihkiskâwasâkay *pl.* **sîpihkiskâwasâkaya** (NI) A coat that stretches, i.e.: a cardigan.

sîpihkiskâwascocinis *pl.* **sîpihkiskâwascocinisa** (NI) A toque. *(Plains). Alt.* **sîstakwastotin** *(Northern).*

sîpihkiskâwasikan *pl.* **sîpihkiskâwasikanak** (NA) A stretchy stocking or sock.

sîpihkitâs *pl.* **sîpihkitâsak** (NA) A pair of stretch pants, i.e.: resilient. *(Northern). Alt.* **sipekipayiwitâs** *(Plains).*

sîpihkosiw *pl.* **sîpihkosiwak** (VAI) S/he *or* it is blue. *(Northern). Alt.* **askihtakwâw** *(Plains).*

sîpihkotahtahkwanew *pl.* **sîpihkotahtahkwanewak** (VAI) S/he *or* it has blue wings.

sîpihkwasâkay *pl.* **sîpihkwasâkaya** (NI) A blue coat, jacket, or dress.

sîpihkwasiw *pl.* **sîpihkwasiwak** (VAI) S/he has the stamina to remain awake.

sîpihkwaskosiya (NI) Blue grass.

sîpihkwâw *pl.* **sîpihkwâwa** (VII) It is blue. *(Plains)*

sîpihkwekan *pl.* **sîpihkwekanwa** (VII) It is blue in color. *(Northern). Alt.* **sipihkwâw** *(Plains).*

sîpihkwekin *pl.* **sîpihkwekinwa** (NI) A piece of blue cloth.

sîpihkwekisiw *pl.* **sîpihkwekisiwak** (VAI) It is blue in color. *(Northern). Alt.* **sipihkosiw** *(Plains).*

sîpihtakwaskâw *pl.* **sîpihtakwaskâwa** (VII) The grass is blue.

sîpikihkâw *pl.* **sîpikihkâwak** (VAI) S/he resists the ravages of age; s/he is old but strong. *(Northern). Alt.* **sipikihkâw** *(Plains).*

sîpikihkâwin *pl.* **sîpikihkâwina** (NI) Being aged; antique.

sîpinew *pl.* **sîpinewak** (VAI) S/he resists pain; s/he can endure pain.

sîpinewin *pl.* **sîpinewina** (NI) The act of being able to resist pain; being impassive.

sîpiniskeyiw *pl.* **sîpiniskeyiwak** (VAI) S/he has the stamina to hold her/his arms up for a long time.

sîpisiw *pl.* **sîpisiwak** (VAI) S/he has a tireless character.

sîpiw (VTA) S/he stretches herself/himself.

sîpiyawesiwin *pl.* **sîpiyawesiwina** (NI) Anger that lasts for a long period of time.

sîpiyâsk *pl.* **sîpiyâska** (NI) A long, dry pole.

sîpiyâw *pl.* **sîpiyâwa** (VII) A vast expanse of sparsely growing trees.

sîpîkiskâw *pl.* **sîpîkiskâwa** (VII) It is stretchy.

sîpîhkân *pl.* **sîpîhkâna** (NI) An imitation river, i.e.: a canal.

sîpîsis *pl.* **sîpîsisa** (NI) A creek.

sîpîsisihkân *pl.* **sîpîsisihkâna** (NI) A homemade ditch.

sîpîwan *pl.* **sîpîwana** (VII) It becomes a river.

sîpîwiw *pl.* **sîpîwiwa** (VII) It has become a river.

sîpîy *pl.* **sîpîya** (NI) A river.

sîpohtew *pl.* **sîpohtewak** (VAI) S/he has the stamina to walk a long distance; s/he is tough and has staying power when walking.

sîsîkan (VII) It hails. *(Plains). Alt.* **sîsîkwan** *(Northern).*

sîsîkanihtaw *pl.* **sîsîkanihtawak** (VAI) It is hailing. *(Northern). Var.* **miskwamiy pahkisin** *(Plains).*

sîsîkocipicikewin *pl.* **sîsîkocipicikewina** (NI) The act of ejaculating; ejaculation. *(Northern). Alt.* **metawâkâtisowin** *(Plains).*

sîsîkwan (VII) It hails. *(Northern). Alt.* **sîsîkan** *(Plains).*

sîsîkwan *pl.* **sîsîkwanak** (NA) A rattle for religious ceremonials.

sîsîkwanis *pl.* **sîsîkwanisak** (NA) A rattle for a baby.

sîsîp *pl.* **sîsîpak** (NA) A duck.

sîsîpaskihk *pl.* **sîsîpaskihkwak** (NA) An iron kettle with a spout shaped like a duck's neck.

sîsîpaskihkos *pl.* **sîsîpaskihkosak** (NA) A small iron kettle with a spout shaped like a duck's neck.

sîsîpâwi *pl.* **sîsîpâwa** (NI) A duck egg.

sîsîpihkân *pl.* **sîsîpihkânak** (NA) A decoy.

sîsîpipimiy *pl.* **sîsîpipimiya** (NI) Duck grease.

sîsîpisis *pl.* **sîsîpisisak** (NA) A duckling.

sîskawakomewewin *pl.* **sîskawakomewewina** (NI) Having sniffles. *(Plains). Alt.* **iskoyikomiwâyâwin** *(Northern).*

sîstakwastotin *pl.* **sîstakwastotina** (NI) A toque. *(Northern). Alt.* **sîpihkiskâwascocinis** *(Plains).*

sîtawahikan *pl.* **sîtawahikana** (NI) Something that stiffens thing, i.e.: starch.

sîtawahwew (VTA) S/he starches them.

sîtawaham (VTI) S/he starches it.

sîtawahikew (VTI) S/he starches things.

sîtawâskohtin *pl.* **sîtawâskohtinwa** (VII) It is supported by being wedged between two trees.

sîtawâskosimew (VTA) S/he supports her/him or it by placing her/him or it between two trees.

sîtawâskohtâw (VTI) S/he supports it by placing it between two trees.

sîtawâskohcikew (VTI) S/he supports things by placing them between two trees.

sîtawâskosin *pl.* **sîtawâskosinwak** (VAI) S/he is supported by being wedged between two trees.

sîtawâskosiwin *pl.* **sîtawâskosiwina** (NI) Being rigorous; being supportive.

sîtawâw *pl.* **sîtawâwa** (VII) It is stiff.

sîtawekin *pl.* **sîtawekinwa** (NI) A starched linen. *(Plains). Alt.* **pikiwekin** *(Northern).*

sîtawihew (VTA) S/he makes her/him stiff.

sîtawitâw (VTI) S/he makes it stiff.

sîtawihiwew (VTA) S/he makes people stiff.

sîtawicikew (VTI) S/he makes things stiff.

sîtawisiw *pl.* **sîtawisiwak** (VAI) S/he is stiff.

sîtawisiwin *pl.* **sîtawisiwina** (NI) Being rigid; rigidity.

sîtonew (VTA) S/he holds her/him up.

sîtonam (VTI) S/he holds it up.

sîtoniwew (VTA) S/he holds people up.

sîtonikew (VTI) S/he holds things up.

sîtoskâkewin *pl.* **sîtoskâkewina** (NI) The act of supporting or bracing someone.

sîtowihew (VTA) S/he is mildly afraid of her/him.

sîtowihtâw (VTI) S/he is mildly afraid of it.

sîtowihhiwew (VTA) S/he is mildly afraid of people.

sîtwahew (VTA) S/he supports her/him by leaning her/him against something.

sîtwastâw (VTI) S/he supports it by leaning her/him against something.

sîtwahiwew (VTA) S/he supports people by leaning them against something.

sîtwascikew (VTI) S/he supports things by leaning them against something.

sîtwahpicikan *pl.* **sîtwahpicikana** (NI) A bracket or splint.

sîtwâskwahikan *pl.* **sîtwâskwahikana** (NI) A support column, i.e.: a pillar.

sîtwâskwahwew (VTI) S/he supports it with a pillar.

sîtwâskwaham (VTI) S/he supports it with a pole.

sîtwâskwahikew (VTI) S/he supports things with a pole.

sîwakamisikan *pl.* **sîwakamisikana** (NI) Sweetened boiled water, i.e.: birch sap.

sîwakamow *pl.* **sîwakamowa** (VII) The liquid is sweet.

sîwanos *pl.* **sîwanosa** (NI) Sweet food. *(Plains). Alt.* **sîwâyi** *(Northern).*

sîwapoy *pl.* **sîwapoya** (NI) A sweetened water, i.e.: pop or juice.

194

sîwascikewin *pl.* **sîwascikewina** (NI) The act of fermenting; fermentation.

sîwatew *pl.* **sîwatewak** (VAI) S/he is very hungry; s/he has an empty stomach.

sîwâkamihtâw (VAI) S/he makes the liquid sweet.

sîwâkamisew (VTA) S/he sweetens it by boiling it.

sîwâkamisam (VTI) S/he sweetens it by boiling it.

sîwâkamisikew (VTI) S/he makes sweetened water.

sîwâsiw *pl.* **sîwâsiwak** (VAI) The sun is shining in her/his eyes. *(Plains). Alt.* **cakâsiw** *(Northern).*

sîwâstew *pl.* **sîwâstewa** (VII) The glare of the sun is bright on the eyes.

sîwâw *pl.* **sîwâwa** (VII) It is sour or sweet.

sîwâyi *pl.* **sîwâyiya** (NI) Sweet food. *(Northern). Alt.* **sîwanos** *(Plains).*

sîwepayihew (VTI) S/he rings it by shaking it, i.e.: a bell. *(Northern). Alt.* **sewepayihew** *(Plains).*

sîwepayitâw (VTI) S/he makes it ring by shaking it.

sîwepayicikew (VTI) S/he makes things ring by shaking them.

sîwihtâkan *pl.* **sîwihtâkana** (NI) Salt.

sîwihtâkanisâposikan *pl.* **sîwihtâkanisâposikana** (NI) Epsom salts.

sîwihtin *pl.* **sîwihtinwa** (VII) It has gone sour, i.e.: milk.

sîwinikan *pl.* **sîwinikana** (NI) Sugar. *(Plains). Alt.* **sesipâskwat** *(Northern).*

sîwipak *pl.* **sîwipakwa** (NI) One stalk of rhubarb or acid leaves.

sîwisiw *pl.* **sîwisiwak** (VAI) S/he or it is sweet.

sîwisiwin *pl.* **sîwisiwina** (NI) Being sweet; sweetness.

sîwiskâtâsk *pl.* **sîwiskâtâskwak** (NA) A sweet carrot.

sîyâpitestawew (VTA) S/he snarls and bares her/his teeth at her/him. *(Plains). Alt.* **seyâpitestawew** *(Northern).*

sîyâpitestam (VTA) S/he snarls and bares her/his teeth at her/him.

sîyâpitestakew (VTA) S/he snarls and bares her/his teeth at people.

sîyâpitew *pl.* **sîyâpitewak** (VAI) S/he snarls and bares her/his teeth. *(Plains). Alt.* **seyâpitew** *(Northern).*

sîyâpitewin *pl.* **sîyâpitewina** (NI) The act of snarling and baring one's teeth. *(Plains). Alt.* **seyâpitewin** *(Northern).*

sohkaciw *pl.* **sohkaciwak** (VAI) S/he tolerates the cold well. *Var.* **sîpaciw**.

sohkahcâhkwew *pl.* **sohkahcâhkwewak** (VAI) S/he has an inner strength; s/he has a strong spirit.

sohkahcâhkwewin *pl.* **sohkahcâhkwewina** (NI) The act of having inner strength or a strong spirit.

sohkahew (VTA) S/he places her/him solidly.

sohkastâw (VTI) S/he places it solidly.

sohkascikew (VTI) S/he places things solidly.

sohkahpinewin *pl.* **sohkahpinewina** (NI) The act of having inner strength to endure pain; impassivity.

sohkan *pl.* **sohkanwa** (VII) It is strong, solid, powerful.

sohkapewiw *pl.* **sohkapewiwak** (VAI) He is a muscular man. *(Northern). Alt.* **maskawisiwiyiniwiw** *(Plains).*

sohkapiskâw *pl.* **sohkapiskâwa** (VII) It is a solid piece of steel.

sohkaskihew (VTA) S/he plants them solidly or firmly.

sohkaskhitâw (VTI) S/he plants it solidly.

sohkaskcikew (VTI) S/he plants something solidly.

sohkaskisiw *pl.* **sohkaskisiwak** (VAI) The tree is solid; s/he is well rooted.

sohkaskitew *pl.* **sohkaskitewa** (VII) It stands solid, i.e.: a pole.

sohkastwâw *pl.* **sohkastwâwak** (VAI) S/he has resilience.

sohkastwâwin *pl.* **sohkastwâwina** (NI) The act of having resilience; placidity; stolidity.

sohkatamowin *pl.* **sohkatamowina** (NI) The act of singing strongly or loudly.

sohkatâmow *pl.* **sohkatâmowak** (VAI) S/he sings strongly or loudly.

sohkatin *pl.* **sohkatinwa** (VII) It tolerates the cold well.

sohkâkamiw (VII) It is a powerful liquid.

sohkâkinew *pl.* **sohkâkinewa** (VTI) S/he reinforces the bow and makes it difficult to bend it.

sohkâpekan *pl.* **sohkâpekanwa** (VTI) The rope is very strong.

sohkâpekisiw *pl.* **sohkâpekisiwak** (VIA) The thread or yarn is strong.

sohkâpew *pl.* **sohkâpewak** (NA) A muscular or strong man. *(Northern). Alt.* **omaskawisiwiyiniw** *(Plains).*

sohkâpisk *pl.* **sohkâpiskwa** (VII) A solid piece of steel.

sohkâsiw *pl.* **sohkâsiwak** (VAI) The tree stands solid even with the strong wind.

sohkâskosiw *pl.* **sohkâskosiwak** (VAI) It is a huge tree; solid.

sohkâskwan *pl.* **sohkâskwanwa** (VII) It is a strong railing or pole.

sohkâtan *pl.* **sohkâtanwa** (VII) It is powerfully built, i.e.: a bridge.

sohkâtisiw *pl.* **sohkâtisiwak** (VAI) S/he is physically tough.

sohkâtisiwin *pl.* **sohkâtisiwina** (NI) The act of being physically tough, i.e.: roughness.

sohkâyâwin *pl.* **sohkâyâwina** (NI) Having fortitude or stamina; intensity; poise; stability.

sohkeciwan *pl.* **sohkeciwanwa** (VII) It has a strong current, i.e.: river; a strongly flowing river.

sohkehkasiw (VTI) S/he has a massive, deep burn, i.e.: a third-degree burn.

sohkehkasam (VTI) S/he gave it a massive, deep burn.

195

sohkehkasikew (VTI) S/he gives something a massive, deep burn.

sohkehtâkosiw *pl.* **sohkehtâkosiwak** (VAI) S/he has a loud voice.

sohkehtâkwan *pl.* **sohkehtâkwanwa** (VII) It is a story blown out of proportion; it has a loud noise.

sohkekan *pl.* **sohkekanwa** (VII) It is a strong fabric or cloth, i.e.: heavy canvas. *(Northern). Var.* **maskawekiniwiw** *(Northern); Alt.* **maskawekiniwiw** *(Plains).*

sohkekin *pl.* **sohkekinwa** (NI) A strong piece of fabric or cloth. *(Northern). Var.* **maskawekin** *(Northern); Alt.* **maskawekin** *(Plains).*

sohkekisiw *pl.* **sohkekisiwak** (VAI) It is a durable pair of pants. *(Northern). Var.* **maskawekisiw** *(Northern); Alt.* **maskawekisiw** *(Plains).*

sohkekocin *pl.* **sohkekocinwak** (VAI) S/he is speeding; s/he drives fast or travels fast.

sohkesicikewin *pl.* **sohkesicikewina** (NI) The act of enforcing.

sohkesihcikâsowin *pl.* **sohkesihcikâsowina** (NI) Being brawny.

sohkewesin *pl.* **sohkewesinwak** (VAI) S/he falls with a loud thud.

sohkeyawesiw *pl.* **sohkeyawesiwak** (VAI) S/he is screaming angry. *(Northern). Var.* **kîskweyawesiw** *(Northern); Alt.* **kîskweyawesiw** *(Plains).*

sohkeyawisowin *pl.* **sohkeyawisowina** (NI) The act of screaming in anger. *(Northern). Var.* **tepweyawesiw** *(Northern); Alt.* **tepweyawesiw** *(Plains).*

sohkeyâskwahikewin *pl.* **sohkeyâskwahikewina** (NI) The act of having leverage.

sohkeyihtam *pl.* **sohkeyihtamwak** (VAI) S/he has made up her/his mind very firmly; drastic.

sohkeyihtamowin *pl.* **sohkeyihtamowina** (NI) The act of thinking courageously; an affirmative resolution.

sohkeyihtâkosiw *pl.* **sohkeyihtâkosiwak** (VAI) S/he is honoured, praised, respected, highly thought of.

sohkeyihtâkwan *pl.* **sohkeyihtâkwanwa** (VII) It is well-regarded; it is highly thought of; it is strong, resistant.

sohkeyimew (VAI) S/he has firm views of her/him.

sohkeyitam (VTI) S/he has firm views of it.

sohkeyimiwew (VTA) S/he has firm views of people.

sohkeyicikew (VTI) S/he has firm views of things.

sohkeyimitowin *pl.* **sohkeyimitowina** (NI) The act of being in favor of solidarity.

sohkeyimohiwewin *pl.* **sohkeyimohiwewina** (NI) Being brazen or emboldened.

sohkeyimow *pl.* **sohkeyimowak** (VAI) S/he is brave and courageous, or has strong expectations.

sohkeyimowin *pl.* **sohkeyimowina** (NI) Being courageous; the act of having strength, courage, bravery; having nerve; brazen.

sohkihew (VTA) S/he makes her/him or them strong; s/he gives her/him strength.

sohkitâw (VTI) S/he makes it strong.

sohkihiwew (VTA) S/he makes people strong or tough.

sohkicikew (VTI) S/he makes things strong or tough.

sohkikâpawiw *pl.* **sohkikâpawiwak** (VAI) S/he stands firmly or with feet well planted.

sohkikâtew *pl.* **sohkikâtewak** (VAI) S/he has large, strong legs.

sohkipimosinewin *pl.* **sohkipimosinewina** (NI) The act of hurling something.

sohkipitonew *pl.* **sohkipitonewak** (VAI) S/he has strong, powerful arms.

sohkisihcikâsowin *pl.* **sohkisihcikâsowina** (NI) Being well-built, burly, or sturdy.

sohkisiw *pl.* **sohkisiwak** (VAI) S/he is robust or stout.

sohkisiwekocin *pl.* **sohkisiwekocinwak** (VTA) It has a loud ringing sound.

sohkisiwin *pl.* **sohkisiwina** (NI) Being robust or stout.

sohkiskâkewin *pl.* **sohkiskâkewina** (NI) The act of confirming power on someone; confirmation.

sohkistikwânew *pl.* **sohkistikwânewak** (VAI) S/he has a firm mindset (literally means "a strong head").

sohkitehew *pl.* **sohkitehewak** (VAI) S/he has a strong, brave heart.

sohkitehewin *pl.* **sohkitehewina** (NI) The act of being brave; having a strong heart.

sohkiwaniskânikewin *pl.* **sohkiwaniskânikewina** (NI) The act of upheaving or uplifting someone's spirits.

sohkiwehtin *pl.* **sohkiwehtinwa** (VII) It rattles loudly.

sohkiyawew *pl.* **sohkiyawewak** (VAI) S/he is well built; s/he has a robust, sturdy, powerful body.

sohkîsihcikew *pl.* **sohkîsihcikewak** (VAI) S/he fortifies.

sohkîsihcikewin *pl.* **sohkîsihcikewina** (NI) The act of fortifying; fortification; stabilization.

sokopocikâsow *pl.* **sokopocikâsowak** (VAI) It is cut up, i.e.: tobacco. *(Plains). Alt.* **sikopocikâsow** *(Northern).*

sonesâkahikanihk (LN) Along the lake shore; along shore. *(Northern). Alt.* **sisonesâkahikanihk** *(Plains).*

soneskanâhk (LN) It is on the roadside. *(Northern). Alt.* **sisoneskanâhk** *(Plains).*

soniyawat *pl.* **soniyawata** (NI) A purse or wallet. *(Northern). Alt.* **sônîyâwiwat** *(Plains).*

soniyawiw *pl.* **soniyawiwak** (VAI) It is made of gold, silver, or money.

soniyâhkâkew (VAI) *or* (VII) S/he makes money with it.

soniyâhkâtam (VAI) *or* (VII) S/he makes money from it.

soniyâhkâsiwew (VAI) S/he makes money with people.

sonîsîpîhk (LN) Along the riverside. *(Northern). Alt.* **sisonesîpihk** *(Plains).*

sopahcikâkan *pl.* **sopahcikâkana** (NI) A blotter.

sopâcikan *pl.* **sopâcikana** (NI) A nozzle.

sopâcikewin *pl.* **sopâcikewina** (NI) The act of saturating.

sopeham (VTA) S/he paints it. *(Northern). Alt.* **sisopeham** *(Plains).*

sopehowew (VTA) S/he paints people.

sopehikew (VTI) S/he paints things.

sopekahikâkan *pl.* **sopekahikâkanwa** (NI) A large paint brush, i.e.: for painting a house. *(Northern). Alt.* **sisopekahikâkan** *(Plains).*

sopekahikan *pl.* **sopekahikana** (NI) Paint.

sopekinikan *pl.* **sopekinikana** (NI) Ointment.

soskoceskowakisin *pl.* **soskoceskowakisinwak** (VAI) S/he slips and slides on the slippery mud.

soweyakan *pl.* **soweyakanak** (NA) A bell. *(Northern). Alt.* **sewiyâkan** *(Plains).*

sôminapohkew *pl.* **sôminapohkewak** (VAI) S/he makes wine.

sôminâhtik *pl.* **sôminâhtikwak** (NA) A grape vine.

sôminâhtikokistikân *pl.* **sôminâhtikokistikâna** (NI) A field of grape vines.

sôminâpoy *pl.* **sôminâpoya** (NI) Wine; sherry.

sôminis *pl.* **sôminisak** (NA) A raisin.

sôniskwatahikew *pl.* **sôniskwatahikewak** (VAI) S/he is skating.

sôniskwâyaham *pl.* **sôniskwâyahamwak** (VAI) S/he skates.

sôniskwâyahikan *pl.* **sôniskwâyahikana** (NI) An iceskate.

sôniyawahkesîs *pl.* **sôniyawahkesîsak** (NA) A silver fox.

sônîyâs *pl.* **sônîyâsak** (NA) A piece of silver money, i.e.: a quarter; a coin.

sônîyâw *pl.* **sônîyâwak** (NA) Paper money; dollars.

sônîyâwasinahikan *pl.* **sônîyâwasinahikana** (NI) A cheque.

sônîyâwikamik *pl.* **sônîyâwikamikwa** (NI) A bank.

sônîyâwikimâw (NA) An Indian agent or government representative to the band.

sônîyâwiwacis *pl.* **sônîyâwiwacisa** (NI) A change purse.

sônîyâwiwat *pl.* **sônîyâwiwata** (NI) A purse or wallet. *(Plains). Alt.* **soniyawat** *(Northern).*

sôpahcikan *pl.* **sôpahcikana** (NI) Something that absorbs.

sôpahcikewin *pl.* **sôpahcikewina** (NI) The act of absorbing; absorbency.

sôpamew (VTI) S/he sucks on them.

sôpahtam (VTI) S/he sucks on it.

sôpamiwew (VTA) S/he sucks on people.

sôpacikew (VTI) S/he sucks on things.

sôskohew (VTI) S/he makes them slippery.

sôskohtâw (VTI) S/he makes it slippery.

sôskohcikew (VTI) S/he makes things slippery.

sôskohtakisin *pl.* **sôskohtakisinwak** (VAI) S/he slips on a slippery floor.

sôskonew (VTA) It slips from her/his hand.

sôskonam (VTA) It slips from her/his hold.

sôskoniwew (VTA) They slip from her/his hold.

sôskonikew (VTI) Something slips from her/his hold.

sôskonikosiw *pl.* **sôskonikosiwak** (VAI) S/he is a shifty or slippery person.

sôskonikosiwin *pl.* **sôskonikosiwina** (NI) Being a shifty or slippery person.

sôskopayihew (VTA) S/he makes it slide down with ease; s/he makes it slide on the ice; s/he swallows it with ease, e.g.: a fish.

sôskopayihtaw (VTI) S/he makes it slip.

sôskopayihiwew (VTA) S/he makes people slide.

sôskopayihcikew (VTI) S/he makes things slide.

sôskopayiw *pl.* **sôskopayiwa** *or* **sôskopayiwak** (VII) *or* (VAI) It *or* s/he slips and slides.

sôskosikwâw *pl.* **sôskosikwâwa** (VII) It is icy and slippery.

sôskosin *pl.* **sôskosinwak** (VAI) S/he slips, i.e.: on a greasy floor.

sôskosiw *pl.* **sôskosiwak** (VAI) It is slippery, i.e.: a toboggan.

sôskwaciwew *pl.* **sôskwaciwewak** (VAI) S/he slides down the hill.

sôskwaciwewepinew (VTA) S/he sends her/him sliding down a hill.

sôskwaciwewepinam (VTI) S/he sends it sliding down a hill.

sôskwaciwewepiniwew (VTA) S/he sends people sliding down a hill.

sôskwaciwewepinikew (VTI) S/he sends things sliding down a hill.

sôskwaciwewepinkewin *pl.* **sôskwaciwewepinkewina** (NI) Something used to slide items down, i.e.: a chute.

sôskwaciwewin *pl.* **sôskwaciwewina** (NI) A sliding place.

sôskwahikan *pl.* **sôskwahikanak** (NA) An iron for clothes.

sôskwahwew (VTI) S/he irons them.

sôskwaham (VTI) S/he irons it.

sôskwahikew (VTI) S/he irons things.

sôskwakamiw *pl.* **sôskwakamiwa** (NI) Slimy water.

sôskwakonesin *pl.* **sôskwakonesinwak** (VAI) S/he slides on the slippery snow.

197

sôskwawew *pl.* **sôskwawewak** (VAI) The fur is smooth and shiny.

sôskwâpekan *pl.* **sôskwâpekanwa** (VII) It is smooth and slippery, i.e.: a rope.

sôskwâpekisiw *pl.* **sôskwâpekisiwak** (VAI) S/he has slippery skin.

sôskwâskwan *pl.* **sôskwâskwanwa** (VII) The pole is slippery.

sôskwâw *pl.* **sôskwâwa** (VII) It is slippery or smooth.

sôskwekin *pl.* **sôskwekinwa** (NI) A smooth cloth, i.e.: velvet.

sôskwekisiw *pl.* **sôskwekisiwak** (VAI) It is made of smooth cloth; it has a smooth texture, i.e., smooth fur on beaver.

sôsôwatim *pl.* **sôsôwatimwak** (NA) A donkey; an ass; a mule.

sôsôwatimowiw *pl.* **sôsôwatimowiwak** (VAI) S/he is a mule or an ass.

swepayihcikewin *pl.* **swepayihcikewina** (NI) The act of spreading throughout or permeating.

swepekatahikewin *pl.* **swepekatahikewina** (NI) The act of splashing the surface of water.

swescikewin *pl.* **swesikewina** (NI) The act of strewing or scattering.

t

tahcikatew *pl.* **tahcikatewak** (VTA) S/he advises her/him to hide it elsewhere. *(Northern). Alt.* **ahcikatew** *(Plains).*

tahcipicikewin *pl.* **tahcipicikewina** (NI) The act of disconnecting. *(Plains). Alt.* **tasipicikewin** *(Northern).*

tahkahcikakanistikwân *pl.* **tahkahcikakanistikwâna** (NI) A spearhead. *(Plains). Alt.* **cîstâskwânostikwân** *(Northern).*

tahkahcikan *pl.* **tahkahcikana** (NI) A stabbing weapon; a knife; a spear. *(Plains). Alt.* **cîstaskwan** *(Northern).*

tahkamâpoy *pl.* **tahkamâpoya** (NI) Cold water. *(Northern). Alt.* **tahkikamâpoy** *(Plains).*

tahkamew (VTA) S/he stabbed her/him.

tahkahtam (VTA) S/he stabs it.

tahkamiwew (VTA) S/he stabs someone.

tahkahcikew (VTA) S/he stabs things.

tahkamow (VII) The water is cold. *(Northern). Alt.* **tahkikamiw** *(Plains).*

tahkapiw *pl.* **tahkapiwak** (VAI) It has gone cold or it has cooled off, i.e.: freshly baked bread. Literally, "it sits cold".

tahkastew *pl.* **tahkastewa** (VII) It has gone cold or cooled off, i.e.: soup.

tahkâpawahew (VTA) S/he reduces her/his vitality by throwing cold water on her/him.

tahkâpawatâw (VTA) S/he reduces its vitality by throwing cold water on it.

tahkâpawahiwew (VTA) S/he reduces their vitality by throwing cold water on people.

tahkâpawacikew (VTA) S/he reduces their vitality by throwing cold water on things.

tahkâpiskâw *pl.* **tahkâpiskâwa** (VII) The steel is cold.

tahkâpiskisow *pl.* **tahkâpiskisowak** (VAI) The stove is cold.

tahkâskwan *pl.* **tahkâskwanwa** (NI) A log or stick that is cold to the touch.

tahkâw *pl.* **tahkâwa** (VII) It is cold to the touch.

tahkâyâw (VII) It is chilly outside.

tahkikamâpohkew *pl.* **tahkikamâpohkewak** (VAI) S/he is making the water cold.

tahkikamâpoy *pl.* **tahkikamâpoya** (NI) Cold water. *(Plains). Alt.* **tahkamâpoy** *(Northern).*

tahkikamiw (VII) The water is cold. *(Plains). Alt.* **tahkamow** *(Northern).*

tahkikwayawew *pl.* **tahkikwayawewak** (VAI) S/he has a cold neck.

tahkinew (VTA) S/he cooled her/him down with her/his hand.

tahkinam (VTI) S/he cools it with her/his touch.

tahkiniwew (VTA) S/he cools someone with her/his hand.

tahkinikew (VTI) S/he cools things with her/his hand.

tahkipayihew (VTA) S/he causes her/him to cool off.

tahkipayitâw (VTI) S/he causes it to cool off.

tahkipayihiwew (VTA) S/he causes someone to cool off.

tahkipayihcikew (VTI) S/he causes things to cool off.

tahkipayiw *pl.* **tahkipayiwa** *or* **tahkipayiwak** (VII) *or* (VAI) It *or* s/he got chilled.

tahkipeyâw (VII) It is rainy and cold.

tahkipiskwanew *pl.* **tahkipiskwanewak** (VAI) S/he has a cold back.

tahkipiskwanewaciw *pl.* **tahkipiskwanewaciwak** (VAI) Her/his back is chilled.

tahkipitonew *pl.* **tahkipitonewak** (VAI) S/he has a cold arm.

tahkisimew (VTA) S/he let her/him cool off.

tahkititâw (VTI) S/he lets it cool off.

tahkisimiwew (VTA) S/he lets someone cool off.

tahkihcikew (VTI) S/he lets things cool off.

tahkisiw *pl.* **tahkisiwak** (VAI) S/he is cold to the touch.

tahkisiwin *pl.* **tahkisiwina** (NI) Being cold.

tahkiskawew (VTA) S/he kicks her/him.

tahkiskam (VTI) S/he gives it a kick.

tahkiskâkew (VTA) S/he gives people a kick.

tahkiskâcikew (VTI) S/he gives something a kick.

tahkiskâcikew *pl.* **tahkiskâcikewak** (VAI) S/he kicks.

tahkiskâcikewin *pl.* **tahkiskâcikewina** (NI) The act of kicking.

tahkiyawehikewin *pl.* **tahkiyawehikewina** (NI) The act of ventilating; ventilation. *(Northern). Alt.* **tahkiyowepahikewin** *(Plains).*

tahkiyowepahikewin *pl.* **tahkiyowepahikewina** (NI) The act of ventilating; ventilation. *(Plains). Alt.* **tahkiyawehikewin** *(Northern).*

tahkiyowepayiw *pl.* **tahkiyowepayiwak** (VAI) The air became chilly.

tahkiyowew (VII) It is chilly, i.e.: air.

tahkocihtin *pl.* **tahkocihtinwa** (VII) It fits on top.

tahkocikâpawistawew (VTA) S/he stands above her/him.

tahkocikâpawistam (VTA) *or* (VTI) S/he stands above it.

tahkocikâpawistâkew (VTA) S/he stands above people.

tahkocikâpawiw *pl.* **tahkocikâpawiwak** (VAI) S/he stands on top.

tahkocisin *pl.* **tahkocisinwak** (VAI) S/he lays on top.

tahkohtaciwew *pl.* **tahkohtaciwewak** (VAI) S/he arrives at the top or summit.

199

tahkohtahew (VTA) S/he places her/him on top.

  tahkohtastâw (VTA) S/he places it on top.

  tahkohtahiwew (VTA) S/he places people on top.

  tahkohtascikew (VTI) S/he places things on top.

tahkohtastâw (VTI) S/he places it on top.

  tahkohtasscikew (VTI) S/he places things on top.

tahkohtâmaciwew *pl.* **tahkohtâmaciwewak** (VAI) S/he climbed onto the top of the hill.

tahkohtâmatin *pl.* **tahkohtâmatinawa** (VII) It is the summit or top of the hill or mountain.

tahkonew (VTA) S/he carries or holds her/him.

  tahkonam (VTI) S/he carries or holds it in her/his hand.

  tahkoniwew (VTA) S/he carries or holds someone on her/his knees.

  tahkonikew (VTI) S/he carries or holds something.

tahkonikan *pl.* **tahkonikana** (NI) Something to hold or carry.

tahkonikewin *pl.* **tahkonikewina** (NI) The act of toting or carrying.

tahkopicikanâpisk *pl.* **tahkopicikanâpiskwa** (NI) A wire to tie things.

tahkopicikâkana (NI) Something used for tying things down, i.e.: strap.

tahkopisiw *pl.* **tahkopisiwak** (VAI) S/he is tied up.

tahkopitew (VTA) S/he tied her/him up.

  tahkopitam (VTI) S/he tied it up.

  tahkopisiwew (VTA) S/he ties people up.

  tahkopicikew (VTI) S/he ties things up.

tahkoskâtew (VTA) S/he stepped on her/him.

  tahkoskâtam (VTI) S/he stepped on it.

  tahkoskâsiwew (VTA) S/he stepped on people.

  tahkoskâcikew (VTI) S/he stepped on things.

tahkoskew *pl.* **tahkoskewak** (VAI) S/he stepped.

tahkoskewin *pl.* **tahkoskewina** (NI) A step.

tahkwaham *pl.* **tahkwahamwak** (VAI) S/he steers it, i.e.: a canoe.

tahkwahamowapoy *pl.* **tahkwahamowapoya** (NI) A paddle used to steer a canoe. *Var.* **apoy.**

tahkwahamowâkanâhtik *pl.*
  tahkwahamowâkanâhtikwa (NI) A pole used to manoeuvre a canoe.

tahkwahikew *pl.* **tahkwahikewa** (VTI) S/he is steering the canoe or boat. *(Northern). Alt.* **pimiskâw** *(Plains); Var.* **pimiskâw** *(Northern).*

tahkwahkew *pl.* **tahkwahkewak** (VAI) S/he bites.

tahkwahkewin *pl.* **tahkwahkewina** (NI) The act of biting.

tahkwahtamôhew (VTA) S/he made her/him bite it.

  tahkwahtamôhtâw (VTI) S/he made it bite.

  tahkwahtamôhiwew (VTA) S/he made people bite.

tahkwamew (VTA) S/he bites her/him.

tahkwatam (VTI) S/he bites it.

tahkwamiwew (VTA) S/he bites people.

tahkwacikew (VTI) S/he bites at some things.

tahtakosiw *pl.* **tahtakosiwak** (VAI) It has a flat and level surface.

tahtakowâc (IPC) Simutaneously; successive. *Var.* **takowâc.**

tahtakwahcâw *pl.* **tahtakwahcâwa** (NI) An area of even or level ground.

tahtakwaskamikâw *pl.* **tahtakwaskamikâwa** (VII) It is level ground.

tahtakwâw *pl.* **tahtakwâwa** (VII) It is flat and level.

tahtapipimohtewin *pl.* **tahtapipimohtewina** (NI) The act of following the same course or trail.

tahtaskosehikakan *pl.* **tahtaskosehikakana** (NI) A stoker or poker used in the fire. *(Northern). Var.* **yahkisehikâkan** *(Northern); Alt.* **yahkisehikâkan** *(Plains).*

tahtatâmosin *pl.* **tahtatâmosinwak** (VAI) The fall induces her/him to catch her/his breath.

tahtinew (VTA) S/he unhooks it, i.e.: a button. *(Plains). Alt.* **tasinew** *(Northern).*

  tahtinam (VTI) S/he unhooks it.

  tahtiniwew (VTA) S/he unhooks people.

  tahtinikew (VTI) S/he unhooks things.

tahtinikan *pl.* **tahtinikana** (NI) Something to be unhooked, i.e.: a button. *(Plains). Alt.* **tasinikan** *(Northern).*

tahtonisk *pl.* **tahtoniskewina** (NI) A Cree unit of measurement from chin to fingertip, i.e.: one yard.

tahtoniskesiw *pl.* **tahtoniskesiwak** (VAI) A Cree expression of measurement used to describe length, i.e.: "it is that many arm lengths."

tahtoniskeyâw *pl.* **tahtoniskeyâwak** (VAI) A Cree expression of measurement used to describe length, i.e.: "this is how many yards it is."

tahtotipiskâw (IPC) Nightly; every night.

tahtweyak (LN) At each place.

takahkatim *pl.* **takahkatimwak** (VAI) It is a good or nice dog or horse.

takahkayi *pl.* **takahkaya** (VII) It is a good and useful thing.

takahkeyimew (VTA) S/he thinks postively of her/him.

  takahkeyitam (VTI) S/he thinks positively about it.

  takahkeyimiwew (VTA) S/he thinks positively about people.

  takahkeyicikew (VTI) S/he thinks positively about things.

takahkeyimitowin *pl.* **takahkeyimitowina** (NI) The act of adoring one another; adoration.

takahkeyimow *pl.* **takahkeyimowak** (VAI) S/he has positive thoughts about herself/himself.

takahkeyimsowin *pl.* **takahkeyimsowina** (NI) The act of adoring oneself; self confidence; pert.

takahkeyitamohew (VTA) S/he makes her/him feel positive.

takahkeyitamohiwew (VTA) S/he makes people feel positive.

takahkeyitamohewak (VTA) They make her/him or them feel positive.

takahkîwin *pl.* **takahkîwina** (NI) Being skilled. *(Plains).* *Alt.* **miyowin** *(Northern).*

takahkatim *pl.* **takahkatimak** (NA) A good or nice dog or horse.

takocimew *pl.* **takocimewak** (VAI) S/he arrives by canoe or boat. *(Plains and Northern variant). Alt.* **takwaskow** *(Northern).*

takohtâmaciwewin *pl.* **takohtâmaciwewina** (NI) The act of climbing to the crest; crested.

takohtew *pl.* **takohtewak** (VAI) S/he arrived on foot.

takokâpawiw *pl.* **takokâpawiwak** (VAI) S/he arrives to stand in line.

takomiyew *pl.* **takomiyewak** (VTA) S/he gives her/him a bit more.

takonamakewin *pl.* **takonamakewina** (NI) The act of augmenting or giving a bit more.

takonamawew (VTA) S/he gives her/him an additional amount.

takonamakew (VTA) S/he gives people some more.

takopayiw *pl.* **takopayiwak** (VAI) S/he arrives by car or horse.

takopiciw *pl.* **takopiciwak** (VAI) S/he arrived from her/his camping trip.

takosin *pl.* **takosinwak** (VAI) S/he has arrived.

takosiniwin *pl.* **takosiniwina** (NI) An arrival.

takotâpew *pl.* **takotâpewak** (VAI) S/he arrived pulling something, i.e.: sled.

takôsihcikewin *pl.* **takôsihcikewina** (NI) The act of supplementing; supplemental.

takwahastohew *pl.* **takwahastohewak** (IPC) It flaps its wings as a mating call, i.e.: refers to a prairie chicken.

takwahew (VAI) S/he puts more of them on top.

takwastâw (VAI) S/he puts more of it on top.

takwahiwew (VAI) S/he puts more people on top.

takwascikew (VAI) S/he puts more things on top.

takwahikan *pl.* **takwahikana** (NI) Something used to hold or pin something down, i.e.: a holder or clip.

takwahiminân *pl.* **takwahiminâna** (NI) A chokecherry.

takwahiminânâhtik *pl.* **takwahiminânâhtikwak** (NA) A chokecherry tree or bush.

takwamohcikan *pl.* **takwamohcikana** (NI) A tool used to hold something, e.g.: a clamp. *(Northern). Var.*

akwamohcikan *(Northern); Alt.* **akwamohcikan** *(Plains).*

takwascikewin *pl.* **takwascikewina** (NI) The act of including; augmentation; installation; inclusion.

takwaskow *pl.* **takwaskowak** (VAI) S/he arrives by canoe or boat. *(Archaic Cree; Northern). Var.* **takocimew** *(Northern); Alt.* **takocimew** *(Plains).*

takwawew (VTA) S/he pins her/him between two things.

takwaham (VTI) S/he pins it between two things.

takwahowew (VTA) S/he pins people between two things.

takwahikew (VTI) S/he pins something between two things.

takwâkin (VII) It is autumn or fall time.

takwâkohk (IPC) Last fall or autumn.

takwâsiw *pl.* **takwâsiwak** (VTA) S/he has arrived with the wind; the wind blew her/him towards us.

tamasaskonew (VTA) S/he will confiscate it from her/him.

tamasaskonam (VTI) S/he will confiscate it completely.

tamasaskoniwew (VTA) S/he will take people all away.

tamasaskonikew (VTI) S/he will confiscate everything completely.

tamâskahpinasiw *pl.* **tamâskahpinasiwak** (VTA) S/he will cripple someone.

tamâskahpinew *pl.* **tamâskahpinewak** (VAI) S/he will be crippled by sickness.

tanisetokwe (IPC) An expression meaning "I do not know."

tanisi (IPC) An expression meaning "how are you?" *Var.* **tân'si**.

taniwâ (IPC) Where is s/he?

taniwehkâk (IPC) Where are they? (animate)

tapahcikâpawiw *pl.* **tapahcikâpawiwak** (VAI) S/he stands low to the ground.

tapahtakocin *pl.* **tapahtakocinwak** (VAI) It hangs low.

tapahtakotew *pl.* **tapahtakotewa** (VII) It hangs low.

tapahteyihtâkosiw *pl.* **tapahteyihtâkosiwak** (VAI) S/he is believed to be a low, vile or base character.

tapahteyihtâkwan *pl.* **tapahteyihtâkwanwa** (VII) People have a low opinion of it; it is believed to be base or vile.

tapahteyimew (VTA) S/he has a low opinion of her/him.

tapahteyitam (VTI) S/he has a low opinion of it.

tapahteyimiwew (VTA) S/he has a low opinion of people.

tapahteyicikew (VTI) S/he has a low opinion of things.

tapahteyimisiw *pl.* **tapahteyimisiwak** (VAI) S/he is humble; s/he has a low opinion of herself/himself.

tapahteyimisiwin *pl.* **tapahteyimisiwina** (NI) Humility; being humble; having low self-esteem.

tapahteyimisôstawew (VTA) S/he humbles or abases herself/himself before her/him.

tapahteyimisôstam (VTI) S/he humbles herself/ himself before it.

tapahteyimisôstâkew (VTA) S/he humbles herself/ himself before people.

tapahteyimohew (VTA) S/he causes her/him to humilate herself/himself.

tapahteyimohiwew (VTA) S/he causes people to humilate themselves.

tapahtisiw *pl.* **tapahtisiwak** (VAI) S/he is low.

tapahtiskweyestawew (VTA) S/he bows her/his head before her/him.

tapahtiskweyestâkew (VTA) S/he bows her/his head to others.

tapahtiskweyiw *pl.* **tapahtiskweyiwak** (VAI) S/he bows her/his head down, i.e.: ready to pray.

tapapistamawew (VII) S/he is representing them. *(Plains). Alt.* **nokosistamawew** *(Northern).*

tapapistamakew (VAI) S/he is representing people.

tapapistawew (VTA) S/he replaces her/him or takes her/ his place.

tapapistakew (VTA) S/he takes people's places.

tapapiw *pl.* **tapapiwak** (VAI) S/he replaces someone.

tapasihew (VTA) S/he flees from her/him; s/he runs away from her/him.

tapasitâw (VTI) S/he flees from it.

tapasihiwew (VTA) S/he flees from someone.

tapasicikew (VTI) S/he flees from something.

tapasihtahew (VTA) S/he flees with her/him.

tapasihtatâw (VTI) S/he flees with it.

tapasihtahiwew (VTA) S/he flees with someone.

tapasihtahcikew (VTI) S/he flees from something.

tapasihtâwin *pl.* **tapasihtâwina** (NI) Something to flee from or run away from.

tapasinahikewiyiniw *pl.* **tapasinahikewiyiniwak** (NA) A sketch artist.

tapasiyâmiw *pl.* **tapasiyâmiwak** (VAI) S/he flees or runs away in fear.

tapasiyâmohew (VTA) S/he flees with her/him.

tapasiyâmotâw (VTI) S/he flees with it.

tapasiyâmohiwew (VTA) S/he flees with someone.

tapasiyâmohcikew (VTI) S/he flees from something.

tapasîstawew (VTA) S/he avoids her/him.

tapasîstam (VTI) S/he avoids it.

tapasîstâkew (VTA) S/he avoids people.

tapasîw *pl.* **tapasîwak** (VAI) S/he fled from her/him; s/he ran away; s/he scampered away.

tapasîwin *pl.* **tapasîwina** (NI) The act of fleeing; flight.

tapasîyâmowin *pl.* **tapasîyâmowina** (NI) The act of fleeing in fear.

tapaskwahwew (VTA) S/he hooks the fish with a gaffe.

tapaskwaham (VTI) S/he hooks it with a pole.

tapaskwahikew (VTI) S/he hooks something with a pole.

tapiskawew (VTA) S/he wears them around her/his neck.

tapiskam (VTI) S/he wears it around her/his neck.

tapiskâkew (VTI) S/he wears something around her/ his neck.

tapowesimew (VAI) S/he maintains the rhythm with them.

tapowetitâw (VAI) S/he maintains the rhythm with it.

tapowecikew (VAI) S/he maintains the rhythm with things.

tapwewakeyimew (VTA) S/he believes in her/him.

tapwewakeyitam (VTI) S/he believes in it.

tapwewakeyimiwew (VTA) S/he believes in people.

tapwewakeyicikew (VTI) S/he believes in things.

tapwewin *pl.* **tapwewina** (NI) The act of telling the truth; being frank; veracious.

tapweyihtâkosiw *pl.* **tapweyihtâkosiwak** (VAI) S/he is veritable, authentic.

tasamanihkewin *pl.* **tasamanihkewina** (NI) The act of making a smudge for horses or cattle. *(Northern). Alt.* **atisamanihkwewin** *(Plains).*

tasamaw *pl.* **tasamawak** (VAI) S/he stands by the smudge or smoke to keep bugs away. *(Northern). Alt.* **atisamânihkew** *(Plains).*

tasamân *pl.* **tasamâna** (NI) A smudge. *(Northern). Alt.* **atisamân** *(Plains).*

tasamânihkawew (VTA) S/he makes a smudge for them. *(Northern). Alt.* **atisamânihkawew** *(Plains).*

tasamânihkew (VTI) S/he makes a smudge.

tasamânihkâkew (VTI) S/he makes a smudge with it.

tasihew (VTA) S/he is doing busy work with them.

tasitâw (VTI) S/he is doing busy work with it.

tasikew (VTA) S/he does busy work.

tasihcikew (VTI) S/he is doing busy work with things.

tasihkawew (VTA) S/he is preoccupied with busy work over her/him.

tasihkam (VTI) S/he is preoccupied with busy work over it.

tasihkâkew (VTA) S/he is preoccupied with busy work over people.

tasinastimwew *pl.* **tasinastimwewa** (VTI) S/he unhooks a team of horses; s/he takes the harness off. *(Northern). Var.* **âpahastimwew** *(Northern); Alt.* **âpahastimwew** *(Plains).*

tasinew (VTA) S/he unhooks it, i.e.: a button. *(Northern). Alt.* **tahtinew** *(Plains).*

tasinam (VTI) S/he unhooks it.

tasiniwew (VTA) S/he unhooks people.

tasinikew (VTI) S/he unhooks things.

tasinikan *pl.* **tasinikana** (NI) Something to be unhooked, i.e.: a button. *(Northern). Alt.* **tahtinikan** *(Plains).*

tasipicikewin *pl.* **tasipicikewina** (NI) The act of disconnecting. *(Northern). Alt.* **tahcipicikewin** *(Plains).*

tasiw (VAI) S/he stretches.

taskamaham *pl.* **taskamahamwak** (VAI) S/he cuts across the lake in a boat; s/he takes a short cut.

taskaman *pl.* **taskamanwa** (VII) It is shorter across, i.e.: a short cut.

taskamihâw *pl.* **taskamihâwak** (VAI) S/he flew the short cut.

taskamipayiw *pl.* **taskamipayiwa** *or* **taskamipayiwak** (VII) *or* (VAI) It *or* s/he drove via the short cut.

taskamiskohtew *pl.* **taskamiskohtewak** (VAI) S/he cuts across the ice.

taskamohtew *pl.* **taskamohtewak** (VAI) S/he cuts straight across.

taskamohtewin *pl.* **taskamohtewina** (NI) A short cut on a trail.

taskapîstawew (VTA) S/he sits spread eagle in front of her/him. *Alt.* **taskapîstawew.**

taskapîstam (VTI) S/he sits spread eagle in front of it.

taskapîskew (VTA) S/he sits spread eagle in front of people.

taskapîstâkew (VTA) S/he sits spread eagle in front of everyone.

taskinikewin *pl.* **taskinikewina** (NI) The act of splitting.

taskisikopayiw *pl.* **taskisikopayiwa** *or* **taskisikopayiwak** (VII) *or* (VAI) Ice is cracked on the lake.

tasokâpawiw *pl.* **tasokâpawiwak** (VAI) S/he stands straight.

tasonew (VTA) S/he straightens them up.

tasonam (VTI) S/he straightens it up.

tasoniwew (VTA) S/he straightens people up.

tasonikew (VTI) S/he straightens things up.

tasopayiw *pl.* **tasopayiwa** *or* **tasopayiwak** (VII) *or* (VAI) It *or* s/he straightens out.

tasopitew (VTA) S/he pulls them straight.

tasopitam (VTI) S/he pulls it straight.

tasopicikew (VTI) S/he pulls things straight.

tasotâw *pl.* **tasotâwa** (VII) S/he caught it in the trap.

tasoteskanew *pl.* **tasoteskanewak** (VAI) Her/his horns are straight.

tasotew *pl.* **tasotewa** (VII) It is caught in a trap.

tasôhew (VTA) S/he caught it in a trap.

tasôtâw (VTI) S/he caught it in a trap.

tasôhiwew (VTA) S/he caught someone in a trap.

tasôhikew (VTI) S/he caught fur bearing animals in her/his traps.

tasôsiw *pl.* **tasôsiwak** (VAI) S/he is caught in a trap.

tasôwin *pl.* **tasôwina** (NI) The act of stretching.

tastakiskweyiw *pl.* **tastakiskweyiwak** (VTA) S/he stretches or cranes her/his neck.

tastapayâwin *pl.* **tastapayâwina** (NI) The act of being swift or moving quickly; swiftness. *(Northern). Alt.* **cacâstapiwin** *(Plains).*

tastasâpiw *pl.* **tastasâpiwak** (VAI) S/he looks up.

tastawahikan *pl.* **tastawahikana** (NI) A pole used for a teepee frame; a teepee pole.

tastawahokew *pl.* **tastawahokewak** (VAI) S/he sets up a teepee frame.

tastawasakay *pl.* **tastawasakaywa** (NI) A web.

tastawâpiteyâw *pl.* **tastawâpiteyâwa** (VII) It has spaces between the teeth, i.e.: a harrow.

tastawâskohtâw *pl.* **tastawâskohtâwak** (VAI) S/he puts something in the space between two trees.

tastawâw *pl.* **tastawâwa** (VII) A space between two walls, i.e.: a corridor or walkway.

tastawâyâw (IPC) There is space between.

tastawâyihk (IPC) In between.

tastawikamâw *pl.* **tastawikamâwa** (NI) The channel between two adjoining lakes.

tastawikapawîstawew *pl.* **tastawikapawîstawewak** (VAI) S/he stands between them.

tastawisiw *pl.* **tastawisiwak** (VAI) S/he is between.

taswahew (VTI) S/he stretches them out.

taswastâw (VTI) S/he stretches it out.

taswacikew (VTI) S/he stretches things out.

taswâskiw *pl.* **taswâskiwak** (VAI) S/he stretches and straightens up to her/his full height.

taswâskopayihiw *pl.* **taswâskopayihiwak** (VAI) S/he lays down and stretches out to her/his full length.

taswekahew (VTI) S/he lays them out and stretches them.

taswekastâw (VTI) S/he lays it out and stretches it.

taswekascikew (VTI) S/he lays things out and stretches them.

taswekan (VII) It lays spread out, i.e.: a moosehide.

taswekapiw *pl.* **taswekapiwak** (VAI) S/he sits spread eagle.

taswekascikewin *pl.* **taswekascikewina** (NI) The act of splaying.

taswekastew *pl.* **taswekastewa** (VII) It sits spread eagle.

taswekatahwew (VTA) S/he splits them open and they spread all over the place.

taswekataham (VTI) S/he splits it open and it spreads all over the place.

taswekatahikew (VTI) S/he splits things open and they spread all over the place.

taswekinew (VTI) S/he lays them out in her/his hand.

taswekinam (VTI) S/he lays it out in her/his hand.

taswekinikew (VTI) S/he lays things out in her/his hand.

203

taswekinkewin *pl.* **taswekinkewina** (NI) The act of spreading out, i.e.: a map; unwrinkle.

taswekipayiw *pl.* **taswekipayiwa** *or* **taswekipayiwak** (VII) *or* (VAI) It *or* s/he fell down open and spread out, i.e.: a teepee.

taswekipitew (VTA) S/he pulls and rips them apart; s/he opens or spreads them out.

taswekipitam (VTI) S/he lays it spread out.

taswekipisiwew (VTA) S/he lays people spread out.

taswekipascikew (VTI) S/he lays things spread out.

taswekisimew (VTA) S/he lays them spread out.

taswekihtitâw (VTI) S/he lays it spread out.

tasweksimiwew (VTA) S/he lays people spread out.

taswekascikew (VTI) S/he lays things spread out.

taswekisiw *pl.* **taswekisiwak** (VAI) S/he is wide, i.e.: fat. *(Northern). Alt.* **âyakaskisiw** *(Plains).*

tawahcâw *pl.* **tawahcâwa** (NI) A ravine.

tawapîstawew (VTA) S/he makes a space for another person to sit down.

tawapîstam (VTI) S/he makes space for it.

tawapîstâkew (VTA) S/he makes space for someone to sit down.

tawatinâw (NI) A gap between hills.

tawâpitew *pl.* **tawâpitewak** (VAI) There is a gap between her/his teeth.

tawâskweyâw *pl.* **tawâskweyâwa** (NI) A path or gap or opening amongst the trees.

tawâw *pl.* **tawâwa** (VII) It has an opening.

tawikahikâsiw *pl.* **tawikahikâsiwak** (VAI) It is cut clear.

tawikahikâtew *pl.* **tawikahikâtewa** (VII) It is cut clear.

tawikahikew *pl.* **tawikahikewak** (VAI) S/he cuts a clearing with an axe.

tawikahwew (VTA) S/he cuts it to make a clearing.

tawikaham (VTI) S/he cuts an opening to it.

tawikahowew (VTA) S/he cuts an opening to someone.

tawikahikew (VTI) S/he cuts an opening to something.

tawinamawew (VTA) S/he makes a space or room for her/him.

tawinamâkew (VTA) S/he makes a space or room for people.

tawinew (VTI) S/he opened it or them.

tawinam (VTI) S/he opens it.

tawiniwew (VTA) S/he opens people.

tawinikew (VTI) S/he opens things.

tawisiw *pl.* **tawisiwak** (VAI) S/he has an opening.

tawisiwin *pl.* **tawisiwina** (NI) The act of having an opening.

tawîstawew (VTA) S/he makes space or room for her/him.

tawîstam (VTI) S/he makes space or room for it.

tawîstâkew (VTA) S/he makes space or room for people.

tawpaskwâw *pl.* **tawpaskwâwa** (NI) A glade or open prairie.

tawpayiw *pl.* **tawpayiwak** *or* **tawpayiwak** (VII) *or* (VAI) It *or* s/he opened up.

tâcikwetotawew (VTA) S/he cries out for her/him.

tâcikwetotam (VTI) S/he cries out to it.

tâcikwew *pl.* **tâcikwewak** (VAI) S/he screams.

tâcikwewin *pl.* **tâcikwewina** (NI) The act of screaming; the act of making a loud outcry; vociferous expression.

tâhcipohew *pl.* **tâhcipohewak** (VTA) S/he fattens her/him; s/he makes her/him gain weight.

tâhcipow *pl.* **tâhcipowak** (VAI) S/he fattens up; s/he gains weight.

tâkohkahtew *pl.* **tâkohkahtewa** (VII) It will be burnt onto a pot or pan.

tâpahew (VTA) S/he replaces what is missing; s/he adds to the shortfall.

tâpastâw (VII) S/he replaces the missing thing or amount.

tâpahiwew (VAI) S/he replaces the missing people.

tâpascikew (VAI) S/he replaces the missing things.

tâpahkohtowin *pl.* **tâpahkohtowina** (NI) The act of replacing a deceased child by adopting in name another child the same age; or of friendship.

tâpahkomew (VAI) S/he is related or considered part of the family because s/he was given the name of the deceased person.

tâpahkotam (VTI) S/he relates to the name of the deceased person's family.

tâpahkomiwew (VTA) S/he relates to someone's family.

tâpahkocikew (VTA) S/he relates to people's families.

tâpahkomiwew *pl.* **tâpahkomiwewak** (VTA) S/he is related.

tâpahkomowewin *pl.* **tâpahkomowewina** (NI) The act of adopting a brother or sister.

tâpakwan *pl.* **tâpakwana** (NI) A snare.

tâpakwawew (VTA) S/he puts a wire snare around someone's neck. *(Northern). Alt.* **tâpakwâtew** *(Plains).*

tâpakwaham (VTI) S/he puts a snare around it.

tâpakwahikew (VTI) S/he puts a snare around something.

tâpakwâtew (VTA) S/he snared her/him; s/he puts a wire snare around someone's neck. *(Plains). Alt.* **tâpakwawew** *(Northern).*

tâpakwâtam (VTI) S/he snared it; s/he puts a snare around it.

tâpakwâcikew (VTI) S/he snared something.

tâpakwew *pl.* **tâpakwewak** (VAI) S/he sets up a snare.

tâpasinahikan *pl.* **tâpasinahikana** (NI) A sketch.

tâpasinahwew (VAI) S/he makes a sketch of her/him.
tâpasinaham (VTI) S/he makes a sketch of it.
tâpasinahowew (VTA) S/he makes a sketch of people.
tâpasinahikew (VTI) S/he makes a sketch of things.

tâpastâw (VAI) S/he replaced something; a replacement for something lost; replacing, i.e.: to renew.

tâpastew *pl.* **tâpastewa** (VII) It replaces or fits in place of something else.

tâpâhkohtowak (VTA) They are related to each other by adoption.

tâpâskohtin *pl.* **tâpâskohtinwa** (VII) It is replaced or fitted into, i.e.: an axe handle. *(Northern). Var.* **tâpihtin** *(Northern); Alt.* **tâpihtin** *(Plains).*

tâpâskosimew (VTA) S/he puts another in place of her/him, i.e.: a log on a log house.
tâpâskotitâw (VTI) S/he puts another in place of it, i.e.: an axe handle on an axe.
tâpâskocikew (VTI) S/he replaces handles on things.

tâpâskosin *pl.* **tâpâskosinwak** (VAI) It is replaced, i.e.: a house log.

tâpeyihtamowin *pl.* **tâpeyihtamowina** (NI) The act of judging or reckoning correctly.

tâpeyimew (VTA) S/he judges her/him correctly; s/he had her/him or them figured out.
tâpeyitam (VTI) S/he judges it correctly.
tâpeyimiwew (VTA) S/he judges others correctly.
tâpeyicikew (VTI) S/he judges things correctly.

tâpihtehpisiw *pl.* **tâpihtehpisiwak** (VAI) S/he wears an earring.

tâpihtehpison *pl.* **tâpihtehpisonak** (NA) An earring.

tâpihtin *pl.* **tâpihtinwa** (VII) It is replaced or fitted into, i.e.: an axe handle. *(Plains and Northern variant). Alt.* **tâpâskohtin** *(Northern).*

tâpinawew (VTA) S/he thinks s/he looks just like someone else.
tâpinam (VTI) S/he thinks it looks just like something else.
tâpinakew (VTA) S/he thinks people look just like others.

tâpinâkosiw *pl.* **tâpinâkosiwak** (VAI) S/he looks just like her/him.

tâpinâkwan *pl.* **tâpinâkwanwa** (VII) It looks just like it.

tâpipayiw *pl.* **tâpipayiwak** *or* **tâpipayiwa** (VII) *or* (VAI) It *or* s/he clicks into place.

tâpisahiminew *pl.* **tâpisahiminewa** (VTI) S/he threads or strings beads into a necklace.

tâpisawew (VTI) S/he threads them.
tâpisaham (VTI) S/he thread it.
tâpisahikew (VTI) S/he threads things.

tâpisikoskawew (VTA) S/he puts her/his foot in them.
tâpisikoskam (VTI) S/he puts her/his foot in it, i.e.: a stirrup.

tâpisikoskâcikan *pl.* **tâpisikoskâcikana** (NI) A stirrup on a saddle.

tâpisimew (VAI) S/he fits them in place, i.e.: wheels.
tâpihtitâw (VTI) S/he fits it in its place, i.e.: an axe handle.
tâpisimiwew (VTA) S/he fits people in their places.
tâpihcikew (VTI) S/he fits things in their places.

tâpisiminew *pl.* **tâpisiminewa** (VTI) S/he threads beads.

tâpisin *pl.* **tâpisinwak** (VAI) It falls into place.

tâpisiskoskâcikaneyâpiy *pl.* **tâpisiskoskâcikaneyâpiya** (NI) A strap used to hold the stirrup.

tâpiskâkan *pl.* **tâpiskâkana** (NI) A neck scarf or neckerchief.

tâpiskâkanemin *pl.* **tâpiskâkaneminak** (NA) A large bead used for making a necklace.

tâpiskoteyihcikan *pl.* **tâpiskoteyihcikana** (NI) A premonition; an awareness about a coming event.

tâpiskoteyimew (VTA) S/he has a premonition about them; s/he has insights about them.
tâpiskoteyitam (VTI) S/he has a premonition about it.
tâpiskoteyimiwew (VTA) S/he has a premonition about people.
tâpiskoteyicikew (VTI) S/he has a premonition about things.

tâpitaweyihtamwak (VAI) They constantly have the same ideas or thinking. *(Northern). Alt.* **pâhpeyakwan** *(Plains).*

tâpitaweyihtowak (VTA) They constantly think of each other. *(Northern). Alt.* **mâmâmitoneyihtowak** *(Plains).*

tâpitaweyimew (VTA) S/he thinks of her/him constantly.
tâpitaweyitam (VTI) S/he thinks of it constantly.
tâpitaweyimiwew (VTA) S/he thinks of people constantly.
tâpitaweyicikew (VTI) S/he thinks of things constantly.

tâpitawipayiw *pl.* **tâpitawipayiwa** *or* **tâpitawipayiwak** (VII) *or* (VAI) It *or* s/he runs constantly or nonstop.

tâpitonehpicikan *pl.* **tâpitonehpicikana** (NI) A bridle.

tâpitonehpicikanâpisk *pl.* **tâpitonehpicikanâpiskwa** (NI) A bridle bit.

tâpitonehpicikaniyâpiy *pl.* **tâpitonehpicikaniyâpiya** (NI) A bridle strap; a rein.

tâpitonehpisiw *pl.* **tâpitonehpisiwak** (VAI) S/he is bridled; s/he wears a bridle.

tâpowew *pl.* **tâpowewak** (VAI) S/he sings the correct melody.

tâpowewin *pl.* **tâpowewina** (NI) The act of being able to sing the proper melody; assonance.

tâpwe (IPC) It is true.

tâpwe hetoke (IPC) An expression meaning "I guess it is true" or "you can say that again."

205

tâpwehtam *pl.* **tâpwehtamwak** (VTA) S/he believes it.

tâpwehtamowin *pl.* **tâpwehtamowina** (NI) The act of believing.

tâpwehtawew (VTA) S/he believes her/him.

    tâpwehtam (VTI) S/he believes it.

    tâpwehtâkew (VTA) S/he believes people.

tâpwehtâkawiw *pl.* **tâpwehtâkawiwak** (VAI) S/he is to be believed.

tâpwehtâkwan *pl.* **tâpwehtâkwanwa** (VII) It is to be believed.

tâpwemakan *pl.* **tâpwemakanwa** (VII) It tells the truth.

tâpwew *pl.* **tâpwewak** (VAI) S/he tells the truth.

tâpwewakeyihmowewin *pl.* **tâpwewakeyihmowewina** (NI) The act of being loyal; loyalty.

tâpwewakeyihtamohew (VAI) S/he believes something is good for her/him.

tâpwewakeyihtamowin *pl.* **tâpwewakeyihtamowina** (NI) A belief or hope; assertion; a verity.

tâpwewakeyihtâkwan *pl.* **tâpwewakeyihtâkwanwa** (VII) It is truthful or believable.

tâpwewiniwiw *pl.* **tâpwewiniwiwa** (NI) Something that tells the truth; truth-telling thing, i.e.: the Bible.

tâsahikan *pl.* **tâsahikana** (NI) A sharpener. *Var.* **kînipocikan**.

tâsahwew (VTA) S/he sharpens them.

    tâsaham (VTI) S/he sharpens it.

    tâsahikew (VTI) S/he sharpens things.

tâskahkatosiw *pl.* **tâskahkatosiwak** (VAI) It dries and splits open, i.e.: a tree.

tâskahkatotew *pl.* **tâskahkatotewa** (VII) It dries and splits open.

tâskamew (VTA) S/he bites it or them open.

    tâskatam (VTI) S/he bites it open.

    tâskahcikew (VTI) S/he bites things open.

tâskatahikewin *pl.* **tâskatahikewina** (NI) The act of splitting or tearing apart violently.

tâskatahimihtew *pl.* **tâskatahimihtewak** (VAI) S/he is splitting wood.

tâskatahwew (VTA) S/he hits them and splits them in half.

    tâskataham (VTI) S/he hits it and splits it in half.

    tâskatahikew (VTI) S/he hits them and splits things in half.

tâskâw *pl.* **tâskâwa** (VII) It is split.

tâskihkotew (VTA) S/he cuts them in half.

    tâskihkotam (VTI) S/he cuts it in half.

    tâskihkocikew (VTI) S/he cuts things in half.

tâskikahwew (VTA) S/he chops them in half.

    tâskikaham (VTI) S/he chops it in half.

    tâskikahikew (VTI) S/he chops things in half.

tâskikawew (VTI) S/he chops them loose; s/he splits them in half.

tâskikaham (VTI) S/he chops it loose.

tâskinew (VTA) S/he splits them open by hand.

    tâskinam (VTI) S/he splits it open by hand.

    tâskiniwew (VTA) S/he splits people open by hand.

    tâskinikew (VTI) S/he splits things open by hand.

tâskipayiw *pl.* **tâskipayiwak** *or* **tâskipayiwak** (VII) *or* (VAI) It is split in half.

tâskipitew (VTA) S/he pulls or tears them in half.

    tâskipitam (VTI) S/he pulls or tears it in half.

    tâskipisiwew (VTA) S/he pulls or tears people in half.

    tâskipicikew (VTI) S/he pulls or tears things in half.

tâskipocikan *pl.* **tâskipocikana** (NI) A sawmill.

tâskipocikâkan *pl.* **tâskipocikâkana** (NI) A band saw.

tâskipocikew *pl.* **tâskipocikewak** (VAI) S/he saws wood into lumber.

tâskipocikewikamik *pl.* **tâskipocikewikamikwa** (NI) A sawmill shack.

tâskipohew (VTA) S/he saws them all up, i.e.: logs.

    tâskipotâw (VTI) S/he saws it in half.

    tâskipohiwew (VTA) S/he saws someone in half.

    tâskipocikew (VTI) S/he saws lumber in half.

tâskisikwâw *pl.* **tâskisikwâwa** (VII) There is an opening on the ice.

tâskisiw *pl.* **tâskisiwak** (VAI) S/he split.

tâskiswew (VTA) S/he cuts them in half with a knife.

    tâskisam (VTI) S/he cuts it in half with a knife.

    tâskisikew (VTI) S/he cuts things in half with a knife.

tâstapipayiw *pl.* **tâstapipayiwa** *or* **tâstapipayiwak** (VII) *or* (VAI) It *or* s/he goes very swiftly; it moves rapidly. *Var.* **câstapipayiw**.

tâstapiw (VAI) S/he is swift; s/he is agile.

tâstapîwin *pl.* **tâstapîwina** (NI) Being sleight or having dexterity. *(Northern).* *Alt.* **câstapiwin** *(Plains).*

tâstapîwin *pl.* **tâstapîwina** (NI) The act of being swift or agile.

tâstapwaskawewin *pl.* **tâstapwaskawewina** (NI) The act of being nimble or very fast movement. *(Northern).* *Alt.* **câstapiwaskawîwin** *(Plains).*

tâtopayiw *pl.* **tâtopayiwak** *or* **tâtopayiwak** (VII) *or* (VAI) It *or* s/he is torn, i.e.: any kind of cloth.

tâtopitew (VTA) S/he tears her/his clothes.

    tâtopitam (VTI) S/he tears a piece of cloth.

    tâtopisiwew (VTA) S/he tears someone's clothes.

    tâtopicikew (VTI) S/he tears something off.

tâwahwew (VTA) S/he hits her/him, i.e.: with an arrow.

    tâwaham (VTI) S/he hits it, i.e.: with an arrow.

    tâwahowew (VTA) S/he hits people, i.e.: with an arrow.

    tâwahikew (VTI) S/he hits things, i.e.: with an arrow.

tâwaskâw *pl.* **tâwaskâwa** (NI) A path or gap in the tall grass.

206

tâwatiw *pl.* **tâwatiwak** (VAI) S/he opened her/his mouth wide; s/he yawned.

tâwâkonakâw *pl.* **tâwâkonakâwa** (NI) A path or gap in the snow.

tâwicihcan *pl.* **tâwicihcana** (NI) The middle finger.

tâwiciwan (VII) It flows in the middle.

tâwihtin *pl.* **tâwihtinwa** (VII) It falls in the middle.

tâwisin *pl.* **tâwisinwak** (VAI) S/he falls in the middle.

tâwistikwanehwew (VTA) S/he hit her/him on the head with something.
  tâwistikwaneham (VTI) S/he hits it on the head.
  tâwistikwanehowew (VTA) S/he hits someone on the head.
  tâwistikwanehikew (VTI) S/he hits something on the head.

tâwkihtin *pl.* **tâwkihtinwa** (VTI) It bumps against something.

tâwkipayihtowak (VAI) They collide.

tâwkisimew *pl.* **tâwkisimewak** (VTA) S/he bumps her/him against something.

tâwkisin *pl.* **tâwkisinwak** (VTA) S/he bumps against something.

tâwkiskaw (VTA) You accidently bump her/him or run into her/him. *(Plains). Alt.* **tâwskawew** *(Northern).*
  tâwkiskam (VTI) S/he accidently bumps or runs into it.

tâwkiskâtowin *pl.* **tâwkiskâtowina** (NI) The act of bumping against one another; impinge.

tâwkiskâkew (VTA) S/he accidently bumps or runs into people.

tâwpiskwaewew (VTA) S/he hit her/him in the back, i.e.: with something.
  tâwpiskwaneham (VTI) S/he hits it on the back.
  tâwpiskwanehowew (VTA) S/he hits people on the back.
  tâwpiskwanehikew (VTI) S/he hits something on the back.

tâwskawew (VTA) S/he accidently bumps her/him or runs into her/him. *(Northern). Alt.* **tawkiskaw** *(Plains).*
  tâwskam (VTI) S/he accidently bumps or runs into it.
  tâwskâkew (VTA) S/he accidently bumps or runs into people.

tehcikwâskohtiw *pl.* **tehcikwâskohtiwak** (VAI) S/he jumps on it.

tehciwepinew (VTA) S/he throws her/him on top of something.
  tehciwepinam (VTI) S/he throws it on top.
  tehciwepiniwew (VTA) S/he throws someone on top.
  tehciwepinikew (VTI) S/he throws things on top.

tehcohpâtew (VTA) S/he jumps on top of her/him.
  tehcohpâtam (VTI) S/he jumps on top of it.

tehcohpâcikew (VTI) S/he jumps on top of things.

tehtahew (VTA) S/he places her/him on top of something, i.e.: a table.

tehtastâw (VTI) S/he places it on top of something.

tehtahiwew (VTA) S/he places people on top of something.

tehtascikew (VTI) S/he places things on top of something.

tehtapâmew *pl.* **tehtapâmewak** (VTA) S/he sits on top of her/his back, i.e.: horse. *(Plains). Alt.* **tehtapâtew** *(Northern).*

tehtapâtew *pl.* **tehtapâtewak** (VTA) S/he sits on top of her/his back, i.e.: horse. *(Northern). Alt.* **tehtapâmew** *(Plains).*

tehtapiw *pl.* **tehtapiwak** (VAI) S/he sits on top of something.

tehtapiwin *pl.* **tehtapiwina** (NI) The act of sitting on top of something; a chair.

tehtapîhew (VTA) S/he gives her/him a horseback ride.
  tehtapîhowew (VTA) S/he gives someone a horseback ride.

tehtapîwatim *pl.* **tehtapîwatimwak** (NA) A saddle horse.

tehtapîwitâsak (NA) A pair of chaps.

tepahkamikan *pl.* **tepahkamikanwa** (VII) The activity is monotonous.

tepahkamikisiw *pl.* **tepahkamikisiwak** (VAI) S/he is tired of moving around; tired of doing the same thing.

tepakeyihtakosiw *pl.* **tepakeyihtakosiwak** (VAI) S/he is worthy of it.

tepakeyihtâkwan *pl.* **tepakeyihtâkwanwa** (VII) It is worthy of it.

tepakeyimiw *pl.* **tepakeyimiwak** (VAI) S/he expresses a willingness to undertake it.

tepakeyimowin *pl.* **tepakeyimowina** (NI) The act of expressing a willingness to undertake a task.

tepakohpimitanaw (IPC) Seventy.

tepamohew (VTA) S/he makes them all fit in. *(Northern). Alt.* **tepiskamohew** *(Plains).*
  tepamohtâw (VTI) S/he makes it fit.
  tepamohiwew (VTA) S/he makes people fit.
  tepamohcikew (VTI) S/he makes things fit.

tepamow *pl.* **tepamowa** *or* **tepamowak** (VII) *or* (VAI) It *or* s/he fits just right; there was enough space.

tepapekinkewin *pl.* **tepapekinkewina** (NI) The act of taking a measurement or dimensions. *(Northern). Alt.* **tipahikewin** *(Plains).*

tepapiw *pl.* **tepapiwak** (VAI) There is enough space or room for her/him to sit.

tepapîstawew (VTA) S/he sits with her/him long enough.
  tepapîstam (VTI) S/he sits with it long enough.
  tepapîstâkew (VTA) S/he sits with people long enough.

207

tepaskinahew (VTA) S/he makes her/him fit; s/he makes enough space or room for her/him or them.

tepaskinahtâw (VTI) S/he makes it fit.

tepaskinahiwew (VTA) S/he makes people fit.

tepaskinahcikew (VTI) S/he makes things fit.

tepaskinew *pl.* **tepaskinewak** (VAI) S/he fits inside; there is enough space or room for her/him inside.

tepaskinewin *pl.* **tepaskinewina** (NI) The act of fitting inside; having enough space or room to be inside.

tepastew *pl.* **tepastewa** (VII) It fits; there was enough space or room for it.

tepâcimow *pl.* **tepâcimowak** (VAI) S/he is tired of telling stories.

tepâcimowin *pl.* **tepâcimowina** (NI) The act of being tired of telling stories.

tepakohp (IPC) Seven.

tepakohpimitanaw (IPC) Seventy.

tepakohpimitanawâw (IPC) Seventy times, seventieth time.

tepakohposâp (IPC) Seventeen.

tepakohposâpwâw (IPC) Seventeen times, seventeenth time.

tepakohpwâw (IPC) Seven times, seventh time.

tepakohpwâw mitâtahtomitanaw (IPC) Seven hundred.

tepâskonew (VTA) S/he is able to put her/his arms around her/him.

tepâskonam (VTI) S/he is able to put her/his arms around it.

tepâskoniwew (VTA) S/he is able to put her/his arms around people.

tepâskonikew (VTI) S/he is able to put her/his arms around everything.

tepâskwahwew (VTA) S/he coils her/him around a stick.

tepâskwahâm (VTI) S/he coils it around a stick.

tepâskwahikew (VTI) S/he coils things around a stick.

tepâsteskawew (VTA) S/he meets with her/him on time.

tepâsteskam (VTA) S/he arrives on time.

tepâsteskâkew (VTA) S/he arrives on time for people.

tepekinew (VTA) S/he has enough to wrap them up.

tepekinam (VTI) S/he has enough to wrap it up.

tepekiniwew (VTA) S/he has enough to wrap people up.

tepekinikew (VTI) S/he has enough to wrap things up.

tepesin *pl.* **tepesinwak** (VAI) S/he fits just right.

tepeyihtam *pl.* **tepeyihtamwak** (VAI) S/he is tired of it; s/he is fed up with it.

tepeyihtâkwan *pl.* **tepeyihtâkwanwa** (VII) It is considered monotonous; they have had enough of it.

tepeyimew (VTA) S/he is tired of her/him.

tepeyimiwew (VTA) S/he it tired of people.

tepeyicikew (VTI) S/he is tired of everything.

tepeyimow *pl.* **tepeyimowak** (VAI) S/he agrees.

tepeyimowin *pl.* **tepeyimowina** (NI) An agreement; acquiesce.

tepeyitâkosiw *pl.* **tepeyitâkosiwak** (VAI) Others are tired or disgusted with her/his actions.

tepihkwâmiw *pl.* **tepihkwâmiwak** (VAI) S/he has enough sleep.

tepihtawew (VTA) S/he is tired of hearing her/him.

tepihtam (VTI) S/he it tired of hearing it.

tepihtâkew (VTA) S/he is tired of hearing people.

tepihtin *pl.* **tepihtinwa** (VII) It fits just right; it fits.

tepimâkosiw *pl.* **tepimâkosiwak** (VAI) S/he fills the place with her/his odor.

tepimâkwan *pl.* **tepimâkwanwa** (VII) It filled the place with its odor.

tepimew (VTA) S/he is tired of speaking to her/him.

tepimiwew (VTA) S/he has spoken enough to people.

tepihcikew (VTA) S/he has done enough.

tepinamawew (VTA) S/he gives her/him a sufficient amount.

tepinamakew (VTA) S/he gives people a sufficient amount.

tepinew (VTA) S/he reaches her/him.

tepinam (VTI) S/he reaches it.

tepiniwew (VTA) S/he reaches people.

tepinikew (VTI) S/he reaches things.

tepipayihew (VAI) S/he has a sufficient amount for her/him.

tepipayitâw (VAI) S/he has a sufficient amount for everyone.

tepipayihiwew (VAI) S/he has a sufficient amount for everybody.

tepipayicikew (VTI) S/he has a sufficient amount for everything.

tepipayiw *pl.* **tepipayiwak** (VAI) S/he has a sufficient amount; s/he has enough.

tepipayowin *pl.* **tepipayowina** (NI) The act of having a sufficient amount; adequacy; sufficiency.

tepipew *pl.* **tepipewak** (VAI) S/he has had a sufficient amount to drink; s/he has had enough to drink.

tepiskamohew (VTA) S/he makes them fit. *(Plains). Alt.* **tepamohew** *(Northern).*

tepiskamohtâw (VTI) S/he makes it fit.

tepiskamohiwew (VTA) S/he makes people fit.

tepiskamohcikew (VTI) S/he makes things fit.

tepiskawew (VTA) S/he fits into it or them.

tepiskam (VTI) S/he fits into it.

tepitotawew (VTA) S/he has done a sufficient amount for her/him; s/he has done enough for her/him.

tepitotam (VAI) S/he has done a sufficient amount.

tepitotâkew (VTA) S/he has done a sufficient amount for someone.

tepitôtam *pl.* **tepitôtamwak** (VAI) S/he keeps her/his word or promise.

tepitôtamowin *pl.* **tepitôtamowina** (NI) The act of keeping one's word or promise.

tepwâtew (VTA) S/he hollers at her/him.
  tepwâtam (VTI) S/he hollers at it.
  tepwâsiwew (VTA) S/he hollers at people.
  tepwâcikew (VTI) S/he hollers at things.

tepwepicikan *pl.* **tepwepicikana** (NI) A car horn or a whistle. *(Northern). Alt.* **pôtâcikan** *(Plains).*

tepwew *pl.* **tepwewak** (VAI) S/he hollers or shouts.

tepwewin *pl.* **tepwewina** (NI) The act of hollering or shouting; outcry.

tepweyawesiw *pl.* **tepweyawesiwa** (NI) The act of screaming in anger. *(Plains and Northern variant); Alt.* **sohkeyawisowin** *(Northern).*

tetipahpitew (VTA) S/he ties a rope around her/him.
  tetipahpitam (VTI) S/he ties a rope around it.
  tetipahpisiwew (VTA) S/he ties a rope around people.
  tetipahpicikew (VTI) S/he ties a rope around things.

tetipeweham *pl.* **tetipewehamak** (VAI) S/he circle around along the edge, i.e.: a lake.

tetipeweskawew (VTA) S/he circles around her/him.
  tetipeweskam (VTI) S/he circles around it.
  tetipeweskâkew (VTA) S/he circles around people.
  tetipeweskâcikew (VTI) S/he circles around things.

tetipeweskâkewin *pl.* **tetipeweskâkewina** (NI) The act of enveloping; envelopment.

tetipewew *pl.* **tetipewewak** (VAI) S/he circles all the way around it.

tetipiskawew (VTA) S/he walks circling around her/him.
  tetipiskam (VTI) S/he walks circling around it.
  tetipiskâkew (VTA) S/he walks circling around people.
  tetipiskâcikew (VTI) S/he walks circling around things.

teyaskikanew *pl.* **teyaskikanewak** (VAI) S/he has an ache in her/his chest.

teyehtawakayewin *pl.* **teyehtawakayewina** (NI) Having an earache. *(Northern). Alt.* **mihtawakayâspinewin** *(Plains).*

teyipitonew *pl.* **teyipitonewak** (VAI) S/he has an ache in her/his arm. *(Northern). Alt.* **teyisipitonew** *(Plains).*

teyisipitonew *pl.* **teyisipitonewak** (VAI) S/he has an ache in her/his arm. *(Plains). Alt.* **teyipitonew** *(Northern).*

teyisiw *pl.* **teyisiwak** (VAI) S/he is aching.

teyistikwânew *pl.* **teyistikwânewak** (VAI) S/he has an ache in her/his head; s/he has a headache.

teyistikwânewimaskihkiy (NI) Aspirin; Tylenol.

teyistikwânewin (NI) A headache.

tihkahcâw (VII) The ground has thawed.

tihkapiskisiw *pl.* **tihkapiskisiwak** (VAI) The metal has thawed.

tihkapiskiswew (VTI) S/he melts them, i.e.: something metallic.
  tihkapiskisam (VTI) S/he melts it.
  tihkapiskisikew (VTI) S/he melts things.

tihkastew *pl.* **tihkastewa** (VII) It is thawed by the sun.

tihkâpawahew (VAI) S/he thaws something with water.
  tihkâpawahtâw (VAI) S/he thaws it with water.
  tihkâpawahiwew (VAI) S/he thaws someone with water.
  tihkâpawahcikew (VAI) S/he thaws things with water.

tihkâpawew *pl.* **tihkâpawewak** *or* **tihkâpawewa** (VAI) *or* (VII) It is thawed with the aid of water.

tihkâpiskâw *pl.* **tihkâpiskâwa** (VII) The metal has melted.

tihkâpiskisikan *pl.* **tihkâpiskisikana** (NI) Something used to melt iron.

tihkâstew *pl.* **tihkâstewa** (VTI) It is melted by the sun.

tihkâw *pl.* **tihkâwa** (VII) It is melted, i.e.: butter.

tihkinew (VTI) S/he thaws them with her/his hands.
  tihkinam (VTI) S/he thaws it with her/his hands.
  tihkiniwew (VTA) S/he thaws people with her/his hands.
  tihkinikew (VTI) S/he thaws things with her/his hands.

tihkipayiw *pl.* **tihkipayiwa** *or* **tihkipayiwak** (VII) *or* (VAI) It *or* s/he is thawed; dissolved.

tihkipâw *pl.* **tihkipâwa** (VII) It is slightly melted or it is softened. *(Northern)*

tihkipestew *pl.* **tihkipestewa** (VII) It is melted into a liquid.

tihkipeswew (VTA) S/he melts them into a liquid form, i.e.: water.
  tihkipesam (VTI) S/he melts it into a liquid form, i.e.: water.
  tihkipesikew (VTI) S/he melts things into a liquid form.

tihkisamawew (VTA) S/he melts it out for her/him.
  tihkisamakew (VTA) S/he melts it for people.

tihkisikan *pl.* **tihkisikana** (NI) Some metal that can be used for melting.

tihkisiw *pl.* **tihkisiwak** (VAI) S/he has thawed out.

tihkiskawew (VTA) S/he thaws her/him out with body heat.
  tihkiskam (VTI) S/he thaws it out with body heat.
  tihkiskâkew (VTA) S/he thaws someone out with body heat.

tihkiswew (VTA) S/he melts them.
  tihkisam (VTI) S/he melts it.
  tihkisowew (VTA) S/he thaws people.
  tihkisikew (VTI) S/he melts things.

209

tihkitew *pl.* **tihkitewa** (VII) It is slightly melted or it is softened; it has thawed out or defrosted. *(Plains).*

tihtipahpinewin *pl.* **tihtipahpinewina** (NI) The act of writhing in pain.

tihtipayiw *pl.* **tihtipayiwak** (VAI) It is rolling, i.e.: a wheel in motion. *(Northern). Alt.* **tihtipipayiw** *(Plains).*

tihtipâkonepayiw *pl.* **tihtipâkonepayiwak** *or* **tihtipâkonepayiwa** (VII) *or* (VAI) It *or* s/he rolls in the snow.

tihtipâpihkesimew *pl.* **tihtipâpihkesimewak** (VTA) S/he rolls them up into a ball, i.e.: yarn.

tihtipinatowân *pl.* **tihtipinatowânak** (NA) A soccer ball. *(Northern). Alt.* **pâkahtowân** *(Plains).*

tihtipinatowew *pl.* **tihtipinatowewak** (VAI) S/he plays football. *(Northern). Alt.* **pâkahtowew** *(Plains).*

tihtipinew (VTA) S/he rolls her/him over.
  tihtipinam (VTI) S/he rolls it over.
  tihtipiniwew (VTA) S/he rolls people over.
  tihtipinikew (VTI) S/he rolls things over.

tihtipinikan *pl.* **tihtipinikana** (NI) A rolling pin; a roller.

tihtipipayihew (VTA) S/he makes them roll.
  tihtipipayitâw (VTI) S/he makes it roll.
  tihtipipayicikew (VTI) S/he makes things roll.

tihtipipayihow *pl.* **tihtipipayihowak** (VAI) S/he rolls herself/himself around on the ground or floor.

tihtipipayiw *pl.* **tihtipipayiwak** *or* **tihtipipayiwa** (VII) *or* (VAI) It is rolling, i.e.: a wheel in motion, *or* s/he is rolling. *(Plains). Alt.* **tihtipayiw** *(Northern).*

tihtipipitew (VTA) S/he pulls and makes her/him roll around.
  tihtipipitam (VTI) S/he makes it roll around.
  tihtipipisiwew (VTA) S/he makes people roll around.
  tihtipipicikew (VTI) S/he makes things roll around.

tihtipisimew (VTA) S/he rolls her/him around, i.e.: in the dust.
  tihtipihtitâw (VTI) S/he rolled it around, i.e.: in the dust.
  tihtipisimiwew (VTA) S/he rolled someone around, i.e.: in the dust.
  tihtipicikew (VTI) S/he rolled things around, i.e.: in the dust.

tihtipisin *pl.* **tihtipisinwak** (VAI) S/he rolls over in a fall.

tihtipitapânâsk *pl.* **tihtipitapânâskwak** (NA) A cart. *(Plains). Alt.* **newokâtew** *(Plains); Var.* **tihtipitâpânâsk** *(Northern).*

tihtipitâpânâsk *pl.* **tihtipitâpânâskwak** (NA) A wagon. *(Northern). Alt.* **newokâtew, tihtipitapânâsk** *(Plains).*

tihtipiw *pl.* **tihtipiwak** (VAI) S/he rolls over, i.e.: an animal.

tikinewin *pl.* **tikinewina** (NI) The state of being out of one's mind, i.e.: unconsciousness. *(Northern). Alt.* **waneyihtamowin** *(Plains).*

timaskâw (VII) The grass is deep, high or long.

timâkonakâw (VII) The snow is deep all over. *(Northern). Var.* **timikoniw** *(Northern); Alt.* **timikoniw** *(Plains).*

timikoniw (VII) The snow is deep. *(Plains and Northern variant). Alt.* **timâkonakâw** *(Northern).*

timîw (VII) It is deep, i.e.: water.

tipahamawew (VTA) S/he pays her/him or them.
  tipahamakew (VTA) S/he paid everyone.

tipahamâkestamawew *pl.* **tipahamâkestamawewak** (VTA) S/he pays her/his way for her/him. *(Northern). Alt.* **tipahikestamawew** *(Plains).*

tipahamâkew *pl.* **tipahamâkewak** (NA) Someone who pays.

tipahamâkewin *pl.* **tipahamâkewina** (NI) A payment.

tipahamâkosiw *pl.* **tipahamâkosiwak** (VAI) S/he has been paid.

tipahamâkosiwin *pl.* **tipahamâkosiwina** (NI) The act of receiving a payment; being paid.

tipahamâtowin *pl.* **tipahamâtowina** (NI) The act of paying a bounty; treaty rights.

tipahaskân (NI) An Aboriginal Reserve; a reservation.

tipahaskewin *pl.* **tipahaskewina** (NI) A cut line.

tipahâkâtew (VTA) S/he imitates her/him; s/he follows someone else's ideas.
  tipahâkâtam (VTI) S/he imitates it.
  tipahâkâsiwew (VTA) S/he imitates people.
  tipahâkâcikew (VTI) S/he imitates everything.

tipahikan *pl.* **tipahikana** (NI) An hour; a unit of measurement equaling a yard.

tipahikanâhtik (NI) A measuring device, i.e.: a ruler.

tipahikepayihcikan *pl.* **tipahikepayihcikana** (NI) Retribution.

tipahikepayihcikewin *pl.* **tipahikepayihcikewina** (NI) The act of paying someone back; vengence; retribution.

tipahikepayihtâwin *pl.* **tipahikepayihtâwina** (NI) The act of imposing a punishment, tax, or duty; imposition.

tipahikestamawew *pl.* **tipahikestamawewak** (VTA) S/he pays her/his way for her/him. *(Plains). Alt.* **tipahamâkestamawew** *(Northern).*

tipahikestamâkewin *pl.* **tipahikestamâkewina** (NI) The act of posting bail for someone; bailable; providing a bond.

tipahikew *pl.* **tipahikewak** (VAI) S/he pays.

tipahikewin *pl.* **tipahikewina** (NI) The act of paying; the act of compensating.

tipahikewin *pl.* **tipahikewina** (NI) The act of taking a measurement or dimensions. *(Plains). Alt.* **tepapekinkewin** *(Northern).*

tipahikwewin *pl.* **tipahikwewina** (NI) The act of paying amounts due; remittance.

tipahipîsimwân *pl.* **tipahipîsimwâna** (NI) A monthly calendar.

tipahwew (VTA) S/he has sufficient resources for all of them; s/he makes a measurement sufficient to her/his size.
  tipaham (VTI) S/he has enough for all of it.
  tipahowew (VTA) S/he has enough for all of the people.

tipahwew (VTA) S/he measures her/him or it by the arm length (i.e.: Cree measurement system). *Alt.* **tipiniskâtew** *(Northern).*
  tipahtam (VTI) S/he measures it by the arm length.
  tipahsiwew (VTA) S/he measures people by the arm length.
  tipahcikew (VTI) S/he measures things by the arm length.

tipahwew (VTI) S/he paid it for her/him.
  tipaham (VTI) S/he paid it for it.
  tipahowew (VTI) S/he paid it for others.
  tipahikew (VTI) S/he paid it for everyone.

tipakimew (VTA) S/he totals them all up.
  tipakihtam (VTI) S/he totals all of it up.
  tipakimiwew (VTA) S/he totals all of the people up.
  tipakihcikew (VTA) S/he totals all of everything up.

tipakimow *pl.* **tipakimowak** (VAI) S/he judges or condemns.

tipaweham *pl.* **tipawehamwa** (VTI) S/he curls it.

tipawehamawew *pl.* **tipawehamawewak** (VTA) S/he curls her/his hair.

tipawehamâkan *pl.* **tipawehamâkana** (NI) A hair curler or roller.

tipâham *pl.* **tipâhama** (VTI) S/he pays for it.

tipâhamakestamakewin *pl.* **tipâhamakestamakewina** (NI) The act of paying the way for someone.

tipâhâkew *pl.* **tipâhâkewak** (VAI) S/he mimicks her/him; s/he follows her/his actions.

tipâhew (VTA) S/he acts according to her/his influence.
  tipâtâw (VTI) S/he acts according to its influence.
  tipâhiwew (VTA) S/he acts according to others' influence.

tipâpân *pl.* **tipâpâna** (NI) A line for measuring. *(Northern). Alt.* **tipâpâniyâpiy** *(Plains).*

tipâpâniyâpiy *pl.* **tipâpâniyâpiya** (NI) A line for measuring. *(Plains). Alt.* **tipâpân** *(Northern).*

tipâpâtew (VTI) S/he measure them with a string or line, i.e.: fish nets.
  tipâpâtam (VTI) S/he measures it with a tape measure.

tipâpâsiwew (VTA) S/he measures people with a tape measure.

tipâpâcikew (VTI) S/he measures things with a tape measure.

tipâpekinikan *pl.* **tipâpekinikana** (NI) A measure of length.

tipâpeskohew (VTI) S/he weighs them.
  tipâpeskohtâw (VTI) S/he weighs it.
  tipâpeskohiwew (VTA) S/he weighs people.
  tipâpeskohcikew (VTI) S/he weighs things.

tipâpeskôcikan *pl.* **tipâpeskôcikana** (NI) A scale.

tipekisimew (VAI) S/he lays her/him down all wrapped up.
  tipekihtitâw (VTI) S/he lays it down all wrapped up.
  tipekisimiwew (VTA) S/he lays someone down all wrapped up.

tipekisin *pl.* **tipekisinwak** (VAI) S/he lies all wrapped up.

tipekîw *pl.* **tipekîwak** (VTA) S/he wraps herself/himself up, i.e.: in a blanket.

tipeyicikew *pl.* **tipeyicikewak** (VAI) S/he is owner of everything and everyone.

tipeyicikiwina (NI) Assets. *(Northern). Var.* **pamihowina** *(Northern); Alt.* **pamihowina** *(Plains).*

tipeyicikîwin *pl.* **tipeyicikîwina** (NI) The act of owning something; domain. *(Northern). Var.* **pamihowina** *(Northern); Alt.* **pamihowina** *(Plains).*

tipeyihtam (VTI) S/he owns it.
  tipeyimiwew (VTA) S/he owns people.
  tipeyicikew (VTI) S/he owns things.

tipeyihtamawew (VTA) S/he owns it for her/him.
  tipeyihtamakew (VTI) S/he owns it for everyone.

tipeyihtâkosiw *pl.* **tipeyihtâkosiwak** (VAI) S/he is owned.

tipeyimew *pl.* **tipeyimewak** (VTA) S/he owns her/him.

tipeyimisiw *pl.* **tipeyimisiwak** (VAI) S/he owns herself/himself; s/he is her/his own boss; s/he is free.

tipeyimisowin *pl.* **tipeyimisowina** (NI) The act of being one's own boss.

tipeyimowew *pl.* **tipeyimowewak** (VAI) S/he owns everyone.

tipeyitamohew (VTA) S/he gives her/him ownership.
  tipeyitamohtâw (VTI) S/he gives it ownership.
  tipeyitamohiwew (VTA) S/he gives people ownership.
  tipeyitamohewak (VTA) They give her/him or them ownership.

tipeyitâkwan *pl.* **tipeyitâkwanwa** (VII) It is owned.

tipihew (VTA) S/he is her/his equal; s/he keeps up with her/him; s/he is even with her/him, or tied with her/him, i.e.: race.
  tipitâw (VTI) S/he is its equal.
  tipihiwew (VTA) S/he is their equal, i.e.: people.

211

tipihtwâw *pl.* **tipihtwâwak** (VAI) S/he has equal
capabilities; s/he is able to keep up.

tipikwâcikan *pl.* **tipikwâcikana** (NI) A hem.

tipikwâsiw *pl.* **tipikwâsiwak** (VAI) S/he sews a hem.

tipikwâtew (VTA) S/he hems it.

   tipikwâtam (VTI) S/he hems it.

   tipikwâcikew (VTI) S/he hems things.

tipinahokân *pl.* **tipinahokâna** (NI) A shelter from the
cold. *(Northern)*. *Alt.* **tipinawâhokân** *(Plains)*.

tipinawahikan *pl.* **tipinawahikana** (NI) A shelter from
wind.

tipinawâham *pl.* **tipinawâhamwa** (VTI) S/he shelters it
from wind.

tipinawâhew (VAI) S/he makes shelters for others.

   tipinawâham (VII) S/he makes shelters for it.

   tipinawâhowew (VAI) S/he makes shelters for people.

   tipinawâhikew (VII) S/he makes shelters for things.

tipinawâhokân *pl.* **tipinawâhokâna** (NI) A shelter from
the cold. *(Plains)*. *Alt.* **tipinahokân** *(Northern)*.

tipinawâsimiw *pl.* **tipinawâsimiwak** (VAI) S/he stays
some place sheltered free of cold and wind.

tipinawâsimowin *pl.* **tipinawâsimowina** (NI) The act of
staying some place where it is sheltered.

tipinawâw (VII) It is a sheltered area away from the wind
and cold.

tipiniskâtew (VTA) S/he measures her/him or it by the
arm length (i.e.: Cree measurement system).
(Northern). *Alt.* **tipahwew** *(Plains)*.

   tipiniskâtam (VTI) S/he measures it by the arm length.

   tipiniskâsiwew (VTA) S/he measures people by the
   arm length.

   tipiniskâcikew (VTI) S/he measures things by the arm
   length.

tipiskâw (VII) It is night.

tipiskâw pîsim (NA) The moon.

tipiskâwimîcisiw *pl.* **tipiskâwimîcisiwak** (VAI) S/he has
a meal at night.

tipiskâwimîcisiwin *pl.* **tipiskâwimîcisiwina** (NI) A night
meal.

tipiskisiw *pl.* **tipiskisiwak** (VTA) S/he stayed overnight.

tipiskisowin *pl.* **tipiskisowina** (NI) The act of staying
overnight.

tipiskocahew (VTA) S/he evens them up. *(Northern)*. *Alt.*
tipiskôtahew *(Plains)*.

   tipiskocastâw (VTI) S/he puts it even.

   tipiskocascikew (VTI) S/he puts things even.

tipiskocihew (VTA) S/he makes her/him an equal; s/he is
even with her/him.

   tipiskocihiwew (VTA) S/he makes people equal; s/he
   is even with people.

   tipiskociascikew (VTA) S/he makes things equal.

   tipiskocitâw (VTI) S/he is even with it.

tipiskocipayihew (VTA) S/he makes her/him even.

   tipiskocipayitâw (VTI) S/he makes it even.

   tipiskocipayihiwew (VTA) S/he makes people even.

   tipiskocipayicikew (VTI) S/he makes things even.

tipiskohk (LN) Last night.

tipiskôcipayiw (VII) It comes out even; it went evenly.

tipiskôtahew (VTA) S/he evens them up. *(Plains)*. *Alt.*
tipiskocahew *(Northern)*.

   tipiskôtastâw (VTI) S/he puts it even.

   tipiskôtascikew (VTI) S/he puts things even.

tipiyaw nîcisân (NA) A full sibling; a full brother or
sister.

tipiyawehew (VAI) S/he has sufficient to give to him/
her.

   tipiyawehtâw (VII) S/he has sufficient to give to it,
   i.e.: a dog.

   tipiyawehiwew (VAI) S/he has sufficient to give to
   people.

tipiyawehew (VTA) S/he makes her/him the owner.

   tipiyawetâw (VTI) S/he makes it the owner.

   tipiyawehiwew (VTA) S/he makes people the owner.

tipiyawehiw *pl.* **tipiyawehiwak** (VAI) S/he has her/his
own.

tipiyawehona (NI) Belongings.

tipiyawehowisowin *pl.* **tipiyawehowisowina** (NI) An
ownership. *(Plains)*. *Alt.* **tipiyawesowin** *(Northern)*.

tipiyawesowin *pl.* **tipiyawesowina** (NI) An ownership.
(Northern). *Alt.* **tipiyawehowisowim** *(Plains)*.

tipiyicikîw *pl.* **tipiyicikîwak** (VAI) S/he owns things.
(Northern). *Var.* **pamihow** *(Northern)*; *Alt.*
pamihow *(Plains)*.

tîyapiw *pl.* **tîyapiwak** (VAI) S/he has aching eyes.

tîyâpitew *pl.* **tîyâpitewak** (VAI) S/he has a toothache;
s/he has an aching tooth.

tocikatew *pl.* **tocikatewa** (VII) It is done.

tocikâsiw *pl.* **tocikâsiwak** (VAI) It was done to her/him.

tohiw *pl.* **tohiwak** (VAI) It lands, i.e.: a bird; alights. *Var.*
itwehiw.

tohkapiw *pl.* **tohkapiwak** (VAI) S/he sits with her/his
legs spread out.

tohkinew (VTI) S/he spreads them out.

   tohkinam (VTI) S/he spreads it out.

tohkipayiw *pl.* **tohkipayiwa** *or* **tohkipayiwak** (VII) *or*
(VAI) It *or* s/he falls spread eagle.

tohototawew (VTA) S/he lands or descends on or near
her/him, i.e.: a bird.

   tohototatam (VTI) S/he lands on it, i.e.: a bird on a
   nest.

   tohototatâkew (VTA) S/he lands on someone, i.e.: a
   bird.

tohtôsâpoy *pl.* **tohtôsâpoya** (NI) Milk.

tohtôsâpowahtik *pl.* **tohtôsâpowahtikwak** (NA) A common milkweed. *Var.* **totosapowatik**.

tohtôsâpowikamik *pl.* **tohtôsâpowikamikwa** (NI) A milk shed or dairy.

tohtôsâpowipimihkew *pl.* **tohtôsâpowipimihkewak** (VAI) S/he is making butter.

tohtôsâpôwipimîy *pl.* **tohtôsâpôwipimîya** (NI) Butter.

tostokan *pl.* **tostokanwa** (NI) A marshy area.

tômacâpinew *pl.* **tômacâpinewak** (VTA) S/he applies oily or greasy cosmetics to her/his eye.

tômacâpinisiw *pl.* **tômacâpinisiwak** (VAI) S/he applies oily or greasy cosmetics to her/his own eyes.

tômapiskinew (VTI) S/he greases it, i.e.: a frying pan.

  tômapiskinam (VTI) S/he greases it, i.e.: a knife.

  tômapiskinikew (VTI) S/he greases things.

tômaskwan *pl.* **tômaskwana** (VII) It is greasy.

tômastenew (VTA) S/he rubs grease all over the other person's body.

  tômastenam (VTA) S/he rubs grease all over it.

  tômasteniwew (VTA) S/he rubs grease all over people.

  tômastenikew (VTA) S/he rubs grease all over bodies.

tômâpohkew *pl.* **tômâpohkewak** (VAI) S/he makes a greasy soup.

tômâskonew (VTA) S/he greases the whole length of it.

  tômâskonam (VTI) S/he greases the whole length of it.

  tômâskonikew (VTI) S/he greases the whole length of things.

tômâw *pl.* **tômâwa** (VII) It is greasy or oily.

tômicihcenew (VTA) S/he greases someone's hands.

  tômicihceniwew (VTA) S/he greases people's hands.

  tômicihcenikew (VTA) S/he greases hands.

tômicihcenisiw *pl.* **tômicihcenisiwak** (VTA) S/he greases her/his own hands.

tômihew (VTI) S/he makes them greasy.

  tômihtâw (VTI) S/he makes it greasy.

  tômihiwew (VTA) S/he makes people greasy.

  tômihcikew (VTI) S/he makes things greasy.

tômihiw *pl.* **tômihiwak** (VTA) S/he makes herself/himself greasy.

tômihkwenew (VTA) S/he greases someone else's face.

  tômihkwenam (VTI) S/he greases the face of it.

  tômihkweniwew (VTA) S/he greases the face of someone.

  tômihkwenikew (VTI) S/he greases the face of things.

tômihkwew *pl.* **tômihkwewak** (VAI) Her/his face is greasy, or s/he is applying lotion.

tôminew (VTA) S/he greases them; s/he anoints them.

  tôminam (VTI) S/he greases it.

  tôminiwew (VTA) S/he greases someone.

  tôminikew (VTI) S/he greases things.

tôminikan *pl.* **tôminikana** (NI) A grease or an ointment; a lubricant; a salve.

tôminikâkan *pl.* **tôminikâkana** (NI) A lubricator.

tôminikâkew *pl.* **tôminikâkewak** (VTA) S/he greases it with something.

tôminisiw *pl.* **tôminisiwak** (VTA) S/he applies salve to herself/himself.

tômisitenew (VTA) S/he greases her/his feet.

  tômisiteniwew (VTA) S/he grease peoples' feet.

  tômisitenikew (VTA) S/he greases feet.

tômisitenisiw *pl.* **tômisitenisiwak** (VTA) S/he greases her/his own feet.

tômisiw *pl.* **tômisiwak** (VAI) S/he is greasy.

tômistikwanâkan *pl.* **tômistikwanâkana** (NI) A hair grease or cream.

tômistikwanenew (VTA) S/he greases her/his head.

  tômistikwanenam (VTI) S/he grease the head of it.

  tômistikwaneniwew (VTA) S/he greases the head of people.

  tômistikwanenikew (VTA) S/he greases the head of others.

tômistikwânenisiw *pl.* **tômistikwânenisiwak** (VTA) S/he greases her/his own head.

tômistikwânew *pl.* **tômistikwânewak** (VAI) Her/his head is greasy.

tôneyâw *pl.* **tôneyâwa** (VII) It is open, i.e.: a shirt collar.

tôskwahikewin *pl.* **tôskwahikewina** (NI) The act of prodding.

tôtam *pl.* **tôtamwak** (VAI) S/he does it.

tôtamawew (VTA) S/he does it for her/him.

  tôtamakew (VTA) S/he does it for others.

  tôtamawewak (VTA) They do it for her/him or them.

tôtamâkewin *pl.* **tôtamâkewina** (NI) The act of doing it for others; react.

tôtamohiwewin *pl.* **tôtamohiwewina** (NI) The act of forcing someone to act.

tôtawew (VTA) S/he does it to her/him.

  tôtatâkew (VTA) S/he does it for people.

twahipanihkew *pl.* **twahipanihkewak** (VAI) S/he is making a hole in the ice.

twahipew *pl.* **twahipewak** (VAI) S/he made a hole in the ice.

twawew (VTA) S/he is chopping a hole in the ice to get it out, i.e.: a beaver in a trap under the ice.

  twaham (VTA) S/he chops a hole in the ice.

  twahikew (VTA) S/he is making a hole in the ice.

twâhikan *pl.* **twâhikana** (NI) Something used to make a hole on ice; an auger.

twâhipâkan *pl.* **twâhipâkana** (NI) Needlepoint.

twâhipân *pl.* **twâhipâna** (NI) A hole drilled in the ice; a blow hole.

twâkonehwew (VAI) S/he makes a hole in the snow for someone. *(Northern). Alt.* **nitwakonewew** *(Plains).*

213

twâkoneham (VAI) S/he makes an opening or pathway in the snow.

twâkonehowew (VAI) S/he makes an opening in the snow for people.

twâkonehikew (VTI) S/he makes an opening in the snow for things.

twâkonesin *pl.* **twâkonesinwak** (VAI) S/he fell through the crusty snow.

twâsimew (VTA) S/he caused something or someone to fall through the ice.

twâsimiwew (VTA) S/he caused people to fall through the ice.

twâsicikew (VTI) S/he caused things to fall through the ice.

twâsin *pl.* **twâsinwak** (VAI) S/he fell through the ice.

W

wacask *pl.* wacaskwak (NA) A muskrat.

wacaskomicisowin *pl.* wacaskomicisowina (NI) Sweet flag or rat root.

wacaskowâtih *pl.* wacaskowâtiha (NI) A muskrat hole.

wacaskwayân *pl.* wacaskwayânak (NA) A muskrat skin.

wacihkameyihtam *pl.* wacihkameyihtamwak (VAI) S/he has unrestrained enthusiasm about something.

wacihkameyimew (VTA) S/he thinks of her/him as unrestrained.

wacihkameyitam (VTA) S/he thinks in an undisciplined manner.

wacihkameyimiwew (VTA) S/he has an unorthodox conception of people.

wacihkamisiw *pl.* wacihkamisiwak (VAI) S/he is off the wall, i.e.: unrestrained.

wacihkamisiwin *pl.* wacihkamisiwina (NI) The act of being off the wall, i.e.: unrestrained.

wacikâpahkitek (NA) An exploding mountain, i.e.: a volcano.

waciston *pl.* wacistona (NI) A bird nest. *(Plains). Alt.* wacistwan *(Northern).*

wacistonihkew *pl.* wacistonihkewak (VAI) S/he makes a nest; s/he is nesting. *(Plains). Alt.* wacistwanihkew *(Northern).*

wacistwan *pl.* wacistwana (NI) A bird nest. *(Northern). Alt.* waciston *(Plains).*

wacistwanihkew *pl.* wacistwanihkewak (VAI) S/he makes a nest; s/he is nesting. *(Northern)*

waciwahtik *pl.* waciwahtikwak (NA) A mountain ash tree. *(Northern). Alt.* maskominânâhtik *(Plains).*

waciwaskiy *pl.* waciwaskiya (NI) Upland.

waciy *pl.* waciya (NI) A mountain.

wacîwiw *pl.* wacîwiwya (VII) There is a mountain.

wahkepinewin *pl.* wahkepinewina (NI) Being vulnerable; vulnerability. *(Plains). Alt.* kakecisayawin *(Northern)*

wahkewisiw *pl.* wahkewisiwak (VAI) S/he is highly temperamental; s/he is skitterish.

wahkewisowin *pl.* wahkewisowina (NI) Being highly temperamental; fragility; sensitivity.

wahkewiyawesiw *pl.* wahkewiyawesiwak (VAI) S/he has a quick temper.

wahkewiyawesowin *pl.* wahkewiyawesowina (NI) Being hot-tempered; having a quick temper.

wahkohtahew (VTA) S/he makes him part of the family.

wahkohtahiwew (VTA) S/he makes people part of the family related.

wahkohtahisiw *pl.* wahkohtahisiwak (VTA) S/he makes herself/himself part of the family.

wahkohtowak (VAI) They are related to each other.

wahkohtowin *pl.* wahkohtowina (NI) The act of being related to each other; offspring or descendant.

wahkomâkan *pl.* wahkomâkanak (NA) A cousin; a relative; a kinsman.

wahkomew (VTA) S/he is related or connected to her/him.

wahkotam (VTA) S/he is related or connected to the family.

wahkomiwew (VTA) S/he is related or connected to the people.

wahkomowewin *pl.* wahkomowewina (NI) The act of being a relative.

wahwanahew (VTA) S/he is continually misplacing her/him.

wahwanastâw (VTI) S/he is continually misplacing it.

wahwanahiwew (VTA) S/he is continually misplacing people.

wahwanascikew (VTI) S/he is continually misplacing things.

wahwâkamiw *pl.* wahwâkamiwa (VII) It curves a lot, i.e.: the road; it is winding.

wahwâkasinahikewin *pl.* wahwâkasinahikewina (NI) The act of squiggling or curving.

wahwâkihtin *pl.* wahwâkihtinwa (VII) It curves a lot, i.e.: river.

wahwâkistikweyâw *pl.* wahwâkistikweyâwa (VII) The river has a lot of curves or bends.

wahwâyahcâw *pl.* wahwâyahcâwa (NI) An area of ground with many dips.

wakinew (VTA) S/he bends her/him.

wakinam (VTI) S/he bends it.

wakiniwew (VTA) S/he bends people.

wakinikew (VTI) S/he bends things.

wanamiw *pl.* wanamiwak (VAI) S/he flees the wrong way.

wanaskocihcân *pl.* wanaskocihcâna (NI) The tip of a finger.

wanaskocihcew *pl.* wanaskocihcewak (NA) The tip of a hand.

wanaskwatanask *pl.* wanaskwatanaskwak (NA) A tree top.

wanaskwâhtak *pl.* wanaskwâhtakwa (NI) The tip or top of a pole or piece of wood.

wanastew (VII) It is misplaced or not in its proper place.

wanâhew (VTA) S/he disrupts her/him.

wanâtâw (VTI) S/he disrupts it.

wanâhiwew (VTA) S/he disrupts people.

wanâhcikew (VTI) S/he disrupts things.

215

wanâhikowin *pl.* **wanâhikowina** (NI) Being bewildered; bewilderment.

wanâhiwewin *pl.* **wanâhiwewina** (NI) The act of being bewildered by someone; being beguiled; becloud; confusion; engross.

wanâmew (VTA) Her/his talking disrupts her/him.
  wanâtam (VTA) S/he disrupts the speech.
  wanâmiwew (VTA) S/he disrupts the people.
  wanâhcikew (VTI) S/he disrupts the things.

wanâmowin *pl.* **wanâmowina** (NI) The act of running or fleeing the wrong way.

wanâpamew (VTA) S/he loses sight of her/him.
  wanâpahtam (VTI) S/he loses sight of it.
  wanâpahkew (VTA) S/he loses sight of people.
  wanâpahcikew (VTI) S/he loses sight of things.

wanehkâtew *pl.* **wanehkâtewak** (VTA) S/he miscalls her/him, i.e.: uses the wrong name.

wanew *pl.* **wanewak** (VAI) S/he is amusing; mischievious.

wanewin *pl.* **wanewina** (NI) Having an amusing character.

wanewisâyâwin *pl.* **wanewisâyâwina** (NI) Being jocular.

wanewitonâmowin *pl.* **wanewitonâmowina** (NI) The act of chatting; blithering; joking.

waneyihtam *pl.* **waneyihtamak** (VAI) S/he is at a loss; s/he does not know what to do. *(Plains). Alt.* **waneyimiw** *(Northern).*

waneyihtamohiwewin *pl.* **waneyihtamohiwewina** (NI) The act of deranging or perplexing; peplexity.

waneyihtamowin *pl.* **waneyihtamowina** (NI) The act of thinking in a baffling manner; bafflement; the state of being out of one's mind, i.e.: unconsciousness. *(Plains). Alt.* **tikinewin** *(Northern).*

waneyimew *pl.* **waneyimewak** (VAI) S/he is at a loss with her/him; s/he does not know what to do with her/him. *(Northern). Alt.* **wâneyihtamihik** *(Plains).*

waneyimiw *pl.* **waneyimiwak** (VAI) S/he is at a loss; s/he does not know what to do. *(Northern). Alt.* **waneyihtam** *(Plains).*

wanihew (VTA) S/he loses her/him or them.
  wanihiwew (VTA) S/he loses people.
  wanihcikew (VTI) S/he loses things.

wanihikamawew *pl.* **wanihikamawewak** (VTA) S/he sets a trap for her/him or them.

wanihikan *pl.* **wanihikana** (NI) A trap.

wanihikew *pl.* **wanihikewak** (VAI) S/he sets traps.

wanihitowin *pl.* **wanihitowina** (NI) The act of losing each other.

wanihow *pl.* **wanihowak** (VAI) S/he lost her/his way.

wanihowin *pl.* **wanihowina** (NI) The act of being lost; disappearance.

wanihtam *pl.* **wanihtamak** (VAI) S/he heard it the wrong way.

wanihtin *pl.* **wanihtinwa** (VII) It is misplaced.
  wanastew *pl.* **wanastewa** (VII) It does not belong.

wanikiskisiw *pl.* **wanikiskisiwak** (VAI) S/he forgot.

wanikiskisiwin *pl.* **wanikiskisiwina** (NI) The act of forgetting.

wanikiskisototawew (VTA) S/he forgot all about him.
  wanikiskisototam (VTI) S/he forgot all about it.
  wanikiskisototâkew (VTA) S/he forgets people.

wanimestinikewin *pl.* **wanimestinikewina** (NI) The act of misspending.

wanimetawew *pl.* **wanimetawewak** (VAI) S/he makes the wrong move or misplays.

wanimitimew *pl.* **wanimitimewak** (VAI) S/he is lost and follows the wrong trail.

waninawew (VTA) S/he mistakes her/him for someone else; s/he is amusing.
  waninam (VTI) S/he mistakes it.
  waninâkew (VTA) S/he mistakes people.

waninewâtisiw *pl.* **waninewâtisiwak** (VAI) S/he is an amusing character.

wanipayihcikewin *pl.* **wanipayihcikewina** (NI) The act of mixing everything up; a mix-up.

wanipicikewin *pl.* **wanipicikewina** (NI) The act of deviating from the set course; deviation.

wanipîkiskwewin *pl.* **wanipîkiskwewina** (NI) The act of speaking incorrectly; misspoken.

wanisihcikewin *pl.* **wanisihcikewina** (NI) The act of defacing; defacement.

wanisihew (VTI) S/he bungles them.
  wanisihtâw (VTI) S/he bungles it.
  wanisihiwew (VTA) S/he bungles with people; s/he makes them go the wrong way.

wanisimew *pl.* **wanisimewak** (VTA) S/he makes her/him lose her/his way.

wanisin *pl.* **wanisinwak** (VAI) S/he is lost.

wanisinowin *pl.* **wanisinowina** (NI) The act of losing one's way; being lost.

wanisitohtamowin *pl.* **wanisitohtamowina** (NI) The act of misunderstanding.

waniskam *pl.* **waniskamwak** (VAI) S/he makes too many tracks.

waniskânamawew (VTA) S/he lifts it up for him, i.e.: a telephone pole.
  waniskânamakew (VTA) S/he lifts it up for people.

waniskânew (VTA) S/he assists her/him in sitting up from bed; s/he assists her/him in getting set up in business.
  waniskânam (VTI) S/he assists it in sitting up.
  waniskâniwew (VTA) S/he assists people in sitting up.
  waniskânikew (VTI) S/he assists them in sitting up.

waniskâw *pl.* **waniskâwak** (VAI) S/he rises; s/he gets up out of bed.

waniskâwin *pl.* **waniskâwina** (NI) The act of rising or getting up out of bed.

wanitipiskanohk (LN) In the dark.

wanitipiskâw (VII) It is dark outside.

wanitipiskinam *pl.* **wanitipiskinamwak** (VAI) S/he makes it go dark; s/he turns the light off; s/he blacked out.

wanitipiskinamawew *pl.* **wanitipiskinamawewak** (VTA) S/he makes it dark for him.

wanitipiskipayiw (VII) It went dark suddenly.

wanitipiskisiw *pl.* **wanitipiskisiwak** (VAI) It went dark on her/him.

wanitôtam *pl.* **wanitôtamwak** (VAI) S/he does the wrong thing, i.e.: makes a mistake.

wanitôtamowin *pl.* **wanitôtamowina** (NI) The act of doing the wrong thing, or a mistake; a wicked doing or action, i.e.: a misdeed.

waniyiw *pl.* **waniyiwak** (VAI) S/he makes a mistake.

wanîkâsowin *pl.* **wanîkâsowina** (NI) The act of using a false name.

wanohtahiwewin *pl.* **wanohtahiwewina** (NI) The act of getting someone lost, i.e.: misleading.

wanotinikewin *pl.* **wanotinikewina** (NI) The act of making a mistake or having a misdealing.

wanowew *pl.* **wanowewak** (VAI) S/he provides incorrect facts, i.e.: a slip of the tongue.

wanowewin *pl.* **wanowewina** (NI) The act of providing incorrect facts, i.e.: "a slip of the tongue"; misquote; misleading statement.

wapahtihew (VTA) S/he shows it to her/him.
 wapahtihiwew (VTA) S/he shows it to people.

wapahtihikosiwin *pl.* **wapahtihikosiwina** (NI) The act of being shown something; a lesson.

wapahtihiwewin *pl.* **wapahtihiwewina** (NI) The act of displaying or showing; demonstration; display; rendition.

wapahtowak (VTA) They see each other.

wapakâw *pl.* **wapakâwa** (VII) It is flattened. *(Plains). Alt.* **samakâw** *(Northern).*

wapiwin *pl.* **wapiwina** (NI) The act of seeing; vision.

wapîhew (VTA) S/he makes her/him see.
 wapîhiwew (VTA) S/he makes people see.

wasakay *pl.* **wasakayak** (NA) A piece of skin. *(Northern). Alt.* **masakay** *(Plains).*

wasakânew (VTA) S/he builds a fence around them.
 wasakânam (VTI) S/he builds a fence around it.
 wasakâniwew (VTA) S/he builds a fence around people.
 wasakânikew (VTI) S/he builds a fence around things.

wasakânikanpiwâpisk *pl.* **wasakânikanpiwâpiskwa** (NI) Barded wire.

wasas *pl.* **wasasa** (NI) An inlet; a pocket of dead water. *(Northern). Alt.* **pihcâpekos** *(Plains).*

wasaskwecôs *pl.* **wasaskwecôsak** (NA) A pinecone.

wasaskwetiw *pl.* **wasaskwetiwak** (NA) A fungus on a tree.

wasepescan *pl.* **wasepescanak** (NA) A meadowlark. *(Northern). Alt.* **opîscîwâcikwasow** *(Plains).*

wasihkopayowin *pl.* **wasihkopayowina** (NI) Being radiant; radiance; resplendance; scintillation.

wasihkwekahwew (VAI) S/he blazes a trail through the bush; s/he places indicating marks on the trees.
 wasihkwekaham (VTI) S/he blazes it.
 wasihkwekahikew (VAI) S/he blazes a trail through them.

waskatamiw *pl.* **waskatamiwak** (NA) A yellow pond lily.

waskatay *pl.* **waskataywa** (NI) The skin around the stomach of an animal. *(Plains). Alt.* **waskatayekin** *(Northern).*

waskatayekin *pl.* **waskatayekinwa** (NI) The skin around the stomach of an animal. *(Northern). Alt.* **waskatay** *(Plains).*

waskawâkamipayiw *pl.* **waskawâkamipayiwa** (VII) The water moves, i.e.: around a beaver house.

waskawinew (VAI) S/he moves her/him or them.
 waskawinam (VTI) S/he moves it.
 waskawiniwew (VTA) S/he moves people.
 waskawinikew (VTI) S/he moves things.

waskawipayihew (VTA) S/he makes her/him move by shaking her/him.
 waskawipayitâw (VTI) S/he makes it move by shaking her/him.
 waskawipayihiwew (VTA) S/he makes people move by shaking them.
 waskawipayihcikew (VTI) S/he makes things move by shaking them.

waskawipayiw *pl.* **waskawipayiwa** *or* **waskawipayiwak** (VTI) *or* (VTA) It *or* s/he moves.

waskawipitew (VTA) S/he moves her/him by shaking her/him.
 waskawipitam (VTI) S/he move it by shaking it.
 waskawipisiwew (VTA) S/he moves people by shaking them.
 waskawipihcikew (VTI) S/he move things by shaking them.

waskawîhew (VTA) S/he makes her/him move herself/himself.
 waskawîtâw (VTI) S/he makes it move itself.
 waskawîhiwew (VTA) S/he makes people move themselves.
 waskawîhcikew (VTI) S/he makes things move on their own.

waskawîw *pl.* **waskawîwak** (VAI) S/he moves.

waskawîwin *pl.* **waskawîwina** (NI) The act of being active; activity; motion.

217

waskewceses *pl.* **waskewcesesak** (NA) A two-year-old bull moose.

waskicicowan *pl.* **waskicicowanwa** (VII) It flows on top.

waskicipekinam *pl.* **waskicipekinamwak** (VAI) S/he walks on top of the water.

waskicipicikan *pl.* **waskicipicikana** (NI) A jersey; a turtleneck shirt; a sweater.

waskitahew (VTA) S/he places her/him on top.

waskitastâw (VTI) S/he places it on top.

waskitahiwew (VTA) S/he places people on top.

waskitascikew (VTI) S/he places things on top.

waskitahipewin *pl.* **waskitahipewina** (NI) Being bouyant; bouyancy.

waskitapiw *pl.* **waskitapiwak** (VAI) S/he sits on top.

waskitaskamik (IPC) On top of the earth.

waskitastew *pl.* **waskitastewa** (VII) It sits on top.

waskitatenikwan (NI) Crusty snow.

waskitatewenam *pl.* **waskitatewenamwak** (VAI) S/he walks on top, i.e.: of hard snow.

waskitateweyâw (NI) The time of year when one can walk on top of the snow crust.

waskitipew *pl.* **waskitipewa** (VII) It floats on top.

waskiwâkinam *pl.* **waskiwâkinamwa** (VTI) S/he is able to move or bend it into a circle.

waskîw *pl.* **waskîwak** (VAI) S/he turns.

waskotepayiw (VII) There is lightening. *(Northern). Alt.* **wâsaskotepayiw** *(Plains).*

waskôw *pl.* **waskôwa** (NI) A cloud; skies.

waskway *pl.* **waskwayak** (NA) A birch tree.

waskwayahtikoskâw (VII) There are lots of birch in this area.

waskwayakan *pl.* **waskwayakana** (NI) A bowl made from birch bark. *(Northern). Alt.* **waskwayiwiyâkan** *(Plains).*

waskwayâhtik *pl.* **waskwayâhtikwa** (NI) Birch wood.

waskwayâhtik *pl.* **wakwayâhtikwak** (NA) Birch tree.

waskwayâpoy *pl.* **waskwayâpoya** (NI) Birch sap.

waskwayiskâw *pl.* **waskwayiskâwa** (NI) A birch covered area.

waskwayiwiyâkan *pl.* **waskwayiwiyâkana** (NI) A bowl made from birch bark. *(Plains). Alt.* **waskwayakan** *(Northern).*

waskwayosih *pl.* **waskwayosiha** (NI) A birch bark canoe.

waspawehew (VTA) S/he makes a noise and wakes her/him up.

waspawehiwew (VTA) S/he makes a noise and wakes people up.

waspawehiwewin *pl.* **waspawehiwewina** (NI) The act of rousing someone; awakening; rousing.

waspâwemew (VTA) Her/his talking wakes her/him up.

waspâwewitam (VTA) Her/his talking wakes everyone up.

waspâwemiwew (VTA) Her/his talking wakes people up.

waspâwepayiw *pl.* **waspâwepayiwak** (VAI) S/he wakens suddenly.

waspâwepayowin *pl.* **waspâwepayowina** (NI) The act of feeling wakeful, i.e.: insomnia. *(Plains). Alt.* **waspâwisâyâwin** *(Northern).*

waspâwisâyâwin *pl.* **waspâwisâyâwina** (NI) The act of feeling wakeful, i.e.: insomnia. *(Northern). Alt.* **waspâwepayowin** *(Plains).*

waspekahikewin *pl.* **wasepekahikewina** (NI) The act of white-washing something.

waspitew (VTA) S/he laces her/him.

waspitam (VTI) S/he laces it up.

waspisiwew (VTA) S/he laces people.

waspihcikew (VTI) S/he laces things.

watakamisiw *pl.* **watakamisiwak** (VAI) S/he is hot tempered; s/he is easily riled.

watakamisiwin *pl.* **watakamisiwina** (NI) The act of being easily riled; being hot tempered; being tempermental.

watapiwât *pl.* **watapiwâta** (NI) A container made from roots, i.e.: a basket.

watapiwinipewinis *pl.* **watapiwinipewinisak** (NA) A bed made with roots, i.e.: a basinette.

watapiy *pl.* **watapiya** (NI) A tree root.

watapîwiw *pl.* **watapîwiwak** (VAI) It has lots of roots.

watihkân *pl.* **watihkâna** (NI) A cellar.

watihkwan *pl.* **watihkwana** (NI) A limb on a tree.

watihkwaniwiw *pl.* **watihkwaniwiwa** (VII) The tree has plenty of limbs.

watokisiw *pl.* **watokisiwak** (VAI) It is clotted, i.e.: blood on fur.

watow *pl.* **watowak** (NA) A blood clot; clotted blood.

watowiw (VAI) The area has plenty of holes.

wawesihcikewin *pl.* **wawesihcikewina** (NI) The act of making ornaments; ornamentation.

wawesihew (VTA) S/he dresses her/him up; s/he is decorating her/him.

wawesitâw (VTI) S/he dresses it up.

wawesihiwew (VTA) S/he dresses people up.

wawesihcikew (VTA) S/he dresses things up.

wawesihowak *pl.* **wawesihowakak** (VAI) They are dressed up.

wawesihowâkew *pl.* **wawesihowâkewa** (VTI) S/he uses it to dress up.

wawesihtamawew *pl.* **wawesihtamawewa** (VTI) S/he dresses it up for her/him.

wawesihtâw *pl.* **wawesihtâwa** (VTI) S/he decorates it.

wawesiwasâkay *pl.* **wawesiwasâkaya** (NI) A suitcoat; dress-up clothes.

wawesîw *pl.* **wawesîwak** (VAI) S/he dresses up.

wawesîwin *pl.* **wawesîwina** (NI) The act of dressing up.

wawikankan *pl.* **wawikankana** (NI) A backbone; one vertebrae.

wawisihcikan *pl.* **wawisihcikana** (NI) An ornament.

wawitehkasikan *pl.* **wawitehkasikana** (NI) An omelette.

wawiyasasinahikewin *pl.* **wawiyasasinahikewina** (NI) The act of writing funny things.

wawiyasihew (VTA) What s/he did to her/him was deserved.

wawiyasihtâw (VTI) What s/he did to it was deserved.

wawiyasihiwew (VTA) What s/he did to people was deserved.

wawiyasimew (VTA) What s/he said to her/him was deserved.

wawiyasihtam (VTI) What s/he said to it was deserved.

wawiyamiwew (VTA) What s/he said to people was deserved.

wawiyasinawew (VTA) S/he sees her/him as being odd looking.

wawiyasinam (VTI) S/he sees it as being odd looking.

wawiyasinâkew (VTA) S/he sees people as being odd looking.

wawiyatisiw *pl.* **wawiyatisiwak** (VAI) S/he deserves it; serves her/him right.

wawiyatisowin *pl.* **wawiyatisowina** (NI) The act of deserving some negative action.

wawiyâpiskâw *pl.* **wawiyâpiskâwa** (VII) It is circular or round steel.

wawiyâpiskisiw *pl.* **wawiyâpiskisiwak** (VAI) S/he is circular or round.

wawiyehew (VTA) S/he gets her/him ready.

wawiyehtâw (VTI) S/he gets it ready.

wawiyehiwew (VTA) S/he gets people ready.

wawiyesiw *pl.* **wawiyesiwak** (VAI) S/he is round.

wawiyesiwin *pl.* **wawiyesiwina** (NI) Being round.

wawiyesîcikewin *pl.* **wawiyesîcikewina** (NI) The act of doing preparatory work.

wawiyestew *pl.* **wawiyestewa** (VII) It sits in a round or circular shape.

wawiyeyâpiskinew (VAI) S/he makes it round, i.e.: iron.

wawiyeyâpiskinam (VAI) S/he makes it round.

wawiyeyâpiskinikew (VAI) S/he makes iron or steel round.

wawîyew *pl.* **wawîyewak** (VAI) S/he gets ready.

wawîyewin *pl.* **wawîyewina** (NI) The act of getting ready, i.e.: preparation; packing.

wayakay *pl.* **wayakaya** (NI) A fish's scale. *(Northern).* *Alt.* **kinosewayakay** *(Plains).*

wayakesk *pl.* **wayakeskwak** (NA) Tree bark.

wayakeskomanicôs *pl.* **wayakeskomanicôsak** (NA) A bark beetle.

wayasit *pl.* **wayasitak** (NA) A hoof.

wayatew *pl.* **wayatewa** (VII) It is in flames. *(Northern).* *Var.* **kwahkotew** *(Northern)*; *Alt.* **kwahkotew** *(Plains).*

wayawepinikewin *pl.* **wayawepinikewina** (NI) The act of ejecting or pushing out; ejection.

wayawihtahew (VTA) S/he takes her/him outside.

wayawihtâw (VTI) S/he takes it outside.

wayawihiwew (VTA) S/he takes people outside.

wayawihcikew (VTI) S/he takes things outside.

wayawîpahtâw *pl.* **wayawîpahtâwak** (VAI) S/he runs outside.

wayawîpayiw *pl.* **wayawîpayiwa** *or* **wayawîpayiwak** (VII) *or* (VAI) It *or* s/he falls to the outside.

wayawîpitew (VTA) S/he pulls her/him outside.

wayawîpitam (VTI) S/he pulls it outside.

wayawîpisiwew (VTA) S/he pulls people outside.

wayawîpicikew (VTI) S/he pulls things outside.

wayawîskawew *pl.* **wayawîskawewak** (VTA) S/he pushes her/him out with her/his body.

wayawîstawew (VTA) S/he went outside for her/him.

wayawîstam (VTI) S/he went outside for it.

wayawîstâkew (VTA) S/he went outside for people.

wayawîtimâyihk (LN) On the outside.

wayawîtimihk (LN) Outside.

wayawîtisahwew (VTA) S/he sends her/him outside.

wayawîtisaham (VTI) S/he sends it outside.

wayawîtisahowew (VTA) S/he sends people outside.

wayawîtisahikew (VTI) S/he sends things outside.

wayawîtisinew (VTA) S/he hands it to someone on the outside.

wayawîtisinam (VTI) S/he hands it to someone on the outside.

wayawîtisiniwew (VTA) S/he hands people to someone on the outside.

wayawîtisinikew (VTI) S/he hands things to someone on the outside.

wayawîw *pl.* **wayawîwak** (VAI) S/he went outside.

wayawîwepahwew (VTA) S/he sweeps it or them outside.

wayawîwepaham (VTI) S/he sweeps it outside.

wayawîwepahowew (VTA) S/he sweeps them outside.

wayawîwepahikew (VTI) S/he sweeps things outside.

wayawîwepinew (VTA) S/he throws her/him to the outside.

wayawîwepinam (VTI) S/he throws it to the outside.

wayawîwepiniwew (VTA) S/he throws people to the outside.

wayawîwepinikew (VTI) S/he throws things to the outside.

wayawîwin *pl.* **wayawîwina** (NI) The act of going outside.

219

wayawîyahkinew (VTA) S/he pushes her/him outside.

wayawîyahkinam (VTI) S/he pushes it outside.

wayawîyahkiniwew (VTA) S/he pushes people outside.

wayawîyahkinikew (VTI) S/he pushes things outside.

wayawîyâmiw *pl.* **wayawîyâmiwak** (VAI) S/he escapes to the outside.

wayawîyâpahtew *pl.* **wayawîyâpahtewa** (VII) The smoke goes outside.

wayâhiwewin *pl.* **wayâhiwewina** (NI) The act of flustering someone; bestir; invigoration; upheaval.

wayân *pl.* **wayânak** (NA) A piece of fur.

wayesâpiw *pl.* **wayesâpiwak** (VAI) S/he has an eye sickness, i.e.: cataracts.

wayesâpowin *pl.* **wayesâpowina** (NI) An eye sickness, i.e.: cataracts.

wayesihew (VTA) S/he cheats on her/him; s/he betrays her/him.

wayesitâw (VTI) S/he cheats about it.

wayesihiwew (VTA) S/he cheats on people.

wayesihcikew (VTI) S/he cheats about things.

wayesihisiw *pl.* **wayesihisiwak** (VTA) S/he cheats on or betrays herself/himself; s/he is not true to herself/himself.

wayesihisowin *pl.* **wayesihisowina** (NI) The act of cheating on or betraying oneself.

wayesihitowin *pl.* **wayesihitowina** (NI) The act of gyping or cheating someone else.

wayesihiwew *pl.* **wayesihiwewak** (VTA) S/he cheats on or betrays others.

wayesihiwewin *pl.* **wayesihiwewina** (NI) The act of cheating on or betraying others; deception.

wayesihtâwin *pl.* **wayesihtâwina** (NI) The act of pretending to be working hard; simulation.

wayesimew (VTA) S/he cheats on her/him with a lie.

wayesimiwew (VTI) S/he cheats people by means of a lie.

wayesitôtawew (VTA) S/he does some cheating things to her/him.

wayesitôtam (VTA) S/he does some cheating.

wayesitôtâkew (VTA) S/he does some cheating things to people.

wayeskaneyitâkosiw *pl.* **wayeskaneyitâkosiwak** (VAI) S/he is thought of as a mental case.

wayeskanihew (VTA) S/he really confused her/him mentally.

wayeskanihtâw (VTI) S/he really confused it mentally.

wayeskanihiwew (VTA) S/he really confused people mentally.

wayeskâneyimew (VTA) S/he thinks of her/him as a mental case.

wayeskâneyitam (VTI) S/he thinks of it as being mental.

wayeskâneyimiwew (VTA) S/he thinks of people as being mental.

wayeskâneyihcikew (VTI) S/he thinks of things as being mental.

wayeskânihiwewin *pl.* **wayeskânihiwewina** (NI) The act of demobilizing someone.

wayeskânimew (VTA) What s/he said to her/him mentally disturbed her/him.

wayeskânimiwew (VTA) What s/he said about people mentally disturbed them.

wayeskânisiw *pl.* **wayeskânisiwak** (VAI) S/he is mentally confused.

wayeskânisiwin *pl.* **wayeskânisiwina** (NI) The act of being mentally confused.

wâcistakâc (IPC) An exclamation of surprise or disappointment, i.e.: "wow, how about that!" or "oh, my goodness!"

wâhkwan *pl.* **wâhkwanak** *or* **wâhkwana** (NA) *or* (NI) A fish egg.

wâhyaw (IPC) Far away; afar.

wâhyaweskamik (IPC) Far, far away, quite a distance.

wâkâpiskâw *pl.* **wâkâpiskâwa** (VII) The metal is bent.

wâkâpiskisiw *pl.* **wâkâpiskisiwak** (VAI) It is uneven or warped, i.e.: something made of metal such as a frying pan.

wâkâs *pl.* **wâkâsak** (NA) A banana.

wâkâsiw *pl.* **wâkâsiwak** (VAI) It is made crooked by the wind.

wâkâskisiw *pl.* **wâkâskisiwak** (VAI) It goes crooked.

wâkâtewin *pl.* **wâkâtewina** (NI) Being bow-legged. *(Northern). Var.* **wâkikâtewin** *(Northern); Alt.* **wâkikâtewin** *(Plains).*

wâkâyiwew *pl.* **wâkâyiwewak** (VAI) S/he has a crooked tail.

wâkicîkahikan *pl.* **wâkicîkahikana** (NI) A crooked axe.

wâkikâtewin *pl.* **wâkikâtewina** (NI) Being bow-legged. *(Plains and Northern variant). Alt.* **wâkâtewin** *(Northern).*

wâkikihkâw *pl.* **wâkikihkâwak** (VAI) S/he is bent with age.

wâkikocesîs *pl.* **wâkikocesîsak** (NA) A wading bird, i.e.: a curlew.

wâkinâkan *pl.* **wâkinâkanak** (NA) A tamarack tree.

wâkinâkanâhtik *pl.* **wâkinâkanâhtikwa** (NI) Wood from a tamarack.

wâkinâkaniskâw *pl.* **wâkinâkaniskâwa** (VII) There are many tamaracks; it is a tamarack swamp, i.e.: wet muskeg.

wâkinikan *pl.* **wâkinikana** (NI) Something that was bent.

wâkinokew *pl.* **wâkinokewak** (VAI) S/he makes a shelter with bent sticks.

220

wâkipayiw *pl.* **wâkipayiwa** *or* **wâkipayiwak** (VII) *or* (VAI) It *or* s/he bends on its *or* her/his own.

wâkipiskwanew *pl.* **wâkipiskwanewak** (VAI) S/he has a hunched back.

wâkipitew (VTI) S/he bends them by pulling.
  wâkipitam (VTI) S/he pulls it till its bends.
  wâkipisiwew (VTA) S/he pulls people till they bend.
  wâkipicikew (VTI) S/he pulls things till they bend.

wâkisiw *pl.* **wâkisiwak** (VAI) S/he is bent or stooped; s/he is crooked or untrustworthy.

wâkiteskanew *pl.* **wâkiteskanewak** (VAI) S/he has crooked horns.

wâkîw *pl.* **wâkîwak** (VAI) S/he bends her/his own body.

wânahahtew (VTI) S/he loses the tracks s/he was following.
  wânahahtam (VTI) S/he loses its track.
  wânahahcikew (VTI) S/he loses their tracks.

wânahamew *pl.* **wânahamewak** (VAI) S/he took the wrong trail and s/he loses her/his way.

wâneyihtam *pl.* **wâneyihtamwak** (VAI) S/he is worried; distracted.

wâneyihtamasowewin *pl.* **wâneyihtamasowewina** (NI) The act of being arbitrary or random.

wâneyihtamâyâwin *pl.* **wâneyihtamâyâwina** (NI) The act of being desperate; fanciful.

wâneyihtamihew (VTA) S/he makes her/him confused.
  wâneyihtamihiwew (VTA) S/he makes people confused.
  wâneyihtamihcikew (VTI) S/he makes things all confused.

wâneyihtamihik *pl.* **wâneyihtamihikak** (VAI) S/he is at a loss with her/him; s/he does not know what to do with her/him. *(Plains)*. *Alt.* **waneyimew** *(Northern)*.

wâneyihtamimew (VTA) Her/his words make her/him confused.
  wâneyihtamiyitam (VTA) S/he is confused.
  wâneyihtamimiwew (VTA) S/he confuses others with her/his speech.
  wâneyihtamihcikew (VTI) S/he makes things all confused.

wâneyihtamisâyâwin *pl.* **wâneyihtamisâyâwina** (NI) The act of being strange; uncanny.

wâneyihtamisiwin *pl.* **wâneyihtamisiwina** (NI) The act of being peculiar.

wâneyihtamowin *pl.* **wâneyihtamowina** (NI) The act of worrying; puzzlement.

wâninâkosiw *pl.* **wâninâkosiwak** (VAI) S/he is fading away or becoming hard to see.

wâninâkwan *pl.* **wâninâkwanwa** (VII) It is getting hazy or becoming hard to see.

wâpahcikewin *pl.* **wâpahcikewina** (NI) The act of inspecting or examining things; inspection; seeing.

wâpahki (IPC) Tomorrow.

wâpamâwasiw *pl.* **wâpamâwasiwak** (VTA) S/he sees her/his children; she gives birth to a child.

wâpamâwasiwin *pl.* **wâpamâwasiwina** (NI) The act of seeing children; the act of giving birth.

wâpamew (VTA) S/he sees him/her.
  wâpatam (VTI) S/he sees it.
  wâpakew (VTA) S/he sees people.
  wâpahcikew (VTI) S/he sees things, i.e.: pictures.

wâpamisiw *pl.* **wâpamisiwak** (VTA) S/he sees herself/himself.

wâpamiw *pl.* **wâpamiwak** (VTA) S/he looks in the mirror and sees herself/himself.

wâpamon *pl.* **wâpamona** (NI) A mirror.

wâpamonâpisk *pl.* **wâpamonâpiskwa** (NI) Glass; a glass pane. *Var.* **wâsenamawinâpisk**.

wâpan (VII) It is morning.

wâpanacahkos (NI) The morning star.

wâpanapowin *pl.* **wâpanapowina** (NI) The act of remaining awake all night, i.e.: a vigil.

wâpanosip *pl.* **wâpanosipsak** (NA) A butterball duck.

wâpapiskâw *pl.* **wâpapiskâwa** (VII) The metal is white.

wâpasakew *pl.* **wâpasakewak** (VAI) It is white, i.e.: a prime animal skin. *(Plains)*. *Alt.* **wâpiksiw** *(Northern)*.

wâpask *pl.* **wâpaskwak** (NA) A polar bear.

wâpaskâw (VII) The Cree name for the settlement of Wabasca means "white meadow or grass."

wâpaskweyâw *pl.* **wâpaskweyâwa** (NI) An area covered with white colored trees, i.e.: birch or white poplars.

wâpastim *pl.* **wâpastimwak** (NA) A white horse or white dog.

wâpaswew (VAI) S/he fades them to a paler or lighter color.
  wâpasam (VTI) S/he fades it to a paler or lighter color.
  wâpâsowew (VTA) S/he fades people to a paler or lighter color.
  wâpâsikew (VTI) S/he fades things to a paler or lighter color.

wâpatihk *pl.* **wâpatihkwak** (NA) A white goat; mountain sheep; domestic sheep.

wâpaskihk *pl.* **wâpaskihkwak** (NA) A white pail, i.e.: a bed pan.

wâpawew *pl.* **wâpawewak** (VAI) It has white fur.

wâpayomin *pl.* **wâpayominak** (NA) A grain of rice.

wâpapiskisiw *pl.* **wâpapiskisiwak** (VAI) It is white, i.e.: iron or metal.

wâpasiw *pl.* **wâpasiwak** (VAI) S/he has light coloured or pale skin.

wâpasiwin *pl.* **wâpasiwina** (NI) Having light coloured or pale skin.

wâpekihew *pl.* **wâpekihewak** (NA) A white eagle.

wâpekin *pl.* **wâpekinwa** (NI) A white hide. *(Northern).* *Alt.* **wâpiskipahkekin** *(Plains).*

wâpihtakahikan *pl.* **wâpihtakahikana** (NI) White wash for a house.

wâpiksiw *pl.* **wâpiksiwak** (VAI) It is white, i.e.: a prime animal skin. *(Northern).* *Alt.* **wâpasakew** *(Plains).*

wâpikwanew *pl.* **wâpikwanewa** (NI) A flower. *(Northern).* *Alt.* **nepihkân, wâpikwaniy** *(Plains).*

wâpikwaniwan *pl.* **wâpikwaniwanwa** (VII) It has flowers.

wâpikwanihkân *pl.* **wâpikwanihkâna** (NI) An artificial flower.

wâpikwaniy *pl.* **wâpikwaniya** (NI) A flower. *(Plains).* *Var.* **nepihkân** *(Plains);* *Alt.* **wâpikwanew** *(Northern).*

wâpimahkâskâw (VII) The lake is full of whitecaps. *(Northern).* *Alt.* **mâmahkâskâw** *(Plains).*

wâpimîkis *pl.* **wâpimîkisak** (NA) A white bead. *(Plains).* *Alt.* **wâpimin** *(Northern).*

wâpimin *pl.* **wâpiminak** (NA) A white bead. *(Northern).* *Alt.* **wapimîkis** *(Plains).*

wâpimitos *pl.* **wâpimitosak** (NA) An aspen; a white poplar.

wâpinesiw *pl.* **wâpinesiwak** (VAI) S/he is pale.

wâpisitew *pl.* **wâpisitewak** (VAI) S/he has white feet or paws.

wâpisiw *pl.* **wâpisiwak** (NA) A white swan.

wâpiskahikewin *pl.* **wâpiskahikewina** (NI) The act of blanching.

wâpiskakohp *pl.* **wâpiskakohpa** (NI) A white blanket.

wâpiskasâkay *pl.* **wâpiskasâkaya** (NI) A white dress; a priest's white garment, i.e.: a vestment.

wâpiskasiniy *pl.* **wâpiskasiniyak** (NA) A white rock.

wâpiskaskosiy *pl.* **wâpiskaskosiya** (NI) A white onion.

wâpiskaskwa *pl.* **wâpiskaskwawa** (NI) An area of white grass.

wâpiskatim *pl.* **wâpiskatimwak** (NA) A white dog. *(Plains)*

wâpiskâw *pl.* **wâpiskâwa** (VII) It is white in colour.

wâpiskawes *pl.* **wâpiskawesa** (NI) A white-gray hair.

wâpiskayiwinisew *pl.* **wâpiskayiwinisewak** (VAI) S/he has her/his white clothes on.

wâpiskekin *pl.* **wâpiskekinwa** (NI) A white cloth.

wâpiskekisiw *pl.* **wâpiskekisiwak** (VAI) It has white, prime fur. *(Northern).* *Alt.* **wâpiwayanew** *(Plains).*

wâpiskihew (VTA) S/he makes her/him white.

wâpiskihtâw (VTI) S/he makes it white.

wâpiskihiwew (VTA) S/he makes people white.

wâpiskihcikew (VTI) S/he makes things white.

wâpiskikâtew *pl.* **wâpiskikâtewak** (VAI) S/he has white legs.

wâpiskikihew *pl.* **wâpiskikihewak** (NA) A white eagle.

wâpiskipahkekin *pl.* **wâpiskipahkekinwa** (NI) A white hide. *(Plains).* *Alt.* **wâpekin** *(Northern).*

wâpiskisiw *pl.* **wâpiskisiwak** (VAI) S/he is white.

wâpiskiyâpekan *pl.* **wâpiskiyâpekanwa** (VII) The entire length of it is white.

wâpiskiyâpekisiw *pl.* **wâpiskiyâpekisiwak** (VAI) The entire length of her/him is white.

wâpistan *pl.* **wâpistanak** (NA) An adult marten. *Var.* **wâpiscânis**.

wâpistânis *pl.* **wâpistânisak** (NA) A little or baby marten.

wâpistikwân *pl.* **wâpistikwâna** (NI) A white head.

wâpistikwânew *pl.* **wâpistikwânewak** (VAI) S/he has a white head.

wâpistikwanewikiseyiniw *pl.* **wâpistikwanewikiseyiniwak** (NA) A white haired old man.

wâpiw *pl.* **wâpiwak** (VAI) S/he sees.

wâpiwayanew *pl.* **wâpiwayanewak** (VAI) It has white, prime fur. *(Plains).* *Alt.* **wâpiskekisiw** *(Northern).*

wâpos *pl.* **wâposwak** (NA) A rabbit.

wâposos *pl.* **wâpososak** (NA) A bunny.

wâposwayân *pl.* **wâposwayânak** (NA) A rabbit skin.

wâsahikamâw *pl.* **wâsahikamâwa** (NI) A bay.

wâsakahew (VTA) S/he places them around something.

wâsakastâw (VTI) S/he places it around something.

wâsakahiwew (VTA) S/he places people around something.

wâsakascikew (VTI) S/he places things around something.

wâsakahtew *pl.* **wâsakahtewak** (VAI) S/he walks around something.

wâsakanikan *pl.* **wâsakanikana** (NI) A fence. *Var.* **menikan**.

wâsakâkâpawistawew *pl.* **wâsakâkâpawistawewak** (VTA) S/he is standing around her/him or them.

wâsakâkâpawiw *pl.* **wâsakâkâpawiwak** (VAI) S/he is standing around.

wâsakâm (IPC) All around; around along the shore.

wâsakâmepiwak (VAI) They sit around in a circle.

wâsakâmew *pl.* **wâsakâmewak** (VAI) S/he goes around along the shore of a lake.

wâsakâmewin *pl.* **wâsakâmewina** (NI) The act of going around in areas, i.e.: shore; bush.

wâsakânikanipîwâpiskos *pl.* **wâsakânikanipîwâpiskosa** (NI) A piece of barbed wire. *(Plains).* *Alt.* **wâsakânikanyâpiy** *(Northern).*

wâsakânikanyâpiy *pl.* **wâsakânikanyâpiya** (NI) A piece of barbed wire. *(Northern).* *Alt.* **wâsakânikanipîwâpiskos** *(Plains).*

wâsakâpayis *pl.* **wâsakâpayisa** (NI) A carousel.

wâsakâpayiw *pl.* **wâsakâpayiwa** *or* **wâsakâpayiwak** (VII) *or* (VAI) It *or* s/he is going around.

wâsakâpayîstawew (VTA) S/he goes all around them.
  wâsakâpayîstam (VTI) S/he goes all around it.
  wâsakâpayîstakew (VTA) S/he goes all around people.
  wâsakâpayîscikew (VTI) S/he goes all around things.

wâsakâpiwak (VAI) They are sitting around.

wâsakâpîstamwa (VTI) They are sitting around it.

wâsakâpîstâtowak (VTA) They are sitting around each other.

wâsakâsimew (VTA) S/he lays them around something.
  wâsakâhtitaw (VTI) S/he takes it around.

wâsakâskawew (VTA) S/he goes around her/him.
  wâsakâskam (VTA) S/he goes around it.
  wâsakâskâkew (VTA) S/he goes around people.

wâsaskotenamawew (VTA) S/he shines a light for her/him; s/he lights a lamp for her/him.
  wâsaskotenamakew (VTA) S/he shines a light for people.

wâsaskotenikan *pl.* **wâsaskotenikana** (NI) A lamp.

wâsaskotenikanâhtik *pl.* **wâsaskotenikanâhtikwa** (NI) A candlestick.

wâsaskotenikanâpisk *pl.* **wâsaskotenikanâpiskwa** (NI) A globe for a lamp.

wâsaskotenikewin *pl.* **wâsaskotenikewina** (NI) Illumination; lighting.

wâsaskotepayihew (VTI) S/he makes them give off light.
  wâsaskotepayitâw (VTI) S/he makes it give out light.
  wâsaskotepayihiwew (VTA) S/he makes light for people.

wâsaskotepayiw (VII) There is lightning. *(Plains)*. *Alt.* **waskotepayiw** *(Northern)*.

wâsaskotepayiw *pl.* **wâsaskotepayiwa** (NI) Lightning; electricity.

wâsaskotepicikan *pl.* **wâsaskotepicikana** (NI) A flashlight.

wâsaskotew *pl.* **wâsaskotewa** (VII) It gives off light.

wâsaskotnamâkan *pl.* **wâsaskotnamâkana** (NI) A tool that gives off light.

wâsâkonastew (VII) The fresh snow is clean and shiny.

wâsâsin *pl.* **wâsâsinwa** (NI) A cove.

wâsenamawin *pl.* **wâsenamawina** (NI) A window.

wâsenamawinekin *pl.* **wâsenamawinekinwa** (NI) A cloth used in place of glass for a window pane.

wâsesikwâw (VII) The ice is clear.

wâseskosîw *pl.* **wâseskosîwa** (NI) A red hot coal.

wâseskwan (VII) It is clear weather; the sky is clear.

wâseskwastan (VII) The wind has cleared the sky.

wâsewew *pl.* **wâsewewak** (VAI) S/he has a high pitched voice. *(Northern)*. *Alt.* **wâswewew** *(Plains)*.

wâsewewin *pl.* **wâsewewina** (NI) Having a high pitched voice. *(Northern)*. *Alt.* **wâswewewin** *(Plains)*.

wâseyâpiskâw *pl.* **wâseyâpiskâwa** (VII) It shines, i.e.: something made of metal.

wâseyâpiskisiw *pl.* **wâseyâpiskisiwak** (NA) The metal pan is glowing.

wâseyâpiskitew *pl.* **wâseyâpiskitewa** (NI) The metal is glowing red hot.

wâseyâw *pl.* **wâseyâwa** (VII) It is light outside; it is bright or shiny.

wâsihkwahikan *pl.* **wâsihkwahikana** (NI) Alabaster.

wâsihkwahikâkan *pl.* **wâsihkwahikâkana** (NI) Something used for shining, i.e.: a buffer.

wâsihkwapiskâw (VII) It is shining.

wâsihkwastew *pl.* **wâsihkwastewa** (VII) It is sitting there and shining.

wâsihkwekahikew *pl.* **wâsihkwekahikewak** (VAI) S/he blazes a trail.

wâsisiw *pl.* **wâsisiwak** (VAI) S/he shines.

wâsitew *pl.* **wâsitewa** (VII) It shines.

wâsîs (IPC) Especially.

wâskahikan *pl.* **wâskahikana** (NI) A house.

wâskahikanihk (NI) The Cree name for the settlement of Grouard. *Var.* **ocinâsihk**.

wâskahikanihkawew (VTI) S/he built a house with something.
  wâskahikanihkâkew (VTI) S/he makes a house with it or for others.

wâskahikanihkew *pl.* **wâskahikanihkewak** (VAI) S/he is building a house.

wâskahikanihkewiyiniw *pl.* **wâskahikanihkewiyiniwak** (NA) A house builder; i.e.: a contractor. *(Northern)*
  mistikonâpew *pl.* **mistikonâpewak** (NA) A carpenter.

wâskamâyâw *pl.* **wâskamâyâwak** (VAI) S/he is now aware of things, i.e.: sobering up.

wâskameyihtakosiwin *pl.* **wâskameyihtakosiwina** (NI) The act of being thought of as aware or clear headed.

wâskameyihtam *pl.* **wâskameyihtamwak** (VAI) S/he is more aware; s/he is thinking clearer.

wâskameyihtâkosiw *pl.* **wâskameyihtâkosiwak** (VAI) S/he is thought of as being aware of things, i.e.: clear headed.

wâskameyihtâkwan *pl.* **wâskameyihtâkwanwa** (VII) It is thought of as being aware.

wâskameyimew (VTA) S/he thinks of him as being more aware.
  wâskameyimiwew (VTA) S/he thinks of people as being more aware.

wâskamisiw *pl.* **wâskamisiwak** (VAI) S/he is becoming more aware, i.e.: sobering up.

223

wâskamisiwin *pl.* **wâskamisiwina** (NI) The act of becoming more aware.

wâskâkonekwâcikan *pl.* **wâskâkonekwâcikana** (NI) Something sewn around a moccasin.

wâskâmehtew *pl.* **wâskâmehtewak** (VAI) S/he walks around the lake shore.

wâskâpihcihkan *pl.* **wâskâpihcihkana** (NI) Fish jerky.

wâskitanâskan *pl.* **wâskitanâskana** (NI) A blanket that is on top, i.e.: a bed spread.

wâskitoy *pl.* **wâskitoya** (NI) The buttocks.

wâskitskohtew *pl.* **wâskitskohtewak** (VAI) S/he walks now on top of ice. *(Northern). Var.* **pimiskohtew** *(Northern)*; *Alt.* **pimiskohtew** *(Plains)*.

wâskwetin *pl.* **wâskwetinwa** (VII) It ricochets. *(Northern). Alt.* **kwâskwehtin** *(Plains)*.

wâsnamawinâpisk *pl.* **wâsnamawinâpiskwa** (NI) A window pane.

wâspisiw *pl.* **wâspisiwak** (VAI) S/he is laced up in a moss bag.

wâspison *pl.* **wâspisona** (NI) A pack for babies, i.e.: a moss bag.

wâspisonâhtik *pl.* **wâspisonâhtikwa** (NI) A cradleboard.

wâspitâpân *pl.* **wâspitâpâna** (NI) Something laced onto a toboggan.

wâstahamawew (VTA) S/he waved at her/him.
wâstahamakew (VTA) S/he waves at people.

wâstakamowin *pl.* **wâstakamowina** (NI) The act of swigging.

wâstinikew *pl.* **wâstinikewak** (VAI) S/he waves in a desperate manner.

wâswepekahwew (VTA) S/he splashes water on her/him with something, i.e.: a paddle.
wâswepekaham (VTI) S/he splashes water on it with something.
wâswepekahowew (VTA) S/he splashes water on people with something.
wâswepekahikew (VTI) S/he splashes water on things with something.

wâswewew *pl.* **wâswewewak** (VAI) S/he has a high pitched voice. *(Plains). Alt.* **wâsewew** *(Northern)*.

wâswewewin *pl.* **wâswewewina** (NI) Having a high pitched voice. *(Plains). Alt.* **wâsewewin** *(Northern)*.

wâti *pl.* **wâtahi** (NI) A hole in the ground, i.e.: a lair.

wâtihkew *pl.* **wâtihkewak** (VAI) S/he digs a hole.

wâtihkewin *pl.* **wâtihkewina** (NI) The act of burrowing; making a hole.

wâwâkastew (VII) It zig-zags.

wâwâskesiw *pl.* **wâwâskesiwak** (NA) An elk; a reindeer; a wapiti.

wâwâskesiwisâkahikan (NI) The Cree name for the town of Lac La Biche meaning "elk lake."

wâwâskesowîsopiy *pl.* **wâwâskesowîsopiya** (NI) An elk gall bladder.

wâweyiyahtik *pl.* **wâweyiyahtikwa** (NI) A round log. *(Plains). Alt.* **notimâhtik** *(Northern)*.

wâweyiyâw (VII) It is round. *(Plains). Alt.* **notimâw** *(Northern)*.

wâwi *pl.* **wâwa** (NI) An egg.

wâwipahkwesikan *pl.* **wâwipahkwesikanak** (NA) A cake. *(Plains). Alt.* **siwpahkwesikan** *(Northern)*.

wâwiyatisihkew *pl.* **wâwiyatisihkewak** (VAI) S/he is playing tricks on others.

wâwiyâskosiw *pl.* **wâwiyâskosiwak** (NA) It is circular in shape, i.e.: a pole.

wâwiyâskwan *pl.* **wâwiyâskwanwa** (NI) A circular or round shaped stick.

wâwiyepayiw *pl.* **wâwiyepayiwa** *or* **wâwiyepayiwak** (VII) *or* (VAI) It *or* s/he went round.

wâwiyisiw *pl.* **wâwiyisiwak** (VAI) S/he is round.

wâyahcâw *pl.* **wâyahcâwa** (NI) A dip in the ground.

wâyatinâw *pl.* **wâyatinâwa** (NI) A bowl-like valley, i.e.: between mountains.

wâyâpiskatahwew (VTA) S/he made a dent or dip on her/him.
wâyâpiskataham (VII) S/he made a dent or dip on it, i.e.: a car fender.
wâyâpiskatakew (VII) S/he made a dent or dip on something.

wâyinokiwewin *pl.* **wâyinokiwewina** (NI) The act of regressing; regression. *(Northern). Alt.* **wâyiniwin** *(Plains)*.

wâyinowin *pl.* **wâyinowina** (NI) The act of regressing; regression. *(Plains). Alt.* **wâyinokiwewin** *(Northern)*.

wâyipiyaw *pl.* **wâyipiyawa** (NI) A pool of water, i.e.: a dug out; a water hole.

wâyipîyâs *pl.* **wâyipîyâsa** (NI) A small puddle.

wâyisiw *pl.* **wâyisiwak** (VAI) It is dented.

wâyisiwin *pl.* **wâyisiwina** (NI) The act of being dented.

wecâtoskemâkan *pl.* **wecâtoskemâkanak** (NA) A co-worker.

wecâtoskemew (VTA) S/he works with her/him or them.
wecâtoskemiwew (VTA) S/he works with people.

wecâtoskeyâkan *pl.* **wecâtoskeyâkanak** (NA) A work helper, i.e.: an assistant.

wecâyamihâmew (VTA) S/he prays with her/him or them.
wecâyamihâmiwew (VTA) S/he prays with people.

wehcihiw *pl.* **wehcihiwak** (VAI) S/he does it the simple or easy way.

wehcihiwewin *pl.* **wehcihiwewina** (NI) The act of being pliant.

224

wehcihowin *pl.* **wehcihowina** (NI) The act of doing it
the easy way; pliability.

wehcihôpayiw (VAI) It is easy to approach.

wehcinatew (VTA) S/he has an easy time in attaining it
or them.

wehcinatam (VTI) S/he has an easy time in attaining
it.

wehcinasiwew (VTA) S/he has an easy time in
attaining them.

wehcinahcikew (VTI) S/he has an easy time in
attaining things.

wehcipihtokwewin *pl.* **wehcipihtokwewina** (NI) The act
of being easy to enter, i.e.: accessibility.

wehcipîkopayiw *pl.* **wehcipîkopayiwak** (VAI) It breaks
easily.

wehkesk *pl.* **wehkeskwak** (NA) A medicine root or a
musquash root or a ginger root. *(Plains). Alt.*
manitoskâtâsk *(Northern).*

wehtakihtew *pl.* **wehtakihtewa** (VII) It is cheap or
inexpensive.

wehtakimew (VTA) S/he is selling them cheap.

wehtakitam (VTI) S/he sells it cheap.

wehtakihcikew (VTI) S/he sells things cheap.

wehtakisiw *pl.* **wehtakisiwak** (VAI) It is cheap or
inexpensive.

wehtisiw *pl.* **wehtisiwak** (VAI) S/he is easy to get along
with.

wehtisowin *pl.* **wehtisowina** (NI) Being easy to get along
with.

wehwepisiw *pl.* **wehwepisiwak** (VAI) S/he is going to
swing. *(Northern). Alt.* **wîwewepisiw** *(Plains).*

wehwew *pl.* **wehwewak** (NA) A small goose.

wekahpitew (VTA) S/he wraps her/him up into a bundle.
(Northern). Alt. **wewekahpitew** *(Plains).*

wekahpitam (VTI) S/he makes a bundle with it.

wekahpisiwew (VTA) S/he bundles up the people.

wekahpihcikew (VTI) S/he bundles up the things.

wekinikan *pl.* **wekinikana** (NI) Wrapping paper or
anything used for wrapping; sheathing. *(Northern).*
Alt. **wewekinikan** *(Plains).*

wekistikwanew *pl.* **wekistikwanewak** (VAI) S/he wraps
up her/his head, i.e.: scarf. *(Northern). Alt.*
wewekistikwânew *(Plains).*

wemahtewin *pl.* **wemahtewina** (NI) The act of detouring
or walking around something; a by-pass.

wemâhceskanâs *pl.* **wemâhceskanâsa** (NI) A by-path.

wemâhteskanaw *pl.* **wemâhteskanawa** (NI) A by-road.

wemâhtew *pl.* **wemâhtewak** (VAI) S/he detours or walks
around it.

wemâskawew (VTA) S/he detours or walks around her/
him.

wemâskam (VTI) S/he detours or walks around it.

wemâskâkew (VTA) S/he detours or walks around
people.

wemâskâcikew (VTI) S/he detours or walks around
things.

wemâskâcikan *pl.* **wemâskâcikana** (NI) Something to be
avoided; avoidance.

wemâskâcikewin *pl.* **wemâskâcikewina** (NI) The act of
evading; evasion.

wemistikosiwâhtik *pl.* **wemistikosiwâhtikwak** (NA)
Oak tree. *Var.* **mistikominâhtik, maskawahtik.**

wemistikôsiw (NA) A French person.

wemistikôsînâhk (NI) A French area; Quebec.

wepahamawew *pl.* **wepahamawewak** (VTA) S/he sweeps
for her/him or them.

wepahaskwân *pl.* **wepahaskwâna** (NI) A sling used to
propel stones at things.

wepahaskwâtew (VTA) S/he tosses a sling at her/him.

wepahaskwâtam (VTI) S/he tosses a sling at it.

wepahaskwâsiwew (VTA) S/he tosses a sling at people.

wepahaskwâhcikew (VTI) S/he tosses a sling at things.

wepahaskwew *pl.* **wepahaskwewak** (VAI) S/he uses a
sling to propel stones.

wepahâkonâkan *pl.* **wepahâkonâkana** (NI) A snow
shovel.

wepahâkonâtew (VTA) S/he shovels the snow off her/
him or it.

wepahâkonâtam (VTI) S/he shovels the snow off it.

wepahâkonâsiwew (VTA) S/he shovels the snow off
people.

wepahâkonew *pl.* **wepahâkonewak** (VAI) S/he shovels
snow.

wepahikan *pl.* **wepahikana** (NI) A broom.

wepahikanâhtik *pl.* **wepahikanâhtikwa** (NI) A
broomstick.

wepahikanihkew *pl.* **wepahikanihkewak** (VAI) S/he
makes brooms.

wepahikew *pl.* **wepahikewak** (VAI) S/he sweeps.

wepahok (IPC) S/he is gored by a bull.

wepahwew (VTA) S/he swept them.

wepaham (VTI) S/he sweeps it.

wepahowew (VTA) S/he sweeps people.

wepahikew (VTI) S/he sweeps things.

wepapakow *pl.* **wepapakowak** (VAI) S/he is swept away
by the current. *(Northern). Alt.* **wepâhokiw**
(Plains).

wepâhokiw *pl.* **wepâhokiwak** (VAI) S/he is swept away
by the current. *(Plains). Alt.* **wepapakow**
(Northern).

wepâpotew *pl.* **wepâpotewa** (VII) It is swept away by the
current.

wepâsiw *pl.* **wepâsiwak** (VAI) S/he is blown away.

wepâstan *pl.* **wepâstanwa** (VII) It is blown away.

225

wepâstimew (VTI) S/he tosses it away.
> **wepâstimiwew** (VTA) S/he tosses people away.

wepâyowew *pl.* **wepâyowewak** (VTA) S/he wags her/his tail.

wepehtowin (NI) The act of intercourse; sleeping together.

wepeyimowin *pl.* **wepeyimowina** (NI) The act of rejecting one's own existence.

wepeyitamawew (VTA) S/he rejects the existence of another person.
> **wepeyitamakew** (VTA) S/he rejects the existence of another person.

wepinam (NI) Something thrown away; disown. *(Northern). Alt.* **wepinamowin** *(Plains).*

wepinamawew (VTI) S/he throws it away for her/him.
> **wepinamakew** (VTI) S/he throws it away for someone.

wepinamowin (NI) Something thrown away; disown. *(Plains). Alt.* **wepinam** *(Northern).*

wepinâsiw *pl.* **wepinâsiwak** (VAI) S/he offers a sacred sacrifice.

wepinâsiwin *pl.* **wepinâsiwina** (NI) The act of offering a sacred sacrifice; immolate.

wepinâskwewin *pl.* **wepinâskwewina** (NI) The act of casting something away.

wepinâsôstamawew (VTA) S/he offers a sacred sacrifice for someone.
> **wepinâsôstamakew** (VTA) S/he offer a sacred sacrifice for people.

wepinâsôstawew (VTA) S/he offers a sacred sacrifice to the deity.
> **wepinâsôstam** (VTI) S/he offers a sacred sacrifice to it.
> **wepinâsôstâkew** (VTA) S/he offers a sacred sacrifice to someone.

wepinew (VTA) S/he throws them away; s/he leaves her/his mate.
> **wepinam** (VTI) S/he throws it away.
> **wepiniwew** (VTA) S/he throws people away.
> **wepinikew** (VTI) S/he throws things away.

wepinikan *pl.* **wepinikanak** (NA) A castaway; riddance.

wepinikâsiw *pl.* **wepinikâsiwak** (VAI) S/he was thrown away; her/his spouse left her/him.

wepinikâtew *pl.* **wepinikâtewa** (VII) It was thrown away.

wepinikewin *pl.* **wepinikewina** (NI) The act of being banished; banishment; dereliction; turfed.

wepinikewina *pl.* **wepinikewinawa** (NI) Discarded material, i.e.: garbage; leavings.

wepinisiw *pl.* **wepinisiwak** (VTA) S/he throws herself/himself away; s/he has given up on herself/himself.

wepinisiwin *pl.* **wepinisiwina** (NI) The act of throwing oneself away or giving up on oneself.

wepiniskâtew *pl.* **wepiniskâtewak** (VTA) S/he throws a punch at him.

wepiniskew *pl.* **wepiniskewak** (VAI) S/he throws a punch.

wepiniskwewew *pl.* **wepiniskwewewak** (VTA) S/he throws away her/his relationship; s/he leaves her/his spouse.

wepiskweyistawew (VTA) S/he shakes her/his head at her/him in disagreement.
> **wepiskweyistam** (VTI) S/he shakes her/his head at it in disagreement.
> **wepiskweyistâkew** (VTA) S/he shakes her/his head at people in disagreement.

wepiskweyiw *pl.* **wepiskweyiwak** (VTA) S/he shakes her/his head in disagreement. *(Northern). Alt.* **wewepiskweyiw** *(Plains).*

wepison *pl.* **wepisona** (NI) A swing or hammock. *(Northern). Alt.* **wewepison** *(Plains).*

wepitawasiwin *pl.* **wepitawasiwina** (NI) The act of rocking a baby. *(Northern). Alt.* **wewepitâwasowin** *(Plains).*

wepitew (VTA) S/he swings her/him in a swing or hammock. *(Northern). Alt.* **wewepitew** *(Plains).*
> **wepitam** (VTI) S/he swings it in a swing or hammock.
> **wepisiwew** (VTA) S/he swings people in a swing or hammock.

weposkâw *pl.* **weposkâwa** (NI) A burned out piece of land, i.e.: an old burn; a fire burning underground. *(Northern). Alt.* **pahkwatiteskâw** *(Plains).*

wesakakamow (VII) It is a bitter taste.

weskwamotayew *pl.* **weskwamotayewak** (NA) A five-year-old bull moose.

weskawâhiwewin *pl.* **wekawâhiwewina** (NI) The act of being caught unawares.

weskwasiw *pl.* **weskwasiwak** *or* **weskwasiwa** (VAI) *or* (VII) S/he *or* it is tanned.

weskwastew *pl.* **wekwastewa** (VII) It is tanned.

weskwaswew (VTA) S/he tanned her/him.
> **weskwasam** (VTI) S/he tanned the hide.
> **weskwasowew** (VTA) S/he tanned the people.
> **weskwasikew** (VTI) S/he tanned the hides.

wespâkamicewâpôs (NI) Coffee. *(Plains). Alt.* **pihkahtewâpoy** *(Northern)*, **pihkahcewâpos** *(Plains).*

wespinac (VII) It is tragic.

wespinaciyawehew (VTA) It is tragic that s/he upsets her/him.

wespinaciyawesiw *pl.* **wespinaciyawesiwak** (VAI) It is tragic that s/he is upset.

wespinaciyawesiwin (NI) The act of being tragically upset.

wetaskehtowak (VAI) They live in the same part of the country.

wetaskehtowin *pl.* **wetaskehtowina** (NI) The act of living in the same part of the country.

wetaskemâkan *pl.* **wetaskemâkanak** (NA) A person living in the same country, i.e.: countryman.

wetaskemew (VAI) S/he lives in the same part of the country as her/him.

wetasketam (VAI) S/he lives in the same part of the country as it.

wetaskemiwew (VAI) S/he lives in the same part of the country as them.

wetokemew (VTA) S/he lives or dwells with her/him or them.

wetoketam (VTI) S/he lives or dwells with it.

wetokemiwew (VTA) S/he lives or dwells with people.

wewekahpitew (VTA) S/he wraps her/him up into a bundle. *(Plains). Alt.* **wekahpitew** *(Northern).*

wewekahpitam (VTI) S/he makes a bundle with it.

wewekahpisiwew (VTA) S/he bundles up the people.

wewekahpihcikew (VTI) S/he bundles up the things.

wewekinâwasowin *pl.* **wewekinâwasowina** (NI) The act of swaddling, i.e.: a baby. *(Plains). Alt.* **wikinâwasowin** *(Northern).*

wewekinew (VTA) S/he wraps her/him up. *(Plains). Alt.* **wikinew** *(Northern).*

wewekinam (VTI) S/he wraps it up.

wewekinew (VTA) S/he wraps people up.

wewekikew (VTI) S/he wraps things up.

wewekinikan *pl.* **wewekinikana** (NI) Wrapping paper or anything used for wrapping; sheathing. *(Plains). Alt.* **wekinikan** *(Northern).*

wewekinkewin *pl.* **wewekinkewina** (NI) The act of enveloping or wrapping.

wewekistikwânew *pl.* **wewekistikwânewak** (VAI) S/he wraps up her/his head, i.e.: scarf. *(Plains). Alt.* **wekistikwanew** *(Northern).*

wewepiskweyiw *pl.* **wewepiskweyiwak** (VTA) S/he shakes her/his head in disagreement. *(Plains). Alt.* **wepiskweyiw** *(Northern).*

wewepiskweyow *pl.* **wewepiskweyowak** (VTA) S/he shakes her/his head.

wewepison *pl.* **wewepisona** (NI) A swing or hammock. *(Plains). Alt.* **wepison** *(Northern).*

wewepitâwasowin *pl.* **wewepitâwasowina** (NI) The act of rocking a baby. *(Plains). Alt.* **wepitawasiwin** *(Northern).*

wewepitew (VTA) S/he swings her/him in a swing or hammock. *(Plains). Alt.* **wepitew** *(Northern).*

wewepitam (VTI) S/he swings it in a swing or hammock.

wewepisiwew (VTA) S/he swings people in a swing or hammock.

wewow *pl.* **wewowak** (VAI) He has a wife.

weyotan *pl.* **weyotanwa** (VII) It is abundant.

weyoteyimew (VTA) S/he thinks s/he is rich.

weyoteyitam (VTI) S/he thinks it is rich.

weyoteyimiwew (VTA) S/he thinks people are rich.

weyoteyimiw *pl.* **weyoteyimiwak** (VAI) S/he thinks herself/himself as being rich.

weyotisehew (VTA) S/he makes her/him rich.

weyotisetâw (VTI) S/he makes it rich.

weyotisehiwew (VTA) S/he makes people rich.

weyotisihiwewin *pl.* **weyotisihiwewina** (NI) The act of making someone rich; enrichment.

weyotisiw *pl.* **weyotisiwak** (VAI) S/he is rich.

weyotisiwin *pl.* **weyotisiwina** (NI) Being rich.

wicehtowak (VAI) They have a partnership or friendship.

wicehtowin *pl.* **wicehtowina** (NI) The act of having a partnership or friendship; spousal; unity.

wicewâkan *pl.* **wicewâkanak** (NA) A partner or a friend; a comrade.

wicewâkanihew (VTA) S/he makes them partners or friends; s/he pairs them up.

wicewâkanitâw (VTI) S/he pairs it to something else.

wicewâkanihiwew (VTA) S/he pairs people to something else.

wicewâkanihcikew (VTI) S/he pairs things to something else;

wicewâkanihtowak (VAI) They are partners or friends.

wicewâkanihtowin *pl.* **wicewâkanihtowina** (NI) Being partners or friends; conformation; cooperation.

wicewâkanikahew (VTA) S/he makes partners or friends for her/him.

wicewâkanikâkew (VTI) S/he make partners or friends with it, i.e.: using something.

wicewâkanimew (VAI) S/he is partners or friends with her/him.

wicewâkanitam (VTI) S/he is partners or friends with it.

wicewâkanimiwew (VTA) S/he is partners or friends with people.

wicewew (VTA) S/he accompanies her/him.

wicimîcisomew (VTA) S/he eats with her/him or them.

wicimîcisomiwew (VTA) S/he eats with people.

wicisanitowin (NI) Having siblings. *(Plains). Alt.* **wîtisânitowin** *(Northern).*

wihayotôtemiw (VTA) S/he is friendly.

wihcekan *pl.* **wihcekanwa** (VII) It stinks.

wihcekaskociy *pl.* **wihcekaskociya** (NI) An onion.

wihcekihtin *pl.* **wihcekihtina** (NI) A moose hide that is starting to stink.

wihcekisiw *pl.* **wihcekisiwak** (VAI) S/he stinks.

wihcekisiwin *pl.* **wihcekisiwina** (NI) The act of stinking.

wihcekitâpânâsk *pl.* **wihcekitâpânâskwak** (NA) A stinking machine; a vehicle that runs by itself, i.e.: a car. *(Northern). Alt.* **sehkepimipayîs, sehkes** *(Plains).*

227

wihcikâsiw *pl.* **wihcikâsiwak** (VAI) S/he is mentioned by name.

wihcikâtew *pl.* **wihcikâtewa** (VII) It is mentioned by name.

wihew (VTA) S/he names her/him or them; s/he calls her/him by name.
  witam (VTI) S/he names it.
  wihiwew (VTA) S/he names people.

wihikimâstew *pl.* **wihkimâstewa** (VII) It produces a pleasant aroma.

wihkasin *pl.* **wihkasinwa** (VII) It is tasty, i.e.: soup, stew, water.

wihkimâkohew (VTA) S/he puts perfume on someone.
  wihkimâkotâw (VTI) S/he puts perfume on it.
  wihkimâkoh'wew (VTA) S/he puts perfume on people.

wihkimâkohow *pl.* **wihkimâkohowak** (VAI) S/he puts on perfume.

wihkimâkohowin *pl.* **wihkimâkohowina** (NI) The act of putting on perfume.

wihkimâkosiw *pl.* **wihkimâkosiwak** (VAI) S/he smells pleasant or perfumed.

wihkimâkosiwin *pl.* **wihkimâkosiwina** (NI) The act of smelling pleasant; being perfumed; aromatic.

wihkimâkwahon *pl.* **wihkimâkwahona** (NI) A perfume; balm; a powder.

wihkimâkwan *pl.* **wihkimâkwanwa** (VII) It smells perfumed.

wihkimâmew (VTA) S/he likes the smell of someone.
  wihkimâtam (VTI) S/he likes its smell.
  wihkimâmiwew (VTA) S/he likes peoples' smell.

wihkimâsawew *pl.* **wihkimâsawewak** (VAI) S/he makes a pleasant aroma from what s/he is burning.

wihkimâsawewin *pl.* **wihkimâsawewina** (NI) The act of making a pleasant aroma by burning something.

wihkimâsikan (NA) A fungus that grows on willow trees that produces a pleasant aroma when lit, i.e.: a ceremonial smoke fungus.

wihkimâsiw *pl.* **wihkimâsiwak** (VAI) It produces a pleasant aroma, i.e.: sweetgrass.

wihkipew *pl.* **wihkipewak** (VAI) S/he enjoys drinking, i.e.: pop.

wihkipewin *pl.* **wihkipewina** (NI) The act of enjoying drinking, i.e.: pop.

wihkipiw *pl.* **wihkipiwa** (VTI) S/he enjoys eating, i.e.: meat.

wihkipiw *pl.* **wihkipiwak** (VTA) S/he enjoys eating, i.e.: fish.

wihkipwew (VTA) S/he enjoys the taste of them.
  wihkipstam (VTI) S/he enjoys the taste of it.

wihkiskwewewin *pl.* **wihkiskwewewina** (NI) The act of being susceptible to women; the act of feeling armorous towards women.

wihkitisiw *pl.* **wihkitisiwak** (VAI) It is tasty, i.e.: fish or bread.

wihkiw *pl.* **wihkiwak** (VAI) S/he exerts power, i.e.: pulling on something.

wihkohkew *pl.* **wihkohkewak** (VAI) S/he hosts or puts on a feast.

wihkohkewin *pl.* **wihkohkewina** (NI) The act of hosting or putting on a feast; invitation. *Var.* **wihkomitowin**.

wihkohtohew (VTA) S/he makes them take part in a feast.
  wihkohtohiwew (VTA) S/he makes a feast for people.

wihkohtow *pl.* **wihkohtowak** (VAI) S/he takes part in a feast.

wihkomew *pl.* **wihkomewak** (VTA) S/he invites her/him or them to a feast.

wihkwacipayiw *pl.* **wihkwacipayiwak** (VAI) S/he breaks free by herself/himself.

wihkwacipitew (VTA) S/he pulls her/him free.
  wihkwacipitam (VTI) S/he pulls it free.
  wihkwacipisiwew (VTA) S/he pulls people free.
  wihkwacipihcikew (VTI) S/he pulls things free.

wihkwaciw *pl.* **wihkwaciwak** (VAI) S/he manages to break free by exerting herself/himself.

wihkwatahwew (VTI) S/he knocks them lose.
  wihkwataham (VTI) S/he knocks it lose.
  wihkwatahowew (VTA) S/he knocks people lose.
  wihkwatahikew (VTI) S/he knocks things lose.

wihkwatinew (VTI) S/he breaks it free with her/his hands.
  wihkwatinam (VTI) S/he breaks it free by hand.
  wihkwatiniwew (VTA) S/he breaks people free by hand.
  wihkwatinikew (VTI) S/he breaks things free by hand.

wihkway *pl.* **wihkwaya** (NI) A balloon.

wihkwâs *pl.* **wihkwâsa** (NI) A small balloon; a mantle used for gas lamp; a condom.

wihkwekwâsiw *pl.* **wihkwekwâsiwa** (VTI) S/he sews around something and closes it up.

wihkwesiw *pl.* **wihkwesiwak** (VAI) It is closed in and has space inside, i.e.: van or a pair of pants.

wihkwesiwin *pl.* **wihkwesiwina** (NI) The act of being closed in and having space inside.

wihkwetinâw *pl.* **wihkwetinâwa** (NI) Hills that surround and close in an area.

wihkweyâw *pl.* **wihkweyâwa** (VII) It is closed in and has space inside, i.e.: a tent.

wihowin *pl.* **wihowina** (NI) A name.

wihpehtowak (VAI) They sleep together.

wihpemew (VTA) S/he sleeps with her/him.
  wihpetam (VTI) S/he sleeps with it.
  wihpemiwew (VTA) S/he sleeps with someone.

wihpikahikan *pl.* **wihpikahikana** (NI) A dugout.

wihpikahwew (VAI) S/he makes a dugout from them.

  wihpikaham (VAI) S/he makes a dugout from it.

  wihpikahikew (VAI) S/he makes a dugout from things.

wihpitwânsip *pl.* **wihpitwânsipak** (NA) A type of mallard. *(Northern). Var.* **iyinisip** *(Northern); Alt.* **iyinisip** *(Plains)*.

wihtam *pl.* **wihtamwak** (VAI) S/he tells.

wihtamawew (VTA) S/he tells her/him or them.

  wihtamakew (VTA) S/he tells people.

wihtamâkew *pl.* **wihtamâkewak** (VTA) S/he tells others.

wihtamâkewin *pl.* **wihtamâkewina** (NI) The act of telling others.

wihtamâtowak (VTA) They told each other.

wihtamâtowin *pl.* **wihtamâtowina** (NI) The act of telling each other; the act of communicating with someone.

wihtamowin *pl.* **wihtamowina** (NI) The act of telling on someone.

wihteyihtam (VTI) S/he thinks it is easy to attain.

  wihteyihmiwew (VTA) S/he thinks people are easy to attain.

  wihteyihhcikew (VTI) S/he thinks things are easy to attain.

wihteyimew *pl.* **wihteyimewak** (VTA) S/he finds her/him easy to get along with.

wihtihp *pl.* **wihtihpa** (NI) A brain. *(Northern). Alt.* **wîyitihp** *(Plains)*.

wihtikiw *pl.* **wihtikiwak** (NA) A person who goes insane and turns to cannibalism, subject of much legendary development in Cree tradition.

wihtikowiw *pl.* **wihtikowiwak** (VAI) S/he eats greedily.

wihtikowiwin *pl.* **wihtikowiwina** (NI) The act of eating greedily.

wihwepâsow *pl.* **wihwepâsowak** (VAI) S/he is going to be blown away.

wihwepâstan *pl.* **wihwepâstanwa** (VII) It is going to be blown away.

wikihto wahkohtowin (NA) An in-law.

wikihtowin *pl.* **wikihtowina** (NI) A traditional Cree permanent relationship, the act of getting married.

wikikwatew *pl.* **wikikwatewa** (VTI) S/he sews it closed.

wikimâkan *pl.* **wikimâkanak** (NA) A spouse or a married partner. *Var.* **owîkitiw**.

wikimâkanimew (VTA) S/he is a spouse to her/him.

  wikimâkanimiwew (VTA) S/he is spouse to someone.

wikimew (VTA) S/he marries her/him.

  wikimiwew (VTA) S/he marries someone.

wikinâwasowin *pl.* **wikinâwasowina** (NI) The act of swaddling or wrapping a baby. *(Northern). Alt.* **wewekinâwasowin** *(Plains)*.

wikinew (VTA) S/he wraps her/him up. *(Northern). Alt.* **wewekinew** *(Plains)*.

wikinam (VTI) S/he wraps it up.

wikiniwew (VTA) S/he wraps people up.

wikinikew (VTI) S/he wraps things up.

winasakâcihp *pl.* **winasakâcihpak** (NA) A groundhog.

wineyihtâkosiwin *pl.* **wineyihtâkosiwina** (NI) Being considered filthy or dirty; disgusting.

wineyihtâkwan *pl.* **wineyihtâkwanwa** (VII) It is considered filthy; disgusting.

wineyimew (VTA) S/he considers her/him filthy.

  wineyitam (VTI) S/he finds it filthy.

  wineyimiwew (VTA) S/he finds people filthy.

  wineyihcikew (VTI) S/he finds things filthy.

wisakahwew (VTA) S/he is painfully abusing her/him, i.e.: sexually.

  wisakahowew (VTA) S/he is painfully abusing people, i.e.: sexually.

  wisakahikew (VTA) S/he is painfully abusing someone, i.e.: sexually.

wiwiw *pl.* **wiwiwak** (VAI) He has a wife.

wiya (PR) She/he, her/him.

wiyahkwew *pl.* **wiyahkwewak** (VAI) S/he is swearing; s/he is using foul language.

wiyakihew (VTA) S/he squandered them unnecessarily.

  wiyakitâw (VTI) S/he squandered it for nothing.

  wiyakihiwew (VTA) S/he squandered people unnecessarily.

  wiyakihcikew (VTI) S/he squandered things unnecessarily.

wiyakisiw *pl.* **wiyakisiwak** (VAI) S/he is squandered; what a waste.

wiyakisiwin *pl.* **wiyakisiwina** (NI) Being squandered unnecessarily.

wiyakiskawew (VTI) S/he is squandering it by wearing it.

  wiyakiskam (VTI) S/he doesn't suit it.

  wiyakiskakew (VTA) S/he doesn't suit people.

wiyanihew *pl.* **wiyanihewak** (VTA) S/he butchers a moose.

wiyanihtâkan *pl.* **wiyanihtâkana** (NI) A butchering place.

wiyanihtâkew *pl.* **wiyanihtâkewak** (VAI) S/he butchers.

wiyanihtâkewikamik (VAI) A butcher shop or butchery.

wiyanihtâkewin *pl.* **wiyanihtâkewina** (NI) The act of butchering.

wiyateyihtâkosiw *pl.* **wiyateyihtâkosiwak** (VAI) S/he is thought of as funny or comical.

wiyateyimew (VTA) S/he thinks of her/him or them as being funny or comical.

  wiyateyitam (VTI) S/he thinks of it as being funny or comical.

  wiyateyimiwew (VTA) S/he thinks of people as being funny or comical.

wiyawihtam *pl.* **wiyawihtamwak** (VAI) S/he hears well.

wiyâkinew (VAI) S/he shapes or repairs them, i.e.: a blacksmith repairing instruments. *(Plains)*

wiyâkiham (VII) S/he shapes or repairs it.

wiyâkihowew (VTA) S/he shapes or repairs them.

wiyakihikew (VII) S/he shapes or repairs things.

wiyâsihkân (NI) Canned meat.

wiyâsimiw *pl.* **wiyâsimiwak** (VAI) S/he has meat.

wiyâsiwan *pl.* **wiyâsiwanwa** (VII) It is beefy or full of meat.

wiyâsowan *pl.* **wiyâsowanwa** (VII) There is meat on it.

wiyetinihan *pl.* **wiyetinihana** (NI) A piece of tobacco twisted in a roll. *(Plains). Alt.* **pîminikan** *(Northern).*

wiyin *pl.* **wiyina** (NI) Fat.

wiyiniw *pl.* **wiyiniwak** (VAI) S/he is fat; s/he has fat on her/his body. *(Plains). Alt.* **wîyinowisiw** *(Northern).*

wiyinohew (VTA) S/he makes her/him fat.

wiyinohiwew (VTA) S/he makes people fat.

wiyinomakan *pl.* **wiyinomakanwa** (VII) It has fat on it.

wiyomew (VTA) S/he tells her/him what to do. *(Plains). Alt.* **oyimew** *(Northern).*

wiyotam (VTI) S/he incites it.

wiyoniwew (VTA) S/he tells people what to do.

wiyonikew (VTI) S/he incites things.

wiyoyow *pl.* **wiyoyowak** (VAI) S/he howls. *(Plains). Alt.* **ôyow** *(Northern).*

wiyoyowin *pl.* **wiyoyowina** (NI) The act of howling. *(Plains). Alt.* **ôyowin** *(Northern).*

wîcehtahew *pl.* **wîcehtahewak** (VTA) S/he assists them in breeding.

wîcihew (VTA) S/he assists her/him or them; s/he participates.

wîcitâw (VTI) S/he assists it.

wîcihiwew (VAI) S/he assists others.

wîcihikowisiw *pl.* **wîcihkowisiwak** (VAI) S/he is helped spirtually.

wîcihikowisiwin *pl.* **wîcihikowisiwina** (NI) The act of receiving spirtual help.

wîcihiwew *pl.* **wîcihiwewak** (VAI) S/he accompanies or tags along with the group.

wîcihiwewin *pl.* **wîcihiwewina** (NI) The act of accompaning or tagging along with the group; participation.

wîcikapesîmew (VTA) S/he camps with her/him overnight; s/he spends the night with her/him.

wîcikapesîtam (VTI) S/he camps with it overnight.

wîcikapesîmiwew (VTA) S/he camps with people overnight.

wîcikâpawistawew (VTA) S/he stands with her/him or them.

wîcikâpawistam (VTI) S/he stands with it.

wîcikâpawistâkew (VTA) S/he stands with people.

wîcimâtomew (VTA) S/he cries with her/him or them.

wîcimâtomiwew (VTA) S/he cries with people.

wîcimetawemew (VTA) S/he plays with her/him or them.

wîcimetawetam (VTI) S/he plays with it.

wîcimetawemiwew (VTA) S/he plays with people.

wîciminihkwemew (VTA) S/he drinks with her/him or them.

wîciminihkwemiwew (VTA) S/he gets drunk with people.

wîcimiyawâtamowmew (VTA) S/he has a happy time with her/him.

wîcimiyawâtamowtam (VTI) S/he has a happy time with it.

wîcimiyawâtamowmiwew (VTA) S/he has a happy time with people.

wîcinikamômew (VTA) S/he sings with her/him or them.

wîcinikamôtam (VTI) S/he sings with it.

wîcinikamômiwew (VTA) S/he sings with people.

wîcinôtinitômew *pl.* **wîcinôtinitômewak** (VTA) S/he fights with her/him. *(Plains). Alt.* **nôtinitomew** *(Northern).*

wîcipihtwâmew (VTA) S/he smokes with her/him.

wîcipihtwâmiwew (VTA) S/he smokes with people.

wîcipîkiskwemew (VTA) S/he talks with her/him or them.

wîcipîkiskwetam (VTI) S/he talks with it.

wîcipîkiskwemiwew (VTA) S/he talks with people.

wîcohkamawew (VTA) S/he helps her/him with something. *(Plains). Var.* **nîsohkamawew**. *Alt.* **ohcikamawew** *(Northern).*

wîcohkamatam (VTI) S/he helps it up.

wîcohkamakew (VTA) S/he helps someone up.

wîhcasin *pl.* **wîhcasinwa** (VII) It is simple or not very hard to do; easy.

wîkihtahew (VTA) S/he marries them.

wîkihtahiwew (VTA) S/he gets people married.

wîkihtiw *pl.* **wîkihtiwak** (VAI) S/he is married to someone.

wîkihtowak (VTA) They are married to each other.

wîkiw *pl.* **wîkiwak** (VAI) S/he lives or inhabits there; s/he dwells there; s/he resides there; s/he has a home there.

wîkîhew (VTA) S/he gives her/him a place to inhabit or live.

wîkîtâw (VTI) S/he gives it a place to inhabit or live.

wîkîhiwew (VTA) S/he gives people places to inhabit or live.

wîkowin *pl.* **wîkowina** (NI) The act of inhabiting; a dwelling.

wînayih *pl.* **wînayiha** (NI) Something gross or foul.

wînâtisowin *pl.* **wînâtisowina** (NI) Being impure, filthy, or dirty; impurity.

wînâw *pl.* **wînâwa** (VII) It is filthy or dirty.

wîncoyesis *pl.* **wîncoyesiswak** (NA) A skunk. *(Plains)*. *Alt.* **sikak** *(Northern)*.

wîneyihtâkosiw *pl.* **wîneyihtâkosiwak** (VAI) S/he is considered filthy or dirty; disgusting.

wînih (NI) Bone marrow.

wînihow *pl.* **wînihowak** (VTA) S/he makes herself/ himself filthy or dirty.

wînihowin *pl.* **wînihowina** (NI) The act of making oneself filthy or dirty.

wînihtak *pl.* **wînihtakwa** (NI) A rotten piece of wood.

wînimâkosiw *pl.* **wînimâkosiwak** (VAI) S/he smells pungent.

wînimâkwan *pl.* **wînimâkwanwa** (VII) It smells pungent.

wînimâsiw *pl.* **wînimâsiwak** (VAI) The smell of it burning is pungent.

wînimâsiwin *pl.* **wînimâsiwina** (NI) A pungent smell.

wînimâstew *pl.* **wînimâstewa** (VII) The smell of it burning is pungent.

wînimâswew (VAI) S/he cooks them and they produce a pungent smell.

  wînimâsam (VAI) S/he cooks it and it produces a pungent smell.

  wînimâsikew (VAI) S/he cooks things and they produce a pungent smell.

wînisîhisowin *pl.* **wînisîhisowina** (NI) The act of appearing to live in squalor.

wîniyisâyâwin *pl.* **wîniyisâyâwina** (NI) The act of being ribald; ribaldry.

wîpac (IPC) Soon. *(Plains)*. *Alt.* **kîyipa** *(Northern)*.

wîpinâkwan *pl.* **wîpinâkwanwa** (VII) S/he is a grayish color.

wîsahkecâhk (NA) The Cree culture hero and the object of many legends and tales.

wîsakahpinew *pl.* **wîsakahpinewak** (VAI) S/he has pain.

wîsakamew (VAI) Her/his bite is causing her/him pain.

  wîsakamîwew (VAI) Her/his bite is causing people pain.

wîsakan *pl.* **wîsakanwa** (VII) It tastes bitter.

wîsakapiw *pl.* **wîsakapiwak** (VAI) S/he is in pain from sitting.

wîsakapiwin *pl.* **wîsakapiwina** (NI) The act of being in pain from sitting.

wîsakasew *pl.* **wîsakasewak** (VAI) S/he has a burning sensation on her/his skin.

wîsakasewin *pl.* **wîsakasewina** (NI) The act of having a burning sensation on one's skin.

wîsakatahwew (VTA) S/he hurts her/him by hitting her/ him.

  wîsakatahikew (VTA) S/he hurts someone by hitting.

wîsakatwemow *pl.* **wîsakatwemowak** (VAI) S/he is crying in pain.

wîsakatwemowin *pl.* **wîsakatwemowina** (NI) The act of crying in pain.

wîsakâpasiw *pl.* **wîsakâpasiwak** (VAI) The smoke is hurting her/his eyes.

wîsakeyihtam *pl.* **wîsakeyihtamwak** (VAI) S/he is in pain because of her/his illness.

wîsakeyitamostamawew (VTA) S/he feels her/his pain; s/he empathizes with her/him. *(Northern)*. *Alt.* **môsihtestamawew** *(Plains)*.

  wîsakeyitamostamatâw (VTA) S/he feels its pain.

  wîsakeyitamostamakew (VTA) S/he feel people's pain.

wîsakeyitamowin *pl.* **wîsakeyitamowina** (NI) Being in pain because of illness; affliction.

wîsakimin *pl.* **wîsakimina** (NI) A low bush cranberry.

wîsakinew (VAI) S/he hurts or injures her/him with her/ his grip; her/his handling of her/him is painful to her/him.

  wîsakiniwew (VAI) S/he hurts or injures people with her/his grip.

  wîsakinikew (VAI) S/he hurts or injures things with her/his grip.

wîsakipayiw *pl.* **wîsakipayiwak** (VAI) She has a painful miscarriage; s/he feels twinges of pain.

wîsakipayowin *pl.* **wîsakipayowina** (NI) A spontaneous abortion or miscarriage.

wîsakipitew (VTA) S/he is hurting her/him by pulling, i.e.: a dentist.

  wîsakipisiwew (VTA) S/he is hurting someone by pulling.

wîsakisimew (VTA) S/he hurts her/him by causing bodily injury.

  wîsakititâw (VTA) S/he hurts her/his sore hand.

  wîsakisimiwew (VTA) S/he hurts people by body contact.

wîsakisin *pl.* **wîsakisinwak** (VAI) S/he is hurt or injured by the fall.

wîsakiskawew *pl.* **wîsakiskawewak** (VTA) S/he is hurting her/him with a bodily injury.

wîsakiskâkiw *pl.* **wîsakiskâkiwak** (VTA) S/he was hurt or injured by something.

wîsakitehenitowin *pl.* **wîsakitehenitowina** (NI) The act of agonizing.

wîsakiteheskâkiw *pl.* **wîsakiteheskâkiwak** (VTA) S/he or it is causing her/him a heartache.

wîsakitehew *pl.* **wîsakitehewak** (VAI) S/he has a heartache; s/he is suffering a broken heart.

231

wîsakitehewin *pl.* **wîsakitehewina** (NI) The act of having a heartache; being hurt emotionally; having a broken heart; poignancy.

wîsakiyawesiwin *pl.* **wîsakiyawesiwina** (NI) The act of being outraged; outrageous.

wîsaksimew *pl.* **wîsaksimewak** (VTA) S/he hurts her/him.

wîsawitam (VTA) S/he invites someone to go along.
  wîsawimiwew (VTA) S/he invites others to go along.

wîsawitamowin *pl.* **wîsawitamowina** (NI) The act of giving an invitation.

wîsâmew *pl.* **wîsâmewak** (VTA) S/he invites her/him to go along.

wîscihkânis *pl.* **wîscihkânisa** (NI) A small haystack.

wîsih (NI) A fat covering found outside the stomach of animals.

wîsinâw *pl.* **wîsinâwa** (NI) A beaver scent gland.

wîskacân *pl.* **wîskacânak** (NA) A whiskey jack, i.e.: a Canada jay. *(Northern)*. *Alt.* **wîskipôs** *(Plains)*.

wîskipôs *pl.* **wîskipôsak** (NA) A whiskey jack, i.e.: a Canada jay. *(Plains)*. *Alt.* **wîskacân** *(Northern)*.

wîsopiwaskimot *pl.* **wîsopiwaskimota** (NI) A gall bladder. *(Northern)*. *Alt.* **wîsopiy** *(Plains)*.

wîsopiy *pl.* **wîsopiya** (NI) A gall bladder. *(Plains)*. *Alt.* **wîsopiwaskimot** *(Northern)*.

wîspâcimew (VTA) S/he says annoying words to her/him. *(Plains)*. *Alt.* **pacimew** *(Northern)*.
  wîspâcimiwew (VTA) S/he says annoying words to others.

wîstaskemâkan *pl.* **wîstaskemâkanak** (NA) Someone who lives in the same part of the country, i.e.: a neighbor.

wîstihkân *pl.* **wîstihkâna** (NI) A hay stack.

wîstihkew *pl.* **wîstihkewak** (VAI) S/he makes haystacks.

wîtapimew (VTA) S/he sits with her/him or them.
  wîtapitam (VTI) S/he sits with it.
  wîtapimiwew (VTA) S/he sits with people.
  wîtapihcikew (VTA) S/he sits with things.

wîtisânitowin (NI) Having siblings. *(Northern)*. *Alt.* **wicisanitowin** *(Plains)*.

wîwahew (VTA) S/he puts a pack on him, i.e.: a horse; s/he puts the blame on her/him.
  wîwataw (VTI) S/he puts a pack on it.
  wîwahiwew (VTA) S/he puts a pack on people.

wîwahow *pl.* **wîwahowak** (VAI) S/he puts a pack on herself/himself.

wîwahowin *pl.* **wîwahowina** (NI) The act of being loaded with a pack; being blamed.

wîwewepisiw *pl.* **wîwewepisiwak** (VAI) S/he is going to swing. *(Plains)*. *Alt.* **wehwepisiw** *(Northern)*.

wîyahkwâtew (VTA) S/he swore at her/him or them.
  wîyahkwâtam (VTI) S/he swears at it.

wîyahkwâsiwew (VTA) S/he swears at people.

wîyahkwew *pl.* **wîyahkwewak** (VAI) S/he swears; s/he uses foul language.

wîyahkwewin *pl.* **wîyahkwewina** (NI) The act of using foul or profane language; the act of swearing.

wîyakan *pl.* **wîyakanwa** (VII) It is an unfortunate squandering.

wîyakihkâkamihtâw *pl.* **wîyakihkâkamihtâwa** (VTI) S/he made it luke warm.

wîyakihkâkamow (VII) It is lukewarm.

wîyakihow *pl.* **wîyakihowak** (VAI) S/he is squandering her/his life unnecessarily.

wîyakihowin *pl.* **wîyakihowina** (NI) The act of squandering one's life unnecessarily.

wîyakimew (VTA) S/he castigates her/him for no reason, i.e.: squandered words.
  wîyakimiwew (VTA) S/he castigates people for no reason, i.e.: squandered words.

wîyasihtawew (VTA) S/he thinks that s/he sounds funny or comical.
  wîyasihtam (VTI) S/he thinks it sounds funny or comical.
  wîyasihtâkew (VTA) S/he thinks people sound funny or comical.

wîyasihtâkwan *pl.* **wîyasihtâkwanwa** (VII) It sounds funny or odd.

wîyatwew *pl.* **wîyatwewak** (VAI) S/he tells funny jokes or stories. *Var.* **wawîyatwew**.

wîyawâw (PR) Them.

wîyawiskâkow *pl.* **wîyaswiskâkowak** (VAI) It builds up her/his body.

wîyâs *pl.* **wîyâsa** (NI) Meat.

wîyâtikosiw *pl.* **wîyâtikosiwak** (VAI) S/he is fun-loving or joyful.

wîyâtikosiwin *pl.* **wîyâtikosiwina** (NI) Being fun-loving or joyful.

wîyâtikwan *pl.* **wîyâtikwanwa** (VII) It is fun-loving or joyful.

wîyâw *pl.* **wîyâwa** (NI) Her/his body.

wîyinowisiw *pl.* **wîyinowisiwak** (VAI) S/he has fat on her/his body. *(Northern)*. *Alt.* **wiyiniw** *(Plains)*.

wîyipapawewin *pl.* **wîyipapawewina** (NI) The act of being sloppy. *(Northern)*. *Alt.* **mâmâsimâciwin** *(Plains)*.

wîyipastim *pl.* **wîyipastimwak** (NA) A chestnut colored horse.

wîyipawew *pl.* **wîyipawewak** (VAI) Her/his fur is dirty.

wîyipayi *pl.* **wîyipayiha** (NI) Something filthy; filth.

wîyipâskosiw *pl.* **wîyipâskosiwak** (VAI) The log is dirty.

wîyipâskwan *pl.* **wîyipâskwanwa** (VII) The pole is dirty.

wîyipâtan *pl.* **wîyipâtanwa** (VII) It is dirty. *Var.* **iyipâtan**.

wîyipâw *pl.* **wîyipâwa** (VII) It has dirt or filth on it.

wîyipicihcew *pl.* **wîyipicihcewak** (VAI) S/he has dirty hands.

wîyipihew (VTA) S/he dirties them.

wîyipitâw (VTI) S/he dirties it.

wîyipihiwew (VTA) S/he dirties people.

wîyipihcikew (VTI) S/he dirties things.

wîyipihkwew *pl.* **wîyipihkwewak** (VAI) S/he has a dirty face.

wîyipinâkosiw *pl.* **wîyipinâkosiwak** (NA) A dark complexion.

wîyipisimew *pl.* **wîyipisimewak** (VTA) S/he dirties them by dragging them, i.e.: socks.

wîyipisiw *pl.* **wîyipisiwak** (VAI) S/he has dirt or filth on her/him.

wîyipisiwin *pl.* **wîyipisiwina** (NI) Having dirt or filth on oneself.

wîyipiskawew (VTA) S/he dirties them with her/his dirty clothes or boots.

wîyipiskam (VTI) S/he dirties it, i.e.: the floor with muddy feet.

wîyipiskâkew (VTA) S/he dirties people with her/his dirty clothing.

wîyipistikwânew *pl.* **wîyipistikwânewak** (VAI) S/he has a dirty head or hair.

wîyitihp *pl.* **wîyitihpa** (NI) A brain. *(Plains). Alt.* **wihtihp** *(Northern).*

wîyocipayiw *pl.* **wîyocipayiwa** *or* **wîyocipayiwak** (VII) *or* (VAI) It *or* s/he comes in abundance.

y

yahkahwew (VTA) S/he gives her/him a push with her/his vehicle.

yahkaham (VTI) S/he gives it a push with her/his vehicle.

yahkahowew (VTA) S/he pushes people with her/his vehicle.

yahkahikew (VTI) S/he pushes things with her/his vehicle.

yahkakihcikewin *pl.* **yahkakihcikewina** (NI) The act of enhancing or incrementing cost or price.

yahkasin *pl.* **yahkasinwa** (VII) It is lightweight.

yahkâpiskaw *pl.* **yahkâpiskawa** (VII) The iron or steel is lightweight.

yahkâskosew *pl.* **yahkâskosewa** (VII) It is a partly burned piece of wood.

yahkâskwan *pl.* **yahkâskwanwa** (VII) It is light, i.e.: a pole.

yahkâstimew (VTA) S/he makes her/him sail.

yahkâstitâw (VTI) S/he makes it sail.

yahkâstimon *pl.* **yahkâstimona** (NI) A sail boat.

yahkâstimonâhtik *pl.* **yahkâstimonâhtikwa** (NI) The pole on a sail boat.

yahkâstimonekin *pl.* **yahkâstimonekinwa** (NI) Material for the sail.

yahkâstimow *pl.* **yahkâstimowak** (VAI) S/he sails.

yahkemohew *pl.* **yahkemohewak** (VTA) S/he makes them increase.

yahkemow *pl.* **yahkemowak** (VAI) S/he increases or generates.

yahkihew *pl.* **yahkihewak** (VTA) S/he makes them lightweight.

yahkikihew (VTA) S/he makes her/him grow light in weight.

yahkikihtâw (VTI) S/he makes it grow light in weight.

yahkikihiwew (VTA) S/he makes people grow light in weight.

yahkikihcikew (VTI) S/he makes things grow light in weight.

yahkikiw *pl.* **yahkikiwak** (VAI) S/he grows light in weight.

yahkinew (VTA) S/he gives them a push.

yahkinam (VTI) S/he gives it a push.

yahkiniwew (VTA) S/he gives people a push.

yahkinikew (VTI) S/he gives things a push.

yahkipitew (VTA) S/he pulls them easily.

yahkipitam (VTI) S/he pulls it easily.

yahkipisiwew (VTA) S/he pulls people easily.

yahkipicikew (VTI) S/he pulls things easily.

yahkisehikâkan *pl.* **yakisehikâkana** (NI) A stoker or poker used in the fire. *(Plains and Northern variant). Alt.* **tahtaskosehikakan** *(Northern).*

yahkisehtâw (VTI) S/he makes it light in weight.

yahkisehtcihikew (VTI) S/he makes something light in weight.

yahkiskawew (VTA) S/he pushes her/him around.

yahkiskam (VTI) S/he pushes it around.

yahkiskâkew (VTA) S/he pushes people around.

yahkiskâtchikew (VTI) S/he pushes things around.

yahkitisawew (VTA) S/he pushes her/him along; s/he tells her/him to keep going.

yahkitisaham (VTI) S/he pushes it along.

yahkitisahowew (VTA) S/he pushes people along.

yahkitisahikew (VTI) S/he pushes everyone along.

yahkitisihew *pl.* **yahkitisihewak** (VTA) S/he makes her/him light in weight.

yahkitisiw *pl.* **yahkitisiwak** (VAI) S/he is light in weight.

yahkitisiwin *pl.* **yahkitisiwina** (NI) Being light in weight.

yahkohtewin *pl.* **yahkohtewina** (NI) The act of moving forward.

yapew *pl.* **yapewak** (NA) A bull moose. *(Northern). Alt.* **iyâpewimôswa** *(Plains).*

yayîpewin *pl.* **yayîpewina** (NI) The act of laying on your side.

yayîpîw *pl.* **yayîpîwak** (VAI) S/he lays on her/his side.

yâhkikin *pl.* **yâhkikinwa** (VII) It grows light in weight.

yâhkipayiw *pl.* **yâhkipayiwa** *or* **yâhkipayiwak** (VII) *or* (VAI) It *or* s/he increases by itself *or* it goes light in weight.

yâhyânam *pl.* **yâhyânamwak** (VAI) S/he swims.

yâhyînamowin *pl.* **yâhyînamowina** (NI) The act of swimming.

yâkwâmeyimow *pl.* **yâkwâmeyimowak** (VAI) S/he believes herself/himself to be reliable. *(Northern). Alt.* **mamisîwâtisiw** *(Plains).*

yâkwâmeyimowin *pl.* **yâkwâmeyimowina** (NI) The act of believing that oneself is reliable.

yâkwâmimew *pl.* **yâkwâmimewak** (VTA) S/he thinks s/he is reliable.

yâkwâmisiw *pl.* **yâkwâmisiwak** (VAI) S/he is reliable.

yâkwâmisiwin *pl.* **yâkwâmisiwina** (NI) The act of being reliable.

yâsâpekinew (VTA) S/he lowers them with a rope.

yâsâpekinam (VTI) S/he lowers it with a rope.

yâsâpekiniwew (VTA) S/he lowers people with a rope.

yâsâpekinikew (VTI) S/he lowers things with a rope.

yâsestawew *pl.* **yâsestawewak** (VTA) S/he slides down to them.

235

yâsewin *pl.* **yâsewina** (NI) The act of sliding down.

yâsinew *pl.* **yâsinewa** (VTI) S/he slides it (inanimate) off.

yâsinew *pl.* **yâsinewak** (VTA) S/he slides it off, i.e.: pants.

yâsipayihew (VTA) S/he makes them slide down.

  yâsipayihtâw (VTI) S/he makes it slide down.

  yâsipayihiwew (VTA) S/he makes people slide down.

  yâsipayitchikew (VTI) S/he makes things slide down.

yâsipayihow *pl.* **yâsipayihowak** (VAI) S/he slides down.

yâsipayiw *pl.* **yâsipayiwa** (VII) It slides down.

yâsipayiw *pl.* **yâsipayiwak** (VAI) It slides down, i.e.: pants.

yâsitisahamawew *pl.* **yâsitisahamawewak** (VTA) S/he sends it down to her/him.

yâsiw *pl.* **yâsiwak** (VAI) S/he is sliding down.

yâwaskenam *pl.* **yâwaskenamwak** (VAI) S/he can barely touch the ground in deep water.

yâwâpamew *pl.* **yâwâpamewak** (VTA) S/he sees her/him at a distance.

yâwâsihtawew (VTA) S/he hears her/him at a distance.

  yâwâsihtam (VTI) S/he hears it at a distance.

  yâwâsihtâkew (VTA) S/he hears people at a distance.

yâwehakwan *pl.* **yâwehakwanwa** (VII) The sound can be heard at a distance. *(Northern)*. *Alt.* **yâwehtâkwan** *(Plains)*.

yâwehtâkwan *pl.* **yâwehtâkwanwa** (VII) The sound can be heard at a distance. *(Plains)*. *Alt.* **yâwehakwan** *(Northern)*.

yâwenawew (VTA) S/he thinks s/he resembles or looks like someone else.

  yâwenâkew (VTA) S/he appears to think that someone looks like someone else.

yâwenâkwan *pl.* **yâwenâkwanwa** (VII) It resembles something; it looks like something. *(Northern)*. *Alt.* **âwenâkwan** *(Plains)*.

yâwew *pl.* **yâwewak** (VAI) It sounds far away.

yâwewin *pl.* **yâwewina** (NI) The act of sounding far away.

yâwihtakosiw *pl.* **yâwihtakosiwak** (VAI) S/he sounds far away.

yâwihtawew (VTA) S/he makes them sound from a long ways. *(Plains)*.

  yâwihtam (VTI) S/he makes it sound from a long ways.

  yâwihtahewak (VTA) S/he makes someone sound from a long ways.

yâwinâkosiw *pl.* **yâwinâkosiwak** (VAI) S/he resembles someone; s/he looks something like her/him. *(Northern)*. *Alt.* **âwenâkosiw** *(Plains)*.

yâwipayihew (VTA) S/he makes them sound from a long ways. *(Northern)*

  yâwipayihtaw (VTI) S/he makes it sound from a long ways.

yâwipayihiwew (VTA) S/he makes someone sound from a long ways.

yâwipayiw *pl.* **yâwipayiwa** *or* **yâwipayiwak** (VII) *or* (VAI) The sound can be heard echoing.

yâyikahwew (VTI) S/he cuts a hole in them, i.e.: a pair of pants.

  yâyikaham (VTI) S/he cuts a hole in it, i.e.: a jacket.

  yâyikahowew (VTA) S/he cuts a hole in people's clothes.

  yâyikahikew (VTI) S/he cuts a hole in everything.

yâyikipayiw *pl.* **yâyikipayiwa** *or* **yâyikipayiwak** (VII) *or* (VAI) It *or* s/he is torn.

yâyikipitew (VTA) S/he tears them up.

  yâyikipitam (VTI) S/he tears it up.

  yâyikipisiwew (VTA) S/he tears someone's clothes up.

  yâyikipitcikew (VTI) S/he tears things up.

yâyiskipitew (VTA) S/he pulls them off the traps.

  yâyiskipitam (VTI) S/he pulls it off the traps.

  yâyiskipisiwew (VTA) S/he pulls people off the traps.

  yâyiskipitcikew (VTI) S/he pulls things off the traps.

yâyiskwenew (VTA) S/he twists her/his head all around.

  yâyiskwenam (VTI) S/he twists its head all around.

  yâyiskweniwew (VTA) S/he twists peoples' heads all around.

  yâyiskwenikew (VTA) S/he twists everyones' heads all around.

yehew *pl.* **yehewak** (VAI) S/he is breathing.

yehewin *pl.* **yehewina** (NI) The act of breathing.

yekâwimaskotew *pl.* **yekâwimaskotewa** (NI) A sandy prairie. *(Northern)*. *Alt.* **iyikawiskâw** *(Plains)*.

yekistikweyaw *pl.* **yekistikweyawa** (VII) The river has forks in it.

yeyihew *pl.* **yeyihewak** (VTA) S/he tempts her/him, i.e.: s/he is a bad example.

yeyimew *pl.* **yeyimewak** (VTA) S/he coaxes her/him to give into temptation.

yeyisiw *pl.* **yeyisiwak** (VAI) S/he is tempted.

yeyisowin *pl.* **yeyisowina** (NI) The act of temptation.

yihkatawâw *pl.* **yihkatawâwa** (NI) A meadow or lea.

yikatekâpawiw *pl.* **yikatekâpawiwak** (VAI) S/he stands off to one side to be out of the way.

yikatepayihowin *pl.* **yikatepayihowina** (NI) The act of dodging.

yikawiskâhk (LN) At the beach; sandy place.

yikawiskâw *pl.* **yikawiskâwa** (VII) It is sandy.

yikâwan *pl.* **yikâwanwa** (VII) It is full of sand.

yikâwâkamiw (VAI) The water is sandy.

yikihcawases *pl.* **yikihcaswasesak** (NA) A one-year-old bull moose.

yikicik *pl.* **yikicikwak** (NA) A clumsy person. *(Northern)*. *Alt.* **onanâtohkonikew** *(Plains)*.

yikihtawamiw *pl.* **yikihtawamiwa** (VII) The road has a fork.

yikihtawipayiw *pl.* **yikihtawipayiwa** (VII) A fork in the road.

yikihtawiteskanew *pl.* **yikihtawiteskanewak** (VAI) The moose has forks on its horns.

yikihtawiyaw *pl.* **yikihtawiyawa** (VII) It has many forks.

yikitchikâwiw *pl.* **yikitchikâwiwak** (VAI) S/he is very slow.

yikitcikâwiwin *pl.* **yikitcikâwiwina** (NI) The act of being very slow.

yikiytawâw *pl.* **yikiytawâwa** (VII) The river has a back channel.

yikopiwipîsim (NA) The frosty moon or month; November. *Var.* **ayikopinipîsim, iyikopiwipîsim.**

yikopîwan (VII) It is frosty, i.e.: rime.

yikwaskwan (VII) It is cloudy.

yiwahikan *pl.* **yiwahikanak** (NA) A piece of dry, pounded moose meat.

yiwahikew *pl.* **yiwahikewa** (VTI) S/he is pounding the meat. *Var.* **iyiwahikew.**

yiwahwew (VTA) S/he pounds her/him. *Var.* **iyiwahwew.**
  yiwaham (VTI) S/he pounds it.
  yiwahowew (VTA) S/he pounds someone.
  yiwahikew (VTI) S/he pounds something.

yiwatahwew *pl.* **yiwatahwewak** (VTA) S/he smashes them up by pounding.

yiwew *pl.* **yiwewa** (VII) It is deflated.

yiwipayiw *pl.* **yiwipayiwa** *or* **yiwipayiwak** (VII) *or* (VAI) It *or* s/he became deflated.

yiyihiwewin *pl.* **yiyihiwewina** (NI) The act of being attracted or tempted; attraction.

yiyikastis *pl.* **yiyikastisak** (NA) A homemade glove.

yiyikâw *pl.* **yiyikâwa** (NI) Something made with fingers on it.

yiyikicihcân *pl.* **yiyikicihcâna** (NI) A finger on your hand.

yiyikisitân *pl.* **yiyikisitâna** (NI) A human toe.

yiyikisiw *pl.* **yiyikisiwak** (VAI) It has fingers, i.e.: a glove.

yîkaw (NI) Sand. *Var.* **iyikâw.**

yîkawaciy (NI) Sandhill.

yîkicikâwohtew *pl.* **yîkicikâwohtewak** (VAI) S/he walks slowly. *(Plains). Alt.* **pekihkâtohtew** *(Northern). Var.* **papwâstahohtew** *(Plains).*

yîkinew (VTA) S/he milks the cow.
  yîkinam (VTI) S/he milks it out.
  yîkiniwew (VTA) S/he milks someone.
  yîkinikew (VTI) S/he milks cows.

yîkinikâkan *pl.* **yîkinikâkanak** (NA) A milker.

yohtehwew (VTI) S/he opens up a can with an instrument.
  yohteham (VTI) S/he opens it up with an instrument.
  yohtehikew (VTI) S/he opens things up with an instrument.

yohtekotew *pl.* **yohtekotewa** (VII) It is open, i.e.: a door.

yohtenamawew *pl.* **yohtenamawewak** (VTA) S/he opens it for her/him.

yohtenew (VTI) S/he opens up a box with her/his bare hands.
  yohtenam (VTI) S/he opens it up with her/his bare hands.
  yohtenikew (VTI) S/he opens things up with her/his bare hands.

yohtepitew (VTA) S/he pulls them open.
  yohtepitam (VTI) S/he pulls it open.
  yohtepicikew (VTI) S/he pulls things open.

yohtewepahwew (VTI) S/he knocks them open.
  yohtewepaham (VTI) S/he knocks it open.
  yohtewepahikew (VTI) S/he knocks things open.

yohteyaskwahikewin *pl.* **yohteyaskwahikewina** (NI) The act of prying open.

yohteyâskisam *pl.* **yohteyâskisamwak** (NI) Burned with a blow torch to open or shot by a gun to open.

yoskahcâw (VII) The ground is soft.

yoskahikan *pl.* **yoskahikana** (NI) Something soft with padding, i.e.: cotton batting.

yoskaskosiy *pl.* **yoskaskosiyak** (NI) A soft piece of grass.

yoskâpiskâw *pl.* **yoskâpiskâwa** (VII) The steel is soft or malleable.

yoskâpiskisiw *pl.* **yoskâpiskisiwak** (VAI) The metal object is soft or malleable.

yoskâskwan *pl.* **yoskâskwanwa** (VII) It is soft, i.e.: a pole.

yoskâtan *pl.* **yoskâtanwa** (VII) It is a soft piece.

yoskâtisiw *pl.* **yoskâtisiwak** (VAI) S/he has a soft-hearted character.

yoskâtisiwin *pl.* **yoskâtisiwina** (NI) Being a soft-hearted person. *(Northern). Alt.* **miyohtwâwin** *(Plains).*

yoskâw *pl.* **yoskâwa** (VII) It is soft.

yoskihew (VII) S/he made it soft, i.e.: bannock.
  yoskihtâw (VII) S/he softened it up, i.e.: moosehide.
  yoskihiwew (VAI) S/he softens people.
  yoskitchikew (VII) S/he softens things.

yoskihtak *pl.* **yoskihtakwa** (NI) A powdery soft wood used for smoking moose hide.

yoskihtakâw *pl.* **yoskihtakâwa** (VII) It is powdery soft.

yoskinew (VTI) S/he made them soft by rubbing.
  yoskinikew (VTI) S/he made things soft by rubbing.

yoskipem *pl.* **yoskipemak** (NA) A plantain.

yoskiskawew (VTI) S/he makes them soft by wearing them, i.e.: pants.
  yoskiskam (VTI) S/he makes it soft by wearing it.

yoskiskowakâw *pl.* **yoskiskowakâwa** (VII) It is soft mud.

yoskisiw *pl.* **yoskisiwak** (VAI) It is soft.

yoskisiwin *pl.* **yoskisiwina** (NI) Being soft; softness.

yoskitehestawew *pl.* **yoskitehestawewak** (VTA) S/he has a soft spot in her/his heart for her/him.

237

yoskitehew *pl.* **yoskitehewak** (VAI) S/he has a soft heart.

yoskitehewin *pl.* **yoskitehewina** (NI) The act of having a soft heart.

yospâtisiw *pl.* **yospâtisiwak** (VAI) S/he act tamed, i.e.: a wild horse. *(Northern). Alt.* **yospisîw** *(Plains).*

yospâtisiwin *pl.* **yospâtisiwina** (NI) The act of being tamed. *(Northern). Alt.* **yospisîwin** *(Plains).*

yospisihew *pl.* **yospisihewak** (VTA) S/he made her/him tame.

yospisiwin *pl.* **yospisiwina** (NI) Being tame, or kind.

yospisîw *pl.* **yospisîwak** (VAI) S/he acts tamed, i.e.: a wild horse. *(Plains). Alt.* **yospâtisiw** *(Northern).*

yospisîwin *pl.* **yospisîwina** (NI) The act of being tamed. *(Plains). Alt.* **yospâtisiwin** *(Northern).*

yôskihtepakwa (NI) The skunk cabbage plant.

yôtin (VII) It is windy.

yôwenam *pl.* **yôwenamwa** (VTI) S/he deflates it or s/he lets the air out of it, i.e.: a balloon.

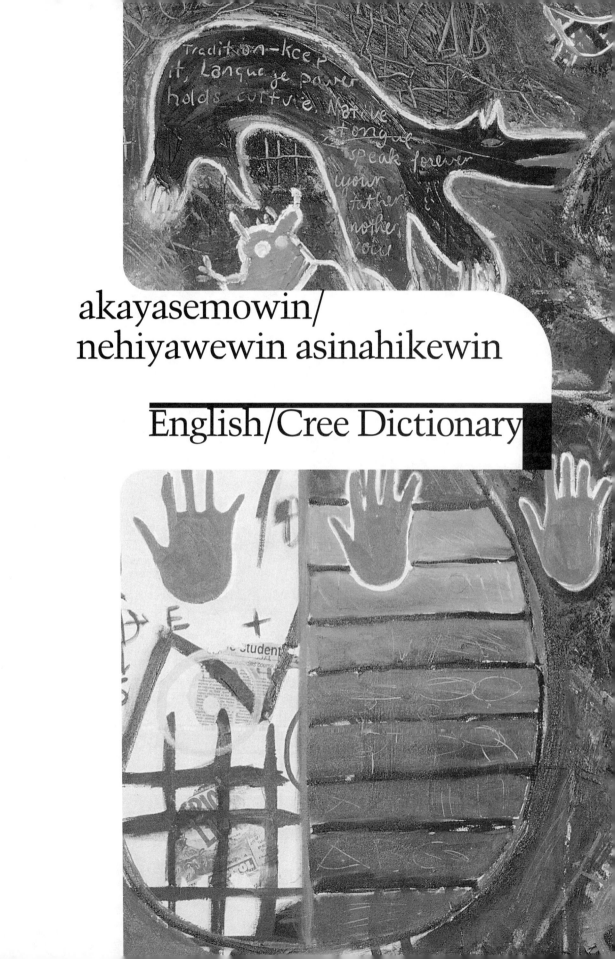

akayasemowin/ nehiyawewin asinahikewin

English/Cree Dictionary

A

aback Taken aback, *mâmaskâtamowin* (NI).

abaft At the back end, *otâhk* (IPC) *(Northern)*; *nâway* (IPC) *(Plains)*.

abandon Throwing something away, *wepinikewin* (NI); s/he abandons herself/himself to her/him, *pakiteyimisôstawew* (VTA); s/he abandons or gives up on herself/himself, *pakiteyimisiw* (VTA); the act of self-abandonment, *pakiteyimisowin* (NI); s/he is unable to get through to her/him and abandons the attempt, *pwâtawihew* (VTA).

abandoned When something has been abandoned, *kakeh wepinamihk*; a lonely and abandoned feeling, *kewâtan*; the act of feeling lonely and abandoned, *kewâteyimowin* (NI).

abase The act of reducing something, *asepicikewin* (NI).

abasement *otâhkipicikewin* (NI).

abash The act of making someone ashamed, *nîpiwihiwewin* (NI); s/he is ashamed, *nîpewisiw* (VAI).

abate *yâhkipayiw* (VAI).

abatement *acôpecikewin* (NI).

abbreviate *acôpekiskwewin* (NI).

abbreviation *acônikewin* (NI); *pakiteyhtamâkewin* (NI).

abcess An abcess or collection of pus, *miyi* (NI); s/he has an abcess, *miyiwew* (VAI).

abcessed *miyiwin* (NI).

abdomen *matay* (NI).

abdominal *matahk* (NI).

abduct *kwâsihiwewin* (NI); *kôtiniht kîmotowin* (NI).

abductor *ôkwâsihiwew* (NA).

aberrance *pîtosâyâwin* (NI).

aberrant *pîtosipayiw* (VII).

aberration *pîtosisiwepinikewin* (NI).

abeyance *nomemeciminikewin* (NI); *misikwâhkotew* (NA); *nemâskohtin* (VII).

abhor *kwâyakeyihcikewin* (NI).

abhorrence *pakwâtamowin* (NI).

abhorrent Something that is abhorrent or loathsome, *kakwâyakan* (NI).

abide *wîcêtowin* (NI)

abiding *wîcâyamtowin* (NI).

ability *kaskihtâwin* (NI).

abject *wâwiyak*.

abjuration *pomemetowin* (NI).

abjure *pômemew* (VTA).

ablate *maskahcihiwewin* (NI).

ablation *mansikâsowin* (NI).

ablaze *kwahkotew* (VII); blazing, *misiwayatew* (VII); raging fire, *misikwâhkotew* (NA); s/he burns them up, *mestihkaswew* (VTA).

able *kaskitâw* (VTA); *kaskihtâwin* (NI).

abloom *sâkipakâw* (VAI).

ably *wîhcasin* (VII).

abnegate *ponihtâwin* (NI).

abnormal *namoya kwayasksâyâwin*.

abnormality *pîtosâyâwin* (NI).

aboard *pôsiwin* (NI); *pôsiw* (VAI).

abode *kihciwikowin* (NI); *owikowin* (NI); one who resides in a certain place, *owikiw* (NA).

abolish *poneyicikew* (VTI); *ponitâw* (VTI).

abominable *nâspicmacîsâyawin* (NI); *naspacinâkwan* (VII).

abominate *kakwâyakeyihtâkwan* (VII).

abomination *kakwayakeyimiwewin* (NI).

aboriginal i.e.: a Cree, *nehiyaw* (NA); s/he is aboriginal, *nehiyâwiw* (NA).

abort *wîsakipayiw* (VAI).

abortion *wîsakipayowin* (NI).

abortive *misiwanâcihcikewin* (NI).

abound *mihcetometanaw* (IPC); *mihcetin* (VII); *mihcetiw* (VAI).

about Almost *nânitâw* (IPC); here and there, around and about, *papâmi* (IPC).

above *tahkoc* (IPC); *ispimihk* (IPC); it fits on top, *tahkocihtin* (VII).

abrade *pâpakopayiw* (VAI).

abrasion *pâpakwasakayesiniwin* (NI).

abreast *tipiskôcihew* (VTA); s/he is even with it, *tipiskocitâw* (VTI).

abrogate *âhtasowewin* (NI).

abrupt *sîsîkocinakinamâkewin* (NI).

abscond *kîmotowin* (NI).

absence *patahamowin* (NI); *pataham* (VTI);

absent-minded *wanikiskisiwin* (NI).

absent S/he is absent, *namoya otâhayaw* (VAI); s/he is absent without a good reason, *otamisipwehtew* (VAI).

absently *waneyawin* (NI); *wanipayihcikewin* (NI).

absolute *metoni* (IPC).

absolutely *metoni sôskwâc*.

absolution *kâsenamâtowin* (NI).

absolve *paketinowewin* (NI); *pakiteyihtamâkewin* (NI); *kâsenamâtowin* (NI).

absorb *mescipicikewin* (NI).

absorbed *mescisôpahcikewin* (NI).

absorbency *sôpahcikewin* (NI).

absorbent *otahcikan* (NA).

absorbing *sohkimamitoniyicikan* (NA); *otahcikewin* (NI).

241

absorption *sôpahcikâkan* (NI).

abstain *ekâ katotamihk*.

abstainer *opakiteyihcikew* (NA).

abstemious *ka poni isayahk*.

abstention *ka ponihtahk*.

abstinence Fasting, *ka ewansehesohk*; the act of fasting, *yiwanisihisiwin* (NI).

abstinent A fasting person, *otiyiwanisihisiw* (NA).

abstract Any old way, *sôskwâc pokowese* (IPC).

abstruse *ka wanohkakohk*.

absurd Being foolish, *kepâtisiwin* (NI).

absurdity *kakepâtinikewin* (NI).

abundance Very much, *metoni mistahi* (IPC); it comes in abundance, *wîyocipayiw* (VII).

abundant In abundance, *namoyacikawasis*; there is lots of, *mihcetin* (VII); it is abundant, *osâmeyatin* (VII); it is abundant, *weyotan* (VII).

abuse The act of abusing someone, *kitimahiwewin* (NI).

abusive Being abusive, *pîwihiwewin* (NI).

abut It is sitting against something, *akwastew* (VAI).

abutment Something sitting against something, *akwascikan* (VII).

abutting The act of placing things against each other, *akwascikewin* (NI).

abysm A bottomless lake, *metoni wanatimew*.

abysmal Bottomless or endless, *mecimwacipayiw* (VII).

abyss *itâmpek* (IPC).

accede Being agreeable to something, *kawicewâkanihk*.

accelerate The act of going faster, *kisiskâpayowin* (NI).

acceleration An increase in speed, *kisiskapayihcikewin* (NI).

accent Emphasising one's speech to be understood, *nisitohtâkosiwin* (NI).

accentual S/he sounds differently or s/he has an accent, *pîtosihtâkosiw* (VAI).

accentuate *nistaweyihtâkosiwin* (NI).

accept The act of accepting something, i.e.: an apology or gift, *miyotinikewin* (NI); *otina*; s/he warmly accepts her/him, *naheyihmew* (VTA); the act of warmly accepting something, *naheyihtamowin* (NI); they warmly accept each other, *naheyihtowak* (VTA); the act of feeling warm acceptance with one another, *naheyihtowin* (NI).

acceptability Taking something in good faith, *miyotinikewin* (NI).

acceptable Taken with a good heart, *metoni miyoteh*.

acceptably Received good heartedly, *miyoteh kîkway ka tôtamihk*.

acceptance Approval, *miyotinikewin* (NI).

accepted S/he is accepted, *miyotinaw* (VAI).

acceptor A person who accepts, *omiyotinikew* (NA).

access The way of approach, *pihtokwepayiw* (VAI).

accessory Someone who helps, *onîsohkamâkew* (NA).

accessibility Easy entering, *wehcipihtokwewin* (NI).

accessible It is easy to approach, *wehcihôpayiw* (VAI).

accession An addition, *tahkonikewin* (NI); the act of adding, *takonamakewin* (NI).

accessory Taking some more, *tahkonikewina* (NI).

accident A sudden mishap, *sisikôc mayinikewin* (NI); a car crash, *tâwikintowin* (NI).

accidental Happening by chance, *wespenâc mayinikewin* (NI).

accidentally Not on purpose, *namoya ohcitâw* (IPC); accidental, not on purpose, unintentionally, *pisci* (IPC).

acclaim A loud applause, *awîyak ka miyosakowatiht*; to applaud by shouting, *miyosakowasiwewin* (NI).

acclivity *nesihkacopahcâw* (NI).

accommodate *ka pesihiwew*; *tawîcihiht* (VAI).

accommodating *ka kapesihiwehk*.

accommodation *kapesihiwewin* (NI).

accompany The act of accompanying someone, *wîcihiwewin* (NI); s/he assists her/him or them, *wîcihew* (VTA); s/he accompanies her/him, *wicewew* (VTA); s/he accompanies or tags along with the group, *wîcihiwew* (VAI); the act of accompanying or tagging along with the group, *wîcihiwewin* (NI).

accomplish *kisâyâwin* (NI); *kispinatam* (VTI).

accomplished *kihkisayaw*; *kesehtawin* (NI).

accomplishment *kesihcikewin* (NI); *kâskitamâsowin* (NI).

accord *miyoteh*; *kîyâsoskwâc* (IPC).

accordance *miyoteh miyitowin*.

according *soskwacisimiyopayekî* (VII).

accordingly *isimeyopayeyik* (VII).

accrue *ka nihtâmiyopayihk*; *ka papewehk* (VAI).

acculturation *mamawi isihcikewin* (NI).

accumulate *ka mâwasakonikehk*; *mâwacitâw* (VTI).

accumulation *mâwasakonikewin* (NI).

accumulator *omâwasakonikew* (NA).

accuracy *metoni kwayaskopicikewin* (NI); *metoni kwayask* (IPC).

accurate *metoni ekota* (IPC); *tâpwew* (VAI).

accursed *wîyahkwatowin* (NI).

accusation *atameyihcikewin* (NI).

accuse The act of accusing, *atameyihcikewin* (NI); s/he is accused, *atameyemaw* (VAI); s/he accuses her/him, *atameyimat* (VTA); s/he accuses someone, *âsteyihcikew* (VAI); s/he accuses others, *misihkemow* (VTA).

accused *nayahtahâw* (VTA).

accustom *nakachitâw* (VTI); *nakâyâskam* (VTI).

accustomed *nakacihtâwin* (NI).

242

ace The highest card in a deck, *misipehikan* (NI); the ace or the number one card in a deck, *peyakopehikan* (NI); s/he plays an ace or s/he has all four aces, *peyakopehikew* (VAI).

ache Having aching bones, *teyisowin* (NI); s/he aches; s/he has aching bones, *teyisiw* (VAI); her/his bones ache right through to the marrow, *pinikanew* (VAI); s/he has an aching tooth, *tîyâpitew* (VAI); s/he has aching eyes, *tîyapiw* (VAI); s/he has an ache in her/his chest, *teyaskikanew* (VAI); s/he has an ache in her/his arm, *teyipitonew* (VAI); s/he has an ache in her/his head or s/he has a headache, *teyistikwânew* (VAI).

achieve *pihkohtew* (VTA).

achievement *pihkohtawin* (NI).

Achilles tendon The tendon attached to the heel bone, i.e.: Achilles tendon, *sikâkwan* (NI).

acknowledge *naskweyasihtam* (VTI).

acknowledgment *or* acknowledgement *mamihcitotamowin* (NI).

acme *metoninîkan* (IPC).

acorn *mistikopâkan* (NA).

acquaint The act of introducing people to each other, *nakayâskamohtahiwewin* (NI).

acquaintance *awîyak ka nakayâskaht; nistawehtowin* (NI).

acquiesce *tepeyimowin* (NI).

acquiescent *ka tepeyimohk* (VAI).

acquire *kahtinikewin* (NI).

acquirement *ka kahtinamihk* (VTI).

acridity *ka wisakispakwak* (VTI).

acrimonious *ka macâtisihk* (VAI).

acrimony *macâtisiwin* (NI).

acrobat *osîsâwew* (NA); *onanâtohkonikew* (NA).

acrobatic *nanâtohkonikewin* (NI).

acrobatics *nanâtohkonikewina* (NI).

across *âsawih* (IPC); going across on an angle, i.e.: crossways, *pîmakâm* (IPC); across the water or lake, *akâmihk* (NI); across the land or overseas, *âkâm'askîhk* (NI); across the room, *âkâmihtak* (NI); across the way, *âkâmâyihk* (NI); a road that leads across, *âsawâkâmemow* (NI); something that you pull across with something on it, i.e.: a ferry, *âsawâkâmepicikan* (NI).

act *ekosi katôtamihk; tôtamowin* (NI).

acting *katôtamihk.*

action *tôtamowin* (NI); *waskawîwin* (NI).

activate *ka sipwepayihtahk* (VTI).

activator *osipwepayicikew* (NA).

active *kakayawatesowin* (NI); happening or active, *itahkamikisow* (NI); *itahkamikan* (NI).

activity *waskawîwin* (NI).

actual *kehcinâhowin* (NI).

actuality *ka kehcinâhohk* (VAI).

actualize *ka kehcinâhtahk* (VTI).

actuate *omacipayihtaw* (NA).

acuity *nakacihtâwin* (NI) *(Plains)*; *kashihcikewin* (NI) *(Northern)*.

acumen *nihtâweyihtamowin* (NI).

acute *metoni ekota* (IPC).

Adam *mawace oskâc* (IPC); *nâpiw oweyowin* (NA) *(Northern)*; *nâpew oweyowin* (NA) *(Plains)*.

adamant *maskaweyihtamowin* (NI); *maskawitehewin* (NI).

Adam's apple *nâpew kohtakan* (NA).

adapt *nahiskamowin* (NI).

adaptability *kanihta nahiskamihk* (VTI).

adaptable *nahiskamowin* (NI).

adaptive *wâhki nakayâskamowin* (NI).

add *mamawih akihcekewin* (NI); *akihta* (NI).

adder *omamawih akihcikew* (NA).

addible *kakeh akihcikatek* (VTI).

addition *takohakihcikewin* (NI).

additional *ayiwâkes* (IPC).

addle *pikiskaciwâwi* (NI).

adduce *kehcinahowin kawapahtehiwehk.*

adduct *ka napopitamihk* (VTI).

adduction *napopicikewin* (NI).

adductor *onapopicikew* (NA).

adept *metoni îyinisowin* (NI); being adept at something, *nahiwin* (NI).

adequacy *tepipayowin* (NI).

adequate *nahiyikohk* (IPC)

adhere *ka sakamohk*; the act of adhering, *akwamohcikewin* (NI).

adherence *pimitisahikewin* (NI).

adherent *opimitisahikew* (NA).

adieu *mina kawapahtonaw* (VTA).

adjacency *cîkahtawâyâhk* (IPC).

adjacent *cîkâhtaw* (IPC).

adjoin *nepem; âniskostew; akwascikewin* (NI).

adjoining *ka nepemâniskostek* (VTI).

adjunct *tako ascikewin* (NI).

adjust Adjusting something, *oyastawin* (NI), *oyascikewin* (NI); s/he adjusts it perfectly, *miyomohew* (VTA) *(Northern)*; *miyamohew* (VTA) *(Plains)*.

adjusted *tîpisin* (VAI).

adjuster *or* adjustor *okwayaskwascikew* (NA).

adjustment *kwayaskascikewin* (NI).

administer *miyew* (VTA); *pisis keyimiwew.*

admirable *metoni tamamicihiwet*; it looks admirable, *mâmaskâcinâkwan* (VII).

243

admiration The act of looking at someone with admiration, **miyokanawâpacikewin** (NI); s/he looks at her/him with great admiration, **kihcinawew** (VTA) *(Northern)*; **kihcinahowakeyimew** (VTA) *(Plains)*.

admire S/he admires her/him, **miyowapamew** (VAI); s/he holds her/him in high regard, **kihceyimew** (VTA).

admirer **omiyowâpahkew** (NA) *(Northern)*; **otakâwâcikew** (NA) *(Plains)*.

admiring **mâhmiyowâpahkewin** (NI).

admit **pihtokahew** (VTA).

admittance **pihtokahakan** (NI).

admix **ka itehamihk** (VTI).

admixture **itehikewin** (NI).

admonish **peyahtik ka kitahamakehk** (VTA).

admonition **peyahtik kitahamakewin** (NI).

adopt Adopting a child, **awâsis koteniht**; s/he adopts him as a son, **okosisimew** (VTA) *(Northern)*; **okosisihkâw** (VTA) *(Plains)*; an adopted child or person, **pikwatôsân** (NA).

adoption The process of adopting a child, **otinawasowin** (NI); the act of replacing a deceased child by adopting in name another child the same age, **tâpahkohtowin** (NI); the act of adopting a brother or sister, **tâpahkomowewin** (NI).

adoptive An adoptive relationship, **tâpahkohtowin** (NI).

adorable **awîyak kosam takahkeyimiht** (VTA).

adoration **takahkeyimitowin** (NI).

adore **kosam sakihiwehk**; **akâwâtew** (VAI).

adorer **osakihiwew** (NA).

adorn **wawesihcikewin** (NI); **wawesihew** (VTA).

adornment **wawisihcikan** (NI).

adrift **ôsi** (NI); **kawepasihk**; **pimâhokow** (VAI).

adulate **ka pâsci mamihtôtamihk** (VAI).

adulation **pâsci mamihcisowin** (NI).

adulatory **pâsci mamihtsewakewin** (NI).

adult **kîsohpikiwin** (NI); s/he is all grown up, **kîsohpikiw** (VAI).

adulterate **kaweyepihtahk** (VAI).

adulterer **nâpew nocihkâkew** (VTA).

adulteress **iskwew nocihkâkew** (VTA); **nocekamakew** (VTA).

adulterous **pisikwâcîsâyâwin** (NI).

adultery S/he commits adultery, **pisikwâcitôtam** (VAI) *(Northern)*; **pisikwatisiw** (VAI) *(Plains)*; the act of committing adultery, **pisikwâcitôtamowin** (NI).

adulthood Maturation, **kîsohpikiwin** (NI).

adumbrate **kicimoyetamowin** (NI).

advance **kanîkânpayhohk**; **yahkohtew** (NI).

advanced **nîkân yahkohtewin nîkânohtew** (VAI).

advancement **nîkânpayihowin** (NI); **nîkânpayiw** (VII) (VAI).

advantage **ayewâkes miyopayowin** (NI).

advantageous **ayewâkes kawehcehopayik** (VII).

advection **kîkway espahkepayik** (VTI).

Advent **niyo ayamihikesikâw pâmayes kanepa ayamihâhk** (NI).

adventitious **episcetôtamihk kîkway** (IPC).

Advent Sunday **ayamihiwkesikâw pâmayes kanepayamihahk** (NI).

adventure **kakocihtâhk** (VTI).

adventurer **okocihtâwiyiniw** (NA).

adventuresome **nihtâkocew**; **papâmacihowin** (NI).

adventurous **kakâyawiyiniw** (NI).

adversary **kapakwâtiht awîyak** (VTA).

adverse **kanaspâcipayik** (VTI).

adversity **naspâcipayowin** (NI).

advert **sisikoc kakweskeyetamihk** (VAI).

advice Giving advice, **kakeskimiwewin** (NI); s/he gives her/him advice, **kakeskimew** (VTA).

advise **kawihtamâtohk** (NI); s/he advises or counsels children, **kakeskimâwasiw** (VTA).

advised **kîhwîhtamâkew** (NA); **kîhwîhtamakawin** (NI).

adviser *or* **advisor** **owihtamâkew** (NA); **omâminomowew** (NA) *(Plains)*.

advisory **etah kawihtamâkehk** (VTA).

affability **miyowicihiwewin** (NI).

afar **wâhyaw** (IPC).

affair **isicikâtowin** (NI).

affairs **oyasiwewin** (NI).

affect **miyomahcihowin** (NI).

affection **miweyehtowin** (NI); **sâkihitowin** (NI).

affectionate **naspic kamiweyetohk**; **sâkihewew** (VAI).

affective **kohespayik kîkway** (VTI).

affiliate **kamâmawintohk** (VTA).

affiliation **mâmawinitowin** (NI).

affinity **moscimiweyihtowin** (NI).

affirm The act of positive thinking, **metoni kehcinâhowin** (NI); s/he affirms it in her/his presence, **pasikôstawew** (VTA).

affirmation **ka kehcinâhohk** (VAI).

affirmative **kehcinâhowinihk** (IPC).

afflict **wîsakeyitamowin** (NI).

affluence **sisikôc mistahi** (IPC).

affluent **sisikôc ka iskepepayek**; **weyotisiwin** (NI).

afflux **ka matâwisicowahk** (VTI).

afford **ka kaskitah** (VAI).

affront **metoni kapewomiht awîyak** (VTA).

afield **pecayihk kistikanihk** (VTI).

afire **ka kwahkotek**; **kwahkotew** (VII).

aflame **ka wayatek**; **cahkaskitew** (VTI); **cahkaskiswew** (VTA).

afloat **waskitahipew** (VII); **pimâhokow** (VAI).

afraid **ka kostâcik**; **sekisiw** (VAI).

afresh **oskihcikewin** (NI).

after Or another time or later, **mwestas** (IPC).

afternoon It is afternoon, *ponapihtakesikaw* (VII); *poni apihtâkisikâw* (VII).

afterward *mwestas* (IPC).

afterwards *mwestases* (IPC).

again Also, and, *mîna* (IPC); all over again, *âsay mîna* (IPC) *(Plains)*; *asaymîna* (IPC) *(Northern)*; *kahkihtwam* (IPC); still, more, some more, again, *keyâpic* (IPC); *eyâpic* (IPC); again, another time, once more, *kawi* (IPC).

against Something leaning against something, *kîkway ka asotihk*; s/he leans it against something, *âsohtitâw* (VTA); the direction is against the wind, *nayiman* (VII).

age Telling how old one is by how many winters, *etahtopiponewin* (NI); telling how old one is by physical appearance, *ispîhtisiwin* (NI); s/he is so many winters old, *itahtopiponiw* (VAI).

aged *kihtehayak* (VII); *kayâsâyiwiw* (VII); s/he is old, aged, ancient, *kihtehayiwiw* (VAI); the act of being old, old age, *kihtehayowin* (NI).

ageless A youthful person, *oskapewin* (NA); it is ageless, i.e.: a tree, *sîpâskisiw* (VAI); it is ageless, i.e.: a cedar pole/an old log house, *sîpâskitêw* (VII).

agglomerate *asascikewin* (NI).

agglomeration *ka asascikehk*.

aggravate *ayiwâkes kakisiwâhiwehk*; *ekisiwâhat*; *kisiwâhew* (VAI).

aggravation *ayiwâkes kisôwâhitowin* (NI).

aggregrate *mâwasako itehikewin*; *mâmawi ka astahk*.

aggression *ka mawineskakehk* (VTA).

aggressive *mawineskâkewin* (NI).

aggressor *omawineskâkew* (NA).

aggrieve *kakakwe kisiwâhiwehk* (VTA).

aggrieved *kakisiwâhikohk* (VTI).

aghast *metoni kasekisihk* (VAI).

agile *kakayawesehk* (VTI).

agility *kakayawesewin* (NI).

agitate *kakisôwitotakehk*.

agitation *kisôtôtâkewin* (NI).

agitator *okisôtôtâkew* (NA).

agleam *kihkâyâsawew* (VAI).

aglow *kihkâyâstew* (VAI).

ago *ka mamiskotamihk kayâs*, right now, a minute ago, *anohc piko* (IPC); a long time ago, *kayâs* (IPC); a little long ago, *kayâsis* (IPC).

agog *nanihkâtisiwin* (NI) *(Northern)*; *nanihkisiwin* (NI) *(Plains)*.

agonize *wesakitehenitowin* (NI).

agony *wisakahpinewin* (NI); *kamositahk wisakeyitamowin* (VTI).

agree S/he agrees, *tepeyimow* (VAI).

agreeability *kanihtâtepeyimohk* (VAI).

agreeable *wahkew tepeyimow* (VAI).

agreed *tepeyimow* (VAI).

agreement *tepeyimowin* (NI); agreeing to something, *katepeyimototamihk* (VTI).

aground *kamesaskehtihk ôsi* (NI).

ahead First or before, *nîkân* (IPC); s/he is put ahead or in front, *nîkânahâw* (VAI); s/he places it ahead of others, *nîkânamohtâw* (VAI); ahead of time, *neyâk* (IPC); *niyâk* (IPC).

aid *nîsohkamâkewin* (NI).

ail *kamâyâyâhk*; *ahkosow* (VAI).

ailment Illness, *mâyâyâwin* (NI); sickness or disease, *âhkosiwin* (NI); s/he has various ailments, *nanâtohkwahpinew* (VAI); the act of having various ailments, *nanâtohkwahpinewin* (NI).

aim S/he aims a gun, *oyâpahcikew* (VAI); s/he aims at her/him, *oyâpamew* (VTA).

aimless *ekâ kîkway* (IPC); *kisâyâhk*.

airily *môcikesâyâwin* (NI).

airiness *kawanewisâyâhk* (VAI).

airing *wayawîtimihk kakocikehk* (VTI).

airless *kaskamôtan* (VII).

aisle *etah katawak pimohtewin ayamihewikamikohk* (NI); a place for walking through, passageway, *sâpohtewin* (NI).

alacrity *metoni kanihpemâyâhk* (VAI).

alarm *kawehtamakohk kîkway*; *kawi espayik*; *sewepicikan* (NI).

alarming *mâmaskâc kîkway* (IPC).

alarmist *omâmaskâsiwew* (NA).

alas *ketimakeyecekewin* (NI).

alcohol *iskotewâpoy* (NI).

alcoholic *ominihkwewâspinew* (NA).

alcoholism *minikwewâspinewin* (NI).

Algonquin Different people, *pîtos nehiyawak* (NA); Algonquin, different language, *pîtos nehiyawpekiskwewin* (NI); *sâkâstenohk ohci* (LN).

alias *waniyikasowin* (NI).

alienate *kapaskepayihohk* (VTI).

alienation *paskepayihowin* (NI).

alight *tohiw* (VAI); *itwehiw* (VAI).

align *kakwayaskastahk* (VTI).

alignment *kwayaskascikewin* (NI)

alike *nâspitâtowin* (NI); *naspitâtowak* (VAI); *mweci peyak* (IPC).

aliment *nâtawiskâkewin* (NI).

alimentary *kîkway kanâtawihtahk* (VTI).

alimentation *kamiyoskâkohk miciwin* (NI).

alive Being alive, *pimâtisiwin* (NI); s/he is alive, *pimâtisiw* (VII); it is alive, *pimâtan* (VII); while s/he was alive, *emekwâpimâtisit* (VAI).

alkali *sîwihtâkan asiskîy* (NI) .

245

all *kahkiyaw* (IPC); together, all at once, *mamawi* (IPC); all over the place or all over the world, *misiweskamik* (IPC); it is all mixed up, *kiyekawe* (IPC); s/he is completely whole; s/he is all in one piece, *misiwesiw* (VAI); it is whole; it is all in one piece, *misiweyâw* (VII); all of everything, *kahkiyaw kîkway* (IPC).

all-around *tetipewew* (VAI).

allay *nome astemosetawin* (NI).

all clear *miyotawâw* (IPC).

allegiance *mistahi etiyetowin* (NI).

alleluia *ayamihâw nikamowin ka âpisisinokâsikak* (NI).

alleviate *ka opahscasihk* (VTI).

alleviation *ohpastawin* (NI).

All Fool's Day *kîyâskiw kîsikâw* (NI).

alliance *miyowicehtowin* (NI).

allied *nîso âskîyah kawicewâkanihtotwaw*.

allocate *masanak kamekihk* (VTI).

allocation *masanak mikowin* (NI) *(Northern)*; *mekowin* (NI) *(Plains)*.

allot *pahpiskic mikowin* (NI) *(Northern)*; *mekowin* (NI) *(Plains)*.

allow *pakitinowewin* (NI); *pakitinam* (VAI); s/he allows *pakitinamâkew* (VAI).

allowable *kapakitinikatek* (VTI).

allowance *pakitinamatowin* (NI); *sônîyâwikameyiht awîyak*.

alloy *kamaskawak pîwâpisk* (NI).

All Saints' Day *okihcetwawsowok ohci kesikaw* (VII).

All Souls' Day *ahcakwak ohci kesikaw* (VII).

all together *mâmawi* (IPC).

allude *kwanta mâmases mâmiskôtowin* (NI).

allure *ka akâwâtamihk; akâwâsowewin* (NI).

allusive *akâwâcikew* (VAI).

ally *kawecewakanpayehohk* (VTA).

almighty *naspic maskawisiwin* (NI); *kimanitominaw* (NA).

almost *metoni kekâc* (IPC); almost, nearly, *kekâc* (IPC).

almsgiver *omekiw* (NA).

almsgiving *kamekihk* (NI).

aloe *maskihkîwahcikos* (NI).

aloft *ispimeskamik* (IPC).

alone Being alone, *ka peyakohk*; s/he is alone or s/he travels alone, *peyakow* (VAI); being alone, *peyakowin* (NI); s/he does it all alone, *peyakosihcikew* (VAI); s/he handles her/him alone or by herself/himself, *peyakohkawew* (VTA); s/he is alone in her/his canoe, *peyakohkam* (VAI).

along *nekanohtewin* (NI); along the side, *sisone* (IPC); all along or along the whole length of, *misakâme* (IPC).

alongshore *sonesâkahikanihk* (LN) *(Northern)*; *sisonesâkahikanihk* (LN) *(Plains)*.

alongside *sisone* (IPC).

aloof *ocakes nawâc* (IPC).

aloud *metoni kakiseweh*.

alphabet *akayasew masinahikewin* (NI); written objects, *masinahikanisa* (NA).

already *sâsay* (IPC) *(Northern)*; *âsay* (IPC) *(Plains)*; already this time, *sâsayekwa* (IPC).

alright *kahkiyaw kwayask* (IPC).

also *mîna* (IPC).

altar A sacrificial altar, *pakitinâsowinâhtik* (NI); a holy offering table, *ayamihew wepinisonahtik* (NI).

alter *acisehtat* (NI).

alteration *meskocascikewin* (NI).

alterative *kanihtâmeskoc ispayik*.

altercate *kakehkâhtohk* (VTA).

altercation *kehkâhtowin* (NI).

alternate *mâmeskoc* (IPC).

alternately Taking turns, *kamâmeskocepayik*; alternately or each in turn, *mâmeskôc* (IPC).

alternation *mâmeskociwepinikewin* (NI).

alternative *nîsowak isi nawasonikewin* (NI).

although *âtâ* (IPC).

altogether *mâmawi* (IPC).

always Only, exclusively, *nayistaw* (IPC) *(Northern)*, *neyistaw* (IPC) *(Plains)*; always or without end, *kâkike* (IPC); it will always be so, *kâkikeham* (IPC); just always and ever, *tahki* (IPC).

amalgamate *kamâmawipicikehk* (VTA).

amalgamation *mâmawipicikewin* (NI).

amass *misci mâwasakonikewin* (NI).

amatory *pisikwâtisowin* (NI).

amaze The act of doing amazing things, *mamaskatamohiwewin* (NI); s/he is amazed with her/him, *koskweyimew* (VTA); it is amazing or astonishing, *koskweyihtâkwan* (VII).

amazed Being surprised, *mâmaskâtamowin* (NI).

amazedly *tesimâmaskâtamihk* (VAI).

amazement *mâmaskâtamowin* (NI); s/he looks at him with amazement, *mâmaskâcinawew* (VTA); s/he looks at it with amazement, *mâmaskâcinam* (VTI); s/he looks at people with amazement, *mâmaskâcinâkew* (VTA).

amazing *tamamaskatamihk* (VAI).

amber *kosawinakwahk* (VII).

ambidexterity *nesokwakanewin* (NI); *âyitawiniskewin* (NI).

ambidextrous S/he uses either of her/his arms or s/he is ambidextrous, *âyitawiniskew* (VAI).

ambition *kakayawisewin* (NI).

ambitious *kakayawatsowin* (NI); *kayawisew* (VAI).

ambivalence *nesoyak isi mâmitoneyihcikan* (VAI).

ambivalent *nesoyak isi wehkowin* (NI).

246

amble *papîyahtiko pîmohtewin* (NI).
ambush *weskawâhiwewin* (NI).
ameliorable *takehkweskesâyahk* (VAI).
ameliorate *kakweskesâyahk* (VAI).
amelioration *kweskesâyâwin* (NI).
ameliorative *nohtekweskisâyâwin* (NI).
amen *êkosi* (IPC)
amenability *kanihtâ kitimâkihtakehk* (VTA).
amenable *kitimâkihtâkewin* (NI).
amend *kakweskesâyahk* (VAI).
amendment The act of making a legal amendment, *kwesketasowewin* (NI) *(Northern)*; *kweskasowewin* (NI) *(Plains)*.
amenity *môcikesâyâwin* (NI).
amiability *kamiyo isayahk*.
amiable *meywâtisowin* (NI).
amicability *metoni miyohtwâwin* (NI).
amicable *miyohtwâwin* (NI) *(Plains)*; *yoskâtisiwin* (NI) *(Northern)*.
amid *mekwânohk* (IPC).
amidst *mekwâyihk* (IPC).
amiss *kapatahamihk* (VAI).
amity *miyowicehtowin* (NI).
among *kiyikawe* (IPC); among a crowd of people, *mekwâcayisiyininâhk* (IPC); *mekwânohk* (IPC).
amongst *kakiyekawepayihk* (VYI).
amorous *wihkiskwewewin* (NI).
amount Totalling everything together, *mâmawi akihcikewin* (NI); that amount of, *itahto* (IPC); just the right amount, *nahiyikohk* (IPC).
ample *metoni ekwaykohk*; *mecetin tepipayow* (VAI).
amplifier *kisewemohcikâkan* (NI).
amplify *ka kisewemohtahk* (VTI).
amplitude *mahkisîhcikewin* (NI).
amply *ayiwâkes* (IPC).
amputate *kamansoht awîyak* (VTA).
amputation *kakîskisawatek miskat* (NI).
amputee *awîyak kakîskikâtet* (NA).
amuck *naspic kîsiwasowin* (NI).
amuse *môcikimisowin* (NI).
amused *ka môcikisihk*; *môcikisowin* (NI).
amusement *môcikihtâwin* (NI).
amusing Having a good time, *kamôcikisihk*; s/he is amusing, *waninew* (VAI); s/he is an amusing character, *waninewâtisiw* (VAI); having an amusing character, *waninewin* (NI).
analyse or **analyze** *koyakihcikehk* (IPC).
analysis *oyakihcikewin* (NI).
analytical *ka oyakihtamihk*.
analytic *oyakihcikewin* (NI).
ancestor *aniskâc wahkomâkan* (NA); *wahkomâkanak* (NA).

ancestral *aniskâc wahkohtowin* (NI).
ancestress *aniskâc kohkominaw* (NA).
ancestry *aniskâc ohcêwin* (NI); *wahkomitowin* (NI).
anchor An anchor made with a rock, *pakitasinâpân* (NI).
ancient *mitonikayâs* (IPC); *kayâsâyiwan* (VII).
anciently *kayâseskamik* (IPC).
angel *okîsikow* (NA).
angelic *tâpiskôc ikîsikosis* (VAI).
anger Being angry, *kisiwâsowin* (NI); anger that lasts for a long period of time, *sîpiyawesiwin* (NI).
angle *kwâskwepicikewin* (NI); s/he angles, i.e.: fishing, *kwâskwepicikew* (VAI).
angle Mathematical term, *ka eyipemok nawâc poko*.
angler *nôcikinosewew* (VAI).
angry Being angry, *kisôwâsiwin* (NI); s/he makes her/him secretly angry, *kîmôciyawehew* (VTA); s/he is hiding her/his anger, *kîmôciyawesiw* (VAI); being secretly angry or seething mad but not showing it, *kîmôciyawesiwin* (NI); s/he made her/him angry, *kisôwâhew* (VTA); the act of making each other angry, *kisôwâhitowin* (NI); s/he gets others mad at her/him, *kisôwâhtwâw* (VTA); the act of making others mad at someone, *kisôwâhtwâwin* (NI); s/he is angry, *kisôwâsiw* (VAI); the act of looking angry, *kisôwinâkosiwin* (NI); s/he looks angry, *kisôwinâkosiw* (VAI); it looks upset, *kisôwinâkwan* (VII); s/he is angry over something, *ohciyawesiw* (VAI); s/he remains angry for a long time, *sîpiyawesiw* (VAI); s/he is screaming angry, *sohkeyawesiw* (VAI); *kîskweyawesiw* (VAI) *(Plains and Northern variant)*; the act of screaming in anger, *sohkeyawisowin* (NI).
anguish *mistahi mamitoneyihcikan* (NA).
anguished *kisôweyihtamowin* (NI).
angular *ka cacihkokanehk* (VAI).
angularity *cacihkokanewin* (NI).
animal Or beast, *pisiskiw* (NA); a huge animal, i.e.: a dog or horse; a wild or untamed animal, *pakwâcipisiskiw* (NA); a one-year-old animal, *piponâskos* (NA); s/he is a one-year-old animal, *piponâskosowiw* (VAI); s/he acts like an animal, *pisiskowisihtwâw* (VAI); s/he is an animal, *pisiskowiw* (VII); acting like an animal, *pisiskowiwin* (NI).
animal spirits *pisiskow acahkwak* (NA).
animate *kîkway kapîmâtisimakahk* (VTI).
animated *kîkway kapîmâtisimakihtahk* (VTI).
animation *pîmâtisimakihtâwin* (NI).
animosity *kakemoci pakwâcikehk* (VAI).
ankle *aniskawkanan mistihk ohci* (VTI).
ankle bone *aniskawkan* (NI).

annex *kakosetahk waskahikanis misiwaskahikanihk* (VTI).

annexation *akosicikewin* (NI).

annihilate *kamisciwipahikehk* (VTA).

annihilation *misciwipahikiwin* (NI); *mestapinatihiwin* (NI) *(Plains)*; *mestahpinasiwewin* (NI) *(Northern)*.

annihilative *kanihtâ misciwipahikehk*.

anniversary *kîkway katôtamihk tahtwaski*; the reminder, *kiskisototâmohiwewin* (NI).

announce *kawihtamihk*; *itwew* (VAI).

announcement *wihcikewin* (NI); *keci kîkway kawihtamihk* (VTI).

announcer *owihcikew* (NA).

annoy That act of irritating one another, *pakwatehtowin* (NI); s/he annoys her/him or them, *mikoskâcihew* (VTA); they annoy one another, *mikoskâcihitowak* (VTA); the act of annoying someone, *mikoskâcihiwewin* (NI); s/he annoys her/him with her/his speech, *mikoskâcimew* (VTA); it makes an annoying or bothersome noise, *mikoskâsihtakwan* (VII); s/he is annoyed to see her/him, *mwestâteyimew* (VTA).

annoyance *ka pakwâciyetohk* (VTA).

annoying The act of being annoying, *mikoskâtisiwin* (NI); s/he has an annoying voice, *mikoskâsihtâkosiw* (VAI); s/he finds her/him annoying, *mikoskâteyimew* (VTA); s/he is annoying, i.e.: a pest, *mikoskâtisiw* (VAI); s/he says annoying words to her/him, *wîspâcimew* (VTA) *(Plains)*; *pacimew* (VTA) *(Northern)*.

annual *tahtwaw peyakaski*; *tahtowaske* (VII).

annually *peyakwâw tahtowaske* (VII).

annul *nakâwew* (VTA).

annulment *nakinamâkewin* (NI).

annunciate *kîkway nîkânes kawihtamihk*.

annunciation *nîkân wihcikewin* (NI).

annunciator *awîyak kawihtahk* (NA).

annoint *tôminitowin* (NI).

anomaly *kapîtosisiwepinikehk* (VTA).

anonymity *kayesâyâwin* (NI).

anonymous *ekâ kanohte kiskiyetakosihk kiskeyihtâkosiwin* (NI).

another *or* **another one** *kotak* (VII); differently, in another way, *pîtos* (IPC); from one to another, *ayâsawi* (IPC); *ayâsaw* (IPC).

answer The act of responding or answering someone, *naskwewasimowin* (NI); s/he is answering a moose call, *kîsistohtawew* (VAI) *(Northern)*; *naskwewasihtawew* (VAI) *(Plains)*; the act of responding to or answering one another, *naskohtowin* (NI); they respond to or answer each other, *naskohtowak* (VTA); s/he responds or answers her/him or them, *naskweyasimew* (VTA); s/he responds or answers, *naskwewasimow* (VAI).

ant *ayikos* (NA); *eyik* (NA), *ikos* (NA); *eyikos* (NA), *iyikos* (NA).

antagonism Being angry, *kisôweyecekewin* (NI); having antagonism, *pimâmeyitamowin* (NI).

antagonist *okisowâhiwew* (VAI).

antagonistic Making someone angry by antagonizing them, *nihtakisiwahiwewin* (NI); s/he is antagonistic towards her/him *pimâmeyimew* (VTA); s/he looks at her/him with antagonism, *pimâminawew* (VTA).

antagonize *ohtaw kisiwâhitowin* (NI).

antelope *paskwâw apiscimosos* (NA); *apiscacihkos* (NA).

anthem *nîkânikamowenis* (NI).

ant hill *ayikowistih* (NA) *(Northern)*; *eyikosisti* (NA) *(Plains)*.

antic *môcohkâsowin* (NI).

anticipate *ka asoweyitamihk* (VTI).

anticipation *ka kwayace asoweyitamihk* (VTI).

antipathy *pakwâteyihcikewin* (NI).

antiquarian S/he lives long enough to see her/him, i.e.: an antiquarian, *otisâpamew* (VTA).

antique *ka kanawiyehtamihk kayasi kîkway*.

antiquity *kayâs mâmitoniyehtamowin* (NI).

antler Horn, *miteskan* (NA) *(Plains)*; *oteskan* (NA) *(Northern)*.

antlered *kôtîskanit* (NI) *(Northern)*; *koteskanit* (NA) *(Plains)*.

anxiety Being anxious, *papâseyihtamowin* (NI); anxiety *pîkweyihtamowin* (NI).

any *poko* (IPC), *piko* (IPC).

anybody *pokawîyak* (IPC); just anybody, *poko tana* (IPC).

any more Not any more, not necessary or not needed any more, *namoyakatâc* (IPC); an expression that indicates a change of mind, "don't bother anymore, or any longer, or any more", *nitawâc* (IPC).

anyone *piko ana* (IPC); *pikotana* (IPC).

anyplace *pikwita* (IPC).

anything *pikokîkway* (IPC); just anything, *piko tanima* (IPC).

anytime *pikwîspi* (IPC).

anyway *pikotansesih* (IPC); *pikwisi* (IPC); anyway, in any case, regardless of what is said or done, *kihtohkan* (IPC).

anywhere *piko iteh* (IPC); *pikotanta* (IPC); *pikwite* (IPC).

Apache *pîtos nehiyaw* (NA).

apart Apart from, *piskihc piskis* (IPC); s/he takes it apart, *nanânistinew* (VAI).

apathetic *ekâ omôsihtawinihk* (VAI).

apathy *namakîkway môsihtawin* (NI).

apology *mihtâteyehtamowin* (NI).

appal *or* **appall** *nâspic sekihtakosowin* (NI).

appalling *metoni âstamihk kîkway* (VII).

appaloosa A real light brown or sand colored horse, *ewâpinakosit osâwastim* (NA).

apparatus *âpacicikan natohk etapatahk*; a kind of tool, *âpacihcikan* (NI).

apparel *ayiwinisa* (NI).

apparent *pakahkam* (IPC).

apparently *ahpô etoki* (IPC).

apparition *cîpay nokosiwin* (NI).

appear To appear, *kanokosihk*; *penôkosiw* (VAI); s/he appears out of the bush or wood, *matâwisiw* (VAI); s/he appears in the distance and is headed this way, *pecinâkosiw* (VAI); it appears in the distance and is headed this way, *pecinâkwan* (VII); s/he appears to be nearby, *pesonâkosiw* (VAI); it appears to be nearby, *pesonâkwan* (VII); s/he appears or looks sneaky, *kimôcinâkosiw* (VAI).

appearance To make an appearance, *nokosiwin* (NI); s/he appears or looks that way, *isinakasiw* (VAI); it appears or looks that way *isinakwan* (VII); s/he is clear or easily recognizable, *kihkanakosiw* (VAI); it is clear or easily recognizable, *kihkanakwan* (VII).

appease S/he has appeased her/his hunger, *kîspiw* (VAI).

appeasement *naheyeyihtamowin* (NI).

append *akwamohcikewin* (NI).

appetite *nohtehkatewin* (NI).

applaud *sâkowewin* (NI).

applause *awîyak ka sâkowestamaht*; *pakamicicihamatowin* (NI).

apple *picikwâs* (NA).

applicant *osâkaskinahtamohiwew* (NA).

applied *kîkway ka akwamohtahk* (VTI).

apply *akwamohcikewin* (NI).

appoint *awîyak kameyeht nîkânapiwin* (NI); s/he chooses him/her, *nawasonew* (VTA).

appointee *onîkânapîhiwew* (NA).

appointment S/he makes an appointment with her/him, *kiskimew* (VTA); the act of making an appointment, *kiskimowin* (NI); s/he makes an appointment with something, *kiskitam* (VTI); s/he makes an appointment with someone, *kiskimiwew* (VTA); s/he makes an appointment with everyone, *kiskihcikew* (VTA)

appreciable *kîkway ka atamihikohk* (VTI).

appreciate *ka ataminahk* (VAI).

appreciation *ataminâwin* (NI).

appreciative *atamihikowin* (NI).

apprehend *moyehcikewin* (NI).

apprehension *ka moyetamihk*.

apprehensive *moyetamowin* (NI).

approach *ka pîkiskwatitiht awîyak kîkway isihcikewin* (NI); *petâstamohtew* (VAI); meeting, approaching from both sides, *âyîtaw ohci* (IPC).

approachability *miyo isihcikatitowin* (NI).

appropriate Appropriation or to take exclusive possession of things, *manâhowin* (NI); s/he helps herself/himself to things, i.e.: after a death, *manâhow* (VAI); s/he unjustly appropriates it for herself/himself, *otinamâsiw* (VTA); the act of unjust appropriation or taking something without consent, *otinamâsiwin* (NI).

approval *ka mamihtitamihk* (VTA).

approve *tepeyemototamowin* (NI); *katâpwehtamihk*.

approximate *cîkâhtaw* (IPC).

approximately *nawâc poko cîkâhtaw* (IPC); about, approximately, *nânitâw* (IPC).

approximation *cîkâhtaw akihcikewin* (NI).

April The frog moon or month, *ayîkiwipîsim* (NI); *ayikîpîsim* (NI) *(Plains)*.

April Fools' Day *kakiyaskew kisikak* (NI).

apron *aspastakanis* (NI); *aspastakan* (NI).

apron strings *aspastakan yapîya* (NI).

apt *kîkway kanahipayik* (VTI).

aptitude *nahiwepinikewin* (NI).

arbiter *awîyak kanihtâ oyastat isihcikewin*.

arbitrage *etah kakîhtwam atâwakihk kîkwaya* (VTI).

arbitrary *wâneyihtamasowewin* (NI).

arbitress *okwayaskosihcikew iskwew* (NA).

arc *ka nomiwaweyeyak* (VTI).

arch *ka waweye apahkwâtek wâskahikan* (VTI).

archaic *metoni nestokâyâs kîkway* (VII).

archangel *metoni ka nîkânapit okisikow*; a very special angel, *kihcikokisikow* (NA).

archenemy *awîyak metoni ka mayi wiciwiht*.

archer A person who shoots arrows well, *awîyak ka nihtâ pimotahkwew atosah*; an archer, *opimotahkwew* (NA).

archery *eta kasesawihk pimotahkwewin* (NI).

archway *sîpâhtewin* (NI).

ardent *metoni naspic itamahcihiwin* (NI).

ardor *or* ardour *metoni kapapâseyihtamihk* (VAI).

arduous *metoni kasemacak amacowewin* (NI).

area *ayesawih eta ka tepapekinikatek*; there is burned area, *weposkâw* (NI); *paskwâskitew* (VAI); there is burned over area where growth, grass and weeds have started again, *oskâpôskitew* (VAI); there is an area where trees have fallen one on top of the other, *kawihtakaw* (NI); there is spongy area, soil, *pîswehcâw* (NI).

argue The act of arguing, *kihkâhtowin* (NI); they are arguing *kihkâhtowak* (VAI); s/he is known for arguing or s/he likes to argue, *kihkâwitaskiw* (VAI).

argument *awîyak kawîcikehkâhtomiht* (VTA).

argumentation *kosihtâhk kehkâhtowin* (NI).

argumentative *awîyak kakehkâwtaskit* (VAI).

arise *waniskâwin* (NI); *waniskâw* (VAI).

arithmetic *akihtâsowinah kanakacitahk*; *akecikewin* (NI); *akihcikewin* (NI).

arithmetical *akihtâsowepinikewin* (NI).

arm *mispiton* (NI); s/he has a deformed arm, *mâskipitonew* (VAI); her/his arms are bare, *mosisepitonew* (VAI); s/he has only one arm, *napatepitonew* (VAI); her/his arms are tired, *nestopitonew* (VAI); her/his arm is bent, *pihkipitonew* (VAI); s/he has strong, powerful arms, *sohkipitonew* (VAI).

armband *iskwanakwepson* (NI).

armful *sâkaskini spihtasenikewin* (NI).

armistice *ka poninôtinitohk* (VTA).

armpit *mitihkôkan* (NI).

aroma Something that has a pleasant aroma, *kîkway ka wihkimâkwahk*; s/he makes a pleasant aroma from what s/he is burning, *wihkimâsawew* (VAI); the act of making a pleasant aroma by burning something, *wihkimâsawewin* (NI); it produces a pleasant aroma; *wihkimâstew* (VII); it produces a pleasant aroma, i.e.: tobacco, *wihkimâsiw* (VII).

aromatic *wehkimâkosowin* (NI).

around *wâsakâm* (IPC); in a circle, *wâska*; completely turned around, *kweskîwin* (NI); s/he places them around something, *wâsakâhew* (VTA); s/he walks around something, *wâsakâhtew* (VAI); they are standing around her/him or them, *wâsakâkâpawistawewak* (VTA); they are standing around, *wâsakâkâpawiwak* (VAI); around along the shore, *wâsakâm* (IPC); s/he walks around the lake shore, *wâsakâmehtew* (VAI); they sit around in a circle, *wâsakâmepiwak* (VAI); s/he goes around along the shore of a lake, *wâsakâmew* (VAI); the act of going around along the shore of a lake, *wâsakâmewin* (NI); s/he goes all around them, *wâsakâpayîstawew* (VTA); it is going around, *wâsakâpayiw* (VAI); they are sitting around it, *wâsakâpîstamwak* (VTI); they are sitting around each other, *wâsakâpîstâtowak* (VTA); s/he lays them around something, *wâsakâsimew* (VTA); s/he goes around her/him, *wâsakâskawew* (VTA); something sewn around a moccasin, *wâskâkonekwâcikan* (NI).

arouse *kasisikocehiht awîyak*; *koskon* (VAI).

arrange The act of arranging, *kanahawâscikehk* (VTI).

arrangement *nahawâscikewin* (NI).

array *ka nihtâ nahawâscikehk* (VAI).

arrest *simâkansak kotenewitwaw*; *otinaw* (VAI).

arrested *otiniwewin* (NI).

arrival *takosinowin* (NI).

arrive Somebody arriving, *katakosihk awîyak*; s/he arrives, *takosin* (VAI)); they arrive at the same time, *kesiskotâtowak* (VAI); the act of arriving at the same time, *kesiskotâtowin* (NI); s/he arrives by boat or

canoe, *misakâw* (VAI) *(Northern)*; *kapâw* (VAI) *(Plains)*; s/he arrives at the top or summit, *tahkohtaciwew* (VAI); s/he arrived from her/his camping trip, *takopiciw* (VAI); s/he arrives to stand in line, *takokâpawiw* (VAI) s/he arrives by car or horse, *takopayiw* (VAI); s/he has arrived; *takosin* (VAI); s/he arrives pulling something, i.e.: sled, *takotâpew* (VAI); s/he arrived on foot, *takohtew* (VAI); s/he has arrived with the wind or the wind blew her towards us, *takwâsiw* (VTA).

arrogance Thinking you are better than everyone, *mistahi iteyemesowin mistakeyimisowin* (NI); an arrogance that respects no one, *ayiwâkeyimisowin* (NA); s/he thinks herself/himself as superior, *ayiwâkeyimototawew* (VTA); s/he is arrogant, *ayiwâkeyimow* (VAI); being arrogant, *ayiwâkeyimowin* (NI).

arrogate *awîyak kamisteyimisot* (NI).

arrow *akask* (NA); *acosis* (NA).

arrowhead *ostikwân akaskos* (NI).

arrowroot *akaskocepihk* (NI).

arrow-wood *akaskwahtik* (NI); red willow, *atospiy* (NA).

art *naspasinahikewin* (NI).

artery *mihkoyapiy* (NA).

artesian well *môhkicowanipek kosihtâhk*; *kakipihcipayik* (NI); a well that stops and goes according to pressure, *mônahipân* (NI), *nipekakahkipihcipayik* (NI).

articulate *awîyak metoni kanihtawet* (VAI).

artifice *ka kayesew îyinisiwin* (NI).

artificer *owayesihiwew* (NA); *môhcohkâsowewin* (NI).

artificial *kîkway emosci osihtahk* (VTI).

artificiality *kîmôtâtisiwin* (NI).

artisan *awîyak kanihtâ osihciket.*

artist *onihtâwasinahikew* (NA) *(Northern)*; *otâpasinahikew* (NA) *(Plains)*.

artistic *onihtâwasinahikew* (NA) *(Northern)*; *otâpasinahikew* (NA) *(Plains)*.

artistry *awîyak naspasinahikewin* *kakiskinohamasosit* (VTI).

artless *awîyak ekâ kîkway kakaskihtat* (VTI).

ascend *amacowew* (VTI).

ascendance *ka amacowinekanehk* (VTI).

ascendancy *amacowinekanewin* (NI).

ascendant *awîyak okihcinekanew* (NA).

ascending *amacowewin* (NI).

Ascension Day A Christian celebration, *ohpiskâwikîsikâw* (NI).

asexual *ekâ ka pisikwâcî ayisiyiniwihk.*

ash Ashes, *pihkoh* (NI); s/he is covered with ashes, *pihkowiw* (VAI); it is covered with ashes, *pihkowan* (VII).

ashamed S/he is ashamed to look at her/him, *nepewisîstawew* (VTA); s/he is ashamed of herself/himself, *nepewakeyimiw* (VAI); the act of being ashamed of oneself, *nepewakeyimowin* (NI).

ashcan *pihkoyakanis* (NI) *(Northern)*; *pakicipihkoweyâkanis* (NI) *(Plains)*.

ashen An ashen colour, *kîkway ewâpinakwahk* (VTI).

ashen A person who looks pale, *awîyak metoni ka wâpinesit* (VAI).

ashes *mistahi pihkoh misiponikewnihk ohci*; there is ash or ashes, *pihkowiw* (VAI); *pihkowan* (VII).

aside *pimicayihk* (IPC); aside, away from river or road, *nohcimayik* (IPC).

asinine *môhcohisâyâwin* (NI).

asininity *ka môco isâyahk* (VAI).

ask Asking or inquiring, *kakwecihkemowin* (NI); s/he asks, *kakwecihkemow* (VAI); s/he asks her/him, *kakwecimew* (VTA); s/he asks or requests in a ritual manner for a spiritual ceremonial, *nâspitohtawew* (VAI).

askew *kîkway kawahwakak* (VTI).

aslant *kîkway ka iyipestek* (VTI).

asleep *ka pôsahkwâmihk* (VAI).

aspen *wâpimitos* (NA).

aspirin *teyistikwânewimaskihkiy* (NI).

aspire *metoni sohki kîkway kanohtihayahk*.

ass A donkey or a mule, *sôsôwatim* (NA); s/he is an ass or mule, *sôsôwatimowiw* (VAI).

assail *ka sikotatahikehk* (VTA).

assailant *osikotatahikew* (NA).

assault *notinikewin* (NI).

assemblage *mâmawinikewin* (NI).

assemble S/he gets them together, *mâmawahew* (VTA); s/he calls them together for the assembly, gathering or meeting, *mâmawinâtomew* (VTA); s/he assembles them, *mâmawinew* (VTA); s/he puts things all together, *mâmawinikew* (VAI); they assemble themselves, *mâmawinitowinak* (NI); s/he orders for it all at one, *mâmawinâtisaham* (VAI); it comes together all by itself or assembles itself, *mâmawipayiw* (VAI); s/he drives them together, i.e.: horses or cattle, *mâmawitisawew* (VTA); they assemble themselves to help one another, *mâmawohkamâtowak* (VTA).

assembly An organized meeting or assembly, *mâmawapowin* (NI); an informal gathering of people, *mâmawipayowin* (NI).

assent *kîyamketeyihtamihk* (VAI).

assert *kîkway katâpwehtamihk* (VTI).

assertion *tâpwewakeyihtamowin* (NI).

assertive *metoni tâpweyihcekewin* (NI).

assess *koyakihtamihk kîkwaya* (VTI).

assessment *oyakihcikewin* (NI).

assessor *otôyakihcikew* (NA).

asset *awîyak katipeyihtahk kîkway* (VTI).

assets *tipeyicikiwina* (NI) *(Northern)*; *pamihowina* (NI) *(Plains)*.

assiduity *ka kâyawatisowin* (NI).

assiduous *awîyak ekâkayawatisit*.

assign *nîkânapîhiwewin* (NI).

assignation *kîmôc sakihitowin* (NI).

assignee *awîyak kanîkânapîhiht* (VTA).

assignment *nîkânapiwin* (NI).

assignor *onîkânapîhiwew* (NA).

assimilate *awîyak kayeniht* (VTA).

assimilative *oyiniwewin* (NI).

Assiniboine *nehiyawak asinipotak kîsiyekasotwaw*.

assist *kanîsohkamakehk*; s/he procures it for others, *ohcestamâkew* (VTA); the act of procuring something for someone, *ohcestamâkewin* (NI); s/he procures it for her/him, *ohcestamâwew* (VTA); s/he assists her/him in sitting up in bed, *waniskânew* (VTA); s/he assists her/him, *wîcihew* (VTA).

assistance A form of help, *nîsohkamâtowin* (NI); s/he runs to her/him for assistance, i.e.: help or protection, *nâtâmototawêw* (VTA).

assistant A helper, *onîsohkamâkew* (NA); a work helper, i.e.: assistant, *wecâtoskeyâkan* (NA).

assize *kihciwiyasowewin* (NI).

associate *otôtemow* (VAI); *otôtemiw* (VAI).

association *mâmawih otôtemihtowin* (NI); *mâmawintowin* (NI).

assonance *tapowewin* (NI).

assort *ka piskihtastahk* (VTI).

assorted *kakeh piskihtascikehk* (VTI).

assortment *nanâtohk piskihtascikewina* (NI).

assuage *nîkimôsihtâwin* (NI).

assume *ahpô* (IPC).

assumed *ahpô etikwe* (IPC).

assumption *moscitâpeyihtamowin* (NI).

assurance *metoni kehcinâhowin* (NI); *kecinâhowinihk* (IPC).

assure *kehcinâ* (IPC).

assured *kehcinahetowin* (NI).

assuredly *tânsi tacikohoinahohk* (VAI).

astir *ka kâyawâyâwin* (NI).

astonish *mâmaskâc* (IPC); *mâmaskâtamowin* (NI).

astonishing *kamâmaskâtamihk* (VAI).

astonishment *mâmaskâteyihcikewin* (NI); astonishment, admiration, wonderment, wonderful, *mâmaskâc* (IPC).

astound *nâspic kamâmaskâtamihk* (VAI).

astray *kawanisinihk*; *kawanisihk*; becoming lost, *wanisinowin* (NI).

astride *katastawahamihk kîkway* (IPC).

251

astute *iyinisowin* (NI).

Athabasca The Cree name for the settlement of Athabasca, *kapâwin* (NI).

athlete *awîyak ka sîsawet nanâtohk isi metawewina* (NA).

athletic *nanâtohk isi metawe wisâyâwin* (NI).

atop *tahkôc* (IPC).

atrocious *kihci maci isâyâwin* (NI).

atrocity *misimacîtôtamowin* (NI).

attach Attaching something, *akwamohcikewin* (NI); s/he attached it to something, *kikamohew* (VTI); it is attached to something, *kikamow* (VII); s/he attached things, *kikamocikew* (VTI) s/he attaches them securely i.e.: used to refer to a car wheel, *sanaskamohew* (VTI); it is securely attached, *sanaskamow* (VII); it is attached underneath, *sekwamow* (VII).

attachment *akwamohcikan* (NI); an attachment, *ânaskohpicikâkan* (NI).

attack *sisikoc moskestakewin apô sisikôc ahkosowin ka otihtikohk* (VTI).

attain *kîkway kamiyokaskihtahk* (VTI).

attainability *miyokaskihcikewin* (NI).

attainable *kîkway takeh miyo kahtinamihk.*

attainment *kahtinikewin* (NI).

attempt The act of trying hard, *sohkahacikocewin* (NI); s/he attempts or tries to do something, *kociw* (VAI); s/he attempts or tries to sing, *kocinikamiw* (VAI); s/he attempts or tries to speak, *kocipîkiskwew* (VAI); an attempt to talk, *kocipikiskwewin* (NI); an attempt or act of trying, *kociwin* (NI).

attend Attending to someone, *kawîcihiwehk*; s/he attends to her/him, *pamihew* (VTA); s/he attends to herself/himself, *pamihisiw* (VTA); the act of attending to oneself or the act of self care, *pamihisiwin* (NI); the act of attending to someone or taking care of someone, *pamihiwewin* (NI); s/he looks after her/him, *paminew* (VTA).

attendance *wîcihiwewin* (NI); *kamâmawâyâtihk* (VAI).

attendant *awîyak kawîcihiwet* (VTA).

attention *nâkateyihcikewin* (NI); *natohtamok*; careless by, without attention, by heart, *pakwaniw* (VAI); with care, slowly, with attention, *peyahtik* (IPC).

attentive *ka nihtâ nâkateyihtamihk* (VAI).

attest *pîkiskwestamâkewin* (NI).

attestation *ka pîkiskwestamâkehk* (VTA).

attitude *tansi keteyihtamihk kîkway* (VAI).

attract *ka kakwayiyihihit awîyak* (VTA).

attraction *yiyihiwewin* (NI).

attractive It is attractive, *miyonâkwan* (VII); s/he is beautiful or attractive, *katawasisiw* (VAI); s/he finds her/him attractive, i.e.: beautiful or handsome, *miyonawew* (VTA); it is very attractive or it looks very fine, *miwasin* (VII) *(Northern)*; *miywâsin* (VII) *(Plains)*.

attributable *miyokiskinwahikewin* (NI).

attribute *ka kiskinwahamihk kîkway apô awîyak* (VTA).

attribution *kiskinawâteyihcikan* (NI).

attributive *ka nihtâ kiskinwaheket awîyak.*

auburn *kaskitewmihkosiw* (VAI).

audacious *mistakeyimisowin* (NI).

audacity *kostanakeyemowin* (NI).

aucibility *awîyak ka kisiwet* (VAI).

audible *kisewewin* (NI); clearly audible, clearly heard, *kihkâwihtâkosiw* (VAI); *kihkâwihtâkwan* (VII); sound good, well, *miyohtâkosiw* (VAI); *miyohtâkwan* (VII); sounds bad, *mayihtâkosiw* (VAI); *mayihtâkwan* (VII); sounds shy, ashamed, *nepewihtakosiw* (VAI); *nepewihtakwan* (VII); loud voiced, loud "noised", *sohkihtakosiw* (VAI); *sohkihtakwan* (VII); comes through as voice, as noise, *sâpohtakosiw* (VAI); *sâpohtakwan* (VII); loud enough, *tepihtâkosiw* (VAI); *tepihtâkwan* (VII); too far to be heard, *yâwihtakosiw* (VAI); *yâwihtakwan* (VII).

audience *ayeseyenowak ka penâtohtahkwaw*; listeners, *natohtamakewak* (NA).

audio *kîkway ka pihtâkwahk* (VTI).

auditory *metoni ka wiyawihtamihk* (VAI).

augment *ka takwastahk kîkway* (VTI).

augmentation *takwascikewin* (NI).

augmented *takonamakewin* (NI).

August The flying moon or month, *ohpahowipîsim* (NA) *(Northern)*; *ohpahopîsim* (NA) *(Plains)*.

aunt My aunt (or my mother-in-law), *nitosis* (NA); my father's sister or paternal aunt, *nisikos* (NA); my mother's sister or maternal aunt, *nimamasis* (NA); your aunt, *kesikos* (NA); *kimamasis* (NA); someone's parent's sister, *awîyak osikosa* (NA); *awîyak omamasisa* (NA); *awîyak otôsisa* (NA); someone's father's sister, *awîyak osokisa* (NA); someone's mother's sister, *awîyak okawîsa* (NA).

aura *kâwehmoyehtamihk* (VAI).

aural *metoni nahihtamowin* (NI).

Aurora Borealis The ghost dancing in the skies, *epayak ka nimihitotwâw*; *kânîmihitocik* (NA) *(Plains)*.

auspicious *miyo asotamakewin* (NI).

austere *macihtwâwin* (NI).

austerity *macihtwâwisâyâwin* (NI).

authentic A reliable person, *metoni ka sohki mamsehk*; when it was first made, *nistam kake osehtahk*; s/he is veritable or authentic, *tâpweyitakosiw* (VAI).

authenticate *kihcipikiskwewin* (NI).

authenticity *miyo mâmiskomewewin* (NI).

authoritative *okimâwakeyimisowin* (NI).

authority *okimâwapiwin* (NI).

authorization *okimâwahiwewin* (NI).

authorize *awîyak ka okimâwahiht.*

authorized *awîyak kakeh okimâwahiht.*

autumn It is fall time or autumn, *takwâkin* (NI)
(Plains); autumn, the season of falling leaves,
pinâskiw (NI) *(Northern)*; last fall or autumn,
takwâkohk (IPC); this fall or autumn, *anohcitakwâkin*
(IPC), *takwâkiki* (IPC).

autumnal *ka mâcitakwâkihk.*

auxiliary *tako nîsohkamâkewin* (NI); giving support to
people, *mâmawihkahwecihiwehk* (NI).

avail *nehpemayawin* (NI).

availability *kanihta nehpemayahk* (VAI).

available *kakeki nehpemapowin; ihtakon* (NI).

avaricious *nâspic sasâkisiwin* (NI).

avast *ka sisikoc nakehk.*

avenge *nâtamâkewin* (NI).

aver *kihcipikiskwewin* (NI).

average *tipakicikewin* (NI); not too bad, well enough,
eyiwek (IPC).

averse *kweskiwepinikewin* (NI).

aversion *ka kweskiwepinikehk* (VAI).

avert *kîkway kaponihtahk* (VTI).

avid *ka papâseyihtamihk* (VAI).

avidity *papâseyihtamowin* (NI).

avocation *ka pîmatisahamihk kîkway ka
miweyihtamihk* (VAI).

avoid Avoiding someone, *awîyak ka wemâskaht;* s/he
avoids her/him, *tapasîstawew* (VTA).

avoidable *kanihta wemâskamihk* (VTI).

avoidance *wemâskâcikan* (NI).

avow *metoni tâpwewin* (NI).

avowal *misimisowin* (NI).

avowed *ka moscimisimsohk* (VAI).

avowedly *ka kihcipikiskwehiwehk* (VTA).

await *pehowin* (NI).

awake Insomnia, *waspâwisâyâwin* (NI); s/he awakes,
koskopayiw (VAI).

awaken *koskonowewin* (NI).

award *kîkway ka kîspinatamihk* (NI).

aware The act of awareness, *nistaweyecikewin* (NI);
s/he senses his total personal support, *nistâseyimew*
(VTA); s/he is aware of being supported, *nistâseyimow*
(VAI); the act of being aware of being supported,
nistâseyimowin (NI); s/he provides her/him with a
sense of support, *nistâsiskawew* (VTA); s/he is now
aware of things, i.e.: sobering up, *wâskamâyâw* (VAI);
s/he is thought of as being aware of things, i.e.: clear
headed, *wâskameyihtâkosiw* (VAI); the act of being
thought of as being aware or clear headed,
wâskameyihtakosowin (NI); it is thought of as being
aware, *wâskameyihtâkwan* (VII); s/he is more aware
or s/he is thinking clearer, *wâskameyihtam* (VAI); s/he
thinks of her/him as being more aware,
wâskameyimew (VTA); s/he is becoming more aware,
i.e.: sobering up, *wâskamisiw* (VAI); the act of
becoming more aware, *wâskamisiwin* (NI).

away *namoya ikotah; wahiyawes* (IPC); away from the
water or a road, *nohcimik* (IPC); aside, away from river
or road, *nohcimayik* (IPC).

awe *mâmaskâteyihcikewin* (NI).

awesome *kôsâme mâmaskâteyihtamihk* (VAI).

awe-struck *kôsâmeyitamohiht awîyak* (VTA).

awful *ka kwâyakih; mâmaskâc* (IPC).

awfully *waweyak kakwâyakih* (IPC).

awhile *nômanak* (IPC); *kanakes* (IPC).

awkward Someone being awkward and clumsy,
kayekicikawihk (VAI); s/he does something awkward
or clumsy, *mâyinikew* (VAI); the act of awkwardness
or clumsiness, *mâyinikewin* (NI).

awl A tool for punching holes in leather or moosehide,
oskâcihk (NA); s/he has an awl, *oskâcihkow* (VAI).

awning *âkawâstehikan* (NI); a sun shade, *âkawâstehon*
(NI).

axe or **ax** *cîkahikan* (NI); a broad axe, *napakicîkahikan*
(NI); an axe for squaring timber, i.e.: a broad axe,
pasahikewicîkahikan (NI); a crooked axe,
wâkicîkahikan (NI).

axe handle *cîkahikanâhtik* (NI).

azure It looks like sky blue, *sipihkonakwan* (NI).

253

B

babe *apisisisit* (NA); *oskawâsis* (NA).

baby *apiscawâsis* (NA); *awâsis* (NA).

babyhood *apiscawâsisiwiwin* (NI).

babyish *peyakwan apiscawâsis* (VII).

baby-sit *kanaweyimâwasowin* (NI).

baby-sitter *okanaweyimâwasiw* (NA).

bachelor An unmarried or single man, *môsâpew* (NI).

bachelorhood *môsâpewiwin* (NI).

back *mispiskwan* (NI); in the back or behind, *otâhk* (IPC) *(Northern)*; *nâway* (IPC) *(Plains)*; s/he stands with her/his back towards her/him, *atamikâpawiw* (VTA).

backache *teyipiskwaniwin* (NI).

back and forth *kahkekwask* (IPC).

backbone *wawikankan* (NI); *mâwikan* (NI).

backbreaking *kaskawkanipayowin* (NI).

backhanded *asepakamahikewin* (NI).

backing *nîsohkamâkewin* (NI).

backscratching *cîhcikaw kaneniwewin* (NI).

backset *otâhkipicikewin* (NI).

backslide *aseyâpoyowin* (NI).

backtrack Backtracking tracks, *asihacikewin* (NI); s/he backtracks on the trail, i.e.: retracing steps, *asihtamew* (VAI).

backward *nepewisiwin* (NI).

backwards *teyakwâc otâhkisih* (LN); the water is flowing backwards, *aseciwan* (VII).

backwoods *sakâsihk* (NI).

backwoodsman *sakâyiyiniw* (NA).

bacon *kohkôsiwiyin* (NA).

bad Having bad character, *macihtwâwin* (NI); s/he has a bad character, *macihtwâw* (VAI); s/he plagues herself/himself with bad luck, *pâstamow* (VTA).

badger *mistanask* (NA).

badly *metoni namoyakwayask* (IPC).

bad-tempered *nâspic macihtwâwin* (NI).

baffle *ekâ kanistaweyihtâmihk* (VAI).

bafflement *waneyihtamowin* (NI) *(Plains)*; *tikinewin* (NI) *(Northern)*.

baffling *kawaniyihtamihk kîkway* (VTI).

bag *maskimot* (NI); a cloth bag, *ayiwinisekin* (NI).

bagging *asowacikewin* (NI).

bail An expression meaning bailing someone out of jail or bailing water out of a canoe or boat, *ihkahipewin* (NI); *tipahikestamâkewin* (NI).

bailable *tipahikestamâkewin* (NI).

bait *mîcimihkahcikan* (NI).

bake *pahkwesikanihkewin* (NI).

balance Something well balanced, *kwayask kîkway* (IPC); a balanced personality, *ayâtisowin* (NI); s/he is a well balanced person, *ayâtisiw* (VAI).

bald *paskostikwânewin* (NI); *paskostikwânew* (VAI).

bald eagle *paskostikwânewkihew* (NA); *mikisow* (NA).

bald head *paskostikwân* (VAI); s/he has a bald head, *paskostikwânew* (VAI).

baldheaded *paskwâtihpewin* (NI).

bald prairie *maskotew* (NI).

bale A bale of hay, *tahkopicikewin* (NI).

bale The act of bailing out a boat, *ihkahipewin* (NI).

baleful *macîteyihcikewin* (NI).

balk *ka sisikoc nakipayehohk* (VAI).

balky *macistikwânewin* (NI).

ball A ball for games, i.e.: a baseball or soccer ball, *pâkahtowân* (NA) *(Plains)*; *tihtipinatowân* (NA) *(Northern)*; s/he plays ball, i.e.: football, *pâkahtowew* (VAI) *(Plains)*; *tihtipinatowew* (VAI) *(Northern)*.

balm *wihkimâkwahon* (NI).

balmy *wihkimakosowin* (NI).

balsam fir *napakâsihta* (NA).

balsam pitch *or* **balsam gum** *napakâsihtipikiw* (NA).

balsam poplar *mâyimitos* (NA).

ban *nakinikewin* (NI).

banal *kîkway kâsewak* (VTI).

banality *kîkway ka sewihtihk* (VTI).

band An adhesive, *akohpisiw* (VAI); a group of people, i.e.: a tribe, *ka mâmawîpayetwâw ayisiyinowak* (NA).

bandage *akohpisowin* (NI); s/he has a bandage on, *akohpisiw* (VAI); s/he places a bandage on her/him, *akohpitew* (VTA).

bandana *or* **bandanna** *misihtâpiskâkan* (NI).

bandit *okimotiw* (NA); *kîmôtis* (NA).

banditry *kîmôto isâyâwin* (NI).

band saw *tâskipocikâkan* (NI).

bang A sound made by a gun shot, *matwewew* (VAI); something that fall down with a loud sound, *kîkway ka mistowihtihk*; it bangs against something, *pakamihtin* (VII).

banish *ka wepinamihk*; *wayawepinikewin* (NI).

banishment *wepinikewin* (NI).

bank *sônîyâwikamik* (NI)

bannock *pahkwesikan* (NA); *napakinikan* (NA); s/he makes bannock, *pahkwesikanihkew* (VAI).

banquet To make a big banquet, *asahkewin* (NI); a big banquet, *isihcikewin* (NI); s/he makes a big

255

banquet or feast or do, *isihcikew* (VAI); eating, *micisowin* (NI).

bantam *apisisisit pisiskîwayîs* (VAI).

banter *nanoyatiwewin* (NI).

baptise The act of pouring water over someone or the act of performing a baptism, *sîkahahtakewin* (NI); s/he is baptised, *sîkahahcikâsiw* (VAI); s/he pours water over her/him or s/he baptised her/him, *sîkahahtawew* (VTA); s/he pours waters over someone or s/he performs a baptism, *sîkahahtakew* (VAI).

baptism A ritual bath, i.e.: a baptism, *sîkahahcikasiwin* (NI); s/he performs a quick baptism, *kiskinowâtâpâwahew* (VTA).

Baptist *pîtosâyamihâwin* (NI).

bar *minihkwewikamik* (NI).

barbed *awîyak ka nihtâkihsiwâhtwat* (VTA).

barbed wire *wâsakânikanipiwâpisk* (NI) *(Plains)*; *wâsakânikaniyâpiy* (NI) *(Northern)*.

barbwire *wâsakânikaniyâpiy* (NI).

bare The act of being nude, *moseskatewin* (NI); bare, uncovered, *môstasewin* (NI); s/he is nude, *môstasewin* (NI).

256

bareback *môstaw kanehikewin* (NI).

barefisted *ka moscecihcehk* (VAI).

barefoot Being barefoot, *sâsâkihtiwin* (NI); s/he is barefoot, *sâsâkihtiw* (VAI) *(Plains)*; *mosesitew* (VAI) *(Northern)*.

barehanded *ka sâsâkincihcehk* (VAI).

barelegged *sâsâkinikâtew* (VAI).

barely *metoni itahtâw* (IPC); *itatiw* (IPC); *itahto* (IPC); just about, well enough, barely enough, *tîpiyak* (IPC); *kisâstaw* (IPC); *kitisk* (IPC).

bareness *môstâpekasewin* (NI).

bargain *wehtakihcikewin* (NI).

bark It barks, *mikisimow* (VAI); the act of barking, *mikisimowin* (NI); it barks at her/him, i.e.: a dog, *mikitew* (VAI).

bark Tree bark, *wayakesk* (NA); the bark comes off easily, *pahkwenew* (VTA).

bark beetle *wayakeskomanicôs* (NA).

barkeeper *osîkinikew* (NA).

barley *iskwesisihkân* (NA).

barn *mistatimokamik* (NI); an animal house, *pisiskiwikamik* (NI); an animal keeping house, *kanawipisiskiwikamik* (NI); cow barn, *mostosokamik* (NI).

barn dance *mistati emokamikohk kanimihitohk* (VAI).

barn raising *mâmawihisicikewin* (NI).

barn swallow *omîcaskosîs* (NA).

barnyard *ka wâsakânikatek mistatimokamik* (NI).

barrel *mahkahk* (NI); a sugar barrel, *sesipâskwatômahkahk* (NI); a gun barrel, *pâskisikanâpisk* (NI).

barrelful *ka sâkaskinek mahkahk* (NI).

barricade *ka nakinamihk kîkway*.

barrier S/he puts a barrier up to prevent her/him from proceeding, *nakâhowew* (VTA).

barroom *pehcayihk menihkwewkamikohk*; *minihkwewkamik* (NI).

bartender *ominahiwew* (NA).

barter *mosci meskotonamâtowin* (NI); *meskotonamâkewin* (NI).

base *opascikewin* (NI).

bash *misi môcikihtâwin* (NI).

basic *ka macipayik kîkway* (VTI).

basically *tânsi kesi macipayik kîkway* (VTI).

basin *kâsîhkweweyakan* (NI); s/he washes her/his own face, *kâsîhkwew* (VTA).

basinette A bed made with roots, *watapiwinipewinis* (NI).

basis A place or thing from which a solid foundation is built, *ayâtaskisiw* (VII).

bask *ka astamastepihk* (VAI).

basket Made from roots, *watapiwât* (NI); a type of basket used for a collection plate, *pihcipoyâkan* (NI).

basketry *etah kosihtâhk watapew weta* (VTI).

basket weave *ka pihkatamihk watapîwiwatah* (VTI).

basketwork *etah kosihtâhk watapîwiwatah* (VTI).

bass *metoni ka kihtewenikamohk*; the act of sounding deep-throated, *kihtewewin* (NI).

bass drum *ka kihtewet mistikwaskihk* (NA).

bastard *kîminîcâkan* (NA).

bat A small flying mammal, *apahkwaces* (NI); a baseball bat, *pâkahatowânahtik* (NI).

batch *pakwesikanihkewin* (NI).

bath *kisipekastewin* (NI); *pakâsimow* (VAI); s/he is washing her/him, *kisipekinew* (VTA).

bathe *ka kisipekastehk* (VTI).

batter Making batter, i.e.: for bread or bannock, *pahkwesikanihkewin* (NI).

batting Making something soft with padding, i.e.: cotton batting, *yoskahikan* (NI).

battle *nôtinikewin* (NI); *nôtinew* (VTA); *wîcinôtinitômew* (VTA).

battle dress *nôtinikew sihowin* (NI).

bawl *kamisematohk*; *mâtow* (VAI); the act of animals calling out, *kitowin* (NI).

bay *wâsahikamâw* (NI).

beach *yikâwiskâhk* (LN).

bead *mîkis* (NA); a large bead used for making a necklace, *tâpiskâkanemin* (NI); a white bead, *wâpimin* (NA) *(Northern)*; *wapimîkis* (NA) *(Plains)*.

beaded *ka mîkisihkahcikatek kîkway* (VTI).

beading *ka mîkisihkahcikehk* (VTI).

beadwork The act of doing beadwork, *mîkisihkahcikewin* (NI).

beak *pîwâyisisokot* (NI) *(Northern)*; *piyesisikot* (NI) *(Plains)*.

beam A wooden beam, *ka asawâskwastahk* (NI); *wâskahikanahtik* (NI); *wâwikanahtik* (NI).

bean *peswîmin* (NA) *(Northern)*; *miyîcîmin* (NA) *(Plains)*; *pîmiciwacis* (NA); a bean stalk, *miyîciminahtik* (NA).

beanpole *kanwaskweyinew* (NA).

bear S/he makes her/him bear something on her/his back, *nayahtahew* (VTA); s/he makes people bear something, *nayahtahiwew* (VTA); a person who bears things on her/his back, *nayahcikewiyiniw* (NA).

bear *maskwa* (NA); a male bear, *nâpemaskwa* (NA); a female bear, a mother bear, *nôsemaskwa* (NA); a one-year-old bear, *opacawanisîs* (NA); a two-year-old bear, *kihtemaskwa* (NA); a brown bear, *osâwask* (NA); a very large old bear; a grizzly bear, *okistatowan* (NA); *mistahaya* (NA); a polar bear, *wâpask* (NA).

bearable *ka nîpawistamihk* (VTI).

bearberry *maskomin* (NI); bearberry bush, i.e.: a mild poison, *maskominanahtik* (NA).

beard *miyastowân* (NI); having a beard, *miyastowanewin* (NI); he has a beard, *miyastowew* (VAI).

bearded A long bearded person, *komiyastowânit* (NA).

bearer A carrier, *onayahcikew* (NA); Cree origin of Carrier Indians.

bearing *âspamohcikan* (NI).

beast An animal, *pisiskiw* (NA).

beat To win over someone else, *paskiyawew* (VTA); the act of disciplining a child, *nôcihâwasowin* (NI).

beaten *ka paskeyâht awîyak* (PR); *paskiyakewin* (NI).

beater *opaskîyâkew* (NA); s/he slaps faces, *opasihkwetahikew* (NA).

beatific *kîkway ka saweyehtakwahk* (VTI).

beatification *saweyihcikewin* (NI).

beatify *ka saweyehtamihk* (VTI).

beating The act of disciplining a child, *nôcihâwasowin* (NI).

beatitude It is well respected, *kihkâteyihtâkwan* (VII) *(Northern)*; *kihceyihtâkwan* (VII) *(Plains)*.

beau *kîcimos* (NA).

beauteous *metoni kâmiwasik*.

beautiful S/he is beautiful, *katawasisiw* (VAI); s/he looks lovely, *mîyosiw katawasisiw* (VAI); it looks beautiful, *katawasisin* (VII); it looks very fine; it is attractive, *miwasin* (VAI) *(Northern)*; *mîywâsin* (VII) *(Plains)*; the beautiful one, *omiyosiw* (VAI).

beautify Making something beautiful, *miyosihcikiwin* (NI); s/he beautifies her/him, *miyonâkohew* (VTA).

beauty *miyosiwin* (NI).

beauty spot *masinâsiwin* (NI).

beaver *amisk* (NA); beaver house, *amiskowestih* (NI); beaver dam, *oskwatim* (NI); beaver pelt, *amiskwayan* (NI); beaver castors, i.e.: used in medicine, *amiskowesinâw* (NI); a two-year-old beaver, *patamisk* (NA); a one-year-old beaver, *poyawesis* (NA); a family of 10–15 beaver, *okikacimewak* (NA).

Beaver Lake The Cree name for the settlement of Beaver Lake, *amiskosâkahikan* (NI).

Beaver Mountain House The Cree name for the city of Edmonton, *amiskwaciwâskahikan* (NI).

becalm *kâmwâtisowin* (NI).

becalmed *awîyak kakâmwâtsit* (VAI).

became *ekosi kakehispayik* (VAI).

because *eyoko ohci* (IPC).

beckon *nitohkemowin* (NI).

becloud *wanahiwewin* (NI).

becoming *metoni miyonâkosiwin* (NI).

bed *nipewin* (NI); s/he makes a bed, *nipewinihkew* (VAI); a bed frame or a head board, *nipewinâhtik* (NI).

bedazzle *môhcohkâsowewin* (NI).

bedbug *nipewinihk manîcosak* (NA); *napak manîcos* (NA).

bedclothes *nipâwayiwinisa* (NI).

bedding S/he arranges the bedding or makes up a bed, *nahastâsiw* (VAI); the act of arranging bedding, *nahastâsiwin* (NI).

bedfellow *awîyak kâmiyo wetsinomiht* (VTA).

bedlam *metoni wâyâpayowin* (NI).

bedridden *mecimwâtisinowin* (NI).

bedrock *ka ayisko aseniskak* (VTA).

bedside *ka iskwâstek nepewin* (NI).

bedspread A blanket that is on top, *wâskitanâskan* (NI).

bedstead *nipewinâhtik* (NI).

bedtime *nipâwin* (NI).

bee *âmô* (NA); a bee hive, *âmowaciston* (NI).

beech *metoni maskawâhtik* (NA).

beef Meat, *mostosowîyâs* (NI).

beefy *wiyâsiwan* (VII).

257

beer *iskwesis âpoy* (NA).

beeswax *âmôwak ka watistwanihkaketwaw.*

beet *mihkoskatask* (NA).

beetle A water bettle, *amiskosîs* (NA); a lightening bug or beetle, *pîwâpiskomanicos* (NA).

befit *ka nahisinihk etah* (LN).

befitting *nahiskamowin* (NI).

before First, ahead, *nîkân* (IPC); before time, *pâmayes* (IPC) *(Plains)*; *mayes* (IPC) *(Plains)*; *namic* (IPC) *(Northern)*; right now, without delay, before doing anything else, *kesâc* (IPC); before, ere, *kayahte* (IPC).

beforehand Ready, *kwayaci* (IPC).

befriend Feel sorry for, *kitimâkinâtowin* (NI).

beg S/he begs her/him, *pakosihew* (VTA).

beggar A person who begs for things, *onâtotamaw* (VAI); an asker, *natotamâsk* (NA); a beggar, *pakosihtâwiyiniw* (NA).

begin *mâcihtawin* (NI); *mâcihta* (VAI).

beginner *omâcitaw* (NA); *nistam mâcihtawin* (NI).

beginning Where something begins, *etah ka mâcipayik kîkway* (IPC); in the beginning, at first, *oskac* (IPC).

begrudge *sawânakeyimowin* (NI).

beguile *wanâhîwewin* (NI).

behave *peyahtikisâyâwin* (NI).

behavior *or* **behaviour** Someone's conduct, *awîyak otsâyâwin* (NI); s/he acts with good behavior or s/he (is well-behaved) behaves well, *miyowâyihtiw* (VAI).

behest *awîyak ka sihkimiht* (VTA).

behind From behind, *otâhk ohci* (LN); back or behind, *otâhk* (IPC) *(Northern)*; *nâway* (IPC) *(Plains)*; s/he places them behind, *otâhkahew* (VTA); s/he is behind or running late, *otâhkowiw* (VAI) *(Northern)*; *otâhkesin* (VAI) *(Plains)*.

beholden *mâmeskoc miyotôtatowin* (NI).

behoove *ka nahiskamomakahk kîkway* (VTI).

beige *kîkway ka osâminakwahk* (VII).

being *ayâwin* (NI); *nânitâw ka ayâhk* (LN).

belch *ka pekatehk*; *pekatew* (VAI).

belie *kîmôcisâyâwin* (NI).

belief Something believable, *ka tâpwewakeyihtamihk kîkway* (VAI); a belief or hope, *tâpwewakeyihtamowin* (NI).

believe The act of believing, *tâpwehtamowin* (NI); s/he believes her/him to express sacred power or to be divine, *manitoweyimew* (VTA); s/he believes her/him to express the good spirit power in the universe, *kisemanitokatew* (VTA); s/he is to be believed, *tâpwehtâkowiw* (VAI); it is to be believed, *tâpwehtâkwan* (VII); s/he believes it, *tâpwehtam* (VTA); s/he believes her/him, *tâpwehtawew* (VTA); s/he believes in her/him, *tâpwewakeyimew* (VTA);

s/he believes something is good for her/him, *tâpwewakeyihtamohwew* (VAI).

believer *otâpwehtam* (NA).

belittle *acowihisiw* (VTA).

bell *sewiyâkan* (NA) *(Plains)*; *soweyakan* (NA) *(Northern)*.

bellicose *awîyak ka nôtinikeskit* (VTA).

belligerence *ayiwâkeyimowin* (NI).

belligerency *ka ayiwâkeyimohk* (VAI).

belligerent *kostanakeyimowin* (NI).

bellow *sâkowewin* (NI).

belly Stomach, *matay* (NI).

bellyache *kisôwaskatewin* (NI).

belong Belonging somewhere, *kiscâyâwin* (NI).

belongings *tipiyawehona* (NI).

beloved *awîyak mistahi ka sâkihiht* (VTA).

below *capasis* (IPC); just a little bit below, *nehîcâyihk nawâc* (IPC); below or downwards, *nehîcâyihk* (IPC).

belt *pakwahtehon* (NI); *pakwatihon* (NI); s/he makes belts, *pakwahtehonihkew* (VAI); s/he wears a belt, *pakwahtehiw* (VAI); s/he puts a belt on her/him, *pakwahtehwew* (VTA).

belted *awîyak kapakamahoht* (VTA).

bemoan *mihtâtamowin* (NI).

bemuse *sohki kamâmetoneyihtamihk* (VAI).

bench *îkinwak tehtapowin* (NI); *tehtapowinis* (NI).

bend Bending something, *ka wakinamihk kîkway* (VTI); bending over, *wakisowin* (NI); s/he bends her/him many different ways, *ayapakinew* (VTI); s/he makes it bend by applying heat, *pihkihkaswew* (VTI) *(Northern)*; *pihkaswew* (VTI) *(Plains)*; s/he bends her/his knee for her/him, *pihkikestawew* (VTA); s/he bends her/his own knee, *pihkikeyiw* (VAI); s/he bends her/him or them, *pihkinew* (VTA); s/he bends them by pulling, *pihkipitew* (VTA); s/he bends her/his arm by pulling, *pihkipitonepitew* (VTA); s/he bends it with a kick, i.e.: a pail, *pihkiskawew* (VTA); s/he is bent over, *pihkisiw* (VAI) *(Northern)*; *pihkiw* (VAI) *(Plains)*; it is bent over, *pihkâw* (VAI); s/he bends her/his own body, *wâkîw* (VAI); s/he bends her/him, *wakinew* (VTA); s/he is bent with age, *wâkikihkâw* (VAI); something that was bent, *wâkinikan* (NI); s/he makes a shelter with bent sticks, *wâkinokew* (VAI); it bends on its own, *wâkipayiw* (VII); s/he bends them by pulling, *wâkipitew* (VTI); s/he is bent or stooped, *wâkisiw* (VAI).

bender *ka minihkwewâhkamekahk* (VII).

beneath *sekwayihk* (IPC); *sihpa* (IPC).

benediction *otâkwan ayamihâwin* (NI).

benefice *ayamihewiyiniw opimâtisowin* (NI).

beneficence *mistahi kisewâtisowin* (NI).

beneficent *awîyak ka kisewatesit* (VAI).

beneficial *kîkway takeh ohci miyopayihk* (VII).

beneficiary *sônîyâw nîsohkâmatowin* (NI).

benefit *ka mekihk sônîyâw* (NA); *wîcîtowin* (NI).

benevolence Kindheartedness, *osâm kisewatesiwin* (NI); s/he looks at her/him with benevolence, *miyokanawâpamew* (VTA).

benevolent Lots of kindness, *mistahi miyohtwâwin* (NI).

benevolent action *miyotôtamowin* (NI); being kind, *kisewatisowin* (NI).

benign *kamiyo kâmwâci ayisiyinikehk* (VAI).

benignancy *mistahi miyotehewin* (NI).

benignant *awîyak miyotehet* (VAI).

benignity *miyotehewin* (NI).

berate *awîyak ka pewomiht* (VAI).

bereave *nakataskewin* (NI); the act of losing someone in death, *mâyipayiwin* (NI).

bereaved *kakaskeyihtamaskatiht awîyak* (VTA).

bereavement *kaskeyihtamowin* (NI).

bereft *peyakwaskatitowin* (NI).

berry A wild berry, *mînis* (NI); a cluster of berries, *mihcetominakâw* (NA) *(Northern)*; *mînisiskâw* (NA) *(Plains)*; a dried berry, *pâsiminân* (NI).

berserk *môhcopayowin* (NI).

berth *nîpawin pôsowenihk* (NI).

beseech Pleading with someone, *kîskwe kakwecihkemowin* (NI); s/he beseeches them for something, *natotamâwew* (VTA); the act of beseeching or imploring, *natotamâwin* (NI).

besetting *misiwe ohtehkiniwewin* (NI).

beside *mecim ekotah* (IPC); *sisone* (IPC).

besides *kotak kîkway mina* (IPC).

besiege *ka askamacikehk* (VTA).

besmirch *kamisiwanâcitâhk kîkway* (VTI).

besot *sâkocihikowin* (NI).

besotted *kasâkocihikohk kîkway*; *sâkocihikowin* (NI).

bespread *kîkway kaswestâhk* (VTI).

best *mâwaci kâmewasik* (VII).

bestial *kapisiskiw isâyahk* (VAI).

bestiality *pisiskiw isâyâwin* (NI).

bestir *wayâhiwewin* (NI).

bestow *kihtâwihiwewin* (NI); the act of bestowing, *okihcitâwihiwewin* (NI).

bestowal *okihcitâwihiwewin* (NI).

bestride *tastawahikewin* (NI).

bet Making a bet, *astowatowin* (NI); s/he bet her/him, *astowew* (VTA).

betake *nânitâw kitohtahisohk* (VTI).

bethought *kiskisopayowin* (NI).

betimes *kîyepa nawâc* (IPC).

betook *kakeh itohtahisohk* (VTI).

betray *awîyak kamayetotâht* (VTA); s/he betrays her/him, *kwayakihew* (VTA).

betrayal *mâyitôtâtowin* (NI).

betroth *mîkiwin* (NI).

betrothal *mîkiskwewewin* (NI).

better Something better than something else, *nawâc* (IPC); better looking, *nawâckâmewasik* (VAI); feeling better, *miyomahcihowin* (NI); more, better, *ayiwâk* (IPC); a little better, less bad, *sîyâkes* (IPC); s/he makes him feel better, *âstewepawew* (VTA)

betterment *nawâc miyopayowin* (NI).

bettor *or* **better** *awîyak ka astwaket* (VTI).

between In between, *tastawâyihk* (IPC); between two points, *nayewâc* (IPC); s/he puts something in the space between two trees, *tastawâskohtâw* (VAI); there is a space between, *tastawâyâw* (IPC); a space between two walls, i.e.: a corridor or walkway, *tastawâw* (VII); s/he is between, *tastawisiw* (VAI).

beverage *menihkwewin* (NI); *minihkwewin* (NI).

beware *ka asweyihtamihk* (VAI).

bewilder *wanâhiwewin* (NI).

bewildering *ka wanâhikohk kîkway* (VTI).

bewilderment *wanâhikowin* (NI).

bewitch *sâkoteyimowewin* (NI).

bewitched *awîyak ka sâkocihiht* (VTA).

bewitching *osâkoteyimowew* (NA).

beyond *wâhyaw neyâk* (IPC).

bias *namoya metoni kwayask* (IPC).

biassed *or* **biased** *mâyisihcikewin* (NI).

bib *awâsis aspaskanipîsowin* (NI); *awâsisaspastakawinis* (NI).

bible The Holy Bible, *manitowimasinahikan* (NI); the great book, *kihcimasinahikan* (NI).

biceps *ka maskawpetonehk* (VAI).

bicker *kîhkâhtowin* (NI).

bicuspid *kâmi sakimepita* (VAI).

big Being big, *misikitiwin* (NI); s/he is big, *misikitiw* (VAI); it is big or large, *misâw* (VII); much or lots, *mistahi* (IPC); s/he makes it bigger or larger, *mahkisîhew* (VTA); s/he makes herself/himself bigger than the other person, *ayiwâkiskam* (VAI).

Big Dipper *misikwapahikan* (NI).

big-hearted *awîyak metoni ka miyotehet* (VAI).

bighorn A mountain sheep or goat, *mahkiteskanew âcikosak* (NA); *mâyatihk* (NA).

big shot *metoni mistikimaw* (NA).

big time *misi isihcikewin* (NI).

bilious *ohpanahpinewin* (NI).

bilk *mecimwâtasinahikewin* (NI).

billion *kesipâkihtâsowin* (NI).

259

billow *ka mahkâskâk sakahikanihk* (VTI).

bin *asowacikan* (NI).

bind *asahpicekewin* (NI).

binder *otasahpicikew* (NA).

binder twine *asahpicekew pîminahkwânis* (NI).

binding *ka asahpicikehk* (VTI).

binge *môcikihtâwipewin* (NI).

birch A birch tree, *waskway* (NA); birch wood, *waskwayâhtik* (NI); a birch covered area, *waskwayiskaw* (NI); there are lots of birch in this area, *waskwayahtikoskâw* (VII); *waskwayiskâw* (NI); birch sap, *waskwayâpoy* (NA); *sîwakamisikan* (NI).

bird A small bird, *pîwâyisis* (NA) *(Northern)*; *pîyesîs* (NA) *(Plains)*; a bird of prey i.e.: a falcon, *onôtayikowew* (NA) *(Plains)*; *onocayikowiw* (NA) *(Northern)*.

bird call *pîwâyiskitohâcikan* (NI) *(Northern)*; *pîyesîsikitowin* (NI) *(Plains)*.

birdseed *pîwâyisisomîciwin* (NI) *(Northern)*; *pîyesîsimîciwin* (NI) *(Plains)*.

bird watcher *pîwâyisis okanaweyihcikew* (NA).

birth *nihtâwikiwin* (NI); she gives birth, *nihtâwikihew* (VAI); she gives birth to an illegitimate child, *pikwatôsew* (VAI) *(Northern)*; *kiminicâkanihkew* (VAI) *(Plains)*; she gives birth to a child or s/he sees her/his children, *wâpamâwasiw* (VTA); the act of giving birth to a child or the act of seeing one's children, *wâpamâwasiwin* (NI).

birthday *nihtâwikew kisikâw* (NI); *tipiskamowin* (NI) *(Plains)*.

birthmark Being born with a birthmark, *nihtâwikew masinâsowin* (NI); a spot on the body, i.e.: a birthmark, *masinâsowin* (NI).

birthplace *etah ka nihtâwikihk* (LN).

biscuit *siwpahkwesikanis* (NI) *(Northern)*; *wâwipahkwesikanis* (NI) *(Plains)*.

bisection *âpihtâw pahkwenikewin* (NI).

bishop The great holy father, *kihci ayamihewiyiniw* (NA) *(Northern)*; *pahkwâyaminewiyiniwiwin* (NA) *(Plains)*.

bison A prairie cow, *paskwâwimostos* (NA); *maskotewimostos* (NA).

bit A drilling bit for steel, *pîwâpiskopayipahikan* (NI); a drilling bit for wood, *payipihtakahikan* (NI); quite a bit, *mistahi* (IPC).

bitch A female dog or a Cree slang for a prostitute, *kiskânak* (NA); a swear word: son of a bitch, *kiskânak kosisan* (NA); a small female dog or a Cree slang for a prostitute, *kiskânakos* (NA).

bite The act of biting, *tahkwahkewin* (NI); s/he bites her/him accidently, *pistamew* (VTA); s/he bites her/him right through, *sâpwamew* (VTA); s/he bites,

260

tahkwahkew (VAI); s/he made her/him bite it, *tahkwahtamôhew* (VTA); s/he bites her/him, *tahkwamew* (VTA).

biting *tahkwahkewin* (NI).

bitter Something that tastes bitter, *kîkway kawîsakahk* (VTI); *âhkospakwan* (VII); it is a bitter taste, *wîsakakamow* (VII); it tastes bitter, *wîsakan* (VII).

bizarre *metoni mâmaskâc kîkway* (IPC); *mâmaskâcihkin* (VII).

blab *misayekitonewin* (NI).

black Something black, *kakaskitewak* (VII); it is black, *kaskitewâw* (VII); s/he is black, *kaskitesow* (VAI); black horse, *kaskitewastim* (NA); s/he blackens her/his face, *kaskitewihkwenew* (VTA); s/he is black faced, *kaskitewihkwew* (VAI); a black-haired person, *kaskitewistikwan* (VAI); a dark person, *kaskitewiyâs* (NA).

black bear *kaskitew maskwa* (NA); *maskwa* (NA).

blackberry *kaskitew mînis* (NI).

blackbird *cahcahka* (NA) *(Northern)*; *cahcahkayiw* (NA) *(Plains)*.

blackboard *masinahikewinâhtik* (NI).

blacken *ka kaskitew isihtâhk* (VTI).

black eye *ka kaskitew acapihk* (VAI).

blackfly Horsefly, *misisâhk* (NA).

Blackfoot *kaskitew ayasit* (NA); the Plains Cree people use it to describe the Blackfoot people, *ayahciyiniw* (NA).

blacking *kaskitewahikewin* (NI).

blackness *kaskitesowin* (NI).

blacksmith A shaper of metal, i.e.: a blacksmith, *oyahisiw* (NA); a blacksmith shop, *oyahisiwikamik* (NI); s/he shapes or repairs them, i.e.: a blacksmith repairing implements, *oyawew* (VAI) *(Northern)*; *wiyâkinew* (VAI) *(Plains)*.

black spruce *napakasihta* (NA); *maskekosihta* (NA); *maskekwâsihta* (NA).

bladder *sikihwat* (NI); *wihkway* (NI).

blade *môhkomanihkan* (NI).

blame S/he lays blame, *atâmeyimew* (VTA); s/he lays blame on her/him, *âsteyimiwew* (VTA); s/he blames another person for her/his misfortune, *pakamimew* (VTA) *(Northern)*; *atâmeyimew* (VTA) *(Plains)*.

blameworthy *awîyak takeh atameyimiht* (VTA).

blanch *wâpiskahikewin* (NI).

bland It is bland, *piyekwan* (VII) *(Northern)*; *pihekwâw* (VII) *(Plains)*.

blandish *miyohtwâwisâyâwin* (NI).

blank *metoni namoya kîkway* (IPC) *(Northern)*; *metoni namakîkway* (IPC) *(Plains)*.

blanket *akohp* (NI); a white blanket, *wâpiskakohp* (NI).

blare *kitow* (VAI).

blasphemy Speaking irreverently of sacred things or God, *manito kawîyahkwatiht* (VTA) *(Northern)*; *manitow kawîyahkwatiht* (VTA); s/he curses or swears, *wîyahkwew* (VAI).

blast *pahkisawewin* (NI); *pahkitew* (VAI).

blasted *kîkway kapahkisamihk* (VTI).

blatant *ka kisewe kehkâwtamihk* (VTA).

blaze A large and bright fire, *ka kihkawayatek* (VTI); s/he blazes a trail, *wâsihkwekahikew* (VAI); s/he blazes a trail through the trees or s/he places indicating marks on the trees, *wasihkwekahwew* (VAI).

bleak *metoni ka kisinyotihk* (VTI).

blear-eyed *ka mihkwâskapimohk* (VTI).

bleat *kâketôt mâyacihkosis* (NA).

bled *ka kehmihkowihk* (VAI).

bleed *mihkowiwin* (NI).

bleeder *awîyak ka nihtâmihkowit*.

bless When you bless something, *saweyihcikewin* (NI).

blessed The state of being blessed, *saweyihtâkosiwin* (NI); s/he had blessed her/him, *kehsaweyimew* (VTA); s/he is blessed, *saweyihcikâsiw* (VAI); it is blessed, *saweyihcikâtew* (VII); s/he blesses, *saweyihcikew* (VAI); the act of blessing someone, *saweyimiwewin* (NI); s/he has been blessed; *saweyihtâkosiw* (VAI); it has been blessed, *saweyihtakwan* (VII); s/he blesses her/him, *saweyimew* (VTA); s/he is favored by the spirits or s/he is blessed by God, *saweyimikosiw* (VAI); the act of being favored by the spirits, *saweyimikowisiwin* (NI).

Blessed Virgin *kihcitwâwmare* (NA).

blessing An act of blessing, *saweyihcikewin* (NI); a blessing of something, *saweyihtamowin* (NI).

blew *ka kihyotihk* (VTI); it blew out or cracked open, ie: a car tire, *pâstisin* (VII).

blight *kîkway kamisiwanâtâhk* (VTI).

blind Being blind, *pâskâpiwin* (NI); s/he is blind, *pâskâpiw* (VAI); s/he hits her/him and makes her/him blind, *pâskâpahwew* (VTA).

blinders *âkohkwepicikana* (NI).

blink S/he makes her/him blink when s/he pretends to hit her/him, *pasahkapehew* (VTA); s/he blinks her/his eyes, *pasahkapiw* (VAI).

bliss *naspic kamiweyihtamihk* (VAI).

blissful *metoni kamôcekâyâhk* (VAI).

blister S/he gave it a blister, *pihtopekinew* (VTA); s/he is blistered, *pihtopekipayow* (VAI) or (VII); having a blister or a blister, *pihtopekipayowin* (NI).

blizzard *kîwetin* (NI); a drifting wind, *kapewanyotihk* (VTI); a storm with wind and snow,

misponyotin (VAI); a sudden and heavy snowfall; a blizzard, *pakihtakonakâw* (NA) *(Northern)*; *mahmahkâkonepayiw* (NA) *(Plains)*.

bloat An animal with a bloated belly, *pisiskiw kapakatayepayet* (VAI).

bloated A bloated stomach, *pakatayepayowin*; s/he or it is bloated or swollen, *pîswepayiw* (VII) or (VAI); the act of being bloated, *pôtawipayowin* (NI).

block Wood block, *mistik* (NI); sawed off wood block, *kakeskipotek*; s/he blocks my view, *âokôpawiw* (VTA); s/he sits blocking others, *kipapiw* (VAI); it sits blocking others, *kipastew* (VTI); the act of standing in the way or blocking others, *kipiskâkewin* (NI); *kipiskamowin* (NI); s/he is standing in her/his way, *kipiskawew* (VTA); *kiposkawew* (VTA).

blonde *kosawinakwahk* (VII).

blood *mihko* (NI); her/his breath smells like blood, *mihkowatâmow* (VAI); s/he has blood on her/him, s/he is bloody, *mihkowiw* (VTA); s/he is dripping blood, *pihkwâkew* (VAI).

blood brother *tipiyaw wîtsanihtowin* (NI).

bloodletting *ka mekihk mihko* (VTA).

blood relation Or relative, *tipiyaw wahkohtowin* (NI).

bloodshed *mistahi kanôtintohk* (VTA).

bloodstained *kîkway kamihkowik* (VTI).

bloodsucker *akahkway* (NA).

blood vessel *mihkoyapiy* (NA).

bloody Making something bloody, *mihkowihtcikewin* (NI); it is bloody, there is blood on it, *mihkowan* (VII); s/he has a bloody face, *mihkowihkwew* (VAI); s/he has bloody feet, *mihkowisitew* (VAI); s/he makes her/him bloody, *mihkowihew* (VAI).

blooming *kamacinokwahkwaw nepihkâna* (NI) *(Plains)*; *wâpikwanew* (NI) *(Northern)*.

blooper *awîyak kâmâyinekeskit* (VAI).

blossom *ka maci ohpikihkwaw nepihkâna* (NI) *(Plains)*; *wâpikwanew* (NI) *(Northern)*

blotch *kamayisicikehk* (VAI); *kîkway ka atihtek* (VTI).

blotchy *mâyisihcikewin* (NI), *atihtowayih* (NI)

blotter *sopahcikâkan* (NI).

blouse *pihcones* (NI).

blow A blow to the head, *pakamahotowin* (NI); s/he blows on something, *pôtacikew* (VAI); the act of blowing, *pôtacikewin* (NI); something you blow, *pôtâcikan* (NI); s/he blew on her/him, *pôtatew* (VTA).

blower A mechanical blower or fan, *pôtâcikan* (NI).

blowfly *ôcew* (NA).

blowhole *twâhipân* (NI).

261

blown Affected by wind, *pimâstan* (VII); blown backwards on water, *aseyâhokiw* (VTA), *aseyâhotew* (VTI); blown across expanse of water, *âsawahôkiw* (VAI); *âsiwahôtew* (VAI); blown back home while paddling, *kiweyâhokow* (VTA), *kiweyatew* (VTI); blown into a heap, a pile, *asasiw*; *asastan*; blown back, backwards, *aseyâsiw* (VAI); *aseyâstan* (VTI); blown across the water, open space, *asawâsiw* (VAI) *(Northern)*; *asawepâsiw* (VAI) *(Plains)*; *asawâstan* (VII) *(Northern)*; *asawepâstan* (VII) *(Plains)*; s/he or it is blown down by the wind, i.e.: a tree, *kawâsiw* (VAI); it is blown down by the wind, i.e.: a house, *kawâstan* (VTI); blown away, *wepâsiw* (VAI); *wepâstan* (VII); it is blown upwards, *ohpâstan* (VII); s/he is blown upwards, *ohpâsiw* (VAI); being blown by the wind towards the speaker, *petâsiw* (VAI); *petâstan* (VII); it is blown to shore, *akwâhotew* (VII); *akwâyastan* (VTI); s/he is blown across, *asawâsow* (VAI) *(Northern)*; *asawepâsow* (VAI) *(Plains)*; it is blown across, *asawâstan* (VII) *(Northern)*; *asawepâstan* (VII) *(Plains)*; it is all blown out like snow, *mestâsiw* (VII); s/he is blown by the wind towards shore, *nâtakâmeyâsiw* (VTA); it is blown towards shore, *nâtakâmeyâstan* (VII); it is blown from that side, *ohtâstan* (VII); s/he is blown from that side, *ohtâsiw* (VAI); s/he is blown all over the water, *papâmâpahokow* (VAI); it is blown all over the water, *papâmâpotew* (VII); s/he is blown here and there by the wind, *papâmâsiw* (VAI); it is blown here and there by the wind, *papâmâstan* (VII); it is blown crooked by the wind, *pimâsiw* (VII); being blown crooked by the wind, *pimâsiwin* (NI); it is blown and scattered about by the wind, *piwâstan* (NI); it is blown or carried by the wind, *pimâstan* (VII); it is blown off, *pinâstan* (VII); s/he is blown away by the wind, *sipweyâsiw* (VAI); it is blown away by the wind, *sipweyâstan* (VII); s/he is going to be blown away, *wihwepâsiw* (VAI); it is going to be blown away, *wihwepâstan* (VII); s/he is blown away, *wepâsiw* (VAI); it is blown away, *wepâstan* (VII).

blow-up Or rage, *sisikôc ka kisôwipayihk* (VAI).

blowy *ka yotinayasik* (VTI).

blubber *wiyin ka otinamihk misikinosew ohci* (VTI).

bludgeon *nôtinikakanahtik* (NI).

blue Something blue, *ka sîpihkwak* (VII); s/he or it has blue wings, *sîpihkotahtahkwanew* (VAI); s/he or it is blue *sîpihkosiw* (VAI) *(Northern)*; *askihtakwâw* (VAI) *(Plains)*; it is blue in color, *sîpihkwekan* (VII) *(Northern)*; *sîpihkwâw* (VII) *(Plains)*; it is blue in color, *sîpihkwekisiw* (VAI) *(Northern)*; *sipihkosiw* (VAI) *(Plains)*.

bluebell *ka sîpihkwakwâw nîpihkansa* (NI).

blueberry A domestic (high) blueberry, *niskimin* (NI) *(Northern)*; *iyinimin* (NI) *(Plains)*; a wild blueberry, *nikoman* (NI).

bluebird *sîpihkopiwâyisîs* (NA) *(Northern)*; *sîpihkopiyesîs* (NA) *(Plains)*.

bluebonnet *sîpihko astotinis* (NI).

bluebottle *sîpihko môteyâpisk* (NI).

bluefish *sîpihko kinosew* (NA).

bluegrass *sîpihkwaskosiya* (NI).

blue ribbon *sîpihko sînipân* (NI) *(Northern)*; *senipân* (NI) *(Plains)*.

blues *kaskeyihtamowin* (NI).

bluff *pwasitisahikewin* (NI); *pihtokwepayihiwewin* (NI).

blur *ekâ ka kihkânâkwahk kîkway* (VTI).

blurt *osâmitonewin* (NI).

blush S/he blushes or her/his face reddens, *mihkohkwepayiw* (VAI).

bluster *ka pahpahkihtowestihk* (VTI).

blustery *ka pahpahkihtowestinpayik* (VTI).

boar *nâpekohkôs* (NA).

board A thin board or plank, *napakihtak* (NI).

boast When one is boasting about oneself, *ka mamihcimohk* (VAI); the act of flaunting or singing praises, *mamihcimowin* (NI); s/he flaunts herself/himself or sings herself/himself praises, *mamihcimow* (VAI); s/he boasts about herself/himself, *mamihcimisiw* (VTA); s/he flaunts her/him or sings her/him praises, *mamihcimew* (VTA); s/he is highly praised, *mamihcimikosiw* (VAI); s/he boasts about it, *mamihtôtam* (VTI).

boastful Being boastful in a vain way, *ka mamihcimisoskihk* (VAI); boastfulness or self-promoting, *mamihcimisowin* (NI).

boat *ôsi* (NI); *cîman* (NI).

boat dock *kapâwin* (NA) *(Plains)*; *onikewin* (NA) *(Northern)*; *kapâwinihk* (LN) *(Plains)*.

boatload *sâkaskineposihtâsowin* (NI).

boatman *posihtâsohwiniw* (NA).

bob The action of bobbing for objects in the water, *kahkihtwampekopewin* (NI).

bob The act of cutting hair in a short blunt style, *paskwahamakewin* (NI); *paskwatahikan* (NI).

bobcat A large male cat, *misinâpeminôs* (NA).

bobskate *ka kociwakehk sôniskwâtahikana* (NI).

bobsled *sôskwaciwew* (VAI); *capanaskos* (NI); *pipontâpânâsk* (NI) *(Northern)*; *pehkokawân* (NI) *(Plains)*.

bobtail *kiskayôs* (NA).

bode *ka kiskiwehikihk* (VAI).

bodiless *ekâ ka oweyawihk* (VAI).

bodily *sohki kotastenitowin* (NI).

body *miyaw* (NI); someone's body, *awîyak wîyaw* (NI); s/he has a huge body, *mihcâskoyawew* (VAI); her/his body is tired, *nestoyawew* (VAI); my body, *niyaw* (NI); s/he has a swollen body, *pâkiyawew* (VAI); inside of a body, *pihtâkiyaw* (NI); her/his body, *wîyâw* (NI); it builds up her/his body, *wîyawiskâkiw* (VAI); s/he has fat on her/his body, *wîyinowisiw* (VAI) *(Northern)*; *wiyiniw* (VAI) *(Plains)*.

bog *katostokahk* (NI).

boggy *ka akohtenowahcak* (VTI).

boil Something that boils, *kapakâhtek* (VTI); it is boiling, *ohtew* (VII); s/he makes it boil, *osôhew* (VTA); it boils, *osow* (VAI); s/he boiled it, *osowew* (VII); it is boiled, *oswâw* (VAI); s/he cooks something in water or s/he boils something, i.e.: stew or soup, *pakâhtâkohkew* (VAI); the act of cooking in water or boiling food, i.e.: soup or stew, *pakâhtâkohkewin* (NI); s/he boils it, *pakâhtâw* (VTI); it is boiled, i.e.: meat of an animal, *pakâhtew* (VII); s/he boils them in water, *pakâsimew* (VTA); it is boiled, i.e.: fish, *pakâsiw* (VAI); it boils over, i.e.: a pot, *pastâciwasiw* (VAI); it boils over, i.e.: water, *pastâciwahtew* (VII); it boils and spills over, *sîkaciwahtew* (VII); it boils and spills over, *sîkaciwasiw* (VAI).

boil *sihkihp* (NI); having a boil, *kosihkihpemihk* (VAI); s/he has a boil, *osihkihpimiw* (VAI).

boisterous *kakâh kestinpayik*.

bold *kostanakeyimowin* (NI); *ahkotonamiw* (VAI).

boll weevil *manîcos ka misiwanâcitat kiscikânsa* (NA).

bolster *kasîtwâskwahamihk kîkway* (VTI).

bolt *kapemastehamihk misisâkahikan* (NI).

bonanza *ka misi miyosoneyahkehk* (VAI).

bond *awîyak ka tipahikestâmaht* (VTA).

bondage *tipahikestamâkewin* (NI).

bone *oskan* (NA); a deformed bone, *mâskikan* (NI); her/his bone is deformed, *mâskikanew* (VAI).

bone-dry *metoni kapâstek* (VII).

bone meal *oskan miciwin* (NI).

boner *ka naspâtakamikisihk*.

boney S/he is boney, i.e.: a fish, *oskaniwiw* (VAI).

bonfire *pônamowin* (NI); *kotawân* (NI).

bonnet *astotinis* (NI).

bony *kîkway ka oskaniwik* (VII).

book Or letter to someone, *masinahikan* (NI); a book done in Cree language, *nehiyawimasinahikan* (NI).

boom *nepehk ka asahpitihtwâw mistekwak* (VTI) *(Northern)*.

boon *kitimâkenatowin* (NI).

boorish *peyahtikesâyâwin* (NI).

boost *kakihcimowin* (NI).

booster *awîyak mamihcimisoskit* (NA).

boot Or shoe or a wooden mocassin, *mistikwaskisin* (NI); a winter boot, *piponaskisin* (NI); a pair of stretchy footwear, i.e.: a rubber boot, *sîpekaskisin* (NI) *(Northern)*; *pahkopewaskisin* (NI) *(Plains)*.

booth *micisowikamik piskiht apiwin* (NI).

booze *kîskwepewâkan* (NI).

bore S/he bores a hole in them, *payipahwew* (VTA).

boredom The act of being bored, *kaskamocisâyâwin* (NI); s/he is bored of that food, *saskatahtam* (VAI).

borer *payipahikan* (NI).

born The act of being born, *nihtâwikiwin* (NI); s/he is born, *nihtâwikiw* (VAI).

borrow *ka nitahtâmohk* (VTA); *nitahtâmiw* (VAI).

borrowing *nitahtâmowin* (NI).

bosom *iskwew tôhtôsimak* (NA); *tôhtôsim* (NA); *mitohtôsim* (NA).

boss A leader on a job site, *okimâw* (NA); the boss's wife, *okimâskwiw* (NA); the boss's hat, *okimâwastotin* (NI); s/he thinks of her/him as the boss, *okimâweyimew* (VTA); s/he is thought to be worthy of being boss, *okimaweyihtâkosiw* (VAI); the boss house, *okimâwikamik* (NI); s/he is boss, *okimâwiw* (VAI); the act of being boss, *okimâwiwin* (NI); the boss's son, *okimâwikosisan* (NA).

both Both of them, *nânapo* (IPC); both sides, *âyîtaw* (IPC).

bother The act of being bothersome, *âyimisowin* (NI); s/he bothers her/him, *kiyomâhew* (VTA); s/he bothers her/him unceasingly, *kiyomâskawew* (VTA).

bothersome The act of being bothersome, *môstatahkamkisowin* (NI); s/he finds her/him bothersome, *kiyomâyeyimew* (VTA).

bottle *môteyâpisk* (NI).

bottom From under, *etamihk* (IPC); at the base of the stairway, *nehîcâyihk* (IPC).

bottomless *ka kaskatemek* (VII).

bough *sihta anaskakanah mîkowâhpihk* (NI).

bought *kîkway kakih atâwehk* (VTI).

boulder *mistasiniy* (NA).

bounce Something bouncing, *ka kahkwâskwehtihk kîkway* (VTI); it bounces up and down, *kwâskwehtin* (VII) *(Plains)*; *wâskwetin* (VII) *(Northern)*; it rebounds, *kwâskwepayiw* (VII).

bouncing *kakah kwâskwesinihk* (VTI).

bound *kwâskwepayehowin* (NI); bounding, resilient, *kwâskwepayiw* (VAI); *kwâskwepayin* (VII); very tightly bound, *mâhkwahpisiw* (VAI); *mâhkwahpitew* (VII).

263

boundary *etah iskopaywin tipahaskân* (NI); *kecitipahaskan* (NI).

boundless *ekâ ka kisipâyik* (VTI).

bounteous *ka weyocipayik kîkway* (VTI).

bountiful *weyotsemakan* (NI).

bounty *tipahamâtowin* (NI).

bouquet *nepihkân wawisihcikan* (NI).

bout *mawinehotowin* (NI).

bow An instrument for launching an arrow, *pimotahkwakan* (NI); *ahcapiy*; s/he reinforces the bow and makes it difficult to bend it, *sohkâkinew* (VTI).

bow S/he bows her/his head or s/he bends her/his neck downwards, *patapiskweyiw* (VAI); s/he bows her/his head before her/him, *tapahtiskweyestawew* (VTA); s/he bows her head, i.e.: preparing for prayer, *tapahtiskweyiw* (VAI).

bowel *misiwiyâpiy* (NI).

bowl A round bowl, *wâwiyakan* (NI); a bowl made from birch bark, *waskwayakan* (NI) (Northern); *waskwayiwiyâkan* (NI) (Plains).

bowleg *wâkâtew* (Northern); *wâkikâtew* (Plains).

bowlegged *wâkâtewin* (NI) (Northern); *wâkikâtewin* (NI) (Plains); *awîyak ka wâkikâtet* (VAI).

bowler *ometawew* (NA).

bowls *maskosiskâhk metawewin* (NI).

bowshot *ahcapew pîmotahkwakan* (NI).

bowstring *ahcapew pîminahkwânis* (NI).

box A wooden box, *mistikowat* (NI); a cardboard or paper box, *masinahikanekinowat*; s/he boxes for sport, *pakamahikew* (VAI); the act of boxing for sport, *pakamahikewin* (NI).

boy *nâpesis* (NA).

boyhood *nâpesisowin* (NI).

boyish *nâpesis isâyâwin* (NI).

brace *miciminkan payepocikan ohci* (NI); a brace for using and drilling wood, *payipihkocikanâhtik* (NA).

bracelet *kispison* (NI); a dressy bracelet, *wawisihcikan* (NI); a very fancy or ornate bracelet, *kiskinawacihokispison* (NI).

bracing *sîtoskâkewin* (NI).

bracken *kisâstaw masânâhtik* (NA).

bracket *sîtwahpicikan* (NI).

brag Bragging or vain glory, *mamihcimowin* (NI).

braggart *okakihcimiw* (NA).

braid The act of braiding, *apîhkewin* (NI); s/he braided it, *apihkâtam* (VTI); s/he makes braids or it is braided, *apihkâtew* (VAI); s/he braids her/his own hair, *sekipatowew* (VAI); a braid of hair, *sekipatwân* (NI); s/he has braids, i.e.: may be used to identify a person of Chinese descent, *sekipatwâw* (VAI).

braided They are braided, *apihkâtewa* (VTI).

brain *wihtihp* (NI) (Northern); *wîyitihp* (NI) (Plains).

bran *kohkôsimicowin* (NI).

branch *îyikihtawaskwan* (NI); there is branch, knot, *sakahkwan* (NI) or *sakikwaniwiw* (VAI); there are branches, *wacikwaniwiw* (VAI); branches stick out over trail, *sakâskweyaw* (VII); it branches off in another direction, *paskeyâw* (VII).

brand Branding iron, *masinâskisikan* (NI); the act of branding animals, *masinâskisikewin* (NI); s/he brands the animal, *masinâskiswew* (VTA).

brand-new *metoni oskâyi* (VII).

brash *mâmâsisihkewin* (NI).

brat A big brat, *mestatew* (NA); a little brat, *mescacesis* (NA); a spoiled brat, *otipeyimisiw* (NA).

brave The act of being brave or courageous, *nâpihkâsiwin* (NI); *sohkeyimow* (VAI); s/he is brave, *nâpihkâsiw* (VAI); a brave or a warrior, i.e.: used when referring to an older person, *nâpehkâsowiyiniw* (NA); a brave or warrior, i.e.: used when refering to a younger person, *onâpehkâsowiyinîs* (NA).

bravery *nâpihkâsiwin* (NI); *sohkeyimowin* (NI)

brawl *ka tepwe kehkâhtohk* (VTA); *nôtinitowak* (VAI).

brawn *sohkâpewiw* (VAI) (Northern); *maskawisiwiyiniwiw* (VAI) (Plains).

brawny *sohkesihcikâsowin* (NI).

bray *sôsôwatim kakitot* (VAI).

brazen *sohkeyimowin* (NI).

breach *kweskî wepenikewin* (NI).

bread A loaf of bread, *ohpayihcikan* (NI); a soft, spongy loaf of bread, *pîswepahkwesikan* (NI).

breadcrumb or **bread-crumb** *ohpayihcikan* (NI); *pîwipecikansah* (NI); *pîwahcikan* (NI).

break S/he breaks up the beaver lodges, *iskew* (VTI); breaking something or ploughing the ground, *pîkopicikewin* (NI); s/he makes her/him break off or detach by shaking, *kîskipayihew* (VTA); s/he snaps it off with her/his hands, *kîskipitew* (VAI); s/he breaks her/his teeth in a fall, *kaskâpitesin* (VTA); s/he breaks her/his neck by wrestling, *kaskikwepitew* (VTA); s/he breaks her/his neck in a fall, *kaskikwesin* (VTA); s/he breaks her/his arm in a fall, *kaskipitonesin* (VTA); s/he breaks it in, i.e.: a horse for riding, *nakâyâhew* (VTA); s/he breaks it apart with something heavy, i.e.: an axe, *nâtwâham* (VTI); s/he breaks them, i.e.: snowshoes, *nâtwâsimew* (VTA); s/he breaks it with her/his weight, i.e.: a tree, *nâtwâskawew* (VTA); it breaks from the wind, *nâtwâyâstan* (VII); s/he breaks off a piece by striking it, i.e.: with a hammer, *pahkwehwew* (VTA); s/he breaks a piece from

them with her/his hands, **pahkwenew** (VTA); a
broken off piece, **pahkwenikan** (NI); it breaks off in
pieces, **pahkwepayiw** (VII) *or* (VAI); a piece breaks
off, **pahkwesin** (VII); a thing is broken off,
pahkwesiw (VAI); when it falls a piece breaks off,
pahkwehtin (VII); it breaks and now it has a piece
missing, **pahkweyâw** (VII); s/he breaks it off by
pulling, i.e.: a thread, **paskipitew** (VTA); s/he
breaks it off, i.e.: a rope, **paskâpew** (VAI); s/he
breaks or smashes them into pieces,
pikinatahwêw (VTI); it falls and breaks into small
pieces, **pîkinihkoswew** (VII); s/he breaks them into
piece with force, **pîkinsimew** (VTI); it breaks into
many pieces, **pîkinipayiw** (VII) *or* (VAI); s/he breaks
them into small pieces, **pîkinipitew** (VTI); it is
broken into small pieces, **pîkinisiw** (VAI); s/he
breaks them into small pieces by hitting them,
pîkiniwepahwew (VTI); they break into pieces,
pîkinisinwak (VTI); it breaks after a fall, i.e.: a
person's leg or an axe handle, **pîkohtin** (VII); s/he
breaks her/him, i.e.: financially, **pîkonew** (VTA);
s/he breaks or destroys things, **pîkonikew** (VAI);
the act of breaking or destroying things,
pîkonikewin (NI); s/he breaks it when she drops it,
pîkosimew (VTA); it breaks when it falls, i.e.: a
clock, **pîkosin** (VII); s/he steps on them or kicks
them and breaks them, **pîkoskawew** (VTI); something that became broken when it was hit,
pîkwatahikan (NI); s/he breaks them by striking
them, **pîkwatahwew** (VTA); it broke right off, i.e.: a
hammer of axe handle, **nâtwâtin** (VII) *(Plains)*;
kaskacihtin (VII) *(Northern)*.
breakable **nihtâpekopayiw** (VTI).
breakage **pîkopicikewin** (NI).
breaker *ka nâtakâme mahkâskâk* (VTI).
breakfast Or eating breakfast, **kîkisepâ mîcisowin**
(NI); when you are eating breakfast, *ka kekisepaw*
metisohk (VAI).
breakfast food **kîkisepâ mîcowin** (NI).
break of day **petâpan** (VAI).
breakthrough **sohki sâpohtewin** (NI).
break-up *ka pîkopayîk wîkîhtowin* (VII);
poniwicewew (VTA).
breast **mitohtôsim** (NA).
breastfeed The act of breastfeeding, **nôhawasowin**
(NI); she breastfeeds, **nôhawasiw** (VTA); she
breastfeeds her/him, **nohew**; she ceases
breastfeeding her/him, **poninôhew** (VTA).
breath The act of breathing, **yehewin** (NI); her/his
breathing is dry, **pâhkwatahtam** (VAI); her/his
breath is dry, **pâhkwatâmiw** (VAI); feverish, heated,
dry breath, **pâhkwatâmowin** (NI); the fall induces

her/him to catch her/his breath, **tahtatâmosin** (VAI);
s/he is breathing, **yehew** (VAI).
breathe The act of breathing, **kayehehk** (VAI); s/he
breathes easily, **nahiyehew** (VAI).
breather **astetahtamowin** (NI).
breathing **yehewin** (NI); s/he is breathing, **yehew**
(VAI).
breathless **nîpâhatahtamowin** (NI).
breathtaking **kakipwatâmopayahk** (VAI).
breathy **sepatahtamowîn** (NI).
breed **ohpikihewewin** (NI).
breeder **otohpikihiwew** (NA).
breeding Breeding animals, **kohpikihihtwâw**
pisîskowak (VTA); s/he assists them in breeding,
wîcehtahew (VTA).
breeze It is starting to stir or blow, **maciyotin** (NI); a
slight breeze, **yôtisin** (NI); a warm breeze,
sâwaniyowew (NI) *(Northern)*; **kisopwemyocisin**
(NI) *(Plains)*.
breezy **kayôtinayasik** (VTI).
brew **etakamascikan** (NI).
bridge **âsokan** (NI); s/he makes a bridge,
âsokanihkew (VAI); the act of walking on a bridge,
âsokewin (NI); s/he walks on the bridge, **âsokew**
(VTI).
bridging **âsokanihkewin** (NI).
bridle **tâpitonehpicikan** (NI); a bridle strap,
tâpitonehpicikaniyâpiy (NI); a bridle bit,
tâpitonehpicikanâpisk (NI); s/he is bridled or s/he
wears a bridle, **tâpitonehpisiw** (VAI); s/he bridled
her/him, **tâpitonehpitew** (VTA).
brief **âciyaw poko** (IPC); **kanakes** (IPC).
bright Something bright, **kawâsihkwak kîkway** (VII);
it is bright, **wâseyâw** (VII).
brighten **wâsihkonakwan** (VII).
brilliance **iyinisowin** (NI).
brilliancy **iyinisiwâyâwin** (NI).
brilliant One who is brilliant, **awîyak ka iyinisit**
(NA); **iyinisiwâyâwin** (NI)
brimful **kapâstapoweskinacikehk** (VTI).
bring S/he is bringing something here, **petâw** (IPC);
s/he is bringing someone or her/him here, **pesowew**
(VTA); s/he is bringing a bunch of things, **pecikewin**
(NI); s/he quickly brings her/him over, i.e.: by car,
papahew (VTA); s/he brings things home,
pekîwehcikew (VAI); s/he brings her/him home,
pekîwehtahew (VTA); s/he brings it for her/him,
petamawew (VTA); s/he brings her/him down the
hill, **penâsipehtahew** (VTA).
brink **metoni iskweyânihk** (IPC).
brisk **katâstapehk** (VTI).

bristle *kasîtawâkwâw mestakaya* (NI) *(Northern)*; *mescaka* (NI) *(Plains)*.

bristly *sîtawâw âniskwewin* (NI).

brittle Something brittle, *kakâspak kîkway* (VTI); something that is dry and brittle, *kaspihkasikanis* (NA) *(Plains)*; it is brittle, i.e.: cast metal, *kâspâw* (VII); it is dry and brittle, i.e.: toast, *kâspisiw (Northern)* (VAI); s/he fries it crispy, i.e.: bacon, *kâspihkaswew* (VTI); it is bone dry, i.e.: a loaf of bread, *kaspakatosiw* (VAI); it is bone dry, i.e.: ground or soil, *kaspakatotew* (VII).

broad *kayakaskâhk kîkway* (VTI).

broadaxe *or* **broadax** A trimming axe, *pasahikewicîkahikan* (NI).

broadcloth *pakowayanekin* (NI).

broaden *kayakaskinâmihk kîkway* (VTI).

broadminded *kihte mâmitoneyihcikan* (NA).

broil *kanawacihk* (VTI).

broke Being broke, *pîkopayowin* (NI); it broke or it is broken, *pîkopayiw* (VII) *or* (VAI); it broke off by itself, *kîskipayiw* (VAI); it broke right off, i.e.: a hammer or axe handle, *kaskacitin* (NI); s/he broke it off with her/his hands, *kîskinew* (VTA); it broke once and for all, *nâspicipikopayiw* (VII); it all broke off, *masaskopayiw* (VII); it broke when it fell, i.e.: a wood product like a pencil, *nâtwâhtin* (VTI); it broke in half, i.e.: a pencil or tree, *nâtwâpayiw* (VTI); s/he breaks it apart with something heavy, i.e.: an axe, *nâtwâham* (VTI); it broke when it fell, i.e.: a tree, *nâtwâsin* (VAI); it broke apart, i.e.: rope, *paskipayiw* (VII) *or* (VAI); it broke open on its own, *pâskipayiw* (VII) *or* (VAI).

broken Something that breaks, *kîkway kapekopayik* (VTI); it is broken off or part of it is gone, *kîskâw* (VII); it is completely broken off, *masaskohtin* (VII); they are completely, totally broken off, *masaskosinwak* (NA); it was broken by the wind, i.e.: a tree, *nâtwâyasiw* (VAI); it lays broken on the ground, i.e.: a dead tree or pole, *nâtwâyâskohtin* (VTI); it lays broken on the ground, *nâtwâyâskosin* (VTI).

broken-hearted *wîsakitehewin* (NI).

broken-winded *mistatim kapâskâtahtahk*.

bronco *or* **broncho** *môhcohkânewatim* (NA); *pikwatastim* (NA) *(Northern)*; *pakwatastim* (NA) *(Plains)*.

brooch A dress up pin, *wawesîw aniskamân* (NI).

brood *pîwayisis ka pâskâwehot* (VTA).

brooding *kâmekwa pâskâwehotwâw sîsîpak* (VTA).

brook *sîpîsis* (NI).

brook trout *sîpîsis namekosak* (NI).

broom *wepahikan* (NI); s/he makes brooms, *wepahikanihkew* (VAI).

broomstick *wepahikanâhtik* (NI).

broth *micimâpoy* (NI); the broth from a roast, *nawaciwapiy* (NI).

brother The eldest brother, *ostesimâw* (NA); younger brother (or sister), *osîmimâw* (NA); my brother (or sister), *nîtisân* (NA); *nîcisân* (NA); my older brother, *nistes* (NA); my younger brother (or sister), *nisîmis* (NA); sisters say my brother, *nîtisân* (NA); brothers say my brother, *niciwam* (NA); someone's male sibling, *awîyak nâpew wîtisana* (NA); he is the eldest brother, *ostesimâwiw* (VAI); s/he has him as a brother, *nâpew owîtisânimew* (VAI).

brotherhood *ostesihtowin* (NI); *ociwâmihtowin* (NI).

brother-in-law My brother-in-law, *nîstâw* (NDA); men say my sister's husband, *nîstâw* (NA); women say my sister's husband, *nîtim* (NA); someone's brother-in-law, *awîyak wîstâwa* (NA); *awîyak wîtîmwa* (NA).

brotherly *peyakwan kostesihtohk* (VTA).

brought S/he brought it, *petâw* (IPC).

brow *miskahtik* (NI).

brown Light brown, *wapâsowew* (VTA).

brown bear *osâwask* (NA).

brown bread *osâwipahkwesikan* (NI).

brownish *osâwnakwan* (VII).

brown rice *osâw wâpayominak* (NI).

brown sugar *osâw sesipâskwat* (NI) *(Northern)*; *osâw sîwinikan* (NI) *(Plains)*.

bruin *maskwa* (NA).

bruise *âpihtipayowin* (NI).

brunch *ka mîtisohayasihk*.

brunette *ka kasketew osâwakwâw mestakaya* (NI) *(Northern)*; *mescaka* (NI) *(Plains)*; *kaskitewâniskwe*w (NA).

brunt *ka kiscipakamahoht awîyak* (VTA).

brush A big paint brush, i.e.: for painting a house, *sopekahikâkan* (NI) *(Northern)*; *sisopekahikâkan* (NI) *(Plains)*; a floor or scrubbing brush, *sinikohtakahikan* (NI); a hair brush, *pinawehikan* (NI); s/he brushes against her/him, *pisoskawew* (VAI); a rubbing brush or cloth used for shining or polishing, *sinikwahikan* (NI); a shaving brush used to brush on foam, *sinikwastowehikan* (NI); s/he brushes her/his own face with a soap brush, *sinikwastowehosiw* (VTA); s/he brushes his beard with a soap brush, *sinikwastowehwew* (VTA).

brushup *kasesawihk* (VAI).

brushwood *sakâw mihta* (NI).

brushy *kaskisakasihk* (VAI).

brutal *macîsâyâwin* (NI).

brutality *kamacâyiwihk* (VAI).

brutalize *macitôtâtowin* (NI).

brutish *ka pisîskohatisihk* (VAI).

bubble *kisipekinikan ka wihkwe pôtatamihk* (VTI).

bubbly *wihkwe isâyâwin* (NI).

buck A horse that is bucking, *kamohkawkanepayehot mistatim* (NA).

buck A male deer, *yapew apiscimosos* (NA).

buckboard *ocâpâsôwâyis* (NI) *(Northern)*; *napakahcikowâyis* (NI) *(Plains)*.

bucket *askihk* (NA).

buckle A belt fastener, *pakwahtehon sakicihcikan* (NI).

bucksaw *kîskipocimihtâkan* (NI).

buckshot *niskasiniy* (NI).

buckskin *ka kîsekinkateh môsopahkekin* (NI); *moswekin* (NA)

buckthorn *okâminakasîwâhtik* (NA).

bucktooth *kâmâyâpitehk* (VAI).

bucktoothed *mâyâpitewin* (NI).

buckwheat *kisepamicowin* (NI).

bud A leaf bud, *osimisk* (NA).

buddy *awîyak katowîcewâkanihk* (VTA).

buff *kawâsihkwahamihk kîkway* (VTI).

buffalo *paskwâw mostos* (NA) *(Northern)*; *paskwâwimostos* (NA) *(Plains)*.

buffalo berry *mihkominsa*.

buffer *wâsihkwahikâkan* (NI).

buffet *oyâkanikamik* (NI); *akocikan* (NI); *oyâkanikamikos* (NI).

buffoon *awîyak ka môhcohkâsoskit* (VAI); *môhcohkâsoskiwin* (NI)

buffoonery *môhcohkâsoskiwin* (NI).

bug *manicôs* (NA).

bug-eyed *mâyaskâpôwin* (NI).

build *osihcikewin* (NI).

builder *otôsihcikew* (NA).

building A big building, *misiwâskahikan* (NI); the interior of a building, i.e.: a house, *pihtokamik* (LN).

build-up Inertia through build-up in an enclosure, *kaskamocâyâwin* (NI).

built Building a house, *wâskahikanihkew* (VAI); it is securely built, *sanaskâw* (VII); built for shade, *âkawâstehikin* (VAI).

bulk *misikitiw* (VAI).

bulky *awîyak ka wiyinot* (VAI); *misikitiwin* (NI).

bull *nâpemostos* (NA), *îyâpewimostos* (NA).

bullet *môsisinîy* (NI).

bullfinch *pîwâyisis ekosi isiyihkasot* (NA) *(Northern)*; *pîyesîs ekosi isiyihkasot* (NA) *(Plains)*.

bullfly Place with many bullflies, *misisâhkoskâw* (NI).

bullfrog *nâpemayokwatay* (NA); a large bullfrog, *pikwatehtew* (NA); *mayokowatay* (NA).

bullock steer *ayihkwew* (NA).

bull moose *yapew* (NA) *(Northern)*; *iyâpewimôswa* (NA) *(Plains)*.

bullwhip *pasastehikan* (NI).

bully *awîyak ka aspihat wecayah* (VTA).

bullrush Ocean grass, *kihcikamewaskwah* (LN); a part of a bullrush, i.e.: a cattail *pikwanâhtik* (NI); *otâwask* (NI).

bumble *kamâyinikeskihk* (VAI).

bumblebee *mistahamo* (NA); *âmô* (NA).

bump S/he bumps herself/himself on something roughly, *pakamisimisiw* (VTA); s/he bumps herself/himself roughly, i.e.: falling down, *pakamisin* (VTA); s/he bumps against her/him roughly, *pakamiskawew* (VTA); s/he bumps her/him against something, *tâwikisimew* (VTA); s/he bumps against something, *tâwikisin* (VTA); it bumps against something, *tâwikihtin* (VTI); s/he accidently bumps her/him or runs into her/him, *tâwiskawew* (VTA) *(Northern)*; *tâwikiskaw* (VTA) *(Plains)*; s/he bumps against something or someone, *akopayihiw* (VAI).

bumpy *mahmâyahcâw* (NI).

bunch S/he bunches it together, *mâwasakonam* (VTI).

bundle *mâmawipicikewin* (NI); a ceremonial bundle, *kaskahpicikan* (NI); s/he bundles it up securely, *kaskahpitew* (VTA); s/he wraps her/him up into a bundle, *wekahpitew* (VTA).

bung *kipaskwahikan* (NI).

bungle S/he bungles them or s/he makes them the wrong way, *wanisihew* (VTI).

bunny *wâposos* (NA).

buoy *ka kiskinowacicikakehk nipehk kîkway* (VTI).

buoyancy *waskitahipewin* (NI).

buoyant *kawaskitahipek* (VTI).

burble *ka matwecowahk sîpîsis* (NI).

burden *kosokonayahcikewin* (NI); the act of being burdened, *sihtiskosowin* (NI).

burdensome *awîyak mistahi ka âyimitasot* (VTA).

burial *nahinowowin* (NI); a building where burials take place, i.e.: a funeral home, *nahinowewikamik* (NI).

burial ground *kihkwahaskânsa ka yakwaw* (LN).

burlap *ayiwinisekin* (NI).

burly *sohkisihcikâsowin* (NI).

burn A burned out piece of land, i.e.: an old burn, *weposkâw* (NI) *(Northern)*; *pahkwatiteskâw* (NI) *(Plains)*; a burn, *kîsisowin*; it burns off, *kîskihkasiw*; s/he is all burned off, *masaskohkasiw* (VAI); s/he burns her/him or them completely,

267

masaskohkaswew (VTA); it is completely burned off, i.e.: grass, *masaskohkahtew* (VII); s/he is all burned, *mestâskisiw* (VAI); s/he burns her/him or them or it all, i.e.: tobacco in a pipe, *mestâskiswew* (VTA); it is all burned off, i.e.: from a forest fire, *mestâskitew* (VII); s/he burns them up, *mestihkaswew* (VTA); burning something up, *kamestihkasikehk* (VTI); the act of being burned up, *mestihkasowin* (NI); a newly burned off area, *oskâpôskitew* (VII); s/he burns them off something else, *pawihkaswew* (VTA); s/he burns the prairie grass, *pasisâwew* (VTA); s/he is burned out by a bush fire, *pasisiw* (VAI); s/he was burned by a spark, *paskisiw* (VAI); s/he burns or reduces them to ashes, *sekohkaswew* (VTA); it is burned to ashes, *sekohkahtew* (VII); s/he or it has burned to ashes, *sekohkasiw* (VAI); s/he has a massive, deep burn, i.e.: a third degree burn, *sohkehkasiw* (VTI).

burner *kîsisikakan* (NI).

burning *kîsisikewin* (NI); water is burning hot, *kisâkamitew* (VTI); the act of burning off, *kîskihkasowin* (NI); the act of having a burning sensation on one's skin, *wîsakasewin* (NI).

burnish *kosawihkasamihk kîkway* (VTI).

burnout *mestikasowin* (NI).

burns It is burned or cooked, *kîsitew* (VTI); the sun burns right overhead, *kisastew* (VII); s/he burns her/him off, *kiskihkasiw* (VAI); something poorly burned, *kwâtakihkahtew* (VTI); *kitimâkihahtew* (VTI).

burnt Having been burnt, *kakehkesohk* (VTI); it is burnt onto the pot, *akohkahtew* (VII); it burnt off, *kîskihkahtew* (VTI); it will be burnt onto a pot or pan, *tâkohkahtew* (VII).

burnt offering *macostehikewin* (NI).

burp The act of burping, *pekatewin* (NI); s/he burps, *pekatew* (VAI).

burr *or* **bur** A small burr, *pîmascehikanis* (NI).

burrow *wâtihkewin* (NI).

burrower *owâtihkew* (NA).

bury Burying something in the ground, *kanâhinamihk kîkway* (VTI); s/he buries her/him, *nahinew* (VTA); *ayahcinew* (VTI); it is buried or hidden, *ayipayiw* (VII) *or* (VAI); s/he buries her/him in the ground, *ayahwew* (VTI); s/he buries or covers her/him with snow, *ayâkonehwew* (VTI).

bush In the bush, *sakahk* (LN); there are clumps of shrubs or trees in succession, *ayapâskweyâw* (VAI); a wild bean bush, *pîmahopak* (NA); the bushes are thick with leaves, *kaskipakiw* (VAI).

bushed *ka sakaw îyinewihk* (VAI).

bush partridge A grouse, *iyintopihew* (NA).

bushy *ka kispakanskwehk* (LN); *sakasin* (LN).

busied *ka otamiyohk* (VAI).

busily Uncontrolled, *ka kîskwehkamiksihk* (VAI).

bustle Agitation, *kisôtôtâkewin* (NI).

busy The act of being busy, *otamiyowin* (NI); busy with something else, *kotamiyohk* (VAI); s/he is busy, *otamiyiw* (VAI); right now, busy at it, happening right now, *mekâc* (IPC); thing are very busy, *ayapahkamikan* (IPC); s/he is preoccupied with busywork over her/him, *tasihkawew* (VTA).

busybody *otayâhkonikew* (NA).

but Or although, *âtâ* (IPC); but, *mâka* (IPC).

butcher Someone who cuts meat, *ka mansahk wîyâs awîyak* (NA); s/he butchers a moose, *wiyanihew* (VTA); a butchering place, *wiyanihtâkan* (NI); s/he butchers, *wiyanihtâkew* (VAI); the act of butchering, *wiyanihtâkewin* (NI).

butchery A butcher shop or butchery, *wiyanihtâkewikamik* (VAI).

butt Someone's behind, *awîyak osôkan* (NI).

butt The act of butting heads, i.e.: rams, *ostikwânahikewin* (NI).

butte *kaskatinâw* (VII).

butter *tohtôsâpôwipimîy* (NI); s/he is making butter, *tohtôsâpowipimihkew* (VAI).

butterball *wâpanosipsak* (NA).

buttercup *sîpihko nepehkans* (NI).

butterfat *manahikan* (NI).

butterfingered *kitiskinikeskowin* (NI).

butterfingers *ka kitiskinikeskihk* (VAI).

butterfly Small butterfly, *kamâmakos* (NA); a large butterfly, *kamâmak* (NA).

buttermilk *manahikan tohtôsâpoy* (NI).

buttocks Buttocks or rearend, *misôkan* (NI).

button S/he buttons her/him, *aniskamâtew* (VTA); s/he buttons herself/himself, *aniskamatisiw* (VTA); a button, *aniskamân* (NI).

buttonhole *aniskamân sakâskwahon* (NI).

buxom *iskwew ka takakiyawet* (VAI).

buy Buying something, *katawehk kîkway* (IPC); s/he buys, *otinikew* (VAI).

buyer *otatâwew* (NA).

buzz *ka sewepitamaht awîyak* (VTA).

buzzer *sewepicikanis* (NI).

by and by *mwestas* (IPC).

bygone *kayas pece otâhk* (IPC) *(Northern)*; *kayas pece nâway* (IPC) *(Plains)*.

by-pass *wemahtewin* (NI); s/he by-passes something, *âsteskan* (VTI).

by-path *wemâhceskanâs* (NI).

by-road *wemâhteskanaw* (NI).

bystander *okanawâpahkew* (NA).

C

cabbage *otehipak* (NI).

cabin A camping cottage, *kapesiwkamkos* (NI); a wooden cabin or loghouse, *mistikokamik* (NI).

cabinet *oyâkanikamik* (NI); *akocikan* (NI); *âpacihcikan kamikos* (NI).

cabinetwork *oyâkanikamikohkewin* (NI).

cable A steel rope or cable, *pîwâpiskopîminahkwan* (NI).

cache *astahcikon* (NI).

cackle *pahkahahkwan ka kitot* (NI); *pahkahahkwan okitowin* (NI).

cacophony *ka nanâtohkîhtakosihk* (VAI).

cactus *môstâskamkahk kohpikihk* (NI).

cagey *kemoc iyinisowin* (NI).

cairn *asiniw kiskinowâcihcikan* (NA).

cajole *mamihcimitowin* (NI).

cajolery *kamamihcimowihk* (VAI).

cake *siwpahkwesikan* (NI) *(Northern)*; *wâwipahkwesikanak* (NI) *(Plains)*.

calamitous *metoni wisakahpinewin* (NI).

calamity *metoni ka misimayahkamkahk*; *misiwanâcipayowin* (NI).

calcify *ka asinîhkahtek kîkway* (VTI).

calculate *ka akihcikehk* (VAI).

calculating *kamekwa akihtamihk* (VTI).

calculation *akihcikewin* (NI).

calculative *ka akihcikewayahk* (VTI).

calendar Monthly calendar, *tipahipîsimwân* (NI).

caldron *mistaskihk* (NI).

calf *moscosis* (NA); a newborn calf, *oskimoscosis* (NA).

calfskin *moscosis apihkan* (NA); *moscosisowayân* (NA).

Calgary The Cree name for Calgary meaning "at the elbow", *otôskwanihk* (LN).

calico *ayapasinâstewekin* (NI).

calibre *pâskisikanis* (NI).

call Calling someone, *tepwâslwewln* (NI); it is called this, *isiyihkâtew* (VII); s/he is called or named, *isiyihkâsow* (VAI); s/he calls, i.e.: to an animal, *kitohew* (VAI); s/he makes an animal call, *kitohâcikew* (VAI); s/he or it called, i.e.: moose or other animals call out, *kitow* (VAI); the act of animals calling out, *kitowin* (NI); s/he calls him by several names, *mihcetweyihkâtew* (VTA); s/he calls out and makes it come towards her/him, i.e.: calling a moose, *pecimew* (VTA).

caller *otepwew* (NA).

Calling Lake The Cree name for the settlement of Calling Lake, *kitow sâkahikan* (NI).

calm A person being calm, *kâmwâtisiwin* (NI); it is calm or the wind ceases, *aywâstin* (VII).

calve *kôcawâsimisihk mostos* (NA); *ociwâsimisiw* (NA).

calves *mihcet mostosisak* (NA).

camaraderie *nâspic ka miyowicehtohk* (VTA).

camel A hump back animal, *piskwâwikanewatim* (NA) *(Plains)*; *pikwâwikanewipisiskiw* (NA) *(Northern)*.

camisole *iskwew pihcones* (NI).

camomile *maskihkîy lite or lite* (NI) *(Northern, French/ Cree)*; *maskihkiwâpoy* (NI) *(Plains)*.

camouflage *ka wanisihohk* (VAI).

camp Or resting spot, *kapesiwin* (NI); s/he camps for the night or s/he stays at a hotel, *kapesiw* (VAI); s/he prepares a place to camp, *kapesowinihkew* (VAI); the act of preparing a campground, *kapesowinihkewin* (NI); s/he camps with her/him overnight, *wîcikapesîmew* (VTA).

campfire A campfire pit, *kotawân* (NI); an old campfire site, *pônamowin* (NI).

campground *kapesiwin* (NI).

campsite *etah ka kapesihk* (VTI); *kapesiwin* (NI)

can *pîwâpiskos* (NI).

Canada balsam spruce *sihcisis* (NA); *napakasihta* (NA).

Canada goose *niska* (NA).

Canada jay *wîskacân* (NA) *(Northern)*; *wîskipôs* (NA) *(Plains)*.

cancel *nakinikewin* (NI).

cancellation *nakinamôwewin* (NI).

candid *ka nihtâpîkiskwîhk* (VAI).

candle *wâsaskocenikanis* (NI).

candleholder *wâsaskotenikan miciminikan* (NI).

candlelight *mosci wâsaskotenikewin* (NI).

candlestick *wâsaskotenikanâhtik* (NI).

candy *maskihkîs* (NA).

cane *saskahon* (NI); something used to assist someone to walk, *saskahohtakan* (NI); s/he walks with a cane, *saskahotew* (VAI); s/he uses a cane, *saskahiw* (VAI).

canister *ascikakan* (NI).

canker *kapiskopayihk picâyihk mitônihk* (VTI).

canned *kaskapowioiltowin* (NI) *(Northern)*; *kaskâpiskahikewin* (NI) *(Plains)*; s/he cans it, *kaskâpiskahikew* (VTI) *(Plains)*; *kaskapowehikew* (VTI) *(Northern)*.

cannibal Legendary eater of humans, *wihtikiw* (NA).

cannon *misipaskisikan* (NI).

canoe *ôsih* (NI); a big canoe, *mistahôsih* (NI); a wooden canoe, *mistikôsih* (NI); a birch bark canoe, *waskwayosih* (NI); canoeing, *ka pimiskahk* (VAI); birchbark canoe making, *astoyewin* (NI); *waskwayosihkewin* (NI).

269

canon *ayamihewiyniw* (NI); *ayamihewiyasiwiwin* (NI).

canopy A cover for something, *akwanahikan* (NI).

canter S/he is cantering, i.e.: a horse, *nisihkepayiw* (VAI); the act of cantering, *nisihkepayowin* (NI).

canvas Sheltering material *apahkwânekin* (NI) *(Northern)*; *apahkwâsonekin* (NI) *(Plains)*.

canyon *ka poskatinak*; *posiskaw* (NI); *kaskatinâw* (NI).

cap *astotin* (NI); *la palet* (NI) *(French Cree)*.

capability *kaskihcikewin* (NI) *(Northern)*; *nakacihtâwin* (NI) *(Plains)*.

capable *kaskihtâwin* (NI).

capacity *ispîhcipîsâkwahk* (IPC).

cape There is a point or cape, *neyâw* (VII) *(Plains)*; a point advancing in water, *miniwatimiwiw* (VII) *(Plains)*; *miniwatim* (LN).

capitulate *âyitaw ohci naheyeyihtamowin* (NI).

capitulation *âyitaw naheyeyihtamowin* (NI).

caprice *ka sekôc kweskeyetamihk* (VAI).

capricious *ekâ kâmamsehk* (VTA).

capsize S/he capsizes, *kotapîw* (VAI) *(Northern)*; *kwatapîw* (VAI) *(Plains)*; s/he capsizes the canoe when someone is paddling with her/him, *kotapâhoyew* (VTA) *(Northern)*; *kwatapâhohew* (VTA) *(Plains)*; s/he makes her/him capsize, *kotapîhew* (VTA) *(Northern)*; *kwatapîhew* (VTA) *(Plains)*; s/he turns her/him over while s/he is in the boat, *kotapinew* (VTA) *(Northern)*; *kwatapinew* (VTA) *(Plains)*.

captain *onîkâniw* (NA); *nâpihkwânihk okimâw* (NA).

captivate *awîyak ka otiniht* (VTA).

captivation *otiniwewin* (NI).

captive *awîyak koteniht* (VTA).

captivity *otiniwewin* (NI); *otinikewinihk* (IPC).

capture *kahtinikewin* (NI) *(Northern)*; *kahtitinikewin* (NI) *(Plains)*; *kâcitinew* (VTA)

caravan *mamawih pimpecowin* (NI); *opiciwak* (NA).

carbuncle *sihkihp* (NI).

card A playing card, *pakesan* (NI).

cardinal *mawaci kihci ayamihewiyiniw* (NA) *(Northern)*; *pahkwâyamihewiyiniwiwin* (NA) *(Plains)*.

cardinal bird *mihko pîwâyesis* (NA).

care Caring for someone, *awîyak kanakateyimiht* (VTA); s/he cares for her/him, *pisiskeyimew* (VTA); the act of caring for someone, *pisiskeyimiwewin* (NI); someone worthy of being cared for, *pisiskeyihtâkosowin* (NI); s/he is worthy of care, *pisiskeyihtâkosiw* (VAI); it is worthy of care, *pisiskeyihtâkwan* (VII); care and attention, *pisiskeyihtamowin* (NI).

careful Being very careful, *metoni kanakateyehtamihk* (VAI); carefully or with caution, *kâkitâw* (IPC) *(Northern)*; *peyahtik* (IPC) *(Plains)*.

careless Being very careless, *metoni ekâ ka nâkateyihtamihk* (VAI); s/he just doesn't care, *namoya*

nâkatohkew (VAI); careless by, without attention, by heart, *pakwanaw* (NI); without concern or conscience, done carelessly, *mâmâsîs* (IPC); the act of carelessness, *mâyinikeskiwin* (NI).

caress S/he caressed her/his private parts, *kîminew* (VTA); s/he is caressing someone's private parts, *kîminikew* (VTA); s/he is fondling or caressing herself/himself, *kîminisiw* (VTA); the act of fondling or caressing oneself, *kîminisiwin* (NA); they are fondling or caressing each other, *kîminitowak* (VTA); the act of fondling or caressing each other, *kîminitowin* (NI); s/he caresses her/him, *metawâkâtew* (VTA).

carful *sâkaskineposiwin* (NI).

caribou *atihk* (NA).

caribou hide *atihkwayân* (NI).

carnage *ka kwespanâci nîpâhitowin* (NI); *nipahtâkewin* (NI).

carnal *akâwâtihtowin* (NI).

carol *nîpâyamihâwin nikamona* (NI) *(Northern)*; *nîpâyamihâw nikamowin* (NI) *(Plains)*.

carouse *môcikihtâwipewin* (NI).

carousel *wâsakâpayis* (NI).

carp *kinosew* (NA).

carpenter *mistikonâpew* (NA); *owaskahikanihkew* (NA).

carpentry The act of being a carpenter, *mistikonâpewiwin* (NI).

carpet *aspitahkoskewin* (NI).

carriage *ocâpâsôwâyis* (NI) *(Northern)*; *napakahcikowâyis* (NI) *(Plains)*; *otâpânâskos* (NI).

carrier One who carries packs or the name for Carrier people, *onayahcikew* (NA) *(Plains)*; *onîkâtew* (NA) *(Northern)*.

carrot *oskâtâsk* (NA); a sweet carrot, *sîwiskâtâsk* (NA).

carry The act of carrying something in one's arms, *tahkonikewin* (NI); s/he carries her/him everywhere, *papâmohtahew* (VTA); s/he carries her/him along, *pimoyiw* (VTI); s/he carries or holds her/him, *tahkonew* (VTA); something to hold or carry, *tahkonikan* (NI).

cart *yahkinikan* (NI); *tihtipitapânâsk* (NA) *(Plains)*; *newokâtew* (NA) *(Plains)*; *tihtipitâpânâsk* (NA) *(Northern)*.

carter *opapâmohcicikew* (NA).

carton *masinahikanekin watapiwât* (NI).

cartwheel *emisikitit otihtipipayiw* (NA).

carve S/he carves it or planes it, *môhkotew* (VTA); s/he carves them with a knife, *oyihkotew* (VTA); s/he scratches or carves grooves on them with a knife, *pesihkotew* (VTA).

carver *omansikew* (NA); *omôhkocikew* (NA).

carving *manisikewin* (NI); *môhkocikewin* (NI).

case *peyak mistikowatis* (NI).

casing *pîwâpiskos akwanahikan* (NI).

cask *mistikomahkahkos* (NI); *mahkahkos* (NI).

cast *kâwepinâskwehk* (NI); *kâwepinamihk* (NI); *wepinam* (NI) *(Northern)*; *wepinamowin* (NI) *(Plains)*.

castaway *wepinikan* (NA).

casting *wepinâskwewin* (NI).

castor oil *saposikan* (NI).

castrate *ayihkwehiwewin* (NI); a castrated cow, i.e., a steer, *ayihkwew* (NA); *iyâpesisemanisoht* (NA) *(Plains)*.

cat *minôs* (NA).

catastrophe *mâyipayowin* (NI).

catch Grabbing or catching someone, i.e.: rape, *otihtinkiwin* (NI); s/he catches her/him, *kâcitinew*; s/he catches it in midair or s/he catches the bus, *nawatinew* (VTA).

catching *ka otihtihnamihk kîkway*; *kacitinamawew* (VTA).

catechism *ayamihâw kiskinohamâsiwin* (NI).

categorization *oyahowewin* (NI).

categorize *ka oyahowehk* (VAI).

categorical *kwayaskwahitowin* (NI).

caterpillar *mihyawimohtiw* (NA) *(Northern)*; *mohtew* (NA) *(Plains)*; *mwapokwesiw* (NA).

Catholic The Catholic religion, *pâhkwayamihâwin* (NI); a Catholic priest, *pahkwâyamihewiyiniwiwin* (NA) *(Plains)*; *ayamihewiyiniw* (NA) *(Northern)*.

catholicism *kapahkwayamihâhk* (VAI).

cat-tail A part of a bulrush, *pikwanâhtik* (NI); *otâwask* (NI).

cattle *mostoswak* (NA).

caught Somebody being caught, *awîyak ka kahtitiniht* (VTA); s/he is caught on something, *sakicin* (VAI).

cause *awîyak weyah otôtamowin* (NI); *kîkway ohci* (IPC).

caution *nâkateyihcikewin* (NI); with care, slowly, with attention, with caution, *kâkitaw* (IPC) *(Northern)*; *peyahtik* (IPC) *(Plains)*.

cautious S/he is a cautious person, *peyahtikowatisiw* (VAI); s/he considers her/him to be a cautious person, *peyahtikweyimew* (VTA); s/he is cautious, *peyahtikweyihtam* (VAI); s/he is very cautious, *kwespanâtisiw* (VAI) *(Plains)*; being cautious, *peyahtikweyihtamowin* (NI).

cave *kawihkwehcipayik*; a hole in the ground, *wâti* (NI).

cavern *kawatowahcak sôniyamatih* (NI) *or* (LN).

cease When things stop, *kaponâhkamkahk* (VTI); s/he ceases to think about her/him, *poneyimew* (VAI); s/he ceases to be here or s/he ceased having it, *poni-ayâw* (VAI); s/he ceases to bother her/him or s/he leaves her/him alone, *ponihew* (VTA); it ceases, i.e.: a meeting, *ponipayiw* (VAI); s/he ceases to live, *poni-pimâtisiw* (VAI); s/he ceases to live with her/him or s/he separates from her/him, *poniwicewew* (VTA); s/he cease being angry, *pôniyawesiw*; the wind has ceased, *pôniyotin* (VII); s/he ceases arguing with her/him, *pônowemew* (VTA); s/he ceases talking, *pônowihtam* (VAI).

cedar *mâsikes* (NA); *minisihkes* (NA); a place where there are many berries, *mînisihkeskâw* (NI).

cedar bird *sihtipiwâyisis* (NA) *(Northern)*; *mâsikeskopiyesîs* (NA) *(Plains)*.

celebrate *môcikihtâwin* (NI).

celebration *môcikihtâwinihkewin* (NI).

celibate Being a bachelor, *môsâpewiwin* (NI).

cemetery A burying spot, grave, *kihkwahaskân* (NI).

central *âpihtaw ayihk* (IPC).

centre *or* **center** *metoni âpihtaw* (IPC); in the centre room, middle place, *âpihtâwâyihk* (NI).

cereal Or porridge, *kîkisepâ mîcowin* (NI).

ceremonial *kihci isihcikewin* (NI).

ceremony *isihcikewin* (NI).

certain *metoni kehcinâhowin* (NI); certainly, sure, *kehcinâ* (IPC).

certainly *kehcinâkîkway kîspayik* (VII); *kehcinâhowinihk* (IPC); sure, *kehcinâ* (IPC).

271

chafe *pinipocikewin* (NI).

chaff *pawâtahikana* (NA) *(Northern)*; *piwihtakahikana* (NA) *(Plains)*.

chain *sakâpihkan* (NI).

challenge The act of challenging someone, *mawineskâkewin* (NI); s/he challenges her/him or them, *mawineskawew* (VTA); s/he challenges or s/he stands up to her/him, *nîpawistawew* (VTA).

champion *opaskiyakew metawewenihk* (NA); *otahowew* (VTA).

chance Something good happening by chance, *mameskawimiyopayowin* (NI); by chance, unintentionally, *keswân* (IPC); it happens by chance, *mameskawipayiw* (IPC).

change The act of changing, *meskocipayiwin* (NI); the act of changing something, *meskociwepinikewin* (NI); changing, in lieu of, one instead of the other, *meskoc* (IPC); s/he changes her/his shirt, *meskocipakowayânew* (VAI), it changed on its own, *meskocipayiw* (VII) *or* (VAI); s/he changes shoes, *meskotaskisinew* (VAI); s/he changes her/him, *meskotônew* (VTA); the act of changing direction, *paskewin* (NI).

channel The water runs right through, *ka sâpostekwîyak* (LN); a channel between two adjoining lakes, *tastawikamâw* (NI); the river has a back channel, *yikihtawâw* (VAI); the river has forks in it, *yekistikweyaw* (VAI)

chant *ka nikamowayasihk* (VAI); *pihtâkosiwak* (VAI).

chap A little boy, *nâpesis* (NA).

chapel A small church, *ayamihew kamikos* (NI).

chapped Her/his hands are chapped, *kîspicihcew* (VAI); her/his skin is chapped, *kîspisiw* (VAI).

chaps A pair of chaps, *tehtapîwitâsak* (NI).

char It is charred, *pihkahtew* (VII) *(Plains)*; *pihkihkahtew* (VII) *(Northern)*; s/he charred them, *pihkaswew* (VTA).

character *isâyâwin* (NI); Native characteristics or native culture, *nehiyawihtwawin* (NI); s/he is a solid character, *ayâtisiw* (VAI); s/he finds her/him to have a good character, *kohkwâwâteyimew* (VTA); s/he has a good character, *kohkwâwâtisiw* (VAI); the act of having a good character, *kohkwâwâtisiwin* (NI).

characterize *isâyâhiwewin* (NI).

charcoal *iskwâskisew* (NI).

charge Buying on credit, *akihtâmakewin* (NI); s/he is in charge of someone, *kanaweyimew* (VTA); s/he charges more, *ayiwâkakihcikew* (VAI); s/he over charges her/him, *ayiwâkakimew* (VTI); s/he charges at someone, e.g.: moose or bull, *môskestâkew* (VTA); s/he charges at her/him, *môskestawew* (VTA).

charging *kamekwa akihtâmakehk* (VTA).

charitable Being charitable, *kakisewâtisihk* (VAI); s/he is very kind and charitable, *kisewâtisiw* (VAI).

charity *kisewâtisowin* (NI); *mekiwin* (NI); friendship, *wîcîtowin* (NI).

charm Being charming towards someone, *miweyihtamohiwewin* (NI).

charmed *ka meweyîtamohiht awîyak* (VTA).

charmer *omiweyihtamohiwew* (NA).

charming *miweyihtâkosiwin* (NI).

chase S/he chases her/him out of the water, *kapatetisawew* (VTA); s/he chases them together, *mawasakotisawew* (VTA); s/he chases after her/him in a canoe, *nawawew* (VTA); s/he runs or chases her/him into the woods, *kospitisawew* (VTA); s/he chases after her/him or them, *nawaswâtew* (VTA); they chase after each other, *nawaswâtitowak* (VTA); s/he chases her/him or them, *nawaswew* (VTA); the act of chasing someone, *nawaswewin* (NA); s/he chases her/him in a different direction, *pasketisawew* (VTA); s/he chases them all away, *pawitisawew* (VTA) *(Northern)*; *mestâmohkew* (VTA) *(Plains)*; s/he chases them into the woods, *seskitisawew* (VTA).

chaser *onawaswew* (NA).

chasm *misiwâti* (NI).

chaste *metoni kanâtisowin* (NI).

chatter S/he likes to chatter, *kakihcimow* (VAI); a chatter box, *osâmitôn* (NA); s/he is a chatterer, *osâmitonew* (VAI).

cheap The act of being a cheap person, *sasâkisiwin* (NI); it is cheap or inexpensive, *wehtakihtew* (VII); s/he is selling them cheap, *wehtakimew* (VTA); it is cheap; inexpensive, *wehtakisiw* (VAI).

cheat The act of cheating; deceit, *kakayesiwin* (NI); s/he cheats, *kakayeyisiw* (VAI); s/he acts improperly by cheating her/him, *kakayesitotawew* (VTA); s/he cheats her/him, *kakayesihew* (VTA); s/he suspects her/him to be a cheater, *kakayesiyimew* (VTA); s/he cheats on or betrays, her/him, *wayesihew* (VTA); s/he cheats or betrays herself/himself, *wayesihisiw* (VTA); the act of cheating or betraying oneself, *wayesihisowin* (NI); s/he cheats on or betrays others, *wayesihiwew* (VTA); the act of cheating on or betraying others, *wayesihiwewin* (NI); s/he cheats on her/him with a lie, *wayesimew* (VTA); s/he does some cheating things to her/him, *wayesitôtawew* (VTA).

check A sudden stoppage, *sisikoc nakinikewin* (NI).

cheek A cheek on the face, *manaway* (NI); *monaway* (NI).

cheer *sâkowestamakewin* (NI); *miyotôtâkewin* (NI).

cheerful *môcikâyâwin* (NI).

cheery *môcikeyihtam* (VAI).

cheese Something cooked hard; something pressed together, *mâkwahikan* (NI) *(Plains)*; *maskawihkasikan* (NI) *(Northern)*.

cherish S/he keeps it in memory of the past, *kasispowihew* (VTI).

cherry *mihko mînis* (NI); chokecherry, *takwahiminân* (NI).

chest *maskan* (NI); *maskikan* (NI).

chestnut *kosawinakwah kîkway* (VTI).

chew The act of chewing gum, *misimiskowewin* (NI); s/he chews on something, *mâmâkwahcikewin* (NI); s/he chews it, *misimew* (NA); s/he chews gum, *misimiskowew* (VAI).

chickadee *picikîskisîs* (NI).

chicken *misimisihew* (NA); *pahkahahkwan* (NA) *(Northern)*; *pahpahahkwân* (NA) *(Plains)*; a large chicken, *misipahkahahkwân* (NA) *(Northern)*; *misipahpahahkwân* (NA) *(Plains)*; a prairie chicken, *âhkiskiw* (NA).

chief A leader of a clan or tribe, *okimahkân* (NA); s/he makes her/him chief, *okimahkânihkew* (VTA).

chieftain *onîkânîw* (NA).

chieftainship *okimahkâniwiwin* (NI).

child *awâsis* (NA); a newborn child, *oskawâsis* (NA); the youngest child, *osîmimâw* (NA); my child, *nicawâsimis* (NA); the first-born child, *nistamôsân* (NA); s/he is the first-born child, *nistamôsaniwiw* (VAI).

childbearing *ayâwâwasowin* (NI).

childhood *awâsisîwiwin* (NI).

childish Acting innocent like a child, *awâsisihkasowin* (NI); acting like a child, i.e.: immature, *awâsisikasiw* (VAI); s/he is childish or showing immaturity, *kaketawatisiw* (VAI); s/he responds reluctantly because of his childish immaturity, *kaketâweyimew* (VAI).

childishness *awâsis sinkewin* (NI).

childlike *awâsisihkasowin* (NI).

children Lots of children, *mihcet awâsisak* (NA); my children, *nicawâsimisak* (NA); *nitawâsimisak* (NA).

chilled Cooling something off or chilled, *kâtahkastahk kîkway* (VTI); it or s/hc was chilled, *tahkipayiw* (VAI); her/his back is chilled, *tahkipiskwanewaciw* (VAI).

chilly It is chilly outside, *tahkâyâw* (VII); the air became chilly, *tahkiyowepayiw* (VII); it is chilly, i.e.: air, *tahkiyowew* (VII).

chin *mitâpiskan* (NI); a jaw, *mikwâskonew* (NI).

chink *sihtawahikewin* (NI).

chinook *kîsopweniyotin* (NI) *(Northern)*; *saskan* (NI) *(Plains)*.

chip A wood chip, *pîwikahikan* (NI); a wood chip used by beavers in their houses for bedding, *pahtehikan* (NI).

Chipewyan *ocepwayanew* (NA).

chipmunk *sâsâkawâpiskos* (NA).

chisel An instrument for carving a wood groove, *pasihkocikan* (NI); s/he chisels a groove on a piece of wood, *pasihkocikew* (VAI); the act of chiselling a groove on a piece of wood, *pasihkocikewin* (NI); s/he chisels a groove on them, *pasihkotew* (VTA).

choice *nawasôh* (IPC).

choir Ensemble, *ka mâmawinikamohk* (VTA).

choke The act of choking on something, *kipihkitonipayewin* (NI); s/he chokes on something, *atohow* (VAI); s/he is choking from the smoke, *kipwatâmâpasiw* (VAI); the act of choking from smoke, *kipwatâmâpasiwin* (NI); s/he chokes her/him with smoke, *kipwatâmâpaswew* (VTA); s/he chokes up and can't breathe, *kipwatâmopayiw* (VAI); the act of choking up and not breathing, *kipwatâmopayowin* (NI).

chokecherry A chokecherry tree or bush, *takwahiminânâhtik* (NA); a chokecherry, *takwahiminân* (NI).

choose The act of making a choice, *nawasonikewin* (NI); s/he chooses her/him, *nawasonew* (VTA); s/he chooses her/him by looking at her/him, *nawasowâpamew* (VTA).

chop Splitting wood, *tâskatahimihtewin* (NI); s/he chops something with an axe, *cîkahikew* (VTI); s/he chopped her/him with an axe, *cîkahwew* (VTA); it is chopped off, i.e.: a tree, *kîskatahikâsiw* (VAI); it is chopped off, i.e.: fence post, *kîskatahikâtew* (VTI); the act of chopping oneself off, *kîskatahosîwin* (NI); s/he chops it off, *kîskatahwew* (VTI); s/he chops the tail off, *kîskâyowetahwew* (VTA); s/he chops them off with an axe, *manikawew* (VTI); s/he chops them all up, *mescikawew* (VTA); s/he chops it into shape, *oyikahwew* (VTA); s/he chops off a piece of them, *pahkwekawew* (VTA); s/he chops them up, *pîkokahwew* (VTI); s/he chops them into small pieces, i.e.: wood chips, *pîwihtakahwew* (VTA); s/he chops them into chips, *pîwikahwew* (VTA); s/he chops them loose, *tâsikahwew* (VTI) *(Northern)*; s/he chops them loose, *tâskikawew* (VTI) *(Plains)*.

chore A small chore, *acoskewinis* (NI).

chorus *mâmawinikamowin* (NI).

christen *ka sîkahahtaht awâsis* (NA).

christening *sîkahahtakewin* (NI).

Christian Someone who prays; a religious person, *otayamihâw* (NA).

Christmas *nîpâyamihâwin* (NI); Christmas time, *ka mekwâ nîpâyamihahk* (VTI); the Lord's Day, *manito okesikam* (NI).

Christmas day *ka nîpâyamihawkesikaw* (NA).

Christmas tree *nîpâyamihewisihta* (NA).

chubby *pitikosiw* (VAI).

chuckle *kiyakahpowin* (NI); *pahpisiw* (VAI); *pâhpowin* (NI).

chum *wîcîwâkan* (NA).

chunk *pahkwenikan* (NI).

church *ayamihekamik* (NI); *ayamihewikamik* (NI).

churn *tohtôsâpopimihkew* (VAI); a machine for making homemade butter, *tohtôsapopimihkakan* (NI).

chute *metoni kehcinâhowin* (NI).

cinder *iskwâskisewa* (NI); a burned up piece of wood, *sikohkasikan* (NI); *mestâskitew* (NI).

circle Drawing a circle, *wawiyasasinahikewin* (NI); in a circle, *wâsakâm* (IPC); s/he circles or surrounds her/him, *pihciskawew* (VTA); s/he circles around her/him, *tetipeweskawew* (VTA); s/he circles around along the edge, i.e.: a lake, *tetipeweham* (VAI); s/he circles all the way around it, *tetipewew* (VAI); o/he walks circling around her/him, *tetipiskawew* (VTA).

circular Something circular, *notimâw* (VII) *(Northern)*; *wâweyiyâw* (VII) *(Plains)*; *kîkway ka wâwiyak* (VII); it is circular in shape, *wâwiyâskosiw* (NA).

circulate *ka papâmipicimohk* (VAI).

cistern *mônahipânihkân* (NI).

civil *peyakopemacehowin* (NI).

civility *metoni manâcisowin* (NI).

civilize Teaching, *miyokiskinohamâkewin* (NI).

claim S/he homesteads, *otinaskew* (VAI).

273

clam *esis* (NA).

clamber *kîhcikosiw* (VAI).

clamp *sakicihcikan* (NI).

clan *etah ka ohtâskanesihk* (VTA).

clap *pakamicicihamawin* (NI); *pakamiciciw* (VAI).

clarification *nisitohtamohiwewin* (NI).

clarify *ka nisitohtamohewehk*; S/he makes her/him understand, *nistotamohew* (VTA); the act of clarification or interpretation, *nisitohtamohiwewin* (NI).

clasp *sakicihcikan* (NI).

class *papiskihc ayâwin* (NI).

classification *piskihc akimowewin* (NI).

classify *ka piskihcakihcikehk* (VTI).

claw *wâskases* (NA); *maskasiy* (NA).

clay *maskawâsiskîy* (NI); *asiskîy* (NI); there is mud, sticky clay, *pasakoskowakâw* (VAI).

clean Something clean, *kîkway kakânatahk* (VII); it is pure and clean, *kanâtan* (VII); s/he is pure and clean, *kanâtisiw* (VAI); cleanliness, *kanâcihiwin* (NI); s/he cleans her/him, *kanâcihew* (VTA); s/he is neatly dressed or tidy, *kanâcihow* (VAI); s/he lives a clean life, i.e.: morally, *kanâcipimâtisiw* (VAI); purity of life (morally), *kanâcipimâtisowin* (NI); s/he has a clean or pure soul, *kanâtahcâkwew* (VAI); having a clean or pure soul, *kanâtahcâkwewin* (NI); it is neat and clean, *kanâtan* (VII); s/he considers her/him of faultless, pure, umblemished character, *kanâteyimew* (VTA); being considered faultless, *kanâteyihtâkosowin* (NI); s/he is considered faultless, *kanâteyihtâkosiw* (VAI); it is considered faultless, *kanâteyihtâkwan* (VII); s/he cleans the snow off something, *pânahikew* (VTA); s/he cleans or clears the snow off her/him, *pânahwew* (VTA); s/he cleans the snow off the trees, *pawahtakinew* (VTA); the tree becomes clean of snow, *pawahtakipayiw* (VAI); it is all cleaned off by the wind, i.e.: a spruce tree, *pawâsiw* (VAI); it is cleaned off by the wind, i.e.: a road blown free of snow, *pawâstan* (VII).

cleanse *kanacicikewin* (NI).

clear Something that looks clear, *wâsenakwan* (VII); clearly, in the open; exactly, *memohc* (IPC); s/he can be seen plainly or clearly, *kihkânâkosiw* (VAI); s/he sees her/him clearly or recognises her/him, *kihkânâwew* (VTA); it is seen plainly or clearly, *kihkânâkwan* (VII); the fish has a clear or distinct taste, *kihkâspakosiw*; (VAI) the meat has a clear or distinct taste, *kihkâspakwan* (VII); s/he can be heard plainly or clearly, *kihkâwihtâkosiw* (VAI); the act of being heard plainly or clearly, *kihkâwihtâkosowin* (NI); it can be heard plainly or clearly, *kihkâwihtâkwan* (VII); s/he hears her/him plainly, *kihkâwihtawew* (VTA); the

light is bright or clear, *kihkâyâsawew* (VAI); there is bright moonlight, *kihkâyâstew* (VAI); it is clear weather or the sky is clear, *wâseskwan* (VII); the wind has cleared the sky, *wâseskwastan* (VII).

clearance *paspîwin* (NI).

click It clicks into place, *tâpipayiw* (VII).

cliff *kîskatinâw* (NI); a rocky cliff, *kîskâpiskâw* (NI); a dirt or earth cliff, *kîskahcâw* (NI); a cut bank, *kîskatawahkâw* (NI).

climb The act of climbing or going up a ladder or stairs, *kîhcikosiwin* (NI); s/he is climbing the ladder, *amaciwihâhtawew* (VAI); s/he climbs up stairs or a ladder, *kîhcikosiw* (VAI); s/he takes her/him up a ladder or stairs, *kîhcikositahew* (VTA); s/he chases her/him up the ladder or stairs, *kîhcekosîtisawew* (VTA); s/he climbed over, i.e.: a hill or mountain, *pasitâmacowew* (VAI); s/he climbed over, i.e.: a fence, *pasitâhtawiw* (VTI); s/he climbed onto the top of the hill, *tahkohtâmaciwew* (VAI).

climber *otâmaciwew* (NA).

clincher An instrument for cinching a load of wood, i.e.: a clincher, *sihcipayihcikan* (NI).

clinic *maskihkîwikamik* (NI).

clip *kipwâskwahonis* (NI).

clipper *paskosikâkan* (NI).

cloak *miskotâkay* (NI); a cover for the body, *akwanahon* (NI).

close Close to or near, *cîkâhtaw* (IPC); closer to the edge, *cîkayihk* (IPC); close to water, *cîkipek* (IPC); s/he closes it for her/him, *kipahamawew* (VTA); s/he is closed in or locked up, i.e.: jail, *kipahikâsiw* (VAI); the act of being closed in or locked up, i.e.: jail, *kipahikâsiwin* (NI); it is closed or shutdown, i.e.: store, *kipahikâtew* (VII); s/he closes her/him in, *kipawew* (VII); it is closed in and has space inside, i.e.: a van or pair of pants, *wihkwesiw* (VAI); the act of being closed in and having space inside, *wihkwesiwin* (NI); it is closed in and has space inside, i.e.: a tent, *wihkweyâw* (VII).

closer Close by, *kisiwâk* (VII); a little close by, *kisiwâkis* (VII); close by, very near: also for time, quality and quantity, *cîkâhtaw* (IPC).

clot It is clotted, i.e.: blood on fur, *watokisiw* (VAI); a blood clot or clotted blood, *watow* (NA).

cloth *ayiwinis* (NI); cloth bag or cloth for making clothes, *ayiwinisekin* (NI) *(Plains)*; *ayiwinisihkakanekin* (NI) *(Northern)*; durable pair of pants, *sohkekisiw* (VII); a strong piece of cloth, *sohkekin* (NI) *(Northern)*; *maskawekin* (NI) *(Plains)*; slippery, even, *sôskwekisiw* (VII); something soft with padding, *sôskwekan* (VII); soft, *yoskisiw* (VII); *yoskahikan* (NI); thick, *kispakekisiw* (VAI); *kispakekin*

(NI); a special cloth used in sacred ceremonies, i.e.: in priests' vestments, **manitowekin** (NI); a red cloth or material, **mihkwekin** (NI); the cloth is yellow, **osâwekan** (VII); yellow cloth, **osâwekin** (NI); a cotton cloth, **pakowayanekin** (NI); a single layer of cloth, **peyakwekan** (NI); it has a fine texture, i.e.: cloth, **sanaskekan** (VII); a fine texture cloth, **sanaskekin** (NI); the cloth is blue, **sîpihkwekan** (VII) *(Northern)*; **sîpihkwâw** (VII) *(Plains)*; a piece of blue cloth, **sîpihkwekin** (NI); smooth cloth, i.e.: velvet, **sôskwekin** (NI); it is made of smooth cloth, **sôskwekisiw** (VII); it is a strong cloth, i.e.: heavy canvas, **maskawekiniwiw** (VII) *(Plains and Northern variant)*; **sohkekan** (VII) *(Plains)*; s/he puts clothes on her/him, **postayiwinisahew** (VTA) *(Plains)*; **kikayiwinsahew** (VTA) *(Northern)*; s/he puts on her/his own clothes, **postayiwinisew** (VAI) *(Plains)*; **kikayiwinsew** (VAI) *(Northern)*.

clothes A suit of clothes, **ayiwinisa** (NI).

cloud **waskôw** (NA); it is cloudy, **yikwaskwan** (VII); a huge cloud, **mahkaskwâw** (NI).

cloudy It is cloudy, **yikwaskwan** (VII); **ikwaskwan** (VII); the clouds have broken up and scattered across the sky, **pawaskwew** (VAI) *(Northern)*; **pesakâstew** (VAI) *(Plains)*.

clover **mostosmecewin** (NI); **maskosiya** (NI).

club **mistik** (NI).

clump Clumps of trees in succession; **ayapâskweyâw** (VAI); there is a clump of bushes, **ministikwâskweyâw** (VAI); a clump of spruce trees, **ministikosihtiskâw** (NI); **ministikominâhikoskâw** (NI)

clumsy A clumsy person, **onanâtohkonikew** (NA) *(Plains)*; **yikicik** (NA) *(Northern)*.

cluster A cluster of berries, **mihcetominakâw** (NA) *(Northern)*; **mînisiskâw** (NA) *(Plains)*.

coach **okimâw tapan** (NA).

coagulate It congeals, **misiwepayiw** (VII).

coal A piece of black coal, **kaskitehkan** (NI).

coat Or jacket or dress, **miskotâkay** (NI); a new coat or dress, **oskasâkay** (NI); s/he has a coat or jacket, **oskotâkâw** (VAI); a blue coat, dress or jacket, **sîpihkwasâkay** (NI); a woolen coat, i.e.: a sweater, **sîpihkiskawasâkay** (NI) *(Plains)*; **sestakwasâkay** (NI) *(Northern)*.

cob of corn **mahtâmin** (NA).

cocky The act of being cocky, **mâmaskâtikohkâsowin** (NI); s/he is cocky, **mâmaskâtikohkâsiw** (VAI).

cod **kecikamew kinosew** (NA).

coffee **pihkahtewâpoy** (NI) *(Northern)*; **pihkahcewâpos** (NI) *(Plains)*; **wespâkamicewâpôs** (NI) *(Plains)*.

coil S/he coils her/him around a stick, **tepâskwahwew** (VTA).

coin **sônîyâs** (NA).

cold It is cold, i.e.: refers to the weather, **tahkâyâw** (VII); being numb with cold, **kiskimâskaciwin** (NI); it is cold, **kisin** (VII); it feels cold, **kisinâw** (VII); it is kind of cold, **kisinayaw** (VII); s/he has cold hands, **kawacihcewaciw** (VAI); s/he has cold feet, **kawacisitewaciw** (VAI); s/he is cold, **kawaciw** (VAI); s/he makes her/him cold, **kawatimew** (VTA); it has gone cold or it has cooled off, i.e.: freshly baked bread, **tahkapiw** (VII); a stick or log is cold to the touch, **tahkâskwan** (NI); it has gone cold or it has cooled off, i.e.: soup, **tahkastew** (VII); it is cold to the touch, **tahkâw** (VII); the water is cold, **tahkikamiw** (VII) *(Plains)*; **tahkamow** (VII) *(Northern)*; s/he is making the water cold, **tahkikamâpohkew** (VAI); s/he has a cold neck, **tahkikwayawew** (VAI); s/he has a cold back, **tahkipiskwanew** (VAI); s/he has a cold arm, **tahkipitonew** (VAI); being cold, **tahkisiwin** (NI); s/he is cold to the touch, **tahkisiw** (VAI); s/he reduces his vitality by throwing cold water on her/him, **tahkâpawahew** (VTA); cold water, **tahkamâpoy** (NI) *(Northern)*; **tahkikamâpoy** (NI) *(Plains)*.

colic **kisôwaskatewin** (NI).

collapse **pîkopayiw** (VAI); **kipatâhtam** (VAI).

collar Something to wear around the neck, **tâpiskâkan** (NI).

collect S/he gathers or collects, **mâwasakonam** (VTI); s/he collects or s/he saves, **mâwacihcikew** (VAI); the act of collecting, **mâwacihcikewin** (NI); s/he collects them or saves them, **mâwacihew** (VTA).

collection **mâwacihcikewin** (NI); the act of collecting, **mâwasakonikewin** (NI).

collide **tâwikipayihitowak** (VAI).

colon The large intestine, **misitaksiyapiy** (NA).

color *or* **colour** The color it has, **ketasinastek** (VII); it has distinctive colors, **pakaskasinâstew** (VII).

colorful *or* **colourful** **mamiywasinâstew** (VII).

colt **miscacimosis** (NA).

comb **sîkahon** (NI); a fine comb for combing lice, **pinahihkwâkan** (NI); a fine comb, **pinahihkwân** (NI); s/he combs the hair on it, **sîkaham** (VAI); s/he combs her/his own hair, **sîkahow** (VTA); s/he combs her/his hair for her/him, **sîkahwew** (VTA).

come S/he comes from that direction, **ohcipayiw** (VAI); s/he makes her/him come from a different direction, **ohcipayihew** (VTA); s/he comes from there, **peyohcipayiw** (VAI); s/he comes here by train or canoe, **petâpoyiw** (VAI); s/he comes in this direction because s/he is being blown by the wind, **petâsiw** (VAI); it comes in this direction because it is being blown by the wind, **petâstan** (VII); s/he makes her/him come to her/him by her/his thoughts, **peteyimew** (VTA); s/he comes running down the hill, **penâsopwepahtâw**

275

(VAI); s/he comes down the hill on horseback, **penâsipepayiw** (VAI).

comfortable **miyopiw** (VAI).

command S/he commands or orders her/him to hurry up, **nanihkitisawew** (VTA); s/he commands or orders everyone to hurry up, **nanihkowitam** (VTA).

commence S/he commences working on her/him for a while, **nomehkawew** (VTA); s/he commences working on it for a while, **nomehkam** (VTI); s/he commences work on her/him for a while and then stops, **nomihew** (VTA); s/he commences whittling on them for a while, **nomihkotew** (VTA); s/he commences making them for a while and then stops, **nomisîhew** (VTA).

commend **mamihcimowewin** (NI).

common spruce **sihta** (NA); **minahik** (NA).

commotion **âyimipayiwin** (NI).

communal Living together, **mâmawiwikowin** (NI).

communicate **wihtamâtowin** (NI).

communion S/he receives communion or s/he puts food in her/his mouth, **saskamiw** (VAI); the act of receiving communion or putting something in the mouth, **saskamowin** (NI).

community Living in a community, **mâmawâyâwin** (NI); **mâmawinitowin** (NI).

companion **wîcîwâkan** (NA); s/he makes her/him her/his companion, **owîcewâkanimew** (VTA); s/he has companions, **owîcewâkaniw** (VAI).

compassion S/he has a heart or compassion, **otehiw** (VAI); compassion or goodness of heart, **otehiwin** (NI).

compatible S/he is compatible with her/him, **nahiskawew** (VTA).

compensate **tipahikewin** (NI).

compete S/he competes, **mawinehikew** (VAI); s/he competes against her/him or them, **mawinewew** (VTA).

competition **mawinehikewin** (NI).

complete **kahkiyâw** (IPC); all in one piece, complete, **misiweyâw** (VII).

compliment **mamihcimowewin** (NI); **mamihcimôw** (IPC)

complimentary Bragging, **mamihcimowin** (NI).

composed It is composed of many kinds of things, **nanâtohkîkway** (VII); her/his heritage is composed of various ethnic groups, **nanâtohkôskânesiw** (VAI).

comprehensible S/he is comprehensible, **kwayaskweyihtamoyicikâsiw** (VAI); s/he is thought to be comprehensible, **kwayaskweyihcikâsiw** (VAI); it is thought to be comprehensible, **kwayaskweyihcikâtew** (VII); it is comprehensible, **kwayaskweyihtamoyicikâtew** (VII).

comrade A friend, **wîcîwâkan** (NA).

conceal **kâtaw** (VTI).

concentrate **mâmitoneyihcikewin** (NI).

concern **pîkweyihtam** (VTI).

conclude **ka kesihtahk kîkway** (VTI); **kesihtâw** (VTI); **ponipayiw** (VII).

conclusion **kesihcikewin** (NI).

concrete **asinîwipayihcikewin** (NI) *(Plains)*; **asinîhkahcikewin** (NI) *(Northern)*.

concur **ka pisci nîsopayihk** (VTA).

concurrence **nîsopayihcikewin** (NI).

concurrent **nîswesihcikewin** (NI).

concussion **kîskweyâpamowin** (NI); **kîskwesin** (VAI).

condemn **weyasowasowewin** (NI); **oyasowatâw** (VTA); **oyasowewin** (NI)

condensation **acowinikewin** (NI).

condense **kaconamihk kîkway** (VTI).

condensed **acowisihcikewin** (NI).

condescend **ka miyo otôtemihk** (VTA).

condescending **awîyak ka nihtâ otôtemit** (VTA).

condescension **miyo otôtemihtowin** (NI).

condition **tânsi isâyâwin** (NI); **isâyâwin** (NI).

conditional **kwayaskosihcikewin** (NI).

condolence **kitimâk mâmitoneyihtamowin** (NI).

condone **keyam ka iteyihtamihk** (VAI).

conduct **kîkway ka nîkaniskamihk** (VAI); **itâtisiwin pimipayitâw** (VTI).

confederation **mâmawinitowin** (NI).

conference **ka mâmawpekiskwehk** (VTA); **mamawapowin** (NI).

confess **ka âcimisohk** (VAI); **âcimisowin** (NI).

confessed **awîyak ka âcimisot** (VAI).

confession **âcimisowin** (NI); a confession to a priest, **âcimsostâkewin** (NI).

confessor **otâcimisohiwew** (NA).

confide **mamisîwin** (NI).

confidence S/he has confidence in people, **mamisîtotakew** (VTA); s/he has confidence in it, **mamisîtotam** (VTI); s/he has utmost confidence in her/him, **mamisîwakeyimew** (VTA).

confident Being confident in a general sense, believing, **tâpwehtamowin** (NI); being confident in one's abilities or skills, **sohkeyimowin** (NI).

confidential Keeping something to oneself, **kanaweyihtamâsowin** (NI).

confine **kipahikewin** (NI).

confinement **kipahikâsiwin** (NI).

confirm **ayiwâk kasohkisihtaht** (VAI).

confirmation **sohkiskâkewin** (NI).

confirmed **awîyak kasohkiskâht** (VAI).

confiscate S/he will confiscate it from her/him, **tamasaskonew** (VTA).

confiscation **ka maskahcihiwehk** (VTA).

conflagration A flaming fire, *iskotew* (NI); *kwakotew* (VAI).

conflict *nôtinitowin* (NI); *nôtinicowinis* (NI); *mâyiwecehtowin* (NI).

conform *kowicewâkanihk* (IPC).

conformation *wicewâkanihtowin* (NI).

conformist *owîcewâkanihiwew* (NA).

confound *ekâ kakeh nistawenamihk* (VAI).

confuse *ka wanâhitohk* (VTA).

confused *awîyak ka wanâhiht* (VTA).

confusion *wanâhiwewin* (NI).

congest *kiposkatowin* (NI).

congratulation *mamihcimowewin* (NI).

congregate They all get together, *mâmawipayiwak* (VAI).

congregation The act of getting together, *mâmawipayiwin* (NI); *mâmawi ayamihâwin* (NI).

conjure *ka mâmaskâsâpamohewehk* (VTA).

conjurer A spirit world guide, *omamâhtâwisiw* (NA); a conjurer or shaman, *okosâpahcikew* (NA).

connect *ka âniskômohcikehk* (VTI); *âniskotâw* (VTI).

connected *âniskômiw* (VTI).

connection *âniskômohcikewin* (NI).

conquer *awîyak ka sakocihiht* (VTA).

conqueror *osâkocihiwew* (NA).

conquest *sâkocihiwewin* (NI); s/he wins, *otahowew* (VTA).

conscience *mâmitoneyihcikan* (NA).

conscentious *kwayask mâmitoneyihcikewin* (NI).

conscious S/he is conscious, *pakahkamâyâw* (VAI); the act of making people conscious, *astâhiwewin* (NI)

consciousness *apâhkawâyâwin* (NI); s/he regains consciousness, *pakahkameyihtam* (VAI).

consecrate *kîkway kasaweyihcikatek* (VTI).

consecration *saweyihcikewin* (NI).

consecutive *nâhnâway isihcikewnah* (VTI); consecutively, from generation to generation, *âniskac* (IPC).

consent *pakiteyimowin* (NI).

consequence *kisipâyowin* (NI).

conserve *nahascikewin* (NI).

consider The act of thinking, *mâmitoneyihcikewin* (NI); s/he considers her/him spiritually powerful, *mamâhtâkweyimew* (VTA); s/he is considered to be more important, *nîkâneyihtâkosiw* (VAI); the act of being considered as being more important, *nîkâneyihtâkwan* (VII).

consideate *manâtisiwin* (NI).

consideration *nâkateyihcikewin* (NI).

considering *mâmitoneyihtamowin* (NI).

consistency *âhkameyihtamowin* (NI).

consistent *awîyak kâhkameyihtahk* (VAI).

consolation *kehcinahetowin* (NI).

console Consoling someone, *awîyak ka kâkecihiht* (VTA); the act of consoling, *kâkecihiwewin* (NI); s/he consoles her/him, *kâkecihew* (VTA); s/he speaks consolingly to her/him, *kâkecimew* (VTA).

consolidate *maskawâw isihcikewin* (VTI).

constant *tâpitawipayiw* (VAI).

constantly They constantly think of each other, *sôskwâc tâpitaweyihtowak* (VTA) *(Northern)*; *mâmâmitoneyihtowak* (VTA) *(Plains)*; s/he thinks of her/him constantly, *tâpitaweyimew* (VTA).

constipation Being bound up, *kisipikahcîwin* (NI).

constitute *nîkânapîhiwewin* (NI).

construct *osihcikew* (VAI); the act of making something; construction, *osihcikewin* (NI).

consult *kakwecikemowewin* (NI); *kakwecihkemowin* (NI).

consultation *pîkiskwâsowewin* (NI).

consume *mîciw* (VAI); *kitâw* (VTI).

contact *nakiskâtowin* (NI).

contain *nahascikewin* (NI).

container Something to hold materials, *asowacikan* (NI).

contaminate *misiwanâcihcikew* (VAI); s/he makes it poisonous, *piscipohtâw* (VTI).

contamination *misiwanâcihcikewin* (NI).

contemplation *kâkitaw mâmitoneyihtamowin* (NI) *(Northern)*; *peyahtik mâmitoneyihtamowin* (NI) *(Plains)*.

contemplative *awîyak peyahtik kamâmitonetahk* (VAI).

contemptible S/he finds her/him contemptible, *kohpâteyimew* (VTA); s/he is thought of as being contemptible, *kohpâteyitakosiw* (VAI); the act of being thought of as contemptible, *kohpâteyitâkosiwin* (NI); it is considered contemptible, *kohpâteyihtâkwan* (VII); s/he is considered contemptible, *maceyihtâkisiw* (VAI); the act of being contemptible, *maceyihtamowin* (NI); it is contemptible, *mâyeyihtâkwan* (VII).

contemptuous *opîweyecikew* (VAI).

contend *naskwâwin* (NI); *ohcinatew* (VTA).

content *naheyihtowin* (NI), *naheyihtam* (VTI).

contented *ka naheyihtamihk* (VAI).

contention *nahiwin* (NI).

contentment The act of contentment, *miweyihtamowin* (NI).

contents *mâwatascikewina* (NI).

contest *mawinehotowin* (NI).

contestant *omawinehikew* (NA).

continual *kîkway âhkami kîspayik* (VTI); *âhkameyihtam* (VTI).

277

continually *sôskwâc tâpitawipayiw* (VAI); it or s/he runs continually, *tâpitawipayiw* (VAI).

continuation *âhkam isihcikewin* (NI).

continue *âhkam etotamowin* (NI); *âhkameyihtamowin* (NI).

continuous *neyistaw* (IPC) *(Plains)*; *nayistaw* (IPC) *(Northern)*.

contort *mâyihkweyowin* (NI).

contour *cikâstesinowin* (NI).

contradict *pahpitos etacimowin* (NI); the act of making a liar out of yourself, *kiyâskehisowin* (NI); contradictory, *naspâciwepinikewin* (NI).

contrary *pîtosâyâwin* (NI); to the contrary, *tiyahkwac* (IPC).

contrast *naspâciwepinikewin* (NI).

contribute *pakitinikew* (VTI).

contribution *mekiwin* (NI).

contributor *omekiw* (NA).

contrite *mihtâtamowin* (NI); with sorrow, regretfully, with contrition, *kîsinâc* (IPC).

contrive *osihcikewin* (NI).

control The act of controlling, *paminkewin* (NI); s/he controls it, *paminam* (VTI); s/he has total control over her/him or them, *paminew* (VTA).

controller *opaminikew* (NA).

controversy *ka mâyeyihcihewehk* (VTA); blaming each other, *atâmeyimtowin* (NI).

controversialist *omâyipayihcikew* (NA).

convene *mâmawipayowin* (NI).

convenient *nahipayiw* (VAI), (VTI) *or* (VII).

conventional *ka isinahiskamomakahk* (VII).

conversation *âcimostatowin* (NI); *âcimostakewin* (NI).

conversational *ka âtotamihk kîkway* (VAI).

conversion *meskoc isihcikewin* (NI).

convert *kweskâyamihâw* (NA).

convey *awatamakewin* (NI); giving someone or something a ride, *pôsihew* (VTA); *pôsitâw* (VTI).

convince S/he convinced her/him to do something, *kâskimew* (VTA); the act of convincing someone, *sâkocihiwewin* (NI).

convincing *sâkocihiwewin* (NI).

cook *okîstepiw* (NA); s/he cooks it, *kîsiswew* (VTA); s/he cooks it, *kîsisam* (VTI); s/he cooks, *kîstepiw* (VAI) *(Northern)*; *piminawasiw* (VAI) *(Plains)*; the act of cooking, *kîstipowin* (NI); s/he cooks for her/him or them, *kîstipohew* (VTA) *(Northern)*; *piminawatew* (VTA) *(Plains)*; it is cooked or burned, *kîsitew* (VII); it is cooked hard by fire, *maskawihkahtew* (VAI); it is cooked hard by fire, *maskawihkasiw* (VTA); s/he cooks it hard, i.e.: bannock, *maskawihkaswew* (VTA); it is cooked on the inside and its outside peels off, i.e.: a baked potato, *pehtohkasiw* (VII); s/he cooks them on the inside, *pehtohkaswew* (VTA).

cool Being a little cool, *ka cakayasik* (VII); it is a little bit cool, i.e.: weather, *cahkayasin* (VII); it is kind of cool, *kisinayaw* (VII); it is nice and cool, *miyotahkayâw* (VII); s/he cooled her/him down with her/his hands, *tahkinew* (VTA); s/he causes her/him to cool off, *tahkipayihew* (VTA); s/he lets them cool off, *tahkisimew* (VTI).

cooperate *ka wicewâkanihtohk* (VTA).

cooperation *wicewâkanihtowin* (NI).

co-operative Being willing to co-operate, *miyowicehtowin* (NI).

coordinate *ka nîsohkamakehk* (VTA).

coordination *nîsohkamâkewin* (NI).

cope *kîkway ka nîpawistamihk* (VTI).

copulate *ka nîswamohk* (VTI).

copy The act of copying, *naspasinahikewin* (NI); writing the same way, *tâpasinahikan* (NI).

cord A long cord, *kinwâpekisiw* (NA); *kinwâpekan* (NI); strong cord, *maskawâpekisiw* (NA); *maskawâpekan* (NI); flattened, *napakâpekisiw* (NA); *napakâpekan* (NI); twisted, *pimâpekisiw* (NA); *pimâpekan* (NI); a small cord, *apistapekisiw* (NA); *apistapekan* (NI); short, *cimâpekisiw* (NA); *cimâpekan* (NI); a cord of firewood, *pâsimihtân* (NI); a piece of small twine or string, *pîminahkwânis* (NI).

cork A bottle cover, *kipahikan* (NI).

corn One ear of corn, *mahtâmin* (NA).

corner *wihkwehtakâw* (LN).

cornfield *mahtâmin kistikân* (NI).

cornflower *mahtâminwapekonis* (NI).

corpse *miyaw* (NI).

corral A horse fence, *mistatim wasakanikan* (NI); *mistatim menikan* (NI); a fenced in area for keeping horses, i.e.: a corral, *kanawastimwân* (NA).

correct It is right or correct, *kwayask* (IPC); it is okay, *ekosi* (IPC); doing something correctly, *kâtawahk*; s/he places it correctly, *kwayaskwahew* (VTI); s/he has a correct opinion, *kwayaskweyihtam* (VAI); conceptually correct, *kwayaskweyihtamowin* (NI).

corrected *kîkway ka kwayaskwastahk* (VTI).

correction *kwayaskwasihcikewin* (NI).

correspond The very same, *pahpeyakwan* (IPC); the act of corresponding or letter writing, *masinahamâtowin* (NI).

corresponding *pahpeyakwan itôtamowin* (NI).

corrode *ka kipomesiyapisak* (VTI).

cost What something costs, *tansi ka etakihtek* (VII); it costs, *itakihtew* (VII); s/he costs, *itakisiw* (VAI); it costs a lot or plenty, *mistakihtew* (VTI).

costly *kîkway emistakihtek* (VII); it is costly, *mistakihtew* (VTI).

costume *wawesihowin* (NI); *wawesiwasâkay* (NI).

cosy *ka kîsowak* (VTI).

cot *peyakohkwamiw nipewinis* (NI).

cottonwood *mâyimitos* (NA).

cougar *misipisiw* (NA) *(Northern)*; *misiminôs* (NA) *(Plains)*; *pakwaciminôs* (NA) *(Plains)*.

cough *ostostotamowin* (NI); s/he coughs, *ostostotam* (VAI); a cough syrup or remedy, *ostostotamômaskihkîy* (NI).

coughing *ka ostostotamihk* (VAI).

could *kaskihtâwin* (NI).

coulee *ka misiwayatinak* (LN); *misiwâti* (NI).

counsel *opîkiskwestamâkew* (NA).

count *akihcikewin* (NI).

country Land, *askîy* (NI); somebody's homeland, *awîyak otaskehk* (VAI); *awîyak otaskiw* (VAI).

countryman A person living in the same country, *wetaskemâkan* (NA).

couple *ka nesihk* (VTA); *enesihk* (VTA).

courage *ka sohkeyimohk* (VAI).

courageous *sohkeyimowin* (NI); *nâpihkâsiwin* (NI).

course *tahtapipimohtewin* (NI).

courteous *ka manâtisihk* (VAI).

courtesy *manâcihiwewin* (NI).

courtship *nitawâpamiskwewewin* (NI).

cousin *wahkomakan* (NA); my first cousin, *nistes* (NA); *nimis* (NA); *niciwam* (NA); *nîtim* (NA); second cousin, a man calls a man, *nîscas* (NA); second cousin, a man calls a woman, *nîcimos* (NA); *nîtim* (NA); second cousin, a woman calls a man, *nîcimos* (NA); *nîtim* (NA); second cousin, a woman calls a woman, *nîcakos* (NA); your cousin, *kiciwam* (NA); he is a cousin, *ociwâmimâw* (VAI); she is a cousin, *ociwâmiskwemâw* (VAI); they are cousins, *ociwâmihtowak* (VAI); being cousins, *kôciwamihtohk* (NI); being cousins or a cousin relationship, *ociwâmihtowin* (NI).

cove *wâsâsin* (NI).

cover Or lid, *akwanâpowehikan* (NI); a blanket, *akohp* (NI); s/he covers her/him with evergreen branches, *ayasihtakinew* (VTA); s/he covers her/him with hay, *ayaskosiwepinew* (VTI); s/he covers her/him with earth, *ayahcinew* (VTI); s/he covers her/him with snow, *ayâkonehwew* (VTI); s/he hides it in the ground, *ayahcinam* (VTI); s/he covers it over with earth, *ayahcinam* (VTI); s/he covers a body, *nahinew* (VTA); s/he covers it, *akwanaham* (VTI); s/he is covered up, *akwanahiw* (VAI); it is covered over by some material, *ayipayiw* (VAI) (VII).

covered *akwanâpowehikewin* (NI); openly, visibly, not hidden or not covered up, *mosis* (IPC).

covering *akwanahikan* (NI); a waterproof covering for a shelter, i.e.: a tarpaulin, *apahkwâsonekin* (NI) *(Plains)*; *apahkwânekin* (NI) *(Northern)*.

covet *akâwâsowewin* (NI); the act of coveting, *akâwâcikewin* (NI).

cow *mostos* (NA); *nôsemostos* (NA) *(Northern)*; *onîcâniw* (NA) *(Plains)*; plains buffalo, *paskwâwimostos* (NA) *(Plains)*; woods bison, *sakâwmostos* (NA); a castrated cow, *ayihkwewimostos* (NA); a prairie cow, *maskotewimostos* (NA).

coward *awîyak kakostâciskit* (VAI); *sâkotehesk* (NA).

cowardliness *ka nipahitehehk* (VAI).

cowardly *nipahitehewin* (NI).

cowhide *mostoswekin* (NA); *mostosowayân* (NA).

coy *nepewisiskiwin* (NI).

coyote A big coyote, *mîstacakan* (NA); a little coyote, *mîscacâkanis* (NA) *(Northern)*; *mescacâkanis* (NA) *(Plains)*.

cozy *kîsowâsin* (NI).

crack A crack in the floor, *tawihtakaw* (VII); it cracks, *tawipayiw* (VII); it is a crack, fissure, or crevice in the ground, i.e.: in a field, *pasahcipayiw* (VAI); s/he cracks it with her/his teeth, *paskamew* (VAI); s/he cracks them with her/his fingers, *pâstinew* (VTA); it or s/he cracks on its or her/his own, i.e.: an egg, *pâstipayiw* (VAI); it blew out or it cracked open, i.e.: a car tire, *pâstisin* (VII); it cracks when it falls, i.e.: a globe from a lamp or an egg, *pâstihtin* (VII); s/he cracks open someone's head and gives her/him a scar, *pîkostikwânewew* (VTA); s/he falls and cracks her/his head, *pîkostikwânesin* (VTA).

crackle Fire crackling, *iskotew kapâhpaskitek* (VTI); it is crackling, *papaskitew* (VII); the fire cracks, sparks audibly, or sizzles while cooking, *cowehkahtew* (VII); it is so cold you can hear it crackle, i.e.: ice, *matweyaskatin* (VII).

cradle A pack in which native women place babies, *wâspison* (NI); a swinging cradle, *wewepisowinis* (NI); s/he is laced up in a mossbag, *wâspisiw* (VAI); a baby swing, *awâsisowepisin* (NI).

cradleboard *wâspisonâhtik* (NI).

craft *ka nihtâosihcikehk* (VAI); *osihcikewin* (NI).

craftiness *nihtâwosihcikewin* (NI).

craftsman *atoskatamowin* (NI); a person good at making things, *otôsihcikew* (NA).

crafty *nihtâwihcikewin* (NI).

crag *ka sisikoc kîskâpiskâk* (LN).

cram *ka kipwaskenahcikehk* (VTI).

cramp Having cramps, *kocipitikoskihk* (IPC); the act of cramping, *ocipitikowin* (NI); s/he has cramps, *ocipitikiw* (VAI).

cranberry A low bush cranberry, *wîsakimin* (NA); a high bush cranberry or mooseberry, *môsômin* (NI); *nîpiniminân* (NI).

279

crane Or a long legged bird, *ocicâhk* (NA); a crane of a machine for lifting, *ohpahpekipicikan* (NI)

cranky *kisôweyihtam* (VAI).

crash *ka tâwahototwaw otâpânâskwak* (NA).

crate A wooden box, *mistikowatihkân* (NI).

crawl The act of crawling, i.e.: on one's knees, *pimitâcimowin* (NI); s/he crawls, i.e.: on her/his knees, *pimitâcimow* (VAI); s/he crawls around everywhere, *papâmitâcimow* (VAI); s/he crawls right through, i.e.: a hole, *sâpoyahkiw* (VAI); s/he crawls or creeps underneath something, *sekow* (VAI); s/he makes her/him crawl underneath, *sekoyahkîhew* (VTA) *(Northern)*; *sikoyahkinew* (VTA) *(Plains)*; s/he crawls under, i.e.: blankets, *sekoyahkiw* (VAI).

crazy Being crazy, *ka môhcowihk* (VAI); s/he acts crazily, *kakepatisihkâsow* (VAI) *(Northern)*; *mohcohkâsow* (VAI) *(Plains)*; *kakepatisihkew* (VAI) *(Northern)*; *kakepâcâyihtiw* (VAI) *(Plains)*; s/he is crazy, *keskwew* (VAI); fool! crazy fool, *kîskwehkan* (NA); s/he makes her/him go crazy or wild, *kîskwehew* (VTA); s/he gets into everything, *kîskwehkamikisiw* (VAI); the act of being wild, crazy, uncontrolled, *kîskwehkamikisiwin* (NI); her/his talking makes her/him act wild or crazy, *kîskwemew* (VTA); the act of going crazy or mad, *kîskwewin* (NI); a crazy character, *kîskweyâtisowin* (NA); s/he has a wild character or personality, *kîskweyâtisiw* (VAI); s/he is going crazy over something, *kîskweyeyihtam* (VAI); s/he is seen as wild or crazy, *kîskweyihtâkosiw* (VAI); it is thought of as crazy, *kîskweyihtâkwan* (VII); s/he is a crazy type or character, *môcowâtisiw* (VAI); craziness or foolishness, *môcowâtisowin* (NI); s/he thinks she/he or they are crazy or foolish, *môcoweyimew* (VTA); s/he is crazy or foolish, *môcowiw* (VAI); the act of craziness or foolishness, *môcowiwin* (NI); a wild, crazy, and insane person, *okîskwiw* (NA).

creak *ka kiceskihtakak* (VTI); *kiceskwew* (VTI).

cream *manahikan* (NI).

create When something is given life; *kanihtâwihtahk kîkway* (VTI).

creation *nihtâwihcikewin* (NI).

creator A maker of people, *otôsihiwew* (NA); a creator of things, *otôsihcikew* (NA).

creature *pisiskiwâyis* (NA).

Cree An aboriginal language, i.e.: Cree, *nehiyawemowin* (NI) *(Northern)*; *nehiyawewin* (NI) *(Plains)*; the Cree people, *nehiyawak* (NA); a Cree person, *nehiyaw* (NA).

creed *tâpwewakeyihtamowin* (NI); a believing prayer, *tâpwehtamowin* (NI); *ayamihawin* (NI); *âpateyihtamowin* (NI).

creek *sîpîsis* (NI).

creep *ka nâciyôscikehk* (VAI); *papâmitâcimow* (VAI); the act of crawling on hands and knees, *papâmitâcimowin* (NI).

crest *takohtâmatin* (VII).

crested *tahkohtâmaciwewin* (NI).

crew A group of working men, *atoskeweyiniwak* (NA).

crib *apiscawâsis onipewinis* (NI); a baby bed, *awâsisonipewinis* (NI).

cricket *kwâskocisîs* (NA).

cries It cries, *mâtow* (VAI).

crimp *nânapwekinkewin* (NI)

crimson *mihkwâw* (VII); *mihkonâkwan* (VII).

cringe *ka waneyehtamamohk* (VAI).

crinkle *ka nâhnâtohkwekinkehk* (VTI).

cripple Being crippled, *ka mâskisihk* (VAI); s/he is crippled, *mâskisiw* (VAI); the act of being crippled, *mâskisowin* (NI); s/he will be crippled by sickness, *tamâskahpinew* (VAI); s/he will cripple someone, *tamâskahpinasiw* (VTA).

crisis *astâmipayiw* (VAI).

crisp *ka kâspâk* (VTI); *kâspâw* (VII); *kâspisiw* (VII) *(Northern)*; *kâspihkasikanis* (VII) *(Plains)*.

crisply *ka kâspayak*.

critical *awîyak koyotahk kahkeyakîkway* (VTI).

criticism *âyimwewin* (NI); talking about people, *âyimomiwewin* (NI).

criticize *awîyak kahastemiht* (VTA).

croak *mayokwatay ka kitot* (VAI); *kitow* (VAI).

crock *mîkisiyâkan* (NI).

crockery *asiskîwîyâkana* (NI).

crook *wawakisiw* (NA) *or* (VAI).

crooked A dishonest person, *awîyak kâwâksit* (VAI); something crooked or warped, *wâkaw* (VII); it went crooked, *wâkipayiw* (VII) *or* (VAI); it went crooked, *wâkipayin* (VII); it is crooked and twisted or warped, i.e.: something metallic such as a frying pan, *pîmâpiskisin* (VAI); *wâkâpiskisiw* (VII); it is crooked and twisted or warped, i.e.: something metallic such as a car door, *pîmâpiskihtin* (VAI); it is crooked and twisted, i.e.: a tree, *pîmâskisiw* (VAI); it is crooked and twisted, i.e.: a pole, *pîmâskwan* (VII); it is crooked or slanted, *pîmâw* (VII); s/he makes them crooked, *pîmisîhew* (VTI); s/he wears it crooked or cockeyed, i.e.: a hat or s/he found it on her/his way up, *pîmiskam* (VII); s/he wears it crooked or cockeyed, i.e.: shirt or s/he found her/him or them on her/his way up, *pîmiskawew* (VTA); s/he is crooked or slanted, *pîmisiw* (VII); it goes crooked, *wakâskisiw* (VAI); it is made crooked by the wind, *wâkâsiw* (VII).

crop *ohpikihcikewin* (NI); *kistikewin* (NI).

cross A Christian cross, *ayamihewâhtik* (NA); s/he makes her/him cross the road, *pîmiskanawehew* (VTA)

(Northern); *âsowakâmetisahwew* (VTA) *(Plains)*; s/he crosses the road, *pîmiskanawew* (VAI) *(Northern)*; *âsowakamehtew* (VAI) *(Plains)*.

crossroad Where the roads cross, *ayamihewâhtikopayiw meskanaw* (NI).

crossways Going across on an angle, i.e.: crossways, *pîmakâm* (IPC); s/he goes crossways over the water to the other shore, *pîmakâmeham* (VAI); s/he places her/him crossways, *pimitahew* (VTA); s/he sticks them on crossways, *pimitamohew* (VAI); it is extended crossways, *pimitamiw* (VII); s/he is seated crossways, *pimitapiw* (VAI); s/he hangs them crossways, i.e.: on a pole, *pimitaskwahew* (VTI); s/he extends them crossways, i.e.: on a road, *pimitaskwamohew* (VTI); it extends crossways onto the road, *pimitaskwamiw* (VII); it is placed crossways, *pimitastew* (VII).

crossing *âsiwahonân* (NI).

crotch *micicâskâhk* (NI).

crouch The act of crouching down, *ka samakehk* (VTI); s/he crouches down suddenly, *samakipayihow* (VAI).

crow The raven, *kahkakow* (NA) *(Northern)*; *âhâsiw* (NA)

crowd *ka mihcetihk* (VTA).

crowded *kosâmiyatihk* (NI).

crucifix *ayamihewâhtik* (NA).

crucify *cestahaskwasiwewin* (NI).

cruel The act of being cruel, *kâmacatisihk* (NI); being cruel, *kitimahtâsowin* (NI); s/he is cruel to someone, *kitimahtâsiw* (VTA).

cruelty *macâtisiwin* (NI) .

crumb *pîwahcikan* (NI); s/he is dropping crumbs while eating, i.e.: bread, *pîwamew* (VAI).

crumble *napiwekinikewin* (NI).

crumbly *ka napwekak kîkway* (VTI).

crumple *ka pitikonamihk kîkway* (VTI).

crunch Eating something with a crunching noise, *ka kakâspahcikehk* (VTI); s/he eats it with a crunching noise, *kâspahtam* (VTI); s/he breaks it with a crunchy noise, *kaspinew* (VTI).

crush *ka sikwahamihk kîkway* (VTI); *sikona* (VTI); *sikwataha* (VTI); s/he crushes them with her/his hands, *sikonew* (VTI); s/he crushes her/him with her/his foot, *sikoskawew* (VTA); s/he crushes them to pieces by striking them, *sikowepawew* (VTI); s/he crushes them, *sikwahwew* (VTI); s/he is crushed or smashed to pieces, *sikwatahikâsiw* (VAI); it is crushed or smashed to pieces, *sikwatahikâtew* (VII); s/he crushes or grinds them to pieces, *sikwatahwew* (VTA).

crust *ka maskawihkasot pahkwesikan* (NA).

crusty *ka kâspihkahtek kîkway* (VTI).

crutch *kwâskweyâskwahoswâkan* (NI); a walking cane, *saskahotakan* (NI); *saskahon* (NI); s/he walks with crutches, *kwâskweyâskwahosiw* (VAI).

cry S/he cries, *mâtow* (VAI); s/he can be heard crying from a distance, *matwemâtiw* (VAI); s/he makes her/him cry, *mohew* (VTA); *môskohew* (VTA); s/he cries over something sad, *môskweyihtam* (VAI); s/he cried herself/himself to sleep, *nipahimiw* (VAI); s/he goes crying here and there, *papâmatwemow* (VAI); s/he cries with her/him, *wîcimatomew* (VTA).

crying *mâtowin* (NI).

cub *maskosis* (NA).

cucumber "Our late grandmother", *kohkomin* (NA) *(Northern)*; *kohkompaninawak* (NA) *(Plains)*.

cuddle *metoni ka sihtintohk* (VTA).

cue *ka kiskisohiwehk* (VTA).

cuff *kispison* (NI).

cull A rejected item, *asenikewin* (NI).

culmination *metoni kisipipayowin* (NI).

culprit *awîyak otôtamowin* (NI); *nipahtâkew* (VTA); *mâyitôtâkew* (VTA).

cultivate *ka sikwahcahikehk* (VTI); smashing up ground, *sikwahcahikewin* (NI).

cultivated *ka sikwahcahamihk* (VTI).

cultivation *sikwahcahikewin* (NI).

culture *tansi kesihtwahk* (VAI); *isihtwâwin* (NI); *isipimâtisiwin* (NI).

cunning *metoni îyinisiwin* (NI).

cup *minihkwâcikanis* (NI) *(Northern)*; *minihkwewîyâkanis* (NI) *(Plains)*; a drinking cup, *minihkwâcikan* (NI).

cupboard A place for dishes, *oyâkanikamik* (NI); *akocikan* (NI).

curable *ka nihtâ nâtawihohk* (VAI).

curative *nâtawihwâkan* (NI).

cure The act of recuperation, *âstepayowin* (NI); s/he cure her/him, *âstewew* (VTA); s/he makes her/him feel better, *âstihwew* (VTA) ; s/he is cured, *âstepayiw* (VAI); the act of curing, *âpacihiwewin* (NI).

curl S/he curls her/his own hair, *tipawehamaw* (VTA); s/he curls it, *tipaweham* (VTI); s/he curls his hair, *tipawehamawew* (VTA).

curler A hair curler or roller, *tipawehamâkan* (NI).

curling *asinîwepinikewin* (NI).

curly *makotowepayowin* (NI).

currant berry A black currant, *manitômin* (NA); a black currant bush, *manitominâhtik* (NA).

current *sîpî ka pimcowahk* (VTI); *pimicowan* (VII); heaped up, piled up by water, *âsapokîw* (VAI); *âsapotew* (VII); carried backwards, back by current, *aseyâpokiw* (VAI); *aseyâpotew* (VII); driven off by a current, *mahâpokow* (VAI); *mahâpotew* (VII); it flows, *nihtâciwan* (VII); it flows in the middle, in the middle of the current, *tâwiciwan* (VII); the current comes from there, *ociciwan* (VII); the current turns in a round, a funnel, *wâwiyeciwan* (VII); you can hear the

281

current, water flow, **matweciwan** (VII); there is a strong current, **sohkeciwan** (VII).

currently **mekwâcoma** (IPC).

curse S/he invokes a curse on her/him, **pâstamew** (VTA); s/he curses herself/himself or plagues herself/himself with bad luck, **pâstâmiw** (VTA); the act of cursing oneself or plaguing oneself with bad luck, **pâstâmowin** (NI); s/he is being cursed by someone, **pâstâmâw** (VAI); s/he puts a curse on him, **asomew** (VTA); the act of placing a curse on someone, **mayakwamitowin** (NI)

cursed S/he is cursed, **pâstâpâyiw** (VAI); **pâstamâw** (VAI).

curve A road with curves or bends, **ka wâkamok meskanaw** (VTI); it is curved, **wakamon** (VII); it curves a lot, i.e.: a road, **wahwâkamiw** (VAI); it curves a lot, i.e.: a river, **wahwâkihtin** (VII); the river has a lot of curves and bends, **wahwâkistikweyâw** (VAI).

curved **kîkway ewakak** (VTI).

cushion **aspapowin tehtapiwinihk** (NI).

cuss **wîyahkwew pîkiskwewin** (NI).

custom **nakâyâtotamowin** (NI); **isihtwawin** (NI).

customarily **nakayâtotamowinihk** (IP).

customary **ka nakâyâtotamihk** (VAI).

cut Cutting something, **kamansamihk kîkway** (VTI); s/he cuts the model out, **naspisâwâtew** (VTA); it is cut off, i.e.: pants, **kîskisikâsiw** (VTI); it is cut off, i.e.: rope or wire, **kîskisikâtew** (VII); the cut off or detached thing, **kîskisikan** (NI); s/he cuts herself/himself off from people or hanging up on the phone, **kîskisosiw** (VTA); the act of cutting one's self off from people or on the phone, **kîskisosiwin** (NI); s/he cuts it off, **kîskiswew** (VTI); s/he cuts or severs the face from her/his picture, **kîskihkweswew** (VTA); s/he cuts the tail off, **kîskâyoweswew** (VTA); s/he cuts it off with a knife, **kîskihkotam** (VTI); s/he cuts the joints of an animal, **kotokiswew** (VTA); s/he cuts hay with a scythe, **manaskosiwew** (VTA); the act of cutting hay with a scythe, **manaskosiwewin** (NI); s/he cuts off the neck or its neck with a knife, **manikwayaweswew** (NA); s/he cuts her/him or them off, **manisawâtew** (VTA); an instrument for cutting, i.e.: a sickle, **manisikâkan** (NI); the act of cutting crops or grain, **manisikewin** (NI); s/he cuts off her/his head or their heads, **manistikwâneswew** (VTA); s/he cuts her/him or them with scissors or a knife, **maniswew** (VTA); it is cut flat, **napakihkotew** (VTI); s/he cuts them off, **paskiswew** (VTI); s/he cuts her/his hair off, **paskoswew** (VTA); s/he cuts a hole in them, **payipiswew** (VTI); s/he cuts them into small pieces, **pîkinsâwâtew** (VTI); s/he cuts them into pieces or bits, **pîkoswew** (VTI); s/he cuts them all up, **pîwihkotew** (VTA); s/he leaves remnants of them cut up, **pîwiswew** (VTI); machine for cutting things up, **sikopocikan** (NI); it is cut up, i.e.: tobacco, **sikohkosiw** (VII) *(Northern)*; **sokopocikâsow** (VII) *(Plains)*; s/he cuts them up into small pieces, **sikohkotew** (VAI); s/he cuts them in half, **tâskihkotew** (VTA); s/he cuts them in half with a knife, **tâskiswew** (VTA); s/he cuts a clearing with an axe, **tawikahikew** (VAI); it is cut clear, **tawikahikâsiw** (VAI); it is cut clear, **tawikahikâtew** (VII); s/he cuts it to make a clearing, **tawikahwew** (VTA); s/he cuts a hole in them, i.e.: a pair of pants, **yâyikâhwew** (VTI).

cutting **ka mekwâmansikehk** (VTI).

D

dab *apisis* (IPC).

daily *tahto kîsikâw* (VII).

daintiness *osâm miyonâkosiwin* (NI).

dam A beaver dam, *oskwatim* (NI).

damage *pîkonikewin* (NI).

damp Dampness or being moist, *miyamawisowin* (NI) *(Northern)*; *miyimawisiwin* (NI) *(Plains)*; it is damp and humid, *miyamawâw* (VII) *(Northern)*; *miyimawâw* (VII) *(Plains)*; s/he or it is damp or moist, *miyamawisiw* (VAI) *(Northern)*; *miyimawisiw* (VAI) *(Plains)*.

dampen Wet; it is dampened by water, *miyamâpawew* (VII); s/he dampens it, *miyamawinew* (VAI); *miyimawinew* (VAI).

dance *nîmihitowin* (NI); *nimihtowin* (NI); the opening dance, *mâcisimowin* (NI); tea dance or lame dance, *mâskisimowin* (NI); s/he dances, *nîmihitow* (VAI); a dance hall, *nîmihitowikamik* (NI); a trance-inducing ceremonial dance, *nipâhkwesimowin* (NI).

dancer *onîmiheto* (NA); s/he is an excellent dancer, *nihtâwisimow* (VAI).

dandelion *osâwâpikones* (NI).

danger *ka kostamihk kîkway*.

dangerous Being thought of as dangerous, *kakwespaneyihtâkosiwin* (NI); s/he is afraid of her/him and thinks of her/him as dangerous, *kakwespâneyimew* (VTA); s/he is considered dangerous by everyone, *kakwespâneyihtâkosiw* (VAI); it is thought of as dangerous, *kakwespâneyihtâkwan* (VII).

dangle *ka akotek kîkway* (VTI); something hanging, *kosâwekotew* (VII); *kosâwekocin* (NI).

dare *nâpihkâsiwin* (NI).

daring *ka nâpehkâsohk* (VAI).

dark *ka kaskitipiskak*; it is dark in color, *kaskitewâw* (VII); in darkness, *tipiskanohk* (IPC); in deep darkness, *kaskitipiskanohk* (IPC); it is very dark, *kaskitipiskâw* (VII); it is pitch dark, *wanitipiskâw* (VII); it is getting dark, *ati tipiskâw* (VII); s/he makes it go dark or s/he turns the light off, *wanitipiskinam* (VII); in the dark, *wanitipiskanohk* (LN); it went dark suddenly, *wanitipiskipayiw* (VII); it went dark on her/him, *wanitipiskisiw* (VAI); s/he makes it dark for her/him, *wanitipiskinamawew* (VTA).

darn *mîsahasikanewin* (NI).

dart *pîmosenacikewepinkansa* (NI).

date *kiskimowin* (NI); at that time, *ekospi* (IPC).

daughter *mitânisimâw* (NA); *otânisimâw* (NA); someone's daughter, *awîyak otânsa* (VTA); my daughter, *nitânis* (NA); s/he has her for a daughter, *otânisimew* (VTA); *otânisihkâw* (VTA) *(Plains)*; s/he has a daughter, *otânisiw* (VAI).

daughter-in-law *nahâkaniskwem* (NDA); *nistim* (NA).

daughter *otânisimâw* (NA); my daughter, *nitânis* (NA); someone's daughter, *awîyak otânsa* (NA); s/he has her for a daughter, *otânisihkâwew* (VTA) *(Plains)*, *otânisimew* (VTA) *(Northern)*; s/he has a daughter, *otânisiw* (VAI).

daughter-in-law *ostimâw* (NA); *nahâkaniskwem* (NDA); my daughter-in-law (or sister's daughter), *nistim* (NA); my daughter-in-law, *ninahâkaniskwem* (NDA); *ninahâhkisîm* (NA) *(Plains)*.

dauntless *nâpihkâsiwin* (NI).

dawdle S/he is dawdling on the way, *pemâmitâwew* (VAI).

dawn *naspikeksepa* (VAI); *petâpan* (VAI).

day It is daytime or day or daylight, *kîsikâw* (VII); *kîsikaki* (VII); day after tomorrow, *awasiwapahki* (VII); it is full day, *ispîhkisikâw* (VII); it is a nice day, good weather, *miyokîsikâw* (VII); it is a bad day, bad weather, *mâyikisikâw* (VII); it looks like it is going to be a nice day or it has to be a nice day, *nohtemiyokîsikâw* (VII); it will be a nice day, *wimiyokîsikâw* (VII); all day, *kapekîsik* (IPC); on a moonlight night, the moon shines like the daylight, *kîsikayastew* (VII); s/he spends the whole day, *kîsikanisiw* (VAI); the act of spending the whole day somewhere, *kîsikanisowin* (NI); it is daytime right now, *mekwâkîsikâw* (VII); sometime during the day, *nayewac kîsikâw* (VII).

daybreak When daylight comes, *ka petâpahk* (VII); daylight is incoming, i.e.: daybreak, *peciwâpan* (VAI) *(Northern)*; *petâpan* (VAI) *(Plains)*; the dawn begins to appear, i.e.: daybreak, *petâpan* (VAI).

daylight *kâ kîsiwâpahk* (VII); it is daylight, *wâpan* (VII); daylight just starts, first light of day, *petâpan* (VAI) *(Plains)*; *peciwâpan* (VAI) *(Northern)*; *petâpaw* (VAI) *(Plains)*.

daylong The whole day, all day long, *kapekîsik* (IPC).

daytime *ka mekwa kîsikak* (VII).

daze S/he dazed her/him by pounding her/his head on something *kîskwesimew* (VTA); s/he is stunned or dazed, *kîskwesin* (VAI).

dead Someone who is dead, *awîyak kanepit* (VAI); it is dead, i.e.: a plant, *nipemakan* (VII); s/he is dead, *naspicinipiw* (VAI) *(Northern)*; *pônipimâtisiw* (VAI) *(Plains)*; *nipiw* (VAI) *(Plains)*; her/his spirit life is dead, *nipowatisiw* (VAI).

283

deadly Without life, *nipahâyâwin* (NI).

deaf Being deaf, *kipihtewin* (NI); a deaf ear, *kipihtawakay* (NI); s/he is deaf, *kipihtew* (VAI).

deafen *kipihtehowewin* (NI).

deal *isihcikatitowin* (NI).

dealing *isihcikewin* (NI).

death The end of living, *poni pîmâcisiwin* (NI); a sudden death from an illness, *kîyipahpinewin* (NI); s/he has a death in the family, *mâyipayiw* (VAI); the act of having a death in the family, *mâyipayiwin* (NI).

debark *kapawin osihk ohci; misakâw* (VAI) *(Northern)*; *kapâw* (VAI) *(Plains)*.

debate *kîkway ka mâmiskotamihk* (VAI); debating or engaging in an argument, *pîkiswacikewin* (NI).

debauch *misiwanâcihcikewin* (NI).

debility Being weak, *nesowisiwin* (NI).

decapitate *awîyak ka kaskwesawatiht* (VTA).

decay *ka misiwanâtahk kîkway* (VTI).

decease *nipowatisiw* (VAI).

deceased *awîyak ka poni pîmâtisit* (VTA).

deceit Doing something crooked, *kayesiwin* (NI).

deceitful Very crooked behavior or deceit; *kakayesiwin* (NI); deceitful conduct, *kakayesihtwâwin* (NI); s/he is deceitful, *kakayesihtwâw* (VAI).

deceive The act of telling lies, *kakeyaskiskowin* (NI); one who deceives people by her/his actions, *cîsihiwew* (NA); one who lies to fool people, *cîsihkemiw* (VAI); a teller of fibs, *cîsimiwew* (NA); delusion, error, deceptive talk, falsehood, *cîsimiwewin* (NI); s/he deceived her/him or told her/him a fib, *cîsimew* (VTA); s/he deceives her/him, *kakayesihew* (VTA); s/he deceives her/him by pretending to be someone else, *cîsihew* (VTA); deceiving people, *cîsihiwewin* (NI); s/he is mistaken, mistaking one for someone else, *cîsihiw* (VAI); being mistaken, *cîsihowin* (NI); s/he speaks deceitfully, *kakayesipikiskwew* (VAI); s/he is considered deceitful or misleading or dishonest, *kakayesiyihtâkosiw* (VAI).

deceiver *ocesihiwew* (NA).

December The tree cleaning moon or month, *pawahcakinasîs* (NA); drift cleaning moon or month, *pawahcakinasîs* (NA) *(Plains)*; God's moon or month, *manitow kîsikan pîsim* (NI).

decency *kwayaskwesâyâwin* (NI).

decent *kwayaskwâtisiwin* (NI) *(Plains)*; *kwayaskwesâyawin* (NI) *(Northern)*.

deception *wayesihiwewin* (NI).

deceptive *wayesihiweskiwin* (NI).

decide *keseyehtamowin* (NI); *keseyihtam* (VTI).

decision *kese isihcikewin* (NI).

declamation *âyimwewin* (NI).

declaration *ka wehtamihk kîkway* (VAI).

declare *kwayask wîhtamowewin* (NI).

decline *asipayihowin* (NI).

decompose *ka mestatitihk kîkway* (VTI); *misiwanâtan* (VII).

decorate *wawesihtâw* (VTI); making something look good, *wawesehcikewin* (NI).

decoration A room decoration, *kiskinowâcihcikan* (NA); a dress-up decoration, i.e.: a brooch, tie, or bracelet, *wawisihcikana* (NA); s/he decorates her/him, *kiskinowâcihew* (VTA).

decorative *kîkway ka wawesiwnakwahk* (VTI).

decoy *sîsîpihkan* (NI).

decrease *pahkwenam* (VTI).

decree *kihci wiyâsowewin* (NI).

dedicate *awîyak ka nîkamostamaht* (VTA).

dedication *nîkamostamakewin* (NI).

deed *tôtamowin* (NI).

deem *mosci iteyihtamiwin* (NI).

deep It is very deep, *metoni timîw* (VII); it is deep, i.e.: water, *timîw* (VII); the snow is deep all over, *timâkonakâw* (VII) *(Northern)*; *timikoniw* (VII) *(Plains and Northern variant)*; the grass is deep, high, or long, *timaskâw* (VII); the snow is deep, i.e.: refers to one area only, *timikoniw* (VII).

deer *âpisimôsos* (NA) *(Northern)*; *âpiscimôsis* (NA) *(Plains)*.

deerberry *atihkomin* (NI).

deface *ka wanisihtahk kîkway*.

defacement *wanisihcikewin* (NI).

defamatory *mâyimâmiskomowewin* (NI).

defame *awîyak ka mâyimâmiskomiht*.

default *ka patahamihk isihcikewin*.

defeat The act of defeating someone, *paskiyâkewin* (NI); s/he defeats her/him, *paskiyawew* (VTA); s/he defeats her/him decisively, *misinocihew* (VTA).

defecate S/he defecates on her/him, *micitew* (VTA); s/he defecates or has a bowel movement, *mîsîw* (VAI).

defect Something spoiled, *kîkway kamisiwanatahk* (VTI).

defence *or* **defense** *naskwâwin* (NI).

defenceless *or* **defenseless** *ekâ konaskwawnihk* (VTA).

defend Defending someone, *kispewâsowewin* (NI); s/he defends her/him, *kispewâtew* (VTA); *kispewew* (VTA); the act of defending someone, *kispewewin* (NI); s/he defends herself/himself, *naskwâw* (VAI).

defender Or errand boy, *onâtamâkew* (NA).

deference An act of deference or submission out of respect, *kâketôkâsiwin* (NI); s/he acts in great deference to herself/himself, *kâketôkâsiw* (VTA); s/he acts in deference to her/him, *kâketôkawew* (VTA).

defiance *naskwâwin* (NI); a gesture of defiance, *nemah* (NA).

define A mutual understanding, *kwayaskohtowin* (NI).
definite *metoni kehcinâ* (IPC).
definitely *metoni ka kehcinâhohk* (VAI).
definition *kwayask mâmiskocikewin* (NI).
definitive *kakesipayik kîkway* (VTI).
deflate It is deflated, *yiwew* (VII); it became deflated,
yiwipayiw (VII); s/he deflates it or lets the air out of it,
i.e.: a balloon, *yôwenam* (VAI).
deform *mâskisiwin* (NI).
deformation *mâskihiwewin* (NI).
deformed S/he grows deformed, *mâskikiw* (VAI);
awîyak kamâskisit (VAI); a deformed bone, *mâskikan*
(NI).
deformity The act of being deformed, *mâskisiwin* (NI);
being born with a deformity, *mâskinihtâwikiwin* (NI).
defy *mawineskâkewin* (NI).
degenerate Demote; passing from a better to a lower
state, *astamopayowin* (NI).
degrade S/he has a degrading or demoralizing lifestyle,
pîwâcihiw (VAI); the act of having a degrading or
demoralizing lifestyle, *pîwâcihowin* (NI).
dehydrate S/he is dehydrated, *nohteyâpakwew* (VAI);
dehydration, *nohteyapâkwewin* (NI).
deification *manitoweyimowewin* (NA).
deify *ka manitoweyimiht awîyak* (VTA).
deity *kihcitwâweyicikewin* (NI).
dejected *pomewin* (NI)
dejection *pomehiwewin* (NI).
delay Something held back, *otâhkipicikewin* (NI); s/he
is delayed, *otâhkepayiw* (VAI); right now, without
delay, before doing anything else, *kesâc* (IPC); s/he is
delayed by the wind or bad weather, *kicistinahokiw*
(VAI); a delay caused by a big wind, *kicistinahokowin*
(NI); s/he delays them, *otâhkipitew* (VTA); s/he delays
him with her/his talking, *otamimew* (VTA).
delicacy *kîkway metoni ka wehkasik* (VII).
delicate *wahkewisowin* (NI); *nesowisiw* (VAI);
manâtisiw (VAI); *manâtan* (VII).
delicious *mistahiwekasin* (VII); *wihkitisiw* (VAI);
wihkasin (VII).
delight *meyawâtamohiwewin* (NI); *meyawâyâmowin*
(NI) *(Northern); mîywâtamowin* (NI) *(Plains).
delighted *metoni ka meyawâtamihk* (VAI).
delightful *omiyawâtamôhiwew* (VTI).
delirious *kîskweyâpamowin* (NI).
deliver *ka petamakehk kîkway* (VTA).
deliverance *paspîhiwewin* (NI).
delivered *pecikâtew* (VII).
deluge *ka sekipestak* (VII); it is pouring rain,
sekipestâw (VII).
delusion *pateyihcikewin* (NI).
demand *sohki ka natotamahk kîkway* (VAI);
natotamâwew (VTA).

demeanour Certain behavior, *itâtisiwin* (NI).
demobilize *wayeskânihiwewin* (NI).
demolish *pîkonikewin* (NI).
demon *macimanito* (NA).
demonic *ka macimanitowihk* (VAI).
demonism *macimanito tâpwewakeyihtamowin* (NI).
demonstrable *ka nihtâ wapahtihiwehk* (VTA).
demonstrably *nihtâwapahtamohiwewnihk* (IPC).
demonstrate *ka wapahtihiwehk; wapahtihiwew* (VTI).
demonstration The act of showing, *wapahtihiwewin*
(NI).
demote S/he demotes herself/himself to a lower rank,
âstamahisiw (VTA); s/he is demoted, *astâmapiw* (VAI)
(Northern); asehâw (VAI) *(Plains).
demure *metoni kâmwâc ayisiyiniw* (NA).
den *maskowatih* (NI); *wati* (NI).
denial *ânwehtamowin* (NI).
denied *ânwehtam* (VAI).
denote *kîkway ka wihtamomakahk*; to point out and
identify, *kiskeyihtamohiwewin* (NI).
denounce *ka pomemiht awîyak*.
denouncement *pomemetowin* (NI).
dense It is dense or thick bush, *kaskisâkasihk* (IPC); it
is dense and leafy, *sâkipakâw* (VAI).
dent S/he made a dent or dip on it, i.e.: a car,
wâyâpiskatahwew (VAI); it is dented, *wâyisiw* (VAI).
denude *môstâpekasewin* (NI); *môstâpekasew* (VAI).
denunciation *ka wehtamihk kapoyohk*.
deny Denying something, *ka ânwehtamihk kîkway*;
s/he denies, *ânwehtam* (VAI); a denial,
ânweyihtamowin (NI); s/he denies what the other
says, *ânwehtawew* (VAI).
depart *ka sipwehtehk*; s/he departs or s/he left,
sipwehtew (VAI); s/he departed riding in a vehicle or
riding a horse, *sipwepayiw* (VAI).
departed Her/his souls have departed or s/he dies,
sipweyahcahkwew (VAI).
departure The act of departure, *sipwehtewin* (NI).
depend Depending on someone, *ka mamisehk* (VTA);
s/he depends only on one person, *mamisîw* (VTA);
peyakohew (VAI).
dependability *mamisîtotâkewin* (NI).
dependable *mamisîwakeyimew* (VTA).
dependence *ka mamisîtotâkehk* (VTA).
dependency *paminowewin* (NI).
deplete *sîkawihew* (VTA) *(Northern); sîkonew* (VTA)
*(Plains).
deplore *kwetaweyecikewin* (NI).
deprave *ka macîsâyahk* (VAI).
depraved *macîsâyâwin* (NI).
depreciate S/he depreciates her/his own ability or s/he
puts herself/himself down, *acowihisiw* (VTA).
depress *kaskeyihtamâyâwin* (NI).

285

depressed *awîyak ka kaskeyihtamâyat* (VAI).

depression *ka kaskiyihtamâyâhk* (VAI); *kitimâkisowin* (NI).

deprive Witholding something from someone, *sâkihtamakewin* (NI); s/he deprives her/him of everything completely, *masaskonamawew* (VTA); s/he takes it away from her/him, *masaskonew* (VTA); s/he deprives her/him of everything in a game, *masaskoyawew* (VTA).

depth *taneyikohk iskwahtimew* (VTI); *wâyatimew* (VTI).

derail It derailed or slid off, i.e.: a train or car or s/he misses her/his chance, *pacipayiw* (VAI).

derange *waneyihtamohiwewin* (NI).

derelict *kîkway kawepinikâtek.*

dereliction *wepinikewin* (NI).

deride *pahpihiwewin* (NI).

derive *kahtinikewin* (NI).

derogatory *okakihcimiw* (NA).

descend The act of descending, *nihtaciwewin* (NI); s/he descends from heaven to the earth, i.e.: Christ, *peyâsaskew* (VAI); s/he descends from the air to the ground, i.e.: a bird, *peyâsew* (VAI).

descendant *aniskac ohcîwin* (NI); *wahkohtowin* (NI).

describe Describing someone, *awîyak ka kiskinwahoht* (VTA); s/he is describing someone, *kiskinowâwew* (VTA).

description *kiskinowahekiwin* (NI).

desert Dried ground, i.e.: a desert, *pâhkwataskamikâw* (NI); an area where nothing grows, i.e.: a desert, *pikwataskamik* (NI); it is desert-like, *pikwataskamikâw* (VII); wild or untamed country where nothing grows, *pikwataskiy* (NI).

desert Abandoning someone, *awîyak ka wepiniht.*

deserve Deserving something postive to happen, *ka kîspinatamâsohk* (VAI); what s/he did to her/him was deserved by her/him, *wawiyasihêw* (VTA); what s/he said to her/him was deserved, *wawiyasimew* (VTA); s/he deserves it or it serves her/him right, *wawiyatisiw* (VAI); the act of deserving some negative action, *wawiyatisowin* (NI).

deservedly *kîspinatamâsowenihk* (VAI).

deserving *kîspinatamâsowin* (NI).

designate *oyahiwewin* (NI).

desirable *kîkway ka akawâtamihk* (VAI).

desire The act of wishing for something, *akawâcikiwin* (NI); s/he desires her/him on seeing her/him or s/he is sexually attracted to him, *môstawinawew* (VTA).

desist Stopping a relationship, *pôniwâhkohtowin* (NI).

desolate *kewâtan* (NA).

despair The act of being discouraged or giving up, *pomewin* (NI); it is despairing, *osâmeyihtâkwan* (VII);

s/he thinks in desperation, *osâmeyihtam* (VAI); the act of thinking in desperation, *osâmeyihtamowin* (NI).

desperate *wâneyihtamâyâwin* (NI).

desperation *ka wâneyihtamâyâhk* (VAI).

despise Looking down on someone, *awîyak kapakwâteyemiht* (VTA); s/he despises her/him, *maciyimew* (VTA); the act of despising someone, *maciyimiwewin* (NI); s/he is despised, *mâyeyihtâkosiw* (VAI).

despite *misawâc* (IPC).

despondent *metoni kapomewakeyemohk* (VAI).

destination *nânitâw ka eteyemohk* (VAI).

destiny *tansi poko kaweh ispâyehk* (VII); *ohcitâw* (IPC).

destitute *metoni micimohowin* (NI); *kitimâkisiw* (VAI); being poor or unhappy, *kitimâkisowin* (NI).

destroy Destroying things, *misiwanâcihcikewin* (NI); s/he destroys, *misiwanacitâw* (VTI); s/he destroyed it completely, *kîsiyiw* (VTI); the act of destroying something completely, *kîsiyiwin* (NI); s/he destroys or ruins herself/himself, *pîkonisiw* (VTA).

destructible *misiwanâcihcikewin* (NI).

destruction Destroying things, *misiwanâcihcikewin* (NI); the act of self-destruction, *pîkonisiwin* (NI).

detain S/he detains or keeps it, *kisâtinam* (VTI); stopping someone from doing something, *nakinowewin* (NI); s/he detains her/him, *kitinew* (VTA); s/he is detained by her/his hunger, *otâmâkatisiw* (VAI); s/he detains her/him with her/his visit, *otâmapistawew* (VTA).

detail *ka oyahiwehk* (VTA).

detect *ka miskawâhtâhk* (VTI).

detectable *miskawâhtâwin* (NI).

detection *miskawâhtâwin* (NI).

deteriorate *ka mescipayik* (VTI).

deterioration *mescipayowin* (NI); *misiwanâtisiwin* (NI).

determination *âhkameyihtamowin* (NI).

determine *kakakwi kwayaskweyihtamihk* (VAI).

detest *kapakwatamihk kîkway* (VAI); the act of being detested, *pakwâtikosiwin* (NI) *(Plains)*; *kakwâyakeyihtâkosowin* (NI) *(Northern)*; disliking something, *pakwâtam* (VTI).

detestation *pakwâcikewin* (NI).

detour S/he bypasses it, *wemâskam* (VTI); s/he detours or walks around it, *wemâhtew* (VAI); the act of detouring or walking around something, *wemâhtewin* (NI); s/he detours or goes around her/him, *wemâskawew* (VTA).

detriment *kamayitôtaht awîyak* (VTA).

detrimental *mâyitôtamowewin* (NI).

devastate *ka misiwanâcipayik* (VTI).

devastation *misiwanâcipayowin* (NI).

develop *ka osihcikehk* (VAI).

development *osihcikewin* (NI).

deviate *ka wanipicikehk* (VAI).

deviation *wanipicikewin* (NI).

device *osihcikewenis* (NI); *miskweyitamowin* (NI).

devil *macâya* (NA); the wicked god, *macimanito* (NA).

devilish *ka macâyowihk* (VAI).

devious *macîsâyâwin* (NI).

devise *ka oyeyihtamihk* (VAI); *oyeyihtam* (VAI).

devoid *kîkway ka mescipayik* (VTI).

devote *ka pakitinsohk* (VTA).

devotion *sâkihitowin* (NI); *ayamihâwin* (NI).

devotional *naspic miyotehewin* (NI).

devour *ka kitâpayihtahk kîkway* (VTI).

devout *tâpwewakeyihtamowin* (NI).

dew *akosipayaw* (NI).

dewberry *kisâstaw ayoskanak* (NA); a red currant berry, *miskîsikomin* (NA).

dewy *ka akosipeyak* (VII).

dexterity *metoni nahiwin* (NI); *tâstapiwin* (NI) *(Northern)*; *câstapiwin* (NI) *(Plains)*.

diabolical *ka mosci macâyowihk* (VAI).

diaper *âsîyân* (NI).

die The act of dying, *nipowin* (NI); s/he loses her/his whole family from illness, *mescinew* (VAI); they all died from illness, *mescinewak* (VAI); the act of one person losing her/his whole family from illness, *mescinewin* (NI); s/he died or s/he is dead, *nipiw* (VAI); s/he feints death to people, *nipohkâsototawew* (VAI); s/he died, *naspicinipiw* (VAI) *(Northern)*; *pônipimâtisiw* (VAI) *(Plains)*; *nipiw* (VAI) *(Plains)*;

differ *pîtos* (IPC).

difference *namoya pahpeyakwan* (IPC).

different Being of a different personality, *pîtosisâyâwin* (NI); differently or in another way, *pîtos* (IPC); separated from, *pahkan* (VII); of many different kinds, in many different ways, *nanâtohk* (IPC); in a different way, *pîtos isi* (IPC); placed all differently, or of different lengths and sizes, *kahtapahew* (VTI); in a different area or just around the corner, *kweskâyihk* (IPC); it is a different kind, *pîtosâya* (VII); s/he acts different, *pîtosâyihtiw* (VAI); s/he is different, *pîtosîsâyâw* (VAI); s/he finds her/him different, *pîtoseyimew* (VTA); s/he understands her/him in a different manner, *pîtosihtawew* (VTA); the act of looking or appearing to be different, *pîtosinâkosowin* (NI); s/he looks different, *pîtosinâkosiw* (VAI); it looks different, *pîtosinâkwan* (VII); s/he sees her/him in a different way, *pîtosinawew* (VTA); it becomes different, *pîtosipayiw* (VII); s/he thinks differently, *pîtoteyihtam* (VTI); a different kind of thought, *pîtoteyihtamowin* (NI); they have a difference of opinion of each other, *pîtoteyihtowak* (VAI); s/he finds

her/him to be different or changed, *pîtoteyimew* (VTA); altogether different, *ayasâwâc* (IPC) *(Plains)*.

differentiate *pîtosinâkwan* (VII).

differentiation *pîtosinâkohcikewin* (NI).

difficult *ka nayihtawahk*; it is difficult or hard times, *âyiman* (VII); a difficult time period, *âyimahkamikan* (IPC); in a difficult place, *âyimanohk* (IPC); s/he finds her/him difficult, *âyimeyimew* (VTA); s/he gives him a hard or rough time, *âyimihew* (VTA); s/he is difficult to handle, *âyimihiwew* (VAI); s/he needlessly gives herself/himself a hard time, *âyimihisiw* (VTA); the act of giving oneself a hard time, self-destruction, *âyimihisowin* (NI); it is difficult or hard to do, *nayihtâwan* (VII); s/he has a difficult or hard time, *nayihtâwew* (VAI); having a difficult or hard time, *nayihtâwewin* (NI); s/he thinks of her/him as difficult or hard to get along with, *nayihtâweyimew* (VTA); people think of her/him as being difficult or hard to get along with, *nayihtâweyihtâkosiw* (VTA); something that is thought of as being difficult or hard to understand, *nayihtâweyihtâkwan* (VII); s/he thinks it is too difficult or it is hard to do, *nayihtâweyihtam* (VAI); the act of thinking of something as being too difficult or hard to do, *nayihtâweyihtamowin* (NI); s/he makes it difficult or hard for her/him, *nayihtâwihew* (VTA); s/he finds it difficult or hard to listen, *nayihtâwihtawew* (VTA); s/he looks difficult, hard, rough, *nayihtâwinâkosiw* (VAI); it looks difficult, hard, rough, *nayihtâwinâkwan* (VII); s/he is difficult to get along with, *nayihtâwisiw* (VAI); being difficult or hard to get along with, *nayihtâwisiwin* (NI).

difficulty *nayihtâwewin* (NI); *âyimihisowin* (NI).

dig The act of digging a hole, *wâtihkewin* (NI); the act of digging in the ground, *monahikewin* (NI) s/he digs it, *mônaham* (VTI); s/he digs the ground with it, *mônahîkakew* (VAI); s/he digs a well, *mônahipew* (VAI); s/he digs them out, *mônahwew* (VTA); s/he unearths or digs her/him or it up, *mônahatihkâtew* (VTA).

digest *ka mecihk mîciwin* (VTI).

digestion *mîciwin kamiyoskâkohk* (VTI).

digestive *mîciwin ka pimohte makahk* (VTI); the act of digesting food, *mîciwin kawepinamihk* (NI).

digit *peyak akihtâson* (NI).

dignify *mamihcimowewin* (NI).

dignity *mamihcâyâwin* (NI).

digression *ka wanowetamihk* (VAI).

dike Building a rock dam, *oskwatimihkewin* (NI).

dilapidated *kayâsâyiwan* (VII); an old broken down thing, *kayâsayi* (IPC).

dilate *mahkisîhcikewin* (NI).

287

diligence *ayâhkweyihtamowin* (NI).
diligent *awîyak ka ayâhkweyihtahk* (VAI); s/he is persistent, *âhkameyimiw* (VAI).
diligently S/he never stops trying, *âhkameyihtam* (VTI).
dilute S/he dilutes it, *takopataw* (VTI).
dim *itâtaw ka nôkwahk*.
dimension *tîpapekinkewin* (NI).
diminish *ka acôsehcikehk* (VTI); *acôwpayiw* (VAI); making something smaller, *acôwinikewin* (NI).
dimple *ocisikwaskonewin* (NI); *masinâsiwin* (NI).
dine *kihcimetsowin* (NI); s/he eats, *mîcisiw* (VAI).
dinner *âpihtâkîsikan mîcisowin* (NI) (i.e.: eating at lunchtime).
dings It rings, *sewepayiw* (VII).
dinnertime *âpihtâkîsikan* (NI).
dip A dip in the ground, *wâyahcâw* (NI); using a dipper and dipping something, *kwapahikewin* (NI); s/he sinks her/him with a pole or stick, *kihtawew* (VTA); s/he dips her/him/it under water, i.e.: during a baptism, *kihtânew* (VTA); s/he dips water out for her/him, *kwapahamawew* (VTA); s/he dips it out, i.e.: fish, *kwapahwew* (VTA).
dipper A tool for dipping water or liquid, *kwâpahikan* (NI).
dire *ka misiwanâtahkamikahk* (VII).
direction Indicating direction, *kiskinwahikewin* (NI); in all directions, *nanânisk* (IPC); many different directions or manners, *mihcetweyak* (IPC); four directions, *newayak* (IPC).
directly *mweci ekotah* (IPC).
dirt *asiskîy* (NI); accumulated dirt, *wîyipayih* (NI); there is dry soil, dry dirt, *pâhkwacaw* (NI); a lump on the ground, *piskwahcâw* (NI); there is soft dirt, *yoskacaw* (NI); it is full of dirt, *asiskîwan* (VII).
dirty When something is dirty, *ka wîyipak kîkway* (VTI); it is dirty, *wîyipatan* (VII); *iyipâtan* (VII); it is dirty, *iyipâtisiw* (VII); s/he dirties her/him, *iyipâcihew* (VTA); s/he finds her/him dirty, *iyipâteyimew* (VTA); s/he gets her/him dirty with her/his hands, *iyipâtinew* (VTA); s/he tramps mud or dirt on her/him and makes her/him muddy or unclean, *iyipâtiskawew* (VTA); s/he is dirty or untidy, *kokosiwiw* (VAI); the act of being dirty or untidy, *kokosiwiwin* (NI); s/he dirties them by dragging them, i.e.: socks, *weyipisimew* (VTI); s/he has dirt or filth on her/him, *wîyipisiw* (VAI); having dirt or filth on oneself, *wîyipisiwin* (NI); it has dirt or filth on it, *wîyipâw* (VII); her/his fur is dirty, *wîyipawew* (VAI); s/he has dirty hands, *wîyipicihcew* (VAI); s/he dirties them, *wîyipihew* (VTA); s/he has a dirty face, *wîyipihkwew* (VAI); s/he dirties them with her/his clothes or boots, *wîyipiskawew* (VTA); s/he has a dirty head or hair, *wîyipistikwânew* (VAI).

disability *eka ka kaskihohk* (VAI).
disable *eka ka kaskihtahk* (VAI).
disabled *metoni kistapiwin* (NI).
disadvantage *âyimihowin* (NI).
disadvantageous *ka âyimihohk* (VAI).
disaffected *mâyiwecehtowin* (NI).
disaffection *ka mâyiwecehtohk* (VTA).
disagree *petos ka iteyihtamihk* (VAI); *pîtosihtam* (VTI).
disagreeable *ka pîtoteyicikehk* (VAI).
disagreement Each thinking differently, *pahpîtoteyihtamowin* (NI); *pîtoteyicikewin* (NI); s/he shakes her/his head in disagreement, *wewepiskweyiw* (VTA) *(Plains)*; *wepiskweyiw* (VTA) *(Northern)*.
disallow *eka kapakitinowehk* (VTA); *namoyapakitinam* (VTI).
disappear *ka namatakohk* (VAI).
disappearance *wînihowin* (NI)
disappeared *namatakon* (VII); *namatakon* (VAI).
disappoint *ka kisiwâhiht awîyak* (VTA).
disappointed *kisôweyihtamowin* (NI).
disappointment *kisiwâhiwewin* (NI); *pomehiwewin* (NI); the act of quitting in disappointment, *pomeyihtamowin* (NI).
disapproval *eka ekose iteyihtamowin* (NI).
disapprove *eka ekose ka iteyihtamihk* (VAI).
disarm *masaskoniwewin pâskisikan* (NI).
disarrange *mâyascikewin* (NI).
disaster *mâyipayiwin* (NI).
disastrous *misi mâyipayiwin* (NI).
disbelief *ânwehtamowin* (NI).
disburden *ketowatenowewin* (NI).
discard *wepinkewin* (NI); disown, *wepinanowin* (NI) *(Plains)*; *wepinam* (VTI) *(Northern)*.
discern *koyemiht awîyak* (VTA).
discernment *oyecikewin* (NI).
discipline A disciplinary conduct, *kwayaskwâtisiwin* (NI).
discharge *pakitinowewin* (NI).
discharged *pakitinaw* (VAI).
disciple *otaskokew* (NA).
discipleship *askôkewin* (NI).
disciplinaran *okwayaskwahiwew* (NA).
disciplinary *ka kwayaskwahiwehk* (VTA).
discipline Good discipline, *kwayaskwâtisewin* (NI); being brought up the right way, *kwayaskohpikiwin* (NI); the act of correcting someone, *kwayaskwahiwewin* (NI); s/he corrects or disciplines her/him, *misawihew* (VTA); s/he has been disciplined or s/he has learned her/his lesson, *misawiw* (VAI); the act of having been disciplined or having learned a lesson, *misawewin* (NI).

288

disclaim *kîkway ka pakiteyihtamihk* (VAI).

disclose *ka nôkohtahk* (VTI); *nôkohtâw* (VTA).

disclosure *nôkohtâwin* (NI).

discolor *or* discolour *pîtos sopekahikewin* (NI).

discontended The act of not liking something,
pakwâtamowin (NI).

discomfort *mâyimahcihowin* (NI).

disconcert *mâyipicikewin* (NI).

disconnect *ka tasipitamihk kîkway* (VTI); *âpihkonam*
(VTI); the act of disconnecting, *tasipicikewin* (NI)
(Northern); *tahcipicikewin* (NI) *(Plains)*.

discontent *eka ka nahîsayahk* (VAI).

discontented *pîkweyihtamowin* (NI).

discontinue Discontinuing something, *kaponihtak
kîkway* (VTI); s/he discontinued it, *ponitâw* (VTI); s/he
discontinues because s/he is apprehensive of her/him,
nakîstawew (VTA); discontinuing something,
ponitawin (NI).

discontinuity It is continuous and then has a sudden
break, *âstehtin* (IPC).

discord *mâyiwecehtowin* (NI).

discordant *ka mâyiwecihiwehk* (VTA).

discourage S/he is discouraged, *pomew* (VAI); s/he
discourages her/him, *pômemew* (VTA); the act of being
discouraged or giving up, *pomewin* (NI); s/he is
discouraged with her/him, *pomeyimew* (VTA).

discouragement *pomehiwewin* (NI).

discourse *pîkiskwewin* (NI).

discourtesy *pîwitôhtâkewin* (NI).

discover *ka miskamihk kîkway* (VTI); *miskam* (VTI).

discovery *miskamowin* (NI).

discredit *mayahiwewin* (NI).

discrete *pîtos mâmitoneyicikan*.

discuss Discussing, *mâmiskôcikewin* (NI); having a real
heated discussion, *kihkihtowin* (NI), they have a
heated discussion, *kihkahtowak* (VAI).

discussion *mâmiskôtamakew* (VTA); talking about
something, *mâmiskôcikewin* (NI).

disdain Regarding someone with disdain,
pîweyihcikewin (NI); thinking in a disdainful manner,
mâyeyihtamowin (NI).

disease A sickness, *âhkosowin* (NI); s/he has a chronic
sickness i.e.: diabetes, *katohpinew* (VAI); the act of
having a bad disease and generally refers to
gonorrhoea, *macâspinewin* (NI); s/he has a bad disease
and generally refers to gonorrhoea, *macâspinew* (VAI).

disembard S/he disembarks by boat or canoe, *misakâw*
(VAI) *(Northern)*; *kapâw* (VAI) *(Plains)*.

disenchant *pomemowewin* (NI); *awîyak ka pomemiht*
(VTA).

disentangle *âpihkonam* (VTI).

disfigurement *pîtosisihiwewin* (NI).

disgrace *nepewihowin* (NI); *nepewâkâc* (VAI).

disgraceful *nîpewihiwewin* (NI).

disgruntle *kisôwisâyâwin* (NI).

disguise *ka wanisihohk* (VTI).

disgust *kisewahiwewin* (NI).

dish Or plate; *oyakan* (NI).

dishcloth *kasihakanakan* (NI).

disheartened S/he gives up, *sâkweyimow* (VAI).

dishonest *eka ka kwayaskwâtisihk* (VAI); *kîyâskiw*
(VAI).

dishonor *or* dishonour *mâyiwehyowin ka yahk* (VAI).

dishonorable *or* dishonourable *maceyihtâkwan* (VII).

dishpan *kisipekinyakanewayakan* (NI).

dishrag *kisipekinyakanewayanis* (NI).

dishtowel *pâhkwahyakanakan* (NI).

disillusionment *pomehiwewin* (NI).

disintegration *mosci mescipayiwin* (NI).

disjoint It is out of joint, *kotokopayiw* (VII).

disjointed *mamases kakikamok kîkway* (VTI).

disk *or* disc *asiski sekopicikan* (NI).

dislike *pahkwacikewin* (NI); *pakwâtam* (VTI).

dislocate *kotokosiniwin* (NI).

dislodge Driving from a special habitation,
ohpimetsahikewin (NI).

disloyal *kîmôtâtisiwin* (NI).

dismal *kâmwâtisiwin* (NI); it looks lonely,
pîkiskacinâkwan (VII).

dismantle S/he is dismantling her/his teepee,
pâskinokew (VTI).

dismay *kostaciwâyâwin* (NI); s/he frightens her/him,
sîkihew (VTA).

dismember *pahpiskihtinikewin* (NI).

dismiss S/he lets her/him go; *pakitinew* (VTA).

dismount *nihtakosîwin* (NI).

disobedient S/he is disobedient, *sasepihtam* (VTI);
disobedience, *sasepihtamowin* (NI).

disobey Not listening, *eka ka nitohtamihk* (VTA); s/he
disobeys her/him, *sasepihtawew* (VTA).

disorder It is out of order, *apotastew* (VII).

disordered *namoyakwayask* (IPC).

disorderly *metoni mamases* (IPC).

disorganize *namoyu kutawuhk* (VII).

disown *wepinam* (NI) *(Northern)*; *wepinamowin* (NI)
(Plains).

dispatch *or* despatch *ka sipwetesahamihk kîkway*
(VTI); s/he sends it away, *sipwetisaham* (VTI).

disperse Spreading something out, *siwescikewin* (NI);
s/he disperses it or s/he carefully drops bits of
something, i.e.: seeds, *pîwipitew* (VTI).

dispirit *pomêyihtamohiwewin* (NI).

displace *ohpimeteh kâyâhk* (VTA).

display *wapahtihiwewin* (NI).

289

displease *ka pakwâteyihtâmohiwehk* (VTA).

displeased *kisîwâsiw* (VAI)

disprove *môstawikanehowewin* (NI).

dispute *kehkâhtowin* (NI).

disregard *eka ka pisiskeyihtamihk* (VAI).

disreputable *awîyak ka astameyemiht* (VTA).

disrespect *pîwihiwewin* (NI); s/he treats her/him with disrespect, *pîwihew* (VTA).

disrobe S/he takes her/his clothes off, *ketayiwinisew* (VTA).

disrupt Disrupting something, *ka wanâhtahk kîkway*; s/he disrupts her/him, *wanâhew* (VTA); her/his talking disrupts her/him, *wanâmew* (VTA).

dissatisfaction Rejection, *âtaweyihtamowin* (NI).

dissect *ka wiyanihiht moswa* (VTI).

dissection *kîkway ka pahpiskihtastahk* (VTI).

dissent *naspâc isâyâwin* (NI).

dissolve *tihkipayiw* (VII).

dissuade *ka kweskeyihtamohiwehk* (VTA).

distance S/he thinks the distance is too great, *pehteyihtam* (VAI); s/he thinks s/he is a long ways away, i.e.: a great distance, *pehteyimew* (VTA); the act of thinking that the distance is too far, *pehteyitamowin* (NI); it is quite a distance across, i.e.: a lake, *pehtikamâw* (VAI).

distant *pihcâw* (VII).

distaste It tastes sour, *âhkospakwan* (VII).

distasteful *mâyispakwan* (VII).

distil or **distill** *ka itâkamascikehk* (VTI).

distilled *itâkamascikan* (NI).

distiller *otâkamascikew* (NA).

distinct S/he looks at her/him distinctly, *pakahkâpamew* (VTA); s/he appears very distinctly, *pakahkinâkosiw* (VAI); it appears very distinctly, *pakahkinâkwan* (VII); s/he sees it very distinctly, *pakahkinam* (VTI); s/he sees her/him very distinctly, *pakahkinawew* (VTA).

distinction *pakaskowehikewin* (NI).

distinguish To recognize something, *nistawinâmowin* (NI)

distinguishable *ka pakaskinakwahk kîkway* (VII).

distort It is distorted by fire, *pihkihkahtew* (VII) (Northern); *pihkatew* (VII) (Plains); it is distorted by fire, *pihkihkasiw* (VAI) (Northern); *pihkasiw* (VAI) (Plains).

distract Diverting someone's attention, *wanâhiwewin* (NI).

distracted *wâneyihtam* (VAI).

distress *mâyâyâwin* (NI).

distressed *kakwâtakihtâwin* (NI).

distribute *ka papâmi mekihk*; *mâhmekiw* (VAI).

distribution *papâmimekiwin* (NI); the act of giving, *mekiwin* (NI).

distributor *awîyak ka papâmimekit* (VTA).

disturb *mikoskâcihiwewin* (NI).

disturbance *wanâhiwewin* (NI).

ditch A makeshift ditch, *sîpesisihkan* (NI).

dive The act of diving, *kokîwin* (NI); s/he dives, *kokiw* (VAI); s/he makes her/him dive, *kokîhew* (VTA).

diver A person who dives, *okokiw* (NA).

diverse *pahpitos kîkway* (IPC).

diversion *pîtosispayecikewin* (NI).

divert *ka pîtos ispayehtahk* (VTI).

divest *masaskoniwewin* (NI).

divide Break off a chunk, *pahkwenikewin* (NI); s/he divides them into small pieces, *pahpiskihtahew* (VTI).

divided It is divided, i.e.: a split road, *nîswayakan* (VII).

divine *kihcihtwâwesowin* (NI).

divisible *ka nihtâ pahkwepayik* (VTI).

division *pahpiskihc âyâwin* (NI).

divulge *misihkemowin* (NI); *wihtam* (VAI).

dizzy Being dizzy, *kîskweyâpamowin* (NI); s/he is made dizzy by smoke, *kîskwesiw* (VAI); s/he is dizzy, *kîskweyâpamiw* (VAI).

do *itôtâ*; the act of doing, *itôtâmowin* (NI); s/he does, *itôtam* (VAI); *tôtam* (VAI); s/he does it for her/him, *itôtamawew* (VTA); s/he does it for others, *itôtamakew* (VTA); the act of doing it for others, *itôtamakewin* (NI); s/he does it to her/him, *itôtawew* (VTA); it was done to her/him, *itôtawâw* (VII) (Plains); *itôcikasiw* (VII) (Northern); the act of doing something for one's own good, *âpacihowin* (NI); s/he does miraculous acts, *mamâhtâwitôtam* (VAI); s/he does it all wrong, *mâyitôtam* (VAI); the act of doing things all wrong, *mâyitôtamowin* (NI); s/he does it all done, *peyakosihcikew* (VAI); s/he does it, *tôtam* (VAI); s/he does it for others, *tôtamâkew* (VTA); s/he does it for her/him, *tôtamâwew* (VTA); the act of doing it for others, *tôtamâkewin* (NI); s/he does it to her/him, *tôtawew* (VTA).

dock A landing, *kapâwin* (NI) (Plains); *kapâwinihk* (LN) (Plains); *onikewin* (NI) (Northern).

doctor Someone who heals illness, i.e.: doctor or medicine man or shaman, *maskihkîwiyiniw* (NA); *onatawehiwew* (NA).

doctrinal *ka keskihkemowin* (NI).

doctrine *ka kâkeskihkemohk* (VTA).

dodge *yikatepayihowin* (NI).

doe *nôse âpisimôsosis* (NA).

doer *awîyak ka tôtâhk* (VTA); one who does things for others, *itôtamâkew* (NA).

doeskin *apiscimososowayânis* (NI).

dog *atim* (NA); toy dog, statue of dog, *atimôhkan* (NI); strange dog, *ayahcatim* (NA); pack dog, *nayacikewatim* (NA); a sled dog, *otapewatim* (NA); retriever, *onatahisipewatim* (NA); small female, *kiskânakos* (NA); male, *napistim* (NA); shaggy, *pekwaskawewatim* (NA); dark, *kaskitewastim* (NA); newborn dog, *acimosisis* (NA); s/he has dogs or horses, *otemiw* (VAI); it is a good or nice dog or horse, *takahkatim* (NA); a white horse or white dog, *wapâstim* (NA) *(Plains)*.

dogfight *atimahpinatowin* (NI).

dogged *ka âhkameyihtamihk* (VAI).

dogrib *atimospikay* (NA).

dogsled *atimotâpânâsk* (NI).

dogwood *mihkwâpimakwahtik* (NA); dogberry, *mihkwâpimakomina* (NA).

doll An imitation baby, *awâsisihkân* (NI); a small doll, *awâsisihkânis* (NI).

domain *tipeyicikîwin* (NI); *pamihowin* (NI).

dominant *ka kostanakeyimohk* (VAI).

dominate *awîyak ka pimpayihciket* (VTA).

domination *pimipayihiwewin* (NI).

domineer *opimipayihcikew* (NA).

donate *ka mikih* (VTI).

donation *mikowin* (NI) *(Northern)*; *mekowin* (NI) *(Plains)*.

done It was done, *itôcikâtew* (VII); it was done to her/him, *itôcikasiw* (VTA); it is all done or finished, *kesâyâwin* (NI); it was done to her/him, *tôcikâsiw* (VAI); it was done, *tôcikâtew* (VII).

donkey Or ass or mule, *sôsôwatim* (NA); s/he is an ass or mule, *sôsôwatimowiw* (VAI).

don't *kâya* (IPC).

doom *misiwanâcipayowin* (NI); *iskweyâc oyasiwewin* (NI).

dormant *nipowayâwin* (NI).

doormouse *mistâpakosîs* (NA).

dot A large dot or Cree syllabic consonant, *cahkipehikan* (NI); a small dot, *cahkipehikanis* (NI); s/he makes a dot on her/him, *cahkasinahwew* (VTA); s/he writes, makes sign, marks, dots or diagrams, *cahkipehwew* (VAI).

dote *ka kepâcikihkasihk* (VAI).

doting *ka môconkeskihk* (VAI).

dotted *cakipehikewin* (NI).

doubled *nîswamiw* (VII).

doubly *nîswayak isi* (IPC)

doubt *ânwehtamowin* (NI).

dough *ohpayecikan* (NI); *mamakonikan* (NI).

douse *âstaweyâpâwacikewin* (NI).

dove *mehmew* (NA).

dowdy Being dowdy; *kitimâkiskwewewin* (NI); being poorly dressed, *kitimâkisehowin* (NI).

down A soft, fluffy feather, i.e.: down, *pîswepiway* (NI); fluffy down, i.e.: goose down, *mestanipewayan* (NI); it leads downward, *nâsipemiw* (VII); s/he takes her/him or them down the hill to the water, *nâsipehtahew* (VTA); going down the hill to the water's edge, *ka nâsipetimihk* (VTA); s/he sends her/him or them down the hill to the water's edge, *nâsipetisahwew* (VTA); s/he goes down the hill to the water's edge, *nâsipew* (VAI); the act of going down the hill to the water's edge, *nâsipewin* (NI); s/he fell down the hill, *nihtaciwepayiw* (VAI); s/he goes down, i.e.: a hill or a stairway, *nihtaciwew* (VAI); the act of going down a hill or stairway, *nihtaciwewin* (NI); s/he lets her/him down with a rope, *nihtâpekinew* (VTA); it blew off or down, i.e.: a diaper off a clothes line, *nihtâsiw* (VAI); it blew off or down, i.e.: a facecloth off a clothesline, *nihtâstan* (VII) s/he takes her/him down, *nehtinew* (VTA); it leads down, i.e.: a road down a hill, *penasipemon* (NI); s/he goes down the hill, *penâsipew* (VAI); s/he is coming down, i.e.: stairs or a hill, *penihtaciwew* (VAI); s/he climbs down, i.e.: a pole or tree, *penihtâskiw* (VAI).

downcast *pîkweyihtam* (VTI).

downfall *mayinikewin* (NI).

downgrade Running down hill, *nihtâmatinâw* (NI).

downhearted *metoni wesakitehewin* (NI).

downward Downstairs, *nîhcâyihk* (IPC); *nehcîcâyihk* (IPC).

dowry *kîkway âsawemeyitowin* (NI).

doze S/he dozed, *nanipâsiw* (VAI); the act of dozing, *nipepayisiwin* (NI) *(Plains)*; *ninipâsiwin* (NI) *(Northern)*.

drab *kîkway ka kaskitewosawak*; it has a dull color, *wîpinâkwan* (VII).

drafty *ka tahkiyowek wâskahikanihk*.

drag Dragging something, *kapimtapihk* (NI); s/he drags it from the water, *akwâpinam* (VTI); s/he drags her/him from the water, *awâpitew* (VTA).

dragonfly *cohkanapises* (NA).

drain S/he drains it, *sekohkiciwunihew* (VAI); s/he empties it, *ehkinam* (VAI); a draining of something, *ehkinamowin* (NI).

drainage *sekawicowanihcikewin* (NI).

drake A male duck, *nâpesip* (NA); *iyinisip* (NA) *(Plains and Northern variant)*; *wihpitwânsip* (NA) *(Northern)*.

drank *awîyak ka kehminihkwet* (VTI).

drastic *sohkeyihtam* (VAI).

draw S/he draws water from here, *ohtahipew* (VAI); s/he draws them out of the water with a stick or pole, *otâskwahwew* (VTA).

drawing Drawing a sketch, *naspasinahikewin* (NI); s/he draws her/him, *naspasinahwew* (VTA).

drawknife *poyakeskinkewihkomân* (NI).

drawn Tired, *metoni ka nestomahcihohk* (VAI).

dread Being very much afraid, *kostâciwisâyâwin* (NI); fear, *astâsiwin* (NI); s/he dreads her/him, *kospaneyimew* (VTA); s/he is to be dreaded or feared, *kospaneyihtâkosiw* (VAI); it is to be dreaded or feared, *kospaneyihtâkwan* (VII).

dreadful *metoni ka kostâmihk*; *kostâtikwan* (VII).

dream The act of dreaming, *pawâtamowin* (NI) *(Plains)*; *pawatamowin* (NI) *(Northern)*; the act of dreaming of an encounter with the tribal totem, *powatamowin* (NI); s/he dreams about it, *powatam* (VAI) *(Northern)*; *powâtam* (VAI) *(Plains)*; s/he has a spirit of dream about her/him/her, *powatew* (VAI) *(Northern)*; *pawatew* (VAI) *(Plains)*.

dreamer *opowatam* (VAI); *opawamow* (NA), a dream of spirits.

dreamland *powatamowaskîhk* (NI).

dreamy *nanâtohk ka isi akâwâtamihk*.

dreary It feels lonesome, *kaskeyihtakwan* (VII).

dregs *iskwâpohkahcikan* (NI) *(Northern)*; *sîkawâcowasikan* (NI) *(Plains)*.

drench *ka sîkanâpâwehk* (VTI); *sîkanâpâwewin* (NI).

dress *miskotâkay* (NI); a woman's dress, *iskwewasâkay* (NI); a new coat or dress, *oskasâkay* (NI); a blue dress, coat, or jacket, *sîpihkwasâkay* (NI); a white dress, *wâpiskasâkay* (NI); s/he dresses her/him up, *wawesihew* (VTA); they are dressed up, *wawisihowak* (VAI); s/he uses it to dress up, *wawesihowâkew* (VTI); s/he dresses it up for her/him, *wawesihtamawew* (VTA); s/he dresses it up, *wawesihtâw* (VAI); s/he dresses up, *wawesîw* (VAI); the act of dressing up, *wawesîwin* (NI).

dressing *akohpisiwâkan* (NI).

dressmaking *iskwew asâkayihkewin* (NI).

dressy *ka wawesîw isehohk* (VTI); *wawesîw* (VAI).

dribble *ka pâhkawik nepe* (VTI); *ohcikawiw* (VII).

dried It is dried out, i.e.: a tree, *pâstewâhkatosiw* (VAI); it is dried out or parched, i.e.: ground, *pâstewâhkatotew* (VII); it is dried out, i.e.: a leaf, *pâstewipak* (VII); s/he or it is dried, i.e.: by the sun, *pâsow* (VAI) *(Plains)*; *pâhkosiw* (VAI) *(Northern)*.

drift Something drifting, i.e.: water, *ka pimâpakohk kîkway* (VTI); it drifts ashore, *akwâyapâyew* (VTI); snow drift, *papestin* (NI); s/he drifts down stream, *mahâpokow* (VAI); it drifts down stream, *mahâpotew* (VII); the action of drifting down stream in a canoe, *mahâpoyiwin* (NI); s/he drifts around, i.e.: in a river, *papâmâpahokow* (VAI); it drifts around, i.e.: in a river, *papâmâpotew* (VII); it is drifting, i.e.: snow, *pîwan*

(VII); s/he drifts along in the water, *pimâhokow* (VAI); it drifts along in the water, *pimâpotew* (VII); s/he makes her/him drift along with the current, *pimâpohew* (VTA).

driftwood A piece of driftwood, *akwâwahonihtak* (NI).

drill The act of exercising or practicing, *sesawewin* (NI); a machine for boring holes, *payipahikan* (NI); a bracing bit handle, *payipihkocikanâhtik* (NI).

drink Having a drink, *minihkwewin* (NI); s/he gives her/him a drink, *minahew* (VTA); s/he drinks, *minihkwew* (VAI); s/he makes her/him drink, *minikwahew* (VTA); s/he sells it to buy drinks, *minihkwâtew* (VTI); the act of drinking, *minihkwewin* (NI); s/he drinks to excess, *osâmipew* (VAI); s/he drinks with her/him, *wîciminihkwemew* (VTA); s/he enjoys drinking, i.e.: alcoholic beverages, *wihkipew* (VAI); the act of enjoying drinking, i.e.: alcoholic beverages, *wihkipewin* (NI); s/he is sick from drinking alcohol, *âhkosepew* (VAI); s/he has drank enough or s/he is satisfied, *tepipew* (VAI); s/he is angry or mad while drinking alcohol, *kisôwipew* (VAI); s/he is sobering up after drinking alcohol, *âstepew* (VAI); s/he drinks a hot broth or soup, *kisâkamitehkwew* (VAI); the act of drinking a hot broth, *kisâkamitehkwewin* (NI).

drip It drips, *pahkikawiw* (VII); s/he makes it drip, *pahkikawihew* (VTI); s/he makes her/him or it drip by squeezing, *pahkikawinew* (VTA); the act of dripping, *pahkikawiwin* (NI); s/he is dripping blood, *pihkwâkew* (VAI).

drizzle *ka kaskawanpescasik* (VTI); *kimowasin* (VII).

drop The act of dropping something, *kitiskinikewin* (NI); s/he dropped it, *kitiskinam* (VTI); s/he dropped her/him, *kitiskinew* (VTA); s/he dropped her/him accidently, *kitiskipayihew* (VTA).

drown The act of drowning, *nistâpâwewin* (NI); s/he drowned, *nistâpawew* (VAI); s/he drowned her/him, *nistâpâwahew* (VTA); s/he drowned herself/himself, *nistâpawayisiw* (VTA).

drowsy A sense of being drowsy, *nohtihkwasiwâyâwin* (NI); *nohtehkwasiwin* (NI); s/he is extremely drowsy, *nipahihkwasiw* (VAI); s/he is drowsy, *pawinekwasiw* (VAI).

drum An aboriginal drum, *mistikwaskihk* (NA); a starting drum for a celebration, *mâtowehikan* (NA); a steel barrel, *pîwâpiskomahkahk* (NI); a wooden barrel, *mistikomahkahkos* (NI); s/he beats the starting drum in a celebration song, *mâtowetahikew* (VTA).

drummer One who beats the drum, *opakahamâw* (NA).

drumstick *pakamahâkanis* (NI).

drunk Being drunk, *kîskwepewin* (NI); s/he is drunk, *kîskwepew* (VAI); s/he got her/him drunk, *kîskwepâhew* (VTA).

drunken *ka kîskwepehk* (VAI).

drunkeness *kîskwepewin* (NI).

drunkness A person feeling drunk, *okîskwepewayaw* (VAI) .

dry When it is dry, *ka pâstek* (VTI); it is dry, *pâstew* (VII); s/he dries moose meat, *akwâwew* (VAI); s/he or it becomes dry, *pâhkopayiw* (VAI); there is little humidity of it is kind of dry, *pâhkwayâw*; s/he dries them, *pâhkwahwew* (VTI); it is dried up or parched, *pâhkwastew* (VII); s/he or it is dried, i.e.: by the sun, *pâhkosiw* (VAI) (Northern); *pâsow* (VAI) (Plains); s/he dries a moosehide, *pâsekinwew* (VAI); s/he dries berries, *pâsiminew* (VTI); s/he dries clothes for her/him, *pâsinâsikew* (VTA); s/he dries her/his own clothes, *pâsinâsiw* (VTA); s/he dries leaves, *pâsipakwew* (VTI); s/he made her/him dry off, *pâsohew* (VTA); s/he is dry, *pâsiw* (VAI); s/he dries her/him, *pâswew* (VTA); s/he dries meat, *pâswewokwew* (VTI); her/his face is dry, *pahkohkwehow* (VAI) (Plains); *pâhkohkwakanew* (VAI) (Northern); s/he drys her/his hands for her/him, *pahkocihcewew* (VTA) (Plains); *pâhkocihcenew* (VTA) (Northern); her/his eyes are dry, *pâstewacâpiw* (VAI) (Plains); *pâstewiskisikwew* (VAI) (Northern).

dubious Doubting someone, *eka ka mâmisîtotakehk*; s/he does it without believing it will succeed or s/he is dubious, *pakwanawâhtaw* (VAI); s/he acts in a dubious manner, *pakwanawisiw* (VAI); an uncertain action or being dubious, *pakwanawisiwin* (NI); s/he speaks to her/him in a dubious manner, *pakwanawimew* (VTA).

duck *sîsîp* (NA); a male duck or a drake, *nâpesip* (NA); a female duck, *nôsesip* (NA).

duck *ka tapahcipayihohk* (VAI); s/he ducks, *kahtapipayiw* (VAI).

duck egg *sîsîpâwi* (NI).

ducklings *sîsîpisisak* (NA).

due *ka ihtateyimiht awîyak* (VTA).

duel *mawineskâtowin* (NI).

dugout A boat, *wihpikahikan* (NI); s/he makes a dugout for them, *wihpikahwew* (VTA).

dull Something dull, *kîkway ka asâhtihk* (VTI); it is dull, *asâhtin* (VII).

dumb Not being able to speak, *namoya nihtâwew* (VAI); s/he thinks s/he is dumbfounded, *kepâteyimew* (VTA).

dummy *môhcohkân* (NA).

dump *wepinikewenihk* (NI).

dumpling *pakasimihkewin* (NI).

dunce *metoni ka kepâcâyeniw* (NA); *môcoweniw* (NA).

dung *mostosomiy* (NA).

duplicate *ka naspisihtahk kîkway* (VTI); *tatâpiskôc* (IPC).

duplication *naspisihcikewin* (NI).

durability *sîpâyâwin* (NI).

durable Something durable, *kîkway kâsepahk* (VTI); it is durable or strong, *maskawâw* (VTI); it is durable or longlasting, *sîpâyâw* (VII).

during *mekwâ* (IPC); *mekwâc* (IPC).

dusk *ka waninakwahk* (VII).

dusky *ka atihwaninakwahk* (VII).

dust Dust flying up, *kohpweyapahtek asiskîy* (NI); s/he dusts her/him off with a shake, *pahpawinew* (VTA); s/he dusts them off her/him by banging them on something, *pahpawisimew* (VTA); s/he dust it off by shaking it, *pahpawiwepinew* (VTA); s/he dusts or brushes them off, *pawahwew* (VTA).

duster *kanâcihcikakan* (NI); *pahpawahikan* (NI).

dusty *asiskîwan* (VII); *asiskîwiw* (VII).

dutiful *kwayaskwâtisiwin* (NI); the act of listening to someone's wishes, *nahihtamowin* (NI).

duty *kwayask ka tôtamihk* (VAI); s/he does her/his duty, *tipitôtam* (VAI); a moral obligation, *tipitôtamowin* (NI).

dwarf *apisciyenis* (NA); a small person, *apiscinis* (NA).

dwarf spruce *sihcisis* (NA) (Plains).

dwell Staying in one place for good, *ka kisci ayâhk nânitâw*; s/he dwells, *ayâw* (VAI).

dwelling *wîkowin* (NI); a permanent dwelling, *kisciwîkowin* (NI); a house, *waskiyikan* (NI); s/he has only one dwelling or home, *peyakokamikwew* (VAI).

dwindle *acôwipayiw* (VAI); shrinking in size, *acôwipayowin* (NI).

dye *atisikan* (NI).

dyeing *ka atisamihk kîkway* (VTI).

dying *athilpowin* (NI); the act of dying, *nipowin* (NI).

293

E

each *peyako* (IPC); separated, each in its own place or spot, in its own wrapping, etc., *piskihc* (IPC); *pahpiskihc* (IPC); at each place, *tahtweyahk* (LN).

eager *nanihkeyehtamowin* (NI); *sohkihatoskatam* (VTI).

eagle *kihew* (NA); *mikisiw* (NA); a big eagle, *misikihew* (NA); an eagle feather, *kihêwatanîy* (NA); a white eagle, *wâpiskikihew* (NA); *wâpikihew* (NA).

ear *mihtawakay* (NI).

ear ache *teyehtawakayewin* (NI) *(Northern)*; *mihtawakayâspinewin* (NI) *(Plains)*.

early *nawac* (IPC); *mâtayak* (IPC); *kîyipa* (IPC) *(Northern)*; *wîpac* (IPC) *(Plains)*.

earn The act of earning, *kîspinacikewin* (NI); s/he earns it, *kîspinatam* (VTI); the act of earning for someone, *kîspinatamâkewin* (NI); s/he earns it for herself/ himself, *kîspinatamâsiw* (VTA); s/he earns it for her/ him, *kîspinatamawew* (VTA).

earnest *sâpweyihtamowin* (NI).

earring *tâpihtehpison* (NA); s/he wears an earring, *tâpihtehpisiw* (VAI).

earth *askîy* (NI); the world or the whole earth, *misiwe askîy* (NI); over the whole earth, the whole universe, *misiweskamik* (IPC); on bare earth, *môstaskamik* (IPC); on the side of the earth, *pimitaskamik* (IPC); close to earth, *cîkaskamik* (IPC); there is dirt, earth, edge of cliff, *kîskahcâw* (NI); rough earth, dirt, soil, *pipikwahcâw* (VAI); *piskwahcâw* (NI); there is valley, plain, bowl shaped earth, *wâyahcâw* (NI).

earthenware *asiskîwîyâkan* (NI).

earthquake An expression used to indicate an earthquake and means "the ground trembles", *nanamaskipiyiw* (IPC) *(Plains)*; *nanamahcipayiw* (IPC) *(Northern)*

earwax *miskihtekom* (NA).

ease *ka wehcitahk* (VAI); easily or at ease, *wetinahk* (IPC).

easily *ka wehcepayik* (VTI).

easiness *wehce isâyâwin* (NI).

east Or towards the sunrise, *sâkâstenohk* (IPC); east towards the dawn, *wâpanotahk* (IPC).

easterly *sâkâstenohk etehki* (IPC).

eastern *eteh ka sâkâstek* (VII).

easy Something easy or not hard to do, *ka wihcasik* (VII); it is easy or simple, *wihcasin* (VII); s/he does it the easy or simple way, *wehcihiw* (VAI); the act of doing it the easy way, *wehcihowin* (NI); s/he has an

easy time attaining them, *wehcinatew* (VTA); it breaks easily, *wihcipîkopayiw* (VII); s/he finds her/him easy to get along with, *wihteyimew* (VTA); s/he thinks it is easy to attain, *wihteyihtam* (VTI); s/he is easy to get along with, *wehtisiw* (VAI); being easy to get along with, *wehtisowin* (NI).

eat Act of eating, *micisowin* (NI); s/he has had her/his fill, *kîspiw* (VAI); s/he eats, *micisiw* (VAI); having enough to eat, *kîspowin* (NI); s/he has given her/him enough to eat, *kîspohew* (VTA); s/he is satisfied after eating, *kîsposkoyiw* (VAI); s/he ate up all of the other person's food, *kitâmawew* (VAI); s/he ate everything up, *kitânawew* (VAI); the act of eating up everything, *kitânawewin* (NI); s/he ate it up, *kitâw* (VTI); s/he is eating right now, *mekwâmîcisiw* (VAI); s/he eats the sap of the trees, *mestasiw* (VAI); s/he makes her/him eat, *micisohew* (VTA); s/he eats it, *miciw* (VAI); s/he pretends to eat, *mîtisohkâsiw* (VAI); s/he eats berries from the fruit tree, *môminew* (VAI); s/he eats snow, *mowâkonew* (VAI); s/he eats them, *mowew* (VTA); s/he overeats and is sick, *osâmiskoyiw* (VAI); s/he eats marrow from a bone, *pâstasiw* (VAI); the act of eating marrow from a bone, *pâstasiwin* (NI); s/he eats with her/him, *wicimîcisomew* (VTA); s/he enjoys eating, *wihkipiw* (VAI); s/he eats greedily, *wihtikowiw* (VAI); the act of eating greedily, *wihtikowiwin* (NI); cannibal or insane person, *wihtikiw* (NA).

eavesdrop S/he is eavesdropping on them or her/him, *kîmihtawew* (VAI).

echo It echoes, *cistâwew* (VAI) *(Plains)*; the place echos, *cistâwepayiw* (VAI) *(Northern)*; the place is full of echos, *cistâweyâw* (VII); her/his dropping her/him created an echo, *cistâwesimew* (VTA); it is creating echos, *cistâwehtin* (VII); s/he or it makes an echoing sound, *ciwepayiw* (VAI); s/he causes or makes her/him echo, *cistâwehew* (VTA); s/he is creating echoes, *cistâwesin* (VAI); it echoes when s/he strikes it, *cistawetahwew* (VTI); state of echoing, *ciwew* (NI).

ecstasy *miyomahcihowin* (NI).

ecstatic *ka meyowatamopayihk* (VII); *miyawâyâmowin* (NI).

edge Right at the edge, *eskwayak* (IPC); along the edge, *sisone* (IPC); s/he edges this way, *pecipayiw* (VAI).

edgy *kisôwâyawin* (NI).

edible *ekâ ka manamecihk* (VTI); *ka mecihk* (VTI).

Edmonton The Cree word for Edmonton meaning "beaver mountain house", *amiskwaciwâskahikan* (NI).

educate *ka kiskinohamâkehk* (VTA); *kiskinohamâw* (NA).

education The act of teaching, *kiskinohamâkewin* (NI).

educational *kiskinohamakosiwinihk ohci* (LN).

295

educator *okiskinohamâkew* (NA).
effect *kisipayihcikewin* (NI).
efficiency *miyopayihcikewin* (NI).
efficient *ka miyopayihtahk* (VAI).
effort *sohki kociwin* (NI); *kociw* (VAI); *sohki atoskatam* (VAI).
effortless *nama kîkway sihciwin* (NI).
egg *wâwih* (NI); rotten egg, *asâwih* (NI); raw egg, *askâwih* (NI); s/he eats raw eggs, *askâwew* (VAI); a duck egg, *sîsîpâwih* (NI); a fish egg, *wâhkwan* (NI).
eider *sîsîp omekwana ka yoskâyekwâw* (NA); *kîsôwahohp* (NI).
eight *ayinânew* (IPC); eight each, *ahayinânew* (IPC); eight times, *ayinânewâw* (IPC); eight of a kind, *ayinânewayih* (IPC); eight different kinds, *ahayinânewayih* (IPC); in eight places or eight directions, *ayinânewayak* (IPC); in eight different places, *ahayinânewayak* (IPC); s/he is number eight or eighth, *ayinânewiw* (VAI).
eight hundred *ayinânewâw mitâtahtomitanaw* (IPC).
eighteen *ayenânewosâp* (IPC); eighteen times, *ayinânewosâpwâw* (IPC).
eighteenth *mweci ayinânewosâp* (IPC); eighteenth time, *ayinânewosâpwâw* (IPC); eighteenth of the month, *ayinânewosâp akimâw pîsim* (IPC).
eighth *mweciayinânew* (IPC); eighth time, *ayinânewâw* (IPC); eighth of the month, *ayinânew akimâw pîsim* (IPC).
eightieth *mweciayinânewomitanaw* (IPC); eightieth time, *ayinânewomitanawâw* (IPC).
eighty *ayinânemitanaw* (IPC); eighty times, *ayinânemitanawâw* (IPC).
either *pakotanima* (IPC); either one, *nikotwâw* (IPC).
ejaculate S/he ejaculates, *metawâkew* (VAI) (Plains).
ejaculation The act of ejaculation, *sîsîkocipicikewin* (NI) (Northern); *metawâkâtisowin* (NI) (Plains).
eject *ka wayawepinamihk kîkway*.
ejection *wayawepinikewin* (NI).
elaborate *ka âhkwatisik* (VAI).
elaboration *âhkwatisowin* (NI).
elate *ka miyawatamohiwehk* (VTA).
elation *miyawatamohiwewin* (NI); *miywâtamowin* (NI) (Plains); *meyawâyâmowin* (NI) (Northern).
elbow *mitôskwan* (NI).
elder *kihtehayah* (NA); *ostesimâw* (NA); *omisimâw* (NA); old man, *kiseyiniw* (NA).
elderly *ka kihtehayewihk* (VTA); *kihtehayowin* (NI).
eldest brother *ostesimâw* (NA).
elegance *kihkâc isâyâwin* (NI).
elegant *ka kihkâc ayâhk* (VAI).
elevate The act of elevating, *ohpastawin* (NI).

eleven *peyakosâp* (IPC); *mitâtaht peyakosâp* (IPC); eleven times, *peyakosâpiwâw* (IPC); there are eleven of them, *peyakosâpowiwak* (VII) (Northern); *peyakosâyihtasiwak* (VII) (Plains).
eleven hundred *peyakosâpwâw mitâtahtomitanaw* (IPC).
eleventh *mwecipeyakosâp* (IPC); eleventh time, *peyakosâpwâw* (IPC); eleventh of the month, *peyakosâp akimâw pîsim* (IPC).
eligible *kaskihtâwin* (NI).
eliminate *ponipayihcikewin* (NI).
elk *wâwâskesiw* (NA); an elk gall bladder, *wâwâskeswîsopiy* (NI).
elm *kisâstaw mîtosahtik* (NA).
elope Eloping, *kemoci sipwehtewin* (NI); s/he elopes with her/him, *kwâsihew* (VTA); he elopes with a woman, *kwâsihiskwewew* (VTA); elopement, *kwâsihiskwewewin* (NI); the act of eloping, *kwâsihiwewin* (NI).
eloquent *ka nihtâwtonamohk* (VAI).
else Where else, *tânte asci* (IPC); *tânte mîna* (IPC).
elsewhere *ohpime* (IPC).
elucidate *kwayask ka wihtamihk kîkway*.
elude *wemâskâcikewin* (NI).
emaciate *ka sihkacîhiwehk*.
emaciation *sihkacîhiwewin* (NI).
emanate *etah ka macipayik kîkway*.
embark Embarking onto a big ship, *ka posihk mistahôsihk*; s/he embarks onto a vehicle, *pôsiw* (VAI); the act of embarking onto a vehicle, *pôsiwin* (NI); s/he gets on something, *pôsiw* (VAI).
embarrass S/he embarrasses her/him, *nepewihew* (VTA); the act of embarrassing someone, *nepewihiwewin* (NI); s/he embarrassed her/him with her/his words, *nepewimew* (VTA); the act of being embarrassed, *nepewisiwin* (NI); s/he is embarrassed, *nepewisow* (VAI); s/he is embarrassed by her/him, *nepewakeyimew* (VTA); it is thought of as embarrassing, *nepewakeyihtâkwan* (VII); her/his description of it is embarrassing, *nepewotam* (VAI); s/he makes her/him embarrassed, *nepewihew* (VTA).
embarrassed *nepewokeyimow* (VAI).
embarrassing It is embarrassing, *nepewâkâc* (VAI); s/he has an embarrassing sickness, *nepiwaspinew* (VAI); the act of having an embarrassing sickness, *nepiwaspinewin* (NI).
embarrassment *ka nepewihiwehk* (VTA).
embellish *tako kiskinowâcihcikewin* (NI).
ember A piece of red hot charcoal, *iskoces* (NI).
embitter *kisôwâhitowin* (NI); *kisôweyihtam* (VAI).
embody *ka wiyawihtahk kîkway* (VTI).
embolden *sohkeyimohiwewin* (NI).

embrace *âkwaskitinitowin* (NI).

embroider Embroidery or ornamental sewing, *masinistahikewin* (NI); s/he embroiders, *masinistahamâkew* (VAI); s/he embroiders it, *masinistawew* (VTA).

emend *kwayaskwastâw* (VTI).

emerge *môskîw* (VAI).

emit *mekiwin* (NI),

emotion *mâmitoneyihcikan* (NA); *mosihowin* (NI).

emotional *mistahi ka iteyihtahk awîyak* (VAI).

emotive *mâmitoneyitamowin* (NI).

empathize S/he empathizes with her/him, *môsihtestamawew* (VTA) *(Plains)*; *wîsakeyitamostamawew* (VTA) *(Northern)*.

emphasis *ispahâkeyimowin* (NI).

emphasize *ka ispahâkemohk* (VAI).

empty Something empty, *ekâ kîkway kasowatek* (VTI); her/his stomach is empty, *iyiwatew* (VAI); it sits empty, *pisisikwâstew* (VII); it is empty, *pisisikwâw* (VII); s/he empties or evacuates the place, *sîkawiw* (VTA); s/he empties her/him, *sîkawihew* (VTA) *(Northern)*; *sîkonew* (VTA) *(Plains)*; s/he evacuates everything or s/he empties everything out, *sîkawihow* (VAI) *(Northern)*; *sîkonikew* (VAI) *(Plains)*; the act of evacuating everything or emptying everything out, *sîkawihowin* (NI) *(Northern)*; *sîkonikewin* (NI) *(Plains)*; s/he empties or drains it, i.e.: a pail, *sîkiwepinew* (VTA); s/he empties or cleans out the buckets, *sîkinew* (VTI).

emulate *ka kakwe atihkimohk* (VAI).

enable *niso kamakewin* (NI).

enchant *môcikihiwewin* (NI).

enchanting *ka môcikihiwehk* (VTA).

enchantment *môcikihitowin* (NI).

encircle Encircling something, *ka wâsakâmiskamihk* (VTI); encircling a specific area, i.e.: the territory of a moose, *pihciskanawew* (VAI); s/he goes all around it, *wâsakâmeskam* (VAI).

enclose *ka kipaskinahcikehk* (VTI).

encompass *ka wasakameskamihk kîkway* (VTI).

encounter A chance encounter or meeting, *sîsîkoc nakiskâtowin* (NI); s/he meets her/him by chance, *mekwaskawew* (VTA).

encourage S/he encourages her/him verbally, *sihkimew* (VTA).

encumber *ka micimpicikehk* (VTI).

encumbrance *micimipicikewin* (NI).

end Where it ends, *etah ka iskopayik* (VII); at the end, *ka iskweyanihk* (VII); at the very end, i.e.: end of a hallway, *kisipâyihk* (LN); at the very end, i.e.: a pole or tree, *wanaskowâhtak* (NI); in the end, finally, *piyisk* (IPC); this is the end, *kisipan* (VII); it is the end of a piece of land, *kisipaskamik* (NI); where the muskeg ends, *kisipaskamikâw* (NI); the end of the timber line, *kisipâskweyaw* (NI); where the hills end, *kisipatinâw* (NI); it has an end, *kisipâw* (VII); the end of a lake, *kisipikamâw* (NI); it has an end, *kisipisiw* (VAI); the end of a river flow, *kisipistikweyâw* (NI); s/he ends it, i.e.: a road, *nakamohtâw* (VAI); it ends or doesn't go any further, *nakamiw* (VII); *kisipayiw* (VII).

endear *naspic sâkihiwewin* (NI).

endeavor or **endeavour** *ka kocihtotamihk* (VAI); s/he tries, *kociw* (VTI).

ending *ponipayiw* (VII).

endless *ekâ kakisipak nâspicipayiw* (VII).

endurance *nipawiscikewin* (NI).

endure Enduring something, *ka nipawistamihk kîkway* (VTI).

enduring It is enduring, *nipawiscikewin* (NI).

enemy *ka pakwâteyimiht awîyak* (VTA).

energetic *ka kakâyawsehk* (VAI).

energy *kakâyâw ayâwin* (NI); *mâskâwatisowin* (NI).

enforce *sohkesicikewin* (NI).

engage *ka atoskemakihtahk kîkway* (VTI).

English *âkayâsimowin* (NI).

engross *wanâhewewin* (NI).

enhance *yahkakihcikewin* (NI).

enjoy The act of enjoying, *meyawâtamowin* (NI); s/he enjoys, *mîyowâtam* (VAI).

enjoyable *ka meweyihtamihk kîkway* (VAI).

enjoyment Or happiness, *cîhkeyihtamowin* (NI).

enlarge *mahkisehcikewin* (NI); s/he made an extension on her/his house, *âniskôsetâw* (VAI).

enlighten *kiskisohiwewin* (NI).

enliven *môcikihiwewin* (NI).

enmity The act of hating one another, *pakwâteyimetowin* (NI); s/he is at enmity with her/him, *ohteyimew* (VTA).

enormous *metoni mistahi kîkway* (IPC) or (VII); a real large size, *nipahimisâw* (VII).

enough *îkwayekohk* (IPC); *ekwayikok* (IPC); not too bad, well; enough, *îyiwek* (IPC); *îkwayikohk* (IPC); just enough, just right, *nahiyikohk* (IPC); enough, barely enough, *tipiyak* (IPC).

enrage *kisiwâsowin* (NI).

enrapture *miweyehtamohiwewin* (NI).

enrich *ka weyotisihiwehk* (VTA); s/he is rich, *weyotisiw* (VAI).

enrichment *weyotisihiwewin* (NI).

ensemble *mâmawinikewin* (NI).

ensnare *nakwâcikewin* (NI).

ensue *kîkway ka askôkemakahk* (VTI).

ensure *kehcinahiwewin* (NI).

entail *ka askôkehiwehk* (VTA).

297

entangle *ka wanâhipihkepayik kîkway* (VTI).

enter The act of entering into, *pihtokewin* (NI); s/he
enters into a hole, *kwayastew* (VAI); s/he becomes part
of her/his psyche, i.e.: guardian spirit,
pihcitahcahkoweskawew (VAI); s/he enters or fills
her/his heart, *pihciteheskawew* (VAI); it enters her/his
mouth, *pihcitonewkawew* (VTA); s/he enters into
someone's house, *pihtokwawew* (VTA); it enters or
leads into it, i.e.: railroad tracks going into a tunnel,
pihtokemow (VII); s/he enters, *pihtokwew* (VAI); it
enters into something, *pihtokwepayiw* (VAI).

enterprising *macipayihcikewin* (NI).

entertain The act of entertaining by an instrument, *ka
metawestamakehk* (VTA); s/he shows or gives them a
good time, *miyowatamohew* (VTA); s/he entertains
her/him, *pahpakwacihew* (VTA).

entertainer *ometawestamâkew* (NA).

entertaining Making music for someone,
miyometawestamâkewin (NI).

entertainment *kosehtahk metawewin* (VTI);
miyowatamowin (NI); the act of giving a good time,
miyawatamohiwewin (NI).

enthuse *ka îyehitohk* (VTA).

enthusiasm *îyehitowin* (NI).

enthusiastic *ka îyeyehsihk* (VAI).

entice *akâwâtamowin* (NI).

enticement *akâwâtamohiwewin* (NI).

entire *kahkiyaw* (IPC).

entirely *kahkiyaw ohci* (IPC).

entity *ka pîmâtisimakahk kîkway* (VTI).

entomb *nahinowewin* (NI).

entrail The insides of an animal, *otamyawa
pesiskowak ohci* (NI); an intestine or entrail,
mitakisiyâpiy (NI).

entrap *ka micimtisahoht awîyak* (VTA).

entreat *ka kâkesimototaht awîyak* (VTA).

entry *pihtokwewinihk* (NI).

entwine *pitikwahpicikewin* (NI).

envelop *wewekinkewin* (NI).

envelopment *tetipeweskâkewin* (NI).

enviable *ka sawânakeyemototaht awîyak* (VTA).

envious S/he would like to have it, *akâwâtam* (VAI);
s/he is envious of her/him, *sawânakeyimew* (VTA);
s/he acts envious towards her/him,
sawânakeyimotatawew (VTA); s/he is envious,
sawânakeyimiw (VAI); being envious,
sawânakeyimowin (NI).

envisage *oyehcikewin* (NI).

envision *neyâk kiskiwehikewin* (NI).

envy *sawânakeyimowin* (NI).

enwrap *koskohiwewin* (NI).

enwreathe *ka sweyapahtek* (VTI).

epistle *manito masinahikewin* (NI).

epitaph *masinahikewin ka kiskisohekohk kîkway* (NI).

equal All the same amount, *pahpeyakwan iyikohk*
(IPC); equal, level, or even, *papeyakwan* (IPC); s/he is
her/his equal, *tipihew* (VTA); s/he has equal
capabilities, *tipihtwâw* (VAI); s/he makes her/him an
equal, *tipiskocihew* (VTA); all the same, *pahpeyakwan*
(IPC).

equalize *pahpeyakwan mekiwin* (NI).

equally *peyakwan iyikohk* (IPC).

equate *ka kwayaskwakihcikehk* (VAI).

equip *ka nehpemascikehk* (VTI).

equipment *âpacihcikan* (NI).

equivalence *metoni tipahwan iyikohk* (VII).

equivalent *pahpeyakwaniyikohk* (IPC).

eradicate Eradicating sickness, *metoni kanipahtahk
âhkosowin* (VTA); the act of eradicating,
mescihtâniwan (NI); s/he eradicates them or kills
them off, *mescihew* (VTA); s/he eradicates everyone,
mescihtâsiw (VTI); to destroy completely,
mescihtâwin (NI).

eradication Or total destruction, *mescihtâsiwin* (NI).

erase Erasing something, *kîkway kâkasehamihk* (VTI);
s/he erases it for her/him, *kâsîhamawew* (VTA); s/he
erases them, *kâsinew* (VTI); it erases by itself,
kâsepayiw (VTI); the act of self-forgiveness, i.e.:
erasing sins or a pardon for oneself, *kâsnamasowin*
(NI); s/he forgives herself/himself, i.e.: erases her/his
sin, *kâsnamasiw* (VAI); s/he forgives her/him,
kâsnamawew (VTA).

erect *ka cimatahk kîkway* (VTI).

erection *cimacikewin* (NI); *mânokewin* (NI).

erode *ka mescipayik kîkway* (VTI).

erosion *ka mosci mecayak askîy* (VTI); *pikwapotek*
(VII).

erotic S/he has erotic thoughts about her/him,
pisikwâciteyîmew (VAI).

err *ka naspâtahkamiksihk* (VAI).

errand *kîkway ka tôtamâkehk* (VTA); a special job
entrusted to someone, *tôtamâkewin* (NI).

erratic *nanâtohkonikewin* (NI).

erroneous *ka kîyâskiskihk* (VAI).

error *patahamowin* (NI); *wanitotamowin* (NI).

erupt *ka pâstipayik askîy* (VTI); *pahkitew* (VII).

eruption *pâstipayowin* (NI); *môskipayiwin* (NI);
pahkitewaciy (NA).

escape The act of successfully escaping or eluding
danger, *paspîwin* (NI); s/he runs away, *tapasîw* (VAI);
s/he escapes into the hole, *kwayasteyâmiw* (VAI); s/he
has successfully escaped or eluded the danger, *paspîw*
(VAI); *paspînam* (VAI).

escarpment *ka kahkihtwam kîskâpiskâk waci* (VTI).

eschew *kîkway ka ponihtâhk* (VTI).

escort *awîyak ka kiskinohtahiht* (VTA).

especially *wâwîskîspin* (IPC).

essence *kîkway ka osihesomakahk* (VTI).

essential *ka mana patahamihk kîkway* (VTI); *poko ka âpacetahk* (VTI); it is of good use, *miyohapatan* (VII).

establish *miyo picikewin* (NI); s/he started something, *macihtaw* (VAI).

esteem Holding someone in high regard, *mistahi awîyak ka itiyimiht*; s/he has great esteem for her/him, *kihceyimew* (VTA); s/he is venerable, in high esteem, *kihceyitâkosiw* (VAI); esteem or great consideration, *kihceyitâkosowin* (NI) *(Northern)*; *kihceyihtâkosowin* (NI) *(Plains)*; it is venerable, *kihceyihtâkwan* (VAI); it is esteemable, *kihkâteyihtâkwan* (VAI) *(Northern)*; *kihceyihtâkwan* (VAI) *(Plains)*.

estimate Estimating the value of something, *koyakihcikehk* (IPC); s/he estimates her/his value, *oyakimew* (VTA); s/he estimates its value for her/him, *oyakihtamawew* (VTA); counting how much, *taniyikohk* (IPC).

estimation *oyakihcikewin* (NI).

estrange *ka kisestâtohk* (VTA); *wepinitowin* (NI); the act of hating one another, *pakwâtitowin* (NI).

estrangement *kisestâtowin* (NI).

etch *kîkway metoni keskwayak itah* (VII).

etching *iskosihcikewin* (NI).

eternal *ekâ wehkac ka ponipayik* (VII).

eternally *namakîkway iskopayiwin* (NI).

Eucharist God's bread, *manitopahkwesikan* (NI).

eulogize *awîyak ka mamihcimiht* (VTA).

eulogy *mamihcimowewin* (NI).

euphoria *miyomahcihowin* (NI).

euphoric *ka miyomahcihohk* (VAI).

evacuate *sisikoc nakacikewin* (NI); *tapasihtâwin* (NI); *tanakatamihk* (VTI); *tasipwitehk* (VTI); s/he evacuates everything or s/he empties everything out, *sîkawihow* (VAI) *(Northern)*; *sîkonikew* (VAI) *(Plains)*; the act of evacuating everything or emptying everything out, *sîkawihowin* (NI) *(Northern)*; *sîkonikewin* (NI) *(Plains)*.

evacuation *nakatâmotocikewin* (NI).

evade *kîkway ka wemâskâmihk* (VTI).

evader *awîyak ka nihta wemâskâhk* (NA).

evaluate *kîkway koyakihtamihk* (VTI).

evaluation *oyakihcikewin* (NI).

evangel *sohkâyamihâwin* (NI).

evangelical *pitôs sohkâyamihâwin* (NI).

evangelist *awîyak ka sohkâyamihât* (NA).

evangelize *pitôs sohkâyamihew kiskinohamâkewin* (NI).

evaporate *ka mestâpahtek*; *mescipayiw* (VAI).

evaporation *mestâpahtepayiwin* (NI).

evasion *wemâskâcikewin* (NI).

even Equal, *metoni pahpeyakwan* (IPC); s/he evens them up, *tipiskocahew* (VTA) *(Northern)*; *tipiskôtahew* (VTA) *(Plains)*; s/he is even with her/him, *tipiskocihew* (VTA); s/he makes her/him even, *tipiskocipayihew* (VTA); it comes out even, *tipiskocipayiw* (VII).

evening It is evening, *otâkosin* (VII); s/he has run out of time or the sun is going down, i.e.: evening, *otâkwanisiw* (VAI); tonight, this evening, *otâkosiki* (IPC); last night, last evening, *otâkosehk* (IPC).

event *kîkway ketahkamekahk* (VTI); some kind of happening, *ispayiwin* (NI).

eventful *nanâtohk ketahkamikahk* (VTI).

eventual *peyisk kîspayik kîkway* (VII).

ever *wehkac* (IPC); habitually and ever, *tahki mâna* (IPC); just always and ever, *tahki sôskwâc* (IPC).

evergreen *sihta* (NA);. *minahik* (NA).

everlasting Lasting forever, *kahkike* (IPC).

every *kahkiyaw ohci* (IPC); *tahto* (IPC).

everybody *kahkiyaw itasiyek* (IPC); *kahkiyaw awîyak* (IPC); *tahto awîyak* (IPC).

everyday *tahtokîsikâw* (IPC).

everyone *kahkiyaw ohci awîyak* (NA); *kahkiyaw etasiyek* (IPC); as many as there are, any one, every one, everything, *tahto* (IPC).

everything *kahkiya kîkway* (IPC); *kahkiyaw* (IPC); *kahkiyaw kîkway* (IPC); *tahtokîkway* (IPC); as many as there are, any one, every one, everything, *tahto* (IPC).

everywhere *misiweyita* (IPC); it goes everywhere, *misiweyispayiw* (VII); all over the place or everywhere, *papâmih* (IPC).

evident *kîkway ka kihkânâkwahk* (VTI).

evidently *peyisk ka tâpwepayik* (VAI).

evil *maci*; being an evil person, *macâtisowin* (NI); s/he is evil, *macâtisiw* (VAI); s/he does evil, *macayiwiw* (VAI); the act of doing evil, *macâyiwiwin* (NI); s/he has an evil face, *macihkwew* (VAI); an evil son, *macikosisân* (NA); he is an evil son, *macikosisaniwiw* (VAI); evil mind, *macimâmitoneyihcikan* (NI); s/he has an evil mind, *macimâmitoneyitam* (VTI); s/he has evil thought about her/him or them, *macimâmitoneyimew* (VTA); it appears evil, *macinâkwan* (VII); s/he speaks evilly, *macipikiskwew* (VAI).

evildoer *awîyak ka macitôtahk* (NA).

evildoing *macitôtamowin* (NI).

evil eye *maci kanawapahkewin* (NI).

evince *kihkâyapamohiwewin* (NI).

299

evocation *netawecikewin* (NI).

evocative *kanihta netawecikehk* (VTA).

evoke *ka kiskisohiwehk* (VTA).

ewe A female sheep, *nôsemayatihk* (NA).

exact *mweci ekotah* (IPC); *mweci* (IPC); just enough, the exact quantity, *nahiyikohk* (IPC).

exacting *metoni kwayask* (IPC).

exactly *metoni katawahk* (IPC); *metoni* (IPC); exactly there, on the exact spot, *mwehci* (IPC).

exaggerate S/he says too much, *ayîwak itwew* (VAI); s/he exaggerates her/his speech about her/him, *osâmimew* (VTA); s/he says too much, *ayiwâkitwew* (VAI).

exaggeration *kwanta ayîwak tôtamowin* (NI).

exalt *mistahi ka iteyimowehk* (VTA).

exaltation *misteyihcikewin* (NI).

exam *ka koteyimiht awîyak* (VTA).

examination *koteyimowewin* (NI); asking questions as a test, *nitosahikewin* (NI).

examine The act of being examined, *wâpamowewin* (NI); s/he examines what s/he does with great care, *nâkatâpamew* (VTA).

example *nâspitôtamowin* (NI).

exasperate Making someone frustrated, *kisowayawihewewin* (NI); s/he is exasperated by her/him, *osameyimew* (VTA).

exceed *pasciwepinikewin* (NI); *osam mistah ayîwak*; too much, *osamistahi* (IPC).

exceeding Goes over the top, *metoni pascipayew* (VII).

exceedingly *pasciwepinikewenihk* (IPC); *pasciwepinikewin* (NI).

excel *nîkânîwin* (NI).

excellence *metoni nekânapiwin* (NI); *nahîwin* (NI).

excellent *metoni ka nahihk* (VAI); *ka miyotôtamihk* (VAI); it is very good, *mitonimiwasin* (VII).

except *kîkway poko* (IPC).

excepting *ka otinkîstamakehk kîkway* (VTA).

exception *piskihtascikewin* (NI).

exceptional *piskihtakihcikewin* (NI).

excess *metoni mistahi* (IPC); too much of something, *ayiwâkipayiw* (VAI).

excessive Too much, *waweyak mistahi* (IPC); s/he has an excessive character, *ayiwâkâtisiw* (VAI); excessiveness, *osâmihisiwin* (NI).

excessively *pasciwininekewinihk* (IPC); *pasciwepinikewin* (NI).

exchange Exchanging something, *meskotonikewin* (NI); *mestotonamâkewin* (NI); in exchange or in return, *meskoc* (IPC); s/he exchanges her/his or its place, *meskotahew* (VTA); they exchange things, *meskotonamâtowak* (VAI); s/he exchanges it with her/

him, *meskotonamâwew* (VTA); the act of exchanging, *meskotonamâtowin* (NI).

exchangeability *ka nihtâ meskotônikehk* (VTI).

exchangeable *meyomeskotônkewin* (NI).

excitability *ka môcikihiweskihk* (VTA).

excitable *omôcikihiwew* (NA).

excitation *môcikihiwewin* (NI).

excite *ka môcikihiwehk* (VTA).

excitement *môcikâyâwin* (NI); *meyowâtamowin* (NI); a little too much excitement or movement, *osâmahkamik* (IPC).

exclaim *sisikôc ka tepwehk* (VAI).

exclamation *sisikôc tepwewin* (NI).

exclude *ka piskiht astâhk* (VTI).

exclusion *piskiht ascikewin* (NI).

exclusive *piskiht akihcikewin* (NI).

excommunicate *ayamehâwin ka ponihtahk* (VTI).

excommunication *poni-ayamehâwin* (NI).

excrement Waste matter eliminated from the human body, *meyih* (NI); it smells like excrement, *meyakan* (VII) *(Plains)*; *miyakan* (VAI) *(Northern)*; s/he smells like excrement, *meyakisiw* (VAI) *(Plains)*; *miyakisiw* (VAI) *(Northern)*.

excremental *miciwin ka wepinamihk meyâwihk ohci* (VTI).

excrete *maci kîkway ka wepenamihk* (VTI).

excretion *wepinikewin* (NI); discharging of the feces, *kamisehk* (VAI).

excruciating *ka nâspic wesakahpinehk* (VAI).

excuse *kasenamakewin* (NI); *kwetawe itwewin* (NI).

execute *awîyak ka akotiht* (VTA); s/he is killed, *nipahaw* (VAI).

exemplary *naspî sayahiwewin* (NI).

exemplification *meyohayesinâkewin* (NI).

exemplify *kamiyo ayesinâkehewehk* (VTA).

exempt *ekâ ka akihtâmakehk* (VTA).

exercise Active performance for the purpose of training, *sesawewin* (NI).

exert S/he exerts herself/himself, *sihciw* (VAI); s/he exerts power, i.e.: pulling on something, *wihkiw* (VAI); s/he manages to break free by exerting herself/himself, *wihkwaciw* (VAI).

exertion The act of trying your hardest, *sihciwin* (NI); moving, *ka waskawehk* (VAI).

exhale S/he exhales or s/he lets her/his breath out, *pakitatâhtam* (VTA); the act of exhaling, *pakitatâhtamowin* (NI).

exhaust The act of using something up, *mescipayicikewin* (NI); s/he is exhausted or totally used up, *mescipayiw* (VAI).

300

exhausted The act of being exhausted, *nohtesinowin* (NI); s/he exhausts her/him, *nohtesimew* (VTA); s/he is exhausted, *nohtesin* (VAI).

exhaustion *ka nipahinestosihk* (VAI).

exhaustive *kîkway ka nestomakahk* (VTI).

exhaustless *ekâ konestosowenihk* (VAI).

exhibit *ka wapahtehiwehk kîkway* (VTI); s/he is showing something, *wapahtihiwew* (VTI).

exhilarate *ka sohki payihcikehk* (VAI).

exhilaration *sohki payihcikewin* (NI).

exhort *ka asweyihtamihk* (VAI).

exhortation *asweyihcikewin* (NI).

exist *pemâtisiwin* (NI); *ihtaw* (VAI).

existence Being in a place, *ayâwin* (NI); the act of making a living, *pimâcihowin* (NI); s/he has three elements to her/his existence, *nistwayakihiw* (VAI).

existent *kîkway ka pimâtahk* (VAI).

exit *otahk wayawewin* (NI).

exodus *mamawisipwehtewin* (NI).

exorcise *ayamihâwin ohci ka yikatetisahoht macâhcâhk* (VTA).

exorcism *ayamihestamakewin* (NI).

exotic *môstâpekasewesimowin* (NI).

expand *ka mahki sehcikehk* (VTI); *ayiwâk* (IPC); *micit nawac* (IPC).

expanse *ka pihcak kîkway* (VII).

expansion *mahkisihcikewin* (NI).

expansive *ka pihcikamak sakahikan* (VII).

expect *ka ihtateyihtamihk; pakoseyimow* (VAI).

expectancy *ihtateyihcikewin* (NI).

expectant *awîyak ka ihtateyimiht* (VTA).

expectation *ka ihtateyicikehk* (VAI); *âsawapowin* (NI).

expectorate S/he spits, *sihkiw* (VAI).

expediency *akâwâcikewin* (NI).

expedient *ka akâwâcikehk* (VAI).

experience *kiskinohamâsiwin kîkway ka tôtamihk* (VTI).

experienced *awîyak ka nakacihtat* (VTA).

explain *kwayask ka wehtamihk* (VTA); *mâmiskôtam* (VTI); *kwayaskwîhtam* (VAI).

explanation *kwayask wehtamowin* (NI).

explicit *metoni ka kihkâpekiskwehk* (VAI).

explode It explodes, *pahkitew* (VII); it explodes, i.e.: a car blew up, *pahkisiw* (VAI); being exploded, *pahkisiwin* (NI); s/he is struck by an explosion set off by someone else, *pahkiswâw* (VAI); s/he blew her/him up, i.e.: with an explosive, *pahkiswew* (VTA).

exploit *ka awahkanihkehk* (VTA).

exploitation *awahkanihkewin* (NI).

exploration *netawaskewin* (NI).

explore *ka netawaskehk* (VTI).

explorer *onetawaskeweyeniw* (NA).

explosion *pahkisikewin* (NI); it explodes, there is an explosion, *pahkisiw* (VAI); *pahkitew* (VII).

explosive *ka pahkitek kîkway* (VTI); *pahkisikakana* (NI).

expose Exposing something, *mosenikewin* (NI); s/he exposes, *nôkohisiw* (VAI); s/he exposes all kinds of things about her/him, *nanâtohkomew* (VTA); s/he exposes it, *nôkotaw* (VTI); s/he exposes herself/himself to them, *nôkohosestawew* (VTA); s/he is exposed, *nôkohow* (VAI); the act of exposing, *nôkohtawin* (NI).

exposure *mosis wapahtihiwewin* (NI); s/he opens it up or uncovers it, *môskinam* (VTI).

expound *kwayask wehtamâkewin* (NI).

express *kâkwayask kowehk* (VAI).

expression *kwayaskowewin* (NI).

expressive *kwayask kîkway kîsayak* (VII).

expressly *kwayaskonikewin* (NI).

exquisite *ka osam miyo nakwahk* (VII).

extend Extending something, *yahkascikewin* (NI); s/he extends her/his hand to her/him, *awicicestawew* (VTA) *(Northern) isiniskestawew* (VTA) *(Plains)*; s/he extends her/his arms, *awiniskew* (VAI); s/he extends her/his arm towards her/him, *awiniskestawew* (VTA); s/he extends her/his hands, *awicicew* (VAI) *(Northern)*; *isiniskestakew* (VAI) *(Plains)*.

301

extended *ka yahkâstahk* (VTI); already extended, *ka kîsiyakastahk* (VTI).

extension *yahkâstaw* (VTI); *ka kinosetahk* (VTI); *ka yahkisetahk* (VTI).

exterior *wayawîtimâyihk* (LN); from the outside, *wayawîtimiyihk* (LN).

external *wayawîtimihk ohci* (VII); *wayawîtimâyihk* (LN).

extinguish *âstawehikewin* (NI); s/he puts out the fire, *âstaweham* (VAI).

extortion *ka natotsahamihk tipahamâtowin* (VTI).

extra *ayiwâkes* (IPC).

extract *kîkway ka manapicikatek* (VTI); s/he pulls it out, *wehkwacipitam* (VAI).

extraction *manapitepicikewin* (NI); *mepit ka ocipitamihk* (VTI).

extraordinary *nâspic miyo kîkway* (IPV).

extravagance *môhco mestinikewin* (NI).

extravagant *ekâ ka manâcihiht sôniyâw* (VTI); *nihtamestinikew* (VAI).

extreme More than, *ayîwak* (IPC); s/he goes to extremes, *nânôsamâcipayiw* (VAI); s/he makes them go to extremes, *nânôsamâciwihew* (VTA); s/he goes too far or s/he is extreme, *ôsamipayiw* (VAI).

extremely *naspic* (IPC); very, very much, *metoni mistahi* (IPC); the highest, greatest, slowest, etc., *mamawâyas* (IPC).

extremity *metoni isko iskweyâc* (IPC); at the end, on the extremity, *wanaskoc* (IPC).

extricate *ka tahtapihkenikehk* (VTI).

exuberance *môcikeyihtamowin* (NI).

exude *ka wayawîyâpahtek* (VTI).

exult *misteyihcikewin* (NI).

exultation *misteyimowewin* (NI).

eye *miskîsik* (NA); the eye berry or red currant (found in the muskeg), *miskîsikomin* (NI); s/he rubs her/his own eyes, *mimikwapiw* (VTA); s/he has swollen eyes, *pâkacapiw* (VAI); her/his eyes close, *pasakwapipayiw* (VAI); s/he closes her/his eyes, *pasakwâpiw* (VAI); the act of closing the eyes, *pasakwapiwin* (NI); her/his eyes are dry, *pâstewacapiw* (VAI); the eyes on her/him are dry, *pâstewiskisikwew* (VTA); s/he has something in her/his eyes, *pisin* (VAI); s/he sticks something in her/his eye, *pisinihew* (VAI); having something in the eye, *pisinowin* (NI); s/he is able to keep her/his eyes open for a long time, *sâsepatawapiw* (VAI); s/he applies oily or greasy cosmetics to her/his eyes, *tômacâpinew* (VTA); s/he applies oily or greasy cosmetics to her/his own eyes, *tômacâpinisiw* (VAI); s/he has an eye sickness, i.e.: cataracts, *wayesâpiw* (VAI); an eye sickness, i.e.: cataracts, *wayesâpowin* (NI).

eyeball *pihcâyihk ohci miskîsik* (NI).

eyebrow *masinihcapowinan* (NI).

eyeful *awîyak ka miyonâkosit* (VII).

eyelash *mîsapowinân* (NI).

eyelid *kipaskapowinan* (NI) *(Northern)*; *pasakwâpiwinân* (NI) *(Plains)*.

eyeopening *tohkaskapayowin* (NI).

eyesight *wapiwin* (NI); having good eyesight, *nahâpiwin* (NI); s/he has good eyesight, *nahâpiw* (VAI).

eye socket *oskîsikokanân* (NI).

eyetooth *kinwâpicikanân* (NI).

F

fabric It is strong fabric or cloth, i.e.: heavy canvas, *sohkekan* (VII) *(Plains)*; *maskawekiniwiw* (VII) *(Northern)*; a strong piece of fabric or cloth, *sohkekin* (NI) *(Northern)*; *maskawekin* (NI) *(Plains)*; a cloth for making dresses, i.e.: gingham, *miskotâkayekin* (NI).

fabulous *naspic ka mewasik* (VII).

face *mihkwâkan* (NI); s/he has a disfigured face, *mâyihkwew* (VAI); s/he makes faces, *mâyihkweyiw* (VAI); s/he has a pleasant face, *miyohkwenakosow* (VAI); s/he faces her/him, *otiskawiskawew* (VTA); her/his face is dry, *pâhkohkwakanew* (VAI); s/he dries her/his own face, *pâhkohkwihiw* (VAI); s/he has a swollen face, *pâkihkwipayiw* (VAI); her/his face is stained, *atihtewihkwew* (VAI).

face cloth *pahkohkwehonis* (NI).

faceless *ekâ ka ohkwakanihk* (VAI).

facile *ka wehciyohk* (VAI).

facing *ka ohtiskawkapawihk* (VAI).

fade *kîkway ka wapastek* (VII); *wapastew* (VII).

fail *ka sâkohikohk* (VTI); *namoya kaskitâw* (VTI).

failing *sâkohikowin* (NI).

failure *ka sâkocihikohk* (VTI); *pîkopayiw* (VII).

faint A fainting spell, *kipatâhtamowin* (NI); s/he fainted, *kipatâhtam* (VAI).

fair Even-handed and moral, *kwayaskwâtisiwin* (NI); s/he has light colored skin, *wâpâsiw* (VAI).

fair-haired *ka wâpâstehanskwehk* (VAI).

fairly *kwayaskopayihcikewin* (NI).

faith *tâpokeyihtamowin* (NI); s/he has faith in her/him, *âpateyimew* (VTA) articles of faith (creed), *âpateyihtamowin* (NI); having faith, *tâpwewokeyihtamowin* (NI).

faithless Not believing in religion, *eka kayâmihahk* (VAI); *eka ka tâpokeyihtamihk* (VAI).

faithful *metoni ka tâpokeyihtamihk* (VAI).

falcon *onocayikowiw* (NA) *(Northern)*; *onôtayikowew* (NA) *(Plains)*.

fall The act of falling, *pahkisiniwin* (NI); it falls down, *pahkihtin* (VII); what a stumbling fool, *pakisinohkan* (NA); s/he falls with legs splayed, *kahkapepayiw* (VAI); s/he falls asleep, *kawihkwasiw* (VAI); s/he falls down, *kawipayiw* (VAI); s/he pulls her/him and s/he falls down, *kawipitew* (VTA); s/he makes her/him go to bed, *kawisimôhew* (VTA); retiring, falling or going to bed, *kawisimowin* (NI); s/he goes to bed, *kawisimiw* (VAI); s/he collapses from the weight, *kawiskosiw* (VAI); it collaspes from the load, *kawiskotew* (VII); it falls off accidently, *kitiskipayow* (VII); s/he falls upside down, *otihtapihtin* (VAI); s/he drops her/him, *pahkisimew* (VTA); s/he falls down, *pahkisin* (VAI); it falls on the ice roughly, *pakamiskohtin* (VII); s/he falls on the ice roughly, *pakamiskosin* (VAI); s/he makes her/him fall into the water, *pakastawewew* (VTA); s/he falls in the water, *pakastawepayiw* (VAI); it falls off the shelf, *pinipayiw* (VII); s/he or it falls in, *pôsipayiw* (VAI) (VII); it falls into place, *tâpisin* (VII); it falls in the middle, *tâwihtin* (VII); s/he falls in the middle, *tâwisin* (VAI); s/he caused something or someone to fall through the ice, *twâsimew* (VTA).

fall It is fall or fall time, *takwâkin* (VII) or (NI); the fall of the leaves, i.e.: fall time, *pinâskiw* (VII); when all the leaves have fallen, *mestaskiw* (VII); this fall, *oma ka takwâkik*; fall is starting or "fall is young and new", *oskitakwakin* (NI).

fallacy *kîmôtâtisiwin* (NI).

fallen *kîkway ka kehpahkihtihk* (VTI); it falls down, *pahkihtin* (VII); it is lying propped up, *âsosin* (VAI); *âsohtin* (VII); tired no longer, rested after laying down, *âstesin* (VAI); lying thus, fallen this way, *isisin* (VAI); *ishtin* (VII); tired of laying down, *iskisin* (VAI); *iskihtin* (VII); dizzy from falling, *koskwesin* (VAI); *koskwehtin* (VII); blocking the way lying down, fallen, *kipisin* (VAI); *kipihtin* (VII); pricked, (hurt) wounded after puncturing foot, *kisisin* (VAI); heard falling, *matwesin* (VAI); *matwehtin* (VII); well laid, it fits well, *nahisin* (VAI); *nahihtin* (VII); fallen in two pieces, *nâtwâsin* (VAI); *nâtwâhtin* (VII); dead tired, needing to lay down, *nohtesin* (VAI); hitting something while falling, *pakamisin* (VAI); *pakamihtin* (VII); fallen, falling, *pakisin* (VAI); *pakihtin* (VII); a part came off falling, *pahkwesin* (VAI); *pahkwehtin* (VII); split while falling, *pâstisin* (VAI); *pâstihtin* (VII); hurt by a fall, *wisakisin* (VAI); *wisakihtin* (VII); hurt while hitting the ice falling, *pahkamiskosin* (VAI); *pahkamiskohtin* (VII); from a whole, comes off on its own, *manipayiw* (VAI); *manipayin* (VII); I am falling or I have fallen, *nipahkisinin* (VAI); you are falling or you have fallen, *kipahkisinin* (VAI), o/he or it is falling or has fallen, *pahkisin* (VAI); we are falling or have fallen, *nipahkisininan* (VAI); we are falling or have fallen, *kipahkisininaw* (VAI); you are falling or have fallen, *kipahkisininawaw* (VAI); they are falling or have fallen, *pahkisinwak* (VAI).

false *kiyâskiwin* (NI); *naspâc* (IPC); s/he amplifies her/his false accusation, *ayiwâkimew* (VTA).

falsehood *kiyâskiwayawin* (NI); the telling of lies, *kahkiyâskowin* (NI).

falsify *kiyâskew isehcikewin* (NI).

303

falsity *ka kakiyâskiskihk* (VAI).

falter *piswahcahikewin* (NI).

famed *kiskeyihtâkosiwin* (NI).

familiar Being familiar with something, *ka nakacihtahk* (VAI); s/he is familiar with her/him, *nakacihew* (VTA); s/he knows her/him well, *nistaweyimew* (VTA); s/he is familiar with hearing her/his voice, *nakayâhtawew* (VTA).

familiarity *ka nakacihtamowayahk* (VII).

familiarize *nakacihtamohiwewin* (NI).

family All in one family, *ka peyakoskânewihk* (NA); one family, one bond; one tribe; one nation, *peyakôskan* (NA); s/he is with her/his own family, *kikosew* (VAI); the act of being with family, i.e.: a family setting, *kikosewin* (NI); s/he is together with the entire family, *kistôtew* (VAI); being together with the entire family, *kistôtewewin* (NI); s/he has a large family, *mihcetiw* (VAI); they are one family, one tribe, one nation, *peyakoskânesowak* (VAI).

famish *metoni nohtehkatewin* (NI).

famous *kihci isâyâwin* (NI); being well-known, *kiskeyihtâkosiwin* (NI).

fan They fan out to different places, *nanânistohtewak* (VAI); the act of fanning out to different places, *nanânistohtewin* (NI).

fanciful *wâneyihtamâyâwin* (NI).

fancy *awîyak ka miweyimiht* (VTA).

fang *atim mepit* (NI) *(Northern)*; *atim mipit* (NI) *(Plains)*.

fantastic *kakoskohikohk kîkway* (VTI).

fantasy *ka isi akâwâtamihk*; an unrestrained imagination, coveting, *akâwâcikewin* (NI).

far *wâhyaw* (IPC); quite a ways, *wâhyawîs* (IPC); too far, *osam wâhyaw* (IPC); not quite far enough, lacking, short or mark, *nohtâw* (VII); it is far or a long way, *pihcâw* (VII).

faraway *wâhyaweskamik* (IPC).

fare *pôsiwin ka tipahamihk* (VTI).

farewell *iskwayac atamiskâtowin* (NI).

farther *wâhyaw nawâc* (IPC); *wahiyawes nawâc* (IPC); farther off that way; *awastisi* (IPC); farther away "than where you are", *awasita* (IPC); in a room farther way, next room, *awasayik* (IPC).

farthermost *metoniwâhyaw* (IPC).

farthest *ayîwak wâhyaw* (IPC).

fascinate People are intrigued by you, *ka mâmaskâteyihtâmohiwehk* (VTA); s/he is fascinated by it or s/he is attracted to it, *mâmaskâtikosiw* (VAI).

fascination Being a fascination for other people, *mâmaskâteyihtamohewewin* (NI); being fascinated, *mâmaskâtikosiwin* (NI).

fast The act of being fast, *kîyipewin* (NI); fast or quick, *katastapehk* (VII); s/he is fast, *kîyipiw* (VAI); too fast or too soon, *osâm kîyipa* (IPC); it happens fast or quickly, *kîyipan* (VII); s/he uses them up fast or quickly, *kîyipinew* (VTA); it is moving fast, i.e.: a bullet, *kisekotew* (VII); it is moving fast, i.e.: a car, *kisiskâpayiw* (VAI); s/he runs fast, *mihkawikew* (VAI).

fast S/he fasts, *iyiwanisihisiw* (VAI); s/he makes her/him fast, *iyiwanisihisohew* (VTA); the act of fasting, *iyiwanisihisowin* (NI).

fasten Tying something up securely, *ayâtâhpecikewin* (NI); s/he fastens them firmly together, *sanaskinew* (VTA); s/he fastens is firmly, *ayîtahpisiw* (VAI) *(Plains)*; *ayâtâhpisiw* (VAI) *(Northern)*.

fastening *sakâskwahikewin* (NI).

fastness *kweyahowin* (NI).

fat *wiyin* (NI); being fat, *wiyinowin* (NI); s/he is fat, i.e.: used to refer to animals which are ready to be slaughtered or hunted, *paskonew* (VAI); the fat covering found outside the stomach of animals, *wîsih* (NI); s/he makes her/him fat, *wiyinohew* (VTA); it has fat on it, *wiyinomakan* (VII); s/he is fat, *wiyiniw* (VAI) *(Plains)*; *wîyinowisiw* (VAI) *(Northern)*.

fatal *kîkway ka nipohikohk* (VTI); *nipowin* (NI).

father *ohtâwîmâw* (NA); *opâpâmâw* (NA); my father, *nohtâwiy* (NA), *nipâpâ* (NA); someone's father, *awîyak ohtâwîmâh* (NA); *awîyak opâpâmâh* (NA); he is her/his surrogate father, *ohtâwiskawew* (VAI); he becomes her/his father, *ohtâwihkawew* (VAI).

father-in-law *osisimâw* (NA); my father-in-law (or uncle), *nisis* (NA); someone's father-in-law, *awîyak osisisa* (NA); he is a father-in-law, *osisimâwiw* (VAI); s/he has a father-in-law, *osisiw* (VAI).

fatherless *kewâtisowin* (NI).

fatigue *nestowayawin* (NI); the act of being tired, *nestosowin* (NI).

fatten Fattening an animal, *pisisko ka weyinohiht* (VTA); s/he has fattened or s/he gains weight, *tâhcipiw* (VAI); s/he fattens her/him or s/he makes her/him gain weight, *tâhcipohew* (VTA).

fatty It is fatty, *paweyaw* (VII); *weyinowiw* (VII).

fault *awîyak otôtamowin* (NI).

favor or favour *miyo tôtakewin* (NI); *ohcestamâkewin* (NI).

favorable or favourable *take miyopayik keteyihtakwahk* (VII).

favorably or favourably *ka isi miyopayik kîkway* (VII).

favored or favoured *awîyak ka nawasoniht* (VTA).

favorite or favourite *awîyak ka ayîwakeyemiht* (VTA); one who is loved, *sâkihakan* (NA).

fawn *oskâyisis apisimosos* (NA); *apisimososis* (NA).

fear *kostamowin* (NI); feeling fearful, *ka
kostaciwâyâhk* (VAI); being scared, *sîkisowin* (NI);
being fearful of someone, *kosiwewin* (NI); being
fearful, *kostâciwin* (NI) *(Plains)*; *kostaciwâyâwin* (NI)
(Northern); s/he is regarded as being fearful or
dreadful, *kostâteyihtâkosiw* (VAI); it is to be feared or
dreaded, *kostâteyihtâkwan* (VII); s/he is to be feared or
dreaded, *kostâtikosiw* (VAI); it is fearful or dreadful,
kostâtikwan (VII); s/he fears her/him, *kostew* (VTA);
s/he is afraid to talk to her/him, *kostonâmew* (VTA);
s/he is afraid to speak, *kostonâmiw* (VAI); being fearful
to speak, *kostonâmowin* (NI).

fearful Being fearful, *kostâciwâyâwin* (NI) *(Northern)*;
kostâciwin (NI) *(Plains)*; s/he is fearful, *kostâciw* (VAI);
s/he finds her/him fearful, *kostateyimew* (VTA).

fearless *ka nâpehkâsohk* (VAI); *sohkitehew* (VAI).

fearsome *kostânakeyimowin* (NI).

feast A group feast, *mâmawimitsowin* (NI); s/he hosts
or puts on a feast, *wihkohkew* (VAI); s/he makes them
take part in a feast, *wihkohtohew* (VTA); s/he takes
part in a feast, *wihkohtow* (VAI); s/he invites her/him
to a feast, *wihkomew* (VTA); the act of hosting or
putting on a feast, *wihkohkewin* (NI).

feast day *wihkohtowikisikaw* (NI).

feat *ka tôtamihk kîkway* (VTI).

feather *mekwan* (NA); a duck feather, *sîsîp pîwây* (NA).

feathered *kîkway kopiwawik* (VAI).

feathery *ka opiwayâyik wiyaw* (NI).

feature Having different features, *nâtohkonakosowin*
(NI); s/he has no visually distinguishing features,
nanâtohkonakosiw (VAI).

featureless *ekâ ka mamoyinakosihk* (VAI).

February The eagle moon or month; the bald eagle
moon or month *(Plains)*, *mikisowipîsim* (NI).

feeble *nawac poko ka nipowâyâhk*; being weak,
nesowisowin (NI).

feed Feeding cattle, *pisiskowak kasamihtwaw*; s/he
feeds her/him, *asâmew* (VTA); cattle feed,
asâmastimwewin (NI); s/he feeds people or s/he share
her/his food, *manasahkew* (VAI); s/he feed them bland
food, *peyekoskohew* (VTA).

feel S/he feels for her/him, *mosihow* (VTA), s/he feels,
itamahcihiw (VAI); s/he feels bad, i.e.: health-wise,
mayimahcihow (VAI); s/he feels for her/him with her/
his hands, *miskonew* (VTA); s/he feels her/his
presence, *mosihew* (VTA); s/he feels her/his pain,
môsihtestamawew (VTA) *(Plains)*;
wîsakeyitamostamawew (VTA) *(Northern)*.

feeling How someone is feeling, *itamahcihiwin* (NI);
s/he is not feeling well, *mâyâyâw* (VAI); the act of not
feeling well, *mâyâyâwin* (NI); intuition or feeling,
mosihowin (NI); a physical sensation or feeling,

mosihtâwin (NI); the way one feels, health,
itamahcihiwin (NI).

feet *misita* (NI).

feign *mwecitapwi* (IPC).

felicitous *ka môcikimisohk* (VAI).

felicity *môcikimisowin* (NI).

fell Someone who fell, *awîyak ka kehpahkisihk* (VTI);
s/he fell off, *nehcipayiw* (VAI); it fell off or slid off to
one side, *patotepayiw* (VII); it fell when s/he dropped
it, *pahkihtâw* (VAI); s/he fell and landed on her/his
back, *sâsakicipayiw* (VTA); s/he fell through the crusty
snow, *twâkonesin* (VAI); s/he fell through the ice,
twâsin (VAI).

felling *kawipocikewin* (NI).

fellow *awîyak ka miyowiceht* (VTA); a person,
ayisiyiniw (NA).

felt *ka miskonikehk* (VAI); *meskonam* (VAI); *yoskikin*
(NI).

female *nôsehaya* (NA); a woman, *iskwew* (NA).

feminine *iskwewayi* (NA); *iskwewow* (NA); being a
female, *iskwowowin* (NI).

fence *wâsakanikan* (NI); s/he builds a fence around
them, *wasakânew* (VTA); a fenced in place or a
structure for closing around land, *wâsakanikan* (NI).

fend *ka yikatetahamihk kîkway* (VTI).

ferment *ka sîwâstek* (VTI); the liquid is working or
boiling like home brew, *atoskemakan* (VII).

fermentation *sîwascikewin* (NI).

fern *masânâhtik* (NA).

ferny *kîkway ka masânâhtikowik* (VTI).

ferocious *ka sohkâtisihk* (VAI).

ferocity *kîkway ka sohkikotek* (VTI).

ferret *âkâmaskew minôs* (NA); a big weasel, *misisihkôs*
(NA).

ferry Something you pull across with something on it,
âsiwakamipicikan (NI); something that takes things
across, i.e.: a ferry, *âsiwahôcikan* (NI); s/he ferries her/
him across the water, *âsiwahoyew* (VTA); a crossing
over a river, *âsowahonân* (NI).

fertile *ka miyokihcikemakahk askîy* (VTI);
weyotisemakan (NI); soil good for growing vegetables,
miyo ohpilihoikowaolûy (NI).

fertility *miyokihcikewin* (NI).

fester *ka miyewpayik eta komikehk* (VTA); it is full of
mucus, *miyewan* (VII).

festival *môcikihtâwnihkewin ka nîpâyamihahk* (NI); a
good time, *miyowâtamowin* (NI).

festivity *ka môcikihtâwnihkehk* (VTA).

fetch *ka petâhk*; *nâtamawew* (VTA).

fetching *pecikewin* (NI).

fever *ka kisisohk* (VAI); *kisisowin* (NI).

fevered *kisisohiwewin* (NI).

305

feverish *kisisowâyâwin* (NI).

fever-root *kisisocipihk* (NI).

few *âtiht* (IPC); a few, small quantity, *cikawâsis* (IPC); a few times, *cikawâsiwâw* (IPC); a very few times, *âskaw poko* (IPC); quite a large number, quite a few, *mihcecis* (IPC); s/he takes a few off, *cikawâsisihew* (VAI); s/he is of a smaller number, *cikawâsisiwiw* (VAI); few in number, *cikawâsisiwan* (VII).

fib *kîyâskowin* (NI).

fidget *ekâ kakih koskwâwâtapihk* (VAI).

fidgety *namoya koskwâwâtapiw* (VAI); s/he can not keep still, *kîskwepayiw* (VAI).

field *ka wâsakânkatek askîy* (VTI); a place for growing crops, *kistikân* (NI).

fiend *awîyak ka macimantowit* (VAI).

fiendish *metoni maci isâyâwin* (NI).

fierce *macâyiwiwin* (NI); difficult, *âhkwatisowin* (NI).

fiery *kîkway ka kwahkotewnakwahk* (VII); *watakamisiw* (VAI).

fifteen *nîyânanosâp* (IPC); *neyânanosâp* (IPC); fifteen times; *nîyânanosâpwâw* (IPC).

fifteenth *mwecinîyânanosâp* (IPC); *mwecineyânanosâp* (IPC); fifteenth time, *nîyânanosâpwâw* (IPC); fifteenth of the month, *nîyânanosâp akimâw pîsim* (NI).

fifth *mwecinîyânan* (IPC); fifth time, *nîyânanwâw* (IPC); fifth of the month, *nîyânan akimâw pîsim* (NI).

fiftieth *mwecinîyânanomitanaw* (IPC); fiftieth time, *nîyânanomitanawâw* (IPC).

fifty *nîyânanomitanaw* (IPC); fifty times, *nîyânanomitanawâw* (IPC); s/he is number fifty or fiftieth, *nîyânanomitanowiw* (VAI).

fight *nôtinitowin* (NI); s/he fights, *nôtinikew* (VAI); s/he fights with her/his horses, *nôtinastimiwew* (VAI); s/he fights her/him, *nôtinew* (VTA); *nôtinitomew* (VTA) *(Northern)*; *wîcinôtinitômew* (VTA) *(Plains)* they fight each other, *nôtinitowak* (VAI); s/he contends against her/him for it, *ohcinatew* (VTA).

figure *akihtâson* (NI).

file The act of making a file, *kiskimanihkewin* (NI); a sharpener, *kiskiman* (NI).

fill Filling something up, *ka sâkaskinahtâhk*; it is filled or full, *sâkaskinew* (VII); s/he fills them up with liquid, *sâkaskinepahew* (VAI).

filth *wîyipâyi* (NI).

filthy Something very dirty, *kîkway metoni ka wîyepâtahk* (VII); it is filthy or dirty, *wînâw* (VAI); s/he is considered filthy or dirty, *wîneyihtâkosiw* (VAI); being considered filty or dirty, *wîneyihtâkosiwin* (NI); s/he considers her/him filthy or dirty, *wîneyimew* (VTA); s/he makes herself/himself filthy or dirty, *wînihow* (VAI); the act of making oneself filthy or dirty, *wînihowin* (NI); it is considered filthy, *wîneyihtâkwan* (VII).

fin *kinosew osikwanâs* (NI).

final *eyoko iskwâyac* (IPC).

finally *piyisk âtaweya* (IPC); finally, in the end, at last, *piyisk* (IPC).

finch *okimowanahkes* (NI); *osâwpewayisis* (NI).

find Finding something, *ka miskamihk kîkway* (VTI); s/he finds a horse, *miskawastimwew* (VTA); s/he finds eggs, *miskawâwew* (VAI); s/he finds her/him or them or it, *miskawew* (VTA); s/he finds ways to do something, *miskosihcikew* (VAI); s/he finds a way to deal with her/him, *miskweyimew* (VTA).

finder *miskamakew* (NA).

fine *miyo isâyâwin* (NI).

fineness *ka miyo isâyâhk* (VII).

finger One finger, *peyak micices* (NI); the middle finger, *tâwicihcan* (NI); the tip of a finger, *wanaskocihcan* (NI); it has fingers, i.e.: a glove, *yehyikisow* (VII); a finger on your hand, *yehyikitchitchân* (NI); something made with fingers on it, *yehyikaw* (VII).

fingermark *ka ayesihtihk micices* (NI).

fingernail *maskasiy* (NI).

fingertip *wanaskocicanihk* (NI).

finish The act of finishing, *kesihtawin* (NI); the happening or event is all over or finished up, i.e.: a dance or party: it is over, *kesahkamikan* (VII); the act of finishing the happening or event, *kesahkamikisiwin* (NI); s/he is finished with it, *kesahkamikisiw* (VAI); s/he finishes with them, *kisipayihew* (VTA); finishing something, *kesihcikewin* (NI); s/he completed it for her/him, *kesihtamawew* (VTA); when referring to a meeting or business, i.e.: it is over or finished or done with, *kisipayiw* (VII); s/he is finished blessing her/him, *kisisaweyimew* (VAI); s/he is finished with or done with her/him, *kesihew* (VTA).

finished Something finished or the final, completed product, *kisehcikewin* (NI); s/he finished it or completed the final product, *kesihtâw* (VII); s/he finished her/his house or putting up her/his teepee, *kîsokew* (VAI); when referring to a completed product, i.e.: it is all finished, *kîsihcikâsiw* (VAI); when referring to a completed product, i.e.: it is all finished, *kîsihcikâtew* (VII).

finite *itâh kîskopayik* (VTI).

fir *soni okihcikamehk kohpikit sihta* (NA).

fire *iskotew* (NI); destroyed by fire, *mistihkahtew* (VII); it is affected by fire, *itihkahtew* (VII); it is affected by smoke, *itapahtew* (VII); warming by the fire, *awasowin* (NI); s/he is burning or on fire, *kwahkosiw* (VAI); s/he has sparks on her/him, *paskisiw* (VAI); it dried by the fire, *pahkosow* (VAI); s/he dried by the fire, *pahkohtew* (VII); shooting sparks from the fire, *papaskisiw* (VAI); *papaskitew* (VII); a fire started by nature, i.e.: a thunderstorm, *pasitew* (VII); a fire started by humans, *pasawew* (VII); a ground fire, *pâhkwahcitew* (NA) *(Plains)*; *pahkwahtew* (NA) *(Northern)*; fire water or liquor, *iskotewâpoy* (NI); s/he sets fire to her/him, *kwahkoswew* (VTA); it is on fire, *kwahkotew* (VII); it started burning, *kwahkosiw* (VAI); a ground fire, *pahkwahtew* (VII); the fire throws sparks, *paskwâskitew* (VII); s/he makes a fire, *pônam* (VAI); s/he makes a fire for her/him, *pônamowew* (VTA); s/he makes a fire with it, i.e.: wood, *pônew* (VAI); s/he is stoking up the fire for them, *ponihkahtew* (VTA); it is on fire, *kwahkotew* (VAI) *(Plains and Northern variant)*; *wayatew* (VAI) *(Northern)*.

fireweed *ihkapaskwa* (NI).

firewood One piece of firewood, *mihtih* (NI); a cord of firewood, *pâsimihtân* (NI); one piece of dried firewood, *pâstew mihtih* (NI).

firm *metoni ka asanak* (VTI); s/he places it firmly, *âyâtahew* (VTI) *(Northern)*; s/he tightens it securely, *âyâtamohew* (VTI); s/he has made up her/his mind very firmly, *sohkeyihtam* (VAI); s/he has firm views of her/him, *sohkeyimew* (VTA).

first Or ahead or before, *nîkân* (IPC); the first time, initially, or originally, *nistam* (IPC); at first, for the first time, in the first place, *ekwayâc* (IPC); in the beginning, at first, firstly, first, *oskac* (IPC); it is first, *nistaman* (VII); first, *mwecipeyakwâw* (IPC); first time, once, *peyakwâw* (IPC); first of the month, *peyak akimâw pîsim*.

firstborn *oski nihtâwkowin* (NI); *nistamôsân* (NA).

firstly *nîkân peta* (IPC).

fish *kinosew* (NA); a dried, smoked fish, *namestek* (NI); a male fish, *nâpemek* (NA); a female fish, *nôsemek* (NA).

fish eagle *misi kîyâsk* (NA).

fisher A carnivorous mammal of the weasel family, *ocek* (NA).

fish egg *wâhkwan* (NI).

fisherman *opakitahwâw* (NA); *pakitawâwiyiniw* (NA).

fish-hawk *pîwâyisis kinosewa kohtacihot*.

fishing The act of fishing, *nôcikinosewewin* (NI); s/he is fishing, *nôcikinosewew* (VAI).

fish oil *kinosewpimiy* (NI).

fish scale *wayakay* (NI) *(Northern)*; *kinosewayakay* (NI) *(Plains)*.

fish tail *osikwanâs* (NI) *(Northern)*; *osikwanay* (NI) *(Plains)*.

fishy *ka kinosewaksihk*; *kinosewakan*.

fist The act of making a fist, *pâpitikoniskewin* (NI); s/he rolls her/his hand into a fist, *pitikoniskew* (VAI); s/he makes a fist, *pâpitikoniskew* (VAI).

fit *ka tepiskamihk*; it fits well, *nahihtin* (VII); s/he makes it fit into something, *nahisimew* (VAI); s/he fits into something, *nahisin* (VAI); it fits in the groove, *nepitetin* (VII); it fits on top, *tahkocihtin* (VII); s/he fits them in place, i.e.: wheels, *tâpisimew* (VTA); s/he makes them fit, *tepâmohew* (VTA) *(Northern)*; *tepiskamohew* (VTA) *(Plains)*; it fits or there was enough space for it, *tepamiw* (VII) *or* (VAI); s/he makes her/him fit or s/he makes enough space or room for her/him, *tepâskinahew* (VTA); s/he fits inside or there is enough space or room for her/him inside, *tepâskinew* (VTA); the act of fitting inside or having enough space or room to be inside, *tepâskinewin* (NI); it fits or there was enough space or room for it, *tepâstew* (VII); it fits just right, *tepihtin* (VTI); s/he fits just right, *tepisin* (VAI); s/he fits into it or them, *tepiskawew* (VTA).

fitful *kocipitikoskihk* (IPC).

fitting *ka nahiskamihk*; *tepisin* (VAI); *tepihtin* (VII).

five *nîyânan* (IPC); five each, *nahnîyânan* (IPC); five times, *nîyânanwâw* (IPC); five of a kind, *nîyânanwayih* (IPC); five different kinds, *nahnîyânanwayih* (IPC); in five places or five directions, *nîyânwayak* (IPC); in five different places, *nahnîyânwayak* (IPC); s/he is number five or fifth, *nîyânanowiw* (VAI).

fivefold *nîyânanwâw* (IPC).

five hundred *nîyânanwâw mitâtahtomitanaw* (IPC).

fix Something fixed or in one place, *kosihtâhk* (VTI).

fixed *ka kesihtâhk* (VTI).

fizz *ka cowehkahtek* (VTI).

flabby Someone big and fat, *ka mistikamohk* (VAI).

flagrant *ka kihkânâkwahk* (VII).

flaky *ka wâsakâmakahk* (VTI).

flame Something in flames, *ka wayatek*; it is a high reaching flame, *cahkaskitew* (VII); it is in flames, *wayatew* (VAI) *(Northern)*; *kwahkotew* (VAI) *(Plains and Northern variant)*.

flaming *ka mekwâ wayatek* (VTI).

flank *pisiskow âpihtâwisiyaw* (NI); *wâskitoya* (NA).

flannel A piece of flannel, *pîsweweyân* (NI); a soft fluffy piece of cloth, *pîsweweyân* (NI).

flap *kîkway ka akwanamok* (VTI).

flare *ka sisikockwahkotek* (VTI); *kwahkotes* (NI).

flare-up *ka wayatepayik* (VTI).

flash *ka wâsiskotepayik* (VTI); lightning, *waskotepayiw* (VAI) *(Northern)*; *wâsaskotepayiw* (VAI) *(Plains)*.

flashy *ka mâmaskâtikonkeskihk* (VAI).

flask *napakâpiskos* (NI); *napakmoteyapiskos* (NI).

flat Something flat, *ka napakâk* (VAI); it is flat, *napakâw* (VAI); it is flat, *napakisiw* (VAI) *(Plains)*;

307

samakisiw (VAI) *(Northern)*; s/he makes her/him flat, *napakihew* (VTA); it is flat, i.e.: a wooden floor, *napakihtakâw* (VII); it has a flat, wooden surface, *napakihtakisiw* (VAI); it is flat, i.e.: a pole, *napakâskwan* (VII); the tree grows flat against an outcropping, *napakâskisiw* (VAI); s/he goes flat, i.e.: a tire, *samakipayiw* (VII).

flatten The act of flattening something, *napakâtahikewin* (NI); s/he flattens it, *napakâtaham* (VAI); s/he flattens it with her/his hands, *napakinam* (VTI); s/he flattens her/him by holding her/him down by the head, *samakinew* (VTA); s/he flattens her/him by settling on top of her/him, *samakiskawew* (VTA); s/he is flattened, *samakisiw* (VAI) *(Northern)*; *napakisiw* (VAI) *(Plains)*; it is flattened, *samakâw* (VII) *(Northern)*; *wapakâw* (VII) *(Plains)*.

flatter *ka mamihcimowehk* (VTA).

flattery *mamihicimowewin* (NI).

flatulence *pwekitiw* (VAI); the act of being flatulent or passing intestinal gas, *pwekitowin* (NI).

flaunt *ka mamihtsewakehk* (VTI).

flavor or **flavour** *ka pahpitos ispakwahk* (VTI).

flaw *mâyesihcikewin* (NI).

flay *poyakeskinkewin* (NI).

flea *okwaskwepayihos* (NA); dog lice, *atimotihkoma* (NA).

flea-bitten *ka tahkwahketwaw okwaskwepayihosak* (VTA).

fleck *ka masinâsohk nânitâw* (VAI).

flee The act of running away, *tapasetamowin* (NI); s/he flees or runs here and there, *papâmamiw* (VAI); s/he flees in this direction, *pîtamiw* (VAI); s/he flees from her/him, *tapasihew* (VTA); something to flee or run from, *tapasihtâwin* (NI); s/he flees with her/him, *tapasihtahew* (VTA); *tapasiyâmohew* (VTA); s/he fled from her/him, *tapasîw* (VTA); the act of fleeing or flight, *tapasîwin* (NI); s/he flees or runs away in fear, *tapasiyâmiw* (VAI); the act of fleeing in fear, *tapasiyâmowin* (NI); s/he flees the wrong way, *wanamiw* (VAI); the act of fleeing the wrong way, *wanâmowin* (NI).

fleece *mâyatihkos owayan* (NI); sheep hair, *mâyatihkopiway* (NI).

flesh All kinds of raw meat, *nanâtohk isiweyâs* (NI); meat, *wîyâs* (NI); s/he fleshes it with a bone, i.e.: a beaver hide, *mihkitew* (VTA); s/he fleshes them with a knife, *pihtoswew* (VTA).

fleshy *ka wîyâsowik kîkway* (VAI).

flew *kâke pimihahk* (VAI).

flex *ka pihkinamihk kîkway* (VTI).

flexibility *ka wahkew pihkipayik* (VTI).

flexible *nanâtohk ka etakinamihk* (VTI).

flick *kîkway ka pasastehikewepenamihk* (VTI).

flicker *ka ati sîkaw astawek iskotew* (VTI).

flightless *ekâ kâke pimihahk* (VAI).

flighty *ekâ ka mamsîwisayahk* (VTA); *wahkewisowin* (NI).

flimsy *metoni mâmâsisihkewin* (NI); *papakâsin* (VII).

flinch *metoni ka kakwesepinehk* (VAI).

fling *metoni ka sohki wepinamihk kîkway* (VTI); *kwaciwepinam* (NI).

flint *sikisehikan* (NI) *(Plain)*; *paskitewasiniy* (NI) *(Northern)*; *cahkisehikan* (NI) *(Plains)*.

flinty *peyakwan cahkisehikan kesayak kîkway* (VII).

flip *ka kwâskwi wepinamihk kîkway* (VTI).

flippant *ekâ ka ayâhkweyihtamihk*.

flirt *pisikwâtsowin* (NI); s/he is flirting with her/him, i.e.: someone else's spouse, *nôcihkawew* (VTA).

flirtation *ka pisikwâcehtotamihk* (VAI); *pisikwâcitôtamowin* (NI)

flirtatious *pisikwâcîsâyâwin* (NI).

float *ka waskitahepek* (VTI); floats ashore, *akwâyapotew* (VII); a float for a gill net, *ayapâhtik* (NI); s/he has floated ashore (on a river), *akwâyapakiw* (VAI); it floats ashore, i.e.: driftwood, *akwâyapotew* (VII); it is on the shore, i.e.: driftwood, *kapâhotew* (VAI); s/he floats across from shore to shore, *âsawahokiw* (VAI); it floats around, i.e.: in a lake; *papâmâhotew* (VII); s/he floats around, i.e.: in a lake, *pahpâmâhokow* (VAI).

floats Drifting, *pimahokow* (VAI); it floats or it is floating, *pimâpakiw* (VAI); *pimâpotew* (VII); floating away, carried away, *wepâpakow* (VAI) *(Northern)*; *wepâhokiw* (VAI) *(Plains)*; *wepâpotew* (VII); it floats across the current, *asawâpotew* (VII); it floats to the surface and reveals itself, *môskipew* (VII).

floating Something floating along, *kapemapotek kîkway* (VTI), s/he floats things across; s/he is floating across by the current, *âsawâpakiw* (VAI); it is floating across by the current, *asawâpotew* (VII).

flock *ka mâmawi pîmeyatwaw pîwâyisak* (VTA); a flock of birds, *kamâmawipayitwaw pîwâyisak* (NA).

flog *awîyak mistik ka pakamahekaket* (VTI).

flood When it is flooded, *ka iskipek* (VTI); the act of flooding, *iskipewin* (NI); water reaches high, up to there, or a flood, *iskipew* (VII); indicating how high the water is, *iskopew* (VII); it flooded over or the water flooded or overflows, *pastipew* (VII).

flop *ka môstahtakihkwamihk* (VAI); *sohkipahkisin* (VAI).

floppy *kîkway ekâ ka sâpahk* (VII).

flounce *wawisihcikan iskwewasakahk* (NI).

flounder *mistahi ka mâyinikeskihk* (VAI).

308

flour Or raw bread, ***askipahkwesikan*** (NI); bannock, ***pahkwesikan*** (NA).

flourish *awîyak ka miyowepiniket* (VAI).

floury *kîkway ka askipahkwesikanowik* (VTI).

flow When it is flowing, ***ka pemicowahk***; flowing along, ***pimiciwan*** (VII); the water is flowing backwards, ***aseciwan*** (VII); it flows off in another direction, i.e.: a river, ***patoteciwan*** (VII); it is flowing this way, i.e.: a river, ***peciciwan*** (VAI); water flowing down the hill or mountain, i.e.: from a spring, ***penâsipeciwan*** (NA); it is flowing, i.e.: a river, ***pimihtin*** (VII); it flows right through, ***sâpociwan*** (VII); it flows in the middle, ***tâwiciwan*** (VII).

flower ***wapikwanew*** (NI) *(Northern)*; ***wâpikwaniy*** (NI) *(Northern)*; ***nîpihkân*** (NI) *(Plains)*; ***nepihkân*** (NI) *(Plains)*; an artificial flower, ***wâpikwanihkân*** (NI); it has flowers, ***wapikwaniwan*** (VAI).

flowered *ka nîpihkanihtahk* (VTI).

flowery *ka nîpihkanowik* (VAI).

flowing *ka mekwâ pemicowahk* (VTI).

fluent *metoni kanisitohtamihk* (VAI).

fluff The fluff from plants or trees, ***mestanpeway*** (NI); it is fluffy, ***pîswesow*** (VAI); a piece of soft, fluffy material, ***pîsweyekin*** (NI); it is fluffy, ***pîsweyâw*** (VII).

fluid *kîkway ka nipewâkamik* (VTI); water that puts one to sleep, i.e. an anaesthetic, ***nipewâpiy*** (NI).

flung *kake pimosinehk kîkway* (VTI).

flunk *kîkway ka sâkocihikohk* (VTI).

flurry *misponipayiw* (VII).

flush *ka nâtapawacekewin* (NI); *kanâcipayiw* (VII).

fluster *wayahiwewin* (NI).

flute *pipikwanis* (NI) *(Plains)*; *pikwan* (NI) *(Northern)*.

flutter *sîsîp ka pahpawet* (VAI).

flux *ka tihkisamihk pîwâpisk* (VTI).

fly The act of flying in a plane, ***pimeyawin*** (NI); s/he flies, ***pimihâw*** (VAI); s/he flies away, i.e.: like a bird, ***ohpahow*** (VAI); s/he flies all over the place, ***papâmiyâw*** (VAI) *(Northern)*; ***papâmihâw*** (VAI) *(Plains)* s/he flies this way, s/he comes flying, or s/he arrives by plane, ***pâpiyâw*** (VAI); s/he flies past, ***pimihâw*** (VAI); s/he flies right through, ***sâpoyâw*** (VAI) *(Northern)*; ***sâpohâw*** (VAI) *(Plains)*.

fly A type of insect, ***ôcew*** (NA).

flying The act of flying, ***pimihawin*** (NI); a bird flying south, ***kîweham*** (VAI);

flying squirrel *asaniskwahtawesiw* (NA).

foal *miscacimosis* (NA).

foam *pîstew* (NI); it boiled until it was foaming, ***pîstewâciwasiw*** (VAI); s/he boils them until they were foaming, ***pîstewâciwaswew*** (VTA); it boiled until it was foaming, ***pîstewâciwahtew*** (VII); s/he is foaming at the mouth, ***pîstewatâmiw*** (VAI); the act of foaming at the mouth, ***pîstewatâmowin*** (NI).

foamy *ka pîstewâyak kîkway* (VII).

focal *kisewewin* (NI).

focalize *ka kisewehtâkosihk* (VAI).

focus *nahâpahcikewin* (NI).

fog It is foggy, ***kaskawahkamiw*** (VII) *(Northern)*; ***kaskawahkamin*** (VII) *(Plains)*; a mist ***kaskawahkamin*** (NI) *(Northern)*; ***iyikopiwan*** (NI) *(Plains)*; there is fog or it is kind of foggy, ***kaskawan*** (VII); it is a misty, foggy day, ***pîkiseyâw*** (VII); there is a thick, dense, misty fog, ***pîkiseyâpahtew*** (VII).

foggy When it is foggy, ***ka kaskawahkamik*** (VII).

foist *wayesih isihcikewin* (NI).

fold S/he folds them, ***nahawekinew*** (VTA); s/he folds them, ***napwekinew*** (VTA); s/he folds them up, i.e.: pants, ***oyekinew*** (VTI); s/he folds them in two, ***pihekinew*** (VTI); s/he folds her/his own hands, ***pihkicihceyiw*** (VTA); s/he fold it up, ***nânapwekinew*** (VTA) *(Plains)*; ***oyeyimew*** (VTA) *(Northern)*.

foliage Foliage is dense, ***sâkipakaw*** (VAI); ***sihkwepakaw*** (VAI); ***kaskipakâw*** (VAI); a bunch of leaves, ***nîpîya*** (NI).

folk *tân'ta ka ohtoskanisit ayisîniw* (VAI); *ayisîniwak* (NA); *wahkomâkanak* (NA).

follow Following behind, ***askôkewin*** (NI); s/he follows her/him closely, ***kanoskawew*** (VTA); s/he follows her/him at a distance, ***kihtaskowew*** (VTA); s/he follows the road or path, ***mitimew*** (VAI); the act of following or trailing something, ***nânôsawi*** (VAI); following after, ***nôsawih*** (IPC); s/he follows in the tracks, ***nâwayimâtam*** (VTI); s/he follows her/him afterwards, ***nâwayimâtew*** (VTA) *(Northern)*; s/he follows afterwards, ***nâwayimew*** (VTA) *(Plains)*; s/he follows behind her/him, ***pimitisahwew*** (VTA); the act of following behind someone, ***pimitisahikewin*** (NI).

follower *otaskôkew* (NA).

following *askôkewin* (NI); s/he is following behind everyone, ***pimitisahikew*** (VTA); following, in a line, continuous like generation, from generation to generation, ***aniskac*** (IPC); ***aniski*** (IPC).

folly *ka kakepatinikteoktiht* (VAI), *kakepâcihtwâwin* (NI) *(Northern)*; *kakepâtinikewin* (NI) *(Plains)*

fond *ka sâkihiht awîyak* (VTA); *sâkihew* (VAI); *sâkihtaw* (VAI).

fondle *âkwaskitinkewin* (NI).

food *mîciwin* (NI); s/he has food, ***omîciwiniw*** (VAI); one who share food, ***omekinawew*** (NA); sweet food, ***sîwâyi*** (NI) *(Northern)*; ***sîwanos*** (NI) *(Plains)*.

fool A foolish person, ***kakepâtis*** (NA); s/he is a fool, ***kepâtis*** (NA).

foolish Being foolish, *ka kakepatisihk* (VAI); the act of being foolish or acting like a clown, *kakepatisihkewin* (NI); s/he behaves foolishly towards her/him, *kakepatisihkasostawew* (VTA); foolish conduct or behavior, *kakepâcihtwâwin* (NI) *(Northern)*; *kakepâtinikewin* (NI) *(Northern)*; s/he acts foolishly, *kakepatisihkew* (VAI) *(Northern)*; s/he is foolish, *kakepâtisiw* (VAI).

foot *misit* (NI); at the foot of stairs, *nehcayihk* (IPC); s/he has a deformed foot, *mâskisitew* (VAI); a crippled foot, *mâskisit* (NI); s/he is bare footed, *mosesitew* (VAI); *sâsâkihtiw* (VAI); s/he is two footed, *nîsositew* (VAI); s/he has a swollen foot or feet, *pâkisitew* (VAI); s/he has lacerated feet, *papakositesin* (VAI); s/he has white feet or paws, *wapisitew* (VAI).

footfall *ka petowesinihk*.

foothill *iskwamatinâw* (NI); it is elevated ground, i.e.: foothills, *oseskamikâw* (VII).

foothold *kahtaskenikewin* (NI).

footing *ka kistaskenikewin* (NI).

footless *ekâ kîkway ka ositihk* (VTI).

footloose Not taking on any responsibilities, *nanâtohk isâyâwin* (NI); s/he is footloose, *papâmeyimiw* (VAI); the act of being footloose, *papâmeyihtamowin* (NI).

footpace *ka tipitakoskehk* (VAI).

footprint A footprint or tracks, *ayetiskowin* (NI); *ayetiskiw* (NI).

footrest *aspitahkoskewin* (NI).

footsore *ka pâpakostesinihk* (VTA).

footwear A pair of stretchy footwear, i.e.: rubber boots, *pahkopewaskisin* (NI) *(Plains)*; *sîpekaskisin* (NI) *(Northern)*.

for From, with, for that, *ohci* (IPC).

forbade *kakeh nakinamâkehk* (VTA).

forbear *ekâ kawakew kisewasihk* (VAI).

forbid Stopping someone from doing something, *ka nakinowehk* (VTA); forbidding other from going or the act of forbidding entrance, *kipotisahikewin* (NI); s/he forbids her/him from coming, *kipotisawew* (VTA); stopping someone, *kitahamakewin* (NI).

forbidden *ka nakinamihk* (VTI).

forbidding *nakinkewin* (NI).

force The act of using force or physical strength, *maskawisîwin ka âpacitahk* (VTA); *ka tôtamohiwehk kîkway* (VTA).

forceful *tôtamohiwewin* (NI).

forcible *maskawisîwin ka âpatahk* (VTI).

ford *ka âsawâkâmeyâtakahk sepe* (VTI); walking across a stream, *âsawâkâmeyâtakâwin* (NI).

fore *nîkânisi kîkway* (IPC).

forearm *nîkânisi mispiton* (NI).

forebear *anskac wahkohtowin* (NI).

foreboding *neyak kîkway ka wâpahtamihk* (VAI).

forefather *anskac kimosom* (NA); *kayâs wahkotowin* (NI); *kiseyinipan* (NA).

forefinger *itwahikanicicanis* (NI); *itwahikancican* (NI).

foregone *neyâk wâpahcikewin* (NI).

forehead *miskahtik* (NI).

foreleg *nîkânkât* (NA).

forelock *nîkân kaskihtakahikewin* (NI).

foremost Way in the front, *mâwacinikan* (IPC).

forepaw *minôs onîkânsitana* (NI).

foresee *nekan wapahcikewin* (NI).

forest *sakâw* (NA).

forestall *neyak ka nakinamihk kîkway* (VAI).

foretell *pakwanawihtam* (VAI).

forethought *neyak mâmitoneyihtamowin* (NI); *nekan mâmitoneyihtamowin* (NI).

forever *kâkike* (IPC).

forevermore *metoni kâkike* (IPC).

forgave *kakeh kâsenamakehk* (VTA).

forget *wanikiskisowin* (NI); *wanikiskisiw* (VAI).

forgetful *ka wanikiskisiskihk* (VAI).

forgetfulness *wanikiskisiskew isâyâwin* (NI).

forgive The act of forgiving or forgiveness, *kâsinamakewin* (NI); *kâsinamâtowin* (NI); s/he forgives her/him, *poneyihtamawew* (VTA) *(Plains)*; *kâsînamawew* (VTA) *(Northern)*.

forgiven *awîyak ka kâsinamaht* (VTA).

forgiveness *kâsînamawew* (VTA) *(Northern)*; *poneyihtamawew* (VTA) *(Plains)*.

forgiving *ka kâsinamakehk* (VTA); *kisewatisiw* (VAI); *kisewatan*.

forgot The act of forgetting, *ka wanikiskisihk* (VAI); s/he forgot all about her/him, *wanikiskisototawew* (VTA); s/he forgot, *wanikiskisiw* (VAI); the act of forgetting, *wanikiskisiwin* (NI).

forgotten *ka wanikiskisototaht awîyak* (VTA).

fork A small table fork, *cîstahisîpwâkanis* (NI); a fork in a road, *yikihtawipayiw* (VII); a fork in a river, *paskestikweyaw* (VII); the road has a fork, *yikihtawamiw* (VII); it has many forks, *yikihtawisiw* (VII); the moose has forks on its horns, *yikihtawiteskanew* (VAI); the river has forks on it, *yikistikweyaw* (VII).

forked A forked road, *nîswayakemow* (NI).

forlorn *kîkway ka wepinamihk* (VTI); s/he looks pitiful, *kitimâkinâkosiw* (VAI); *kaskeyihtamâyâwin* (NI).

form *tansi kîsenakwahk kîkway* (VII).

formal Dressing formally, *kwayaskosihowin* (NI).

formality *kwayaskonikewin* (NI).

formalize *kwayaskosecikehk* (VTI); *kwayaskosihcikewin* (NI).

formation *kwayaskwascikewin* (NI).

310

former *oskâc awîyak* (IPC).

formerly *ekotihoci* (IPC); before that time, *awâsispeh* (IPC).

formidable *kîkway ka âyimihikohk* (VAI).

formless *kîkway ekâ ka oyastek* (VTI).

fornicate S/he fornicates, *pisikwatisiw* (VAI) *(Plains)*; *pisikwâcitôtam* (VAI) *(Northern)*.

fornication Immorality, *pisikwâtisowin* (NI).

forsake *wepinwewin* (NI); *wepinew* (VTA); *wankiskisitotawew* (VTA); s/he forsakes her/him, *pakiteyimew* (VTA); the act of forsaking, *pakiteyihtamowin* (NI).

forsaken Being discarded, *wepinkâsowin* (NI); s/he finds herself/himself forsaken, *kewâteyimow* (VAI); s/he is thought of as being forsaken, *kewâteyihtâkosiw* (VAI); the act of being of thought of as forsaken, *kewâteyihtâkosiwin* (NI).

Fort McMurray The Cree name for Fort McMurray meaning "the merging of three rivers", *nistawâyâw* (NA).

forthcoming *ka ihtateyecikehk; papayiw* (VAI).

forthright *kwayaskohtowin* (NI).

fortieth *mwecinemitanaw* (IPC); fortieth time, *nemitanawâw* (IPC).

fortification *sohkîsihcikewin* (NI).

fortify *sohkîsihcikew* (VAI).

fortitude Or stamina, *sohkâyâwin* (NI).

fortunate Being very lucky, *metoni miyopayowin* (NI); s/he is lucky, *papewew* (VAI).

forty *nemitanaw* (IPC); forty times, *nemitanawâw* (IPC).

forward *yahkohtewin* (NI).

forwardness *ka nihtâ nîkânehk* (VAI).

foster *ka kanaweyimiht awâsis* (VTA).

fought *kakeh nôtinkehk* (VTA).

foul *wînayih* (NA).

found Something that has been found, *kakeh miskamihk kîkway* (VTI); s/he found it, *miskam* (VAI).

four *newo* (IPC); four each, *nahnewo* (IPC); four times, *newâw* (IPC); four of a kind, *newayih* (IPC); four different kinds, *nahnewayih* (IPC); in four places or four directions, *newayak* (IPC); in four different places, *nahnewayak* (IPC); s/he is number four or fourth, *newiw* (VAI).

fourfold *newâw* (IPC).

four-footed *newo misita ka ayâhk* (VTI).

four hundred *newâw mitâtahtomitanaw* (IPC).

foursome Four players, *neyometawewak* (IPC).

fourteen *newohsâp* (IPC); fourteen times, *newosâpwâw* (IPC).

fourteenth *mwecinewosâp* (IPC); fourteenth time, *newosâpwâw* (IPC); fourteenth of the month, *newosâp akimâw pîsim* (IPC).

fourth *mwecinewo* (IPC); fourth time, *newâw* (IPC); fourth of the month, *newâw akimâw pîsim* (IPC).

fowl *nanâtohk pewayisak* (NA); a pullet, *pâkahakwan* (NA).

fox *mahkesîs* (NA); a red fox, *osâwahkesîs* (NA); a silver fox, *soniyawahkesîs* (NA).

foxberry *mahkesîsîmina* (NI).

foxhole *mahkesîs owati* (NI).

foxy *kaskamoc iyinisowin* (NI).

fragile It is fragile, *nesowan* (VII); s/he has a fragile constituion, *nesowâtisiw* (VAI); having a fragile constitution or being weak after an illness, *nesowâtisiwin* (NI).

fragility *wahkewisowin* (NI).

fragment *ketisk pahki kîkway* (VII) or (NI); *pahkwenikan* (NI); just a part of it, *pahki* (IPC).

fragmentary *ka pahpiskiht astahk kîkwaya* (VTI).

fragrance *wihkimâkohowin* (NI).

fragrant *kîkway ka wihkimâhwahk* (VII); it smells good, *wihkimâkwan* (VII).

frail Being frail, *nesowâtisiwin* (NI); everything s/he does looks frail, *nesowinâkohcikew* (VAI); her/his condition is frail, *nesowisiw* (VAI); being in a frail condition, *nesowisiwin* (NI).

frailty *nesowâyâwin* (NI).

frank *tâpwewin* (NI).

frantic *kîskweyeyihtam* (VAI).

frazzle *ka mosci nohtesinihk* (VAI).

freak Being goofy, *môhcowisâyâwin* (NI); *kîkwayihkan* (NA).

free The act of being free to act as one wishes, *peyakotipiyimisiwin* (NI); s/he is free and independent, *tipiyimisiw* (VAI); s/he frees herself/himself by breaking away or breaking loose, i.e.: a horse, *pihkohow* (VII); the act of becoming free, *pihkohowin* (NI); s/he breaks free by herself/himself, *wihkwacipayiw* (VAI); s/he pulls her/him free, *wihkwacipitew* (VTA); s/he breaks it free with her/his hands, *wihkwatinew* (VTI).

freedom *ka peyakotipiyimisohk* (VAI); one's own boss, *tipiyimisiwin* (NI).

freeze *ka âhkwacihk* (VAI), *âhkwatin* (VII), *âhkwatihtâw* (VII).

freeze-up It freezes up, *kaskatin* (VII); freeze-up month or moon, October, *kaskatinowipîsim* (NI).

French A French person, *wemistikôsiw* (NA); French country, *wemistikôsînâhk* (NI).

frenetic *kîkway ka kisiwâhikohk* (VTI).

frenzy *sîsîkoc kisiwâsowin* (NI).

frequent *kahkiyipa* (IPC).

frequently *kahkiyipa nawac* (IPC).

fresh *ka oskâyak kîkway* (VII).

311

freshen *oskihcikewin* (NI).

fret *ka kisôwisâwâyahk* (VAI).

fretful *kisôwâyâwin* (NI).

Friday It is Friday, *nîyânano kîsikâw* (VII).

friend My friend, *nitotem* (NA); s/he regards her/him as a friend, *otôtemimew* (VTA); s/he makes friends, *otôtemiw* (VAI).

friendless *peyakowicihiwewin* (NI).

friendly Everyone is friendly with her/him, *miyotôtemimaw* (VTA); s/he is friendly to her/him, *ototemihkâtew* (VTA) *(Northern)*; *otôtemiw* (VTA) *(Plains)*; the act of being friendly, *otôtemiwewin* (NI) *(Northern)*; *otôtemihtowin* (NI) *(Plains)*; s/he is friendly, *wihayotôtemiw* (VTA).

friendship *otôtemihtowin* (NI).

fright *sekisowin* (NI); *sekisiwin* (NI).

frighten *sekihiwewin* (NI).

frightened *ka sekihikohk* (VAI); *sekisiw* (VAI).

frightening *sekihiwewin* (NI); *sekihtasowin* (NI).

frightful *ka sekihtasoskihk*; *kostâcinakwan*.

frigid It is very cold, *mistahikisin* (VII).

frigidity *pônosewin* (NI).

frill *akostahikewin* (NI); *masinkwacikewin* (NI).

fringe *ka iskosakak* (VII).

frisk *ka metawepayit mistatim* (VAI).

frivolity *môcikisowin* (NI).

frivolous *awîyak ka môciksit* (VAI).

fro To and fro from here to there, *kahkekwask* (IPC).

frock *ka yahkisehot iskwew* (VTI); *iskwewasakay* (NI).

frog A large frog, *mistayek* (NA); big bull frog, *mayokowatay* (NA); *pikwatehtew* (NA).

frolic *môcikihtawin* (NI).

from For, with, for that, *ohci* (IPC); from where, *tânti ohci* (IPC); from one to another, *ayâsawih* (IPC).

front From the front, *nîkan ohci* (IPC); in front, *âkwask* (IPC); in front or face to face, *ohtiskaw* (VII).

frost *yikwatin* (NI); it is full of frost, *iyikwatin* (VII); frosty month or moon, November, *iyikopiwipesim* (NI).

frosted *wâsenamawin ka kipaskatihk* (VTI).

frosty *kîkway ka iyikwatihk*.

froth Foam, *pîstew* (NI).

frothy *ka pîstewik* (VTI).

frown *kisôkanawapahkewin* (NI).

froze *kakeh âhkwacihk* (VAI).

frozen It is frozen, *âhkwatin* (VII); *ka âkwacihk* (VAI); frozen stiff, *kaskaskaciw* (VAI); *kaskaskatin* (VII); frozen into one block, piece frozen to the depth, completely frozen, *misiweyâskaciw* (VAI); it freezes, *âkwatin* (VII); it is thinly frozen, i.e.: ice, *papakatin* (VII); frozen thick, ice, *kispakaciw* (VAI); *kispakatin* (VII); frozen hard, *maskawaciw* (VAI); *maskawatin*

(VII); it is frozen and splits because of the cold, *pâstaskaciw* (VAI); tolerates the cold, *sohkaciw* (VAI); *sohkatin* (VII).

fruit Wild fruit, *mînis* (NI); a wild fruit tree, *mînisâhtik* (NI); it bears fruit, i.e.: a fruit tree, *mînisiwiw* (VAI); it bears fruit, *mînisiwan* (VII); domestic berries, i.e.: grapes, *mînisihkân* (NI).

fruitful *ka mînisowik* (VAI); *mînisiwinwa* (VAI).

fruitless *ekâ ka mînisowik*; it has no fruit, *namoyamînisowiw* (VAI).

frustrate *kosamyawesihk* (VAI).

frustration *osamyawesowin* (NI); *pîkweyihtam* (VAI).

fry Cooking in grease, *pemehk ka kîstepohk*; s/he fries the fat to make grease, i.e.: sirloin fat, *sâsipimâtew* (VTI); s/he fries or melts fat to make grease, *sâsipimew* (VAI).

frying pan *napwen* (NA) *(Plains)*; *seseskihkwân* (NA) *(Archaic Cree)*; *lapewel* (NA) *(French Cree)*.

fulfil *or* **fulfill** *ka kesihtahk* (VTI).

fulfilment *or* **fulfillment** *kisihcikewin* (NI).

full *ka sakaskinek*; it is full, *sakaskinew* (VII); full of water, *sakaskinepew*; s/he is full and can't fit her/him in, *notaskinahew* (VTA); there is no room for her/him, *notaskinew* (VTA).

full grown *kîsohpikew* (VAI); he is a full grown man, *kîsâpewiw* (VAI); she is a full grown woman, *kisôskinikiskwewiw* (VAI); being a fully grown man, *kesâpewiwin* (NI); being a full grown woman, *kisôskinîkiskwewiwin* (NI); referring to a prime fur bearing animal: "her/his fur is full grown", *kîsawew* (VAI); having full grown fur, *kîsawewin* (NI); the leaves are full grown, *kîsipakaw* (VII).

fullness *pesakosowin* (NI).

fully *mitoni* (IPC).

fulsome *kwanta ayîwak mamihcimowewin* (NI).

fumble *ka patinamihk kîkway* (VTI); *kitiskinew* (VTA).

fume *ka petâpahtek kîkway* (VTI); to smell, *pasiwin* (NI).

fume As smoke, *kaskâpahtew* (VII); s/he smells like smoke, *kaskâpahtewaksiw* (VAI).

fumed *kaskâpasowin* (NI).

fun The act of laughing, *pahpowin* (NI); having plenty of fun, *môciketâwin* (NI); s/he is fun-loving or joyful, *wiyatikosow* (VAI); being fun-loving or joyful, *wîyâtikosiwin* (NI); it is fun-loving or joyful, *wîyâtikwan* (VII).

fungus A red fungus, *mihkwatow* (NI); a fungus on a tree, *wasaskwetiw* (NI); a fungus that grows on willows that produce a pleasant aroma when lit, i.e.: a ceremonial fungus, *wihkimâsikan* (NI).

funny The act of being funny or comical, *waweyasinikewin* (NI); it is funny or comical, *wawiyasitakwan* (VII); s/he thinks of her/him as being funny or comical, *wiyateyimew* (VTA); s/he is though of as funny or comical, *wiyateyihtâkosiw* (VAI); it sounds funny or odd, *wîyasihtâkwan* (VII); s/he thinks that s/he sounds funny or comical, *wîyasitawew* (VTA); s/he tells funny jokes or stories, *wîyatwew* (VAI).

fur A piece of fur, *wayân* (NI); furs that are sold, i.e.: squirrel, beaver, etc., *âhtayak* (NI); a piece of fur or a piece of body hair, *opîway* (NI); the fur is thick and prime, *sanaskatowew* (VII); the fur is smooth and shiny, *sôskwawew* (VII).

furbish *ka wâsihkwahikehk* (VTI).

furious *kôsâmiyawesihk* (VAI); *kisiwâsiw* (VAI); *kisiwâsowin* (NI).

furnish *ka ohtinamakehk* (VTA); furnishing something, *ohtinamatowin* (NI).

furor *wîsakiyawesowin* (NI).

furred *ahcâs ka akokwatiht nânitaw* (VAI).

furrow Plowed ground, *asiskîy ka pîkopetamihk* (VTI); s/he makes a furrow in the ground, i.e.: a fireguard, *pasahcisikew* (VAI); digging a furrow, *mônahcahikan* (NI).

furry Something furry that is saleable, *ka âhtawik kîkway* (VAI); it has nice fur, *ka takahkawet* (VII); s/he is furry, *mîhyawesiw* (VAI); it is furry, *mîhyaweyaw* (VII).

further *wâhyawîs nawâc* (IPC).

furthermore *kiyapic* (IPC).

furthermost *mawaci wâhyaw* (IPC).

furthest *ayîwak wâhyaw* (IPC).

fury *osâm yawesowin* (NI); *mistahikisiwasiw* (VAI).

fuss *ka pakwâteyihtamihk kîkway* (VAI).

futile *ekâ ka kaskihtahk* (VTI).

futility *ekâ kaskihowin* (NI).

future *oteh nîkân* (IPC); *nîkânote* (IPC).

fuzz *opîwayâyi* (IPC).

fuzzy *kopîwayâyak* (NI).

313

G

gab *kwantapekiskwewin* (NI).

gadflys *âmôsisak* (NA); a horsefly, *misisâhk* (NA).

gaff A barbed fishing spear, *kapateyâskwahikan* (NI); s/he draws her/him out of the water with a gaft, *kapateyâskwahwew* (VTA).

gag *kepihketonepayowin* (NA); to gag, *kipotonenew* (VTA); stopping the mouth of someone, *kipotonenkewin* (NI).

gaiety *metoni ka môcikahk* (VII); *môcikeyihtamowin* (VII).

gaily *metoni miyoteh* (VAI).

gain *kotahowehk* (VAI); *ohtisiwin* (NI); increase, *pihkotaw* (VTI).

gainful *papewewin* (NI).

gait *isipimotewin* (NI).

gale *ka kestihk* (NI).

gall *wîsopi* (NI).

gallant *metoni ka napehkâsohk* (VAI); s/he is tough and strong, *sohkâtisiw* (VTA).

gallantry *napehkâsiwin* (NA).

gall bladder *wîsopiwaskimot* (NI) *(Northern)*; *wîsopiy* (NI) *(Plains)*.

gallon *tipâhopan* (NI); half a gallon, *âpihtawtipâhopan* (NI).

gallop A horse race, *kociskâwewin* (NI); s/he gallops, *kociskâwew* (VAI); s/he gallops slowly or canters, *nisihkepayiw* (VAI).

galore *mihcetinwa* (VTI); it is abundant, *mihcetin* (VTI).

gamble *astwatowin* (VTI).

gambler *otascikew* (NA).

gambling *astwatometawewin* (VTI).

game *metawewin* (NI).

gander Or male goose, *nâpeniska* (NA).

gangly S/he is gangly, *sâsâskosiw* (VTA).

gangling *napew ka sekwâpeksit* (VTA).

gap A small opening or crack in the wall, *ka tâwihtakak* (VII); it is a small opening, *tawâsin* (VII); a path or gap in the snow, *tâwâkonakâw* (VII); a path or gap in the tall grass, *tâwaskâw* (VII); a path or gap among the trees, *tawâskweyâw* (VII); a gap between the hills, *tawatinâw* (NI).

gape *tâwtoni mâmaskâsâpahkewin* (NI).

garb Clothes, *ayiwinisa* (NI).

garbage Discarded material, *wepinikewina* (NI).

garble *pîtos tônamowin* (VAI).

garden *ka kiscikesihk*; a vegetable garden, *kiscikânis* (NI) *(Plains)*.

gardener A person who sows vegetables, *kistikewenow* (NA); *awîyak ka kiscikesit* (NA).

gargle *ka senkonewehk* (VTA).

garish *ka ayahkonakwahk kîkway* (VTI).

garland *wawesiwakana ka tâpiskamihk* (NI); *wawesihcikewin* (NI).

garment *ka kiskamihk ayiwinisa* (NI); *ayiwinis* (NI); any kind of clothes, *ayiwinisa pokwetowa* (NI).

garner *ascikew kamik kistikân ohci* (NI); *kistikânikamik* (NI).

garter *seskepison* (NI); s/he puts garters on her/him, *seskepitew* (VTA).

garter snake A small snake, *kinepikos* (NA).

gash *kakwâyakisawâtisowin* (VII).

gasoline *pahkitewipimiy* (NI) *(Plains)*.

gasp The last gasp before death, *kîskwatamopayihk* (VAI); s/he gasps her/his final breath, *pakitatamiw* (VII).

gate *iskwâhtem wâsakanikanihk* (NI); *iskwâhtemis* (NI).

gather Gathering things or money, *ka mâwasakonkehk* (VTI); s/he gathers or picks up pitch from spruce, i.e.: spruce gum, *manahiskwew* (VTI); the act of gathering or picking up pitch from spruce trees, *manahiskowewin* (NI); s/he gathers or picks eggs, *manâwew* (VTA); a place where eggs are gather, i.e.: a slough, *manâwânis* (NI); hunting and gathering eggs, *manâwewin* (NI); they gather together, *mâwacihitowak* (VTA); s/he gather them up, *mâwasakonew* (VTA); s/he gathers them together in a hurry, *mâwasakopitew* (VTA); s/he gathers furs, *mâwatahew* (VTI).

gathering *mâwacihitowin* (NI); a gathering of people, *mâmawihitowin* (NI); an informal gathering of people, *mâmawipayowin* (NI); an organized gathering, meeting or assembly, i.e.: a business meeting, *mâmawapowin* (NI).

gaudy *ka mosci miyonakwahk kîkway* (VII); looking bright and gay, *âhkonakosiw* (VTI).

gaunt *sihkacepayowin* (NI); being skinny, *sihkaciwin* (VTA).

gawk *ka kepâtinakosowin* (VAI).

gawky *ka kakepâtnakosihk* (NA).

gay *môcikâyâwin* (NI); s/he has a good time, *miyowatam* (VII).

gayly *môcikisowin* (VAI).

gaze *mecimwâtapisinowin* (NI); *sohkikânawapiw* (VII).

geese *niskak* (NA).

geld *nâpestim ka mansikâsot* (NA).

gelding *ayihkwewatim* (NA); a castrated horse or cow, *ayihkwew* (NA).

generality *kihciyemowewin* (NI).

generalization *ka kihciyemowehk* (VTA).

315

generalize *awîyak ka kihciyemiht* (VTA).

generally *osâmpoko* (IPC).

generate *kîkway kosihtâhk* (VTI); *nihtâwitâw* (VTI); to start an organization, *sipwepayihcikewin* (VTI).

generative *opikihitowin* (VAI).

generosity *miyoteh nesohkamakewin* (NI); *mistahimekowin* (NI); being generous, *miyotehewin* (NA).

generous *ekâ ka sasâkisehk* (VAI); *namoyasasakisew* (VAI); *kisewâtisiw* (VAI); *kisewâtan* (VII); s/he is kind and generous, *kisewâtisiwayaw* (VTA).

genial *ka miyohtwahk* (VAI).

geniality *metoni miyohtwawin* (NI).

genital *awâsis sihkakan* (NA).

gentle *manâtisiwin* (NI).

gentleness *manâtisîwâyâwin* (NI).

gently *peyahtik* (IPC).

genuflect *kocihcikwanipayihohk* (VAI).

genuflection *ocihcikwanipayihowin* (NI).

genuine *metoni ekotah* (IPC); something real, *kihcikîkway* (NI).

geranium *nepihkân* (NI); *wâpikwaniy* (NI).

germinate *kamâci ohpikihk kîkway* (VTI); *ohpikiwin* (NI).

gestation *ayâwâwasowin* (NI).

gesticulate *ka mosci isinskeyihk* (VAI).

gesticulation *mosci isinskewin* (NI).

gesture *mosci itwahekewin* (NI).

get S/he gets some wood, *nâcimihtew* (VAI); s/he fetches or gets people, *nâsiwew* (VTA); s/he fetches or gets her/him with a canoe, *nâtâhoyew* (VTA); s/he fetches or goes to get some moss, *nâtaskew* (VTA); s/he fetches or goes to get some hay, *nâtaskosiwew* (VTA); s/he goes to get, see, or check her/his snares, *nâtakwew* (VAI); s/he goes and gets her/him, *natew* (VTA); s/he goes to get some red hot coals for a fire, *nâtiskotawew* (VTA); s/he goes to get refreshments, i.e.: pop, beer, etc., *nâtopew* (VAI); s/he comes and gets her/him, *penâtew* (VTA).

getter *onâcikew* (NA).

ghastly *kakwâyakahkamiksowin* (NI).

ghost *cîpay* (NA); a ghost or haunted house, *cîpayikamik* (NI); a ghost bag, *cîpayiwat* (NI).

ghostly The act of looking like a ghost, *cîpay nakosowin* (NI).

gibber *ka ayahkotonâmohk* (VAI).

gibberish *ayahkotonâmowin* (NI).

giblet *pîwâyis otamiyawa* (NI).

giddy *kîskweyâpamohiwewin* (NI); sickness from smoking, dizzy, *kîskwesiw* (VAI).

gift Something you give away, *kîkway kâmekihk* (VTI); things that you give away, *mekiwina* (NI); something given, *mekiwin* (NI).

gifted Someone with a special gift or the way you are, *isihtwawin* (NI); naturally gifted, *ka isimeyekowesihk* (VAI); s/he is gifted with spiritual power, *mamahtâwisiw* (VAI); character, *isâyâwin* (NI).

gigantic *ka kâkwayakispehcak* (VII).

giggle *papihkâsowin* (NI); *kîyakahpisiw* (VAI).

giggly *papihkâsohâyâwin* (NI).

gild *wayesih miyonâkohcikan* (NI).

gill *kinosew yehewakanah* (NI).

ginger A ginger root or musquash root, *wehkesk* (NI) *(Plains)*; *manitoskâtâsk* (NI) *(Northern)*.

gingerly *metoni ka nâkateyihtamihk* (VAI).

gingham *miskotâkekin* (NI).

girdle *sihtahpison* (NI).

girl *iskwesis* (NA); a bad girl, *macitwawiskwesis* (NA); a Cree girl, *nehiyawiskwesis* (NA).

girlhood *ka iskwesisowihk* (VII).

girlish *iskewesisâyâwin* (NI).

girth The strap of a saddle, i.e.: the girth, *paskitatayepicikan* (NI); *sihtatayepicikan* (NI).

gist *metoni kehcinâhowin* (NI).

give The act of giving, *mekiwin* (NI); s/he gives, *mekiw* (VAI); s/he gives her/him a horse, *mekastimwâtew* (VTA); the act of giving a gift or present, *mekinawewin* (NI); things that you give away, i.e.: gifts or presents, *mekiwina* (NI); s/he gives it to her/him, *miyew* (VTA); s/he simply gives it to her/him, *moscimiyew* (VTA); s/he gives her/him a little bit more, *takomiyew* (VTA); s/he gives her/him an additional amount, *takonamawew* (VTA).

given Something given, *kamekihk kîkway* (VTA); s/he is given something, *meyâw* (VTA); the spiritual power given, *mâmatâwihikowin* (NI); s/he is given special spiritual gifts for doing extraordinary things, *mamatâwihikosisiw* (VAI).

giver *omekiw* (NA).

gizzard *mitisiy* (NI).

glad *ka meweyihtamihk* (VII).

gladden *ka atamihitohk* (VTA).

glade *tawipaskwaw* (NI).

gladly *metoni ka isimeweyihtamihk* (VII).

glamor or **glamour** *ka miyonâkosihk* (VII); *wawesîwin* (NI); an alluring charm, *wawesîwinakosowin* (NI).

glamorize *ka miyonâkohcikehk* (VAI).

glamorous *miyonâkosowin* (NI).

glance *kîskâw ketapipayihohk* (VAI).

gland *miyîkwak* (NI) *(Plains)*; *oyihk* (NI) *(Northern)*; a small gland, *îyihkos* (NA); a big gland, *îyihkwa* (NI); her/his gland, *wiyihkwa* (NI); a beaver gland, *wîsinâw* (NI).

glare *ka kihkâyâstek* (VII); *sewastew* (VII).

glaring *ka kihkâyâsowek* (VII).

316

glass *wâpamonâpisk* (NI); *wâsenamawinâpisk* (NI); a
window glass, *wâsenamawnâpisk* (NI).

glassful *ka sâkaskinek wâpamonâpiskoyakanis* (VII).

glasspane *wâpamonâpisk* (NI).

glassy *ka wâpamonâpiskowik kîkway* (VII).

glaze *wâpmonâpisk kosihtâhk* (VTI).

glazing *ka akamohtahk wâpamonâpisk* (VTI).

gleam *ka yâweyastek iskotew* (VII).

glean *ka mâwasakonamihk iskopocikana* (VTI).

glee *pahpihiwewin* (NI); *pahpiwin* (NI).

gleeful *ka pahpihiweskihk* (VAI).

glide S/he glides to a landing, *sawahkew* (VAI).

glimmer *ketisk ka wâsaskocesik* (VII).

glimmering *ka wâhwastepayik* (VII).

glimpse *ketisk kahtapahkewin* (NI); *kanak
niwapamaw* (VAI).

glisten *cahkâstenekewin* (NI); *wâsihkopayiw* (VAI).

glitter *ka miyonakohtahk kîkway* (VTI).

glittery *ka wâsihkonakwahk kîkway* (VII).

globular *ka wawîyâk kîkway* (VII); it is round,
wawiyâpiskisiw (VAI).

gloom *nawac poko ka kisisomahcihohk* (VII).

gloomy *kisôwâyawin* (NI); *pîkiskâteyihtâkwan* (VII).

glorification Idolizing someone, *ka
manitoweyimowehk* (VII); glorification or exaltation,
mamâhtâkosiwin (NI).

glorify The act of glorifying someone,
manitoweyimowewin (NI); s/he glorifies her/him,
mamâhtâkomew (VTA); s/he is glorified or exalted,
mamâhtâkosiw (VAI).

glorious It is glorious or exalted, *mamâtâkwan* (VII); it
is very beautiful, *mistahimewasin* (VII).

glory *metoni misteyihcikewin* (NI).

gloss *âyimwewin* (NI); it is shining, *wâsihkwapiskâw*
(VII).

glove A homemade glove, *yehyikastis* (NA); a mitten or
glove, *astis* (NA).

glowing *ka wâsihkwak* (VII).

glue Or paste, *pasakwâhikan* (NI); *pasakoskiwâcikan*
(NI); it sticks, it is sticking, it is holding tight, or it is
glued, *akopayiw* (VTI); *akopayin* (VTI); it is glued on
something, *pasakohtin* (VTI).

gluey *ka akopayik kîkway* (VTI).

glum *ka kamwatnakosihk* (VII).

glut *ka ayiwâkaskinahcikehk* (VAI).

glutton Somebody that eats excessively, *awîyak
kanipahaskatet* (VAI); a glutton or greedy eater,
okâsak (NA).

gluttonous Being gluttonous, *kawehtekowaskatehk*
(VII); s/he is gluttonous, *kâsakew* (VAI).

gluttony Over eating, *kâsakewin* (NI).

gnarl *ka wâkihk mistik* (NI).

gnarled *ka wahwâkikihkwâw miciciya* (VTI).

gnash *ka kiceskapitehk* (VAI).

gnat *pihkosisak* (NA); *ayîkosis* (NA).

gnaw Chewing on something, *ka mâmâkwahtamihk
kîkway* (VTI); s/he chews on it, *mâmâkwacikew* (VAI);
s/he gnaws on it for her/him, i.e.: a dog on a rope,
paskamew (VTA); s/he gnaws a hole in the ice, i.e.:
such as a beaver who breaks through the ice and
creates a breathing hole, *pîkwatamow* (VAI); the act of
gnawing a hole in the ice, *pîkwatamowin* (NI).

gnawn *mâmâkwahcikewin* (NI).

go S/he goes ahead, *nekanipayiw* (VAI).

goal *ka cawihk metawewnihk* (VAI); *kipahotowkamik*
(NI).

goat *nâpemayacikos* (NA); *wâpatihk* (NA); a mountain
goat, *pikiwayastak* (NA) *(Plains)*; *asiniwaciwacihkos*
(NA) *(Northern)*.

goatherd *ka mâmawiyatwâw mâyacihkosak* (NA).

goatskin *mâyatihkowayân* (NA).

gobble *ka kitapayihcikehk* (VAI); *mamisiwepayitâw
mîciwin* (VTI).

God The great postive good force in the universe,
kisemanito (NA); *manito* (abbreviation) (NA); the basic
mysterious quality in the universe, *manitow* (NA)
(Plains); s/he is the great spirit or God,
kisemanitowiw (NA); the quality of having the great
spirit or being God, *kisemanitowiwin* (NI); he is the
son of God, *kisemanitowokosisâniwiw* (NA); son of
God, *manitowikosisân* (NA).

goddaughter My goddaughter, *nitanisihkawin* (NA);
your goddaughter, *kitansihkawin* (NA).

godfather My godfather, *nohtawehkawin* (NA); your
godfather, *kikohtawe* (NA); *kohcawes* (NA).

god-given *manitomekowin* (NA).

godhead *manitowiwin* (NI).

godlike *peyakwan manito* (VII).

godmother My godmother, *nikawihkawin* (NA); your
godmother, *kikawe* (NA); *kikawes* (NA).

godson My godson, *nikosihsikawin* (NA); your godson,
kikosisihkawin (NA).

goggle *mîsikohkâna* (NI).

going The act of going away, *ka wehsipwehtehk* (VAI);
goes all the way or right through, *misakâme* (IPC); s/he
goes all the way from shore to shore, *misakameham*
(VTI); s/he goes right through them all,
misakamehwew (VTA); s/he goes all the way to the
end of the road, *misakamepayiw* (VAI); s/he bypasses
them, *misakâmeskawew* (VTA); s/he goes towards her/
him by swimming or paddling a canoe, *nâtâhwew*
(VTA); s/he goes towards shore by swimming or
paddling a canoe, *nâtakâmeham* (VTI); s/he goes
against the wind, *nayimiskam* (VAI); s/he goes out into

the open, i.e.: onto a lake or into town, *nimitâsiw* (VAI); they are going far out in the water, i.e.: a lake, *nimitâwahamwak* (VAI); s/he goes and gives her/him a drink, *nitawiminahew* (VTA); s/he goes and kills an animal for food, *nitawiminahiw* (VTA); the act of going to kill something, i.e.: a moose, *nitawiminahowin* (NI); s/he goes under something, i.e.: a fence, *sîpâsiw* (VAI); s/he goes into the woods or bush, *seskisiw* (VAI); s/he rides along side, *sisonepayiw* (VAI).

gold *osâwisôniyâw* (NA); gold nuggets, *osâwsôniyâwak* (NI).

gold dust *ka môsahkiniht osâwisôniyâw* (VTA).

golden *ka osâwsôniyâw nakwâhk kîkway* (VII); it has the color of gold, *osâwsôniyâwnakwan* (VII).

golden eye *napakikinosew* (NA).

goldeye *kokîsip* (NA).

goldfinch *pîwâyisis ka naweyemakan* (NA); *osâwâpîwâyisis* (NA).

gone S/he walked away or left, *sepwehtew* (VAI); s/he is not there anymore, *namatew* (VAI); s/he is gone or has left, *namatakiw* (VAI); s/he has gone across, *âsowaham* (VAI); s/he goes across for her/him, *âsowahamawew* (VTA); s/he goes across the water for her/him, *âsowahamwestamawew* (VTA); it is all gone, *namatakon* (VTI).

good It looks good, *miwasin* (VII); s/he is good natured, *mîyohtwâw* (VAI); s/he looks good, *mîyosiw* (VAI); it is good, *mîwâsin* (VTI); they are good, *mîwâsina* (VTI); I am good looking, *nimiyosin* (VAI); you are good looking, *kimîyosin* (VII); we are good (a group), *nimîyosinan* (VII); we are good (two people), *kimîyosinaw* (VII); they are good, *mîyisiwak* (VII); s/he is kind of good, *miyosewayâw* (VII); it is good because it is tough, durable, solid, *kakâyawâtan* (VII); s/he finds her/him a very good worker, *kakâyawâteyimew* (VAI); s/he is an energetic person, *kakâyawâtisiw* (VAI); s/he works well, *kakâyawâtoskew* (VAI); s/he is a good rower, *kakâyawicimew* (VAI); s/he is a hard worker, *kakâyawisîw* (VAI); s/he is a good walker, *kakâyawohtew* (VAI); a morally good act, *miyowâyihtowin* (NI); a good story or good news, *miywâcimowin* (NI) *(Plains)*; *miyowâcimowin* (NI) *(Northern)*.

good-bye *ka wâpamitinasamena* (VTA).

good evening *miyo takosin* (NI).

Goodfish Lake The Cree name for Goodfish Lake meaning "where the fish are good", *kâmiyosicik kinosewak* (NA).

good-hearted Kind heartedness, *miyotehewin* (NI); s/he has a good or kind heart, *miyotehew* (VAI).

good humor or **good humour** (person) *ka waninehk* (VII).

goodhumored or **goodhumoured** *owaninewiyiniw* (NA).

goodly Being of good character, *miyowâtisiwin* (NI).

goodness *miyow isâyâwin* (NI).

good night *ka wihmeyotipiskisin* (IPC).

goods *âpacitawna* (NI).

goose *niska* (NA); a small goose, *wehwew* (NA); a male goose or gander, *nâpeniska* (NA); a female goose, *nôseniska* (NA).

gooseberry *sâpomin* (NI); gooseberry bush, *sâpominâhtik* (NA).

gopher *miscanaskos* (NA); *mistanikwacas* (NA).

gore *ka pôskwaskocinihk* (VAI).

gored *wepahok* (VTA).

gorge *ka pôsiskatinak* (VII).

gorgeous *naspic miyonâkosiwin* (NI); good looking, *miyosiw* (VAI).

gosling *niskisisak* (NA); *niskisis* (NA).

gospel *manito masinahikan* (NI); *ayamihâwin* (NI); preaching the gospel, *kîskihkemowin* (NI).

gossip The act of gossiping, *ayimwewin* (NI); s/he gossips, *ayimwew* (VAI); s/he gossips about her/him, *ayimomew* (VTA); s/he gossips maliciously about her/him, *macayimomew* (VTA); malicious talk of false gossip, *macayimwewin* (NI); her/his gossip about her/him is unsubstantiated, *pakwanaw ayimomew* (VTA).

gossipy *ka ayimweskihk* (VAI).

got *ka ayâhk kîkway* (VTI).

gobuge A tool to gouge, *môhkotâkan* (NI).

gout *oskanahpinewin* (NI); *misisitân pakipayiwin* (NI).

grab Grabbing something, *kotihtinamihk* (VTI); s/he grabs her/him, *otihtinew* (VTA); s/he grabs her/him from the water, *akwâpinew* (VTA); land grab, *otinaskiwin* (NI); s/he grabs her/him, *kahcipitew* (VTA); s/he grabs her/him with her/his teeth when s/he passed by, *nawatamew* (VTA); s/he grabs her/his neck, *sakikwenew* (VTA).

grace *ka nahâwehk* (VAI).

graceful *nahâkeyawewin* (NI) *(Northern)*; *mamihtâkiyawiwin* (NI) *(Plains)*.

graceless *ekâ ka nahâwesihk* (VAI).

gracious *metoni manâtisowin* (NI); *miyowisihtwâwin* (NI).

gradual The act of being gradual, *nisihkâcâyawin* (NI); s/he acts in a slow and steady manner, *nisihkâcâtisiw* (VAI).

grain All kinds of grain, *nanatohkisi kistikân* (NA); grain, i.e.: wheat, barley, etc., *kistikân* (NA).

grand *ka kihciyetakwahk kîkway* (VII).

grandchild My grandchild, *nôsisim* (NA); having a grandchild, *kosisimihk* (NA).

grandchildren My grandchildren, *nôsisimak* (NA); having lots of grandchildren, *mihcet kosisimihk* (VAI).

granddaughter My granddaughter (or grandson), *nôsisim* (NA); my granddaughter, *nôsisim iskwesis* (NA); having a granddaughter (or grandson), *iskwew kosisisimihk* (NA).

grandfather *omosômimâw* (NA); my grandfather, *nimosôm* (NA); our grandfather, *nimosôminan* (NA); her or his grandfather, *omosôma* (NA); their grandfather, *omosômiwâwa* (NA); your grandfather, *kimosôm* (NA); *kimosômiwâw* (NA).

grandfatherly *kihtenapew isâyâwin* (NI).

grandma My grandma, *nohkôm* (NA); your grandma, *kokôm* (NA).

grandmother *ohkomimâw* (NA); my grandmother, *nohkôm* (NA); our grandmother, *nohkomnan* (NA); his or her grandmother, *ohkoma* (NA); their grandmother, *ohkomwâwa* (NA); your grandmother, *kohkom* (NA); *kohkomwâw* (NA).

grandmotherly *notokwew isâyâwin* (NI).

grandnephew My grandnephew, *nôsisim* (NA).

grandniece My grandniece, *nôsisim* (NA).

grandpa *omosômimâw* (NA); my grandpa, *nimosôm* (NA).

grandson My grandson (or granddaughter), *nôsisim* (NA), *nicicim* (diminutive) (NA); my grandson, *nôsism napesis* (NA); having a grandson (or granddaughter), *iskwew kosisisimihk* (VTA).

grand uncle My grand uncle, *nimosôm* (NA).

granny or **grannie** My granny or grannie, *nohkôm* (NA).

grape A raisin, *sôminis* (NA).

grasp *kahtinikewin* (NI); *otihtinam* (VTI); *miciminam* (VTI).

grasping *kahkamesakinamihk kîkway* (VTI).

grass A piece of grass or hay, *maskosiy* (NI); the grass stands high, *ispaskâw* (VII); the grass is deep, *timaskâw* (VII); it is grassy or there is plenty of grass or hay, *maskosiskâw* (VII); a grasshead, *maskosiwistikwân* (NI); a shelter made of grass or hay, i.e.: a straw house, *maskosiwikamik* (NI); brome grass or bone grass, *oskanaskosiy* (NI); new spring grass or fresh grass, *oskaskosiy* (NI); having the appearance of fresh grass, *oskaskosiwinakwan* (NI) *(Plains)*; the grass is blue, *sîpihtakwaskâw* (VII), an area of white grass, *wâpiskaskwa* (LN).

grasshopper A grasshopper, *kwâskocisîs* (NA).

grassland Or prairie, *maskotew* (NI); a whole piece of grassland, *misiwepaskwaskâw* (LN) *(Northern)*; *misiwepaskwâw* (LN) *(Plains)*.

grassy *ka maskoskâk*; *maskosiskâw* (VII).

grateful *mistahi atamihitowin* (NI); being grateful or thankful, *nanaskomow* (VAI); s/he is grateful to be cured, *nanâtaweyimow* (VAI).

gratification *atamihiwewin* (NI).

gratify *ka atamihiwehk* (VTA).

grating *oyaskenahcikewin* (NI).

gratitude *ataminâwin* (NI); *nanâskomowin* (NI).

grave *kihkwahaskân* (NI).

graven *kîkway koyihkotamihk* (VTI).

gravestone *kihkwahaskân asinîy* (NA).

graveyard *kihkwahaskâna kayâkwâw* (LN).

gravy *pahkwesikanâpoy* (NI); making gravy or soup, *micimâpohkewin* (NI).

gray or **grey** A murky color, *wîpinâkwan* (VII); s/he is gray, *pihkonâkosiw* (VAI); it is gray, *pihkonâkwan* (VII).

grayling *cahcahkinosiw* (NA).

grayish A grayish color, *wîpinâkwan* (VII).

grease Or oil, lard, *pimiy* (NI); s/he renders fat to grease or s/he makes a native delicacy of dry meat mixed with moose fat, *pimihkew* (VTI); the act of rendering fat to grease, *pimihkewin* (NI); it is full of grease, *pimiwan* (VII); duck grease, *sîsîpipimiy* (NI); s/he greases it, i.e.: a frying pan, *tômapiskinew* (VTA); s/he greases the whole length of her/him, *tômâskonew* (VTA); s/he rubs grease all over the other person's body, *tômastenew* (VTA); s/he greases someone's hand, *tômicihcenew* (VTA); s/he greases her/his own hands, *tômicihcenisiw* (VAI); s/he greases someone else's face, *tômihkwenew* (VTA); s/he greases them, *tôminew* (VTA); s/he greases it with something, *tôminikâkew* (VAI); grease or ointment, *tôminikan* (NI); s/he greases herself/himself, *tôminisiw* (VAI); s/he greases her/him feet, *tômisitenew* (VTA); s/he greases her/his own feet, *tômisitenisiw* (VAI); a hair grease or cream, *tômistikwanâkan* (NI); s/he greases her/him head, *tômistikwanenew* (VTA); s/he greases her/his own head, *tômistikwânenisiw* (VAI); her/his head is greasy, *tômistikwânew* (VTA).

greasy It is greasy, *pasweyâw* (VII); *pimiwiw* (VII); it smells greasy or oily, *pimiwakân* (VII); the pole is greasy, i.e.: a pole, *tômaskwan* (VII); it is greasy or oily, *tômâw* (VII); s/he makes them greasy, *tômihew* (VTA); her/his face is greasy, *tômihkwew* (VAI); s/he makes herself/himself greasy, *tômihiw* (VAI); s/he is greasy, *tômisiw* (VAI).

great Greatest, *kihci* (IPC); something great, *metoni kihci kîkway* (IPC); much, greatly, big, *mistahi* (IPC); greater, *ayiwâk* (IPC) *(Plains)*; *ayiwâk ohci* (IPC) *(Northern)*; a little more or greater, *ayiwâkes* (IPC).

great-aunt *otanskotapan* (NA); my great-aunt, *nohkôm* (NA).

great-grandchild *otanskotapan* (NA); my great-grandchild, *nôsisim* (NA); *nitanskotapân* (NA).

great-granddaughter *otanskotapan* (NA); my great-granddaughter, *nôsisim* (NA).

319

great-grandfather *otanskotapew* (NA); *omosômâw* (NA); my great-grandfather, *nimosôm nitanskotapan* (NA).

great-grandmother *otanskotapew* (NA); *okômâw* (NA); my great-grandmother, *nohkôm nitanskotapan* (NA).

great-grandparent *otanskotapew* (NA); *onekihikomâw* (NA); my great-grandparent, *nitanskotapân* (NA).

great-grandson *otanskotapan* (NA); my great-grandson, *nôsisim nitanskotapan* (NA).

great-nephew *otanskotapan* (NA).

great-niece *otanskotapan* (NA).

great-uncle *otanskotapew* (NA); *omosômâw* (NA).

grebe A diving bird, i.e.: a grebe, *sihkihp* (NA).

greed *ka wihtikowatsihk* (VAI); *nohtekatew* (VAI).

greedy *kâsakew* (VAI).

greediness *kâsakewin* (NI).

green It is green, *askihtakwâw* (VII); it is green, *askihtakosiw* (VAI).

greenish *asketakonakwan* (VII).

greet *ka atamiskâtohk* (VTA); *atamiskâw* (VTA).

greeting *atamiskâkewin* (NI); *atamiskâtowin* (NI).

grew *kakih ohpikihk* (VTI).

grey goose *cahkipases* (NA).

greyish *wîpinâkwan* (VII).

griddle *kîstepowâpisk* (NI).

grief *wîsakitehewin* (NI); *kewâteyimowin* (NI).

grieve *mihtâcikewin* (NI).

grievous *kîkway ka mihtâtamihk* (VTI); *kwâtakeyihtakwan* (VII).

grill *sohki ka natotsahikehk* (VAI); *nawaciwakan* (NI).

grim *kostâcinakwan* (VII).

grimace *ka mâyihkweyihk ka wîsakahpinehk* (VAI); *mâyihkwepayiw* (VAI).

grime *wîyipayi* (NI); *yipatisiwin* (NI).

grimy *kîkway ka wîyipatahk* (VII).

grin A broad smile on a face, *pahpiwinâkosowin* (NI); s/he grins, *pahpiwinâkosiw* (VAI).

grind Grinding something, i.e.: meat or wheat, *ka sikopocikehk* (VAI); s/he grinds, *pinepocikew* (VAI); s/he grinds or gnashes her/his teeth, *kiciskâpitew* (VAI); s/he grinds or crushes them up, i.e.: wheat into flour, *pîkinipohew* (VTA); s/he grinds, *pinipocikew* (VAI); it is ground or milled, *piniposiw* (VAI); it is ground or milled, *pinipotew* (VTI); s/he grinds it, i.e.: wheat, *pinipoyew* (VTA).

grip *maskawinkewin* (NI); a tight grip, *sohki miciminam* (NI).

gripe *tahkiskâcikew pîkiskwewin* (NI).

gripping *ka tahkiskâcikew pîkiskwehk* (VAI).

grisly *ka kakwâyakinakwahk kîkâw* (VII).

grist *ka sikwatahoht kistikân* (VTI).

gristle *otamiskay* (NI).

gristly *ka otamiskawik pahkikin* (NI).

grit *îyikaw* (NI); *yekaw* (NI).

gritty *kîkway ka pihekwak* (VII).

grizzly *okistatowan* (VII); *mistahaya* (NA).

groan *mahpinewin* (NI); *mamâpinew (vai)*.

groggy *ka ayâhpayihk* (VAI).

groin *âpihtawisiyaw* (NI); *mit'soway* (NI); *micicâskâhk* (LN).

groom Well-groomed, *miyosihowin* (NI).

groove *napakihtak ka pasipotek* (VII).

grope *ka natomeskonkihk* (LN).

gross *wâwiyak* (IPC).

grossness *wâwiyak wîniyisâyâwin* (NI).

grotesque *nanâtohk konikewin* (NI).

grouch *ka macihtwât awîyak* (VAI).

grouchy *macihtwâwin* (NI).

ground Dirt, *asiskîy* (NI); close to the ground, *cîkaskamik* (VII); a large area of rough ground, *mahmâyahcâw* (VII); rough and uneven ground, *mâyahcâw* (VII); rocky ground, *asiniwahcâw* (VII); there is high ground, *ispahcâw* ; there is high, hard ground, *ispatawohkâw* (VII); the ground is frozen, *âhkwatacâw* (VII); right on the ground, *astâskamik* (LN); when something is ground, e.g.: meat, *kasikopotahk kîkway* (VTI); solid ground, *kistahcâw* (VII); spongy ground, i.e.: dry muskeg, *mâyaskamikâw* (VII); s/he touches the ground or bottom in the water with her/his feet, *misaskenam* (VTI); better ground, *miyoskamikâw* (VII); on the ground, *mohcihk* (LN); the ground is dry, *pâhkwahcaw* (VII); as the snow melts in the spring time the ground or earth begins to appear, *pânâkohtew* (VTA); s/he misses touching the ground or bottom in the water with her/his feet, *pataskenam* (VTI); rough ground, *pîkwahcâw* (VII); a soft, spongy piece of ground, *pîswecâw* (VII); an area of even and level ground, *tahtakwahcâw* (VII); it is level ground, *tahtakwaskamikâw* (VII); the ground has thawed, *tihkahcâw* (VII); an area of ground with many dips, *wahwâyahcâw* (VII); a dip in the ground, *wâyahcâw* (VII); s/he can barely touch the ground in deep water, *yâwaskenam* (VTI); the ground is soft, *yoskahcâw* (VII).

groundhog *winasakâcihp* (NA).

groundless *ekâ tahkâskenekewin* (NI).

ground squirrel *anikwacâs* (NA).

groundwork Digging in the ground, *monahikewin* (NI).

group *ka mâmawyatihk* (VAI).

grouping *mâmawinitowin* (NI).

grouse Or wood partridge, *pihew* (NA).

grove *ka nepiteskisotwâw sihtak* (VTA); *metos pisiwaskwayiskâw* (NA).

grovel *ka pimitâcimohk* (VAI).

grow Growing things, *kohpikihcikehk* (VAI); it grows, *ohpikiw* (VAI); s/he grows things, i.e.: vegetables or

grain, *kistikew* (VAI); it grows crippled or deformed,
i.e.: a bone, *mâskikin* (VTI); s/he grows crippled or
deformed, *mâskikiw* (VAI); the tree grows at an angle,
naweskisiw (VAI); it grows crooked or bent out of
shape, *pihkikow* (VAI); it grows crooked or bent out of
shape, *pihkikin* (VII).

grower *otohpikihcikew* (NA).

growing Born, *nihtâwikiw* (VAI); s/he grows up,
ohpikiw (VAI); it grows up, *ohpikin* (VTI); the act of
growing up, *ohpikowin* (NI); sprouting, coming out,
sakikiw (VAI); *sakikin* (VAI); grown enough, big
enough, *tepihkiw* (VAI); *tepihkin* (VAI); grow deformed,
mâskikiw (VAI); *mâskikin* (VAI); growing lighter,
yahkikiw (VAI); *yahkikin* (VAI).

growl A dog growling at someone, *atim ka
nemototaket* (VAI); s/he growls, i.e.: a dog, *nemow*
(VAI); the act of growling, *nemowin* (NI).

grown Something that grows, *kîkway ka ohpikihk*
(VTI).

grown-up Being all grown-up, *kîsohpikiwin* (NI); s/he is
all grown-up, *kîsohpikiw* (VAI).

growth *kîkway ka ohpikihk* (VTI); *ohpikiwin* (NI).

grub Slang for food, *mîciwin* (NI); *nemawin* (NI).

grub *ôcew* (NA); *ohces* (NA).

grudge Being angry at someone, *ka kisôweyimiht
awîyak* (VAI); s/he holds a grudge, *pimâmeyimow*
(VAI); the act of holding a grudge, *pimâmeyimowin*
(NI).

gruesome *ka kakwâyakihkowit awîyak* (VII).

gruff *mâyihtâkosiw* (VAI).

grumble Pout, *mihtawewin* (NI); *mihtawew* (VAI).

grumpy *ka mihtaweskihk* (VAI); *kisôwisâyâwin* (NI).

grunt *mamâpinew* (VAI).

guard A keeper of something, i.e.: a game warden,
okanaweyihcikew (NA); s/he is guarding against it,
i.e.: a fire warden in the forest; a doorkeeper,
okanawiskwahtawin (NI) *(Plains)*; s/he guards at
night, *okanawitipiskwew* (NA); a security guard or a
house guard, *okanawiwaskahikanew* (NA); a prison
guard, *okipahowew* (NA).

guarded *ka kanaweyihtamihk* (VTI).

guess The act of guessing, *pakwanaweyihtamowin*
(NI); guesswork, *pakwanaw* (IPC); s/he takes a guess
about her/him, *pakwanaweyimew* (VTA).

guest *okehokew* (NA); an invited person, *wihkomakan*
(NA).

guffaw Laughing out loud, *kiseweyahpowin* (NI).

guidance *kiskinohtahiwewin* (NI).

guide *okiskinohtahiwew* (NA); s/he guides,
kiskinohtahiwew (VTA); s/he guides her/him or shows
her/him where to go, *kiskinohtahew* (VTA).

guile *kîmôc îyinisiwin* (NI).

guileful *kîmôtâtisiwin* (NI).

guileless *kepâcâyâwin* (NI).

guilt *macâtisiwin* (NI).

guilty Truthful, *tâpwemowewin* (NI); suspected,
atâmeyimâw (VTA).

guise *tansi ka isehohk* (VAI).

gulch *ka wâyatinâk* (VII); a big valley, *tawâtinâw* (VII).

gulf *ka wihkwekamak* (VII); a large bay on an ocean,
kiciwasaw (NI).

gull *kîyâsk* (NA); *kîyâskos* (NA).

gullet The throat, *mikohtâkan* (NI).

gullibility *wahkew tâpwehtâkewin* (NI).

gullible *ka wahkew tâpwehtâmihk* (VAI).

gully *ka pôskatinak* (LN); *pasahtawahkâw* (VII); there
is a gully, *pasahcâw* (VII).

gulp *kohcipayihcikewin* (NI).

gum *pekes* (NA); there is gum, *pikiwiw* (VAI); a piece of
chewing substance, *pikiw* (NA).

gummy Something gummy with pitch, *kîkway ka
pikiwik* (VTI); it is gummy, i.e.: full of spruce pitch,
pikiwan (VII); it is gummy, *pikiwiw* (VAI).

gun *pâskisikan* (NI); a gun barrel, *pâskisikanapisk* (NI);
a gun stalk, *pâskisikanatik* (NI); a small gun,
pâskisikanis (NI).

gunman *opâskisikew* (NA).

gunpowder Gun powder, *kaskitew* (NI).

gunshot *kamatwewek* (VII); the gun shot can be heard,
matwewew (VII).

gunsight *oyâpahcikan* (NI).

gunstock *pâskisikan âhtik* (NI).

gurgle *ka kisipekikonewehk* (VAI);
kitoweyakamipayiw (VAI).

gush *ka misi wayawecowahk* (VTI); *kwâskweciwan*
(VTI).

gushing *ka sohkicowahk* (VTI).

gust *ka pahkihtowestihk* (LN); *yôtinipayiw* (VAI).

gut Cutting, *pakohcenekewin* (NI); s/he guts it,
pakohcenew (VTA) *(Northern)*; *pikohcenew* (VTA)
(Plains); an intestine, *mitakiseyape* (NI).

guzzle *kisiskâ minihkwewin* (NI).

gyp *wayesihitowin* (NI).

gyrate *ka wâsakâpayihk* (VTI).

321

habit *kahkihtwam katohtamihk* (VAI).
habitable *takeh wîkinanowik* (VAI).
habitation *tasicikewin* (NI).
habitual *ekâ kakeh nakehk kîkway* (VTI); habitually and ever, *tahki mana* (IPC).
hack *ka pasahikehk* (VAI).
hackle *nâpepâhkahahkwan ostikwan mekwana* (NI).
hacksaw *pîwâpiskokîskipocikan* (NI).
haggard *niponakosiwin* (NI); looking very sick, *âhkosiwinakosiwin* (NI).
hail It hails, *sîsîkwan* (VII) (Northern); *sîsîkan* (VII) (Plains); it is hailing, *sîsîkanihtaw* (VII) (Northern); *miskwamiy pahkisinak* (VII) (Plains); *miskwamiy pahkisin* (VII); *ka atamiskâkehk* (VTI).
hailstone Or little ice, *miskwamîs* (NI); when it is raining hailstones, *ka sîsîkwahk* (VTI).
hailstorm *ka sîsîkwahk* (VTI).
hair One strand of hair on the head, *mestakay* (NI) (Northern); *mescaskas* (NI) (Plains); a mane of hair, *mescakasa* (NI) (Northern); *mescakasa* (NI) (Plains); a body hair, *opîway*; a white-gray hair, *wâpiskawes* (NI).
hairbrush *sîkahwakan* (NI).
haircut Having a haircut, *paskwahamâwin* (NI); s/he has a haircut, *paskwahamâw* (VAI) (Northern); *kîskahamâw* (VAI) (Plains); s/he gives her/him a haircut, *paskwahamâwew* (VTA) (Northern); *kiskahamawew* (VTA) (Plains).
hairless Being bald, *ka paskwâtihpehk* (VAI); *paskwâtihpewin* (NI); it is hairless or it has no fur, *paskosiw* (VAI).
hairy Being hairy, *opîwâwisiwin* (NI).
hale *ka miyomahcihot kihtehaya* (VAI); *sohkâtisiw* (VAI).
half *âpihtaw* (IPC); a little half, *âpihtawes* (IPC); a wee little half, *âpihcawises* (IPC); a half, *mînâpihtaw* (IPC).
half-and-half *ahâpihtaw* (IPC).
half-blooded *âpihtaw wetisanihtowin* (NI).
half-breed *âpihtaw kosisan* (NA).
half brother *âpihtaw kostesihk* (NA); *âpihtaw kisemis* (NA).
half-hour *âpihtaw tipahikan* (IPC).
half sister *âpihtaw kimis* (NA); *âpihtaw kisemis* (NA).
halfway *âpihtawiskoh* (LN).
halibut A flat fish, *napakikinosew* (NA).
hallow *kihcitwâweyimowewin* (NI).
halo *pesimoyapiy* (NI).
halt *ka nakîhk* (VAI); *nakîw* (VAI); *nakinew* (VTA).

halve *metoni âpihtaw* (IPC); *âpihtawihtaw* (VAI).
ham *kohkôsepoms* (NI); *kohkôsowiyâs* (NI).
hammock *wewepison* (NI) (Plains); *wepison* (NI) (Northern).
hamstring *ka cîsiyiwakwehk* (NI).
hand *micihciy* (NI); a hand towel, *kâsecihcâkan* (NI); s/he has a deformed hand, *mâskicihcew* (VAI); s/he has red hands, *mihkocihcew* (VAI); s/he has bloody hands, *mihkowicihcew* (VAI); with one hand, *napateniskew* (IPC); her/his hands are dry, *pâhkocicew* (VAI); s/he drys her/his hands for her/him, *pâhkocihcenew* (VTA); s/he has a swollen hand or hands, *pâkicihcew* (VAI); s/he has only one hand, *peyakocihcew* (VAI); the tip of a hand, *wanaskocihcew* (NA).
hand game S/he plays the Cree hand game, *pakesiw* (VAI); the act of playing the Cree hand game, *pakesîwin* (NI).
handful *sâkaskinecicehk* (VAI).
handgrip *ka nâpew atamskâtohk* (VII).
handhold *ka sakicicentohk* (VII).
handle *miciminikan* (NI).
handmade *moscôsehcikewin* (NI) (Northern); *iyinitoyishihcikewin* (NI) (Plains).
handshake *atamiskâkewin* (NI).
handsome *ka katawasihk* (VII); *miyowâpewiw* (VAI).
handwork *meciciya ka atoskakehk* (VAI).
handy It is real handy, *metoni nehpemayaw* (VII); something close at hand or handy, *nehpem* (IPC).
handyman *otatoskew* (NA).
hang *kâkotek kîkway* (VAI); it hangs from one side, *napatemiw* (VII) or (VAI); it hangs at an angle, *nawemow* (VAI).
hanging It is hanging, *akotew* (VII); s/he hangs it, *akotaw* (VTI); hanging something, *akocikewin* (NI); hanging from or suspended, *akocin* (VAI); hanging without touching the ground, *nemakocin* (VAI); *nemakotew* (VII); hanging, flying close to the ground, *tapahtakocin* (VAI); *tapahtakotew* (VII); freshly hung, i.e.: new moon, *oskakocin* (VTA); something that hangs with something else, i.e.: a hat and coat, *kikakotew* (VII); s/he or it is hanging by a rope, *kosâwekocin* (VAI); it is hanging by a rope, *kosâwekotew* (VII); s/he packs her/him hanging down, *kosâwenew* (VTA); suspended in air, death by hanging, *kosâwehpisiwewin* (NI) (Northern); *akotitowin* (NI) (Plains); s/he hangs her/him up with a rope, *kosâwehpitew* (VTA) (Northern); *akotew* (VTA) (Plains); it is newly hung, *oskakotew* (VII).
hangout *mâmawâyâwin* (NI).
hangover *âhkosepewin* (NI).
hang-up Detesting something, *pakwâcikewin* (NI).
hank *peyak kwahpetew sestak*.
hanker *kîkway ka akâwâtotamihk*.

323

hankering *akâwâtohcikewin* (NI).

hapless *mayakosiwin* (NI).

happen *kîkway kîspayik* (VII); it happens, *ihkin* (VII); *ispayiw* (VII); it happens in a wonderful fashion, *mâmaskâcihkin* (VII).

happening *kîkway ka wehispayik* (VII); *ispayiwin* (NI); going on, happening, *itahkamikisiw* (VAI); *itahkamikan* (VII); dirtying herself/himself by moving about, doing a job, *iyepatahkamikisiw* (VAI); *iyepatahkamikan* (VII); moving all over the place making things happen, *papâmahkamikisiw* (VAI); *papâmahkamikan* (VII); stops moving around all over the place making things happen, *ponâhkamikisiw* (VAI); *ponâhkamikan* (VII); too much of moving around, *osâmahkamikisiw* (VAI); *osâmahkamikan* (VII); enough, sufficiently of, *tepahkamikisiw* (VAI); *tepahkamikan* (VII).

happily Make everyone happy, *kesimiyawâtamihk* (VAI).

happiness Having a good time, *meyawâtamowin* (NI) *(Northern)*; *miywâtamowin* (NI) *(Plains)*.

happy Being happy, *kamiyawâtamihk* (VAI); s/he is happy with her/him, *cîhkeyimew* (VTA); people are happy with her/him, *cîhkeyihtâkosiw* (VTA); s/he is happy with it, *cîhkeyihtam* (VAI); being in the good books with everyone, *cîhkeyihtâkosiwin* (NI); people are happy with it, *cîhkeyihtâkwan* (VTI); s/he has a happy time with her/him, *wîcimiyawâtamowmew* (VTA).

harass *awîyak ka mekoskâcihiht* (VTA).

harassment *mekoskâcihiwewin* (NI).

harbor *or* **harbour** *ka wihkwekamak* (LN).

hard Something hard or strong, *kamaskawak kîkway* (VII); it is hard or strong, *maskawâw* (VTI); a hard wood, i.e.: oak, *maskawâhtik* (NA); it is a hard, strong tree, *maskawaskosiw* (VAI); it is a hard piece of wood or pole, *maskawâskwan* (VII).

hard-bitten *ka maskawâtsihk* (VAI).

hard-boiled *ka maskawâtcowasikehk* (VTI).

hardbound *ka maskawekinkatek* (VTI).

harden Something that hardens, *kamaskawipayik* (VTI); it hardens, *maskawpayiw* (VAI); there is stiffened, hardened soil, gum, etc., *maskawiskowew* (VII); s/he is hardened by the cold or frozen stiff, *maskawâskaciw* (VAI); s/he makes it hardened by the cold or s/he freezes it, *maskawâskatimew* (VTI); it is hardened by the cold or it is frozen, i.e.: a creek or lake, *maskawatin* (VII); hardened or crusty snow, *maskawâkonakâw* (VII); hardened mud, *maskawiskowakâw* (VII).

hardhead *maskawistikwan* (VII); *maskawistikwanew* (VAI).

hardiness *maskawâyâwin* (NI).

hard labor *or* **hard labour** *sihtatoskewin* (NI).

hardly *namoya tâpwe* (IPC); *namoyaceskwa* (IPC).

hardship *âyimihowin* (NI); *âyimisiwin* (NI).

hardy *maskawâyâwin* (NI); *maskawâtisiw* (VAI).

hare *misiwâpos* (NA).

hark *peyahtik ka natohtamihk* (VAI).

harken *natohtam* (VTI).

harm *mayitôtâkewin* (NI); *kitimahew* (VTA).

harmful *ka mayitôcikeskihk* (VAI).

harmless *miyo isâyâwin* (NI); *yoskatisiw* (VTA).

harness A horse harness, *otâpâniyâpiy* (NI); *otâpâniyâpiya* (NI); s/he harnesses her/him, *oyâhpitew* (VTA); s/he takes the harness off, *âpahastimwew* (VTI) *(Plains and Northern variant)*; *tasinastimwew* (VTA) *(Northern)*.

harried *nayawihitowin* (NI).

harsh *namakîkwây kitimâkinakewin* (NI).

has *awîyak kîkway kayat*; s/he has it on them, *ayâw* (VTA); s/he has them, *ayâwew* (VTA); s/he is at a certain place, *ayâw* (VII); having a possession or place where one stays, *ayâwin* (NI); s/he doesn't have it, *namakîkway ayâw* (VAI); s/he has lots of moose meat, *mistahi ayâw môsowîyâs* (VII); s/he has a mother, *omâmâw* (VAI); s/he has an older brother, *ostesiw* (VAI); s/he has a smaller brother or sister, *osemisiw* (VAI); she has a child, *otawasimisiw* (VAI); s/he has a horse or dog, *otemiw* (VAI); s/he sure has a smaller brother, *osemisiw* (VAI); s/he has her/his own pail, *otaskikomiw* (VAI); s/he has ducks, *osîsîpimiw* (VAI); s/he has cattle, *omostosomiw* (VAI).

haste *nanihkisiwin* (NI); making haste, *nanihkisiwin* (NI) *(Plains)*; *nanihkâtisiwin* (NI) *(Northern)*.

hasten *ka nanihkihewehk* (VTA); *nanihkitisawew* (VTA); moving fast, *kisiskâwaskawewin* (NI).

hastener *onanihkihewew* (NA).

hasty *ka nanihkisiskihk* (VAI); *papasihew* (VTA).

hastily *kîsiskâw* (IPC); very fast, *kisiskâpayonihk* (IPC).

hat *astotin* (NI); red hat, *mihko astotin* (NI); rain hat, *kimowanastotin* (NI).

hatch The act of hatching, *pâskâwihowin* (NI); it hatches, i.e.: an egg, *pâskâwehow* (VAI).

hate Hating one another, *pakwâtitowin* (NI) *(Plains)*; *kakwâyakeyihtâkosowin* (NI) *(Northern)*; s/he hates her/him, *pakwâtew* (VTA); being hated greatly, *kakwâyakeyihtâkosowin* (NI); it is hated greatly, *kakwâyakeyihtâkwan* (VII); s/he hates her/him greatly, *kakwâyakeyimew* (VTA); a hated item, *pakwâcikan* (NI); the act of hatred, *pakwâsowewin* (NI); the act of being thought of as being hateful or detestible, *pakwateyitakosowin* (NI); s/he is hated, *pakwâteyihtâkosiw* (VAI); it is hated, *pakwâteyitâkwan* (VII); s/he hates the situation, *pakwâteyitam* (VTI); the act of being hated or detested, *pakwâtikosiwin* (NI); it is hateful, *pakwâtikwan* (VII); the act of having a mutual hatred for one another, *pakwâtitowin* (NI); s/he finds her/him distasteful or s/he is unsure of her/him, *pakwâteyimiwew* (VTA).

hateful S/he is hateful or detestible, *pakwâtikosiw* (VAI).

hatful *ka sâkaskinek astotin* (VAI).

hatred *pakwâtowin* (NI); *pakwâsiwewin* (NI).

haughtiness *ka mamihtsewayahk* (VAI).

haughty *misteyimisowin* (NI).

haul The act of hauling, *âwacikewin* (NI); when you pull something, *kocipîtamihk* (VTI); s/he hauls water for her/him, *kwâpikawew* (VTA); s/he hauls water, *kwâpikew* (VAI); the act of hauling water by buckets, *kwâpikewin* (NI); s/he hauls her/his moose meat, *nakwâtisiw* (VAI); s/he hauls them here, i.e.: cattle, *petâwahew* (VTA).

haunch *kakwaskohtapihk* (NI); straight up, straighten, on her/his haunches, *simaciw* (VAI); the back side, *misôkan* (NI).

haunt *ka amâtsostakehk* (VTA).

haunted *ka amâtsostamihk* (VAI).

have *ka ayâhk kîkway* (VAI); *ayâw* (VII); s/he has more than s/he needs, *ayiwâkipayiw* (VAI).

havoc *ka mâyahkamkahk* (VII); causing destruction, *nisiwanacicikewin* (NI).

haw *namahtinihk* (LN); *namahtinihkisi* (LN).

hawk *onocayikowiw* (NA); *kiskinowâtascikewin* (NA).

hay Or grass, *maskosiy* (NI); a hay pile or hay bale, *maskosiya* (NI); dry grass, *pastew askoseya* (NI); there is plenty of grass or hay, *maskosiskâw* (VII); a shelter made of grass or hay, i.e.: a straw house, *maskosiwikamik* (NI); one piece of hay, *askaskosiy* (NI).

hazard *mayanohk kastahk kîkway* (VAI); *âyiminakwan* (VII); something dangerous or an obstacle, *âyimisehcikewin* (NI).

hazardous *mayanohk ascikewin* (NI).

haze *ka pîkihtek* (VTI); *pekiseyâhk* (VII); it is hazy, *pekiseyâw* (VII).

hazy *ka pîkihtenakwahk* (VII).

head *mistikwan* (NI), a red head, *mihkostikwan* (NI), her/his head is bare, *mosestikwânew* (VAI); a bare or uncovered head, *sâsâkinistikwan* (NI); s/he has a firm mindset, i.e.: literally means "a strong head", *sohkistikwânew* (VAI); a white head, *wâpistikwan* (NI); s/he has a white head, *wâpistikwânew* (VAI); a white haired old man, *wâpistikwânewikiseyiniw* (NA).

headache Having a headache, *teyistikwânewin* (NI); s/he has a headache, *teyistikwânew* (VAI).

head-dress *mekwan astotin* (NI); *pisiskwepisowin* (NI).

headfirst *ostekwanahikewin* (NI); *acicipayiw* (VAI).

headless *nama kîkway mistikwan* (VAI).

headman *onîkânîw* (NA).

head start *ka nîkân sipwehtehk* (VAI).

headstone *kehkwahaskanihk asinîy kahiht* (VTI).

headstrong *maskawestikwânewin* (NI); *maskawistikwânew* (VAI).

headway *tahkâyewak nîkânewin* (NI); *yahkemowin* (NI).

headwork *kostikwanahoht kwâskwenitowan* (VAI).

heady *minihkwewin ka kîskweskakohk* (VAI).

heal The act of healing a sore, *kîkîwin* (NI); her/his sore is healed, *kîkîw* (VAI).

healer *âstehowew* (NA); *otiyinihiwew* (NA) *(Plains)*.

health *miyomahcihowin* (NI); *isimahcihowin* (NI).

healthful Conducive to health, *miyoskakowin* (NI).

healthy *kâmiyomahcihohk* (NI).

heap *ka cahkastek kîkway* (VTI); on a heap, heaped up, piled up, *asipayiw* (VAI); *asipayin* (VAI); heaped, on a pile, *asîyâs* (IPC).

hear The act of hearing, *pehtamowin* (NI); s/he hears, *pehtam* (VAI); s/he hears her/him clearly, *pakaskihtawew* (VTA); s/he hears her/him, *pehtawew* (VTA); s/he hears her/him nearby, *pesohtawew* (VTA); s/he hears well, *wîyawihtam* (VAI); s/he hears her/him at a distance, *yâwâsihtawew* (VTA).

heard When you have heard something, *kakeh pehtamihk kîkway* (VTI); her/his voice is heard in the ground or earth, *askîhk pehtakosiw* (VAI); an audible or heard sound, *pehtâkwan* (VII); s/he can be heard coming in this direction by her/his drumming, *petoweham* (VAI); it can be heard coming in this direction, i.e.: hail, *petowehtin* (VII); s/he is heard walking in this direction, *petowenam* (VAI); s/he is heard coming in this direction, *petowesin* (VAI); s/he can be heard coming in this direction by her/his talking, *petowitam* (VAI); s/he heard it the wrong way, *wanihtam* (VAI); s/he hears it coming, *petowehtam* (VAI).

hearing *ka mekwa natohtamihk* (VAI); *pehtamowin* (NI).

heart *miteh* (NI); *mitiy* (NI); s/he has a kind, good heart, *miyotehew* (VAI); kind heartedness or good heartedness, *miyotehewin* (NI); s/he has a weak heart, *nesowitehew* (VAI); having a weak heart, *nesowitehewin* (NI); s/he has a strong, brave heart, *sohkitehew* (VAI); the act of being brave or having a strong heart, *sohkitehewin* (NI).

heartache S/he or it is causing her/him a heartache, *wîsakiteheskâkiw* (VTA); the act of having a heartache or being hurt emotionally or having a broken heart, *wîsakitehewin* (NI); s/he has a heart ache or s/he is suffering a broken heart, *wîsakitehew* (VAI).

heartbeat *pâhkahokowin* (NI).

325

heartbreak *pîkotehewin* (NI).

heartbreaking *ka pîkotehehk* (VAI).

heartbroken *pîkotehewin* (NI).

hearten *ka kîhtwam sîhkiskâkewin* (NI).

heartfelt *metoni mitehihk ohci ka mosihtâhk* (VAI).

hearth *asiskew kotawânâpisk* (NI).

hearthstone *asiskîy ka asiniwpayik* (VTI).

heartily *metoni mâhmiyoteh* (VII).

heartiness *miyotehewin* (NI).

heartless *ekâ kotehihk* (VII); *namoya otehiw* (VAI).

heartsick *metoni kaskiyetamowin* (NI).

heartsore *ka wîsakitehehk* (VAI).

heartstricken *ka nestohtehehk* (VAI).

heat Burned on, soldered, caked on, *akohkasiw* (VAI); *akohkahtew* (VII); hot enough to sweat, sweating, *apwehkasiw* (VAI); *apwehkatew* (VII); crimped by heat, sun, *ihkihkasiw* (VAI); *ihkihkatew* (VII); brittle from heat, sun, smoke, *kaskihkasiw* (VAI); *kaskihkatew* (VII); burned to powder, small pieces, *pikinihkasiw* (VAI); *pikinihkatew* (VII); cut in two by fire, *kiskihkasiw* (VAI); *kiskihkatew* (VII); fire hardened, sun baked, *maskawihkasiw* (VAI); *maskawihkatew* (VII); it is heated, i.e.: a house, *kisowehkahtew* (VII) *(Northern)*; *kîsowihkahtew* (VII) *(Plains)*; s/he heats the place up, *kîsowihkasam* (VTI); s/he heats the water up for someone, *kisâkamisamawew* (VTA); the kettle is heated up, *kisakamisiw* (VAI); s/he heats up the water, *kisakamisiwew* (VAI); s/he heats up the frying pan, *kisâpiskisamowew* (VTI); s/he heats it up for her/him, *kisisamawew* (VTA).

heatedly *ka kisôpekiskwehk* (VAI).

heater *awasokocawânâpiskos* (NI) *(Plains)*; *awaswâkan* (NI) *(Northern)*.

heat wave *kawahwesakastek* (NI); there are heat waves, *nanahtew* (VII) *(Northern)*; *nânâtehtew* (VII); heat waves distort things, make things unclear, *wanastew* (VII); *wanakwanastew* (VII); *nânâtehitew* (VII).

heave *ka pimosenehk kîkway* (VTI).

heaven *kihcikîsik* (NA).

heavenly In heaven, *kihcikisikohk* (LN).

heavenwards *kihcikisikohk itehke* (LN).

heavy Something heavy, *kakway ka kosikwahk* (VTI); s/he is heavy, *kosikwatiw* (VAI); it is heavy, *kosikwan* (VII); s/he makes her/him heavy with a load, *kosikohew* (VTA); s/he makes her/him heavy with a pack, *kosikoskohew* (VTA); s/he figures her/him to be heavy, *kosikwateyimew* (VTA); s/he is regarded as being heavy, *kosikwateyihtâkosiw* (VAI); it is regarded as being heavy, *kosikwateyihtâkwan* (VII); being heavy, *kosikwatowin* (NI).

heckle *ka kipotonehowewin* (NI); s/he bothers, annoys someone, *mikoskâcihew* (VTA).

hectic *kîskwehkamikisiwin* (NI); *âyiman* (VII).

heed *ka nâkateyihtamihk*.

heedful *nâkateyicikewin* (NI).

heedless *ekâ kîkway nâkateyicikewin* (NI); *namoya nâkatohkew* (VTA); s/he is neglectful to other people, *namoyanâkotohkew* (VTA).

heel *mahkwan* (NI).

heeled *maskisin ka mahkwanowik* (VTI).

heft *kosikwatiwin* (NI).

hefty *ka kosikwatihk* (VTI).

heifer *oskimoscosis* (NA); a "dry" cow, *onîcaniw* (NA).

height *taniyikohk ka iskosihk* (VAI).

heighten *ka ispinamihk nawâc* (VTI).

held *awîyak ka miciminiht* (VTA).

hell The devil dwelling, *macimanitonahk* (LN).

hello *atamiskâtowin* (NI); *tanisi* (IPC); how are you?, *tanisi* (IPC); *tân'si* (IPC).

help The act of helping one another, *nîsohkamâtowin* (NI); being of help to someone, *nîsohkamâkewin* (NI); s/he helps her/him, *nîsohkamawew* (VTA); they help each other, *nîsohkamâtowak* (VTA); s/he helps her/him with something, *ohcikamawew* (VTA) *(Northern)*; *nîsohkamawew* (VTA) *(Plains)*; *wîcohkamawew* (VTA); they are helping one another or several people are helping one another, *mihcetohkamâtowak* (VTA); s/he is helped spiritually, *wîcihikowisiw* (VAI); the act of receiving spiritual help, *wîcihikowisiwin* (NI).

helper *onîsohkamakew* (NA).

helpful Being helpful, *nihtânîsokamakew* (VTA); somebody that helps, *awîyak kanîsohkamaket* (VTA).

helping Helping right now, *mekwânesohkamâkewin* (NI).

helpless *micimoyowin* (NI); s/he is frail, *nesowisiw* (VAI).

helplessness *micimopicikewin* (NI).

hem *tipikwâcikan* (NI); hemming something, *ka tipekwâtamihk kîkway* (VTI); the act of hemming something, *tipikwâcikewin* (NI); s/he sews a hem, *tipikwâsiw* (VAI); s/he hems it, *tipikwâtew* (VTA).

hemlock *soni okihcikamehk kohpikitwâw sihtak* (NA); water hemlock "poison" ginger, *manitoskâtâsk* (NA).

hen A female chicken, *nôsepahkahahkwan* (NA).

her *wiya* (IPC).

herd A big herd of animals, *mihcet pisiskowak* (NA); s/he herds them altogether, *mawasakopayihew* (VTA); they are in a bunch, *âsîyâtowak* (VAI).

here From here, *ôta ohci* (IPC); here, closer than, farther away than, *ôte* (IPC); *ôta* (IPC); here s/he is, *awita* (IPC); *awa ita* (IPC); here it is, *omita* (IPC); *oma ita* (IPC); here and there, *âhaspehtaw* (IPC); an expression used when

326

handing something over to someone, "here", **na** (IPC); in this place right here, **omatowihk** (IPC); here it is, **ometeh** (IPC).

hereby *mâcika omisiy* (IPC).

hero A brave person, *onâpehkâsiw* (NA); s/he is brave, *nâpehkâsiw* (VAI).

heroic *nâpehkâsototamowin* (NI); having recoursed to extreme daring, *nâpehkâsiwin* (NI).

heroine *nâpehkâsiw iskwew* (NA).

heroism *napehkâsiwin* (NI).

heron *ekinwapek kotet pewayis* (NA); a water bird with long legs, neck and beak, *misimohkahasiw* (NA).

he *wiya* (IPC).

hesitance *nawacpoko îyîsac* (IPC).

hesitancy *îyîsac ka tôtamihk* (VTI).

hesitant *awîyak ka pomet* (VAI).

hesitate *kwantah îyîsac* (IPC); s/he gives up, *sâkweyimow* (VAI).

hesitation *îyîsac isehcikewin* (NI).

hew Shaping with an axe, *ka oyikahikehk* (VAI); the act of hewing with a broad axe, *pasahikewin* (NI); s/he hews timber with a broad axe, *pasahikew* (VAI); s/he hews logs, *pasahwew* (VTI); s/he hews with a broad axe, *pasahiket* (VAI).

hewer One who squares timber, i.e.: a hewer, *pasahikewiyiniw* (NA).

hex Putting a hex on someone, *ka mayakwamiht awîyak* (VAI); the act of putting a curse or hex on someone, *mayasowasowewin* (NI); s/he puts a hex on her/him, *mayasowatew* (VTA).

hiccup *sikokatâwin* (NI); s/he has hiccups, *sikokahtâw* (VAI).

hiccough *ka sikokahtâhk* (VAI).

hickory *pîtosemistik* (NI); *pakânâhtik* (NI).

hid *ka kehkâcikehk* (VAI).

hidden Something hidden, *kâcikewin* (NI); openly, visibly, not hidden or covered up, *mosis* (IPC); *mosise* (IPC); in a hidden, *kimoc* (IPC); in a surreptitious way, *kîsinâc* (IPC); hidden from view, *âkawâyihk* (IPC); s/he is hidden, *kâcikâsiw* (VAI); it is hidden, *kâcikatew* (VII).

hide A moose hide, *pahkekin* (NI); a bear hide, *maskwayân* (NI); a dog hide, *atimwayân* (NI); a horse hide, *mistatimowayân* (NI); a cow hide, *mostoswekin* (NI); raw hide, *askekin* (NI).

hide To hide, *kâsowin* (NI); s/he hides it in the ground, *ayahcinam* (VTI); s/he hides from her/him or others, *kâsostawew* (VTA); s/he hides, *kâsiw* (VAI); s/he hides it from her/him, *kâtamawew* (VTA); s/he hides her/him, *kâtew* (VTA); s/he hides it somewhere else, *ahcikatew* (VTA) *(Plains)*; *tahcikatew* (VTA) *(Northern)*.

hideaway *kâcikewin* (NI).

hideous *nâspic mâyâtisiwin* (NI); *kwâyakeyitâkwan* (VII); hideous to look at, *kwâyakinakwan* (VII).

hiding *ka mekwâ kâsohk* (VAI); tanning hides, *pahkekinohkewin* (NI).

high It is high, *ispâw* (IPC); highest or great, *kihci* (IPC); way up, *ispimihk* (IPC).

highly *misteyimisowin* (NI); *kisteyimâw* (VAI); s/he thinks highly of her/him, *ayiwâkeyimew* (VTA).

high noon *ka akwakesikak* (IPC).

High Prairie The Cree name for the settlement of High Prairie, *maskotewisipiy* (NA) *(Northern)*; *maskotehk* (NA) *(Plains)*.

high priest *ka nîkânapit ayamihewiyeniw* (NA).

high-sounding *ka sohkehtâkwahk* (VII).

high-spirited *ka môcikeyihtamihk* (VAI).

high spirits *môcikâyâwin* (NI).

hike *sîsawohtewin* (NI); *pimohtewin* (NI).

hilarious *kikac mosci nipahâhpowin* (NI).

hilarity *misi wawiyasinikewin* (NI).

hill There are lots of hills, *ayapatinâw* (VII); there is an uneven or rough hill, *pipikwatinâw* (NI); hilltop, *tahkohtâmatinâw* (NI); there is a crooked, winding hill, *wâwakatinâw* (NI); there is a bare, unwooded, literally prairie-hill, *paskwatinâw* (NI); there is a steep hill, *cahkâmatinâw* (NI); a long, elevated hillside, *osetinâw* (NI); indent in a hill, *wihkwetinâw* (NI); *wihkwetinahk* (LN); high hill, *ispatinâw* (NI); down the hill, *nihtâmatin* (LN); hills that surround and close in an area, *wihkwetinâw* (NI).

hillside *ayapeyamatin* (NI).

hilltop *tahkohtâmatin* (NI).

hilly *ka ayapamatinak* (VII); it is hilly, rolling terrain, *ayapatinâw* (VII).

hilt *metoni eskwayak* (IPC).

him *wiya* (IPC).

himself *wiya poko* (IPC).

hind *otâhisi kîkway* (VAI).

hinder *otâhkipisowewin* (NI); s/he impedes her/his action, *otamihew* (VTA).

hindmost *ayiwâkes otâhk* (IPC).

hindquarter *opwâm* (NI); *otâhkekat* (NI).

hindrance *otamihiwewin* (NI).

hindsight *pecikayas kîsiwapahtamihk* (VAI).

hinge *iskwâhtemapisk ka sakamocikakehk* (NI).

hinged *ka sakamohtahk iskwâhtem* (VTI).

hint *ka kakwi îyimiht awîyak* (VAI).

hip *mitôkan* (NI).

hipbone *mitokanikan* (NI).

hire Putting someone to work, *atoskahiwewin* (NI); s/he hires her/him or s/he makes her/him write, *masinahikehew* (VTA); s/he hires herself/himself, *masinahikehisiw* (VTA).

327

his *wiya* (IPC).

hiss *kinepik ketih takosit* (VII).

hit Hitting something, *katawahamihk kîkway* (VTI); s/he succeeds in hitting her/him, *kâcitawew* (VTA); s/he hits both in one shot, *nîsostahwew* (VTA); s/he hits her/him in the eye, *pakamacâpahwew* (VTA); s/he hits her/his children, *pakamahâwasiw* (VTA); s/he is hit or beaten, *pakamahikâsiw* (VAI); it is hit or beaten, *pakamahikâtew* (VII); s/he hits or beats her/him, *pakamawew* (VTA); s/he hit her/him, i.e.: with an arrow, *tawahwew* (VTA); s/he hit her/him in the middle of the back, i.e.: with something, *tâwipiskwanewew* (VTA); s/he hit her/him on the head, i.e.: with something, *tâwistikwanewew* (VTA).

hitch *ka sakicihtahk* (VTI).

hive *âmowaciston* (NI).

hoard *ka nahastahk* (VTI); store up beyond one's own needs, *mâwatascikewin* (NI).

hoarding *nahascikewin* (NI).

hoarfrost *ka yikwatihk kîkway* (VTI); hoarfrost and everything is icy freezing rain, *iyikopiwan* (NI); *iyikopestaw* (VII); the grey frost on something, *yiyekwatin* (VII); it is frosty, *yikopîwin* (NI).

hoarse *ka pâskekohtakanehk* (VAI); *mâyitakosiw* (VAI).

hoary *maci wapistikwanewin* (NI).

Hobbema The Cree name for the settlement of Hobbema meaning "bear mountain", *maskwacîs* (NI).

hobble Putting the hobbles on a horse, *ka nânapwahpetiht mistatim* (VTA); s/he is hobbled, *nânapwahpisiw* (VAI); something used to tie legs together, i.e.: to hobble a horse, *nânapwahpitew* (VTA).

hoe A vegetable hoe, *ayahcahikakanis* (NI); a grubb hoe, i.e.: used for removing tree roots, *mônahikâkan* (NI).

hog *nâpekohkôs* (NA).

hoist *kîkway ka ohpipitamihk* (VTI); *ispâkepitam* (VAI).

hold Holding, *miciminkewin* (NI); s/he holds the door shut on her/him, *kipohtenew* (VTA); s/he holds her/his mouth shut, *kipotonenew* (VTA); s/he holds her/him under water with her/his hands, *kokinew* (VTA); s/he holds her/him awkwardly, *mâyinew* (VTA); s/he holds on for support, *miciminew* (VTA); s/he holds onto something, *micimiw* (VII); s/he holds her/him while s/he is nude, *môstasenew* (VTA); s/he holds them together, *naponew* (VTA); s/he holds her/him at an angle, *nawenew* (VTA); s/he holds her/him down with her/his hands, *patakonew* (VTA); s/he holds her/him down with something heavy, *patakwahwew* (VTA); s/he holds her/him up, *setonew* (VTA); s/he holds her/him upright, *simatinew* (VTA); s/he carries or holds her/him, *tahkonew* (VTA); something to hold or carry,

tahkonikan (NI); a tool used to hold something together, *takwamohcikan* (NI).

holder Or potholder, *miciminkakan* (NI); something used to hold or pin something down, i.e.: a holder, *takwahikan* (NI).

holding *miciminkewin* (NI).

hole A hole in the ground, *watih* (NI); it has a hole in it, i.e.: like a straw, *payipaw* (VII); it has a hole in it, i.e.: a pipe, *payipisiw* (VAI); refers to a hole that develops after hitting something solid, i.e. ; a canoe against a rock, "it has a hole in it", *poskohtin* (VII); s/he makes a hole in them with her/his hands, *pôskonew* (VTA); there is a hole in it, *poskopayiw* (VII); s/he tore a hole in them, *poskopitew* (VTI); s/he cuts holes in it or them, *pôskosâwâcikew* (VTI); s/he makes a hole or incision on her/him, *poskosawâtâw* (VTA); s/he makes a hole in them when s/he throws or drops them down, *pôskosimew* (VTI); refers to a hole that develops after hitting something solid, i.e.: a tire against a nail, "it has a hole in it", *poskosin* (VAI); s/he made a hole in them by kicking them, *pôskoskawew* (VAI); s/he cuts an opening or a hole in them with scissors, *pôskoswew* (VAI); s/he pierces a hole into them with something sharp, *pôskwahwew* (VTA); s/he has a hole in her/his shoe, *pôskwaskisinew* (VTA); s/he made a hole in her/his head by hitting her/him, *pôskwatihpehwew* (VTA); s/he has a hole in her/his head, *pôskwatihpew* (VAI); a hole in something, i.e.: a garment, *pôskwâw* (VAI); s/he pierces a hole in them by hitting them, *pôskwatahwew* (VTA); something used to used to make a hole on ice, *twâhikan* (NI); a hole drilled in the ice, i.e.: a waterhole, *twâhipân* (NI); s/he is making a hole in the ice, *twahipanihkew* (VAI); s/he made a hole in the ice, *twahipew* (VAI); s/he is chopping a hole on the ice to get it out, i.e.: a beaver in a trap under the ice, *twawew* (VTA); s/he makes a hole in the snow for someone, *twâkonehwew* (VTA); s/he digs a hole, *wâtihkew* (VAI); the area has plenty of holes, *watowiw* (VAI).

holiness *kihcihtwâwisiwin* (NI); being holy, *kihcihtwâwisiwin* (NI).

holler The act of hollering or shouting, *tepwewin* (NI); s/he hollers at her/him, *tepwâtew* (VTA); s/he hollers or shouts, *tepwew* (VAI).

hollow Something hollow, *kîkway kawayak* (VII); it is hollow, *wehpaw* (VAI); it is deeply hollowed out, *pôsiskaw* (VAI); s/he makes them hollow, *posiskihew* (VTI); it is hollow or concave, *pôskisiw* (VAI).

holly *kiskinowâcihcikan ka nîpâyamihahk* (NI); *manito kîsikâw wawesihcikewin* (NI).

holster *aspîkinâkan* (NI).

328

holy *kihcihtwâwan* (VII); something holy,
kakihcitwâwik (VAI); it is holy, *kihcihtwâwan* (VII);
s/he thinks of her/him as holy, *kihcihtwâweyimiwew*
(VTA); s/he is thought of as holy,
kihcihtwâweyitakosiw (VAI); it is thought of as holy,
kihcihtwâweyihtâkwan (VII); s/he is dressed holy or
venerably, *kihcihtwâwisihow* (VAI); s/he makes her/
him holy or saintly, *kihcihtwâwisihew* (VTA); s/he is
holy, *kihcihtwâwisiw* (VAI); being holy,
kihcihtwâwisiwin (NI); it is like God, *manitowan*
(VII).

holy day *ka kihcitwâw kîsikak* (IPC).

holy orders *kihcitwâwasowewina* (NI).

home Or dwelling, *wîkowin* (NI); a house, *wâskahikan*
(NI); when speaking to a singular person use "your
home", *kîki*; when speaking to a group of people use
"your home", *kîkiwaw*; the act of going home,
kîwewin (NI); s/he went home, *kîwew* (VAI); in your
own home, *kîkihk*; my home or those, *nîkihk*; having
a home, *wîkowin* (NI).

homelike *peyakwan kîkihk.*

homely *ka mâyatsihk; mâyatisiw* (VAI).

homemade *moscôsehcikewin* (NI); *iyinitoyisihcikewin*
(NI); something homemade, *ka moscôsehtahk kîkway*
(VTI); a homemade item, *osihcikan* (NI).

homemaking *ka nânapâcitahk wîkowin* (NI).

homesick *kaskeyihtamowin* (NI).

homespun *ka moscôsehiht sestak* (VTI); *tipiyawi*
osihcikan (NI).

homestead The act of homesteading, *otinaskewin* (NI);
s/he homesteads, *otinaskew* (VAI); s/he cuts down
trees and clears the land, i.e.: for a homestead,
paskwatahikew (VAI).

homeward *awîyak wekihk itehke* (IPC).

homework *ka atoskasohk* (VAI).

homey *metoni ka miyo wîkihk* (VAI).

hone *asinis ka kanâcicikakehk* (VTI).

honest Doing honest business, *kwayaskwesihcikewin*
(NI); s/he has an honest character, *kwayaskâtisiw*
(VAI); it is honest, i.e.: business, *kwayaskâtan* (VII);
having honest character, *kwayaskâtisiwin* (NI).

honesty *ka kwayaskwesihcikewinihk* (VAI).

honey *âmômey* (NI).

honeybee A bee, *âmô* (NA); queen bee,
okimâskwewâmô (NA); king bee (drone), *okimâwâmô*
(NA); worker bee, *otatoskewâmô* (NA).

honeycomb Inside a bee hive, *pecayihk*
âmowatistwanihk (LN); what the bees make, *âmô*
osihcikana (NI).

honeyed *or* **honied** *âmow aspahcikewin* (NI).

honeysuckle Nice smelling leaves, *owihkimâkopakwa*
(NA).

honk *niska ka ketot* (VAI); the sound of a goose call,
niska otepwewin (NI).

honor *or* **honour** Honoring someone, *awîyak mistahi*
kiteyemiht (VAI); s/he is thought of as honorable,
kisteyihcikâsiw (VAI); it is honored, *kisteyihcikâtew*
(VII); s/he is honorable, *kiteyihtâkosiw* (VAI); the act of
being honored, *kiteyihtâkosiwin* (NI); it is honorable,
kiteyihtâkwan (VII).

honorary *mistahî iteyihtakosiwin* (NI).

honorable *or* **honourable** *mistahi kiteyehtakosihk* (VAI);
an honourable seat, *mistahi itâpowin* (NI).

hoof *wayasit* (NI).

hoofed *mistatim ka tahkiskâket* (VTA).

hook A fishing hook, *kwâskwepicikan* (NI); a wall
hook for clothes, *akocikan* (NI); a gaff hook,
ocikwâcikan (NA); s/he hooks or snares her/him,
nakwâtew (VTA); a long pole with a hook to pull
something out of the water, i.e.: a dead beaver,
ocipicikan (NI); s/he hooks the fish with a gaffe,
tapaskwahwew (VTA).

hooks S/he is caught on a hook, *nakwâsiw* (VAI).

hop *ka ayahcikihk; iskwesapoyipakwa* (NI).

hope The act of hoping, *pakoseyimowin* (NI); s/he
hopes to get something from her/him, *pakoseyimew*
(VTA); s/he has hope, *pakoseyimiw* (VAI); s/he brings or
provides hope, *pakoseyihtâkosiw* (VAI); something
that brings or provides hope, *pakoseyihtâkwan* (VII);
s/he hopes or wishes, *pakoseyihtam* (VAI); hoping for
something, *pâkoseyihtamowin* (NI).

hopeful *pakoseyihtamowin* (NI); *pakoseyimiw* (VTA).

hopeless *ekâ ka pakoseyimohk* (VAI).

hopper *otayahcikiw* (NA); *napatekwâskohtiw* (NA)
(Plains).

horde *mâmawinitowin* (NI).

horizon *wâhyaw kesenokwahk* (VII); *eskonakwahk*
(VII).

horn An animal's horn or antler, *eskan* (NA); *miteskan*
(NA); a car horn or a whistle, *kitôpicikân* (NI); s/he has
crooked horns, *wâkiteskanew* (VAI).

horned *kôtîskanihk* (VAI); *koteskanit* (VAI).

horny A sharp horn, *oteskan* (NA); *miteskaw* (VAI).

horrendous *ka sikihtakwahk âcimowin* (VII).

horrible *ka kakwâyakatahk* (VII); s/he is very disliked,
môstateyimikosiw (VTA).

horrid *ekâ ka kisewâtisihk* (VTA).

horrify *ka sikihtakehk* (VTA); *sikihiwehk* (VTA).

horrified S/he is scared, *sikisiw* (VAI).

horror *mistahi sikisowin* (NI).

horse *mistatim* (NA); a spotted horse, i.e.: a pinto,
masinâsowatim (NA); a stud or male horse, *nâpestim*
(NA); a young horse, i.e.: usually refers to a yearling,
oskastim (NA); a harness horse or a work horse,

329

otâpahâkan (NA); s/he has horses or dogs, *otemiw* (VAI); an untamed horse, *pikwatastim* (NA) *(Northern)*; *pakwatastim* (NA) *(Plains)*; it is a good or nice horse or dog, *takahkatim* (NA); a white horse or white dog, *wapâstim* (NA); a saddle horse, *tehtapîwatim* (NA).

horseback *mistatim ka tehtapihk* (VTA).

horse chestnut *weyipasatim* (NA); *wîyipastim* (NA).

horseflesh *mistatimowiyâs* (NI).

horsefly *misisâhk* (NA); a big horsefly, *misimisisâhk* (NA); a place with lots of horseflies, *misisâhkoskâw* (NI).

horsehair *mistatimopewaya* (NA); *mistatimopiway* (NA).

horseless *ekâ kotemihk* (VTA).

horseman *mistamweyeniw* (NA); *mistatimopamehiwew* (VAI).

horsemanship *ka mistatimwiyenewihk* (VAI).

horseshoe *piwapiskwahikana* (NI); *mistatimopiwapiskwahikan* (NI).

horsetail *mistatimwâyo* (NA).

horsewhip *mistatim opasastehikan* (NI); *pisastehikan* (NI).

horsewoman *mistatim iskwew* (NA).

horsy *mistatimwâyâwin* (NI).

hose *iskwew asikanak* (NI); *asikanis* (NI).

hospitable *ka nihtâ nitôhkimohk* (VAI); happy to welcome guests, *miyotôtâkewin* (NI).

hospitality *miyo otôtemowin* (NI).

host *saskamowin* (NI); *pamihiwew* (NA); host for communion, *manito pahkwesikan* (NA); *okehokew* (NA).

hostess *ka pihtokahiwet iskwew* (NA).

hostile *ka kisôweyihtamihk* (VAI); *namoya miyotôtemiw* (VAI).

hostility *kisôwâyâwin* (NI).

hot It is a hot, *kisitew* (VII); it is hot weather, *kisâstew* (VII); it is burning hot, *âhkwastew* (VII); it is sweating hot, *apweyaw* (VII); it is hot, i.e.: soup or water, *kisâkamitew* (VII); it is hot, i.e.: iron or pot or frying pan or drum, *kisâpiskisiw* (VAI); it is a hot piece of iron, *kisâpiskitew* (VII); it has lots of heat or it is hot, i.e.: a hot stove, *kisiskotewakisiw* (VII); the fire is hot, *kisiskotewahkan* (VII); s/he is hot or s/he has a fever, *kisisiw* (VAI); the act of having a fever, *kisisowin* (NI).

hot-blooded Hot-tempered, *wahkewiyawesiwin* (NI).

hound *onôcicikew atim* (NA).

hour *tipahikan* (NI); one hour, *peyak tipahikan* (NI); one hour measured by a clock, *pîsimohkantipahikan* (NI) *(Northern)*; *peyaktipahikan* (NI) *(Plains)*.

house *wâskahikan* (NI); *wâskayikan* (NI); it is housed, *wâskahikaniwiw* (NI); s/he built a house with something, *wâskahikanihkawew* (VTI); s/he is

building a house, *wâskahikanihkew* (VAI); a house builder, *wâskahikanihkewiyiniw* (NA); *mistikonâpew* (NA).

housefly *misi kaskitew* (NA); *ôcew* (NA).

household *mâmawi wîkowin* (NI); all the permanent residents of a house, *mihcetowekiwin* (NI).

housekeeping Keeping the house, *ka pamihtahk wîkowin* (NI).

hover *awîyak ekâ kakeh nâkatiht* (VTA).

how How are you?, *tân'si* (IPC); *tanisi* (IPC); how is your son, *tanisi kikosis*; how many?, *tân'tahto* (IPC); how many times?, *tantahtwaw* (IPC); how many places? of how many kinds?, *tantahtwayi* (IPC); *tân'tahtwayak* (IPC); for how much?, *tanimayikohk* (IPC); how should it be done?, *tanisi isi* (IPC); *tanisisi* (IPC).

however *tân'sipoko* (IPC).

howl The act of howling, *ôyowin* (NI) *(Northern)*; *wiyoyowin* (NI) *(Plains)*; s/he howls, *ôyow* (VAI) *(Northern)*; *wiyoyow* (VAI) *(Plains)*.

howler *awîyak ka ôyot* (NA).

huckleberry A cranberry, *nîpiminân* (NI).

huddle *kîskâw mâmawapowin* (NI).

huff *ka sohki pôtâcikehk* (VAI).

hug *âkwaskitinkewin* (NI); s/he is hugging her/him, *âkwaskitinew* (VTA).

huge *ka misâk* (VII); *misâw* (VII); it is a huge tree, *sohkaskisiw* (VAI).

huh *natohtamowin* (NI).

hulk *ka pônâpatahk misinâpihkwan* (NI).

hulking *mistiyeniw ka mâyinkeskit* (VAI).

hull *mistahôsih weyawihkan* (NI).

human A human being, *ayisiyiniw* (NA); being human, *îyinewiwin* (NI); it is like a human being, *ayisiyiniwan* (VAI); s/he is a human being, *ayisiyiniwiw* (VAI); humanity, *ayisiyiniwiwin* (NA).

humble Feeling humble, *ka kakwâtakeyemohk*; s/he humbles or abases herself/himself before her/him, *tapahteyimisôstawew* (VTA); s/he is humbles, *tapahteyimisiw* (VAI).

humid *ka akosepeyak* (VTI); it is humid, *miyamawâw* (VII) *(Northern)*; *miyimawâw* (VII) *(Plains)*.

humidity *ka akosepewayak* (VTI).

humiliate Making someone ashamed, *ka nepewehiwehk* (VTA); s/he causes her/him to humiliate herself/himself, *tapahteyimohew* (VTA); s/he is made ashamed, *înepewihiht* (VTA).

humiliation The act of making someone ashamed, *nepewihiwewin* (NI).

humility *peweyimowin* (NI); being ashamed of oneself, *nepewâyawin* (NI); humility or being humble or having low self-esteem, *tapahteyimisiwin* (NI).

330

hummingbird *âmopewayisîs* (NA) *(Northern)*; *âmopiyesîs* (NA) *(Plains)*.

humor *or* **humour** *ka waninehk* (VAI).

humorous *waninew isâyâwin* (NI).

hump *ka piskwâhcak* (VAI); *piskwâcaw* (VAI).

humpy *ka pahpiskwâhcak* (VAI).

hunch *ka moyehcikehk* (VAI).

hundred One hundred, *mitâtahtomitanaw* (IPC); a hundred times, *mitâtahtomitanawâw* (IPC); several hundred, *mihcetomitanaw* (IPC); it is number one hundred or one hundredth, *mitâtahtomitanawiw* (VII).

hundreth One hundreth, *mwecimitâtahtomitanaw* (IPC); hundreth time, *mitâtahtomitanawâw* (IPC).

hung Something that has been hung, *kakeh akotahk kîkway* (VTI).

hunger *nohtehkatewin* (NI).

hungry The act of being hungry, *nohtehkatewin* (NI); s/he is hungry, *nohtehkatew* (VAI); s/he makes her/him go hungry, *nohtehkatehew* (VTA); s/he is very hungry or s/he has an empty stomach, *sewatew* (VAI).

hunk *ka pahkwesawatek opwâm* (NI).

hunt Trapping, *nocicikewin* (NI); s/he goes hunting on horse back, *mâcîpayowin* (NI); s/he goes on a moose hunting trip, *mâcîpiciw* (VAI); s/he hunts her/him up, *mâcîstawew* (VTA); s/he hunts, *mâcîw* (VAI); s/he hunts for ducks, *notsipew* (VTA).

hunter A trapper, *onocicikew* (NA); a moose hunting person, *mâciweniw* (NA); a moose hunter, *omâciw* (NA).

hunting *ka mekwâ nocicikehk* (NI).

hurdle *kwaskweyâskwahowin* (NI).

hurl *sohkipimosinewin* (NI).

hurrah *sâkowestamakewin* (NI); *sâkowewin* (NI).

hurried Being hurried, *ka nanihkihewehk* (VAI); *kweyâhow* (VAI).

hurry The act of hurrying, *kakweyâhiwin* (NI); hurrying up, *kakweyâhohk* (VAI); s/he hurries or rushes, *kakweyâhiw* (VAI); *kweyâhiw* (VAI); s/he hurries her/him up, *nanihkihew* (VTA); the act of being in a hurry or being rushed for time, *nanihkisiwin* (NI);

s/he is in a hurry, *nanihkisiw* (VAI); s/he is in a hurry, *papaseyitam* (VAI); the act of being in a hurry or making haste, *papaseyitamowin* (NI); s/he makes her/him hurry, *papasihew* (VTA); s/he tells her/him to hurry or make haste, *papasimew* (VTA); s/he does things in a hurry, *papasîw* (VAI); the act of doing things in a hurry, *papasîwin* (NI); the act of being in a hurry, *nanihkisiwin* (NI) *(Plains)*; *nanihkâtisiwin* (NI) *(Northern)*.

hurt The smoke is hurting her/his eyes, *wîsakâpasiw* (VAI); s/he hurts her/him by hitting her/him, *wîsakatahwew* (VTA); s/he hurts her/him with her/his grip, *wîsakinew* (VAI); s/he is hurting her/him by pulling, i.e.: a dentist, *wîsakipitew* (VTA); s/he hurts her/him with bodily injury, *wîsakisimew* (VTA); s/he is hurt or injured by the fall, *wîsakisin* (VAI); s/he was hurt or injured by something, *wîsakiskâkiw* (VTA); s/he is hurting her/him by bodily injury, *wîsakiskawew* (VTA); s/he hurts her/him, *wîsaksimew* (VTA).

hurtle *ka sohki astimsohk* (VAI).

husband My husband, *ninâpem* (NA); my marriage partner, *niwîkimâkan* (NA); someone's husband, *awîyak onâpima* (NA); she has a husband, *onâpemiw* (VAI).

hush *awîyak ka wihtamaht tâponi kisewehtat* (VAI).

husk *ka âkwanahamihk kîkway*.

husky *mistâpewiwin* (NI).

hustle *ka yâwatsowin* (NI); *kweyahiwin* (NI).

hut *apisci wâskahikanis* (NI); *kitimâkikamikos* (NI).

hymn *ayamihew nikamon* (NI); a holy song, *ayamihewnikamowin* (NI).

hymnal A hymn book, *ayamihew nikamomasinahikan* (NI).

hyperactive S/he is hyperactive, *kakeskwew* (VAI); being hyperactive, *kakeskwewin* (NI); a person acting in a hyperactive manner, *kakeskwiwiyiniw* (NA).

hysterical *ka koskweyihtamihk* (VAI).

hysterics *koskweyihtamowina* (NI); *kîskweyihtamowina* (NI) *(Plains)*.

331

I

I *niya* (IPC); I am, *niya* (IPC).

ice *miskwamiy* (NA); there is ice, *miskwamiwiw* (VAI); it is frozen or it freezes, *âhkwatin* (VTI); the ice is thick, *kispakatin* (VAI); broken and refrozen ice, *akoyesikwâw* (VAI); the ice is well frozen even or smooth, *miyosikwâw* (VII); the ice is badly frozen or rough, *mayisikwâw* (VII); the ice is rough, *piskosikwâw* (VII); ice breaks up in spring, *âskawew* (VTA); honeycombed ice, i.e.: rough ice which is usually formed during the spring break-up, *pîkwacipayiw* (VAI); there are holes that formed in the ice in spring, *pîkwataskawew* (VTA); ice gets thin, *papakiskwatin* (VAI); it is lumpy ice, *piskosikwâw* (VII); the ice is slippery, *sôskosikwâw* (VII); there is a crack in the ice, *tâskisikopayiw* (VAI); there is an opening on the ice, *tâskisikwâw* (VII); the ice is clear, *wâsesikwâw* (VII).

iced *âhkwatihcikan* (NI).

ice-fisherman *miskwamîhk kâ paktahwât awîyak* (NA).

ice fishing *miskwamihk ka kwâskwepicikehk* (VTA).

icicle *ka miskwamewatihk wasakam apahkwânihk* (VTI); *yiweyaskatin* (VAI).

icy *ka sôskosikwâk* (VII); *miskwamewan* (VII); *sôskwâw* (VII).

idea Thinking about something, *kîkway kiteyehtamihk* (VAI); a kind of thinking, *iteyihtamiwin* (NI); s/he has a fixed idea about her/him or them, *micimeyimew* (VTA).

ideal *kîkway ka nahipayik* (VII).

idealize *awîyak ka takahkeyemiht* (VAI); to regard as ideal, *ayiwâkeyimew* (VTA).

identical *metoni pahpeyakwan kîsnakwahkwaw* (VII); equal, *pâpeyakwan* (IPC); looking the same, *naspitâtowin* (NI).

identification An identification card, i.e.: driver's license, *masinahikanis kohci kîskemiht awîyak* (NI); an identification mark, *kiskinawâc* (NI).

identify *kiskeyimowewin* (NI); *nistaweyimowewin* (NI); s/he identifies it with her/him, *akweyimew* (VTA); s/he identifies it as belonging to her/him, *akweyitamawew* (VTA); knowing or recognizing someone, *nistaweyihtakewin* (NI).

identity When a person is identifiable, *etah kohkiskeyihtakosihk* (VAI); s/he makes a postive identification of her/him, *nahapamew* (VTA); s/he has a distinctive identity, *nahâpaminâkosiw* (VAI); it has a distinctive identity, *nahâpaminâkwan* (VII); knowing what a person is, *nistaweyihtakosiwin* (NI).

idiocy *naspic ka kepâtisowin* (NI).

idiot *metoni ka kepâciyeniw* (NA); *môhcwa* (NA).

idiotic *metoni ka kakepâtisihk* (VAI).

idle *kwanta ayiyawin* (NI); a lazy bones, *kihtimikan* (NA).

idleness *kihtimiwin* (NI); s/he is lazy, *kihtimiw* (VAI).

idol *ayisiyinihkân ka manitoweyimiht* (NA); a statue, *ayisinihkân* (NI).

idolater *omanitoweyihcikew* (NA).

idolatress *iskwew ka manitoweyihciket* (NA).

idolatrous *manitoweyihcikewin* (NI).

idolatry *ka manitoweyihcikehk* (VAI).

idolize *awîyak mistahi kiteyemiht* (VTA); *âkawatam* (VAI); *sakihew* (VTA); s/he idolizes her/him, *omanitomiw* (VTA); something that is worshipped, *âhkwateyihcikan* (NI).

if *kîspin* (IPC); if only, *kîspinesa* (IPC) *(Plains)*; *kîkoc* (IPC) *(Archaic Northern Cree)*; as if, quite similar, or like exactly the same; you'd say it is the same, etc., *mwehci* (IPC); if, in case, when, *kîspin* (IPC).

ignite It flames up, *saskitew* (VII).

ignorance *môhcowisâyâwin* (NI); *kakepâtisiwin* (NI); having little or no knowledge, *kakepâtisiwin* (NI).

ignorant S/he is ignorant, *kakepâtisiw* (VAI); *awîyak ka môhcowisâyât* (VAI).

ignore *ekâ ka papisiskeyehtamihk kîkway* (VTI); s/he ignores her/him, *namoya nâkateyimew* (VTA); s/he ignores it, *namoya nâkateyitam* (VAI).

ill *mistahi ka isâyâhk* (VAI); *âhkosiw* (VAI).

illegitimacy *kîminîcâkanihkewin* (NI).

illegitimate Being an illegitimate child, *kakîminîcâkanowihk* (NA), *kîminîcâkan* (NA); the act of fathering a child out of wedlock, *kîminîcâkanihkewin* (NI); s/he has an illegitimate child, *kîminîcâkanihkew* (VAI) *(Plains)*; *pikwatôsew* (VAI) *(Northern)*.

illness A sickness, *âhkosiwin* (NI); her/his illness makes her/him depressed or s/he is tired of being sick, *pîkiskâtahpinew* (VAI); s/he has a sudden, fatal illness, *sisikotahpinew* (VAI).

illuminant *kîkway ka wâsaskotek* (VTI).

illuminate *ka wâsaskotenikehk* (VAI); lighting up, *wâskotenikewin* (NI); *wâsaskotenikewin* (NI).

illumination *wâsaskotenikewin* (NI).

illusive *ka nihtâpaspet* (VAI).

illustrate *kiskinowâpahtehiwew* (VTA).

illustrious *ka nihtâ wapahtihiwehk* (VAI).

image *ka tâpinâkosihk* (VAI); an image or representation, *naspisihcikan* (NI).

333

imaginable *kîkway ka kakwetâpeyihtamihk* (VAI); *iteyihtamowin* (NI).

imaginary *mosci ka kakwe tâpeyihtamihk* (VAI); *iteyimew* (VTA).

imagination *mâmitoneyihtamowin* (NI).

imagine *mâmitoneyihcikewin* (NI).

imbalance *ekâ pahpeyakwan îyikohk* (VII).

imbecile *mamitoneyihcikan ekâ ka tawah kastek* (VII); frail condition, debility, *nesowisiwin* (NI).

imbed *kwayask kanahastahk kîkway* (VTI).

imitate Imitating someone, *ka ayisinâkehk* (VTA); s/he imitates and mocks others, *ayisinâkew* (VTA); s/he follows their example, *ayisinâwew* (VTA); s/he mimicks her/his words, *ayisitohtawew* (VTA); the act of imitating in order to learn, *kiskinowâpahkewin* (NI); s/he imitates her/him in order to learn, *kiskinowâpamew* (VTA); s/he imitates her/him, *tipâhakatew* (VTA).

imitation *ayisinâkewin* (NI).

imitator *otayisinâkew* (NA).

immaculate *metoni kânatsowin* (NI); it is very clean, *metonikânatan* (VII).

immature *namoya kaketâwâtisiw* (VAI); *awâsisiwiw* (VAI); s/he has not matured, *namoya kesi ohpikow* (VAI).

immediacy *nanihkisiwin* (NI) *(Plains)*; *nanihkâtisiwin* (NI) *(Northern)*.

immediate *semak* (IPC); *sîmâk* (IPC) *(Northern)*.

immediately *metoni semak* (IPC); *kesâc* (IPC); *semak* (IPC) *(Plains)*; *sîmâk* (IPC) *(Northern)*; right now, immediately, without delay (as an adverb of time), *sôskwâc* (IPC).

immense *metoni mistahi* (IPC); it is very large, *mistahimisâw* (VAI).

immensity *kîkway ka mahkipayik* (VTI).

immerse *ekâ ka nokosihk* (VAI); inside, in "immersed in, closed in", *atâmik* (LN); *itâmik* (LN); in, deeply in "but from the outside", *akwâc* (LN); it went underwater, *kehtapayiw* (VAI).

immersion *ayopayowin* (NI).

imminence *kehcinâ kaweh ispayik* (VII).

imminent *kehcinâhowin* (NI).

immobilize *ka wayeskanihiwehk* (VAI).

immoderate *pasci isihcikewin* (NI).

immodest *ekâ konepewsowenihk* (VAI); s/he is indecent, *pisikwâtisiw* (VAI).

immodesty *ekâ konakewnihk* (VAI).

immolate *wepinâsiwin* (NI).

immoral A person leading a base, unethical or immoral life, *ekâ ka ayisiyiniwayahk* (VII); the act of leading an unethical or immoral life, such as a prostitute, *pisikwâcisowin* (NI); s/he thinks s/he is immoral, *pisikwâteyimew* (VAI); s/he acts immorally or unchastely or s/he fornicates, *pisikwâtisiw* (VAI); s/he speaks immorally or unchastely, *pisikwâtonamiw* (VAI); the act of speaking immorally or unchastely, *pisikwâtonâmowin* (NI).

immorality Not conforming to moral law, *ekâ kwayask ketatisihk* (VAI); fornication or immorality, *pisikwâtisowin* (NI).

immortal *kakîke ka pîmatahk* (VII).

immortality *kakîke pîmatesowin* (NI).

immovability *ekâ kakeh waskawinamihk* (VTI).

immovable *ekâ ka waskawimakahk kîkway* (VTI).

immutable *ekâ kakeh kweskiniht awîyak* (VAI).

imp *macâtisiwin* (NI); *macâwasis* (NA).

impact *sohki tawahotowin* (NI); *pakamiskatowin* (NI).

impair *ekâ kwayask ka wapahtamihk* (VAI); s/he is weak or damaged, *nesowisiw* (VAI).

impairment *ekâ kwayask ka wapahtamihk* (VAI).

impale *ka sâpwâskocitahk misit* (VTI).

impart *nîsohkamâkewin* (NI); s/he gives to someone, *miyew* (VTA); *mekiw* (VTA).

impartial Not biased, equitable, just, *pahki nîsohkamakewin* (NI); *peyakwan paminikewin* (NI); *peyakwan tôtakewin* (NI).

impartiality *pahki ka nîsohkamakepayik* (VII).

impassible *ekâ omôsihtawinihk* (VAI).

impassioned *mistahi ka mâmitoneyihtamihk* (VAI).

impassive *sîpinewin* (NI).

impassivity *sohkahpinewin* (NI).

impatience *nanihkisiwin* (NI) *(Plains)*; *nanihkâtisiwin* (NI) *(Northern)*.

impatient *ka nanihkisayahk* (VII); s/he is in a hurry, *papâseyihtam* (VAI).

impede The act of hampering or obstructing progress, *nakinowewin* (NI); the wind impedes her/his progress, *nakâyâsiw* (VTI); the act of being impeded by the wind, *nakâyâsowin* (NI).

impediment *nakinowewin* (NI).

impel *kîkway ka yahkiskakohk* (VTA).

impend *kaweh ispayik kîkway* (VTI).

impending *kîkway ka nehpemastek* (VII).

impenetrability *ekâ kehcinâ ka kîhnistohtamihk* (VAI).

impenetrable *ekâ kakeh sawitsahoht awîyak* (VAI).

impenitent *ekâ ka mihtâtamihk ka pâstahohk* (VAI).

imperative *ekâ nanitâw kakeh isi wemâskamihk* (VAI).

imperceptible *ekâ nîkân kîkway ka kiskeyihtamihk* (VAI).

imperfect Not just right, *namoya kwayask* (IPC); something that is faulty, *mamaskayi* (NI); it is imperfect, not reliable, or faulty, *mâskâw* (VII); faulty, defective, incomplete, *mâmas kayi* (NI).

imperfection *nawâc poko mâmâsîs* (IPC).

imperil *kîkway ka sekihikohk* (VAI).

imperious *kwanta ayîwak ka tôtamihk* (VAI).

imperishability *ekâ ka nihtâ misiwanâtahk* (VII).

imperishable *ekâ kakeh misiwanâtahk* (VII).

impermanence *ekâ ka micimwâci isihcikehk* (VAI).

impermanent *kîkway ekâ ka micimwâtahk* (VII).

impermeable *ekâ ka swepayik kîkway* (VTI).

impersonal *ekâ kohkwâwâc isâyâwin* (NI).

impersonality *ekâ ka kohkwâwâtsihk* (VAI).

impersonate *awîyak ka ayisinaht otôtamowina* (VAI); play the role of, *ayisinâkew* (VAI).

impersonation *ayisinâkewin* (NI).

impersonator *otayisinâkew* (NA).

impertinence *âyimomiwewin* (NI).

impertinent *awîyak ka âyimwet* (VAI).

imperturbabiliy *ekâ ka mamahtiyecikehk* (VAI).

imperturbable *peyahtik ka ayâhk* (VII).

impetuosity *wahkew îyisowin* (NI).

impetuous *ka îyiyehikohk kîkway* (VII).

impiety *ka macitôtamihk* (VII).

impinge *tawikiskatowin* (NI).

impingement *ka tawikiskatohk* (VTA).

implacability *ekâ ka mahteyehtamihk* (VAI).

implacable *peyahtik ka ayâhk* (VII).

implausibility *ekâ tâpwehtamowin* (NI).

implausible *ekâ ka tapwehtamihk* (VAI).

implicate *ka kiyikawepayihiwehk* (VAI).

implication *kiyikawepayihiwewin* (NI).

implied *acîyaw ka pîkiskwâtamihk* (VTI).

implore *ka kâkesomototaht awîyak* (VTA).

imply *ka kiskisomowehk* (VTA).

impolite *ekâ ka manâtsihk* (VAI).

importance *mistahi ispihteyehtakosowin* (NI).

important *awîyak mistahi ispihteyehtakosit* (VAI).

importune *sohki ka natotamahk* (VAI).

importunity *natotamâwin* (NI).

impose *ka pakosihtahk* (VAI).

imposing *mosci pakosihtâwin* (NI).

imposition *tipahikepayihtâwin* (NI).

impossibility *ekâ takehispayik* (VII).

impossible *ekâ kakeh ispayik* (VII).

impotence *âyimisowin ka nukutikohk* (NI).

impotency *poni âyimisowin* (NI).

impotent *awîyak ekâ kakeh isihcikatat iskwewak* (VII); lacking strength, power or virility, *nesowan* (VII); *nesowisiw* (VAI).

impoverish *ka maskahcihiwehk* (VTA).

impoverished *awîyak ka maskahcihiht* (VTA).

impoverishment *maskahcihiwewin* (NI).

impracticable *kîkway ekâ ka âpatahk* (VII); it is of no use, *namoya âpatan* (VII).

impractical *kîkway ekâ kakehapacitahk* (VTI); *namoya âpatan* (VII).

imprecate *awîyak ka mayakwamiht* (VTA).

imprecation *mayakwamtowin* (NI).

imprecise *namoya mwehci ekosi* (IPC).

impregnability *metoni mânatôtamowin* (NI).

impregnable *ka mâna tahkinamihk kîkway* (VTI).

impregnate *ayâwâwasowin* (NI).

impregnation *awîyak ka ayâwâwasohiht* (VTA).

impress *ka miyo wapahtihiwehk tânsi isi kaskihtahk* (VTA).

impression *miyo wapahtihiwewin* (NI); taking impressions by branding, *masinâskisikewin* (NI).

impressive *awîyak ka miyo wapahtihiwet* (VTA).

improbability *mwehci ekâ ekosi takehispayik* (VII).

improbable *ka âymahk kîkway tatâpwehtamihk* (VAI).

improper *namoyakwayask* (IPC).

impropriety *ekâ kwayask ka tôtamihk* (VAI).

improve *ayîwak kwayask* (IPC); improve in health, *astamihk isâyâw* (VAI).

improvement *ayîwak kwayask ka tôtamihk* (VAI).

improvidence *ekâ neyak ka mâmitoneyihtamihk* (VAI).

improvident *awîyak ekâ nîkân ka mâmitoneyihtahk* (VAI).

improvisation *kiskâw osihcikewin* (NI).

improvise *kîkway ka kiskâw osihtahk* (VTI).

imprudence *ekâ peyahtik ka mâmitoneyihtamihk* (VAI).

imprudent *awîyak ekâ peyahtik ka mâmitoneyihtahk* (VAI).

impudence *ekâ kîkway nakîwin* (NI).

impudent *ekâ konakîwinihk* (VAI).

impulse *sisikôc iteyihtamowin* (NI); *sisikôc tôtamowin* (NI).

impulsive *awîyak ka sisikôteyihtaskit* (VAI).

impure Something unclean, *ekâ ka kanatahk* (VII); it is not good, *namoya miwasin* (VII); it is not clean, *namoya kanatan* (VII); s/he is unchaste or impure, *pisikwâtisiw* (VAI); it is unchaste or impure, *pisikwâtan* (VII); in an impure way or fashion, *pisikwâc* (VII); an impure or unchaste mind, *pisikwâcimâmtoneyicikan* (NI), an impure or unchaste thought, *pisikwâciteyihcikan* (NI).

impurity *wînâtisowin* (NI).

in *pihcâyihk* (IPC); *pihci* (IPC).

inability *ekâ ka kaskihohk* (VAI); *namoyakasketâw* (VAI); *pwatawihtâw* (VAI).

inaccessibility *âyimotihtamowin* (NI).

inaccessible *kayimahk totihtamihk* (VAI); its hard to get or find, *âyimantapehtokwehk* (VAI); *âyimantamiskamihk* (VTI).

335

inaccuracy *namoya mwehci ekota* (IPC).

inaccurate *namoyakwayask* (IPC); *naspâc* (IPC); not right, *namoyakwayask* (VII).

inaction *ekâ ka waskawehk* (VAI).

inactive *peyakwanohk ka ayâhk* (VII); *namoya waskawew* (VAI); *kihtimiw* (VAI).

inactivity Sedentary, *peyakwanohk ayâwin* (NI).

inadequacy *nawâc poko nôhcâwîs* (VII).

inadequate *namoya ikwayekohk* (VII); it is too little, *osâm apisis* (VII).

inadvertent *pisci ka tôtamihk kîkway* (VTI).

inadvisability *awîyak ekâ kakeh wihtamaket* (VAI).

inadvisable *kîkway ekâ kakeh wihtamakehk* (VAI); *kaya ekosi itota* (IPC).

inane *kwanta kîkway* (VII).

inanimate *kîkway ekâ ka pimâtsemakahk* (VII); something with no life, *îkakapimatahk* (VII).

inanity *ekâ kîkway kispehtaweyihtakwahk* (VII).

inapplicability *ekâ kakeh takwastahk kîkway* (VTI).

inapplicable *ka aymahk takwascikewin* (NI).

inappreciable *ekâ ka atamihikohk kîkway* (VII).

inappropriate *kîkway ekâ mekwâc takeh ispayik* (NI); not that kind, *namoya ekotowa* (VII).

336

inapt *ka yikicikawihk* (VAI).

inaptitude *ekâ ka nahisinihk nânitâw* (VAI).

inarticulate *ekâ kwayask kakeh pîkiskwehk* (VAI).

inattention *ekâ ka nâkatohkehk* (VAI).

inattentive *ekâ ka nâkateyihtamihk* (VAI).

inaudible *ekâ ka nisitohtâkosihk* (VAI).

inaugural *koskipihtokahiwehk nânitâw* (VAI).

inaugurate *awîyak ka pihtokahiht* (VTA).

inauguration *pihtokahiwewin* (NI).

inauspicious *nawâcpoko ka mayipayihk* (VAI).

inborn *tipiyaw kohcopikihk* (VAI).

inbound *pekiwewin* (NI).

inbred *tipiyaw wahkohtowin* (NI).

inbreed *pahpeyakwan etah ka ohci ohpikitâhk kîkway* (VII).

incalculable *ekâ kakeh tâpeyimiht awîyak* (VAI).

incapability *ekâ kakaskihohk* (VAI).

incapable *ekâ kakaskihtahk* (VAI); *pwâstawew* (VAI); *namoya sohkâtisiw* (VAI).

incapacitate *ka wayeskânihiwehk* (VTA).

incapacity *ka nohtepayihk kîkway* (VTI).

incase *ka kipâpoweskenahtahk kîkway* (VTI).

incasement *kipâpoweskenahcikewin* (NI).

incense *wihkimâsikan ayamihâwenihk ka âpatahk* (NI); *wihkimâkasikan* (NI).

incensed *kisôweyitamowin* (NI).

incentive *oyisehcikewin* (NI).

inception *pihtokwepayihcikewin* (NI).

incessant *ka âhkampayik kîkway* (VTI); continuing without interruption, *tâpitawi* (IPC).

inch *peyak lipos* (NI) *(Northern)*; *misicihcân* (NI); *lipos* (NI) *(Northern)*.

incidence *kîkway kîspayik* (VII).

incident *kîkway ketahkamikahk* (VTI).

incidental *ka nihtâ ispayik* (VII).

incinerate *ka mestihkasekehk* (VAI).

incipient *ka oskimacipayik âhkosiwin* (NI).

incise *ka mansamihk kîkway* (VTI).

incision *mansikâsowin* (NI).

incisive *ka kotâw sawasowehk* (VTA).

incisor *ka sikwahcikakehk mîpit* (NI); a front tooth, *nîkânimîpit* (NI).

incite *ka miskawâsomiht awîyak* (VTA).

incitement *miskawâsihiwewin* (NI).

incivility *kisôwih ka tôtamihk kîkway* (VTI).

inclemency *namakîkway kitimakinatowin* (NI).

inclement *awîyak ekâ ka kitimakinaket* (VTA).

inclination *ita mahcihowin* (NI); s/he is bent over it, *nawakîstam* (VTI).

incline *tansi kitamacihohk* (VAI); *amaciwecâw* (VII).

inclined *ekose kitamahcihohk* (VAI).

include *ewakomîna* (IPC).

inclusion *takwascikewin* (NI).

inclusive *kîkway katakwastahk* (VAI).

incoherence *nanâtohk itâtamowin* (NI).

incoherent *nanâtohk kitacimohk* (VAI).

incoming *awîyak ka petâcimiht* (VTA).

incommunicable *ekâ awîyak kakeh pîkiskwâtiht* (VTA).

incomparable *awîyak ekâ kakeh âstakimiht* (VTA).

incompatability *ekâ peyakwan isâyâwin* (NI).

incompatible *awîyak ekâ peyakwan kesayat* (VAI); unable to live together with harmony, *mâyiwecehtowin* (NI).

incompetence *namoyamamisîwin* (NI).

incompetent *ekâ ka mamisitotaht awîyak* (VTA).

incomplete *ekâ ka kesihtahk* (VAI).

incompletely *ekâ kakesihtahk kîkway* (VTI).

incomprehensibility *ekâ nisitohtamowin* (NI).

incomprehensible *ekâ kakeh nisitohtamihk* (VAI).

inconceivability *ekâ tâpwehtatowin* (NI).

inconceivable *ekâ ka tâpwehtamihk* (VAI).

inconclusive *ekâ ka kisipayihcikehk* (VAI).

incongruous *kîkway ekâ ka wicewâkanpayik* (VII).

inconsequent *ekâ kîkway kiteyihtakwahk* (VII).

inconsiderable *metoni ekâ mistahi* (IPC).

inconsiderate *ekâ mistahi ka iteyemowehk* (VTA); *wanikiskisototawew* (VTA).

inconsistency *pahpîtos isâyâwin* (NI).

inconsistent *pahpîtos ka isâyâhk* (VAI).

inconsolable *ekâ kakeh ka kecihiwehk* (VAI).

inconspicuous *ekâ ka nâkatohkehk* (VTA).

inconstant *ekâ pahpeyakwan ka tôtamihk* (VAI).

incontestable *ekâ kakeh mawineskamihk* (VAI).

inconvenience *ekâ wetnah ka ayâhk* (VII); *âyimipayiwin* (NI); put to trouble, *âyimisiwin* (NI); *âyiman kîspayik* (VII).

inconvenient *kîkway ekâ metoni ka nahipayik* (VII).

inconvertibility *ekâ kakeh meskoc sihcikehk* (VAI).

inconvertible *ekâ kakeh meskotoniht sônîyâw* (VTI).

incorporate *mamawîsihcikewin* (NI).

incorrect *ekâ kwayask* (IPC); *naspâtisiw* (VAI); s/he provides incorrect facts, i.e.: a slip of the tongue, *wanowew* (VAI); the act of providing incorrect facts, i.e.: a slip of the tongue, *wanowewin* (NI).

incorrigibility *ekâ kakeh kwayaskopayihcekehk* (VAI).

incorrigible *ekâ kakeh kwayaskpayihtahk* (VAI).

incorrupt *ekâ ka macâtisihk* (VAI).

incorruptible *ekâ nânitâw kîsimacîsâyahk* (VAI).

increase S/he receives an increase, *ayiwâkimeyâw* (VAI); s/he makes them increase, *yakemohew* (VTA); it increases, *yahkemow* (VAI); it increase by itself, *yahkipayiw* (VAI).

increasingly *tahki ayîwak* (IPC).

incredibility *mwehci ekâ takehispayik* (VII).

incredible *kîkway ka mâmaskâteyihtâkwahk* (VII); *ayiwâkikin* (IPC); *namoya tatâpwehtamihk* (VAI).

incredulity *ekâ ka tâpwehtamihk kîkway* (VTI).

incredulous *ânweciyihikewin* (NI).

increment *yahkakihcikewin* (NI).

incriminate *awîyak ka nayahtahiht kîkway wiyâsowewnihk* (VAI).

incubate *pahkahahkwan ka mahtakoskahk wawah tâpâskawehohtat* (VTI); *pâskâwehow* (VAI); *wîtapitam* (VAI).

incubation *pâskâwehocikewin* (NI).

incur *ka pakitinsohk* (VAI); *wiya itôtamasiw* (VAI).

incurability *ka ayimahk tâstiwepahowihk* (VTA).

incurable *ekâ kakeh âstepayihk* (VII).

incurious *ekâ ahkwac ka nohte kiskeyitamihk* (VAI).

incursion *sisikôc ka tâwkintohk* (VTA).

incursive *ka nihtâ tâwiskâkehk* (VTA).

indecency *ekâ kwayaskesayahk* (VAI).

indecent *ekâ kwayaskwesâyâwin* (NI).

indecision *ekâ kakeh kîsiyehtamihk* (VAI).

indecisive *ekâ ka kîsipayihtahk* (VAI).

indeclinable *ekâ kakeh ponihtahk* (VAI).

indeed *metoni tahtapwe* (IPC).

indefatigable *ekâ konestosowenihk* (VAI).

indefensible *ekâ konaskwawenihk* (VAI).

indefinite *namoya kinwes* (IPC); *tânispî etikwe* (IPC).

indelibility *ekâ ka nihtakâsepayik* (VII).

indelible *ka micemwaci masinahikepayik* (VTI); it does not erase, *namoyakâsepayiw* (VAI).

indelicate *nawâcpoko ka kepâtisihk* (VAI).

indent *ka kicikatahamihk mistik* (VTA); *wâwâkimasinahikewin* (NI); *wâyipiyaw* (NI).

indentation *kicikatahikewin* (NI).

independence *peyako isihcikewin* (NI); *pimâcihowin* (NI).

independent *ka peyako isihcikehk* (VAI); *pamihisiw* (VTA); separated, independent, alone, or loose, *peyakiw* (VAI).

indescribable *ekâ takeh mâmiskôtamihk* (VAI); unable to describe, *namoya tawehtamihk* (VAI).

indestructibility *metoni sohkîsihcikewin* (NI).

indestructible *ekâ ka kehpekonkatek* (VTI); *maskawâw* (VTI); *sohkan* (VII).

indeterminable *ekâ ka kwayaskweyihtamihk* (VAI).

indeterminate *kîkway ekâ kehcina* (IPC).

indetermination *kîkway ekâ kakeh kîsiyihtamihk* (VAI).

indian summer *nehiyaw nîpin* (NI); *nehiyawinipin* (NI).

indian tobacco *nehiyaw cistemaw* (NA).

indicate *kiskeyihtamohiwewin* (NI).

indication *ka kiskeyihtamohiwehk* (VTA).

indicative *ka kiskeyihtakwahk* (VII).

indicator *kîkway kohkiskeyihtamihk* (VAI).

indifference *ekâ ka ayâhkwateyihtamihk* (VAI).

indifferent *pîtos ka isâyâhk* (VAI).

indigent *metoni kitimâkisowin* (NI).

indigestible *kîkway ka kisipikahciskakohk* (VTI); hard to digest, *mâyiskakowin* (NI).

indigestion *kisipikahcîwin* (NI).

indignant *ka kisôweyihtamihk kîkway* (VII); *kisôweyihtam* (VAI).

indignation *kisôweyihtamowin* (NI).

indignity *nepewihiwewin* (NI); *mâyitôtakewin* (NI).

indigo *sîpîhkonakwan* (VII); its color is blue, *sîpîhkonakosiw* (VAI); s/he or it is blue, *sîpîhkosiw* (VAI).

indirect *namoya kwayask* (IPC); *namoya kwayaskwamiw* (VAI).

indiscreet *ekâ ka nihtaweyihtamihk* (VAI).

indiscretion *ekâ ka nâkatohkehk* (VTA).

indiscriminate *ekâ kwayask ka nâkateyihtamihk* (VTA).

indispensable *ekâ kakeh wepenamihk kîkway* (VTI).

indispose *ka pomehikohk kîkway* (VTI); *mâyimahcihowin* (NI).

indisposed *pomehiwewin* (NI); not feeling good, *mâyimahcihowin* (NI).

indisposition *kwanta ka âhkosewayasihk* (VAI).

indisputable *soskwac ekâ nânitâw takeh isi ânwehtamihk* (VAI).

indissoluble *kîkway ekâ wihkac takeh pekopayik* (VTI).

337

indistinct *ka âyimahk takehcinahohk kîkway* (VAI).
indistinguishable *ekâ ka kihkânâkwahk* (VII).
individualist *opeyakweyimisiw* (NA).
individualistic *ka peyakweyimsoskihk* (VAI).
individuality *peyakweyimisowin* (NI); the act of being alone, *peyakowin* (NI).
individualize *ka peyakwakimiht awîyak* (VAI).
individually *ka pahpeyakohk* (VAI).
indivisible *ekâ kakeh pahkwenamihk* (VTI).
indolence *manasihciwin* (NI).
indolent *ka manasihtatoskehk* (VAI).
indoor *pihtokamik* (LN); *pihcâyihk* (LN); *pihtokwekamikohk* (LN).
induce *sâkocimew* (VTA); persuasion, *sihkiskâkewin* (NI).
indulge *miyotôtâkewin* (NI); *ayiwâkeyihtam* (VTI).
indulgence *ka miyotôtâkehk* (VTA).
indulgent *awîyak enihtâ miyotôtâket* (VAI); *miyohtwâw* (VAI).
industrious *kakâyawisiwin* (NI); s/he is a good worker, *kakâyawisiw* (NA).
industry *atoskewin* (NI).
inebriate *ka kîskwepehk* (VAI).
inebriation *kîskwepewin* (NI).
inedible *ekâ kakeh mecihk* (VTA); *namoya tamecihk* (VTA).
ineffective *ekâ nânitâw ketapatahk* (VTI); *namoya mîyopayiw* (VAI).
ineffectual *ekâ kwayask kakeh ispayik* (VII).
inefficiency *ekâ metoni ka nakacihtâhk* (VAI).
inefficient *awîyak ekâ metoni ka nakacihtat* (VAI); *pwâtawihew* (VTA); s/he can't do it, *namoya kasketâw* (VAI).
inelegant *ekâ ka nahehk* (VAI).
ineligible *ekâ ka nahesinihk* (VAI).
inept *ka mohcowisâyâhk* (VAI).
ineptitude *mohcowisâyâwin* (NI).
ineradicable *kîkway ekâ kakeh kweskinamihk* (VTI).
inescapable *ekâ kakeh wemâskamihk kîkway* (VII).
inestimable *ekâ kakeh tepeyimiht awîyak* (VAI).
inevitability *ekâ kakeh nakinamihk kîkway* (VTI).
inevitable *ohcitaw peyisk tespayik* (VII).
inexact *namoya metoni ekota* (IPC); *namoya kwayask* (IPC).
inexcusable *namâkîkway kwetateh etwewin* (NI); *namoya tatapwetaht* (VAI).
inexhaustibility *ekâ konestosowenihk* (VAI).
inexhaustible *sîpâyâwin* (NI); s/he never gets tired, *sîpisiw* (VAI).
inexorable *ekâ awîyak kakeh îyihiht* (VAI).
inexpediency *ka pomehiwehk* (VTA).
inexpedient *pomehiwewin* (NI).

inexpensive *ekâ ka mistakihtek* (VII); it is cheap, *wehtakihtew* (VII).
inexperience *ekâ ka nakacihtâhk* (VAI).
inexperienced *awîyak ekâ ka nakacihtat* (VAI); s/he can't do it right, *namoyanakacihtâw* (VAI).
inexpert *ekâ kîkway ka kaskihtahk* (VAI).
inexplicable *ekâ kwayask kakeh wehtamihk* (VAI).
inexpressible *ekâ nânitâw kakeh isi mâmiskôtamihk* (VAI).
inexpressive *ekâ ka moynakosihk* (VII).
inextinguishable *ekâ kakeh âstawehamihk* (VTI).
infallible *ekâ wehkac ka patahamihk* (VTI).
infamous *metoni mîyapowin* (NI).
infancy *ka apiscawâsisiwihk* (VII); being an infant, *apiscawâsisiwiwin* (NI).
infant *apiscawâsis* (NA); *awâsis* (NA).
infatuated Loving on the sly, *kîmôcisâkihitowin* (NI).
infer *ka kakwe tâpwehk* (VII).
inferior *nawâc âstamihk kîkway* (VII); *ayaskôc* (IPC); *namoya nîkânîw* (VAI).
inferiority *astameyemowin* (NI).
infernal *kîkway ekâ kakeh nîpawistamihk* (VII).
infidelity *pesikwatsowin* (NI); *kakayeyisiwin* (NI); *namoya ayamihâw* (VAI).
infinite *ekâ ka kisipipâyik* (VTI); *kihcimanitowiw* (VAI).
infinitely *ekâ kisipipayihtawin* (NI).
infinity *ekâ kakisipahk* (VII).
infirm *ekâ ka maskawâyâhk* (VII); s/he is weakly, *nesowâtisiw* (VAI).
infirmity *nesowâtisiwin* (NI).
inflame *nâspic kîsiwasowin* (NI); *saskitew* (VII); *saskaha* (VTI).
inflammability *ka nihtâ saskitek kîkway* (VTI).
inflammation *pakicipayowin* (NI); *wesakeyihtamowin* (NI).
inflammatory *ka saskahikehk* (VTI).
inflate *ka pihci pôtatamihk kîkway* (VTI).
inflation *wawîyak ka mistakihcikehk* (VAI).
inflect *koyastahk kîkway* (VTI).
inflection *oysihcikewin* (NI); *sihciwin* (NI).
inflexible *ekâ poko isi kesihtahk* (VII); it can not be bent, *namoya wâkinikatew* (VAI).
inflict *ohcitaw ka tôtakehk* (VTA).
infliction *ohcitaw tôtakewin* (NI).
influence S/he acts according to her/his influence, *tipâhew* (VTA).
influential *awîyak ka kiskinowâpahtehiwet* (VTA).
inform Informing, *ka wehtamakehk* (VTA); telling one another, *âcimostatowin* (NI); s/he correctly informs her/him, *kwayaskomew* (VTA); s/he informs against others, i.e.: a stoole pigeon, *omisihkemow* (VAI); the act of informing against someone, *misihkemowin* (NI).

informal *ekâ ka kihcisâyâhk* (VAI).

informality *ekâ kihcisâyâwin* (NI).

information Correct information, *kwayaskomowewin* (NI).

informational *âcimostakewin* (NI).

informative *kîkway ka âcimomakahk* (VTI).

informer *otâcimostâkew* (NA).

infrequency *wawîyak aspihtaw ekâ kahkiyipa* (IPC).

infrequent *ekâ kahkiyipa* (IPC); *namoya mwasi* (IPC); just once in a while, *ayâspehtâw* (IPC); *ayâspîs* (IPC).

infringe *sôskwac kotinamasohk* (VTI).

infuriate Causing someone to become enraged, *ka kisiwâhtwahk* (VTA); s/he infuriated her/him very quickly, *sasoyawehew* (VTA) *(Northern)*; *sascoyawehew* (VTA) *(Archaic Plains Cree)*; s/he became infuriated very quickly, *sasoyawesiw* (VAI) *(Northern)*; *sascoyawesiw* (VAI) *(Archaic Plains Cree)*; the act of becoming infuriated very quickly, *sasoyawesowin* (NI) *(Northern)*; *sascoyawesiwin* (NI) *(Archaic Plains Cree)*; s/he is mad, *kisiwasiw* (VAI).

infuse S/he infuses liquid into her/him, i.e.: an enema, *pihtâpawahew* (VTA).

infusion *sihkiskakewin* (NI).

ingenious *ka nahehk* (VAI); s/he shows cleverness, *mamâtawisiw* (VAI).

ingenuity *metoninahiwin* (NI).

ingenuous *ekâ nânitâw ka isinahehk* (VTA).

ingest *ka kitâpayihcikehk* (VAI).

inglorious *namoya takeh mamihtsewakehk* (VAI).

ingrain *metoni ka sohkeyihtamihk* (VAI).

ingratiate *kamiyo ahisohk* (VAI).

ingratitude *namâkîkway atamihewewin* (NI).

ingredient *kîkway ka kastahk* (VTI); *ka mâmawinamihk* (VTI).

ingrowing *maskasiy ka pihtokekit masakahk* (VTA).

inhabit The act of inhabiting, *wîkowin* (NI); s/he gives her/him a place to inhabit or live, *wîkîhew* (VTA); s/he lives or inhabits there or s/he dwells there or s/he resides there or s/he has a home there, *wîkiw* (VAI).

inhabitable *metoni takehwekihk* (VAI).

inhabitant *awîyak ekota kawekit* (VAI).

inhalation *otatâhcikewin* (NI)

inhale Breathing something in, *kotatâhtamihk* (VTI); s/he inhales the smoke, *kohcipastewew* (VTI) *(Archaic Cree)*; s/he inhales the pipe smoke, *ocipihkwew* (VAI); *otamew* (VAI).

inhaler *awîyak kotatâhciket* (VAI).

inherence *astakimsowin* (NI).

inherent *awîyak ka astakimsot* (VAI).

inhibit The act of inhibiting or stopping someone or something, *nakinowewin* (NI); it is inhibited or prevented from going any further, *nakahtin* (VII); s/he

inhibits or blocks her/him, *nakâhwew* (VTA); s/he inhibits or stops her/him, *nakânew* (VTA); s/he is inhibited or prevented from going any further, *nakâsin* (VAI).

inhibition *nakinowewin* (NI).

inhibitor *onakinôwew* (NA).

inhospitable *awîyak ekâ kamiyo otôtemit* (VTA).

inimical *ka kostanakeyimohk* (VAI).

iniquity *ka kwayakatisowin* (NI).

initial *wihyowin ka mâtastek* (VII); *nîkânisi* (LN).

initially *metoni nîkân* (IPC).

initiate The act of initiating, *nakayâskamohtahiwewin* (NI); s/he initiates her/him into something, *miskawahew* (VTA).

initiation *ka nakayâskamohtahiwehk* (VTA).

initiative *kîkway ka âhkameyihtamihk* (VAI).

inject *ka cîstahikasohk*.

injection *cîstahikâsiwin* (NI).

injudicious *ekâ ka nihtâweyihtamihk* (VAI).

injure *awîyak ka wîsakahoht* (VAI); *wîsakisin* (VAI).

injury *wisakahosowin* (NI); *wîsakeyihtamowin* (NI).

inlaid *masinatahikew kiskinowâcicihkewin* (NI).

inland *akwâcayihk* (LN); in the bush, *nôhcimihk* (LN).

in-law *wikihto wahkohtowin* (NI).

inlet *ka pihcitawpeyak sakâhikanihk* (LN); a small bay, *wasaw* (NA) *(Northern)*; *pihcâpekos* (NA) *(Plains)*.

in memoriam *kiskisototâkewin* (NI).

inmost *mâmawiyas pihcâyihk* (LN).

inner *kîkway pihcâyihk ohci* (LN); *peci* (IPC).

innermost *pihcâyihk* (LN).

innocent *ekâ nânitâw ka tôtamihk* (VAI); *miyowâtisiw* (VAI); *kanâtisiw* (VAI).

innocuous *peyahtik isâyâwin* (NI).

innovate *ka ahtsihtahk kîkway* (VTI).

innovation *ahtisihcikewin* (NI).

innumerable *wawîyak ekâ kakeh akihtamihk kîkway* (VTI).

inoffensive *ekâ ka nihtâ kisôwâhtwâhk* (VAI); s/he is kind, *miyohtwâw* (VAI).

inopportune *kîkway ekâ ka nahipayik* (VII); at a bad time, *mayanohk* (LN).

inordinate *ka kepâtisiwin* (NI)

inquire *ka kwecihkemowin* (NI); s/he asks, *kakwecihkemow* (VAI).

inquisitive When you are always asking questions, *ka kakwecihkemoskihk* (VAI); obsessively inquisitive or curious, *ayapinikesk* (VTA).

insane *môhcowisâyâwin* (NI); *kîskwew* (VAI).

insanity *ka môhcowihk* (VAI).

insatiable *ekâ kakeh atamihiht awîyak* (VAI).

inscrutability *kîkway ekâ ka nisitohtamihk* (VII).

339

inscrutable *ekâ ka nisitohtakwahk masinahikewin* (NI).

insect *manicôs* (NA).

insecure *ekâ wetna ka ayâhk* (VAI).

insecurity *ekâ wetna ayâwin* (NI).

insensibility *ekâ ka omosihtâwnihk* (VAI).

insensible *ekâ kanakatohkehk kîkway* (VAI).

insensibly *sôskwâcpoko isi ka tôtamihk* (VTI).

insensitive *ekâ ka moysihk* (VAI).

insensitivity *namâkîkway mosihtâwin* (NI).

inseparability *ekâ kakeh paskehk* (VTI).

inseparable *ekâ kakeh paskewehitohk* (VTA); *namoya paskewitowak* (VTA).

insert *ka pihtastahk kîkway* (VTI).

insertion *pihtascikewin* (NI).

inside *pihcâyihk* (LN); inside the house, *pihtokamik* (LN); it is inside out, *âpoceyâw* (VII); *âpocâw* (VII); s/he or it is inside, *asiwasiw* (VAI); it is inside, *asiwatew* (VAI); s/he puts her/him inside a bag, inside of something, *pohcih* (VTA); s/he placed her/his finger inside the hole, *pohtâtakinam* (VAI); s/he holds her/him in, *pohtinew* (VTA).

insider *kakeki pihcâyihk kayâhk* (VTI).

insight *neyak kîkway ka wapahtamihk* (VTI); *nisitihtamowin* (NI).

insignificance *kîkway ekâ mistahi espehtaweyihtakwahk* (VII).

insignificant *awîyak ekâ mistahi espehteyihtakosit* (VAI).

insincere *awîyak ka kîmôtâtisit* (VAI); you can not depend on her/him, *namoya tamâmisehk* (VTA).

insincerity *kîmôtâtisiwin* (NI).

insinuate *nisihkâc ka yiyimiht awîyak* (VTA).

insinuation *nisihkâc yiyimowewin* (NI).

insipid *ka peyahtiko ayâhk* (VAI).

insipidity *peyahtiko ayâwin* (NI).

insist *ka âhkamowitamihk* (VAI).

insistence *âhkameyihtamowin* (NI).

insistent *awîyak metoni ka âhkameyetahk* (VAI).

insobriety *ekâ metoni ka waskamayahk* (VAI).

insole *kakihtwâmaskinahtahk maskisinihk* (VTI).

insolence *pîweyihcikewin* (NI).

insolent Someone who has no respect for others, *awîyak ka pîweyihciket* (VAI).

insolubility *ekâ kakeh nistohtakehk* (VTA).

insoluble *kîkway ekâ kakeh nistohtamihk* (VAI).

insolvent *awîyak ekâ kakeh kîstipahiket* (VAI).

insomnia *ekâ kakeh nipahk* (VTI); *namoya kînipaw* (VAI).

inspect *ka wâpahcikehk* (VTI); *kwayask kahkitapahtam* (VTI).

inspection *wâpahcikewin* (NI).

inspector *owâpahcikew* (NA) *(Northern)*; *onitawâpenikew* (NA) *(Plains)*.

inspiration An inspirational discourse, *sihkiskâkewin* (NI); s/he is constantly providing inspiration or s/he aids in initiating, *sihkiskâkew* (VAI); inspiration of the spirit power, *manitowatâmowin* (NI); s/he inspires her/him to act, *sihkiskâwew* (VTA).

inspirational *ka sihkiskakehk* (VTA).

inspire Giving inspiration to someone, *awîyak kasehkimiht* (VTA); s/he speaks inspired by the spirit power, *manitowatâmiw* (VAI).

instability *ekâ ka sohkimamsehk* (VTI) or (VAI); never in one place, *papâmacihowin* (NI).

install *kîkway ka takwastahk* (VTI).

installation *takwascikewin* (NI).

instalment or **installment** *ahapsis ka tipahikehk* (VTI).

instance *ka wapahtehiwehk tansi kîkway* (VTI).

instant *metoni semak* (IPC).

instantaneous *semak kispayik kîkway* (VTI).

instantly *sisikoc* (IPC).

instead *meskoci iwepinkewin* (NI); *meskoc* (IPC).

instep The inside part of the foot, *picâyihk misit* (LN).

instigate Causing a happening, *macipayihiwewin* (NI).

instigation *ka macipayihtahk kîkway* (VTI).

instigator *omacipayihcikew* (NA).

instil or **instill** *nisihkâc awîyak ka îyiyimiht* (VTA).

instillation *ka tako osihcikehk* (VTI).

instinct *moyehcikewin* (NI).

instinctive *ka nihtâ moyeyihcikehk* (VAI).

instrument A tool, *kîkway ka osihcikakehk* (NI); a musical instrument, *kitohcikan* (NI).

insubstantial *ekâ tâpwe kîkway* (VII).

insufferable *ka osâm wîsakahpinehk* (VAI).

insufficient *namoya ekwaykohk*; that is not enough of, *nohtepayiw*.

insulate *ka kesonamihk wâskahikan* (VTI); insulate it, *pihtawina* (VTI).

insult Insulting someone, *kapewomiht awîyak* (VTA); s/he says something which insults her/him indirectly, *kitihkimew* (VTA).

insuperable *kîkway ekâ kakehk paskeyatamihk* (VTI).

insupportable *ekâ ka nihtâ nîsohkamâkehk* (VAI).

insurable *awîyak takeh nîsohkamaht* (VTA).

insure *awîyak ka nâkateyihtamaht kîkway* (VTA).

insusceptible *ekâ ka mamahcehikohk kîkway* (VII).

intact *peyakwan ka ayetastek kîkway* (VII).

intake *ka pihtokwepayik kîkway* (VTI).

integral The whole thing, *kahkiyaw* (IPC).

integrate *ka pihtokâhiwehk askîhk* (VTA).

integration *pihtokwâhiwewin* (NI).

integrity *metoni miyo isâyâwin* (NI); *kwayaskwâtisiwin* (NI); being honest, *kwayaskwâtisiwin* (NI).

intellect *awîyak otiyinisowin* (NI).

intellectual *ka iyinisihk* (VAI); *kwayask mâmitoneyihtam* (VAI); being intelligent and informed, *kwayasmâmitoneyihtamowin* (NI).

intelligence *iyinisowin* (NI).

intelligent *awîyak ka iyinisit* (VAI).

intelligible Having a good understanding of something, *kamiyo nisitohtamihk kîkway* (VTI); the sound is very intelligible, *pakaskihtâkwan* (VII).

intend *ka sâpweyihtamihk kîkway* (VII).

intended *sâpweyihtamowin* (NI).

intense *metoni sohki kîkway* (IPC); *sohki* (IPC).

intensely *sohki ka kocehk* (VAI).

intensify *tahki ayîwak sohki* (IPC).

intensity *sohkâyâwin* (NI).

intensive *metoni sohki kîkway ka tôtamihk* (VTI); *kwayask nisitotam* (VAI); very acute, *metoni kwayask* (IPC).

intent *sohki kociwin* (NI).

intention *sâpweyihtamowin* (NI).

intentional *ohcitaw ka tôtamihk* (VAI); on purpose, *ohcitaw* (IPC).

intercede *ka otamihiht awîyak* (VTA).

intercept *ka kipipayihohk* (VTA); s/he stops something, *nakinam* (VTI); *kipihtinam* (VTI).

intercession *awîyak ka ayamihestamaht* (VTA).

intercessor One who prays for people, i.e.: an intercessor, *otayamihestamakew* (NA).

interchange *ka mâhmeskwatascikehk* (VAI).

interchangeable *ka mâhmeskwatastahk kîkway* (VTI).

intercourse Reciprocal social or commercial dealing between individuals, *iyinew wecehtowin* (NI); s/he sleeps with her/him, *wihpemew* (VAI); the act of sleeping together, *wihpehtowin* (NI).

interdependence *ka wicehsihcikemtohk* (VTA).

interest *kîkway ka miywanamihk* (VII).

interested *awîyak ka miywanahk* (VAI).

interesting *awîyak ka miywanakohciket* (VAI); *pisiskapamaw* (VAI).

interfere *kôtamihtâsohk* (VTA).

interference *ôtamihtâsowin* (NI).

interior Inside of, *pihcâyihk* (LN).

interlude *ka nomepoyohk* (VAI).

intermarriage *kisowak kawahkohtohk wikihtowin* (NI).

intermarry *awîyak tipeyaw ka wikihtot* (VAI); *papiskic ohci wikitowak* (NA); marrying within the limits of a family, *tipyawikihtowin* (NI).

intermediate *apihtawayihk nânitâw* (VII); situated between two extremes, *tastawâyihk* (IPC).

interminable It is interminable, *sîpan* (VII); an interminable speaker, *kwanta ka kwahtonamohk* (VAI).

internal *pihtâkiyaw* (NI).

interpenetrate *ka sâponistohtatohk* (VTA).

interpret *ka isinistohtamihk* (VAI).

interpretation *nistohtamohiwewin* (NI).

interpretative *ka nistohtamohiwehk* (VTA).

interpreter *ôtitwestamâkew* (NA).

interrupt *kakeskiniht awîyak* (VTA); *wanimew* (VAI).

interruption *kakeskinamihk pîkiskwewin* (VTI).

intersect Splitting, *taskinikewin* (NI).

intersection *meskanawa ka ayamihewâhtikopayekwâw* (NI); a point where two roads meet, *nakiskâtomeskanawa* (NI).

intersperse *nânatohk isi ka mamawascikehk* (VTI).

interval *aciyawes kapoyohk* (VAI); in between times, *tastawâyihk* (IPC).

intervene *ka nakinamihk kîkway* (VTI); s/he stops it, *nakinam* (VTI).

intervention *nakinikewin* (NI).

interweave *ka apihkâtamihk kîkway* (VTI).

interwoven *apihkâcikewin* (NI).

intestine An intestine or entrail, *mitakisiyâpiy* (NI).

intimacy *sâkihitowin* (NI).

intimate *sâkihitowin* (NI); *sâkihew* (VTA); a close relationship, *ka miyowicewâkanihk* (VAI).

intimidate Trying to scare or intimidate someone, *awîyak kakakwe sekimiht* (VTA); s/he intimidates her/him, *sasehkimew* (VTA); s/he is not intimidated by her/him, *mayeyimew* (VTA).

into *kîkway ka pihtokepayik* (VTI).

intolerable *ekâ kakeh nîpawistamihk* (VAI); *maceyihtâkisiw* (VAI).

intolerance *nihtâ nîpawiscikewin* (NI).

intoxicate *awîyak kakîskwepahiht* (VTA); drunk, *kîskwepew* (VAI).

intoxication *kîskwepewin* (NI).

intransitive A verb that does not need an object, i.e., "It is hot," *pîkiskwewin kâwihtamômakahk tânsi etâpatahk* (VII).

intrepid *nâpehkâsiwin* (NI).

intricate *nanâtohk isâyâwin* (NI).

intrigue *ka kîmôc isihcikehk* (VAI); *kîmôc sâkihitowak* (VTA).

introduce Introducing someone to someone else, *nakayaskamohtahiwewin* (NI); s/he introduces her/him to someone, *nakayaskamohtahew* (VTA).

introduction *nakayaskamohtahiwewin* (NI).

introductory *nakayaskamohtahetowin* (NI).

intrude *ka môstatahkamiksihk* (VAI).

intrusion *môstatahkamiksowin* (NI).

341

intrusive *awîyak ka nihtâ môstatahkamekisit* (VAI).
intuition *semak kanistawenamihk* (VAI).
intuitive *awîyak ekâ ka wâneyihtahk* (VAI).
invade *sôskwac ka pihtokwehk* (VAI).
invalid *awîyak ekâ ka kaskihot* (VAI).
invalids They are sick, *âhkosowak* (VAI);
  okatohpinewak (NA).
invaluable *ekâ mistahi kîspeteyihtakwahk* (VII);
  namoya mistahi iteyihtakwan (VII); it is very valuable,
  mistahi iteyihtakwan (VII).
invariable *pahpitos kesayak* (VAI).
invasion *soskwac pihtokahesowin* (NI); *nôtinitowin*
  (NI).
invent *ka osihcikehk* (VTI); *miskweyihtamowin* (NI).
inventive *awîyak ka osihciket* (VAI).
invert You turn it over, *kwetipina* (VTI).
invest *atâwewin* (NI).
investigate *natonikewin* (NI).
invigorate *awîyak ka wayâhiht* (VTA).
invigoration *wayâhiwewin* (NI).
invincible *kâ kakeh wapahtamihk* (VAI).
invisible *ekâ ka nôkwahk* (VTI); *namoya nôkwan* (VTI).
invitation *wihkohkewin* (NI); *wihkomitowin* (NI).
invite Inviting someone, *awîyak ka wîsâmiht* (VTA);
  the act of inviting, *wekohkiwin* (NI); s/he invites her/
  him to go along, *wîsâmew* (VTA); the act of giving an
  invitation, *wîsawitamowin* (NI); s/he invites someone
  to go along, *wîsawitam* (VTA).
inviting A place that looks inviting, *miywanohk* (LN).
invoke *ka kisemototakewin* (NI).
involuntary *ka pisci tôtamihk kîkway* (VTI).
involve *ka kiyikawepayihk* (VTI).
involvement *kiyikawepayiwin* (NI).
invulnerability *nihtâ miyopayowin* (NI).
inward *pihcâyihk nawâc* (LN).
inwardly *pihtâkiyaw* (NI).
inwardness *kihcitwâw isâyâwin* (NI).
irate *kisôpayowin ka kisônakosihk* (VAI); *kisôwipayiw*
  (VAI); it is loud, *kisiwew* (VAI).
ire *kisôwâsiwin* (NI).
irksome *ka mikoskâcihiwehk* (VTA).
iron An iron for clothes or a clothing iron,
  sôskwahikan (NA); *piwâpisk* (NI); *kinowapiskisiw*
  (VAI); *kinowapiskâw* (VAI); the iron or rock has a flat
  surface, *napakâpiskisiw* (VAI); round bar, pipe,
  notimâpiskisiw (VAI); *notimâpiskâw* (VAI); copper,
  osâwâpiskisiw (VAI); *osâwâpiskâw* (VII); strong,
  sohkâpiskisow (VAI); *sohkâpiskâw* (VAI); cold,
  tahkâpiskisiw (VAI); *tahkâpiskâw* (VAI); short,
  cimâpiskisow (VAI); *cimâpiskaw* (VAI); crooked, bent,
  wakapiskisow (VAI); *wakapiskaw* (VAI); twisted,
  pimâpiskisiw (VAI); *pimâpiskaw* (VAI); the iron is full

of dents, *mâyâpiskâw* (NI); a poorly made iron,
mâyâpiskinikan (NI); iron or steel that is bent out of
shape, *mâyâpiskisiw* (NI); it is a big piece or iron, i.e.:
a railroad rail or steel pole, *mihcâpiskâw* (VII); it is
yellow iron, *osâwâpiskâw* (VII); the iron is yellow,
osâwâpiskisiw (VAI); it has a thin surface, i.e.: an iron,
pakâpiskisiw (VAI); nothing but iron, *pisisikwâpisk*
(NI).
iron S/he irons them, *sôskwahwew* (VTI).
Iroquois *onatowew* (NA).
irrecoverable *kîkway ekâ kakeh kwayask astahk* (VTI).
irredeemable *ka micimwaci mekihk* (VTA).
irrefutable *ekâ kakeh sâkotonamowehk* (VTA).
irregular *ahaspihtaw* (IPC); *namoyatahki* (IPC).
irregularity *aspihtaw iyikohk* (IPC).
irremovable *ekâ kakeh mahtinamihk* (VTI).
irreparable *ekâ kakeh nânapâcihtahk* (VTI).
irreplaceable *ekâ kakeh meskotastahk* (VTI).
irrepressible *awîyak ekâ kakeh micimiht* (VTA).
irreproachable *awîyak ekâ kîkway takeh ohci*
  kehkâmiht (VAI).
irresistible *ekâ kakeh nakinsohk* (VAI); *osâm*
  maskawâtisiw (VAI); something hard to turn down,
  osâm akâwâcikan ().
irresolute *ekâ ka kecinâhohk tansi iwihtotamihk* (VAI).
irresolution *ekâ kehcinâhowin* (NI).
irrespective *ekâ ka manatsihk* (VAI).
irresponsible *ekâ ka mamsehk* (VTA); *namoya*
  tamamisehk (VTA); undependable, *namoya*
  tamamisehk (VTA).
irretrievable *ekâ kawe kakeh kahtinamihk* (VTI).
irreverence *ekâ kîkway manâtsiwin* (NI).
irreverent *ekâ ka manâtsihk* (VAI).
irreversible *ekâ kakeh kweskînkatek* (VTI).
irrevocable *ekâ kakeh mamisîtotamihk* (VTA).
irritable *ka wahkewyawesihk* (VAI).
irritant *kîkway ka kisiwâhikohk* (VTI).
irritate Making someone angry, *kisiwâhiwewin* (NI);
  her/his teasing irritates her/him, *niweyacihew* (VTA);
  s/he irritates her/him, *kisiwâhew* (VTA); s/he irritates
  her/him in a threatening way, *makohew* (VTA).
irritation *kisôweyihtamowin* (NI).
island *ministik* (NI); there is an island, *ministikowiw*
  (VAI); it is a rocky island, *ministikwâpiskâw* (NI); there
  is a wooded island, *ministikwâskweyâw* (VAI); there is
  a sandy island, *iyîkawawahkâw* (VII); archipelago, a
  chain of islands, many islands, *ayapiministikweyâw*
  (VII).
isle *miniscikos* (NA).
islet A small island, *miniscikos* (NA).
isolate When someone is put alone in one place, *ka*
  piskihtaskenek (VTI); an isolated place, *kwanteteh*

(LN); s/he thinks s/he is all alone or isolated, *peyakweyimow* (VAI); the act of thinking of oneself as being isolated, *peyakweyimowin* (NI); s/he feels isolated, *pîkiskâtamacihow* (VAI); it is isolated or it is depressingly alone, *pîkiskâtan* (VII).

isolation *piskihtaskinewin* (NI).

it *eyoko* (IPC); *ômah* (IPC); *anima* (IPC); *ewako* (IPC).

itch *ka kîyaksihk* (VAI); *kîyakisiwin* (NI).

itchy The itchy skin sickness, *kîyakasewin* (NI); the act of being itchy, *kîyakisewin* (NI); s/he is itchy, *kîyakisiw* (VAI); s/he rubs herself/himself against something because s/he is itchy, *kîyakisimow* (VTA).

item *peyak kîkway* (IPC); an item, *ekwanima* (IPC).

itself *ka peyakwahk* (NI) or (IPC).

ivy *ka piscipomakahk mistikwacekos* (NI).

J

jab *sâponikan ohci ka cîstahosohk* (VTI).

jack Or something used to lift things up, *ohpahikakan* (NI); s/he jacks it up, *ohpahikew* (VAI); s/he jacks them up, *ohpawew* (VTA).

jackass *ka kepâciyinow* (NA).

jacket Coat or dress, *miskotâkay* (NI); a small jacket, coat or dress, *miskocâkasis* (NI); s/he has a coat or jacket, *oskotâkâw* (VAI); a winter jacket, *piponasâkay* (NI); a small coat, *miskotâkasis* (NI); a new coat or dress, *oskasâkay* (NI).

jackfish *iyinikinosew* (NA).

jack rabbit *mistâpos* (NA).

jack pine *oskâhtak* (NA); a jack pine ridge, *oskâhtakaw* (VII).

jail cell *kipahitowikamik* (NI) (Plains); *kipahikâsowikamik* (NI) (Northern).

January The elder moon or month (Northern); the cold moon or month (Plains), *kisepîsim* (NI).

jar To jar something, *kwâskwesin* (VTI).

jaunt *kantâw môcikihtâhk* (VAI); a pleasure trip, *môcikih papâmohtewin* (NI).

jaw *mitapiskan* (NI).

jawbone *otâpiskanikan* (NI).

jay Canada jay or whiskey jack, *wîskacân* (NA) (Northern); *wîskipôs* (NA) (Plains).

jealous S/he is envious, *sawânakeyimow* (VAI); when someone is jealous of someone else who is better, *kâsawânakeyimohk* (VTA); they are jealous of each other, *kahkweyihtowak* (VTA); s/he is jealous of her/him, *kahkweyimew* (VTA); being jealous over a spouse, *kahkweyihtamowin* (NI); s/he is jealous, *kahkweyihtam* (VTA).

jealousy *sawânakeyimowin* (NI).

jeer *ka pahpihiht awîyak* (VTA).

jeeringly *pahpihiwewinihk* (VII).

jell *ka misiwepayik* (VTI).

jeopardize *mâyanohk ka ahiwehk* (VTA).

jeopardy *mâyapowin* (NI); the state of being exposed to danger, *paspinasowewin* (NI).

jerk *ka sisikocipetamihk* (VAI); it jerks, *koskwepitam* (VTI).

jerky Dried meat, *pâstew wiyâsis* (NI); s/he jerks or bounces, *kahkwaskwepayiw* (VAI).

jersey A sweater, *waskicipicikan* (NI).

jest *ka waninehk* (VAI); *pahpowin* (NI).

jiffy Just a little while, *kanakes* (IPC).

jigger Used to pull fish nets underneath ice, *sîpâpicikan* (NI) (Northern); *sîpâwepahikan* (NI) (Plains).

jingle *ka sîwepayihk* (VTI); s/he rings it, *sîwepitam* (VTI).

job *atoskewin* (NI).

jocular *nanoyacimowewin* (NI).

jocularity *ka nihtâ noyacimowehk* (VAI).

jocund *ka waninayahk* (VAI).

jocundity *waninisâyâwin* (NI).

jog *ka sesawpahtahk* (VAI); s/he jogs, *pimipahtasiw* (VAI); the act of running, *pimipahtâwin* (NI).

joggle *ka kwâskwewepinkesihk* (VTI).

join Joining two things together, *kaneswamohtahk kîkwayah* (VTI); s/he joins or ties them together, *aniskopitam* (VTI); s/he joins them firmly together or s/he glues them together, *sanaskihew* (VTI); it is firmly joined, *sanaskisiw* (VAI).

joint A knuckle, *anskawkanan* (NI); a bone joint, knuckle, *piskokanân* (NI).

jointly *ka wicewâkanihtohk* (VTA).

joist *anaskanihtakwa etah ka sakahamihk* (NI).

joke Telling a joke, *wanew âcimowin* (NI); the act of joking or talking lightheartedly, *wâwiyatwewin* (NI); s/he is joking with her/him, *nanoyacimew* (VTA); the act of joking with each other, *nanoyacihtowin* (NI); s/he is telling jokes, *nanoyatwew* (VAI); the act of telling jokes, *nanoyatwewin* (NI).

joker *mâwaci ka maskawiset pakesan* (NA); s/he tells jokes, *wawiyatwew* (VAI).

jollity *môcikisowin* (NI).

jolly *awîyak ka môcikisit* (VAI); s/he has an attractive voice, *miyohtâkosiw* (VAI).

jolt *ka sisikôc nakiptiht awîyak* (VTI).

josh *ka nanoyacehiht awîyak* (VTA).

jostle *ka yahkiwepinowehk* (VTA); the act of being shoved and pushed around in a crowd, *tôskinikewin* (NI).

jounce *ka sohki pakamisimiht awîyak* (VTA).

journey *nânitâw ka etohtehk* (VTI); walking, *pimohtewin* (NI).

jovial *metoni ka môcikisihk* (VAI); s/he is a happy person, *môcikisiw* (VAI).

joviality *môcikisowin* (NI).

jowel *otâpiskanikan* (NI).

joy The act of celebrating joyfully, *miyawâtamowin* (NI).

joyful S/he is joyful, *miyawâtikosiw* (VAI); the act of being joyful, *miyawâtikosowin* (NI); s/he is full of joy, *môcikeyihtam* (VAI).

joyless *ekâ kîkway môcikisowin* (NI).

345

joyous S/he is joyous, ***miyawatam*** (VAI); the act of celebrating joyfully, ***miyawâtamowin*** (NI); having a good time, ***miyowâtamowin*** (NI).

jubilance *mistahi ka môcikihtâhk* (VAI).

jubilant *môcikisowin* (NI).

jubilation *metoni ka môcikisihk* (VAI).

jug *asnew tipahopan* (NI); a gallon jug, *tipahopan* (NI).

juggle *mistikwa ka metawâke wepinamihk* (VTI).

juggler *ometawew* (NA).

jugular vein *misihkwâniyâpiy* (NAZ) *(Northern)*; *misihkwân* (NA) *(Plains)*.

juice A sweet drink, ***sîwiminihkwewin*** (NI); a yellow liquid, i.e.: orange juice or lemonade, ***osâwâpoy*** (NI); berry juice, ***mîmisâpoy*** (NI).

July The moulting moon or month, ***opaskowipîsim*** (NI).

jumble *nanâtohkwascikewin* (NI).

jump The act of jumping, ***kwâskohtowin*** (NI); s/he jumps over, ***pascikwâskotiw*** (VAI); s/he jumps by, ***pimikwâskohtow*** (VAI); s/he jumps on it, ***tehcikwâskohtiw*** (VTI); s/he jumps on top of her/him, ***tehcohpâtew*** (VTA); s/he jumps up, ***ohpiw*** (VAI).

jumper *okwâskohtow* (NA); sleigh, *pipontâpânâsk, iskwewasakay* (NI).

jumpy *ka kwâskohcesâyahk* (VAI).

June The egg hatching moon or month, ***opâskahopîsim*** (NA) *(Plains)*; ***opâskâwehopîsim*** (NA) *(Northern)*; ***opâskâwewowipîsim*** (NA) *(Northern)*.

juniper *mihkwâpemakwahtik* (NA); a medicine spruce tree, *maskihkîwahsihta* (NA).

junk *wepinikewina* (NI); a pile of garbage, weeds, *macikwanasa* (NA).

just *ketisk* (IPC); being fair or just, *kwayaskosowin* (NI); it is just or fair, *kwayask* (IPC).

justifiability *ka kwayaskwasowehk* (VAI).

justifiable *awîyak kakwayaskwasowet* (VAI).

justify *kwayaskâtotamihk* (NI).

jut *ka sâkamok kîkway* (VTI).

K

keel *osihk mâwikanihkan* (NI).

keen *ka nahihk* (VAI); *âhkameyimiw* (VTA).

keenness *nahiwin* (NI).

keep The act of keeping and guarding the house, *kanawapokewin* (NI); the act of keeping horses, *kanawastimwewin* (NI); s/he keeps or guards the house, *kanawâpokew* (VAI); s/he keeps or guards horses, *kanawastimwew* (VTA); s/he keeps or guards her/his cows, *kanaweyimostoswew* (VTA); s/he keeps or guards her/him or s/he takes care of her/him, *kanaweyimew* (VTA); s/he keeps it, *kanaweyihtam* (VTI); s/he keeps it for herself/himself, *kanaweyihtamâsiw* (VTA); the act of keeping something for oneself, *kanaweyihtamâsowin* (NI); s/he keeps or tends the animals, *kanawipisiskiwew* (VTA); s/he keeps her/him inside, *kipinew* (VTA).

keeper *okanaweyihcikew* (NA).

keeping *ka kanaweyihtamihk* (VTI); *kanaweyicikewin* (NI).

keg *mahkahkos* (NI); a small barrel or tub, *mahkahkos* (NI).

kept *ka kehkanaweyihtamihk* (VTI).

kernel *kisâstaw pâkânis mînsihk ohci* (NI); *mînis* (NI).

kettle An iron kettle with a spout shaped like a duck's neck, *sîsîpaskihk* (NA); a small iron kettle with a spout shaped like a duck's neck, *sîsîpaskihkos* (NA); a pail, *askihk* (NA).

kick The act of kicking, *tahkiskacikewin* (NI); s/he succeeds in kicking her/him, *kahtiskawew* (VTA); s/he is kicking the breathe out of her/him, *kipihtamiskawew* (VTA); s/he kicks a part of it off, *pahkweskawew* (VTI); s/he kicks her/him accidently, *pistiskawew* (VTA); s/he kicked them and they spilled, *sîkiskawew* (VTI); s/he kicks, *tahkiskacikew* (VAI); the act of kicking, *tahkiskacikewin* (NI); s/he kicks her/him, *tahkiskawew* (VTA).

kicker *otahkiskacikew* (NA).

kid Baby moose, *oskâyis* (NA).

kidnap *ka kîmôc sipwehtahiwehk*; the act of taking without consent, *kimotamakewin* (NI).

kidney *otihtekosew* (NA); *mititihkôsiw* (NA).

kill Killing someone or something, *nipahtâkewin* (NI); s/he kills someone of great value, *kichi aspinatew* (VTA); s/he made a great kill, *kihci aspinasiw* (VTA); s/he kills wild game, *minahow* (VTA); the act of killing wild game, *minahowin* (NI); s/he kills herself/himself on impact, *nâspitisin* (VTA); s/he killed her/him, *nipahew* (VTA); s/he killed her/him on impact or in a collision, *nipahisimew* (VTA); s/he was killed in an accident, *nipahisin* (VAI); s/he kills her/him by falling on her/him, *nipahiskawew* (VTA); s/he kills her/him by feeding her/him too much, *nipahiskohew* (VTA); s/he kills herself/himself by overeating, *nipahiskoyiw* (VTA); s/he kills herself/himself, *nipahisiw* (VAI); the act of killing oneself, *nipahisiwin* (NI); s/he dies while giving birth, *nipahôsew* (VTA); s/he just barely missed killing them, *paspinasiw* (VTA); s/he just about killed them, *paspinatew* (VTA).

killdeer A bird which announces the rain, i.e.: a type of snipe such as a killdeer, *pacaskahask* (NA) *(Northern)*; *kimonanahasîs* (NA) *(Plains)*; a bird with a black stripe around its neck, *capiskakaneses* (NA).

killer Murderer, *onipahtâkew* (NA).

killing *awîyak ka nipahtaket* (VAI).

kin A relationship, *etah kohtaskanesihk* (VTA); s/he is kin with or related to, *itâhkômow* (VTA).

kind Of that kind, *ekotowa* (IPC); of the same kind as that there, *omatowahk* (IPC); I am of the kind, *niya itowa* (IPC); I am of that kind, *niya ekotowa* (IPC); Are you a Cree? Yes I am! I too!, *nehiyaw ci kiya? ekotowa! nista!*; one of a kind, *peyakwayihk* (IPC).

kind S/he is kind to her/him and giving her/him tender, loving care, *kisewâtotawew* (VTA); s/he thinks of her/him as being very kind, *kisewâtisiwokeyimew* (VTA); s/he thinks of herself/himself as being kindly, *kisewâtisiwokeyimow* (VAI); the act of thinking that oneself is very kind, *kisewâtisiwokeyimowin* (NI); s/he is kind, *kisewâtisiw* (VAI); the act of being kind, *kisewâtisowin* (NI); s/he thinks of her/him in a kindly way, *kisewateyimew* (VTA).

kind-hearted *kisewâtisowin* (NI).

kindle *ka pônamihk* (VTI).

kindliness *ka kisewâtisihk* (VAI).

kindling A piece of kindling, *pâwihkotâkan* (NI); kindling for a fire, *pîwihkotâkana ka pônkakehk* (NI); a knife used for cutting kindling for a fire, i.e.: shavings, *pîwihkocikan* (NI); a piece of kindling made by an axe, i.e.: a wood chip, *pîwihtakcahihkan* (NI).

kindly S/he is kindly, *kisewâtotakew* (VTA); s/he treats her/him kindly or s/he does her/him a good turn, *miyotôtawew* (VTA).

kindness *miyohtwâwin* (NI); *kisewâtisiwin* (NI).

kindred *peyak oskan ohci* (IPC).

kinfolk *or* **kinsfolk** *aniskâc ohcewin* (NI); *wahkomâkanak* (NA).

kingfisher *okeskimanasiw* (NA).

kink *pimâstepayiw* (VTI); there is a kink in the wire, *pihkapiskopayiw* (VTI).

347

kinnikinnick *mihkwâpemakwa ka pihtwâtamihk* (NI).

kinsman A relative, *wahkomakan* (NA).

kiss The act of kissing, *ocehtowin* (NI); s/he kisses her/him, *ocemew* (VTA); they are kissing, *ocehtowak* (VTA); the kissing day or New Year's Day, *ocehtokîsikâw* (NI); s/he kisses, *ocemiwew* (VTA).

kisser Someone who likes kissing, *awîyak ka ocehcikeskit* (VTA).

kite *ohpâscikan*, a flying kite, *ohpahascikan* (NI).

kitten *minôsis* (NA).

knack *ka nihtâ kiskisihk* (VAI); a talent, *nihtâwetamowin* (NI).

knead *ka mamakoniht pahkwesikan* (VTA); *mamakonew* (VTA); kneading bread, *mamakonew* (VTA).

knee *mihcikwan* (NI).

kneecap *mikitik* (NA).

kneel The act of kneeling down, *kocihcikwanapihk* (VTI); the act of kneeling, *ohcikwanapowin* (NI); s/he kneels before or in front of her/him, *ohcikwanapestawew* (VTA); s/he kneels, *ohcikwanapiw* (VAI).

kneeler *awîyak kahki kocihcikwanapit* (VAI).

kneepad *yoskahikana mihcikwana ohci* (NI).

knell *ka netohkemohk soyakan ohci* (VTI); a ringing for a funeral, *onipow sewepitamakewin* (NI).

knelt *kakeh ocicikwanapihk* (VTI).

knife *môhkomân* (NI); s/he defends herself/himself with a knife, *manihkomânew* (VTI); a large knife, *mistihkomân* (NI); machete or large bladed knife, *mistâpiskihkomân* (NI); a small knife, *môhkomânis* (NI); *môhkomânis* (NI); a carving knife, *môhkotâkan* (NI).

knife edge *peyakwan môhkomân* (NI).

knit *asikanihkewin* (NI); knitting, *apihkewin* (NI).

knitting *ka asikanihkehk* (NI).

knitting needle *asikanihkâkan* (NI).

knives *môhkomâna* (NI).

knock Knocking on the door, *pakamihtakahikewin* (NI); s/he knocks the tree or her/him or it down, *kawawew* (VTI); s/he punches her/him and knocks her/him down, *kawepahwew* (VTA); s/he knocks her/him dead, *nâspitawew* (VTA); s/he is knocking or shooting at something while it is in midflight, i.e.: duck hunting or hitting a baseball, *nawatahikew* (VTA); the act of knocking or shooting something at something while it is in midflight, *nawatahikewin* (NI); s/he knocked or shot it or them while they were in midflight, i.e.: ducks, *nawatahwew* (VTA); s/he knocks her/him down off something, *nihciwepawew* (VTA); s/he came up and knocked her/him backwards, *peyasiwepahwew* (VTA); s/he knocks her/him into something, *posiwepawew* (VTA); s/he knocks her/him flat onto her/his back, *sâsakiciwepawew* (VTA); s/he knocks them lose, *wihkwatahwew* (VTA).

knoll It is an elevated hillside, i.e.: a knoll, *osetinâw* (NI); a small hill, *piskwatinâw* (NI).

knot *ka tahkoptamihk pîminahkwân* (VTI).

knothole *napakihtak ka watowahk* (VTI); *watihkwaniwâtis* (NI).

knotted *ka kahkihtwam tahkopitek pîminahkwân* (VTI).

knotty *ka sâkatihkwanowit mistik* (VAI).

know The act of knowing, *kiskeyitamowin* (NI); s/he knows, *kiskeyitam* (VAI); something you know, *kiskeyihcikan* (NI); s/he knows her/him, *kiskeyimew* (VTA); s/he lets her/him know, *kiskeyitamohew* (VTA); s/he knows her/him before everyone else, *nîkânikiskeyimêw* (VTA); s/he knows about her/him, *nistaweyimew* (VTA).

knowing *ka kiskeyihtamihk* (VAI).

knowledge *kiskeyitamowin* (NI); *kiskitamawin* (NI).

knowledgeable Being smart or wise, *iyinisowin* (NI).

known The act of knowing, *kiskeyihcikewin* (NI); s/he is known, *kiskeyimâw* (VAI) *(Northern)*; *nistaweyimâw* (VAI) *(Plains)*; s/he is well known, *nistaweyihtâkosiw* (VAI); it is well known, *nistaweyihtâkwan* (VII); s/he knows her/him, s/he knows about her/him, *nistaweyimew* (VTA) *(Plains)*; *kiskeyimew* (VTA) *(Northern)*.

knuckle *aniskawkanan mecicehk* (NI); *piskokanân* (NA) *(Plains)*; *piskokanân* (NA) *(Northern)*.

knucklebone *pahpiskokanân* (NA) *(Northern)*; *piskokanân* (NA) *(Plains)*.

L

labor *or* **labour** The act of working hard, *sohkatoskewin* (NI); work or labor, *atoskewin* (NI); s/he makes her/him or it labor, *misamihew* (VTA); s/he labors, *misamew* (VAI); the act of laboring, *misamewin* (NI).

labored *or* **laboured** *iskwew ka maci wesakeyihtahk* (VTI).

laborer *or* **labourer** *osohkâtoskew* (NA); *atoskew* (VAI).

laborious *awîyak kakâyawiset* (VAI).

Labrador tea A white muskeg flower, *maskêkopak* (NI).

lace A lace made from moosehide, *cîstanihkwânaniyapiy* (NI); a moccasin string or lace, *cistanihkwânân* (NI); something with which you tie your boots, *mistikwaskisina kâtahkoptamihk* (VTI); baby moss bag, *waspison* (NI); a baby tied or laced in a moss bag, *waspitew* (VTA); s/he laces it or them, *askimâtew* (VTA); s/he laces snowshoes for her/him, *askimâtamawew* (VTA); s/he is lacing snowshoes, *askimew* (VAI); s/he puts laces on her/his moccasins for her/him, *cîstanikwanâtew* (VTA); s/he laces the racquet, *pisimâtew* (VTA); s/he is lacing, i.e.: a racquet, *pisimew* (VAI); s/he laces her/him in firmly, i.e.: in a toboggan, *sihtwaspitew* (VTA); something laced onto a toboggan, *wâspitapan* (VII); s/he laces her/him, *waspitew* (VTA).

lacerate S/he cuts it all up, *mamanisam* (VTI); it is lacerated, *pâpakopayiw* (VAI); torn up skin, *pâpakosiniwin* (NI).

laceration *pâpakosiniwin* (NI).

lack *ka nohtepayihk kîkway* (VAI); *kwetamâw* (VAI).

lacking *nohtepayiwin* (NI).

Lac La Biche The Cree name for the settlement of Lac La Biche meaning "Elk Lake", *wawaskesiwisakahikan* (NI).

lacrosse *metawewin* (NI).

lad *oskinîkeweyenes* (NA); *oskinîkos* (NA), *oskâpow* (NA).

ladle Taking food out of a pot with a spoon, *ka kapateskwakehk emihkwan* (VAI); s/he takes fish from the pot, *kapâtehiwew* (VTA); s/he serves herself/himself from the cooking pot, *kapateskwew* (VAI).

ladybug *nôsemanicôs* (NA); a small bug, *manicôsis* (NA).

lady's slipper An orchid, *wâpakwaniy* (NA); the Blessed Virgin's shoe, *kihcitwâmarie omaskisin*.

lag *otâhk ka ayâhk* (VTI); falling behind in progress, *otâhkepayiw* (VAI).

lagging *ka otâhkisimohk* (VAI).

lagoon A body of dead water, *pihtapek* (NI).

lair A hole in the ground, *wâti* (NI).

lake *sâkâhikan* (NI); the lake is stormy, very rough there are large waves, *mamahkâskâw* (VII); a dirty lake, *winakamew sâkâhikan* (NA); a dirty shoreline, *winikamâw* (VII); there is a channel in between two lakes, *tastawikamâw* (VII); there is a series of lakes separated by narrow strips of land or there are plenty of inlets on the lake, *ayapikamâw* (VII); there is a lake of such a form or laying in such a direction, *isikamâw* (VII); there is a big lake, *mahkikamâw* (VII); it is a long lake, *kinokamâw* (VII); there is round lake, *wawiyekamâw* (VII); there is big lake, *misikamâw* (VII); sea, ocean, *kihcikamew* (NA); area is all lake, slew became a lake, *sakahikaniwiw* (VTA); open water in a lake, *askâwew* (VTA); a large lake, *misisâkahikan* (NI).

lake herring *otônipiy* (NA) *(Northern)*; *ocônipes* (NA) *(Plains)*.

lake shore Along the lake shore, *sisonesâkahikanihk* (LN) *(Plains)*; *sonesâkahikanihk* (LN) *(Northern)*.

lake trout *namekos* (NA).

lamb *mâyacihkosis* (NA); a small sheep, *mâyatiskos* (NA).

lambkin A baby sheep, *mâyatikosis* (NA).

lambskin *mâyacihkos owayân* (NI).

lame *mâskihiwewin* (NI); s/he is lame, *maskipayiw* (VAI).

lament *nikamowin ka kaskeyihtamihk* (NI); *mâtow* (VAI); crying, *mâtowin* (NI).

lamentable Someone who can sing sad and lonely songs, *awîyak ka nihtâ kaskeyihtamonikamot* (IPC); it is lamentable, *pekiskatikwan* (VII); bemoan, *mihtâtamowin* (NI).

lamentation Expression of regret, *kwâtakatâmiw* (VAI).

lamp *wâsaskotenikan* (NI); a globe for a lamp, *wâsaskotenikanâpisk* (NI); something that gives light, *wâskotenikan* (NI).

lamplight *waskotenkewin wâhyaw kohnokwahk* (NI).

land *askîy* (NI); in a distant land, long ago, far away, *wayaweskamik* (IPC); there is rolling high land, *oseskamikaw* (VII); aboriginal land or territory, *nehiyawaskiy* (NI); s/he has land, *otaskew* (VAI); barren land, *pakwataskamik* (NI); uninhabited land, *pakwataskiy* (NI); in the virgin land, *pâtosahk* (VAI); it lands, i.e.: a bird, *tohow* (VAI); s/he lands or descends on or near her/him, i.e.: a bird, *tohototawew* (VAI).

landing *kapawin* (NI).

landscape *wâsakâm wîkiwinihk ka wawesihtahk askiy* (NA); *ka isinakwâhk* (NA).

landslide *asiskîy ka pinacipayik* (VII).

349

language A person's way of speaking, *tansi ka isipîkiskwehk* (VAI); the act of talking, *pîkiskwewin* (NI).

languish ka *kaskiyihtamayahk* (VAI).

languishing *kaskeyetamâyâwin* (NI).

languorous *mistahi ka mamitoneyihtamihk* (VTI).

lank S/he is skinny, *sihkaciw* (VAI).

lanky *kâkwâhtâskosihk* (VAI).

lantern A night lamp, *nîpâwâsaskotenikan* (NI).

lap *kwapatetam* (NI); *kakahkîhtwamastahk kîkway* (VTI).

lapse *ka nomih wanikiskisihk* (VAI); *asepayiw* (VAI).

larch *waskway ahtik* (NA).

lard *pîme* (NI); *kokosiweyin* (NI).

large Something large, *kamesak kîkway* (IPC); quite a large number, quite a few, *mihcices* (IPC); many, a large number, or a big lot, *mihcet* (IPC); the act of making a large footprint, *mahkiskamowin* (NI); it is large, i.e.: a tree, *mihcâskosiw* (VAI); s/he gave birth to a large family, *mihcetosew* (VAI); it is big or large, *misâw* (VII); the lake is large, *misikamâw* (VII); s/he is large, *misikitiw* (VAI); being a large size, *misikitiwin* (NI).

larva *manicosak opimatisiwinwâw* (NA); becoming a moth or butterfly, *mohtew ohpikowin* (NA).

larynx Or trachea, *mikohtaskway* (NI); the throat, *mikohtâkan* (NI).

lash *pasastehowewin* (NI).

lashing *ka pasastehowehk* (VAI).

last *iskwayâc* (IPC); at last, for the last time, in the last place, *iskwiyâc* (IPC); at last, finally, in the end, *piyisk* (IPC); at long last, *piyiskâtaweya* (IPC).

lasting *kîkway ka sîpahk* (IPC).

lastly *eyoko iskwayâc* (IPC).

last rites *iskwayâc tômintowin* (NI).

latch *kaskihtakipicikan* (NI); a door opener, *tahatapiskinikan* (NI).

late *mwestasipayowin* (NI); not as soon as, late, or too late, *mwesiskam* (NI); running late, *otâhkesin* (VAI) *(Plains)*; *otahkowiw* (VAI) *(Northern)*.

lately *anohcîke* (IPC).

later *mwestas* (IPC); a little later, *mwestasis* (IPC).

lather *pîstew kosihtâhk* (VAI); soap suds, *pîstew* (NI).

latter *tanima kîskwayacepayik* (VII); the last, *iskwayac* (IPC).

laud *mamihcimowewin* (NI).

laudable *awîyak takeh mamihcimiht* (VAI).

laudatory *ka mamihcimowehk* (VAI).

laugh *pâhpowin* (NI); laughing, *ka pâhpihk* (VAI); s/he laughs, *pâhpow* (VAI); s/he laughs at her/him, *pâhpihew* (VTA).

laughable *ka pahpiw mahcihohk* (VAI).

laughing *ka mekwâwahpihk* (VAI).

laughter *pahpowin* (NI).

launch Placing a boat in the water, *ka pakastawehamihk ôsi* (VTI).

launder *ka kisipekinkehk* (VAI); *kisipekina* (VAI); the act of washing clothes, *kisipekinkewin* (NI).

lava Exploding mountain, *pahkitewaciy* (NA).

lavish *ekâ ka manamekihk kîkway* (VAI).

lax *metoni peyahtik ka ayâhk* (VAI); lacking in structures, *namoya âyimisiw* (VAI).

laxative A laxative medicine of any kind, i.e.: castor oil, *sâposikan* (NI) *(Plains)*; *kanâcihcikan* (NI) *(Northern)*.

laxity *peyahtikwesayâwin* (NI).

lay When you lay or put something away, *kîkway kanahastahk* (VTI); s/he lays down from a sitting position or s/he stretches out fully, *kipiw* (VAI); s/he lays in the same row as the group, *nepitesin* (VAI); s/he lays them all in a row, *nepitesimew* (VAI); s/he lays inside, *pihcisin* (VAI); s/he lays her/him down, *pimisimew* (VTA); s/he is laying down, *pimisin* (VAI); she lays her eggs, *pinâwew* (VTA); the act of laying eggs, *pinâwewin* (NI); s/he lays on top, *tahkocisin* (VAI); s/he lays down and stretches out to her/his full length, *taswâskopayihiw* (VTA); it lays spread out, i.e.: a moosehide, *taswekan* (VII); s/he lays them out and stretches them, *taswekinew* (VAI); s/he lays them spread out, *taswekisimew* (VAI); s/he lays on her/his side, *yayepew* (VAI); the act of laying on your side, *yayepewin* (NI).

layer *peyakwâw kîkway ka pimâstahk* (VAI).

layman A member of a religion, *ayamihâw* (NA).

laze *peyahtik ka ayâhk* (IPC).

laziness *kihtimiwin* (NI).

lazy A lazy person, *awîyak kakihtimit* (VAI); a lazy bones, *kihtimikan* (NA); s/he is lazy, *kihtimiw* (VAI); the lazy one, *okihtimiw* (NA); s/he is a lazy bones, *kihtimikanew* (VAI); being a lazy bones, *kihtimikanewin* (NI); being lazy, *kihtimiwin* (NI).

lea A meadow, *yihkatawâw* (NI).

leach *ka sâpokawihcikehk* (VAI).

lead Walking ahead or leading, *nîkânohtakewin* (NI); leading or being ahead by a slim margin, *nîkânîsiwin* (NI); s/he is leading by a slim margin, *nîkânîsiw* (VAI); s/he is leading, *nîkânîw* (VAI); being in the lead or being ahead, *nîkânîwin* (NI); s/he leads in singing a song, *sipweham* (VTI).

lead Metal for a bullet, *môsisiniwapisk* (NI); iron that makes pellets for a gun, *pitikomôsiniya kosihcikakehk* (VTI).

leaden *kîkway ekosikwahk* (VAI).

leader *onîkânew* (NA); *kiskinohtahiwew* (NA).

leadership *nîkânîwin* (NI).

leading *ka nîkânihk* (VAI).

leaf *nîpiy* (NA).

leafage *ka nîpew pakak* (VII).

leafless *ekâ ka nîpewahk* (VII).

leaflet *masinahikanis* (NI).

leak *ka ohcikâwik* (VII); it leaks, i.e.: a roof, *ohcikawiw* (VII); it leaks, i.e.: a canoe, *ohcistin* (VAI); it all leaked out, *mescikawiw* (VII); it leaks into something, *posikawiw* (VII).

leakage *etah ka ohci ohcikâwik* (VTI).

leaky *ekâ ka poni ohcikâwik* (VTI).

lean Leaning on somewhere, *âsosimowin nânitâw* (NI); s/he leans it against something, *âsohtitâw* (VTI); it leans on something, *âsohtin* (VII); s/he leans on her/him while standing, *âsokâpawîstawew* (VTA); s/he leans something against something, *âsosimew* (VTI); s/he leans on something, *âsosimiw* (VAI); s/he leans it up against something, *âswastâw* (VAI); the act of leaning on something while lying down, *âsosinowin* (NI); s/he is leaning on something, *âsosin* (VAI); someone who is not fat, *awîyak ekâ kâweyenot* (NA); something leaning, *ka âsohtihk kîkway* (VAI); it leans to the side, *naweyâskohtin* (VII); it leans to the side, *naweyâskwamiw* (VAI); it leans against something, *naweyâskosin* (VAI); it is built on an angle, *naweyâw* (VII).

lean-to *ka âkosehtahk wâskahikan* (VTI); *nawekamik* (NI).

leap *ka kwâskwepayihohk* (VAI); *kwaskwepayihow* (VAI).

leapt *awîyak kakeh ohpît* (VAI).

learn *ka kiskinohamâkosihk* (VAI).

learned *kîkway ka kiskeyihtamihk* (VTI); *kiskeyitam* (VTI).

learner *kiskinohamâkan* (NA) *(Northern)*; *kiskinohamawâkan* (NA) *(Plains)*.

learning *mekwa kiskinohamâkosiwin* (NI); *macikiskeyitam* (VTI).

learnt *metoni ka îyinisihk* (VAI).

leash *sakâpihkinkan* (NI); *pîminahkwânapiskos* (NI).

least *âstamihk mâwaci* (IPC); *metoni apisis* (IPC).

leather *apihkun* (NI); *pahkekin* (NI).

leathern It is made of animal hide, *pahkekinowan* (VII).

leathery *peyakwan apihkan* (VII).

leave When someone leaves, *awîyak kâsepwehtet* (VAI); s/he leaves her/him behind in the canoe race, *nakatahwew* (VTA); s/he leaves others and runs away by herself/himself, *nakatâmototawew* (VTA); s/he leaves this world or s/he died, *nakataskew* (VAI); s/he leaves her/him, *nakatew* (VTA); s/he leaves her/him and goes in another direction, *pâskewiyew* (VTA); s/he leaves her/him alone or by herself/himself, *peyakwaskatew* (VTA).

leaven *kîkway ka ohpâyihcikakehk* (VAI).

leaves *nîpiya* (NI); the leaves start, *ati sâkipakâw* (VII); the leaves come out, *sâkipakâw* (VII); the leaves are full grown, *kisepakâw* (VII); there are large summer leaves, *nîpinipakâw* (VII); the leaves are thick, in a thick layer, *kaskipakâw* (VII); the tree is fully leafed out, *nîpeskâw* (VII); a dried out leaf, *pâstewipak* (NI).

leavings *wepinikewina* (NI).

lecher *awîyak kakohkôsatisit* (VAI).

lecherous *ka kohkôsatisihk* (VAI).

lechery *kohkôsatsowin* (NI); *pisikwâtsowin* (NI).

led *awîyak kakeh nîkânohtaket* (VAI).

ledge *kakahkihtwam kîskâpiskak* (VII).

lee On the other side, out of sight, away from, *âkawâyâhk* (VII).

leech A blood sucker, *akahkway* (NA).

leer *ka pisikwâci kanawâpahkehk* (VAI); *kayeyisêw nakosiw* (VAI).

leery *nawâcpoko ka kostâcihk* (VAI).

left On the left side, *namahtinihk isi* (LN); someone who has gone, *awîyak kakeh sipwehtet* (VAI).

left hand *namahtin* (NI); with the left hand, *namahtinisk* (VII).

left-handed *namahcîwin* (NI); s/he is left-handed, *namahcîw* (VAI).

leg *miskât* (NI); a front leg, *nîkânikât* (NI); a hind leg, *otâhkekât* (NI); s/he has a deformed or lame leg, *mâskihkâtew* (VAI); s/he or it has several legs, *mihcetokâtew* (VAI); s/he is one-legged, *napatekâtew* (VAI); her/his legs are tired, *nestokâtew* (VAI); s/he is three-legged, *nistokâtew* (VAI); s/he has a swollen leg or legs, *pâkikâtew* (VAI); s/he is bare-legged, *sâsâkinikâtew* (VAI); s/he has large, strong legs, *sohkikâtew* (VAI); s/he has white legs, *wâpiskikâtew* (VAI).

legend A legendary figure, *âtayohkan* (NI); the Cree culture hero and the object of many legends and tales, *wîsahkecâhk* (NA).

legendary *ka âtayohkehk* (VAI).

leggings *mitâsihkanak* (NA); *mitâsak* (NA); *wihkwepân* (NA).

legume A vegetable plant something like a pea or bean, *kiscikânis* (NA).

leisure *papeyahtik ka ayâhk* (VTI); *namoya katosehk* (VAI); *ayiwepiw* (VTI); easy living, *peyahtik pimâtisiwin* (NI).

leisurely *wetinahk ka ayâhk* (VTI).

lend *awihiwewin* (NI); *awi* (VTA); *awihew* (VAI).

length The full length of it, *iskwâpekahk* (VTI); too long, *waweyak kinwâw* (VII).

lengthen *nawâc ka kinosehtâhk* (VAI); *kinohtâw* (VII).

lengthwise *ka iskwâk* (VII); in the longest direction, *esikinwak* (VII).

lengthy *kinwesesnawâc ka ispayik kîkway* (VII); *kinwâw* (VII).

lenient *nawâc poko manâcihiwewin* (NI); *kitimakinâwew* (VTA); s/he is easy on her/him, *kitimakinâwew* (VTA).

lent *îyiwansehisowin* (NI); *awihew* (NI); a day for fasting, *yiwansehisokesikâw* (NI).

less *âstamihk* (IPC); *âstami* (VAI); *âstamik* (VII); *âstameyikok* (IPC); less...than, *astameyikok* (IPC); a little bit, more qualitative than quantitative, *sîyâkes* (IPC).

lessen Reducing something, *astampitamakewin* (NI); make it smaller, *acowina* (VAI); s/he demotes herself/himself to a lower rank, *âstamahisow* (VAI).

lesser *âstam iyikohk* (IPC); *âstamihk mekiw* (IPC).

let The act of letting or permitting, *pakitinamâkewin* (NI).

let's Let's see, let's try, let's go, indicates the softening of a doubt, *mahti* (IPC).

lettuce *nipiya* (NA); eating lettuce, *nepeyah kamecihk* (VTI); a head of lettuce, *nipiya ohtihipak* (NA).

level It is flat or level, *tahtakwâw* (VII); it has a flat and level surface, *tahtakosiw* (VAI).

leverage *sohkeyâskwahikewin* (NI).

lewd S/he acts in a lewd or unchaste manner, *pisikwâcayihtiw* (VAI); the act of being lewd, *pisikwâcayihtowin* (NI); very indecent or obscene language, *macipikiskwewin* (NI).

liar *kîyâskisk* (NA).

liberate *pakitinowewin* (NI).

liberation *ka pakitinowehk* (VAI).

lice *ihkwak* (NA).

lick The act of licking, *nohkwâcikewin* (NI); s/he licks it, i.e.: a plate, *nohkwâcikew* (VAI); s/he licks her/him, *nohkwâtew* (VTA); s/he is licking her/his lips, *pâstakew* (VAI); the act of licking the lips, *pâstakewin* (NI).

lid A cover, *akwanâpowehikan* (NI).

lie Lying verbally, *kîyâskiwin* (NI); s/he lies to her/him, *kakwecisimew* (VTA); *kîyâskîmew* (VTA); s/he told a lie, *kîyâskiw* (VAI); s/he tells a false story, *kîyâskiwâcimow* (VAI); s/he makes her/him tell a lie, *kîyâskîhew* (VTA); a lie or something not true, *kîyâskiwin* (NI).

lie The act of lying down, *pimisinowin* (NI); s/he lies down, *pimisin* (VAI); s/he lies face down, *otihtapisin* (VAI); s/he lies on her/his back, *sâsakicisin* (VAI); s/he makes her/him lie on her/his back, *sâsakitisimew*

(VTA); s/he lies with her/his straight or stretched out, *sâwahtôsin* (VAI).

lied *kîyâskiw* (VAI).

lieu Repetitive, one after the other, in turn, the next taking the place of the first, *mâmeskôc* (IPC).

life *pimâtisiwin* (NI); s/he leads an exemplary life, *miyopimâtisiw* (VAI); the act of leading an exemplary life, *miyopimâtisiwin* (NI); a tree of life, *pimâtisîwâhtik* (NA).

lifeless *nipohâyâwin* (NI).

lifesaver *opimâcihiwew* (NA).

lifesaving *ka pimâcihiwehk* (VAI).

lift The act of lifting, *ohpinikewin* (NI); s/he lifts her/him up with rope or cable, *ohpahpekipitew* (VAI); s/he lifts it up for her/him, *ohpinamawew* (VTA); s/he lifts her/him up, *opinew* (VTA); s/he lifts her/his arm up, *ohpiniskeyiw* (VAI); s/he lifts her/his head, *ohpiskweyiw* (VAI); s/he lifts her/him up with a stick or pole, *ohpaskwawew* (VTA); s/he comes to lift them, *peyohpinew* (VAI); s/he lifts it up for her/him, i.e.: a telephone pole, *waniskânamawew* (VTA).

ligament *ocestatayâpiy* (NI).

light It is light in weight, *ka yahkasik* (VII); it is light in color, *waseyaw* (VII); there is light, *wasaskotew* (VII); the light is red, *mihkwâstew* (VII); s/he lights or sets fire to her/him, *saskiswew* (VTA); s/he lights a fire with a flint stone, *saskisimew* (VAI); s/he is lighted on fire or s/he is in flame, *saskisiw* (VAI); it is lighted on fire or it is in flames, *saskitew* (VII); s/he makes them give off light, *wâsaskotepayihew* (VTA); s/he shines a light for her/him, *wâsaskotenamawew* (VTA); it gives off light, *wâsaskotew* (VII); the iron or steel is lightweight, *yahkâpiskaw* (VII); it is lightweight, *yahkasin* (VII); it is light, i.e.: a pole, *yahkâskwan* (VII); s/he makes her/him grow in weight, *yahkikihew* (VTA); it grows light in weight, *yahkikin* (VII); s/he grows light in weight, *yahkikiw* (VAI); s/he makes it light in weight, *yahkisehtâw* (VII); s/he makes her/him light in weight, *yâhkitisihew* (VAI); being light in weight, *yahkitisiwin* (NI); s/he is light in weight, *yahkitisiw* (VAI); s/he makes them lightweight, *yahkihew* (VAI).

light It is daylight, *kawâseyâk* (VII); a tool that gives off light, *wâsaskotenamâkan* (NI); a flashlight, *wâsaskotepicikan* (NI); it is light outside, *wâseyâw* (VII).

lighten *ka yahkisehtâhk* (VII); *yahkisehtâw* (VII).

lighter Something to light a fire with, i.e.: a lighter, *saskahikâkan* (NI) *(Northern)*; *saskicepicikanis* (NI) *(Plains)*; a type of lighter used to spark a fire, i.e.: a flint stone, *saskihcikan* (NI) *(Northern)*; *cahkisehikanasiniy* (NI) *(Plains)*.

lighting *wâsaskotenikewin* (NI).

lightly *metoni papeyahtik* (IPC).

lightness *yahkitisiwin* (NI).

lightning Or electricity, *wâsaskotepayiw* (NA); there is lightning, *waskotepayiw* (VII) *(Northern)*; *wâsaskotepayiw* (VII) *(Plains)*; lightning strikes on earth or between clouds, *piyesiwok pâskisikewok*; lightning strikes the earth, literally: fire falls, *pakihtin iskotew*.

likable *ka miweyihtâkosihk* (VTI); *takahkeyimâw* (VII); *takahkeyihtakosiw* (VTI).

like Something alike, *mwecipeyokwan* (NI); as if, quite similar, like exactly the same, you'd say it is the same, *mweci* (IPC); the act of liking one another, *miweyihtowin* (NI); s/he likes her/him or them, *miweyimew* (VAI).

likelihood Maybe, *ahpôyetikwe* (IPC).

likely *maskoc* (IPC); *ahpô* (IPC); *tapweyihtikwe* (IPC).

likeness *peyakwan îsâyâwin* (VII); *naspitâtowin* (NI); *tâpiskôc* (IPC).

likewise *ayisinâkewin* (NI); *kîstamena* (IPC).

liking *kîkway kameweyihtakwahk* (VTI).

lilac *nîpisîsa ka wâpikwanekiy* (NA).

limb A limb on a person, *awîyak oskat* (NI); *mispiton* (NI); a limb on a tree, *watihkwan* (NI); the tree has plenty of limbs, *watihkwaniwiw* (VAI).

limit *isko iskwâyâc* (IPC).

limitation *kîkway ka iskopayik* (VII).

limited *iskopayiwin* (NI).

limp *ka maskipayihk* (VAI); *maskipayow* (VAI).

line A fishing line, *kwâskwepicikanyapiy* (NI); a clothes line, *akohcikanyapiy* (NI); a line for measuring, *tipâpân* (NI); *tipâpekinikan* (NI).

linen A starched linen, *sîtawekin* (NI) *(Plains)*; *pikiwekin* (NI) *(Northern)*.

line-up *or* **lineup** Standing in line waiting your turn or queing, *ka askôkapawihk* (VAI); being lined up or being lined up in a row, *nâhnâway* (LN).

linger Standing in one place, *kisâcikapawewin* (NI); lingering, *kisâci* (VAI); s/he is hanging or lingering around her/him, *kisâtam* (VTA); s/he does not want to leave her/him and s/he lingers, *kisâteyimew* (VTA).

liniment *sopekinikan* (NI); a soothing medicine for bones, *sopekahoswakan* (NI).

lining The inside lining for clothes, *pihtawinikan* (NI).

lint Gauze, *akohpisiwâkan* (NI).

lip There is no common word for lip instead the word for "a mouth" is usually used, *mitôn* (NI); s/he has dry lips or s/he has a dry mouth, *pâstewitonew* (VAI); putting lipstick on, *mihkotonehowin* (NI).

lipped *awîyak ka otônahoht* (VAI).

liquefy *ka nipewihkahtamihk* (VTI); adding water, *takopata* (VAI).

liquid *nipey* (NI); *apiy* (NI); it is a bitter liquid, *akwâkamow* (VAI); it is a strong liquid, i.e.: alcohol, *maskawâkamow* (VAI); a pure or good liquid, *miyowakamiw* (VII); it is red liquid, *mihkwâkamiw* (VII); it is dirty, *pekakamiw* (VII); it is spiced, sweetened, sour, vinegar, *siwâkamow* (VAI); it is even, unruffled, calm, glassy water, *sôskwakamow* (VII); it is cold, cool, *tahkakamow* (VAI); *tahkikamow* (VAI); it is clear, *wasekamow* (VAI); yellow liquid, i.e.: orange juice, *osâwâpoy* (VII); a sticky liquid, i.e.: honey, *pasakwâpoy* (NI); it is a powerful liquid, *sohkâkamiw* (VII); some kind of liquid, *nepewapoy* (NI).

liquor Or fire water, *iskotewâpoy* (NI).

lisp Good pronouncing, *miyowipîkiskwew* (VAI); *ekâ kwayask ka pîkiskwehk*; *mâyipîkiskwew* (VAI).

list *masinahikansihk kastahk*; *ka masinahikâtek* (VAI).

listen The act of listening, *nitohtamowin* (NI); s/he listens to her/his teaching, *kiskinowâsohtawew* (VTA); s/he listens to her/him with wonderment, *mâmaskasitawew* (VTA); they are annoying to listen to continuously, *mwestâsihtâkosiwak* (VAI); it is annoying to listen continuously, *mwestâsihtâkwan* (VII); s/he is an effective listener, *nahihtam* (VTI); *nanahitam* (VTI); the act of being an effective listener or listening well, *nahihtamowin* (NI); s/he listens to her/him very carefully, *nâkasohtawew* (VTA); s/he listens to it, *natohtam* (VTI).

listless *ekâ ka tataspayahk* (VII); *nesowâtisiw* (VAI); s/he is listless, *nesowâtisiw* (VAI).

lit *kakeh waskotenkehk* (VAI).

litany A group of prayers, *ayamihâwina* (NI).

lithe *ka sekwâpeksit awîyak* (VAI); it is soft and easily bent, *yoskâw* (VII).

litter *wepinkewnah* (NI); *nokohawasowin* (NI); *pisiskew* (VAI).

little Somebody little, *ka apisîsisit awîyak* (VAI); s/he is little, *apisîsisiw* (VAI); something little, *apisâsisin* (VII); too little, *osâm apisis*; quite a little bit, *miscahes* (IPC); a little too much, *wawiyak* (IPC); a little more (IPC), *ayiwâkes* (IPC); a little, *apisis* (IPC).

liturgical *ayamihâwin ka mâsihtahk* (NI).

liturgy *ayamihewâyi* (NI).

livable *ka miyo wekihk* (VAI).

live The act of living, *pimâtisiwin* (NI); s/he lives, *pimâtisiw* (VAI); s/he lives or dwells alone, *peyakokew* (VAI); s/he makes her/him lively, *pimâtisîskawew* (VTA); s/he lives for her/him, *pimâtisîstawew* (VTA); someone who lives in the same part of the country, i.e.: a neighbor, *wîstaskemâkan* (NA); they live in the same part of the country, *wetaskehtowak* (NA); the act

353

of living in the same part of the country,
wetaskehtowin (NI); s/he lives in the same part of the
country as her/him, ***wetaskemew*** (VTA); s/he lives or
dwells with her/him, ***wetokemew*** (VTA).

livelihood *pimâcihowin* (NI); a life, *pimâtisiwin* (NI).

lively *kâyawisiwin* (NI); it is lively, unrestrained, i.e.: a
horse, *wacihkamisew* (VAI).

liven *ka weskawâhtahk kîkway*; *môcikihew* (VTA).

liver *miskwan* (NI).

livestock A group of animals, *pisiskowak* (NA).

livid *ka âpihtepayihk nânitâw* (VII).

living It lives, *pimâtan* (VII); s/he makes a good living,
pimâcihow (VAI); the act of making a good living,
pimâcihowin (NI).

lizard *osikiyâs* (NA).

load The act of loading something, i.e.: a vehicle or
wagon, *posihtâsiwin* (NI); s/he is loading the
container, *asiwatâsiw* (VAI) *(Northern)*; *asowacikew*
(VTI) *(Plains)*; it is loaded, i.e.: a gun, *kikapowehtin*
(VII); s/he loads her/his gun, i.e.: a muscle loader,
pihcipihkwew (VAI); s/he loaded her/his gun, i.e.: a
rifle, *pihtâsiw* (VAI); the act of loading a gun,
pihtâsiwin (NI); s/he loads into a vehicle, *pôsihew*
(VAI); s/he is loading things into a vehicle, *pôsihtâsiw*
(VAI); s/he loads the toboggan for her/him,
postâpanihkawew (VTA) *(Northern)*; *posihtasôs* (VTA)
(Plains).

loaded *sihtiskosowin* (NI).

loaf *peyak ohpayihcikan* (NA); *peyak pahkwesikan*
(NA).

loath The act of hating someone, *pakwâsowewin* (NI).

loathsome Abhorrent or loathsome, *kakwâyakan* (VTI);
s/he sees her/him in a loathsome way or sight, i.e.: in
a dream or visually, *kakwâyakâpamew* (VAI).

loathing *kapakwasowehk* (VAI).

loaves *mihcet ohpayihcikanak* (NA).

locate *miskâcikewin* (NI); the act of locating,
miskâkewin (NI) *(Plains)*; *miskâcikewin* (NI)
(Northern).

lock *kaskihtakahikan* (NI); s/he locks everything,
kaskihtakahikew (VAI); s/he locks her/him up,
kaskihtakahwew (VTA).

locomotive A train, *iskotewitâpân* (NA) *(Plains)*;
pîwâpiskomeskanaw (NA) *(Northern)*.

lodge *ka pesewkamkos* (NI).

lodgepole pine *oskâhcakosak* (NA).

lodging *ka pesowin* (NI).

log *mistik* (NI); wood, tree, log, *askosow* (NI); *askwan*
(NI); it is long, *kinowâskisiw* (VAI); *kinowâskwan* (VII);
it is solidly planted, hard to pull out, *ayâtaskisiw*
(VAI); *ayâtaskitew* (VTA); it is strong, *maskawâskosiw*
(VAI); *maskawâskwan* (VII); it is narrow, strip of wood,

sâkawaskosiw (VAI); *sâkawâskwan* (VII); it is light,
not heavy, *yahkaskosow* (VAI); *yahkaskwan* (VII); it is
soft, *yoskaskosow* (VAI); *yoskaskwan* (VII); it is short,
cimâskosiw (VAI); *cimâskwan* (VII); it is crooked or
bent, *wâkâskosiw* (VAI); *wâkâskwan* (VII); a round log,
notimâhtik (NI) *(Northern)*; *wâweyiyahtik* (NI)
(Plains).

loin *opwâmowiyâs* (NI).

loincloth *otâsiyânahpisowin* (NI).

loiter *ka kisâtamihk nânitâw* (VII).

lone *peyakowin* (NI).

lonely When you are lonely, *kakaskeyihtamihk* (VTI); it
feels lonely, *kaskeyihtâkwan* (VII); s/he died of
loneliness, *nipaheyihtam* (VII); the act of dying of
loneliness, *nipaheyihtamowin* (NI); it looks lonely,
pîkiskacinâkwan (VII); loneliness or feeling alone,
pîkiskâteyitamowin (NI).

loner *ka nihtâ peyakohk* (NA).

lonesome Being lonesome, *kaskeyihtamowin* (NI); s/he
is lonesome for her/him, *kaskeyimew* (VTA); s/he is
lonesome, *kaskeyitam* (VII).

lone wolf *ka peyakot mahihkan* (NA).

long Something too long, *kîkway kâkinwak*; it is too
long, *kâspohtin* (VII); it sticks out too long, *kâspomiw*
(VII); a long time ago, *kayâs* (IPC); a very, very long ago,
kayâsîskamik (IPC); s/he made them too long,
kinohtâw (VAI); the house has a long floor,
kinohtakâw (VII); it has a long floor, i.e.: a trailer,
kinohtakisiw (VII); s/he has long legs, *kinokâtew* (VAI);
s/he makes it too long, *kinositâw* (VAI); s/he is long
and skinny, *kinowâpekisiw* (VAI); s/he has a long
body, *kinowâpekiyawew* (VAI); it is a long piece of
steel or gun barrel, *kinwapiskâw* (VII); it is long,
kinwâw (VII); it is long, i.e.: a bolt of cloth, moosehide,
kinwekan (VII); it is long, i.e.: deerhide or cariboohide,
kinwekisiw (VII); a long time, *kinwes* (IPC); a long log
or a tall person, *kinwaskosiw* (NA).

longbow *ekinosit ahcapiy* (NA).

long house *kakinwak wâskahikan* (NI).

longing *kîkway ka akâwâtamihk* (VAI).

longways *metoni wâhyaw*.

look Looking, *ka itapihk* (VAI); s/he looks after or
nutures herself/himself, *nâkateyimisiw* (VAI); the act
of looking after oneself or nuturing oneself,
nâkateyimisowin (NI); s/he looks at her/him with
amazement, *mâmaskâcinawew* (VTA); s/he looks at
her/him and thinks s/he is ugly, *mâyinawew* (VTA);
s/he looks at her/him, *kanawâpamew* (VTA); s/he
looks at her/him from the wrong side, *naspâtâpamew*
(VTA); s/he looks upwards, *ispimihkitapow* (VAI); s/he
looks just like her/him, *tapinakosow* (VAI); it looks
just like it, *tapinakwan* (VII); s/he thinks s/he looks

354

just like someone, *tâpinawew* (VTA); s/he looks up,
i.e.: across from, *tâstasapiw* (VAI).

lookout *âsawâpowin* (NI); *peyahtik* (IPC).

looks S/he looks that way, *isinakosiw* (VAI); it looks
that way, *isinakwan* (VII); s/he looks mad,
kisôwinâkosiw (VAI); it looks mad, *kisôwinâkwan*
(VII); s/he looks bad, *mâyinâkosiw* (VAI); it looks bad,
mâyinâkwan (VII); s/he looks good, *miyonâkosiw*
(VAI); it looks good, *miyonâkwan* (VII); s/he does not
look right, *naspacinâkosiw* (VAI); it does not look
right, *naspacinâkwan* (VII); s/he looks shy or ashamed,
nepewinâkosiw (VAI); something to be ashamed of,
nepewinâkwan (VII); s/he looks transparent,
sâponôkosiw (VAI); it looks transparent, *sâponôkwan*
(VII); s/he looks dazzling, *mâmaskacinâkosiw* (VAI); it
looks dazzling, *mâmaskâcinâkwan* (VII); s/he looks
ashamed, *nepewinâkosiw* (VAI); it looks ashamed,
nepewinâkwan (VII).

loon *mâkwa* (NA).

loop *ka wihkwehpitamihk pîminahkwân* (NI);
wawiyâpekamon (NI).

loose *pihkoho* (IPC); untie, *apehkon* (VII); it comes
loose, *apehkopayo* (IPC); separated, independent,
alone, loose, *piyako* (VAI); s/he chops it loose,
itâsikahwew (VAI); *tâsikahwew* (VAI).

loosen Loosening something, *pahkwatinikewin* (NI);
loosening a rope or string, *apehkona apisis*; s/he
loosens the rope on her/him, *pahkihtapekinew* (VTA).

lope *atim kakewahet* (VAI).

lopsided *pîmâw* (VII).

loquacity *pahpayakitonewin* (NI).

Lord God, *kisemanito* (NA); *ohtâwimâw* (NA) *(Plains)*;
s/he is Lord of all, *tepeyicikew* (NA).

Lord's Prayer *nohtawenan ka etwehk ayamihâwin.*

lose Losing count, *ka wanakihcikehk* (VAI); losing
something, *ka wanihtahk* (VII); s/he makes her/him
lose sight of it, *patâpahtamohew* (VTA); s/he makes
her/him lose her/his place, i.e.: a chair,
patapitisahwew (VTA); s/he loses the tracks s/he was
following, *wânahahtew* (VAI); s/he took the wrong
trail and s/he loses her/his way, *wânahamew* (VAI);
o/he looco oight of her/him, *wânapamew* (VTA).

loss The act of being at a loss or not knowing what to
do, *waniyihcikewin* (NI); s/he is at a loss with her/
him, *waneyimew* (VTA) *(Northern)*; *wâneyihtamihik*
(VAI) *(Plains)*; s/he is at a loss, *waneyimiw* (VAI)
(Northern); *waneyihtam* (VAI) *(Plains)*.

lost The act of losing one's way or being lost,
wanisinowin (NI); s/he lost her/his way, *wanihow*
(VAI); s/he is lost, *wanisin* (VAI); it is misplaced,
wanihtin (VII); s/he lost her/him or them, *wanihew*
(VTA); they lost each other, *wanihitowak* (VAI); the act

of losing each other, *wanihitowin* (NI); the act of being
lost, *wanihowin* (NI); s/he is lost and follows the
wrong trail, *wanimitimew* (VAI); s/he makes her/him
lose her/his way, *wanisimew* (VAI).

lot *ôtenaw askîhkanis* (NI); *tipahaskanis* (NI).

lotion *wehkimakwahon* (NI); a shaving lotion,
sopekahoswakan kaskipasowinihk (VAI).

loud Being loud or loudness, *kisiwewin* (NI); s/he or it
is loud, *kisiwew* (VAI); it has a loud ringing sound,
sohkewekocin (VII); s/he falls with a loud thud,
sohkewesin (VAI).

louse *ihkwa* (NA); full bellied louse, *mistatayew ihkwa*
(NA); a nit or head louse, *cîkinâhk* (NA); a small nit,
cîkinahkos (NA).

lout *môhcohkan* (NI).

lovable *awîyak ka sâkihekosit*; *sâkihikosiw* (VAI).

love The act of being in love, i.e.: a mutual love,
sâkihitowin (NI).

loveless *awîyak ekâ ka sâkihekosit* (VAI).

loveliness *miyonâkosiwin* (NI).

lovely *katawasisowin* (NI); *katawasisiw* (VAI).

lover *awîyak ka miyokapawihk*; *sâkihakan* (NA);
nicimos (NA).

loving *ka sâkihiwehk*; *sâkihiwew* (VTA).

low Under or down low, *capasis* (LN); the act of lowing
or calling out, *mostosokitowin* (NI); s/he stands low to
the ground, *tapahcikâpawiw* (VAI); it hangs low,
tapahtakocin (VAI); it hangs low, *tapahtakotew* (VII);
it is low, *tapahtisiw* (VAI).

lower A little lower, *nawâc capasis*; *nawâc nîhcayihk*;
s/he lowers her/him down with a rope,
pakitapihkenew (VTA); s/he lowers them with a rope,
yâsâpekinew (VAI).

lowland *ka tapahtak askîy*; *tapahcahk* (NI).

loyal *awîyak ka tâpwewokeyemiht*; *tâpwewiniwiw*
(VAI).

loyalty *tâpwewakeyihmowewin* (NI).

lubricant Something for oiling, *tôminikan* (NI).

lubricate S/he oiled it, *tôminam* (VTI); *ka tôminamihk
kîkway*.

lubricator *tôminkâkan* (NI).

lucid *ku pukuskihtûkusihk* (VAI).

luck Having good luck or a success; the act of having
luck, *papewewin* (NI); having bad luck, *mayakosiwin*
(NI); s/he brings her/him luck, *papiweskawew* (VTA).

luckily *miyopayowenihk*.

luckless *ekâ kîkway miyopayowin*; s/he is unlucky,
mayakosiw (VAI).

lucky Being lucky, *kanihta miyopayihk* (VAI); s/he is
fortunate or lucky, *miyopayiw* (VAI); s/he makes her/
him lucky, *papiwihew* (VTA); s/he makes her/him

lucky with her/his words, **papiwemew** (VTA); s/he is a lucky person, **papewew** (VAI).

ludicrous *ka pîwahpihiwehk* (VAI).

lukewarm Lukewarm water, *nîpîy ka wîyakihkâkamitek* (VAI); a warm liquid, *kîsowakamik* (NI); s/he made it lukewarm, *wîyakihkâkamihtâw* (VAI); it is lukewarm, *wîyakihkâkamow* (VII).

lull *ka cistomwehk*; *cistomawasowin* (NI).

lullaby *ka cistomawasohk* (NI); s/he sang her/him to sleep, *cistomew* (VTA).

lumber *napakihtakwa* (NI); it is long, *kinohtakâw* (VII); it is sheet-like, plank, flat, *napakihtakisiw* (VII); *napakihtakaw* (VII); a bunch of boards, *napakihtakwa* (NI).

luminescence *kaskitipiskâhk ka wâsiskotek* (VII).

luminescent *kaskitipiskâhk ka nôkwahk* (VII).

luminous *pîsimohkanis wanitipiskâhk ka nokosit* (VAI); it lights up, *wâsaskopayiw* (VII).

lump *piskosiwin* (NI); s/he has a lump, i.e.: in one place, *piskosiw* (VAI); s/he has lumps, i.e.: all over, *piskopayiw* (VAI); a lump or hump in the ground, *piskwahcâw* (VII); there is a lump in the snow, *piskwâkonakâw* (VII); there is a lump on it, *piskwâw* (VII); s/he has a lump on her/his back, i.e.: a hunchback person, *piskwâwikanew* (NA); s/he piles them in a lump, *piskwahew* (VAI).

lumpy Something full of lumps, *kapah piskwâk* (VII); it is lumpy, *pahpiskwâw* (VII); s/he is lumpy, *pahpiskosiw* (VAI).

lunacy The act of going insane, *kîskwewin* (NI).

lunatic *kakîskwet* (NA).

lunch *ka micosihk apisis*; *nemâwin* (NI); *âpihtâkîsikan mîcisowin* (NI).

lung *ohpan* (NA).

lunge *ka nikankwâskohtihk*; *kwâskwetotawew* (VAI).

lurch *awîyak sôskwâc ka nakatiht âymanohk*.

lure A scent used to lure, *mîcimihkahcikan* (NI).

lurid *ka sîkinakosihk* (VAI).

lurk *askamacikewin* (NI); *papâmikasow* (VAI).

luscious *mistahi miyos pakwan*; it tastes very good, *mistahimiyospakwan* (VII).

lush *maskosiya ka miyokihkwâw*; *mitoni miyokowin* (NI).

lust *ka pisikwâtisihk* (VAI); being inticed, *akâwâtamowin* (NI).

lustful *pisikwâtisowin* (NI).

lustre *or* **luster** It is shiny, *wâsihkopayiw* (VII).

lustrous *kîkway ewâsihkonakwahk* (VII).

lusty *kîkway ka môstasihtakwahk* (VII).

luxuriance *ka miyokihcikehk* (VAI).

luxuriant *kîkway ka miyokihk*; it grows well, *miyokin* (VII).

luxuriate *miyomahcihowin* (NI).

luxurious *ka miyomahcihohk* (VAI).

lye Something used to whiten clothes, *wâpiskinkan* (NI); lye, *pihkwâpoy* (NI).

lying Telling a fib, *kiyâskiwin* (NI); s/he is lying down, *pimisin* (VAI); s/he is lying or fibbing, *kiyâskiw* (VAI); it is lying down on the ground, i.e.: a pole, *pimâskohtin* (VII); it is lying on the ground, i.e.: a tree, *pimâskosin* (VII).

lynx *pisiw* (NA); *misipisiw* (NA) *(Northern)*; *misiminôs* (NA) *(Plains)*; *pakwaciminôs* (NA) *(Plains)*.

356

M

mad *ka kisiwâsihk* (VAI); *kisôwâsiw* (VAI).

madden *kisiwâhiwewin* (NI).

made Something finished, *kîkway kakeh osehtahk* (VTI); s/he made repairs along the way, *naskwewosihew* (VAI); s/he made an image or likeness of someone, *naspisihew* (VAI); s/he made an image or likeness of herself/himself, *naspisihisiw* (VAI); the act of making an image or likeness of oneself, *naspisihisowin* (NI).

madly *kisiwâsiwinihk* (VAI).

madness *kisôwâsowin* (NI).

magic *ka mamahtâw tôtamihk* (VTI).

magical *mamahtâwisiwin* (NI).

magician *awîyak ka mamahtâwsit* (VAI); *mamahtâwinikew* (NA); s/he performs magic, *mamahtâw kaskihtâw* (VAI).

magnificence *naspic ka miyonâkwahk* (VII).

magnificent *naspic miyosiwin* (VII); splendid and brilliant, *osâmkatawasisik* (VII).

magpie *apisci kakakes* (NA); *apistikakakes* (NA).

maim *ka wanihtahk miskat ahpô mispiton* (VAI); *maskipitew* (VAI); *cistipitew* (VAI); disable by wounding, *maskipitew* (VAI); *cistipitew* (VAI).

main *eyoko kihcina* (IPC); *kecikîkway* (IPC).

mainly That's why, *eyoko oci* (IPC); mainly, principally, chiefly, *osâmpoko* (IPC).

maintain *ka nânapâcihtahk kîkway* (VII).

maintenance *nânapâcihcikewin* (NI).

make The act of making something, *osihcikewin* (NI); making something, *kîkway ka osehtahk* (VTI); s/he makes, *osihcikew* (VAI); s/he makes it for her/him, *osihtamawew* (VTA); s/he makes them, *osihew* (VAI); s/he makes her/him that way, *isihew* (VTA); s/he makes it or her/him or them strong, *maskawisihew* (VTA); s/he makes her/him strong of heart, *maskawitehew* (VTA); s/he makes a bag, *maskimotihkew* (VAI); s/he makes footwear for her/him, i.e.: shoes or mocassins, *maskisinihkawew* (VTA); s/he makes footwear, i.e.: shoes or moccasins, *maskisinihkew* (VAI); s/he makes grass or hay, *maskosihikew* (VAI); s/he makes or prepares a sweat bath, *matotisânihkew* (VAI); s/he makes her/him red, *mihkohew* (VTA); s/he makes her/him bloody, *mihkôwihew* (VTA); s/he makes her/him a lunch to take with her/him, *nimâhew* (VAI); s/he makes lunches, *nimawinihkew* (VAI); s/he makes two out of them, *nîsohew* (VAI); s/he makes four of them, *newihew* (VAI).

maker Or creator, *otosihcikew* (NA).

making *ka mekwâ osihcikehk* (VAI).

malady *nânatohk isi mâyâyawin* (NI); *âhkosowin* (NI).

male *nâpewiwin* (NI).

malevolence *ka nihtâ mâyitôtâkehk* (VTA).

malevolent *mâyitôtâkewin* (NI).

malice *ekâ ekosi ka eteyimiht awîyak* (VTA).

malicious *pakwâteyimowewin* (NI); *pakwâsowewin* (NI).

malign The act of making false or misleading statements about someone with the intent to injure, *macâyimwewin* (NI); s/he maligns other people, *macâyimomiwew* (VAI).

mallard Drake, *iyinisip* (NA) *(Plains and Northern variant)*; *wihpitwânsip* (NA) *(Northern)*.

malleability *pewapisk ka oyatahamihk* (VTI).

malleable *awîyak ka nihtâ oyiniht* (VTA).

maltreatment *ekâ kwayask ka totaht awîyak* (VTA).

mama *or* **mamma** *komâmâhk* (NA); *kokâwîhk* (NA).

man *napew* (NA) *(Plains)*; *napîw* (NA) *(Northern)*; a large man, *mistapew* (NA); a male mannequin, *napewihkan* (NI); he is a handsome man, *miyowapewiw* (VAI); an unmarried or single man, *môsâpew* (VAI); he is a man, *nâpewiw* (VAI); s/he feels manly, *nâpewâyâw* (VAI); s/he talks like s/he is a man or s/he talks bravely, *nâpemow* (VAI); a young man, *oskâpew* (NA); a muscular or strong man, *sohkapew* (NA).

manage *ka nakateyehtamihk kîkway* (VII); *pimpayihtâw* (VII).

manageability *nihtâ paminikewin* (NI).

manageable *kîkway ka miyopayihtahk* (VTI).

mane *mestakaya* (NI).

mangle *ayiwinsa ka sôskwahikakehk* (VTI); *sôskwahikewin* (NI); *kîkway metoni ka sikwatahamihk* (VTI).

mangy *ka pîkwaskawet atim* (VAI).

manipulate *kîkway kamiyopayihtahk* (VTI); *nihtâpaminam* (VTI); handle with care, *nihtâpaminikewin* (NI).

manipulation *miyopayihcikewin* (NI).

manipulative *ka nihtâ miyopayihtahk* (VTI).

mankind *ayisiyinowak* (NA); *ayisininahk* (NA).

manlike *nâpewinakosowin* (NI).

manly *ka nâpewihk* (VAI); *nâpehkâsiw* (VAI).

manner *tansi kesâyahk* (VAI).

mannered *isâyâwin* (NI).

mannerless *ekâ ka manâtisihk* (VII).

mannerly *manâtisiwin* (NI).

357

manoeuvrability *or* **maneuverability** *ka nihtâ waskawenamihk kîkway* (VTI).

manoeuvre *or* **maneuvre** *katawahk kesiwaskawehk* (VAI); the act of manoeuvring something, *ispayihcikewin* (NI).

manure *mostos omiy* (NI); *mistatim omiy* (NI).

many A large number, or a big lot, *mihcet* (IPC); *mihcetiw* (IPC); there are many of it, *mihcetin* (VII); too many, *osâmeyatiw* (VII); *osâmeyatin* (VII); many people, *mihcet awîyak* (NA); many things, *mihcet kîkway* (NI); as many as there are, any one, every one, or everything, *tahto* (IPC); as many as needed, *tepitahto* (IPC); referring to lots of something, "there are lots of....", *misahci* (IPC); indicating a whole bunch, "there are many of....", *misahkamik* (IPC).

maple tree Or sugar cane, *sesipâskwatâhtik* (NA); there are many maple trees or there are many sugar canes, *sesipâskwatâhtikoskâw* (VTA).

maple leaf *sesipâskwatâhtikonîpîy* (NA).

mar *ka mâyesehtahk kîkway* (VTI).

march *kîspahkenkehk pimohtewin* (NI).

March The goose moon or month, *niskipîsim* (NA).

mare *kiskisis* (NA); a female horse, *nôsestim* (NA); s/he is a mare, *kiskisisiwiw* (VAI).

mark Making a mark on something, *masinihcikewin* (NI).

marked *awîyak ka masinahoht* (VTA).

marking Stamping, typing, *masinatahikewin* (NI).

marmot *miscanaskos* (NI).

marriage *wîkihtowin* (NI).

marriageable *ka nohte wîkihtohk* (VAI).

married *ka kihci wîkihtohk* (VAI).

maroon It is reddish in color, *mihkonâkwan* (NI).

marrow Bone marrow, *wînih* (NA); bone marrow or grease, *oskanipimiy* (NI).

marrowbone *ka pâstasohk oskan* (NI).

marry The act of performing a marriage ceremony, *ka wîkihtahiwehk* (VAI); the act of getting married or a marriage, *wîkihtowin* (NI); s/he marries them, *wîkihtahew* (VTA); s/he is married to someone, *wîkihtiw* (VAI); they are married to each other, *wîkihtowak* (VAI); s/he marries her/him, *wîkimew* (VTA).

marsh *ka paskwaskekak* (NI).

marshland *kayas paskwaskekâw* (NI).

marshy Marshy ground, *ka tostokahk askiy* (NI); a marshy area, *tostokan* (NI).

marten *wapistan* (NA); *wâpiscânis* (NA).

martyr *awîyak ka nipôstamâket* (VAI).

martyrdom *nîpostamâkewin* (NI).

marvel *mâmaskâtam* (VTI); *sisikoteyitam* (VTI).

marvellous *or* **marvelous** *kîkway kosam mewasik* (VII); *mâmaskâteyihtâkwan* (NI); being moved by wonder, *tamâmaskâtamihk* (VTI).

masculine *nâpewiwin* (NI).

masculinity *ka nâpew sihcikasohk* (VAI).

mash *ka sikwahamihk* (VTI); it crushes something, *sikwaham* (VTI).

mask An imitation face, *mihkwâkanihkan* (NI); something that hides the face, *âkohkwehon* (NI).

mass *ayamihewiyinow ka ayamihat* (NA); a special praying, *ayamihâwin* (NA).

massive *kîkway ka sohkahk* (VAI); *kwayakimisâw* (VII).

masterful *awîyak ka nihtâpaminwet* (VAI); authoritative or attributable, *meyokiskinohamakew* (VAI).

masterly *awîyak ka nihtâ paminahk kîkway* (VAI).

mastery *nakacihtâwin* (NI).

masticate *metoni ka sikwahamihk kîkway* (VTI); chew into a pulp, *mâmâkwahtam* (VTI).

mat *aspitahkoskewin* (NI).

match *kocawâkanis* (NI); they match well, *miyoskotatowak* (VAI); a matching pair, *kamiyo nahiskatohk* (VTA).

matchless *ekâ kakeh nanakahiht awîyak* (VTA).

mate The act of making friends, *wicewâkanihtowin* (NI); a bullmoose searching for a mate, *kîwahohtew* (VAI); they are mating, i.e.: animals, *nôcihitowak* (VAI).

material *kîkway ka osihcikakehk* (VTI).

materialize *kîkway ka tâpwepayihtahk* (VTI); *tâpwe ispayow* (VII); assume a material form of existence, *tâpwepayiw* (VII).

materially *tapwepayihcikewnihk* (NI).

maternal *pahpeyakwan komâmâhk* (VTA).

maternity *pâmayes ocawasimsit iskwew* (NA).

mathematical *akihtasowenihk ka akihtek* (NI).

mathematics *akihtasona ka kiskinohamakosihk* (NI); working with numbers, *akihcikewin* (NI).

matrimonial *kihci wikihtowin* (NI).

matrimonially *kihci wikihtonihk* (NI).

matrimony *ka kihciwikihtohk* (VAI); getting married, *wikihtowin* (NI).

matted *aspitakoskewin kastahk pehcayihk* (NI); *maskawipayiw* (VII); *mâmawipayiw* (VII).

matter *kîkway kohcispayik* (VII); *meyewiwin* (NI).

maturation *kîsohpikiwin* (NI).

mature Being mature in the physical sense, *kakîsohpikihk* (NI); s/he is full grown or mature, *kîsohpikiw* (VAI); s/he acts mature, *kîsohpikewatisiw* (VAI); s/he thinks s/he is mature, *kîsohpikiweyimew* (VTI).

maturity *awîyak ka kîsohpikit* (VAI).

maul *cistiniwewin* (NI).

mauve It is dark purple in color, *kaskitewimihkwâw* (VII).

maximize *metoni kisipipayihcikewin* (NI).

maximum *metoni kisipanohk* (NI); the greatest amount possible, *namoyayîwak* (IPC).

May The egg laying moon or month, *opiniyâwewipîsim* (NA) *(Plains)*; the leaf budding moon or month, *sâkipakâwipîsim* (NA) *(Northern)*; *apiniyâwepîsim* (NA).

maybe *etoke* (IPC); maybe, or a fair degree of certitude, *ahpô* (IPC); perhaps or maybe, *mâskôc* (IPC); maybe, it could easily be or might happen, *ahpôtapwe* (IPC); maybe, perhaps, *ahpô mina itoke* (IPC); maybe, often a very polite no, but not always: *matwanci* (IPC); maybe I should, should I? *ahpô ci* (IPC); maybe, more possibly, *ahpô etikwe* (IPC).

me *niya* (PP); me too, *nîsta* (PR).

meadow *yihkatawâw* (NI).

meadowlark *wasepescan* (NA) *(Northern)*; *opîscîwâcikwasow* (NA) *(Plains)*.

meadowy *ka mâhmâskotewahk* (VII).

meagre *or* **meager** *namoya mitoni ekwayikohk* (VII); *tipiyahk* (VII); without fullness or scanty or lean, *tipiyahk* (VII).

meal *asahkewin* (NI); *micisowin* (NI); *kistikan sikopocikan* (NA).

mealtime *mitsowin* (NI).

mealy *ka wâpanesihk* (VAI).

mean Having a mean character, *macihtwâwin* (NI); being mean, *macâyiwewin* (NI); s/he is mean, *macihtwâw* (VAI); cruel, hard to get along with, *âhkwatisow* (VAI).

meander *wâwâkamon* (NI); pursue a winding course, *wâwâkohtewin* (NI).

meaning *ocitaw ka tôtamihk* (VII).

meaningful *kîkway ka sohkeyihtamihk* (VII).

meaningless *ekâ kîkway kispehtaweyihtawahk* (VII); hard to understand, *namoya nistotâkwan* (VII).

meanness *maci isâyâwin* (NI).

meant *ka sapweyihtamihk kîkway* (VII).

meantime Than, *ispîhci* (IPC).

meanwhile In the interval, *mekwâc* (IPC).

measurable *ka tipowakeyihtamihk kîkway* (VTI).

measure The length or depth of something, *tipâpekinikan* (NI); something used for measuring, *tipahikakan* (NI); *tipâha* (VTI); s/he measures the depth of the water, *kotaskeham* (VTI); a line for measuring, *tipâpân* (NI) *(Northern)*; *tipâpâniyâpiy* (NI) *(Plains)*; s/he measures them with a string or line, i.e.: fish, *tipâpâtew* (VAI); s/he measures her/him or it with her/

his arms, *tipiniskâtew* (VAI); a unit for determining extent, *tipahikan* (NI).

measured *kîkway ka tipâpekinamihk* (VTI); *tipahikatew* (VAI); regulated by measure, *tipahikatew* (VAI).

measureless *ekâ kakeh tipahamihk* (VII).

measurement Measuring with a tape measure, *tipâpekinkewin* (NI); measuring something, *tipahikewin* (NI); false measurement, *kakayesitipahikan* (NI); the act of measuring or paying or the act of taking a measurement or dimensions, *tipahikewin* (NI); *tepapekinkewin* (NI) *(Northern)*.

meat *wîyâs* (NI); raw meat, *askiwiyâs* (NI); moose meat, *môsowiyâs* (NI); s/he makes pemican, *îwahikanihkew* (VAI); a piece of dried meat, *kahkewak* (NI); fresh meat, *oskiwîyâs* (NI); s/he has meat, *wiyâsimiw* (VAI); it has meat on it, *wiyâsiwiw* (VAI); there is meat on it, *wiyâsowan* (VII); canned meat, *wiyâsihkan* (VII).

meaty *ka wiyâsowik* (VII).

meddle *ka môstatahkamiksihk* (VAI).

meddlesome *môstatahkamkisowin* (NI); disposed to interfere unjustifiedly, *sâminikeskow* (NI).

medicate *nâtawehowin* (NI).

medicine A healing potion or a medicine gift that has spirit power benefits, *maskihkîy* (NI); a medicine root or musquash root, *manitoskatask* (NA) *(Northern)*; *wehkesk* (NA) *(Plains)*; medicine water or spirit power liquid, *maskihkiwâpoy* (NI); medicine leaves or herbs with spirit power benefits, *maskihkiwopakwa* (NI); medicine vapor, aroma, or odor, *maskihkîwakan* (NI); that characteristic that all great medicine possesses, *maskihkîwan* (NI); healing medicine, *nâtawihowin* (NI); the act of providing healing medicine, *nâtawihiwewin* (NI); s/he provides the healing medicine for her/him, *nâtawihew* (VAI); s/he provides healing medicine for herself/himself, i.e.: boiling roots, *nâtawihisiw* (VAI).

medicine bag A bundle that contains sacred power objects, *maskihkîwiwat* (NI); *mewat* (NI); s/he makes a medicine bag or a bundle that contains sacred power objects, *mîwatihkew* (VAI).

medicine man Someone who knows Cree medicine, *awîyak kakiskeyihtâhk neheyaw maskihkîy* (NA); medicine woman or nurse, *maskihkiwiskwew* (NA); someone who treats illness, i.e.: medicine man, shaman, or doctor, *maskihkîwiyiniw* (NA); s/he has many spirit power gifts or s/he is a shaman, *maskihkîwiyiniwiw* (VAI); a medicine person who uses the good spirit to offset evil spirits, *nanatawihiwewiyinow* (VAI).

medicine root *wehkesk* (NA) *(Plains)*; *manitoskâtâsk* (NA) *(Northern)*.

meditation *ka ayamihew mâmitoneyihtamihk* (VTI).

medium *âpihtaw iyikohk* (IPC); *âpihtaw isi* (IPC); about halfways, *âpihtawisi* (IPC).

meek *metoni peyahtik isâyâwin* (NI).

meet Meeting someone, *awîyak kanakiskaht* (VTA); they meet, *nakiskâtowak* (VAI); s/he meets her/him, *nakiskawew* (VTA); s/he meets with her/him on time, *tepâsteskawew* (VTA).

meeting An organized meeting or assembly, i.e.: a business meeting, *mamawapowin* (NI); they are having a meeting, *mâmawapowak* (VAI); s/he sits and holds meetings here and there, *pahpapamapiw* (VAI) *(Northern)*; *papâmimâmawopiw* (VAI) *(Plains)*; *pahpapamapi mâmawaponihkew* (VAI).

melancholic *ka kakwâtakeyimohk* (VAI).

melancholy Feeling of low spirits or depression, *kwâtakeyimowin* (NI); sad thoughtfulness, *pîkiskâteyihtam* (VTI); a state of melancholy or sadness, *koskwâwâtahkamikan* (NI); a state of depression, *pîkiskâtan* (NI).

mellow *awîyak ka kitimâkeyimowet* (VAI).

melt Something that melts, *ka tihkitek* (VII); it is melting, *tehkitew* (VII); the metal has melted, *tihkâpiskâw* (VII); something used to melt iron, *tihkâpiskisikan* (NI); s/he melts them, i.e.: something metallic, *tihkâpiskiswew* (VAI); it is melted by the sun, *tihkâsiw* (VAI); it is melted, i.e.: butter, *tihkâw* (VII); it is melted into a liquid, *tihkipestew* (VII); s/he melts them into a liquid form, i.e.: water, *tihkipeswew* (VAI); s/he melts it for her/him, *tihkisamawew* (VTA); some metal that can be melted, *tihkisikan* (NI); s/he melts them, *tihkiswew* (VAI); it is kind of melted or it is softened, *tihkipâw* (VII); make or become a liquid through heat, *tihkitew* (VTI); *tihkisam* (VTI); it is slightly melted or thawed, *tihkitew* (VII) *(Plains)*.

membrane *tahkôc wasakay* (NI).

memorable *ekâ ka wanikiskisihk awîyak* (VTA) *or* (VTI); worthy of remembering, *kiskisototawaw*.

memorize *nitawi kiskisowin* (NI).

memory *ka kiskisihk kîkway* (NI); *mamitoneyicikan* (NI); *kiskisiwin* (NI).

men *mihcet nâpewak* (NA).

mend The act of mending, *mîsahikewin* (NI); s/he mends it for her/him, *mîsahamawew* (VTA); s/he mends the net, *mîsahayapiw* (VAI); s/he mends it or them, *mîsawew* (VTA).

mendacious *ka kîyâskiskowin* (NI).

mendacity *ka kîyâskiskihk* (VAI).

menfolk *mihcet nâpewak* (NA).

menial *otatoskew* (VAI).

menstrual *iskwew âhkosiwin* (NI).

menstruate A woman's monthly period, *kâwepinahk mihkoh tahto pîsim iskwew* (VTA); she is menstruating, *mihkowâspinew* (VAI).

menstruation A woman's monthly "sickness", *pîsim âhkosiwin iskwew ohci* (VTA); she has her monthly menstruation, *pîsimwaspinew* (VAI); the act of menstrating, *pîsimwaspinewin* (NI); her menstruation is finished or she is well again, *ponâhkosiw* (VAI).

mental The mind, *mâmitoneyihcikan* (NI); a thinking activity, *ka mâmitoneyihtamihk* (VTI); s/he thinks of her/him as a mental case, *wayeskâneyimew* (VTA); s/he is thought of as a mental case, *wayeskaneyitâkosiw* (VAI); s/he really confused her/him mentally, *wayeskanihew* (VTA); what s/he said to her/him mentally disturbed her/him, *wayeskânimew* (VAI); s/he is mentally confused, *wayeskânisiw* (VAI); the act of being mentally confused, *wayeskânisiwin* (NI).

mentality *awîyak omâmitoneyihcikan* (NA).

mentally *ka mâmitoneyihcikanihk* (VAI).

mention Mentioning something to someone, *mâmiskôtamâkewin* (NI).

merciless *ekâ kokitimâkinakewnihk* (NI).

mercy *kitimakinâwew* (VAI).

mere *metoni ketisk* (IPC).

merely *etatâw* (IPC); *ketisk* (IPC).

merge *ka wicewâkanipayihk* (VII).

merriment *môcikihtâwin* (NI).

merry *ka môcikihsihk* (VAI); *môcikeyitam* (VTI).

merrymaking *môcikihtâwinihkewin* (NI).

mesmerism *sâkoteyimowewin* (NI).

mesmerize *awîyak ka sâkoteyimiht* (VTA).

mess *ka wînâscikehk* (VTI); *mâmawimecisowin* (NI); it is filthy, *wînâw* (VII).

message *masinahikanis ka itsahamatohk* (VAI).

messenger *awîyak ka pimohtatamaket masinahikanis* (NI); *twestamakew* (VAI).

messy *wenascikewin* (NI); *yepatan* (VII).

met *awîyak kakeh nakiskaht* (VTA); *nakiskâtowak* (VAI).

metal Iron material, *pîwâpiskwayih* (NI); it is long, *kinowâpiskisiw* (VAI); *kinowâpiskâw* (VAI); it is flat, *napakâpiskisiw* (VAI); *napakâpiskâw* (VAI); it is round, bar, pipe, *notimâpiskisiw* (VAI); *notimâpiskâw* (VAI); it is copper, *osâwâpiskisiw* (VAI); *osâwâpiskâw* (VAI); it is strong, *sohkapiskisow* (VAI); *sohkapiskaw* (VAI); it is cold, *tahkapiskisow* (VAI); *tahkapiskaw* (VAI); it is short, *cimâpiskisiw* (VAI); *cimâpiskâw* (VAI); it is crooked, bent, *wâkâpiskisiw* (VAI); *wâkâpiskâw* (VAI); it is twisted, *pimapiskisow* (VAI); *pimapiskaw* (VAI); a piece of metal broken off, i.e.: a sawed off shotgun, *kîskâpiskâw* (NI); a smooth metal, *miyowâpiskâw* (NI); a fine metal with a smooth surface, i.e.: a clothes iron, *miyowâpiskisiw* (NI); it is a flat metal, *napakâpiskâw* (NI); it consists of two pieces of metal, i.e.: a double-barreled shotgun, *nîswâpiskâw* (VII); metal, i.e.: iron or steel, *pîwâpisk* (NI); a piece of metal, *pîwâpiskos* (NI); the metal is white, *wapâpiskâw* (VII).

metallic *ka pîwâpiskowik kîkway* (VII).

meticulous *awîyak ka nahihtahk* (VAI).

mew *minôs kâkitôt* (VAI); *minôsis okitowin* (NI).

mid *âpihtâwayihk* (NI).

midair or **mid-air** *nayewâc ka pîmakotek* (VTI).

midday *ka âpihtâkîsikâk* (VII); it is midday, *âpihtâkîsikâw* (VII).

middle Right in the middle, *metoni âpihtâw* (IPC); in the centre room or middle place, *âpihtâwayihk* (NI); middle of the current, *mekwacowanohk* (NI); in the middle of or among, *mekwânohk* (NI); in the middle of the forest, *mekwâsakâhk* (NI); in the centre, *tastawayihk* (NI).

middle-aged The start of old age, *kâmacipayik kihte ayiwewin* (NI); s/he is getting to be an old person, middle-aged, *atikiseyinewiw* (VAI).

midland *âpihtâwayihk askehk* (NI).

midnight When it is midnight, *ka âpihtâtipiskak* (VII); it is midnight, *âpihtâtipiskâw* (VII); it is past midnight, *poni âpihtâtipiskâw* (VII).

midrift *kipahon* (NI).

midst *ka kîyi kawisinihk* (VTA); *kîyikawipayowin* (NI); a control or middle position, *kîyikawe* (IPC).

midstream *âpihtâwakam* (NI).

midsummer *ka âpihtânepihk* (IPC); *âpihtânepin* (VII).

midway *mweci âpihtâw* (IPC).

midweek *ka nisto kîsikahk* (IPC).

midwinter *ka âpihtâpipohk* (IPC); *âpihtâpipon* (VII).

midyear *ka âpihtâwpayik peyak askîy* (NI).

might Strength, *ka ispîhcehk* (VAI).

might Possibly, *ahpô etikwe* (IPC).

mightily *metoni sohki* (IPC).

mightiness *sohkâtisiwin* (NI).

mighty *awîyak ka sohkâtisit* (VAI); *maskawâtisiw* (VAI).

mild *ka kîsopwek* (VII); "It is warm out", *kîsopwew* (VII).

mile One mile, *peyak mistik* (NI); stick, road, tree, *mistik* (NI).

mileage Every mile, *tânimatahtomistik* (NI); *ka akihtamihk tahtomistik' tânimatahtomistik* (LN).

militancy *ayiwâkeyimowin* (NI).

militant *ka ayiwâkeyimohk* (VAI); a fight, *nôtinitowin* (NI).

milk *tohtôsâpoy* (NI).

milker *yîkinikâkan* (NA).

milking The act of milking, *yîkinikewin* (NI); s/he milks the cow, *yîkinew* (VAI).

milky *ka tohtôsâpowahk* (VII).

million One million, *peyakwaw kisipakihtasowin* (IPC).

mimic *ka ayisinâkehk* (VAI); *kiskinowâpamew* (VAI); s/he mimics her/him; s/he follows her/his actions, *tipâhakew* (VAI); *ayisinawew* (VTA) *(Plains)*; the act of mocking someone, *ayisinâkewin* (NI).

mimicry *ayisinâkewin* (NI).

mince Smashing or cutting something into smaller pieces, *kasikosawatamihk kîkway* (VTI); s/he minces it up, *kaskihkotew* (VAI).

mind *mâmitoneyihcikan* (NI); a one-track mind, *nâspiciteyihcikan* (NI); s/he has a one-track mind, *nâspiciteyihtam* (VTI); the act of having a one-track mind, *nâspiciteyihtamowin* (NI).

minded *tansi mâmitoneyihcikan ketastek* (VII).

mindful *sohki mâmitoneyihcikan* (NI).

mindless *ekâ komâmitoneyecikanihk* (VII); *namoya mâmitoneyihtam* (VTI).

mine *niya* (PR); *kîkway ka tepeyihtamihk* (VTI).

mine A hole in the ground, *wâtîkan* (NI); an explosive mine, *pakisikan* (NI)

mingle *ka kîyikawipayehohk* (VTA); *kikawipayihiw* (VAI).

miniature *ka apiscisehcikesihk* (VAI).

miniaturize *apiscisehcikanis* (NI).

minister A member of the clergy, *ayamihewiyiniw* (NA).

ministerial *ka ayamihewiyiniwihk* (NA).

ministery *tansi ka isi ayamihahk* (VAI).

mink *sâkwes* (NA).

minnow *apisci kinosesis* (NA); *kinosesis* (NA).

mint *ka tahkeyawepayesik* (VAI).

minus *ka otinamihk pahki* (VTI); *pahki otinamakewin* (NI); less than ordinary, *astamihk* (VTI).

minutely *tâhtwâw peyak cipahikanis* (IPC).

miracle *mamâhtâw kîkway kîspayik* (VII); *mamâhtâw payiwin* (NI); an act of supernatural power, *mamâhtâwpayowin* (NI).

miraculous A miraculous happening, *mamâhtâw ketahkamikahk* (VII); it happens in a miraculous way or manner, *mamâhtâwipuyiw* (NI).

mirage *ka nanahtek* (VII).

mire It is slimy or muddy, *pasakoceskowakâw* (VII).

mirth *môcikihtâwin* (NI); amusement, celebrating joyfully, *miyawâtamowin* (NI).

mirthful *ka môcikisihk* (VAI).

mirthless *namakîkway môcikisowin* (NI).

misadventure *mâyakopayowin* (NI).

misalliance *ekâ kwayask ka wicehtohk* (VAI).

misapply *ekâ kwayask ketapacitahk kîkway* (VAI).

misapprehension *ka wani nisitohtamihk* (VTI).

361

misbehave *ka naspâtahkamekisihk* (VAI); *namoya kwayask tâtisowin* (NI).

misbelief *ekâ ka tâpwehtamihk* (VII).

miscalculate *ekâ kwayask ketakihcikehk* (VAI); s/he miscounted, *wânakicikew* (VAI).

miscall *wâneyihkâtew* (VAI).

miscarriage The act of miscarrying, *osikowin* (NI); s/he makes her miscarry by having a car crash, *osikosimew* (VAI); she miscarries after falling, *osikosin* (VAI); she causes her own miscarriage, *osikow* (VAI); she has a painful miscarriage, *wîsakipayiw* (VAI).

miscarry *awîyak ka wîsakipayit* (VAI).

miscellaneous Consisting of a mixture, *nanâtohk kîkway* (NI); *mihcetkîkwâya* (NI).

mischief *ka waninewahkamiksihk* (VAI); *waninewin* (NI); *wanitôtamowin* (NI).

mischievious *waninew* (VAI).

misconduct *mâyitôtamowin* (NI); improper conduct, *mâyitôtamowin* (NI).

misdeed *wanitôtamowin* (NI); a wicked doing or action, *wanitôtamowin* (NI).

misdirect *wanitisahwew* (VAI); giving wrong directions, *wanitisahowewin* (NI).

misdoing *naspâctôtamowin* (NI); going the wrong thing, *naspâctôtamowin* (NI).

miserable *nanâtohk isâyâwin* (NI); *kitimâkisiw* (VAI).

misery *ka kwâtakihtâwin* (NI); *kakwâtakihtâwin* (NI); *kitimâkisowin* (NI).

misfire *kâcakapiskihtihk pâskisikan* (VTI).

misfit Clothes that do not fit, *ekâ kanahiskamihk* (VTI); it does not fit, *namoyatepihtin* (VAI).

misfortune Having bad luck, *nayihtâwpayowin* (NI); being unlucky, *mayakosiwin* (NI); s/he brings her/him misfortune, *kîsinâcihew* (VAI); s/he brings misfortune upon herself/himself, *kîsinâcihiw* (VAI); the act of bringing misfortune upon oneself, *kîsinâcihowin* (NI); extreme misfortune is happening, *kîsinâtahkamikan* (NI); s/he is causing extreme misfortune, *kîsinâtahkamikisiw* (VAI); the act of causing extreme misfortune, *kîsinâtahkamikisiwin* (NI).

misgive *ka pisci mekihk* (VTA).

misgiving *pisci mekiwin* (NI); *wawâneyihtakwan* (NI).

misguide *wansimowewin* (NI); misleading someone, *wanimowewin* (NI).

misguided *awîyak ka wansimiht* (VTA).

mishandle *ekâ kwayask ka paminamihk kîkway* (VTI).

mishap *mâyipayiwin* (NI); *âyimipayiw* (VAI).

mischievous *nanâtohk isâyâwin* (NI).

misconceive *ka wani nisitohtamihk* (VTI).

misconception *wani nisitohtamowin* (NI).

misconduct *mâyitôtamowin* (NI); *kakepâcihtwâwin* (NI).

misconstruction *ka wani isihcikehk* (VAI).

misconstrue *ka wanâmowehk* (VAI).

miscount *wanakihcikewin* (NI); s/he miscounted them, *patakimew* (VAI).

misdeal *wanotinikewin* (NI).

misdeed *ka wanitôtamihk* (VTI); *wanitôtamowin* (NI).

misdirect *ka wanikiskinohamakehk* (VAI); *wânahamew* (VAI).

misinform *wani wihtamâkewin* (NI).

misinformation *ka waniwihtamâkehk* (VAI).

misinterpret *wanitônamiw* (VAI).

misjudge Misjudging someone's character, *kawaneyimiht awîyak* (VTA); s/he judged her/him incorrectly, *wanâsowatew* (VTA); something misjudged, goes beyond proper limits, *kâspopayiw* (VAI); s/he has an unjust opinion, *waniyimew* (VAI).

mislay *wanascikewin* (NI); *wanastâw* (VII).

mislead Getting someone lost, *wanohtahiwewin* (NI).

misleading Leading someone astray, *wanohtahiwewin* (NI); regarding a misleading thought, i.e.: it sounds suspicious and it may not be true, *kakayesiyitakwan* (NI).

mismatch When people are not suited for each other, *ekâ kanahiskatohk* (VAI); s/he does not fit in with her/him or is not suited for her/him, *mâyiskawew* (VTA).

misname *ekâ kwayask ka wehiht awîyak* (VTA).

misplace *wanastew* (VAI); s/he misplaced it or lost track of it, *wanastacikiw* (VAI); it is misplaced or does not belong, *wanihtin* (VII); s/he is continously misplacing her/him, *wahwanahew* (VTA).

misplay *wanimetawew* (NI).

mispronounce *ekâ kwayask ka wihtamihk* (VTI); pronounce incorrectly, *wanipîkiskwewin* (NI).

misquote *wanowewin* (NI).

misread *ka wanâyamihcikehk* (VAI).

misrepresent *ekâ kwayask ka nepawestamaht awîyak* (VTA); represent falsely, *wanitapapiw* (VAI).

misrule *ka waniwihtamâkehk* (VAI).

miss S/he misses her/him or longs for her/him, *kwetaweyimew* (VTA); s/he misses her/him by arriving too late, *mwesiskawew* (VTA); s/he misses her/him by firing too late, *mwestawew* (VTA); s/he arrives too late to eat, *mwestamew* (VTA); s/he misses her/him when trying to catch her/him, *mwestinew* (VTA); s/he misses her/his road or trail, *patahamew* (VTA); s/he makes her/him miss her/his target, *patahikehew* (VTA); s/he misses her/his target, *patahikew* (VAI); s/he misses her/him, i.e.: with an arrow or gun, *patahwew* (VAI); s/he misses grabbing it with her/his teeth, *patamew* (VAI); s/he makes her/him miss her/his chair, *patapehew* (VTA); the act of missing one's chair, *patapiwin* (NI); s/he misses her/

his chair, *patapiw* (VAI); s/he misses singing the right pitch, *patatâmiw* (VAI); s/he misses catching it, i.e.: a ball, *patinew* (VAI); s/he misses her/him, i.e.: either a planned or unplanned encounter, *patiskawew* (VTA).

misshape *pîmâw* (VII).

misshapen *kîkway ka mayikihk* (VAI).

missing *ka namatakohk kîkway* (VTI); *namatakiw* (VAI).

mission *awasisak ka kanaweyimihtwaw etah ayamihewikamikohk* (NI); a church, *ayamihewikamik* (NI).

missionary *ayamihewiyiniw ka papâmohtet* (VAI); one who performs a religious duty, *ayamihewâtoskewin* (NI).

misspeak *ka wanâtamohk* (VTI).

misspell *ka wanasinahikehk* (VAI).

misspend *wanimestinkewin* (NI).

misspoke *awîyak kakeh wanipîkiskwet* (VAI).

misspoken *wanipîkiskwewin* (NI).

misstatement *wanowewin* (NI).

misstep *mâyitahkoskewin* (NI); *mâyitahkoskew* (VAI); s/he stumbled making a bad step, *mâyitahkoskew* (VAI).

mist *kaskawahkamin* (NI) *(Northern)*; *iyikopiwan* (NI) *(Plains)*.

mistakable *ka nihtâ waninamihk* (VTI).

mistake Taking something by mistake, *wanotinikewin* (NI); the act of mistaken, *cîsihowin* (NI); s/he mistakes her/him for someone else, *waninawew* (VTA); s/he does the wrong thing, i.e.: a mistake, *wanitôtam* (VTI); the act of doing the wrong thing, i.e.: a mistake, *wanitôtamowin* (NI); s/he makes a mistake, *waniyiw* (VAI).

mistaken *kakeh wanotinmihk* (VTI); *wanotinam* (VTI).

mistakenly *pisci kotinamihk* (VTI).

mistreat *ekâ kwayask awîyak kapaminiht* (VTA); *kitimahew* (VAI).

mistrust *awîyak ekâ ka mamsehk* (VTA); *atâmeyimew* (VAI).

misty *kaskawahkami* (NI); *pîkiseyâw* (VII); it is misty or moist, *kaskawacamiw* (VII); there is a misty rain, *kuskawunipestâw* (VII).

misunderstand *ka waninisitohtamihk* (VTI); *waninisitohtam* (VTI).

misunderstanding *wanisitohtamowin* (NI).

misunderstood *kakeh waninisitohtamihk* (VTI).

misuse *ka wanapacitahk* (VAI); *misiwanâcitâw* (VII).

mitt Glove, *astis* (NA).

mitten Something for the hands, i.e.: a pair of mittens (modern term), *astisak* (NA); mittens, *wihkwestisak* (NA).

mix S/he mixes them or blends them with something else, *kîyikawisimew* (VAI); it mixes wells or it fits

into, *kikihtin* (VII); s/he mixes them with something else, *kikinew* (VAI); s/he mixes or blends them together, *kîyikawahew* (VAI); s/he mixes or blends together, *kîyikawinew* (VAI) *(Plains)*; everything comes together by itself or everything mixes together, *mawasakopayow* (NI); s/he mixes them up, *mawasakwahwew* (VAI).

mixed The act of mixing, *itehikewin* (NI); it is all mixed up, *kikawepayiw* (VAI); things are very busy, *ayapahkamikan* (VII); something mixed with something else, *kîyikawi* (IPC); something mixed in the water with something else, *kikakohtin* (VAI); something mixed, *kîyikawi* (IPC).

mixture *kîkway ketehamihk* (VTI); the result of mixing, *mâmawinikan* (VII).

mix-up The act of mixing everything up, *wanipayihcikewin* (NI).

moan The act of moaning with pain, *mahpinewin* (NI); s/he moans with pain, *mahpinew* (VAI).

mob *macâyiseyinowak ka mâmawintotwâw* (VAI); a "mob"—spoken derogatively, *micetiwak* (NA).

mobile *sehki ka pimpayik* (VTI); it is moving or movable, *waskawîmakan*.

mobility *sehki pimpayowin* (NI).

moccasin A moose hide shoe, *pahkekinweskisin* (NI); a moccasin, *maskisin* (NI); a wooden moccasin, a shoe or boot, *mistikwaskisin* (NI).

moccasin flower A beaded flower on a moccasin, *pahkekinweskisin nîpihkan* (NI) *(Modern Cree)*.

mock *ka ayisinâkehk* (VAI).

mockery *ayisinâkewin* (NI).

mocking *awîyak ka ayisinâket* (VAI).

model *ka naspisihtâhk* (VAI); *naspisihcikewin* (NI); *tapisehtawin* (NI); model, pattern, *ayisicikan* (VII); s/he mimics others, *ayisitohtawew* (VAI).

modelling or **modeling** *ka wapahtehiwehk ayiwinsah* (VTI).

moderate *nawâc poko peyahtik* (IPC); it is temperate, *kîsowâw* (VII).

moderation *namoya metoni sohki* (IPC).

modest *ekâ kwanta ayîwak kesayahk* (VAI).

modesty S/he is shy, *nepewisiw* (VAI); *nîpewisiw* (VAI).

modification *ka ahtsihcikehk* (VAI).

modify *kîkway ka ahtsihtahk* (VAI); changing the form of, *ahcisihtawin* (NI).

modular *nîkinikan* (VII).

modulate *ka nîkinamihk* (VTI).

modulation *nîkinkewin* (NI).

Mohawk *petos nehiyaw* (NA).

Mohican *mahihkan nehiyawak* (NA).

moist *ka ahkostihk kîkway* (VAI); *miyamawâw* (VII); s/he or it is moist, *miyimawisiw* (VAI) *(Plains)*; *miyamawisiw* (VAI) *(Northern)*; being moist,

363

miyimawisiw (NI) *(Plains)*; *miyamawisiwin* (NI) *(Northern)*.

moisten *kîkway ka ahkostatahk* (VAI); *miyamawina* (VII).

moisture *ka akosipiyak* (VAI); *kamiyamawâk* (VII).

molar *mepitah ka sikwahcikâkehk* (NI).

mold S/he molds her/him the way s/he wants, *oyiskowakinew* (VAI).

mole *ka ohpikihk kîkway masakahk* (NA).

molehill *asiskîy ka cahkastahk* (LN).

mollify *ka nîkinamihk kesîwasiwin* (NI).

molt S/he is molting, i.e.: a duck, *paskow* (VAI); the act of molting or shedding of plumage or feathers, *paskowin* (NI).

molten *ka tihkâpiskisamihk pîwâpisk* (VTI).

mom *komâmâhk* (NA); *kokâwîhk* (NA).

moment *aciyawes poko* (IPC); *kanakes* (IPC); at the moment itself, right now, right then, *mwehci* (IPC); a moment, short time, *aciyâw* (IPC); a moment, *kanak* (IPC); *nômanak* (IPC); *nomihpiko* (IPC); a short moment or wait a minute!, *nomes* (IPC).

momentarily *metoni kîskâw* (IPC); a moment, wait a second, *ceskwa pita* (IPC).

momentary Just, *ketisk* (IPC); a little while, *kîskâw* (VII).

momentous *mistahi ka itahkamkahk* (VII).

Monday *ka poni ayamihewkîsikak* (NI); *peyak kîsikâw* (VII); it is Monday, *poni ayamihewikîsikaw* (VII); *nistamkîsikâw* (VII).

monotonous Something that becomes monotonous, *ka kihtimeyihtakwahk kîkway* (VII); it is always the same, *osam tahki peyakwan* (IPC); it becomes monotonous, *saskateyihtakwan* (VII); the activity is monotonous, *tepahkamikan* (NI); it is considered monotonous or they have had enough of it, *tepeyihtâkwan* (VII); it gets tiresome, *saskateyihtakwan* (VII).

monotony *kihtimeyihcikewin* (NI).

monster *maci pisiskiw* (NI); *kostâcinakos* (NI).

monstrous *ka misteyimohk* (VTI); s/he looks frightful, *kostâsinâkosiw* (VAI).

month Or the sun, *pîsim* (NA); this month, *awa pîsim* (NA); middle of the month, *ehâpihtaw akimiht pîsim* (IPC); beginning of the month, *emâtakimiht pîsim* (VTA); the end of the month, *emestakimiht pîsim* (VTA); last month, *awa otâhk pîsim* (IPC) *(Northern)*; *awa nâway pîsim* (IPC) *(Plains)*; used when inquiring about a baby's age, "how many months old?", *tân'tahto pîsimwew* (VTA).

monthly *tahtopîsim* (NI).

monumental *kiskisohiwewin* (NI).

mood *tansi ka itamahcihohk* (VAI); *isâyâwin* (VII).

moody *pahpetos itamahcihiwin* (NI); *kâmwâtisiw* (VAI).

moon *tipiskâw pîsim* (NA); the moon sets, *pakisimow* (VAI); there is part moon/sun, an eclipse, or just a quarter moon, *pahkwesiw pîsim* (VAI); there is full moon, *kesâpiskisiw* (VAI); it is a new moon, *oskakocin* (VAI); the moon is coming up, *petâstew* (VAI).

moonbeam *pîsim wasisowin* (NI); a light from the moon, *nîpâyâstew* (VAI).

moonlight There is moonlight, *nîpâyâstew* (VAI).

moonlit *ka nîpâwâseyastek* (VII); *nîpâwâsaskotenikewin* (NI).

moonstruck *kakemôc akâwâtiht awîyak* (VTA).

moony Beside oneself with envy, *akâwâteyihtamowin* (NI).

moorage *etah ka mani kapahk* (LN).

mooring *etah ka tahkopitamihk osih* (VTI); a boat stopping place, *kapâwin* (VAI).

moose *môswa* (NA); bull moose, *yâpew* (NA); a big bull moose, *mistiyâpew* (NA); a one-year-old bull, *yikihcawases* (NA); a two-year-old bull, *waskewceses* (NA); a three-year-old bull, *okinomwacayeses* (NA); a four-year-old bull, *oskoweskwamotayew* (NA); a five-year-old bull, *weskwamotayew* (NA); a six-year-old and older bull, *mistakwanakotew* (NA); a female moose, *onîcaniwmôswa* (NA); a mother moose with one calf, *nôses* (NA); a mother moose with two calves, *onîswaskomew* (NA); a dry cow, i.e.: used when referring to a female moose, *onîcaniw* (NA); a young moose or baby moose, *oskâyis* (NA).

mooseberry Or a high bush cranberry, *môsômino* (NI).

moose bird *môsopiwayisîs* (NA) *(Northern)*; *mosopiyesîs* (NA) *(Plains)*.

moosehide *môswekin* (NI).

moosemilk *môsotohtosapoy* (NI); metaphor for bootleg liquor, *îtakamascikan* (NI).

moose nose *oskowan* (NI); *môsoskowan* (NI) *(Plains)*.

mope *ka pomehk* (VAI).

mopish *pomewisâyâwin* (NI).

moral A person with a good reputation, *miyowihowin ka ayâhk* (NI); *miyowâtisiwin* (NI); her/his face reflects a moral purity, *miyohkwew* (VAI).

morale *kwayask ka mâmitoneyihtamihk* (VTI); a moral or mental condition as in regards to courage or confidence, *maskawâtisiwin* (NI).

morality *kwayask isi waskawewin* (NI); quality of being moral, *kwayaskâtisiwin* (NI).

moralize *kwayask kîkway ka mâmiskôtamâkehk* (VAI).

morally Moral thinking, *katawah kaisi mâmitoneyihtamihk* (VTI); s/he is morally upright, *miyohtwâw* (VAI); being morally upright, *miyohtwâwin* (NI).

morbid *ka kîskwehk*; *mayimacihow* (VAI).

morbidity *mâmitoneyihcikan ekâ kwayask kastek* (NI).

more *ayiwâk* (IPC) *(Plains)*; *ayiwâk ohci* (IPC) *(Northern)*; some more, also, and, again, *mîna* (IPC); more than, *ayiwâkeyikohk* (IPC); a little more, *ayiwâkes* (IPC); still more, *keyapic* (IPC); for more, much more, some more, *ayiwâkohcih* (IPC); more than necessary, *awaseyikohk* (IPC); a tiny bit more, a touch more, *ayiwâkesis* (IPC); s/he chops it or her/him longer than necessary, *ayiwâkahwew* (VTA); s/he overcharges her/him, *ayiwâkakihcikew* (VTA); s/he accuses her/him of more than is just, *ayiwâkimew* (VTA); s/he gives her/him more than is needed, *ayiwâkimiyew* (VTA); s/he has some left over, more than is required, *ayiwâkipayihew* (VAI); s/he drinks more than is needed, *ayiwâkipew* (VAI); s/he cuts it or her/him more than is necessary, e.g.: moose, *ayiwâkisâwâtew* (VTA); s/he says more about her/him than she should, *ayiwâkimew* (VTA); s/he favors her/him more, *ayiwâkeyimew* (VTA); s/he is taller than her/him, *ayiwâkiskawew* (VTA); surpassing or harder worker, *ayiwâkispihtisiw* (VAI); s/he has an excessive character, *ayiwâkâtisiw* (VAI); exceeding quality, *ayiwâkan* (VAI).

moron A stupid person, *kakepâtis* (NA).

morning In the morning or tomorrow morning, *kîkisepâ* (NI); this past morning, *kîkisep* (NI); it feels like early morning, *kîkisepâyâw* (VII); it is morning, *wâpan* (VII).

morning star *wâpanacahkos* (NA).

morose *ekâ tapwe ka otôtemihk* (VTA).

morrow *kîhtwam kesikaw*; *wâpahki* (NI).

morsel *peyak saskamowin miciwin* (NI).

mortal *kîkway ka nipahikohk* (NI); *nipahiwewin* (NI).

mortality *nipowin ka mâmiskôtamihk* (VTI).

mortally *ka kesahpinatiht awîyak* (VTA); *nipahaw* (VTA).

mortification *ka nepewihiwehk* (VAI).

mortify *awîyak ka nepewihiht* (VTA); *kwâyakeyihtam* (VTI); s/he humilates someone, *nâpewihew* (VTA).

mosquito *sâkimes* (NA); *sakimew* (NA); there are lots of mosquitos, *sâkimeskâw* (VII).

moss Ground moss, *astâskamkwa* (NI); muskeg moss, i.e.: used in diapers, *askiya* (NI); ceremonial moss, i.e.: sweetgrass, *wihkimâsikan* (NI).

mossy *ka astâskamkwahcak* (VII).

most *nâspic* (IPC); more, *ayîwak* (IPC); part of, *pahki* (IPV); the most or above all, *mâmawiyask* (IPC); mostly, *mâwaci* (IPV).

mostly *ayiwâkes* (IPC); *kekâc kahkiyaw* (IPC).

moth *môhtew* (NA); a thunderbird louse, *pehesew tihkom* (NA).

mother *okâwîmâw* (NA); *omâmâwaw* (NA); my mother, *nikâwiy* (NA); *nimâmâ* (NA); someone's mother, *awîyak okâwîmâh* (NA); *awîyak omâmâwah* (NA); she has a mother, *okâwîm* (VAI); *omâmâw* (VAI); s/he has her as a mother, *okâwîmew* (VTA); *omâmâmew* (VTA).

motherhood *ka ocawâsimisihk* (VAI); *komâmâwiwihk* (VAI).

mother-in-law Or paternal aunt, *osikosimâw* (NA); my mother-in-law (or aunt), *nisikos* (NA); s/he has a mother-in-law, *osikosiw* (VAI).

motherly *nâspic kisewâtsowin* (NI).

motion *waskawîwin* (NI).

motionless *ekâ kawaskawehk* (VAI).

motivate *ka yîyihtasohk* (VAI).

motivation *îyiyihewewin* (NI); *îyiyihtasowin* (NI).

motivational *ka îyihtasomakahk* (VAI).

mottle *nanâtohk ka isi sopekahamihk kîkway*; *mâmâsinastew* (VAI); *mâmâsinasow* (VAI); marked with different colors, *nanâtohkwasinastew* (VAI).

mould *or* **mold** S/he molds her/him, *oyiskowakinew* (VTA); it is mouldy, *akwâkohtin* (VII).

moulder *or* **molder** Or a potter, *otoyiskowakinikew* (NA) *(Northern)*; *owîceskoyakinikew* (NA) *(Plains)*.

moulding *or* **molding** *ka tetipewi cîpinasihk masinipayiwin* (NI).

mouldy *or* **moldy** *kîkway ka akwâkohtik* (VII).

moult *or* **molt** *sîsîp ka paskot* (VAI); the act of growing new feathers, *paskowin* (NI).

mound *piskwatastew* (NI).

mount *ka tehtapihk mistatim* (VTA).

mountain *waciy* (NI); it is a steep, rugged mountain, *câkâmatinâw* (NI); there is a mountain, *wacîwiw* (VII); a rough, rugged hill, *mâyatinâw* (NI); a bare mountain, *paswaciy* (NI).

mountain ash Also used by Northern Cree for red willow from which kinnikinik is made, *maskominânâhtik* (NA) *(Plains)*; *waciwahtik* (NA) *(Northern)*; *kamihkwaciwasot* (NA).

mountain goat *asiniwaciwacihkos* (NA) *(Northern)*; *pikiwayastak* (NA) *(Plains)*.

mountain lion *asiniwacew* (NA); *mistahkesiw* (NA).

mountainous *ka' ayapatnak asiniwaoo* (VAI).

mountaintop *metoni tahkohtâmatin* (VII).

mounted *ka tapihtahk mistatim* (VTA).

mounting *kîkway ka tapihcikakehk* (VTA).

mourn *kaskeyihtamowin* (NI); *mawihkasowewin* (NI); *wesakitehewin* (NI).

mourner *awîyak kakike kakaskeyihtahk* (VAI).

mournful *awîyak ka nihtâ kaskeyiktahk* (VAI); *pekiskateyihtâkwan* (NI).

mourning *kaskeyimowewin* (NI); *wesakitehewin* (NI); *kwâtakimowin* (NI).

365

mouse *âpakosîs* (NA).

mouser *onôcâpakosîsiwew* (NA).

moustache *or* mustache Whiskers, *meyastowâna* (NI).

mouth *mitôn* (NI); s/he has a swollen mouth, *pâkitonew* (VAI); s/he has a dry mouth or s/he has dry lips, *pâstewitonew* (VAI); interior or inside of the mouth, *pihcikonew* (VAI).

mouthed *awîyak kotonit* (VAI).

mouthful Having a mouthful, *ka sakaskinekonewehk* (VTI); one mouthful, *peyakokonewin* (NI); a mouthful, *peyakokonew* (NI).

mouthless *ekâ kakeh pîkiskwestamâsohk* (VAI).

mouthwash *kisipekikonewakan* (NI); s/he had a mouth wash, *kisipekikonewew* (VAI).

mouthy *awîyak ka pîkiskweskit* (VAI).

movability *kîkway ka nihtâwaskawimakahk* (VAI).

movable *âhtascikan* (VII).

move S/he moves, *waskawiw* (VAI); the thing is moved to another place, *âhtastew* (VAI); move to sit in a different location, *âhtapiw* (VAI); s/he moves against something or someone or s/he bumps against something or someone, *akopayihiw* (VTA); the act of moving to a different place, *ahcipicowin* (NI); s/he moves all over the place, i.e.: her/his home, *papâmipiciw* (VAI); the act of moving all over the place, i.e.: a home, *papâmipiciwin* (NI); s/he moves her/his belongings a little at a time, *picitwâw* (VAI) *(Northern)*; *piciwak* (VAI) *(Plains)*; the act of moving one's belongings a little at a time, *picitwâwin* (NI); s/he moves and makes her/his home elsewhere, *piciw* (VAI); the act of moving one's home to a new area or the act of relocating, *picitwâwin* (NI) *(Northern)*; *picîwin* (NI) *(Plains)*; s/he is in the process of moving, *pimipiciw* (VAI); the act of being in the process of moving, *pimipiciwin* (NI); the water moves, *waskawâkamipayiw* (VII); s/he able to move or bend it into a circle, *waskiwâkinam* (VTI); s/he makes her/him move herself/himself, *waskawîhew* (VTA); s/he makes her/him or them move, *waskawinew* (VTA); s/he makes her/him move by shaking her/him, *waskawipayihew* (VTA); it moves, *waskawipayiw* (VII); s/he moves her/him by shaking her/him, *waskawipitew* (VTA).

movement *waskawêwin* (NI); someone undergoing action or becoming, *waskawepayiw* (NI); something undergoing action, *waskapayin* (VII).

moving *ahcipicowin* (NI); passing by, *pimipayow* (VTI); *pimipayin* (VTI).

mow *ka manaskosowehk*; *manisikew* (VAI).

much Or lots of, *mistahi* (IPC); a little too much, a little too..., *wawiyak* (IPC); too, too much, *osâm* (IPC); too much, *osâm mistahi* (IPC); as much...as,

ekoyikok...eyikok (IPC); as much as possible, *espihci* (IPC).

muck Sticky mud, *pasakoceskowakâw* (NI); it is sticky mud, i.e.: on a mucky road, *micimoskowakâw* (VII).

mucus *mîyîy* (NI).

mud *asiskîy* (NI); when wet ground turns to mud, *asiskîy ka sapopek* (VII); there is mud, sticky clay, *pasakoskowakâw* (VII); there is mud, *asiskîwiw* (VII); it is soft mud, *yoskiskowakâw* (VII).

muddle *ka nanâtohkwascikehk* (VAI).

muddler *onanâtohkwascikew* (NA).

muddy When something is full of mud, *ka asiskîwik kîkway* (VTI); it is muddy, *asiskiwiw* (VII); being muddy, *asiskîwiwin* (NI); it is gummy, gluey mud, i.e.: on a road, *pasakoceskowakâw* (VII); it is muddy, i.e.: a field, *pasakoskowakâw* (VII).

mud hen *cakek* (NA).

muffle *ka wekinamihk kîkway osâm kakisewek* (VII).

mulch *kîkway ka âhkoscikakehk* (VAI).

mule Or a donkey, an ass, *sôsôwatim* (NA); s/he is an ass or mule, *sôsôwatimowiw* (VAI).

mule deer *cimâyos âpiscimôsos* (NA).

mulish *awîyak ka sasepihtahk* (VAI).

mull *kantawi mâmitoneyihtamihk kîkway* (VTI).

multicolored It is multicolored, *nanâtohkonâkwan* (VII).

multitude There is a huge crowd, *misahci mihcetinanowan* (NI).

multiple *ka mihcetweyakimakahk kîkway* (VII).

multiplication *mâmawi akihcikewin* (NI); the act of multiplying, *mihcetowakihcikewin* (NI).

multiplicity *ka mâmawi akihcikehk* (VAI).

multiply *ka mâmawi akihtâmihk* (VTI); s/he multiplies something, *mihcetohtâw* (VAI).

mum *kipitonew* (VAI).

mumble *namoya nistohtâkosiw* (VAI).

mumbling *papehtâkopayiw* (VAI).

mummy *kayâs onipiw* (NI).

munch *miciw* (VTI).

munificent *ekâ ka manamekihk kîkway* (VTI).

murder The act of murdering someone, *nipahtâkewin* (NI); s/he murders someone, *nipahtâkew* (VAI); s/he murders people, *nipahiwew* (VTA); a murderer, *onipahtakew* (NA).

murky Something you can not see through, *ekâ kakihkânâkwahk* (VII); s/he makes the water murky by walking in it, *pekâkaminam* (VTI); s/he makes the water murky by swimming in it, *pekâkamihtaw* (VAI); it is murky water, *pîkâkamiw* (VII).

murmur *kwanta itâtamowin* (NI); *pehtâkosisiw* (NI).

muscle *micistatayâpiy* (NI) *(Northern)*; *omakohkew* (NI) *(Plains)*.

muscular *ka sohkâpewihk* (VAI); a muscular or strong person, *omaskawisiwiyiniw* (NI) *(Plains)*; *sohkâpew* (NI) *(Northern)*; s/he is a muscular or strong person, *sohkâpewiw* (VAI) *(Northern)*; *maskawisiwiyiniwiw* (VAI) *(Plains)*.

mushroom "A frog sucker," *ayîkinônâcikan* (NA); "bullfrog food," *pîkwatehtewmiciwin* (NI).

mushy *kîkway ka pasakwak* (VII).

music Making music or playing an instrument, *kitohcikewin* (NI); s/he makes music, *kitohcikew* (VAI).

musical It sounds like music, *kitohcikewitâkwan* (NI); *ka miweyihtamihk kitohcekewin* (NI).

musician *okitohcekeweyinow* (NA); a person who plays music, i.e.: on a stereo or instrument, *okitocikew* (NA); a person who plays music, *kitohcikeweniw* (NA).

musk Glans that produce musk, *amiskowesinâw* (NI).

muskeg *maskek* (NI); there is muskeg, *maskekowiw* (NI); it is a muskeg, *maskekowan* (VII).

muskeg spruce *maskêkosihta* (NA); *maskekwâsihta* (NA).

muskeg tea A leaf that grows in the muskeg, herbal tea (medicinal), *maskekopak* (NI).

musket *ka mosci pihtâsohk pâskisikan* (NI); *maskohcikwan* (NI) *(slang)*.

muskrat A muskrat in water, *wacask* (NA); a muskrat on dry ground, *pâhkwacask* (NA); a muskrat skin, *wacaskwayân* (NI); a muskrat hole, *wacaskowâtih* (NA).

musky *ka wesinâwmakosihk* (VAI).

muss *iyipâtascekewin* (NI); *yipâcitâw* (NI).

mussy *ka iyipâtascekehk* (VAI).

must *kîkway kehcina takehtôtamihk* (VTI).

mustang A wild horse, *pakwatastim* (NA).

mustard *maskihkiw akohpison awâsisimeyis kîsiyihkatek* (NI); *ako pisowin* (NI); a mustard plaster, *kotawahkân* (NI).

muster *ka mâwasakonikehk* (VAI).

musty *ka akohtenowakahk kîkway* (VII); *akwâkohtin* (VAI).

mutability *ka nihtâ kweskîsayahk* (VII).

mutable *kweskîsayawin* (NI).

mute Not being able to talk, *ekâ kakehpîkiskwehk* (VAI); a slang word for someone who is unable to talk, i.e.: a mute, *kipocihkân* (NA); *kipoc* (abbreviation) (NA).

mutilate *metoni ka yawastahk kîkway* (VTI); s/he cut some off, *pahkwepitew* (VAI).

mutilation *metoni yawatahikewin* (NI).

mutter *kîmôc pekiskwewin* (NI); *kîmôcipîkiskwew* (VAI); *kimwew* (VAI).

mutton Sheep meat, *mâyatihkowiyâs* (NI).

mutual *metoni nahiskatowin* (NI).

mutuality *awîyak miyoteh ka isihciket* (VAI).

muzzle *paskisikanihk etah kohwayawekotek môsisinîy* (NI).

my *kîkway ka tipiyihtamihk* (VTI).

myself *neya poko* (PR); *niyatipiyawiy* (PR).

mysterious *ka âyimahk nistohtâkewin* (NI).

mystery *mâmaskâc kîkway* (IPC).

mystic *awîyak ka mamâhtâwsit* (VAI); *kapekîskwatat manitowa* (NA); believing in mystery or mysticism, *mâmaskâtamowin* (NI).

mystical *mamâhtâwisiwin* (NI).

mysticism *mamâhtâw isowin* (NI).

mystification *mamâhtawehiwewin* (NI).

mystify *awîyak ka mamâhtâw apimohiht* (VTA); bewildering someone, *wâneyihtamohiwewin* (NI).

mystique *omamâhtâwsiw* (NA).

367

N

nab *otiniwiwen; otihtinew.*

nag An aged horse, *kiseyinewatim* (NA).

nail *sakahikan* (NI); a finger nail, *maskasiy* (NA); s/he is nailed onto something, *cestahaskwâsiw* (VAI); s/he speared her/him onto something, *cestahaskwâtew* (VTA); s/he is nailed shut, *kipihtakahikâsiw* (VTA); it is nailed shut, *kipihtakahikâtew* (VII); s/he nails her/him shut, *kipihtakawew* (VTA); a slender, pointed piece of steel, *sakahikan* (NI).

naive *ka kepâtisewâyâwin* (NI).

naked Being nude, *môstâpekasewin* (NI); s/he is naked, *moseskatew* (VAI); s/he makes her/him naked, *moseskatenew* (VTA); nakedness, *moseskatewin* (NI).

name *wihowin* (NI); your name, *kiwihowin* (VAI); s/he is mentioned by name, *wihcikâsiw* (VAI); it is mentioned by name, *wihcikâtew* (VII); s/he names her/him or s/he calls her/him by name, *wihew* (VTA).

nap *kakîsikâwihkwamsihk* (VAI).

nape The back of the neck, *otahk ohci mikwayaw* (NI); *otahk mikwayaw* (NI).

narrate The telling of something, *ka âtiwehtamihk kîkway* (VAI).

narrow Something narrow, *kîkway ka sâkawâsik* (NI); it is narrow, *sâkawâsin* (VAI); it is a narrow or slender piece of metal, *sâkawâpiskisiw* (VII); it is a narrow or slender piece of wood, *sâkawâskwan* (VAI); it is narrow or slender, *sâkawâw* (VAI).

nasal *kîkway mekot ohci* (NI); *miskowan* (NI); the nose, *mikot* (NI) *(Plains)*; *paswâkan* (NI) *(Northern)*.

nasty *metoni mâyekîkway* (IPC).

natal *nihtâwkowin* (NI); *nehtâwikowin* (NI).

natality *kôcawâsimsihk* (NA).

native *awîyak askehk etah ka ohci ohpikit* (NA).

nativity *manito kakeh nihtâwkit* (NI); *manito nihtâwikowin* (NI).

natural *kisclkîkway* (IPC) or (IPV).

naturally *sehki kîkway ka ispayik* (VII); *piko* (IPC); true enough, of course, naturally, *mânamaka* (IPC).

nature *askehk kîkway ka ohcimakahk.*

naughty *ekâ ka natohtamihk* (VII); evil, *macâtisiw* (VAI).

nausea *pwâkomowin* (NI); *mâyimahcohowin* (NI).

nauseate *ka pwâkomohiwehk* (VAI).

nauseated Getting sick and throwing up, *pwâkomowin* (NI).

nauseous *ka nohte pwâkomohk* (VAI).

navigability *ka nihtâ pimâpoyohk* (VAI).

navigable *sîpîy takeh miyo sâpwâpoyohk.*

navigate Going by boat or canoe, *pîmiskawin* (NI).

navigation *ka papâmiskahk* (VAI).

navigational *ka pîmiskatôtamihk* (VTI).

navigator *awîyak ka papâm pîmiskat* (VAI).

near *cîki* (IPC).

nearby It is not far, *kisôwak* (IPC); in a room, in the area, in a place close by, *cikayihk* (IPC); an ancient Cree way of saying "it is nearby or not that far away", *pîswasin* (VII); s/he is thought to be nearby, *pîsweyihtakosiw* (VAI); it is thought to be nearby, *pîsweyihtakwan* (VII).

nearly Or just about or almost, *kekâc.*

neat Or being clean, *kanâtsowin* (NI); it is clean or neat, *kanâtan* (VII); it is neat or orderly, *nahawâw* (VII); s/he is neat and tidy, *nahâwisiw* (VAI) *(Northern)*; *kanâcihow* (VAI) *(Plains)*.

neatness *kanâtisiwin* (NI).

necessarily *peyisk kîkway ka wehispayik* (VII).

necessary *ohtâw takehispayik kîkway* (VII); *nitaweyitakwan* (VII).

necessitate *ekâ kakeh wemâskamihk* (VTI).

necessity *kîkway kanitaweyihtamihk* (VTI).

neck *mikwayaw* (NI); the neck broke off in a fall, i.e.: a bottle, *kîsiskewhtin* (VII); s/he broke her/his own neck in a fall, *kîskwesin* (VAI).

necklace *kîkway ka tâpiskâkehk* (VAI); beads worn around the neck, *tâpiskâkaniminak* (NA).

need Needing something, *kîkway kanitaweyihtamihk* (VTI); s/he needs, *nitaweyitam* (VTI); s/he is in need or short on necessities, *kwetamâw* (VAI).

needful Needing something, *nitaweyihcikewin* (NI).

needle *sâponikan* (NI); a small needle, a sewing needle, *sâponikanis* (NI).

needle point *twahipakan* (NI).

needler *omoscikwâsôw* (NA).

needless *namoya ahkwâc* (IPC).

needlework *moscikwasowin* (NI); doing embroidery work, *masinistahikewin* (NI).

need not *namoya katâc* (IPC).

needs *awîyak ka kwetamat kîkway* (VAI).

needy *kwetamâwin* (NI).

negate *soneyawasenahikan ka nakinamihk* (VII).

negation *nakinikewin* (NI).

negative *ekâ kakehcinahohk* (VAI); *ânwehtamowin* (NI); not expressing the positive, *naspâteyihtamowin* (NI).

neglect *ekâ ka papisiskeyimiht awîyak* (VTA); *wanikiskisitotawew* (VTA).

neglectful *ka wanikiskisitotakehk* (VAI); *namoya pisiskeyimew* (VAI); very careless, *namoyapisiskiyicikew* (VAI).

369

negligence The act of not caring for others, *wanikiskisitotakewin* (NI); the act of carelessness or neglience, *mâyinikeskiwin* (NI).

negligent Someone who neglects things or people, *awîyak ekâ ka pisiskeyehciket* (VAI); s/he has a habit of doing things carelessly or being negligent, *mâyinikeskiw* (VAI).

neigh *ka mistatimowkitohk* (VAI); *mistatim okitowin* (NI).

neither *namoya nikotwâw* (VAI).

nephew *otikwatimâw* (NA); *tehkwatim* (NA) (slang); my nephew (or my stepson), *nicosim* (NA); men say my brother's son, *nitôsim* (NA); *nikosis* (NA); women say my brother's son, *nitikwatim* (NA); men say my sister's son, *nitikwatim* (NA); women say my sister's son, *nitôsim* (NA); someone's nephew, *awîyak otihkwatimah* (NA).

nerve Being courageous, *sohkeyimowin* (NI).

nervous *ekâ ka nahayahk* (VAI).

nest A bird nest, *wacistwan* (NI); s/he makes a nest or s/he is nesting, *wacistwanihkew* (VAI).

nestle *akosimowin* (NI).

nestling *pîwâyisisis* (NA) *(Northern)*; *piyesîsis* (NA) *(Plains)*.

net A gill net, *ayapiy* (NI); s/he makes nets, *ayapihkew* (VAI); s/he visits or checks her/his nets, *nâtayapiw* (VAI); the act of visiting or checking nets, *nâtayapiwin* (NI); s/he sets fishing nets, *pakitahwâw* (VAI); s/he sets fishing nets for her/him, *pakitahwestamawew* (VTA); the act of fishing by setting nets, *pakitahwâwin* (NI).

netting *ayapihkewin* (NI).

nettle *masân* (NA); a bunch of nettles, *masânâk* (NA).

never *mohkâc* (IPC) *(Northern)*; *moywihkâc* (IPC) *(Northern)*; *namawihkâc* (IPC) *(Plains)*; *namoyawihkâc* (IPC) *(Plains)*.

new *oskâyi* (IPV); it is new, *oskâyiwan* (VII).

newborn A newborn human, *ôskawasisis* (NA); a newborn calf, *ôskimoscosisis* (NA).

newcomer *ôskitakosin* (NA).

newly *anohc poko* (IPC) *(Plains)*; *anohc piko* (IPC) *(Northern)*.

news Tidings of recent public events or news, *âcimowin* (NI); bad news, *mâyâcimowin* (NI); good news, *miyowâcimowin* (NI).

New Year's Day Or kissing day, *ocehtokîsikâw* (NI).

next *kîhtwam* (IPC); *kotak* (IPC); repetitive, one after the other, in turn, the next taking the place of the first, etc., *mâmeskoc* (IPC); following, again, *kîhtwam* (IPC); in a room farther way, next room, *awasayik* (IPC).

nibble *kinosew ka nahnome cahkwahcasit kwâskwepicikan.*

nice Something that looks nice, *kîkway kâmiyonakwahk* (VII).

nick *kakwây kacîkahasihk mistik.*

nicotine Tobacco juice that congels around a pipe stem, *pasakwaskican* (NA).

niece *ostimimâw* (NA); my niece (or stepdaughter), *nitanisihkawin* (NA); men say my brother's daughter, *nitôsimiskwem* (NA); women say my brother's daughter, *nistim* (NA); men say my sister's daughter, *nistim* (NA); women say my sister's daughter, *nitôsimiskwem* (NA); someone's niece, *awîyak ostima* (NA).

nigh *ispimihk* (VII).

night It is night, *tipiskâw* (VII); last night or last evening, *otakosihk* (IPC); *otakosik* (IPC); last night, *tipiskohk* (IPC); in the night "place", *tipiskanohk* (IPC); all night, *kapetipisk* (VII); it is a pitch dark night, *kaskitipiskâw* (VII); it is a pleasant night, *miyotipiskâw* (VII); during the night, *nîpâtipisk* (VII); s/he has a meal at night, *tipiskâwimîcisiw* (VAI); a night meal, *tipiskâwimîcisiwin* (NI).

nightfall When it is really dark, *metoni kakesitipiskâk* (VII); it is getting dark, *ati tipiskâw* (VII); when it is dusk, *wâninâkwan* (VII).

nighthawk A night bird, *pîskwa* (NA).

nightlighting *nîpâwâsaskotenikewin* (NI).

nightlong *kapetipisk* (VII); the whole night, all night long, *kapetipisk* (VII).

nightly *tahtotipiskâw* (VII).

nightmare *kîskwehkwasiwin* (NI).

nighttime *or* **night-time** *kâmekwâtipiskâk* (VII); it is nighttime right now, *mekwâtipiskâw* (VII).

nil *namakîkway* (IPC).

nimble *tastap waskawewin* (NI).

nine *kîkâmitâtaht* (IPC); *kekâymitâht* (IPC) *(Plains)*; nine each, *kahkîkâmitatahtwâw* (IPC); nine times, *kîkâmitatahtwâw* (IPC); nine of a kind, *kîkâmitâtahtwayih*; nine different kinds, *kahkîkâmitâtahtwayih*; in nine places or nine directions, *kîkâmitâtahtwayak*; in nine different places, *kahkîkâmitâtahtwayak*; s/he is number nine or ninth, *kîkâmitâtahtowiw* (VAI).

nine hundred *kîkâmitâtahtwâw mitâtahtomitanaw* (IPC).

nineteen *kîkâmitâtahtosâp* (IPC); nineteen times, *kîkâmitahtatosâpâw* (IPC).

nineteenth *mwecikîkâmitahtatosâp* (IPC); nineteenth time, *kîkâmitahtatosâpâw* (IPC); nineteenth of the month, *kîkâmitahtatosâp akimâw pîsim.*

nintieth *mwecikîkâmitâtahtomitanaw* (IPC); nintieth time, *kîkâmitâtahtomitanawâw* (IPC).

ninety *kîkâmitâtahtomitanaw* (IPC); ninety times, *kîkâmitâtahtomitanawâw* (IPC).

ninth *mwecikîkâmitâtaht* (IPC); ninth time, *kîkâmitâtahtwâw* (IPC); ninth of the month, *kîkâmitâtaht akimâw pîsim.*

nip *kakotciscasihk minihkwewin* (NI).

nipple An artificial nipple or soother, *ococôsimihkânis* (NI); the sucking thing or baby bottle, *nônâcikan* (NI); breast nipple, *micohcôsimis* (NA); *micohcôsimihkânis* (NA).

nit *cîkinâhk* (NA).

no *namoya* (IPC); but no! disappointment, *maka ekâ* (IPC); *makekâ* (IPC).

nobody *namâwîyak* (IPC).

nod The act of nodding, *nânâmiskweyowin* (NI); s/he nods her/his head, *nânâmiskweyiw* (VAI).

nodding *nânâmiskwestâkewin* (NI).

noel Christmas time, *nîpâyamihâwin* (NI).

noise The act of making a loud noise, *kisewehtâwin* (NI); having a loud noisy voice, *kisewehtâkosiw* (VAI); the act of making a muffled noise, *kîyakihtâwin* (NI); s/he makes a muffled noise, *kîyakinam* (VTI).

noiseless *ekâ ka kisewehtâhk* (VII).

noisy S/he is noisy, *pitihkohtaw* (VAI).

nonchalance *namakîkway mawineskâkewin* (NI).

nonchalant *ekâ kanihta mawineskamihk* (VTA).

none *namâkîkway* (IPC) *(Plains); namoya kîkway* (IPC) *(Northern).*

nonsense *môcowesâyâwin* (NI).

nook *wehkwehcakasihk* (NI).

noon It is noon, *âpihtâkîsikâw* (VII); this noon, next noon, at noon, *âpihtâkesikaki* (VII); middle of the day or high noon, *âpihtâkîsikanohk* (VII).

no one or **no-one** *namâwîyak* (DPR).

noose *tâpakowepinkan pemnahkwan* (NI); *tâpakwan* (NI).

no place *namânanitâw* (IPC).

nor *namoya nikotwâw* (IPC); *namâ* (IPC).

norm *mweci ekosi* (IPC).

normal *kwayask kîkway* (IPC), *peyakwan sâyaw* (IPC); but, it's only normal, natural, *mâka* (IPC).

normally *kwayask kwesâyâwnihk* (VAI).

north Up north or in the north, *kewetinohk* (NI); *kîwetinohk* (NI); north or towards north, *kiwetinotâhk* (NI); in the north, *kîwetinohk* (NI).

northbound *kîwetinohk kesîsîpwehtehk* (NI).

northerly Towards north, *kîwetenohk isi* (NI); in a northerly direction, *kiwetinokisin* (VII).

northern Up the northern way, *kîwetinotahk* (NI).

northerner *kîwetinohk ohci* (NI) or (IPC).

northern lights The Cree word means "the ghosts are dancing", *cîpiyak nîmehitowak; kîwetinohk kacakastek*; there are northern lights, i.e.: literally means the deceased are dancing, *cîpayak nîmitowak.*

nose A human nose, *mikot* (NI) *(Plains); paswâkan* (NI) *(Northern)*; an animal nose, *miskowan* (NI); a moose nose, *oskiwan* (NI).

nosebleed Having a nosebleed, *kipistanewin* (NI); s/he has a nosebleed, *kipistaniw* (VAI); s/he gives her/him a nosebleed with her/his hand, *kipistanehew* (VTA).

nosey or **nosy** *awîyak kahkeyaw kîkway ka kakwekiskiyihtahk* (VAI).

nostril *miteyikom* (NA).

not *sôskwâc namoya* (IPC); not usually, not likely, *namoya mwasi* (IPC); not true, it is not true, *ekama* (IPC); not any more, not needed or wanted any more, or changed her/his mind later, *nitawâc* (IPC); not yet, *nameskwa* (IPC); *namoyaceskwa* (IPC).

notch The act of making a notch, *kicikikahikewin* (NI); having a notch, *kicikisiwin* (NI); it has a notch, *kicikâw* (VII); it has a notch made with a knife, *kicikihkotew* (VII); it has a notch, *kicikisiw* (VAI); s/he makes notches with an axe, *kicikikahwew* (VAI); a nick or slot in the edge of something, *kicikihkocikan* (VII).

noted *awîyak ka kiskeyihtâkosit* (VAI).

nothing *namakîkway* (DPR) *(Plains); namoya kîkway* (IPC) *(Northern)*; for no reason, senseless, with no results, for nothing, *kwanta* (IPC).

nothingness *ka namâkîkwawihk* (VAI).

notice Giving an advanced warning of something, *kîkway kakiskeyihtâmohiwehk* (VAI).

noticeable *kîkway ka kihkânâkwahk* (VAI); something perceived, *kihkânâkwan* (NI).

noticeably *ka kihkânâkohtahk kîkway* (VAI).

notify *wehtamakewin* (NI); *kiskeyitâmohaw* (VAI); the act of informing someone, *kiskeyitâmohiwewin* (NI).

notion *ka nohtetôtamihk kîkway* (VTI); *iteyitamowin* (NI).

notoriety *metoni kiskeyihtâkosiwin* (NI); state of being notorious, *kihcehkawisowin* (NI).

notorious *wahyaw isko ka nistaweyihtâkosihk* (VAI), widely but not favorably known, *pimâmeyihtakosowin* (NI).

nourish *ka pimâcihiwehk* (VAI).

nourishment *pimâcihiwewin* (NI).

November The frosty moon or month, *iyikopiwipîsim* (NI).

now *sîmâk* (IPC) *(Northern); semak* (IPC) *(Plains)*; right now, now is the time, let's go, come on, ready, *ekwa* (IPC); right now, a minute ago, *anohc piko* (IPC) *(Northern); anohc poko* (IPC) *(Plains)*; now and then,

371

sometimes, *âskaw* (IPC); an expression meaning "for now" or "for the time being", *nakisk* (IPC).

no way *sôskwâc namoya* (IPC); *namânanitâw* (IPC).

nowhere *namoya nânitâw* (IPC); no place, no where, *namananitaw* (IPC).

nozzle *sopâcikan* (NI).

nude The act of being nude or without clothes, *môstâpekasewin* (NI); s/he is nude or has no clothes on, *môstâpekasew* (VAI).

nudge *ka tôskwahoht awîyak* (VAI).

nudity *môstâpekasewin* (NI).

nuisance *môstâtahkamkisowin* (NI); an annoying person, *pakwatikosow* (VAI).

numb Being numb, *ekâ komosihtawnihk* (VAI); s/he is numb, *kîskimisow* (VAI); her/his hands are numb, *kîskimicihcew* (VAI); her/his feet are numb, *kîskimisitew* (VAI); feeling numb, *kîskimisiwin* (NI); s/he is feeling numb, *kîskimipayiw* (VAI); being numb with cold, *kîskimâskaciwin* (NI); s/he is numb with cold, *kîskimâskaciw* (VAI); her/his feet are numb with cold, *kîskimistewaciw* (VAI).

number *akihtâson* (IPC); counting numbers, *akihtâsowin* (NI).

numberless *ekâ kîkway akihtâson*; too many to number or countless, *osâm mihcetwâksowak*.

number one *peyak ispîhtakihcikewin* (NI).

numbness *kîskimipayowin* (NI).

numerable *takeh akihtâmihk kîkway*.

numeral *akihtâson* (IPC); a symbol denoting numbers, *akihcikewina* (NI).

numerate *kîkway ka akihtâmihk*.

numeration *akihcikewin* (NI).

numerous *okistakewi* (IPC) *(Northern)*; *mihcet* (IPC) *(Plains)*; lots of something, *ka mihcitihk kîkway*

(VAI); there are lots of them, *mihcetinwa* (VII); there are lots of it, *mihcetin* (VTI); too numerous, *osâmeyatow* (VAI); *osâmeyatin* (VII); having a numerous family, *mihcetowin* (NI); s/he has a large family, *mihcetiw* (VAI); they are in the canoe or numerous people are in the canoe, *mihcetohkamwak* (VTA); they are helping one another or numerous people are helping one another, *mihcetohkamâtowak* (VAI); they sleep together or numerous people sleep together, *mihcetohkwâmiwak* (VAI); it is divided into numerous parts, *mihcetweyakan* (VII); s/he divides them into numerous parts or classes, *mihcetweyakihew* (VAI); they are divided in numerous or many different ways, *mihcetweyakisiwak* (VAI); a numerous group of people, *okistakew ayisiyiniwak* (NA); they are numerous, *okistakeweyatowak* (VAI) *(Northern)*; *mihcetiwak* (VAI) *(Plains)*.

nun *ayamihewiskwew* (NA); a holy woman, *ayamihewiskwew* (NA).

nunnery A home for nuns, *ayamihewiskwewkamik* (NI); *ayamihewiskwewak wekiwâw* (NI).

nuptial *ka kihciwekihtohk* (NI); getting married, *wekihtowin* (NI).

nurse Or medicine woman, *maskihkiwiskwew* (NA) *(Northern)*; *maskikiwiskiw* (NA) *(Plains)*.

nursing *mohawasowin* (NI).

nurture *kîkway ka ohpikihtâhk*; rearing or training a child, *opikihâwasiwin* (NI).

nut *pâkân* (NI) *(Northern)*; a nut tree or shrub, *pakânâhtik* (NI).

nutshell *etah ka asowasot pâkân* (NI).

nutty *ka môhcowisâyâhk*.

nuzzle *ka yahkewepahikakehk mikot*.

O

oak tree *mistikominâhtik* (NI).

oar A paddle for rowing, *apiy* (NA).

obduracy *maskâwtehewin* (NI).

obdurate *ka maskâwtehehk* (VII).

obedience *ka nihtâ nahihtamihk* (VII).

obedient *awîyak ka nanahihtahk* (VAI); *nahihtam* (VAI).

obese *awîyak ka mistikamot* (VAI).

obesity *mistikamowin* (NI); *weyinowin* (NI).

obey The act of obedience, *nahihtamowin* (NI); s/he obeys her/his directions without complaint, *nahihtawew* (VTA).

object S/he objects to it, *pimâmeyihtam* (VAI).

objection *ekâ ka tâpwehtamihk kîkway* (VAI); *kipihtinamakewin* (NI).

objective *kîkway ka kocitôtamihk* (VII).

objectivity *kociwin* (NI).

obligate *awîyak ka sihkiskaht kîkway tatotahk* (VAI).

obligation *sihkiskakewin* (NI); *asotamakewin* (NI); the state of being bound to do something, *ka totamihk asotamakewin* (NI).

obligatory *poko tatôtamihk kîkway* (VAI).

oblige *awîyak ka sihkiskaht* (VAI).

obliging *ka nihtâ sihkiskakehk* (VII); s/he is accommodating or courteous, *miyotôtâmakew* (VAI).

obliterate *metoni ka wansihtahk kîkway* (VAI).

oblivion *metoni ka wanikiskisihk* (VII); the state of being forgotten, *wanikiskisoytotâkewin* (NI).

oblivious *ekâ ka nâkatohkehk* (VII).

oblong *kîkway ayiwâk ka kinwak eyikohk ka ayakaskak* (VII); *kinwâw nawâc* (VII); longer than wide, *isikinwak* (VII).

obnoxious *ka macihtwâhk* (VAI).

obsequious *ka peyahtiko isâyâhk* (VAI).

obscure *ekâ kakihkânâkwahk* (VII); *âkawâyaw* (VII); remote, hidden, *kâtanohk* (LN).

obscurity *nawâc poko âkawâyhk* (LN).

observable *kîkway ka nâkatâpahtamihk* (VAI).

observance *nâkatâpahkewin* (NI).

observant *awîyak ka nâkatâpahtahk kîkway* (VAI).

observation *nâkatâpacikewin* (NI).

observational *ka nihtâ nâkatâpahtamihk* (VAI).

observe *ka nawâpahcikewin* (NI); *nâkateyihtam* (VAI); *wapahtam* (VAI).

observing *ka kanawâpahcikehk* (VTI).

obsess *ekâ kakeh wanikiskisihk* (VAI); s/he is obsessed with one thought, *peyakweyihtam* (VAI); s/he is obsessed with her/him, *peyakweyimew* (VTI).

obsession When something gets the best of you, *kîkway ka sâkocihikohk* (VAI); an obsessive thought, *peyakweyitamowin* (NI).

obsessive *kîkway ka sâkocihiwemakahk* (VII).

obstacle *kôtamihikohk kîkway* (VTI).

obstinacy *macistikwânewin* (NI).

obstinate *awîyak ka matstikwânet* (VAI).

obstreperous *ka tepwekehkawtamihk* (VAI).

obstruct *ka kipastahk kîkway* (VTI); s/he is in the way, *kipiskam* (VAI); block so as to prevent passing, *kipastew* (VTI).

obstruction *kipascikewin* (NI).

obstructive *ka nihtâ kipascikehk* (VTI).

obtain Obtaining something, *kakahtinamihk* (VTI); s/he takes it, *otinam* (VAI); s/he obtains or purchases it for her/him, *otinamawew* (VTA).

obtrude *ka mâmaskâtikonikeskihk* (VAI).

obtrusion *mâmaskâtikonikewin* (NI).

obtrusive *ka nihtâ mâmaskâtikonikehk* (VAI).

obtuse Or absurd, *ka kepâtisowin* (NI).

obvious *kîkway ka kihkânakwahk* (VII).

occasion *ka itahkamkahk kîkway* (VII); *ispayiwin* (NI).

occasional *âhâpîhtaw* (IPC); *âskaw* (IPC); *namoya tahki* (IPC).

occasionally *âhâspîhtawiyikohk* (LN).

occupy The act of occupying someone's time with a job, *atoskahewewin* (NI); s/he is busy or occupied, *otamiyiw* (VAI); the act of being busy or occupied, *otamiyowin* (NI).

occur *ka ispayik kîkway* (VII); *ispayow* (VII).

occurrence Something that is happening, *kîkway ketahkamkahk* (VII).

ocean A very large body of water, i.e.: ocean or sea *kihcikamiy* (NA) *(Plains)*; *kicikamiw* (NA) *(Northern)*.

o'clock *tahto tipahikan* (NI); hour, at the clock, o'clock, *tipahikan* (NI); a minute, *tipahikanis* (NI); a second, *tipahikanisis* (NI); a.m., *kikisep* (NI); p.m., *ponapihtakisikak* (NI); before, or minutes before the hour, *nohtaw* (VII); after, *miyaskam* (VAI); minutes after the hour, *ayiwâk* (VII).

October The freeze-up moon or month, *kaskatinowipîsim* (NI).

odd *kîkway ekâ kowicewâkanpayik* (VII).

odds *namoya metoni kehcinâhowin* (NI).

odious *ayiwâkeyimowin* (NI).

odor *or* odour *ka pecimakwahk kîkway* (VTI); *isimakwan* (VII); it has a smell or it has an odor, *isimakosiw* (VAI); *isimakwan* (VII); *isimasow* (VAI); *isimastew* (VAI); it has a strong cooking odor, *kihkâmahtew* (VAI); it has a strong odor, *kihkâmâkwan* (VII); it has a strong odor, i.e.: a peace pipe, *kihkâmâsiw* (VAI); it has a strong smokey odor, *kihkâmâstew* (VAI); s/he has a pleasant smell,

373

miyomakosow (VAI); s/he fills the place with her/his odor, *tepimakosow* (VAI); it fills the place with its odor, *miswetepimakwan* (VII).

of course Only, it has to be that, naturally, *poko* (IPC); true enough, of course, naturally, *mânamaka* (IPC).

off *wâhyawîs keyâpic* (IPC); *patoti* (IPC).

offence *or* **offense** *kisiwâhitowin* (NI).

offend *kisowâhiwewin* (NI).

offender *okisowâhiwew* (NA).

offensive The state of being the attacker, *onotinkew* (NA).

offer Offering something, *kîkway ka mekihk* (VTI); the offering or giving, *mâtinamâkewin* (NI); s/he offers her/him something, *mâtinamawew* (VTA); s/he offers or gives, *mâtinawew* (VTA); the act of offering something, *mâtinawewin* (NI); s/he offers a sacrifice for her/him, *pakitinâsôstamawew* (VTA); s/he offers a sacrifice to her/him, *pakitinâsôstawew* (VTA); s/he offers a sacrifice, *pakitinâsiw* (VAI); the act of offering a sacrifice, *pakitinâsiwin* (NI).

offering *mekowin* (NI); *pakitinikewin* (NI).

often *kahkiyipah* (IPC); *mihcetwâw* (VII); not usually, not commonly, not too often, *namoya mwasi* (IPC).

oftentimes *mihcetwâw* (VII).

oil *pimiy* (NI); a liquid grease, *tominkan pimiy* (NI);

oilskin *awîyak ka tômâsakayet* (VAI); *pimiwekin* (NI).

oily It is an oily liquid, *pimitew* (VTI); it tastes greasy or oily, *pimiwakan* (NI).

ointment An ointment or liniment, *sopekinikan* (NI); a grease or ointment, *tominikan* (NI).

Ojibwa *or* **Ojibway** *ocepwayanew* (NA).

okay *âw* (IPC); okay then, *âw mâka* (IPC); something that goes all right, *kîkway kakwayaskopayik* (VII); saying it is okay about something, *kîyâm* (IPC); it is okay or there is nothing wrong, *namananitaw* (IPC).

old An old thing, *kayâsâyi* (NI); it is old, aged or ancient, *kayâsâyiwiw* (VAI); s/he is old and ancient, *kihtehayiwiw* (VAI); acting old, *kihtehyâtisiwin* (NI); s/he acts old, *kihtehyâtisiw* (VAI); the act of being an old person, *kiseyinewiwin* (NI); s/he thinks of her/him as being an old person, *kiseyinewakeyimew* (VAI); s/he thinks herself/himself as an old person, *kiseyinewakeyimow* (VAI); an old person, *kiseyiniw* (NA); s/he is old but strong, *sipikihkâw* (VAI) *(Plains)*; *sîpikihkâw* (VAI) *(Northern)*.

old age *kihtehayowin* (NI).

olden *kayâsowanwa* (NI); in olden times, in the far away past, in former days, *kayâhte* (IPC); *oye* (IPC); anciently, *kayâseskamik* (LN).

older brother *nistes* (NA); *ostesa* (NA).

older sister *nimis* (NA); *omisa* (NA).

oldish *nawâcpoko ka kiseyinewihk* (VII).

omen A sign prophesying the future, *mosihowin* (NI).

ominous *ka nihtâ sekihtasohk* (VII).

omit *ka micimnamihk kîkway ekâ ka masinahamihk* (VII).

omelette *wawitehkasikan* (NA).

on On top, solidly placed, touching squarely, *tahkôc* (IPC); *tahkohc* (IPC); on the surface, *waskicayik* (LN); on the other side "area", *akamayik* (LN); *kweskâyihk* (LN).

once One time, *peyakwâw* (VII); once each, *pahpeyakwâw* (VII).

one *peyak* (IPC); *piyak* (IPC); one each or one by one, *pahpeyak* (IPC); one time, *peyakwâw* (IPC); of one kind, *peyakwayihk*; each in its own place, *pahpeyakwayak*; in one place, the same area, *peyakwayak*; s/he is number one or first, *peyakow* (VAI); from one to another, *ayâsawi* (IPC); *ayasâwâc* (IPC); s/he is one, alone, *peyakow* (VAI).

one another *kanesihk* (VII).

one day Or Monday, *peyak kîsikâw* (NI).

one-hundred thousand *mitâtahtomitanowâw kihci mitâtahtomitanaw* (IPC).

oneself Thinking only of oneself, *peyakweyimisowin* (NI).

one-sided *aspihiwewin* (NI).

one-time *peyakwâw poko* (IPC).

one-way *peyakwayak isi* (IPC).

onion Or stinking grass, *wihcekaskosiy* (NI); a white onion, *wâpiskaskosiy* (NI).

onlooker *okanawâpahkew* (NA).

onlooking *ka kanawâpahkehk* (VTI).

only *poko*; only that one, or that's the only way, *eyoko poko* (IPC); *ahpônâni* (IPC); if only it was like that; *kîspinesa* (IPC); if only, *piko* (IPC); only, purely; exclusively, continuously, always, *nayistaw* (IPC) *(Northern)*; *neyistaw* (IPC) *(Plains)*; precisely that, *pisisik* (IPC).

onto *katahkohtastahk* (VTI).

onward *semakohtewin* (NI); *atimohtew* (VAI).

ooze *kîkway ka kwâyakocowahk* (VTI); *wayaweciwan* (VTI).

oozy *ka ahkamohcikawik* (VTI).

open Something that has been opened, *ka yohteyak* (VII); s/he opens it, i.e.: a jar, *pâskapowenew* (VTA); s/he opens her/his mouth, *pâskitonew* (VTA); s/he opened her/his mouth wide or s/he yawned, *tâwatiw* (VAI); it has an opening, *tawâw* (VII); s/he opened it or them, *tawinew* (VTA); it opened up, *tawipayiw* (VAI); s/he has an opening, *tawisiw* (VAI); the act of having an opening, *tawisiwin* (NI); it is open, i.e.: a shirt collar, *tôneyâw* (VII); s/he opens up a can with an instrument, *yohtehwew* (VTA); it is open, i.e.: a door, *yohtekotew* (VII); s/he opens up a box with her/his bare hands, *yohtenew* (VTI); s/he pulls them open, *yohtepitew* (VTI) *or* (VTA); s/he opens them, *yohtenew* (VTA); s/he knocks them open, *yohtewepahwew* (VTA); s/he opens it for her/him, *yohtenamawew* (VTA).

opening The act of opening a box, *kîkway ka yohtenamihk* (VTI).

openly Visible, not hidden or covered up, *mosis* (IPC); *mosisiy* (IPC).

openness *ekâ manâtisiwin* (NI).

operate *kîkway ka pimipayihtahk* (VTI); s/he runs it, *pimipayitâw* (VAI); it operates quickly, *kakweyâhomakan* (VII).

operation *pimipayihcikewin* (NI).

operational *kîkway ka pimipayihesomakahk* (VII).

opinion The act of having an opinion, *tansi isimâmitoneyihcikewin* (NI); an opinion, *iteyihtamiwin* (NI); s/he has a correct opinion of her/him, *kwayaskweyimew* (VAI); s/he has a poor opinion of her/him, *kwâtakeyimew* (VTA); people have a low opinion of her/him or s/he is believed to be low, vile, or base character, *tapahteyihtâkosiw* (VAI); people have a low opinion of it or it is believed to be base or vile, *tapahteyihtâkwan* (VII); s/he has a low opinion of her/him, *tapahteyimew* (VTA).

opinionated *ekâ kakeh kweskinamihk mâmitoneyihcikan* (VII).

opponent *nôtinâkan* (NA); a challenger, *omawineskâkew* (NA); someone to fight with, *nôtinitomâkan* (NA).

opportune *ka nahipayik kîkway* (VII); timely, *nahipayiw* (VII).

opportunism *nihtâ kahtinikewin* (NI).

opportunist *awîyak ka nihtâkahtiniket* (VAI).

opportunity A favorable occasion, *kanahipayik* (VII); *nahipayiwin* (NI).

opposable *pîtoteyihcikewin* (NI).

oppose *kîkway ka nôtinamihk* (VTI); *namoya tepeyimow* (VAI).

opposite *pahpîtos kîkway* (VII); in the other room, the opposite place, area, *atâmayik* (LN).

opposition *pîtos mâmitoneyihcikan* (NI).

oppress *awîyak kakwâtakehiht* (VAI).

oppression *kwâtakihiwewin* (NI).

oppressor *okwatakihiwew* (NA).

opt *ka nawasonkehk* (VTI).

optimism *miyo mamitoneyihcikan* (NI).

optimist *awîyak ka miyo akâwâceket* (VAI).

optimistic *miyo akâwâcikewin* (NI).

option *nawasonikewin* (NI).

optional *takeh nawasonamihk kîkway* (VTI).

opulence *osâm wiyotisiwin* (NI).

opulent *metoni ka wiyotisihk* (VII).

or *ahpô* (IPC).

oracle *ka kîskihkemowin* (NI).

oral *namoya masinahikâtek* (VTI); the act of talking, *pekiskwewin* (NI) (*Northern*); *pîkiskwawewin* (NI) (*Plains*).

orally *pîkiskwewenihk* (LN).

orange A fruit, *osâwâs* (NA); it is orange or yellow, *osâwâw* (VII); it is orange or yellow, *osâwisiw* (VAI).

oration *pîkiskwestamâkewin* (NI).

orator *opîkiskwestamâkew* (NA).

oratorical *ka sohkâyamihahk* (VII).

oratory *ka acikipahamihk etah ka ayamihahk* (NI).

ordain *ayamihewinow kosehiht awîyak* (VAI); confer holy orders upon, *ayamihewenihkaht* (VAI).

ordeal *kîkway ka kocetôtamihk* (VTI); *kecinahowin* (NI).

order An order to purchase something, *kanatocikehk* (VAI); s/he orders or sends for it, *natôtam* (VAI); ordering something by mail, *natisahikewin* (NI).

orderly *ôtahkosowah ka nîsohkamawat* (NA); *atoskewiyakan* (NA); it is neat or orderly, *nahâwastew* (VII) (*Plains*).

ordinarily *ka nakaya ispayik kîkway* (VII); usually, *osâmpoko* (IPC).

ordinary *kîkway ekâ kwanta ayiwâk* (VII).

ore *pîwâpisk* (NI).

organ A church instrument, *kitohcikan ayamihekamkohk* (NI); an instrument with pedals, a large musical instrument played by releasing air, *mâmakoskacikan* (NI); an internal organ, *itâmiyaw* (NI).

organist *okitohcikew ayamihewkamkohk* (NA).

organize Putting things in place, *kwayaskascikewin* (NI); that's how s/he places it, *isâstâw* (VAI); s/he organizes an opening dance, *mâcisimowinihkew* (VTA); s/he organizes or arranges things in a box, *oyaskinahtâw* (VAI); s/he organizes or arranges her/him with care, *oyinew* (VTA).

orgiastic *mâmawipesikwatsowin* (NI).

orgy *ka mâmawipesikwatsihk* (VII).

orientate *sakastenohk ka isi ohtiskawascikehk* (VTI).

orientation *ka nahâwisehcikehk* (VTI).

orifice *ka yohteyak kîkway peyakwan metoni* (VII).

origin Where you originated, *tantah kohoohk* (VAI), the origin, *ohcîwin* (NI).

original *ka yahte ohci* (IPC); *nistamoci* (IPC); *kayas ohci* (IPC).

original sin *oskâc pâstâhowin* (NI).

originate *etah ka ohcimakahk kîkway* (VII); *ohcîwin* (NI).

origination *etah ka ohcipayihk* (LN).

ornament *wawisihcikan* (NI); something that beautifies, *sakâskwahon* (NI); *wawisicikan* (NI).

ornamentation *wawesihcikewin* (NI).

ornate *metoni ka wawesihtahk kîkway* (VTI).

375

ornery *macistikwânewin* (NI).

orphan An orphan child, *kewâcawâsis* (NA); an adult orphan, *kewâciyinîs* (NA); s/he is an orphan, *kewâtîsiw* (VAI); s/he is orphaned, *kewâtisiw* (VAI); s/he thinks of her/him as an orphan, *kewâteyimew* (VAI); s/he made an orphan out of her/him, i.e.: a moose calf, *kewâcihew* (VTA); God makes her/him an orphan, *kewâcihikowisiw* (VTA).

ostensible *kîkway ka kihkânâkwahk* (VII).

ostensibly *ka nokohtahk kîkway* (VII).

ostentation *kîkway ka mamihtsewakehk* (VTI).

ostentatious *awîyak kamamihtsiskit* (VAI).

ostracism *meciminowewin* (NI).

ostracize *awîyak ka meciminiht ekâ towecewakanit* (VAI).

other Another, *kotak* (IPC); *kotakak* (IPC); *kotaka* (IPC); one after the other, in turn, or the next taking the place of the first, *mâmeskôc* (IPC); on the other side "area", *akamayihk* (LN); in the other room, the opposite place, area, *kweskâyihk* (LN).

otherwise *pîtos ka eteyihtamihk* (VII); *ahpô etikwe* (IPC).

otter An otter skin, *nikikowayân* (NA).

ouch *mawmowin* (NI).

ounce *peyak kohcipayihcikan* (NI).

our *nîyanân eyoko* (VII).

ours *nîyanân* (VII); us, *kîyânaw* (VII).

ourself *ketisk nîyanân* (VII).

ourselves *nîyanân poko* (VII); *nîyanân tipiyawe* (VII).

oust *ka maskahtwehk* (VTI); *wayawewepin* (VTA).

ouster *omaskahtwew* (NA).

out Or outside, *wayawîtimihk* (LN).

outburst *ka sekotahkamkisihk* (VAI).

outcast *pîkwaciyiniw* (NA); *sipwetsahikan* (NI); s/he treat her/him like an outcast, *ayahteyimew* (VAI).

outcry *tepwewin* (NI).

outdoors In the outdoors, *wayawîtimihk* (LN); on the outside, *wayawîtimâyihk* (LN).

outfit *ka mâwasakwayahk kîkwaya* (NI); *ayowinisa* (NI).

outhouse *misiw kamikos* (NI).

outing *kwanta papamohtewin* (NI); *papampayiw* (VTA).

outline A rough sketch or drawing, *masinipehikewin* (NI); a dark outline in the distance, *nihcikâw* (NI); her/his outline is in the distance, *nihcikisiw* (VAI).

outnumber *ayiwâkeyatowin* (NI).

outpour *ka sekipestâhk* (VTI).

outpouring *ka mekwâ sekipestâhk* (VTI).

outrage *ka wîsakayawesihk* (VII); *kisiwâsowin* (NI); *kwayikiyawesiw* (VAI).

outrageous *wîsakayawesiwin* (NI).

outran Outrunning someone, *awîyak ka nakacipahiht* (VTA); s/he outran her/him or them or s/he leaves them behind, *nakacipahew* (VTA).

outside *wayawîtimihk* (LN); on the outside, *wayawîtimâyihk* (LN); s/he takes her/him outside, *wayawihtahew* (VTA); s/he sends her/him outside, *wayawîtisahwew* (VTA); s/he pushes her/him outside with her/his body, *wayawîskawew* (VTA); s/he takes things out, *wayawihcikew* (VAI); s/he hands it to someone on the outside, *wayawîtisinew* (VTA); s/he went outside, *wayawîw* (VTA); s/he pushes her/him outside, *wayawîyahkinew* (VTA); the smoke goes outside, *wayawîyâpahtew* (VAI); s/he runs outside, *wayawîpahtâw* (VAI); s/he falls to the outside, *wayawîpayiw* (VAI); s/he pulls her/him outside, *wayawîpitew* (VTA); s/he went outside for her/him, *wayawîstawew* (VTA); s/he knocks her/him outside, *wayawîwepahwew* (VTA); s/he throws her/him to the outside, *wayawîwepinew* (VTA); the act of going outside, *wayawîwin* (NI); s/he escapes to the ouside, *wayawîyamiw* (VAI).

outsider *wayawîtimâyihk ohci* (LN); *ohpimiy ohci* (IPC).

outsmart *ayiwâk iyinisowin* (NI).

outtalk *ka ayiwâk tônamohk* (VAI).

oval *kîkway peyakwan wawih kesicikatek* (VII).

over Or on top, *pasci* (VII); refers to a direction, "over on the other side", *pascayihk* (LN); it goes over, *pascipayiw* (VTI).

overact *ayiwâk ka tôtamihk* (VAI).

overboard *ka pakastawepayihk* (VTI); s/he fell overboard into the water, *nipîhkpahkisin* (VTI).

overcast *ka yekwaskwahk* (VII); it is very cloudy, *yekwaskwan* (VII).

overcharge S/he overcharges her/him, *ayiwâkakimew* (VAI).

overcoat *waskitasakay* (NI); *piponasâkay* (NI); a winter coat, *piponasâkay* (NI).

overcrowd *ka ayiwâkaskinehk nânitâw* (VTI).

overdo Overextending oneself, *ayiwâk katôtamihk* (VAI); the act of playing oneself out, *kesihowin* (NI); s/he overdid it and played herself/himself out, *kesihow* (VAI); *osamehtaw* (VAI); the act of overdoing it, *nôsamâcihisowin* (NI); overdoing, *nôsamâc* (IPC).

overdress *wâwiyak kispakesihowin* (NI).

overestimate *wâwiyak kasohkimamsehk* (VII).

overflow *kîkway kapascowahk* (VTI).

overgrow *kîkway ka pascopikihk* (VTI).

overgrown *ka pascopikihcikehk* (VTA).

overhear *ka pisci pehtamihk kîkway* (VTI).

overheard *pisci pehtam* (VAI); the hearing of something, *pehtamowin* (NI).

overhung *kîkway ka pâstakotek* (VTI).

overjoy *pasci miweyihtamowin* (NI); *ayiwâkeyitam* (VAI).

overjoyed S/he is overjoyed, *ayiwâkmiweyihtam* (VAI).

overladen *wâwiyak ka pwâwâtehk* (VTI).

overlain *wâwiyak ka iyipeyak* (VII).

overland *ka sâpokaskewehk* (VII).

overlap *ka kîhtwam ascikehk* (VAI); *âhkwetawastew* (VTI).

overlay *ka tahtahkohtascikehk* (VAI).

overload *ka ayiwâk askinahtahk* (VTI); *osâmposi cikewin* (NI); s/he overloads her/him, *pwâwâtahew* (VTA); s/he overloads it, *pwâwâtahtâw* (VTI); s/he is overloaded, *pwâwatew*; being overloaded, *pwâwatewin* (NI).

overlook *ka asweyapahtamihk*; *patâpahtam* (VAI).

overly *wâwiyak* (IPC).

overnight Staying overnight, *ka katikonihk*; s/he stayed over for one night, *peyakotipiskwew*; the act of staying overnight, *tipiskisowin* (NI); s/he stayed overnight, *tipiskisow*.

overplay *ka pasci metawehk* (VAI).

overpower *ka sâkocihiwehk* (VII); *otahowew* (VAI); *paskiyatam* (VAI).

overprice *wâyiwak akihcikewin* (NI).

overproduce *ka ayiwâk osihcikehk* (VTI).

overproduction *wâyiwak osihcikewin* (NI).

overrate *ayiwâk etakihcikewin* (NI).

overreach *ayiwâk ka tôtamihk* (VAI).

override *ka ayiwâk tâpâsohk* (VTI).

overrun *ka pascipayihk* (VAI).

oversee *ka nâkateyihtamihk kîkway* (VTI).

overseer *onâkateyihcikew* (NA).

overshadow *ka paskeyakehk* (VII); *cikâsteskawew* (VTA).

overshoe *waskitaskisin* (NI); *âhkwetaweskisin* (NI).

overshoot *ka pasci pâskisikehk* (VAI).

overshot *ka pâstahamihk kîkway* (VTI).

oversight *ka asweyapahtamihk* (VII); *patâpahtamowin* (NI).

oversize *ayiwâk kîspehcak* (VII).

oversleep *osâmihkwâmihk* (VAI).

overstep *ka pastahkoskehk* (VTA).

overstock *ka ayiwâk astahk* (VTI).

overstuff *ka ayiwâk sihtaskinahcikehk* (VAI).

oversupply *ka ayiwâk epayihk* (VII).

overt *ekâ ka kâtahk kîkway* (VII).

overtake S/he overtakes her/him, *otihtew* (VTA); s/he catches up to her/him, *atimew* (VTA).

overtask *wâyiwak atoskehk* (VAI).

overtone *ka paskastehamihk kitohcikan* (VTI).

overtook *ka atimiht awîyak* (VTA).

overtop *ka patakopayihcikehk* (VTA).

overview *kakeh twam wâpahtamihk* (VTA).

overwhelm *osâmeweyihtamohiht awîyak* (VII).

overwhelming *osâmeweyihtamohiwewin* (NI).

overwork Overworking, *ka kosâmatoskehk* (VAI); s/he is played out, *nohtesin* (VAI); s/he overworks her/him, *osâmihew* (VTA); s/he overworks herself/himself, *osâmihisiw* (VAI); the act of overworking oneself, *osâmihisiwin* (NI); overworking oneself, *osâmihowin* (NI).

overwrought *ka nipahinohtesinihk* (VAI).

owe The act of owing a debt or writing a letter, *masinahamâkewin* (NI); the act of corresponding with someone or owing a debt to someone, *masinahamâtowin* (NI); s/he owes her/him or is in debt to her/him or s/he writes for her/him, *masinahamawew* (VTA); s/he owes a debt or s/he writes, *masinahikew* (VAI).

owing *ka masinahikehk* (VAI).

owl *ôhô* (NA).

owlet *ôhôsis* (NA).

owlish *ôhôsisâyâwin* (NI).

own *ka tipeyawehohk* (VII); separated, each in its own place or spot, or in its own wrapping, *piskihc* (IPC); *pahpiskihc* (IPC); s/he has them or owns them, *ayâwew* (VTA); a possession or place where one stays, *ayâwin* (NI); s/he has it, *ayâw* (VAI); s/he gives her/him something to own, *tipiyawehew* (VTA); s/he has her/his own, *tipiyawehiw* (VAI); s/he owns things, *tipiyicikew* (VAI) *(Northern)*; *pamihow* (VAI) *(Plains and Northern variant)*; the act of owning something, *tipeyicikîwin* (NI) *(Northern)*; *pamihowin* (NI) *(Plains and Northern variant)*; s/he owns it, *tipeyihtam* (VAI) or (VII); s/he owns her/him, *tipeyimew* (VAI); s/he owns everyone, *tipeyimowew* (VAI); s/he owns herself/himself or s/he is her/his own boss or s/he is free, *tipeyimisiw* (VAI); the act of being one's own boss, *tipeyimisiwin* (NI); s/he is owned, *tipeyihtâkosiw* (VAI); s/he owns it for her/him, *tipeyihtamawew* (VTA); it is owned, *tipeyitâkwan* (VII).

owner The owner of something, *awîyak ka tipiyihtahk* (VAI); s/he is the owner, *tipiyicikîw* (NA); s/he makes her/him the owner, *tipiyawehew* (VTA).

ownership *tipiyawesowin* (NI) *(Northern)*; *tipiyawehowisowin* (NI) *(Plains)*; s/he gives her/him ownership, *tipeyitamohew* (VTA).

ox *ayihkwew mostos* (NA); *yapemostos* (NA); a male cow, *yapemostos* (NA).

oxblood *mostos mihko* (NI).

oxcart *mostos ocâpânaskos* (NI).

oxen *ayihkwew mostoswak kotapîtwaw* (NA).

oyster *esis* (NA).

P

pace One pace or step, *peyak tahkoskewin* (NI).

pacify *ka kihcihiwewin* (NI); s/he make her/him happy, *naheyihtamohew* (VTA).

pack A pack sack, *nayahcikan* (NI); s/he goes for her/him and packs her/him on her/his back, *nâtowatâmew* (VTA); s/he goes for it and packs it on her/his back, *nâtowatew* (VAI); s/he packs or carries her/him or it on her/his shoulders, *onîkâtew* (VAI); s/he packs or carries on her/his shoulders, *onîkew* (VTA); s/he packs or carries it under her/his arm, *pîmoyiw* (VAI); the act of packing or carrying something under the arm, *pîmoyowin* (NI); s/he puts a pack on her/him, i.e.: a horse, *wîwahew* (VTA); s/he puts a pack on herself/himself, *wîwahow* (VAI); the act of being loaded with a pack, *wîwahowin* (NI).

package *wewekahpecikewin* (NI); a small wrapped bundle, *wewekahpicikan* (NI).

pack animal *nayahcikew pisiskiw* (NA).

packboard *nayahcikâkan* (NI).

packet *miscekowets* (NI); a package of cigarettes, *peyak miscekowets sekaretsak* (NI); a tiny wrapped bundle, *wewekahpicikanis* (NI).

pack horse *onayahcikewatim* (NA).

packing *wawîyewin* (NI).

pack mule *sôsôwatim ka nayahciket* (NA).

packsaddle *aspapowin ka yoskak; aspascikan* (NI).

padding *yoskahikan* (NI); *yoskascikewin* (NI).

paddle *apiy* (NA); *apoy* (NA); a paddle used to steer a canoe, *tahkwahamowapiy* (NA); *tahkwahamowapoy* (NA).

paddling S/he is paddling a canoe or rowing a boat, *pimiskaw* (VTA); s/he paddles down stream in a canoe, *mâham* (VTA); the act of paddling down stream, *mâhamowin* (NI); s/he paddles up stream, *nâtaham* (VAI); s/he paddles against the wind, *nayimaham* (VAI); s/he is paddling towards us, i.e.: a person in a canoe or a muskrat in the water, *pecastamiskâw* (VAI); *peciskâw* (VAI) *(Plains)*; the act of paddling a canoe or rowing a boat, *pimiskâwin* (NI) *(Northern)*; s/he paddles her/his canoe into shore, *seskaham* (VTI); *kapatewpaham* (VTI) *(Plains)*; s/he paddles the canoe along the shoreline, *sisonecimew* (VAI).

paid *ka kîstepahikehk* (VTI).

pail *askihk* (NA); a large pail, *mistaskihk* (NA); a drum, a wooden pail, *ikwaskihk* (NA); a flat pail or pot, *napakaskihk* (NA); a metal pail, *pîwâpiskwaskihk* (NA); a bed pan, *misiwiyakan* (NI).

pailful *ka sâkaskinet askihk* (NA).

pain The act of being in pain, *wesakahpinewin* (NI); the act of moaning in pain, *mâmahpinewin* (NI); the act of hurting or being hurt, *wîsakeyihtamowin* (NI); s/he has pain, *wîsakahpinew* (VAI); s/he is painfully abusing her/him, i.e.: sexually, *wîsakahwew* (VTA); her/his bite is causing her/him pain, *wîsakamew* (VAI); s/he is in pain from sitting, *wîsakapiw* (VAI); the act of being in pain from sitting, *wîsakapiwin* (NI); the act of crying in pain, *wîsakatwemowin* (NI); s/he is crying in pain, *wîsakatwemow* (VAI) ; s/he is in pain because of her/his illness, *wîsakeyihtam* (VAI); being in pain because of illness, *wîsakeyitamowin* (NI); s/he feels her/his pain or s/he empathizes with her/him, *wîsakeyitamostamawew* (VAI).

pained *awîyak ka wîsakahpinehiht* (NA) *or* (VTA).

painful *âhkwan* (VII); very painful, *metoni kâhkwahk* (VII).

painless *ekâ kawesakahoht awîyak* (VTA).

painstaking *metoni kanâkateyihtamihk* (VTI).

paint *sopekahikan* (NI); s/he paints or colors her/his face, *masinihkwehosiw* (VAI); s/he paints her/his face, *masinihkwewew* (VTA); s/he paints or draws her/him, *masinipewew* (VTA); s/he paints it, *sopeham* (VTA) *(Northern)*; *sisopeham* (VTA) *(Plains)*; s/he paints her/him, *sopekahwew* (VTA).

paint brush A large paint brush, i.e.: for painting a house, *sisopekahikâkan* (NI) *(Plains)*; *sopekahikâkan* (NI) *(Northern)*.

painter *osopîkahikiw* (NA) *(Northern)*; *osisopekahikew* (NA) *(Plains)*.

pair One pair, *peyakwayihk* (IPC).

pal *awîyak ka miyowicihiwîht* (NA) *or* (VII).

palatable *kîkway ka miweyihtamihk* (VII).

palate *pehcayihk metonihk etah kohnistospecikehk* (VTA); the roof of the mouth, *wayakask* (NI).

pale Being pale, *ka wâpinesihk* (VTI); s/he is pale, *wâpinesiw* (VAI); s/he has light colored or pale skin, *wâpâsiw* (VAI); having light colored or pale skin, *wâpâsiwin* (NI); s/he fades them to a paler or lighter color, *wapâswew* (VTA).

paleface *ka wâpiskihkwehk* (IPC).

pall *wâpiskayans ka apacitahk ayamihawinihk* (VTA); black clothes for a coffin, *kaskitewekin* (NI).

pallid S/he is pale, *wâpinesiw* (VAI).

pallid *ka wâpanesihk* (VII); *wâpinakosiw* (VAI).

pallor *awîyak ka wâpânepayit* (VII); being pale, *wâpinesowin* (NI).

palm The inside of the hand, *wayicecan* (NI); *pehcayihk ohci mecici* (VII).

palpability *ka nahâpahtamihk kîkway* (VAI).

palpable *ka kihkânâkwahk* (VTI).

palpably *kihkânâkosowinihk* (LN).

379

380

palpitate *ka cîhcîpitehehk* (VTA).

palpitation *cîhcîpitehewin* (NI).

paltry *kwanta apsis kîkway* (IPC).

pamper *ekâ ka ponekaht awîyak* (VTA).

pan Or plate, *yakan* (NI); just too much, i.e.: panning something, *wâwiyakan* (IPC).

pander *macikîkway awîyak ka paminahk* (VAI).

pang *ka sisikôc teyistikwânehk* (VAI); *nohtekatewin* (NI).

panic *sasopayowin* (NI); *mistahi sekisowin* (NI).

panicky *ka nihtâ sasopayihk* (VAI).

panorama *cikâstepayihcikewin* (NI).

panoramic *kîkway ka cikâstepayihtahk* (VTA).

pant *ka nestwatâmihk* (VAI); breathing heavily, *yehesiwin* (NI).

pants A pair of pants, *mitâs* (NA), *wihkwepan* (NA) *(Archaic Cree)*; a pair of pants with legs cut off, i.e.: cutoffs, *kîskitâs* (NA); s/he makes her/him a pair of pants, *mitâsihkawew* (VTA); s/he makes a pair of pants, *mitâsihkew* (VTA); a pair of stretchy, woolen pants, *sepekiskawitas* (NA); a pair of stretch pants, i.e.: resilient, *sepihkitas* (NA); it is a durable pair of pants, *sohkekisow* (VAI); *maskawekisiw* (VAI) *(Plains)*; s/he puts pants on; s/he puts on her/his own pants, *postitâsew* (VAI) *(Plains)*; *kikitâsew* (VAI) *(Northern)*.

panty *or* **panties** *iskwew casisak* (NI).

papa *awîyak opâpâwa* (NA); *ohtâwîmâw* (NA).

papal *mâmawiyas kihci ayamiheweyeniw otôsihcikewna* (VAI); the Roman Catholic religion, *pâhkwayamihâwin* (NI).

paradise In the spirit world; in heaven, *kisemanitonahk* (NA).

paralyse *or* **paralyze** When your limbs are dead to feeling, *ka nipopayihk* (VAI); s/he is paraplegic, *kistapiw* (VAI); the act of being paraplegic, *kistapiwin* (NI); s/he is totally paralyzed, *nipowisiw* (VAI) *(Northern)*; *nipômakisiw* (VAI) *(Plains)*; the act of being totally paralyzed, *nipowisiwin* (NI) *(Northern)*; *nipômakisiwin* (NI) *(Plains)*.

paralysis *nipowipayowin* (NI).

paralytic *ka nipowisihk* (VAI).

paranoia *atâmeyimowewin* (NI).

parch *ka pasamihk kîkway* (VTA); so dry lightning starts a fire, *pasitew* (VTA).

pardon *poneyihtamâkewin* (NI); they pardon each other, *poneyihtamâtowak* (VAI); s/he pardons her/him, *poneyihtamawew* (VAI).

pardonable *kâsenamâtowin* (NI).

pare *ka poyakisamihk kîkway* (VTA).

parent *onekihikomâw* (NA) *(Northern)*; *onîkihikomâw* (NA) *(Plains)*; my parents, *ninîkihikwak* (NA); someone's parents, *awîyak onekihikwa* (NA); s/he has parents, *onekihikiw* (VAI).

parentage *ka onekihikohk*; our parents, *kinîkihikonawak* (NA).

parental *awîyak onekihikomaw ka iteyimsot* (VAI).

parenthood *onekihikomâwiwin* (NI).

paring *ka mekwâ poyakisamihk* (VTA); *pweyakisikewin* (NI).

parish *ayamihewiyiniwkamik* (NI); the property under a clergyman's office, *ayamihewitipeyicikewin* (NI).

parishioner A member of a church parish, *ayamihewiyinehkan* (NA); *awîyak ka wekit ayamehewikamkohk* (NA).

parson *âkayâsiw ayamihewiyiniw* (NA); an Anglican priest, *âkayâsiwayamihewiniw* (NA).

parsonage A residence of the Anglican priest; *âkayâsiw ayamihewiyiniw wekih* (NI).

part Not all of it, *namoya kahkeyâw* (IPC); a part or portion of, *pahki* (IPC).

partake *ka wîcihiwehk* (VTA); s/he takes a part of it, *pahkwenam* (VTA).

partial *pahki* (IPC); affecting a part only, *pahkweyâw* (VII).

partially *pahkipoko* (IPC).

participant *awîyak ka wîcihiwet* (NA).

participate *ka wîcihiwehk* (VTA); *wîcihiwew* (VTA).

participation *wîcihiwewin* (NI).

particular *peyak kîkway poko* (IPC).

particularity *peyakohtawin* (NI).

particularize *ka peyakohtahk* (IPC).

particularly *wâswîs kîspin* (IPC).

parting *ka nakatohk* (VTA), *awîyak ka nakatiht* (VTA).

partly *pahkipoko* (IPC); a part, *pahki* (IPC).

partner Or a friend, *wicewâkan* (NA); my partner, *niwicewâkan* (NA); having a partner, *ka wiciwâkanihk* (VAI); s/he makes them partners or friends, *wicewâkanihew* (VTA); they are partners or friends, *wicewâkanihtowak* (VAI); being partners or friends, *wicewâkanihtowin* (NI); s/he makes friends for her/him, *wicewâkanikawew* (VTA); s/he is partners or friends with her/him, *wicewâkanimew* (VAI).

partnership *wiciwâkanihtowin* (NI).

partridge A wood partridge or grouse, *pihew* (NA).

party *mâmawi môcikihtâwin* (NI); having a good time, a benevolent action, *miyowâtamowin* (NI).

pass The act of passing by someone on the road, *awîyak kamiyaskaht* (VTA); s/he passes by it, *miyaskam* (VTI); s/he passes by her/him on the road, path or trail, *miyaskawew* (VTA); s/he passes her/him over the top, *pâstinew* (VTA); s/he hands or passes her/him through an opening, *paspitisinew* (VTA); the act of passing by, *pimipayowin* (NI); s/he passes by, *pimipayiw* (VAI); s/he passes right by them, *pimisâposkawew* (VTA); s/he passes by while holding

her/him or it in her/his arms, *pimitahkonew* (VTA);
s/he passes by on horseback, *pimitehtapiw* (VAI); s/he
hears her/him pass by, *pimowehtawew* (VTA).

passable *miyo pimohtewin* (NI).

passage A path that goes right through, *sâpohteskanaw*
(NI); there is an opening that leads right through, i.e.: a
passage, *sâpostawâw* (VII); having a passageway or a
passage, *sâpostawisowin* (NI); there is a passage, i.e.:
an opening right through, *sâpostawisiw* (VAI); it has a
passage or an opening, *sâpostawiyâw* (VII).

passageway *sâpohtewin* (NI).

passerby *osâpohtew* (NA).

passing *awîyak ka sâpohtet* (NA) or (VTA).

passion *kwâtakihiwewin* (NI); *môsihtawin* (NI).

passionate *kitimâkeyimowin* (NI).

passionless *ekâ omôsihtawin* (NI).

Passion Sunday *peyak ayamihiwikîsikâw pamayes ka
âpisisinokîsîkak* (NI).

Passion Week *peyak ayamihiwikîsikâw manito
okwâtakihtâwin ka kiskisototamihk* (VTA) or (NA).

passive *awîyak kakwâtakeyimot* (VTA).

passivity *kwâtakeyimowin* (NI).

past *ka miyaskamihk* (VTA); *miyas kamo payiw* (VAI);
in the past, *otak isi* (IPC); in the olden times, in the far
away past or in former days, *kayahte; oye*.

paste *ka pasakoskiwahtahk* (VTA); *pasakwahikan* (VII).

pastor *ayamihewiyiniw kanakateyihtahk ayamihawin*
(NA).

pastoral Duties of a pastor, *ayamihewiniw tôtamowin*
(NI); *etah ka ohpikihihtwâw pisiskowak* (NA).

pasty *pasakosiw* (VAI).

pat *ka pakamiskwanehowehk* (VTA).

patch The act of patching or repairing, *mîsahikewin*
(NI); s/he patched it with tar or spruce pitch,
pikihkâtam (VTI); it is patched with tar or spruce
pitch, *pikihkâtew* (VII).

patchy *mîsahikana kamisiwestekwâw* (VTI).

paternal *ohpikihâwasiwin* (NI); related through a
father, *ohtâwimaw* (NA).

paternalism *ka kakwe ophpikihâwasohk* (VTA).

paternalistic *kwayask ka kakwe pimpayihtahk askiy*
(VTA).

path S/he makes a well beaten path, *kistatamohtâw*
(VAI); a minor walking path, *pimohceskanas* (NI); a
little road, *meskanas* (NI); a path or road that is well
travelled, *kistatamiw* (VAI); a major walking path,
pimohteskanaw (NI).

pathetic *ka kitimâknakohcikehk* (VAI); unfortunate
state of affairs, *kitimâkan* (VII).

pathetical *ka kitimâkipayihk* (VAI).

pathfinder *onîkânohtâkew* (NA).

pathway *pimohceskanas* (NI); a short cut pathway,
taskamohteskanas (NI).

patience The power to wait calmly, *ekâ kîkway ka
mamâhteyihtamihk* (VAI); s/he patiently sits for long
periods, *sîpapow* (VAI); s/he is patient, *sîpeyicikew*
(VAI); *sâsîpeyihtam* (VAI) (Plains) s/he is patient with
her/him, *sîpeyimew* (VAI); *sâsîpihkeyimew* (VAI)
(Plains) the act of being patient, *sîpeyitamowin* (NI).

patient *awîyak papeyahtik ka ayat* (NA) or (VAI);
sîpeyihtam (VAI); the sick one, the patient, *otâhkosiw*
(NA).

patter *ka matwetahikehk* (VTA).

pattern A pattern for making clothes, *nâspoyesikan*
(VII) or (NI); a stamp, *ayîsihcikan* (NI) (Northern);
aspisâwâcikan (NI) (Plains).

pause *nomenakîwin* (NI); *kipihciw kanakes* (IPC).

pavement *asiniw mesakanow* (NI) (Plains);
asiniwipayihcikewin (NI) (Plains).

paw An animal's foot, *minôs ocihce* (NI); *misit* (NI).

pay S/he pays her/his way for her/him,
tipahikestamawew (VTA) (Plains);
tipahamâkestamawew (VTA) (Northern).

pea *mîcîmin* (NI); *lepwa* (NI) (French Cree); little things
that are wrapped up, *wewekapisosak* (NI).

peace *peyahtikeyimowin* (NI); after the war, *ka poni
nôtinitohk*.

peaceable *peyahtik ka ayâhk* (VAI).

peaceful *metoni papeyahtik ayâwin* (NI);
kîyamiyohtakwan (VII).

Peace River The Cree name for the settlement or town
of Peace River, "the mouth of a river", *sâkitawâhk*
(NA).

peak *kîmôtâpiwin* (NI).

peaked *awîyak ka kîmôtâpit* (VTA).

peanut Or a nut, *pâkân* (NA).

peanut butter *anikwacâsîciwin* (NI) (Plains);
pakânipimiy (NI) (Northern).

pebble *asinisy* (NI).

pebbly *ka asineskasik* (VII) or (VAI).

peck Woodpecker, *pahpahscîs kamatwetahiket* (NA);
s/he pecks at her/him with her/his beak, *cahkatawew*
(VTA).

pecker *pahpahscîs omatwetahikakan* (NI).

peculiar *awîyak ka wâneyihtamsit* (NA);
wîyasihtâkwan (VII); *wîyasinakosiw* (VAI).

peculiarity *wâneyihtamisiwin* (NI).

peek Peeking, i.e.: Peeping Tom, *kîmôtâpiwin* (NI); s/he
peeks at her/him, *kîmâpamew* (VTA); s/he is peeping
out, *kîmâpahkew* (VTA).

peel The act of peeling something, *poyakinkewin* (NI);
s/he peels them by pulling, i.e.: the skin off a banana,
poyakipitew (VTA); s/he peels them with an axe,
poyakawew (VTA); s/he peels them with her/his teeth,
poyakamew (VTA); s/he peels them, *poyakinew* (VTA);
s/he peels them with a knife, *poyakiswew* (VTA); s/he

381

peels it off by pulling, i.e.: the skin off a banana; s/he skins it, i.e.: usually used to refer to small fur bearing animals such as muskrat or beaver, *pihtonew* (VTA) *(Plains)*; *pihtôpitew* (VTA) *(Northern)*.

peeling *ka poyakinkehk* (VTA).

peep *cawihcakasik kohwapahtamihk* (VII) or (VAI); *kîmôtâpiw* (VAI).

peer S/he peers at her/him, *kanawâpamew* (VTA); s/he peers at the window, i.e.: looking out or in, *paspâpiw* (VAI).

peerless *ekâ takehpaskeyatamihk* (VAI).

peevish *ka pîkiskweskihk* (VTA); fretful or irritable, *nayihtâwisiw* (VAI).

peg A tent or teepee peg, *cîstîkahikan* (NI); s/he pegs it into the ground, *cistikaham* (VTA).

Peigan A Peigan person, *pekâniwiyiniw* (NA).

pellet *niskasiniy* (NA); *môsisinîy* (NI).

pelt A beaver pelt, *amiskwâyan* (NA); it is worth just one pelt, *peyakwâhtayeyaw* (VII); *âhtay* (NA).

pelvis *mitokan* (NI).

pemmican Moose tallow, a bag of pemmican, or a native delicacy from dry moose meat and moose fat, *pimihkân* (NI); s/he makes a stew from pemmican, *pimihkânâpohkew* (VTA); *cîsâwânâpohkew* (VTA); pemmican soup or stew made from pemmican, *pimihkânâpoy* (NI); *cîsâwânâpoy* (NI); a bag or container for pemmican made from a moose bladder, *pimihkâniwat* (NI); *wihkway* (NI).

penance *kîkway ka tepahikepayihtahk* (VAI); a self-inflicted punishment for sin, *kisinâteyihtamowin* (NI).

pending *kîkway ka pihomakahk* (VII); *namoya kîseyihtamwak* (VAI).

pendulous *kâkwayawekotek kîkway* (VAI).

penetrable *ka nihtâpihtokwemakahk* (LN) or (VAI).

penetrate Going into something, *ka pihtokwetôtamihk kîkway* (VTA); it went right through, *sâpopayiw* (VAI); the water penetrates or the canoe takes on water, *ohcistin* (VTA).

penetrating *pihtokwepayowin* (NI).

penetration Enter and become part of, *pihtokwepayihiwin* (NI).

penetrative *pihtokwepayihiwewin* (NI).

penis *mitakisiy* (NI); *nâpewsikewakan* (NI) *(Northern)*; *nâpewâpacihcikan* (NI) *(Plains)*.

penitence *mihtâtamowin* (NI).

penitent *awîyak ka mihtâtahk* (VAI).

pensive *peyahtik kamâmitoneyihtamih*k (VAI).

pent *ka kaskamotaskinehk* (VTA).

pent-up *kaskamotaskinewin* (NI).

people *ayisiyinowak* (NA); *ayisiniwak* (NA); there are lots of people, *ayisiyineskaw* (VII).

pep *macikastewin* (NI).

pepper *kahkominakâk* (NI) *(Northern)*; *papeskomina* (NI) *(Plains)*.

peppermint *ka tahkiyawepaysik* (NI).

peppery *âhkwatsowin* (NI).

peppy *macikastewin* (NI).

perceive *ka nihtâ moyeyihtamihk kîkway* (VAI); the act of perceiving, *moyehcikewin* (NI); the act of being sceptical, *moyeyihtamowin* (NI).

percept *ka kakwe tâpeyihtamihk* (VAI).

perceptibility *nihtâ tâpeyihtamowin* (NI).

perceptible *ka nihtâ tâpeyihtamihk* (NI).

perception *mosci tâpeyihtamowin* (NI).

perch Or type of fish, *asâwesis* (NA); the act of sitting on a tree, *akosewin* (NI).

percipience *moyehcikewin* (NI).

perdition *metoni ka misiwanâcihcikehk* (VTA) or (VAI).

peremptory *ekâ ka asenamihk* (VAI).

perfect *metoni kwayask* (IPC); perfect, generous, charitable, forgiving, *kisewâtisiw* (VAI).

perfectibility *kwayaskwesâyâwin* (NI).

perfectible *kakwayaskwesâyahk* (VAI).

perfection *namoyah ayiwâk isi kwayask* (IPC); complete in every detail, *metonikwayask* (VII).

perfectly *metoni ekotah* (IPC) or (LN).

perform Performing, *kîkway katôtamihk* (VAI); s/he performs spiritually powerful acts, *mamahtawisihcikew* (VAI); a gift of performing powers, *mamatâwihikowisiwin* (NI); s/he performs religious rites, *manitohkasiw* (VAI); s/he performs perfectly, *miyow* (VAI).

performance *tôtamowin* (NI); the act of performing, *metawewin* (NI); the act of doing, *itôtamowin* (NI).

performer *awîyak kîkway ka totahk* (VTA).

perhaps *ahpô etoki* (IPC); perhaps or maybe, *mâskôc* (IPC); sometimes, some day it could happen, some day maybe, or not likely but possibly, *kitahtawi* (IPC); perhaps or probably, *pakahkam* (IPC).

peril Nearly killed, *paspinasiwin* (NI); the act of taking a big risk or danger, *sohki paspinewin* (NI); the act of sensing peril, *kostâciwin* (NI) *(Plains)*; *kostaciwâyâwin* (NI) *(Northern)*.

perilous *kostaciwâyâwin* (NI).

period *iskwew opîsimwaspinêwin* (NI); time period like right now, *mekwâc* (IPC).

periodic *aspihtaw* (IPC).

periodical *aspihtaw iyikohk* (IPC); once in a while, *ahaspihtaw* (IPC).

perish Sudden death, *sikocnipowin* (NI).

permanence *ka kiscâyâhk* (VAI).

permanency *kiscâyâwin* (NI).

permanent *kîkway ka kistastek* (VAI).

permissible *kîkway ka pakitinkatek* (VAI); the act of allowing something to happen, *pakitinamâkewin* (NI).

permission *pakitinowewin* (NI).

permit S/he permits or s/he allows, *pakitinamâkew* (VAI); s/he permits or allows her/him, *pakitinamawew* (VTA); s/he permits her/him, *pakitinew* (VTA).

pernicious *ka pîkonkeskihk* (VTA).

perpetrate Perpetuating a downfall, *mayinikewin* (NI).

perpetual *ka tâptawakotek kîkway* (VII); all the time, *tâpitawi* (IPC).

perpetually *tâptaw'payihcikewinihk* (LN).

perpetuate *kîkway ka tâptawipayihtahk* (VTA).

perplex *ekâ kakeh nisitohtamihk* (VII); *wâneyihtamowin* (NI).

perplexity *wâneyihtamohiwewin* (NI).

persecute *awîyak ka wiyâsowatiht* (VTA).

persecution *wiyâsowatowin* (NI); the act of being made to suffer for divergent principles, *kwâtakihiwewin* (NI).

perseverance To persist in something undertaken, *âhkameyihtamowin* (NI).

persevere *ka âhkameyihtamihk* (VAI) or (VTI); s/he is persistant, *âhkameyihtam* (VTI).

persist *âhkameyimowin* (NI).

persistence *ekâ kîkway ka papomehikohk* (VTI).

persistency *metoni sâpweyihtamowin* (NI).

persistent *metoni ka sâpweyihtamihk* (VTI); s/he is at it all the time, *tâpitawitotam* (VTI).

person Person or human being, *ayisiyiniw* (NA); a white person, *moniyâw* (NA); s/he is a white person, *mônîyâwiw* (VAI); first person, *nistam ayisiyiniw* (NA); a greedy person, *okâsakiwiyiniw* (NA); a kind-hearted person, *okisewâtisiw* (VAI).

personable *miyow ayisiyiniwiwin* (NI).

personal *tepeyawihowin* (NI); *tipiyawe tipeyihtamowin* (NI).

personality The way a person is, *tansi ka isi ayisiniwihk* (VAI); she has a beautiful personality, *miyoskwewiw* (VAI); a personality, *isâyâwin* (NI); s/he has multiple personalities, i.e.: schizophrenia, *nanâtohkwisâyâw* (VAI) or (VII); s/he has a double personality, *nîswayakisiw* (VAI); s/he has four personalities, *newayakisiw* (VAI); a distinctive character, *Isâyâwin* (NI).

personalize The act of stamping something, *masinatahikewin* (NI).

personally *tipiyaw keya* (IPC).

personify *ka powâmihk* (VII) or (VAI).

perspiration *apwesiwin* (NI).

perspire *ka apwesihk* (VII); s/he perspires, *apwesiw* (VAI).

persuade The act of persuading, *sîhkimwewin* (NI); s/he persuades her/him, *sîhkimew* (VAI).

persuasive S/he is persuasive, *sihkihkemiw* (VAI); s/he is a persuasive type or s/he is always encouraging, *sihkimowew* (VTA); the act of being a persuasive type, *sihkimowewin* (NI).

persuasion *sihkihkemowin* (NI); the act of convincing someone, *sâkocihiwewin* (NI).

pert *takahkeyimsowin* (NI).

pertain *kîkway ka wicewâkanpayik* (VAI).

pertinacity *ekâ ka papoyohk* (IPC).

pertinence *ekâ kîkway wahwima* (IPC).

pertinent *ekâ kîkway kahkwetateh itwewin* (NI).

perturb *awîyak ka mikoskâcihiht* (NA); the act of disturbing greatly, agitation, *mikoskâcihiwewin* (NI).

perusal *awîyak ka astâhiwet* (VTA).

peruse *astâhiwewin* (NI).

pervade *kîkway misewi kîspayihtahk* (VAI).

pervasion *swepayihcikewin* (NI).

pervasive *kîkway ka sâpopayik nânitâw* (VAI).

perverse *ohcitâw ka mayitôtamihk* (VAI).

perversion *pîtos mâmitoneyihtamowin* (NI).

perversity *pisikwâtsowin* (NI).

pervert *awîyak ka pisikwâtsit* (NA).

pesky *kakike kamayiwecihiwehk* (VAI).

pessimism *naspâteyihcikewin* (NI); expecting the worst, *mayimamitoneyihtamowin* (NI).

pessimist *awîyak ka naspâteyihcikeskit* (NA).

pessimistic *naspâteyihcikeskiwin* (NI).

pest *awîyak kamostatahkamkisit* (NA) or (VTA).

pester *mikoskâcihiwewin* (NI).

petal *peyak nîpis* (NI); *nîpehkansihk ohci*.

pettish *ka mihtaweskihk* (VTA).

petty *apisis kîkway* (IPC).

petulance *pîkiskweskiwin* (NI).

petulant *ekâ kakeh naheyihtamihk* (VII) or (VAI).

pheasant *ekinwâpekayowet pewayis* (NA); prairie chicken, *ahkiskow* (NA).

phenomena *ka mâmaskâsâpimohk* (VAI).

phenomenal *mâmaskâsâpahcikewin* (NI).

phenomenon *kîkway ka mâmaskâsâpahtamihk* (VAI).

phlegm *osâwâpân* (NI); s/he has phlegm, *osâwâpew* (VAI).

physical S/he is physically tough, *sohkâtisiw* (VAI); the act of being physically tough, *sôhkatisiwin* (NI).

pick A tool for picking roots, *mônahicepihkakan* (NI), the act of picking, *môsahkinkewin* (NI); s/he picks berries, *mawisiw* (VAI); the act of picking berries, *mawisowin* (NI); s/he picks berries from the trees, i.e.: apples, *mawiswatew* (VTA); s/he picks them up, *mosahkinew* (VTA); s/he picks it up along the way, *naskwenam* (VTA); s/he is picking up old spruce boughs from a teepee, *pewahtakinew* (VTA).

pickaxe or **pickax** *napakcîkahikan* (NI).

picked *kakeh môsahkinkehk* (VTA).

picker *omôsahkinkew* (NA).

383

pickerel *okâw* (NA).

pickings *môsahkinikewina* (NI).

picky *ka nawasonkîskihk* (NI).

picture *masinipayiwin* (NI).

piece *pahki* (IPC); a piece of something, *pahkih kîkway* (IPC).

pierce Something pierced, *kasâpostahamihk* (VTA); s/he pierces her/him or it through with a spear, *cîpacistahwew* (VTA); s/he pierces it through with a spear, *cîpacistaham* (VTI); s/he pierces it, *pakonehwew* (VTA); s/he pierces a hole with her/his hands, *pakonenew* (VTA); s/he makes a hole or pierces it by throwing it against something, i.e.: the ground, *pakonesimew* (VAI).

pierced It is pierced, *pakonesin* (VAI); it is pierced, *pakonehtin* (VII); it has a hole, i.e.: a shirt or tent, *pakoneyâw* (VII); s/he has a hole, i.e.: a water pail, *pakonisiw* (VAI).

piercing *sâpostahikewin* (NI).

piety *ayamihewâyâwin* (NI); a reverence for God, *manitowatisiwin* (NI).

pig *kohkôs* (NA).

piggyback Carrying a baby on one's back, *nayâwasiwin* (NI).

piglet *kohkôsis* (NA).

pigskin *kohkôsowayân* (NA).

pike A big pike or jackfish, *mistahi iyenkinosew* (NA); a smaller jackfish, *iyenkinosesis* (NA).

pile The act of piling, *asascikewin* (NI); heaped up or piled up, *asipayow* (VII); *asipayin* (VII); heaped, on a pile, *asastew* (VTA); s/he piles them together, *mawasakwahew* (VTA); s/he piles things together, *mâwasakwascikew* (VTA).

pilgrimage *wahyaw ohci kantawi ayamihahk* (VTA); a journey to a holy place, *nitawe ayamihâwin* (NI).

pillage The act pillaging or of taking goods by force, *maskahcihiwewin* (NI); s/he pillages, *maskahtwew* (VTA); s/he plunders her/him, *maskamew* (VTA); the act of taking things away, *maskahtwewin* (NI).

pilot *opimihâw* (NA) *(Plains)*; *opimiyaw* (NA) *(Northern)*.

pimple *mohtew* (NA).

pimpled *ko mohtemihk* (VTA).

pimply *omohtewihkwewin* (NI).

pin Brooch, button or badge, *sakâskwahon* (NI); a safety pin for diapers, *sakâskwahonis* (NI); s/he pins her/him or it down, *micimaskwahwew* (VTA); a straight or head pin, *ostikwânisâponikan* (NI); s/he pins them securely, *sanâskwahwew* (VTI) *(Northern)*; *sakâskwawew* (VTI) *(Plains)*; s/he holds her/him down with something heavy, i.e.: a log, *patakwahwew* (VTA); a small needle, *sâponikanis* (NI); s/he pins her/him between two things, *takwahwew* (VTA).

pinch *awîyak ka takwaseniht* (VTA).

pine *oskâhtak* (NA); there is pine covered area, sandy area, *oskâhtakaw* (VII).

pine S/he pines for someone, *nipaheyihtam* (VAI).

pine-cone *wasaskwetiw* (NA).

pine family *pahpitos oskâhtakwak* (NA).

pine needle *oskâhcakos sihtapihkwanah* (NI).

pinfeather *oskimekwanis* (NA).

ping *ciweyapiskihcikewin* (NI).

pinhead *sakâskwahikan oscikwanis* (NI).

pinhole *sâposcahikewinis* (NI).

pink *kokenewapikoneyak* (VII); it is pink, *wâpikwaniwinâkosiw* (VAI); it is pink, *wâpikwaniwinâkwan* (VII).

pinkish *kokinewapikonewnakwahk* (VII).

pious *sohkâyamihâwin* (NI); s/he is a holy person, *ayamihewatisiw* (VAI).

pipe *ospwâkan* (NA); a stone shaped into a pipe, *ospwâkanasiniy* (NA); a pipestem, *oskiciy* (NI); a homemade pipestem, *oskiciyahtik* (NI).

pipeful *peyak ospwâkan iyikohk* (IPC).

pique *kisôtôtâkewin* (NI).

pistol *apisci pâskisikanis* (NI); *pâskisikanis* (NI).

pit *misiwâtihkân* (NI); cellar, *watihkân* (NI).

pitch Loading hay with a pitch fork, *ka posaskwahamihk maskosiya* (VTA); s/he pitches it, i.e.: like hay, *kwâskweyâskwaham* (VTI).

pitch Spruce gum, *sihtipikiw* (NA); *pikiw* (NA).

pitch pine *oskâhtakopikîs* (NA).

pitchy *ka pasakoskowek kîkway* (VAI).

piteous *kitimâkinakewin* (NI); it is arousing pity, *kitimâkiyihtakwan* (VII).

pithy *pehcayihk ohci masakahk tapiskôc otamiskay* (VAI).

pitiable *ka miskamihk kitimâkinatowin* (NI).

pitiful *awîyak ka kitimâkinâkosit* (VAI); *kitimâkan* (VII).

pitiless *awîyak ekâ ka kitimâkinâket* (VAI).

pity Sympathizing with someone or offering compassion, *kitimâkinatowin* (NI); pitying, *kitimâkinakewin* (NI); s/he pities her/him, *kitimâkiyimew* (VAI).

placable *ka kâmwâciyiniwihk* (VAI).

placate *kâkecihiwewin* (NI).

place *otâh* (LN); *nita* (IPC); *anitah* (IPC); sitting, placed, *apiw* (VAI); *âstew* (VII); someplace else, in another place, *ohpime* (IPC); in an open place, between, *tastawih* (IPC); *tastawinohk* (IPC); in a good spot, place, *miyonohk* (IPC); at a certain place on the inside, *pecayihk* (IPC) *or* (LN); on the outside, *wayawitimayihk* (LN); s/he places them on both sides, *âyitawahew* (VTA); s/he places it firmly, *ayâtâhew* (VTI); at each place or a number of places, *itahtwayak*

(IPC); s/he places them here and there, i.e.: staggered, **kahtapahew** (VTI); it moves out of place, **kahtapipayiw** (VII); s/he places her/him solidly, **maskawahew** (VTA); s/he places things solidly, **maskawascikew** (VAI); it is placed improperly, **mâyastew** (VII); s/he places it on a slant, **nawestâw** (VAI); s/he places them all in a row, **nepitehew** (VTA); some other place, **ohpime** (IPC); it moves to another place, **ohpimepayiw** (VII); in only one place, **peyakwanohk** (LN); s/he places it on top, **tahkohtastâw** (VAI); s/he places her/him on top, **tahkohtahew** (VTA); s/he places her/him solidly, **sohkahew** (VTA); s/he places her/him on top of something, i.e.: a table, **tehtahew** (VTA).

placement *oyahiwewin* (NI).

placid *ekâ kakeh kisiwâhiht awîyak* (VAI).

placidity *sohkastwâwin* (NI).

plain A wide open, grassy space of land, **paskwâw** (NI); a prairie, **maskotew** (NI); a hollow in the ground, **wayacâw** (NI).

Plains Cree Being Plains Cree, **paskwâw nehiyawewin** (NI); a Plains Cree person, **paskwâwiyiniw** (NA).

plainsman *paskwâw iyinowak* (NA).

plan *oyeyihcikewin* (NI).

plant Vegetable plant, **kiscikânis** (NA); s/he plants or grows, **kistikew** (VAI); an industrial plant, **misi atoskewkamik** (NI); s/he is planting the garden, **nihtâwikihcikew** (VAI); the act of planting a garden, **nihtâwikihcikewin** (NI).

planted Also staked, **pakitinkewin** (NI); it has been planted long, **kinohwaskisiw** (NA); **kinowaskitew** (NA); it is solidly rooted, **ayâtaskisiw** (VII); **kistaskisiw** (VII); **kistaskitew** (VII); planted slanted, **pîmâskitew** (VII); newly planted, **oskaskisiw** (VII); **oskaskitew** (VII).

plaster *pemoskowahcikewin* (NI); a remedy spread on cloth and applied to the body, **akohpisowin** (NI).

plate An eating plate, **metsoyâkan** (NI); a flat plate, **napakiyâkan** (NI); a porcelain or glass plate, **mîkisiyâkan** (NI); a plate, **oyâkan** (NI); s/he makes plates, **oyâkanikew** (VAI); an iron or metal plate, **pîwâpiskoyâkan** (NI); a type of basket used as a collection plate, **pihcipoyâkan** (NI); a flat plate, **napakiyâkan** (NI).

plateful A full plate, **ka sâkaskinahtahk oyâkan** (VAI); four servings or platefuls of something, **newoyâkan** (NI); three servings or platefuls of something, **nistoyâkan** (NI).

platitude *ka kakwe wayesihkemohk* (VAI).

plausibility *kîmôtâtisiwin* (NI).

plausible *awîyak ka kîmôtâtisit* (VAI).

play Playing a game, **kametawehk** (VAI); s/he plays or sports with her/him, **metawâkâtew** (VTA); s/he plays or sports, **metawâkew** (VAI); s/he plays or amuses

herself/himself, **metawew** (VAI); s/he came to play, **pemetawew** (VTA); s/he plays with her/him, **wîcimetawemew** (VTA).

playable *kîkway takeh metawakehk* (VTI).

player *ometawew* (NA).

playful *ka metaweskihk* (VAI); *metaweskiw* (VAI).

pleasance *miweyihtamowin* (NI).

pleasant Liking something, **kîkway ka miweyihtamihk** (VII); it is pleasant, **meyawatikwan** (VII); it is very pleasant, **metoni meyawatikwan** (VII).

please Would you please? **mahti** (IPC).

pleasing *miweyihcikewin* (NI).

pleasurable *kîkway ka miyowâtamohikohk* (VAI).

pleasure *meyawâtamowin* (NI).

plenteous *kîkway ka pîsâkwahk* (NI).

plentiful *ka kwâyakahkamik* (IPC); s/he makes them plentiful, **pîsâkopayihew** (VTI); the act of being plentiful or in abundance, **pîsâkopayowin** (NI); s/he finds them plentiful, **pîsâkweyimew** (VTI); it is plentiful or in abundance, **pîsâkopayiw** (VAI) *or* (VII).

plenty Something that is plentiful, **kîkway ka pîsâkopayik** (VAI) *or* (VII); there is plenty or enough, **tepipayiw** (VAI) *or* (VII); that is enough or plenty, **ekwayikohk** (VAI) *or* (VII); there is plenty of something, **micetin** (VAI); having plenty of space or room, **pîsâkosiwin** (NI); it contains a great deal of space or room, **pîsâkosiw** (VAI); it contains a great deal of space or room, **pîsâkwan** (VII).

pliability *wehcihowin* (NI).

pliable *kîkway ka wehcipayik* (VII); flexible material, **yoskâw** (VII).

pliancy *awîyak ka wehcisit* (VAI).

pliant *wehcihiwewin* (NI), *wehcisâyâwin* (NI).

plight *mâyakopayowin* (NI).

plod *nisihkâc pimohtewin* (NI).

pluck The act of plucking, **paskopicikewin** (NI); s/he plucks it, i.e.: removes the feathers, **paskopitew** (VTA); s/he plucks it, i.e.: weeds from a garden, **paskopitam** (VTI).

plucky *otameyawa kotnamihk* (VTA); *nâpehkâsiw* (VAI).

plug The act of plugging something, **kipunuskuhikewin** (NI); it is plugged or clogged, i.e.: a pipe, **kipsiw** (VAI); a wooden plug, **kipahikan** (NI); something plugged or clogged, **kipwâw** (VII).

plumage *sîsîp pewaya* (NI); *mekwanak* (NA).

plume *misi mekwan ka wawesihcikakehk* (NA).

plump *awîyak nahiyikohk ka weyinot* (VAI) *or* (NA).

plumy *awîyak ka mehawesit* (NA).

plunder Taking things away from people by force, **masaskoniwewin** (NI); s/he plunders her/him or them, **manawatew** (VTA).

plunge *kîkway ka tahkahtamihk* (VAI).

plunk *ka mistowehtahk kîkway* (VAI).

plus *mâmawakihcikewin* (NI); something additional, *mina* (IPC).

plush *metoni ka yoskekahk ayanis* (VII); a fabric like velvet, *sôskwekin* (NI).

ply *awîyak kahkamwemiht* (VAI).

pocket A pouch inserted in a garment, *asiwacikan* (NI).

pocketful *asiwacikan ka kipwâskinek* (VII).

pockmark *ocikisiwin* (NI) *(Plains)*; *ocesiwin* (NI) *(Northern)*; *kocesisihk nânitâw* (VAI); s/he has a scar, *ocesisiw* (VAI) *(Northern)*; *ocikisiw* (VAI) *(Plains)*.

pockmarked *ocesisiwin* (NI).

pod *payipahikan* (NI).

podgy *awîyak ka picikokamosit* (VAI).

poignancy *wîsakitehewin* (NI).

poignant *awîyak ka wîsakitehet* (VAI) or (VII).

point When pointing to something, *ketwahamihk kîkway* (VAI); s/he points to her/him, *itwahwew* (VTA).

point Or cape, *miniwatim* (NI); at the point advancing in water, the cape, *miniwatimik* (NI); there is a point or cape, *miniwatimiwiw* (VII) *(Northern)*; *neyâw* (VII) *(Plains)*; a wooded point, i.e.: on a lake, *nimitâweyâskweyâw* (VII).

point-blank Shooting at something at a close distance, *metoni ka kistahamihk kîkway* (VAI); s/he shoots her/him point blank, *kistahwew* (VTA).

pointed Something pointed, *kîkway kacîpwak* (VII); s/he is pointed, *cîposiw* (VAI); it has grown pointed, *cîpwaskisiw* (VAI); it is standing pointed, i.e.: teepee, *cîpwaskitew* (VII); it has a pointed shape, *cîpwâw* (VII); it is pointed and sharp, i.e.: knife, *kînikâw* (VII); s/he sharpens it to a point with a knife, i.e.: sticks or poles, *kenikîhkohtew* (VTA); s/he chops it to a point with an axe, *kînikikahwew* (VTA); a pointed nose, *kînikikotew* (NA); it is pointed, i.e.: a rock, *kinikisiw* (VAI).

pointer *itwahikakan* (NI).

pointless *kwanta tôtamowin* (NI).

poise *sohkâyâwin* (NI).

poison *piscipowin* (NI); it is poisononous, *piscipowiniwiw* (VAI); s/he took poison, *piscipiw* (VAI); s/he poisons her/him on purpose, *piscipohew* (VTA); s/he poisons herself/himself, *piscipoyisiw* (VAI); a poisoner, *piscipoyiwiwiyiniw* (NA).

poke Poking, *cahkahikewin* (NI); poking with a needle, *cîstahikewin* (NI); s/he poked her/his eye, *cahkâpawew* (NA); a branch poked her/his eye, *cahkâpicin* (VAI); s/he got poked with a sharp object, *cahkicin* (VAI); s/he burns with a flaming stick, *cahkaskiswew* (VTA); an innoculation needle, *cîstahikan* (NI); s/he poked her/him with something sharp, i.e.: needle, *cîstahwew* (VTA).

poker A stoker used in the fire, *yahkisehikâkan* (NI) *(Plains and Northern variant)*; *tahtaskosehikakan* (NI) *(Northern)*.

pole *kacimahiht mistik pewapiskos ohci* (VAI); a fence pole, *wâsakanikanahtik* (NA); a house pole, *wâskahikanatik* (NA); a tent pole, *apasoyâhtik* (NA); a pole for a boat, *kwakosonâtik* (NA); poling upstream, *kwakosowin* (NI); it is a large round pole, *mihcâskwan* (VAI) or (VII); it is a good pole, *miyowâskwan* (VAI) or (VII) *(Northern)*; *miywâskwan* (VAI) or (VII) *(Plains)*; a long, dry pole, *sîpeyâskwan* (VAI) or (VII); a pole used for a teepee frame, *mîkowâhp apasiy* (NI).

polite Kind, *yospisiwin* (NI); *manâtisiw* (VAI).

pomp *katâwasisowin* (NI); a showy display of something, *katâwasisin* (VAI) or (VII).

pomposity *mistahi iteyimisowin* (NI).

pompous Being a show-off or being stuck up, *misteyimisowin* (NI).

pond *wâyipîyâs* (NA); *sâkahikanis* (NA); a small body of water, *ka wâyipîyâsik* (NA).

ponder *mâmitoneyihtam* (VAI); pondering, *mâmitoneyihtamowin* (NI).

ponderable *awîyak ka tâpeyimiht* (VAI).

ponderous *mawiyas kihci ayamihewiyeniw* (NA).

pontifical *kihci ayamihewiyeniw ka ayamihat* (VTA).

pontificate *kihci ayamihewiyeniw ka nîsohkamaket ayamihawnihk* (VAI).

pony *tehtapîwatimos* (NA); *miscacimosis* (NA).

pool Pooling money for something, *ka mâmawascikehk sôniyâw* (VTA); a pool of water, i.e.: a dugout, *wâyipiyaw* (NI) or (VII).

poor Being poor, *kitimâkisowin* (NI); a poor person, *kitimâkis* (NA); *okitimâkisiw* (NA); s/he is poor or lacking possessions, *kitimâkisiw* (VAI).

poorly *ka kitimâksehcikehk* (VAI).

pope The highest holy father, *mâmawiyas kihci ayamihewiyeniw* (NA); the highest priesthood, *mâmawiyas kihci ayamihewiyiniw* (NA).

poplar *mitos* (NA); white poplar, *sôskomitos* (NA); black poplar, *mâyimitos* (NA).

popular *ka miweyihtakosihk* (VAI).

popularity *miweyihtakosiwin* (NI).

porcupine *kâkwa* (NA); porcupine quill, *kâkwiy* (NA).

pore *metoni peyahtik ka mâmitoneyihtamihk* (VAI).

pore *ka payepisit masakay* (NA).

pork *kohkôsiwiyâs* (NI).

porky *wiyin* (NI).

porker *kohkôsis ka wiyinohiht* (NA).

porridge *kîkisepâ mîcowin* (NI).

port Wine drink, *sôminâpoy* (NI); embarcation point, *nakîwin* (NI).

portable *apiscikîkwas* (NI).

portage *onikewin* (NI); packing something across land, *kaskewetowatewin* (NI); a portage trail, *kaskewewin* (NI); s/he portages, *kaskewew* (VTA).

portend Something foretold, *ka neyak wihtamâkehk* (VII).

portion *ketisk pahki* (IPC); *pahki* (IPC).

portly *mistatayewin* (NI).

portray *naspasinahikewin* (NI).

pose *kwayask kapihk kaweh masinipayihk* (VTA); *nahawapiw* (VAI).

posh *metoni okimawâyâwin* (NI).

position *awîyak tansi ka itâpit* (VAI).

positive S/he is sure or positive, *kehcinâhiw* (VAI); s/he thinks positively of her/him, *takahkeyimew* (VAI); s/he has positive thoughts about herself/himself, *takahkeyimow* (VAI); s/he makes her/him feel positive, *takahkeyitamohew* (VTA).

possess Owning something, *ka ayâhk kîkway* (VAI); s/he owns her/him, *ayâwew* (VTA); it possesses or enters her/his body, *pehciyaweskawew* (VTA); having one's own property, *ayâw* (VTA).

possessed *kîkway ayâwin* (NI); under influence of evil forces, *awîyak kakikiskakot maci kîkway* (VAI).

possession *ka tipeyawehohk kîkway* (VAI); the act of having something as your own, *ayâwin* (NI).

possessive *ka tipeyihtamohkasohk* (VAI).

possessor *otipeyihcikew* (NA).

possibility *mâskôc ahpô takeh ispayow kîkway* (IPC), *mâskôcetikwe* (IPC); it could happen that way, *takehihkin* (IPC).

possible *kîkway ka pakoseyimohk* (VAI); *tapwe mâskôc* (IPC); as much as possible, *ahpô etikwe tespayiw* (IPC).

possum A small animal, *pisiskîs* (NA).

posterity *nîkân mamitoneyihcikewin* (NI).

postpone *ka âhtastahk isihcikewin* (NI) or (VAI).

postponement *âhtsehcikewin* (NI); "wait for now", to indicate you're not quite ready, *ceskwa pita* (IPC).

pot A soup making pot, *pakâhcikewaskihk* (NI); a little pot or pail, *askihkos* (NI); a flat pot or pail, *napakaskihk* (NI).

potato *uskipwâw* (NI); *lupatuk* (NI) *(French Cree)*.

potbellied *awîyak ka mistatayet* (VAI).

potbelly *mistatayewin* (NI).

potency *miyomahcihowin* (NI); male strength, *nâpewâyâwin* (NI).

potent *kîkway ka maskawâk* (VAI); potent liquid, alcohol, *maskawâkamow* (VII).

potential *kekâc kakehcinâhohk* (VII) or (VAI).

potentiality *kekâc kehcinâhowin* (NI).

potentially *kekâc kehcinâhowenihk* (VAI).

potion *maskihkiwapiy* (NI) *(Plains)*; (swamp soup) *maskekew pakâhcikewin* (NI).

potter *owîceskoyakinikew* (NA) *(Plains)*; *otoyiskowakinikew* (NA) *(Northern)*.

potted *pakâhcikan* (NI).

pouch A tobacco pouch, *cistemâw ahpihtis* (NI); a little bag, *maskimotis* (NI); a pouch for carrying gunpowder, *pihcipihkwan* (NI); a pouch for carrying gun pellets, *pihtasinân* (NI).

pouchy *ka pitikohkwakanet awîyak* (VAI).

poultice *kotahcikemakahk akohpisowin* (NI); a medicine man's technique for sucking out poison, *otahcikewimaskihkiy* (NI); a mustard plaster, *kotawahkân* (NI).

poultry *pahkahahkwan wiyâs* (NI); pullet, *pâpahakwan* (NA).

pounce *ka sikôc otihtinamihk kîkway* (VAI); *kwâskwehtotawew* (VTA).

pound One pound, *peyak kosikwan* (NI); pounded dried meats, *iyiwahikanak* (NI).

pound Smashing something up, i.e.: dry meat, *ka sikwatahikehk* (VAI); s/he pounds her/him, *yiwahwew* (VTA); s/he is pounding the meat, *yiwahikew* (VTA); s/he smashes them up by pounding, *yiwatahwew* (VTA); a piece of dry, pounded moose meat, *yiwahikan* (NI).

pour The act of pouring, *sîkinkewin* (NI); it has poured out or spilled, *sekipayiw* (VTA); it has poured out or spilled, *sekipayin* (VAI); s/he pours her/him a cup of something, *sîkinamawew* (VTA); s/he pours them out or empties them, i.e.: a pail of something, *sîkinew* (VTA).

pout The act of pouting, *mihtawewin* (NI); s/he pouts at her/him, *mihtawamew* (VTA); s/he pouts because s/he does not have enough, *mihtawew* (VTA).

pouter *awîyak ka mihtaweskit* (VAI) or (NA).

pouty *ka mihtawehk* (VII).

powder *wihkimâkwahon* (NI).

powdery *metoni ka pikinak* (NI) or (VAI).

power Being powerful, *maskawisewin* (NI); strongly, with power, or strength, *sohki* (IPC); *sohkahâc* (IPC); a spirit power, *mamahtâwisiwin* (NI); the object embodying sacred power or spirit power, *manitohkân* (NA); s/he makes her/him a spirit power, *manitohkew* (VTA); to see in a concrete form sacred power, *manitohkewin* (NI); it is the expression of spirit power, *manitowan* (VII); it has spirit power or it is religious, *manitowâtan* (VII); s/he has medicine power or sacred power, *manitowiw* (VAI); the act of expressing sacred power or divinity, *manitowiwin* (NI).

powerful A powerful person, *awîyak kamaskawiset* (VAI); s/he is powerful, *maskawâtisiw* (VAI); s/he is spiritually powerful, religious, devout, *manitowâtisiw* (VAI); the act of being spiritually powerful or devout,

387

manitowâtisiwin (NI); it is powerfully built, i.e.: a bridge, *sohkâtan* (VII).

powerfully *maskawisewnihk ohci* (VII); s/he is powerfully built or robust, *sohkisiw* (VAI).

powerless *ekâ kîkway maskawisewin ka yahk* (VII).

powwow *maskisimowin* (NI).

practicability *ka wehcihômakahk kîkway* (VII).

practicable *kîkway ka wehcihôpayik* (VII).

practical *ka nakacihtâhk kîkway* (VII); *tahki âpatan* (IPC); useable and useful, *miya âptan*.

practically *kekâc poko* (IPC).

practice *sîsawewin* (NI); *kahketwamitôtamowin* (NI).

practise *or* **practice** Someone doing the same thing every day, *awîyak pahpeyakwan katotahk tahto kîsikâw* (VAI); the act of practicing spirit rites, *kosâpahtamowin* (NI); *kosâpahcikewin* (NI).

practictioner S/he is a practioner of spirit rites, *kosâpahtam* (NA) *or* (VII).

prairie *maskotew* (NI); it is prairie, *maskotewan* (VII); a big meadow, *paskwâhk* (NI); there is a big meadow, *paskwâw* (VII); there are wood islands in the prairie, *ayapâskweyâw* (VII); woods advance into prairie, *neyâskweyâw* (VII); *neyâskwâw* (VII); *pimâskweyâw* (VII); there is space, prairie, open land in between, *tâstawayâw* (VII); high trees on the edge of woods and prairie, *ispâskweyâw* (VII); there is a prairie, *maskotewiw* (VAI); a prairie man, *maskotewiyiniw* (NA); an endless prairie vista, *pihtaskoteweyâw* (VII).

prairie chicken *âhkiskiw* (NA); it flaps its wings as a mating call, i.e.: refers to prairie chickens, *takwâstoyew* (NA).

prairie dog *pasowahkesîs* (NA); *paskwâwatimosis* (NA).

praise Praising someone, *mamihcimowewin* (NI); s/he praises it, *mamihtôtam* (VAI); s/he praises her/him or s/he speaks approvingly of her/him, *mamihcîmew* (VTA) *(Plains)*; *kâkihcimew* (VTA) *(Northern)*; s/he praises herself/himself, *kakihcimow* (VAI); the act of praising or adulating oneself, *kakihcimowin* (NI).

praiseworthy Someone who is deserving of praise, *awîyak ka kîspinatahk tamâmihcimiht* (VAI) *or* (VTA); s/he is praiseworthy, *mâmihteyihtakosiw* (VAI); the act of being praiseworthy, *mâmihteyihtakosiwin* (NI).

prance *mistatim ka sahsimacet* (VTA).

prank Playing a prank, *nanoyacihiwewin* (NI).

prankish *ka nanoyacihiweskihk* (VAI).

prankster *nanoyacihiwesk* (NA).

prattle *pahpayakitonewin* (NI).

pray Christian praying, *ayamihâwin* (NI); s/he prays to God, *ayamihâw* (VTA); *kâkesimow* (VTA); s/he supplicates to the spirits with humility, *kâkesimow* (VTA); when you pray to God, *kâ ayamihâhk* (VTA); s/he communicates with the spirit world or s/he prays to her/him, *kâkesimototawew* (VTA); s/he finishes praying or s/he completes her/his prayers, *poni ayamihâw* (VTA); s/he prays with her/him, *wîcâyamihâmew* (VTA).

prayer Communion with the spirits, *kakesimowin* (NI); Christian prayer, *ayamihâwin* (NI); *kakesimowin* (NI); people who pray, *otayamihâwak* (NA); *okakesimowâk* (NA); s/he is at prayer or doing spiritual devotions, *mekwâ ayamihâw* (VTA).

prayer book *ayamihew masinahikan* (NI).

prayerful *awîyak kanihtâ ayamihat* (VTA) *or* (VII).

prayer meeting *mâmawi ayamihâwin* (NI).

preach *ka keskihkemowin* (NI).

preacher *okakeskihkemiw* (NA); *okakeskimiwew* (NI).

preaching *ka kâkeskihkemohk* (VII).

preachy *awîyak ka nihtâ ka keskihkemot* (VII).

prearrange *kakwayatascikehk* (VTA).

precarious *ekâ metoni kakecinahohk* (IPC); *wâneyihtôtamowin* (NI); insecure and uncertain, *wanâyâwin* (NI).

precaution Taking precaution, *asweyihtamowin* (NI); s/he is on the look out for it, *asweyihtam* (NI); s/he takes precaution against her/him, *asweyimew* (VAI); prudent foresight, *nâkateyihtamowin* (NI).

precautionary *kîkway ka asweyihtamihk* (VAI).

precede *kîkway ka nîkânispayik* (VAI); going before in place or time or rank, *nîkânohtew* (VAI).

preceding *nîkân sihcikewin* (NI).

precious *mistahi kîspehteyihtakwahk* (VAI); held in great esteem, *ayiwâkiteyihtakwan* (VII).

preciously *miyotôtamowinihk* (VII).

precipice *ka sikôc kîskâpiskâhk waci* (VAI); an overhanging cliff or cut bank, *kîskatinâw* (NI).

precipitous *kîkway ka ayiminakwahk* (VAI); a steep hill, *kîskahcâw* (NI).

precise *metoni kwayask* (IPC); *mweci* (IPC).

precisely *metoni kekâc kwayask* (IPC).

precision *metoni kwayaskopayowin* (NI).

preclude *kîkway ka nakinikemakahk* (VAI).

preclusion *nakinikewin* (NI).

precocious *awâsis ka keyipi kiskeyihtahk* (VAI).

predatory *awîyak ka nocitâsot* (VAI) *or* (VTA).

predetermine *nîkân kwayaskosihcikewin* (NI).

predicament *wâneyihtamipayowin* (NI); a trying or dangerous situation, *âyimihowin* (NI).

predict *neyak wihtamowin* (NI); *pakwanaw wihtamowin* (NI).

prediction *kwayaci wihcikewin* (NI).

predictive *ka kihkânâkwahk kîkây îwihispâyik* (VAI).

predispose *ka nehpemascikehk* (VTA).

predisposition *nehpemascikewin* (NI).

predominant *ka oyinamihk kîkway* (NI).

predominate *oyinikewin* (NI).

pre-eminent *awîyak ka cacotasot* (VTA).

388

pre-emption *cacowihiwewin* (NI).
preen *kânâcihiw* (VAI).
prefer *pîtos kîkway kantaweyihtamihk* (VAI);
ayiwâkeyitam (VAI).
preferable *ka nîkân astahk* (VAI).
preferably *nîkân ascikewin* (NI).
preference *kotak kîkway nawac* (IPC); the act of
prefering, *nawasonikewin* (NI).
pregnancy *ayâwâwasowin* (NI).
pregnant *iskwew ka ayâwâwasot* (VTA); she is
pregnant, i.e.: refers to pregnant animals, *pwawew*
(VAI); *pwawewahcesiw* (VAI); he made her pregnant
with an illegitimate child, *kîminîcâkanihkawew*
(VTA).
preliminary *kwayacesihcikewin* (NI); leading up to
something more important, *nistam katôtamihk* (VAI).
premonition *oywâscikewin* (NI); telling something
ahead of time, *nîkân wihtamâkewin* (NI); s/he has a
premonition about her/him, *oywâstawew* (VTA); a
premonition or a thought about a coming event,
tapiskoteyicikan (VII); s/he has a premonition about
them or s/he has thoughts about them,
tapiskoteyimew (VAI); a foreboding, i.e.: as of
impending danger, *moyehtamowin* (NI); a psychic,
otoywâscikew (NA).
premonitory *ka nîkân wihtamihk* (VAI).
preoccupation *otameyihtamowin* (NI).
preoccupy S/he is preoccupied with her/him,
otameyimew (VAI); it is preoccupying,
otameyihtâkwan (VII).
preparation Getting ready, *wawîyewin* (NI).
preparative *kîkway ka wawiyestamihk* (VTA) *or* (VAI).
preparatory *wawiyesicikewin* (NI).
prepare Preparing for something, *ka wawiyehk* (VAI);
s/he prepares it ahead of time, *kwayacisihtâw* (VII);
s/he prepares her/his pipe, *oyaskinahew* (VTA); s/he
prepares a pipe for her/him, *oyaskinatowew* (VTA).
preparedness *kakiki ka wawiyestamihk* (VII).
prepay *ka nîkân tipahikehk* (VTA).
preponderance *paskeyâkewin* (NI).
preponderant *ka paskeyâkehk* (VTA).
prepositional *nîkân îsihcikasowewin* (NI).
prepossess *akâwâcikewin* (NI), *akâwâsowewin* (NI).
prepossessing *kwayaci otintowin* (NI).
prepossession *kwayaci ka otinamihk kîkway* (VAI).
preposterous *kîkway ka mâyenakwahk* (VII); contrary
to common sense, foolish, *ka kepâtisiwin* (NI).
presage *neyakoci wihtamâkewin* (NI); the act of giving
a warning before hand, *neyakoci wihtamâkewin* (NI).
presence *wîcihiwewin* (NI).
present Being present, *ka wîcihiwehk* (VAI) *or* (VTA);
s/he is present, *otahayaw* (VAI); something you give

away, *kîkway kamekihk* (VAI); things that you give
away, i.e.: presents or gifts, *mekiwina* (NI).
presentable *ekâ ka manawâpahtehiwehk* (VAI) *or* (VTA).
presently *mekwâc ôma* (IPC).
preservation *manâcihcikewin* (NI).
preserve *micowin ka nahastahk* (VTA).
preserver *onahascekew* (NA).
press *ka makwahamihk* (VAI).
pressing *ka makwahikehk* (VTA).
pressure Applying pressure or pressing something down
with force, *makwahikewin* (NI); s/he puts pressure on
her/him or s/he forces her/him, *sihcihew* (VAI)
(Plains); s/he puts pressure on herself/himself or s/he
forces herself/himself, *sihciw* (VAI); *sihcihew* (VAI)
(Plains) the act of putting pressure on oneself or the
act of forcing oneself, *sihciwin* (NI); feeling pressure,
sihtamahcihowin (NI) *(Plains)*; *sihcîsâyâwin* (NI)
(Northern).
prestige *miyowihowin* (NI).
prestigious *metoni ka mamisehk* (IPC).
persuasion *sihkiskâkewin* (NI) *(Plains)*; *sihkihkemowin*
(NI) *(Northern)*.
presumable *mosci tâpiyihtamowin* (NI).
presumably *ahpô etoki keteyihtamihk* (VAI).
presume *ka mosci kakwe tâpeyihtamihk* (VAI);
iteyihtam (VAI); taking for granted or assuming,
iteyihtamiwin (NI).
presumption *kwanta pitoskiteyihtamihk* (VAI).
presumptive *kwanta iteyihcikewin* (NI).
presuppose *kwayaci ka mâmitoneyihtamihk* (VAI).
presupposition *kwayaci mâmitoneyihcikewin* (NI).
pretence *or* pretense *mweci tapwi ka tôtamihk* (VAI); a
sham or false profession, *kîmôtâtisiwin* (NI).
pretend The act of pretending, *kwanta katôtamihk*
(VTA); s/he pretends to pray, *kakayesi ayamihâw* (VAI).
pretended *awîyak ka wayesihtât* (VTA).
pretender *owayesihtâw* (NA).
pretentious *ka nihtâ wayesihtâhk* (VAI).
pretty *katawasisiw* (VAI).
prevail *paskeyâkewin* (NI); being victorious, *sakôcihew*
(VTA).
prevailing *kîkway ka paskeyâkomakahk* (VII).
prevalence *paskeyâkepayowin* (NI).
prevalent *awîyak ka paskeyâket* (VAI).
prevent *ka kitinamihk* (VAI); *nakinam* (VTA).
preventable *kitinikewin* (NI).
preventative *kîkway ka kitinikakehk* (VAI); preventing
or precautionary, *kipihtinikewin* (NI).
prevention *kitinikewin* (NI).
preventive *kîkway ka kitinamihk* (VAI); *ka
nakinamihk* (VAI); *kakipihtinamihk* (VAI).

389

previous *awaspeh kîkway kake ispayik* (VII); prior or earlier or foregoing, *âstamispeh* (IPV).

prey *pisiskow ka nipahat weci pisiskowa* (VTA); *minahowin* (NI).

prick *ka cîstahowehk* (VTA).

prickle *keyakistahikewin* (NI).

prickly *nepeyah ka cîstahikemakahkwaw* (VII).

pride Taking pride of oneself, *mâmihteyimisowin* (NI); having vain pride, *kisteyimowin* (NI).

priest *ayamiheweyiniw* (NA); a holy father, *ayamiheweniw* (NA).

priestess *ayamihewiskwew* (NA).

priesthood *ayamiheweyiniwiwin* (NI) *(Northern)*; *pahkwâyamihewiyiniwiwin* (NI) *(Plains)*.

priestly *ka ayamihewiyiniw isayahk* (VII) *or* (VAI).

prim *mistahi ka iteyemisohk* (VAI).

primacy *ka okimâw apsihk* (VAI).

primarily *nîkânpayowenihk* (VII).

primary *kîkway ka macipayik* (VII); from the start, *nistamoci* (VII).

primate A high ranking bishop, *ayamihewiniw otapiwin* (NI).

prime *metoni ka nâpew ayâhk* (VII); *kîsopikiwin* (NI); *maskawatisowin* (NI).

prior *pâmayes* (IPC).

priority *kîkway ka nîkâneyihtakwahk* (VII).

pristine *kîkway ka oskayowik* (VII).

privacy *peyakowin* (NI).

private *kapahpeyakohk* (VAI).

privilege *miyopayowin* (NI); *pakitinamâkewin* (NI).

prize *kîkway kakispinatamihk* (VAI); *kîspinatamâsowin* (NI).

probable *apô etoki takeh ispayow* (IPC); *takihkin* (IPC).

probe *kîkway ka wapahcikakehk pehcayihk meyawihk* (VAI); *natonikew* (VAI).

problem *ka âyimahk* (VII); *âyimisiwin* (NI); s/he gives her/him problems, *âyimihiwew* (VTA).

problematic *âyimahkamikan* (VII).

problematical *âyimahkamikisowin* (NI).

procedure *mâtakamikisowin* (NI).

proceed *mâtakamikisiw* (VAI).

process *nahascikewin* (NI).

proclaim *kîkway ka wihtamihk* (VAI); *wihtam* (VAI); declare publically, *wihtamakewin* (NI).

procreate *kohpikihâwasohk* (VTA).

procreation *ohpikihâwasowin* (NI).

procure *kakahtinkatek kîkway* (VAI); obtaining something, *otinkewin* (NI).

procurement *kahtinikewin* (NI) *(Northern)*; *kahtitinikewin* (NI) *(Plains)*.

prod *tôskwahikewin* (NI).

produce *ka wapahtehiwehk* (VTA); produce from a good garden, *nihtâwikihcikan* (NI).

producible *kîkway ka miyo mekihk* (VAI) *or* (VTA).

product *kîkway kosihtâhk ahpô kohpikihtahk* (VTA).

production *osihcikewin* (NI).

productive *ka nihtâ osihcikehk* (VII).

productivity *nihtâ osihcikewin* (NI).

profess *ka wihtamihk kîkway* (VAI).

professed *awîyak ka wihtahk* (VTA).

proficient *metoni takahkiwepinkewin* (NI).

proficiency *metoni ka kaskihtahk* (VAI).

profile *tansi kesinakosit awîyak* (VII); a side view of the face, *sinakosowin* (NI).

profound *metoni sohkeyihtamowin* (NI); intense or deeply felt, *itamihk mosihtâwin* (NI).

profuse *ekâ ka mana mekihk kîkway* (VAI); abundant or liberal to excess, *mistahi miyowicihtowin* (NI).

progeny Offspring or descendants, *wahkohtowin* (NI).

program *or* **programme** *kîkway isihecikewin* (NI).

progress *ka nîkânehk* (VAI) *or* (VTA); *yahkotewin* (NI).

progression *nîkânewin* (NI).

progressive *ka nihtâ nîkânehk* (VII); *yayahkotew* (VTA).

prohibit *ka nakinamâkehk* (VTA).

prohibition *nakinamâkewin* (NI).

prohibitive *ka nakinamihk* (VAI).

project *oyesehcikewin* (NI); *kamamawi osihtahk* (VAI) *or* (VTA).

projection *ka semakamok kîkway* (VAI).

proliferate *ka kisiskâ ohpikihk kîkway* (VAI).

proliferation *kisiskâ ohpikihcikewin* (NI).

prolific *kisiskâ ohpikihitowin* (NI).

prolong *ka pîsâkohcikehk* (VII); *kinohtâw* (VTA); extent in time or length, *kinosihcikewin* (NI).

prolongation *ka aniskosihcikehk* (VTA).

promentory A rocky promontory, *neyâpiskâw* (NI); a wooded promontory, *neyâskweyâw* (NI); a promontory covered with jackpines, *neyâhtakâw* (NI).

prominence *mistahi iteyihtakosowin* (NI).

prominent *awîyak kakihceyihtâkosit* (VAI); really distinguished, *misteyihtakosiwin* (NI).

promise *asotamowin* (NI); the act of making a promise, *asotamakewin* (NI); s/he made a promise, *asocikew* (VAI); s/he promises, *asotam* (VAI); s/he has promised something to someone, *asotamakew* (VAI); s/he promises her/him, *asotamawew* (VTA); s/he puts a curse on her/him, *asomew* (VTA).

promising *kekâc kehcinahowin* (NI).

promote Starting something, *ka sipwepayihcikehk* (VTA); s/he promotes her/him ahead of everybody, *nânekâminew* (VAI); s/he promotes herself/himself over everyone else, *nânekâmisiw* (VAI); the act of

390

promoting oneself over everyone else, **nânekamisowin** (NI).

prompt *awîyak ka ahkamowemiht* (VTA); quick to eat, **semaktôtam** (VAI).

prone *ka otihtapisinihk* (VTA).

proneness *ka wahkew tôtamihk kîkway* (VAI).

prong A sharp horn, **oteskan** (NI).

pronghorn *apiscacihkos* (NA).

pronounce *kihkapekiskwewin* (NI); s/he said something, **itwew** (VTA).

pronounced *awîyak ka kihkapekiskwet* (VTA).

pronounciation The act of pronouncing words, **nihtâwewin** (NI).

proof *ka kehcinâhohk* (VAI); **kehcinâhowin** (NI).

prop Helping something to stand up, **kasimataskwahamihk kîkway** (VAI); a support from falling over, **sîtwâskwahikan** (NI).

propagate *ka kîyiposehk* (VTA).

propagation *kîyiposewin* (NI).

propel Drive forward by force, **sipwepayihcikewin** (NI).

proper *katawahk* (VII).

properly *metoni kwayask* (IPC).

prophecy *oteh nîkân ka kiskeyihtamihk* (VII); a prediction of the future, **nîkân wehtamowin** (NI).

prophesy *nîkân kiskowehikewin* (NI).

prophet *okakiskihkemow* (NA); one who predicts the future, **okiskiwehikew** (NA).

prophetic *awîyak ka nihtâ ka kiskihkemot* (NA).

proportion *ka tipowakeyihtamihk kîkway* (VAI); how much?, **tânimayikohk** (IPC).

proportionable *miyo tipowakeyihcikewin* (NI).

proportional *pahpeyakwan eyikohk ka ayâhk* (VII).

proportioned *awîyak ka nihtâ tipowakeyihtahk* (VII) or (NA).

proposal *nitomiskwewewin* (NI).

propose *awîyak ka nitomiskwewet* (VTA).

proposition *isihcikâsowewin* (NI); **kamâmitoneyihtamihk** (VII).

prospect *kîkway ka pakoseyihtamihk* (VII); **nocisoniyawewin** (NI).

prospective *pakoseyimowin* (NI).

prospectively *pakoseyimowinihk* (VII).

prosper *ka sônîyâhkepayihk* (VII).

prosperity *miyopayowin* (NI).

prosperous *ka miyopayihk* (VII).

prostitute *pisikwât iskwew* (NA); **omanisônîyâwew** (NA).

prostrate *ka pimâpekastesimiht awîyak* (VTA); s/he is lying flat, **samakisin** (VTA); **sâsakitisin** (VTA) *(Plains)*.

prostration *pimâpekastesimowewin* (NI).

prosy *ekâ ka nihtâ pikiskwet awîyak* (VAI) or (VII).

protect *kanaweyimowewin* (NI).

protectingly *nâkateyimiwewnihk* (VII).

protection Keeping something from harm, **ka nâkateyimiwehk** (VTA); s/he has protection from a charm, **kanawisimow** (VAI); something which offers protection, i.e.: a bear claw, **kanawisimowin** (NI); it is a protective charm, **kanawisimowiniwin** (NI).

protective Something that is protective, **ka kanaweyicikemakahk** (VAI).

protector A protective person, **onâkateyimowew** (NA).

protest *ka pekiskwatamihk kîkway* (VTA); formally objecting to, **ânwehtamowin** (NI).

Protestant *âkayâsiw ayamihâw* (NA).

protestantism *âkayâsiw ayamihâwin* (NI).

protrude Something sticking out of something, **kakwayakwamok kîkway** (VAI); it is sticking out, **sakamow** (VAI); her/his tail is up in the air, **cahkâyowew** (VTA); it protrudes upwards, e.g.: a boil, **câhkipayiw** (VAI); it sticks out, **sâkamow** (VAI).

protrusion *kwayakwamohcikewin* (NI).

protuberance *pôtawipayowin* (NI).

protuberant *ka pôtawipayihk* (VII).

proud Being proud, **mamihtisowin** (NI); s/he is proud of her/him, **mamihteyimew** (VAI); s/he is proud, **mamihtisiw** (VAI); s/he makes people proud of her/him/her, **mamihcihiwew** (VTA).

prove *kecinahiw* (VAI).

proven *kehcinahowin* (NI).

provide Providing for someone, **ka ohtinamakehk** (VTA); s/he gives it to her/him, **meyew** (VAI); s/he provides sustenance for her/him, **ohtacihew** (VTA).

provided *ohtinamakewin* (NI).

provider Or saviour, **opimâcihiwew** (NA).

providence Divine care from God, **kanaweyihtâkosowin** (NA).

provident *ka nîkân mamitoneyihtamihk* (VII).

providential *ka nihtâ miyopayihk* (VII).

providing *ka pamihiwehk* (VTA).

provision Predisposition, **pamihiwewin ka nehpemascikehk** (VTA).

provoke *kisiwâhew* (VAI).

prowl *natonikewin* (NI).

proximately *kesewak ohci* (IPC).

proximity *kesewak wahkohtowin* (NI).

prude *awîyak ka peyahtikoyisâyat* (VAI).

prudence *peyahtikoyisâyâwin* (NI).

prudent *peyahtik mâmitoneyihcikan* (VII).

prudish *peyahtikowisowin* (NI).

pry Prying something up by force, **kohpâskwahamihk** (VTA).

prying Lifting something up by force, **ohpâskwahikewin** (NI).

psalm *ayamihâwin* (NI); a religious way, **nikamon ayamihâwinihk** (NI).

391

psalmbook *ayamihew masinahikan* (NI).
psyche S/he becomes part of her/his psyche
   pihtâkoyaweskawew (VAI) *(Plains)*;
   pihcitahcâhkoweskawew (VAI) *(Northern)*.
ptarmigan *wapîhew* (NA).
puberty *metoni kesohpikowin* (NI).
pubic *kopewahk* (NI); pubic hair, *opîwâwin* (NI)
   (Northern); *miyacowân* (NI) *(Plains)*.
public *kahkiyaw awîyak* (NA).
publicly *metoni mosis ka tôtamihk* (VAI).
pucker *ka ocipotonehk* (VTA).
puddle *ka wâyipeyâsik* (NI).
pudgy *apisciyenîs ka weyenot* (VAI) *or* (NA); a person
   short and stubby, *pitikosiw* (VAI).
puff The act of breathing hard, *nestwatâmowin* (NI).
puffy S/he is puffy or swollen, *pôtawipayiw* (VAI).
pull Pulling something, *ocipicikewin* (NI); s/he pulls
   her/him ashore, *akwâpitew* (VTA); *kapatenew* (VTA);
   s/he pulls them together, *ascipitew* (VTA); s/he pulls it
   off accidently, *kitiskipitew* (VTA); s/he pulls her/him
   quickly underwater with her/his hands, *kokipitew*
   (VTA); s/he pulled them off, *manipitew* (VTA); s/he
   pulled them all off, *masaskopitew* (VTA); s/he pulls off
   all her/his clothes, *moseskatepitew* (VTA); the act of
   pulling off all clothing, undressing,
   moseskatepitsowin (NI); s/he pulls her/him or it into
   view, *moskipitew* (VTA); s/he pulls it or her/him to a
   stop, *nakipitew* (VAI); s/he pulls from one side,
   napateyapew (VAI); s/he pulls her/him toward shore,
   natakamepitew (VTA); s/he pulls her/him down off
   something, i.e.: from a shelf, *nihcipitew* (VTA); s/he
   pulls her/him, *ocipitew* (VTA); s/he drags or pulls a
   sleigh behind her/him, *otâpew* (VAI); the act of pulling
   or dragging something behind oneself, *otâpewin* (NI);
   s/he pulls it off the wall, *pahkwacipitew* (VTA); s/he
   pulls her/him down with a rope, *pahkihtapekipitew*
   (VTA); s/he pulls the cover off her/him, i.e.: a blanket,
   pâskipitew (VTA); s/he pulls them towards herself/
   himself, *pecipitew* (VTA); s/he came and pulled her/
   him or them down, *peyasipitew* (VTA); s/he pulls from
   one end to the other, *pimisâkâmepicikew* (VAI); s/he
   pulls her/him down flat, *samakipitew* (VTA); s/he pulls
   them together securely, *sanaskipitew* (VTA); s/he pulls
   them underneath, *sîpâpitew* (VTA); s/he pulled her/his
   net under the ice, *sîpâskopitew* (VTA); s/he pulls her/
   him into shore, *sîskipitew* (VTA); s/he pulls them or
   tears them in half, *tâskipitew* (VTA); s/he pulls them
   straight, *tasopitew* (VTA); s/he pulls and rips them
   apart, *taswekipitew* (VTA); s/he pulls them easily,
   yahkipitew (VTA); s/he pulls them off the traps,
   yâyiskipitew (VTA).
pullet *pâpahahkwan* (NA).

pulpit *kîskihkemowinâhtik* (NI).
pulsation *pâhkahamowin* (NI).
pulse A person with a pulse, *ayisiyiniw ka pâhkahahk*
   (VAI); the act of having a pulse, *pâhkahokowin* (NI);
   s/he has a pulse, *pahkaham* (VAI) *(Northern)*;
   pâhkahokow (VAI) *(Plains)*; s/he feels her/his pulse,
   pahkahokohew (VTA); s/he feels a pulse,
   pâhkahokohew (VTA); a pulsation or pulse,
   pâhkahokowin (NI).
pulverize The act of pulverizing, *sikwatahikewin* (NI);
   it is pulverized, *pîkinâw* (VII); s/he pulverizes them
   with her/his hands, *pîkinew* (VTA).
puma *misipisiw* (NA).
punch *awîyak ka pakamahoht* (VTA);
   sewminihkwewnis (NI).
punctual *takosiniwin etah ka kiskimohk* (NI).
punctuality *ka nihtâ takosinihk* (NI).
punctually *nihtâ takohtewenihk* (VII).
puncture The act of puncturing, *pôskotahkahcikewin*
   (NI); s/he made her/him puncture herself/himself, i.e.:
   stepping on a nail, *kisisimew* (VAI); s/he stepped on a
   nail and punctures her/his foot, *kisisin* (VAI).
pungency *ekâ ka manâcimiht awîyak* (VAI).
pungent S/he smells pungent, *wînimâkosiw* (VAI); it
   smells pungent, *wînimâkwan* (VII); the smell of it
   burning is pungent, *wînimâsiw* (VAI); the smell of it is
   burning is pungent, *wînimâstew* (VII); s/he cooks
   them and they produce a pungent smell, *wînimâswew*
   (VAI).
punt *kwaskwenitowan ka tahkiskâht* (VAI).
pup *acimosis* (NA).
pupil *ka kiskinwâhamaht awâsis* (NA); *miskesik* (NI).
puppy Young dog, *oskascimos* (NA).
pure *naspic ka kanâtahk* (VII); *kanâtan* (VII); pure,
   clean, *kanâtisiw* (VAI); *kanâtan* (VII).
purgative *kanâcihcikan* (NI).
purgatorial *kâsenamâkewin* (NI).
purgatory *kâsenamâkew iskotew* (NA).
purge *awîyak ka kâsenamaht* (VAI); *saposikan* (NI).
purification *kanâcicikewin* (NI).
purify *ka kanâcitahk kîkway* (VAI).
purist *okanâcicikew* (NA).
purity *kanâtisiwin* (NI); purity, cleanliness,
   kanâcihowin (NI).
purple *ka âpihtimihkwak* (VII).
purplish *ka âpihtinakwahk* (VII).
purpose *kîkway kohtôtamihk* (VAI); *kîkwayohci* (IPC);
   on purpose, planned or according to plan,
   consequently, *ohcitâw* (IPC).
purposeful *ohcitâw ka tôtaskit awîyak* (VII) *or* (NA).
purposeless *kwantatôtamowin* (NI).
purposely *ohcitâw ka tôtamihk* (VII).

392

purse *sônîyâwiwat* (NI) *(Plains)*; *soniyawat* (NI) *(Northern)*.

pursue Taking after something or someone, *nawaswewin* (NI); s/he follows her/him, *pimitisawew* (VTA); s/he runs after her/him, *nawaswâtew* (VTA); he pursues her or tries to get her for a girlfriend, *nocihiskwewâtew* (VTA).

pursuit *ka pimâmohkehk* (VAI).

pus An abcess or collection of pus, *mîyî* (NI).

push The act of pushing something, *yahkinikewin* (NI); s/he pushes her/him under or into something, *kotâwinew* (VTA); s/he pushes her/him through an opening, *paspinew* (VTA); s/he pushes her/him or it underneath or in between, *sekoyahkinew* (VTA); s/he gives them a push, *yahkinew* (VTA); s/he pushes her/him around, *yahkiskawew* (VTA); s/he gives her/him a push with her/his vehicle, *yahkahwew* (VTA); s/he pushes her/him along or s/he tells her/him to keep going, *yahkitisawew* (VTA).

pussy *minôs* (NA).

pussy willow *acimosihkansak* (NA).

put S/he puts her/him aside, *âhtahew* (VTA); s/he puts them away, *nahahew* (VTA); it is put away, *nahastew* (VII); s/he puts her/him in the wrong place, *naspâtahew* (VTA); s/he puts two people together, *nîswahew* (VTA); s/he is put ahead or in front, *nîkânahâw* (VTA); s/he puts her/him ahead or in front, *nîkânihew* (VTA); s/he puts her/him first, *nistamahew* (VTA); s/he puts her/him over the top, *pasitahew* (VTA);

s/he puts them in their place, *postamohew* (VTA); putting clothes on, *postayiwinisewin* (NI); s/he puts clothes on her/him or s/he dresses her/him, *postayiwinisahew* (VTA); s/he puts clothes on her/him, *kikayiwinsahew* (VTA); s/he puts on her/his own shoes, *postaskisinew* (VTA); s/he puts her/his own apron on, *postaspastakanew* (VTA); s/he puts gloves on her/him, *postastisahew* (VTA); s/he puts on her/his own clothes, *postayiwinisew* (VTA); s/he puts a coat on her/him, *postasakahew* (VTA); s/he puts on her/his own coat, *postasâkew* (VAI); s/he puts on her/his own snowshoes, *postasâmew* (VAI); s/he puts shoes on her/him, *postaskisinahew* (VTA); s/he puts on her/his own footwear, *postaskisinew* (VAI); s/he puts a hat on her/him, *postastotinahew* (VTA); s/he puts on her/his own cap or hat, *postastotinew* (VTA); s/he puts a pair of pants on her/him, *postitâsahew* (VTA); s/he puts on her/his own pants, *postitâsew* (VAI); s/he puts something in the other person's mouth, *saskamohew* (VTA); s/he puts her/him underneath, *sekwahew* (VTI); s/he puts more of them on top, *takwahew* (VTI); s/he puts her/his foot in them, *tâpisikoskawew* (VTA); s/he is able to put her/his arms around her/him, *tepâskonew* (VTA).

put-up S/he plants a tree, s/he puts it up, i.e.: a post, *cimahew* (VTA).

putrefy *ka pikiskatihcikehk* (VAI).

putrid *kîkway ka pikiskatihk* (VII).

puzzlement *wâneyihtamowin* (NI).

393

Q

quack *sîsîp kakitot* (NI).

quail *opâspaskow* (NA); *pihesîs* (NA).

quake *ka namahcipayik* (LN).

qualm *ka mayakeyawehk* (VAI).

quarrel *kehkâhtowin* (NI).

quarrelsome *kehkâhtoskiwin* (NI).

quash *ka nakinamihk weyasowewin* (NI).

quaver *koskoskopayow* (VAI).

queer *waneyihtamisâyâwin* (NI).

quell *nakinikewin* (NI); *âstaweham* (VTI).

quench *kastawehamihk iskotew* (VTI); *âstaweham* (VTI).

querulous *ka pikiskweskihk* (VAI).

query *kakwecikemowin* (NI).

quest *ka natonamihk kîkway* (VTI); *nitawi natonikewin* (NI).

question *kakwecikemowin* (NI).

questionable *namoya kehcinâ* (IPC).

quibble *atâmeyihcikewin* (NI).

quick The act of being quick, *câstapiwin* (NI); s/he is quick, *câstapiw* (VAI).

quicken *ka kiskapayihtahk* (VAI).

quickly *kisiskâc* (IPC); the act of moving quickly, *cacâstapiwin* (NI) *(Plains)*; *tastapayâwin* (NI) *(Northern)*.

quiet A very quiet atmosphere, tranquil, *kakâmwâtahk* (VII); it is tranquil or peacefully quiet, *kâmwâtan* (VII); soothing, quiet speech, *kâmwâcipikiskwewin* (NI); s/he is calm and quiet, *kâmwâcihtakosiw* (VAI); being thought of as very quiet, *kâmwâteyihtâkosiwin* (NI); it is a quiet isolated place, *kâmwâtan* (VII); being quiet and sneaky, *kîmôtisiwin* (NI); the act of being quiet, *kîyamâtisiwin* (NI); s/he is a quiet person, *kîyamâtisiw* (VAI); s/he finds her/him very quiet, *koskwâwâteyemew* (VTA) *(Northern)*; *kâmwâteyimew* (VTA) *(Plains)*.

quieten *kâmwâcihiwewin* (NI).

quietude Melancholic, *kâmwâtisiwin* (NI).

quill *ôkawiy* (NA).

quip *nanoyacitowin* (NI).

quit The act of quitting, *poyiwin* (NI); s/he quit or s/he ceased to work, *poyiw* (VAI).

quits *awîyak ka poyot* (VTI).

quitter *opoyow* (VTI); one who abandons a task through fear, *opomew* (NA).

quiver *kîkway ka nampayik* (LN); a shutter or tremor, *cîhcîpipayaw* (VII); a case for holding arrows, *pihtahcâpân* (NI) *(Northern)*; *pihtatwan* (NI) *(Plains)*.

395

R

rabbit *wâpos* (NA); there are many rabbits, *wâpososkâw* (VII); a rabbit skin, *wâposwayân* (NI).

rabble Unprincipled people, *kîskweweniwak* (NA).

rabid *atim âhkosowin ka ayâhk* (VTI); *tahkwahkew* (VTA); furious and fanatical, *macihtwâwin* (NI).

raccoon *ocikomsis* (NA); a small animal, *pisiskîs* (NA).

race A contest, *kotaskatitowin* (NI); a certain kind of people, *tantowahk ayisiyinowak* (NA); *peyakôskân* (NA).

rack *akocikan* (NI); an open framework for holding articles, *akotascikan* (NI).

racket *kisewehtâwin* (NI).

racy *nanihkisiwin* (NI).

radiance *wâsihkopayowin* (NI).

radiant *ka wâsihkwak kîkway* (VAI); it looks beautiful, *katawasisin* (VII).

radiate *kîkway misiwi ka isiwepahikemakahk* (VII).

raft A flood raft, *mihtot* (NI).

rag *ka sehtakahikan* (NI); *ayanis* (NI).

rage *ka kisowipayihk* (VAI); *kisiwâsowin* (NI).

raging A raging fire, *misikwâhkotew* (NI).

ragged *awîyak ka sikwacipayit* (VTA); dressed in wornout clothes, *tatopayiw* (VAI).

ragweed *macikwanasa* (NI).

rain It is raining, *kimowan* (NI); it is pouring rain, *sekipestâw* (VII); it stops raining, *ponikimowan* (VAI); there is a fine rain, *pîsipestaw* (VII); it is rainy, it rains lightly, *kimowanâyâw* (VII); it is kind of rainy, a very fine steady rain, *kimowanâyâsin* (VII); it will rain or it is going to rain soon, *wehkimiwan* (VII); it looks like it is going to rain or it wants to rain, *nohtekimiwan* (VII); there is a misty rain, *kâskawanipestâw* (VAI); it is raining right now, *mekwâkimowan* (VII); rainwater, *kimowanapoy* (NI); s/he makes it rain, *kimowanihtâw* (NI); a slight, gentle rain at the start of a storm, *pahkipestâw* (VII); it is rainy and cold, *tahkipeyâw* (VII).

rainbow *pîsimoyâpiy* (NI).

raindrop *ka pahkipestâk* (VII); a few raindrops fall, *pakipestâw* (VII).

rainfall *ka misikimowahk* (VAI); when it rains, *kakimowahk* (VII).

rainstorm *ka sikipestâk* (VAI).

rain water *kimowanâpoy* (NI).

rainy *kakah kimowahk* (VII).

raise An increase in wages, *kayahki tipahamâkehk* (VTA); s/he raises children, *ohpikihâwasiw* (VAI); the raising of children, *ohpikihâwasiwin* (NI); s/he brings up or raises her/him, *ohpikihew* (VTA).

raised It is raised ground, *ohpahcaw* (VII).

raisin *sominis* (NI).

ram A male bighorn, *wapemâyatihk* (NA); a mountain sheep, *asiniwaciwacihkos* (NA).

ramble *ka papâmâtcihohk* (VAI); roaming all over, *ayapohtewin* (NI).

rambling *papâmitohtew* (VAI); the act of wandering about, *papâmohtew* (VAI).

ramp *pimohtewin kosihtâhk* (VAI); *âsokanis* (NI); a sloping bridge on a lake shore, *âsokan* (NI).

rampage *sisikociyawesowin* (NI).

rampant *metoni ka kisiwasihk* (VII); raging and unchecked, *wacihkamisiw* (VAI).

ran *awîyak kakeh pimipahtât* (VAI); s/he runs, *pimpataw* (VAI).

rancid Or spoiled food, *miciwin kamisîwanatahk* (NI); it is sour, *sîwâw* (VII); it is rancid, i.e.: grease or something with fat, *sâstehtin* (VII) (*Northern*); *sâsteyâw* (VII) (*Plains and Northern variant*); it is rancid, i.e.: grease or something with fat, *sâstesin* (VAI); it went rancid, *sâstesiw* (VAI); it went rancid, *sâsteyâw* (VII); having a rank or tainted smell or taste, *sîwihtin* (VAI).

random By heart, haphazardly or by guesswork, *pakwanaw* (IPC).

rankle *awîyak ka kisimiht* (VAI).

range *ka misipaskwak* (VII); stove, *kotawânâpisk* (NI).

ransack *apotascikew* (NA).

rascal *awîyak nanoyatisiskit* (NA).

rascality *nanoyatisiskowin* (NI).

rascally *nanoyatisiskowenihk* (VII).

rant *kwanta kwahcitonamowin* (NI).

rap *ka pakamihcakahikesihk* (VAI).

rapacious *ka asiskonâtisihk* (VII).

rapacity *asiskonâtisowin* (NI) (*Northern*); *asponâtisowin* (NI) (*Plains*).

rape *otihtinkewin* (NI); s/he rapes her/him or s/he seizes or grabs her/him, *otihtinew* (VTA).

rapid Moving very fast, *metoni kisiskâc* (IPC); it is flowing rapidly, *kiseciwan* (VII) or (VTI).

rapidity *kisiskâtôtamowin* (NI).

rapid *pawistik* (NI); it has rapids, *pawistikowiw* (VAI).

rapt *osâmôcikeyihtamowin* (NI); ecstatically engrossed or bemused, *miweyihtamowin* (NI).

rapture *metoni ka môcikâyahk* (VII).

rarity *aspîs kîkway* (NI).

rash Like measles, *ka mihkwasepayihk* (VAI); *môskipayowin* (NI).

rashness *mâmâsihkewin* (NI).

rasp *mistikow soskopocikakan* (NI); a file, *kiskiman* (NI).

397

raspberry *ayoskan* (NA).

rat *âpakos* (NA); there are many rat houses, *wistiskaw* (VII); a muskrat, *wacask* (NA).

rational *ka nihtâweyihtamihk* (VII).

rationality *nihtâweyihcikewin* (NI).

rationalize Envisage, *kwayask oyehcikewin* (NI).

rattle A rattle for religious ceremonies, *sîsîkwan* (NA); s/he rattles it, *kitowepayihew* (VTA); it rattles, *kitowepayiw* (VTI); it rattles loudly, *sohkiwehtin* (VAI).

rattler A baby rattle, *sîsîkwanis* (NA).

rattlesnake *misi kinepik wâhyaw kohpehtakosit* (NA); a poisonous snake, *piscipokinepik* (NA).

rattling *sîsîkwan ka metawâkehk* (VII).

ravage *metoni ka misowanâcicikehk* (VTA); s/he ruins her/his reputation, *misiwanâcihtaw* (VTA).

rave *mamihcimitowin* (NI); s/he is talkative, *kakihcimow* (VAI).

ravel *apihkewin* (NI); *apihkopayiw* (VAI).

ravelling *or* **raveling** *ka apihkâtamihk kîkway* (VTI).

raven *kahkakiw* (NA) *(Plains)*; a crow, *âhâsiw* (NA) *(Northern)*.

ravenous *awîyak ka osâm nipahaskatet* (VAI); *kâsakew* (VAI).

ravine It is a ravine, *pasahcâw* (VII); there is a rocky ravine, i.e.: in the mountains, *pasâpiskâw* (VII); a ravine, *tawahcâw* (VII).

ravish *awîyak ka osâm ka tawasisit* (VAI); seize and carry off, rape, *otihtinkewin* (NI).

ravishing *kîkway metoni ka mîwasik* (VII).

raw It is raw, *askâw* (VII); it is raw, i.e.: meat, *askitin* (VAI); it is raw, i.e.: bread or bannock, *askitiw* (VAI); when it is raw, *kâ askak* (VII); s/he makes her/him eat something raw, *askipohew* (VTA); s/he eats something raw, *askipiw* (VAI).

raw-boned *ka cacihkokanehk* (VAI).

rawhide A piece of raw hide, *askekin* (NI).

ray *ka cahkâstek* (VII); *pîsim nokosiw* (VTA).

raze *kîkway ka mescihtâhk* (VTI); *kwahkotew* (VTA).

razor *kâskipason* (NI).

reach Attaining or reaching something, *kîkway kotihtamihk* (VAI); s/he reaches it, *tepinam* (VTI); s/he reaches or arrives on foot, *takohtew* (VAI); s/he reaches her/him, *tepinew* (VTI).

react *tôtamowin* (NI).

reaction *kîkway ka tôtamihk* (VAI).

read S/he reads, *ayamihtâw* (VAI); when s/he reads, *ka ayamihcikehk* (VAI); s/he reads, *ayamihcikew* (VAI); reading material, *ayamihcikewin* (NI).

readable *kihka ayamihcikêwin* (NI).

readily *sôskwâc semak* (IPC).

readiness *kakike nehpem ayâwin* (IPC).

reading S/he is reading, *ayamicikew* (VAI).

re-adjust *meskotastâw* (VAI); *pîtostôtam* (VAI); s/he rearranges, *meskotastâw (vai)*.

ready Being already finished or being ready, *kesâyâwin* (NI); *kesâyâw* (VII); *wawiyew* (VAI); ready, waiting, ready beforehand, *kwayaci* (IPC); now is the time, let's go come on, or ready, *ekwa* (IPC); a little postponement to indicate you're not quite ready, *ceskwa pita* (IPC); s/he is ready or set to go, *nehpemew* (VAI); the act of being ready or set to go, *nehpemewin* (NI); s/he gets ready, *wawiyew* (VAI); s/he gets her/him ready, *wawiyehew* (VTA).

real *metoni kehcina kîkway* (IPC); *tâpwehtâkwan* (VII).

realization *peyisk ka kiskeyihtamihk* (VAI).

realize *moyehcikewin* (NI); *kiskeyihtamowin* (NI).

really *tahtâpwe* (IPC); really!, or an exclamation of big surprise such as "oh my that is terrible" as in "you're kidding!" *ayiwâkehkin* (IPC).

realm *kihci wîyâsowewin* (NI); *tipeyicikîwin* (NI).

reap *ka mâwasakonamihk kistikânsa* (VTI); *manisam* (VTA); *manisikew* (VAI).

reappear *asaymîna takosin* (VAI); *kîhtwam nôkwan* (VII).

rear *otahk ohci* (LN); *otahkisi* (LN); s/he rears or raises her/him or s/he brings her/him up, *ohpikihew* (VTA).

rearrange *meskotascikewin* (NI); *meskotastâw* (VAI).

reason *tanehki kîkway ka ispayik* (VII); for no reason, senseless, with no results, for nothing, *metoni kwanta* (IPC); without reason, *konta* (IPC) *(Plains)*; *kwanta* (IPC) *(Northern)*.

reasonable *kîkway ka kwayaskopayik* (VII); *nahinakwan* (VII).

reassemble *kahkîhtwam mâwasakwascikehk* (VAI).

reassurance *metoni kehcinahowewin* (NI).

reassure *awîyak ka kehcinamiht* (VTA); being reassured, *kehcinâhowin* (NI).

rebel Someone who is willing to fight, *onaskwâw* (NA); s/he rebels against someone, *mâyeyihcikew* (VAI); the act of rebelling, *mâyeyihcikewin* (NI); the act of fighting back, *naskwâwin* (NI).

rebellious *awîyak ka nihtâ naskwat* (NA) *or* (VII).

rebound *mînowin* (NI).

rebuff *ka aseniht awîyak* (VAI).

rebuild *kîhtwam osihcikewin* (NI); *ahcisetaw* (VAI); *ahcimanokwew* (VTA).

rebuilt *ka mînosihtâhk kîkway* (VTI).

rebuke The act of telling someone off, *awîyak kâkwayaskomiht* (VAI); s/he rebukes her/him, *kitotew* (VAI).

recall *kîhtwam tepwâcikewin* (NI); remembering something, *kiskisiwin* (NI).

recapture *ka kîhtwam kahtinwehk* (VAI); s/he is recaptured, *kîhtwam kahtinaw* (VAI).

recast S/he rebuilds, *ahcisetaw* (VAI).

recede *ka aseptamihk kîkway* (VTI); withdraw or fall away, *yihkipayiw* (VAI).

receive *kîkway ka kahtinamihk* (VTI); *otihtikow* (VII).

recent *namoya kayâs* (IPC).

recently Just recently, *mastaw* (IPC).

recess *nomes ayiwepiwin* (NI); a small rest, *ayowepiwinis* (NI).

recessional A hymn sung ending a church service, *poyonikamowin ayamihâwinihk* (NI).

recite *kîhtwam itwewin* (NI); recitation by heart, *pakwanaw itwewin* (NI).

reckless *ka nihtâ pîkonikehk* (VAI).

reckon *iteyihtam* (VAI).

reckoning *tapeyihtamiwin* (NI).

reclaim *ka kawôtinamihk* (LN); *kawôtinikew* (VAI).

reclamation *kawôtinikewin* (NI).

recline *metoni miyosiniwin* (NI); lying down for a rest, *ayiwepiwin* (NI).

recluse The act of being a loner, *ka nihtâpeyakohk* (VAI); the act of being alone or reclusive, *kewâcihowin* (NI); s/he lives like a recluse, *kewâcipimatisiw* (VAI); a solitary person, i.e.: a recluse, *pikwaciyiniw* (NA).

recognizable *awîyak kawahkew nistawnaht* (VAI).

recognize The act of recognizing someone, *nistawinâkewin* (NI); s/he recognizes it, *nistawinam* (VTI); s/he recognizes her/him, *nistawinawew* (VTA); s/he recognizes the taste of it, *nistospitam* (VAI); s/he recognizes her/his type of character, *pakaskinawew* (VTA).

recoil *kîkway ka tahkiskâcikepayik* (VTI).

recollect *kiskisopayowin* (NI); *kiskisiw* (VAI); *kiskisototâwew* (VTA).

recollection *ka kiskisopayihk* (LN); *kiskisiwin* (NI).

recommend *awîyak ka mamihcimiht* (VAI); *pîkiskwestamâwew* (VTA).

recommendation *miyo mâmiskomiwewin* (NI); s/he recommends her/him, *pîkiskwestamâkew* (VAI).

recommit *ka kîhtwam ahiwehk nânitâw* (VII).

recommitment *kîhtwam ahiwewin* (NI).

recommittal *ka kîhtwam ahiwehk* (VII).

recondition *ka pîtosinâkohtahk* (VII).

reconsider *ahcimâmitoneyihtam* (VAI).

reconstruct *ka pîtosihtâhk* (VAI).

record *kitohcikewin kosihtâhk* (VAI).

re-count *kîhtwam akihcikewin* (NI); re-counting, *ahciyakecikewin* (NI).

recourse *nâtâmototamowin* (NI).

recover *ka kîhtwam kahtinamihk* (VTI).

recovery *mînowin* (NI).

recreate *môcikihtâwin kosihtâhk* (VTI).

recreation *môcikihtâwin* (NI); a game, *metawewin* (NI).

recreational *kîkway ka môcikihtâwakehk* (VTI).

recriminate *kakîhtwam mâyahiwehk* (VII).

recrimination *kîhtwam mâyahiwewin* (NI).

rectal *wayawiwinihk* (NI) or (LN)

rectify *kîkway ka tipahikepayihtahk* (VAI); s/he corrected it, *menwastaw* (VTI).

rector *ayamihewiyiniw* (NA); a Protestant minister, *âkayâsimow ayamihewiniw* (NA).

rectory *ayamihiwiyiniw wîkih* (NI).

rectum *wayawiwin* (NI).

recumbent *ka pimsinihk* (VII).

recuperate *ka âstepayihk* (VII); s/he is getting better, *astepayiw* (VAI).

recuperation *âstepayiwin* (NI).

recur *kakîhtwam nokwahk* (VII); all over again, *asaymîna* (IPC).

recurrence *kîhtwam nokosiwin* (NI).

recurrent *kakah kîhtwam papayik* (VAI).

red It is red, *mihkwâw* (VII); s/he has a red face, *mihkohkwew* (VAI); a red berry, *mihkomin* (NI); s/he becomes red, *mihkopayiw* (VAI); s/he has red feet, *mihkositew* (VTA); s/he is red, *mihkosiw* (VAI); being red, *mihkosiwin* (NI); it is red liquid, *mihkwâkamiw* (NI); a red river, *mihkwâkamiwisipoy* (NI); s/he has red skin i.e.: a sunburn, or s/he has measles, *mihkwasew* (VTA); red water, *mihkwâpoy* (NI); it is red, *mihkwâw* (VII).

redbird *mihkoh pîwâysis* (NA).

red-blooded *awîyak ka mihkwayik omihkoh* (VII).

redbreast *ka mihkwaskanet* (VAI).

red cedar *mihkwâsiht* (NA).

Red Deer *mihkwâpisimosos* (NA).

redden It turned red, *mihkopayiw* (VAI).

reddish *ka mihkonâkwahk* (VII); it looks red, *mihkonâkwan* (VII).

redeem *kâwi kahtinkewin* (NI).

redeemable *kâwi ka nihtâ kahtinamihk* (VAI).

redeemer *okîhtwam kahtinkew* (NA); *opimâcihiwew* (NA) *(Plains)*.

redemption *pimâcihiwewin* (NI).

redevelop *kîhtwam osihcikewin* (NI).

red fox *osâwahkesîs* (NA).

redhead *mihkostikwân* (NI).

redheaded *awîyak ka mihkostikwânet* (VII).

redistribution *kîhtwam mekiwin* (NI).

redo *kakîhtwam osihcikehk* (VAI) or (VTI).

redness *mihkopayiwin* (NI); being red, *mihkopayiwin* (NI).

red pine *mihkoskahtak* (NA).

red squirrel *mihkwânikwacâs* (NA).

redress *meskotsehowin* (NI).

reduce *nîkinkewin* (NI); s/he reduced her/him in size or cut her/him down, *acôwihew* (VTA).

399

reduction *nîkinkewin* (NI); the act of making lesser,
acowinikewin (NI); the act of reducing costs,
mestinikewin (NI) *(Plains)*; *nîkimestinkewin* (NI)
(Northern).

reduplicate *kakah kîhtwamasinahamihk masinahikan*
(VTI).

red willow *mihkwâpemak* (NA).

redwing black bird *mihko tahtahkwan* (NA).

redwood *mihkwâhtik* (NA).

re-echo *ka kahkîhtwam cistâwek* (VII).

reed *aniskowihkaskwah* (NI); a tall grass that grows
near water, *aniskowask* (NI).

reef A low rocky or sandy ridge near the water line,
piskwapiskâw (NI) *or* (VII).

reek *ka sokemakohcikehk* (VAI); it stinks, *wihcekan*
(VII).

reel *pîminahkwân tipastehikan* (NI); a dance,
nîmihitowin (NI); *kayâs mônîyâwisimowin* (NI).

re-establish *or* **reestablish** *kîhtwam oyahiwewin* (NI).

refine Crushed, *ka sikwatahikehk* (VAI); bring or reduce
to a pure state, *miyosihtawin* (NI).

refined S/he made it pure, *miyosihtaw* (VAI); *ka
sikwatahamihk* (VTI).

refinement *sikwatahikewin* (NI); elegance, *miyosiwin*
(NI).

refit *kahkîhtwam kotascikehk* (VAI).

reflection *cahkâstesinowin* (NI); it casts a shadow,
cikâstehtin (VTI).

reflective *kîkway ka cahkâstek* (VTI).

reflex *ka kayawâyâwin* (NI).

reform *kîkway ka mînosehtahk* (VTI); s/he is reformed,
kweskâtisiw (VAI).

reformation The act of being reformed, *kweskâtisiwin*
(NI); *mînosehcikewin* (NI).

refrain *asepayihowin* (NI); s/he holds herself/himself
back; s/he stops, *kipihciw* (VAI).

refresh *awîyak ka miyomahcihot* (VII); *astesin* (VAI).

refreshing *kîkway ka miyomahcihowakehk* (VTI).

refusal *asenamâkewin* (NI); *ânwehtamowin* (NI).

refuse *awîyak ka asenamâht kîkway* (VAI); *ânwehtam*
(VAI).

refuse *asenamâkew* (NI).

refutable *ekâ ka tâpwehtamihk* (VII).

refutation *ekâ tâpwehcikewin* (NI).

refute *awîyak ekâ katâpwehtaht* (VAI).

regain *kîhtwam kahtinikewin* (NI); *kawi kâcitinam*
(VAI).

regale *môcikehiwewin* (NI).

regard The act of holding someone in high regard,
miyokanawapahkewin (NI); s/he regards it,
pisiskeyihtam (VAI); s/he regards her/him with awe,
mâmaskâtapamew (VTA).

regarding *awîyak ka miyomâmitoneyihtahk* (VAI).

regardless *pikwesih kîsimamitoneyihtamihk* (VII);
pisiskeyihtakosiw (VAI).

regress In retreat, *kâwaynohtehk* (VAI).

regression *wâyinokiwewin* (NI) *(Northern)*; *wâyinowin*
(NI) *(Plains)*.

regret Being sorry about losing something,
kamihtâtamihk (VII); s/he regrets it, *mihtâtam* (VAI);
s/he regrets her/his behavior, *kîsinateyimew* (VAI);
s/he regrets or repents her sins and s/he feels humble
about herself/himself, *kîsinateyimisiw* (VAI); the act of
repentance, *kîsinâteyimisiwin* (NI); s/he regrets losing
her/him, *mihtâtew* (VAI).

regretful *ka nihtâ mihtatamihk* (VII); *kîsinateyihtam*
(VAI); with sorrow, regretfully, or with contrition,
kîsinâc (IPC).

regrettable *mihtâcikewin* (NI).

regular *sôskwâc tâpitawi* (IPC); *peyakwan* (VII).

regulate *kwayaskwascikewin* (NI).

regularity Frequently, *kahkiyipa nawâc* (IPC).

regularly *sôskwâc kahkiyipa* (IPC).

regurgitate S/he regurgitates it, *pâpayihew* (VTA);
pwâkomow (VAI).

rehash *kakahkîhtwamsehtahk* (VTI).

reindeer Elk, *wâwâskesiw* (NA).

reinforce *ayiwâkes ka maskawsihtahk kîkway* (VTI);
s/he makes it stronger, *maskawisehtâw* (VTI).

reinforcement *ayîwak maskawsihcikewin* (NI).

reins *menoskwepicikaneyapeya* (NI).

reinsure *kîhtwam miyowihowenihk ka apihk* (VII).

reiterate *kahkîhtwam pîkiskwewin* (NI); s/he repeats
herself/himself, *kahkîhtwamitwew* (VAI).

reject Something refused, *ka asenamihk kîkway* (VTI);
s/he rejects it, *âtaweyihtam* (VTI); s/he rejects her/
him, *âtaweyimew* (VTA); the act of rejecting one's own
existence, *wepeyimowin* (NI); s/he rejects the
existence of another person, *wepeyitamawew* (VTA).

rejection *âtaweyihtamowin* (NI).

rejoice *môcikihtâwin* (NI); s/he has a good time,
miyowâtam (VAI); *môcikihtâw* (VAI).

rejoicing *ka mekwâmôcikihtâhk* (VII).

rejoin *kawi wîcihewewin* (NI); s/he rejoins her/him,
nakiskawew (VTA); s/he rejoined the party, *kîhtwam
wîcihiwew* (VTA).

rejoinder *ka naskweyasimohk* (VII).

rejuvenate *oskinâkohcikewin* (NI).

relapse *kahkîhtwam âhkosihk* (VAI); s/he had a relapse
with her/his sickness, *ayiwâkisâyaw* (VII).

relate S/he tells, *ka wihtamâkehk* (VAI); *wihtam* (VAI);
âcimow (VAI).

related Being related, *ka wahkohtohk* (VII); they are
related to each other by adoption, *tâpâhkohtowak*
(VAI); s/he is related or considered part of the family
because s/he was given the name of the deceased

person, *tâpahkomew* (VAI); s/he is related,
tâpahkomiwew (VAI); s/he makes her/him part of the
family or related, *wahkohtahew* (VTA); s/he makes
herself/himself part of the family or becomes related,
wahkohtahisiw (VAI); they are related to each other,
wahkohtowak (VAI); the act of being related to each
other, *wahkohtowin* (NI); s/he is related or connected
to her/him, *wahkomew* (VAI).

relation *wahkomâkan* (NA).

relationship A good relationship, *miyo wicehtowin* (NI).

relative Being related to someone, *awîyak ka
wahkomiht* (VAI); her/his relatives are very diverse,
nanatohkwakomew (VTA); a relative, *wahkomâkan*
(NA); the act of being a relative, *wahkomowewin* (NI).

relatively *miyo wahkohtowenihk* (LN).

relax *ka ayiwepihk* (VAI).

relaxation *miyo ayiwepiwin* (NI).

relay *ka âsawnamatohk* (VTI).

release S/he is released, *pakitinâw* (VAI); s/he releases
herself/himself, *pakicîw* (VAI); the act of releasing,
pakicîwin (NI); s/he releases her/him hastily or
quickly, *pakiciwepinew* (VTA).

relegate *ka sipwetsahikehk* (VTA).

relent *kitimâkinâkewin* (NI); feeling compassion or to
soften or to yield, *pakiteyimowin* (NI).

relentless *namakîkway kitimâkinâtowin* (NI).

relevance *kwayaskweyihcikewin* (NI).

relevant *kîkway ka kwayaskweyihtamihk* (VII).

reliability *mamisîtotâkewin* (NI).

reliable Someone who is dependable, *awîyak
kamamisîhk* (VAI); s/he believes herself/himself to be
reliable, *yâkwâmeyimow* (VAI) *(Northern)*;
mamisîwâtisiw (VAI) *(Plains)*; the act of believing
oneself to be reliable, *yâkwâmeyimowin* (NI); s/he
thinks s/he is reliable, *yâkwâmimew* (VAI); s/he is
reliable, *yâkwâmisiw* (VAI); the act of being reliable,
yâkwâmisiwin (NI).

reliance *ka miyomamsîhk awîyak* (VTA).

reliant *miyo mamisîwin* (NI); it is to be trusted,
mamiseweyihtâkwan (VII).

relic *ka yasikîkway ka kanaweyihtamihk* (VTI);
kayâsayiwiw (VII); a very old religious accoutrement,
kayâsikîkway (NI).

relief *nîsohkamâtowin* (NI).

relieve S/he relieves her/him or takes her/his place,
nâtamawew (VTA); s/he is relieved that it happened as
it did, *peyaseyimow* (VAI); the act of being relieved
after an occurrence, *peyaseyimowin* (NI); s/he feels
relieved about it, *peyaseyihtam* (VAI); the act of feeling
relieved, *peyaseyihtamowin* (NI).

religion A Christian religion, *ayamihâwin* (NI); a
different religion, *pîtos ayamihâwin* (NI); Catholic
religion, *pahkwayamihâwin* (NI); a wrong religious

tradition, *naspacâyamihâwin* (NI); s/he follows the
wrong religious tradition, *naspâcayamihâw* (VAI).

religious A religious person, *otayamihâw* (NA).

relinquish *kîkway ka ponihtâhk* (VTI); giving
something up, *kawimekowin* (NI).

relinquishment *ponihtâwin* (NI).

relish *kîkway kawihkistamihk* (VAI); s/he enjoys her/
his food, *miyoskoyow* (VAI).

relocate S/he makes her/him relocate, *ahcipicihew*
(VTA).

reluctance *iyisâc kîkway ka tôtamihk* (VTI).

reluctant *iyisâc* (IPC); s/he reluctantly speaks about her/
him, *nanihkâcimew* (VAI); s/he sounds reluctant,
nanihkâtowew (VAI); the act of sounding reluctant,
nanihkâtowewin (NI); s/he is telling a story
reluctantly, *nanihkâcacimow* (VAI); the act of telling a
story reluctantly, *nanihkâcacimowin* (NI); s/he is very
reluctant, *sâkweyimow* (VAI).

rely Depending on someone, *aspeyimowin* (NI);
aspeyimow (VAI).

remain *ka iskopayik kîkway* (VII).

remainder Leftovers, *iskopayihcikan* (NI).

remark *awîyak ka kitihkimiht* (VAI).

remarkable *ka sohki kaskihtat awîyak* (VII); it is
worthy of notice, *mâmaskâtikwan* (VII).   401

remedy *nâtawihowin* (NI).

remember The act of remembering, *kiskisiwin* (NI);
s/he remembers, *kiskisiw* (VAI); s/he remembers while
on her/his way, *pîkiskisiw* (VAI); s/he tries to
remember, *nitawikiskisiw* (VAI); s/he would like to
remember, *nohtekiskisiw* (VAI); s/he tries to
remember, *kakwekiskisiw* (VAI); s/he will remember,
wehkiskisow (VAI); s/he starts to remember,
atikiskisiw (VAI); s/he stops remembering,
ponikiskisiw (VAI); s/he finishes remembering,
kisikiskisiw (VAI); s/he has a good memory or s/he is
good at remembering, *nihtâkiskisiw* (VAI); s/he forgets
or s/he is at a loss remembering, *wînikiskisiw* (VAI);
s/he helps her/him to remember, *kiskisohew* (VTA);
s/he remembers her/him, *kiskisototawew* (VAI).

remembrance *ka kiskisototakehk* (VAI) *or* (VII); the act
of remembering, *kiskisiwin* (NI).

remind When you remind someone about something,
awîyak ka kiskisomiht (VAI); s/he reminds her/him by
telling her/him, *kiskisomew* (VAI); s/he makes a
mental note of her/him, *kiskinowâteyimew* (VAI).

reminder The act of reminding someone,
kiskisomtowin (NI); something used as a reminder,
i.e.: a date book, *kiskiwehikan* (NI).

reminiscence *kayâs kiskisiwin* (NI); recall the past to
mind, *ka kiskisopayihk* (VII).

reminiscent *kayâs kîkway ka mâmiskotamihk* (VAI);
ka kiskisopayihk (VAI).

remiss *ka patahamihk isihcikewnihk* (VTI);
mâyipamehiwewin (NI).

remission Or abatement, i.e.: of sins,
pakiteyihtamâkewin (NI); s/he grants remission for
her/him, *pakiteyihtamawew* (VTA); the act of
forgiving or a pardon, *kâsenamâkewin* (NI).

remit *ka tipahikehk* (VAI); s/he makes less intense,
âstamapitam (VAI).

remittance *tipahikwewin* (NI).

remnant Something leftover, *ka iskonamihk kîkway*
(VTI); a remnant or leftover piece of cloth, *pîwisikan*
(NI).

remonstrance *ekâ ekosi keteyihtamihk* (VII).

remonstrant *pîtoteyihcikewin* (NI).

remonstration *ka pîtoteyihtamihk* (VAI).

remonstrative *awîyak ka nihtâ pîtoteyihtahk* (VAI).

remorse *kîkway ka mihtâtamihk* (VAI); *mihtâtam* (VAI);
the act of thinking something is remorseful,
kîsinâteyihtamowin (NI); s/he thinks it is remorseful,
kîsinâteyihtam (VAI).

remorseful *awîyak ka nihtâ mihtâtahk kîkway* (VAI).

remorseless *awîyak ekâ komihtâtamowinit* (VAI); the
act of remorse, *mihtâtamowin* (NI).

remote *metoni pâtosâyihk* (LN).

remount *ka kîhtwam tehtapihk* (VTI).

removal *âhtascikewin* (NI).

remove Moving something to another place, *ka
âhtastahk kîkway* (VTI); s/he removes them off with
her/his hand, *maninew* (VTA); it comes off on its own,
manipayiw (VTI); the bull moose removes the velvet
off its horns, i.e.: by scraping, *nimitaham* (VAI) *or* (VTI).

removed *kîkway kakeh âhtastahk* (VTI); it has been
removed and planted elsewhere, *âhtaskehaw* (VTI).

rend *ka nanânistinamihk kîkway* (VTI); tear apart
violently, *pîkopitam* (VTI).

rendezvous *ka kiskihtohk* (VTA).

rendition *wapahtihiwewin* (NI).

renew *kîhtwam sihcikewin* (NI); a replacement,
tâpastâw (VTI).

renounce *ka pakitinamihk kîkway* (VTI); abandon,
wepinam (VTA); *wepinew* (VTA).

renown *ka kiskeyihtâkosihk* (VII); a great reputation for
achievements, *kihciteyitâkosiwin* (NI).

renowned *awîyak ka kiskeyihtâkosit* (VAI).

renunciate *ka pakiteyimohk* (VAI).

renunciation *pakiteyimowin* (NI).

reopen *ka kîhtwam yohtenamihk* (VTI).

repaint *kakîhtwam sopekahamihk* (VTI).

repair The act of repairing something,
nânapâcihcikewin (NI); s/he repairs it, *nânapâcihtaw*
(VTI); s/he repairs it for her/him, *nânapâcihtamawew*
(VTA); restore to good condition, *mîsahikewin* (NI);
s/he shapes or repairs them, i.e.: a blacksmith

repairing instruments, *wiyâkinew* (VAI) *(Plains)*; s/he
shapes or repairs it, *wiyâkiham* (VII) *(Plains)*; s/he
shapes or repairs them, *wiyâkihowew* (VTA) *(Plains)*;
s/he shapes or repairs things, *wiyakihikew* (VII)
(Plains).

reparable *takeh nânapâcihcikatek kîkway* (VII).

repass *kakah kîhtwam meyaskatohk* (VTA).

repast *ka kitânawehk* (VAI).

repeat *kahkîhtwam kîkway ka tôtamihk* (VII) *or* (VAI).

repeated *kahkîhtwam tôtamowin* (NI).

repeatedly *kahkîhtwam tôtamowenihk ka ayâhk* (VII).

repeater *awîyak kahkîhtwam kîkway ka tôtahk* (NA).

repel *ka yikatetsahikehk* (VTA).

repent *ka mihtâtamihk* (VII); s/he regrets or does
penance, *kîsinâteyihtam* (VAI).

repentance *mihtâtamowin* (NI).

repentant *awîyak ka mihtâtahk kîkway* (VAI).

repercussion *ka cistâwehtihk kîkway* (VTI).

repetition *kahkîhtwam kîkway ka tôtamihk* (VAI);
kîhtwam itwewin (NI); *kîhtwam tôtamowin* (NI);
doing over, *kîhtwamitwewin* (NI);
kîhtwamtôtamowin (NI).

repetitious *kahkîhtwam kîkway kîspayik* (VII).

rephrase *pîtos ka isi pîkiskwehk* (VAI).

repine *pîkiskweskiw* (VAI).

replace Replacing something, *ka meskotascikehk* (VTI);
s/he replaces the missing amount, *tâpahew* (VTA); s/he
replaces her/him or takes her/his place, *tapapistawew*
(VTA); s/he replaces someone, *tapapiw* (VAI); it is
replaced, i.e.: an axe handle, *tâpâskohtin* (VAI)
(Northern); *tâpihtin* (VAI) *(Plains and Northern
variant)*; s/he replaces her/him or s/he puts another
thing in place of her/him, i.e.: a log on a log house,
tâpâskosimew (VTA); it is replaced, i.e.: a house log,
tâpâskosin (VTI); it replaces or fits in place of
something else, *tâpastew* (VTI).

replacement *meskotascikewin* (NI).

replay *kakîhtwam metawehk* (VAI).

replenish *kakîhtwam sâkaskinahtahk* (VTI); s/he
replaces something, *tâpastâw* (VAI).

replenishment *kîhtwam sâkaskinahcikewin* (NI).

replete *metoni ka sâkaskinek* (VAI).

repletion *metoni sâkaskinahcikewin* (NI).

reply *ka naskwewasimohk* (VAI).

report *âcimowin* (NI).

reportable *kîkway ka atôtamihk* (VTI).

repose *miyo ayiwepiwin* (NI); s/he rests, *ayiwepiw*
(VAI).

reprehensible *awîyak ka nihtâ atameyimiht* (VAI).

represent S/he is representing them, *tapapistamawew*
(VII) *(Plains)*; *nokosistamawew* (VII) *(Northern)*; s/he is
representing people, *tapapistamakew* (VAI) *(Plains)*;
nokosistamakew (VAI) *(Northern)*.

repress *ka patakonamihk kîkway* (VII).

repression *patakonkewin* (NI).

repressive *awîyak ka patakonweskit* (VAI).

reprieve *ka nomi nakinamihk kîkway* (VTI).

reprimand *ayâhkwemowin* (NI); when someone is given an easier sentence, *awîyak kamanâtasowatiht* (VAI); the words spoken to her/him are very strong, *ayâhkwemâw* (VTA); reprove severely, *kehkâmaw* (VTA); *kehkâmew* (VTA).

reprisal *naskwâwin* (NI).

reproach *peyahtik ka wihtamâht awîyak ekâ kwayask ka tôtaket* (VTA); charge with shame or disgrace, *nepewâkâc* (IPC).

reproachful *peyahtik wihtamâkewin* (NI).

reproachless *awîyak ekâ kapapekiskwet* (VAI).

reproduce The act of multiplying or having children, *ka âhkami ohpikihitohk* (VTA); showing something once again, *kîhtwam wapahtehiwewin* (NI); s/he reproduces her/him in her/his mind, i.e.: an artist's subject, *naspapamew* (VTA); s/he reproduces the scene through painting, *naspasinahikew* (VAI); the act of reproducing a scene through painting, *naspasinahikewin* (NI).

reproductive *kîkway ka âhkami osihcikemakahk* (VTI).

reproof *kweskâsowewin* (NI).

reprovable *kîkway ka kweskâsowatamihk* (VTI).

reproval *awîyak ka kweskâsowatiht* (VTA).

reprove *kâkweskasowehk* (VAI).

repudiate *kîkway ka ânwehtamihk* (VII).

repudiation *ânwehtamowin* (NI).

repugnance *ka pîtosisâyâhk* (VAI); being disliked, *pakwâtikosiwin* (NI).

repugnancy *pîtosisâyâwin* (NI).

repulse *kîkway ka asenamihk* (VTI); *macâtisiwin* (NI); s/he is repulsed by what others say, *pisiskihtawew* (VTA); being bad, *macâtisiwin* (NI).

repulsion *asenikewin* (NI).

repulsive *awîyak ka nihtâ aseniket* (VAI); s/he is thought of as being offensive, *maceyihtakosiw* (VAI).

reputable *miyo wehyowin ka ayâhk* (VTA); *mîywacimaw* (VTA); s/he is well-liked, *miweyimaw* (VTA).

reputation *awîyak omiyowehyowin* (NI); *kayat miyowâcimikosiwin* (NI).

repute *awîyak ka miyo mamiskomiht* (VTA); *kisketakwan* (VII); s/he has a good reputation, *miweyihtakosiw* (VAI).

reputed *miyomamiskomwewin* (NI).

request The act of asking, *natohtamawin* (NI); s/he requests it, *natohtam* (VAI); s/he requests medicine from her/him, *nâcinehamawew* (VTA); s/he makes a request for medicine, *nâcinehikew* (VAI); s/he makes a request, *natohtamaw* (VTA).

require *kîkway ka nohti ayâhk* (VTI); s/he requires it, *nitaweyihtam* (VTI).

requirement *nohti âyâwin* (NI).

requisite *ahkwac kîkway takeh ayâhk* (VAI); something indispensable, *kwetamâwin* (NI).

requite *kîkway ka tipahikipayihtahk* (VTI).

rescue *pimâcihiwewin* (NI).

reseat *kîhtwam apihiwewin* (NI).

resemblance *naspitâkewin* (NI); being resembled, *naspitâkosiwin* (NI).

resemble Resembling someone, *awîyak ka naspitaht* (VTA); s/he resembles or looks like her/him, *naspitâwew* (VTA); it resembles something else, *naspitâtômakan* (VII); they resemble one another, *naspitâtowak* (VTA); s/he sort of resembles someone or s/he looks something like her or him, *yawinâkosiw* (VAI) *(Northern)*; *âwenâkosiw* (VAI) *(Plains)*; it sort of resembles it or it looks like something like it, *yâwenâkwan* (VII) *(Northern)*; *âwenâkwan* (VII) *(Plains)*; s/he thinks s/he resembles or looks like someone, *yâwenawew* (VAI).

resent *ka pakwâteyihtamihk kîkway* (VTI); *pakwâtam* (VAI).

resentful Being enraged, *kisiwâsiwin* (NI); *kisôwasiwin* (NI).

resentment *kisôweyihtamowin* (NI); the act of being mad, *kisiwâsowin* (NI).

reserve Saving something for future use, *iskonikan* (NI); a Native Reserve, *tipahaskân* (NI).

reserved *kîkway kakeh manâcihtamakehk* (VTI); cache, *astahcikon* (NI).

reset *kîhtwam oyascikewin* (NI).

reshape *ka pîtos nakohtahk kîkway* (VTI).

reside Living at one place for a long time, *etah kawikihk* (LN); s/he lives, *wîkiw* (VAI); s/he lives or resides for good, *kistokew* (VAI); s/he lives there permanently, *kiscâyâw* (VAI).

residence *awîyak owîkowin* (LN); *wâskahikan* (NI); a place of residence, *wîkiwin* (NI).

residency *wîkowenihk* (LN).

resident *owîkiw* (NA).

resilience S/he has resilience, *sohkastwâw* (VII), the act of having resilience, *sohkastwâwin* (NI).

resiliency *nihtâ mînowin* (NI).

resilient It is resilient, *sîpihkâw* (VII); s/he is resilient, *sîpihkisiw* (VAI).

resist S/he resists, *nanakestam* (VAI); s/he resists the ravages of age or s/he is old but strong, *sîpikihkâw* (VAI); s/he resists pain, *sîpinew* (VAI); s/he resists the cold temperature, *sîpâcow* (VAI).

resistance *nakinisowin* (NI); *maskawisiwin* (NI).

resistant *kîkway ka nakiniswakehk* (VTI).

403

resistibility *ka nihtâ nakinisohk* (VAI).

resistible *kîkway ka nakinisomamahk* (VII).

resistless *nama kîkway nakinisowin* (NI).

resole *mîsahaskisinewin* (NI).

resolute When the mind is made up, *kasâpweyihtamihk* (VAI); s/he is resolute or firmly decided, *maskaweyihtam* (VAI).

resolution Making up one's mind, *sapweyihtamowin* (NI); a decided or strong resolution, *maskaweyihtamowin* (NI); an affirmative resolution, *sohkeyihtamowin* (NI).

resolve *kîkway ka miyopayihtahk* (VTI); a determine decision expressed as a resolution, *ahkameyihtamowin* (NI).

resolved *miyopayihcikewin* (NI).

resolvedly *miyopayihcikewinihk* (LN).

resort *môcikihtâw ka pesowin* (NI).

resound *ka cistâwehtihk* (VII); s/he falls with a resounding noise, *cistâwesin* (VAI).

resource *isihcikewin* (NI).

resourceful *ka nihtâ isihcikehk* (VAI).

respect Having respect for someone, *manâtcihiwewin* (NI); something respected, i.e.: religion, *manâtan* (VII); it is well respected, *kihkâteyihtakwan* (VII) *(Northern)*; *kihceyihtâkwan* (VAI) *(Plains)*; s/he is well respected, *kihkâteyihtâkosiw* (VAI) *(Northern)*; *kihceyihtâsosiw* (VAI) *(Plains)*; s/he respects her/him, *manâcihew* (VAI); s/he respects it, *kihceyihtam* (VTA) *(Plains)*; *kihkâteyihtam* (VTA) *(Northern)*; a respected in-law, *manâcimâkan* (NA); s/he is respectful or polite, *manâtisiw* (VAI); the act of being respectful or polite, *manâtisiwin* (NI); s/he treats her/him or them with respect or esteem, *manâtôtawew* (VTA); s/he is honored, praised, repected, or highly thought of, *sohkeyihtâkosiw* (VAI); it is highly thought of or it is strong or resistant, *sohkeyihtâkwan* (VII); the act of showing respect, *kihceyihtâkosowin* (NI) *(Plains)*; *kihceyimikosowin* (NI) *(Northern)*.

respectability *manâtisiwin* (NI).

respectable Having respect, *kamanâtsihk* (VAI); s/he is respectable, *miyotôtâmakew* (VAI).

respectful *awîyak kamanâtcihewet* (VTA); *miyopikihaw* (VTA); s/he is a respectful person, *manâtisiw* (VAI); s/he has a respectful feeling for her/him, *kihkâteyimew* (VAI); s/he holds others respectfully, *nâkatohkew* (VAI).

respecting *kîkway ka manâtcitahk* (VTI).

respective *pahpiskihc ohci* (LN).

respectively *tânsi ka atetapihk* (VAI).

respiration The act of breathing, *yihewin* (NI).

respiratory *iyihewnihk ohci kîkway* (VTI).

respire *ka iyohehk* (VAI); s/he breathes, *yehew* (VAI).

respite Call for a delay or a little respite, *ceskwa pita* (IPC).

resplendence *wâsihkopayowin* (NI).

resplendency *ka wâsihkopayihk* (VAI).

resplendent *kîkway ka wâsihkwak* (VII); shining, *wâsihkopayowin* (NI).

respond *ka naskweyasimohk* (VAI); *naskomow* (VAI).

respondent *awîyak ka pîkiskwestamasot* (VAI).

response *wehtamakewin* (NI).

responsibility *nâkateyimowewin* (NI); the act of looking after something, *nâkateyihcikewin* (NI).

responsible *kîkway ka nâkateyihtamihk* (VTI).

responsive *awîyak ka nihtâ nâkatohket* (VAI).

rest The remainder or something leftover, *iskonikewna kîkwaya ka iskonamihk* (NI); s/he is resting, *ayiwepiw* (VAI); a nap or a place to rest, *ayiwepowin* (NI); s/he makes her/him rest, *ayiwepihew* (VTA).

restate *pîtos ketastahk pîkiskwewin* (VTI).

restful *papeyahtikwesâyâwin* (NI); *miyo ayowepowin* (NI).

restive *mistatim ka macikastet* (VAI).

restless *ekâ kakeh ayiwepihk* (VAI); *papâmahkamikisiw* (VAI).

restock Installation, *ka takwascikehk* (VTI).

restore *ka mînosihtahk* (VTI).

restrain *ka miciminwehk* (VAI); *nakinam* (VAI); s/he stops her/him, *nakinew* (VTI).

restraint *ka nakinwehk* (VTA); the act of stopping, *kipihtinikewin* (NI).

restrict *nome isko ka pakitinowehk* (VTA); the act of attaching limitations to, *nakinamakewin* (NI).

restrictive *kîkway ka kîskinamakehk* (VTI).

restring *ayapiy ka ahtahpitiht* (VTI).

result *tânsi ka isiponpayik* (VII); *ispayow* (VII); for no reason, senseless, with no results, or for nothing, *kwanta* (IPC).

resume *kakîhtwam macipayik* (VII); *macihtâw* (VAI).

resumption *kîhtwam macihtâwin* (NI).

resurrect *ka âpisimiht awîyak* (VTA).

resurrection The act of resurrection, *âpisinowin* (NI).

retain *kanaweyihcikewin* (NI); s/he keeps it, *kanaweyihtam* (VAI).

retake *kawi otinikewin* (NI).

retaliate *ka naskwâstamâsohk* (VAI).

retaliation *naskwâstamâsowin* (NI).

retaliative *awîyak ka naskwâstamâsot* (VAI).

retard *ka otâhkipitamihk kîkway* (VTI); s/he moves slow or slower, *otamihtâsow* (VAI).

retarded *kakepâtisiw* (VAI); *nawacpoko ka môhcowisâyâhk* (VAI).

retardation *otâhkipicikewin* (NI).

retch *ka nohti pwakomohk* (VAI).

retention *kawi kahtinikewin* (NI); s/he is kept inside, *kanaweyimaw* (VTA).

reticence *ekâ ka papîkiskweskihk* (VAI).

reticent S/he has a reticent personality, *nanihkâtisiw* (VAI); being reticent, *nanihkâtisiwin* (NI); s/he is disposed to be silent, *kâmwâtisiw* (VAI).

retire S/he stopped, *nakîw* (VAI).

retired *ekâ ayîwak katoskehk* (VAI); *pônâpatisowin* (NI).

retiring Someone who retires or quits working, *awîyak ka ponatosket* (VAI); s/he retires or goes to bed, *kawisimiw* (VAI); the act of retiring or going to bed, *kawisimowin* (NI).

retort *kisowi tepwasowewin* (NI); return a retaliatory remark, *kisowipîkiskwewin* (NI).

retouch *kakîhtwam sopekahikehk* (VTI); s/he repaints it, *acimasinpeham* (VTI).

retrace *kantawahtahk tânsi peci otâhk* (VTI).

retread *ka nânapâcihiht otihtipipayew* (VTI).

retreat In retreat, *kâwayinohtehk* (VII).

retrench *ka nîkimestinkehk* (VAI).

retrenchment *nîkimestinkewin* (NI).

retribution *tipahikepayihcikewin* (NI).

retributive *kîkway ka tipahikepayik* (VII).

retrieval *nâcikewin* (NI).

retrieve *ka nâtamihk kîkway* (VTI); s/he retrieves ducks, *nâtahîsîpew* (VTA).

return *kawi pecikewin* (NI).

returnable *kawi kapetahk kîkway* (VTI).

returned Returned home, *pekiwew* (VAI).

reunite *kawi nîsopayowin* (NI); *kawi wicehtowak* (VTI).

reveal The act of telling, *kiskeyihtamohiwewin* (NI); s/he shows or reveals it, *wapahtihiwew* (VTA); s/he uncovers and reveals her/him, *moskinew* (VTA); s/he reveals or shows herself/himself, *moskîw* (VAI); s/he reveals herself/himself to them, *nokosistawew* (VTA); s/he is revealed, *nokosiw* (VAI); the act of being revealed, *nokosiwin* (NI); it is revealed, *nokwan* (VII).

revel *ka môcikihtâhk* (VAI); join in merry making, *môcikeyitamowin* (NI).

revelation *kîkway ka wihtamihk* (VII).

revelatory *kîkway ka wihtamomâkahk* (VII).

revelry *môcikihtâwnihkewin* (NI).

revenge The act of revenge, *apehowin* (NI).

revengeful *ka nihtâ apehohk* (VAI).

reverberate *ka kisewehtakwahk* (VII).

revere *mistahi iteyemowewin* (NI); regard with deepest respect, *kihceyihtamowin* (NI).

reverence *mistahi iteyihtakosowin* (NI); the act of showing reverence, *kihceyihtâkosowin* (NI) *(Plains)*; *kihceyimikosowin* (NI) *(Northern)*.

reverend *ayamihewiyiniw* (NA); s/he is deserving of respect, *kihciyimaw* (VTA).

reverential *kihceyihtakosiwin* (NI).

revert Going back to a former position, *kweskîwin* (NI).

reversal *kweski isi* (IPC).

reverse *otâhk isi* (LN); *kweskastew* (VTI).

reversely *asipayowin* (NI); *asepayowin* (NI) *(Plains)*.

reversibility *asipayiwinihk isi* (LN).

reversible *kweskiwepinikewin* (NI).

reversion *ka kweskowepinikehk* (VAI).

revert *kawi ka kiwetôtamihk* (VAI).

revery *powatam* (VAI); *nanâtohk kaisi akâwâtamihk* (VAI).

review *ka ahci ka nawapahtamihk kîkway* (VTI); s/he reads it over, *aciyayamihtâw* (VTI).

revile *kapew mâmiskomiht awîyak* (VTA); s/he finds her/him contemptible, *kohpâteyimew* (VTA).

revilement *pîwâcihiw* (VAI); *mâmiskomowewin* (NI); considered contemptible, *kohpâteyitâkwan* (VII).

revise *ka meskotsehtahk* (VTI); it has been revised, *kwayaskwastaniwan* (VII).

revival *pimâcihiwewin* (NI); the effect of restoration, *kweskatisiwin* (NI).

revive *ka pimâcihtahk kîkway* (VTI); *pimâcihew* (VTA).   405

revocable *kîkway ka nakinamihk* (VTI).

revocation *nakinamâkewin* (NI).

revocatory *kîkway ka nihtâ nakipayik* (VII).

revolting *ka mawineskâkehk* (VAI).

revolve *peyakwanohk ka wâsakakotek* (VTI); *wâsakâpayiw* (VTI).

revolver A small firearm, *pâskisikanis* (NI).

revulsion *ka sisikôc kweskeyihtamihk* (VAI).

rhythm Maintaining proper rhythm, *pahpiyakwan kîsiwepinkehk* (VAI); s/he maintains the rhythm with them, *tâpowesimew* (VTA); having good rhythm in singing, *takahkihtakosiwin* (NI).

rhythmic *pahpiyakwan isiwepinkewin* (NI).

rib *ospikay* (NI); a rib bone, *mispikekan* (NI).

ribald The act of being ribald, *wîniyisâyâwin* (NI).

ribaldry *wînisâyâwin* (NI).

ribbed Teasing, *nanoyacihtowin* (NI).

ribbon *senipân* (NA); a piece of ribbon, *senipân* (NA).

rice A grain of rice, *wâpayômin* (NA); a grain of wild rice, *pikwaciwâpayômin* (NA).

rich Being rich, *wiyotisiwin* (NI); s/he is rich, *wiyotisiw* (VAI); s/he thinks s/he is rich, *wiyoteyimew* (VTA); s/he thinks of herself/himself as being rich, *wiyoteyimiw* (VAI); s/he makes her/him rich, *wiyotisihew* (VTA); s/he is rich, *wiyotisiw* (VAI).

riches *wiyotisowina* (NI).

ricochet A bullet that ricochets, *môsisinîy ka kwâskwehtihk* (VTI); it ricochets, *wâskwetin* (VII); (Northern); *kwâskwehtin* (VII) *(Plains)*.

rid *kîkway ka wepinamihk* (VTI).

riddance *wepinikan* (NI).

ridden *kakeh tehtapihk* (VTI).

riddle *ekâ ka nisitohtakwahk* (VII).

ride A ride in a vehicle, i.e.: a bus, train, or car, *pôsiwin* (NA); s/he rides her/his horse ahead of her/him, *nîkânipayîstawew* (VTA); s/he goes for a ride, *otâpâsiw* (VAI); s/he gives her/him a ride, *otâpâtew* (VTA); s/he comes riding, *pâpayow* (VAI).

rider Passenger, *oposiw* (NA).

ridge A long ridge of ground, *osihcâw* (NI).

ridicule *âyimwewin* (NI).

ridiculous *namoya kohkwâwâc kîkway* (VII); s/he ridicules people with laughter, *ipahpihiwet* (VTA).

rife *mistahi ka apatahk kîkway* (VTI); the act of talking for nothing, *kwantapîkiskwewin* (NI).

rifle Repeater rifle, *mihcet omacwewes* (NI); *môsisinîy pâskisikan* (NI); opening something with rifle shot, *yohtepaskisam* (VTI).

rift An opening made by splitting, *ka taskinamihk kîkway* (VTI).

right *kihtiniskehk isi* (LN); just enough, just right, *nahiyikohk* (IPC); right, correctly, *kwayask* (IPC); right now, busy at it, happening right now, *mekwâc* (IPC); *mekwâ* (IPC); at the moment itself, right now, right then, *mwehci* (IPC); right now, without delay, or before doing anything else, *kesâc* (IPC); immediately or right now, *semak* (IPC); right now, at this time, or as of now, *mekwâc* (IPC); right in the centre, *mekwayik* (IPC); on the right hand side, *kiciniskehk* (LN); s/he makes it go right for her/him, *kwayaskopayihew* (VTA); it goes right or well, *kwayaskopayiw* (VTI); her/his right hand, *okihcinisk* (LN).

righteous *awîyak ka kwayask isâyât* (VAI); the act of being righteous, *kwayaskwâtisiwin* (NI) *(Plains)*; *kwayaskwesâyâwin* (NI) *(Northern)*.

righteousness *kwayaskwesâyâwin* (NI).

rightful *kakeki kwayask* (IPC).

rightfully *kwayask kîspayihtahk kîkway* (VTI).

right hand *kihcinisk* (LN).

right-handed *awîyak kakihcinisket* (VAI); s/he is right-handed, *kîciniskew* (VAI).

rightly *tipiyawi* (IPC).

rigid *ka sîtawak kîkway* (VII).

rigidity *sîtawsiwin* (NI).

rigor *or* **rigour** *ka sîtawsihk* (VAI).

rigorous *sîtawâskosowin* (NI).

rim *ka pîmâpiskamok wayawîtimâyihk ohci* (VTI); all around, *wâsakâm* (LN).

rime It is frosty, *yikopîwan* (VII).

rind *mîniswasakay* (NA); the outer covering, *pihtôpicikan* (NI).

ring It is ringing, i.e.: a bell, *sîwepayiw* (VTI); her/his ears are ringing, *coweskihtew* (VAI); a steel ring, *pîwâpiskwahcanis* (NI); s/he rings it by shaking it, *sîwepayihew* (VTI); s/he rings the bell, *sîwepitew* (VTI).

ring A finger ring, *ahcanis* (NA).

ringlet *tipawehkasamawin* (NI); s/he has curly hair, *makotawestikwanew* (VAI).

rinse Rinsing the soap off, *kakîhtwam apawacikehk* (VAI); s/he rinses it, *mimikopâtinew* (VTI).

riotous *ka nihtâ mâyipayihtahk* (VAI).

rip Ripping something off with force, *katâtopitamihk kîkway* (VTI); s/he rips it off, *tâtopitam* (VTI); s/he rips the seams apart with care, *kâskiskipitew* (VTA); s/he rips the face off someone from a picture, *keskihkwepitew* (VTA); s/he is ripping things up or s/he plows the ground, *pîkopicikew* (VAI); the act of ripping things up or plowing the land, *pîkopicikewin* (NI).

ripe *ka atihtek kîkway* (VTI).

ripen *mînisa ka atihtekwaw* (VTA).

ripple *ka yotinpeyasik* (VTI).

rise Something that rises up, *kîkway kohpipayik* (VTI); s/he rises or gets up, i.e.: out of bed, *waniskâw* (VAI); it rises up, *ohpipayiw* (VAI); s/he rises up in the air, *ohpiskâw* (VAI); the act of rising or getting up, i.e.: out of bed, *waniskâwin* (NI).

risen *kakeh waniskat awîyak* (VAI).

riser *owaniskâw* (NA).

rising *ohpipayiwin* (NI).

risk *ka koteyihtamihk* (VAI).

risky *nawac poko ka kostamihk* (VAI).

rite Rites or religious ceremonies, *manitohkâsowin* (NI).

rival *awîyak omawineskaht* (NA).

rivalry *mawineskakewin* (NI).

rive *taskatahikewin* (NI).

riven *ka taskatahamihk* (VAI).

river *sîpîy* (NI); water flows outside of river bed, *patoteciwan* (VTI); river source, *peciciwan* (VTI); it flows through, *sâpociwan* (VTI); there is a strong current, *sâpiciwan* (VTI); a strong flowing river, *sohkeciwan* (VTI); it is a river, *sîpîwiw* (VAI); it becomes a river, *sîpîwan* (VII).

riverside *sonîsîpîhk* (LN) *(Northern)*; *sisonesîpihk* (LN) *(Plains)*.

roach *manicôs* (NA).

road *meskanaw* (NI); there is a summer road, *nipinmeskanaw* (NI); there is a winter road, *piponmeskanaw* (NI); a trail or road goes in such a direction, *itamiw* (VTI); there is a road branch or a road

406

branches off, ***paskemow*** (VTI); there is road straight
between a point, ***kaskaman*** (VTI); the road is crooked,
winding, ***wawakamow*** (VTI); a road leading into the
woods or a road going up a hill, ***kospamiw*** (VTI); a road
leading down stream, ***mahohteskanaw*** (NI); there are
many roads, ***mihcetôskanawa*** (NI); the road leads
toward the river, ***nâsipeskanaw*** (NI); a road that forks
off from the main road, i.e.: a secondary road,
naskweskanaw (NI) *(Northern)*; ***iyitomeskanaw*** (NI)
(Plains); the road behind, ***otâskanaw*** (NI); a minor
road that branches off the main road, ***paskemow*** (VTI);
a road which branches, forks, or divides,
pâskeskanaweyâw (VII); off to the side of the road,
patoteskanaw (NI); the road is crooked or something is
off kilter, ***pîmamiw*** (VTI); it runs right through, i.e.: a
road, ***sâpwamiw*** (VTI).

roadside Along the side of the road, ***sisone meskanâhk***
(LN); it is on the roadside, ***soneskanâhk*** (LN)
(Northern); ***sisoneskanâhk*** (LN) *(Plains)*.

roadway *etah ka meskanahkehk* (VAI).

roam *papâmacihowin* (NI).

roar S/he yells or shouts, ***tepwew*** (VAI).

roaring Yelling, ***tepwewin*** (NI).

roast Roasting meat, ***ka nawacihk weyâs*** (VTI); cooking
the whole piece, i.e.: a roast, ***misiwekasikan*** (NI); s/he
roasts it, ***nawaciw*** (VAI); roasting something,
nawacîwin (NI).

rob ***ka kimotihk*** (VAI); ***kimotamawew*** (VTA); s/he
pillages, ***maskahtwew*** (VTA).

robber *okimotow* (NA).

robbery *kimotiwin* (NI).

robe A priestal robe, ***kinwâpekasakay*** (NI); a cow or
buffalo robe, ***mostosowayân*** (NI).

robin *pihpihciw* (NA).

robus Being robust and strong, ***sohkâtisiwin*** (NI); s/he
is robust or stout, ***sohkisiw*** (VAI); being robust or
stout, ***sohkisowin*** (NI).

rock ***asinîy*** (NI); a big rock, ***mistasinîy*** (NI); there is a
rock outcropping, ***mistasiniskaw*** (VII); a rocky outcrop
in the hillside, ***oseyâpiskâw*** (VII); a white rock,
wapiskasinîy (NI).

rock Rocking a baby, ***wepitawasiwin*** (NI) *(Northern)*,
wewepitâwasowin (NI) *(Plains)*.

rocky *kamistasiniskak* (VII); a rocky boat, ***koskoskwâw***
(VII).

rod *kwâskwepicikanahtik* (NI); a fishing rod,
kwâskwepicikan (NI).

rodent *pesiskîs kowatit* (NA); a member of the gnawing
mammals with sharp teeth, i.e.: a beaver, ***amisk*** (NA).

rogue *maci ayiseyeniw* (NA).

roguish *awîyak ka macayowit* (VAI).

roll The act of rolling something, i.e.: a barrel,
tihtipinikewin (NI); s/he rolls them, ***pâpitikonew***

(VTA); s/he rolls it up, ***pitikonam*** (VTI); s/he rolls her/
him into a ball, ***pitikonew*** (VTA); something rolled
into a ball, ***pitikonikan*** (VII); s/he rolls in the snow,
tihtipâkonepayiw (VAI); s/he rolls them up into a ball,
i.e.: yarn, ***tihtipâpihkesimew*** (VAI); s/he rolls over, i.e.:
an animal, ***tihtipew*** (VAI); s/he rolls her/him over,
tihtipinew (VTA); s/he makes them roll,
tihtipipayihew (VTA); s/he rolls herself/himself around
on the ground or floor, ***tihtipipayihow*** (VAI); it rolls,
tihtipipayiw (VII) or (VAI) *(Plains)*; ***tihtipayiw*** (VII) or
(VAI) *(Northern)*; s/he pulls and makes her/him roll
around, ***tihtipipitew*** (VTA); s/he rolls her/him around,
i.e.: in the dust, ***tihtipisimew*** (VTA); s/he rolls over in a
fall, ***tihtipisin*** (VAI).

roller *tihtipinikan* (NI).

rollick *môcikihtâwin* (NI).

rollicking *ka môcikihtâhk* (VAI); having fun,
môcikeyihtamowin (NI).

rolling *tihtipipayiwin* (NI); ***ayapatinâw tihtipisin***;
tihtipihtin (VTI).

romance Being in love, ***sâkihitowin*** (NI).

romantic *ka sakihitohk* (VTA); s/he likes being in love,
sakihitoskiw (VAI).

romp *môcikâyâwin* (NI); ***metawew*** (VAI).

rood A cross, ***ayamihewâhtik*** (NA).

roomy *ka pesakwahk wîkowin* (VII); lots of room,
tawâw (VII).

rooster A male chicken, ***nâpepâkahahkwân*** (NA).

root A stringy root, ***wacapîs*** (NI); a tap root, ***ocepihk***
(NI); there are many roots, ***watapeskâw*** (VII); it has a
root, ***ocepihkiw*** (VTI); it has roots, ***ocepihkowan*** (VII);
a tree root, ***watapîy*** (NA); a container made from roots,
watapiwât (NI); it has lots of roots, ***watapîwiw*** (VTI).

rope *pîminahkwân* (NI); a long rope, ***kinwâpekan*** (NI); a
strong rope, ***maskawâpekan*** (NI); flattened rope,
napakâpekan (NI); a twisted rope, ***pimapekahikan***
(NI); a small cord, ***apistâpekasin*** (VII); a white rope,
wâpiskiyâpekan (NI); a short rope, ***cimâpekasin*** (VII); a
measuring rope, ***tipâpekinikan*** (NI); a form of rope to
lace up a toboggan, ***cîstâpâniyâpîy*** (NI); a rope or cord
made of moose hide, ***pîsâkanâpîy*** (NI); a rope for
passing the fish net under the ice,
sîpâskopicikaneyâpîy (NI); the rope is very strong,
sohkâpekan (VII).

rosary *ayamiheminak* (NI).

rose *okinewâpikonew* (NI); a rosehip or tomato, ***okinîy***
(NA); the Alberta rose bush, ***okâminakasîwâhtik*** (NA);
a rosehip bush, ***okiniwâhtik*** (NA).

rosy *kîkway ka okinewâpikonewik* (VII).

rot *ka misiwanâtahk kîkway* (VII).

rotate *ka mâhmeskwatascikehk* (VAI).

rotation *meskwatascikewin* (NI).

rotational *mâhmeskwatascikewinihk* (LN).

407

rote *ka mosci tâpiyihcikehk* (VAI).

rotten Something rotten, *kîkway ka pikiskatihk* (VII); it smells rotten, *wehcekan* (VII); s/he makes things go rotten, *pikiskacihcikew* (VAI); it is rotten or spoiled, *pikiskatin* (VII); s/he makes it rot or spoil, *pikiskatihtâw* (VTI); a rotten egg, *piskâc wâwi* (NI) *(Plains)*; *asâwi* (NI) *(Northern)*.

rotund Someone rotund, *awîyak ka pitikosit* (VAI); s/he is rotund, *pôtawisiw* (VAI); *pitikosiw* (VAI).

rough Area of rough ground, *mahmâyacâw* (VII); rough or dry skin, *kâspisiw* (VAI); rough character, *metoni sohkâyâwin* (NI); s/he is giving her/him a rough time, *âyimihew* (VTA); it is rough to the touch, *kâwaw* (VII); it is rough to the touch, *kawisiw* (VAI).

roughen *kakakiciksehtahk kîkway* (VTI).

roughing *awîyak kakisowimetawet* (VAI).

roughness The act of being physically tough, *sohkâtisiwin* (NI).

round Something round, *kawawîyak kîkway* (VII); it is round, *wawiyeyaw* (VII); it is rounded, i.e.: a heating stove, *notimâpiskisiw* (VAI); it is round and tall, i.e.: a telephone pole or tree, *notimâskosiw* (VAI); it is round in shape, *notimâskwan* (VII); it is round, *notimâw* (VII) *(Northern)*; *wâweyiyâw* (VII) *(Plains)*; s/he is round in shape, *notimisiw* (VAI); it is circular or round, *wawiyâpiskâw* (VII); s/he is circular or round, *wâwiyâpiskisiw* (VAI); it is circular or round in shape, i.e.: a pole, *wâwiyâskosiw* (VAI); a circular or round shaped stick, *wâwiyâskwan* (VII); it went round, *wâwiyepayiw* (VTI); being round, *wâwiyisiwin* (NI); s/he is round, *wâwiyesiw* (VAI); it sits in a round or circular shape, *wâwiyestew* (VTI); s/he makes it round, i.e.: iron, *wâwiyeyâpiskinew* (VTA); a round log, *notimâhtik* (NI) *(Northern)*; *wâweyiyahtik* (NI) *(Plains)*.

roundish *wâwiyisowin* (NI); it is round in shape, *wâwiyiyaw* (VII).

rouse *awîyak ka waspawehiht* (VTA); s/he wakes someone up, *koskonew* (VTA).

rousing *waspawehiwewin* (NI).

rout *nanihki tapasiwin* (NI); s/he drives people away, *sipwetisahikew* (VTA).

routine *tahki peyakwan ka tôtamihk* (VAI); something done every day, *tahtokesikâw tocikewin* (NI).

rove *papâmi môcikihtâwin* (NI); just walking around, *papâmohtewin* (NI).

row *kîhkahtowin* (NI); rowing a boat, *pimiskâwin* (NI).

rowdy *ka macihtwat ayisiyiniw* (VII).

rowdyish *ka macihtwahk* (VII).

rub Or liniment, *sopekahoswakan* (NI); the act of stroking or lightly rubbing, *sinikoniwewin* (NI); s/he rubs it or them off, *pawinew* (VTA); it rubs right off, *pawipayiw* (VTI); s/he rubs them off, *pawisimew*

(VTA); s/he rubs or wipes her/his eyes for her/him, *sinikwacâpinew* (VTA); s/he rubs or wipes her/his own eyes, *sinikwacapinisiw* (VTA); s/he rubs it, i.e.: pants or a diaper, *mimikonew* (VTA); s/he rubs her/him, *sinikonew* (VTA); s/he rubs her/him against the ground, *sinikosimew* (VTA); s/he rubs herself/himself against something, *sinikosimiw* (VAI); s/he rubs her/his body against her/him, *sinikoskawew* (VTA); s/he rubs her/him with a brush, *sinikwastowehwew* (VTA); s/he rubs or smears them, *sinikwahwew* (VTA); s/he rubs ointment on her/him, *sopekinew* (VTA); s/he rubs her/him with mud or with whitewash, *soskowakinew* (VTA).

rubbing *ka sinkonowehk* (VTA); a rubbing tool used to soften a hide, *sinikopocikan* (NI); s/he uses a rubbing tool to soften a hide, i.e.: a beaver skin, *sinikopohew* (VTA); a place where horses rub themselves, i.e.: a post or tree, *sinikosimowin* (NI).

rubbish *wepinikewina* (NI); house garbage, *macikwanasa* (NI).

rucksack *nayahcikaniwat* (NI).

ruckus *kisewehtawin* (NI).

rudder *osihk menwahikakan* (NI).

ruddy Reddish in color, *mihkonakwan* (VII); *mihkiwâw* (VII).

rude *macisâyâwin* (NI).

rue *mihtâtamowin* (NI).

rueful *ka nihtâ mihtâtamihk* (VAI).

ruff *kîkeskinamakehk metawewnihk* (VAI).

ruffed-grouse *îyintopihew* (NA).

ruffle *ka mâwasakokwâtek kîkway* (VTI); *ocipopicikan* (NI).

rugged *ka ayapahcak* (VII); *mamâyatinâw* (VII).

ruin *ka mesiwanâcitah kîkway* (VTI); *misiwanâcihtâw* (VTI).

ruination *misiwanâcihcikewin* (NI).

ruinous *kîkway ka misiwanâtahk* (VII).

rule *ka weyasowatamihk kîkway* (VTI); *tipahikan* (VII).

ruler Someone who governs, *otoyasowew* (NA); s/he is the ruler or owner, *otipeyihcikew* (NA); a measuring device, i.e.: a ruler, *tipahikanâhtik* (NI).

ruling *oyasowacikewin* (NI); *weyasowewin* (NI).

rumble *ka pitihkwek kîkway* (VTI); making a noisy sound, *pitihkohtawin* (NI).

ruminate Chewing or gnawing, *mâmâkwahcikewin* (NI).

rummage *ayapinikewin* (NI).

rumor *or* **rumour** *kwanta âcimowin* (NI); *papâmacimowin* (NI).

rumple *mâwasakwascikewin* (NI); s/he made her hair all messed up, *sehkwestikwanepitew* (VTA).

rumpus *kisewehtâwin* (NI).

run The act of running, i.e.: in a race or election, *pimpahtawin* (NI); s/he runs swiftly, *kîyasiw* (VAI); the act of running swiftly, *kîyasowin* (NI); s/he runs into the woods, *seskipahtâw* (VAI); running headlong into the woods, *seskisowin* (NI); it does not run right, i.e.: a motor, *mâyipayiw* (VAI); it runs well, i.e.: a motor, *miyopayiw* (VAI); s/he runs downwards, *nâsipepahtâw* (VAI); s/he has run away for good or forever, *nâspitamiw* (VAI); the act of running away for good, *nâspitâmowin* (NI); s/he runs out onto the road, *nimitâsipahtâw* (VAI); s/he runs out from somewhere into the open, i.e.: horse, *nimitâsipayiw* (VAI); s/he runs into the water, *pahkopepahtâw* (VAI); s/he runs everywhere, *papâmipahtâw* (VAI); the act of running everywhere, *papâmipahtâwin* (NI); s/he comes running, *pâpahtâw* (VAI); s/he runs inside, *pihtokwepahtâw* (VAI); s/he runs, i.e.: in a race or an election, *pimpahtâw* (VAI); s/he runs along with it, *pimipahtwâw* (VTI); s/he runs her/him, i.e.: a vehicle, *pimipayihew* (VTA); it runs constantly or nonstop, *tâpitawipayiw* (VAI).

runaway *tapasîwin* (NI).

rung A step, *tahkoskewin* (NI).

running *pimipahtâwin* (NI).

runt *apisciyinîs* (NA).

rupture *ka pôskwatayepayihk* (VTI); *pôskwatayewin* (NI).

ruse *wayesihiwewin* (NI); some kind of trickery, *mahtawinikewin* (NI).

rush S/he is charging ahead, *môskescikew* (VAI); rushing someone, *awîyak kapapasihiht* (VTA); s/he is rushed for time, *canawiw* (VAI); s/he is always in a rush, *nanihkipayiw* (VAI); the act of always being in a rush, *nanihkipayowin* (NI).

rusk Crusty cake, *siwpahkwesikan* (NI).

rust *misiyâpiskâw* (VII).

rustic *kîkway ka misiyâpiskâk* (VTI).

rustle *ka kîmôc atâwakehk kîkway* (VTI).

rustling A rustling sound, *kitoweyâskocin* (VAI).

rusty *ka misiyâpiskâk* (VII).

rut *ka watowahcak* (VII).

ruthless *ekâ ka kitimakinâket awîyak* (VAI); *metoni sohkâyâwin* (NI).

409

S

sabbath It is Sunday, i.e.: praying day, *ayamihewikîsikâw* (NI).

sack An ordinary sack, *maskimot* (NI); a little sack, *maskimotis* (NI); a gunny sack, *kâsecihcâkaniwat* (NI); a seamless sack made from bear skin, *maskwemotas* (NI).

sackful *tesakaskinek maskimow* (VII).

sacking *maskimotihk ka asowacikehk* (VAI); *maskimotekin* (NI).

sacrament *kihcitwâw isihtwawin* (NI); the sacrament of communion, *saskamowin* (NA).

sacramental *kîkway ka kihcitwâwahk* (VII).

sacred *kihcitwâw kîkway* (NI); *kihcihtwâwisiwin* (NI).

sacrifice The act of offering a sacred sacrifice, *wepinâsiwin* (NI); s/he offers a sacred sacrifice, *wepinâsôstamawew* (VTA); s/he offers a sacred sacrifice to the deity, *wepinâsôstawew* (VAI); s/he offers a sacred sacrifice, *wepinâsiw* (VAI).

sacrificial *ka wepinâsôstakehk*.

sacrilege *ka misiwanâcitahk ayamihekamik*.

sad Being sad, being melancholic, *kâmwâtisiwin* (NI); really taciturn or quiet and depressed, *pîkiskâtam* (VII); feeling depressed and quiet, *pîkiskâtikwan* (NI); s/he looks sad or depressed, *kâmwacinâkosiw* (VAI); it looks sad or depressing, *kâmwacinâkwan* (VII); it is a sad sound, *kâmwâcihtâkwan* (VII); it is depressing or melancolic, *kâmwâtan* (VII); s/he is thought of as sad and depressed, *kâmwâteyihtâkosiw* (VAI); it is thought of as being depressing, *kâmwâteyihtâkwan* (VII); s/he finds her/him depressed or sad, *kâmwâteyimew* (VTA); s/he is melancholic, depressed or sad, *kakwâtisiw*; s/he makes her/him sad and lonely, *kâmwâcihew* (VTI); s/he looks sad and lonely, *kâmwacinâkosiw* (VAI); s/he sounds sad and lonely, *pîkiskacinâkosiw* (VII); it sounds sad and lonely, *pîkiskâsihtâkwan*; s/he becomes sad and lonely when s/he hears her/him, *pîkiskâsihtawew* (VTA); it is sad, lamentable, depressing, *pîkiskâteyihtâkwan* (VII); s/he feels sad and lonely, *pîkiskâteyihtam* (VTA); s/he finds her/him melancholic *pîkiskâteyimew* (VII); people think of her/him as sad and depressed, *pîkiskâteyihtâkosiw* (VAI); the act of being thought of as being sad and depressed, *pekiskateyitakosiwin* (NI); s/he is sad and depressed, *pîkiskâtikosiw* (VAI); the act of sadness and depression or dejection, *pîkiskâtikosiwin* (NI); the act of being melancholic, *pîkiskâtisiwin* (NI); s/he is a melancholic person, or character, *pîkiskâtisiw* (VAI).

sadden Being sadden, *kâmwâcihiwewin* (NI); s/he saddens her/him with her/his words, *kâmwâcimew* (VTI).

saddle A riding saddle, *aspapowin* (NI).

saddlebag *aspapowiniwat* (NI).

saddlecloth *aspâwikanehikan* (NI).

saddle horse *tehtapîwatim* (NA).

Saddle Lake The Cree name for the settlement of Saddle Lake, *onihcikiskwapiwinihk* (NI).

sadness The act of feeling sad, *kitimâkimamitoneyîhcikan* (NI).

safe *miyonohk ka ayâhk* (VTI).

safeguard *ka miyo nâkateyimiwehk* (VTA).

safekeeping The act of safekeeping something for someone else, *kanaweyihtamâkewin* (NI); s/he retains it from safekeeping for her/him or for others, *kanaweyihtamawew* (VTA); s/he confides it to her/him for safekeeping, *kanaweyihtamohew* (VTI).

safety *miyonohk âyâwin* (NA).

sag *kîkway ka nîkipayik* (VTA).

sagacious *îyinisiwin* (NA); the act of being wise, *nihtâweyihtamowin* (NA).

sagacity *ka îyinisihk* (NA).

said *kîkway ka itwehk* (VTA); it is said, *itwewin* (NA).

saint *okihcihtwâwisiw* (NA).

saintly *kihcihtwâw isâyâwin* (NI).

sake *awîyak ohci ka tôtamihk kîkway* (VTA); her/his sake, *weya ohci* (VTA).

salacity *macimâmitoneyihcikan* (NA).

saliva *sihkowin* (NA).

salivary *kîkway ka sihkowinowik* (NA).

salivary gland *eyihkosak sihkowin ohci* (VTA).

salivate *ka ohcikawisihkwahk* (VTA).

salivation *ohcikawisihkwawin* (NA).

sallow *ka pâhkwâk* (VTA).

salmon *mistamek* (NA) *(Northern)*; *misiwâpamek* (NA) *(Plains)*.

salt *sîwihtâkan* (NI); s/he makes salt, *sîwihtâkanihkew* (VTA); epsom salt, *sîwihtâkansaposikan* (NA).

salted *kîkway ka sîwihtâkanowik* (NA).

saltish *ka sîwihtâkanakahk* (NA).

salutation Greeting someone by shaking hands, *atamiskâkewin* (NA).

salvage *kîkway ka pimâcitahk* (VTA); picking up scrap, *môsahkinikewin* (NA).

salvation *pimâcihiwewin* (NA).

salve *tôminikan* (NA); *maskeki*; *tôminikewin* (NI).

salver A flat dish or salver, *napakiyâkan* (NI).

same *peyakwan* (VII); even or equal, *pahpeyakwan* (VII); in one place, *peyakwayak* (VTA); the same area, *peyakwanohk* (VTA).

sameness *peyakwan isâyâwin* (VTA); the same, *mwehci* (NI).

411

sample *ka koteyihtamihk* (VAI).
sanctification *kihcihtwâwihkewin* (NI).
sanctify *ka kihcihtwâwihtahk kîkway* (VII).
sanctimonious *ka kihcihtwâwihkâsohk* (VAI).
sanctimony *kihcihtwâwihkâsowin* (NI).
sanctity *kihcihtwâwsowin* (NI).
sand *yikâw* (NA): *iyikâw* (NA); there is a sand bar, *yikâwahkaw*; the water is sandy, *yikâwâkamiw* (VAI); it is full of sand, *yikâwan* (VAI); it is a sandy prairie, *yikâwimaskotew* (VTA); it is sandy, *yikâwiskâw* (VAI).
sandals *maskisinihkanisa* (NI).
sandfly *pihkos* (NA); there are lots of sandflies, *pihkosiskâw* (NA).
sandy *kîkway ka yikâwihk*; *yikâwiskâw* (NA); sandy cliff, sandy cut bank, *kiskatawahkâw* (NI); there is sandy area, *iyikawahcaw* (NI); it is sandy, *iyikawiskâw* (VII) *(Plains)*; *yekâwimaskotew* (VII).
sane *ka nihtâweyihtamihk* (VTA).
sank *kîkway kakikosâpek*.
sap Tree sap, *mestan* (NA); the sap stops flowing, *ahsanew* (VAI); it is full of sap, *mestaniwiw* (NA).
sapling *oskimetosis* (NA).
sarcasm *mamihcimowin* (NI).
sarcastic *awîyak ka mamihcimoskit* (VTA).
Sarcee *pitos nehiyaw* (NA).
saskatoon A saskatoon berry, *misâskwatômin* (NA); the wood of a saskatoon shrub, *misâskwatwâhtik* (NA) *(Northern)*; *misâskwatominaht* (NA) *(Plains)*.
Satan Negative power in universe, *macimanito* (NA).
sate *ka tepeyih tamohiht awîyak* (VTA).
satiate *ayiwâkeyihtamohiwewin* (NI).
satiety *awîyak ka ayiwâkeyihtahk kîkway* (VTA); *ayiwâkeyâtowin*.
satisfaction *atamihewewin* (NI).
satisfactory *ka atamihikohk kîkway*; acceptance of one another, *naheyihtamowin* (NI).
satisfy *awîyak ka atamihiht*.
saturate *ka sopâtamihk kîkway* (VTA).
saturated Soaking wet, *sîkanâpâwew* (VTA).
saturation *sopâcikewin* (NA).
Saturday It is Saturday, *nikotwâsik kîsikâw* (NI).
saunter *peyahtik ka papâmohtehk* (VTA); a happy stroll, *mocikeh papâmohtewin* (NA).
savage *pikwaciyiniw* (NA).
savagery *awîyak ka pikwaciyiniwit* (VTI); *pikwacayiwiw* (VII).
save Being saved, *pimâtcihwewin* (NA); kept aside or hoard, *nahascikewin* (NA); s/he saves it for her/him or them, *manâcihtamawew* (VTA); s/he saves her/him or helps her/him get through, *pihkohew* (VTA); the act of saving people or helping people get through, *pihkohiwewin* (NI); s/he saved her/him or s/he supports her/him, *pimacihew* (VTA).

saving *sôniyâw ka nahahiht*.
savior *or* **saviour** A provider, *opimâcihtasow* (NA); someone that saves, *opimâcihiwew* (NA).
savor *or* **savour** *pîtos kîspakohtahk kîkway* (VTA).
savory *or* **savoury** *ka wihkasik kîkway*; it is good tasting, *wihkasin* (NI).
saw *kîskipocikan* (NI); a large saw, *misikeskipocikan* (NI); the act of sawing, *kîskipocikewin* (NA); one who uses a saw, *kîskipocikewiyînow* (NA); something sawed off, *kîskipotâwin* (NI); s/he saws them off, i.e.: logs, *kîskipohew* (VTA); s/he saws wood into lumber, *tâskipocikew* (VTA); s/he saws them all up, *tâskipoyew* (VTA).
saw Something you have seen, *kîkway kakehwâpahtamihk* (VTI); s/he saw her/him, *wâpamew* (NA).
sawn *kîkway ka tâskipotek* (VTA).
say S/he said, *itwew* (VII); say it again, *kîhtwam itwe* (VII).
saying Saying something, *itwewin* (NI); s/he is saying, *pekiskwew* (NA); s/he is saying the wrong things, *naspâtowew* (NA); the act of saying the wrong things, *naspâtowewin* (NI).
says S/he says, *ekosi itwew* (VTI); s/he says it or s/he belongs to her/him, *ascimew* (NI); s/he says annoying words to her/him, *kitihkimew* (NI).
scab A crusted sore, *omikiy* (NA); s/he has scabs, *omikîw* (VTA); having sores, *omikîwin* (NI).
scabby *awîyak ka omikaset* (VTA).
scald *ka kîsisohk ohtewapoy ohci* (VTA).
scale The act of scaling fish, *peyahikinosewewin* (NA); a fish's scale, *wayakay* (NI); s/he scales them, i.e.: fish, *peyahwew* (VTA); scaling a mountain, *tahkohtamacowewin* (NI).
scalp *ostikwân pâskatihkway* (NA); the scalp, *paskwatipepicikan* (NI).
scalloped Cutting material in a wavy line, *yihyekisawacikewin* (NI).
scaly *ka omikasehk* (VTI).
scamp *awîyak ka niweyatsit* (VTA).
scamper *ka sipweyamohk* (VTA).
scampered S/he ran away, *tapasîw* (VTA).
scan *peyahtik ka papamiwâpahcikehk* (VTA); *natonam* (VTI); *natonikew* (VTA).
scant *metoni apisis* (IPC); *namoya mistahi* (IPC).
scanty *apisis poko* (IPC).
scar *ocesiswin* (NI) *(Northern)*; *ocikisiwin* (NI) *(Plains)*; being scarred, *ka ocesihk nânitâw* (VAI); s/he has a scar on her/his face, *ocesihkwew* (VTA); the act of many scars on the face or a scarface, *ocesihkwîwin* (NI); s/he has a scar, *ocesisiw* (VAI) *(Northern)*; *ocikisiw* (VAI) *(Plains)*.
scarce *namoya mistahi* (IPC).

412

scarcely *nawâcpoko itahtwaw* (VII).

scare Being scared or frightened, *sekisiwin* (NI); scared of being alone, the bush, the night, spirits, etc., *sekisiw* (VAI); *kostâcow*; s/he scares it away so that it will not come close to others, *âmahâmawew* (VTA); s/he scares it away, i.e.: wild geese, *amâhew* (VTA); her/his talking scares her/him away, *amâmew* (VTA); her/his chopping has scared everything away, *amâwekahikew* (VTA); s/he scares things away with her/his shots, *amâweswew* (VTA); a big scare, *makweyimowin* (NI); s/he scares her/him away, *mîwihew* (VTA); s/he scares the game away, *osahikew* (VTA); s/he scares it, *osahwew* (VTA); s/he scares her/him away, *osiskawew* (VTA); s/he scares them away, i.e.: game, and does not leave any for the next person, *pawitisahamawew* (VTA) *(Northern)*; *sekihtamawew* (VTA) *(Plains)*; in that area, all the game has been scared away, *pawitisahikâtew* (VII); s/he scares or frightens her/him, *sekihew* (VTA); her/his talking scares her/him, *sekimew* (VTA) *(Northern)*; *sekihiwew* (VTA) *(Plains)*; s/he looks scared, *sekinâkosiw* (VAI); s/he thinks s/he is scared or frightened, *sekiseweyimew* (VTA); s/he is scared or frightened, *sekisiw* (VAI); s/he is a little frightened of her/him, *setowiyew* (VAI).

scarf *kesowahpison* (NI); something tied around the head, *pasiskwehpison* (NI); a neck scarf or neck kerchief, *tâpiskakan* (NI); a silk neck scarf, *senipânitâpiskâkan* (NI).

scarification *sikosawacikewin* (NI).

scarify *asiski ka sikosawatamihk* (VTA).

scary Being scared, *kostâciwin* (NI); used when looking at something and saying "it looks scary", *koskonâkwan* (NA); *kostâsinâkwan* (NA).

scat *kisiskâyâmowin* (NI).

scathe *awîyak ka mewakacimiht* (VTI).

scatheless *awîyak ekâ ka mikoskâcitasot* (VII).

scathing *mikoskâcihiwewin* (NI).

scatter S/he scatters the pieces all over, *nanânistahew* (VTA); s/he scatters them in tiny pieces, *pîkinipayihew* (VTA); it is scattered about, *pîwastew* (VII); it scatters, *pîwipayiw* (VTA); s/he scatters or flings it about/ around like powder, *pîwiwepinew*; s/he scatters it about, *saswepayihew* (VTA); it scatters about, *saswepayiw* (VII) *(Northern)*; *siswepayiw* (VII) *(Plains)*; it scatters about into pieces, *saswesin* (VAI) *(Northern)*; *isiwesin* (VAI) *(Plains)*; it scatters about into pieces, *saswetin* (VII); *siswehtin* (VII) *(Northern)*; *isiwehtin* (VII); s/he sends them scattering in every direction, i.e.: cattle, *saswetisahwew* (VTA); s/he scatters it by tossing it, i.e.: grain, *saswewepinew* (VTI).

scattered Scattered here and there, placed here and there, *papâmi* (IPC).

scattering *ka papâmâscikehk* (VTI).

scenic *ka takahkinakwahk askîy* (VAI); it is good looking country, *katawasisin askîy* (VAI).

scent *mîcimihkahcikan* (NA).

scentless *ekâ ka picimakwahk* (VII).

sceptic or **skeptic** *awîyak ekâ ka nihtâ tâpwehtahk* (VAI); an unbelieving person, *ânwehtask* (VAI).

scepticism or **skepticism** *ânwehtamowin* (NI).

scheme *kwayacisehcikewin* (NI); the planning of something, premeditation, *oyeyitamowin* (NI).

scheming *awîyak kakwayacisehciket* (VAI).

scintillate *peyakwan acahkos ka wâsihkopayiht* (VAI).

scintillation *wâsihkopayowin* (NI).

scoff Deriding something or someone, *pakwatamowin* (NI); *ayisinâkewin* (NI).

scold Scolding, *kîhkâmwewin* (NI); s/he is scolding, *kîhkâwitam* (VAI); s/he nags her/him and makes her/him nervous, *kîhkihew*; s/he gives her/him a good talking to, *kîhkimew*; s/he scolds her/him, *kîhkâmew*.

scoop *asipicikewin* (NI); *kwapahikan* (NI).

scoopful *ka sâkaskine asipicikehk* (VTI).

scoot *ka sisikôc sipwepayihk* (VTI).

scorch *naspic ka wesakihkasohk* (VAI).

score *ka cawihk* (VTA).

scorn Being scornful of something, *kîkway ka pîweyihtamihk* (VII) s/he voices to her/him her/his scorn or disapproval of her/him, *pîwimew* (VTA); s/he feels scornful of herself/himself, *pîwinakohow* (VII); the act of being self-scorning, *pîwinâkohowin* (NI); s/he looks scornful, *pîwinâkosiw* (VAI); it looks scornful, *pîwinâkwan* (VII); s/he looks at her/him with scorn, *pîwinawew* (VTA); s/he voices to other people her/his disapproval of her/him, *pîwomew* (VTA).

scornful *awîyak ka pîweyihciket* (VTA).

scoundrel *awîyak ka nepewinâkohciket* (VTA).

scour *ka kanâtapawatahk oyakana* (VTA).

scourge *pasastehowewin* (NI).

scout *onîkânohtew* (NA); s/he scouts her/him from a safe distance, *nososkawew* (VTA).

scouting *ka nîkânohtakehk* (VTA).

scowl *ka kisôkanawapamiht awîyak* (VAI).

scraggly *ayiwâk ka cacihkokanewnakosit* (VAI).

scraggy *ayiwâk ka cacihkokanet* (VAI).

scram Taking off in a hurry, *kisiskâsipwehtewin* (NI).

scramble *ka pimâtacimopahtahk* (VTA).

scrap A scrap of paper, *ka wepinamihk masinahikanekin* (VTI); a fight, *nôtinitowin* (NI).

scrape Scraping something, *kakâskahamihk kîkway* (VTI); s/he scrapes it, i.e.: a moosehide, *mâtaham* (VTA);

413

s/he scrapes the hair off, *mâtahikew* (VTI); *paskwahikew* (VTI); the act of scraping the hair off mooosehide, *mâtahikewin* (NI); s/he scrapes her/his face in a fall, *sinkohkwesin* (VTA); her/his scraping makes it swell up, *pâkâtâham* (VTA); s/he scrapes the fur from the skin, *paskwahwew* (VTI).

scraper *kâskahikakan* (NA); a scraper that removes the flesh from the hide or a sharp bone (stone) for fleshing hide, *mihkihkwan* (NI); a scraping instrument or piece of steel for scraping the fur off the skin or hide, *mâtahikan* (NI).

scraping *kâskahikewin* (NI); *mâtahikewin* (NI).

scrappy *ka nihtânotinkehk* (VTA).

scratch Scratching, *cistinkewin* (NI); the act of scratching an itch, *cîhcîkîwin* (NI); s/he scratched her/him briefly, *cîhcîkipitew* (VTA); s/he scratched her/him when s/he was itchy, *cîhcîkînew* (VTA); s/he scratched her/him with her/his nail, *cîstipitew* (VTA); s/he pinched her/him with her/his nail, *cîstnew* (VTA); a scratch mark, *kaskipicikewin* (NI); s/he makes scratch marks, *kaskipitam* (VTI); s/he scratches her/his itch, *cîhcîkîw* (VTA); s/he scratches her/his face with her/his nails, *cîstihkwepitew* (VTI); s/he accidently scratched herself/himself, *piscicestinsiw*.

scratchy *kîkway ka kicîskwek* (VII).

scrawl *mâhmâses masinahikewin* (NI).

scrawny *awîyak ka sihkacewapeksit*; being skinny, *sihkaciwin* (NI).

scream S/he screams, *tâcikwew* (VTA); s/he screams or cries out for her/him, *tâcikwetotawew* (VTA); the act of screaming, *tâcikwewin* (NI); the act of screaming in anger, *tepweyawesiw* (NI) *(Plains and Northern variant)*; *sohkeyawisowin* (NI) *(Northern)*.

screaming *ayiwâk ka câcikwet*.

screech *ka coweskihtehtakwahk kîkway*.

screechy *ka coweyapiskihtakwahk* (VTI).

screen *etah ka cikâstepayihcikehk* (VTA).

screening *cikâstepayihiwewin* (NI).

screw The act of screwing something in, *pîmâstehikewin* (NI); a small metal screw, *sakamohcikanis* (NA); it is screwed into place, *pîmâpiskahwâw* (VTA); s/he screws them into the metal, *pîmâpiskahwew* (VTA); s/he screws it into the wood, *pîmihtakahwew* (VTI); s/he screws them on by hand, *pîmihtakinew* (VTI).

scribble *ka masinahikehkasohk* (VAI).

scrimp *sasâkisiwin* (NI).

scrimpy *ka sasâkisiwayahk* (VII).

scrounge *ka papâmihmosahkinkehk* (VAI).

scrub Scrubbing the floor, *kisipekihtakinkewin* (NI); scrubbing on a washboard, *sinikohcikewin* (NI); s/he scrubs it with a brush, i.e.: a floor, *sinikohtakahwew* (NA).

scrubby *metoni ka sakâk*.

scruff *otâhk ohci mikwayaw*.

scruffy *nawâc poko ka mâyinakosihk*.

scrumptious *môcikâyâwin* (NI).

scrunch *ka petowenamihk* (VTA).

scrupulous *metoni kwayaskwatisiwin* (NI).

scrutinize *kîkway kahkîhtwam ka nâkateyihtamihk* (VTI); the act of observing closely, *nâkatâpahtamowin* (NI).

scrutiny *nâkateyihcikewin* (NI).

scuff *nestohtewin* (NI).

scuffle *ka mâmawi notintohk* (VTA).

scum *awîyak ekâ kîkway ka ispîhteyihtakosit* (VII).

scummy *maci kîkway ka waskitahipek* (VTA).

scurrilous *ka nihtâ kisiwâhtwahk* (VTI).

scurry *tapasîyâmowin* (NI).

scuttle *mistikowat kaskitihkan ka asowayiht*.

sea A very large body of water, i.e.: an ocean or a sea, *kihcikamiy* (NA) *(Plains)*; *kicikamiw* (NA) *(Northern)*.

seal The act of sealing up something, *kaskâpiskahikewin* (NI) *(Plains)*; *kaskapowicikewin* (NI) *(Northern)*; s/he seals up something, *kaskâpiskahikew* (VTI) *(Plains)*; *kaskapowehikew* (VTI) *(Northern)*; someone is sealed in, *kaskâpiskawâw* (NA) *(Plains)*; *kaskapowesin* (NA) *(Northern)*; s/he stored them in sealers, *kaskâpiskawew* (VTA) *(Plains)*; *kaskapowehsimew* (VTA) *(Northern)*.

sear *ka osâwihkahtek kîkway* (VTI); s/he burns it brown, *osâwikasam* (VTI).

search S/he searches for it, *natonam* (VTI); s/he searches for her/him on horseback or in a car, *natopayistawew* (VTA); s/he searches for beaver, *nitawamiskwew* (VTA); s/he searches for bear, *nitawaskwew* (VTA); s/he searches for horses, *nitawastimwew* (VTA); s/he searches for cattle, *nitawimostoswew* (VTA); s/he searches for signs or tracks, *nitwahâhcikew* (VTI); s/he searches for something in an optimistic way, *nitawâhtâw* (VTA).

searching *natonikewin* (NI).

seat Firmly seated, *ayâtapow*; a seat or a place to sit, *apiwin* (NI).

seating *apiwinihkewin* (NI).

seclude *ka kipahoht awîyak* (VTA).

secluded *peyakwaskinewin* (NI).

seclusion *ka peyakwaskinahiwehk* (VTA).

seclusive *peyakwaskinahiwewin* (NA).

second *mweci nîso* (IPC); second time, *nîswâw* (IPC); second of the month, *nîso akimâw pîsim*.

secondary *mwehcinîso ka masinahikatek* (VTA).

secondly *mweci nîswâw* (IPC); *kîhtwam* (IPC); the next one, *kîhtwam* (IPC).

414

secrecy Being secretive or underhanded, *kîmôtisiwin* (NI).

secret *ka kaskamoci kanaweyihtamihk pîkiskwewin* (NI).

secrete *ka pakicipayihtahk kîkway* (NA).

secretion *pakicipayowin* (NI).

secretive *kîkway ka pakcipayik* (NI).

secure *sohkastew* (VII).

sedate *peyahtikwesâyâwin* (NI).

sedentary *ka mecimwâtapihk* (VTA).

seduce *iskwew ka isihcikatiht masowewin* (NA); s/he leads her away from chasity, *wayesimew* (VTI).

seducement *ka isihkaht iskwew* (VTA).

seducible *awîyak poko ispî kesihcikatiht* (VAI).

seduction *masowewin* (NA).

seductive *pisikwâtisowin* (NI).

sedulous *peyahtik kesimâmitoneyihtamihk* (VII).

see The act of seeing, *wâpiwin* (NI); s/he sees, *wâpiw* (VAI); seeing something, *kawâpahtamihk* (VTI); s/he sees her/him and finds her/him hideous, *kakwâyakinawew* (VTA); s/he is used to seeing her/him, *nakayânawew* (VTA); s/he sees with only one eye, *napatehkapiw* (NA); s/he sees her/him in the wrong way or manner, *naspacinawew* (VTA); s/he goes to see her/him, *nitawâpamew* (VTA); s/he sees her/him clearly or distinctly, *pakaskâpamew* (VTA); s/he sees her/him nearby, *pîswâpamew* (VTA); s/he just happens to see her/him, *pisiskâpamew* (VTA); s/he sees her/him right through something, *sâponawew* (VTA); s/he can be seen right through it, *sâponôkosiw* (VAI); it can be seen right through it, *sâponôkwan* (VII); s/he is fading away or becoming hard to see, *wâninâkosiw* (VAI); it is getting hazy or becoming hard to see, *wâninâkwan* (VII); they see each other, *wapahtowak* (VTA); s/he sees her/his children or s/he gives birth to a child, *wâpamâwasiw* (VTA); the act of seeing one's children or giving birth to a child, *wâpamâwasiwin* (NI); s/he sees her/him, *wâpamew* (VTA); s/he sees herself/himself, *wâpamisiw* (VTA); s/he looks in the mirror and sees herself/himself, *wâpamiw* (VTA); s/he makes her/him see, *wapîhew* (VTA); s/he sees her/him as being odd looking, *wiyasinawew* (VTA); s/he sees her/him at a distance, *yâwâpamew* (VTA).

seed *pakitinikan* (NI); a vegetable seed for planting in the ground or a vegetable, *kiscikânis* (NI) *(Plains)*; *pîwi kistikân* (NI) *(Northern)*; s/he seeds or plants or sows, *pakitinikew* (VTI).

seedy *mihcet kiscikânsa kayamakahkwâw* (VII).

seeing *wâpahcikewin* (NI).

seeking *natonikewin* (NI).

seem *tapiskoc ekosi* (IPC); *iteyihtakwan*; it seems, perhaps, it seems true, *pakahkam* (IPC).

seeming *mweci ekosi takeh ispayik* (IPC).

seen Someone who is seen, *awîyak ka kîhwapamiht* (NA); s/he can be seen approaching, *penôkosiw* (NA); it can be seen approaching, *penôkwan* (NI).

seep It seeps, *pihtikweciwan* (VTA).

seer *okiskowehikew* (NA).

seeress *otiyinesew iskwew* (NA).

seesaw Playing see-saw, *cahkâskwahotowin* (NI); s/he suspends her/him in the air on a see-saw, *cahkâskopayihew* (VTA); s/he is suspended on air on a see-saw, *cahkâskopayiw* (NA).

seethe *metoni kisiwâsowin* (NI).

segment *ka pahkwenamihk kîkway*; a cut off part, *pahkwenikan* (NI).

segmental *ka pahpiskihtahk kîkway* (VTA).

segmentary *ka pahpiskihtascikehk*.

segmentation *pahpiskihtascikewin* (NI).

seize Seizing or claiming something, i.e.: a car, *ka masaskonikehk* (VTA); s/he seizes or grabs her/him or s/he rapes her/him, *otihtinew* (VTA); they seize or grasp each other, *otihtinitowak* (VTA); the act of seizing or grasping one another, *otihtinitowin* (NA).

seizing *masaskonikewin* (NI).

seldom *metoni ayâspîs* (IPC); *namoya mwasi* (IPC); very seldom, *askâw* (IPC); once in a while, *ayâspîs* (IPC).

select The act of selecting, *nawasonikewin* (NI); s/he selects it, *nawasonam* (VTA); s/he selects one from a large group, *nawasoyâpamiw* (VTA); the act of selecting one from a large group, *nawasoyâpamowin* (NI).

selection *nawasonikewin* (NI).

selective *ka nihtâ nawasonikehk* (VTA).

selectivity *nihtâ nawasonikewin* (NI).

selector *onawasonikew* (NA).

self *tipiyaw awîyak wiyapoko* (NA).

self-centred *or* **self-centered** Thinking only of oneself, *ka peyakweyimsohk* (VII); s/he is self-centred, *peyakweyimisiw* (VAI).

self-confidence *ka takahkeyimsohk* (VTA).

self-confident *takahkeyimsowin* (NI).

self-conscious *kiskeyimsowin* (NI).

self-control *nâkateyimsowin* (NI).

self-defence *or* **self-defense** *naskwâstamâsowin* (NI).

self-developing Or it builds up by itself, i.e.: a storm, *osihomakan* (NI).

self-discipline *kiskinohamâsiwin* (NI); *kwayaskwâtisiwin* (NI).

self-destruction The act of self-destruction, *pîkonisiwin* (NI).

self-interest *mâmitoneyimisowin* (NI).

selfish *ka sasâkisihk* (VTA).

selfishness The act of thinking only of one's own self, *peyakweyimisowin* (NI).

415

semblance *ka naspitâtohk* (VTA).

semen *kîkway nâpew ka ayât ka ohpikihisomakaneyek* (NA) *or* (VAI).

semicircle *âpihtâw waweyiyaw* (VTI).

semicircular *âpihtâw ka waweyiyak* (VTI); half a circle, *âpihtawaweyaw* (VTI).

send Sending something somewhere, *ka itsahamakehk kîkway* (VTA); s/he sends something away, *sipwetisaham* (VTA); s/he sends back what is sent, *kîwetisaham* (VTA); s/he sends her/him ahead, *nîkânitisawew* (VTA); s/he sends her/him here, *petisawew* (VTA); s/he sends her/him away, *sipwetisahwew* (VTA); s/he sends it down to her/him, *yâsitisahamawew* (VTA).

senior Being an old person, *kiseyenewiwin* (NA); s/he is old, *kihtehayiwiw* (VTA).

sensation *mosihitowin* (NI); the act of feeling, *mosihtâwin* (NI); *petamahcihowin* (NI).

sense Perceiving through the senses, *nisitohtamowin* (NI).

senseless *awîyak ekâ ka nisitohtaht; kakepâtisiw* (VAI); *wanikiskisiw* (VAI); for no reason, senseless, with no results, for nothing, *kwanta* (IPC); s/he is without reason, *kakepâtisiw* (VAI).

sensibility The sensing of one's self, *mosihowin* (NI).

sensible Someone with good sense or decency, *awîyak ka kwayaskwesâyat* (VAI); s/he finds her/him sensible, *pakahkeyimew* (VTA).

sensibly *metoni kwayask ka tôtamihk* (VTA).

sensitive *ka wahkewsihk; nesowâtisiw* (VAI); *watakamisiw* (VAI); s/he has a weak ability, *nesowâtisiw* (VAI).

sensitivity *wahkewisowin* (NI).

sensual A state of being sensual, *omôsihtawin* (NI).

sensuous *ka mosihtâwnihket awîyak* (VTI).

sent *ka sipwecisahikehk* (VTA).

sentiment *tansi kesimosihtâhk*; being emotional, *pekweyihtamowin* (NI).

sentinel *awîyak ka kanaweyihciket*.

sentry Military sentry, *simakansihkanak ka kanaweyihciketwaw*; a horse sentry, *okanawastimwew* (NA); an animal sentry, *okanawepisiskiwew* (NA).

separability *nihtâ paskewin* (NI).

separable *ka nihtâpaskehk* (NA).

separate Or apart from, *piskis* (IPC); the act of separating something, *piskihtinikewin* (NI); separated, independent, alone, each in its own place or spot, *pahpiskihc* (IPC); it is separated into pieces, *piskihtisiw* (VTA); s/he separates or divides it into compartments, *piskihcikipaham* (VTA); it is separated or divided into compartments, *piskihcikipahikâtew*

(VTA); it is separated or divided, *piskihcasin* (VTI); it is separated or divided into compartments, *piskihcâyâw* (VTI); s/he separates her/him, *piskihcihew* (VTA); s/he separates herself/himself, *piskihcihow* (VTA); it is divided or separated into rooms, *piskihcikipahikâtew* (VTA); s/he separates it or pulls it apart, *piskihtinam* (VTA); s/he separates it or pulls it apart for her/him, *piskihtinamawew* (VTA); s/he speaks a separate or different language, *piskihtowew* (VTA); a separate or different language, *piskihtowewin* (NI).

separately *pahpiskihc* (IPC); separately, *piskic* (IPC).

separation *paskewin* (NI).

September The mating moon or month, *onôcihitowipîsim* (NA).

serene Sad, quiet surroundings, *kâmwâtan* (VII).

sermon Or the act of preaching a sermon, *kakîskihkemowin* (NI); preaching a sermon, *kîskihkemowin* (NI).

serve S/he serves herself/himself from the cooking pot, *kapateskwew* (VTA).

servile *ka awahkâtiht awîyak* (VTI).

servility *awahkâsowewin* (NI).

servitude *awahkewin* (NI).

set Setting something up or preparing, *koyascikehk* (VTA); s/he sets her/him up, i.e.: s/he starts her/him out, *oyahew* (VTI); s/he sets it up, *pasikotisaham* (VTA); s/he sets up or pitches a tent for someone else, *mânokatew* (VTA); s/he sets up or pitches a tent, *mânokew* (VTA); the act of setting up or pitching a tent, *mânokewin* (NI); s/he sets up a teepee frame, *tastawahokew* (VTA).

setting *oyascikewin* (NI).

settle Settling a bill, *kwayaskosihcikewin* (NI); s/he settles it, i.e.: a bill, *kwayaskastâw* (VTA); after a big wind and the water is calm, *âsteyakamin* (VTI); s/he settles or lays on top of her/him, *mahtakoskawew* (VTA); s/he settles on top of her/him and holds her/him down, *patakoskawew* (VTA).

seven *tepakohp* (IPC); seven each, *tahtepakohpwâw* (IPC); seven times, *tepakohpwâw* (IPC); seven of a kind, *tepakohpwayih* (IPC); seven different kinds, *tahtepakohpwayih* (IPC); in seven places or seven directions, *tepakohpwayak* (IPC); in seven different places, *tahtepakohpwayak* (IPC); s/he is number seven or seventh, *tepakopowow* (VAI).

seven hundred *tepakohpwâw mitâtahtomitanaw* (IPC).

seventeen *tepakohposâp* (IPC); seventeen times, *tepakohposâpwâw* (IPC).

seventeenth *mwecitepakohposâp* (IPC); seventeenth time, *tepakohposâpwâw* (IPC); seventeenth of the month, *tepakohposâp akimâw pîsim*.

seventieth *mwecitepakohpomitanaw* (IPC); seventieth time, *tepakohpomitanawâw* (IPC).

416

seventh *mwecitepakohp* (IPC); seventh time,
tepakohpwâw (IPC); seventh of the month, *tepakohp
akimâw pîsim*.

seventy *tepakohpimitanaw* (IPC); seventy times,
tepakohpimitanawâw (IPC).

sever *ka kaskisawatamihk kîkway* (VTA); *kîskisam*;
cutting something off, *kîskisikewin* (NI).

several Quite a few or several, *mihcecis* (IPC); they are
in the canoe or several people are in the canoe,
mihcetohkamwak (VTA).

severe *mistahi kesayahk* (VII); *mistahi ayiman* (IPC).

severity *mistahi isâyâwin* (NI).

sew The act of sewing, *kaskikwâsowin* (NI); s/he sews
or stitches, *kaskikwâsiw* (VTA); a person who sews,
kaskikwâsowiyiniw (NA); s/he sews it, *kaskikwâtam*
(VTA); it is sewn, *kaskikwâtew* (VTI); something sewed
up, *kîpokwâcikan* (VTA); s/he sews things up for them,
kipokwâtamawew (VTA); s/he sews things together for
others, *mawasakokwâcikestamâkew* (NA); s/he sews
them together, i.e.: a pair of pants, *mâwasakokwâtew*
(VTA); s/he sews various materials together or s/he
quilts, *nanâtohkokwâsiw* (VTA); something sewn
using colored materials, i.e.: a quilt,
nanâtohkokwâtew (VTA); s/he makes a quilt,
nanâtohkokwâtam (VTA); s/he sews them on crooked,
pîmikwâtew (VTI); s/he sews them and they are
puckered, *sihpostahwew* (VTI); s/he sews around
something and closes it up, *wihkwekwâsiw* (VTA);
s/he sews it closed, *wikikwâtew* (VTI); s/he sews
something, *kaskikwasiw* (VTI).

sewing *ka kaskwasohk* (VTA).

sewn *kaskwasowin* (NI).

sex *iskwewiwin ahpô nâpewiwin* (NA); a male and
female, *iskwew mena nâpew* (NA).

sexual *nâpew mina iskwew wicehtowin* (NA).

sexually S/he is sexually involved, *nôcihiskwew* (VTA);
the act of being sexually involved, *nôcihiskwewewin*
(NI).

sexy *pisikwâcinâkosiwin* (NI).

shabby *ka kakwâtaksehohk* (VTA); *macinâkwan* (VII);
yiwenakwan (VII).

shack *miscikokamikos* (NA).

shade *âkawâstehikan* (NI); under the shade,
âkawâstesimowin (NI); shady, *âkawâstew* (VTI); s/he
is in the shade, *âkawâsiw* (VAI).

shading *âkawâstehikewin* (NI).

shadow The act of casting a shadow, *cikâstesimowin*
(NI); s/he casts her/his shadow across her/him,
cikâstenew (VTA); its reflection can be seen in the
water, *cikâstepekihtin* (NI); her/his reflection can be
seen in the water, *cikâstepekisin* (NI); s/he casts a
shadow of her/him, *cikâstesimew* (VTA); s/he casts
her/his shadow on her/him, *cikâsteskawew* (VTA);

her/his shadow can be seen, *cikâstesin* (VTA); its
shadow can be seen, *cikâstehtin* (VTA).

shadowy *ka cikâstesenihk* (NA).

shady *ka âkawâstepakak*; *âkawâsteyâw* (VTA).

shaggy *atim ka pîkwaskawet* (VTA).

shake The act of shaking, *koskoskopayowin* (NI)
(Northern); *nanamipayowin* (NI) (Plains); shaking a
blanket or moosehide, *pahpaw wepinikewin* (NI); s/he
shakes her/his head, *kewahiskweyiw* (VTA); it shakes
or rocks or it is not steady, i.e.: a boat or canoe,
koskoskwâw (VII); s/he shakes her/him,
koskowepinew (VTA); s/he is rocking it,
koskoskopayiw (VTI); s/he shakes her/him or them
briskly, *mimikopitew* (VTA); s/he or it shakes,
nanamipayiw (VAI) or (VII) (Plains); *koskoskopayiw*
(VAI) or (VII) (Northern); her/his body shakes,
nanamiyawepayiw (VAI); it shakes its wings,
pahpawahkew (VAI); s/he shakes herself/himself, i.e.:
a dog, *pahpawiw* (VTA); the act of shaking oneself,
pahpawiwin (NI); s/he makes her/him shake herself/
himself, *pahpawihew* (VTA); s/he shakes the dust off
her/him, *pahpawipayihew* (VTA); s/he shakes the dust
off it, *pahpawipayihtâw* (VTI); s/he shakes her/his
head at her/him in disagreement, *wepiskweyistawew*
(VTA); s/he shakes her/his head in disagreement,
wepiskweyiw (VTA).

shaken *kîkway ka pahpawihtahk* (VTA).

shaky Or having vibrations, *nanamipayowin* (NI); it
shakes, *nanamipayiw* (VTA).

shallow *ka pâhkwak*; *pâhkwâw*; *pâhkwasin* (VTI).

sham *kîmôtâtisiwin* (NI).

shaman *awîyak kamamâhtâwisit* (VII).

shamanism *mamâhtâwsiwin* (NI).

shamble *ka mamâyipimohtehk* (VTA).

shambles *kîkway ka yawastek* (VTA).

shame *nepewakâc* (IPC); *nepewisiwin* (NI).

shamefaced *ka nepewisihk* (VII).

shameful *nepewisestakewin* (NI); *nepewinakwan* (VII).

shameless *ekâ konepewsowenihk* (VTI).

shape Your body shape, *tansi kîsiyawehk* (VTA); it is
the way in which s/he shapes her/him, *ayisihew* (VTA).

shapeless *awîyak ka notimaskosit* (VTA).

shapely *awîyak ka takahkisehcikasot* (VTA).

share Two people sharing something,
kanesotipeyihtamihk (VII); s/he gives her/him some of
it, *pahkwinamawew* (VTA).

sharp Something sharp, *kîkway kakâsik* (VTI); it is
sharp, *kâsisin* (VTI); it feels sharp, *kâsapiskâw* (VTI).

sharpen Sharpening something, *kînipocikewin* (NI);
s/he sharpens it for her/him, *kînipotamawew* (VTA);
s/he sharpens it, i.e.: an axe, *kînipotâw* (VTA); s/he
sharpens them, *tâsahwew* (VTA).

sharpener *kînipocikan* (VTA); *tasahikan* (VTA).

417

sharp tailed grouse Or prairie chicken, *âhkiskiw* (NA).

shatter *ka swetahikehk* (VTA); *pîkinipayiw* (VTI).

shave When you are shaving, *ka kâskipasohk* (VTA); the act of shaving, *kâskipasowin* (NI); s/he shaves, *kâskipasiw* (VTA); s/he shaves her/him, *kâskipatew* (VTA); s/he shaves her/his head, *paskwatihpeswew* (VTA); the act of a shave, *kâskipacikewin* (NI).

shaver *kâskipason* (VTI).

shaving While you are shaving, *kamekwâ kâskipasohk* (VTA); s/he is shaving, *kâskipasiw* (VTA).

shawl *akwanahowenis* (NA); a cover-up, *akwanahon* (NI).

shear *mâyacihkos paskosowakan* (VTA); s/he shears them, i.e.: sheep, *paskoswew* (VTA).

shears *emisak paskwahamatowin* (NI).

sheath A case for a knife, i.e.: a scabbard, *pihcihkomân* (VTI).

sheathe *aspîkinâkan* (VTI).

sheathing *wekinikan* (VTI).

sheaves *kistikan tahkopicikana* (VTA).

shed An animal molting, *pisiskiw kapinawet* (VTA); a storage shed, *ascikewikamik* (NI).

sheen *ka wâsihkonakwahk* (VTA); the act of being shiny, *wâsihkopayiwin* (NI).

sheep A small sheep, *mâyacihkos* (NA); a bighorn sheep, *mâyatihk* (NA).

sheepish *kisâstaw kanepewsewayahk* (VII); *môconakosiw* (VAI).

sheepskin *mâyatihkowayân* (NA).

sheer *ka yekatekwaskwetihk kîkway* (VTA); very thin or transparent, *papakekin* (NI).

sheet *anaskan* (NI).

shelf *akotascikewin* (NI); a plank on a wall for holding objects, *akocikan* (NI).

shell Or bullet, *môsisinîy* (NI).

shelter An overhead shelter, roof, cover, *apahkwâson* (NI); shelter from the elements, i.e.: a spruce tree, *ohcistikosimowin* (NI); there is shelter out of the elements, i.e.: a bus shelter, *tipinawaw* (VTA); *ohcistikwân* (NA); in the shelter of a dense forest or wood, *âkawâskweyâhk* (VTA); the spruce tree provides shelter from the rain, *ohcistikosiw*; a shelter from the cold, *tipinawâhokan* (NI) *(Plains)*; *tipinahokân* (NI) *(Northern)*; s/he shelters from the wind, *tipinawâham* (VTI); a shelter from the wind, *tipinawahikan* (NI); s/he makes shelters for others, *tipinawâhew* (VTA); it is a sheltered area away from the wind and cold, *tipinawâw* (VII); s/he stays some place sheltered from the cold and wind, *tipinawâsiw* (VAI); the act of staying some place where it is sheltered, *tipinawâsimowin* (NI); an element shelter, *tipinawihon* (NI).

shelve *ka akotascikehk* (VTA).

shelving *akocikana kosehtahk* (VTA).

shepherd Someone who looks after sheep, *mâyacihkosa ka kanaweyimat* (NA); s/he shepherds her/him along, *nâkateyimew* (VTA).

sherry *sôminâpoy* (NI).

shield An arrow stopper, i.e.: a shield, *nakahaskwan* (NI).

shift Changing locations, *meskoc wepinekewin* (NI); s/he shifts them over to one side, *pasketisinew* (VTA).

shiftless *nipahikanewin* (NI); *kîhtimikan* (NA); useless, *yikitcikâw* (NA).

shifty *sôskon'kosiwin* (NI).

shimmer *ka cahkâsteknipiy* (VTI); it shines brightly, *kihkâyâsawew* (VTI).

shimmery *cahkâsteyâw* (VTI).

shin *maskaskwan* (NI).

shinbone *kiskatikan* (NI).

shine It shines, *wâsitew* (VII); s/he shines the light, *cahkâstenikew* (VTA); the sun is shining in her/his eyes, *cakâsiw* (VAI) *(Northern)*; *sîwâsiw* (VAI) *(Plains)*; there is sun shining or the light is shining brightly, *cahkâstew* (VII); it shines, i.e.: something made of metal, *wâseyâpiskâw* (VII); the metal pan is shining, *wâseyâpiskisiw* (VAI); the metal is shining red hot, *wâseyâpiskitew* (VII); it is bright and shiny, *wâseyâw* (VII); s/he shines, *wâsisiw* (VAI); it is sitting there and shining, *wâsihkwastew* (VTI).

shining *wâsihkwapiskâw* (VII).

shiny Something that is shiny, *ka wâsihkwak* (VTI); a shiny object, *wâsihkopayew* (VTI).

ship *nâpihkwân* (NI).

shirk *kisôw atoskewin* (NI).

shirt *pakowayan* (NI).

shirting *pakowayanekin* (NI).

shiver The act of shivering, *nanamipayowin* (NI) *(Plains)*; *koskoskopayowin* (NI) *(Northern)*; s/he shivers, *nanamâcow* (VAI); s/he shivers with cold, *nanamâskaciw* (VAI); s/he is shivering, *nanamipayiw* (VAI); s/he is so cold that her/his teeth chatter, *nanamipiteyâskaciw* (VAI); s/he or it shivers, *nanamipayiw* (VAI) or (VII) *(Plains)*; *koskoskopayiw* (VAI) or (VII) *(Northern)*;

shivery *nanamâskaciwin* (NI).

shoal *mecet kinosewak* (NA); *piskwahcâw* (VAI).

shock Being shocked or astounded by something, *ka sisikoteyihtamihk* (VTI); s/he was shocked by electricity, *pakamiskakiw* (VTA); s/he is shocked or astounded by her/him, *sisikoteyimew* (VTI); s/he is shocked or astounded, *sisikoteyihtam* (VAI).

shocking *sisikoteyihcikewin* (NI); stacking grain bundles, *cimacikewin* (NI).

shoddy *ka mâyisihcikatek kîkway* (VTA).

418

shoe A wooden moccasin or a shoe or boot, *mistikwaskisin* (NI); a moccasin, *maskisin* (NI); s/he has torn shoes, *pîkwaskisinew* (VTI); footwear, *maskisin* (NI).

shoo *ka sipwecisahikehk* (VTA).

shook *kîkway kakeh namipayik* (VTA).

shoot Shooting at something, *ka pâskisamihk kîkway* (VTA); s/he shoots, *pâskisikew* (VTA); s/he takes a random shot at her/him, *kotahaskwâtew* (VTA); s/he fires a random shot, *kotahaskwew* (VAI); the act of shooting at a target or target practice, *kotahaskwewin* (NI); it shoots accurately over long distances, *ohciskâw* (VTA); s/he shoots over her/him, *pâstâhwew* (VTA); the act of shooting oneself, *pâskisosiwin* (NI); s/he shoots herself/himself, *pâskisosiw* (VAI); s/he shoots her/him, *pâskiswew* (VTA); s/he shoots or launches the arrow, *pimotahkwew* (VTI); s/he shoots an arrow at her/him, *pimwew* (VTA).

shop Buying supplies in a store, *ka papâmatawehk atâwikamikohk* (VTA); a store, *atâwewikamik* (NI); s/he goes shopping, *mahiskam* (VTA).

shopping *ka papâmatawehk* (VTI).

shore The edge of a body of water, i.e.: a river or lake, *eskopeyak* (NI); close to shore, *cikakam* (NI); s/he pulls her/him into shore, *kapatepitew* (VTA) *(Plains)*; *seskipitew* (VTA) *(Northern)*; along the shore, *sisonesâkahikanihk* (LN) *(Plains)*; *sonesâkahikanihk* (LN) *(Northern)*.

shorn *kakeh paskwahamakehk* (VTI).

short Someone short, *awîyak kacimisit* (VAI); it is short, *cimâsin* (VII); s/he is of short stature, *cimisisow* (VAI); short of something, i.e.: money or food, *nohtepayow* (VAI); a pair of shorts, *kîskicâsis* (NI); s/he has a short tail, *cimâyowew* (VAI); s/he has a short hand, *cimicihcew* (VAI); s/he has short legs, *cimikâtew* (VAI); s/he has a short face, *cimihkwew* (VAI); her/his neck is short, *cimikwayawew* (VAI); s/he has a large, short foot, *cimisitew* (VAI); s/he has a little, short foot, *cimisicesiw* (VAI); s/he has a large, short body, *cimiyawew* (VAI); s/he has a little, short body, *cimiyawesiw* (VAI); s/he shortens it by pulling, *cimipitew* (VTA); s/he makes it short by cutting, *cimisâwâtew* (VTA); short of the mark, *nohtâw* (IPC); her/his throw or shot falls short of her/him, *nohtehwew* (VTA); s/he runs short of something, i.e.: money or sugar, *nohtepayiw* (VTI); s/he makes them too short, *cimisihew* (VTA).

shortage *nohtepayiwin* (NI).

short cut It is shorter across, *taskaman* (VTI); s/he cuts across the lake in a boat, *taskamaham* (VTA); s/he cuts across the ice, i.e.: walking, *taskamiskohtew* (VTA); s/he cuts straight across, i.e.: walking, *taskamohtew* (VTA); a short cut, i.e.: a trail, *taskamohtewin* (NI); s/he

drove through the short cut, *taskamipayiw* (VAI); s/he flew the short cut, *taskamihâw* (VAI).

shorten *ka cimsihtahk nawâc* (VTA); s/he shortens it or makes it short, *cimisihtâw* (VTI).

shortly *namoya kinwes* (IPC).

shot Having shot at something, *kakeh paskisamihk kîkway* (VTI); buckshot, *niskasinîy* (NI); s/he has a good shot, i.e.: with a bow and arrow, *nahastwew* (VTA); the act of having a good shot, *nahastwewin* (NI); s/he fires a shot, *pâskisikew* (VTA); the act of shooting oneself, *pâskisosiwin* (NI); s/he is a good shot, *nahâskwew* (VTA); being a good shot, *nahâskwewin* (NI).

should *takeh tôtamihk kîkway* (IPC).

shoulder *mitihtiman* (NI); a shoulder bone, *otihtimankan* (NI).

shoulder blade *otehye* (NI); *mitehye* (NI).

shove Pushing someone away, *awîyak kayahkiwepeniht* (VTA); s/he shoves her/his face aside, *pasihkwenew* (VTA).

shovel *pîwâpiskwapoy* (NA); it is a shovelful, *ka sakâskinet pîwâpiskwapoy* (VTA); a snow shovel, *wepahâkonâkan* (NA); s/he shovels the snow off her/him or it, *wepahâkonâtew* (VTA); s/he shovels the snow, *wepahâkonew* (VTA).

show The act of showing something, *wapahtihiwewin* (NI); s/he shows it to her/him, *wapahtihew* (VTI); the act of being shown something, *wapahtihikosiwin* (NI).

shower *ka sekipestâk* (VTA); *pahkipestâw* (VTI); it is a heavy rain shower, *sekipestâw* (VTA); taking a shower, *kisepekastewin* (NI).

showery *ka pahpimpestak* (VTI).

showing S/he is showing something, *wapahtihiwew* (VTI) *or* (VTA); *nôkwan* (VTI).

shown *kîkway kakeh wapahtamihk* (VTI).

show-off The act of showing off, *mâmaskâcâyihtowin* (NI); s/he acts in a show-off or pompous way, *mâmaskâcâyihtow* (VAI).

showy *kîkway ka miywâsik* (VAI).

shrank *kakeh acopayik kîkway* (VTI).

shred Cutting a clothe to shreds with scissors, *ka sikosamihk ayiwinis* (VTI); s/he shreds it into pieces, *nanânistipitam* (VTA).

shrew A pointed-nose mouse, *cîpokotewapakosis* (NA).

shrewd *naspic îyinisowin* (NI).

shriek *ka ciweyapiskihtakosihk* (VTA); s/he makes a shrill outcry, *tâcikwew* (VTA).

shrift A confession, *âcimsostakewin* (NI).

shrill *ka wâsewesihk* (VTA).

shrilly *ka wâsewehtakosihk* (VTA).

shrine *manito ayisinehkan* (NI); a holy statue, *kihcitwawiyinehkan* (NI).

shrink *ka otehkapawek* (VAI).

419

shrivel *kîkway kotekipayik* (VTI); *nipimakan* (VAI); *pastew* (VTI).

shroud *ka wewekinkatek miyaw* (VTI); *cîpayekin* (NI).

shrub *kohpikihiht miscikos* (VTA); *nîpisewahtikos* (NA); there is a shrub covered area, willow covered, *nîpisihkopâw* (VTA); there is shrub, birch, *waskweskaw* (VTI); there is area covered with small shrubs, *neyâmihkopâw* (VAI); a little willow bush, *nîpisewahtikos* (NA).

shrubbery *ka wawesihcikakehk miscikosak* (VTA); there is small shrubby spruce, *sihtiskâw* (NA); tree transplants, *âhtaskicikewina* (NI).

shrug *kopitihtimanepayihohk ekâ ka kiskeyihtamihk* (VTA).

shrunk *ka otehkipayik kîkway* (VTI).

shrunken *otehkipayihcikewin* (NI).

shudder *paskâc kanampayihk ka osâmyawesihk; nanamipayiw* (VTA).

shuffle *ka itenikehk pakesanak* (VTA).

shun *ka ponihtahk kîkway* (VAI).

shunt *ka ekatenamihk kîkway* (VTI).

shut *ka kipahamihk* (VTI).

shut-out *ekâ ka pihtokahiwehk* (VTA).

shut up S/he shuts up or stops talking, *kipihtowew* (VAI); the act of shutting up or stop talking, *kipihtowewin* (NI); her/his words shuts her/him up, *kipotonehwew* (VTA).

shutter *kîkway ka kipahikâkehk* (VTA); *kipohtenikân* (NI).

shy *ka nepewsihk* (VAI); *nepewisiw* (VAI).

shyly *nepewisowinihk* (VII).

sibling Younger brother or sister, *osîmimâw* (NA); my younger brother or sister, *nisîmis* (NA); my sisters and brothers, *nîcisânak* (NA); a full sibling or a full brother or sister, *tipiyaw*, i.e.: *tipiyaw nîcisân* (NA); having siblings, *wîtisânitowin* (NI) *(Northern)*; *wicisanitowin* (NI) *(Plains)*; s/he is the youngest sibling in the family, *osîmimâwiw* (VAI).

sick Being sick, *ka âhkosihk* (VAI); s/he is sick, *âhkosiw* (VAI); s/he suffers from her/his ridicule, *ohcinew* (VAI); s/he is sick after eating too much fat, *pasweskoyiw* (VAI).

sicken *awîyak ka âhkosehiht* (VTA); *âhkosepayiw* (VAI).

sickening *âhkosehiwewin* (NI).

sickly *katohpinewin* (NI); being weak and sickly for a long time, *nanihkâtâspinew* (VAI); something weak and sickly, *nanihkâc* (IPC).

sickness *âhkosiwin* (NI); immune to sickness, *sepinew* (VAI); stuck with an incurable sickness, *micimahpinew* (VAI); a skin disease, *wasakayaspinew* (VTI); *wesakasew* (VTI); s/he has sores, *omikîw* (VAI); a sickness caused by evil medicine or a suffering caused by ridicule, *ocinewin* (NI).

side From one side, *pimicohci* (VTI); on the side of the road, *patoteyayihk* (VII); mountains on each side, *âyitawatinâw* (IPC); on the other side across, *akâmihk* (VAI); s/he pulls from either side, *âyitawapew* (VTA); either side of the mountain, *âyitawatinâw* (IPC); s/he is firmly in place on both sides, *âyitawisin* (VTA); s/he holds her/him on both sides, *âyitawinew* (VTA); both sides, each side of something, *âyitâw* (VAI); on each side of the water or both sides of the river or lake, *âyitawakâm* (VTI); it fits on both sides, *âyitawihtin* (VAI); just on one side, *napate* (IPC); on one side of, *napatekâm* (VAI); s/he is one-sided, *napatesiw* (VAI); it is one-sided, *napateyâw* (VII); from the side or sideways, *pimic* (IPC); s/he sides with her/him in a fight, *nâtamawew* (VTA).

sidelong Just on one side, *napate* (IPC).

sideways *pimic ohci* (IPC); s/he is travelling crosswind or sideways, *pimicistinoweskam* (VTA).

sidewise *ka pimitastek* (VTI).

sidle *ka pimtohtehk* (VTI).

sieze *masaskonikewin* (NI).

sift S/he sifts them, *sîkawipayihew* (VTA).

sifter *sîkawipayihcikan* (NI); a steel utensil for sifting flour, *piwâpiskosakimewayan sâpopayihcikan* (NA).

sigh *mahkatahtamowin* (NI).

sight The sight on a gun, *oyâpahcikan* (NI); the act of seeing, *wapiwin* (NI); s/he sees her/him in a loathful situation, *kakwâyakâpamew* (VAI); s/he misses sighting her/him, *patâpamew* (VTA); s/he lost sight of her/him, *pônâpamew* (VTA); s/he disappears out of sight, *poninokosiw* (VAI); it disappears out of sight, *poninôkwan* (VII).

sightless *ekâ ka wapihk* (VAI).

sign An identification tag, *kiskinawâcecikan* (NI).

significance *mistahi îtiyihtakosiwin* (NI).

significant *mistahi kîtiyihtakwahk* (VII).

signify Act of suggesting or indicating, *wihtamâkewin* (NI).

silence *ka kâmwâtahk* (VII); s/he stops talking, *kipihtowew* (VTI).

silent Not talking, *ekâ ka papekiskwehk* (VTA); her/his mouth is shut, *kipitonew* (VTA).

silliness *môhcowisâyâwin* (NI).

silly *awîyak ka môhcowisâyât* (VAI).

similar *peyakwan kekâc* (IPC).

similarity *ka naspitâtomakahk kîkway* (VII).

simmer *kekâc ka ohtek* (VAI); *nisihkâc pakâhcikewin* (ni).

simper *pahpihkâsiwin* (NI).

simple Something that is not hard to do, *ekâ kayimahk kîkway* (VAI); it is simple or not hard to do, *wihcasin* (VAI); s/he is a simple or slow person, *kepâtis* (NA).

420

simplicity The act of being slow, *peyahtikwesâyâwin* (NI).

simplification *ka wihcasehtahk* (VTI).

simplify *tesiwihcasik kisehtahk* (VTI).

simply *soskwâc papeyahtik* (IPC).

simulate *mwehci tâpwe ekâ tôtamihk* (VTI).

simulation *wayesihtâwin* (NI).

simultaneous At the same time, *pahpeyakwanita* (IPC).

simultaneously *tahtakowac*; at the same time, *papeyakwan*; *keswanpapeyakwan kespayik*; all at the same, *pahpeyakwan* (IPC).

sin Committing a sin, *pâstâhowin* (NI); s/he sins, *pâstâhow* (VAI); s/he makes her/him commit sinful acts, *pâstâhew* (VAI).

since *âspin* (IPC); since that time, *âspin ekospi* (IPC); just before, *mastaw* (IPC); not often, very seldom, *âspîs* (IPC); once in a while, *âyâspîhtaw* (IPC).

sincere *tâpwewakeyihtâkwan* (VII).

sincerity *tâpwe isâyâwin* (NI).

sinew *astinwan* (NI).

sinewy *peyakwan astinwan* (VTI).

sinful *ka sâkaskineskakohk pâstâhowin* (NI).

sing The act of singing, *ka nikamohk* (VTA); s/he sings with her/him, *naskwahamawew* (VTA); s/he makes her/him sing, *nikamohew* (VTA); s/he sings for her/him, *nikamostawew* (VTA); s/he sings, *nikamiw* (VTA); the act of singing strongly or loudly, *sohkatamowin* (NI); s/he sings strongly or loudly, *sohkatâmow* (VAI); s/he sings the correct melody, *tâpowew* (VAI); the act of being able to sing the proper melody, *tâpowewin* (NI); s/he sings with her/him, *wîcinikamômewew* (VTA).

singe The act of singeing a moose head for eating, *ka pahtamihk mostoskowan* (VTA); it is singed, *paskohkasiw* (NA); *paskohkahtew* (NI).

singer *onikamow* (NA); s/he is an excellent singer, *nihtânikamow* (VTA).

singing The act of singing, *nikamowin* (NI) *(Plains)*; *nikamon* (NI) *(Northern)*; s/he joins in the song, *naskwaham* (VAI); the act of joining in the song, *naskwahamâtowin* (NI).

single *ka môsâpewihk* (VAI); being alone, *peyakowin* (NI).

singleness *pahpeyakowin* (NI); being alone, *peyakowin* (NI).

singly *pahpeyak ohci* (IPC); just once, *peyakwâw* (IPC).

singular *ka peyakomâmiskomiwehk* (VAI); just one thing alone, *ka peyakwâk* (NI).

sinister *metoni matatisowin* (NI); bad or harmful action, *mâyitôtamowin* (NI).

sink The act of sinking or submerging, *kosâpewin* (NI); s/he or it sinks, *kosâpew* (VAI); s/he has sunk into the water, *kosâpepayiw* (VAI); s/he submerges her/him in the water, *kosâpepitwew* (VTA); s/he sinks her/him

into the water with her/his weight, *kosâpeskawew* (VTA); s/he sinks into the water, *kosâpew* (VAI); the act of sinking or submerging, *kosâpewin* (NI); it sinks under, *kotâwipayiw* (VAI).

sinner *pâstâhosk* (NA); a person that commits sin, *opâstâhosk* (NA).

sinuate *kîkway ka pihkipayik* (VTI).

sinuosity *wahkew pihkipayowin* (NI).

sinuous *meskanaw kawahwakamok* (VTI).

sinus *ka wesakastanehk* (VAI); *testikwanewin* (NI).

Sioux A Sioux person, *pwâtiyiniw* (NA); the Sioux language, *pwâtômowin* (NI); s/he is Sioux, *pwâtowew* (NA).

sip *âhapsis ka minihkwesihk* (VTA); *minihkwesiw* (VTA); *kotspitam* (VTA).

sir *nâpiw kesi atamiskâht* (VTA).

sire *miscacimosis tanhi kopapat nâpestimwak* (VTA); a father, *ohtâwimâw* (NA).

sister The eldest sister, *omisimâw* (NA); younger sister (or brother), *osîmimâw* (NA); my sister (or brother), *nîtisân* (NA); my older sister, *nimis* (NA); my younger sister (or brother), *nisîmis* (NA); sisters say my sister, *nitisaniskwew* (NA); brothers say my sister, *nitawemâw* (NA); someone's female sibling, *awîyak iskwewa wetcisana* (NA); she is the eldest sister, *omisimawiw* (VAI); s/he has her as an older sister, *omisimiw* (VAI) *(Northern)*; *omisahkomew* (VAI) *(Plains)*.

sisterhood Organization of religious sisters, *ayamihewiskwewiwin* (NI).

sister-in-law *ocakosimâw* (NA); my sister-in-law, *nîtim* (NDA); women say my brother's wife, *nicahkos* (NA); men say my brother's wife, *nîtim* (NA); their sister-in-law, *ocakosiwawa* (NA); someone's sister-in-law, *awîyak ocakosa* (NA); *awîyak nâpiw wîtimwa* (NA).

sisterly *ayamihewiskwewayâwin* (NI).

sit The act of sitting, *apiwin* (NI); please sit or be at home, *ayapih* (VTA); the act of changing a sitting position or moving to sit in another location, *âhtapiwin* (NI); s/he changes her/his seating position or s/he moves to sit in a different location, *âhtapiw* (VTA), s/he sits firmly, *ayâtapiw* (VTA), *ayâtapow* (VTI) *(Northern)*; *ayitapow* (VTI) *(Plains)*; it is made like a place to sit, *apiwineyâw* (VII); a good place for sitting, *miyowapowineyâw* (VII); s/he sits improperly, *mâyapiw* (VAI); s/he sits down beside her/him, *nahapîstawew* (VTA); s/he sits down, *nahapiw* (VTA); s/he sits on one side, *napatepiw* (VAI); it sits on one side, *napatestew* (VII); it sits facing the wrong way, *naspatastew* (VII); s/he sat facing the wrong way, *naspâtapiw* (VAI); s/he sits in the back, *nawayapiw* (VAI); s/he sits slumped to one side, *nawepiw* (VAI); it sits close at hand, *nehpemastew* (VII); s/he sits raring

421

to go, **nehpemapiw** (VAI); s/he is seated in front of her/
him, **nîkânapîstawew** (VTA); s/he sits in the front,
nîkânapiw (VTA); s/he sits throughout the summer,
nîpinapiw (VAI); there are four of them sitting
together, **newapiwak** (VAI); s/he makes her/him sit in
front of others, or s/he makes her/him boss,
nîkânapîhew (VTA); the act of sitting ahead of others
or the act of being made a boss, **nîkânapiwin** (NI); the
act of sitting first in line, **nistamapiwin** (NI); s/he sits
first in line, **nistamapiw** (VAI); it is first in line,
nistamastew (VII); s/he sits with her/his head down,
otihtapiskwepiw (VAI); it sits here and there,
pahpâmâstew (VII); s/he sits alone there, **peyakwapiw**
(VAI); s/he sits spread eagle in front of her/him,
taskapestawew (VTA); s/he sits spread eagle,
taswekapiw (VAI); it sits spread eagle, **taswekastew**
(VII); s/he sits on top of her/his back, i.e.: a horse,
tehtapâtew (VTA) (*Northern*); **tehtapâmew** (VTA)
(*Plains*); s/he gives her/him a horseback ride,
tehtapîhew (VTA); s/he sits on top of something,
tehtapiw (VAI); the act of sitting on top of something,
i.e.: a chair, **tehtapiwin** (NI); s/he sits with her/him
long enough, **tepapîstawew** (VTA); there is enough
space or room for her/him to sit, **tepapiw** (VAI); s/he
sits with her/his legs spread out, **tohkapiw** (VAI); s/he
sits with her/him or them, **wîtapimew** (VTA); they sit
in a circle, **wâsakâmepiwak** (VTA).

site Camping site, *ka pesowinihk* (NI).
sitter House sitter, *okanawapokew* (NA); baby sitter,
kanawawâsisowew (NA).
sitting *ka ayapihk* (VII); s/he is sitting, **apiw** (VTA);
ayayapow (VTA); s/he is home, **ayapiw** (VAI); sitting
piled up, **asastew** (VII); sitting, placed on top, **aspapow**
(VTA); **aspastew** (NI); solidly placed, hard to move,
ayâtapow (NA); **ayatastew** (NI); piled high, sitting
high, **ispâpow** (NA); **ispâstew** (NI); blocks passage
while sitting, placed, **kipapiw** (NA); **kipastew** (NI);
sitting well, exactly placed, **nahastew** (NI); waiting,
ready, **nehpemapiw** (NA); **nehpemastew** (NI); sitting,
placed first, presiding, honored, **nîkânapiw** (NA);
nîkânastew (NI); in the back, behind, **otâkapow** (NA);
otâkastew (NI); never in one place, restless,
papâmapiw (NA); **papâmâstew** (NI); sitting up,
simatapow (NA); **simatastew** (NI); sitting on your
haunches, **cîpatapiw** (NA); **cîpatastew** (NI); sitting a
long time, **sipapow** (NA); **sipastew** (NI); sitting
endlessly, i.e.: handicapped, **kistapiw** (VAI); on top
rides on horseback, **tehtapow** (VTA); turned around
completely sitting, **kweskâpiw** (NA); **kweskastew** (NI),
sitting alone, placed alone, **peyakwapiw** (NA);
peyakwastew (NI); sitting, placed across, **pimitapiw**
(NA); **pimitastew** (NI); changing of a sitting position,
âhtapiwin (NI); s/he is sitting silently and not talking,

kâmwâtapiw (VAI); the act of sitting silently and not
talking, **kâmwâtapiwin** (NI); s/he is sitting quietly,
koskwâwâtapiw (VAI); s/he is sitting facing someone,
otiskawapiw (VAI); it is sitting facing someone,
otiskawastew (VII); s/he is sitting in a dry spot, i.e.:
during a rain storm, **pâstewapiw** (VAI); s/he is sitting
upright, **simatapiw** (VTA).
situate *tân'ta kosihtâhk wâskahikan* (VTA).
situated *etah kastek kîkway* (VAI).
situation *tansi ketahkamkahk* (VAI); that is the
condition, *ekosi kespayik* (VII).
six *nikotwâsik* (IPC); six each, **nahnikotwâsikwâw**
(IPC); six times, **nikotowâsikwâw** (IPC); six of a kind,
nikotwâsikwayih; six different kinds,
nahnikotwâsikwayih; in six places or six directions,
nikotwâsikwayak; in six different places,
nahnikotwâsikwayak; s/he is number six or sixth,
nikotwâsikowiw (VAI).
sixfold *nikotwâsikwâw* (IPC).
six hundred *nikotwâsikwâw mitâtahtomitanaw* (IPC).
sixteen *nikotwâsosâp* (IPC); sixteen times,
nikotwâsosâpwâw (IPC).
sixteenth *mwecinikotwâsosâp* (IPC); sixteenth time,
nikotwâsosâpwâw (IPC); sixteenth of the month,
nikotwâsosâp akimâw pîsim.
sixth *mwecinikotwâsik* (IPC); sixth time,
nikotwâsikwâw (IPC); sixth of the month, **nikotwâsik
akimâw pîsim**.
sixtieth *mwecinikotwâsomitanaw* (IPC); sixtieth time,
nikowâsomitanawâw (IPC).
sixty *nikotwâsomitanaw* (IPC); sixty times,
nikowâsomitanawâw (IPC).
sizable *kisâstaw ka misâk*; fairly large, **keyiwehk
misâw** (VII).
size The size of something, *taniyekohk kîspehcak*; s/he
is just the right size, **nahetikitiw** (VAI); it is just the
right size, **nahîspihcâw** (VII).
sizzle Red hot iron, *iskotewâpiskitew* (VTI); it sizzles
while cooking, **cowehkahtew** (VII); it makes a sizzling
or whistling sound like a spinning top, **cowehkocin**
(VAI).
skeleton Ghost-like, *cîpay* (NA); *cîpayoskana* (NI).
skeptical *moyeyihtamowin* (NI); s/he is skeptical of
her/him, **moyeyimew** (VTA); the act of being skeptical,
moyesowin (NI); a nonbeliever, s/he denies what
others affirm, **ânwehtawew** (VAI).
sketch *tapasinahikan*; sketch or a quick drawing,
mâhmâses ka taspasinahamihk; a sketch artist,
tapasinahikewiyiniw (NA); s/he makes a sketch of
her/him, **tapasinahwew** (VTA).
sketchy *pahpahki etah ka nistawnakwahk
masinahikewin* (NI); **tapasinastew** (VII).

skew *ka mâyesihcikatek* (VAI).

skewer Something sharp used to skewer meat to cook over a campfire, *cîpatâskwahikan* (NI).

skid *ka sôskwâciwewapoyohk*; the act of sliding along, *sôskwâpoyowin* (NI).

skies *waskôwa* (NI); a cloud, *waskôw* (NI).

skilful *or* **skillful** *metonikanahehk* (VAI).

skilfully *or* **skillfully** Using skill, *nahiwin ka âpacitahk* (VTA); *nakacihtâw* (VAI); s/he is skillful or adept, i.e.: sports, *nahiw* (VAI).

skill Being skilled or adept at something, i.e.: sports, *nahiwin* (NI); being skilled, *miyowin* (NI) *(Northern)*; *takahkîwin* (NI) *(Plains)*.

skilled *awîyak ka nahet*; *nakacihtâw* (VAI); *kaskihtâw* (VAI).

skim The act of skimming off, *ka manahikehk*; s/he skims it, *manaham*; the cream is skimed off, *manahipimâtew*; s/he skims off the grease or the lard, *manahipimew*; the act of skimming off grease, *manahipimewin* (NI).

skimmer *manahikakan* (NI); *manahikanakan* (NI).

skimp *etâtaw pimâcihowin* (NI).

skimpy *etâtaw ka pimâcihohk* (VAI).

skin Human skin, *masakay* (NA) *(Plains)*; *wasakay* (NA) *(Northern)*; a piece of skin, *wasakay* (NA); her/his skin is burned and shrivelled, *ocipwasakayehkasiw* (VTA); s/he skins them, i.e.: usually used to refer to large animals such as a moose or a cow, *pahkonew* (VTA); s/he skins her/his head or s/he takes her/his fur off with her/his hands, *paskwatihpenew* (VTA); s/he skins it and fleshes the inside of the pelt, i.e.: usually used to refer to small fur bearing animals such as a muskrat or beaver, *pihtonew* (VTA); the act of skinning and fleshing a pelt, *pihtonikewin* (NI); her/his skin peels off, *pihtosakepayiw* (VAI); something skinned and fleshed, *pihtosikan* (NI); the skin around the stomach of an animal, *waskatayekin* (NI) *(Northern)*; *waskatay* (NI) *(Plains)*.

skinner One who skins animals, *opahkonikew* (NA).

skinny S/he is skinny, *sihkaciw* (VAI); s/he is skinny and tall, *sâsâkawaskosiw* (VAI); s/he finds her/him skinny, *sihkaceyimew* (VTA); *sihkateyimew* (VTA) *(Plains)*; being skinny, *sihkaciwin* (NI); s/he makes her/him skinny or thin, *sihkatimew* (VTA).

skip The act of skipping, *kwâskohtâpewin* (NI).

skirmish *mâyiwecehtowin* (NI); they have a little fight, *notintowak* (VTA).

skirt *kîskasakay* (NI); a cut-off dress, *kîskasakas* (NI).

skirting *kîskasakayihkakanekin* (NI).

skitter *awîyak ka wawiyasinkeskit* (VTA).

skittish *ka nihtâ wawiyasinkehk* (VTA).

skulk *ka kîmôtisipwehtehk* (VTA).

skull A skeleton's head bone, *mistikwânikan* (NI).

skunk *sikâk* (NA) *(Northern)*; *wîncoyesis* (NA) *(Plains)*; a skunk berry, *sikâkomin* (NI); a skunk pelt, *sikâkwayân* (NA).

skunk cabbage *yôskihtepakwa* (NI).

sky *kîsik* (NI); it is covered, cloudy sky, *iyikwaskwan* (NI); it is clear, a clear sky, *wâseskwan* (NI); the sky is red, *mihkwaskwan* (NI); the morning sky is red, *mihkwâpan* (NI); the sky clears by wind, *wâseskwastan* (NI).

sky blue *ka wâsekwahk*.

slab *napatepocikan* (NI).

slack *ka nîkamok* (VII).

slacken *ka nîkinamihk* (VTI); s/he is slackening or reducing her/his speed, i.e.: a car, *nîkakocin* (VAI); it is slackening or reducing its speed, i.e.: a motorboat, *nîkakotew* (VII).

slain *awîyak ka nipahiht* (VTA).

slake *ka naheyihtamohekohk* (VAI).

slam *iskwâhtem ka kisewehtâhk* (VTI).

slander A lie, *kîyaskowin* (NI); telling lies, *kiyâskimowewin* (NI); s/he slanders her/him, *kitimakimew* (VTA).

slanderous *ka kiyâskihk* (VAI).

slang *pîtos ka isi pîkiskwehk* (VTA); *pîkiskwehkasowin* (NI).

slangy *pîtos pîkiskwewinihk* (VAI).

slant *ka îyipeyak* (VII); across, slanted, slanting, *îyipeyaw* (VII).

slantwise *îyipescikewin* (NI).

slap Slapping someone in the face, *ka pasihkwetahikehk* (VTA); s/he slaps her/his own hands, *pascicehosiw* (VTA); s/he slaps her/his hands, *pascicehwew* (VTA); s/he slaps her/him in the face, *pasihkwehwew* (VTA); s/he slaps her/his mouth, *pastonehwew* (VTA).

slash *paskwatahikewin* (NI).

slat *napakihcakos* (NI).

slather *ka kispakastâhk kîkway* (VTI).

slaughter *ka wiyanihtakehk* (VTA).

slaughterous *awîyak ka nihtâ wiyanihtaket* (VTA).

slavey *ayahciyiniw* (NA).

slaw *ka sikwatahamihk otehîpakwa* (VTA).

slay *ka nipahtâkehk* (VTA).

sleazy *ekâ tâpwe ka miwasik* (IPC).

sled *ocâpânaskos* (NI); *sôskociwiw tâpanaskos* (NI).

sledding *ka sôskwâciwakehk ocâpânaskosak* (VTI).

sleek *ka sôskwawehamahk* (VTI).

sleep The act of sleeping, *nipâwin* (NI); a good sleep, *miyohkwâmiwin* (NI); they sleep together or many of them sleep together, *mihcetohkwâmiwak* (VTA); two of them sleep together, *nîsohkwâmiwak* (VTA); s/he is sleeping, *nipâw* (VTA); s/he likes to sleep, *nipâskiw* (VAI); s/he had to spend the night short of her/his

423

destination, **nohtehkwamiw** (VAI); s/he has a fitful
sleep, **pawinehkwâmiw** (VAI); s/he sleeps alone,
peyakohkwamiw (VTA); s/he sleeps soundly,
pôsahkwâmiw (VAI); they sleep together,
wehpehtowak (VTA); s/he sleeps with her/him,
wehpemew (VTA); the act of sleep, **nipâwin** (NI); s/he
sleeps alone, **peyakohkwamiw** (VTA).

sleeper *ka nipâkehk* (VTA); *nipâsk* (NA).

sleeping *ka nipâhk* (VAI).

sleepless *ekâ kakeh nipâhk* (VTA).

sleepy The act of being sleepy, **nohtehkwasiwin** (NI);
s/he is sleepy, **nohtehkwasiw** (VAI); s/he reduces her/
his sleeping time, **nohtehkwastimew** (VTA); s/he is
sleepy, **nohtekwasiw** (VAI).

sleet *kimowan ka ati âhkwacipayik* (VTI); there is
sleet, **misponipestaw** (VTI).

sleety *ka miskwamewatihk* (VTI).

sleeve *wanakway* (NI); *manakway* (NI).

sleeved *ka manakwayihkehk* (VTI).

sleeveless *ka kîskanakweyak* (VII).

sleigh A horse drawn winter vehicle,
mistatimotâpânask (NI); a winter vehicle,
pipontâpânask (NI) *(Northern)*; **pehkokawân** (NI)
(Plains).

sleighing *ka papâmtapasohk* (VTI); *pipon tapasowin*
(NI).

sleight *tâstapîwin* (NI).

slender Having a slender build, *ka sâsâkosihk* (VAI); it
is slender, i.e.: steel or metal, *sâsâkawâpiskâw* (VAI);
s/he has a slender build, *sâsâkoyawew* (VTA).

slenderize *ka sâsâkosehtahk* (VTI).

slept Someone who slept, *awîyak ka kehnipat* (VTA);
s/he slept right through, *sâpohkwamiw* (VTA).

slew *awîyak kakeh nipahtaket* (VTA).

slice *pâhkwesawacikan* (NI); cutting a slice off
something, *kapahkwesamihk kîkway* (VAI); s/he
slices a piece off, i.e.: bread, *pahkweswew* (VTA); s/he
slices them to pieces, *cîsawatew* (VTA); s/he slices it to
pieces, *cîsawatam* (VTA); s/he slices a piece of bread,
pahkwesâwâtew (VTA); s/he slices them thin,
papakiswew (VTI); s/he sliced it thinly,
papakisâwâtam (VTI); it is sliced thinly,
papakisâwâtew (VTA).

slicer *manisikâkan* (NI).

slick *metoni ka sôskosikwak* (VII); *sôskwâw* (VII).

slid The act of sliding; s/he slides down to them,
yâsestawew (VTA); *ka sôskopayihohk* (VTA); it slid or
rolled underneath something, *sekopayiw* (VII) or (VAI).

sliding The act of sliding down a hill, *soskwacowewin*
(NI); *ka sôskwaciwehk* (VAI); s/he slides her/him
down, i.e.: a chute, *peyâsipayihew* (VTA); it comes
sliding down, i.e.: a chute, *peyâsipayiw* (VII) or (VAI);
s/he makes it slide down with ease or s/he swallows it

with ease, *sôskopayihew* (VTA); s/he sends it sliding
down a hill, *sôskwâciwewepinew* (VTI); s/he slides
down a hill, *sôskwâciwew* (VII); a sliding place,
sôskwâciwewin (NI); s/he slides on the slippery snow,
sôswakonesin (VAI); s/he is sliding down, *yâsiw* (VAI);
s/he slides down to them, *yâsestawew* (VTA); the act
of sliding down, *yâsewin* (NI); s/he slides it off, i.e.:
pants, *yâsinew* (VTI); s/he makes them slide down,
yâsipayihew (VTA); s/he slides down, *yâsipayihow*
(VAI); it slides down, *yâsipayiw* (VII).

slight A little bit, *apisis* (IPC); it is small, *apisasin* (VII);
it is slight, *niyaman* (VII); used when referring to small
items, i.e.: a table, "it is built meagerly", *niyamâsin*
(VAI); used when referring to large items, i.e.: a house,
"it is poorly constructed", *niyamâtan* (VAI); it is tiny
and frail, i.e.: a canoe, *niyamâw*; it is poorly built,
niyamisiw (VAI).

slighting *ekâ kwayask ka tôtamihk* (VAI).

slightly *metoni apsis* (IPC).

slim *ka kinwaskosihk* (VAI); *sihkaciw* (VAI).

slime *ka sôskwak* (VII); *pasakoceskowakâw* (VII).

slimy Something that is hard to grasp, *ka
sôskonkwahk* (VII); slimy water, *sôskwakamow* (VTI).

sling Used to propel stones at things, *wepahaskwân*
(NI); an arm sling or a neckerchief, *tâpiskâkan* (NI);
s/he tosses a sling at her/him, *wepahaskwâtew* (VTA);
s/he uses a sling to propel stones, *wepahaskwew*
(VAI).

slink *ka nâciyôscikehk* (VTA).

slip The act of slipping, *sôskonikewin* (NI); it slips,
sôskopayiw (VII) or (VAI); s/he slips her/him
underneath to hide her/him, *sekonew* (VTI); s/he slips
her/him between the walls, *sekosimew* (VTA); s/he
slips on a slippery floor, *sôskohtakisin* (VAI); s/he slips,
i.e.: on a greasy floor, *sôskosin* (VAI); it slips from her/
his hand, *sôskonew* (VTA); it slips and slides,
sôskopayiw (VII) or (VAI); s/he slips and slides on the
slippery mud, *sôskoceskowaksin* (VTA).

slip Or petticoat, *pihtawesâkan* (NI).

slippery It is icy and slippery, *sôskosikwâw* (VII); s/he is
a slippery person, *sôskon'kosiw* (VAI); s/he makes
them slippery, *sôskohew* (VTI); it is slippery, i.e.: a
toboggan, *sôskosiw* (VAI); it is smooth and slippery,
i.e.: a rope, *sôskwâpekan* (VII); s/he has slippery skin,
sôskwâpekisiw (VAI); the pole is slippery,
sôskwâskwan (VII); it is slippery or smooth, *sôskwâw*.

slit *ka yohtesawatamihk kîkway* (VAI).

slither *ka sôskopayihohk* (VTA).

sliver *ka pahkwepayik napakihtak* (VTI); puncturing
one's foot, *kisisin* (VTA).

slob *ka kohkôsowit awîyak* (VTA).

slobber *awîyak ka ohci kawsihkwat* (VTA);
wînitapiskanew (VAI).

424

slobbery *ohcikawisihkwawin* (NI).

slog *ka sohketahikehk* (VTA).

slop *wîyipapoy* (NI).

slope *ka eyipihcak* (VAI); *yepeyaw* (VAI); there is slope, *nihtâtinaw* (VII).

sloppy *wîyipapawewin* (NI) *(Northern)*; *mâmâsimâciwin* (NI) *(Plains)*.

slouch *metoni pîweyiniw* (NA); *kihtimikan* (NA).

slouchy *ka pîweyiniwihk* (VAI).

slough A little slough, *pihcapekos* (NI); dead water, i.e.: a slough, *pihcapek* (NA).

sloven *awîyak ka kitimâkisehisot* (VTA).

slovenly *kitimâkisowin* (NI).

slow Real slow, *papeyahtik* (IPC); s/he is involved in a long, drawn out, slow process, *nanihkâcipayiw* (VAI); s/he is really slow going or s/he does things slowly, *papîcew* (VAI); s/he finds her/him slow going, *papîcîyimew* (VTA); it is a slow process, *papetan* (VII); s/he goes slowly, *pekihkâciw* (VAI) *(Northern)*; *papwâstawiw* (VAI) *(Plains)*; it goes slowly, *pekihkâcipayiw* (VII); s/he goes there slowly, *pekihkâcitâw* (VII); it is slow coming, *pekihkâtan* (VII); the act of thinking slowly, *pekihkâteyihtamowin* (NI); s/he finds her/him a slow thinker, *pekihkâteyimew* (VTA); s/he is a slow thinker, *pekihkâteyihtam* (VAI); the act of being slow or sluggish, *pekihkâtisiwin* (NI); s/he is slow or sluggish, *pekihkâtisiw* (VAI); s/he is slow moving, *pwâstawiw* (VAI); s/he thinks s/he is slow moving, *pwâstaweyimew* (VTA); it comes real slow, *pwâstawipayiw* (VII); the gun is slow firing, i.e.: a muscle loader, *pwâstawimatwewew* (VII); s/he is slow arriving, *pwâstawitakosin* (VAI); being slow moving, *pwastawîwin* (NI); s/he is very slow, *yîkitchikâwiw* (VAI); the act of being very slow, *yîkitcikâwiwin* (NI); s/he walks slowly, *papwâstahohtew* (VAI) *(Plains)*; *pekihkâtohtew* (VAI) *(Northern)*; *yîkicikâtohtew* (VAI) *(Plains)*; s/he acts in a slow and steady manner or s/he is slow, *peyahtikowisiw* (VAI) *(Plains)*; *nisihkâcâtisiw* (VAI) *(Northern)*; very slowly, *peyahtik* (IPC) *(Plains)*; *kâkitaw* (IPC) *(Northern)*; slow operation, slow or measured, *peyahtikowisowin* (NI) *(Plains)*; *peyahtikoyisâyâwin* (NI) *(Northern)*.

sludge *ka saskanakonakak* (VII).

slug *mohtew mosasiniy* (NI); a snail, *akahkway* (NA).

sluggard *awîyak ka nipahikanet* (VAI).

sluggish S/he is slow moving, *piwastawew* (VAI); *yekicikawiw* (VAI).

slum *kitimâkowekowin ôtenahk* (NI).

slumber *pôsahkwâmowin* (NI); the act of sleeping, *nipâwin* (NI).

slumberous *awîyak ka nihtâ pôsahkwâmit* (VTA).

slump *ka pakastawepayihk* (VTA).

slur *ekâ kwayask ka pikiskwehk* (VTA).

slurp *ka kisewehtonesinihk ka metsohk* (VTA).

slush *ka tihkakonakak* (VII).

slushy *ka tihkisot kona* (VTA).

sly *kîmôtâtisiwin* (NI).

slyly *ke môtâtisowinihk* (VII).

smack *ka napakcicîpakamahoht awîyak* (VTA).

smacker *opasihkwetahikew* (NA).

small It is small, *apisâsin* (VII); when something is small, *kapsasik kîkway* (VII); s/he is small, *apisisiw* (VAI).

small of the back *apiscawikanansihk* (VAI).

smart Being smart, *iyinisowin* (NI); s/he is smart, *iyinisiw* (VAI); s/he makes her/him smart, *iyinisihew* (VTA).

smarten *awîyak ka kiskinohamâht* (VTA).

smash Smashing something, *ka sikwatahikehk* (VTA); s/he dropped it and smashed it into small pieces, *sikohtatâw* (VAI).

smashing *sikwatahikewin* (NI).

smear *ka sinikwahamihk* (VAI).

smeary The act of smearing, *sinikwahikewin* (NI).

smell The act of smelling, *pasowin* (NI); s/he can smell it, *pasow* (VTA); s/he smells it, *miyahtam* (VAI); it has a recognizable smell, *kihkâmâkosiw* (VAI); it has a recognizable smell, *kihkâmâkwan* (VII); the act of smelling pleasant, *miyomâkosiwin* (NI); s/he smells pleasant, *miyomâkosiw* (VAI); it has a pleasant scent, *miyomâkwan* (VII); s/he smells bad, *macimâkosiw* (VAI); it smells bad, *macimâkwan* (VII); it smells like excrement, *miyakan* (VII); s/he smells like excrement, *miyakisiw* (VAI); s/he smells them or her/him, *miyâmew* (VTA); s/he makes her/him smell it, *pasôhew* (VTA); s/he smells perfumed, *wihkimâkosiw* (VAI); s/he makes someone smell pleasant with perfume, *wihkimâkohew* (VTA); the act of smelling pleasant or being perfumed, *wihkimâkosiwin* (NI); it smells perfumed, *wihkimâkwan* (VII); s/he likes the smell of someone, *wihkimâmew* (VTA).

smeller *paswâkan* (NI).

smelly *ka pecimakwahk kîkway* (VTI); bad smelling, *wicekisin* (NA); *wicekihtin* (NI).

smile Smiling, *pahpiw'nâkosiwin* (NI).

smirch *ka atihtek kîkway* (VAI).

smirk *kisonakosowin* (NI).

smite *metoni kanahtakatahikehk* (VAI); *sohketahikehk* (VAI).

smitten *awîyak ka nahtakahoht* (VTA); *sohketahoht* (VTA).

smock *iskwew ayâwawasow asâkay* (NI).

smog *ka kaskâwahkamik* (NI).

smoke Making smoke, *kaskâpahtenkewin* (NI); it is smokey, *kaskâpahtew* (VII); in the smoke, s/he is

425

engulfed in smoke or s/he is smoked, i.e.: fish , *kaskâpasiw* (VAI) *or* (VII); it is smoked, i.e.: moose meat, *kaskâpahtew* (VTI); s/he smokes them, i.e.: fish, *kaskâpaswew* (VTI); s/he smokes pure pipe tobacco, *môstâskosâwew* (VTI); s/he gave her/him a smoke, *pihtwâhew* (VTA); s/he smokes it, i.e.: a pipe, *pihtwatew* (VTI); s/he smokes, *pihtwâw* (VAI); the act of smoking, *pihtwâwin* (NI); s/he smokes with her/him, *wecipehtwamew* (VTA); there is smoke, *kaskapahtew* (VII); smoke passes by, *pimâpahtew* (VTI); the smoke goes up, *ispapatew* (VTI); smoke from a distance, *sakapahtew* (VTI); the smoke drifts down, *nehtapahtew* (VTI); smoke fills it, *sâkaskineyapahtew* (VTI); smoke comes out, *wayawîyâpahtew* (VTI); smoke comes in, *pihtokeyapahtew* (VTI); the smoke is suffocating, (VTI); the act of making a suffocating smoke, *kipwatâmâpasikewin* (NI); there is smoke rising in the distance, *pikihtew* (VTI).

smokeless *ekâ ka kaskâpahtek* (VTI).

smoker *okaskâpasikew* (NA).

smokes S/he smokes, *pihtwaw* (VAI).

smokey Very smokey, *kaskamotâpahtew* (VTI).

smooth It is slippery or smooth, *sôskwâw* (VII).

smote *awîyak kakeh sohkitahikasot* (VAI).

smother *awîyak ka kipahkitoneniht* (VAI).

smoulder *or* **smolder** *kaskâpahtew* (NI).

smudge *tasamân* (NI) *(Northern)*; *atisamân* (NI) *(Plains)*; the act of making a smudge for horses or cattle, *tasamanihkewin* (NI) *(Northern)*; *atisamânihkwewin* (NI) *(Plains)*; s/he makes a smudge, *tasamanihkew* (VTI) *(Northern)*; *atisamânihkew* (VTI) *(Plains)*; s/he makes a smudge for them, *tasamanihkawew* (VTA) *(Northern)*; *atisamânihkawew* (VTA) *(Plains)*; s/he stands by the smudge or smoke to keep bugs away, *tasamaw* (VAI) *(Northern)*.

smudgy *ka pihkahtek kîkway* (VAI).

smug *kanihtâ meweyihtamohisohk* (VAI).

smuggle *ka kimotatawakehk kîkway* (VAI); *kîmôcipihtokwataw* (VTI).

smut *ka wîyipâtahk kîkway* (VII).

smutty *ka kaskitewihkahtek* (VAI).

snaffle *nakayâhastimwew tâpitonehpicikan* (NI).

snag It is snagged on something, i.e.: something floating down the river, *nakâyâhotew* (VAI).

snaggy *mistik ka wâtihkwanowit* (VTA) *or* (NA).

snail Also a blood sucker, *akahkway* (NA).

snake *kinepik* (NA).

snakeroot A piece of snakeroot, *namepin* (NA) *(Plains)*; *kinepikocepihk* (NA) *(Northern)*.

snakeskin *kinepikwasakay* (NI).

snaky *kwanta ka isinamihk* (VAI).

snap Doing something all of a sudden or in a snap, *sisikotcipayowin* (NI); it snaps or breaks off, *pîkopayiw* (VAI); it snaps, *nâtwâpayiw* (VAI).

snapper *awîyak ka nihtâ sikocimowet* (NA); a snapping turtle, *miskinâhk kâtahkwahket* (VTA) *or* (NA).

snappish *sikocâyâwin* (NI).

snappy *ka sisikociyawesihk* (IPC); snappy weather, *sisikoctahkayaw* (VII).

snare *tâpakwan* (NI); s/he is snared, i.e.: by a rope or net, *nakwâsiw* (VAI); s/he snares or hooks it, *nakwâtew* (VTA); s/he puts a snare around someone's neck, *tapakwahwew* (VTA); s/he snared her/him, *tâpakwâtew* (VTA) *(Plains)*; *tâpakwawew* (VTA) *(Northern)*; s/he sets up a snare, *tâpakwew* (VAI).

snarl *atim ka nemot* (VTA); the act of snarling and baring one's teeth, *sîyâpitewin* (NI) *(Plains)*; *seyâpitewin* (NI) *(Northern)*; s/he snares and bares her/his teeth, *sîyâpitew* (VAI) *(Plains)*; *seyâpitew* (VAI) *(Northern)*.

snarly *ka kisôwâyat awîyak* (VAI).

snatch *kîkway kotihtinamihk* (VAI).

snatchy *awîyak ka nihtâ kimotit* (VAI).

snazzy *ka osâm mîwasik* (NI) *or* (IPC).

sneak S/he has sneaky ways, *kîmôtâtisit* (VAI); s/he sneaks up and surprises them, *kîmâhew* (VTA); the act of sneaking away, *kîmiwin* (NI); s/he snuck away, *kîmîw* (VAI); s/he listens in a furtive manner, *kîmihtam* (VTI); that act of being sneaky or devious, *kîmisiwin* (NI); s/he is sneaky or devious, *kîmisiw* (VAI); it is done in a sneaky or underhanded way, *kîmôtahkamikan* (VII); s/he acts sneaky or underhanded, *kîmôtisiw* (VAI); the act of being sneaky or underhanded, *kîmôtisiwin* (NI); s/he sneaks up on her/him, *nâciyôstawew* (VTA).

sneaking *nâciyôscikewin* (NI).

sneaky *ka kîmôtâtsihk* (VAI); on the sly, *kîmôc* (IPC); s/he appears or looks sneaky, *kakayesiwinâkosiw* (NA) *(Plains)*; *kîmôcinâkosiw* (NA) *(Northern)*.

sneer *ka kisôkanawâpahkehk* (VAI).

sneeze The act of sneezing, *ayeyimowin* (NI) *(Northern)*; *câhcâmowin* (NI) *(Plains)*; s/he sneezes, *ayeyimow* (VTA); sneezing powder, *câhcâmosikan* (NI); it makes her/him sneeze, *câhcâmohik* (VTA); s/he makes her/him sneeze with something, i.e.: sneezing powder or pepper, *câhcâmohew* (VTA); s/he sneezes because of sneezing powder or pepper, *câhcâmow* (VAI).

snicker *pahpihkasowin* (NI); *kîmôcipahpiw* (VAI).

snide *macîtwawâyâwin* (NI).

sniff *ka pasôhk* (VAI); *pasiw* (VAI).

426

sniffle *iskoyikomewin* (NI); having sniffles,
iskoyikomiwâyâwin (NI) *(Northern)*;
sîskawakomewewin (NI) *(Plains)*.

snip *paskwahamatowin ohci ka mansamihk* (VTI);
kîskisam (VTA).

snipe A shore bird, i.e.: a snipe, *sesesiw* (NA); a little
bird that walks in the water, *pahkopesis* (NA); a bird
that announces the rain, i.e.: a type of snipe such as a
killdeer, *kimowanahasîs* (NA) *(Plains)*; *pacaskahask*
(NA) *(Northern)*.

snippy *ka nihtâ tahkwahkehk* (VTA).

snivel *ka matohkasohk* (VTA).

snoop Spying on someone, *kîmôtâpiwin* (NI); snooping
around and picking things up, *kîmôci papami
otinikew* (VTA).

snoose *ka kisikawihkwamihk* (VAI).

snoot *awîyak okot* (NI).

snooty *kihceyimowin* (NI).

snooze *ka nomi nipasihk* (VAI).

snore The act of snoring, *kitowehkwamowin* (NI); s/he
is snoring, *matwehkwâmiw* (VAI) *(Northern)*;
kitiwehkwâmiw (VAI) *(Plains)*.

snort *awîyak ka misipotaciket* (VAI); the act of making
noise through the nose, *kitoweyikomew* (VAI).

snot Mucus, *mitakom* (NA); *akik* (NA).

snotty *awîyak kotakikomit* (VAI).

snout *mososkowan* (NI); a human nose, *mikot* (NI).

snow *kôna* (NA); it snows, *mispon* (VII); s/he makes it
snow, *misponihtâw* (VAI); it kind of snows, it snows
lightly, *misponayâw* (VII); it snows lightly, it kind of
snows lightly, *misponayasin* (VII); it snows finely,
pewispon (VII); it snows heavily, *misimispon* (VII); the
snow is deep, *timikoniw* (VII) *(Plains)*; *timâkonakâw*
(VII) *(Northern)*; there is snow on the branches, trees,
akotakonew (VTA); the snow falls from the branches,
pawahamoyâw (VTA); the snow grinds under foot,
sâhkweyaw (VTA); the snow carries, *waskitateweyâw*
(VII), crusty snow, *waskitatenikwan* (VII);
watenikwan (VII); freshly fallen snow which is easy
for tracking, *paskakonakâw* (VII) *(Northern)*;
oskakonakâw (VII); it is freshly fallen snow which
makes for good tracking, *paskâkonakiyâw* (VII); the
snow melts or thaws, *saskânakonakâw* (VII); the snow
is soft, *yoskâkonakâw* (VII); there is room, space in the
snow, *tâwâkonakâw* (VII); the snow has a rough
surface, *piskwâkonakâw* (VII); soil patches show
through snow in spring or during warm spells,
pânakohtew (VAI); *iyihtew* (VAI); the snow glitters at a
distance in the sun, *wâsâkonastew* (VAI); the snow has
melted for good, *kîsiyihtew* (VAI); it is full of snow,
konôwan (VII); there is snow, *konowiw*; there is new
or fresh snow, *oskimispon* (VII); it is soft, fluffy snow
that is falling, *pîsweyâkonakâw* (VII); the snow

becomes slushy, *saskâkonakâw* (VII); the fresh snow is
clean and shiny, *wâsâkonastew* (VII).

snowball *ka pitikoniht kôna* (VAI) or (NA).

snowbank *ka ispakonakak* (NI).

snowbird *pipon pîwâyisis* (NA).

snowbound *ka micimakonehk* (VAI); *kipwakonew*
(VAI); the road is snowbound, *kipwakonakâw* (VII).

snowdrift *ka ayipewanasit kôna* (NA); the snow drifts,
there is driving snow, *pîwan* (VII); *pîwastew* (VAI);
pîwâstan (VAI); a snow drift, *papestin* (NA); having
snow drifting over, i.e.: a road, *papestinowan* (VII).

snowdrop Falling snow, *pakihtakonakâw* (VII).

snowfall *ka mispok* (VII); a sudden and heavy snowfall,
mahmahkâkonepayiw (NA) *(Plains)*;
pahkihtakonakâw (NA) *(Northern)*.

snowflake *peyak pîwâkonis* (NA); soft snowflakes,
yoskikonis (NA).

snowmelt *ka tihkisoht kôna* (VAI); *tihkâkonew* (VAI) or
(VTA).

snowshoe A pair of snowshoes, *asâmak* (NI); harness for
snowshoes, *asâmiyâpiy* (NI).

snowstorm *ka misponyotihk* (VII).

snow water *kônapoy* (NI).

snowy *kîkway ka kônowik* (NI); *konowiw* (VAI).

snub *awîyak ekâ ka nanakatohkehk* (NA).

snubby *awîyak ekâ ka nanakatohkewatsit* (VII).

snuff Chewing tobacco, *kâtahkwamiht cistemâw* (NA);
something to make you sneeze, *câhcâmohkasikan*
(NI).

snuffle *otâkikomow* (VAI); having a bad cold,
otâkikomowin (NI).

snug *wîkowin ka kîsowâk* (NA).

snuggle *ka kîsowiskatohk* (VAI); s/he is cuddling up,
kîsôsimiw (VAI).

soak *ka sâpopatahk* (VTA); *akôhcimew* (VAI); *akôhtitâw*
(VTA).

soap A bar of soap, *kisepekinikan* (NI).

soap bubble *ka pîstewakamik* (VII).

soapsuds *pîstew* (NI).

soapy *mweci kisepekinkan ka ispakwahk* (VII).

soar *ka ispahkepayihk* (VII); flying high in the air,
ispahkepapamihawin (NI).

sob *ka mâtowihtakosihk* (VTA).

sober *âstepewin* (NI); *âstepew* (VAI).

sobriety *kayâs kohastepehk* (VAI).

sociability *otôtemihtowin* (NI).

sociable S/he is sociable, *otôtemimow* (NA).

social acquaintance *otôtemihtowin* (NI).

socialite *otôtemihtowenihk awîyak ka wicihiwet* (NA).

sociality *miyowicihiwewin* (NI).

socialize *kowicewâkan payihohk* (VAI).

socially *miyowicihiwewnihk* (VII).

society *mâmawinitowin* (NI).

427

sock S/he makes her/him socks, *asikanihkawew* (VTA); s/he makes some socks, *asikanihkew* (VAI); a stretchy stocking or sock, *sîpîkiskâwasikan* (NA); a stocking, *asikan* (NA).

sod *ka poyakahcahekehk* (VAI); earth or soil or ground, *asiskîy* (NI).

sodden *ekâ metoni ka pastek keyâpic kahkostihk* (NI); it is soaked right through, *sâpowahkostin* (VII).

soft Something soft, *kîkway ka yoskâk* (VII); it is soft , *yoskâw* (VII); s/he has a soft hearted character, *yoskâtisiw* (VAI); it is a soft piece, *yoskâtan* (VII); it softened, *yoskipayiw* (VAI); the steel is soft or malleable, *yoskâpiskâw* (VII); the metal object is soft or malleable, *yoskâpiskisiw* (VAI); a soft piece of grass, *yoskâskosiy* (NI); it is soft, i.e.: a pole, *yoskâskwan* (VII); being a soft hearted person, *miyohtwâwin* (NI) *(Plains)*; *yoskâtisiwin* (NI) *(Northern)*; it is powderey soft, *yoskihtakâw* (VII); s/he made them soft by rubbing, *yoskinew* (VTA); s/he makes them soft by wearing them, i.e.: pants, *yoskiskawew* (VAI); it is soft, *yoskisiw* (VAI); being soft, *yoskisiwin* (NI); s/he has a soft heart, *yoskitehew* (VII); the act of having a soft heart, *yoskitehewin* (NI); s/he has a soft spot in her/his heart for her/him, *yoskitehestawew* (VTA).

soften *kîkway ka yoskinamihk* (VAI); *yoskihtâw* (VTA).

softness *yoskisiwin* (NI).

softy *awîyak ekâ konâskwawnit* (NA).

soggy *metoni ka sâpwâpawek kîkway* (VII); *sâpowahkostin* (VII).

soil A piece of soil or dirt, *asiskîy* (NI); there is soft soil, *yoskikiwohkâw* (VII); high soil, high ground, *ispacâw* (VII); there is dry soil, dry dirt, *pâhkwacâw* (VII); soil gutted by frost and thaw eroded soil, *pîkwahcâw* (VII); the soil is thawed out, *tihkahcâw* (VII); spongy soil, *piswecaw* (VII); there is area of dry soil, *pâhkwaskamikaw* (VII); rough earth, dirt, soil, *pipikwahcâw* (VII); earth, *asiskîy* (NI); s/he is soiling it, *iyipâcitâw* (VAI); s/he soils it, *misiwanâcitâw* (VAI).

sojourn S/he stayed overnight, *katikoniw* (VAI); s/he went and camped, *kapîsiw* (VAI).

solace *nistasiskakewin* (NI); the act of giving comfort in sorrow, *kâkecihitowin* (NI).

sole *sipa ohci maskisin* (NI); the under part of a shoe, *maskisinaspihcikan* (NI).

solely *peyak kîkway ohci poko* (IPC).

solemn *ka sapweyihtamihk* (VAI); very impressive or solemn, astonishing, *koskweyihtâkwan* (VII).

solemnity Acting with solemnity, *koskweyihtamohiwewin* (NI).

solemnize *ka kihci pekiskwehk* (VAI).

solicitous *awîyak ka nanihkâyat* (VII).

solicitude *ka ayihkeyihtestamaht awîyak* (VII).

solid Something placed permanently, *kîkway kakistastek* (NI); packed together, *mâmawastâw* (VAI); something really solid or strong, *sohkan* (VII); s/he founds or establishes her/him solidly, *kistahew* (VTA); the rock is solid, *kistâpiskâw* (VII); the tree stands solid, *kistahkisiw* (VAI); it is solidly placed or established, *kistastew* (VII); s/he plants them solidly or firmly, *sohkaskihew* (VTA); the tree is solid or s/he is well rooted, *sohkaskisiw* (VAI); it stands solid, i.e.: a pole, *sohkaskitew* (VII); the tree stands solid even with the strong wind, *sohkâsiw* (VAI).

solidarity *sohkeyimitowin* (NI).

solidify *sohki isicikewin* (NI).

solidity *ka sohkahk kîkway* (VII).

solitary *peyakowin* (NI); being alone, *papeyakowin* (NI); a solitary person, *pikwaciyiniw* (NA).

solitude *kaskamoc* (IPC); *pîkiskâtan* (VII); living alone in solitude, *pîkiskâcipematisowin* (NI).

solution *kwayask awihtamihk* (VAI).

solvable *ka miskamihk kîkway* (VAI).

solve *kwayaskweyecikewin* (NI).

sombre *or* **somber** *kîkway ka kaskitewinakwahk* (VII); it is a cloudy day, *yikwaskwan* (VII).

some *âtiht* (IPC); fewer than some, *ayâtiht* (IPC); some people, *âtiht awîyak* (NA); some things, *âtiht kîkway* (NI).

somebody *awîyak* (NA); somebody else, *kotak awîyak* (NA); something else, *kotak kîkway* (NI).

someday *peyak kîsikâw* (VII).

somehow *nânitâw isi* (VII).

someone *awîyak* (NI); someone else, *kotak awîyak* (NI); anybody, *pokwawîyak* (NI).

someplace *nânitâw* (VII).

somersault *ka âpocekwanek* (VAI); s/he rolls over in midair, *âpocikwanew* (VTA).

something Or a thing, *kîkway* (NI); something else, *kotak kîkway* (NI).

sometime *âskaw* (VII).

sometimes *âskaw poko* (IPC); sometimes all of a sudden, *kitahtawi* (IPC).

someway *nânitâw isi* (VII).

somewhat *nawâc poko* (IPC).

somewhere *nânitâw iteh* (VII).

son *okosimâw* (NA); my son, *nikosis* (NA); my first-born son, *nistamôkosisan* (NA); someone's son, *awîyak okosisa* (NA); someone looked upon as a son, *mikosisimâw* (NA).

son-in-law *onahâhkisîmâw* (NA); my son-in-law, *nahâhkis* (NDA).

song *nikamon* (NI) *(Northern)*; *nikamowin* (NI) *(Plains)*.

songbird *ka nikamot pîwâyisis* (NA).

songless *ekâ ka nikamohk* (VAI).

soon *kîyipa* (IPC) *(Northern)*; *wîpâc* (IPC) *(Plains)*; too soon, *osâm kîyipa* (IPC); as soon as, *mayaw* (IPC); in a little while, *kîyipa nawâc* (IPC).

soot *pikahtewayih okohtaskwayihkanihk ohci* (NI).

soothe *kâkecihew* (VAI); the act of soothing someone, *kâkecihiwewin* (NI).

soother *ka kâkecihiwewakehk* (VAI).

sooty *kîkway ka wîyipâtahk* (VII).

sop *katihkakohcimiht pahkwesikan* (VTA).

sophisticate *kwanta ayiwâk kîkway kesihtahk* (VII).

sophisticated *macikastewâyâwin* (NI).

sopping *kîkway ka sîkan napawek* (VII).

soppy *kîkway ka ahkostihk* (VII).

sordid Very dirty, *kaskiweyipaw* (VII); *ka wînipamihohk* (VAI).

sore When it is painful to move, *nânitâw kawîsakeyihtamihk* (VAI); s/he is in pain, *wîsakeyihtam* (VAI); s/he is sore or stiff, *kâkecisiw* (VAI); being sensitive to pain, *kâkecisowin* (NI); her/his sore is healed, *inîwiw* (VAI) *(Plains)*; *kîkîw* (VAI) *(Northern)*.

sorehead *awîyak ka wahkewiyawesit* (NA).

sorrel *wapihk osâwâstim* (NA); *kaskitew mihkwâw* (VII); a light brown horse, *osâwâstim* (NA).

sorrow Mournful, *kaskeyihtâmowin* (NI); s/he thinks it is remorseful or awful, *kîsinâteyihtam* (VAI); with sorrow, regretfully, with contrition, *kîsinâc* (IPC); her/his thoughts of her/him are mournful, *kitimâkeyitamawew* (VTA).

sorrowful Someone full of regret, *awîyak kanihtâ mihtâtahk* (VAI); s/he sounded sorrowful to her/him, *kitimâkitawew* (VTA); her/his thoughts are full of sorrow about it, *kitimâkiyihtam* (VAI).

sorry Being sorry for something, *kamihtâtamihk* (VAI); a sorry state of events, *kitimâkahkamikan* (VII); a sorry or unfortunate situation, *kitimâkan* (VII); s/he feels sorry for everything, *kitimakeyihcikew* (VAI); s/he feels sorry for people, *kitimakinâkew* (VAI); s/he feels sorry for her/him or them for losing it, *mihtâtamawew* (VTA).

sort Sorting material or segmentation, *pahpiskihtascikewin* (NI); what kind? or what sort?, *tântowa* (IPC); sort of or kind of, *kisâstaw* (VII).

sough *ka pîmowestihk* (VII).

sought *awîyak ka nitonaht* (NA).

soul Or spirit, *ahcâhk* (NA); clean soul, *kanâtahcahk* (NA); an evil soul, *macâhcâhk* (NA); s/he has a strong soul, *sohkahcahkwew* (VTA); having strength of soul, *sohkahcahkwewin* (NI).

soulful *ka kâkesimototakehk* (VAI).

soulless *awîyak ka pikwacisayat* (NA); a brute, *pikwaciyiniw* (NA).

sound Something heard, *kîkway kapehtâkwahk* (VII); it sounds far away, *yawew* (VII); it echos far away, *yawehtin* (VII); her/his singing sounds really terrible, *kakwâyakihtakosow* (VAI); s/he sounds sad, *kâmwâcihtâkosiw* (VAI); s/he sounds wonderful, *mâmaskâcihtâkosiw* (VAI); the act of sounding far away, *yâwewin* (NI); s/he makes them sound from a long ways, *yâwipayihew* (VTA); the sound can be heard echoing, *yâwipayiw* (VAI); the sound can be heard at a distance, *yâwihtâkwan* (VII) *(Northern)*; *yâwehtâkwan* (VII) *(Plains)*; s/he sounds far away, *yâwihtakosiw* (VAI); s/he makes them sound from a long ways, *yâwihtawew* (VTA) *(Plains)*.

sounder *pehtâkopicikan* (NI).

sounding *pehtâkopicikewin* (NI).

soundless *ekâ ka pehtâkwahk kîkway* (VII).

soup A homemade soup or broth, *micimâpay* (NI); s/he makes soup with it, *micimâpohkakew* (VAI); s/he makes soup, *micimâpohkew* (VAI); canned soup, *micimâpohkân* (NI); a blood soup or broth, *mihkowâpoy* (NI); s/he makes greasy soup, *tômâpohkew* (VAI).

soupy *ka micimâpowakamik* (VII).

sour When something turns sour, *ka sîwihtihk kîkway* (VII); it is sweet or sour, *sîwâw* (VII); it is sour or sweet, *sîwisiw* (VAI); it has gone sour, i.e.: milk, *sîwihtin* (VII); it is sour, *sîwâw* (VII).

source From where it comes, *itahkohcipayik* (VII); *tanta kohcimakahk kîkway* (VII).

souse *ka sîwihtahk miciwin* (NI).

south *kîsopwenohk* (NI) or (LN) *(Northern)*; *âpihtâkîsikanohk* (IPC) *(Plains)*; towards the south or in a southerly direction, *sâwanohk* (LN) or (NI) *(Northern)*; a sourth wind, *saskaniyotin* (NI) *(Plains and Northern variant)*; *sâwaniyôtin* (NI) *(Northern)*.

southbound *kîsopwenohk ketiyimohk* (LN).

souther *ayiwâk kîsopwenohk* (NA).

southerly *kîsopwenohk etehki* (LN); a little towards the south, *nawâc pokosâwanohk* (LN).

southern *kîsopwenohk isi* (LN).

southerner *awîyak kîsopwenohk kohtohtet* (NA).

southland *kîsopwew askîy* (NA).

southmost *mawaci kîsopwenohk* (LN).

southward Towards the south, *sâwanohk* (LN); *âpihtâkisikanohk* (LN).

souvenir *kîkway ka kasispowitahk* (VAI).

sow S/he sows or plants or seeds, *pakitinikew* (VAI); the act of sowing or seeding, *pakitinikewin* (NI).

sow A female pig, *nôsekohkôs* (NA).

sown *kîkway ka moscikwatek* (NI).

space An open space, *katawak* (VII); it is a small space, *tawasin* (VII); s/he makes space for another person to sit down, *tawapestawêw* (VTA); s/he makes a space for

429

her/him, **tawinamawew** (VTA); s/he makes space or room for her/him, **tawestawew** (VTA); there is space, **tawaw** (VII).

spaceless *ekâ katawak* (VII).

spacious *misitawâw* (VII).

span *tastawayihk* (LN).

spangle *akokwacikan* (NI).

spank *awîyak ka nôcihiht* (NA); *pasaskitoyehwew* (VTA).

spanking *nôcihâwasowin* (NI).

spanless *ekâ ka tawak* (VII).

spar *nôtinew* (VTA).

sparce It is thinly spread, *pîwastew* (VAI).

spare *ka ayiwâkipayik kîkway* (NI); *ayiwâkipayiw* (VAI).

sparing Making something last, *ayiwâkipayihcikewin* (NI); s/he treats her/him sparingly, *nanihkâcihew* (VTA).

spark A spark from the fire, *paskitew* (VAI); it sparks, i.e.: a fire cracker, *paskitepayiw* (VAI); it shoots out red hot sparks, i.e.: a fire, *paskwâskitew* (VAI).

sparkle *metoni ka wâsihkwak* (VII); there is sparkling, *wâsihkwâw* (VII).

sparrow *wâskahikan pîwâyisis* (NA).

sparrow hawk *onocipewayisisowew* (NA) *(Northern)*; *onocipiyesiwew* (NA) *(Plains)*.

sparse *ayâspes* (IPC).

sparsity *aspihtawiyikohk* (LN).

spasm *ociptikowin* (NI).

spastic *ka nihtâ ociptikohk* (VAI).

spat *kakeh kahcosihk* (VAI); being quarrelsome, *kehkâhtoskiwin* (NI).

spatter *pâhpahkawinam* (VAI).

spawn *kinosewak ka amitwâw* (VAI) or (VTA).

spawner *nôsemek;* a female fish, *nôsekinosew* (NA).

spay *nôse pisiskiw ka mansikâsot* (NA).

speak The act of speaking, *pekiskwewin* (NI); s/he speaks English, *âkayâsimiw* (VAI); s/he speaks Sioux, *pwâtimow* (VAI); a speaker for others, *opîkiskwestamâkew* (NA); s/he speaks the truth by swearing on the Bible, *kihcitwew* (VAI); the act of speaking the truth by swearing on the Bible, *kihcitwewin* (NI); s/he speaks poorly of her/him, *kwâtakimew* (VAI); s/he uses provoking speech with her/him, *mâmiwakâcimew* (VAI); s/he uses provocative language, *mâmiwâkâcimow* (VAI); the act of using provocative language, *mâmiwâkâcimowin* (NI); s/he speaks respectfully of her/him or them, *manâcimew* (VAI); s/he speaks many languages, *mihcetopikiskwew* (VAI); s/he speaks to ruin her/his reputation, *misiwanâcimew* (VTA); s/he speaks kindly to her/him, *miyopîkiskwâtew* (VTA); s/he speaks with difficulty, *nayihtâwipîkiskwew* (VAI); s/he is an

excellant speaker, *nihtawew* (VAI); s/he speaks in Ukrainian, *opetatowemow* (VAI); s/he speaks to her/him in an aboriginal language, i.e.: Cree, *nehiyawemototawew* (VTA); s/he speaks in Cree, *nehiyawemow* (VAI); the act of speaking in Cree, *nehiyawemowin* (NI); s/he speaks Cree, *nehiyawew* (VAI); s/he speaks distinctively, *pakaskowew* (VAI); the act of speaking distinctively, *pakaskowewin* (NI); s/he speaks and says the wrong thing, *patowew* (VAI).

speaking The act of speaking, *pîkiskwewin* (NI).

spear An arrow with a handle, *akaskwahtik* (NI); a fishing spear, *kapateyâskwahikan* (NI); s/he draws it out of the water with a spear, i.e.: a gaff, *kapateyâskwahwew* (VTA).

spearhead *acosisostikwan* (NI); *tahkahcikakanistikwân* (NI) *(Plains)*; *cîstâskwânostikwân* (NI) *(Northern)*.

special *kihci kîkway* (NI); *kihci* (VII).

specific *metoni kehcinâ* (IPC); exactly what kind, *mwehcitantowa* (VII).

specifically *kîkway kehcinâ kaweh tôtamihk* (VII).

specify *wihtamkwayask* (VAI); correct expression, *kwayaskwetwewin* (NI).

specimen *kîkway ka misiweyak* (NI); what kind of things, *kîkwaya* (NI).

specious *namoya metoni kehcinâhowin* (NI).

speck *ka masinâsohk* (VII).

speckle *ka cahcahkasnâstek* (VII).

speckled S/he is speckled, *cahcahkasinâsiw* (VAI).

spectacular *takahkinakohcikewin* (NI).

spectacularly *ka takahkinakohcikehk* (VII).

spectator *okanawâpahkew* (NA).

speculate *atâwakew* (VAI); guesswork, *pakwanaw* (VII); the act of speculating, *atâwakewin* (NI).

speech *ka pîkiskwehk* (VAI); the act of talking, *pîkiskwewin* (NI).

speechless *ka kipotonehokohk kîkway* (NI) or (VII).

speechlessly *kipotonehikewnihk* (VII).

speed *ka kisiskâpayihk* (VII); *kweyahowin* (NI); slowing down, diminishing speed, *nîkakotew* (VII); *nîkakocin* (VTA); moving full speed, very fast, *kisîkocin* (VTA); going at great speed, i.e.: a bullet, *sohkekocin* (VTA); *sohkekotew* (VAI).

speedily *kisiskâpayonihk* (LN).

speeding *ka nihtâ sohkekotnihk* (VAI); s/he is speeding or s/he drives fast or travels fast, *sohkekocin* (VAI).

speedy *kisiskâyâwin* (NI).

spell *ka meskocestamakehk* (VAI).

spend Spending all your money, *sônîyâw kamestiniht* (VAI); s/he uses it all up or spends it, *mestinam* (VAI); s/he uses it all up or spends it, *mestinew* (VAI); s/he has spent it all, *mestinikew* (VAI).

spent When you use up all your energy, *metoni kanohtesimsohk* (VAI); s/he spent everything or ruined herself/himself financially, *mestinisiw* (VAI).

sperm *kîkway nâpew ka ayât ka ohpikihisomakaneyek* (VAI) or (NA).

spew *ka pwâkomopayihk* (VAI).

sphere *askîy ka wawiyiyak* (NI); it is round, *wawiyâpiskâw* (VII).

spherical *kîkway ka wawiyesehcikatek* (VII).

spider The bug that makes nets, *ocayapihkes* (NA); a spider (slang), *kohkominaw* (NA); a long-legged spider, i.e.: a daddy long legs, *pispiskocewayik* (NA) *(Plains)*.

spiffy *îyinisewâyâwin* (NI).

spike *mistahi sakahikan* (NI).

spiky *ka nihtâ pisiskihtamihk* (VAI).

spill The act of spilling, *sîkinikewin* (NI); it spills, *sekipayow* (VAI); *sikipayin* (VAI); it is spilled or upset by the wind, i.e.: a pail of grain, *sîkâsiw* (VAI); it is spilled or upset by the wind, i.e.: a pail of water, *sîkâstan* (VII); s/he spills them by pulling or pushing it, *sekipitew* (VAI); s/he stumbles and spills them out, *sekisimew* (VAI); s/he kicked them and they spilled, *sîkiskawew* (VAI).

spillage *etah ka sîkinkehk* (NI).

spilt *kîkway ka taskinamihk* (VAI).

spin *ka kisiskâwasakakotek* (VII).

spinal *mâwkankan* (NI).

spindly *awîyak ka cacikokanet* (NA).

spine *mâwikan* (NI).

spineless *ekâ kanihtâ âhkameyihtamihk* (VII).

spinning *kîkway ka wasakakotek* (NI).

spinous *kîkway kokaminakasiwik* (NI).

spinster *mososkwew* (NA).

spiny *ka nayihtâwehikohk kîkway* (VII).

spiral *kîkway ka pemahtaweyak* (VII).

spire *kakwahci cîpwaskitek* (NI) or (VII).

spirit *ahcâhk* (NA); *manitohkân* (NA); spirit part of aboriginal spirit cult, *manitohkan* (NA); the great negative spirit in the universe (translated by Christians as Satan), *macimanito* (NA); s/he has many spirit power gifts or s/he is a shaman, *maskihkiwiyiniwiw* (VAI); guardian spirit, *powâkan* (NA); it has the spirit of a human being, *ayisiyiniwan* (VII); s/he is the great negative spirit, *macimanitowiw* (VAI); s/he lives in accord with her/his spirit helper, *powahtaw* (VII); s/he has a secret spirit helper, i.e.: an animal identity, *powamow* (VAI); having a secret spirit helper, *powamowin* (NI); s/he has an inner strength or s/he has strong spirit, *sohkahcahkwew* (VTA); the act of having inner strength or a strong spirit, *sohkahcahkwewin* (NI); s/he has a spirit dream, *pawatew* (VAI) *(Plains)*; *powatew* (VAI) *(Northern)*; the spirit helper becomes part of her/his identity,

pihtâkoyaweskawew (VAI) *(Plains)*; *pihcitahcâhkoweskawew* (VAI) *(Northern)*.

spirited *miyomahcihowin* (NI); *wacekamisew* (VAI).

spiritless *pwatawiyiniwiwin* (NI).

spiritual Ritual piety, *ayamihewâyâwin* (NI).

spiritualism Religious thinking, *ayamihew mâmitoneyihcikan* (NI).

spiritualist A spiritually gifted person or an individual who communes with the spirits, *awîyak ka powamit* (NA).

spiritualistic Somebody that feels spiritually gifted, *awîyak ka powamesâyat* (NA).

spirituality *ayamihewâtsowin* (NI).

spit The act of spitting, *ka sihkohk* (VAI); s/he spits, *sihkiw* (VAI); s/he spits blood on it, *mihkoh sihkwatam* (VAI); s/he spits on her/him, *sihkwatew* (VTA); saliva, *sihkowin* (NI).

spite A grudge against someone, *kisestâkewin* (NI); rebellion, *mâyiyihcikewin* (NI).

spiteful *awîyak ka kisestâkeskit* (NA).

spitoon *sihkwacikan* (NI); a spit pail or can, *sihkoyakan* (NI).

spittle *sihkowin* (NI).

431

splash The act of splashing water, *sisweyakamahikewin* (NI); s/he makes a loud splash, i.e.: a beaver with its tail, *camohkaham* (VAI); s/he is making a loud splashing sound, *camohkahikew* (VAI); s/he splashes water on her/him, *siswepekahwew* (VTA); s/he splashes water on her/him with a paddle, *wâswepekahwew* (VTA).

splasher *osweyakamahikew* (NA).

splashy *kîkway ka sohkinakwahk* (NI).

splat *aswapowin tehtapiwenihk* (NI).

splatter Splashing the water's surface, *swepekatahikewin* (NI).

splay The act of splaying, *taswekascikewin* (NI).

splendent *kîkway ka wâsihkwapiskâk* (NI) or (VII).

splendid *kôsâm miyonâkwahk* (VII); *mistahimiwasin* (VII).

splendor or **splendour** *osâm miyonâkosiwin* (NI); it is very beautiful, *mistahikatawasisin* (VII).

splice *aniskomohcikewin* (NI); extending something, *âniskohtawin* (NI).

splint *sîtwahpicikan mispiton* (NI); *miskat ohci* (NI).

splinter *ka itanehtihk mistik* (NI).

splinters Wood chips, *pîwikahikana* (NI).

splintery *misiwi ka itanehtihk* (VII).

split Something you split open, *kîkway ka tâskinamihk* (VAI); s/he splits it with an axe, *tâskataham* (VAI); it dries and splits open, i.e.: a tree, *tâskahkatosiw* (VAI); it dries and splits open, *tâskahkatotew* (VII); s/he is splitting wood, *tâskatahimihtew* (VAI); s/he hits them and splits them

in half, ***tâskatahwew*** (VTA); it split, ***tâskâw*** (VII); s/he
splits them open by hand, ***tâskinew*** (VTA); it is split,
tâskipayiw (VAI); s/he split, ***tâskisiw*** (VAI); s/he splits
them open and they spread all over the place,
taswekatahwew (VTA).

splitting *taskin'kewin* (NI).

splotch *ka nanâtohkopehikehk* (VAI); *masinâstew* (VII);
a large stained spot, *masinâstew* (NI).

splotchy *nanâtohkow sopekahikewin* (NI).

splurge *ka mâmaskâtikonikemistinkehk* (VAI).

splutter *ka tâstapipekiskwehk* (VAI); s/he stutters,
nâhnakowew (VAI).

spoil The act of spoiling things, *misiwanâcihcikewin*
(NI); s/he spoils or damages it or her/him,
misiwanâcihew (VTA); s/he spoiled it, *misiwanâcitâw*
(VAI); s/he spoils things, *misiwanâcihcikew* (VAI); it is
spoiled or rotten, *misiwanâtan* (VII); s/he is spoiled or
rotten, *misiwanâtisiw* (VAI); spoilage, waste, or
deterioration, *misiwanâtisiwin* (NI).

spoiled *sastesin* (VAI); *sastehtin* (VII); spoiled, rendered,
useless, *misiwanâtisiw* (VAI); *misowanâtan* (VII).

spoiler *omisiwanâcihcikew* (NA).

spoilt *awîyak ka misiwanâcihiht* (NA).

spoke *awîyak sâsay kakeh pîkiskwet* (VAI); s/he has
spoken, *kehpekiskwew* (VAI).

spoken *sâsay poni pikiskwewin* (NI).

spoliate *ka patowehk wiyâsowewnihk* (NI) or (LN).

spoliation *ka âhtastahk wiyâsowewin* (NI).

spongy *kîkway ka yoskâk* (VII); it is spongy, *pisweyaw*
(VII).

spontaneity *nakâyâ isâyâwin* (NI).

spontaneous *awîyak ka nakâyâ ihtotahk kîkway* (VII).

spoof *môhcohkâsowewin* (NI).

spook *sekihtasowin* (NI).

spooky *kîkway ka sekinakwahk* (NI).

spool *asapapahcikos* (NI); a wooden spool, *asapapahtik*
(NI).

spoon A small spoon, *emihkwânis* (NA); a wooden
spoon, *mistikowemihkwân* (NA); a metal spoon,
pewapiskowemihkwan (NA).

spoonful *peyakwâw ka sâkaskinet emihkwânis* (VAI).

spoor *meskanaw ka kistatahamihk* (VAI).

sporadic *ekâ ka taptawakotek kîkway* (NI).

sporadical *âhâspîhtaw* (IPC).

sporadically *âspîhtaweyikohk* (VII).

sport *metawewin* (NI).

sportful *ka metaweskihk* (VAI).

sporting *ka miweyihtamihk metawewna* (VAI).

sportive *metawewâyâwin* (NI).

sports *nanatohk isi metawewna* (NI).

sporty *metoni ka wawesihk* (VAI).

spot *cahkipehikanis* (NI); *masinastew* (VAI).

spotless *metoni ka kanâtahk kîkway* (VII).

spotlight *cahkâstenikakan* (NI).

spotted *ka mâhmâsinasohk* (VAI).

spotter *otoyascikew* (NA).

spotty *kîkway ka mâhmâsinastek* (NI).

spousal *wicehtowin* (NI).

spouse A married partner, *owîkitiw* (NA); *wikimâkan*
(NA); my marriage partner or someone you live with,
i.e.: my spouse, *niwîkimâkan* (NA); someone's
marriage partner, *awîyak owîkimâkana* (NA); s/he has
her/him as a spouse, *owîkimâkanimew* (VTA); s/he has
a spouse, *owîkimâkaniw* (VAI); s/he is a spouse to her/
him, *wikimâkanimew* (VAI).

sprain Spraining oneself, *ka kotokonsohk* (VTA); s/he
sprains an ankle or foot by falling, *kotokosin* (VTA);
s/he sprains someone's joints, *kotkonew* (VTA); s/he
sprains an ankle by throwing someone, *kotokosimew*
(VTA); a sprained joint, *kotokosinowin* (NI).

sprang *kîkway kakwâskwekotek* (VII) or (VAI).

sprawl *taswekasinowin* (NI).

spray *sisweyapawacekewin* (NI); *sikahipatam* (VTA);
spraying with water, *sihkahahtapawacikewin* (NI).

spread The act of spreading something out,
taswekascikewin (NI); s/he spreads it, *siswewepinam*
(VTI); s/he spreads them all over, *siswepayihew* (VTA)
(Plains); *saswepayihew* (VTA) *(Northern)*; it fell open
and spread out, *taswekipayiw* (VII) or (VAI); s/he
spreads them out in her/his hand, *taswekinew* (VTI).

spree *mocik minihkwewin* (NI); *minihkwewin* (NI); a
lively celebration, *môcikihtâwin* (NI).

sprig A small branch or twig, *wacihkwanis* (NI).

sprightly *ka kakâyaw payihohk* (VAI).

spring A ground spring, *môskicowanipek* (NI); a coiled
spring, *ka kwâskwekotek kîkway* (NI); spring, the
season, *miyoskamin* (NA); it is spring, *miyoskamiw*
(VAI); it is springtime, *sekwan* (VII); when spring
comes or when it is spring, *miyoskamiki* (LN); next
spring, *sekwahki* (LN); last spring, *sekwanohk* (LN);
miyoskamîhk (LN); it is a fast spring season,
sohkisekwan (VII); the time of the growth of grass,
sâkaskâw (VII); the time leaves come out, *sâkipakâw*
(VII); this spring, *oma ka miyoskamik* (NA) or (LN); to
spring from something, *kwâskwepayowin* (NI).

springtime *ka sekwahk* (VII); it is springtime, *sekwan*
(VII) *(Northern)*; *miyoskamin* (VII) *(Plains)*.

sprinkle *ka sâpopacikehk* (VAI); *sâpopatasiw* (VAI);
sprinkling something with water, *sîkahahcikewin*
(NI).

sprinkling *sâpopacikewin* (NI).

sprint *ka kîyâsohk* (VAI).

sprout *ka osk isakikihk kiscikânis* (NI).

spruce *sihta* (NI).

spruce gum *sihtipikow* (NA); sticky spruce gum, *pasakoskow* (NA); it is sticky with spruce gum, *pasakoskowew* (VAI).

spruce tree *sihta* (NA); *minahik* (NA); there are lots of spruce, *minahikoskâw* (VII); *sihtiskâw* (VII); a spruce needle, *sihtapihkwan* (NA).

sprung *wanihikan ka patskocikemakahk* (VII).

spry *oskimahcihowin* (NI); s/he is spry, *ka kayawayaw* (VAI).

spud *pîwâpiskwapos ahpô la patak* (NI).

spume *pîstew ka pôtatamihk* (VAI).

spun *kîkway kakeh wâsakâkotek* (VII).

spunk *metoni ka sohkeyimohk* (VAI); *sohkeyimowin* (NI).

spunky Courageous, *sohkeyimowin* (NI).

spur *cahkatayeskâcikan* (NI); a spur in the road, *yikihtawipayiw meskanaw* (NI); s/he dug her/his heels in the horse's side, *tahkatayeskawew* (VTA); s/he dug her/his spur on the horse's side, *cahkatayeskawew* (VTA).

spurious *ka kîmenîcâkanowihk* (VII).

spurn *ka kisô asenamihk kîkway* (VAI).

spurred *mistatim ka tahkatayeskaht* (VTA).

spurt *sisikoc kwâskohtowin* (NI).

sputter *kapahpahketehtakosit askihkos* (VTI).

squab *awîyak ka mistikamot* (VAI).

squabble The state of having a tough discussion, *kihkihtowin* (NI).

squalid *kîkway ka wininakwahk* (VII); something dirty and degraded, *wînayih* (VII).

squall *ka pahkihtowestinpayik* (VII); *misiyotinpayiw* (VAI); a sudden violent gust of wind, *pahkihtowestin* (NI).

squally *awâsis ka cacikwematot* (VAI); stormy, *ka mahmayikesikak* (VII).

squalor *wînisîhisowin* (NI).

squander Spending money wastefully, *kwanta ayiwâk mestinikewin* (NI); it is an unfortunate squandering, *wîyakan* (VII); s/he squandered them unnecessarily, *wiyakihew* (VAI); s/he is squandering her/his life unnecessarily, *wîyakihow* (VAI); the act of squandering one's life unnecessarily, *wîyakihowin* (NI); s/he is squandering it by wearing it, *wiyakiskawew* (VTI); s/he is squandered, *wiyakisiw* (VAI); being squandered unnecessarily, *wiyakisiwin* (NI); s/he castigates her/him for no reason, i.e.: squandered words, *wîyakimew* (VAI); s/he likes to spend, *mestinikeskiw* (VAI).

square *kîkway ka ayisaweyak* (VII).

squash *ka napakahamihk kîkway* (VTI); s/he crushes it to pieces, *sikwatahwew* (VTA).

squashy *kîkway ka yoskâpawek* (VII).

squat *cîpatapowin* (NI); *cîpatapiw* (VAI).

squatty *mistatayew nakôsowin* (NI).

squawk *kisôwe tahkiskâcikew pîkiskwewin* (NI).

squeak *ka kiciskwek* (VAI).

squeaky *ka kiciskihtâkwahk* (VII).

squeal *awîyak ka cacikwet* (VAI).

squeamish *ka nihtâ pwâkomohikohk kîkway* (VII).

squeeze *metoni sihtisinowin* (NI); s/he puts her/him between two things, *takwawew* (VTA).

squelch *awîyak kanahtakimiht* (VAI).

squib *metawâkan pahkisawânis* (NA).

squiggle *wahwâkasinahikewin* (NI).

squint *ka pahpiw'nâkosihk* (VII).

squirm *nanâtohk kopayihowin* (NI).

squirrel *ankwacas* (NA); squirrel food or squirrel grease, *anikwacâsimîciwin* (NI) *(Plains)*; *pakânipimiy* (NI) *(Northern)*.

squirrely Someone silly, *awîyak ka môhcowisâyâsit* (VII).

squirt *ka pimocikakehk nîpîy* (VAI); *kwâskwenam* (VAI).

squish *ka astâskoskaht awîyak* (VAI).

stab The act of stabbing, *tahkahtowin* (NI); s/he stabbed her/him, *tahkamew* (VTA); a stabbing weapon, *tahkahcikan* (NI).

stability *sohkâyâwin* (NI).

stabilization *sohkîsihcekewin* (NI).

stabilize *ka sohkîsihtahk kîkway* (VAI).

stable *ekâ kamamahcehikohk kîkway* (VAI); a barn, *mistatimokamik* (NI).

stabling *ka kanaweyimihtwâw mistatimwak* (VTA).

stack The act of stacking, *cahkâscikewin* (NI); s/he stacks them in a pile, *mawasakowepawew* (VTA); a hay stack, *wîstihkân* (NI).

stag *ka papiyakohk* (VAI); a male deer, *yapewapiscimosos* (NA).

stagger When someone staggers around, *ka papâmi ayâhpayihk* (VAI); s/he staggers, *ayâhpayiw* (VAI).

stagnancy *ka wâyaskinek nîpîy* (VII).

stagnant *ka pwektakamihtihk nîpîy* (VII); it does not move, *kistastew* (VII).

stagnate *ekâ ka pimciwahk nîpîy* (VII).

stagnation *kîkway ka mistwanatahk* (VII).

stagy *mâmaskâtikonikewin* (NI).

staid *metoni papiyahtik ka ayâhk* (IPC).

stain Something with a stain, *kîkway ka atihtek* (VII); s/he is stained with different colors, *masinasow* (VAI); it is stained with many different colors, *masinâstew* (VII); her/his face is stained in different colors, i.e.: a clown, *masinastewihkwew* (VAI); it is stained, *atihtew* (VII); s/he is stained, *atihtewisiw* (VAI).

stainless *kîkway ekâ ka atihtehk* (VII).

stake *miscikos kakihtitahikatek* (NI); *cîstahikanis* (NI); a pointed stick, *cîpokahikan* (NI).

433

stale *kîkway ka sewihtihk* (VII); *kayâsâyiwiw* (VAI); rotten and stale, *akwakohtin* (VII).

stalk *otihtimanahtik pâskisikanihk* (NI); *ka nâtwâhahcikehk sakahk* (VTA).

stalky S/he is tall and thin, *kwahtâpekisiw* (VAI).

stall *ka nakipayihk* (VAI); *piskihtaskinahcikan mistatimokamkohk* (NI); stalling someone, *otamihiwewin* (NI).

stallion *nâpestim* (NA).

stalwart *metoni ka sâpweyihtamihk kîkway* (VII); being strong, *maskawisiwin* (NI).

stamina S/he has stamina or lasting strength, *sîpiwisiw* (VAI); having stamina, *sîpiwisowin* (NI); stamina or fortitude, *sohkâyâwin* (NI); s/he has the stamina to remain awake, *sîpihkwasiw* (VAI); s/he has the stamina to hold her/his arms up for a long time, *sîpiniskeyiw* (VAI); s/he has the stamina to walk a long distance, *sîpohtew* (VTA).

stammer *ka yâhyahkatamopayihk* (VTA); *nanakowew* (VTA).

stance *oyikâpawiwin* (NI).

stand Or table, *akocascikewinis* (NI); s/he shifts her/his standing position, *ahcikâpawiw* (VAI); the act of standing, *nîpawiwin* (NI); s/he stands, *nîpawiw* (VAI); s/he stands hidden, *akôkapawiw* (VTA); s/he stands against her/him or it, *akokâpawiw* (VTA); s/he leans against something while standing, *asôkapawiw* (VTI); s/he stands with her/his back to someone else's back, *atimkâpawîstawew* (VTA); s/he stands with her/his back turned, *atimikâpawiw* (VAI); *apamikapawiw* (VAI); they are standing off to one side, *napatekâpawiwak* (VAI); s/he stands in the back of the line, *nâwayikâpawiw* (VTA); s/he stands slumped to one side, *nawekapawiw* (VTA); it stands at an angle, *nawesiw* (VAI); it leans to one side, i.e.: a teepee, *naweskitew* (VII); two of them stand together, *nesokapawiwak* (VTA); s/he makes thing stand up, *nepawascikew* (VTI); s/he makes her/him stand, *nîpawihew* (VTA); s/he stands facing her/him or face to face with her/him, *ohtiskawikapawistawew* (VTA); s/he stands facing this way, *otiskawikâpawiw* (VAI); s/he makes her/him stand up, *pasikohew* (VTA); s/he helps her/him to stand up, *pasikonew* (VTA); s/he stands up very quickly or s/he jumps to her/his feet, *pasikopahtâw* (VAI); s/he makes her/him stand up quickly, *pasikotisahwew* (VTA); s/he makes things stand upright, *nîpawascikew* (VTI); s/he stands up in her/his presence, *pasikôstawew* (VTA); s/he stands up, *pasikow* (VAI); the act of standing up, *pasikowin* (NI); it stands crooked, *pîmâskisiw* (VAI); s/he stands sideways, *pimicikâpowiw* (VAI); s/he stands upright on her/his hind legs, i.e.: a horse, *simacikâpawiw* (VAI); s/he rears up or s/he stands on her/his hind legs,

i.e.: a horse about to mate, *simaciw* (VAI); s/he stands above her/him, *tahkocikapawestawew* (VTA); s/he stands on top, *tahkocikapawiw* (VAI); s/he stands firmly or with feet well planted, *sohkikâpawiw* (VAI); s/he stands straight, *tasokâpawiw* (VAI); s/he stands between them, *tastawikapawîstawew* (VTA); s/he stands with her/him, *wecikapawestawew* (VTA); s/he stands off to one side to be out of the way, *yikatekâpawiw* (VAI).

standard *kîkway ka nîpawemakahk* (VII); *peyakohtawin* (NI).

standardization *katawahk ahiwewin* (NI).

standardize *katawahk kîkway ka astâhk* (VII).

standing It is standing, i.e.: tree, *cimasiw* (VAI); it is standing, i.e.: teepee or house, *cimatew* (VII).

stank *kîkway kakeh wihcekahk* (VII).

star *acahkos* (NA).

starch Something that stiffens things, i.e.: starch, *sîtawahikan* (NI); s/he starches them, *sîtawahwew* (VTA).

starchy *kîkway ka sîtawayak* (VII).

stare *ekâ ka paksapahkehk* (VAI); *sohkikânawapahtam* (VTI).

staring *ekâ paksapahkewin* (NI).

stark *môstasewin* (NI).

starless *ekâ acahkosak kanokostwâw* (VII).

starlight *ka wâsenakwahk acahkosak ohci* (NI); having starlight, *acahkoswasisowin* (NI).

starlike *peyakwan acahkos* (NI).

starred *awîyak kakeh metawet cikâstepayihcikanihk* (VAI).

starry *mesiwe ka nokostwâw acahkosak* (VII).

start Starting something, *macihtawin* (NI); it starts, i.e.: a meeting, *macipayiw* (VAI); s/he makes a great start for her/him, *kihcipayihew* (VTA) *(Northern)*; *miyopayihew* (VTA) *(Plains)*; s/he starts to work, *mâcâtoskew* (VAI); s/he starts to eat, *mâcimîcisiw* (VAI); s/he starts her/him or it, i.e.: a motor, *mâcipayihew* (VTA); spring is starting, *mâcisekwan* (VII); ice starting to move down the river, *mâcistan* (VII); s/he is starting to talk, *mâcipîkiskwew* (VAI); s/he starts dancing, *mâcisimow* (VAI); s/he started trapping or setting taps, *mâciwanehikew* (VTI); s/he starts to be sick, *mâtahpinew* (VTI); the start of a sickness or onset of illness, *mâtahpinewin* (NI); the start or beginning of next month, *mâtakimihci pîsim* (NI); s/he starts to feel pain; s/he starts feeling pain, *mâtamahcihow* (VAI); s/he starts cutting it, *mâtisâwâtew* (VAI); s/he starts to speak, *mâtowitam* (VTI); s/he starts the drumming for the celebration, *mâtoweham* (VTI); it starts from here, *ôtah mâcipayiw* (IPC); s/he starts them, *sipwepayihew* (VTA); *mâcipayihew* (VTA).

434

startle The act of startling someone, *sisikôcihiwewin* (NI); s/he startles her/him, *sisikôcihew* (VTA); s/he startles her/him with her/his speech, *sisikôcimew* (VTA); s/he startle her/him by catching her/him unaware, *sisikôciwihew* (VTA).

startling *kîkway ka sisikôcowiyikohk* (VTI).

starvation *nohtehkatewin* (NI).

starve Starving, *nohtehkatewin* (NI); s/he starved to death, *nipahâkatosiw* (VAI); s/he starves her/him so much s/he can't stand up, *kawahkatosohew* (VTA); s/he is starved to the point where s/he can't stand up, *kawahkatosiw* (VAI); s/he underfeeds her/him, *nohtaskoyew* (VAI).

stash *ka astahcikohk* (VTA).

stated *kîkway masnahikanihk kastahk* (VTI); s/he has stated, *itwew* (VAI).

stately *ka mistikimawnakosihk* (VAI).

statement *pîkiskwehiwewin* (NI); *itwewin* (NI).

stationary *kîkway peyakwanohk ka ayâstek* (VII); always in the same spot, *peyakwanohk* (VII).

staunch *ka nakinamihk mihkoh* (VTA); *ka miyo weciwakanihk* (VAI).

stave From a wooden barrel, *mistikomahkahkos* (NI).

staves *mistikomahkahka* (NI).

stay Staying in one place, *peyakwanohk kâyâhk* (VAI); s/he stays overnight, *katikoniw* (VAI); s/he makes her/him stay, *kisacihew* (VTA); s/he talks her/him into staying longer, *kisâcimew* (VTA); s/he decides to stay for good, *kisâciw* (VAI); s/he stays there forever or permanenetly, *kiscâyâw* (VII); s/he won't leave her/him, *kitisimôtotawew* (VTA); s/he doesn't want to leave, *kitisimow* (VAI); s/he likes staying in one place, *kitisimowâtisiw* (VAI); the act of not wanting to leave, *kitisimowâtisowin* (NI); the act of wanting to stay, *kitisimowin* (NI).

stead *miyowehowin ka ayâhk* (NI).

steadfast *metoni ka sâpweyihtamihk* (VII).

steady The act of being constant, *tâpitawewin* (NI); constantly, *tâpitawi* (IPC); *maskawâtisiw* (VAI); *maskawâtan* (VII).

steak *pîmehk ka kîstek wîyâs* (NI).

steal The act of stealing, *kimotiwin* (NI); s/he steals, *kimotiw* (VAI); in a hidden, stealing, surreptitious way, *kîmôc* (IPC); the act of stealing from someone else, *kimotamakewin* (NI); s/he steals from her/him, *kimotamawew* (VTA); s/he steals horse from her/him, *kimotastimwâtew* (VTA); s/he steals a horse, *kimotastimwew* (VTA); the act of stealing horses, *kimotastimwewin* (NI); s/he steals clothes, *kimotayowinisew* (VTI).

stealthy *awîyak ka nihtâ weskawâhtat* (VAI).

steam *nîpîy kohtek* (NI); boiling water, *ohtewâpoy* (NI).

steamy *kîkway kohtek* (VII).

steed *pîtos wihyowin mistatim ohci* (IPC); a high spirited horse, *wacihkamisiwatim* (NA).

steel Strong metal, *kamewasik pîwâpisk* (NI); it has steel in it, *pîwâpiskowan* (VII); *pîwâpiskowiw* (VAI); the steel is cold, *tahkapiskâw* (VII); a solid piece of steel, *sohkâpisk* (NI); it is a solid piece of steel, *sohkapiskâw* (VII).

steep *ka kino amacoweyak* (VII); *cahkatinâw* (NI); *ka kaskâmatnak* (VII).

steer A castrated cow, *ayihkwew* (NA); *iyâ pesisemanisoht* (NA) *(Plains)*; steering a vehicle, *otâpânâsk ka pamihiht* (VTI); s/he steers it, i.e.: a canoe, *tahkwaham* (VII); a pole used to manoeuvre a canoe, *kwahkosonahtik* (NI); a paddle used to steer a canoe, *tahkwahikan* (NI); s/he is steering the canoe or boat, *tahkwahikew* (VTI).

stem *etah ka pesakikit miscikos* (VTA).

stemless *ekâ konakewnihk* (VII).

stemmed *awîyak ka nakiniht* (VTA).

stench *kîkway ka pecimakawhk* (VII); *wicekimakwan* (VII).

step *tahkoskewin* (NI); the act of stepping, *tahkoskewin* (NI); s/he steps down, i.e.: off of something, *nihtakosew* (VTA); *nihtitahkoskew* (VTA); s/he takes one step, *peyakwawtahkoskew* (VAI); s/he stepped over, *pastahkoskew* (VAI) *(Northern)*; *pascitahkoskew* (VAI) *(Plains)*; s/he is stepping over, *pâstâskow* (VTI); s/he takes small steps, *pesohamew* (VAI); s/he steps right through them, *sapostahkaskâw* (VTA); s/he stepped on her/him, *tahkoskâtew* (VTA); s/he stepped, *tahkoskew* (VAI).

stepbrother My stepbrother or adopted brother, *niciwamihkawin* (NA); his stepbrother or adopted brother, *ociwama* (NA); someone's stepbrother or adopted brother, *awîyak ociwamihkawina* (NA).

stepchild *awâsis ohpime kopâpât ahpô komâmât* (NA).

stepdaughter Or adopted daughter, *otôsimiskwew* (NA); *otanisihkawin* (NA); my stepdaughter or adopted daughter, *nitôsimiskwem* (NA); my stepdaughter (or niece), *nitanisihkawin* (NA).

stepfather *ohkomisimâw* (NA) *(Northern)*; *ohtawihkawin* (NA) *(Plains)*; my stepfather, *nôhkomis* (NA) *(Northern)*; someone's stepfather, *awîyak ohkomisa* (NA) *(Northern)*; *awîyak ohtâwihkawina* (NA) *(Plains)*; *awîyak opâpâsah* (NA).

stepmother Their stepmother, *okawisa* (ob.) (NA); my stepmother, *nikâwîs* (NA); someone's stepmother, *awîyak omâmâsisah* (NA).

step-parent *ohpime ohci konikihikohk* (NA).

stepsister *ohpime ohci komsihk* (NA); my stepsister, *nimisihkawin* (NA).

stepson *ohpime ohci kokosihk* (NA); my stepson (or my nephew), *nitôsim* (NA).

435

sterile *ekâ kakeh ocawasimsihk* (VAI); she is sterile or she cannot give birth to children, *pônosew* (VAI); sterility or the act of not being able to give birth to children, *pônosewin* (NI).

sterility *ka ayihkwewihk* (VII).

sterilize *ka nânapâcihiht iskwew taponoset* (VTA).

stern Being difficult, *âhkwatisowin* (NI).

stew *nanâtohkwâpohkewin* (NI); *pakâhcikewin* (NI).

stick *mistik* (NA); a little stick, *miscikos* (NI); a stick used to cook bannock over an open fire, *pahkwesikanâhtik* (NA); something that sticks to something else, *kîkway ka sakicihk* (VTA); s/he sticks them together with spruce gum, *pasakoskiwahew* (VTA); s/he sticks them together, *pasakwamohew* (VTA); s/he sticks them in underneath, *sekwamohew* (VTA); s/he sticks a knife underneath her/his own belt, *sekwasiw* (VAI).

sticking Sticks, holding tight, glues, *akopayiw* (VAI); *akopayin* (VAI).

sticky Something that is sticky, *ka pasakwak kîkway* (VII); it is sticky , i.e.: molasses, *pasakwâw* (VII); s/he rubs them on something sticky, *pasakosimew* (VAI); it fell on something sticky, *pasakosin* (VTA); it is sticky, i.e.: spruce gum, *pasakosow* (VAI); s/he makes them sticky, *pasakwahwew* (VTA).

stiff Something dried stiff, *ka setawahkatotek kîkway* (VAI); it is stiff, *sîtawâw* (VII); s/he is stiff, *sîtawisiw* (VAI); s/he makes her/him stiff, *sîtawihew* (VTA).

stiffen *kîkway ka sîtawpayik* (VAI); *sîtawâha* (VAI); there is stiffened, hardened soil, gum, etc., *maskawiskowihew* (VTA).

stifle *ka kipwatâmonwehk* (VAI).

stile *tehtitahkoskewin kosihtâhk* (VTI).

still When it is absolutely still or no movement, *metoni ka kâmwâtahk* (IPC); s/he lies still, *kîyâmisin* (VAI); s/he sits still, *kîyâmapiw* (VAI); it sits still, *kîyâmastew* (VII); still, more, longer in or value or quantity also, *keyâpic* (IPC); *eyâpic* (IPC); also: and, some more, again, *mena* (IPC); s/he stands still for her/him, *kîyâmikapawestawew* (VTA); s/he stands very still, *kîyâmikâpawiw* (VAI); alcohol still or firewater maker, *iskotewâpoy kosihcikakehk* (NI); *itakamascikakan* (NI).

stillborn S/he makes her have a stillborn baby, *osikohew* (VTA); she has a stillborn, *osikohow* (VAI); the act of having a stillborn baby, *osikohowin* (NI).

stillness *metoni kâmwâtisiwin* (NI).

stilted *awîyak ka âpacitat pemohtakanah* (VTI).

stimulate *awîyak ka miyomahcihohiht* (VTI); it stimulates her/him, *maskawiskakow* (VAI).

stimulation *miyomahcihowewin* (NI).

stimulative *kîkway ka miyoskâkohk* (VII).

sting *ka cesowet âmô* (VTA); *cesowewin* (NI).

stinger *âmô ocestahikan* (NI).

stingy *ka sasâkisehk* (VAI); *sasâkisew* (VAI).

stink Something that stinks, *kîkway kawihcekahk* (VII); it smells badly, *mayimakwan* (VII); it stinks, *wihcekan* (VII); s/he stinks, *wihcekisiw* (VAI); the act of stinking, *wihcekisiwin* (NI); a moose hide that is starting to stink, *wihcekihtin* (VAI); a car, *wihcek'tâpânâsk* (NI).

stinker *owihcikihcikew* (NA).

stint *ka sâkihtamakehk* (VAI).

stir S/he is stirring, *itehikew* (VTA); s/he stirs up a hornet nest, *ohpwepitew* (VTA).

stirring *itehikewin* (NI).

stirrup On a saddle, *tâpisikoskâcikan* (NI); a foot tie, *tâpisitepison* (NI); a strap used to hold the stirrup, *tâpisikoskâcikaneyâpiy* (NI); a place for the feet, *tâpisikaskâcikan* (NI).

stitch *moscikwasowin* (NI); s/he stitches, *kwaskikwâsiw* (VAI); a stitch, *kaskikwacikan* (NI).

stitching *ka moscikwasohk* (VAI).

stock *pisiskowak* (NI).

stocking *asikan* (NI); a pair of stockings, *asikanak* (NI); s/he has stockings on, *kasikanew* (VTI).

stocky *awîyak ka misikitit* (VAI).

stoke *ka tahtaskosenamihk iskotew* (VTI).

stoker *tahtaskosehikakan* (NI) *(Northern)*; *yahkisehikâkan* (NI) *(Plains and Northern variant)*.

stole A fur cape, *kîsokwayawehon* (NI) *(Northern)*; a stole worn by a priest, *ayamihewitapiskâkan* (NI) *(Plains)*.

stole *kîkway kakeh kimotihk* (VAI).

stolen *kimotiwin* (NI).

stolid *awîyak ekâ kîkway ka mamâhteyihtamohikot* (VAI).

stolidity *sohkastwâwin* (NI).

stomach Or belly, *matay* (NI); s/he has an enlarged stomach, i.e.: from a disease, *mistatayepinew* (VAI); enlarged stomach disease, *mistatayepinewin* (NI); s/he has a large stomach, *mistatayew* (VTI).

stomp *misitah ka sahsokehtahk*; *mistowesinowin* (NI).

stone *asinîy* (NA); there are lots of stones, *asiniskâw* (VII).

stony *asinîpwatsak* (NA).

stood *etah kakeh nîpawihk* (VAI).

stoop *nawakîwin* (NI); s/he bends over, *nawakîw* (VAI); *wakisow* (VAI); *piskihce kamikos wayawetimihk iskawtemihk* (NI).

stop The act of stopping, *kipihciwin* (NI) *(Northern)*; *nakiwin* (NI) *(Plains)*; s/he stops, *kipihciw* (VAI) *(Northern)*; *nakiw* (VAI) *(Plains)*; s/he coaxes her/him to stop, *kipihcimew* (VTA); it or s/he stops suddenly, *kipihcipayiw* (VAI); a sudden stop, *kipihcipayowin* (NI); the act of telling people to stop doing something wrong, *kitahamakewin* (NI); s/he tells her/him to stop doing something, *kitahamawew* (VTA); s/he makes her/him stop, *nakihew* (VTA); s/he stops her/him, *nakinew* (VTA); it stopped by itself, *nakipayiw* (VAI); a stop or place where people embark or disembark, i.e.: a bus stop, *nakîwin* (NI).

stoppage *nakinikewin* (NI); *kipopayiw* (VAI); it is plugged up, *kipopayiw* (VAI).

storm The storm comes closer, *pecimayikesikaw* (NI); a stormy day, *mâyikisikâw* (NI).

stormy *ka mahmâyikisikak* (VII).

story *âcimowin* (NI); an evil story, *macâcimowin* (NI); a good story, *miyowâcimowin* (NI); it is a story blown out of proportion, *sohkehtakwan* (VII).

storyteller *otâcimow* (NA).

storytelling *âcimostakewin* (NI).

stoup *oyâkanis ayamihewâpoy ohci* (NI).

stout *sohkisihcikâsowin* (NI); s/he is stout, *sohkisiw* (VAI).

stow *ka nahascikehk* (VAI); s/he stowed away on the train, *kîmôciposiw* (VAI).

straddle *ka tastawahamihk kîkway* (VTI); s/he stands with legs spread apart, *kahkapekapawiw* (VAI).

straggle *ka papâmacihohk* (VAI); wandering away, *kwahtohtewin* (NI).

straggly *ka wînisîhohk* (VAI).

straight Something that is straight, *kakwayaskwak kîkway* (VII); it is straight or honest, *kwayaskwâw* (VII); straight across, short cut, *kaskam* (VII); straight up, straightened, on her/his haunches, *simâc* (VII); it is straight, rightly placed, *kwayask* (VII); straight up, *simac* (VII); her/his horns are straight, *tasoteskanew* (VAI).

straighten S/he straightened it up, *kwayaskotâw* (VTI); *kakwayaskonamihk kîkway* (VTI); straightened, *kwayaskopayiw* (VAI); *kwayaskopayin* (VAI); s/he straightens their legs out, *sâwahtôhew* (VTA); s/he pulls her/his legs and straightens them out, *sâwahtôpitew* (VTA); s/he straightens her/his own legs out, *sâwahtiw* (VTA); s/he straightens them up, *tasonew*; it straightens out, *tasopayiw* (VAI); s/he stretches and straightens up to her/his full height, *taswâskiw* (VAI).

strain Making oneself work too hard, *wâwiyak sihcihesowin* (NI); straining something with a strainer, *sâpokawihcikewin* (NI); s/he strains it, *sekohkinew* (VTA).

strained *kîkway kakeh sâpokawihtahk* (VTI).

strainer *sekopâtinikan* (NI); *sâpokawihcikan* (NI); s/he puts it through a stainer, *sekopâtinew* (VTI).

strait *kasapotawak itah ka pimakotekwaw mista osah okihcikamehk* (NI).

straiten *okitimâkisiw kosihiht* (VTA).

strand *micimoyowin* (NI); *ka peyakwapekamot sestak* (NI).

strange Someone who is a little bit strange, *awîyak pîtoskesayat* (VAI).

stranger Or outsider, i.e.: Plains Cree use it to describe the Blackfoot peoples and Northern Cree use the word to indicate the Slavey speaking people, *ayahciyiniw* (NA); s/he does not like her/him and treats her/him like an outcast, *ayahteyimew* (VTA); s/he sees her/him as foreign, *ayahcinawew* (VTA).

strap A piece of leather for binding, *apihkan tahkopicikan* (NI); a leather strap, *paskitahpicikan* (NI); a piece of leather, *apihkân* (NI).

strapped Something fastened or strapped on, *kîkway katahkoptek* (VII); s/he is strapped or bound, *paskitahpisiw* (VAI).

strappings *tahkopicikâkana* (NI).

straw *kistikân pawahikewina* (NI); a threshed grain stalk, *pawahikan* (NI).

strawberry A heart berry, *otehimin* (NI).

stray *wanohtewin* (NI); s/he is lost, *wanisin* (VAI).

streak *ka masinâstek* (VII); it is striped, *masinâstew* (VII).

streaky *kakah kîhtwam asinâstek* (VII).

437

stream Flowing water, *nîpîy kapemicowahk* (VTA); a creek, *sepesis* (NI); upstream, *natimihk* (NI); downstream, *mâmihk* (NI).

strength *maskawisiwin* (NI); strength of character, *maskawâtisiwin* (NI); the act of having strength, courage, or bravery, *sohkeyimowin* (NI).

strengthen *ka maskawsehtahk* (VTI).

strenuous *sihtatoskewin* (NI); *nestosiwin* (NI); it is hard work, *âyiman atoskewin* (NI).

stress Being lonesome, *kaskeyihtamâyâwin* (NI); determination, *âhkameyihtam* (VAI); stressing a fact, *meyawakacimowewin* (NI).

stretch The act of stretching, *tasowin* (NI); something that stretches, *kîkway ka sîpekipayik* (VII); it stretched, *sîpekipayiw* (VAI); s/he stretched them by pulling them, *sepekipitew* (VTA); s/he stretches herself/himself, *sîpîw* (VAI); s/he stretches or cranes her/his neck, *tastakiskweyow* (VAI); s/he stretches them out, *taswahew* (VTA).

stretchy A pair of stretchy footwear, i.e.: rubbers, *sîpekaskisin* (NI); it is stretchy, *sîpîkiskâw* (VII); a piece of stretchy material, *sîpekiwayan* (NA); it is stretchy, i.e.: a wool sock, *sîpîkiskisiw* (VAI); *sipihkisiw* (VAI) *(Northern)*; *sipekipayiw* (VAI) *(Plains)*.

strew *swescikewin* (NI).

strewn *kîkway ka swestahk* (VII).

stricken *awîyak kakeh pakamahikâsot* (VTA).

strict *awîyak ka âhkwatsit* (VAI).

stride *kisiskahtewin* (NI); *isi pimohtewin* (NI).

stridence *kiciskihtâkosiwin* (NI).

stridency *ka nihtâ kisiwek* (VAI).

strident *ka kiciskihtâkwahk* (VII).

strife *kehkâhtowin* (NI); a quarrel or conflict, *mawineskâtowin* (NI).

strike A job protest, *atoskewin kanakinamihk* (NI); s/he strikes something noisely, *matwetawew* (VTA); s/he strikes the drum, *pâkahamâw* (VTI); s/he strikes the drum for her/him, *pâkahamawew* (VTA); the act of striking the drum, *pâkahamâwin* (NI); s/he strikes her/his face, *pâkamihkwehwew* (VTA); s/he strikes her/him on the mouth, *pakamitonehwew* (VTA); s/he strikes her/him accidently, *pistahwew* (VTA).

striking *pâkamahikewin* (NI).

strikingly *osâmiyosowenihk* (LN).

string A string for a racquet, *pisimaneyapiy* (NI); a piece of string or small rope, *pîminahkwânis* (NI); *pîsâkanâpiy* (NI) *(Plains)*.

stringency *âhkwatisowin* (NI).

stringent *ka âhkwatsihk* (VAI).

stringy *metoni sihkaciwin* (NI).

strip Stripping off something, *masaskoniwewin* (NI); s/he takes her/his clothes off, *ketayiwinisew* (VAI); s/he strips off all her/his clothes, *môstâpekasenisiw* (VAI).

stripe *ka masinâstehoht awîyak* (VAI); *masinâstew* (VAI) *or* (VII).

striped *masinâstehikâsowin* (NI).

strive *kociwin* (NI).

striven *sohki ka kocehk kîkway* (VTI).

stroke *ka nome nâspicipayihk* (VAI); s/he strokes his beard for him, *sinikwastowenew* (VTA); he strokes his own beard, *sinikwastowenisiw* (VAI).

stroll *sesawohtewin* (NI); s/he walks everywhere, *papâmohtew* (VAI).

strong Strength, *kamaskâwisehk* (VAI); it is strong or hard, *maskawâw* (VTI); strength of character, *maskawatisiwin* (NI); s/he has a strong character or s/he is durable, *maskawatisiw* (VAI); it is durable, *maskawatan* (VII); s/he is strong (in the physical sense), *sohkâtisiw* (VAI); *maskawisew* (VAI); it is strong, i.e.: a car jack, *sohkâtan* (VII); strongly, with power, strength, *sohkâhac* (IPC); *sohki* (IPC); it is a strong liquid, i.e.: alcohol, *maskawâkamow* (VTI); it is a strong cord or rope, *maskawâpekan* (NI); it is a strong bar of iron, *maskawâpiskâw* (VII); it is a strong resistable piece of iron, i.e.: cast iron frying pan, *maskawâpiskisiw* (VAI); a strong piece of steel, iron, or metal, *maskawipîwâpisk* (NI); it is strong, solid, powerful, *sohkan* (VII); a strong railing or pole, *sohkâskwan* (NI); s/he is brave and courageous or has strong expectations, *sohkeyimow* (VAI); s/he makes her/him or them strong, *sohkihew* (VTA).

strop *kâskipâson ka tâsihtahk apihkanihk* (NI); a strap to shape a razor or knife, *tâsahihkoman* (NI).

strove *kîkway kakeh nôtinamihk* (VTI).

struck *awîyak kakeh pakamahoht* (VAI).

struggle *sohki kociwin* (NI); *wawaskawew* (VTA).

strum *ka pakamapekahamihk kitohcikan* (VTI).

strung *pîminahkwân ka pîmapekahpitek* (NI).

strut *ka mâmaskâtikopemohtehk* (VAI); s/he has a dignified walk, *mamihcipimohtew* (VAI).

stub *sikaret iskohkasikanis* (NI); a little stump, *kîskatahikanis* (NI).

stubborn Ornery, *macistikwânewin* (NI); *maskawistikwanew* (VAI).

stubby When someone is short in stature and heavyset, *awîyak kâcimisit mena kasohkisit* (VAI); s/he has a stubby figure, *pitikosiw* (VAI); it is stubby, i.e.: ball shaped, *pitikwâw* (VII).

stuck The act of being stuck, *micimoyowin* (NI); s/he is stuck or run aground or hung up, *micimosin* (VAI); s/he is stuck in the mud, *micimoskowew* (VAI); it is run aground, i.e.: a canoe, *micimohtin* (VTI); s/he is stuck, *micimohiw* (VAI); it is stuck or wedged in between, *sekohtin* (VTI); s/he is stuck or wedged in between, *sekosin* (VAI).

stud A male horse or stallion, *nâpestim* (NA); *ospikekanihkanis ayinânew misit ka iskwak* (NI).

student *okiskinwahamâkosiw* (NA); *kiskinohamâwakan* (NA) *(Plains)*; *kiskinohamâkan* (NA) *(Northern)*; s/he is a student, *okiskinohamâwakaniwiw* (NA); they are her/his students, *okiskinohamâwakanimew* (VTA).

studied *kanitawi kiskeyihtamihk kîkway* (VTI).

studious *sohki kiskinohamâkosiwin* (NI); s/he is a good learning person, *ayamihcikewkiw* (VAI).

study The act of studying, *kiskinwahamâkosiwin* (NI); s/he studies her/him, *nitawikiskeyimew* (VAI); s/he reads it and works at it, *ayamihtâw* (VAI); *atoskatam* (VAI).

stuff Stuffing or filling something up, *ka sâkaskinahcikehk* (VAI); some kind of stuff, *kîkwaya* (IPC); s/he stuffs or packs them with something, *sîpaskwâtew* (VTA).

stuffy *ka kaskamotâhk pehcayihk* (VII).

stumble *ka piswahcahikehk* (VAI).

stump *kîskatahikan* (NI).

stumpy *ka kîskatahikaniskak* (NI).

stun *nome tikinehowewin* (NI)

stung *kakeh cisowet âmô* (VAI).

stunk *kakeh wihcekahk kîkway* (VII).

stunner *otikinehikew* (NA).

stunning *nâspic miyosiwin* (NI).

stunt *mamahtâw kaskihtâwin* (NI); something done to impress people, *mahtâwtôtamowin* (NI).

438

stunted *nome kîskwetahwaw* (VAI).

stupefaction *môhcohiwewin* (NI).

stupefy *ka môhcohiwehk* (VAI).

stupendous *kîkway ka mâmaskâteyihtâkwahk* (VII).

stupid Someone who is stupid or foolish, *awîyak kakepâtsit* (VAI); being stupid, *kakepâtisiwin* (NI); s/he does things in a stupid way, *kepâcâyihtiw* (VAI); it is stupid and foolish, *kepâtan* (VII); s/he is stupid or "not all there", *kepâtisiw* (VAI).

stupidity *kakepâtisiwin* (NI).

stupidly *ka kakepât* (VII); *tahkamiksihk* (VII).

stupor *môhcowisâyâwin* (NI); *wahwankiskisow* (VAI).

sturdy *ka sohksihcikâtek kîkway* (VTI); *sohkinakosiw* (VAI); s/he is well built or s/he has a robust, sturdy, powerful body, *sohkiyawew* (VAI); being strong and sturdy, *sohkâtisiwin* (NI).

sturgeon A type of fish, *namew* (NA).

stutter S/he stutters, *nâhnakowew* (VAI).

sty *kohkôsikamik* (VAI).

style *tânsi ka isinakayâskamihk* (VAI).

stylish *kîkway ka miyonâkwahk* (VII); *miyowâwisew* (VAI).

suave *mistahi miyohtwâwin* (NI).

subdue *ka sâkocihewehk* (VAI); s/he subdues, *sâkohew* (VTA); overcoming by force, *sâkohiwewin* (NI).

subdued *awîyak ka sâkocihiht* (VTA).

subjugate *awîyak ka sâkocihiht* (VTA).

subjugation *sâkocihiwewin* (NI).

submerge When something sinks, *kakosâpek kîkway* (VTI); it sinks underwater, *kosâpew* (VTI).

submergence *kosâpewin* (NI).

submission *pakiteyimowin* (NI).

submissive *ka nihtâ pakiteyimohk* (VAI).

submit *pakiteyihcikewin* (NI).

subsequence *ka askôtomakahk kîkway* (VTI).

subsequent *askôkewin* (NI).

subsequently *askôkewinihk ohci* (LN).

subside *ka nîkipayik* (VII); it went under, *kotâwipayiw* (VAI).

subsidence *nîkipayowin* (NI).

substantial *ka miyo pamihohk* (VAI); it is real or genuine and actual, *tâpwepayiw* (VAI).

substantiality *miyo pamihowin* (NI).

substantiate *miyo payihcikewin* (NI).

substantial *kehcinâhowin* (NI).

substantive *kîkway ka kehcinâhomakahk* (VII).

substitute *ka meskotascikehk* (VAI); supply or serve as a substitute, *meskotascikewin* (NI).

substitution *meskotascikewin* (NI).

substitutional *ka meskotascikakehk* (VAI).

substitutive *meskotascikâkewin* (NI).

subtract The act of taking back, *kawôtinikewin* (NI).

subtle *âyiman tanisitohtamihk* (VAI).

subtlety *ekâ nisitohtamowin* (NI).

subtly *wani nisitohtamowenihk* (LN).

subtract *ka pahkwenikehk* (VII).

subtraction *pahkwenikewin* (NI).

subtractive *kîkway ka pahkwepayihtahk* (VTI).

succeed *ka kaskihtahk kîkway* (VII); *kaskihow* (VAI).

success Being able to succeed, *kaskihowin* (NI); a successful deed, *kaskihtamasowin* (NI); a success or having good luck, *miyopayowin* (NI).

successful *awîyak ka nihtâ kaskihtat kîkway* (NA).

successive *tahtakowâc* (IPC).

successor *otâpapestamâkew* (NA); *meskotapestakew* (VAI).

succinct *metoni katawah* (IPC).

succor or **succour** *nîsohkamâtowin* (NI).

succulent It is juicy, *mînisâpowiw* (VAI).

succumb *metoni pomewin* (NI); *nipow* (VAI); succumbing under a load, *kawiskosiw* (VAI); *kawiskotew* (VAI); give way under pressure, *sâkweyimowin* (NI).

such *ekotowa* (IPC); in such a place, *omatowayihk* (LN).

suck The act of sucking, *nônâcikewin* (NI); s/he sucks them, *nônâtew* (VTA); s/he sucks it out, i.e.: smoke from a pipe, *otahtam* (VTI); s/he sucks them up, *petamew* (VTA); s/he sucks on them, *sôpamew* (VTA).

sucker A type of fish, *namepiy* (NA).

suckle The act of breastfeeding, *nôhawasowin* (NI); s/he suckles, *nôniw* (VAI); she suckles her/him, *nônehew* (VTA).

suckling *awâsis kanohiht* (NA).

suction *otahcikâkan* (NI); *kotâcikemakahk* (VTI); it sucks, *otahcikemakan* (VII).

sudden *sisikôc* (IPC); all of a sudden, *ketahtawe poko* (IPC).

suds *pîstew* (NI); a soapy water, *pîstewâpoy* (NA).

sudsy *ka pîstewak* (VII).

suet *wiyinowin* (NI); fat, *wiyin* (NI).

suety *awîyak ka kwayakikamot* (VAI).

suffer Suffering with pain, *kawîsakahpinehk* (VAI); s/he is suffering, *kwâtakihtâw* (VAI); s/he is moaning with pain, *mamahpinew* (VAI); s/he makes herself/himself suffer, *kakwâtakihisiw* (VAI); the act of mental suffering, *kwâtakeyihtamowin* (NI); s/he suffers for her/him, *kwatakihesôstamawew* (VTA); s/he makes her/him suffer, *kwatakihew* (VTA); the act of personal suffering, *kwâtakihisowin* (NI); the act of suffering, *kwâtakihtawin* (NI); s/he suffers from a burn, *kwâtakihkasiw* (VAI); s/he makes her/him suffer from a burn, *kwâtakihkaswew* (VTA).

sufferable *ka sohkahpinehk* (VAI).

suffering *wîsakahpinewin* (NI); *kakwataketawin* (NI).

suffice *ekwayekohk kîkway* (VII); s/he is fed up, *tepeyihtam* (VAI).

439

sufficiency *tepipayowin* (NI).

sufficient *kîkway ka tepipayihtahk* (VAI); s/he has sufficient resources for all of them or s/he makes measurements sufficient to her/his size, *tipahwew* (VTA); s/he gives her/him a sufficient amount, *tepinamawew* (VTA); s/he has a sufficient amount for everyone, *tepipayihew* (VTA); s/he has a sufficient amount or s/he has enough, *tepipayiw* (VAI); s/he has had a sufficient amount to drink or s/he has had enough to drink, *tepipew* (VAI); s/he has done a sufficient amount for her/him or s/he has done enough for her/him, *tepitotawew* (VTA); it is enough, *tepipayiw* (VAI); s/he has sufficient to drink, *tepipew* (VAI).

sufficiently *tepipayowinihk* (LN).

sugar *sesipâskwat* (VAI) *(Northern)*; *sîwinikan* (NI) *(Plains)*; s/he sweetens them with sugar, *sesipâskwatihkahtew* (VAI); s/he made sugar with it, *sesipâskwatihkâkew* (VTA); s/he made sugar for her/him, *sesipâskwatihkawew* (VTA).

sugary *ka sesipâskwatowik* (LN).

suggest *kîkway kawihtamakihk* (VTI).

suggestion *wihcikewin* (NI); the act of suggesting, *kiskisomowewin* (NI).

suggestive Suggesting something improper, *koyowîtamihk kîkway* (VAI); s/he looks at her/him suggestively, *pisikwâtâpamew* (VTA).

suit *peyakwayiwinis* (NI).

suitability *nahipayowin* (NI).

suitable *kîkway ka nahipayik* (VII); it fits well, *nahipayiw* (VAI).

suit coat *or* **suitcoat** *wawesiwasâkay* (NI).

suite *piskihc wîkowin* (NI).

suiting *aywinsîkin* (NI).

sulk S/he sits and sulks, *kisowapow* (VAI).

sulky *awîyak ka kisôwâyat* (VAI).

sullen *kisôweyihtamowin* (NI); s/he looks mad, *kisôwinâkosiw* (VAI).

sully *ka misowanacihiwehk* (VAI); it is stained, *wepatan* (VII).

sultry *ka âhkwastek* (VII); it is hot, *kisâstew* (VII).

sum *ka mâmawakimiht sônîyâw* (VAI); the act of adding up, *mâmawikecikewin* (NI).

summary *masinahikanihk kastahk* (VII).

summarize S/he summarizes the description in writing, *naspasinahikew* (VAI); the act of summarizing the description in writing, *naspasinahikewin* (NI).

summer *nîpin* (NI); the entire summer, *kapenîpin* (NI); next summer, *kîhtwam nîpihki* (IPC) *(Plains)*; *kîhtwam nîpihkih* (IPC) *(Northern)*; last summer, *nîpinohk* (IPC); it is a good summer, *miyonîpin* (NI); the ground is just like it is in summer, *nîpinaskamikâw* (VII); it feels like summer,

nîpinâyâw (VII); s/he stayed all summer, *nîpinisiw* (VAI); next summer, *nîpihki* (IPC); this summer, *ôma ka nîpihk* (NI).

summertime *ka mekwanîpihk* (IPC).

summery *ka nîpinâyâk* (VII).

summit It is the summit, *tahkohtâmatin* (NI).

summon *ka natohkemohk* (VAI).

sump *ka mâwataskinahtahk nîpîy* (VTI).

sumptuary *ka nâkateyihtamihk mestinikewin* (NI).

sumptuous *miyonâkosiwin* (NI).

sun Or a month, *pîsim* (NA); overcome by sun or heat, *nestwâsiw* (VII); *nestwâstew* (VII); luminous, lit through by sun, *sapwâsow* (VTI); *sapwâstew* (VTI); shining deeply, *sapowâsiw* (VTI); *sapowâstew* (VTI); the glare of the sun hurts her/his eyes, *sîwâsiw* (VAI); the glare of the sun is bright on the eyes, *sîwâstew* (VII); melted by sun, natural heat, *tihkâsow* (VII); *tihkâstew* (VII); whited, discolored by the sun, *wâpâsiw* (VII); *wâpâstew* (VII); darkened by the sun, i.e.: "Indian tan", *pihkasow* (VTI); *pihkahtew* (VTI); sunstroke, killer by sun or heat, *nipahihkasiw* (VAI); the sun burns right overhead, *cakâsikew* (VTI); the sun filtrates through the clouds, *pawaskwew* (VAI) *(Northern)*; *pesâkâstew* (VAI) *(Plains)*; the sun is shining, *pîsimowiw* (VAI).

sunbeam *âstamastew* (VII); *pîsimweyaw* (VII).

Sunday It is Sunday, i.e.: praying day, *ayamihewikîsikâw* (NI).

sunder *ka piskihtinamihk* (VTI).

sundown *ka pahkisimok* (VII); it is sundown, *pahkisimow* (NA).

sung *kakihnikamohk* (VAI).

sunk *kakeh kosâpek kîkway* (VTI).

sunless *ekâ ka nokosit pîsim* (VTA).

sunlight *ka wâsisot pîsim* (VTA).

sunlit *ka wâseyâk pîsimohk ohci* (VII).

sunny *ka wâseskwahk* (VII); *wâseskwan* (VII).

sunrise *ka pîsakastek* (VII); the sun is rising, *sâkâstew* (VII).

sunset When the sun sets, *ka pahkisimok* (VTA); the suns sets, *pahkisimow* (VTA); the sun is setting, *pahkisimon* (VTA).

sunshade *âkawâstehon* (NI).

sunshine *ka wâseskwahk* (VII); the sun is becoming hotter, *pîsimwastew* (VII).

sunshiny *ka wâseskwanayak* (VII).

sun-up *ka oskisâkastek* (VII).

sunward *pîsimohk iteyesih* (IPC).

super *metoni kihcinekan* (VII); it looks super, *miyonakwan* (VII); something to wonder about, *mâmaskâteyihtâkwan* (VII); supermarket, *kecâtâwiwikamik* (NI).

superable *ka nihtâ paskiyaht awîyak* (VAI).

superb *metoni kihci nîkânîwin* (NI).

superior *awîyak ka nîkânet* (VAI); *nekanew* (VAI); s/he thinks herself/himself superior, *ayiwâkeyimototawew* (VAI); s/he is arrogant, *ayiwâkeyimow* (VAI); s/he is head of something, *nîkânîw* (VAI).

superiority *nîkânîwin* (NI).

supernatural Something that is hard to understand, *ekâ metoni ka nistaweyihtâkwahk* (VII); it is thought of as supernatural, *mâmaskâteyihtâkwan* (VII); supernaturally or the godly thing, *manitowakâc* (IPC); it is supernatural, i.e.: a prayer, *mamatâwan* (VII).

superstition *mamahtâw kîkway ka tâpwehtamihk* (VII); *tâpwehtamowin* (NI).

superstitious *awîyak mamahtaw kîkway ka tâpwehtahk* (VAI).

supper Suppertime, *otâkwanimitisowin* (NI); s/he has supper, *otâkwanimitisiw* (VAI); an evening meal, *otâkwan mîcisowin* (NI).

supplant *ka mîweskakehk* (VAI).

supple *miyo waskawîwin* (NI); it is soft, *yoskâw* (VII).

supplement *kîkway ka takwastahk* (VTI); an addition to something, *takwascikewin* (NI).

supplemental *takôsihcikewin* (NI).

supplementation *ka takwastahk kîkway* (VTI).

suppliance *ka kesimototakewin* (NI).

suppliant *awîyak ka kâkesimot* (VAI).

supplicant *awîyak ka kâkesimototaket* (VTA).

supplicate *manito ka kâkesimototaht* (VTA).

supplies Giving supplies, *otinamatowena* (NI); food, *mîciwin* (NI).

supply *miyetowin* (NI).

support Helping someone, *nîsohkamâtowin* (NI); s/he places her/his feet on it for support, *âsostisimow* (VAI); s/he supports her/him by leaning her/him against something, *sîtwahew* (VTA); s/he supports her/him or it by placing her/him or it between two trees, *sîhtawâskosimew* (VTA); s/he is supported by being wedged between two trees, *sîtawâskosin* (VAI); it is supported by being wedged between two trees, *sîtawâskohtin* (VTI); s/he supports it with a pillar, *sîtwâskwahwew* (VTA).

supportable *awîyak ka nîsohkamâket* (VAI).

supporter *onîsohkamâkew* (NA).

suppose I imagine something like this, *kwanta iteyihtamiwin* (NI); I suppose, *etikwe* (IPC); s/he conceives of something, *iteyihtam* (VAI).

supposed *ekosi kakeh iteyihtamihk* (VAI).

supposedly *ka kaspoweyihtamihk kîkway* (VTI).

supposing *kîspin îsa ketahtawe* (IPC).

suppress *ka nakinamihk* (VTI); s/he sits on it, *mahtakoskam* (VTI).

suppressible *kawehci nakinikatek* (VTI).

suppression *nakinikewin* (NI).

suppressive *awîyak ka nihtâ nakinowet* (VTA).

supreme *metoni nîkân* (VII).

supreme being *metoni nîkânîwin* (NI).

sure *kehcinâ* (IPC); *kehcinâhow* (VAI); as sure as can be, *tâpwe poko ani* (IPC); certainly, it is certain, sure, *kehcinâ* (IPC).

surely *kehcinâhowin* (NI).

surety *ka kehcinâhohk kîkway* (VTI).

surf Huge waves or rolling surf, *mahkaskâw* (VII).

surface On top of something, *waskic ohci* (IPC); on top barely touching on the surface, *waskic* (IPC); the act of breaking the surface of the water or appearing out of the water, *pîkopepayowin* (NI); s/he breaks the surface of the water, *pîkopepayiw* (VAI); s/he surfaces from underwater, *pekopew* (VAI); the act of surfacing or rising to the top, *pekopewin* (NI); right on top, *waskic* (IPC).

surfeit *ka osâmskoyohk* (VAI).

surge *mahkâskâw* (VII).

surly *ka wahkewisihk* (VAI).

surmise *kakwi tâpeyihcikewin* (NI); the act of guessing, *oyeyihtamowin* (NI).

surmount *ayiwâk ascikewin* (NI).

441

surpass The act of defeating someone, *paskiyakewin* (NI); s/he trounces her/him, *paskiyawew* (VTA); s/he surpasses, *miyaskawew* (VTA).

surplus *kîkway ka aywâkipayik* (VII); *ayiwâkipayiwin* (NI).

surprise *sikocihiwewin* (NI); *sisikoteyihtam* (VAI); surprise, astonishment, mixed with protest or at least unbelieved, *wâtistakâc* (IPC); it surprises, *sisikoteyihtakwan* (VII); s/he is surprised at the way s/he is now, *mâmaskâtew* (VTA); s/he is surprised by what s/he sees, *mâmaskâtapisin* (VAI); the act of being surprised, *sisikoteyihtamowin* (NI).

surprising *ka sikocihiwehk* (VTA); wonderfully, surprisingly, "wow", *mâmaskâc* (IPC).

surrender S/he surrenders herself/himself, *pakitinisiw* (VAI); s/he surrenders, *pakiteyimow* (VAI); the act of surrendering, *pakiteyimowin* (NI).

surreptitious *ka kimotatsihk* (VAI); in a hidden, stealing, surreptitious way, *kîmôc* (IPC).

surround The act of surrounding something, *tetipeweskâcikewin* (NI); s/he surround it, *wâsakâskam* (VTI); s/he surrounds their path, *pihciskanawew* (VTA); s/he surrounds someone else's trail, *pihciskanawâtew* (VTA).

surroundings *wâsakâm ohci kîkwaya* (NI); *wâsakâskamihtawin* (NI); something all around oneself, *wâsakâmeskakewin* (NI).

survival *paspîwin* (NI).

survive *ka paspîhk* (VAI); *pimâtisiw* (VAI).

survivor *opaspiw* (NA).

susceptibility *kawihkihikohk kîkway* (VTI).

susceptible The act of feeling susceptible to the opposite sex, *wihkiskwewewin* (NI).

suspect Someone who suspects someone, *awîyak ka atâmeyimiht* (VAI); s/he is suspected, *atâmeyimâw* (VAI); s/he suspects her/him, *atâmeyimew* (VAI); s/he suspects it, *atâmeyihtam* (VAI).

suspence Anxious expectation, *pîkweyihtamowin* (NI).

suspend Stopping something for a while, *nome nakinowewin* (NI); it hangs, *akocin* (VTA); s/he receives a suspended sentence, *pakitinâw* (VAI); s/he is leaning over just above the ground or s/he is suspended in midair, *nemâskosin* (VAI); it is leaning over just above the ground, *nemâskohtin* (VII); s/he suspends her/him in midair with a pole, *nemâskwawew* (VTA); s/he holds up a pole, *akotaskwahwew* (VTA).

suspender *pîmakâmehpison* (NI).

suspense *nanihkeyihtamowin* (NI); *pekweyihtamowin* (NI).

suspension *ka nomenakinikatek kîkway* (VTI).

suspicion *atâmeyihcikewin* (NI); s/he suspects her/him, *atâmeyimew* (VAI); the act of suspecting, *atâmeyimowewin* (NI).

suspicious S/he has a suspicious air, s/he suspects it, *atâmeyihtam* (VAI); when you think a person is guilty, *atâmeyimowewin* (NI).

sustain *kîkway ka nâkateyihtamihk ekâ tapahkihtihk* (VTI); s/he sustains herself/himself by that means, *ohtacihow* (VAI).

sustenance *nâkateyihcikewin* (NI).

swaddle *wikinâwasowin* (NI) *(Northern)*; *wewekinâwasowin* (NI) *(Plains)*.

swag The act of stealing, *kimotiwin* (NI).

swagger *okimotiw* (VAI).

swallow *micaskisis* (NA), the act of swallowing, *kohcipayihcikewin* (NI); s/he swallows her/him, *kohcipayihew* (VTA); s/he swallows it, *kohcipayitâw* (VTI); s/he swallows it in one gulp, *misiwepayihew* (VTA); it is rough and hard to swallow, *pihekwâw* (VII) *(Plains)*; *piyekwan* (VII) *(Northern)*

swam The act of swimming, *yâhyânamowin* (NI).

swamp *nipîwaskekahk* (NI) or (LN); a wet swampy spot, *wâkinâkaniskâw* (VII).

swampy The ground is wet, *nepîwahcâw* (VII).

Swampy Cree From the James Bay area, i.e.: the "n" dialect, a Swampy Cree person, *omaskekow* (NA).

swamp spruce *maskekosihta* (NI).

swan *mâyâpisiw* (NA); a white swan, *wâpisiw* (NA).

swank *ka takahkinakwahk kîkway* (VII).

swanky *mistikimaw nakosowin* (NI).

swap The act of swapping, *meskotonamâtowin* (NI); s/he exchanges it with her/him, *meskotonamawew* (VTA).

swarm *ka mâmaweyatwâw âmôwak* (NA).

swarthy *ka wîyipasakayehk* (VII); s/he has a dark complexion, *wîyipinâkosiw* (VAI).

swash The act of white-washing, *wasepekahikewin* (NI).

swat *awîyak ka pakamahoht* (VAI).

swath *peyakwâw ka pimsawehk maskosiya* (VTI).

swathe *kîkway ka wikinamihk* (VTI).

sway The act of staggering, *ayâhpayowin* (NI).

swear The act of swearing or the act of using foul language, *wiyahkwewin* (NI); s/he swears or uses foul language, *wiyahkwew* (VAI); s/he swore at her/him, *wiyahkwâtew* (VTA); using profane language, *wiyahkwewin* (NI).

sweat It is sweating hot, *apweyaw* (VII).

sweater A woolen coat, i.e.: a sweater, *sestakwasâkay* (NI) *(Northern)*; *sîpihkiskawasâkey* (NI) *(Plains)*.

sweat lodge *matotisân* (NI).

sweaty *apweyaw* (VII); perspiration, *apwesiwin* (NI).

sweep The act of sweeping, *wepahikewin* (NI); s/he sweeps for her/him, *wepahamawew* (VTA); s/he sweeps, *wepahikew* (VAI).

sweeper *owepahikew* (NA); a broom, *wepahikan* (NI).

sweeping *ka wepahikehk* (VTI).

sweet *sîwâyi* (NI); it is sweet or sour, *sewâw* (VII); it is sweet or sour, *sîwisiw* (VAI); s/he makes the liquid sweet, *sîwâkamihtâw* (VTI); the act of sweetening something, *sîwinikewin* (NI); the liquid is sweet, *sîwakamow* (VAI).

sweeten Sweetened boiled water, i.e.: birch sap, *sîwakamisikan* (NI); s/he sweetens it by boiling it, *sîwâkamiswew* (VTA); s/he sweetens them, *sewihew* (VTI) *(Northern)*; *siwinew* (VTI) *(Plains)*.

sweetheart *awîyak kowicimosihk* (VAI); a lover, *sâkihakan* (NA).

sweetish *kisâstaw ka sîwâk* (VII).

sweetness *sîwisowin* (NI).

swell S/he or it is swollen, *pâkipayiw* (VAI); s/he causes her/him to swell by her/his grip, *pâkinew* (VTA); s/he makes her/him swell, *pâkipayihew* (VTA).

swelling *pâkipayowin, nânitâw ka pakipayihk* (VTI); swelling goes down, *ihkipayiw* (VAI); *ihkipayin* (VAI).

swelter It is sweltering hot, *nipahikisâstew* (VII).

swept S/he swept them, *wepahwew* (VTA); something that has been swept, *kakeh wepahamihk* (VTI); s/he is swept away by the current, *wepapakow* (VAI) *(Northern)*; *wepâhokiw* (VAI) *(Plains)*; it is swept away by the current, *wepâpotew* (VTI).

swerve *wemâpicikewin* (NI); s/he is alienated, *paskipayow* (VAI).

swift The act of being swift or agile, *tâstapiwin* (NI); *tastapayâwin* (NI) *(Northern)*; *cacâstapiwin* (NI) *(Plains)*; someone who is swift or agile, *otastapiw* (NA); s/he is swift or agile, *tâstapiw* (VAI); it goes very swiftly, *tâstapipayiw* (VAI).

swiftness *tastapayâwin* (NI).

swig *wâstakamowin* (NI).

swill *kohkôsiminihkwewin* (NI).

swim S/he takes a swim, *pakâsimiw* (VAI); s/he swims or paddles in this direction, *pecicimew* (VAI); s/he swims, *yâhyânam* (VAI).

swimmer *awîyak ka yâhyânahk* (NA).

swimming The act of swimming, *pakâsimowin* (NI).

swine A herd of pigs, *kohkôsak* (NA).

swing Or hammock, *wepison* (NI) *(Northern)*; *wewepison (Plains)* (NI); s/he is going to swing, *wehwepisiw* (VAI) *(Northern)*; *wîwewepisiw* (VAI) *(Plains)*; s/he swings her/him in a swing or hammock, *wepitew* (VTA) *(Northern)*; *wewepitew* (VTA) *(Plains)*.

swinish *peyakwan kohkôs* (NI).

swipe *kimotow* (VAI); the act of taking something without consent, *otinamâsiwin* (NI).

swirl *sipi ka apamocowahk* (VTI); *wasakapayow* (VAI).

swish *ka westehikehk* (VAI); it makes a swishing noise, *siswihtakwan* (VII).

swizzle *kitehamihk kîkway* (VTI).

swollen It is swollen, *pâkipayiw* (VAI).

swoon *kipatâhtamowin* (NI); *kipatâhtam* (VAI).

swoop S/he catches her/him, *kacitinew* (VTA).

sword A war knife, *nôtinikewihkomân* (NI); a soldier's knife, i.e.: a sword, *simâkanihkomân* (NI).

swore *ka wîyahkwehk* (VAI).

sworn *ka wîyahkwetôtamihk* (VTA); *wiyâsowewnihk* (LN).

swum *kakeh yâhyânamihk* (VTA).

swung *kakeh wepisohk* (VAI).

syllabic writing *nehiyaw cahkipewasinahikewin* (NI) *(Plains)*; *nehiyawasinahikewin* (NI) *(Northern)*.

sympathetic *ka kitimakinâkehk* (VAI).

sympathetically *kitimâkinakewinihk* (LN) *or* (VII).

sympathize *awîyak ka kitimâkinaht* (VAI).

sympathizer *okitimâkinâkew* (NA).

sympathy *kitimâkinâtowin* (NI); the act of feeling sorry for someone, *kitimâkinâkewin* (NI).

syrup or **sirup** *lamlas* (NI) *(French Cree)*.

syrupy *ka lamlasowik* (VII) *(French Cree)*.

443

T

table *mîcisowinâhtik* (NI).

taciturn *kâmwâtisiwin* (NI).

taciturnity *awîyak ka kakâmwâtsit* (VTI).

tackle *sohki ka otihtinamihk kîkway* (VTA).

tacky *ka pasakwayak kîkway* (VII).

tact *manâtisiwin* (NI).

tactful *awîyak ka manâtisit* (VAI).

tactile *natomeskonikewin* (NI).

tactility *natomahcihowin* (NI).

tactless *awîyak ekâ ka manâtisit* (VAI).

tadpole *ayîkisis* (NA).

tail *misoy* (NI); it has a hairless tail, *cîcikwâyiwew* (VTA); an animal with no tail, *kîskâyiw* (VAI); it has no tail, *kîskâyowew* (VAI); having no tail, *kîskâyowewin* (NI); a beaver tail, *amiskwayiw* (NI); s/he has a crooked tail, *wâkâyiwew* (VAI); a tail, *osoy* (NI).

taint *ka nome misowanatahk kîkway* (VII).

take Taking something, *otinikewin* (NI); s/he takes things across the current in a canoe, *âsawahotâsiw* (VAI); s/he takes it across, *âsawohtâw* (VTI); s/he takes her/him some place, *itohtahew* (VTA); s/he takes it over there, *itohtatâw* (VTI); s/he takes her/him home in a canoe, *kîwehoyew* (VTA); s/he takes her/him to her/his home, *kîwehtahew* (VTA); s/he takes it out, *kwayakonam* (NI); s/he takes her/him down stream in a canoe, *mahâpohew* (VTA); s/he takes her/him down stream, *mahohtahew* (VTA); s/he takes blankets or a sleeping bag with her/him, *nemakohpew* (VTI); s/he takes footwear with her/him, *nemaskisinew* (VAI); s/he gives her/him a weapon to take along, *nemâskwehew* (VTA); s/he takes a weapon with her/him, *nemâskwew* (VAI); s/he takes a lunch with her/him, *nemâw* (VAI); a lunch or food taken along for the trip, *nemâwin* (NI); s/he takes an axe with her/him, *nîmicîkahikanew* (VAI); s/he takes a knife with her/him, *nîmicîkomânew* (VAI); the act of taking a weapon along on a trip, *nemâskwewin* (NI); s/he takes her/him, *otinew* (VTA); s/he takes her/him off to the side of the road, *paskehtahew* (VTA); s/he takes her/him in, *pihtokahew* (VTA); s/he takes her/him by mistake, *pistinew* (VTA); s/he takes her/him right through, *sâpohtahew* (VTA); s/he takes her/him away with her/him, *sipwehtahew* (VTA).

taken *kakeh otinamihk kîkway* (VTI).

taking *kaweh otinamihk kîkway* (VTI).

tale *keyaskew âcimowin* (NI); a ficticious story, *atayohkewin* (NI).

talent *metoni ka kaskihtahk kîkway* (VAI); being talented, *nahewin* (NI).

talented *awîyak kahkiyaw kîkway; ohci ka nahet* (VAI).

talk The act of talking, *pîkiskwewin* (NI); s/he talks poorly of her/him, *kitimâkimew* (VTA); s/he talks about her/him or them, *mâmiskomew* (VTA); s/he mentions it to her/him or them, *mâmiskôtamawew* (VTA); s/he talks about it, *pîkiskwâtam* (VTI); s/he talks to her/him, *pîkiskwâtew* (VTA); s/he talks, *pîkiskwew* (VAI); s/he talks quickly, *câstapowew* (VAI); s/he talks with her/him, *wîcipîkiskwemew* (VTA).

talkative S/he is too talkative, *pîkiskweskiw* (VAI).

talker *nihtâ pîkiskwestamâkew* (VTA).

talky *cikâstepayihcikan ka pekiskwemakahk* (VTI).

tall Being tall, *kinosowin* (NI); s/he is tall, *kinosiw* (VAI); s/he is very tall and slim, i.e.: a long log or tall person, *kinwaskosiw* (VAI); it is standing tall, *kinwâskitew* (VAI); it stands tall, i.e.: a tree, *kinwaskisiw* (VAI); it stands tall, i.e.: a pole, *kinwâskitew* (VII).

taller S/he is taller than her/him, *pasciskawew* (VTA); *ayiwâkiskawew* (VTA) (Northern); *cayôskawew* (VTA) (Plains); s/he is taller than it, *cayoskam* (VTI) (Plains); *pasciskam* (VTI) (Northern); s/he is taller than someone, *cayoskâkew* (VTA) (Plains); *pasciskâkew* (VTA) (Northern); s/he is taller than everything, *cayoskâcikew* (VTI) (Plains); *pasciskâcikew* (VTI) (Northern).

tallow Rendered grease, *ahkwacipimîy* (NI).

tally *ka atih masinahikâtekwaw atiht metawewina* (VTI); counting material or numeration, *akihcikewin* (NI).

talon *misipîwâyis wâskaseya* (NI); a bird's claw, *maskasiy* (NA).

tamarack Wood from a tamarack, *wâkinâkanâhtik* (NI); a tamarack tree, *wâkinâkan* (NA); there are many tamaracks or it is a tamarack swamp, *wâkinâkaniskâw* (VII).

tame The act of taming, *nakâyâhewewin* (NI); s/he is tame, *yospisiw* (VAI); s/he has been tamed, *nakayâsiw* (VAI); s/he acts tamed, i.e.: a wild horse, *yospâtisiw* (VAI) (Northern); *yospisîw* (VAI) (Plains); the act of being tamed, *yospâtisiwin* (NI) (Northern); *yospisîwin* (NI) (Plains); s/he made her/him tame, *yospisehew* (VTA); being tame, *yospisiwin* (NI).

tameless *awîyak ekâ kakeh nakâyâhiht* (VTA).

tamp *ka mahmâkwahcahikehk* (VAI).

tamper *mâmâkwahcahikakan* (NI).

tan The act of tanning hide, *kîsinikowin* (NI); s/he is tanning hide, *kîsinikiw* (VAI); s/he tans deerhide or cariboohide, *kîsinew* (VAI); s/he tans hide,

445

pahkekinohkew (VAI); the act of tanning moosehide, **pahkekinohkewin** (NI); s/he is tanned or darkened by the sun, **pihkasiw** (VAI) *(Plains)*; **pihkihkasiw** (VAI) *(Northern)*; s/he or it is tanned, **weskwasiw** (VAI); it is tanned, **weskwastew** (VII); s/he tanned her/him, **weskwaswew** (VTA).

tangibility The act of being tactile, **natomeskonikewin** (NI).

tangible *ka mosci miskonamihk kîkway* (VII).

tangle *ka wayescikehk; wanâpihkepayiw* (VAI).

tangly *awîyak ka nôtinkeskit* (VAI).

tanner *pahkekinohkakan* (NI); a person who tans hides, **opahkekinohkew** (NA).

tannery *pahkekinohkewikamik* (NI).

tantalize *sohki nanoyatisiwin* (NI); s/he teases people, **nanoyatisiw** (VAI).

tantrum *metoni wahkewiyawesowin* (NI); being very angry, **kisiwâsowin** (NI).

tap *ka pakamihcakahikesihk* (VTI); *nîpiy itah kohwayawekotek.*

taper S/he sharpens it to a point with a knife, **kenikîhkohtew** (VTI); it is pointed, **cîpwâw** (VII).

taping *kîkway ka pihtokepayihtahk* (VTI); **kitohcikanihk** (NI).

taps Strike light blows or rapping audibly, **matwetahikewin** (NI).

tar *kaskitew piko* (VII).

tardily *otâhkepayowin* (NI).

tardy *kîkway kotahkepayik* (VII); s/he misses it by arriving too late, **mwesiskam** (VTI); s/he is moving slowly or sluggishly, **pwâstawiw** (VAI).

target *kotahaskwâcikan* (NI); a target practice, **kotahaskwan** (VII).

tarnish *ka akohamihk kîkway ka waseyak* (VTI); changing color, **pîtosnakosowin** (NI).

tarpaulin A waterproof covering for shelter, **apahkwânekin** (NI).

tarry *kîkway kapikewahk* (VTI); **otâhkepayihowin** (NI); delay or remain for a while, **ihtasehkew** (VAI).

tart *sewipahkwisekanis* (NA).

task Work, a job, **atoskewin** (NI); **atoskewin ka osihtamasohk** (VTI).

taste *nistospicikewin* (NI); it is fine tasting, **wihkitisow** (VAI); **wihkasin** (VAI); tastes like medicine, **maskihkiwakisow** (VAI); **maskihkiwakan** (VII); tastes greasy, fat, **pimewakisow** (VAI); **pimewakan** (VII); strong taste, easily known, **kihkâspakosiw** (VAI); **kihkâspakwan** (VII); tastes bad, **mayispakosiw** (VAI); **mayispakwan** (VII); it tastes like grease, **pimewakan** (VII); s/he tastes it, **kocispitew** (VTI); s/he tastes it, i.e.: fish, **kotamew** (VTA); s/he tastes it, **kocispitam** (VTA); s/he enjoys the taste of the it, **wihkipwew** (VTI).

tasteful *kîkway kakihkaspakwahk* (VTI) *or* (VII).

tasteless *ekâ ka nistospakwahk* (VTI) *or* (VII).

tasty Something tasty, *ka wihkasik kîkway* (VII); it is tasty, i.e.: fish or bread, **wihkitisiw** (VAI); it is tasty, i.e.: such as soup, stew, or water, **wihkasin** (VII).

tatter *ayiwinis ka yewepayik* (VII); a torn piece of cloth hanging from a garment, **kwayawakotew** (VAI).

tattered *kayâs ayiwinsa ka kikiskamihk* (VTI).

tatting *apihkewin* (NI).

tattle *misihkemowin* (NI).

taught Somebody being taught, *awîyak ka kehkiskinwahamaht* (VTA); s/he taught her/him, **kiskinohamawew** (VTA).

taunt *awîyak atâmeyimiht kîkway ohci* (VTA); s/he reproaches her/him scornfully, **nanâtohkomew** (VTA).

taut *ka sehtamahcihohk* (VAI); the rope is drawn tightly, **sehtapitam** (VTI).

tawdry *ekâ metoni ka miwasik kîkway* (VII).

tawny *ka mihko osâwenakwahk kîkway* (VII).

tea *maskihkiwapoy* (NI); *lite* (NI) *(Northern French Cree)*; medicine water or medicine tea, **maskekewapoy** (NI); *lite* (NI) *(Northern French Cree)*.

tea bag *litewatsa* (NI) *(Northern French Cree)*.

tea kettle *ka kisakamsamihk* (VTI); tea kettle or teapot, **litewaskihk** (NI) *(Northern French Cree)*; *lite sesipâskihkohk* (NI) *(Northern French Cree)*.

teach *kiskinwahamâkewin* (NI).

teachability *ka nihtâ kiskinwâhamakehk* (VAI).

teachable *awîyak ka nihtâ kiskinwâhamakosit* (VAI).

teacher *okiskinwahamâkew* (NA); a teaching person, **kiskinohamâkewiyiniw** (NA); s/he teaches, **kiskinohamâkew** (VAI).

teacherage *okiskinwahamâkewak wîkiw* (VAI).

teach-in *ka kiskinwahamâkosihk etah kawîkihk* (VAI).

teaching The act of teaching, **kiskinohamâkewin** (NI); the act of teaching oneself, **kiskinohamâsiwin** (NI).

teal *apisicisip* (NA).

team *peyakwahpitew misitatimwak* (NA); *nîswapisowak* (NA); a team, one pair, **peyakwayihk** (NI).

teapot *litewaskihk* (NI) *(French Cree)* .

tear *mâtowinâpoy* (NI); when your eyes are dripping, **ohcikawâpowin** (NI); s/he sheds tears, **ohcikawâpiw** (VAI); tearing up something, *kîkway katatoptamihk*; s/he tears the face off someone from a picture, **kîskihkwenew** (VTI); a torn off piece, **pahkwepicikan** (VII); s/he tears a piece off, **pahkwepitew** (VAI); s/he tears them into pieces, **nanânistipitew** (VTI); s/he tears them with her/his teeth, **pîkwamew** (VTA); s/he is torn by the wind, **pîkwâsiw** (VAI); it is torn by the wind, **pîkwâstan** (VII); s/he tears them apart, **pîkopitew** (VAI); s/he tears her/his clothes, **tâtopitew** (VTI); it is torn, **yâyikipayiw** (VAI); s/he tears them up, **yâyikipitew** (VTI).

teardrop *pâhkawacapowin* (NI); *ohcikawâpiw* (VAI); shedding tears, i.e.: teardrops, *ohcikawâpowin* (NI).

tearful *ka sâkaskinâcapihk* (VAI).

tearless *awîyak ekâ komatowenit* (VAI).

teary *ka kakwâyakimacitwahk* (VTI).

tease The act of teasing, *nanoyatisiwin* (NI); s/he is teasing her/him, *nanoyacihew* (VTA); they are teasing each other, *nanoyacihtowak* (VTA); s/he is teasing, *nanoyatisiw* (VAI).

teaser *ka nanoyatsiskit awîyak* (VAI).

teat Breast, *mitohtôsim* (NA); *tohtôsim* (NA).

tedious *kîkway ka peyahtikowepayik*; it is tiresome, *nestosemâkan* (VII).

teem *kîkway ka ayiwâk askinek* (VAI).

teeny *metoni apisis* (IPC).

teepee *mîkowâhp* (NA); a teepee pole, *apasoy* (NA) *(Plains)*; *apasoyâhtik* (NA) *(Northern)*.

teeter *ka papame ayâhpayihk* (VAI); move back and forth, i.e.: seesaw motion, *cahkaskwahotowin* (NI).

teeth *mîpita* (NI); s/he has several teeth, *mihcetwâpitew* (VAI); s/he snarls and bares her/his teeth to her/him, *siyâpitestawew* (VTA); s/he snarls and bares her/his teeth, *siyâpitew* (VAI); the act of snarling and baring one's teeth, *siyâpitewin* (NI); there is a gap between her/his teeth, *tawâpitew* (VAI); it has spaces between the teeth, i.e.: a harrow, *tastawâpiteyâw* (VII).

teethe The act of teething, *mîpitihkawin* (NI).

tell The act of telling others, *wihtamâkewin* (NI); s/he tells, *wihtam* (VTA); s/he tells a sad story about her/his life, *kwâtakimiw* (VTI); s/he tells evil stories of her/him, *macâcimew* (VTI); s/he tells an evil story, *macâcimow* (VTI); s/he tells a good story or good news, *miyowâcimow* (VTI); s/he tells her/him to hurry, *nanihkimew* (VTA); s/he goes and tell her/him, *nitawitew* (VTA); s/he tells her/him what to do, *oyimew* (VTA) *(Northern)*; *wiyomew* (VTA) *(Plains)*; s/he tells on her/him, *wihtamawew* (VTA); the act of telling on someone, *wihtamowin* (NI); s/he tells others, *wihtamâkew* (VAI); the act of telling each other, *wihtamâtowin* (NI); they told each other, *wihtamâtowak* (VTI).

tellable *kîkway ka wihtamihk* (VTI).

telling *ka wihtamakehk* (VTA); *papâmiwehtam* (VTA).

tellingly *wehtamâkewinihk* (NI).

temper Having a temper, *macihtwâwin* (NI); being tempermental, *watakamisiwin* (NI); s/he has a quick temper, *wahkewiyawesiw* (VAI); the act of being easily riled or being hot tempered, *watakamisiwin* (NI); s/he is hot tempered or easily riled, *watakamisiw* (VAI).

temperate *kîsowâyâw* (VII).

temperament *ka nihtâ kisôwipayihk* (VAI).

tempermental Being highly tempermental, *wahkewisowin* (NI); s/he is highly tempermental or skitterish, *wahkewisiw* (VAI).

temperate *metoni nahiyikohk* (VAI).

temperately *nahiyikohk nawâc* (VAI).

temperature *tansi isikisikak* (VII).

tempered *pîwâpisk ka maskawâpiskisamihk* (VTI).

tempest *ka kestinpayik* (VII); a violent storm, *misimâyikisikâw* (VII).

tempestuous *ka nihtâ mâyikisikâk* (VII).

temporarily *tepîyâhk nome* (IPC).

temporary *aciyaw poko* (IPC); just a little while, *kanakes* (IPC).

temporize *nisihkâc kîkway ka tôtamihk* (VTI).

tempt S/he is tempted, *yeyisiw* (VAI); s/he coaxes her/him to give into temptation, *yeyimew* (VTA); s/he induces or incites her/him, *kaskimew* (VTA).

temptation Tempting someone, *yeyihiwewin* (NI); the act of tempting someone, *sihkiskakewin* (NI); the act of temptation, *yeyisowin* (NI).

tempter *osihkiskâkew* (NA).

tempting *kîkway ka akâwâtamihk* (VAI).

temptress *iskwew ka sihkiskâket* (NA).

ten *mitâtaht* (IPC); ten each, *mamitâtaht* (IPC); ten times, *mitâtahtwâw* (IPC); ten of a kind, *mitâtahtwayih* (IPC); ten different kinds, *mamitâtahtwayih* (IPC); in ten places or ten directions, *mitâtahtwayak* (IPC); in ten different places, *mamitâtahtwayak* (IPC); s/he is number ten or tenth, *mitâtahtowiw* (VAI); it is in tenth place or there is ten of it, *mitâtahtowan*.

ten thousand *mitâtahtwâw kihci mitâtahtomitanaw* (IPC).

tenable *peyak askîy eyikohk takeh miciminamihk kîkway.*

tenacious *sohki ka miciminamihk kîkway* (VTI).

tenacity *sohki miciminikewin* (NI).

Ten Commandments *manito otitasowewina* (NA).

tend *kîkway ka ohci nakateyihtamihk* (VTI); s/he keeps it, *kanaweyihtam* (VTI); *kîkway ka nihtâ ispayik* (VII).

tendency *pîtos ka nihtâ isiwepinkehk* (VAI); s/he has a tendency, *kîsâstaw* (VAI).

tender It is soft, *yoskâw* (VII); it is cooked until tender, *kaskihkahtew* (VTA); it is cooked until tender, *kaskihkasiw* (VTI); promising help to someone, *ka asotamakehk nehsokamakewin* (NI); someone who looks after something, *onâkateyihcikew* (NA).

tenderize *weyâs ka yoskihkasamihk* (VTI).

tenderloin The softest or most tender meat which is found along the spine of an animal, i.e.: tenderloin, *otastisiwak* (NA); the fat on top of the tenderloin of a moose, *osopew* (NA).

tenderness *yoskisiwin* (NI).

447

tendon A big tendon, *misicestatay* (NI); a tendon, *ocestatay* (NI).

tends S/he looks after it, *kanaweyihtam* (VTI).

tense Uptight, *ka sihtamahcihohk* (VAI); s/he feels tense, *sihtamahcihow* (VAI); the act of being tense, *sihtamahcihowin* (NI) *(Plains)*; *sihcîsâyâwin* (NI) *(Northern)*; tense mark in linguistics, past or present, *tansi ka isi oyastahk pîkiskwewin otâhk mekwâc apôh mwestas* (NI).

tension Feeling tense, *sihtamahcihowin* (NI); *kîkway ka sihcîmakahk* (VII); *âyimeyihtam* (VTI).

tensity *sihcîsâyâwin* (NI).

tent A tent made of tarp, *pakwayankamik* (NI); a tent used in the shaking tent ceremony, *kosâpahcikan* (NA).

tentative *awîyak ka nihtanâkatohket* (VAI).

tenth *mwecimitâtaht* (IPC); tenth time, *mitâtahtwâw* (IPC); tenth of the month, *mitâtaht akimâw pîsim*; s/he is the tenth, *mitatahtowiw* (VAI); it is in tenth place, *mitâtahtowan* (VII).

ten thousand *mitâtahtwâw kihci mitâtahtomitanaw* (IPC).

tenuous *kîkway ka sâponôkwahk* (VTI).

tepid *ka kîsowâkamik nepi* (VTA); it is lukewarm, *weyakihkakamow* (VII).

tepidity *kîsowâyâwin* (VTI).

term *tanta ka kisipipayik nîkânîwin; tanekohk* (IPC); when, *tânispe* (IPC); how much, *tânekohk* (IPC).

terminability *awîyak poko ispehweh poyocih* (IPC).

terminable *poko ispeh ka ponipayik* (VII).

terminal *kîkway etah ka nakemakahk* (VTI); that is the end of it, *kisipipayiw* (VII).

terminate *kîkway ka nakinkatek* (VII); s/he leaves it alone, *ponihtaw* (VTI); s/he is all done, *kesihtâw* (VAI).

termination *nakinikewin* (NI).

terminative *kîkway ka nakinsomakahk* (VTI).

terrible *metoni kakwayaki* (VII); *kostateyihtâkwan* (VII).

terribly *metoni ka kakwayaki patahamihk* (VTI).

terrific *nâspic ka miyotôtamihk* (VTI).

terrifically *metoni kîkway ka miyopayik* (VII).

terrified S/he is terrified by the sight of it, *sekâpamiw* (VTI).

terrify *mistahi sekihiwewin* (NI).

terror *metoni ka sekisihk* (VTI); *sekisowin* (NI).

terrifying Her/his behavior is terrifying or scary, *sekihiweskiw* (VAI).

terrorization *papâmi sekihiwewin* (NI).

terrorize *ka papâmi sekihiwehk* (VAI).

terse *nanihkipayowin* (NI).

test The act of testing, *kocihiwewin* (NI); s/he tests her/him, *kocihew* (VTA); s/he tests her/him mentally, *koteyimew* (VTA).

testament A statement from the Bible, an oath, *kihcipikiskwewin* (NI).

testicle *nâpew isihcikasowin* (NI).

tetchy *ka watakamisihk* (VAI).

tether A rope to restrain a grazing animal, *sakahpitastimwakan* (NA).

texture *ayiwinis tansi ka isâyâk* (VII); it has a strong texture, *sohkekan* (VII).

textured *tansi kesihtahk ayiwinsekin* (VII).

than *ispîhci* (IPC).

thank S/he is thankful, *nanâskomow* (VAI); s/he thanks her/him, *nanâskomew* (VTA); s/he is feeling thankful, *nanâskomowakeyimow* (VAI).

thankful Being thankful, *nanâskomowin* (NI); s/he is thankful to have her/him around, *piyaseyimew* (VTA).

thankfully *nanâskomowinihk* (NI).

thankfulness *ka nanâskomowayahk* (VAI).

thankless *na makekway nanâskomowin* (NI); s/he is not thankful, *namoyananâskomow* (VAI).

thank you *kinanâskomitin* (VTA).

Thanksgiving Day *nanaskomôkîsikâw* (VII).

that *nema* (IPC); that one, *anima* (IPC); that one, *eoko* (IPC); that one, *ana* (IPC); that is her/his, *animiyow* (IPC); that one over there, *nema* (IPC); those ones over there, *nehi* (IPC); that one over there is her/his, *nemiyow* (IPC); that's it or that is enough, *ekosi* (IPC); it is s/he, that is the one, *eoko* (IPC); that's the ones, *eokonik*; (relative) that is the things or those things there, *eokoni* (IPC); thus, that is it, true, amen, *ekosi* (IPC); only, it has to be that, of course, naturally, *piko* (IPC); that's why..., so you see, *matcika* (IPC); that way (direction), *nete isi* (IPC); that one over there, *nâha* (IPC).

thaw The ground is thawing, *tihkahcâw* (VII); it is thawing, *saskahcâw* (VII); s/he thaws something with water, *tihkâpawahew* (VTA); it thawed with the aid of water, *tihkâpawew* (VAI); the metal has thawed, *tihkapiskisiw* (VAI); s/he thaws them with her/his hands, *tihkinew* (VAI); it is thawed, *tihkipayiw* (VII); s/he has thawed out, *tihkisiw* (VAI); it has thawed out or defrosted, *tihkitew* (VII) *(Plains)*; it is thawed by the sun, *tihkastew* (VAI); s/he thaws her/him out with body heat, *tikiskawew* (VTA); it thawed out, *tihkitew* (VAI).

theft *kimotiwin* (NI).

their *wiyawâw* (PR).

theirs *wiyawâw ka tepeyihtahkwâw* (IPC); it is theirs, *wiyawâw* (PR).

them *wiyawâw* (PR).

themselves *kitisk wiyawâw* (PR).

then Or at that time, *ekospi* (IPC).

there Over there, *nete* (IPC); *neta* (IPC); there, closer than, *nete* (IPC); *neta* (IPC); there or farther away than, *neta* (IPC); *nete* (IPC); this thing there, *omote* (IPC); that thing over there, *nemaneta* (IPC); that thing there, over there "farther away", *nemanete* (IPC); s/he is there over there, *nahaneta* (IPC); s/he is way over there, i.e.: "farther away", *nahanete* (IPC); "that right there, *ekota* (IPC) *eoko ita* (IPC); right there, i.e.: "a little farther away", *ekoti* (IPC); *eoko ite* (IPC); there s/he is, *awite* (IPC).

therefore So, *mâcika* (IPC); *ewoko ohci* (IPC); as a result, and so it is, *tâsipwâ* (IPC).

these These ones here, *ohi* (IPC); these here [inanimate in Archaic Cree], *oki* (IPC); these things, *okik* (IPC).

they *wiyawâw* (PR).

thick Something that is thick, *kakispakak* (VII); it is thick, *kispakâw* (VII); s/he is frozen thick, refers to ice, *kispakaciw* (VAI); s/hc piles it thick like hay, *kispakastâw* (VAI); it is on thick, *kispakamow* (VAI); it is frozen thick, i.e.: refers to a whole lake or river, *kispakatin* (VII); the hide or blanket is thick, *kispakekan* (VII); the book is thick, *kispakêkihtin* (VII); a thick hide, *kispakekin* (VII); it has a thick hide, i.e.: referring to a cariboo hide, *kispakekinwekisiw* (VAI); s/he has a thick hide, *kispakekinwew* (VAI); it is thick like a beaver hide, *kispakekisiw* (VAI); s/he has a thick roll of bills, *kispakinew* (VAI); s/he makes her/him or it thick, *kispakisîhew* (VTA); being thick, *kispakaw* (NI); s/he is thick, *kispakisiw* (VAI); s/he cuts it thickly, *kispakisiwew* (VTA).

thicken *ka kispakehtahk* (VTI).

thickening *kispakikihcikiwin* (NI) *(Northern)*; *kispakikihcikewin* (NI) *(Plains)*.

thicket A small jungle, *kaskisakâw* (NI); a thicket or a clump of bushes, *piskohkopaw* (NI); a concentration of shrubs or trees, *sakas* (NA).

thickly *kîkway ka kispakastahk* (VTI).

thickness *taneyikohk ka kispakak* (VII).

thick-set *ka kispakayak* (VII); s/he is stout or heavily built, *pitikosiw* (VAI).

thief *awîyak ka kimotit* (VAI); *kimotisk* (NA).

thieve *okimotiw* (NA).

thievery *awîyak kakocet kimotiwin* (NI).

thieves *okimotiskuk* (NA).

thievish *awîyak ka kimotiskewayat* (VAI).

thigh Hind quarter, *mipwâm* (NI); thigh meat, *opwâmowiyâs* (NI).

thighbone *mipwâmikan* (NI).

thin Something thin, *kîkway kapapakâsik* (VII); it is thin, *papakâsin* (VII); s/he is thin or skinny, *sihkaciw* (VAI); s/he makes them thin, *papakisehew* (VTA); s/he is thin, *papakisiw* (VAI); a thin cloth, *papakekinos* (NI) *(Plains)*; *papakekin* (NI) *(Northern)*; it is whittled until thin, *papkisâwâtew* (VII) *(Plains)*; *pakihkotew* (VII) *(Northern)*.

thing *kîkway* (IPC); it is a good and useful thing, *takahkayi* (VII).

think The act of thinking, *mâmitoneyihtamowin* (NI); thinking, *mâmtoneyihcikewin* (NI); when you think, *kamâmitoneyihtamihk* (VAI); I think, *niteyihten* (VTI); s/he thinks of her/him from the past, *asemamitoneyimew* (VTA); s/he thinks in the past, *asemamitoneyitam* (VTI); s/he thinks only of the past, *asemamitoneyicikew* (VTI); s/he thinks of her/him over and over again, *kîhtwamiyimew* (VTA); s/he thinks her/him to be supernaturally gifted, *mamâhtâweyimew* (VTA); s/he thinks s/he has changed, *mâmaskâteyimew* (VTA); s/he thinks about her/him, *mâmitoneyimew* (VTA); s/he thinks about herself/himself, *mâmitoneyimisiw* (VAI); the act of thinking about oneself, *mâmitoneyimisiwin* (NI); s/he thinks about it, *mâmitoneyihtam* (VTI); thinking about sacred notions, *manitoweyitamowin* (NI); s/he thinks of her/him as embodying sacred power or s/he believes her/him to be God, *manitowokeyimew* (VTA); s/he thinks that the divine resides in her/him, *manitowakeyimew* (VTA); the act of holding oneself to be divine, *manitowakeyimowin* (NI); s/he thinks of her/him as embodying the great spirit, *kisemanitoweyimew* (VTA); s/he thinks of herself/himself as the great spirit of God, *kisemanitowakeyimow* (VAI); the act of thinking of oneself as the great spirit or God, *kisemanitowakeyimowin* (NI); s/he thinks her/him or them is/are strong, *maskawisîweyimew* (VAI); the act of positive thinking, *nanakataweyimowin* (NI); s/he has reservations about her/him, *nanihkâteyimew* (VTA); s/he thinks her/him to be a good person, *nâpewakeyimew* (VTA); s/he thinks of herself/himself as a person, *nâpewakeyimow* (VAI); s/he thinks of her/him with bitterness, *kisôweyimew* (VTA); s/he thinks wrongly of her/him, *naspâciteyimew* (VTA); s/he thinks incorrectly, *naspâciteyitam* (VTI); the act of thinking incorrectly, *naspâciteyitamowin* (NI); s/he thinks of her/him ahead or before others, *nîkâneyimew* (VTA); s/he thinks of herself/himself first, *nîkâneyimisiw* (VAI); s/he thinks ahead, *nîkâneyimiw* (VAI); s/he thinks about what s/he is going to have her/him do, *oyeyimew* (VTA); s/he makes her/his mind up about it, *oyeyitam* (VTI); s/he thinks about what s/he is going to do, *oyeyitamasiw* (VAI); s/he thinks s/he is intelligible or easy to understand, *pakaskeyimew* (VAI); thinking something is intelligible, *pakaskeyitamowin* (NI); they constantly have the same ideas or thinking, *tâpitaweyihtamwak* (VTA); they constantly think of each other, *tâpitaweyihtowak* (VTA); s/he thinks of her/him constantly, *tâpitaweyimew* (VTA).

449

thinkable *ka mâmitoneyihtamihk* (VII).

thinking *mâmtoniyihcikewin* (NI); the way someone thinks, *iteyihtamiwin* (NI).

third *mwecinistwâw* (IPC); third time, *nistwâw* (IPC); third of the month, *nisto akimâw pîsim* (IPC).

thirst Being thirsty, *nohteyâpakwewin* (NI); s/he did not give her/him a drink and s/he is dying of thirst, *nipahâpâkwahew* (VTA); s/he is dying of thirst, *nipahâpâkwew* (VAI); the act of dying of thirst, *nipahâpakwewin* (NI).

thirsty Someone who is thirsty, *awîyak ka nohteyapâkwet* (VAI); s/he is thirsty, *nohteyâpakwew* (VAI).

thirteen *nistosâp* (IPC); thirteen times, *nistosâpwâw* (IPC).

thirteenth *mwecinitosâp* (IPC); thirteenth time, *nitosâpwâw* (IPC); thirteenth of the month, *nistosâp akimâw pîsim* (IPC).

thirtieth *mwecinistomitanaw* (IPC); thirtieth time, *nistomitanawâw* (IPC); thirtieth of the month, *nistomitanaw akimâw pîsim* (IPC).

thirty *nistomitanaw* (IPC); thirty times, *nistomitanawâw* (IPC).

this (inanimate), *omah* (IPC); (animate), *awa* (IPC); this one here, *awa* (IPC); *oki* (IPC); relative, *ohi* (IPC); this way, *ota isi* (IPC); *otisi* (IPC); this thing here, *omota* (IPC); this thing there, *omote* (IPC); this way, i.e.: "closer to where you are", *âstamita* (IPC); this one here, *ôma* (IPC); this way or in this manner, *omisiyisi* (IPC); it is like this, *omisi* (IPC).

thistle *kokaminakasiwit, kakasisiwat* (NI).

thistly *ka wâpanâskak* (VII).

thither *ohpime ohci* (IPC).

thong *mâskisinihkan* (NI); *asâmiyâpiy* (NI).

thorn From a rose bush, *okâminakasiy* (NI).

thorny *ka okâminakasiskak* (VII).

thorough *metoni ka ayâhkwatisihk* (VAI); done completely or perfectly, *mitoni kwayask* (IPC).

those Those or my home, *neki* (IPC); those things over there (inanimate), *anihi* (IPC); those (animate), *aniki* (IPC).

thought Having bitter thoughts, *kisôweyihtamowin* (NI); an incorrect thought, *naspâcîteyihcikan* (NI); a different kind of thought, *pîtoteyihtamowin* (NI); her/his thoughts are full of bitterness, *kisôweyitam* (VTI).

thoughtful *awîyak ka mâmtoniyihtahk* (VTI); s/he is a thoughtful person, *kiskisototâkew* (VAI).

thoughtless *ekâ kîkway ka mâmitoneyihtamihk* (VAI); s/he is thoughtless, *namoyakiskisiw* (VAI).

thousand One thousand, *peyakwâw kihci mitâtahtomitanaw* (IPC).

thousandth One thousandth, *mwecipeyakwâw kihci mitâtahtomitanaw* (IPC); thousandth time, *peyakwâw kihci mitâtahtomitanawâw* (IPC).

thrall *awîyak kamanawahkehk* (VAI).

thrash *ka pawahoht kistikan* (VTI); defeat thoroughly, *misinocihiwewin* (NI).

thread *asapap* (NI); a silk thread, *senipânasapâp* (NA); the thread or yarn is strong, *sohkâpekisiw* (VAI); s/he threads them, *tâpisawew* (VTA); s/he threads beads, *tâpisiminew* (VTA); s/he threads or strings beads into a necklace, *tâpisiminihkew* (VAI).

thready *kîkway ka ayapikwatek* (VAI).

threat *asomiwewin* (NI); *macîsotamawew* (NA).

threaten *awîyak ka asomiht* (VTA).

three *nisto* (IPC); three each, *nahnisto* (IPC); three times, *nistwâw* (IPC); three of a kind *nistwayi* (IPC); of three different kinds, *nahnistwayi* (IPC); in three places or three directions, *nistawayak* (IPC); in three different directions, *nahnistawayak* (IPC); in three different ways, *nistwayakisi* (IPC); s/he is number three or third, *nistow* (VAI); there are three of them, *nistinwaw* (VAI); three of them are doing it or working on it, *nistohkamwak* (VAI); there are three against her/him, *nistohkawewak* (VTA); s/he puts them in threes, *nistwahew* (VTA).

threefold *nistwâw* (IPC).

three hundred *nistwâw mitâtahtomitanaw* (IPC).

three thousand *nistwâw kihci mitâtahtomitanaw* (IPC).

Three Wise Men *nisto eyinesew îyinowak* (NA).

thresh *pawahikewin* (NI); s/he separates the grain from the seeds, *pawahikew* (VAI).

threw *kakeh pimosinehk* (VAI).

thrice *nistâw ka ispayik* (VII).

thrift *manamestinikewin* (NI); economical management, *mawacihcikewin* (NI).

thriftless *ekâ ka manamestinikehk* (VAI); s/he spends everything, *mestinikeskiw* (VAI).

thrifty *ka manâcihcikehk* (VAI); s/he collects and saves, *mâwacihcikew* (VAI).

thrill *kîkway ka mocikihikohk* (NI).

thrive *metoni miyopayowin* (NI).

throat A gullet, *mikohtâkan* (NI); the windpipe, *mikohtaskway* (NI).

throated *kihtewewin* (NI).

throaty *ka kihtewehk* (VAI).

throb *ka pâhkahokohk* (VAI); throbbing, *pâhkahokowin* (NI).

through Right through, *sâpo* (NI); s/he passes through any opening, i.e.: a fence, *paspaham* (VTI); s/he gets through them, i.e.: a crowd, *sâponew* (VAI); s/he passes

450

right through them, *sâposkawew* (VTA); s/he makes thcm go right through, *sâpopayihew* (VTA); it passes right through, *sâpopayiw* (VAI); s/he puts the needle right through her/him, *sâpostahew* (VTA); s/he cuts right through her/him, *sâposawatew* (VTA); s/he feels the air or draught coming right through, *sâpoyowew* (VAI); her/his anger rages on or right through the week(s), *sâpoyawesiw* (VAI).

throw The act of throwing, *pimosinewin* (NI); s/he throws, *pimosinew* (VAI); s/he throws it on the floor noisily, *matwesimew* (VAI); s/he kill her/him by throwing her/him, *naspitisimew* (VTA); s/he throws her/him down off something, *nihciwepinew* (VTA); s/he throws her/him down roughly, *pakamisimew* (VTA); s/he throws her/him down on the ice roughly, *pakamiskosimew* (VTA); s/he throws her/him into the water, *pakastawewepinew* (VTA); s/he throws her/him or it over, *pasciwepinew* (VTA); s/he throws her/him in, *pihciwepinew* (VTA); s/he throws something at her/him, i.e.: stones, *pimosinâtew* (VTA); s/he throws her/him or it into the vehicle, *posiwepinew* (VTA); s/he throws her/him right through, *sapowepinew* (VTA); s/he throws it right through on a pole, *sâpwaskopayihtâw* (VTI); s/he throws her/him down on her/his back, *sâsakiciwepinew* (VTA); s/he throws her/him on top of something, *tehciwepinew* (VTA); s/he throws it away for her/him, *wepinamawew* (VTA); s/he throws them away or s/he leaves her/his mate, *wepinew* (VTA); s/he was thrown away or her/his spouse left her/him, *wepinikâsiw* (VAI); it was thrown away, *wepinikâtew* (VTI); s/he throws a punch at her/him, *wepiniskâtew* (VTA); s/he throws a punch, *wepiniskew* (VAI); s/he throws away her/his relationship or s/he leaves her/his spouse, *wepiniskwewew* (VTA); s/he throws herself/himself away, *wepinisiw* (VAI); the act of throwing oneself away or giving up on oneself, *wepinisiwin* (NI); her/his throw falls short of her/him, *nohtâwew* (VTA) *(Plains)*; *nohtehwew* (VTA) *(Northern)*; her/his throw falls short of it, *nohtâham* (VTI) *(Plains)*; *nohteham* (VTI) *(Northern)*; her/his throw falls short of someone, *nohtâhowew* (VTA) *(Plains)*; *nohtehowew* (VTA) *(Northern)*; her/his throw falls short of something, *nohtâhikew* (VTI) *(Plains)*; *nohtehikew* (VTI) *(Northern)*.

thrown Something thrown away, *wepinam* (NI) *(Northern)*; *wepinamowin* (NI) *(Plains)*; *ka wepinamihk* (VTI).

thrust *sohki yahkowepiskakewin* (NI); push forcibly, *yahkiwepinam* (VTI).

thud *ka mistowehtihk kîkway* (VTI); *matwehtin* (VAI).

thumb *awîyak omicihcin* (NA); *micihcan* (NI); *misicihcân* (NI).

thumbnail *micihcinaskasiy* (NI).

thump *kîkway ka kisewehtatâhk* (VAI).

thumping *kisewesimowewin* (NI).

thunder *piyesiwak* (NA); *pihesiwak ka kitotwaw* (NA) *(Northern)*; it thunders, i.e.: the thunderbird's call, *piyesiwok kitowak* (NA) *(Plains)*.

thunderbird *piyisiw* (NA) *(Northern)*; *pihesiw* (NA) *(Plains)*.

thunderbolt *pihesiwak ka paskisiketwâw* (VTA) *(Northern)*; lightening, *waskotepayiw* (NA); *wâsaskotepayiw* (NA).

thunderclap *ka kisewewasaskotepayik* (VII).

thundercloud *ka ministikwaskwak* (NA).

thundering *pihesowak ka kitotwâw* (VAI).

thunderous *ka pimayikisekawnakwahk* (VII).

thundershower *ka sekipestâk* (VII).

thunderstorm *ka misimâyikisikâk* (VII).

thunderstruck *îyikohk emâmaskâtamihk paskâc ekâ kakepekiskwehk*.

Thursday It is Thursday, *newokisikâw* (VII).

thwack *ka napakicicipakamahoht awîyak* (VTA).

thwart *ka pometisahoht awîyak* (VTA).

tick Moose ticks, *mosotihkomak* (NA); *sîsîpewaya* (NA).

tickle Tickling someone, *kwâyakinowewin* (NI); *kîyakinowewin* (NI); s/he tickles her/him, *kwâyakinew* (VTA); *kîyakinew* (VTA).

tickler *kwâyakinikâkan* (NA).

ticklish *awîyak ka kwâyakisiskit* (VAI); s/he is ticklish, *kwâyakisiw* (VAI).

tidbit *kîkway ka wehkasik* (VTI); something very small, *ka apisâsik* (VII).

tidiness *metoni kanâcihiwin* (NI).

tidings *miyo âcimowin* (NI); good news, *miyo âcimowina* (NI).

tidy *kîkway kakanâtahk* (VII); *nahâwinakwan* (VII); *kanâcinakwan* (NI).

tie Tying something, *kâtahkoptamihk* (VAI); s/he ties them in bunches, *mawasakwahpitew* (VAI); s/he ties her/him down, *micimahpitew* (VTA); s/he ties her/his legs together, *nanapwahpitew* (VTA); something used to tie things together, i.e.: a lash, *napwahpicikan* (NI); s/he ties them together, *napwahpitew* (VII); it is tied on a slant, *nawehpitew* (VAI); s/he ties it on a slant, *nawehpitam* (VTI); s/he ties her/him loosely, *nemahpitew* (VTA); s/he ties them in an upright position, *ohpahpitew* (VAI); s/he ties a band around her/his head, *pasistikwanepitew* (VTA); s/he ties a rope around her/him, *paskitahpitew* (VTA); s/he ties her/him around the stomach, *paskitatayehpitew* (VTA); it is tied crooked, *pîmahpitew* (VAI); s/he ties her/him tightly, *sihtahpitew* (VTA); s/he ties a rope around her/him, *tetipahpitew* (VTA); a necktie, *tâpiskâkan* (NI).

451

tied Bound, bandaged, *tahkopisow* (VAI); *tahkopitew* (VTI); bandaged, *akopisow* (VAI); *akopitew* (VTI); solidly tied, *ayatapisow* (VAI); *ayatapitew* (VTI); very tightly bound, *makwahpisiw* (VAI); *makwahpitew* (VTI); tied stuck or impossible to untie, *mecimwâtahpisow* (VAI); *mecimwâtahpitew* (VTI); cold while tied up, *tahkapisow* (VAI); *tahkapitew* (VTI); tied onto a post, tree, etc., *sahkapisiw* (VAI); *sahkapitew* (VTI); tied on top, *tahkohtahpisiw* (VAI); *tahkohtahpitew* (VTI); bridled, i.e.: already on the horse, *tâpitonehpisiw* (VAI); being put on the horse, *tâpitonehpitew* (VTI); s/he is tied securely, *ayâtâhpisiw* (VAI); s/he ties things well, *âyâtâpitew* (VTI); s/he has retied it, *âhtâhpitam* (VTI); s/he is tied onto something, *akwahpisiw* (VAI); it is tied on, *akwahpitew* (VTI); s/he fastens it firmly, *ayâtâhpitew* (VAI); s/he is tied down, *micimapisiw* (VAI); s/he tied her/him up, *tahkopitew* (VTA); s/he is tied up, *tahkopisiw* (VAI).

tight It is tight, *ayâtan* (VII); s/he places it firmly, *ayâtâhew* (VTA); it is stuck on tight, *âyâtamow* (VAI); something that fits tight, *ka sihtahk* (VII); it is tight on her/him, *sihciskam* (VTI); it is a tight fit, *sihcihtin* (VII); s/he makes them tight, *sihcipayihew* (VAI); s/he fits them tightly together, *sihtamohew* (VAI); they are tight fitting, i.e.: gloves, *sihtiskawew* (VTA); they are fitted tightly together or they are crowded together, *sihtiskotatowak* (VAI); the act of being fitted tightly together, *sihtiskotatowin* (NI).

tighten The act of tightening a bolt or nut, *ka sihtahamihk* (NI); it tightens up, *sihcipayiw* (VAI); s/he tightens them, *sihtahwew* (VTA).

till *ka sikwahcahamihk asiskîy* (VTI).

tillage *sikwahcahikewin* (NI).

tilt It sits tilted, *yepestew* (VAI); s/he tilts her/his head to one side for her/him, *naweskweyistawew* (VTA); s/he tilts her/his head to one side, *naweskweyiw* (VAI); the act of tilting one's head to one side, *naweskweyiwin* (NI).

timber *mistikwak ka otinihtwâw* (VTA) *(Northern)*; a cluster of growing trees, *mistikwak* (NA).

timbered *ka mistikoskak* (VII).

time An hour, *tipahikan* (NI); false time, *kakayesitipahikan* (NI); daytime, *kesikawtipahikan* (NI); a long time, *kinwes* (IPC); *kinowes* (IPC); a little time longer, *kinwesis* (IPC); a moment, a short time, *ahciyaw* (IPC); *aciyawpoko* (IPC); a very short time, *ahciyawesis* (IPC); at the same time, two things happening together, *kisik* (IPC); it is for "round about," a long way, time, it's a long, long time, *awînipan* (IPC); events or time goes fast, *kisiskâpayiw* (IPC); each time or every time, *itahtwâw* (IPC); this is just for a short time, *kanak* (IPC); momentarily, *kanakes* (IPC); next time, *kîhtwam* (IPC); a very, very long time,

452

kinweseskamik (IPC); one of these times, *ketahtawe* (IPC); many times, *mihcetwâw* (IPC); expected time or event, *ocihcipayihowin* (NI); time commences or starting time, *ocihcipayow* (VAI); the time of day, *tipahikan* (NI); used as an indication of time, "in a week's time", *ehispayik* (IPC) *(Plains)*; *ihispayik* (IPC) *(Northern)*; for the first time, *ekwayâc* (IPC) *(Plains)*; *ekwayâk* (IPC) *(Northern)*.

timeless *micimwaci* (IPC).

timely *mitonikeswân* (IPC).

times How many times, *tânimatahtwâw* (IPC); many times, *micetwâw* (IPC).

timid *ekâ ka mamsîtotasohk* (VAI); s/he is weak hearted, *nesowitehew* (VAI).

timidity *ekâ mamisîtotasowin* (NI).

timorous *ka nipahitehehk* (VAI).

tinder *kîkway metoni kapastek*; easily ignited material, *nihtâkwahkotew* (VAI).

ting *ka cewehtihk kîkway* (VAI).

tinge *ka pîtosipehikehk* (VAI).

tingle *ka wîyâsamahcihohk* (VAI).

tinkle *ka seweyapiskahamihk* (VAI); it gives forth a short, metallic sound, *matwesin* (VII).

tiny *apisâsin* (VII).

tip When you give someone inside information or a tip-off, *awîyak kanîkân wihtamâket* (VTA); right at the tip or end, *wanaskôc* (IPC); s/he kicks and tips it over, *kotapiwepiskawew* (VTA); the tip or top of a tree or a piece of wood, *wanaskwâhtak* (NA).

tipsy Slightly intoxicated, *kîskwepesow* (VAI); *takahkipewin* (NI).

tiptoe *ka cihcem pîmohcesihk* (VAI).

tiptop *metoni nîkân ka ayâhk* (VII).

tirade *kinwes kîkway ka pîkiskwâtamihk* (VAI).

tire S/he makes her/him tired, *nestohew* (VTA); being tired, *nestosiwin* (NI).

tired The act of being being tired, *nestosiwin* (NI); s/he is tired, *nestosiw* (VAI); s/he is dog tired or her/his muscles are sore, *ayeskosiw* (VAI); s/he is tired of her/him, *kihtimeyimew* (VTA); s/he is tired of it, *kihtimeyihtam* (VTI); s/he is tired from running in deep snow, *nestwâkonâmiw* (VTI); s/he makes her/him tired of being in pain, *nestwapinew* (VTA); s/he is tired from being in the sun, *nestwâsiw* (VAI); s/he is tired from walking in the water, *nestwâtakâw* (VAI); s/he feels tired, *nestomahcihow* (VAI); s/he is tired of telling stories, *tepâcimow* (VAI); the act of being tired of telling stories, *tepâcimowin* (NI); s/he is tired of moving around, *tepahkamikisiw* (VAI); s/he is tired of it or s/he is fed up with it, *tepeyihtam* (VTI); s/he is tired of her/him or s/he is fed up with her/him, *tepeyimew* (VTA); s/he is tired or digusted with her/his actions, *tepeyitâkosiw* (VAI); s/he is tired of hearing her/him, *tepihtawew* (VTA); s/he is tired of speaking to her/him, *tepimew* (VTA).

tireless *awîyak ekâ konestosowenit* (VAI); *namoya wekâc nestosiw* (VAI); s/he has a tireless character, *sîpisiw* (VAI); never tired, *namoya wekac nestosiw* (VAI).

tiresome *pomeyihmohiwewin* (NI); it is tiresome, *saskateyihtakwan* (VII).

titbit *ka apisâsik* (VII).

tithe *ka tipahikehiwehk ayamihewkamkohk* (VAI).

titillate *awîyak ka kiyakiniht* (VTA).

titillation *kîyakinowewin* (NI).

titter *ka papihkâsohk* (VAI).

toad Or bullfrog, *mayokwatay* (NA); *pikwatehtew* (NA).

toady *peyakwan mayokwatay* (NA).

tobacco A large amount of tobacco, *cistemaw* (NA); a little bag of tobacco, *ciscemas* (NA); a machine that cuts up tobacco plugs for use in a pipe, *kaskikocikan* (NI); a piece of tobacco twisted into a roll, *pîminikan* (NI) *(Northern)*; *wiyetinihan* (NI) *(Plains)*.

toboggan *napakâhtik* (NA) *(Plains)*; *napakitâpânâsk* (NA) *(Northern)*.

today *anohc* (IPC).

toddle *ka mâyipemohtehk* (VAI); walk awkwardly, *mâyipimohtewin* (NI).

toe *yehyikisitan* (NI); the end of the foot, *wanaskoscanis* (NI); a big toe, *misisitân* (NI).

toenail *wanaskostanihk maskasiy* (NI).

tog *metawew ayiwinsa* (NI); garments, *ayiwinisa* (NI).

together All at once, altogether, *mâmawi* (IPC); getting together, *mâmawipayiw* (VAI); *mâmawipayin* (VII); at the same time, together, in the same place or spot, *peyakwayak* (IPC); it comes together, *napopayiw* (VAI); s/he puts them together, *napwahew* (VAI).

togetherness *nihtamâmawâyâwin* (NI).

toil S/he toils, *ka sohkatoskehk* (VAI).

toilet *sikewkamik* (NI) *(Northern)*; *nahapiwikamik* (NI) *(Plains)*; an outhouse, *wayawewkamik* (NI); *mesewikamik* (NI).

toilet paper A piece of toilet paper, *kimisahon* (NI) *(Northern)*; *kimisahwakan* (NI) *(Plains)*.

told *awîyak kakeh wihtamaht* (VTA).

tolerable *ka miyonîpawestakehk* (VAI); endurable with patience, *sipeyihtamowin* (NI).

tolerably *miyonîpawestamakewinihk* (VAI).

tolerant *awîyak ka miyohtwat* (VAI).

tolerate *awîyak ka nîpawistaht* (VTA); s/he let go, *pakitinam* (VTI); s/he tolerates the cold well, *sohkaciw* (VAI); *sîpaciw* (VAI).

tomahawk *pakamâtihpehikakan* (NA); a small axe, *cîkahikanis* (NA).

tomato A rosehip, *okiniy* (NI).

tombstone *asinîy kehkwahaskanihk ohci* (NI); a grave stone, *nahinikewasinîy* (NI).

tomorrow *or* **to-morrow** *wâpahki* (IPC); tomorrow morning, *kikisepa* (IPC); day after tomorrow, *awasiwâpahik* (IPC).

tom-tom A drum, *mistikwaskihk* (NA).

tongue *miteyanîy* (NI).

tonight *or* **to-night** *anohc ka tipiskak* (VII); *anohctipiskaki* (VII); tonight, this evening, *otâkosiki* (VII); tonight later than, *otâkosiki* (VII); *tipiskaki* (VII).

tonsil *îyihkos* (NI).

too Too much, *waweyak* (IPC); me too, *nîsta* (PR); you too (singular), *kîsta* (PR); too many, an excessive amount, *osâmahkamik* (IPC); there is a lot of trouble, *osâmahkamikan* (VII); s/he makes too much fuss or overeacts, *osâmahkamikisiw* (VAI); too little, *osâm apisis* (IPC); s/he is one too many, *osâmeyatiw* (VAI); too many, *osâm mihcet* (IPC); too much, *osâm mistahi* (IPC).

took *ka kehotinamihk* (VAI).

tool *âpacihcikan* (NI); a rubbing tool used to soften a hide, *misipocikan* (NI) *(Plains)*; *sinikopocikan* (NI) *(Northern)*; s/he uses a rubbing tool to soften a hide, i.e.: a beaver skin, *misipohew* (VAI) *(Plains)*; *sinikopohew* (VAI) *(Northern)*; s/he uses a rubbing tool to soften a moose hide, *misipohtâw* (VTI) *(Plains)*; *sinikiopohtâw* (VTI) *(Northern)*; s/he uses a rubbing tool to soften a hide, *misipohcikew* (VTI) *(Plains)*; *sinikopohcikew* (VTI) *(Northern)*.

tooling *masinatahikewin* (NI).

toot *tepwepicikewin* (NI); s/he made it toot, *kitôhew* (VAI).

tooth *mîpit* (NI); one tooth, *peyak mîpit* (NI).

toothache When a tooth hurts, *ka wîsakeyihtamihk mîpit* (VAI); s/he has a toothache or s/he has an aching tooth, *tîyâpitew* (VAI); a tooth disease, *mîpitahpinewin* (NI).

toothed *kîkway ka wîpitemakahk* (VAI).

toothless *mestâpitewin* (NI).

top From the top, *tahkohc ohci* (IPC); on the top, *tahkôc* (IPC); on the topside, *takohcayihk* (IPC); it is the summit or top of the hill or mountain, *tahkohtamatin* (VII); on top, *waskic* (IPC); it flows on top, *waskicicowan* (VII); on top of the water, *waskicipek* (VII); s/he walks on top the water, *waskicipekinam* (VTI); it floats on top, *waskicipew* (VAI); s/he places her/him on top, *waskitahew* (VTA); s/he sits on top, *waskitapiw* (VAI); it sits on top, *waskitastew* (VII); when one can walk on top of the snow crust, *waskitatewenikwan* (VII); on top of the earth, *waskitaskamik* (NI); s/he walks on top, i.e.: hard snow, *waskitatewenam* (VTI); the time of year when one can walk on top of the snow crust,

453

waskitateweyâw (VII); s/he walks on top of a thin layer of ice, *wâskitskohtew* (VAI); a children's toy top, *metawakan tihtipipicikan* (NI); s/he tops off the tall tree, *kîskwatanaskahchew* (VAI).

topple *kîkway ka kepipayik* (VII); *kawipayiw* (VAI).

tops *metoni tahkohc* (IPC).

toque *sîpihkiskâwascocinis* (NI) *(Plains)*; *sîstakwastotin* (NI) *(Northern)*.

torch *cakâstenkan* (NI); something burning and it is carried to give light, *wâskotenikan* (NI).

tore It has been torn, *ka kehtâtopitamihk* (VTA); it tore, *tâtopayiw* (VAI).

torment *ka kwatakihiwewin* (NI).

tormentor *or* **tormenter** *okakwatakihiwew* (NA).

tornado A whirlwind, *pastosewan* (VII); a big whirlwind, *misipastosewan* (VII); there is a tornado or whirlwind, *pastosewow* (VII); a huge whirlwind, *misipisistosiwan*.

torrent *ka misikimowâhk* (VAI); it is pouring rain, *sekipestaw* (VII).

torrid *metoni ka yahkwastek* (VII); it is bone dry, *pastew* (VII).

torso *misokânihkisi miyaw* (NI).

tortoise *miskinâhk* (NA).

torture *awîyak ka wîsakahpinet* (VAI).

torturous *wîsakahpinewin* (NI); full of twists and turns, *wâwâkamow* (IPC).

toss Tossing something back and forth, *ka isiwepinamatohk* (VTI).

tot *awâsisis* (NA).

total A total count, *mâmawi akihcikewin* (NI); s/he totals them all up, *tipakimew* (VAI).

totally *mâmawi akihcikewinihk* (NI).

totem The act of making a totem, *masinihkocikewin* (NI); the act of shaping a totem, *ayisiniw wihkocikewin* (NI); a tribal totem figure encountered in the dream world and subsquently becomes a figure representing spiritual power, *powâkan* (NA) *(Northern)*; *pawakan* (NA) *(Plains)*; a post carved and painted, *naspihkocikewin* (NI).

totter *kahkekâc ka kepipayik* (VII); walk or stagger unsteadily, *yayâhpayowin* (NI).

tottery *ayâhpayowin* (NI).

touch The act of touching, *samikewin* (NI); s/he touches her/him with something, i.e.: a stick, *sâmawew* (VTA); s/he touches her/him with her/his body, *sâmiskawew* (VTA).

touched *metoni kotinkohk kîkway* (VII); touched by water, *samipew* (VAI).

touching *kîkway ka kitimâkihtakwâhk* (VTI).

touchy *awîyak ka wahkewsit* (VAI); s/he is very touchy, *wahkewisiw* (VAI).

tough S/he is difficult to handle, *maskawâtisiwin* (NI); something tough, *maskawâw* (VTA); *âyimihiwew* (VAI).

toughen *ka maskâwsehtahk* (VTI).

tow *kîkway ka otâpehk* (VTI); towing something behind, *otâpewin* (NI).

toward *eteh ketohtehk* (VAI).

towards *eteh kesi otiskawastek* (VII); *ekoti isi* (IPC).

towel A towel or material used for drying or wiping something, *pâhkohkwehon* (NI).

towelling *or* **toweling** *ayiwinis pâhkohkwehona ka osihcikatekwaw* (VTI).

tower *iskotewasawapowin* (NI).

towering *metoni ka ispak kîkway* (VII); away up high, aloft, *ispimeskamik* (NI).

towery A tall tree that towers, *ka kinwâskosit mitos* (VAI).

toy A little toy, *mecawakanis* (NI); a big toy, *metawâkan* (NI).

trace *mistatim ocipcikanyapeya* (NA); horse harness, *otâpâniyâpiy* (NI).

traceability *ka nihtâ natonikehk* (VAI).

traceable *awîyak ka wehcasik tanitonaht* (VTA).

tracer *onatonikew* (NA).

tracery *wapamonapisk nanatohk ka isi îyekwatihk* (VAI).

trachea Throat, *mikohtâkan* (NI).

tracing *ka natonaht awîyak tanti kohcet* (VTA); tracing an outline, *masinipehikewin* (NI).

track Railroad tracks, *piwapiskomeskanâw* (NI); the act of making tracks, *ayetiskiwin* (NI); *nametâwin* (NI); s/he tracks over her/his footprints, *mastamew* (VAI); s/he sees that her tracks are on top of her/his tracks, *mastahtew* (VTA); s/he is tracked, *mâtâhâw* (VAI); s/he finds the footprint, track, trace, trail or s/he arrives on a track of someone, *mâtâhew* (VTA); s/he follows her/his tracks or trail, *mitihtew* (VTA); it is a fresh trail or track, *miyânikwan* (VII); s/he sees tracks, *namehew* (VAI); s/he makes fresh and visible tracks, *namehtâw* (VTI); s/he leaves visible tracks, *nameskanawew* (VAI); s/he leaves her/his tracks everywhere, *papâmiskanawew* (VAI); s/he makes fresh tracks in the snow, *paskâkonakew* (VAI); the act of making fresh tracks in the snow, *paskakonakewin* (NI); s/he makes too many tracks, *waniskam* (VTI).

trackless *awîyak ekâ ka nihtâ pimpahtat* (VAI).

tractable *awîyak ka wahkew tâpwehtâhk* (VTI).

tradition *kayâsohci isitwawin* (VII); *âniskotôtamowin* (NI).

traditional *kayâsohci isitwanihk* (NA).

traditionally *tânsi ka kehpi isipîmâtisihk* (VTA).

traditionary *kiseyinew mâmitoneyihtamowin* (NI).

tragedy *mistahi ka mâyahkamkahk* (VTI).

trail A main trail, *meskanaw* (NI); a little trail, *meskanas* (NI); there is road or trail, *meskanaw* (NI); trail leaves water edge to go inland, *kospamow* (NI); there is trail toward water, *nâsipemiw* (VAI).

train A locomotive, *iskotewitâpân* (NA) *(Plains)*; *pîwâpiskomeskanaw* (NA) *(Northern)*.

trait *ka nakacitâhk kîkway* (VTI); a special feature or quality, *isâyâwin* (VII).

traitor *awîyak ekâ kwayask ketatsit* (VAI).

traitorous *ekâ kwayask itâtisowin* (NI).

tramp *awîyak ka papâminatôtamat* (VAI).

trample *kîkway ka mâmâkoskamihk* (VTA); *napakiskam* (VTA); *tahkoskâtam* (VTA).

tranquil *peyahtik ka ayâhk* (VTI); it is calm, *aywâstin* (VII); *kâmwâtan* (VII).

tranquillity *or* **tranquility** *metoni ka kâmwâtahk* (VTI).

transgress *ka pîkonamihk wiyâsowewin* (NI).

transgression *pâstâhowin* (NI).

transgressor *opâstâhow* (NA).

translucency *sâpwâsiwin* (NI)

translucent S/he is translucent, *sâpwâsiw* (VAI); it is translucent, *sâpwâstew* (VII).

transparence *sâponôkosiwin* (NI).

transparency *kîkway ka sâponôkwâhk* (VTI).

transparent Something transparent or something that can be seen right through, *kîkway ka sâpwâstek* (VII); vision through a solid substance, *sâpwâstew* (VII).

trap *wanihikan* (NA); a wooden trap, *mistikowanehikan* (NA); s/he is trapping, *nôcihcikew* (VAI); the act of trapping, *nocihcikewin* (NI); s/he traps muskrat, *notacaskwew* (VTA); s/he traps bear, *nôtaskwew* (VTA); s/he caught it in a trap, *tasôhew* (VTA); s/he is caught in a trap, *tasôsiw* (VAI); it is caught in a trap, *tasôtew* (VTI); s/he sets a trap for her/him, *wanihikamawew* (VTA); s/he sets traps, *wanihikew* (VAI).

trapline *nôcihcikeskanâw* (NA).

trapped *tasôsiw* (VAI).

trapper *onôcihcikew* (NA).

trash *ekâ ka apatahk kîkway* (VTI); house refuse, garbage, *macikwanasa* (NI).

travel The act of travelling everywhere, *ka papâmohtehk* (VTI); s/he travels all over the place, i.e.: on horseback, *papâmipayiw* (VAI).

travelled *or* **traveled** *awîyak mistahi kakeh papâmohtet* (VAI).

traveller *or* **traveler** A person who travels from place to place, *opapâmohtew* (NA).

traverse *miskanaw ka wâwâkamok* (VII); pass across, over, or through, *sâpohtewin* (NI).

treacherous *ka kostâtikwahk kîkway* (VTI); it is treacherous, *ka kwespanatan* (VII).

treachery *ka kayesowin* (NI).

tread *papeyahtik pimohtewin* (NI).

treat How you treat someone, *tansi ka isi pamihiht awîyak* (VTA); s/he treats her/him that way, *itôtawew* (VTA); s/he treats her/him as a stranger, s/he treats her/him as odd, *ayahteyimew* (VTA); s/he sees her/him as an outsider, *ayahcinawew* (VTA); s/he does not like her/him or treats her/him like an outcast, *ayahteyimew* (VTA); s/he is being treated poorly, *kitimahâw* (VAI); s/he treats her/him poorly, *kitimahew* (VTA); s/he treats herself/himself poorly, *kitimahisiw* (VTA); the act of treating one's self poorly, *kitimahisowin* (NI); s/he treats her/him badly, *mayitôtawew* (VTA); s/he treats her/him like an aboriginal person, *nehiyawitôtawew* (VTA); s/he treats her/him with disrespect or s/he abuses her/him, *pîwihew* (VTA); s/he treats herself/himself disrespectfully, *pîwihiw* (VAI).

treatment *tansi ka isipaminowehk* (VAI); medicine or remedy, *nâtawihowin* (NI).

tree Poplar tree, *mîtos* (NA); spruce, *sihta* (NA); long tree, *kinowaskosiw* (VAI); long pole, *kinoweskwan* (VII); tree solidly planted or hard to pull out, *ayâtaskisiw* (VAI); pole solidly planted, *ayâtaskitew* (VII); hardwood, *maskawâhtik* (NA); it is hardwood, *maskawâskwan* (VII); round tree, *notimâskosiw* (VAI); round pole, *notimâskwan* (VII); it is a narrow strip of wood, *sâkawâskosiw* (VAI); *sâkawâskwan* (VII); light tree, not heavy, *yahkâskosiw* (VAI); light pole, *yahkâskwan* (VII); soft tree, *yoskahtik* (NA); soft pole, *yoskâskwan* (NI); short tree, *cimaskosiw* (VAI); short pole, *cimaskwan* (VII); crooked or bent tree, *wâkâskisiw* (VAI); crooked or bent pole, *wakâskwan* (VII); there are clumps of shrubs, *ayapâskweyâw* (NA); there is lots of wood or plenty of trees, *ayapahtakâw* (NA); green tree, *askâhtik* (NA); a poorly formed tree, *mayâhtik* (NA); a crooked tree, *mayâkisiw* (VAI); a young or new tree, *oskihtak* (NA); a twisted tree, *pîmâhtik* (NA); a dried out tree with the top broken off, *cimanaskwatohtak* (NA); a growth of trees angling across the prairie to provide a wind break, *pîmâskweyâw* (NI); a tall tree that is topped off, *piskwatanaskahikan* (NA); under the tree, *sîpayahtik* (NA); a vast expanse of sparely growing trees, *sîpiyâw* (NI).

tree line *iskwahtakâhk* (NI).

treetop *wanaskwatanask* (NI).

trek *sehci pihkohowin* (NI).

tremble *ka nampayihk* (VAI); *nanampayiw* (VAI).

tremendous *kîkway ka kakwayaki ispehcak* (VII); *kostateyihtâkwan* (NI); *ayiwâkeyihtakwan* (NI); it looks tremendous in size, *kostâsinâkwan* (VII).

tremor The ground trembles, *nanamahcipayiw* (IPC) *(Northern)*; *nanamaskipiyiw* (IPC) *(Plains)*.

455

tremulous *mistahi ka nanamipayihk* (VTI); trembling or unsteady, *nanamipayowin* (NI) *(Plains)*; *koskoskopayowin* (NI) *(Northern)*.

trenchancy *metoni ka iyinisihk* (VTI).

trenchant *iyinisowin* (NI).

trepidation *nawâc poko ka astasihk* (VTI).

tribal *peyakwayih ayisiyinowak* (NA).

tribalism *peyakoskânowin* (NI).

tribalize *ka peyakoskânehiwehk* (VAI).

tribally *peyakoskânowenihk ohci* (NI).

tribe *ka peyakoskânowihk* (VTA); *peyakoskan nehiyawak* (NA).

tribesmen *opeyakoskânesowak* (NA).

tribulation *ka kwâtakihtâwin* (NI); a state cause or instance of suffering, *kwâtakihisowin* (NI).

tributary A creek emptying into a river, *sîpîsis kamâtawsicowahk mistahi sîpihk* (VTA); a branch or fork off a river, i.e.: a tributary, *paskehtin* (VAI); a river that flows into another body of water, *kamatâwsihtihk* (NI).

tribute *miyotôtâkewin* (NI).

trick Playing tricks on someone, *ka wiyasihkamakehk* (VAI); the act of cheating, *wayesihtwâwin* (NI); s/he is playing tricks on others, *wâwiyatisihkew* (VAI).

trickery *wâwiyatisihkewin* (NI); an act of deception, *wayesihiwewin* (NI).

trickle *ketisk ka paspicowasik* (VII); *pimiciwasin* (VII).

trickster *awîyak ka wiyasihkamaket* (VAI); the Cree culture hero and the object of many legends and tales, *wîsahkecâhk* (NA).

tricky *kanihtâ wiyasihkamakehk* (VAI).

tried *awîyak kakehkocet* (VAI).

trifle *metoni apisis kîkway* (VII); something trivial or insignificant, *apiscisehcikanis* (NI).

trifling *kwanta otamiyowin* (NI).

trigger *tahtapiskipicikan* (NI); a trigger on a gun, *tahtapiskinikan* (NI).

trill *ka cistâwehtakosihk* (VAI).

trim *ka kwayaskosâwâtek kîkway* (VTI); *kwayaskosâwâtam* (VTI).

trimmer *kwayaskosâwâcikan* (NI).

trip A holiday, *sipwehtewin* (NI); s/he makes double trips to get her/his possessions, *âhâcinâcikew* (VAI); s/he stumbles, *piswacahikew* (VAI); s/he trips and falls, *cahkatahikew* (VAI); s/he trips over her/him, *piswahwew* (VTA).

tripe The stomach of a cow or moose, *omâw* (NI).

triplets Three babies, *nistôtewak* (NA).

triply *nistwayakihowin* (NI).

tripper *pakiciwepiskâcikan* (NI).

tripping *piswahcahikewin* (NI).

trite *kîkway ka sîwihtik* (VII).

triumph *paskeyâkewin* (NI); a victory, *sakohtwawin* (NI).

triumphal *ka môcikeyihtamihk paskeyâkewin* (NI).

triumphant *ka miyomahcihohk paskiyakewnihk* (VII).

trivial *kîkway ekâ mistahi kespehteyihtakwahk* (VTI); something trivial, *apisis kîkway* (IPC).

triviality *kwanta apisis kîkway kespayisik* (VII).

trod *mosci pîmohtewin* (NI).

trodden *ka kistatahamihk meskanaw* (VTI).

troll Fishing with a moving boat, *kwâskwepicikewin* (NI).

trot *ka kisiskahtehk* (VAI).

troth *ka natomiskwewehk* (VAI).

trotter *pimpatawatim* (NA).

trouble Having problems, *mâyipayiwin* (NI); *âyimipayiwin* (NI); s/he gets her/him into trouble, *misihew* (VAI).

troublemaker *omâyipayihiwew* (NA); s/he gives people a hard time or s/he is a trouble-maker, *âyimihiwew* (VAI).

troublemaking *mâyipayihiwewin* (NI).

troublesome *mâyipayihcikesk* (VII); s/he is causing trouble, *âyimihtasiw* (VAI).

trounce *paskiyakewin* (NI).

trouncing S/he defeats her/him decisively, *misinocihew* (VTA).

trousers *mitâs* (NA).

trout A lake trout, *namekos* (NA).

trudge *wahyaw isi môstohtewin* (NI); walking laboriously or wearily, *sihci pimohtewin* (NI).

true *kîkway ka tâpwemâkahk* (VTI); *tapwe* (IPC); it is true, thus, that's it, true, amen, *ekosi* (IPC); true enough, of course, naturally, *manimâka* (IPC).

truelove *tapwe sâkihiwewin* (NI).

truly *metoni tapwe* (IPC); *tâpwepokwâni* (IPC).

trust Someone very trust worthy, *awîyak metoni kamamisîhk* (VAI); trusting someone, *mamisîwin* (NI); s/he considers her/him to be trustworthy or s/he has the utmost confidence in her/him, *mamisîwakeyimew* (VTA); the act of trusting someone, *mamisîtotâkewin* (NI); s/he trusts her/him, *mamisîtotawew* (VTA); s/he trusts someone, *mamisîw* (VAI); trust, *mamisîwin* (NI).

trustful *mamisîtotâkewin* (NI); a real trustful person, *metoni kamamisîhk awîyâk* (VTA).

trusting *mamisîtotâtowin* (NI); *mamisîwakeyimew* (VTA).

trusty *sohki mamisîwin* (NI).

truth The act of telling the truth, *tapwewin* (NI); it tells the truth, *tâpwemakan* (VTI); s/he tells the truth, *tâpwew* (VAI); something that tells the truth, *tâpwewiniwiw* (VAI).

456

try Trying something, ***kakocihk kîkway*** (VTI); trying or a determined effort, ***kakwe*** (IPC); s/he tries or tests her/him or it, ***kocihew*** (VTA); s/he tries to sing, ***kocinikamow*** (VAI); s/he tries to speak, ***kocipîkiskwew*** (VAI); an attempt to talk, ***kocipîkiskwewin*** (NI); s/he tries it on, i.e.: a stocking, pants, or glove, ***kociskawew*** (VTA); s/he tries or attempts to do something, ***kociw*** (VAI); an act of trying or an attempt, ***kociwin*** (NI).

tub A wash tub, ***mahkahk*** (NI).

tubby ***awîyak ka mistikamot*** (VAI).

tuck ***kiso akwanahiwewin*** (NI); ***kawsimohew*** (VTA).

Tuesday It is Tuesday, ***niso kisikâw*** (VII).

tufted ***asahpicekewina*** (NI).

tug ***kotapîhk*** (VTI).

tumble ***ka tihtipâkocinihk*** (VAI).

tumult ***mâmawetepwewin*** (NI); the uproar or shouting of a crowd, ***mâmawisakowewin*** (NI).

tumultuous ***mihcet ayisiyinowak ka mâmawi kisôtepwetwaw.***

turbid A clouded or muddy liquid, ***pekakamow*** (VAI).

turfy ***wepinikewin*** (NI).

turkey ***onawakohtew*** (NA); ***misihew*** (NA).

turmoil Being annoying, ***mikoskâtisiwin*** (NI).

turn ***ka wasakânamihk kîkway*** (VTA); s/he turn, ***waskîw*** (VAI); ***kweskimeskocipayiw*** (VAI); ***kweskîw*** (VAI); it turns over in the water, i.e.: canoe or raft, ***kotapîw*** (VAI); repetitive, one after the other, in turn, the next taking the place of the first, ***mâmeskôc*** (IPC); s/he turns her/him over while s/he is in a boat, ***kwatapinew*** (VTA) *(Plains)*; ***kotapinew*** (VTA) *(Northern)*; s/he turns the boat over, ***kwatapinam*** (VTA) *(Plains)*; ***kotapinam*** (VTA) *(Northern)*; s/he turns someone over in a boat; s/he turns over, ***kwatapiniwew*** (VTA) *(Plains)*; ***kotapiniwew*** (VTA) *(Northern)*.

turnaround ***kweskîwin*** (NI); ***kweskîw*** (VAI).

turning ***tehtipisin*** (VAI); ***tehtipihtin*** (VAI).

turnip ***otisihkân*** (NI).

turtle ***miskinâhk*** (NA).

tusk A large sized tooth, ***mahkâpit*** (NI).

tustle A small fight or scuffle, ***nôtinicowinis*** (NI).

twaddle ***mamâyipimohtewin*** (NI).

twang ***ka sîweyapiskihtcikehk*** (VAI).

tweak ***ka pîmâseniht awîyak*** (VTA); pinch and twist the skin, ***pîmâsenew*** (VAI).

twelfth ***mwecinîsosâp*** (IPC); twelfth time, ***nîsosâpwâw*** (IPC); twelfth of the month, ***nîsosâp akimâw pîsim.***

twelve ***nîsosâp*** (IPC); twelve times, ***nîsosâpwâw*** (IPC).

twentieth ***mwecinîstanaw*** (IPC); twentieth time, ***nîstanawâw*** (IPC); twentieth of the month, ***nîstanaw akimâw pîsim***; s/he is the twentieth, ***nîstanawiw*** (VAI).

twenty ***nîstanaw*** (IPC); twenty times, ***nîstanowâw*** (IPC).

twenty-five ***nîstanaw nîyânanosâp*** (IPC).

twenty-five cents One quarter, ***peyak sônîyâs*** (NA).

twice ***nîswâw*** (IPC); twice each, ***nahnîswâw*** (IPC).

twiddle ***ka metawâkehk miskihcâna*** (VTI).

twig ***watihkwanis*** (NI).

twilight ***katewaninakwâhk*** (VII); coming daylight, ***pîwâpan*** (VII).

twin ***nîsôtew*** (NA); s/he is a twin to her/him, ***nîsôteskawew*** (VTA); they are twins, ***nîsôtewiwak*** (NA).

twinge ***ka wisakamahcihohk*** (VTI); ***mosihtâwin*** (NI); ***wîsakipayiw*** (VAI).

twinkle ***acahkos ka kihkâyâsawet*** (VAI); ***papasahkapow*** (VAI); sparkle with amusement, ***môcikapisin*** (VII); chirp excitedly, ***kîskwehtakosiw*** (VAI).

twinkling ***acahkosak ka kihkâyâsawetwâw*** (VAI).

twins A set of twins, ***nîsotewak*** (NA).

twirl ***miscikôsa ka wâsakâ wepinamihk*** (VTI).

twist Doing a certain dance, ***ka wahwâkipayihohk*** (VAI); it is twisted out of shape, ***pîmâpiskisiw*** (VAI); s/he twists her/his neck off, ***pîmikwenew*** (VAI); s/he twists or turns her/him, ***pîminew*** (VTA); s/he twists her/his own neck, ***pîmiskweyiw*** (VAI); s/he twists her/his head all around, ***yâyiskwenew*** (VTA).

twit ***onanweyacimiwew*** (NA).

twitch S/he twitches, ***cehcepipayow*** (VAI).

two ***nîso*** (IPC); two each, ***nahnîsow*** (IPC); two times, ***nîswâw*** (IPC); two of a kind, ***nîsôskân*** (NA); two different kinds, ***nîswayi*** (IPC); in two places or two directions, ***nîswayak*** (IPC); two in each place, ***nahnîswayak*** (IPC); s/he is number two or second, ***nîsow*** (VAI); s/he is two winters old, ***nîsowpiponwew*** (VAI); two people in a canoe, ***nîsohkamwak*** (NA); material for two pairs of moccasins or shoes, ***nîsôskisin*** (NI); s/he is gone for two nights, ***nîsotipiskwew*** (VAI); s/he takes on two people, ***nîsohkawew*** (VTA); he has two wives, ***nîsôskwewew*** (VTA); there are two of them, ***nîsowak*** (NA).

two hundred ***nîswâw mitâtahtomitanaw*** (IPC).

two million ***nîswâw kisipakihtasowin*** (IPC).

two thousand ***nîswâw kihci mitâtahtomitanaw*** (IPC).

457

U

udder *mitohtôsim* (NA).

ugly Being ugly, *mâyâtisiwin* (NI); s/he is ugly, *mâyâtisiw* (VAI); it is ugly, *mâyâtan* (VTI).

Ukrainian A Ukrainian person, *opîtatowew* (NA); being a Ukrainian, *opîtatowewiwin* (NI).

ultimate *ka kisipipayik kîkway* (VII); being the last of a series, *iskwayâc* (IPC).

ultra *namoya ayîwak isi; wawîyak mistahi.*

umbilicus *misiwakan.*

un- *ekâ* (IPC).

unable *ekâ ka kâskihtahk* (VAI).

unaccompanied *peyakowin* (NI).

unaccustomed *ekâ ka nakacihtâhk* (VAI); s/he is not acquainted, *namoyanakayâskam* (VAI).

unadvised *awîyak ekâ ka wihtamaht* (VAI); s/he is not told, *namoya wihtamawâw* (VAI).

unadvisedly *ekâ wihtamowinihk* (LN).

unaffected *ekâ ka mâmahcihikohk* (VAI); nothing will happen to her/him, *namoyanânitâw ispayiw* (VAI).

unaffected *ekâ ka mamahteyihtamohikohk* (VAI).

unanswerable *ekâ kakeh naskwewasimotôtamihk* (VII).

unanswered *ekâ ka naskwewasimohk* (VAI).

unapproachable *namoya takeh nâtâmototamihk* (VTI).

unapt *ekâ ka nihtâweyihtamihk* (VII).

unassuming *ekâ ka iteyihtakwahk* (VII).

unattached Unmarried, *môsâpewiwin* (NI).

unattended *peyakwaskasowewin* (NI).

unavoidable *ekâ kakeh wemâskamihk*; it is hard to leave, *âyiman tanakâtamihk.*

unavoidably *ekâ wemâskakewnihk* (LN).

unaware *ekâ ka moyesihk* (VII); s/he does not know, *namoya kiskiyitam* (VAI).

unawares *weskawâhiwewin* (NI).

unbaked *ka askitepohk* (VAI).

unbalance *eka metoni kwayask* (IPC).

unbearable *ekâ kakeh nîpawistamihk* (VAI).

unbeaten *awîyak ekâ wihkâc ka paskeyaht* (VAI).

unbecoming *ekâ kwayask isâyâwin* (NI); it looks bad, *mâyinâkwan* (VII).

unbelief *ekâ ka tapwehtamihk* (VAI).

unbeliever *awîyak ka ânwehtaskit* (VAI).

unbelieving *ânwehtamowin* (NI).

unbend *ka kwayaskonamihk.*

unbending *kwayaskonikewin* (NI).

unbent *kîkway ka tasonamihk* (VTI).

unbidden *ekâ ka tepwatamihk tepwacikewnihk* (VTI).

unbind *ka apihkonkehk* (VAI).

unblemished *ka kwayask kwâscikehk.*

unblessed *ekâ ka saweyihcikatek* (VTI) *or* (VII).

unblushing *ekâ nipewisiwin* (NI).

unbolt *ka yohtenamihk iskwâhtem* (VTI).

unbolted *yohti apiskahikewin* (NI).

unbonneted *ka mosestikwanehk* (VAI).

unbounded *ekâ ka kisipipâyik kîkway* (VII).

unbowed *ekâ ka sâkohikohk kîkway* (VTI).

unbraid *mistakayah ka apihkamihk* (VTI).

unbridled *ekâ tâpitonehpicikan ka âpacitat mistatim* (VAI).

unbroken *ekâ ka pîkonikatek* (VTI).

unbuckle *ka tasinamihk pakwahtehon* (VTI); s/he unbuckles it, *tahtinam* (VTI).

unburden *ketowateniwewin* (NI); *awîyak ka ketowateniht.*

unbutton *ka tasinihtwâw aniskamanak* (VTI).

uncanny *waneyihtamisayawin* (NI).

uncap *ka ketastotineniht awîyak.*

uncaringly *kwanta mâmâsîsihkewin* (NI).

unceremonious *ekâ ka tataspeyihtamihk.*

uncertain *ekâ kakeh cinahohk* (VAI); s/he is not sure, *namoya kehcinâhow* (VAI).

uncertainly *ekâ kehcinâhowenihk* (VII).

uncertainty *kîkway ekâ kakehcinâhohk.*

unchain *ka âpahamihk sâkapihkan*; s/he unchains it, *tasipitam* (VTI).

unchangeable *ekâ kakeh meskotascikehk* (VTI).

unchanged *ekâ pîtos kespayihcikehk* (VII).

uncharted *ka nakinamâkehk kîkway.*

unchaste S/he is unchaste, *pisikwâtisiw* (VTA); it is unchaste, *pisikwâtan* (VTI); an unchaste person, i.e.: a rake, *pisikwâciyiniw* (NA).

unclad *ketayowinisewin* (NI).

unclasp *ka tasinamihk kîkway* (VTI).

uncle My father's brother or paternal uncle, *nôhkômis* (NA); *nipâpâsis* (NA); *nôhcâwîs* (NA); my mother's brother or maternal uncle (or father-in-law), *nisis* (NA); your uncle, *kocawîs* (NA); *kisis* (NA); someone's father's brother, *awîyak ohkomisa* (NA); *awîyak opâpâsisa* (NA); *awîyak ohcawisa* (NA); someone's mother's brother, *osisa* (NA).

unclean *ekâ ka kanâtahk* (VTI); *wepatan* (VTI).

uncleanly *ekâ kwayask kanâcihcikewin* (NI).

unclench *ka tasonamihk micihciya* (VTI).

uncloak *ka kecikonamihk akwanahon* (VTI).

unclothe *ketayiwinsewin* (NI); s/he takes her/his clothes off, *ketayowinisew* (VAI).

uncoil *ka taswâpihkenamihk* (VTI).

uncomfortable *ekâ ka nahayahk* (VAI); s/he feels awful, *kwâtaki macihiw* (VAI).

uncomfortably *ekâ nahayawinihk* (VII).

459

uncommitted *ekâ kopîkiskwewnihk* (VII).

uncommon *ekâ mwasi kespayik* (IPC); not often, *namoya mwasi* (IPC).

uncommonly *kîkway ekâ katawahk kespayik* (VII).

uncommunicative *ekâ ka nihtâ pîkiskwasowehk* (VAI).

uncompromising *ekâ kakwayaskiw sehcikewnihk* (VII).

unconcern *ekâ nâkateyihcikewin* (NI).

unconcerned *ekâ ka nâkateyihtamihk* (VAI); s/he is disrespectful, *namoya nâkatohkew* (VAI).

unconcernedly *sôskwâc poko isi ka tôtamihk* (VAI).

unconditioned *ekâ kwayaskâstek* (VTI).

unconquerable *ekâ kakeh paskeyâtamihk* (VTI).

unconscious Being out of one's mind, *katikinehk* (VAI); s/he knocked her/him unconscious, *cakahkwewepahwew* (VTA); s/he does not think or s/he is out of her/his mind, *namoyamâmitoneyihtam* (VAI).

unconsciousness The state of being out of one's mind, i.e.: unconsciousness, *tikinewin* (NI) *(Northern)*; *waneyihtamowin* (NI) *(Plains)*.

uncork *ka yohtehamihk môteyâpisk* (VTI).

uncounted *ekâ ka akihtamihk* (VII).

uncouth *ka mâmayehk* (VAI).

uncover S/he is uncovered or s/he becomes visible, *mosisepayiw* (VAI); s/he uncovers it or makes it visible, *mosepitam* (VTI); s/he uncovers herself/himself, i.e.: throws off the blankets, *pâskîw* (VAI); the act of uncovering, *pâskîwin* (NI); s/he opens or uncovers it for her/him, *pâskinamawew* (VTA); s/he opens or uncovers them, *pâskinew* (VTA).

undaunted *ekâ kîkway ka sîtostamihk* (VII).

undeceive *ka poni wayesihiwehk* (VAI).

undecided *ekâ kakeh kîseyihtamihk* (VAI); s/he can not make up her/his mind, *wâneyihtam* (VAI).

undefined *ekâ kwayask ka kiskinwahikehk* (VAI).

undeniable *namoya takeh ânwehtamihk* (VII).

undeniably *ekâ ânwehtamowenihk* (LN).

under *sepa* (LN); falls over under a load, *kawiskosiw* (VAI); *kawiskotew* (VAI); breaks in two under a load, *nâtwâskosiw* (VAI); *nâtwâskotêw* (VAI); bends under a load, *nawakeskosiw* (VAI); *nawakeskotew* (VAI); breaks, broken under a load, *pikoskosiw* (VAI); *pikoskotew* (VAI); s/he is or passes under, *sîpâsîw* (VAI); under, underneath, *sîpâyik* (LN).

underarm *mitihkôkanihk* (VII).

underbelly *sîpâmatâhk* (VII).

underbrush *kaskisâkâhk* (VII); a thick underbrush, *kaskisâkâw* (VII).

underclothes *atâmayiwinisa* (NI); clothes in between your skin and top clothes, *pehtawayowinisa* (NI).

undercoat *atamihk miskotâkay* (NI).

undercover *kîmôc isihcikewin* (NI).

undercurrent An undercurrent in a stream, *môhkicowanipek* (NI).

underdone *ekâ metoni ka kesihtahk* (VAI) or (VTI).

underfeed Underfeeding someone, *nohtaw asahkewin* (NI); s/he underfeeds her/him, *nohtâskohew* (VTA); her/his appetite isn't fullfilled, *nohtaskoyiw* (VAI).

underfoot *sîpa mesitihk* (LN).

undergarment *pehtawayiwinis* (NI); a pair of underwear, *pehtawayowinsa* (NI); s/he puts on or wears an undergarment, *postiskawew* (VTI) *(Plains)*; *pihtoskawew* (VTI) *(Northern)*.

undergo *ka tôtamihk kîkway* (VTI).

undergone *kîkway kakeh tôtamihk* (VTI).

underground *atâmaskehk* (VII); in the underworld, *atâmaskamik* (LN).

undergrowth *oskipemakosa* (NI); thick undergrowth, *sakipemakaw*.

underhand *kîmôtatsowin* (NI); *kîmôc* (IPC).

underhanded Underhanded action, *awîyak kakîmôtatsit* (VAI); a sneaky fight, *kîmahpinatew* (VTA).

underhung *kîkway sîpa ka akotek* (VTI).

underlie *sîpa kohsetwastahk* (VAI).

undermine *ayahikewin* (NI); *atâmaskamikohk* (LN); s/he undermines something, *kîmôcihtâw* (VTI).

undermost *mawaci etamihk* (IPC).

underneath Way under, *metoni itâmihk* (LN); *atâmihk* (LN); under, *sîpâ* (LN); underneath something, *sekwayihk* (LN).

undernourish *ekâ kwayask ka metisohk* (VII).

undernourished *awîyak ekâ kwayask ka metisot* (VAI).

undernourishment *ekâ kwayask asahkewin* (NI).

undershirt *etamihk pakowayan* (NI); an undershirt, *pihtawepakowayan* (NI).

underside *sîpa ohci* (LN).

undersized *nawâc poko ka apsasisik* (VII).

underskirt A slip or petticoat, *pihtawesâkân* (NI).

understand The act of understanding, *nisitohtamowin* (NI); s/he understands her/him correctly or perfectly, *kwayaskohtawew* (VTA); s/he makes her/him understand correctly or perfectly, *kwayaskweyihtamohew* (VTA); s/he understands it, *nistohtam* (VTI); s/he makes her/him understand, *nistotamohew* (VTA); s/he understands her/him, *nistohtawew* (VTA).

understandable S/he is understandable, *nistohtâkosiw* (VTA); it is understandable, *nistohtâkwan* (VII).

understanding *awîyak kanisitohtahk* (VAI); a mutual understanding, *kwayaskohtowin* (NI).

understood *kîkway ka nisitohtamihk* (VII).

undertake *ka wehtôtamihk kîkway* (VTI).

460

underwear A man's underpants, i.e.: long johns or underwear, ***pehtawetâsân*** (NA); underclothes, ***pehtawayowinisa*** (NI).

underweight *nohtâw kosikwatiwin* (NI).

underworld In the underworld, *atâmaskamik* (LN).

undesirable *metoni âtaweyihcikan* (NA).

undeveloped *namoya kesihcikewin* (NI).

undisciplined *ekâ kwayask kohpikihawasohk* (VAI).

undisguised *ekâ ka wansihohk* (VTI).

undisputed *kîkway ekâ ka pikiskwâtamihk* (VAI).

undo *ka apihkonamihk kîkway; apihkona* (VTI).

undoubted *namakîkway ânwehtamowin* (NI).

undoubtedly *namoya ânwehtamowenihk isi* (LN).

undress *ketayewinsewin* (NI); s/he takes clothes off, ***ketayowinsew*** (VTA).

unduly *kakwah citôtamihk kîkway* (VTI).

undying *ekâ wihkâc ka nipemakahk* (VII).

unearned *ekâ kakîspinatamihk* (VTI).

unearthly *namoya ôma askiy ohci kîkway* (VII).

uneasy *ekâ kwayask kesâyahk* (VAI); *mikoskâteyitam* (VAI).

unequal *ekâ pahpeyakwan* (VII); all different, ***pahpitos*** (IPC).

unequalled *or* **unequaled** *awîyak ekâ kakeh tipihiht* (VAI).

unerring *metoni kehcinâhowin* (NI).

unessential *ekâ kehcina ka âpatahk* (VII).

uneven When it is not the same, *ekâ pahpeyakwan* (VII); it has an uneven or rough surface, ***pipikosiw*** (VTA); it is uneven or rough ground, ***pipikwahcâw*** (VII); it has a rough or uneven surface, ***pipikwâw*** (VII).

uneventful *ekâ kîkway ketahkamkahk* (VII).

unexceptional *ekâ kwanta ayîwak isihcikewin* (NI).

unexpected *ekâ kâ ihtateyihtamihk* (VII); *ketahtawe* (IPC); all of a sudden, *sisikôc* (IPC).

unexpectedly *metoni sisikôc* (IPC); suddenly, unexpectedly, *sisikôc* (IPC).

unfailing *ekâ wihkâc ka patahamihk* (VAI).

unfailingly *kâkike kâkwayaskopayik* (VII).

unfair *ekâ kwayask ka tôtakehk* (VAI); *namoya kwayask* (IPC); *wanitôtam* (VAI).

unfaithful Deceitful, *kayesowin* (NI); s/he is crooked, *kayesiw* (VAI).

unfamiliar *ekâ ka nakayâskamihk* (VAI); you never know what to expect, *namoya kiskeyitâkwan* (VII).

unfasten *tasinikewin* (NI).

unfavorable *or* **unfavourable** *ka naspâcipayik* (VII); not that way, *namoya ekosi* (IPC).

unfeeling *ekâ omôsihtawinihk* (LN).

unfinished *ekâ kakesihcikatek* (VII); s/he is not finished with it, *namoya kesihtâw* (VTI).

unfit *ekâ ka nahiskamihk* (VAI).

unflinching *metoni kaweh tapwehk kîkway* (VTI).

unfold *taswekinkewin* (NI); s/he unfolds it, ***taswekinam*** (VTI).

unforced *ekâ ka sihkiskaht awîyak* (VAI).

unforeseen *ekâ neyak ka wapahtamihk* (VAI).

unforgettable *ekâ kakeh wanikiskisihk* (VAI).

unformed *ekâ ka oyastahk* (VTI).

unfortunate Having bad luck, ***ka mayakopayihk*** (VAI); ***mayakosiwin*** (NI); it is unfortunate, ***kîsinâc*** (VII); s/he is unlucky, ***mayakosiw*** (VAI); s/he brings her/him bad luck, ***mayakoskawew*** (VTA); s/he puts a bad curse on her/him, ***mayakwamew*** (VTA); it is unlucky, ***mayakwan*** (VTI); s/he makes her/him have bad luck, ***mâyipayihew*** (VTA); s/he has bad or evil luck, ***mâyipayiw*** (VTA); the act of having evil success or bad luck, ***mâyipayiwin*** (NI); s/he is unlucky, ***mayakosiw*** (VAI).

unfounded *kwanta pikiskwewin* (NI).

unfrequented *ayâspîs ka wapahtamihk* (VTI).

unfriendly *ekâ kowîcewâkanihk* (VAI); s/he is unfriendly or anti-social, *ayahteyinewiwin* (NI).

unfurnished *ekâ kîkway ka mekihk* (VTI).

ungainly *ka yikicikawihk* (VAI).

ungenerous *poni miyohtwâwin* (NI).

unglazed *ekâ ka wâsihkwak* (VII).

ungodliness *maci isâyâwin* (NI).

ungodly *metoni ka macâtisihk* (VAI).

ungraceful *ekâ katawah kesâyâhk* (VAI).

ungracious *ekâ ka manatisihk* (VAI).

ungrateful *ekâ ka kiskeyihtamihk atamihitowin* (NI); s/he does not say thank-you, *namoya nanâskomow* (VAI).

ungrudging *poni macihtwâwin* (NI).

unguarded *askihkîw tôminikan* (NI).

unhallowed *awîyak ekâ ayamihâwin katâpwewokeyihtahk* (VAI).

unhand *pakitinam* (VAI).

unhandy It is not easy, *namoya wihcasin* (VII).

unhappily *ekâ meyoteh kîkway ka tôtamihk* (VTI).

unhappy *ekâ ka miweyihtamihk* (VII); *kisôweyihtam* (VAI).

unhealthy *âhkosiwâyâwin* (NI); s/he is sickly, *âhkosiwatisiw* (VAI).

unheard *namoya kiskeyitâkwan* (VII).

unheeded *ekâ ka nâkatohkehk* (VAI).

unhesitating *ekâ ka nâhnaketôtamihk* (VAI).

unhinge *îskwahtemapiskwa ka masaskonamihk* (VTI).

unhitch *ka tasinamihk kîkway* (VTI).

unholy *ekâ ka saweyihtakwahk* (VII); it is unholy or impious, *namoyakihceyihtâkwan* (VII).

unhonored *or* **unhonoured** *awîyak ekâ mistahi keteyihtakosit* (VAI).

unhook S/he unhooks a team of horses, ***tasinastimwew*** (VTA); s/he unhooks it, i.e.: a button,

461

tasinew (VTA) *(Northern)*; ***tahtinew*** (VTA) *(Plains)*; something used for unhooking, i.e.: a button, ***tasinikan*** (NI) *(Northern)*; ***tahtinikan*** (NI) *(Plains)*.

uniformity Well-known all over, ***nistaweyihtâkosiwin*** (NI).

unify ***wicewâkanihiwewin*** (NI); form into one single whole, ***peyakohtâwin*** (NI).

unimportance ***ekâ mistahi kispehteyihtakosiwin*** (NI).

unimportant ***ekâ mistahi kispehteyihtakwahk*** (VII).

uninjured ***ekâ ka wesaksinihk*** (VAI).

uninspired ***ekâ ka tataspiyihtamihk*** (VAI).

unintelligible ***awîyak ekâ ka nisitohtaht*** (VAI).

unintentionally ***keswân*** (IPC).

uninterested ***kîkway ekâ ka âhkwateyihtamihk*** (VAI).

uninterrupted ***ekâ ka nahinakemakahk*** (VII).

unique ***peyakwayak isi poko*** (IPC).

unison ***pahpeyakwan ka tôtamihk*** (VAI).

unit One unit, ***peyak kîkway*** (IPC); a unit of measurement indicating one armful or circa six feet from fingertip to finger tip, ***peyakonisk*** (IPC); referring to a Cree unit of measurement equivalent to six feet, "it is about six feet long, i.e.: a toboggan", ***peyakoniskisiw*** (VAI); referring to a Cree unit of measurement equivalent to six feet, "it is about six feet long, i.e.: a canoe", ***peyakoniskeyâw*** (VII); a Cree unit of measurement from fingertip to chin, ***tahtonisk*** (IPC); a Cree expression of measurement used to describe length, i.e.: "it is that many arm lengths", ***tahtoniskesiw*** (VAI); a Cree expression of measurement used to describe length, i.e.: "this is how that many arm lengths it is", ***tahtoniskeyâw*** (VII).

unite ***ka wîcetahiwehk*** (VAI); combine so as to form one, ***peyakohtâwin*** (NI).

united ***ka wîcehtohk*** (VTA).

unity ***wîcehtowin*** (NI).

unkempt ***ekâ ka nânapâcihcikehk*** (VTI); her/his hair is all messy, ***sehkwestikwanew*** (VAI).

unkind ***ekâ ka kisewâtsihk*** (VAI).

unkindly ***awîyak ekâ ka kisewâtsit*** (VAI).

unknown ***ekâ ka nistaweyihtâkosihk*** (VAI).

unleash ***ka âpihkoniht atim kakeh sakâpisot*** (VTA).

unless ***kîspin poko*** (IPC); if it be not that, ***kîspin ahpô*** (IPC).

unlike ***mwehci ekâ*** (IPC).

unlikelihood ***mwehci ekâ ekosi*** (IPC).

unlikeness ***namoya pahpiyakwan*** (VII).

unload ***nîhtinasowin*** (NI); s/he takes the load off, ***nîhtinasiw*** (VAI).

unlock ***ka apihkokahamihk*** (VTI); s/he unlocked it, ***apihkokwaham*** (VTI).

unloose ***âpahikewin*** (NI); s/he untied it, ***âpihkopitew*** (VTA).

unloosen ***ka nomi âpahamihk*** (VTI).

unlucky Having tough luck, ***mâyakopayowin*** (NI); s/he is unlucky, ***mâyakosiw*** (VAI); it is unlucky, ***mayakwan*** (VII); s/he has no luck, ***miyakosiw*** (VAI).

unmanly ***ekâ ka nâpewâyâhk*** (VII); ***namoya sohkâtisiw*** (VAI).

unmannerly ***ekâ kwayask kesâyâhk*** (VII); impolite, ***namoyakohkwâwâc*** (IPC).

unmarried ***ekâ ka wekihtohk*** (VAI); all alone, ***peyakowin*** (NI).

unmask ***mihkwakanihkan ka kecikonamihk*** (VTI); s/he pulled off her/his mask, ***mosisihkwepitew*** (VTA).

unmatchable ***ekâ kakeh mawinehamihk*** (VTI).

unmeaning ***kaspokîkway ka tôtamihk*** (VAI).

unmeasured ***ekâ ka tipahamihk kîkway*** (VTI).

unmeet ***ekâ ka nakiskâtohk*** (VAI).

unmentionable ***ekâ takehmâmiskôtamihk*** (VAI).

unmerciful ***ekâ kîkway kisewâtisowin*** (NI); s/he is hard to get along with, ***âhkwatisiw*** (VAI).

unmindful ***ekâ kamâmitoneyihtamihk*** (VAI).

umistakable ***ekâ kakeh wâneyihtamihk*** (VAI).

unmixed ***ekâ ketehamihk*** (VTI).

unmoral ***metoni ekâ kwayask*** (IPC).

unmoved ***ekâ ka waskawinamihk*** (VTI).

unnatural ***namoya tâpwe kîkway*** (VII); ***namoya tâpiskôc*** (IPC).

unnecessary ***ekâ kâtac kîkway tatôtamihk*** (VAI); ***namoya nitaweyitâkwan*** (VII); not necessary, ***namoya kâtâc*** (IPC).

unnerve ***awîyak ka misiwanâcihisot papâsipayowin ohci*** (VAI).

unnumbered ***ekâ ka akihcikatek*** (VII).

unobserved ***ekâ ka wâpamowehk*** (VAI).

unoccupied ***ekâ ka atoskehk*** (VAI).

unorganized ***ekâ kwayask kespayik isihcikewin*** (VII).

unpack ***ka sîkawihikehk*** (VAI).

unpaid ***kîkway ekâ ka kîstipahamihk*** (VTI).

unpalatable ***ka atâweyihcikehk*** (VAI).

unparalleled ***ekâ ka nanakahikohk kîkway*** (VTI).

unpin ***ka masaskoniht aniskamân*** (VTI).

unpleasant ***ekâ ka mocikahk*** (VII); s/he is not too pleasant, ***namoya miyawâtamowin*** (NI).

unpleasantness ***ekâ kîkway môcikisowin*** (NI).

unplug ***piwapiskos ka tasipitamihk*** (VTI).

unpopular ***awîyak ekâ ka tataspeyihtakosit*** (VTA); s/he is not liked, ***namoya miweyimaw*** (VTA).

unpopularity ***ekâ tataspeyihtakosowin*** (NI).

unpractical ***ekâ nânitâw ka itâpatahk*** (VII).

unpractised *or* **unpracticed** ***ekâ ka sesawetôtamihk*** (VAI).

unprepared ***ekâ kakesisaweyistamihk*** (VAI); ***namoya waweyew*** (VAI); s/he is not ready, ***namoya kesâyâw*** (VAI).

unprovoked *ekâ ka mamahtiyihtamihk* (VII).

unquestionable *namakîkway kwetatehitwewin* (NI).

unquestionably *metoni sôskwâc kespayik kîkway* (IPC).

unquestioned *ekâ kâtâc kakwecihkemowin* (NI).

unquiet Throwing down with a thump, *kisewehcikewin* (NI).

unravel *ka taswekinkehk* (VTI); the act of unravelling, *âpahikewin* (NI) *(Plains); âpahonikewin* (NI) *(Northern)*.

unreal *namoya tahtâpwe kîkway* (IPC).

unreasonable *ekâ kwayask kespayihtahk* (VTI); *namoya kwayask mâmitoneyitam* (VAI); s/he is unreasonable, *namoyakohkwâwâtisiw* (VAI).

unreasonably *ekâ kwayask ispayihcikewnihk* (LN).

unreasoning *sôskwâc poko isi ka tôtamihk* (VAI).

unreconstructed *ekâ ka ahtisihcikehk* (VAI).

unreflecting *ekâ ka kiskisihk kîkway* (VAI).

unregarded *ekâ kîkway kispehtaweyihtakosihk* (VAI).

unrelenting *ekâ ka pakiteyimohk* (VAI).

unreliability *awîyak ekâ ka mamisîtotahk* (VTA).

unreliable *ekâ ka mamisehk* (VII).

unreligious *awîyak ekâ ka ayamihat* (VII).

unremitting *sôskwâc ka âhkamespayik kîkway* (VTI).

unreserved *awîyak ka mâmâsisihkeskit* (VAI).

unreservedly *mâmâsisihkewinihk* (LN) or (VII).

unripe *ekâ katihtek mînis* (VAI).

unrestrained S/he thinks of her/him as unrestrained, *wacihkameyimew* (VTA); s/he has unrestrained enthusiasm about something, *wacihkameyihtam* (VAI); s/he is off the wall, i.e.: unrestrained, *wacihkamisiw* (VAI); the act of being off the wall, i.e.: unrestrained, *wacihkamisiwin* (NI).

unroll *ka taswapekinkehk* (VTI).

unruffled *kîkway ka sôskwahikatek* (VTI).

unruly *ekâ ka natohtamihk kitahamatowin* (VAI); s/he cause trouble, *âyimihtasiw* (VAI).

unsaddle *mistatim ka âpahoht* (VTA).

unsafe *kîkway ka kostâtikwahk* (VTI) or (VII).

unsaid *ekâ kawihtamihk kîkway* (VAI).

unsatisfactory *ekâ ka atamihikohk kîkway* (VAI).

unsavory or **unsavoury** *ekâ kwayask kesâyähk* (VAI).

unsay *kâwi kotinamihk kîkway ekeh itwehk* (VTI).

unscramble *masinahikewin ka kwayaskwastahk* (VTI).

unscrew *âpahostehikewin* (NI); s/he unscrews it, *âpahonam* (VAI).

unscrupulous *awîyak ekâ kwayask ekehsihciket* (VAI).

unseal *ka ahtinamihk kîkway ekaskamoci kipahikatek* (VTI); s/he undoes the seal, *paskipitam* (VTI).

unseasonable *ekâ kwayask kîsikesikak* (VII).

unseemly *ekâ ka miyonâkohcikehk* (VTI).

unseen *ekâ ka nôkosihk* (VAI); *namoya nôkwan* (VII).

unselfish *ekâ ka sasaksehk* (VAI); s/he likes to give, *nihtamekiw* (VAI).

unsettle *ekâ kwayask itâpowin* (NI).

unsettled *kîkway ekâ kwayask ketastek* (VTI); *namoya keseyitam* (VAI).

unsightly *ka kakwayakinakwahk kîkway* (VTI); it does not look good, *mâyinâkwan* (VII).

unskilful or **unskillful** *ekâ ka nahehk* (VAI); *mamayew* (VAI).

unskilled *awîyak ekâ konahewenit* (VAI); s/he can't do it, *namoya kaskitaw* (VAI).

unsnap Prying open, *yohteyaskwahikewin* (NI).

unsophisticated *ekâ ka misteyimisohk* (VAI).

unsound *nawâc poko ekâ kwayask kesâyâhk* (VAI); it is not strong, *namoya maskawâw* (VII).

unsparing *namakîkway manâcihitowin* (NI).

unspeakable *waweyak ekâ kakeh mâmiskôtamihk* (VAI); not to talk about, *namoya tawihtamihk* (VAI).

unstable *ekâ metoni ka mamisehk* (VTA); s/he can't stay in one place, *papâmayaw* (VAI).

unsteady *ka kecikonamihk kitohcikan yapesa* (VTI).

unstrung *ka nihtâ kisôweyihtamihk* (VAI).

unsubstantial *ekâ ka ayâtâstek kîkway* (VTI).

unsuccessful *ekâ kakaskihtahk* (VAI).

unsuited *ekâ ka nahiskamihk* (VAI).

unsullied *ekâ ka atihtek kîkway* (VTI).

untangle *ka nahawapekinikehk* (VTI); s/he untangles it, *apihkowpitan* (VTI).

unthankful *namakîkway nanâskomowin* (NI).

unthinking *ekâ ka mamitoneyihtamihk* (VAI).

untidy *kohkôsipamihowin* (NI); *namoya kanâtan* (VII); *namoya kanâcinakwan* (VII); s/he is a dirty house keeper, *yepacipamihow* (VAI).

untie *apihkonkewin* (NI).

until *isko* (IPC).

untimely *nanihkipayowin* (NI).

untiring *awîyak ka sîpiwsit* (NI).

untold *ekâ ka atôtamihk* (VTI).

untouchable *ekâ kakeh sâminamihk kîkway* (VTI).

untouched Something not touched before, *ekâ ceskwa kasâminamihk* (VTI); untouched or unspoiled by humans, *kahkan* (VII).

untrue *namoya tapwe* (IPC).

untruth The lack of truthfulness, *kiyâskiwin* (NI).

untruthful *ka kakiyâskiskihk* (VAI).

untwist Unravelling, *âpahonikewin* (NI).

unused *kîkway ekâ ka apatahk* (VII).

unusual *pîtos ka isâyâhk* (VAI); *mamahtâwan* (VII).

unusually *kanihtâ pîtosipayik* (VII).

unwary S/he is not paying attention, *namoya nâkateyitam* (VAI).

unweave *ka âpahonamihk kîkway* (VTI).

unwelcome *ekâ kanitaweyimiht awîyak* (VAI).

463

unwholesome *âhkosiwâyâwin* (NI).

unwieldy *ekâ wetinahk kakeh mâsihtahk* (VAI).

unwilling *ekâ ekosi keteyihtamihk* (VAI); s/he is reluctant or unwilling, *sâkweyimow* (VAI).

unwise *namoya iyinisowin* (NI); stupid, unwise, *kakepâtisiw* (VAI); *kakepâtan* (VTI).

unwitting *kâspokîkway ka tôtamihk* (VTI).

unwittingly *ka kâspopayihtahk kîkway* (VTI).

unworthy *ekâ kakîspinatamihk miyo mâmiskomtowin* (VTI); *namoya tehtakosiw* (VAI); falling short of what is required, *namoya ispeteyihtakosiw* (VAI).

unwound *ka âpahonamihk kîkway* (VTI).

unwove *sestakwasikan ka âpahoniht* (VTI).

unwoven *âpahopicikewin* (NI).

unwrap *pâskinikewin* (NI).

unwrinkle *taswekinkewin* (NI).

up *ispimihk* (LN).

upbringing The upbringing of someone, *kohpikihiht awîyak* (VTA).

upheaval *wayâhiwewin* (NI).

upheave *sohkiwaniskânikewin* (NI).

uphill *amacowemow* (LN).

464

uphold *kwayask ispayihcikewin* (NI).

uplift Lifting something upwards, *ohpinikewin* (NI); s/he uplifts her/him by talking about her/him, *mamihcimêw* (VTA).

upon *tahkôc* (IPC); *waskic* (IPC).

upper *ispimihk nawâc* (IPC) *or* (LN).

upright Something sitting upright, *kîkway ka simatastek* (VTI); s/he straightens up, *simaciw* (VAI); the tree stands upright on the face of the mountain, *ohpâskweyâw* (VII).

uprise *wayâhitowin* (NI).

uprisen *awîyak kakeh wayâhiht* (VAI).

uprising *wayâhiwewin* (NI).

uproar *kisewewin* (NI); *kîskwekamikisiwin* (NI); *kîskweyahkamikan* (VII).

uproarious *ka kisewihtakosihk* (VAI).

uproot The act of uprooting, *mônahicepihkwewin* (NI).

upset The act of tipping a boat over, *kotapîwin* (NI); s/he upsets the boat, *kotapîw* (VAI); s/he upsets her/him with her/his talking, *kisimew* (VTA); the act of being upset with someone, *kisestâkewin* (NI); being upset with each other, *kisestâtowin* (NI); s/he upsets herself/himself by her/his talk, *kisimow* (VAI); her/his illness makes her/him upset and bitter, *kisôwahpinew* (VTA); the act of being upset and bitter because of illness, *kisôwahpinewin* (NI); s/he has an upset stomach, *kisiwaskatew* (VAI); having an upset stomach, *kisiwaskatewin* (NI).

upside down *ka naspâtastek* (VTI); *kotapastew* (VAI) *(Northern)*; *kwatapastew* (VAI) *(Plains)*.

upstairs *ispimihtakohk* (LN); *ispimihk* (LN).

upstanding *metoni kwayask kwâtisowin* (NI).

upstart *mistanakeyimisowin* (NI).

upstream *natimihk sîpehk* (LN); the area upstream, *natimayik* (LN).

upswing *sisikôc ka nîkânehk* (VTI).

upturn *osih kotihtapastahk* (VTI); a turn over, *kweskipayowin* (NI).

upturned *otihtapascikewin* (NI).

upward *ispimihk itehikewin* (NI); *ispimihk isi* (IPC).

upwardly *ispimihk isi nawac* (IPC).

upwards *kîspahkepayik* (VTI).

urge *ka sihkimiht awîyak* (VAI); s/he encourages her/him verbally, *sihkimew* (VTA).

urgency *sohkeyihtamowin* (NI).

urgent *metoni sohki kîkway kanitaweyihtamihk* (VAI).

urgently Requiring immediate attention, *nanihkeyimow* (VAI).

urinate S/he urinates on her/him, *sikitew* (VTA); s/he urinates, *sikow* (VAI).

urine The act of urinating, *sikowin* (NI).

us *kîyânaw* (NA).

usable *âpatan* (VII); something that is useable, *kamiyo âpatahk kîkway* (VII); it works, *âtoskemakan* (VII); something that is well used, *kîkway kanihtâ âpatahk* (VII); it is useful, *âpatan* (VII).

usage The way in which something is used, *ka itâpatahk* (VII); *âpacihcikewin* (NI).

use S/he feels s/he has use for her/him or it, *âpateyimew* (VTA); s/he uses something real fast, *kîyipinew* (VTA); s/he starts to use her/him, *mâcâpacihew* (VTA); s/he uses her/his spiritual power to make them come to her/him, *peciwiyew* (VTA).

used Something that is used up, *kîkway kakeh âpatahk* (VTI); completely used up, *mescipayiw* (VAI); it is used, *âpatan* (VII); s/he has been used or s/he has been cured, *âpacihaw* (VTA); s/he is used to seeing her/him, *nakayâpamew* (VTA) *(Plains)*; *nakayânawew* (VTA) *(Northern)*.

useful S/he is useful, *âpatisiw* (VAI); it is useful, *âpatan* (VII); something useful or being useful, *âpacihcikewin* (NI); one who is given a sense of usefulness, *âpateyitâkosiw* (VAI).

useless *namoyâpatan* (VII); something that you have no use for, *kîkway ekâ nânitâw ketâpatahk* (VII); something that other people do not want, *âtaweyitâkwan* (VII); s/he is useless, *yekicikawow* (VAI); of no practical value, *âtaweyihtâkwan* (VII).

usual *ekosi ispayiw* (IPC).

usually *mâna* (IPC) *(Plains)*; *mânah* (IPC) *(Northern)*; something that happens ordinarily, *tansi kâtesi miyopayik* (VII); not usually, not commonly, not too often, *namoya mwasi* (IPC).

uterus *iskwew ospayawa* (NA).

utilize Something utilized, *kîkway ka âpacitahk* (VTI);
s/he utilizes her/him, *âpacihew* (VTA); s/he uses it,
âpacitaw (VTI); s/he has been utilized, *âpacihaw* (VTA).

utter *ka pîkiskwehk* (VAI); *pîkiskwesiw* (VAI); *metoni
sôskwâc ekâ nânitâw ketâpatahk* (VII).

utterance *pîkiskwewin* (NI).

utterly *sohkahâc* (IPC).

V

vacant *kîkway ka tâwâk* (VII).

vagina *iskwewâpacihcikan* (NA) *(Plains)*; *tastawayakap* (VII) *(Plains)*.

vague *ekâ tâpwe ka kiskisihk* (VAI); *namoya nisitotakwan* (VII).

vain *mistahi kîteyimsohk* (VAI); excessively proud of oneself, *kisteyimow* (VAI).

vainly *mistahi iteyimsowenihk ohci* (VAI).

vale A valley, *wâyatinâw* (VII).

valiant *metoni napehkâsowin* (NI); s/he is a brave person, *nâpehkâsiw* (VAI).

valley *ka tawâtinak* (VII); there is valley, *tawâtinâw* (VII); there is a bowl-like valley, i.e.: between mountains, *wâyatinâw* (VII); there is a narrow valley or ravine, *tawacâw* (VII); a dip in the ground, *wâyacâw* (VII).

valor *or* **valour** Strength of mind in braving danger, *napehkâsowin* (NI); *ekâ ka sâkohtehehk* (VAI).

valorous *ekâ ka kostamihk kîkway* (VTI).

valuable *kîkway ka miyo âpatahk* (VTI); of great value, of great price, *mistakihtew* (VAI).

value The value for which a thing is regarded, *ispehtaweyihtakwahk*; the price of something, *tânsi kitakihtek kîkway* (VII); esteem, *kihcihkawisiwin* (NI); it is of great value, *kihcihkawan* (VII); s/he or it is of great value, *kihcihkawisiw* (VAI).

valued *oyakihcikewin* (NI).

vamp The upper front part of a moccasin, *asesin* (NI).

vanish *ka wanihohk* (VTI).

vanity *mamihcimisowin* (NI); excessive attention to one's appearance, *mistahi mamihcisowin* (NI).

vanquish S/he defeats him in a battle, *sâkohtwâw* (VAI); *sâkohtwawin* (NI).

vapor *or* **vapour** The result of exhaling in cold temperature, i.e.: vapor, *pikihtewatâmowin* (NI); her/his breath is visible, like a vapor, in the cold air, *pikihtewatâmiw* (NI); it is kind of damp, *miyamawâw* (VII).

vaporize Make or become vapor, *miyamawinkewin* (NI).

vaporous *kîkway kakih ka makwahk* (VII).

variability *ka pahpitosipayik* (VII).

variable Tending to change, *meskocipayiw* (VII); *ekâ kakiki peyakwan*

variation *pahpitosipayowin* (NI).

varied *ekâ pahpeyakwan* (VII); it looks different, *pîtosinâkwan* (VII).

variety *pahpitos kîkway* (IPC); *mecet kîkwaya* (IPC); a mixture of different things, *pahpitosikîkway* (IPC).

various Having diverse features, *pîtosâyâwin* (NI); *ahohpimiy ohci*.

vary *pahpitos kîsikesikak* (IPC); *mameskôc*; making different kinds, *mameskôc sehcikewin* (NI).

vast *metoni ka misak askîy* (VII); very great in extent or size, *misâw* (VII).

vastly *metoni mistahi itah* (IPC).

vaunt S/he brags about herself/himself, *mamihcimow* (VAI).

veer Changing direction, *kweskîwin* (VII).

vegetable A vegetable or a vegetable seed for planting in the ground, *kiscikânis* (NA) *(Plains)*; *pîwi kistikân* (NI) *(Northern)*.

vegetate *ohpikin* (VII); grow or live like a plant, *ohpikowin* (NI).

vegetation *ohpikowin* (NI); the act of vegetating, *ohpikicikewin* (NI).

vehemence *macihtwâwin* (NI).

vehement *mistahi ka macihtwâhk* (VAI); showing strength in feeling, *mistahikisiwasiw* (VAI).

vehicle A vehicle that runs by itself, i.e.: a car, *sehkepimipayîs* (NA) *(Plains)*; *sehkes* (NA) *(Plains)*; *wihcekitâpânâsk* (NA) *(Northern)*.

veil *akwanahowenis* (NI); a piece of fabric worn over the face, *âkohkwehon* (NI).

vein *mihkoyapiy* (NA).

venerability *manâcihiwewin* (NI).

venerable Being venerable, *manâtsiwin* (NI).

venerate *kîkway ka manâcitahk* (VII).

veneration *manâcihitowin* (NI).

vengeance *naskwâstamâsowin apô âpehowin* (NI); retributive punishment, *pasastehokowisowin* (NI).

vengeful *ka nihtâ âpehohk* (VAI).

venison One piece of venison, *âpisimôsôweyâs* (NI).

venom *piscipowin* (NI); poison secreted by snakes, *kinepikopiscipowin* (NI).

venomous *ka piscipomakahk kîkway* (VAI).

vent A small outlet, *iskwâhtemis* (NI).

ventilate Let fresh air in, *sâpoyowehtawin* (VII).

ventilation *tahkiyawehikewin* (NI) *(Northern)*; *tahkiyowepahikewin* (NI) *(Plains)*.

venture *kîkway ekostatikwahk ka tôtamihk*; a hazardous enterprise, *ayimanohkitohtew* (NI).

venturesome *ka kostatikwahk* (VII); *okasis* (VII); a venture without real calculation, *astâseyihtakwan* (VII).

venturous *ka kostaciwâyâhk* (VII); attended with risk or danger, *astâsowin* (NI).

veracious The truth as a matter of course, *tâpwewin* (NI).

467

verge *tân'ta kisewaskamok meskanaw* (VII); *metoni tân'ta keskopayik kîkway* (VII).

verity A basic truth of religion, *tâpwewakeyihtamowin* (NI).

vermin *mistahi sihkos* (NA).

versatile *nanâtohk kesinahehk;* possessing various skills, *nanâtohk kaskihowin* (NI).

versatility *nanâtohk isihnahiwin* (NI).

version *awîyak opîkiskwewin* (NI).

vertical It stands straight up, *kwayaskwaskitew* (VII).

vesper *tipiskâw acahkos* (NA).

vespers *ayamihew nikamowina* (NI).

vessel A canoe or boat, *osih* (NI).

vest A sleeveless garment, *kîskanakowayân* (NI).

vestige *kayâs namehtâwin* (NI).

vestment A priest's white garment, *wâpiskasâkay* (NI).

vestry The priest's change room, *meskocewikamikos* (NI).

vex *awîyak ekâ ekosi kiteyimiht* (VTA); to annoy someone, *kisiwâhtwâw* (VAI).

vexation Something that annoys a person, *kisiwâsowin* (NI); *nawâc poko ka pakwatiht awîyak* (NI).

viand Food, *miciwin* (NI).

vibrate *nanamipayiw* (VII) or (VAI) *(Plains)*; *koskoskopayiw* (VII) or (VAI) *(Northern)*.

vibration *nanamipayowin* (NI) *(Plains)*; *koskoskopayowin* (NI) *(Northern)*.

vicar A priest who takes the place of another, *otâpapestamâkew* (NA).

vicinity Around here, *ôtahwâsakâm* (IPC).

vicious *awîyak ka macâyiwit* (VAI).

victim *kitimahakan* (NI); someone who fell victim to suffering, *misiwanacihow* (VAI).

victimize *awîyak ka kitimahiht* (VTA).

victor *awîyak ka sâkohtwat;* a winner, *otôtahowew* (NA).

victorious *ka sâkohiwehk* (VAI).

victory Winning over someone, *sâkohtwawin* (NI); the act of winning, *otahowewin* (NI).

victual A big supply of food and more rarely other provisions, *mîciwina* (NI).

vie Vying for first place, *mawinehotowin* (NI).

view What one can see from where s/he is, *kawâpahtamihk* (VTI); *wâpahcikewin* (NI); coming or being in view: visible, *nokosiw* (VII); *nôkwan* (VII).

viewer *owâpahcikew* (NA).

viewless *ekâ ka nôkwahk kîkway.*

vigil Remaining awake all night, *wâpanapowin* (NI).

vigilant Someone tirelessly on the alert; *awîyak kakike ka asoweyihtahk.*

vigor *or* **vigour** *sohkâyâwin* (NI); physical power, *maskawâtisiwin* (NI).

vigorous *awîyak ka sohkâyat* (VAI).

vile *kîkway ka pakwâtamihk* (VTI); morally hateful, *pakwâtikosiwin* (NI).

villain *awîyak ka nihtâ mâyahkamikisit;* someone capable of evil deeds, *macâtis* (IPC).

villainous The act of being villianous, *macâtsiwin* (NI).

villany Villianous conduct, *mâyitôtamowin* (NI).

vim Vigorous, energetic, *kâyawisiwin* (NI).

vindicate *awîyak ka paspîhiht* (VTA).

vindication *paspîhiwewin* (NI).

vindictive *kîkway ka paspîhiwemakâhk.*

vine A grape vine, *sôminâhtik* (NA); a field of grape vines, *sôminâhtikokistikân* (NA).

vineyard A grapevine garden, *sôminkistikân* (NA).

violence *ka mâyitôtamihk; âhkwatisowin* (NI).

violent *awîyak ka nihtâ mâyitôtahk;* perverted with violence, *macâtisiwin* (NI).

virgin *awîyak ekâ ceskwa ka wicehtot;* a fine young woman, *miyo oskinîkiskwew* (NA).

virginal *metoni kanâcipimâtisowin* (NI).

virginity *iskwew otoskinîkiskwewiwin ka kanaweyihtahk* (VAI).

virtual *metoni ka miyo isâyâhk* (VAI).

virtually *kekâc pokokahkiyaw* (VII).

virtue *micim ohci ka miyohtwâhk;* a quality held to be of great moral value, *kanâtatisowin* (NI).

virtuous *miyo itâtisiwin* (NI).

visage *mihkwâkan* (VII).

visible *ka nôkwahk kîkway; nôkwan* (VII); coming or being view or visible, *nokosiw* (VAI); clear visibility or clear appearance, *pakaskinâkosiwin* (NI); s/he is clearly visible or s/he is in the open, *pakaskinâkosiw* (VAI); it is clearly visible or it is in the open, *pakaskinâkwan* (VII); becoming visible while nearing, *penôkosiw* (VII); *penôkwan* (VII); visible through something, *sâponôkosiw* (VAI); *sâponôkwan* (VAI); openly, visibly, not hidden or covered up, *mosis; mosisiy;* her/his tracks are visible, *nôkwanâhtikosiw* (VAI); it is easy tracking, *nôkwanâhtikwan* (VII); only partially visible or clarity is hampered by an obstacle intervening, *pawâyihk;* s/he doesn't see her/him full, i.e.: not clearly visible, *pawinawew* (VTA); s/he scarcely sees her/him, i.e.: through a fog or thick bush, *pawosimew* (VTA); it can be seen, *nôkwan* (VII).

vision *itapahcikewin* (NI); the ability to see, *wâpwin* (NI).

visit The act of visiting, *kîhokewin* (NI); s/he visits, *kîhokew* (VAI); s/he visits with her/him, *kîhokawew* (VTA) *(Northern)*; *kiyokawew* (VTA) *(Plains)*.

visitor *okîhokew* (NA).

visual *kîkway ka kihkânâkwahk; wâpacikatew* (VAI); used in seeing, *wâpacikakewin* (NI).

visualize *kîkway neyak kawâpahtamihk* (VTI).

visually *kihkawâpahcikewnihk* (NI).

468

vital *kîkway metoni ka âhkwateyihtamihk* (IPC); something essential or necessary in life, *kihcikîkway* (IPC).

vitality Being lively, *metoni kakayawâyâwin* (NI); being strong, *sohkâtisiwin* (NI); s/he has vitality, *sâpikanew* (VAI).

vivacious *metoni ka kayawsewin* (NI); s/he is high spirited and full of life, *kakayawipayihow* (VAI).

vivacity *ka kayaw mâmitoneyihcikan* (VII).

vivid *kîkway ka kihkânâkwahk*; it provides a very strong stimulus to the eye, *kihkânâkwan* (VII).

vixen A female fox, *nôsemahkesîs* (NA).

vocal *metoni ka kisewehk; ka itehtakosihk* (VAI); a voiced sound, *pihtâkosiwin* (NI).

vocalize *ka nikamwatôtamihk kîkway* (VTI).

vocally *nikamowenihk isih*.

vociferous Making a loud outcry, *tacikwewin* (NI).

voice Being heard, *pihtâkosiwin* (NI); her/his voice is amplified by the ground, *askîwatâmiw* (VAI); the sound of someone's voice, *itehtakosiwin* (NI); a voice with an extraordinary tone, *mâmaskâcihtâkosiwin* (NI); s/he has an attractive voice, *miyohtâkosiw* (VAI); singing with an inspiring voice, *miyohtâkosiwin* (NI); her/his voice is intelligible, *pakaskihtâkosiw* (VAI); s/he has a loud voice, *sohkehtâkosiw* (VAI); s/he has a high pitched voice, *wâsewew* (VAI) *(Northern)*; *wâswewew* (VAI) *(Plains)*; having a high pitched voice, *wâsewewin* (NI) *(Northern)*; *wâswewewin* (NI) *(Plains)*; the sound of a voice, *kapehtâkosihk* (VAI).

voiceless *awîyak ekâ kohpehtâkosowenit*.

void *kîkway ekâ ka âpatahk*; it is not useful, *namoya âpatan* (VII).

volatile *kîkway ka nihtâ mestâpahtek*.

volcano An exploding mountain, *wacikâpahkitek*.

vole *pâhkwacaskos* (NA).

volley A gun that shoots a volley of bullets, *mihcetomacwewes*.

voluble *ekâ ka kisipatamohk*; s/he talks with an unhestitating flow of words, *pîkiskweskiw* (VAI).

voluptuous *metoni ka tepmôcekihtahk* (VAI).

vomit The act of vomiting, *pwakomowin* (NI); vomiting blood, *pwâkomohkwewin* (NI); s/he vomits, *pwâkomow* (VAI); s/he vomits it, *papayihew* (VAI); s/he makes her/him vomit, *pwakomohew* (VTA); s/he vomits on it, *pwâkomotôtam* (VTI); a medicine which induces vomiting, i.e.: an emetic, *pwâkomiskan* (VII).

voracious Greedy for food, *kâsakew* (VAI).

vouch *ka nîsohkamâkehk* (VAI); s/he vouches for her/him, *pîkiskwestamâwew* (VTA).

vow *asotamowin* (NI); speaking the truth, *kihci pikiskwewin* (NI); a solemn promise, *kihci itwewin* (NI).

voyage *pimipiciwin* (NI); a long journey, *pamipiciwin* (NI).

voyager *opapâmpiciw* (NA).

vulgar *waweyak ekâ ka manâtisihk* (VAI); offensive to one's finer feelings, *pîweyihcikew* (VAI).

vulgarism *ka nihtâ mikoskâcimowehk* (VAI).

vulgarity *ka mikoskâcitasohk* (VAI).

vulgarize *awîyak ka mikoskâcihiht* (VTA).

vulnerability *kakihcisâyâwin* (NI); *kakecisâyâwin* (NI) *(Northern)*; *wahkepinewin* (NI) *(Plains)*.

vulnerable *metoni ka kakihcisâyâhk* (VII).

469

waddle *sîsîpimohtewin* (NI); s/he walks like a duck, *yâyahpayiw* (VAI).

wade The act of wading in the water, *pimâtakâwin* (NI); s/he wades across, *asawâkâmeyâtakâw* (VAI); s/he wades towards shore, *natakamiyatakaw* (VAI); s/he wades in the water, *pimâtakâw* (VAI).

waft *îspakehamowin* (NI).

wag The act of wagging a tail, *wepâyowewin* (NI); s/he wags her/his tail, *wepâyowew* (VAI).

wagon *tihtipitâpânâsk* (NA) (*Northern*); *tihtipitapânâsk* (NA) (*Plains*); *newokâtew* (NA) (*Plains*).

wagon brace *apasoy* (NI).

wagoner *otihtiptapanaskohkew* (NA).

wagonload *peyakotâpânâsk ka sâkaskinet* (VAI).

waif A child orphan, *kewâcaw* (NA).

waist The middle of the human body, *âpihtawsiyaw* (NI).

waistband *pakwahtehon* (NI).

wait The act of waiting or a waiting place, *pehowin* (NI); wait, s/he is tired of waiting for her/him, *kihtimpehew* (VTA); s/he waits for her/him, *pehew* (VTA); s/he waits, *pehiw* (VAI).

wake The act of waking up, *koskopayowin* (NI); s/he wakes up, *kaskopayow* (VAI); s/he wakes her/him up by making a noise, *koskohew* (VTA); s/he wakes her/him up with her/his talking, *koskomew* (VTA); s/he wakes her/him up, *koskonew* (VTA); s/he shakes her/him awake, *koskopitew* (VTA); a vigil over a corpse before burial, *nepepestamakewin* (NI); s/he stays up late at a wake, *nepepiw* (VAI); s/he makes a noise and wakes up, *waspawehew* (VTA); her/his talking wakes her/him up, *waspâwemew* (VTA); s/he wakens suddenly, *waspâwepayiw* (VAI).

wakeful *waspâwisâyâwin* (NI) (*Northern*); *waspâwepayowin* (NI) (*Plains*).

waken *ka waspâwihiht* (VTA).

walk S/he walks, *pimohtew* (VAI); the act of walking, *pimohtewin* (NA); s/he is walking across on the ice, *âsawiskohtew* (VAI); s/he walks across, *âsawohtew* (VAI); s/he walks by the place where s/he should have been, *âstêhtew* (VAI); s/he walks away, *îyikatehtew* (VAI); s/he missed her/him on the trail, *âsteskawew* (VTA); s/he bypasses someone, *âsteskam* (VTA); s/he walks into the woods, *kospow* (VAI); s/he walks down stream, *mahohtew* (VAI); a walk down stream, *mahohtewin* (NI); s/he walks

with a limp, *mâskipayiw* (VAI); s/he goes on foot, *môstohtew* (VAI); they walk towards each other, *nâtitowak* (VAI); s/he walks up stream, *natahohtew* (VAI); s/he walks against the wind, *nayimohtew* (VAI); s/he walks or travels late into the night, *nîpâhtew* (VAI); the act of walking or travelling late into the night, *nîpâhtewin* (VAI); s/he is tired from walking, *nestohtew* (VTA); the act of being tired from walking, *nestohtewin* (VAI); s/he walks ahead or in front, *nîkânohtew* (VTA); s/he walks first or s/he leads the way, *nistamohtew* (VAI); s/he walks on deep snow without snowshoes, *nôtimew* (VAI); s/he walks till late evening, *otâkwanohtew* (VAI); the act of walking in the late evening or a walk in the late evening, *otâkwanohtewin* (NI); s/he goes or walks into the water, *pahkopew* (VAI); the act of going or walking into the water, *pahkopewin* (NI); s/he walks or travels everywhere, *pahpâmohtew* (VAI); the act of walking everywhere, *papâmohtewin* (NI); s/he walks over, *pastohtew* (VAI); s/he is walking towards us, *pecastamohtew* (VAI); s/he walks slowly, *pekihkâtohtew* (VAI) (*Northern*); *yîkicikâtohtew* (VAI) (*Plains*); *papwâstahohtew* (VAI) (*Plains*); s/he walks from there, *pêyohtohtew* (VAI); s/he walks alone, *peyakohtew* (VAI); s/he walks on top of the ice, *pimiskohtew* (VAI) (*Plains and Northern variant*); *wâskitskohtew* (VAI) (*Northern*); s/he makes her/him walk, *pimohtahew* (VAI); s/he walks through the country, *pimohtâtam* (VTI); s/he continually walks or tread on the same road, *pimohteskanawew* (VAI); s/he walks right through without stopping, *semakohtew* (VAI); s/he walks along the side, *sisonehtew* (VAI); s/he walks along beside her/him, *sisoneskawew* (VTA).

walks S/he walks, *pimohtew* (VAI); s/he is on foot, *mostohtew* (VAI).

walker S/he walks poorly, *mayipimohtew* (VAI); s/he is a real slow walker, *yikicikawow* (VAI); *peyahtikpamotew* (VAI).

wallop To defeat soundly, *pakamawew* (VTA).

wampum *wawesîwina* (NI); shells used and made into ornaments, *wawisihcikana* (NI).

wan S/he is pale, *wâpinesiw* (VAI).

wander *ka kwahtohtehk* (VAI); s/he flies all over the place, *papamiyâw* (VAI).

wane *ka poninôhawasohk* (VAI).

want S/he wants it, *nitaweyihtam* (VTI); s/he wants it for her/him, *nitaweyihtamawew* (VTA); the act of wanting something, *nitaweyihtamowin* (NI); s/he wants her/him, *nitaweyimew* (VTA); s/he wants something for someone else, *nitaweyihtestamawew* (VTA).

471

wanting *nitaweyihcikewin* (NI); running short of things, *kwetamâwin* (NI).

wapiti A reindeer, *wâwâskesiw* (NA).

war *ka misinôtintohk* (VAI); fighting a war, *nôtinikewin* (NI).

warble The act of singing, *nikamowin* (NI); s/he sings, *nikamiw* (VAI); an animal call, *kito* (VAI).

warbler *pewayisis ka takahkihtakosit* (VAI); little warbling bird, *wasepescan* (NA).

war dance *kayâs nehiyaw isihcikewin* (NI).

wardrobe *ka weyot ayiwinisehk* (NI); clothes to wear, *ayiwinisa* (NI).

warfare The act of fighting in a war, *nôtinikewin* (NI).

warily *ka asweyihtamihk* (VTI).

wariness *asweyihcikewin* (NI).

warlike *ka nôtintowinakosihk* (VAI).

warm Being warm, *kîsôsowin* (NI); it is warm, i.e.: house, *kîsowâw* (VII); it is warm out (weather), *kîsopwew* (VII); s/he holds her/him to get her/him warm, *kîsonew* (VTA); s/he is warm, *kesosow* (VAI); s/he sleeps warmly, *kîsowihkwâmiw* (VAI); s/he is warming a drum, *kisâneswew* (VAI); the drum is warmed up, *kisânesiw* (VAI); s/he keeps her/him warm with her/his body, *kîsôskawew* (VTA).

warmish *kisâstaw ka kîsopwek* (VII).

warmth *kîsôsowin* (NI); it feels warm, *kîsowâyâw* (VII).

warm-up Warming up, *awasowin* (NI); s/he warms up, *awasiw* (VAI).

warn *nîkân wihtamâtowin* (NI); *wihtamawew* (VTA).

warning *asweyihtamowin kawihtamâtohk* (NI); *neyak wihtamâkewin* (NI).

warp *ka pemahkatotek mistik* (VII); crooked, warped, *wâkipayiw* (VAI); *wakipayin* (VAI); it is uneven or warped, i.e.: something made of metal such as a frying pan, *wâkâpiskisiw* (VII); to cause wood to become twisted, *pemahkatotew* (VAI).

war paint *nanâtohk kopehikasowin* (NI).

warpath *nôtinkewâyâwin* (NI); *nôtinkeskanâw* (VII).

warrior Or brave, i.e.: used when referring to an older person, *nâpehkâsoweyinew* (NA); a warrior or brave, i.e.: used when referring to a younger person, *onâpehkâsoweyinis* (NA).

wart *ocehcekom* (NI) *(Northern)*; *micihcîkom* (NI) *(Plains)*; s/he has a wart, *ocehcîkomiw* (VAI).

war whoop War cry, *nôtinkew sâkowewin* (NI); s/he shouts out a war whoop, *sâkowew* (VAI); the act of shouting out a war whoop, *sâkowewin* (NI); s/he gives a screeching war whoop, *sâskwatwemiw* (VAI); the act of giving a screeching war whoop, *sâskwatwemowin* (NI).

wary The act of looking out for something, *ka asweyihtamihk* (NI); s/he is wary and leery of him, *seseskeyimew* (VTA).

was *etah kakeh ayâhk* (IPC).

wash The acting of doing laundry or washing clothes, *kisepekinikewin* (NI); s/he is washing her/his hands, *kisipekinicihcenew* (VAI); something to wash the face with, *kâsîhkwâkan* (NI); s/he washes another's face, *kâsîhkwenew* (VTA); s/he washes his/her own face, *kâsîhkwew* (VAI); a cloth used for drying, *kâsehkwehon* (NI); s/he makes her/him wash her/his face, *kâsîhkwehew* (VTA); s/he is washing the floor, *kisipekihtakinikew* (VAI); the act of washing the floor, *kisipekihtakinikewin* (NI); s/he is washing something for her/him, *kisipekinamawew* (VTA); s/he is washing her/him, *kisipekinew* (VTA); s/he soaks it, i.e.: the laundry, *kistâpâwahew* (VAI).

washable *kîkway takeh kisepekinkatek* (VII).

wasp *manicôsak katahkwahketwâw* (NA); *osâwamow* (NA).

waspish *awîyak ka nihtâ mâyiwicehiwet* (VAI).

waste Something that is no longer useful, *ekâ nânitâw ketapatahk kîkway* (VII); s/he makes her/him waste her/his time, *otamihew* (VTA).

wasteful *ka nihtâwepinkehk* (VAI).

wasting *kwanta misiwanacicikewin* (NI).

watchful *nâkateyihcikewin* (NI); *asawapow* (VAI).

water *nîpîy* (NI); rainwater, *kimowanâpoy* (NI); snow water, *konôwâpoy* (NI); slew water, *pihtapekwâpoy* (NI); river water, *sîpiwâpoy* (NI); creek, *sîpîsisâpoy* (NI); lake, *sâkahikanapoy* (NI); fire water, i.e.: whiskey, *iskotewâpoy* (NI); wine, *sôminâpoy* (NI); barley water, i.e.: beer, *iskwesisâpoy* (NI); boiling water, *ohtewâpoy* (NI); ice, *miskwamiwâpoy* (NI); it boils over, *sikahciwasiw* (VAI); *sikaciwatew* (VAI); boils vehemently, *sohkaciwasiw* (VAI); *sohkaciwahtew* (VTI); crimps by boiling or evaporation, *yoskaciwahtew* (VTI); boils down, *ihkacowasiw* (VAI); *ihkaciwatew* (VTI); it is boiling over, *pasitaciwasiw* (VAI); *pastâcowahtew* (VAI); in the middle of the water surface, *âpihtâwokam* (VII); excess of water, *ayiwâkipew* (VTI); water reaches high, up to there, *iskipew* (VTI); *iskopew* (VTI); the water touches, *sâmipew* (VTI); it is wet, *nîpîwâw* (VTI); it is deep, *timew* (VTI); the water is shallow, *pahkwâw* (VTI); there are plenty of water puddles, *nipîskâw* (VTI); stagnant water, *ayisipiy* (NI); red water, *mihkwâpoy* (NI); s/he waters the horses, *minikwahastimwew* (VTA); it is marshy, *nipîwan* (VII); a watery liquid, *nipîwâpoy* (NI); it is watery, *nipewiw* (VTI); a sweetened water, i.e.: pop or juice, *sîwapoy* (NI); salty water, i.e.: ocean brine, *siwihtâkanâpoy* (NI); cold water, *tahkamâpoy* (NI); the water is cold, *tahkamiw* (VII); *tahkamin* (VII); it is hot or boiling water, *kîsowâkamiw* (VII); it is hot, i.e.: soup, *kisâkamitew* (VAI); a very large body of water, i.e.: ocean or sea, *kihcikamiy* (NA) *(Plains)*; *kihcikamis* (NA) *(Northern)*.

watercourse It flows, *pimiciwan* (VII).

waterfall *kiskiciwan* (NI); rapids, *pawistik* (NI); a steep descent of river or stream, *nihtaciwan* (NI); water fall, *nîpîy kapahkihtik* (NI).

waterfowl A mudhen, *cakek* (NA); mallard, *yensep* (NA); duck, *sîsîp* (NA); seagull, *kîyâsk* (NA); Canada goose, *niska* (NA); pelican, *cahcakiw* (NA); loon, *mâkwa* (NA); swan, *wapisiw* (NA); male duck, *nâpesip* (NA); female duck, *nîsesip* (NA); helldiver, *sihkihp* (NA); grey goose, *cahkipasis* (NA).

water hole *wâyipîyaw* (NI).

water-logged *askepekihtak* (VII); it is saturated with water, *sapo ahkostin* (VII).

wave The act of waving one's hands, *wâstahikewin* (NI); s/he waves, *wâstahikew* (VAI); there are waves, *mahkâskâw* (VII); when the lake is stormy or very rough, i.e.: "there is a big wave," *mamahkâskâw* (VII); s/he waved at her/him, *wâstahamawew* (VTA); s/he waves in a desperate manner, *wastinikew* (VAI).

waver *owâstahikew* (NA).

wavy *makotowestikwanewin* (NI); *makotowepayowin* (NI); a person with wavy hair, *makotowestikwan* (VII).

way One way or moving in one direction only, *peyakwayak etah ka pahpimohtehk* (IPC); this way, i.e.: specifying direction, *oteyisih* (IPC); it is a well used way, *kistatamow* (IPC).

wayside On the side of a road, *patoteskanaw* (VII).

we Or us, *kîyânaw* (NA); someone else and me or we, *nîyanân* (NA).

weak Having no physical strength, *ekâ ka maskawisehk* (VAI); s/he is weak, *nesowisiw* (VAI); it is a weak situation, *nanihkâtan* (VII); s/he finds herself/himself too weak to perform, *nesoweyimisiw* (VAI); s/he thinks s/he is weak, *nesoweyimew* (VAI); s/he makes her/him weak, *nesowihew* (VTA); s/he becomes weak, *nesowipayiw* (VAI).

weaken *kîkway ka niyamsehtahk nawac* (VTI); *atinesowisiw* (VAI).

weakling A very weak person, *awîyak metoni ekâ ka maskawiset* (VAI); a weakling, fragile constitution, *nesowâtisiwin* (NI); s/he is a weakling, *nesowisiw* (VAI).

weakly *metoni papeyahtik* (VAI).

weakness *nanihkâtisiwin* (NI).

wealth *metoni ka weyotsihk* (VAI); being rich, *weyotisiwin* (NI).

wealthy *awîyak ka weyotsit* (VAI).

wean *poninohew* (VTA).

weapon Something you fight with, *nôtinkakan* (NI); a defensive weapon, *naskwâkan* (NI); the act of packing a weapon, *nemâskwewin* (NI).

wear Wearing something, *kakikiskamihk kîkway* (VAI); s/he wears it, *kikiskam* (VTI); s/he had pants on, *kikitâsew* (VTA); the act of wearing a holy garmet, *kihcitwasehowin* (NI); s/he has a coat or dress on, *kikasâkew* (VAI); s/he wears snowshoes, *kikasâmew* (VTI); s/he wears socks, *kikasikanew* (VTA); s/he has shoes on, *kikaskisinew* (VTI); s/he has gloves or mitts on, *kikastisew* (VTA); s/he has a hat on, *kikastotinew* (VTI); s/he has clothes on, *kikayowinsew* (VTI); s/he wears an emblem, *kiskiwehow* (VTI); the act of wearing something to be recognized by, i.e.: an emblem, *kiskiwehowin* (NI); s/he is wearing pants, *kitasew* (VTA); s/he wears new clothes, *oskisîhow* (VAI); the act of wearing new clothes, *oskisîhowin* (NI); s/he wears only one shoe, *napateskisinew* (VAI); s/he wears a slip or petticoat, *pihtawesâkew* (VTA); s/he wears underpants, i.e.: long johns or underwear, *pihtawetasew* (VTA); s/he puts on or wears undergarments, *pihtoskawew* (VTI); s/he wears a coat under another coat, *âhkwetawesâkew* (VTI); s/he wears suspenders, *pîmakamehpisiw* (VAI); s/he wears them around her/his neck, *tapiskawew* (VTA).

weariness *nestomahcihowin* (NI).

wearisome *kîkway ka nestohikohk* (VAI); causing physical fatigue, *nestosiwin* (NI).

weary *nestosewâyâwin* (NI); tired and disspirited, *nestwâyâwin* (NI).

weasel *sihkos* (NA).

weaselpelt *sihkosowayân* (NI).

weather This is how the weather is (expression), *tansi kîsikesikâk* (VII); indicating what the weather is like, *isikisikâw* (IPC) *(Northern)*; *isiwepan* (IPC) *(Plains)*; bad weather or a bad day, *mâyikisikâw* (VII).

weave *apihkewin* (NI).

weaver *otapihkew* (NA).

web A spider's web, *ocayapekes ocayapesa* (NA); a web, *tastawasakay* (NA).

webbed A duck or beaver's feet, *sîsîp ahpô amisk ositah.*

webfooted *ayapew sitew* (VAI); s/he has duck feet, *sîsîpisitew* (VAI).

webbing *ka mâmawi apihkâtek kîkway.*

473

wed *ka wikimiht awîyak* (VTA); s/he marries someone, *wîkimew* (VTA).

wedded *awîyak ka wîkihtot*.

wedding *wikihtowin* (NI); a church wedding, *kihci wikihtowin* (NI).

wedge A piece of steel used to split wood, *taskatahikânâpisk* (NI); a wedge, *sihtatahikan* (NI); a steel wedge, *taskihtakahikânâpisk* (NI); s/he wedges it between two objects, *pisohtaw* (VAI); s/he wedges them in, *sihcisimew* (VTI); s/he is wedged in, *sihcisin* (VAI).

wedlock An official wedding, *wîkihtahiwewin* (NI).

Wednesday It is Wednesday, *nistokesikaw* (VII).

wee *apisasisin* (IPC).

weeds *macikwanasa* (NI).

week One week, *peyak ayamihewkîsikâw* (VII); three weeks, *nisto ayamihewkîsikâw* (VII); days of the week, *kisikawa peyak ayamehewkîsikâw (Northern)*; *ohtia kîsikawa (Plains)*

weekly Every week, *tahto ayamihewkîsikâw* (VII).

weekend *ka poni ayamihewkîsikak* (VII).

weekly *tahtwaw peyak ayamihewkîsikâw* (VII).

ween *ka mâmitoneyihtamihk* (VTI).

weep *awîyak ka mâtot* (VAI).

weeper *omâtiw* (NA).

weevil A water beetle, *amiskosîs* (NA).

weigh The act of weighing something, *tipâpeskôcikewin* (NI); s/he is being weighed, *tipâpeskosiw* (VAI); s/he weighs them, *tipâpeskoyew* (VAI); s/he gets weighed, *tipâpeskosiw* (VAI).

weight *taniyikohk ka kosikwatihk* (IPC); how much do you weigh? *ispehtinikwatiwin* (IPC).

weighty *kosikwatiwin* (NI); s/he is heavy, *kosikwatiw* (VAI).

weird *kisâstaw ka môhcowisâyat awîyak* (VII); it looks scary, *kostâcinakwan* (VII).

welcome *miyoteh ka wisamiht awîyak* (IPC); lots of room, *mistahi tawâw* (IPC).

well Being well or in good health, *miyo âyâwin* (NI); s/he is well, *miyo âyâw* (VTI); s/he feels well, *miyomahcihow* (VAI).

well-behaved S/he behaves well, *kwayask isâyâwin* (VAI); s/he is well-behaved, *miyo ayiwiw* (VAI); the act of being well-behaved, *miyo ayiwiwin* (NI).

well-groomed Someone well-groomed or well-dressed, *awîyak ka takahkisehot* (VAI); s/he is well-groomed or well-dressed, *miyosihow* (VAI); the act of being well-groomed or well-dressed in finery, *miyosîhowin* (NI).

well-known *kwayask kiskeyihtakosiwin* (VAI); s/he is well-known, *kiskeyitakosiw* (VAI).

well-mannered *metoni manâtisiwin* (NI).

welt *âhkostahikan* (NI); a strip of leather on the upper part of a shoe, *âhkostahikan* (NI).

went When someone goes somewhere, *awîyak ka sipwehtet* (VAI); s/he went, *sipwehtew* (NI); s/he went to church, *nitawâyamihâw* (NI); s/he went to eat, *nitawimîcisiw* (NI).

wept *awîyak kakeh mâtot* (VAI).

were *etah kakeh ayâhk* (VTA).

west Where the sun sets, *pahkisimôtâhk* (VII); towards the west, *pahkisimownohk* (VII); the west side, *pahkisimôtâhk* (VII).

westerly *pahkisimôtâhk ka ohtihk*; towards the west, *pahkisi môtâhk isih*.

western *pahkisimôtâhk ohci*; a western way of life, *pahkisimôtâhk isitwawin*.

westward *pahkisimôtâhk isih*.

westwardly *nawâcpoko pahkisimôtâhk isih*.

wet *kîkway ka sâpopek* (VII); *ahkostin* (VAI); I am wet, *nisâpopan* (VAI); you are wet, *kisâpopan* (VAI); it *or* s/he is wet, *sapopew* (VII) *or* (VAI); we are wet, *nisâpopanan* (VAI); we are wet, *kisâpopananiw* (VAI); you are wet, *kisâpopanawaw* (VAI); wet up to very high, a flood, *iskopew* (VII); wetness, *sâpopewin* (NI); s/he gets them all wet, *ahkostimew* (VTA) *(Northern)*; s/he soaks them, *akohcimew* (VTA) *(Plains)*; s/he wets them, *sâpopahew* (VTA); it is kind of wet, i.e.: dewy, *sâpopeyâw* (VII); s/he wets the bed, *sikihkwamiw* (VAI).

wetland Land with plenty of water, *askîy mistahi kanipeskak* (VII); it is wetland, *nipewan* (VII).

whack *kîkway ka mistowetahamihk* (VTI).

whale *mistamek* (NA) *(Northern)*; *misiwâpamek* (NA) *(Plains)*.

wham *kîkway ka sohki tahamihk* (VTI).

wharf A landing where ships can be unloaded, *akwanasowin* (NI).

what Used when asking the question, "what", *kîkwây* (IPC); what kind of a thing?, *kîkwâyih* (IPC); what kind of things?, *kîkwâyah* (IPC); why? what for?, *tanekih* (IPC); in what place?, *kîkwanohk* (IPC); what kind of place, *kîkwanohk* (IPC).

whatever *kîkwây poko* (IPC); anything, *pakokîkwây* (IPC).

wheat *iskwesisihkân* (NA); a wheat seed or a grain processed into flour, *pahkwesikanimin* (NA); a wheat straw, *pahkwesikanâhtikwaskosîs* (NI); *pawahikan* (NI).

wheaten *pahkwesikanihkan* (VTI).

wheedle *awîyak ka wayesimiht* (NI); to persuade by flattery, *kaskimowewin* (NI).

wheel *otihtipipayiw* (NI).

wheeled *awîyak ka tihtipiniht* (VTA).

474

wheeze *sihciyehewin* (NI); to breathe with difficulty, *kitowetamowin* (NI).

wheezy *mistatim ka paskatahtahk* (VAI).

whelp A young puppy, *oskascimos* (NA).

whenever Or anytime, *poko ispeh* (IPC); whenever or when, *pahkaci* (IPC).

where *tânte* (IPC); where is your father?, *taniwâ ki papa* (VII); where is the gun?, *tânte pâskisikan* (IPC); where were you last night?, *tânte eyayen tipiskok* (IPC); where is he?, *taniwâ*; where are they?, *taneweka*; where is he or that should be here?, *awînipan*; where are you going?, *tânte etohteyan* (VAI).

whereas Or "and so it is", *tâsipwa* (IPC).

wherever *sôskwâc pokwete* (IPC).

whet S/he sharpens it, *tâsaham* (VTI).

which Which one, *tanima* (IPC); which one, *tana* (IPC); which ones, *tana aniki* (IPC); *tananiki* (IPC); relative, *tana anihi* (IPC); which one, *tana* (IPC).

whichever *poko tanima* (IPC).

while Or during, *mekwâc* (IPC); a while, *nomih* (IPV); a little while, *nomes* (IPV).

whim *iteyihtamiwin* (NI).

whimper *mâtowihtakosowin* (NI).

whimsical *ka môhconikeskihk* (VAI).

whimsy *ka nihtâ môhconikehk* (VAI).

whine *ka pîkiskweskihk* (VAI); *nesowitakosiw* (VAI); *kitimâkitakosiw* (VAI).

whinny *awîyak ka pîkiskweskit, mistatim okitowin* (NI).

whip *pasastehikan* (NI); s/he whips her/him or s/he traps it, *nocihew* (VAI); s/he whips her/his dog team or team of horses, *nocihastimwew* (VTA); s/he cracks or snaps the whip, *pâhkwestehikew* (VAI); the act of cracking or snapping a whip, *pâhkwestehikew* (VAI); the act of cracking or snapping a whip, *pâhkwestehikewin* (NI); s/he whips them loudly or noisily, *pâhkwestewew* (VTA); s/he whips her/his children, *pasastehâwasiw* (VAI); s/he makes a whip with it, *pasastehikanihkâkew* (VAI); s/he makes a whip for her/him, *pasatehikanihkawew* (VTA); s/he makes a whip, *pasastehikanikew* (VAI); the act of whipping children, *pasastehâwasiwin* (NI); the act of whipping someone, *pasastehowewin* (NI); s/he whips her/him, *pasastehwew* (VTA).

whirl *ka wasakakotek kîkway* (VII); *wasakapayiw* (VII).

whirlwind Or tornado, *pastosiwan* (NA); there is a whirlwind or tornado, *pastosiwiw* (NA).

whisk *kisiskâc itehikewin* (NI).

whiskers *meyastowâna*.

whisper The act of whispering, *kîmocipîkiskwewin* (NI) *(Northern)*; *kimwewin* (NI) *(Plains)*; s/he whispers, *kîmocipîkiskwew* (VAI) *(Northern)*; *kimwew* (VAI) *(Plains)*.

whiskey Firewater or alcohol, *iskotewâpoy* (NI).

whiskey jack Or Canada jay, *weskacan* (NA); *wîskacân* (NA) *(Northern)*; *wîskipôs* (NA) *(Plains)*

whistle *ka kweskosehk* (VAI); it whistles past, *cowekotew* (VYI); a whistle, *kitôpicikân* (NI); s/he whistles, *kweskosew* (VAI).

white Something white, *kawâpiskâk* (VII); it is white, *wâpiskâw* (VII); it is white, i.e.: iron or metal, *wâpâpiskisiw* (VAI); an area covered with white colored trees, i.e.: white poplar or birch, *wapâskweyâw*; it has white fur, *wapâwew* (VAI); white hide, *wâpekin* (NI) *(Northern)*; *wâpiskipahkekin* (NI) *(Plains)*; it is white, i.e.: a prime animal skin, *wâpiksiw* (VAI) *(Northern)*; *wâpasakew* (VAI) *(Plains)*; it has white, prime fur, *wâpiwayanew* (VAI) *(Plains)*; *wâpiskekisiw* (VAI) *(Northern)*; s/he has her/his white suit on, *wâpiskayiwinisew* (VAI); a white cloth, *wâpiskekin* (NI); the entire lengthy of it is white, *wâpiskiyâpekan* (VII); the entire length of her/him is white, *wâpiskiyâpekisiw* (VAI); s/he makes him white, *wâpiskihew* (VTA); s/he is white in color, *wâpiskisiw* (VAI); a white dog, *wâpiskatim* (NA) *(Plains)*; a white bead, *wâpimîkis* (NA) *(Plains)*; *wâpimin* (NA) *(Northern)*;

whitecap The lake is full of whitecaps, *wâpimahkâskâw* (VII) *(Northern)*; *mâmahkâskâw* (VII) *(Plains)*.

whitefish *atihkamek* (NA).

whiten *ka wâpiskinamihk kîkway*; s/he really whitens clothes, *wâpiskinam* (VTI).

white spruce *wâpasiht* (NA).

white water *ka mahkâskak* (VII); *wâpacowanâw* (VII).

white willow A wolf shrub, *mahihkanâhtik* (NA).

whitewood *ka wâpihtakak mistik* (NI).

whither *tânte* (IPC).

whittle Whittling something, *ka môhkotamihk kîkway*; it has been whittled down, *acowihkotew* (VII); it is whittled thin, *pakihkotew* (VII); to whittle with a knife, *môhkocikewin* (NI); s/he commences whittling on them for a while, *nomihkahtawew* (VTA) *(Plains)*; *nomihkotew* (VTA) *(Northern)*.

whizz *matwepimipayiw* (VTI).

who *awîna* (IPC); who is your grandmother?, *awîna kohkomin*; who is there or who are you?, *awîna keyah*; who is it?, *awîna awa*; who are they?, *awîniki*; *awîna ewokah*.

475

whoever *awîna poko*; *poko awîyak*.

whole Something in one piece, *kîkway kamisiweyak*; it is whole or in one piece, *misiweyâw* (VII); s/he is whole or complete, *kahkisiw* (VAI); s/he is completely whole or all in one piece, *misiwesiw* (VAI); being whole or all in piece, *misiwesiwin* (NI); all of it, *kahkiyaw* (IPC); the whole way, *misakâme* (IPC).

who will *awîna kaweh totahk*.

wholly *metoni ispehcikaskihtahk* (VII).

whom *awîna ohci*.

whomever *awîna poko*.

whoop *sâkowewin* (NI).

whooping crane *otcak ka sâkowet* (NA).

whore *iskwew ka atâwaket wihpehtowin* (NA); *pisikwâtiskwew* (NA).

whose *awîna ohci*.

why *tânehki* (IPC).

wick A piece of fiber for a coal oil lamp, *waskotenikaneyapiy* (NI).

wicked S/he is wicked, *macayiwiw* (VAI); *awîyak ka macihtwât*.

wickedness *macihtwâwin* (NI).

wide It is wide, *ayakaskaw* (VII); s/he is wide, i.e.: fat, *taswekisow* (VAI) *(Northern)*; *âyakaskisiw* (VAI) *(Plains)*.

widely *ospeh tayakaskak* (VII).

widen *ayakaskisihtâw* (VII).

widow *môsiskwew* (NA).

widower *môsâpew* (NA).

widowhood *awîyak owikimâkana ka wanihat*; being a single woman, *môsiskwewewin* (NI).

wield Wielding something for hitting, *pakamâtihpehikewin* (NI).

wife My married partner, *niwekimakan* (NA); my wife, *nîwah* (NA); he has a wife, *wewow* (VAI); an elderly woman or used when referring to one's wife, *nôcokwîsiw* (NA) *(Northern)*; *nôcikwesiw* (NA) *(Plains)*.

wig Artificial hair, *mestakâhkâna* (NI).

wiggle *mimikowin* (NI).

wiggler *awîyak ka mimikot* (VAI).

wiggly *kanihtâ mimikohk* ().

wigwam *mîkowâhp* (NA).

wild Being untamed or untouched or wild, *pipikwâc isâyâwin*; a loner (in the bush), *pikwaciyiniw* (NA).

wildcat *pikwaciminôs* (NA).

wilderness An isolated country, *pikwacaskîy* (NI).

wild-fire *ka misi wayatek*; to spread like wild fire, *sipweyaskitew*.

wile *awîyak ka nihtâ wayesihkemot*.

wiliness *nihtâ wayesihkemowin* (NI).

will Personal intention, *nakatâmakewasinahikan kosîhtâh*; *kîkway kâwi tôtamihk*.

willed *miyoteh katôtamihk*.

willful *or* **wilful** *ohcitâw ka tôtamihk*.

willfully *or* **wilfully** *awîyak ohcitâw katôtahk*.

willing Doing something willingly, *miyoteh tôtamowin* (NI); s/he expresses a willingness to undertake it, *tepakeyimiw* (VAI); the act of expressing willingness to undertake a task, *tepakeyimowin* (NI).

willow *nîpisîy* (NI); a clump of willows, *nîpisihkopâw* (VII); a willow stick, *nîpisîyâhtik* (NI); a willow bush, *nîpisîy* (NI).

willowy *nîpisîskâw* (VII).

wilt *ka nipemakahk nipîhkanis*; it died out, *nipomakan* (VII).

wily *maci iyinisowin* (NA).

win S/he wins, *otahowew* (VAI); the act of winning, *otahowewin* (NI); s/he wins her/him over, *kaskihew* (VTA); s/he wins from her/him or s/he beats her/him at game, *otahwew* (VTA).

wince *ka asepayihohk* (VAI).

wind *yôtin* (NI); wind on water, *yôtinpeyaw* (VTI); piled up by wind and water, *asahokiw* (VTA); *asahotew* (VTA); broken by the wind, *pîkwâsiw* (VAI); *pikwâstan*; dispersed by the wind, *pîwâstan* (VTI); there is wind from that direction, *ohtin* (VTI); the wind diminishes, *asteyotin* (VTI); the wind falls, there is no more wind, *pôniyotin* (VTI); the wind dies down, *aywâstin* (VTI); a wind that is heard passing by, *pimowestin* (VTI); whirlwind, *apamotin* (NI); there is a cold wind, *kisiniyôtin* (VII); there is a warm wind, i.e.: in winter a chinook, *kisôpweniyôtin* (VII); there is a cool wind, *tahkiyowew* (VII); the wind blows through, there is an air current, *sâpoyowew* (VTI); there is a strong wind, hurricane, *kîstin* (VTI); there is a north wind, *kîwetin* (VTI); you can hear the wind, *matwewestin* (VTI); the wind is beginning to blow, *matowestin* (VTI); the wind is contrary, against us, *nayiman* (VTI); the wind is favorable, with us, *namowan* (VTI); *namowanaw* (VTI); there is a whirlwind or a tornado, *pastosiwew* (NA); a whirlwind or tornado, *pastosiwan* (NA); the wind blows right through it, *sâpwâstan* (VTI); a south wind, *sâwaniyôtin* (NI) *(Plains and Northern variant)*; *kîsopwenyotim* (VTI).

wind The act of winding or cranking, *pîmâstehikewin* (NI); s/he winds it too tight and it broke, i.e.: a clock, *pîkwâstehwew* (VTA); s/he winds or screws them, *pemahwew*; it winds automatically, *pîminikepayiw* (VII).

windbreak *tipinawahikan* (VII); free from wind,
tipinawâw; making a wind break,
tipinawâhikewin (NI).

winded *pâskatahtamowin* (NI);
kipeyihtamahowewin (NI).

winding *wahwâkamiw* (VII).

windpipe A person's windpipe, *kohtaskway* (NI).

windy It is windy, *yôtin* (VII); a huge wind, *miseyotin*
(VII).

wine S/he makes wine, *sôminapohkew* (VAI); raisin
liquid, *sôminâpoy* (NI).

wing *mitahtahkwan* (NI).

wink *ka napatehkâpipayihohk*; *napatehkapiw* (VII).

winker *onapatehkâpipayihiw* (NA).

winner One who wins, *otahowew* (NA).

winnings A bunch of winnings, *otahowewina* (NI).

winnow *ka pawahikehk* (NA).

winter The whole winter, *kapepipon* (VII); it is
winter, *pipon* (VII); next winter, *pipohki*; last
winter, *piponohk* (VII); it is bad winter, *mâyipipon*
(VII); this winter, *ôma kâ pipohk* (VII); it is just like
winter, *piponâyâw* (VII); s/he spends the winter
here, *piponisiw* (VAI); the act of spending the winter
someplace, *piponisiwin* (NI).

wintertime *ka mekwâpipohk* (VII).

wintry *ka tahkâyâk* (VII).

wipe The act of wiping, *kâsehikewin* (NI); the act of
wiping one's own hands clean, *kâsîcihcewin* (NI);
s/he wipes someone else's hands clean,
kâsîcihcenew (VTA); the act of wiping oneself clean
after a bowel movement, *kimisahôwin* (NI); s/he
wipes herself/himself clean after a bowel
movement, *kimisâhow* (VAI); s/he wipes her/his
own hands dry, *pâhkocihcehosiw* (VAI); s/he wipes
her/his hands dry for her/him, *pâhkocicehwew*
(VTA); s/he wipes her/his own feet dry,
pâhkositehosiw (VAI); s/he wipes her/his feet dry for
her/him, *pâhkositehwew* (VTA).

wiry *awîyak ka maskawsiwayat* (VAI).

wisdom *iyinisowin* (NI); s/he imparts wisdom to her/
him, *iyinisikahtew* (VAI); being smart, *iyinisewin*
(NI).

wisdom tooth *awîyak okistapitan* (NA).

wise S/he is wise or intelligent, *iyinisiw* (VAI).

wish *akâwâtamowin* (NI); *akâwâtam* (VTI).

wishbone A lucky bone, *oskanis kapapiwek* (NI); a
wishbone of a bird, *ospasew* (NI).

wishful *ka akâwâcikehk* (VAI).

wisp *ka asahpicekwaw maskosiya*.

wispy *kâskapahtew ka petâpahtepayik*.

wistful *kwanta akawâcikewin* (NI).

wit *iyinisiw mâmitoneyihcikan*; *wiyatwewin* (NI).

witch *kîskwehkan iskwew* (NA); *powâkan iskwew*
(NA); a wonder woman, *mamahtâw iskwew* (NA).

witchcraft S/he performs witchcraft or spiritually
powerful acts, *mamahtawisihcikew* (VAI); *kîkway
ka kîskwehiwemakahk*.

witchery *kîskwehiwewin* (NI); *mamahtâwisiwinihk*
(NI).

with *asici* (IPC); with something else, *kiki* (IPV); with,
for that, from, for, *ohci* (IPC).

withdrew *awîyak kakeh kâwihotiniket* (VAI).

wither *kiscikânis ka nipemakahk* (VII); it is dried up,
pastew (VII).

withheld *kîkway kakeh miciminamakehk* (VAI).

withhold *kîkway ka miciminamihk* (VTI);
kipihtinam (VTI); *kanaweyitam* (VTI); the
withholding of something, *kipihtinkewin* (NI).

within *pehcayihk* (IPC).

without *ekâ ka ayâhk kîkway*; s/he is without,
kwetamâw.

withstand S/he withstands, *nepawestam*; *kîkway
ka nîpawistamihk* (VAI).

withstood *kîkway ka kihnîpawistamihk* (VTI).

witty *awîyak ka nanoyatsiskit* (VAI).

wives *awîyakwak wiwiwawak* (VAI).

wizard A person who performs magic,
mamahtawiyiniw (NA).

wobble Back and forth, *kahkekwask*; *kesayahpayihk*
(VAI).

woe *mâyipayiwin* (NI); *kakwâtakan* (VII).

woeful *mistahi ka mayipayihk* (VAI); a deplorable
person, *kakwâtakemowin* (NI).

woke *awîyak kakeh koskopayit* (VAI).

wolf *mahihkan* (NA); wolfskin, *mahihkaniwayân*
(NI); s/he is a wolf, *mahihkaniwiw* (VAI).

wolverine An adult wolverine, *kihkwahâkew* (NA); a
small wolverine, *kekwahâkes* (NA).

woman *iskwew* (NA); an old woman, *notokew* (NA); a
new woman, *oskeskwew* (NA); a white woman,
mônîyâskwew (NA); an unmarried or single woman,
môsiskwew (VAI); an elderly woman or used when
referring to one's wife, *nôcokwîsiw* (NA) (Northern);
nocɪkwesɪw (NA) (Plains); she has become an old
woman, *nôtokwewiw* (VAI) (Northern); *nôcikwesiw*
(NA) (Plains); a woman from down river, i.e.: a Stony
woman, *omâmihkwew* (NA); a young woman,
oskinîkiskwew (NA); she is a young woman,
oskinîkiskwewiw (VAI); an immoral or unchaste
woman, i.e.: a prostitute, *pisikwâtiskwew* (NA).

womanhood *iskwewowin* (NI).

womankind *iskwewak* (NA).

womanlike *peyakwan iskwew* (IPC).

womanly *awîyak ka miyo iskwewit* (VAI);
iskwewiw; being womanly, *iskwewowin* (NI).

477

womb A woman's womb, *mispayaw* (NA).

women *ayîwak peyak iskwew* (NA); there are many women, *iskweskâw* (NA).

won When something has been won, *kakeh otahowehk kîkway* (VAI); s/he won, *paskeyâkew* (VAI); *otahowew* (VAI).

wonder S/he wonders, *mâmaskâtam* (VTI); s/he achieves awe-inspiring wonders, *mâmaskâcihcikew* (VAI); the act of achieving awe-inspiring wonders or marvels, *mâmaskâcihcikewin* (NI); it is an extraordinary happening, *mâmaskâcihkin* (VII).

wonderful It is wonderful or amazing, *mâmaskâteyihtâkwan* (VII); s/he is wonderful or amazing, *mâmaskateyihtâkosiw* (VAI); an exclamation of surprise: "it is amazing or astonishing", *mâmaskâc* (IPC).

wonderment The act of wondering, *mâmaskâtamowin* (NI).

wonderous *sôskwâc tamâmaskâtamihk* (VTI).

won't Will not, *ekâ kawehtôtamihk* (IPC); *namoya* (IPC).

woo *sâkocihiwewin* (NI); s/he pursues him/her, *nocihiskwewâtew* (VTA).

478

wood One piece of firewood, *mihtih* (NI); a piece of wood, *mistik* (NA); it is a long log, *kinohtakisiw* (VAI); it is a long piece of firewood, *kinohtakâw* (VII); it is a sheet-like, flat plank, *napakihtakisiw* (VAI); it is flat plank, *napakihtakâw* (VII); it is a long piece of wood, *kinowaskosiw* (VAI); it is a long piece of wood, *kinowaskwan* (VII); it is a solidly planted or hard to pull out piece of wood, *ayâtaskosiw* (VTA); it is hard to pull out, *ayâtaskitew* (VTI); it is a strong piece of wood, *maskawâskosiw* (VAI); it is a strong piece of wood, *maskawâskwan* (VII); it is a round log, *notimâskosiw* (VAI); it is a round pole, *notimâskwan* (VII); it is a narrow strip of wood, *sâkawaskosiw* (VAI); it is a narrow strip of wood, *sâkawâskwan* (VII); it is a light piece of wood, i.e.: not heavy, *yahkâskosiw* (VAI); it is a light pole, i.e.: not heavy, *yahkâskwan* (VII); it is a soft piece of wood, *yoskihtakisiw* (VAI); it is a soft piece of wood, *yoskihtakâw* (VII); it is a short piece of wood, *cimaskosiw* (VAI); it is a short piece of wood, *cimaskwan* (VII); it is a crooked or bent piece of wood, *wâkâskosiw* (VAI); it is a crooked or bent piece of wood, *wâkâskwan* (VII); wet wood or green wood, *askipekihtâkaw* (NI); a whole piece of wood, i.e.: a plank or log, *misiwêyahtik* (NI); a dried piece of wood, i.e.: trees, *pâstewahtik* (NI); a rotten piece of wood, *wînihtak* (NI); it is a partly burned piece of wood, *yahkâskosew* (VTI); a powdery, soft wood used for smoking moose hide, *yoskihtâk* (NA).

woodchuck A ground hog, *winasakâcihp* (NA).

woodcock A small brown game bird, *weyikonew* (NA).

woodcutter *onikohtew* (NA).

wooded *ka sakâk* (VII); there are woods, *sakâw* (VII); there is open woods, finely wooded, *sipeyaw* (VII); *sipeyaskweyâw* (VII).

wooden Something made out of wood, *mistik ka ohci osihcikatek*; it is wooden, *mistikowan* (VII); it is wooden, *mistikowiw* (VAI); s/he makes her/him a wooden box, *mistikowatihkawew* (VTA).

woodland *sakâw* (NA); *mistikowaskaw* (VTA); a piece of land with timber, *mistikowaskîy* (NI); *otinahtikwewaskîy* (NI).

woodpecker *pahpahscîs* (NA) *(Northern)*; *pahpahkwecakahikesîs* (NA) *(Plains)*; a small woodpecker, *pahpahscisis* (NA); a large woodpecker, *misipahpahscîs* (NA) *(Northern)*; *opâhpâhkwecakahikesîs* (NA) *(Plains)*.

wood pigeon *sakâwimehmew* (NA).

woodsman A bush man, *sakâwiyiniw* (NA).

wood thrush *okaweyoskesikosîs* (NA).

woodwork A piece of woodwork, *mistikowan atoskewin* (NI).

woody *kîkway ka mistikowik*.

wool Sheep's wool, *mâyacihkos opîwayan* (NI); sheep skin, *mâyatihkowayân* (NI).

woollen *or* **woolen** A woolen article, *sestakwâya* (NI).

woolly Something woolly, *kîkway ka sestakowik* (VII).

word *pîkiskwewinis* (NI); words, *pîkiskwewina* (NI).

wore *kakeh kiskamihk kîkway* (VTI).

work Working, *atoskewin* (NI); s/he works at it, *mâsihtâw* (VTI); it works well, *nahipayiw* (VTI); s/he consistently works hard, *kakâyawisiw* (VAI) *(Northern)*; *ayiwâkispihtisiw* (VAI) *(Plains)* s/he works with her/him, *wecâtoskemew* (VTA).

worker *otatoskew* (NA); an industrious worker, *okâyawisiw* (NA) *(Plains)*; *ayiwâkispihtisiw* (NA) *(Northern)*.

working *ka mekwâ atoskehk* (VAI).

world All over the world, *misiweskamik* (VTA); world, *askîy* (NI); all over the world, *misiweyita askîy* (VTI); in all the world, *misiweskamik* (VTA); the ancient world, *kayâseskamik* (IPC); together with earth, mixed with earth, mixed with world, *asitaskamik* (VTA); on the surface of the world, *waskitaskamik* (VTA).

worm *manicôs* (NA).

wormy *ka manicosowik* (VII).

worn Something that you have worn, *kîkway kakeh kiskamihk*.

worn-out Something you wear out, *kîkway kamestiskamihk*; it is used up or worn-out, i.e.: snowshoes, *mestisin* (VTI); it is all used up or worn-out, i.e.: moccasins; it is entirely worn-out, *mestihtin* (VTI); something that is used up or worn out, *mâskakân* (VII).

worry Someone worrying, *mistahi kamâmitoneyihtamihk* (VTI); s/he is worried, *wâneyihtam* (VTI); s/he cause her/him worries, *mikoskâteyihtamihew* (VTA); s/he worries about her/him, *pîkweyimew* (VAI); s/he makes her/him worry, *wâneyihtamihew* (VTA); her/his words make her/him worry, *wâneyihtamimew* (VTA); the act of worrying, *wâneyihtamowin* (NI).

worse *ayîwak isâyâwin* (VII); s/he is worse, *ayîwak sâyâw*.

worsen *tahki ayîwak kesâyahk*.

worship The act of worshipping, *mawemoscikewin* (NI); the act of praying or worshipping, *ayamihâwin* (NI); s/he worships the sacred, *manitohkâtew* (VAI).

worst *ayîwak ka mâyâtahk* (VII).

worth *kispîhteyihtakwahk* (VII); s/he or it has worth or value, *itakisiw* (VAI); it has worth or values, it costs, *itakitew* (VII).

worthless Something of worthless value, *piwâyi*; s/he is thought as being worthless, *pîweyihtâkosiw* (VAI); it is thought of as being worthless, *pîweyihtâkwan* (VII); the act of thinking of something as being worthless, *pîweyihtamowin* (NI); s/he thinks s/he is worthless or s/he has a low opinion of her/him, *pîweyimew* (VAI); s/he believes herself/himself to be worthless, *pîweyimisiw* (VAI); the act of believing oneself to be worthless or having a low opinion of oneself, *pîweyimisiwin* (NI); the act of believing someone to be worthless, *pîweyimiwewin* (NI); it costs that much, *itakihtew* (VII).

worthy The act of being considered worthy, *ispîteyihtakosowin* (NI); s/he is worthy of it, *tepakeyihtakosiw* (VAI); it is worthy of it , *tepakeyihtâkwan* (VII); it is worth it, *ispîhteyihtâkwan* (VII).

would not *pomewin* (IPC).

wound The act of cutting oneself, *mansosowin* (NI); it is wound or turned, i.e.: like a clock, *pîminikâsiw* (VAI); it is wound or turned, *pîminikâtew* (VII).

wounded A wounded animal or person, *miswâkan* (VII); s/he is wounded or injured, *miswakaniwiw* (VAI).

wrangle *ka paminastimwehk* (VAI).

wrap The act of wrapping, *wewekinkewin* (NI); wrapping paper, *wewekinikan* (NI) *(Plains)*; *wekinikan* (NI) *(Northern)*; s/he is good at wrapping up the baby, *nihtâ wekinawasow* (VAI); being good at wrapping up a baby, *nihtâ wekinawasowin* (NI); s/he removes the wrapping, *pâskekinew* (VAI); the wrapping or covering is removed off of her/him, *pâskekinikâsiw* (VAI); the wrapping is removed off it, *pâskekinikâtew* (VII); s/he has enough to wrap them up, *tepekinew* (VAI); s/he wraps herself/himself up, i.e.: in a blanket, *tipekîw* (VAI); s/he lays her/him down all wrapped up, *tipekisimew* (VTA); s/he lies all wrapped up, *tipekisin* (VAI); s/he wraps her/him up, *wikinew* (VTA) *(Northern)*; *wewekinew* (VTA) *(Plains)*; s/he wraps up her/his head, i.e.: a scarf, *wekistikwanew* (VAI) *(Northern)*; *wewekistikwânew* (VAI) *(Plains)*; s/he wraps her/him up into a bundle, *wewekahpitew* (VTA) *(Plains)*; *wekahpitew* (VTA) *(Northern)*.

wrath *ka wîsakiyawesihk* (VAI); being mad, *kisiwâsowin* (NI).

wrathful *awîyak ka kisiwâsiskit*.

wreck A damaged vehicle, *ka pekosihk otâpânâsk* (NA); s/he wrecked it with a heavy object, i.e.: a hammer or axe, *pîkwawew* (VAI); a total wreck, *sikosin* (VII).

wrest *masaskoniwewin* (NI).

wrestle The sport of wrestling, *mâsihitowin* (NI); s/he wrestles with her/him, *masihew* (VTA); they wrestle, *mâsihitowak* (VAI); s/he wrestles, *mâsihkew* (VAI); the act of wrestling, *mâsihkewin* (NI); s/he wrestles with it or works at it, *mâsihtâw* (VAI).

wrestling *mâsihitowin* (NI); the game of wrestling, *mâsihkewin* (NI).

wretch *macâyis* (IPC); a person in great misfortune, *omâyipayiw* (NA).

wretched *mistahi macihtwâwin* (VII); miserably sad, *kakwâtakeyimow* (VAI).

wriggle *ka mimikohk* (VAI).

wring The act of wringing something out, *sînikewin* (NI); s/he rinses them and wrings them out, *sînew* (VAI); s/he puts them through the automated wringer, *sînipitew* (VAI).

wrinkle *pânahkwasakayewin* (NI); *ocipwâw* (VII).

wrist *mispitonihk ohci âniskawkanan* (NI).

wristband *akokwâcikan manakwahk ohci*; *kispison* (NI).

write Writing or owing a debt, *masinahamâkewin* (NI); the act of corresponding or owing a debt, *masinahamâtowin* (NI); s/he writes for her/him or s/he owes her/him or is in debt to her/him, *masinahamawew* (VTA); s/he writes with it, *masinahikâkew* (VAI); s/he makes her/him write or hires her/him, *masinahikehew* (VTA); it is written, *masinahikatew* (VAI); s/he has a debt, *masinahikew*

479

(VAI); a writing or debit, **masinahikewin** (NI); s/he is historically recorded, **masinahikâsiw** (VAI); s/he writes her/his biography, **masinahwew** (VAI); s/he has written or marked her/him down wrong, **patasinahwew** (VTA); the act of writing funny things, **waweyasasinahikewin** (NI).

writhe The act of writhing in pain, **tihtipahpinewin** (NI).

writing The act of writing, **masinahikewin** (NI).

wrong **naspâc** (IPC); something wrong, **naspâci kîkway**; all wrong, completely wrong, **ayasâwâc**; s/he is wrong, **naspâtisiw** (VAI) *(Northern)*; **mâyitôtam** (VAI) *(Plains)*; the act of being wrong, **naspâtisiwin** (NI) *(Northern)*; **mâyitôtamowin** (NI) *(Plains)*; not right, **naspâc** (IPC).

wrongful **metoni naspâc** (IPC); wrongly, **namoya kwayask**.

wrung **kakeh sînamihk** (VTI).

wry **ka pemkwayawepayihk** (VAI).

X, Y, Z

xerox *ka masinpayitahk masinahikan* (VTI)

x-ray S/he x-rays her/him, *sâpwâpamew* (VTA); s/he x-rays it, *sâpwâpahtam* (VTI); s/he x-rays people, *sâpwâpamiwew* (VTA); s/he x-rays things, *sâpwâpahcikew* (VTI).

yank *ka sikoc ocipitamihk kîkway* (VTI); *sisikoc ocipitam* (VTI).

yap *ka ayahkotonâmohk* (VAI).

yard A unit of measurement equaling a yard, *tipahikan* (IPC); one yard or one hour or one o'clock, *peyak tipahikan* (IPC); if on the road, i.e.: a step, *tahkoskewin* (NI); a measure for cloth, lumber, etc., *tipahikan* (IPC); a yard stick, *tipahikanahtik* (NA).

yarn A skein of yarn for knitting, *sestak* (NI).

yawn *tâwatiw*, (VAI); opening your mouth when you are sleepy, *ka tawatihk ka nohtehkwasihk* (VAI); the act of opening your mouth or yawning, *tâwatowin* (NI).

year One year, also one piece of land, *peyak askîy* (IPC).

yearling A yearling animal, *piponâskos* (NA).

yearly *tahtwawkaskewik* (VII); every year, *tahtwaskîy* (VII).

yearn To be filled with longing, *kaskeyihtamowin* (NI).

yearning *ka kaskeyihtamihk* (VAI).

yellow It is yellow or orange, *osâwâw* (VII); it shines a yellow color, *osâwâskotew* (VAI); the pole has a yellow color, *osâwaskwan* (VII); the sky is yellow, *osâwaskwâw* (VII); being yellow in color, *osâwisowin* (NI); s/he is yellow in color, *osâwisiw* (VAI); yellow jaundice, *osâwâspinewin* (NI).

yellowish It is yellow in color, *osâwnâkwan* (VII).

yellow jacket *osâwâmowak* (NA); a yellow jacket, *osâwâmosis* (NA).

yellow warbler *osâwaskopîwâyisis* (NA) *(Northern)*; *osâwaskopiyesîs* (NA) *(Plains)*.

yelp *atim ka mawmot* (VTI).

yes *îhi* (IPC) *(Northern)*; *ehâ* (IPC) *(Plains)*.

yesterday *otâkosîhk* (IPC); three days ago or two days after yesterday, *kihci awas otâkosîhk* (IPC); day after yesterday, *awastâkosîhk* (IPC).

yet *keyapic* (IPC); *ceskwa* (IPC); not yet, *nameskwa* (IPC); *namoya ceskwa* (IPC).

yield *kohpikihk kîkway* (VTI); to surrender or give something up, *pakitinamakewin* (NI).

yielding *ohpikihcikewin* (NI).

yip *ka mikisimot atim* (VTI).

yoke *mistik kotapaketwaw mostoswak* (NI); a wooden yoke for oxen, *tapiskakanahtik* (NA).

yolk The yellow of an egg, *ka osâwak wawih* (NI); *pehcayihk* (LN).

yonder *awasahcahk* (LN).

you *kîya* (IPC).

young Being young, *koskayowihk* (VII); s/he makes her/him young, *oskâyiwihew* (VTA); s/he is young, *oskâyiwiw* (VAI).

younger brother My younger brother, *nisîmis* (NA).

younger sister My younger sister, *nisîmis* (NA).

youngest brother *osîmimâw* (NA).

youngest sister *osîmimâw* (NA).

youngish *nawâc poko oskâyowiwin* (NA).

youngster *oskâyiseyenow* (NA); young people, *oskâyak* (NA).

your *kîya ôma* (IPC).

you are *or* you're *kîya ketikaweyin* (IPC).

yours This is yours, *kîyawâw ôma* (NI); that is yours, *kîyanima* (NI); this is all yours, *kîyawaw* (NI).

yourself *kîya poko* (IPC); only you or yourself, *kîyatipiyawi* (IPC).

yourselves *kîyawâw poko* (IPC).

youth *oskinîkiw* (NA); he is a young man, *oskinîkowow* (VII); she is a young woman, *oskinîkiskwewiw* (VII); being young, *oskinîkewin* (NI).

youthful S/he is young, *oskinîkowin* (NI); being young, *ka oskâyahk* (VII); being youthful, *oskâyiwiwin* (NI).

youthfully *oskâyowenihk isih* (LN).

Yule The Lord's day, i.e.: Christmas, *manito okîsikam* (IPC); *manitow kîsikâw* (IPC) *(Plains)*.

Yuletide The act of singing yuletide hymns, *nîpâyamihâwin* (NI).

yummy *kâwi kasik kîkway* (VTI).

zap *ka sikotatahoht awîyak* (VTA).

zeal *metoni tapwe wokeyihtamowin* (NI); being full of zeal, enjoyment, *cîhkeyohtamowin* (NI).

zealous Showing lots of zeal, *kakâyawâyâwin* (NI); *awîyak ka sohkitapwewokeyihtahk* (VAI); *ayiwâkeyitam* (VAI).

zero *namahkîway* (IPC).

zest *môcikeyihtamowin* (NI); s/he is happy, *meyawatam* (VAI).

zestful *ka môcikayahk* (VAI).

zig zag *wâwâkastew* (VTI).

zoom *cowehkotew* (VTI).

481

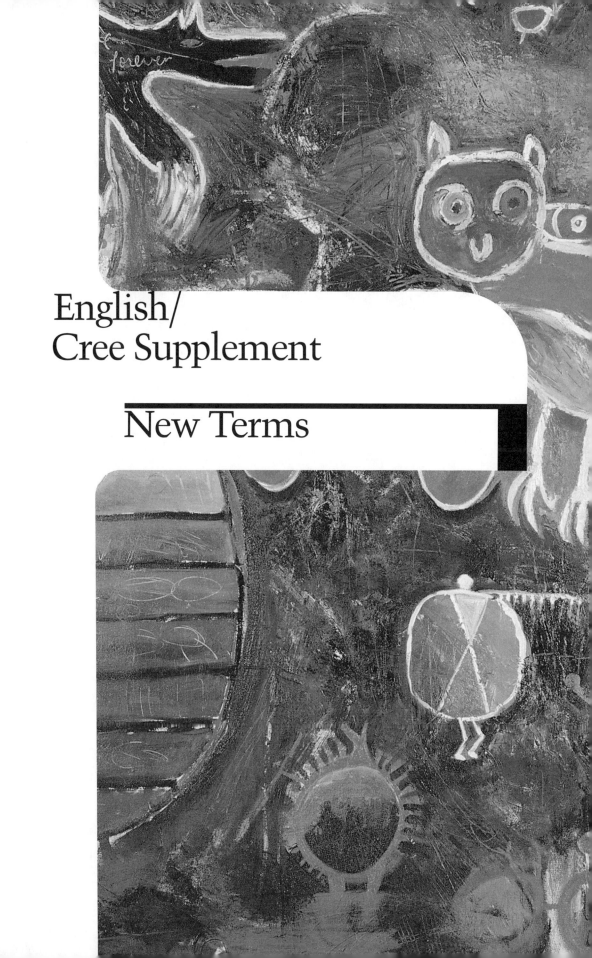

English/
Cree Supplement

New Terms

New Terms

A

abbe *kihce ayamihewiyiniw.*

abbess *kihce ayamehewiskwew.*

abbey *ayamehewekamik.*

abdicate *nehcitakoskewin.*

abdication *pôyôwin.*

able-bodied *sohkapewiwin.*

A-bomb *naspic misipahksawan.*

abolition *ponihtawin.*

abolitionist *oponihtawiyinow.*

aborigines *nistamiyinewak.*

about-face *kweskiwepinekiwin; kweskipayihow.*

about turn *sîsîkoc kweskepayihowin.*

above-board *mosis.*

abridge *cimsecikewin.*

abridgement *or* abridgment *cimsehtawin.*

abroad *wâhyawaskehk; akamaskehk.*

absentee *opataham.*

absenteeism *pahtahamowin.*

absolute alcohol *metoni eskotewapoy.*

absolute monarchy *kihcinekanapowin.*

absolute pitch *metoni ekota.*

absolute zero *metoni namakîkway.*

absolutism *mistikimawewin.*

absolutist *mistikimaw.*

academic The act of learning, *kiskinohamâkosowin.*

academician An academic teacher, *okiskinohamâkiw.*

academy A special school, *kihcikiskinwahamâtokamik.*

accelerator A device for increasing speed, *kisiskapayecikan;* the thing you step on, i.e.: gas pedal, *ka makoskamihk (slang).*

acclamation Someone voted in automatically, *awîyak ka mosci otiniht.*

accompaniment *wehcetawin.*

accompanist *owehcetaw.*

accomplice *onîsohkamakiw.*

accordian The stretch pulling instrument, *kasepekipitamihk.*

account *ka masinahikewapik; sônîyâwimestinikewin;* owing something on account, *masinahamâkewin.*

accountability *miyomasinahikasowin.*

accountable *miyoweyowin.*

accountancy *metonikamamsîhk.*

accountant *omasinahikisis;* a person who looks after accounting, *kihcimasinahikisis.*

accounting *ka masinahikesisowihk.*

accredit *kihcemiyow apowin.*

accredited *kihcemiyow apehaw.*

ace The playing card, *peyakopehikan;* the ace of spades, *mistipek.*

acid Salty liquid, *sewihtakanapoy.*

acidity It is sweet or sour, *sewâw.*

acoustic *ketohcikan katistawek.*

acoustics *ka tistawekwaw (Northern).*

acquittal *pakiteniwewin.*

acquittance *kesitipaham.*

acquitted *pakitinaw ka sîhkitisahot.*

acre *peyakaskekanis; peyak tipahaskân.*

acreage *ayiwâk peyakaskekansa.*

across-the-board *asawahtikohk.*

active voice *kakâyâwatamow.*

activism *weskawahtawin.*

activist *oweskawahtaw.*

actor *metawew nâpew.*

actress *metawew iskwew.*

actuary *masinahikesisihkan.*

acquisition *kahtitinikan.*

adage *kayâs iyinesowin.*

adagio *peyahtikowisiwin.*

adaptation *nakayâskamohtisowin.*

adapter *or* adaptor *pîwâpiskos sa kicihcekans.*

addicted *ekâ kakehpoyohk.*

addiction *sakocih ekowin.*

addictive *metoni kasakohikohk.*

adhesive *akwamohcikan; akwamonihkewin.*

adjective *pekiswewin.*

adjourn *ahtascekewin.*

adjournment *kehtwam ascekewin.*

adjudge *weyasowiw koyastat.*

adjudicate *weyasowiwenihk koyastahk.*

adjuration *sehkitsahikewin.*

adjure *ka sehkiskakehk.*

administration *pimpayecikewin; weyasiwewin ka osehtahk.*

administrator *ka pimpayeciket awîyak.*

admissibility *kamiyo pehtokepahiwehk.*

admissible *miyo pehtokepahiwewin.*

admission *pehtokahiwewin; tipahikewin.*

adobe *asiniw waskahikan.*

adolescence *kakesi opikihk.*

adolescent *kesi ohpikiwin.*

advance poll *kanekan pimpahtahk.*

advertise *masinahikanihk kawapahtehiwehk.*

advertisement *masinahikew wapahtehiwewin.*

485

advertiser *owapahtehiwew.*
advertising *wapahtehiwewin.*
advocate *peyahtik ka nitôtamahk.*
aerobatics *nânatohk kespitamihk pimehakan.*
aeronaut *kanakacîtat pimehakan.*
aeroplane *ka pimeyamakahk; pimehakan.*
aesthete *awîyak kameyonakosehat awîya.*
aesthetic *omeyonakosehiwiw.*
aestheticism *meyonakosehiwewin.*
aesthetics *ka meyonakosehiwehk.*
afforest *kohpikihtahk sakaw.*
afforestation *sihcisisak kohpikihihtwaw (Northern).*
afore *nîkanes nawâc.*
aforesaid *nîkan pekiskwewin.*
aforethought *nîkan mâmitoneyicikan.*
aforetime *nîkan tepahikan.*
afterbirth *aspiskwesimonis.*
after-dinner *poni apihtakisikaki.*
aftereffect *mwestas mositawin.*
afterglow *mwestas ka wasiyak.*
aftergrowth *ka poni ohpikihk.*
after-image *naspitatowin.*
afterlife *poni pimatisowin.*
aftermost *eskweyanihk.*
aftertaste *poni ispakwan.*
afterthought *mwestas mâmitoneyicikan.*
agency *esecikewkamik; paminikewin.*
agenda *kwayaci oyascikewin.*
agent *esecikewiyinow.*
age of consent *kayâs kesiyihtamowin.*
agnostic *awîyak ekâ katapwewokiyihtahk.*
agnosticism *ekâ ka tapwewokiyitamihk.*
agoraphobia *kostiyiniwewin.*
agrarian *awîyak ka tepiyimotôtahk kîkway.*
agrarianism *ka tepiyimôtamihk.*
agricultural *kistikewinihk isi.*
agriculture *kistikewin; ka ohpikihaht kistikan.*
agriculturist *okistikew.*
agrobiology *kistikew kiskiniwahamâkewin.*
agrologist *kistikiw kiskiniwahamakiw.*
air base *tohowin.*
air-borne *ka ohpahohk.*
air-bus *pimehakanis kisiwak ohci.*
air chamber *ka mawasakwaskinek yotin.*
air-condition *tahkiyawehikewin.*
air-conditioned *tahkiyawetiw.*
air conditioner *tahkiyawehikan.*
air conditioning *ka tahkiyawehikehk.*
air-cool *miyotahkiyowiw.*
aircraft *ka pimeyamakahk.*
air drome *tohowin; tohowenihk.*
air drop *pimeyawnehcopewin.*
air-drop *pimeyakan nehciwepenekiwin.*

air express *ka pimohtatahk masinahikana pimyakanihk.*
airfield *tohowenihk.*
airflow *kesiyotihk.*
air force *nôtinikew pimeyawin.*
airframe *pimehakanimeyaw.*
air-freight *pimehakanawatasowin.*
airfreighter *otawatasopimehakanihk.*
airlift *ohpahocikewin.*
air lock *yotin kamecimaskinek nânitâw.*
air mail *pimeyakanik masinahikana kawatahk.*
airman *onotinkewiyinow pimeyakanihk.*
airmattress *aspesinowin ka potatamihk.*
airplane *pimeyakan; pimehakan; pimehiyakan.*
airport The act of landing, **pakicehwin** *(Northern)*; a landing place, **tohowin.**
airpump *potacikan.*
air raid *pimeyakanihk ohci kapahkisawehk.*
air-raid shelter *tohowinihk kakasohk.*
air rights *tohowinihk weyasowiwina.*
airship *pîtosayih pimeyakan.*
airsick *ka keskwetapasohk pimeyakanihk.*
airspace *itakatawak kapimehak.*
airstrip *kwanteteh sakahk; tohowin kosetahk.*
air-to-air *ka pekiskwatitohk pîwâpiskosihk ohci.*
airwoman *opimeyaw iskwew.*
akin *tipeyaw wahkohtowin.*
alarm clock *pîsimohkan ka sewet.*
albatross *mawace ka misikitit pewayis.*
albino *pepekwac iyinow akamaskehk ohci.*
album *eta masinpayiwina ka kanawiyimihtwaw (Northern).*
alcove *piskic nipaw kamikos.*
alderman *peyak onikanapow otenahk; kihci okimâw weyasiwewin ohci.*
ale *ka maskawak eskwesisapoy; iskwesapoyihkan.*
ale house *iskwesisapokamik.*
alfalfa *kohpikitahk maskosiya; maskosiya ka ohpikitahk.*
algebra *pîtos akihcikiwin.*
allegation *ka atamiyimiht awîyak.*
allege *atamiyicikewin.*
alleged *keh atamiyimaw.*
allegorical *kiskowehikewin.*
allegro *kisiska wepenikewin.*
allergic *sîsîkoc ka akosepayihk.*
allergy *kîkway ka ahkosiskakohk.*
alley *sapohteskanâs.*
alleyway *sapohtewin.*
all hail *mamawi mamicemitowin.*
all-out *ka pakitinisohk metoni.*
allowance *ohtinamatosônîyâw.*
all-powerful *naspic maskawisêwin.*

all-purpose *ka nânatohk apatahk.*
all right *kahkiyaw mewasin.*
all-round *misiwewasakam.*
all-star *naspic onihtametawiw.*
all-time *namoyakisipan.*
allusion *ka akawacikehk.*
alma mater *awîyak okiskinomatôkamik.*
almanac *akinkesikwan kakeyaw kîkway kawehtamihk;* a time of day keeper, *nawikesikwan.*
almond *metosis kesopwew askek ohci.*
alter ego *pîtos sâyâwin.*
altitude *ispimehk isi.*
alto *ka kihtewehtakosihk.*
altruism *naspicmeyotwawin.*
altruistic *ka pâscimeyotwahk.*
alum A kind of salty compound, *sewihtakanihkan.*
alumni *awîyak kayâs eta ekeh kiskinohamaht.*
amateur *kwanta ometawew.*
ambassador *onikanew ohpime askehk kanitawi mamawapit;* a special leader, *kihci okimâw.*
ambassadorship *nîkanapestamakiwin.*
ambulance *otâpânâsk otakosowak ohci;* a sickness wagon, *ahkosiw tâpânâsk.*
American *kihcimohkoman; kicimokoman.*
American aloe *kihcimohkomanahtikos.*
American beauty *kihcimohkoman miyonakos.*
americanization *kihcimohkomanehewewin.*
Amerindian *kihcimohkomaninehiyaw.*
ammunition *ka nemaskwehk; paskisikan mina mosisineya.*
amphibious *ka waskitahipet otâpânâsk.*
amphibrous *pimatisowin; nipehk ahpohaskehk.*
anachronism *ka patiyicasihk.*
anachronistic *pateyecikewin.*
anaesthesia *ekâ mosihtawin.*
anaesthetic *awîyak ka nipehiht.*
anaesthetist *onipehiwiw.*
anaesthetization *nipehiwewin.*
anaesthetize *ka nipehiwehk;* s/he is anaesthetized, *nipehaw;* s/he anaesthetizes her/him, *nipehiw.*
analogous *kekâc pahpeyakwan.*
analogue *naspitatowin.*
anathema *macayemohtowin.*
anatomy *kîkway ka isi macesehtahk.*
anchorite *papikwac ayesiyinow.*
anchorman *onekanapo cekastepayicekan ohci.*
ancient history *kayâs acemowin.*
andante *peyahtik waskawewin.*
anemone *wapikwane.*
anew *oskimacitawin.*
angel cake *sewpahkwesikan.*
angelfish *pîtosikinosiw.*
angevin *akamaskiwiyeno.*

angina *sîsîkoc ekâ kakiyehek.*
angina pectoris *metih aspiniwin.*
anglicism *akayâsiw ayâmihawin; wâpiskasakow ayamihâwin* (Plains).
anglicize *akayâsiwehtwawin.*
Anglo-American *akayâsiw kihcimohkoman.*
Anglo-Canadian *akayâsiw otah ohci kanâta.*
Anglo-Catholic *akayâsiw pahkwâyâmehaw.*
Anglo-Catholicism *akayâsiw pahkwâyâmehawin.*
anglomania *akayâsiw isâyâwin.*
anglomaniac *akayâsiw mocowiyenow.*
anglophile *awîyak ka takahkiyimat akayâsêwa.*
anglophilia *akayâsiw takahkiyetowin.*
anglophobe *awîyak ka pakwatat akayâsêwa.*
anglophobia *akayâsiw ka pakwatiht.*
anglophone *akayâsimowin ka âpacitahk kotak askîy.*
angora goat *mayacikos ekinwawet.*
angora rabbit *pîtos wîpos ewasepewayet.*
animalism *pisisko isâyâwin.*
animality *ka pisisko esâyâhk.*
animalize *ka pisiskih kasohk.*
animal kingdom *pisiskiw askîy.*
animism *ka tâpwewokiyetamihk pimatisiwin.*
animist *otâpwewokiyetamohiwiw.*
animistic *tâpwewokiyetamow isâyâwin.*
animus *kîmôci pemamiyetowin.*
ankylose *aniskawkanah enapokihki.*
ankylosis *ka setawkihk aniskawkanan.*
annelid *kîkway mohtew.*
anon *kihcikiyepa.*
answering service *naskomohtowin.*
ante *kanekanascikihk.*
ant-eater One who eats ants, *ayikosakamowat.*
antecedence *aniskac ohci ohcewin.*
antecedent *awîyak aniskac ka ohcet.*
antedate *kayâs aniskac.*
antelope A small caribou, *apistacihkos.*
anthem A special song, *kihcinikamon.*
anteroom *pehokamikos.*
anther *kîkway maskihkiwahtik.*
anthologist *masinahikan omanacicikew.*
anthropological *ka nitawkiskiyetamihk ayesiyinow pimatisiwin.*
anthropology *kiskinohamâkewin iyinew ohci.*
anthropomorphic *ka nitawkiskiyitamihk iyiniwiwin.*
anthropomorphism *ka manito iyitamihk ayesiyiniwiwin.*
anti *ekâ tipiyimowin.*
anti-aircraft *nôtinikakew pimehâkana.*
antibacterial *ka nakinkakihk ahkosowin.*
antibiotic *ahkosêw nakinkakewin.*
antibody *kîkway ka miyoskakemakahk.*
anticlimatic *sîsîkoc pomiyehtamowin.*

487

anticlimax *ka sîsîkoc pomiyehtamihk.*

anticolonialism *ekâ kawicetamihk oyasiwewin.*

antidote *maskihke kanakinkakehk piscipowin; piscipowin natawehowin.*

antifreeze *nipoy ekâ ka ahkwatihk.*

antihero *ekâ ka napekasohk.*

antimony *kîkway pîwâpiskwayih.*

antiphon *âyâmehawinis kanikamohtahk.*

antisocial *ekâ kotôtemakeyimohk.*

antithesis *metoni kapetosisâyâhk.*

antonym *naspace pekiskwewinis.*

aorta *kihcimihkoyape.*

apace *metoni kisiska.*

apartment *wîkowin;* a separated way of living, *piskiciwîkowin.*

apartment block *wîkowina kamamawastekwaw (Northern).*

apartment house *awehowiwkamik.*

ape *ka misikitit ocayesinakes.*

aperiodic *ekâ katapitawakotek.*

aphorism *miyowehtamatowin.*

aphoristic *kamiyowehtamaket awîyak.*

apian *âmôwak ohci.*

apiarist *awîyak ka kanawiyimat âmôwa.*

apiary A bee house, *âmôkamik.*

apiece *pahpeyak akihcikewin.*

apolitical *naskwaw pekiskwewin weyasowewenihk.*

apologist *âyâmihaw onaskwastamakiw.*

apologetic *ka naskwastamakehk âyâmehawin ohci.*

apoplexy *sîsîkoc nipopayiwin.*

apostate *ayamihawin ka wepinamihk.*

apostle *peyak manito ka kinawasonât.*

apostolic *ayamihewemamtoniyecikan.*

apostolic see *ayamihew wapahtamowin.*

apostolic succession *ayamihew kaskihtawin.*

apotheosis *mamihtiyicikewin.*

appeal *ewî âhci wapatamihk weyasiwewin.*

appellant *awîyak ka natôtamat.*

appellate *awîyak kanitohtahk natôtamawin weyasowiwinihk.*

appendicitis *mecakisisa ka paskikihki.*

appendix *iskwâyâc masinahikewin masinahikanihk; mansokahkosowin.*

apperception *metoni nesitohtamowin.*

appetizer *onohtehkatehewiw.*

apple of the eye *awîyak ka akawatiht.*

appliance *pinawasokamik âpacicikan;* a tool of lots of different uses, *nânatôhisêw âpacihcikan.*

applicant *awîyak ka sâkaskinahtat masinahikan.*

application *sâkaskinahtamohewewin.*

appraisal *ka oyakihtamihk kîkway.*

appraise *oyakihcikewin; tanimayikohk.*

appraisement *ka oyakihcikehk.*

appraiser *otoyakihcikew.*

apprentice *okiskinohamakosow atoskewin ohci.*

apprenticeship *kiskinohamakosowin.*

approbation *kîkway ka tepiyimotôtamihk.*

apricot *menisahtikomin; ohcawakas.*

apse *kîkway ekâ metoni kawaweyeyak.*

aqualung *itâmpek iyihewakan.*

aquarium *eta kinosewak kopikihihtwaw* (Northern); the fishes' home, *kinosesisak wîkowaw.*

aquatic *ka nakayâskamihk nipehk.*

aquatint *ka masinaskisamihk kîkway.*

aqueduct *pihcapekos.*

arbitrate *kîkway oyascikewin.*

arbitrator *okwâyâskosihcikew.*

archaeologist *okiskinohamâkew kayâs oskana ohci.*

archaeology *kiskinohamakosowin kayâs kîkway ohci.*

archetype *pahpîtos isihihtwaw ahcapeyak (Northern).*

archives *ka kanawiyihtamihk eta kayâs isecekiwina.*

arc lamp *metoni ekihkayâsowek wasaskotenikan.*

arc light *kihkayâstenikewin.*

arctic *metoni kihci kiwetinohk; kiwetinohk.*

Arctic Circle *peyakwâyâk ekawehkac esakastek.*

aria *mosci yahkowewin.*

arid *metoni epahkowâyâk kîkway.*

aridity *pahko isâyâwin.*

aright *metoni kwayask nisitohtamowin.*

aristocracy *okimâwapowin.*

aristocrat *metoni kokimawapit awîyak.*

aristocratic *okimâw wiyemisowin.*

arithmetician *metoni kanakacitat awîyak akihtasona.*

armature *pîwâpiskosa kapatahkwaw sehkepayesihk (Northern).*

armchair *iyoskapowiniyak tehtapowin.*

armed forces *okiskenohamakosowak nôtinitowinihk; simâkanisihkânak (Plains).*

armor or armour Iron clothes, *pîwâpiskow ahyowinisa.*

armored car or armoured car *pîwâpisk ohci nôtinikiw otâpânâsk.*

armored corps or armoured corps *pîwâpiskow nôtinikewiyenowak.*

armor plate or armour plate *pîwâpiskoyakan.*

armory or armoury *nôtinikakana eta kakanawiyehtamihk.*

army *nôtinitowinihk kawicehiwehk; simakaniseweniwak.*

arraign *ka natomiht awîyak ka wihweyasowatiht.*

arraignment *sehkitsahikewin.*

arrears *mecim watasenahikewin; ekâ katipahamihk masinahikewina.*

arsenal *nôtinikakana ohci ascekewkamik;*
waskahikan; ka osehtahk nôtinitowin ohci; a
storage for army weapons, *nôtintowinihk*
astahcikewkamik.

arsenic *piscepowin.*

arson *ocitâw ka saskahikeh; kapapam saskahamihk*
kîkwaya.

arterial *eta ka macepayek kîkway.*

arthritic *awîyak koskanahpinet.*

arthritis *oskanahpinewin.*

artificial respiration *petahtamowin;* breathing into
someone, *petahtamohiwewin.*

artilleryman *awîyak ka paminahk mesipaskisikana.*

asbestos *kîkway ekâ kasaskitek;* something that does
not catch on fire, *ekâ kakwahkotek.*

asocial *peyakowiyemowin.*

asphalt *ka asinihkahtek meskanaw.*

asphyxia *ekâ ka kehyehehk.*

asphyxiant *kîkway ka kepihketoneskakohk.*

asphyxiate *awîyak ka kepihketonineht.*

aspirate *yahkatamowin.*

aspiration *yahkatamopayowin.*

aspirin *tiyistekwanew maskihki.*

assassin *okemoci nipahtakiw.*

assassination *kîmôci nipahtakewin.*

assault and battery *ka nôtiniht awîyak asci*
kapakamahoht.

assay *ka kocitahk pîwâpisk.*

assembly line *mamawipicikewin.*

assemblyman *omamawipicikiw.*

aster A fall or autumn flower, *takwakin wapikwan.*

asteroid *tapiskoc acakos kîkway nayewac*
epimakotek.

asthma *yehewaspiniwin; ahkosowin.*

asthmatic *awîyak kayehewaspinet.*

astigmatism *oskesikwas pinewin.*

astrologer *okiskenohamakosow acakosak ohci.*

astronaut *ayisiyinow ka pamihtat pimeyakan*
pesemohk katohomakahk.

astronomer *awîyak ka kiskenohamakosit kisikohk*
ohci kîkway.

astronomical *kisikohkoci kîkway ka nakacelal*
awîyak.

astronomy *waskohk ohci kîkwaya ka kiskiyitamihk.*

asunder *ka piskihtinamihk kîkway.*

asylum A mental hospital, *keskwehkosêwikamik.*

asymmetric *awîyak pahpetoskesayat.*

asymmetry *kahkweskesâyâwin.*

athirst *metoni kanohtehâpakwihk; ehakawâtamihk*
kîkway.

athlete's foot *mesitaspeniwin.*

athletics *metawewena nânatohk isi.*

atlas *askewasenahikana.*

atmosphere *ka ispehtaskamik tânsi askîy ka*
isiyowek.

atmospheric *tahtokesikaw tânsi ka atesayak.*

atoll *ka wasahastikweyak sakahikan.*

atom *kîkway ka pahkitek.*

atomic *kihcipahkitewin;* a very large explosion,
kihcipahkisawan.

atomic age *ka otsapahtamihk misipahkisawana.*

atomic bomb *misipahkisawan; misipahkisikân*
(*Plains*).

atomic energy *kîkway pahkisawanihk*
kohsepwepayik.

atomic theory *kiskenohamakosowin pahkitepayew*
ohci mâka namoya ikecinâhohk.

atomizer *sîweypotacikakanis.*

atonement *tepahikepayihtwawin.*

atrophy *ka mosci mesowanatahk kîkway.*

attic *nîpawkamik mawaci ispimehtakohk.*

attorney *pekiskwestamâkew; weyasiwew;*
kihciweyasiwew; a lawyer who does business
transactions for someone, *weyasowew.*

attorney-at-law *weyasowewinihk onatamâkew.*

attorney general *awîyak weyasowewin kapaminahk;*
a high class lawyer, *kiciweyasowew.*

attune *kwayask ka oyastahk kîkway.*

auction *ka tepwacikehk;* a place to sell things by
calling, *tepwacikewin.*

auctioneer A caller for selling materials, *tepwacikew.*

audio frequency *kîkway ka pehtakwahk.*

audio-video *ka pehtakwahk cekastepayecikan.*

audit *ka nakatiyihtamihk masinahikana.*

auditor *awîyak ka nakateyehtahk masinahikana.*

auditor general *kihci omasinahikeses.*

auditorium *misimamawapewikamik;* a place for large
audiences, *mihcetowikamik.*

auger *payipahikan; pemetakinikan;* a tool for making
holes, *pemihtakinikan.*

autarchic *awîyak ka pamenisot.*

autarchy *pamenisowin.*

author *nâpew kamasinahahk masinahikana.*

authoress *iskwew ka masinahahk masinahikana.*

authoritarian *awîyak ka okimâwakiyimiht.*

authoritarianism *okimâwakiyimowewin.*

authorship *awîyak ka kehosihtat masinahekan.*

autobiographical *ka acimso masinahikehk.*

autobiography *acimso masinahikewin.*

auto court *mihcet aseyask kapesêwkamikwa.*

autocrat *awîyak ka macistikwanet.*

autocratic *macistikwanewisâyâwin.*

autograph *kiskenowac masinahikewin;* one's own
writing, *tipiyawemasinahikewin.*

autographic *ka kiskenowac masinahikehk.*

autographical *ka kiskenowac masinahikatek.*

489

automat *âpacicikan sehke ka asahkimakahk.*

automatic *sehke kapimpayehisomakahk kîkway;*
tipiyawe kapimpayik; it runs automatically,
sehkekapimpayik.

automatically *soskwac sehke ka ispayik.*

automatic pilot *sehke kapamihtat pemeyakan.*

automatic transmission *sehke ka meskocipayik.*

automation *sehkepimpayew.*

automobile *sehkepimpayew tâpânâsk.*

automobilist *opamihcikew.*

automotive *ka paminamihk sehke pimpayihcikana.*

autonomic system *kîkway ka pimpayowehiswakehk.*

autonomous *kanihta peyakopaminsohk.*

autonomy *tânsi kesipaminsohk.*

autopsy *meyaw ka wapahtamihk mahte kîkwayo*
kanipahekot; the cutting of a body after death,
kamanisoht awîyak kahponi pimatisit.

avalanche *ka nehtacowepayet kona wacehk ohci;*
wacekasoskopayik.

avenue *ôtenaw meskanaw;* a special road or street,
kihcimeskanaw.

averment *kihcipekiskwewin.*

aviary *pîwâyesak eta ka ohpikihihtwaw (Northern);*
pîyeseswekiwin; a bird house, *pîwâyisisikamik.*

aviation *ka kiskino amakosihk pimeyawin;* the act of
flying a plane, *pimehawin.*

aviator *awîyak pimeyakan kapamihtat;*
pimehawenow; a person that flies a plane,
pimehaweyinow.

aviatrix *iskwew opimehaw.*

aviculture *ka kanawiyimihtwaw ita pîwâyesisak*
(Northern).

aviculturist *okanaw pîwâyesisowew.*

avocado *menis kesopwenohk ohci nânitâw.*

axle *otihtipayewok eta ka akwamotwaw*
otâpânâskohk (Northern); sapomowin; a thing that
turns wheels, *tihtipayewaskapicikan.*

490

B

babe in the wood *or* babe in the woods *sâkaw*
iskwesis.

baboon *otayesinâkes ka misikititwaw etowahk*
(Northern); a large monkey, *mistahi ayisinâkes.*

baby buggy *or* baby carriage *awâsistâpânâskos.*

baby-faced *awîyak ka apiscikwesit.*

bachelor of arts *iyinesowin.*

backbite *awîyak ka ayemomiht.*

backchat *awîyak kanaskwewosemiht.*

back country *askîy metoni akwacayihk.*

backdate *oteh peci otâhk.*

backdoor *otâhk ohci iskwahtem.*

backdrop *akopcikanekin.*

backer *awîyak kamasinahekimekit.*

backfill *asiski kawi ka âyâhikakehk.*

backfire *ka metakwepasawehk eta kapastek.*

backgammon *mawenehotometawewin nîsow*
ayisiyenowak ohci.

background *tânsi ka kehispayik pecitahk.*

backhoe *watihkakan.*

backhouse *wâyâwewkamik.*

back order *ka kehtwam natocikihk.*

backpedal *asepahtawin.*

backroom *otâhk apewkamekos.*

backscratcher *cecekawkanewakan.*

back seat *otahkapowin.*

back-seat driver *otah ohci opamihcikew.*

backspace *katawakotahk ohci.*

backstage *naway ohci.*

back stairs *amacowewin otâhk ohci.*

backstitch *ka kehtwamikwatamihk kîkway.*

backstop *nakinikakan pakahatowanis ohci.*

backstroke *ka asewepahosohk pakasemowenihk.*

back talk *ka naskwewosemohk.*

bacteria *maci kîkway ahkosowin kohispayik.*

bacterial *kîkway ka ahkoseskakohk.*

bacteriologist *okiskinohamakosow.*

bad blood *macimihkoh.*

badlands *askîy eteh ekâ kîkway ka ohpikihk.*

bagel *ewaweyeyak pîwâpisk; ohpipayiw pakwesikan*
ewâwayesit.

baggage *posihcikewena; pimewacikan.*

baggage car *posihcekew tâpânâsk.*

baggageman *oposihcekewiyinow.*

baggagemaster *oposihcekewokimâw.*

bagman *maskemotiyinow.*

bagpiper *opotacekewiyinow.*

baile *awîyak ka tepahikestamaht.*

bailiff *weyasowewokimâw.*

bailment *ka tepahikestamâkehk.*

bailsman *ka pamenahk awîyak tepahikestamakiwin.*

baker *opahkwesekanihkew.*

bakery *pahkwesekanihkewkamik.*

baking *ka pahkwesekanihkehk.*

baking powder An ingredient used to raise bread,
opihkasikan.

baking soda *ka pestewpayik.*

balanced diet *kwayaskometsowin.*

balance of power *kwayaskopayecikewin.*

balance of trade *kwayaskosehcikewin.*

balance wheel *ka kwayaskopayihtahk kîkway.*

bald-faced *wapihkkewmistatim.*

baler *maskosêw tahkopicikakan.*

ball *tihtipinatowan;* a ball for hitting, i.e.: a baseball,
pakahatowan; pâkahtowân (Northern); a bouncing
ball, i.e.: basketball or football, *kwaskwentowan;*

s/he plays with a bouncing ball, *kwaskwentowiw*;
s/he plays with a ball, *tihtipinatowiw*; having a good
time, *metonimocikihtawin*.

ballad *sakihetowinikamonis*; singing, *nikamowin*.

balladeer *onikamow*.

ball-and-socket joint *âpacicikan peko isi ka
etakinamihk*.

ballast *asinîyak ka sikopoyihtwaw (Northern)*.

ballast tube *meskanaw asinehkahcikakan*.

ballerina *onemihitow iskwew*.

ballet *kayâs nemihitowin nânatohk kespayehohk*;
group dancing, *mamawinemihitowin*.

ballistics *ka nakacihtahk paskisikana*.

balloon Something with air in it,
waweyepocacikanis; a small balloon, *wehkwas*.

balloonist *awîyak kosihtat pocacikansa*.

ballot *ka mekihk wehyowin kapimpahtahk*; giving a
name for a vote, *wehowinkamekihk*.

ballot box *mistikowats wehona ka posewepenamihk*.

ballplayer *awîyak ka pakahatowet*.

ball-point or **ballpoint** *masinahekakanis*.

ballroom *mesih nemehetowekamik*.

baloney or **bologna** *palone*; *otakisikan*.

balsa *mistik metoni eyakitisit*.

banana *wâkâs*.

bandbox *mosci masinahikanekinowat*.

bandeau *iskwew pasiskwehpison*.

bandmaster *onekanew ketohcekewnihk*.

bandwagon *ketohcikewtehtiptâpânâsk*.

banister *nosaw mecimewin kehcekosêwnihk*.

banjo *coyapehkehnekiwketohcikan*.

banjoist *ocoyapehkehnekiw*.

bank A money house, *sônîyâwikamik (Northern)*.

banker The money keeper, *okanawsônîyâwiw*.

bank account *sônîyâwkamkohk kahiht sônîyâw*.

bank bill *ka masinahikehk sônîyâwkamkohk*.

bankbook *sônîyâwkamkomasinahekanis*.

banker *okanawsônîyâwiw*.

bank holiday *sônîyâw kamkokihcikisekaw*.

banking *ka ahiht sônîyâw sônîyâwkamkohk*; the
accumulation of money, *sônîyâwkamawacihiht*.

bank note *sônîyâwpehekan*.

bank rate *ka kwayaskopayehiht sônîyâw*.

bankroll *kosônîyâmihk*.

bankrupt *awîyak ka pekopayet*; the act of losing
money, *pekopayowin*.

bankruptcy *pekopayowin*.

banner *kiskenowacecikan*.

bantamweight *ka yahkitsitwaw opakamahotowak
(Northern)*.

barbarian *metoni pikwacayisiyinow*.

barbaric *pikwacayisiyinewowin*.

barbarism *pikwacipekiskwewin*.

barbarity *metoni pikwacisâyâwin*.

barbarous *awîyak ka pikwaciyinewit*.

barbeque *nawâcewinapisk*; outside barbequeing,
wayawetimihk nawâcewin.

barbell *sesawakana*.

barber A hair stylist, *opaskwahamâkew*; a person
who shaves people, *okaskipasowiw*; one who cuts
hair, *opaskosowiw*.

barbershop *paskwahamâkewkamik*.

barge *misti mihtot*.

bargeman *mihtot ka pamenahk awîyak*.

baritone *ka kihtewenekamohk*; singing a certain way,
nikamowin; *itihtakosowin*.

barker *poyakeskinkakan*; auctioneer, *otepwacikew*.

barnstorm *mamawipikiskwewin*.

baron *awîyak ka nekanapit*.

baroness *iskwew ka okimawapit*.

baronet *nâpew ka askowapestahk nîkanapowin*.

barracks *simakanisêw nîpew kamikwa*.

barracuda *misikinosiw okecekamehk ohci*.

barrister *kihci oweyasowiw*; one who tries cases in
court, *oyasiwiw*.

barrow *ka yahkiniht ocâpânâskos*.

basalt *metoni maskaw asinîy*.

baseball *pâkahtowân (Northern)*; playing baseball,
pâkahatowewin; *pâkatwân kapakamahot
(Northern)*; *kwaskwitowan kapakamahoht (Plains)*.

baseboard *kîsihcikâkanisa*; the end of the wall,
kisipihtak.

baseborn *kemenecakan*.

base line *tepahaskan eta kapemepayek*.

basement *ascekewkamik sepa waskahikanihk*; a hole
in the ground, *watihkan*.

basil *kîkway katakwastahk kestepowinihk*.

basketball *metawewin kwaskwentawan ka
posewepeniht*; *pakatwan kapakamisimiht
(Northern)*; *kwaskwitowan kapakamisimiht
(Plains)*.

bass horn *metoni ekihtewek ketohacekan*.

bassinet *watapewet oskawasis ohci*.

bassoon *ka potatamihk ketohcikan*.

bathhouse *kosîpîkastowkamik*.

bathing suit *pakasemo ayowenisa*.

bathrobe *pakasemo asakay*.

bathroom *pakasemokamik*.

bathtub *pakasemomahkahk*.

batter Someone who is hitting the ball, *awîyak
pakahacowansa kakwe tawawat*.

battery *wasaskotepayew pemepayihcekakan*;
waskocipayow; *waskotipayow*.

battleship *nôtinikew napihkwan*.

bazaar Cheap buying, *wehci atawewin*; *ka
atawakehk kîkway*.

491

beachwear *ka pakasemosehohk.*
beagle *onocicekewatim.*
beaker *wapmonapisk oyakan.*
beautician *omeyonakosehewiw.*
beauty shop *meyonakosehewiwkamik.*
beauty sleep *ka kesikawihkwamihk.*
bedchamber *kihci nipawekamik.*
bed chesterfield A sofabed, *misitehtapowin nipewin kosehtahk.*
bedevil *awîyak ka mekoskacehiht.*
bedevilment *mekoskacehewewin.*
bedpan *wayawestamasow askihk.*
bedpost *nipewinahtik.*
bedroom *nipawikamik; nipewikamik.*
bedspring *pîwâpiskonepewin.*
beefsteak *pemehk ka kestek wîyâs.*
beehive *âmô watistwan.*
beekeeper *awîyak ka kanawiyimat âmôwa.*
beeline *metoni kwayaskohtewin; kaskamotewin.*
beet root *mihko otsehkan ocepihk.*
beet sugar *mihkotsehkan sesepaskwat.*
befoul *ka wenihtahk kîkway.*
beget *ka weskawahiht awîyak.*
belfry *ka akocik eta soweyakan;* a wooden tower for a bell, *soyakanahtik.*
bell *soweyakan* (Northern); *soyakan.*
belle *ekatawasisit oskinekiskwew.*
bellyflop *ka otihtap pakesenihk.*
beluga *misikenosêw okihcekamehk ohci.*
benefactor *omeyototakew sônîyâw ohci.*
benefactress *iskwew ka meyototaket.*
bequeath A will, *iskwâyâckecimasinahikan.*
bespectacled *awîyak ka oskesekohkat.*
best man *onepawestamâkew.*
best seller *kîkway kameyow atawakehk.*
better half *awîyak owekemakana.*
bevel *kîkway ka nawîyak.*
beverage room *menihkwewkamik.*
biannually *neswaw peyak askîy isecikewin.*
bibliography *masinahikana kosehtahk.*
bibliophile *awîyak ka mewiyitahk masinahikana.*
bicarbonate of soda *kîkway tapiskoc ohpihkasekan esinakwahk.*
bicultural *neswayak ka isipematesihk.*
bicycle *ocâpânâskos ka tihtipwepiskahtwaw etowa* (Northern); *kawasakawepiskat; kawasakawipiskat nisco wâsakâpayîs.*
bicyclist *awîyak ka tihtipwepiskawat ocâpânâskosa.*
bid *ka astwatohk sônîyâw.*
biddable *ka nihta ascikehk metawewenihk.*
bidder *otascikew iyinow.*
bidding *ka tepwâtamihk tepwâcikewenihk.*
bigamist *onîsoskwewiw.*

bigamous *nîsoskwewewin.*
bigamy *weyasowewenihk ka astahk nîsoskwewewin.*
big game *ka mâcetotahtwaw misi pesiskowak* (Northern).
bigot *awîyak ka peyakwiyimesot.*
bigoted *peyakwiyimowin.*
bigotry *peyakwiyimesow isâyâwin.*
bike *tihtipwepiskacikan.*
bile *wesope;* a yellow secretion, *osawapân.*
bilingual *mihcetwayak ka isi pekiskwehk.*
bilingualism *neswayak isi pekiskewin.*
bill *ka masinahikehk atawikamekohk;* a bill used for money, *nopehikan.*
billboard *akohtakahekewin.*
billfold *sônîyâwiwet.*
billiard *tahkahcikew metawewin.*
billing *mesinahikemekowin.*
billionaire *okihci weyotesew iyinow.*
bill of exchange *esehcikatitowin.*
bill of goods *ka masinahamihk atawakana.*
bill of health *masinahikanihk ka astahk astepayowin.*
bill of rights *weyasowewenihk kastek pekiskwewin.*
bill of sale *ka masinahamihk atawakewin.*
bingo *metawewin ka tepwehk;* the calling of numbers, *katipwatamik akihtasona;* the stamping of numbers, *kacahkatahamihk akihtasona.*
binoculars A pair of looking glasses for distance, i.e.: binoculars, *kanawâpahcikakan;* an instrument to see through for distance, *kanawâpâkân.*
binomial *nîswayak akihcekewin.*
binominal *nîswayak esiyikasowin.*
biochemist *okiskonohamakosow.*
biodegradable *kîkway kamosci mescepayik.*
biographer *awîyak ka masinahahk pematesowin.*
biographic *isi pematesowin ka masinahamihk.*
biography *pematesêw masinahekiwin.*
biopsy *ayisiyenowasakay ka sapwapamiht.*
bipartisan *nîswayak ka isihcekehk.*
biped *nîso ka ositihk.*
biracial *nîswayak ka ohcehk.*
birdbrain *pîwâyisis owetihp.*
bird dog *onatahesipewatim.*
bird's-eye *awîyak metoni ka nahapit.*
birth control *ka nakateyehtamihk âyâwawasowin; pônôsahisowin* (Plains).
bisexual *nîswâyâk ka isâyâhk.*
bisexualism *nîswâyâk isâyâwin; nîswayakisiwin* (Plains).
bitter end *metoni esko iskwâyâc.*
bitumen *kasketiw pikow.*
blackguard *kaskiteweyâs okanawiyicekiw.*

black hole *wantepiskahk ka kipahikasohk.*

black list *kasketew asinahekasowin.*

blackmail *misihkimowin ka kakwey sônîyâkakehk.*

black mark *kaskitew asinahekasowin.*

black market *kîmôc atawakewin.*

black marketeer *okemocatawew.*

blackout *ka naspicepayehk.*

black pepper *kahkominakak.*

black sheep *kaskitew mâyâcikos.*

blackthorn *okaminakasêwahtik.*

blacktop *ka asinehkahtek miskanaw.*

blank cheque or blank check *sônîyâw asinahikan ekâ kapatahk.*

blast furnace *pîwâpisk tihkapiskesikan.*

blazer *ka ayahkwasinastek miskotakay.*

bleach *wâpiskapawacikan.*

bleacher *owâpiskinkew.*

bleaching powder *wâpiskapawacikakan.*

bleeding heart *awîyak ka kitemâkenaket.*

blender *okiyikawapohkahcikew.*

blimp *pemeyakan kamosci pimastahk.*

blind alley *meskanaw ekâ ka sapohtewnowik.*

blind date *pakwanaw ka nakiskatohk.*

block and tackle *ka kosikwahk ohci ohpinikakan.*

blockhead *ka maskawestekwanet awîyak.*

blockhouse *mistikokamik.*

block printing *masinihtcikewin.*

blood bank *ka mawacetahk mihkoh.*

blood count *ka wapahtamihk tantowahk mihkoh.*

bloodcurdling *ka misiwepayik mihkoh.*

blood donor *awîyak kamekit mihkoh.*

bloodhound *ometihcikewatim.*

blood money *ka masinahekihiht awîyak tanipahtaket.*

blood poisoning *ka piscipopayik mihkoh.*

blood pressure *taniyekohk ka sohkepayik mihkoh.*

blood test *mihkoh ka wapahtahk maskihkewiskwew.*

bloodthirsty *awîyak ka natonahk nipahtakewin.*

blood transfusion *mihkoh kamiyiht awîyak.*

blood type *tantowa mihkoh ka âyâhk.*

bloomers *kooktioasioalk ioltwowalk ohci.*

blowgun *pemotahkwew paskisikan.*

blowout *ka pastisihk otihtipayew sehkipayesihk.*

blowtorch *ka kisapiskisikakehk âpacicikan.*

blueprint *ka masinahamihk tânsi ka wehisetahk.*

boarding school *ka kisci âyâhk kiskohamatokamikohk.*

board of control *eta ka oyinamihk isecikewena.*

board of education *eta ka oyastahk kiskinohamâkewin; kiskinohamâkosiwin (Plains).*

board of health *eta ka oyenamihk ahkosowin.*

board of trade *eta ka paminamihk isihcikatowin.*

boardwalk *ka napakihtakohkatek pemohtewin.*

boathouse A house for a boat, *osikamik.*

bobby pin *sakaskwahâmakan.*

bobbysocks *keskasikansak.*

bodyguard *awîyak ka masinahekihiht tanakatiyimowet.*

boiler *nepe ka ohci osamihk.*

boiling point *ka maci ohtek.*

boldface *awîyak ka mistiyimow ihkwehahk.*

bomb *misi pahkisawan; paksikan.*

bombard *ka pahkisikehk.*

bombardier *opahkesawiw.*

bombardment *pahkisawewenihk.*

bombast *mesewanaci pekiskwewin.*

bombastic *ka mesewanacimoskihk.*

bomber *pahkisawew pimeyakan.*

bombsight *pahkisawan oyapahcikan.*

bon-bon A certain type of candy, *maskihkesa.*

bonspiel *ka kakwepaskîyatohk soskwasenewepinkewnihk.*

booby hatch *mohcowekamik.*

booby trap *kimôciwanehikan.*

boodle *ka kakayeseh otiniht sônîyâw.*

bookbinder *awîyak masinahikana ka isikahk.*

bookbindery *eta masinahikana kosehtahk.*

bookbinding *ka mamawahpitamihk masinahikana.*

bookcase *masinahikanah eta ka mawataskenekwaw.*

book club *mamawintowin masinahikanah ohci.*

book end *masinahikan setwascikakan.*

bookie *omasinahikanehkew.*

booking *ka masinahikasohk nânitâw.*

bookkeeper *ka nawiyitahk masinahikanah awîyak.*

bookkeeping *masinahikesisowin.*

bookman *masinahikanewiyinow.*

bookmark *kiskinawacicikan.*

book of matches *masinahikanekinokocowakansa.*

bookrack *masinahikana ka nahawastahk.*

bookseller *awîyak ka atawaket masinahikana.*

bookshelf *masinahikan akocekan.*

bookshop *eta ka atawakehk masinahikana.*

bookwork *ka atoskatamihk masinahikan.*

boondocks *ka apisasisik ôcenas patosayihk.*

booster shot *ka takonamakehk kîkway.*

bootleg *ka kîmôci atawakehk menihkwewin.*

bootlegger *awîyak ka kîmôci atawaket; iskotewapohkew.*

border *eta ka iskwastek askîy.*

borderland *kwanta eteh patosayihk.*

borderline *kîkway eta ka iskwastek.*

bottleneck *kîkway ka nakankimakahk.*

botulism *mîcôwin ka pisciposkakohk.*

bouillon *mecimapoy.*

boulevard A special wide street, *kihcimeskanas.*

493

bourbon *iskotewapoy mahtaminah osihcikakeh.*
boutique *atawkamik kwantakekwasa ohci.*
bovine *pisiskowak; mostosak.*
bowling *ka kawatahamihk miscikosa; pakatowan ohci.*
boxcar *posihtaswakan pîwâpisko meskanahk.*
box elder *kîkway nipisîy kihcimohkomanahk kohpikit.*
boxer *opakamahotowiyinow; pakamahikew.*
boxing The sport of boxing, *pakamahotowin.*
boxing gloves *pakamahotow astisak.*
boycott *ka kipihtinamihk kîkway.*
brace and bit A machine for boring holes, i.e.: a drill, *payipahikan.*
bracer *ka setoskakohk kîkway.*
brackish *ka wenakamik nipîy.*
braille *ekâ kawapitwaw ka ayamihcikaketwaw kîkway* (Northern).
brainless *ka mohcow isâyâhk.*
brain-power *metoni iyinisowin.*
brain storm *ka osam iyinisepayihk.*
brainwash *ka kweskinamihk mamtoniyecikan.*
brain wave *sesikoc iyinisêwpayowin.*
brake *ka nakinkakehk kîkway.*
brake drum *nakinkakanah eta ka pisohtehkwaw.*
brakeman *onakinkewiyinow pîwâpiskomeskanahk.*
brand name *ka mekihk wehyowin.*
brandy *ka maskawak iskotewapoy;* fire water, *iskotewapoy.*
brass *osâw pîwâpisk.*
brassiere *iskew tohtosim setwahpisona.*
brassware *osâwpîwâpiskoyakana.*
brassy *ka mistekimawehtakosihk.*
brazier *awîyak ka atoskatahk osawpîwâpisk.*
breach of faith *keskayamihawin.*
breach of promise *kweski asotamâkewin.*
breach of the peace *kweski isâyâwin.*
bread and butter *ohpayihcikan mina tohtosapopimîy.*
breadbasket *ohpayihcikanwat.*
breadboard *ohpayihcikan aspisawacikanahtik.*
bread winner *awîyak ka nihtâ pimacihot.*
break-in *kîmôc pekonkewin.*
breaking and entering *kîmôc pehtokewin.*
breakneck *naspic ka sohkikocinihk.*
breastpin *nâpew kiskinawacihon.*
breathalyzer *yehewin ka otenamihk.*
breechcloth *kistapiskahikan.*
brewer *awîyak ka itakamasciket.*
brewery *etakamascikewkamik.*
brewing *ka mekwâ etakamascikehk.*
briar or **brier** *kayâs ospwakan.*
bribe *ka kayese isihcikihk.*
bribery *kayesih isihcikewin.*

494

brick *ka yesawesit asinîy.*
bricklayer *awîyak ka oyahat asinîya.*
bricklaying *koyahihtwaw asinîyak* (Northern).
brickyard *eta ka mamawi ahihtwaw asinîyak* (Northern).
bridal *owekihto.*
bridal wreath *wekihto nepehkana.*
bride *owekihto iskwew.*
bridegroom *owekihto nâpew; wekihto.*
bridesmaid *onîpawestamâkew iskwew; nîpawestamâkew.*
bridle path *meskanaw otehtapowak ohci.*
brief case *masinahekanah ohci asowacikan.*
briefing *keskaw pekiskwatowin.*
brigade *kihci mamawintowin.*
brigand *awîyak ka wecihewet kimotowinihk.*
Bright's disease *otihtihkosêw aspinewin.*
brindle *ka wahweyepasinasot awîyak.*
brine *ka sewihtakanowik nipîy;* salty water, *sewihtakanapoy.*
brisket *wîyâs.*
broadcast *ka pekiskweh etowihk;* news to listen to, *kanatohtamihkacimowin.*
broadloom *ka ayakaskak aspitahkoskiwin.*
broiler *nawâcewnapisk.*
bronchitic *awîyak kohpanahpenet.*
bronchitis *ohpanahpinewin.*
broncobuster or **bronchobuster** *onakayahastimwew.*
bronze *osawpisk.*
brothel *pesikwac iskwewkamik.*
browbeat *awîyak ka meywakacimiht.*
brownie *oskinekiskwesis mamawintowin.*
brushoff *ohpimey itesahowewin.*
bubble gum *pekes kawehkwepotatiht.*
bucket seat *pahpiskiht apowena.*
budget *manacicikewin sônîyâw ohci.*
bugle *misipotacikan.*
bugler *opotacikew.*
bulb *waskotenekanapiskos wasiskotepayo ohci.*
bulldog *napakotew atim; mayatisêw atim.*
bulldoze *ka mawasako wepahhikehk;* working with a bulldozer, *kawaskwahikewin; meskanahkew tâpânâsk* (Northern); *otawaskwahikan* (Plains); bulldozer road, *meskanakana.*
bulldozer A machine to push down trees, *kawaskwahikakan; omawasako wepahikew.*
bulletin *acimomasinahikan.*
bulletin board *akohtakahikewin.*
bulletproof *ekâ ka sapopayik mosisinîy.*
bull's-eye *metoni apihtaw; kotahaskwewin.*
bull terrier *omaskawisêwatim.*
bumper *asekwaskwesinowakan.*
bun *waweye pahkwesekanis.*

bungalow *wâskahikanis.*

bunion *ka kespakasakayepayihk misitihk.*

bunk *peyakohkwamew nipewin; nipewinis.*

bunk beds *peyakohkwamew nipewinsa.*

bunker *ascikew kamikos.*

bunkhouse *atoskew kapisêwkamik.*

burbot *ena pakisit kinosêw.*

burden of proof *mistahe kihcinahowin.*

burdock *kîkway kistekanis kamensowik.*

bureau *ayowenis asowacekewin ka wapamonowik.*

bureaucracy *okimanahk isecikewin.*

bureaucrat *otesehcekewiyinow.*

burglarproof *okimotow asweyicikakan.*

burglary *kimotowin.*

burgle *ka nihtâ kimotihk.*

burlesque *ka mostapekasisemohk.*

burning chemical A chemical used to ignite material, i.e.: burning chemicals such as gas or propane, *pahkwehkasikan.*

bursar *awîyak ka nakatiyimat sônîyâwa.*

bursary *eta kohnakatiyimiht sônîyâw.*

bursitis *kisô aspinewin.*

bus *oposihiwew tâpânâsk.*

bushcraft *sâkaw osehcikewna.*

bushel *peyak askihkohkanis.*

bushing *pîwâpisk aspihcikanis.*

bush league *kwanta kametawehk.*

bush line *tepahaskanis.*

bush lot *sakahk kotaskehk.*

bushman *sâkawiyinow.*

bush pilot *sâkaw opimehaw.*

bushranger *sâkaw iskotewkimaw.*

bush telegraph *sâkaw pîwâpiskos.*

bushwhacker *onihtâw sâkawew.*

bushwhacking *nihtâ sâkawewin.*

bushworker *otatoskew sâkahk.*

business *isihcikewin.*

business card *isihcikew asinahikanis.*

business college *isihcikew kiskenohamatokamik.*

businesslike *isihcikew âyâwin.*

businessman *otesehcikewiyinow.*

business school *isihcikew kiskenohamâkewin.*

businesswoman *otesehcikew iskwew.*

busman *onisohkamâkew posêwtâpânâskohk.*

butane *saskaspwakan pimiy.*

butterscotch *eyoskakih maskihkesa.*

by-election *ka kehtwam pimpahtahk.*

by-law *otinaw weyasowewin.*

by-line *ka kiskinowatasenahekasohk.*

by-play *ka kehtwam metawehk.*

by-product *ka pîtos sehtahk kîkway.*

by-street *otenahk wemahtewin.*

byword *ka tâpwemiht awîyak.*

C

cab A pick-up car, *mosahkiniwewtâpânâsk; opemohtahewiw tâpânâsk; otenaw pimpayes.*

cabby *awîyak ka pemohtahiwet.*

cabin A small house, *waskahikanis.*

cabin cruiser *ka waskahikanihkatek osih.*

cabinet A little tool cupboard, *apacicikankamikos;* a filing cabinet, *masinahikan asowacikîwin.*

cabinetmaking *ka osehtahk oyakankamkwa.*

cabinet minister *okimanahk ka nekanapit.*

cable A steel rope, *pîwâpiskopeminahkwan.*

cable television *pîwâpiskos ohci ka pimpayek cikastepayecikan.*

cabman *oposihiwewiyinow.*

caboose *kisisikewotâpânâsk; wâskahikanihkânis.*

cacao *mensihkana koko ka osecekakehk.*

cadaver *ayisiyinow meyaw.*

cafe or cafeteria An eating place, *mecisowikamik.*

caffeine *minihkwewinihk kîkway ekastek.*

cage An animal house, *pisiskewkamik;* eta pisiskesak *ka asowasotwaw ka wapahtehewehk* (Northern).

cake flour *moscipahkwesikan; askipahkwesikan* (Plains).

cake pan *askihkwapisk; nawaciwinapisk* (Plains).

calcimine A paint, *sopekahikan.*

calcium A white wash for a house, i.e.: paint, *wâpiskahikan; ewâpiskak asiski nânatohk etapacitahk asinehkahcikiwenihk;* in the bones, *miskanihk.*

calculator *awîyak ka akihciket.*

calculus *sehki ka akihcikepayek kîkway.*

caldron A large kettle, *misipakahcikewaskihk.*

calendar A day counter, *akinawakesihkwan; kinawakesihkwan;* a monthly calendar, *tipahipesimwan; akinkisihkwan; cakipîsimohsinahikan; pîsimohsinahikan.*

calendar day *ka kihtamihk kesikaw.*

calendar year *ka akihtamihk askîy.*

calibration *pehci tepahhekewin.*

calligrapher *onihtâwasinahikew.*

calligraphic *ka nihtâwasinahikewayahk.*

calligraphy *nihtâw asinahikewin.*

calorie or calory *kîkway kohnakateyehtamihk metsowin.*

camcorder A machine that videotapes pictures, *kanaweyihtomasinipayihcikan.*

camel A hump back animal, i.e.: a camel, *piskwawikanewipisiskow.*

camera A tool for taking pictures, *masinipayihcikan.*

cameraman *omasinpayihcikew.*

camp bed *ka pesêwkamikow nipewin.*

camp chair *ka pesowenihk ohci tehtapowin.*

camper *okapesow.*

camper truck *kapesêw tâpânâsk.*

495

camphor *kapemewakamik maskihki*; a white medicine, *wâpimaskihke.*

campstool *kapesêw tehtapowenis.*

camshaft *pîwâpisk ka sepwepayihcikemakahk sehkipayesihk.*

canary A yellow bird, *osawpîwâyisis.*

cancer A malignant tumor, *maciwîyâsêwin; ka maci wîyâsehk.*

candidacy *nawasonewewin.*

candidate *awîyak ka nawasoniht*; a person who runs for council, *opimpahtaw weyasowewinihk.*

canteen *acawkamkos semakansihkan kamkohk; mecisokamikos.*

canvass *yahkastimon kosecikakehk osihk ohci.*

caper *kahkwaskohtew mocikiyihtamowin.*

capital A leading city, *kihcotenaw; ka nekanastek kîkway; kihci okimânahk.*

capitalize *nîkan mahkasinahekewin.*

capsule *ka mesêwepayehtahk maskihki.*

caption *ka nîkan asinahekatek acimowenihk.*

car Or a smelly vehicle, *wehcektâpânâsk (Northern); wîcîkitâpânâsk*; a vehicle that runs by itself, *sehkepimpayîs*; a Volkswagon, *micihcikepayîs (Northern)*; a vehicle, i.e.: a car, *sihkepayis; sihkîpayis.*

card A spade playing card, *lepek (French Cree)*; a heart playing card, *mitehipehikan; wayinopehikan*; a club playing card, *pehewsit*; a diamond playing card, *ayesawepehikan.*

caravan A moving family of people, *opiciwak.*

carbine An old gun, *kayâsipaskisikan.*

carbuncle An infected boil, *sihkihp kameyewit.*

cardboard *masinahikanekin ka setawak.*

cardigan *waskecipicekan ahpô sestakwasakay.*

career *ka isi pimacihohk.*

caretaker *onakatiyicikew.*

carmel A candy, *maskihkîs.*

carmine *mistahi sihkos.*

carnation *ka okiniwapakoneyak wapikones.*

carnival *ka papamotatahk mociki metawewina.*

carpet *aspitahkoskewin*; a cloth for covering a floor, *anaskewin; moscitakewanaskan; kisô anaskan (Plains).*

carriage A small vehicle, *otâpânâskos.*

carousel A merry-go-round, *wasakapayes; awâsis metawakan.*

cart A Red river cart, *titipitâpânâsk.*

cartoon *pahpewasinahikewin.*

cartoonist *awîyak ka pahpew asinaheket.*

cartridge *pehtasowin.*

cash *sônîyâw.*

cashier *awîyak ka masihat sônîyâwa.*

cash register *sônîyâw asowacikan.*

cashmere God's cloth, *manitowekin.*

casket A burying box, *nahinowew mistikowat.*

casserole A baking dish with a cover, *nawacew oyakanis; ka natohkwapohkehk.*

castaway A discarded person, *wepinikan.*

castle A king's home, *kihci okimâwekih.*

castor oil A laxative, *saposikan.*

catapult *pimosinacikiy wepinkewin.*

cataract Something that grows in the eye, *ka ohpikihk miskesikohk*; s/he has an eye sickness, i.e.: cataracts, *wayesapow*; an eye sickness, i.e.: cataracts, *wayesapowin.*

cathartic *saposikan.*

cathedral *ayamihewkamik.*

cavalry *tehtapew simakanak.*

cavity *ka watowahk mepit.*

ceiling *ispimehk piskihci kipihtakahikan; pihtawapahkwân.*

celebrity *omocikihtawnihkew.*

cell *kipahhotokamikos.*

cellar *watikan.*

cell phone *kâpapâmohtatahk pikiskwâkanis.*

cement Imitation stone, *asinihkan*; a rock that is made, *asinîy kosehiht*; applying cement; *asinihkahcikan*; making cement, *asiniwipayihcikan (Northern).*

censorship *kâsihasinahamihk kîkway.*

census Going around taking count, *papamâkecikewin.*

cent *peyak pîwâpiskos*; little metal, iron, *pîwâpiskos.*

ceramic *asiniw yakanihkewin.*

ceramics *asiniw yakana.*

cereal Morning food, *kekisepa mecowin.*

certificate A special piece of paper, *kihcimasinahikan; masinahikanis ka pemohtahk; kecimasinahikan.*

certification *masinahikanihk ka pihk.*

certified *masinahikewapowin.*

certify *metoni kehcinahowin.*

chairman *nâpew ka nîkan apit.*

chairwoman *iskwew ka nîkanapit.*

chalk A white stick, *wâpahtikos; wâpiskasiniwacikos; wâpiskasiniwahcikos.*

chamber A separate room, *piskihcikamikos.*

chamois A very soft piece of cloth, *yoskekinos; askipahkekin.*

champagne A drink, *minihkwewin; minehkwewin.*

chaperon A guardian, *kanaweyihcikew.*

chaplain A kind of priest, *ayamihewinowikan.*

chapter *pahpiskihtasenahikewin.*

chart *kiskinowatasinahikewin.*

charter *ka kiskenowatasinahamihk kîkway.*

chauffeur A driver, *opamihcikew; pamihiwew.*

cheese Or something cooked hard, *maskawihkasikan* (*Northern*); cheese or something pressed together, *mâkwahikan* (*Northern*).

chef A cook, *kestepowenow; okestepow; kestepowenow.*

chemise An undergarment for women, *petawesakan.*

cheque or **check** *sônîyâwasinahikan.*

cheque book or **checkbook** *sônîyâw asinahikan kosehtahk masinahikanis.*

chess A moving game, *metawewin.*

chicken pox *misiwi ka pahpiskopayisihk.*

chime *ka sewet soweyakan.*

chimpanzee *mistahi ayisinâkes.*

chinchilla A tame rabbit, *wâposohpikihakan.*

chiropractor A rubbing person, *kamamakoniwet.*

chive *kesastaw wehcikaskosehkan.*

chloroform An ingredient to make you sleep, *nipehewakan.*

chocolate *maskihkîsak* (*Northern*); candies made with chocolate, *maskihkîs sakwala.*

cholera An infectious disease, *mayaspinewin.*

chowder A kind of soup, *mecimapoy.*

chronic Born with a disease, *katohpinewin; kayâsoci.*

chrysanthenum A large flower, *misiwapikwan.*

cider A sweet drink, *sewiminapoy.*

cigar *moneyaw pehtwawin* (*Northern*); *titipekinikan;* a "big shot" smoke, *okimâw pehtwawin* (*Northern*).

cigarette A pack of cigarettes, *wiyekinkanisak* (*Plains*); *wikinkanisak* (*Northern*); *picowinisak* (*Northern*).

cinema *cikastepayehcikewkamik.*

circulation *papamohcikewin.*

circumcise *ka mansikasohk.*

circumcision *mansikasowin.*

citizen *ka kisci wekit awîyak;* a member of a nation, *wetaskemakan.*

citizenship *kisci âyâwin.*

city A large city, *mistahôtenaw;* a smaller city, *apiscôcenas;* a town or city, *ôtenaw* (*Northern*); *ôtinaw* (*Plains*).

civilian *ka poni wecihewehk nânitâw tapskoc nôtihtonamihk.*

civilization *meyo kiskinohamakewin; pimatisiwin.*

classroom *piskihcasin kiskenohamakewkamik.*

cleaver A large knife, *misimohkoman.*

clemency *kitimakenakewin.*

clement *ka nihtâ kitemakinakehk.*

climate *ka siwepahk kesikaw.*

clinic A place for sickness check up, *ahkosêw wapahtokamik;* a small medicine house, *akosiwikamikos* (*Northern*); a nurses' hospital, *maskihkewiskiwewkamik* (*Plains*).

clown A crazy funny person, *mohcokân.*

coach A hockey coach, *soniskwâtahikewokimâw.*

cobble *asinikawawiyesit.*

cobra A poisonous snake, *piscipokinepik.*

cockroach *manicos.*

cocktail A sort of drink, *minehkwewin.*

cocoa nut A large nut, *misipâkân.*

coffin A burying box, *nahinowew mistikowat.*

coin Silver money, *sônîyâs;* a coin or change in silver, *pikin sônîyâs.*

coke A drink, *minihkwewinis.*

colander A strainer, *sekopatinikan.*

colic A stomach ache, *kisowaskatewin.*

collie A cattle dog, *kanawpisiskewatim.*

cologne *wehkimakohon.*

colony *apihtowikosan askîy.*

coma A state of stupor, *tikinepayowin.*

comedian A comical person, *owenew; metawesk.*

comet A star, *acahkos.*

comforter An eiderdown blanket, *opewayakohp.*

commodity Food, *meciwin.*

community hall *mamawapewikamik.*

compensate To get paid for getting hurt on the job, *wesakahotow tipahikewin.*

complimentary Giving compliments to someone, *mamihcimowewin.*

computer *kawicikepayik; kahkiyaw kîkway kawicikimakahk; kawicikipayik; kawicikemakahk kisiskâw masinatahikan; cikâstepayihcikew masinatahikâkan.*

concussion Getting knocked out in a collision, *tikinesinowin.*

condom Or a little balloon, *wehkwâs; aspinikâtanis* (*Plains*).

conductor *iskotew tapan okanaweyicikew;* the boss on a train, *pîwâpiskotâpânokimâw.*

cone *wasaskwecos.*

confection *maskikesa;* where candies are made, *maskihkesa kosehtahk.*

confectionery *sewatawikamikos;* a store for sweets, *sewayihatawikamikos;* a small store or confectionery, *acawekamikos* (*Northern*); *acawikamikos* (*Plains*).

conservation *nakatiyicikewin.*

conservationist *okanawiyicikew.*

consort *okimawayis konapemihk.*

consonant Final consonant, *cahkipekanis.*

conspiracy *weci ka kayesehewewin.*

conspire *kîmôc kayesowin.*

constable *masinkwasos; simakanis;* a rookie constable, *oskisimakanis.*

constellation A bunch of stars, *acahkosak.*

contagious *ka asawepayik kîkway.*

contemporary *peyakwanita kohcimakahk.*

497

continent *misiweskamik*; the size of a country, *ispehcakaskîy*.

contract *ka misowe ôtenamihk atoskiwin*.

convalesce *ka menohk ahkosowenihk ohci*.

convalescence *peyahtik astepayowin*.

convalescent *awîyak ka nihtâ menot*; gradually getting better from sickness, *misihkatc astepayowin*.

convention An important meeting, *okimâw nakiskatowin*.

convict *okipahekasow*.

conviction *kipahikasowin*.

convoy *mamawiyatowin*.

convulse *ka ociptikohk*.

convulsion *ociptikowin*.

cookbook *kestepo asinahikan*.

cookhouse A hot lunch kitchen, i.e.: in a bush camp, *piminawasokamik*.

cooler *tahkascikan*.

copper A brown iron, *osawapisk*.

copperhead *misikinepik episcipowenowit*.

cormorant A fish eating duck, *kahkakesip*.

coronation *ka postatotinahiht kihci okimâw*; the making of a king, *kihcokimahkewin*.

corporal A special head of the police force, *simakanisêw okimâw*.

correspondence *pahpeyakwan ketiyihtamihk*.

corrupt *mistahi mayekîkway*.

corruption *mistahi macayowewin*.

cot A small bed, *nipewinis*.

cottage A small house, *waskahikanis*.

cotton *sestak kosehcikakehk*; *pakoyanekin*.

couch *misitehtapowin*; *nipewinis*; a sitting thing, *tehtapowin*.

council *weyasowewin*.

councillor or councilor *otoweyasowew*; *owiyasiwew*; *owiyasowiw*.

counter *akihcikakan*; desk or counter, *masinahikew tihtascikan*.

counterfeit Making false money, *kîmôc sônîyâwehkewin*.

county *ka pahpiskihc tepahaskatek askîy*.

courier *opapamesehcikestamâkew*.

court A law court, *oyasowewin*; a ruling from the highest court, *naspiciwiyasowewin*; s/he takes her/him to court, *oyasowatew*; a court case or a legal judgement, *oyasowewin*.

court house A house where laws are made, *oyasowewikamik*; *wiyasowewikamik (Northern)*; *wiyasowiwikamik (Plains)*.

coverlet A small blanket, *akohpis*.

covert *pesiskesak okasoweniwaw*.

cowbell *mostos soyakan*.

cowbird *mostos pîwâyisis*.

cowboy *otehtapewiyinow*; a riding horse man, *tehtapewenow*.

cowgirl *iskwew ka nihtâ tehtapit*.

cow hand *awîyak mostoswakapaminat*.

cowherd *ka mamawiyatwaw mostoskwak (Northern)*.

co-worker *weci atoskemakan*.

crab A shell fish, *esis*.

crane A machine for lifting, *ohpahpekipicikan*.

crank *peminikan*.

crayon *sopekahikanisa (Northern)*; *sopikahikanacikosak (Plains)*; *masinastewina*.

credit *ka masinahikemekihk*; *awihiwewin*.

cremate It is cremated or reduced to ashes, *pekinihkahtew*; s/he is cremated or reduced to ashes, *pekinihkasow*; s/he cremates them or reduces them to ashes, *pekinihkaswew*.

cremation *ka mestihkasamihk meyaw*.

crematory *mestihkasekewikamik*.

cribbage A card game, *pakesan metawewin*.

cricket A British field game, *akayasew metawewin*.

crime *mayitotamowin*.

criminal *awîyak ka nihtâ mayahkamkisit*; *nipatakew*.

criminality *mayahkamkisowin*.

criminally *mayahkamkisowenihk*.

crochet *ka apihkacikakehk sestak*; a kind of knotting with a hooked needle, *apihkewin*.

crocodile A large greedy lizard, *wehtikowosikiyas*.

crocus *wapikwanes*.

cropland *ohpikihcikew askîy*.

cropper *kistikan ka meyokit*.

crop rotation *ka mahmeskoc kistikehk*.

crown *okimâw astotin*.

cudgel *mistik ka naskwakehk*.

cultivator *sikopocikan*; a ground smasher, *sikwahcahikan*.

curfew *ka kisipipayik tepahikan*.

curlew A bird with a crooked bill, *wakikotesis pîwâyisis*.

curling A sliding rook game, *soskwa sinewepinikewin*.

currant A small raisin, *sominis*.

currency Money, *sônîyâw*.

curriculum A regular course of study, *kiskinohamatowin*; *tânsi ka isikiskinohamakehk*.

curry *kestepwakan weyasihk ohci*.

curtain *akopecikan*; *akopicikewin*.

custody *kipahikasowin*.

cushion Something you sit on, *aspapowin*.

cuspid A tooth, *mepit*.

customer *otatawew*.

curtain *akopicikewin*.

customer *awîyak katawet kîkway*.

cutlery A set of knives, *mohkomana*; *nânatohk isi metsowakana*.

cutlet Soft, tender meat, *yoskiwîyâs*.

cut line *tipahaskewin*; *tipahaskanisa*; *cipahaskanisa*.

cutworm *mohtew*.

cyclone A big whirlwind, *misipastosêwan*.

cypress A special spruce, *minahik*.

cyst *kamiyiwik*.

D

dachshound A short-legged dog, *cimkatis atim*.

daddy long legs *kinokatesiy*; *apehkîs*; a long-legged spider, *kinokatewocayapehkîs*.

daffodil *meyoskamin wapikwan*.

dahlia *wapikwaneya*.

dairy A dairy or milk shed, *tohtosapowikamik*.

daisy *wapiskapikonesa*; *wapikwan*; a yellow flower, *osawak*.

dame *okimaskwew*.

damnation *misiwanâcihisowin*.

damsel A young girl, *oskinekiskwew*.

dandy It looks good, *meyonakwan*.

data *kihcimasinahikan*; a truthful writing, *kihcimasinahikewin*.

daydream *nânatohk akâwâc mâmitoneyihtamowin*.

deathbed *awîyak ka ateponiyehet*.

deathless *kîkway ekâ ka nipemakahk*.

deathwatch *awîyak iskwes kwayac ka wetapemiht*.

debit Owing a debit, *ka masinahikehk*; debit, *masinahikewin*.

debt *ka masinahikepayihk*; owing something, *masinahikewin*.

decentralization *pahpiskihtinkewin*.

decision making *kakwe kisetamowin* (Northern); *ohwipaytahk* (Plains).

decorator *owawesehcikew*.

delegate A chosen person, *nawasonikan*.

delegation The choosing of people, *nawasonitowin*.

delicatessen Prepared food, *mecowina*.

delinquent *omayenikew*; a young offender, *oskimâyinikew*.

delirium Being in a forgetting state, *wawankiskisowin*.

delivery *etohtamâkewin*.

democracy *okimâwiwin*; everybody is here, *mamawi okimâwiwin*.

density *metoni ka kaskisakak*.

dental Something for the teeth, *mepita ohci*.

dentist A tooth doctor, *mepit maskihkiwiyinow*.

dentistry *mepit maskihkiwiyinowin*.

deodorant *wehkimakohcikan*.

department *piskihtapowin isihcikewnihk*.

dependant *awîyak kapamehiht*.

deportation S/he is sent back where s/he came from, *kewetisawaw*.

deposit *ka nahahihtsônîyâw*; putting money away, *sônîyâwkanahahiht*.

deposition *kihci pekiskwewin*.

depositor *onahascikew*.

depository *nahascikewnihk*.

depot *nakewinihk*; a stopping place, *nakewin*.

depressant *maskihki ka sesawiskakohk*.

deputy *semakansihkan*; an assistant, *kihcisimakanis*.

derail It went off the track, *pacipayow*.

desk *apowin kiskinohamatokamkohk*; *kiskinohamatowapowin*; *micisonahtik ita masinahikik*; *masinahikew tihtascikan*.

destroyer *nôtinitonapihkwan*; *omesiwanacicikew*.

detachment *piskihtahewewin*.

detour A road around, *wemaskanaw*.

diadem A king's hat, *kihci okimâw astotin*.

diagram *kiskinowatasinahikewin*.

dial *ka makonamihk akihtasona*.

dialect *pahpîtos isikiswewin*; a certain language, *pekiskwewin*.

diamond A special money stone, *kihcisônîyâw asinîy*.

diarrhea Having an abnormal bowel movement, *saposowin*.

diary *tahtokesikaw tôtamowin*; *tahtokesikaw ka masinahamihk tânsi etôtamihk*; an everyday performance, *tahtokesikawtôtamowin*.

dictionary *otwestamâkewasinahikan*; *masinahikan ka wehtamomakahk tânsi etwemakahk pekiskewin*; a book defining language, *miskwatâmowasinahikan*.

diet *metsowin ka nakatiyihtamihk*; *mecowin ka paminamihk*; a prescribed course of eating, *kiskinowacimetsowin*.

dilemma *waniyihtampicikewin*; a choice between two things equally undesirable, *ayimisiwin*.

dill *ka wesakispakosit menis*.

dime Ten cents, *metataht pewâpiskos*; *mitataht pewâpiskos*.

dimension A measurement, *espicak tipahikewin*.

dimensional *nânatohk ka isi tepapekinkehk*.

dinosaur The first creature, *nistampisiskow*.

diploma *kaskitamasowin*; a certificate given by a school, *kaskitamasowin asinahikan*.

diptheria *mikotaskway ahkosowin*; a throat sickness, *mikohtaskway*.

director *okiskinwahekew*.

discount *nehtakihcikewin*.

discriminate *ka pîtotiyicekehk*.

499

discrimination *pîtos tiyicekewin.*

disinfect *maskihki ka astahk; maskihkewihtaw;* cleaning with medicine, *maskihkewkanacihcikewin.*

disinfectant *ka nipahcikemakahk maskihki.*

disqualify *ka ataweyimiht awîyak.*

distemper *pisiskiw otakosiwin.*

distillery A whiskey making house, *iskotewapokamik; itakamascikewkamik.*

district *peyakwayak ita askehk;* a special land ownership, *asketipeyicikewin.*

division *papiskici sîhcikîwin.*

divorce *ka kihci wepintohk;* a license for separation, *wepinitowasinahikan.*

dock A place for unloading boats, *kapawinkapatenasowin.*

document *kihcimasinakikanis;* a special written script, *kihcimasinahikewin.*

doghouse *atimokamik;* in the doghouse, *mayewicitowin;* a barn or a big doghouse, *misatimokamik.*

dogmatic *sapwiyihtamowin.*

doily A cover for a table top, *aspascikewin.*

dole *sônîyâw ohtenamâkewin.*

dollar One dollar, *peyakwapisk;* four quarters, *newosônîyâs;* a four quarter bill, *newopehikan (Northern).*

domain A land ownership, *asketipeyicikewin.*

domestic *kwayaskopayihcikewin wekowenihk;* a house helper, *atoskeyakan wikowinihk.*

dominion Supreme authority and control of land, *okimâwiwin.*

donation The act of giving, *mekiwin.*

donor *mihko ka mekihk.*

do-nothing *kwanta ka ayapihk.*

doomsday *poni askewkih.*

door A house door, *iskwâhtem;* the door of a teepee, *kistohkan.*

doorbell *iskwahtem soweyakanis.*

doorjamb *iskwahtem tapihtcikan.*

doorkeeper *kanâwiskwatemiwew.*

doorknob *iskwahtem yohtenkan.*

doormat *aspitahkoskewin.*

doorstep *amacowe tahkoskewin.*

dope Evil medicine, *macimaskihkiy.*

dormitory *ispimihtakohk nipawikamik;* a room for sleeping, *nipawikamik.*

dose One dose of medicine, *peyakmaskihkiy mekowin.*

double-barrelled *or* **double-barreled** *kaneswamok kotokohtak.*

double-cross *ka kayesowin.*

double-edged *kaskipasow mohkomansa.*

doughnut A round cooked biscuit, *waweyihkasikan.*

dowager A well off woman, *weyotisêwiskwew.*

dozen *peyak asastew; nisosâp;* twelve of something, *nisosâpkîkway.*

draft *ka kiskinowatasinahamihk atoskewin.*

dramatization *ka mamaskasapamohewehk.*

dramatize *ka tâpwenakwahk cikastepayihcekewin.*

drape *akopicikan.*

drapery A curtain, *akopicikan.*

drawer A wooden container, *mistikowatasiwacikanis.*

dressmaker *awîyak iskewasakaya kosehtat.*

dressing Stuffing for fowl, *aspahcikan.*

drive *pamihcikewin;* s/he drives, *pamihcikew.*

driven *ka pamihtahk.*

driver A person who drives, *pamihcikewenow;* a person who drives a vehicle, *opamihcikew;* a driver, conductor, or chauffeur, *opimohtahiwew.*

drug *maskihki ka keskweskakohk;* a curing medicine, *natawihomaskihkiy.*

dunce A dull witted, stupid person, *kakepaceyinow.*

dungeon A cellar jail house, *watihkankipahotokamik.*

duplicate An exact copy, *tapasinahikewin.*

dynamite An explosive bomb, *pahksikan.*

dynasty *tahtapapestatowin.*

dysentery A stomach disease, *saposowin.*

E

eardrum *pehcayihk mihtawakahk.*

earnings The act of earning, *kespinacikewin.*

ear phones *nitohtamowakana; nihtohtamawikana.*

eccentric *namoya metoni apihtaw.*

eclipse *ka awasiwet pîsim;* there is part moon or sun, *pahkwesiw pîsim;* the moon's disappearance, *kotawew pîsim.*

economic *manacicikewin.*

economical *manacetaw;* it is cheap, *wehtakihtew.*

eczema A disease of the skin, *keyakasêwin.*

edit *acimomasinahikewin.*

editor *omasinahikeses.*

effective *kîkway ka nahipayik.*

effeminate *nâpew ka iskwew isâyât.*

egoism *nakacihesowin.*

egotism Having an exaggerated opinion of oneself, *mistahi kakihcimowin;* s/he thinks highly of herself/himself, *kihciyimow;* the act of thinking highly of oneself, *kihciyimowin.*

egret A big bird that lives in a swamp, *misi mohkahisiw.*

elastic *ka sepekepayik.*

elasticity *ka sepihkak.*

500

elect *ka nawasoniwehk.*

election *nawasoniwewin;* running for election, *wehowina; pimpatawin;* a local election, *kapisasik pimpatawin;* a provincial election, *ka pisasik;* a federal election, *kapimpatahk; kamisak pimpahtawin.*

electric *wasaskotepayow ka ohci pimpayik.*

electricity Or lighting, *wasaskotepayow; pisewiskotew;* something that makes light, *waskotepayicikan;* lighting, *wasaskotenikewin.*

electrify *ka wasaskotepayihtahk.*

elegy *oponi pimatisowak nikamostamakewin.*

element *ka ohci osehtahk kîkway.*

elementary *oski kîkway.*

elementary school *oski kiskinohamatokamik.*

elephant The water spraying animal, *ospackew pisiskow.*

elevate *kîkway ka ohpastahk.*

elevation Up on the hill, a high place on the hill, *ispamatin.*

emancipate *kâwi ka pakitinowehk.*

emancipation *pakitin nowewin.*

embalm *ka wehkimakwahamihk meyaw.*

emblem *kiskowehikan.*

emboss *masinatahikewin.*

emigrant A foreign person, *ayahci ayisiniw.*

emigration *papicowin.*

employ *ka atoskahewehk; atoskehat;* s/he gave her/him a job, *masinahikehat.*

employee A hired person, *atoskewenow.*

employer *otatoskahiwew; nitokimam;* my boss, *nitokimam.*

employment *atoskahiwewin; atoskewin.*

empower S/he empowers her/him to do extraordinary things, *mamatawihew.*

encore Once over again, *asamina peyakwaw.*

endanger *kostacewâyâwin.*

endowment *sônîyâw mekiwin;* giving something away for good, *okihtawihiwewin.*

engaged *asotamatowin tawekihtohk.*

engender *yiyihiwewin.*

engine *iskotewtâpânâsk;* a motor, *askihkos.*

engineer An engine or motor mechanic, *askihkwenow.*

engrave *ka masinaskokahikehk.*

engraving *masinaskokahikewin.*

enigmatical *ekâ kwayaskwiyihcikewin.*

enrol *or* enroll *nânitâw ka wecihiwehk.*

enrolment *or* enrollment *wecihiwewnihk.*

enshrinement *naspisihiwewin.*

enslave *awahkanehiwewin.*

enterprise *kîkway ka macipayihtahk.*

entitle *ka nawapamikowin.*

entrance *eta kohpehtokehk; nîkanpehtikwewin.*

entranceway *pehtokekocinowin.*

enumerate *akihcikewin.*

envelope *masinahikan asowacikan;* a letter pocket, *asiwacikanis.*

environment *ka isi nakayâskamihk;* a way of living, *itatisiwin.*

environmental *isi nakayâskamowin.*

epidemic *ka pimpayik ahkosowin; asoskamatowin.*

epilepsy A muscle disease, *ocipitikowin.*

epileptic *ahkosowin sîsîkoc ka nahnipopayihk.*

epilogue *aniskosehcikewin.*

episode *kîkway ketahkamikahk acimowenihk.*

episodic *kwayaskwacimowin.*

epitome *kiskinowac acimowewin.*

equable *metoni pahpiyakwan.*

equalization *tahtipahwan iyikohk.*

equation *kwayaskwakihcikewin.*

equestrian *awîyak ka pascopehat mistatimwa.*

equine *iyinisêw mistatim.*

equitable *ka kwayas kosecekenehk.*

equity *kwayaskosehcikewin.*

equivocal *nânatohk isi ka nisetohtatohk.*

equivocate *kahkwetateh etwewin.*

equivocation *ka nihtâ kwetateh isi pekiskwehk.*

era *tanta kîkway kohmacipayik; ekospi;* that time or some time ago, *ekospeh.*

eraser *ka sehikakan;* something you rub off, *kasehikan; kâsîwepahikâkan; kâsîwepahikânis; kasiwipahikanis.*

erosive *kîkway ka mesciwepahekemakahk.*

erudite *kwayask kiskinohamakosowin.*

escapism *wanikiskisohiwewin.*

escapist *owanikiskisohiwew.*

espionage *kemotatisiwin kayeyisowin;* the act of spying, *kemotatisiwin.*

espouse *kisci otinowewin.*

essay *acemowin ka masinahamihk.*

establishment *meyo picikewin kosehtahk.*

estate *metoni weyotisowin; tipehtamowina;* a person's posessions, *tipeyihtamowina.*

eternize *kosehtahk ekâ wehkac kisipayowin.*

etiquette Good manners, *meyo sâyâwin.*

ethic *kwayask mâmitoneyicikan.*

ethical *kwayasko mâmitoneyicikewin.*

ethics *kwayasko mâmitoneyicikana.*

ethnic *tanta ka ohtaskanesihk.*

ethos *pahpîtos isihtwawena* (Northern).

etiquette *naspic manatesowin.*

eucliptus A medicine tree, *maskihkewmetos.*

euthanasia *sîsîkoc nipahewewin.*

evacuate Leaving something, *nakacikewin.*

evaporate It turns into vapor, *mestapahtew.*

501

even-tempered *ekâ wawîyak kamacitwahk.*

evict *ka wayawetisahikehk;* s/he chase her/him out, *wayawetisa.*

eviction *wayawetisahikewin.*

evidence *mosepayowin.*

evolutionary *pîtos espayihcikewin.*

evolutionist *awîyak pîtos ka isitapwehtahk.*

evolve *pîtos isihcikewin.*

excavate *watihkewin;* s/he dug it up, *monaham.*

excavation The act of digging up, *monahikewin; ka watihkehk.*

exclamatory *kisewiy pekiskwewin.*

excursion *meseweteh ka papamohtek.*

execution *akosowewin; ka akotiht awîyak;* the act of killing, *nipahitowin.*

executioner *otakosowew.*

executive *onikanapow.*

exemption *ekak akisoh.*

exhibition *wapahtehewewin.*

exhume *ka moskatihkatamihk meyaw.*

exile *awîyak ka nakacipicestahk otaski.*

exorbitance *kakwespanâc isâyâwin.*

exorbitant *metoni ka kakwespanâc isâyâhk.*

expedition *papame picowin.*

expend *kîkway ka pone apatahk.*

expendable *ka ateponapatahk kîkway.*

expenditure *mestinikewin.*

expense *mestinkewin; mistahi ispayow;* charging or something bought, *akihtamâkewin.*

expensive It costs a great deal, *sohkakihtew.*

experiment *kocitawin.*

experimental *kîkway ka kocitahk.*

expert *onakacitaw.*

expire *ka kisipipayik; nipiw;* the act of being no more, *ponipayow.*

expletive *ka mohcotonamohk.*

explosives Exploding material, *pahkisawana.*

exponent *kwayask owehtamâkew.*

expulsion *kawayawiwepinewehk.*

extension Make something larger, *yahkisihcikewin;* a house extension, *aniskohpicikan (Northern); aniskohcikan (Plains).*

exterminate *ka mescihewehk.*

extermination *mescihewewin.*

extinct *ka mescitahk.*

extinction *mescitawin.*

extraction Pulling out a tooth, *mepitka ocipitamihk.*

extravagant S/he likes spending money, *nihtâmestinikew.*

extravaganza *kosam meyonakohcikehk.*

eyestrain *ka nestwacapihk.*

eyewitness *ka wapahcikehk weyasowewnihk.*

502

F

fable *atayohkan;* a fictitious story, *atayohkewin.*

facial *ka nanapacitahk mihkwakan.*

facsimile The copying of an article, *naspimasinahikewin.*

fact *kihcinahowin;* the truth, *tâpwewin.*

factor *kîkway ka ispayihcikemakahk.*

factual *kihci kehcinahowin.*

fainthearted *ka nestotehepayihk.*

fairy tale Or myth, *âtayohkewin.*

fake *mweci tâpwe isâyâwin.*

fallow *ka ayowepehtahk askîy;* the act of turning the soil over, *pekopicikewin.*

false pride *kwanta mamihcisowin.*

false teeth *mipitihkana.*

family allowance cheque *awâsisasinahikan.*

family man *peyak oskanewiyinow.*

famine A poor and hungry time, *nohtekatewin.*

fan A mechanical fan, *tahkeyawepahikan;* a hand fan, *westehikan.*

fanatic *wawîyak isâyâwin.*

fanatical *wawîyak kesayahk.*

farce *wawîyasenikewin cikastepayihcikewnihk.*

farm *kistekew askîy;* land for growing crops and vegetables, *kistikan ohpicihcikewin.*

farmer *okistekewiyinow (Northern); okistikew (Plains).*

farm hand *atoskahakan kistikanihk.*

farmland *askîy ka kistikatamihk.*

far-reaching *wâhyaw metakwi isih.*

far-sighted *wâhyaw ka etapihk; wâhyawisinahapow.*

fashion *pahpîtos kesehohk;* in a suspect fashion, *pisikwâc;* the way one dresses, *isihowin.*

fashionable *anohc tânsi ka mekwa isihohk.*

fatality *awîyak ka nipahiht;* killed in a crash, *nipahisinowin.*

fateful *nânatohk kopayowin.*

fatherland *eta kohtaskanehk; kitaskenew;* our place to live, *kitaskenaw.*

faulty *nayihtawipayow.*

feasible *kîkway ka wehcipayik.*

feather bed *opîway nipewin.*

feather-bedding *opîway akohpa.*

federal *kihci okimanahk.*

federate *okimanahk mamawintowin.*

federation *okimanahk mamawe isihcikewin.*

fee *koyakehtamihk kîkway;* payment of something, *tipahikewin.*

feeble minded Always forgetting, *wanikiskisowin.*

feedbag *metso maskimot.*

feedbox *metso mistikowat.*

feeder *otasahkew.*

feline *noseminôs.*

fellowship *meyo mamawecehtowin.*

felon *ka meyewihk maskasehk.*

felony *misimayenikewin weyasowewnihk;*
committing a major crime, *mayitotamowin.*

feminism *iskwew mâmitoneyicikan.*

feminist *awîyak ka iskwewayat.*

fennel *nepeya ka mecihk.*

fertilization *kameyo kihcikemakihtahk askîy.*

fertilize *ka nesohkamatamihk askîy.*

fetter *ayisiyinew napwapiswakana.*

feud *pahpeyakoskanew mayewecehtowin.*

fiancee *iskwew pamayes wewihtot.*

fibre or **fiber** *asapap ka maskawset.*

fiction *kîyaskiwin;* a person in a fictitous story,
atayohkan.

fictional *ekîyaskimakahk.*

fictitious *kîyaskewacimowin.*

fiddle An instrument, *kitocikan.*

fiddler A person who plays music, *kitocikewenow.*

fidelity *metoni ka peyakohetohk.*

fighter *onôtinikew.*

figment *kwanta acimowin.*

figurate *ka masinatahikehk.*

figuration *masinatahikewin.*

figurative *ka masinatahamihk.*

figured *tânsi ka etakihtamihk kîkway.*

figure skater *ocahkikâtepayihow;* a skater who
dances, *osoniskwâtahikew kanimihitot.*

figurine *aysenehkan kosehiht.*

filbert A small nut, *pâkânis.*

file *masinahikanascikewin.*

filing cabinet *masinahikan asowacikîwin.*

filling *sâkaskinahcikewin.*

film *eta ka masinpayik kîkway.*

filter Something that filters, *ka
sapokawihcikemakahk.*

filtration *sapokawihcikewin.*

finalist *ka iskwayacipayit awîyak.*

finance *sônîyâw;* a money lending business, *sônîyâw
awehiwewin.*

financial *sônîyâw isihcikewin.*

financially *meyo sônîyâhkewnihk.*

financier *sônîyâwah ka awehiwet.*

finding *miskacikewin.*

fine *metoni ka pekinak; ekosi; mewasin.*

finetoothed *pinahihkwan.*

fingerprint *ka ayesihtamohewehk mecicîs.*

fire alarm *iskotew waspawehtaswakan.*

firearms *nânatâhkisi paskisikana; paskisikana.*

fire company *otastaweyapawacikewak.*

fire department *eta kohastaweyapawacekehk.*

fire engine *astaweyapawacikew tâpânâsk.*

fire escape *iskotew paspamowin;* a runaway place in
case of fire, *iskotewtapasêwin.*

fire extinguisher *astaweyapawacikakan.*

firefighter *otastawehikew.*

firefighting *astawehikewin; astawihikiwin.*

fire hall *astawehikewkamik.*

fireman *otastawyapawacikew;* a person who puts out
fires, *otastawehikew.*

fireplace A place where fire is made, *kotawan.*

fire ranger *iskotewokimaw* (Northern); *skotiwikimaw*
(Plains).

fireworks Exploding material, *pahkitepayicikewina.*

fish and wildlife *kinosêw okimâw; kinosiw okimâw.*

fishery *paktahwawnihk.*

fish house *kinosêwikamik.*

fishing hole *eta ka nihtâ ayat kinosêw.*

fish-hook *kwaskwepicikan.*

fishing license *pakitahwawasinahikan.*

fishing line *kwaskwepecikanyapiy.*

fishing pole *kwaskwepecikanahtik.*

fishing tackle *ka mamawatawehk
kwaskwepicikakana.*

fish stick *kinosêwahtik.*

fitter *onahiskamohewew.*

fixer *okesehcikew.*

fixture *osehcikewin.*

flag *kiskowehon.*

flagging *meskanahk nakinowewin.*

flagman *onakinowew.*

flamingo A long-legged bird, *kinokat.*

flammable *ka nihtâ wayatepayik.*

flashing *ka wasiskotepicikehk.*

flask A flat bottle, *napakmoteyapiskos.*

flat-footed *ka napakistehk.*

flight *kohpahohk pimeyakanihk.*

flipper *pakasimwakana.*

floor The flooring of a house, *anaskanihtak;* on the
bare floor, *mohcitak;* double flooring, *nesohtak;* it
has double flooring, i.e.: a trailer, *nesohtakisow.*

floral *wapikwanew tasinastek;* a floral decoration,
wapikonewawesehcikan.

florid *enepehkanakahk kîkway.*

florist A flower person, *wapikonewiyinow.*

floss A kind of yarn, *sestak.*

flowerpot *nepehkan askihkos.*

flu *ahkosowin.*

fluidity *nipewakamihcikewin.*

flute *pikwan.*

flycatcher *pîyesîs.*

flyer An airplane pilot, *pimehawenow.*

foam rubber *apihkanayih ka pestewayak.*

fodder *pastew askoseya; pisiskow mecowin;* cattle
food, *pisiskiwimecowin.*

503

foghorn A ship horn, *napihkwan potacikan.*

folk music *kayâs ketohcikewena.*

folk song *kayâs nikamowena.*

folk tale *kayâs acimowin.*

foodstuff *pimihaweniw; wecinew masinahikan;* some things to eat, *mecowina.*

fool's gold *ka sônîyâwapiskonakosit asinîy.*

footstool *ka tahkohtastahk mesita.*

forage *maskoseya ka samihtwaw pesiskowak (Northern).*

forecast The foretelling of weather or anything else, *kiskowehikewin.*

foreclose *ka kipahamihk isihcikewin.*

foreign *akamaskehk ohci.*

foreign land Another country, *kotak askîy.*

foreknowledge *neyak kiskeyecikewin.*

foreman *awîyak atoskewin ka paminahk; okimâw; okimasis (Northern); okimas (Plains).*

forementioned *nîkan mamiskohtowin.*

forenoon In the morning, *kekisepahk.*

forepart Towards the front, *nîkanisih.*

foreshadow *nîkan cikastesenowin.*

foresight *neyak ka wapahtamihk; nîkan wapahtamowin.*

foresighted *neyak wapahcikewin.*

forestation *sihcisisak kohpikihihtwaw (Northern).*

forestry *sâkaw nakatiyicikewin.*

forestry station *isotewokimawikamik.*

forfeit *katepahikehewehk mayesehcikewin.*

forge *ka oyapiskatahekehk.*

fork An eating fork, *cestahicepwakanis.*

format *kakwayaskwascikehk.*

formative *kakwayaskwascikehewehk.*

formula *oyapohkahcikewin; kehkawenikan;* a mixture of something, *kiyikawenikan.*

forsook *kayâs wepinkewin.*

fort *waskahikan;* a special lookout, *asawapew wasakamehcikan.*

forthcoming Something that arrived, *papayow.*

forthwith *metoni semak.*

fortress *ka sohksehcikatek waskahikan.*

fortune Being rich or well off, *weyotisiwin.*

foul-mouthed *kohkostonamowin.*

foundation *eta waskahikan ka cimatek.*

founder *awîyak ka macipayihciket.*

foundling A discarded child, *wepinikanawâsis.*

fountain A water spring or natural water hole, *mohkicowanpek;* a drinking fountain or a fountain in a public square, *wayaweciwanihkewin.*

fourscore *ayinanewomitanaw askîy.*

foursome Four in a group, *kanahnewihk.*

foxhound A fox hunting dog, *mahkesis nocicikewatim.*

fraction *pahpiskiht akihcikewin;* just a little part of, *pahkipakow.*

fracture Breaking bones of the body, *natwakanepayowin; ka natwatihk oskan; katanetatahk oskan.*

fraternal *kotôtemihk.*

fraternity *mamawi meyowecehtowin.*

fraud *wayesihewewin.*

fraudulent *ka yesew isihcekewin.*

freak An abnormal person, *kîkwayehkan.*

freedom The act of being free, *paspewin.*

freezer A deep freezer, *ahkwacicikan; ahkwatihcikan.*

freight *awatasowin.*

freighter A boat for hauling freight, *awatasowosiw.*

freightage *awatasowena.*

freight car *posihtasotâpânâsk.*

freshman A student for one year, *kiskinohamakan peyakaskîy.*

fricasse A special kind of gravy, *mecimapohkewin.*

friction *ka sinkohtihk kîkway.*

fritter Something toasted, *kaspikasikan.*

frock A woman's dress, *iskwewasakay.*

frond *emahkipakak nipîy.*

frontier *eta ka iskwaste askîy.*

frostbite *nânitâw ka ahkwacihk.*

frostbitten *ahkwacowin.*

frosting *iyikwacowin.*

frying pan *saseskihkwan (Northern); lapwel (Northern, French Cree); nawaciwakan (Plains); napwen.*

fudge *ka moscosehtahkmaskihkes.*

fuel *awaswakan pimiy; pimiy; saskitenikan.*

fugitive *awîyak ka papamamot.*

full moon *ka kesapiskisit tepiskaw pîsim.*

fumes Fumes from a car, *wehcekapasow.*

fumigate Making a smudge with a substance, *maskekewapasikew.*

function *ka pimpayik kîkway.*

functional *pimpayihcikewin.*

fund *ka mawatahiht sônîyâw;* the accumulation of money, *sônîyâwemawacihiht.*

fundamental *ka nihtâ oyesehcikehk.*

funeral A burial, *nahinowewin;* the burying ceremony, *nahinikewin.*

funnel A tool for taking in water or gas, *pecipacikan.*

furlong A measure just about half a mile, *tipahapankekacapihtawmistik.*

furnace *mistahawaswakan;* a big stove heater, *kotawanapisk; kisisikan;* a fuel furnace, *pimewkotawanapisk (Northern); pimiy kotawanapisk (Plains).*

furnishings *ohtenamâkewna.*

furniture *kahkeyaw ohci âpacicikana wekowenihk;* *kesapowina;* house utensils, *âpacihcikana.*
furthermost At the very end, *asonehcac.*
furthermore Just a bit more, *ayiwâkes.*
fuse A fuse for lights on a vehicle, *wasaskotepayihcikan otâpânâskohk.*
fusion *ayetaw ohci saskitihcikan.*

G

gable The end walls at each end of a sloping house roof, *kipihtakahikana.*
gadget *kwanta âpacicikanis.*
gallbladder A sac for bile, *wesopewaskimot.*
galleon A big battle ship, *misinotinikewosih.*
gallery Seats up on top, *ispimehkapowina; ka acikipahekatek apowin metawewkamkohk; ispimehk apewina.*
gallon One gallon, *peyak tipahopan.*
gallows *akocikanahtik.*
galosh An overshoe, *ahkwetawaskisin.*
gamble The betting game, *astwatowin.*
game warden A game keeper, *kanaweyicikew; okanawecikew; okanawicikiw.*
gang *omamawi atoskewak.*
gangrenous *ka maci weyâsehk.*
gangster *onipahtakew;* the member of a lawless gang, *maci ayiseyinow.*
gangway A small bridge, *asokewinis.*
garage A car house, *sehkepimpayesikamik.*
garland Making decorations, *wawesecikewin.*
garner A vegetable cellar, *kistikanikamik.*
garnish *ka nakinamihk tepahikewin;* decorating food, *wawesetaw mecowin.*
garter *seskepison.*
garrison Security soldiers, *kanaweyicikewsimakanisak.*
gasoline *pemewtâpânâskopimiy;* a burning liquid or oil, *pahkitewpimiy.*
gas S/he gases up her/his vehicle, *pehcipimew.*
gas station *eta ka tawakehk pimiy; pimewikamik* (Northern); *otapanaskopimiwikamik* (Plains).
gauntlet A glove, *astis.*
gauze Medicine gauze, *sakimewayan; senipânekin.*
gavel A special hammer, *pakamakanis.*
gazette A small newspaper, *acimo masinahikanis.*
gear *atoskewakana;* a starting gear for a vehicle, *sipwepitamowpicikan.*
gearing *pîwâpiskwa kohpimpayit osehkepayes.*
gearshift *sepwepayihcikan sehkipayesihk.*
gel *kîkway ka misewepayik.*
gem *ka wawesehiht asinîy;* a special money stone, *sônîyâwasines.*

generation *osehcikewin; anskotapan.*
generator *wasaskotepayew kosehcikakehk.*
genius *metoni iyinesowin.*
gentleman A very good man, *takahkinapew; nâpew ka manatsit.*
geography A knowledge of the world, *askekiskeyitamowin.*
germ *ahkosowin kohcemakahk; asoskamatowin.*
germinate Starting to grow, *maci ohpikiwin.*
giant *mistapew.*
giantess *mistapewin.*
gift-wrap *mekowin wekinkakan.*
gimlet A small drill, *payipahikanis.*
gin *iskotewapoy ka nepiw akamik;* a kind of alcoholic drink, *iskotewapoy.*
ginger A herb used for medicine, *wehkesk.*
gingham A piece of dress cloth, *miskotakayekin.*
giraffe A long-necked animal, *kinwapikwayawew atim* (Northern); *kinopik kwayawiw mistatim* (Plains).
girdle A belt, *pakwatehon.*
girl guide *iskwesis isihcikewin.*
girl guides *iskwesisak ka mamawintotwaw* (Northern).
girth A strap on a saddle for tightening, *sehtatayepicikan.*
glasses A term used for buying spectacles, *miskisikokanaw;* referring to goggles or glasses, *oskesikohkana.*
glass eye *mikisacap.*
glen *esakawak tawâtinaw.*
globe *espici waweye askîy ka masinihk.*
glossary *ka ayemwew asinahikehk.*
go-ahead *niya sipwehte; nekanohte.*
goalie *okanawiskwahtawew.*
goblet A drinking cup, *minihkwacikan; minehkwacikan.*
goggles A pair of special glasses, *oskesikohkana.*
goldenrod *ewaposawak nepehkan.*
gong A special disk that sounds when struck, *sewetahikan.*
good-natured *ka meyohtwahk; meyowatisow.*
goose flesh *niskeweyas.*
goshawk A kind of hawk, *kekek.*
goulash A kind of soup or gravy, *mecimapoy.*
govern *pimpayihewewin;* a person who runs things, *pimpayihcikew.*
governess A woman who runs things, *pimpayihcikew iskwew.*
government *kihcokimanahk;* a place from which you run things, *kihci okimanahk.*
governmental *kihcokimanahk ohci.*

505

governor *opimpayehiwew*; a special head man, *kihci okimâw*.

Governor General *kihconekanew*; *kihcokimâw okosisa*.

gown *kinwapekasakay*; a woman's dress, *iskwewasakay*.

gradation *ka tawa ka etah iwehk*.

grade *tantah kayahk masinahikanihk*; making a machine levelled road, *osehtawakahikan*.

grade school *kapsasisik kiskinohamatokamik*.

graduate *ka yahkohtehk kiskinohamâkewnihk*; one who finishes school, *kesikiskinohamakan*.

graduation *ka yahkohtahewehk*.

graft *maskihkewiyinow ka astamaket masakaya*; *akokiwihtahk*; fastening something together, *akokihcikewin*.

grain elevator *kistekan posihtaswakan*.

grainfield *ka wasakankatek kistekewin*.

grammar *akayâsemowin ka kiskenohamakehk*; a way of talking, *isipekeskwewin*.

gramophone An old style winding record player, *kitocikankapemastehamihk*.

granary *eta ka kanaweyemiht kistekan*; a grain house, *kistikanikamik*.

grandsires Special grandparents, *kihci onekihikomawak*; *kihci onekekomimawak*.

grant *pakitinamâkewin*; *meyew*; the giving of something, *mekowin*.

grater *sikopocikan*.

gravedigger *owatihkew kihkwahaskanihk*.

gravel *ka sikwatahoht asinîy*.

graze *eta ka pemacihisot pesiskow*.

grazing *ka metsotwaw pisiskowak* (Northern); *papamimecisowak*.

great-hearted *naspic kesewatsowin*.

great speed *sohkikocinowin*.

greenhorn *askihtakoweskan*.

grenade A small bomb, *pahkisawanis*.

greyhound *atim ka wapinakosit*.

griddle A flat piece of steel for cooking, *kestepowapisk*.

grievance *mawimowin*.

grill A roasting pan, *nawâcewakan*.

grinder A grinder or a grinding mill, *pinipocikan*.

grindstone *kenipocikewasinîy*; a sharpening stone, *kenipocikan*.

grippe *ahkosiwin*; *otakikomowin*; pain in stomach, *kisowaskatew*.

grocer A person who sells groceries, *otatawew*.

grocery *mecowin*; a food store, *atawikamik*.

groom A bride groom, *owekihtow*.

grotto A small chapel, *ayamihew kamikos*.

ground ice *miskwame ka sikwatahoht*.

grosbeak A winter bird, *pipon pîyeses*.

growing pains *ka ahkami wesakahpinehk*.

guardian A guardian for people, *okanaweyimiwew*.

guarantee *kihci kihcinahowin*.

guardian *okanawiyimowew*; *okanawiyimiwew*.

guardianship *ka nawiyimowewin*.

guideline *ka kiskinowatapihkinkehk*.

guidepost *ka kiskinowataskitahk mistik*.

guide word *kiskinowacipekiskwewin*.

guild *mamawi isihcikewin*.

guildsman *awîyak ka akisot isihcikewnihk*.

guitar *petihkwapekahikan*.

gumdrop *misemiskowewin*.

gumption *kwayask mâmitoneyicikan*.

gun cleaner A stick or vine used for cleaning a gun, *kicistapiskahikan*.

gunfight *paskisotowin*.

gunfire *ka pahpaskisekesihk*.

gunning *paskisowewin*.

gunny sack *ka secicakanwat*.

gunsmith *ka nanapacitat paskisikana*.

gusher *ka tapetawecowahk*.

gutter *pakohcenikakan*.

guy *peminahkwan*; *kepacinakos*.

gymnasium A practice room, *sesawewkamik*; *metawewikamik* (Northern); *mitawiwikamik* (Plains).

gymnast *osesawiw*.

gymnastic *ka sesawiwayahk*.

gymnastics *sesawiwna*.

gypsy A roving person, *papamacihosk*.

H

habitat *pisiskow otayawenihk*; *sehtwawin* (Northern).

habitation Taking a homestead, *otinaskewin*.

haemorrhage *nestohkwekawowin*.

haft *mohkomanahtik*.

hairdo *ka wawesehtahk mistakaya*.

hairline *ka iskwamokwaw mistakaya*.

hair net *mistakayah ohci ahyapes*.

hairpin *sakaskwahaman*.

hairsplitting *ka taskepayekwaw miscakasa*.

half moon *ka âpihtaw apiskisit pîsim*.

hall *ka ahci kipahekatek apewikamik*; a dance hall, *namehitokamik*; *nimihtowikamik*; *mamawopewikamik* (Northern); *mamawapiwikamik* (Plains); community hall, *mamawapewikamik*.

hallway A walkway, *pimohtewin*; *ka ahci kipahekatek pemohtewin*.

halter *ayapihkwehpicikan*.

hamburger *ka sikopotek wîyâs.*
hamlet A small town, *ôcenas.*
hammock A baby swing, *wewepison.*
hamper *asahtowin*; a box of groceries, *asatowina.*
handbag *maskimotis.*
handcuff *mahcikwapisona.*
handicap *ekâ kaskihohk*; *maskisowin.*
handicraft *niheyaw osehcikewna*; *osehcikana.*
handiwork *ka moscosehcikehk*; *nihtâwihtaw*; s/he does good work, *nahew.*
handkerchief A silk handkerchief or a neck scarf, *senipânitapiskakan*; a cloth for blowing the nose, *senihkikomakanis.*
hand-picked *ka nawasoniwehk.*
hand-to-hand *asawemiyitowin.*
handwriting *masinahikewin.*
hanger Coat hanger, *akocikakan*; plane hanger, *pimehakan nakewin*; an airplane house, *pimehakanikamik.*
hangman *otâkosowew*; *akocikewenow.*
hangnail *maskasiy kâpahkwepayit.*
happy go lucky *mocikis mocikeyinow*; a happy person, *omocikisow.*
happy hunting ground *mocikimacewnihk.*
hard hat *atoskew astotin.*
hard-hearted *maskawitehewin.*
hardtop *kamaskawak tahkoc.*
hare bell *maskekewan*; a medicine flower, *wapikwaniy.*
harelip *ka pahkewtonehk.*
hark Listen, *natohta.*
harlot *pisikwatsowin.*
harmonic *otôtemowin.*
harmonica *ka potatamihk kicocikans*; a blowing instrument, *pocacikanis.*
harmonious *awîyak kotôtemit.*
harmony *wecewakansimowin.*
harpist *okitohcikew.*
harpoon *misikinosêw tahkahcikan*; a stabbing iron for fish, *tahkahcikan.*
harrow *asiskew sikopicikan*; a tool for harrowing soil, *sikwacipicikan.*
harvest *ka mosakinamihk kistikansa*; cutting grass, *namisikewin.*
harvester *mosahkinkakan.*
harvest home *ascikewikamik.*
harvest moon *takwakin tipiskaw pîsim.*
hash *esekopotek wîyâs.*
hasp A door opener, *tatapiskinikan.*
hassock *ka aspapihk tehtapowenihk.*
hatband *senipân astotenihk kakamot.*
hatchery *paskawewikamik.*
hatchet *napatenskew cikahikanis.*

hatrack *astotin akocikan.*
hawker *okiskinowatascekew.*
hawk-eyed *ka nahapahcikehk.*
hawking *ka nahekohtakanemohk.*
hawthorn *okamnakasêwahtik*; a large size thorn, *misikaminakase.*
haycock A bunch of hay stacks, *westihkanisa.*
hay fever *maskosêwaspinewin.*
hayfield *maskosehkewnihk.*
hayfork Pitch fork, *cestahaskosiwakan.*
haymaker *omaskosehkew.*
hayrack *awataskosowakan.*
haystack *westihkan*; a small haystack, *westihkanis*; s/he makes haystacks, *westihkew.*
haywire Wire for baling hay, *maskosêw tahkopecikan.*
hazel *pâkânahtik.*
hazelnut *pâkân.*
hazel tree *pâkânahtik.*
headband *pasiskwepison.*
headlight *wasaskotenkana.*
head-on *metoni ka mekwahotohk*; *pakamiskotatowak.*
headphone *natohcikakana ka akamokih mihtawakahk.*
headquarters *eta kohpimpayihcikehk.*
headrest *kîkway kaspiskwesimohk.*
headroom *ketisk ka tepapihk posowenihk.*
headset *natohcikakana ka kiskamihk mistekwanihk.*
headwaiter *ka nîkân apit omenahewew.*
hearing aid *pehtamowakana.*
hearsay *kwanta acimowin.*
hearse *kantaw nahenowet otâpânâsk*; a vehicle for hauling bodies, *meyawkapimohtatahk.*
heart attack *miteh ka nakemakahk.*
heartland *metoni tastawayihk askîy.*
heart-rending *metoni ka kitimahiwehk.*
heartstrings *kitimakiyimowewin.*
heart-to-heart *metoni kwayaskohtowin.*
heartwood *apihtawayihk mistekohk.*
heater *awaswâkan.*
heather *sakatihkopemakwahtik.*
heat lightning *kisitew wasaskotepayiw.*
heatstroke *ka nestotehehkasohk.*
heavy-duty *ka sohsehcikatek.*
heavy-handed *ka sohkipaminowehk.*
heavy-hearted *ka mwatsokaskiyihtamowin.*
hedge *ka iskosakasik*; a bunch of thick bushes, *kaskihkopas.*
hedgehog *kohkos akamaskehk ohci.*
heir One who will inherit property, *nanistinamwakan.*
heiress A woman who inherits, *nanistinamwakan.*

507

heirloom Something handed from generation to generation, *aniskomekiwin.*

heist *kimotowin.*

helicopter Dragonfly, *cohkanapises; cokanapisîs; takocihkawaskakotek; takocihkawaskakotik.*

helmet A steel hat, *pîwâpiskowastotin; pîwâpiskastotin;* a hockey helmet, *soniskwâtahikewastotin.*

hemisphere The half of the whole world, *apihtawmisiweskamik.*

hemlock An evergreen tree of the spruce family, *sihtahtik.*

hemorrhage S/he hemorrhages or loses all her/his blood, *mescihkwekawew.*

hemp Some kind of fiberous material, *peminahkwanekin.*

hence *eyoko ohci.*

henceforth *anohc ohci;* from this time onward, *anohc ohci.*

hennery *pahkapahkwanikamik.*

henpecked *nâpew wewa ka taptawikehkamkot.*

herb *maskihkewahtik.*

herbicide *ka nipahcikakehk macikwanasa.*

herd A herd of animals, *aseyatowak pisiskowak.*

herdsman A cattle keeper, *kanawastimwew.*

hereabout *nânitâw ota; otanânitâw.*

hereafter *otah ohci; mwestasoma.*

hereditable *ka nihtâ asawpayik.*

hereditary *ka asawpayik isâyâwin; asoskamatowin.*

heredity *asaw namatowin.*

heresy *nawasoyapimowin.*

heretofore *iskoh anohc.*

herewith *anohc ohci.*

heritability *nakatâmakewin.*

heritable *ka nakatâmakehk.*

heritage *nakatâmatowin.*

hermit *pikwaciyinow; papeyakowekit;* one who always lives alone, *mosapew ayiseyinow.*

hermitage *pikwaciyinewiwin.*

hernia *ka poskwatayepayihk; poskwatayewin;* an abdominal rupture, *poskwatayet.*

hernial *poskwatayepayowin.*

hibernal *ka piponayak.*

hibernation *maskonahapowin.*

hide-and-seek *ka natonatohk metawewin.*

hide-out or hideout *eta ka manikasohk.*

hierarchy *ayamihiwiyinow apowin.*

highborn *kihci ayawenihk ka ohcehk.*

highbred *kihci ayawenihk kohcopekihk.*

highflier *ka kihciyimohk.*

high jinks *kwanta ayiwâk ka tôtamihk.*

high jump *pascohpewin; pascopiwin.*

highland *ka ispahcak;* mountain country, *wacewaskîy.*

highlight *sohkahac kîkway.*

highliner *awîyak ka mistiyimot.*

high-minded *ispimehk kesi mâmitoneyihtamihk.*

high-pitched *metoni ka wasêwehk.*

high-powered *ka maskawsemakahk kîkway.*

high-pressure *sohki yahkiskakewin.*

high-priced *mistakihcikewin.*

high school *ka ispak kiskenohamakewin.*

high-toned *ka wasêwek kitohcikan.*

highway *osehtawahkahikan meskanaw;* a special road, *kihcimeskanaw.*

hinge Steel that holds the door up, *iskwatemapisk.*

hinterland *ka patosak askîy.*

historian *atayohkan; otâcimow.*

historic Some happening of long ago, *kayâsispayowin; kayâsispayiwin.*

historical Something done long ago, *kayâsitotamowin; kayâs kîkway ka atôtamihk.*

history *kayâs acimowin;* old times, *pecinaway;* years from way back, *picotahk.*

hitch-hike *koposipayehohk.*

hither *otehisi;* on that side, *ekoteyisih.*

hithermost *netehisi nawâc.*

hitherto *otâ nawâc.*

hives *kisastaw kiyakasêwin; moskipayiwin.*

hobby *pahpakwac kîkway ka tomihk.*

hobbyhorse A toy horse, *metawakan; mistatimohkan kosehiht.*

hockey *ka soniskwâtahikehk; soniskwâtahkew metawewin;* the act of skating, *soniskwâtahikewin.*

hockey commitee *soniskwâtahikew'kimâwak.*

hockey helmet *soniskwâtahikewastotin.*

hockey knee pads *mihcikwana yôskahikana.*

hockey net *soniskwâtahikewayapiy.*

hockey player *soniskwâtahikew ometawew.*

hockey shirt *soniskwâtahikew pakiwayân.*

hockey skates *soniskwâtahikana.*

hockey socks *soniskwâtahikewasikanak.*

hockey stick *soniskwâtahikewenihk ka apâtahk mistik; soniskwâtahikew mistik.*

hoe A tool for hoeing vegetables, *ayahikakanis.*

hogwash *kwanta pekiskwewin.*

hog-wild *kwahcimohcowin.*

hoisery A large pair of stockings, *asikanak.*

hoist *ispahkepicikan.*

holiday A day of rest, *ayowepew kesikaw; ekâ ka atoskehk.*

homage *kihcitwaw asocikewin* (Northern).

homeland *kitaskenahk.*

homeless *ekanânitâw kawekihk.*

homespun Homespun yarn, *moscosehcikan sestak.*

homestead Taking a homestead, *askekaw otinamihk*.

homicide *nipahetowin; nipahtakewin*; committing a murder, *nipahtahikewin*.

hominy *mahtamin kasikopohiht*.

homogenize *pahpeyakwan itâpohkewin*.

hone A sharpener for a straight razor, *kaskipasotasahikan*.

honeymoon A trip taken by a newly wed couple, *wekihtokwasihitowin; oskiwekihtosipwetewin*.

hood *astotinihkanis*; a warm hat, *kesowastotin*.

hoofbeat *ka petowesihkwaw mistatimwak*.

hoodlum *kitimakayiseyinow*.

hookworm A parasitic worm infecting the intestine, *pehtakeyaw manicos; mohtew*.

hopscotch A child's outdoor game, *awâsisometawewin*.

horde *mecetowak*.

horseman One who looks after horses, *mistatimopamihiwew*.

horticulture Knowledge of growing vegetables, *ohpikihcikiskeyicikewin*.

hose A small sock, *asikanis*.

hospital *âhkosêwkamik; akosiwikamik*.

hostage *ka meciminiht awîyak*.

hostel *okitimakesow kapesêwikamik*; a living place, *kapesowin*.

hotel A resting house, *kapesêwikamik; kapesiwikamik; kapisiwikamik*.

hot-tempered *metoni ka macitwahk*.

hot water bottle *kisakamitewat; kisakamitîwat*.

hour The hour of the day, *tipahikan*.

housebreaking *kiskenohastimwewin*.

housecoat *nipawasakay*.

householder *ka nikanapit mamawekowenihk*.

housekeeper *iskwew wikowin ka pamihtat*.

housemaid A homemaker, *atoskewiskwew*.

housewife *awîyak wewa*.

housework *pehcayihk katoskehk; iskwew atoskewin*; a woman's job, *iskwewatoskewin*.

housing *waskahikanihkewin*.

hub *apihtawayihk otihtipipayew*; a hub for a wagon wheel, *mahkahkos tihtiptâpânâskopipayek*.

humane *ka kisewatotakehk*; treating animals or people with kindness, *kisewatisitotakewin*.

humanism *iyinikewakiyemowin*.

humanist *awîyak ka iyinikewakiyimot*.

humanitarium S/he feels sorry for people, *kitimakinakew*.

humanity *ka ayisiyinewihk*.

humanize *ka ayisiyinekehk*.

humankind *iyinew ayih*.

humidifier *ka tahkiyawepahikemakak*.

hummingbird *âmopîwâyisis*.

humorist *owaninew iyinow*.

humpback *ka piskwawkanehk*.

hunchback *wakahcawkanewin; maskawikan*.

hunting license *macewasinahikanis*.

hurdle Jumping over something, *pascohpewin*.

hurdler *awîyak kakwaskweyaskwahosot*.

hurricane *ka misikestihk*; a very big windstorm, *misikestin; kestin; kakîstihk*.

husbandry *onapimowin*.

hutch *wâposikamikos*.

hyacinth A spring flower, *meyoskamin wapikwaniy*.

hyena *tipiskaw nocicikew pisiskow*.

hygenic Being clean, *kanâtisowin*.

hypnosis *ka nepahiwehk*.

hypnotic *awîyak ka nepahiwet*.

hypnotism *nepahiwewin*.

hypocrisy *kemotatisowin*.

hypocrite *okemotatisow; nanaspâc itotam*.

hypocritical *ka kemotatisiskihk*.

hysteria *koskweyihtamowin*.

I

ibis A long-legged bird, *kinokatewpîwâyisis*.

iceberg *miskwamew waces*.

ice-box or **icebox** *miskwamew mewat*.

icehouse *miskwamewikamik; tahkasicikewikamik*.

idealism *ka kwemeyopayihcikewin*.

idealist *awîyak ka meyopayihtat*.

idealization *ka wapahtehewehk etiyihtamowin*.

ignition The act of igniting something, *saskisikewin*.

igloo *askipow owekih; miskwamewikamik*.

illegal *ekâ weyasowewnihk kastek*; something you should not do, *namoyatatôtamihk*.

illegible Something hard to read, *ayman ayamicikewin*.

illegality *ekâ ka pimitisahamihk weyasowewin*.

illegibility *ekâ kake nesitohtamihk*.

illegible *awîyak ekâ kake nesitohtaht*.

ill-fated *ka nihtâ mayepayihk*.

ill-favored or **ill-favoured** *ka mayatsihk*.

ill-fitting *ekâ kwayask ka tepihtihk*.

ill-founded *ayasawâc kîkway*.

ill-gotten *ka kakayese otenamihk kîkway*.

ill humor or **ill-humour** *macitwawin (Northern)*.

ill-humored or **ill-humoured** *awîyak ka macitwat*.

illicit *kîkway ekâ weyasowewnihk kastek*.

illiteracy *ekâ ayamihcikewin*.

illiterate *awîyak ekâ kayamihciket*; not being able to read, *ekâ kayamihcikehk*.

ill-mannered *ekâ ka manatsit awîyak*.

ill-natured *macesâyâwin*.

ill-spent *kwanta ka mestinkehk*.

509

ill-suited *ekâ ka nahiskatohk.*
ill temper *macitwawin (Northern).*
ill tempered *awîyak ka macitwat.*
ill-timed *ekâ ka kwayaskopayik.*
ill treatment *ekâ kwayask pamihewewin.*
ill-use *ekâ kwayask ka apacitahk.*
illusion *kwanta ketapahtamihk.*
illustrator *owapahtehiwew.*
illustration *kiskinowapahtehiwewin.*
ill will *ekâ ekose ketiyihtamihk.*
immeasurable *ekâ kakeh tipahakatamihk.*
immigrant *akamaskew iyinow; petâpocikan (Plains).*
immigrate *ka ahtaskehk; takwacihowin; oyapowin.*
immigration *ahtaskewin.*
immortal Eternal life, *kakike pimatisowin.*
immune *ekâ wehkâc ka ahkosihk; namoya otehtikow;* someone never sick, *namoya otihtikow ahkosowin.*
immunize *ka cestahikasohk ahkosowin ohci.*
impaired S/he is intoxicated, *keskwepew.*
impaired driver *keskwepew pamihcikewin.*
impeccable *metoni ka meyo isâyâhk.*
imperial *nekanewin.*
impetigo A skin disease, *moskipayiwin.*
implant *wasakay ka astamakehk nânitâw.*
implantation *meskotasmakewin.*
implement *kîkway ka atoskakehk.*
imprison *awîyak ka kipahoht; kipahwaw.*
imprisonment *kipahikasowin.*
impunity *ekâ ka tepahikehiwehk.*
inadmissibility *ekâ pehtokahewewin.*
inadmissible *kîkway ekâ ka pehtokatahk.*
inalienable *ka mecim wacesâyahk.*
inalienability *ka mecimwacesâyâwin.*
incarcerate *ka kaskamotaskenahewehk;* s/he is put in prison, *kipahwaw.*
incarnation *pehtakeyaweskakowin.*
incinerator *mestihkasekakan;* a large burner, *misikotawanapisk.*
incendiary *ohtaw mestihkasekewin.*
incest *tipiyaw ka wecetohk.*
income *sônîyâw kociptiht tahto pîsim;* making money, *kespinacikewin.*
incorporate Organizing into a corporation, *mamawintowin.*
incubator Making eggs hatch, *paskawehowin.*
incumbency *nîkân apihewewin.*
incumbent *awîyak ka nîkân apihiht.*
indebted *ka masinahikepayihk;* owing someone, *masinahikewin.*
indebtedness *masinahikepayowin.*
indemnity *tepahikepayihcikewin.*
indenture A sealed deed or contract, *kihcesehcikewin.*

510

index *eta ka matasinahikehk.*
Indian agent *sônîyâwikimâw (Northern).*
indict *awîyak weyasowewnihk kahiht;* s/he charged her/him with an offense, *sehkitsahewew.*
indictable *awîyak ka nihtâ weyasowatiht.*
indictment *weyasowasowewin.*
indoctrinate *ka kiskinowasomiht awîyak.*
industrial *nânatohk isi atoskewin.*
industrialism *ka nânatohk isihcikehk.*
industry A manufacturing place, *osehcikewin.*
inefficacy *ekâ kwayask ispayihcikewin.*
ineligibility *ekâ ka nahiskamomakahk.*
inequality *ekâ pahpeyakwan kesipamihiwehk.*
inequitable *kitimahiwewin.*
infanticide *awîyak apiscawasisa ka nipahat.*
infantry Soldiers on foot patrol, *simakanisihkanakpimohtewin.*
infect *ka asawmekihk ahkosowin; asoskamawew.*
infection *ka kawacihk ahkosowin; ayiwâksâyâwin.*
infectious *ka nihtâ asawpayihtahk ahkosowin; asoskamakewin.*
inference *kakwe tâpwewin.*
infertile *ekâ kîkway kohpikemakahk.*
infest *kosamyetwaw mencosahk (Northern).*
infestation *osamyatihk kîkway.*
infidelity Being unfaithful, *ka kayeyisiwin.*
infiltration *pahpeyako naceyoscikewin.*
infirmary A small hospital, *ahkosêw kamikos.*
influenza *ka sohkepayik ahkosowin; ka ayimahk;* a highly contagious disease that is very hard to cure, *kamescinehk ahkosowin.*
infraction A violation, *mayitôtamowin.*
infringement *mosci otinamasowin.*
inherit *kîkway ka asawayahk;* s/he is given, *meyaw.*
inheritance Receiving something or the act of giving, *mekiwin; aniskac asawâyâwin.*
inheritor *awîyak ka asawmeyiht kîkway.*
inhuman *ekâ ka aysiniwatsihk; macatisiwin.*
inhumanity *ekâ aysiniwatsowin.*
injection Giving a needle to someone, *cestahowewin.*
injunction *yahkitsahikewin.*
injustice *ekâ kwayask ka totakehk; namoya kwayasmayitôtamowin;* not right, *namoyakwayask mayitôtamowin.*
ink *masinahikewapoy;* a writing liquid, *masinahikanapoy.*
inmate *awîyak nânitâw ka kanawiyimiht; kiphwakan.*
inn *wikowin;* an overnight stop over, *kapihesiwinikamik.*
innate *mecim ohci isâyâwin.*
innermost Inside, *pehcayihk.*
inner tube *ka pehcipotatamihk tihtipipayehk.*

innocence *ekâ nânitâw isimacesâyâwin.*
inoculate *ka cestahekasohk;* giving a needle, *cestahowewin.*
inoculation *cestahekasowin.*
inoperable *ekâ awîyak takeh mansikasot.*
inoperative *kîkway ekâ ka apatahk.*
inquest *natotsahikewin.*
inquiry A search for information, *natotsahikewin.*
inquisitor *onatotsahekew.*
insanitary *ekâ ka kanatsihk.*
inscribe *masinahikanihk ka astahk kîkway; masinaha;* writing something, *masinahikewin.*
inscription *masinahikewin.*
insecticide *manicos maskihkîy.*
insolvent *pekopayowin.*
institute *oysehcikewin.*
institution *ekâ kîkwaya koyastahk.*
instruct *ka kiskenohamakehk; kiskinohamawew.*
instruction *kiskinohamakewin.*
instructional *kiskinohamakewinihk.*
instructive *ka kiskinohamakemakahk.*
instructor *okiskinohamakew.*
instructress *okiskinohamakew iskwew.*
instrument *kitohcikan.*
insubordinate *ekâ ka naheyihtamihk.*
insubordination *pimameyihcikewin.*
insulation *kesowin kakewin.*
inquisition *nitotsahikewin.*
insurance *sônîyâw nesohkamâkewin.*
insurrection *mâneskakewin.*
intangibility *ekâ nistaweyihtowin.*
intangible *awîyak ekâ kakeh nistaweyimiht.*
intemperate *ekâ peyahtik kakeh ayahk.*
intercom *misowetahkwan; misowitahkwan.*
interdenominational *mecetwayak kesi ayamihahk.*
interdepartmental *mecetwayak kesehcikehk.*
interline The lining in clothes, *pehtawekwacikan.*
intermission *nomes ka poyohk;* just a little stop, *kanakesnakewin.*
intern *maskihkewiyinow.*
interment Burial, *nahinowewin.*
international *mecetaskeya ka mamawipayekih;* from all over the country, *misiwete ohci.*
internationalism *ka mamawesehcikehk.*
internship A doctor's internship, *awîyak ka maskihkewiyinehiht.*
interrogate *kakwe miskotsahikewin.*
interrogation *ka kakwe miskotsahikehk.*
interview *kapekiskwasowehk; pekiskwataw;* talking with someone, *pekiskwasowewin.*
intonation *ka pîtosehtakosihk.*
intone *meyohtakosowin.*
intractability *ekâ kowecewakanihk.*

intractable *ka nayihtawsihk.*
introspection *awîyak ka mamtoniyehtamasot.*
introvert *awîyak ka peyakweyimsot.*
invention *osehcikewin.*
inventor *otosehcikew.*
investigation *natonikewin.*
investment *kîkway ka atawehk.*
investor *otatawiw.*
invocation *ka keskihkemowin.*
invoice *masinahikewasinahikanis;* an order catalogue, *natitisahikew masinahikan.*
iodine *maskihki ka kanacicekemakahk.*
iodize *maskihki kastamakehk.*
ironbound *pîwâpisk ka wekinkakehk.*
iron hand *sohke paminowewin.*
ironing board *soskwahekanahtik.*
iron-willed *maskaw isihtwaw (Northern).*
irony *nahnaspaci pekiskwewin.*
irrational *soskwac poko isih.*
irrationality *poko isih ka isâyâhk.*
irreclaimable *ekâ kehtwam kakahtinamihk.*
irrigate *ka sepesisihkehk;* making small creeks, *sepesehkewin.*
irrigation *ka sepesisihkatamihk askîy.*
iterate *kakehtwam ka wehtamihk.*
itinerant *ka papam pecihk.*
itinerary *ka atimasinahamihk kîkway;* a traveling guide book, *papamohtew asinahikan.*
itinerate *papamahcayawin.*

511

J

jack The playing card, *simakan pehikan; simakanis.*
jackal An overseas dog, *akamaskew atimohkan.*
jackdaw An overseas crow, *akamaskew ahasow; ahasis.*
jack-knife *mistihkoman; mohkomanis;* a small knife, *mohkomanis.*
jade A green colored stone, *askihtakow asinis.*
jaguar An American animal of the cat family, *minosihkan.*
jail *kipahotowikamik;* a jail cell, *kipahikasowikamik.*
jailer or **jailor** *okipahowew.*
jam-packed *sehtaskinewin.*
jangle An unpleasant ringing sound, *mostasihtakwan.*
janitor A clean-up person, *kanâcicikewenow; okanâcicikew.*
janitress *iskwew ka kanâciciket.*
Japanese A Japanese person, *capan; sicaskapis.*
Japanese beetle A small beetle, *amiskoses.*
jar A glass container, *moteyapisk asiwacikan; wapmonapisk asowacikan; asiwacikan.*

jasmine A perfume, *wehkimakwahon*.

jasper A piece of stone, *asinîy*.

jaundice *osawapan*; *kosawpayehk*.

jaunty *ka mociksihk*.

jeans *la tweltas* (*Northern, French Cree*); a pair of pants, *mitâs*.

jelly The shaking jam, *kanampayik menisapos*; *ka nampayesik*; *menisapos*.

jester A person who makes people laugh, *waweyatwewiwin*.

jet *kamesak pemeyakan*.

jet-black *naspic ka kasketewak*; it is jet black, *mitonikaskitewaw*.

jetliner *ka kisekotek misipimeyakan*.

jetty A small landing wharf, *kapawin*.

jewel A very special stone, *kihci asinis*; *mistahi ka eteyihtakosit asinis*.

jeweller *or* jeweler *pesimohkansa ka atawaket*.

jewellery *or* jewelery A special ornament made of precious stones, *wawesêwakana*.

jew's harp A mouth instrument, *kitocikanis*.

jig A Métis dance, *apehtaw kosisan onemehitowin*.

jilt Breaking a relationship, *wepiniwewin*; *ka wayesihewehk*; *wepinewosaketowina*.

jobholder *ka nihtâ mecimnahk atoskewin*.

jobless *ekâ ka atoskehk*.

jodhpurs A pair of riding pants, *tehtapewitasak*.

joist Lumber used for a house roof, *apahkwanahtik*.

jot A very small quantity, *mitini apisis*; *mamases ka masinahikesihk*.

journal Writing up the news, *acimomasinahikewin*; *acimo masinahikan*.

journalism *ka acimowasinahikehk*.

journalistic *acimomasinahikewin*.

journeyman *awîyak ka kocehiht atoskewnihk*.

joy ride *mociktapasowin*.

jubilee A fiftieth anniversary, *nîyânanomtanawaske*; *neyânanomitanaw aske kesecekehk*.

judge *kicokimasis*; a law judge, *oyasiwew*; *wiyasowew*; a court judge, *oyasowewiyenow*; *opakicimowew* (*Plains*); a supreme court judge, *kihci weyasowew*; a judge, i.e.: at a contest, *oyasowew*; s/he judges her/him wrongly, *patasowatew*; s/he judges her/him correctly or s/he had her/him figured out, *tapeyimew*; s/he judges or condemns, *tipâkimow*.

judgment *or* judgement A legal judgement or a court case, *oyasowewin*.

judicatory *weyasowasowewin*.

judicature *eta weyasowewin kosehtahk*.

judicial *weyasowewnihk ohci kîkway*.

judiciary *weyasowewin ka atoskatamihk*.

junction Where roads meet, *meskanawah enakiskotatopayikwaw*.

juncture *nesopayowin*.

jungle A really thick bush, *kaskisakaw*.

junior A young boy, *napesis*; *oskinekes*.

junket An excursion trip paid for by someone else, *papamiwapahcikewin*.

juridical *kihci weyasowewna*.

jurisprudence *weyasowew nesohkamatowin*.

jurist *awîyak ka pamnahk weyasowewna*; a special judge, *keci oyasowew*.

juror *awîyak ka kihci pekiskwehewet*.

jury Special high court judges, *kihci oyasowewak*; *aysiyinowak kantohtahkwaw weyasowewnihk*.

justice *kwayaskwasowewin*.

juvenile A young person, *oskaya*; *oskayis ka weyasowatiht*.

K

kayak An Inuit boat, *otaskipow otos*.

keepsake The act of keeping, *kanaweyitamowin*.

kelp Leaves from the bottom of an ocean, *atampekipakwa*.

kennel *atimokamik*.

kerchief A handkerchief, *tapiskakan*.

kerosene Coal oil, *askiw pimiy*.

ketchup An immitation tomato soup, *okinewapohkan*; *aspahcikewin pokokîkway ohci*.

key An unlocker, *apihkokahikan*.

keyhole *apihkokahikanwatis*.

kilt A dancing skirt, *nemihitowasakas*.

kimono A loose fitting coat, *panahkwasakay*.

kindergarten The starting of school, *macikiskinohamakewin*.

king Or grand chief, *kihcokimâw*; the playing card, *okimâw pekikan*.

kingdom *awîyak oweyotisowin*; the big boss's property, *okimâw tipeyicikewin*.

kingly *ka kihcokimâwayahk*.

kit A small boy, *maskimotis*.

kitchen *piminawasowikamik*; a cooking place, *kestepokamik*.

kitchenette A small kitchen, *pinawasokamikos*.

kitchenware *kestepwakana*.

kitty-corner *pimakamiy akamskanaw*.

kleenex *sinihkomakan*.

knap sack A pack sack, *nayacikan*; *nayahcikanwat*.

knee-deep *mihcikwanihk keskopehk*.

knee-high *mihcikwanihk keskosihk*.

knob *iskwahtem apisk*; *miciminikanis*; a door handle, *yohtenkanapisk*.

knockout *tikinetahikewin*.

512

L

label A mark or title of identification, *wehowin kakamohtahk; kiskina watasinahikewin.*

Labor Day or **Labour Day** *atoskew kesikaw; atoskiw kisikaw.*

lace An ornamental fabric, *wawecewapihkacikewin.*

lacework *ka apihkacikehk.*

lacing *kîkway ka tahkopcikakehk;* a cord fastening, *apihkewin.*

lacquer A kind of paint, *sopekahikan.*

lacy *apihkacikewin.*

ladder *kihcekosêwnahtik.*

lady-like *mweci iskwew.*

lady's slipper The Blessed Virgin's shoe, *kihcihtwamarie omaskisin.*

lakefront *kapawin.*

lamppost *akocikan waskotenkan ohci.*

lance *kayâs tahkahcikakan.*

landfill *ka sakaskinewepahamihk asiskiy.*

landholder *awîyak kamciminahk askîy.*

landlady A boss woman, *okimaskwew.*

landless *ekâ kîkway kotaskehk.*

landlord A boss man, *okimâw; awîyak ka tepeyihtahk wekowena.*

landmark A memorable place, *kiskinawataskîy; ka kiskenowateyihtamihk askîy; kanâtawapahtamihk.*

landowner *askew kimaw.*

landownership *ka tepeyihtamihk askîy.*

landscape Beautifying land, *kiskinawatsehcikewin.*

lane *eta ka pimpayihk; meskanas.*

lapel *okwayas miskotakahk.*

larceny The act of stealing, *kimotamâkewin; ka kîmôc otinamihk kîkway.*

larder *tahkascikewikamik; mecowinkamikos;* a storage of food, *mawacimecowininewin.*

large-hearted *ka mahketehehk.*

lariat A lariat rope, *tapekowepinikan.*

lasso *tapekowepinikan; peminahkwan.*

last straw *metoni ka iskwayacipayik.*

latchkey *apihkokahikan.*

laths Roofing boards, *apahkwanihcakosa.*

laughing-stock A person to laugh at, *takahkipahpowin; awîyak ka nihtâ pahpehiht; pahpihaw.*

laundress *okisipekinikewiskwew.*

laundromat *kisipekinikewikamik; kisipikinikiwikamik.*

laundry *kisipekinkewna;* a place for doing washing, *kisepekinikewikamik.*

lavatory A place for washing one's face, *kasehkwewkamikos; wayawewkamik.*

lavender A perfume, *wehkimakohon; mistikwahtikos ewehkimakwahki nepehkansa.*

law A government law, *weyasowewin (Northern); wiyasowewin (Plains); oyasiwewin.*

law-abiding *ka pemitsahamihk weyasowewin.*

lawbreaking *ka pekonamihk weyasowewin.*

lawful *kîkway weyasowewnihk kastek;* allowed by the law, *weyasowewpakitinamatowin.*

lawgiver *awîyak weyasowewin ka mekit.*

lawless *awîyak ekâ ka nakatohket weyasowewin.*

lawmaker *awîyak weyasowewin kosehtat.*

lawmaking *weyasowewin kosehtahk.*

lawn The growing of a small grass area, *maskosesa ka pakitinamihk; maskosesa wayawetimihk kohpekihtahk.*

lawn mower *maskosêw mansikan.*

lawsuit An action for justice in a court of law, *sehkitisahowewin; awîyak weyasowewnihk ka ahiht.*

lawyer A court speaker, *weyasowewnihk opîkiskwestamâkew;* someone who speaks for other, i.e.: a spokesperson or a lawyer, *opîkiskwestamâkew.*

leap year *nitomiskwewiw kesikaw.*

lease *ka nitahtamohk askîy; miciminamasowin;* to obtain the use of a building or land, *nitahtamowin.*

leash *sakahpitastimwakan.*

lecture Giving a lecture, *kakeskikemowin; ka keskimowewin.*

lecturer *okakeskihkemow.*

leek An onion, *wehcekaskosiy.*

leftover *keskwascikehk.*

legacy *nakatamâkewin.*

legal Permitted by law, *weyasowew pakitinamâkewin; ekosi ketastek weyasowewnihk; kihci oyasiwewin.*

legalism *ka nakateyehtamihk tânsi etastek weyasowewin.*

legality *tânsi ketastek weyasowewin.*

legalize *weyasowewnihk kastahk.*

legally *ka mamsitôtamihk weyasowewin.*

legible *kihkawasinahikewin.*

legibility *ka nihtâ nistohtamihk.*

legibly *ayamihcikewnihk ohci.*

legion *kayâs onôtinikewak mamawintowin.*

legislation The enactment of laws, *oyasiwewin ka osetahk.*

legislature A body that prepares and enacts laws, *oyasiwewin ka paminamihk.*

legitimacy *kwayask nihtawkowin.*

legitimate Born to parents legally married, *meyonihtawikiwin.*

legitimize *ka kwayâs kwastahk wekihtowin.*

lemon A sour fruit, *siwimin.*

lemonade A sweet drink, *sewa apoy.*

513

lens *oskisikohkana.*

leper *owapaspinew.*

leprosy *omikiwaspinewin.*

lesson *kiskinohamakewin; kîkway ka kiskinohamakehk.*

lethal *metoni kîkway kamacahk.*

lethargy *namoyacekeyihtam; ka nipowesayahk.*

letdown *ka pomehewehk.*

lettered *ka cahkepehekatek.*

letup *ka nome poyohk.*

levity *wawîyak kayâhki mâmitoneyihtamihk.*

liability *ka kanawapamkohk masnahikewna.*

liaison *kîmôc pesikwatsowin.*

libel *ka ascimiht awîyak kîkway.*

libeller *or* libeler *awîyak kapew mamiskomowet.*

liberal *ekâ ka sasaksehk;* s/he is a good giver, *nehtamekow.*

liberty Being your own boss, *tipeyimisowin; ka paminsohk isihcikewnihk.*

librarian *awîyak masinahikana kapamnahk.*

library *eta masinahikana ka ayamihtahk;* a house for reading material, *masinahikanikamik; ayamicikewina.*

licence *or* license A marriage license, *weketomasinahikan; masinahikan ka mekihk nânatohk isihcikewnah ohci;* a driver's license, *pamihcikew asinahikan.*

lichen *wasaskwetowak metosihk kohpikitwaw* (Northern).

lieutenant A special head soldier, *simakanokimâw.*

lifeblood *ka pimacihekohk kîkway.*

lifeboat A life saving boat, *akwapicikewosi.*

lifelong *isko tapematsihk.*

lifetime *isko tapematsihk.*

lifework *kakiki atoskewin.*

lifter *ka ohpinkemakahk.*

light-fingered *ka nihtâ kemotihk.*

light-foot *yahkiskamaw.*

light-footed *awîyak ka yahkiskamat;* s/he is very light, *yahkitisow.*

light-headed *yahkemâmitoneyihcikan; wankiskisiwin.*

light-hearted *ka mociksit awîyak; mocikeyihtam.*

lily *wapikwan.*

lima bean Large beans which the Cree call "horse beans", *mistatimopensak; kistikanis.*

lime A white wash for houses or fences, *wâpiskahikan.*

limousine *okimâw sehkepimpayes* (Northern); *okimâwitâpânâsk* (Plains).

linchpin *otihtipipayew sakicicikan.*

lineage One line of family descent, *peyakwahkotowin.*

linen A strong white thread, *maskawasapap;* a white sheet, *wâpiskanaskanekin;* a starched linen, *pekewekin.*

linesman One who works on telephone lines, *atoskewenow pîwâpiskosihk;* a hockey linesman, *soniskwâtahikew onakânikew.*

lingerie Women's clothing, *iskwewo ayiwinsa.*

linguist *awîyak nânatohk kesepekiskwet.*

linguistic *nânatohk isipekiskwewin.*

link *askomohcikan.*

linkage *askomohcikewin.*

linoleum A floor covering, *anaskewin; anaskanihtak akwanahikan.*

lion *mistahkesow.*

lipstick *mihkotonehon.*

liqueur *peyakwan iskotew apoy.*

liquid measure *tipahopan.*

liquor *iskotew apoy.*

lisle Knitted with fine linen yarn, *sestakwekin.*

literacy *ayamihcikewin.*

literal *twestamakewin; ka ayamihcikehk.*

literate *ka nihtâ ayamihcikehk.*

literature *kîkway ka ayamihtahk;* different kinds of reading, *papîtosayamicikewina.*

litigation A contest in court, *sehkitsahikewin.*

livelihood *pimacihowin.*

livelong *eskow tapematisihk; aspinohci kapepimatisit.*

lizard A small lizard, *osikiyas.*

llama An old country animal, *pisiskow.*

loafer *awîyak ka papamacihot.*

loam *kaskitew asiskîy.*

loan *awehowewin.*

lobby *piskihcikamikos.*

lobe *pehcayihk mihtawakahk.*

locality *kahkisciwikowin.*

localize *eta ka kisciwekihk.*

locally *micim ohci eta kayahk.*

location *mwehci eta ka kiskeyihtamihk.*

locker *nahascikakan.*

locksmith *awîyak kaskihtakahikana kosehtat.*

locomotion *ka sehkepemakotek kîkway.*

locomotive *sehkepayes; iskotew tâpân.*

logic *ka isi iyinesihk.*

logging *otin nahtikwewin.*

logjam *ka kipwapakotwaw mistekwak* (Northern).

long-distance *wâhyaw kohci pekiskwehk.*

longhorn *ka kinosit oteskan.*

long-range *wâhyaw ohci kîkway.*

long-sighted *wâhyaw neyak ka wapahtamihk.*

long-suffering *kayâs kohwesakahpinehk.*

long-term *kinwes kespayihtahk isihcikewin.*

514

long-winded *ka sepatahtamihk; kinwespekiskwew;* s/he is long winded, *sepatahtam.*

looking glass *wapamon.*

loophole *paspapowenis.*

loose-jointed *ekâ kasapsihk.*

loose-tongued *ka osamtonehk;* gossiper, *osamton.*

lore A store of knowledge about particular subjects, *papetow acimowina.*

lost cause *ka wanihtak isihcikewin.*

lot *ôtenaw askekanis; tipaskanis.*

lottery *sônîyâw metawewin.*

loudmouth *awîyak kakisêwet.*

loudmouthed *awîyak ka mesayektonet.*

lounge A kind of long sofa used as a bed, *nipewinikam.*

love match *nahiskatowin sakihkihitowinihk.*

lovesick *wesaki sakihiwewin.*

loving-kindness *kisewatsow sakihiwewin.*

lowborn *ka kitimak nihtâwkihk.*

lowbred *kitimak ohpikowin.*

lowbrow *pîweyimsowin.*

low-pitched *ekâ ka kisewehk.*

low-pressure *kîkway ekâ ka sohkikotek.*

low-spirited *kapomewayahk.*

low spirits *pomewin.*

lucrative *sônîyâhkipayowin.*

luggage *ka nehpem tahkonamihk ayowinsa;* the act of packing packs or bags, *nemiwatewin.*

lumbering *napakihtakwa kosehtak.*

lunch-room *eta ka nemawnihkehk.*

lupin *wapikwaneya.*

luxury Very rich, *weyotan; kîkway imiwasik ka ayahk.*

lye A solution used for making soap, *pehkwapoy.*

lynch S/he is hung by the neck, *akotaw.*

lyrical *wanewasinahikewin.*

lyricism *ka nânatohk wasinahikehk.*

M

macabre *nipowin ka mamiskotamihk.*

macaroni *oskicisa.*

macaw An overseas bird, *akamaskepîyesîs.*

mace A clublike weapon, *mistikonotinkakan.*

machete *mistapiskihkoman.*

machine *askihkos sehke ka pimakocihk;* a machine for clearing land of trees, *paskwatahikan;* a motor operated engine, *askekokanis.*

machinery Building iron machine, *âpacicikana.*

machine-made *ka osehcikemakahk kîkway.*

machinery *nânatohk âpacicikana.*

machinist *ka pimpayihtat osehcikewnah awîyak.*

madame *mistikosewiskwew.*

mademoiselle A young woman, *oskinekiskwew.*

made-to-order *kwayask ka osehtamâkehk.*

made-up *kwanta mamaseskosehtahk.*

magazine *acimo masinahikan;* reading material, *masinahikan.*

maggot *ociw.*

magistrate *owiyisowew;* a special law enforcer, *kihci oyasiwew.*

magnate *metoni owiyitisêwiyinow;* a person of importance especially in industry, *kihcitipeyicikew.*

magnet *ka ocipcikemakahk pîwâpisk.*

magnetic *ka akopayik pîwâpiskohk.*

magnetism *ka nihtâ peteyemiht aysiyinow.*

magnetize *sakoteyecikewin.*

magnification *ka mahkinakohtahk kîkway.*

magnifier *mahkinakohcikan.*

magnify *ka mahkinakohtahk; mahkipayitaw;* the act of making it larger, *mahkipayitawin.*

magnolia *metoskawapiwanet.*

maid A working woman, *atoskew iskwew.*

maiden A young girl, *oskinekiskwesis; oskeskwew.*

maidenly *peyakwan oskinekiskwew.*

maidenhead *otoskinekiskwewiwin iskwew.*

maidenhood *ka mekwa oskinekiskwewihk.*

maiden name *iskwew owehowin pamayes kawekihtot.*

mail *ka sipwetisahamihk masinahikan;* mail from the post office, *masinahikana.*

mailbox *eta ka posiwepinamihk masinahikana.*

mailman A letter carrier, *masinahikanewiyinow.*

mail-order *ka natsahikehk.*

mainland *kespihtaskewik.*

mainlander *awîyak akwacayihk ka wekit.*

majority *ayiwâk iyikohk; otahowiw;* the greater over the smaller, *ayiwâk.*

make-believe *mweci tâpwe kîkway.*

makeshift *mamases osehcikewin.*

make-up *meyosehisowin.*

maladjustment *ekâ kwayask isâyâwin.*

malady *ahkosowin.*

malaria A feverish disease, *maci ahkosowin.*

malcontent *ekâ ka naheyihtamihk.*

malediction *ka mahyakwamiht awîyak.*

malefaction *awîyak ka mayetotaht.*

malefactor *ka mayetotahk awîyak.*

malice A disposition to inflict injury, *nohtemayitotam.*

malicious Intending harm to someone, *pakwasiwewin.*

malignant *ekâ kakeh astehamihk ahkosowin.*

malinger *ahkosehkasowin.*

mallet *misipakamakan;* a wooden hammer, *mistikopakamahikan.*

515

malnutrition *ekâ kwayask ka metsohk.*

malpractice *ekâ kwasyask ka paminwehk.*

malt *kohkosmecowin; iskwesapohkewin;* grain used to make beer, *iskwesis apohkakan.*

mammal *ayisiyiniwiwin.*

manacle *tahkopswakana kipahotokamkohk;* a hobble or handcuff, *nanapwahpisowin.*

management *ka mamawi paminamihk kîkway;* the act of managing, *pimpayihtawin.*

manager *kapaminahk; awîyak ka paminahk kîkway; katipeyiciket.*

mandarin *apisci osawas.*

mandate *oysehcikewin.*

mandatory *ka oysehcikehk.*

manger *pisikow ometisowakan;* a trough or box for feeding animals, *pisiskow metisoyakan.*

manhandle *ka nâpew otinamihk kîkway.*

manhood *ka kisi nâpewihk; kisâpowiwin (Plains).*

manhunt *nâpew kantonaht.*

mania *macesâyâwin.*

maniac *awîyak ka macayowit.*

maniacal *macayowin ka ayâhk.*

manic *macitwawin (Northern);* a madman, *mohciwa.*

manifest *kîkway ka nokohtahk.*

manifestation *wapahtehewewin.*

mannequin *ayisiyinihkan.*

manpower *nâpew maskawsêwin.*

man-sized *ka nâpew sehcikasohk.*

manslaughter *ka pisci nepahtakehk.*

mantel *akotascikewin.*

mantle A cloak, *akwanahowenis;* a mantle used for a gas lamp, *wehkwas.*

manual *ka mosci osehcikehk.*

manually *moscosehcikewin.*

manual training *ka mosci kiskinohamakehk.*

manufacture *osehcikewin.*

manufacturer *awîyak ka osehciket.*

manuscript *ka mosci masinahamihk masinahikan;* written material, *masinahikewin.*

many-sided *ka mihcetwayaksihk.*

map *askewasinahikan; askiw asinahikan.*

marathon *ka sepahtahk mawinehotowin.*

maraud *ka papami mayahkamkisihk;* going around in search of plunder, *maniwatewin.*

marauder A slick, sneaky murderer, *pakwacinipahtakew.*

margarine *tohtosapopimehkan.*

margin *eta keskwastek.*

marginal *iskwascikewnihk cekih.*

marinate *sewapohk ka akohtahk kîkway.*

marine *onotinkew napihkwanihk ohci.*

marionette A doll, *awasehkan.*

marital *ka kihci wekihtohk.*

maritimes Land on the east coast, *sisonekecikamewaskîy.*

marker *omasenahikew ahpô masinatahikan.*

market *ka atawakehk kîkway;* the selling of food, *meciwina ka atawakehk.*

marketable *kîkway ka meyo atawakehk.*

market place *atawikamikohk.*

market value *wehtakihcikewin.*

marksman *awîyak ka nahepaskiseket; kotahaskwewenow;* a target shooter, *kotahaskweweyinow.*

marksmanship *nahaskwewin.*

marshmellows A confection of gelatin and sugar, *sewahcikana.*

mascaria *iskwew oskesikwa ka sopehahk.*

mascarade Going about under false pretence, *wayesinakohcikewin.*

masking tape *akwamohcikan.*

mascot *ka weyasisihohk;* a person supposed to bring good luck, *meyopayihiwewin.*

masochism *awîyak ka meweyihtahk kwatakihitowin.*

mason *awîyak asiniya ka atoskewaket;* one who builds with brick or stone, *oyasinehikew.*

masonary Stonework, *asiniw osehcikewin; asiniw wawesehcikakewin.*

masquerade *wawesêw nemehitowin.*

massacre *sohki aspinatitowin; nipahitowin.*

massage A treatment of the muscles by rubbing, *sinikonikewin.*

mass meeting *misi mamawapowin.*

mass-produce *ka misi atawahkehk kîkway.*

mass production *misi osehcikewin.*

mast A sail pole, *yahkastimonahtik.*

mastadon An extinct elephant like mammal, *misipisiskew namatewekewa.*

master One who has chief authority or control, *onekanapow; opaminowew.*

masterpiece *ka osam takahkesehcikehk;* a work of surprising excellence, *naspicimewasin.*

mat A piece of fabric used for a door mat, *aspita koskewin.*

matchbox *kocawakaniwats.*

matchmaker *omeyo wecehtahiwew.*

matchmaking *awîyak ka meyo wecehtahiwet.*

matchstick *kocawakan ahcekos.*

mathematician *awîyak ka nihtâwakihciket.*

matinee An afternoon picture show, *poni apehtakesikaw cikastepayicewin.*

matriarch *iskwew metoni ka paminat wecaya.*

matriarchal *iskwew ka nihtâ paminowet.*

matriarchy *iskwew pamihiwewin.*

mattock A tool for digging roots of tree stumps, *monahicepihkakan*.

matter-of-fact *kihcinahowin*.

matting *anaskewin*.

mattress *aspisinowin; anaskasimon;* a thing to sleep on, *anaskason*.

mausoleum *emisak kehkwahaskan*.

maverick *ekâ komamat mostosis*.

maze *kweskeyihtamowin*.

measles *mihkwasêwin;* s/he has measles, *mihkwasêw*.

measuring tape A wooden ruler, *tipahikanahtik;* a steel tape measure, *tipahikaneyapisk;* a cloth measuring tape, *tipahikaneyapiy;* a sewing tape, *masinikwacikaneyapiy;* a steel square, *tipahikanapisk*.

meat packing *ka wewekinamihk wîyâs*.

mechanic *pîwâpiskweyenis;* a machine person, *pîwâpiskwenow*.

mechanical *sehke kapimpayik kîkway*.

mechanics *keskinohamakosowin*.

mechanism A mechanical execution, *sepwepayihicikan; kîkway sehke ka pimpayik*.

medal *kiskowehon ka tapiskaht;* a coin like piece of metal worn around the neck, *tapiskapiskos*.

medial *nawâc poko apihtaw*.

median *pahpeyakwan iyikohk*.

mediate *kwayaskopayihcikewin*.

mediation *kwayaskopayihiwewin*.

medic *maskihkewiyinehkan*.

medical *ka wapamiht maskihkewiyinow;* curative practice, *natawihowin*.

medicinal It has remedy powers, *maskihkewan*.

mediocre *kwanta mamases kîkway*.

medley *ka mamawenikamohk;* a combination of songs, *nanatahk nikamona*.

melodic *awîyak ka nikamoskit*.

melodious It sounds good, *meyohtakwan; ka nihtânikamohk*.

melodist *awîyak kosehtat nekamowena*.

melody *meyo kitohcikewin; nikamowin; meyohtakwan;* a song, *nikamowin*.

member *owecehiwew; paskesiwin*.

membership *wecihewewin; mamawi otinikewin;* a total number of members, *mihcetwapowin*.

memento A reminder, *kiskisopayihiwewin*.

memorandum *masinahikewin ekâ tawanikiskisihk*.

memorial *kiskisitotakewin;* s/he is being remembered, *ka kiskisototaht*.

menace *ka nihtâ mayenikehk*.

menagerie An exhibition of wild animals, *pikwacipisiskowapahtehiwewin*.

meningitis *metihpahkosiwin*.

menswear *nâpewayowinsa*.

menthol An oil of peppermint useful for nasal disorders, *tominikan; etakipayik*.

menu A bill for ordering food, *natotcikewin*.

mercantile Persons who do purchasing, *otatawewak*.

mercenary *ka asponatsihk;* serving only for gain, *sônîyâhkew oyehtamowin*.

merchandise *ayowinsa ka tawakehk;* goods to sell, *atawakana*.

merchant Or salesman, *otatawewiyenow; ocacawes;* a buying person, *otatawew*.

merciful *kesewatsowin; kisewatisow*.

merganser A fish eating duck, *kinosewa ka mowat sîsîp*.

merger *kewecewakanihtohk isihcikewnihk*.

meringue The whites of eggs and sugar to make a coating for pastry, *pestew itehikan*.

merit *ka kespinatamihk kîkway;* the qualities by which someone is evaluated, *kaskitamasowin*.

mermaid *iskwew apihtaw ka kinosewit*.

merman *nâpew apihtaw ka kinosewit*.

merrymaker *omocikihtawnihkew*.

messenger One who goes around with messages, *otwestamâkew papamih; osâkitow; masinahikewpimohcikew*.

meteor A star falling down, *acahkoskapahkisik*.   517

meteoric *ka kisiska nekanet awîyak*.

meteorite *acakos ka pahkisihk askehk*.

meter stick *tipahikanatik*.

method *tânsi ka isi tôtamihk kîkway*.

methodic *metoni peyahtik kamâmitoneyihtamihk*.

methodize *ka kwayaskopayihcikehk*.

microbe A bacterium that starts disease, *ahkosowinkamacipayik*.

microscope Something that magnifies objects, *kamahkipayihcikemakahkapahcikan*.

microwave *keyipihkasikakan (Northern); kipihkasikakan (Plains); yôskihkasikâkan; kihtwâmâciwasikan*.

middleman *tawayihk nâpew;* third party arbiter, *kwayaskwascikew;* the man in the middle, *tastaweyinow*.

middlemost *mawace; apihtaw*.

middle-of-the-road *metoni tawimeskanahk*.

middy A loose fitting blouse, *pehtones kamistayekahk*.

midget *apisciyenes*.

midriff The middle of the body or the diaphragm, *apihtawseyaw*.

midwife A woman who helps in childbirth, *nihtâwikew nesohkamâkew iskwew; kâpamihât iskwew (Plains)*.

midwifery *otinawasowin; nihtâwikihâwasowin* (Plains).

mildew *kîkway ka akwakohtik; akwakohtin.*

milepost Showing every mile, *wapahtihiwewin tahto mistik.*

milestone A stone distance marker on the highway, *kiskinowac asinîy.*

militant One who engages in warfare, *onotinkeweyinow.*

militarize *ka nehpemayahk nôtinitowin ohci.*

military *nôtinitowenihk ka wecihewehk; simakanisihkewin.*

milkman *tohtosapowiyinow.*

mill A grinding mill or a grinder, *pinipocikan;* it is milled or ground (animate), i.e.: wheat, *pinipocikasow;* it is milled or ground (inanimate), *pinipocikatew;* a flour mill, *pinpocikan.*

miller A person who runs a flour mill, *pinipocikewiyinow.*

milliner A person who makes women's hats, *iskwew astotinehkew.*

milling *pahkweskan ka osehiht.*

millstone *pinipocikanasini.*

millwork *sikopocikanihk atoskewin.*

mime *ka wapahtehiwehk metawewin.*

mincemeat *wîyâs kasikopotek;* a kind of mixture, *kekawenikan.*

mindless Thoughtless or heedless, *namoyamâmitoneyihtam.*

mine *asiniw wacek ka watihkehk.*

miner *otatoskew watihkewnihk.*

minimal *apisis kîkway.*

minimize *apiscisihcikewnis.*

minimum *namoya mistahi.*

minimum wage *apisis ka tepahikehk atoskewnihk.*

mining *watehkewin; monahikewin.*

minor *ekâ mistahi kîkway; namoya mistahi kîkway.*

minority The lesser part or number of, *nawâcastamihk; ekâ mihcet; nawâc astamihk.*

mint A cool mint, *katahkeyawepayik.*

minuet *nemihitowin.*

minute *cipahikanis;* one minute, *peyak cipahikanis;* a few minutes, *nomanak; nomanakes.*

mirror *wapamon.*

misappropriation *ka wane isihecikehk.*

misbecome *ka nahipayik kîkway.*

misbegotten *ekâ ekose takehispayik kîkway.*

mischance *waninewin; wanitotamowin;* bad luck, *mayakosowin.*

miserly *peyakwiyimisowin.*

misgovern *ekâ kwayask ka pimpayihcikehk.*

misdemeanor *or* **misdemeanour** *ekâ kwayask etatsowin.*

mismanage *ekâ kwayask pimpayihcikewin;* s/he manages badly, *mayipayihcikew.*

misprint *wanasenahikewin;* s/he writes incorrectly, *wanasinahikew.*

miss A young girl, *oskenekiskwesis;* before a woman is married, *pamwayes kaweketot iskwew.*

misspent S/he squandered money, *metawakew.*

mister *nâpew miscahes keteyihtakosit.*

mistletoe A Christmas decoration, *nepayamihawkiskinowacicikan.*

mistranslate *ekâ kwayask ketwestamakehk.*

mistranslation *ketwestamakewin.*

mistress *ka atoskahihi iskwew;* a boss woman, *okimaskwew.*

mite A small sum of money, *apisis sônîyâs.*

mitigate *ka nekiptamihk kîkway.*

mixer *otitehikew.*

mobilization *sehke pimpayihcikewin.*

mode *tânsi ka itacihohk;* a manner of acting or doing, *isiwepinikewin.*

moderator *awîyak peyaktik kespayihciket.*

modern *anohc kîkway kespayik;* characteristic to present time, *mekwacisihtawin.*

modernize Making something more modern, *ahcisihtahk kîkway.*

modesty Growing up decent, *kwayaskohpikowin.*

module *kîkway ka nikinkakehk.*

molest *kesehkaht awîyak; mikoskacihew.*

molestation *esehkakewin.*

moneylender *otawehiwew sônîyâwa.*

money-maker *osônîyâhkew iyinow.*

money-making *sônîyâhkewin.*

money order *ka sepwetisahoht sônîyâw.*

mongrel *atim mehcetwayakohcet;* a poor dog, *kitimakatim.*

monitor A person who checks things, *kanaweyicikew.*

monkey wrench *apahikan.*

monogamy *peyak aysenow ka wekimiht.*

monogram *ka kiskinowatasinahamihk kîkway.*

monoplane A small plane, *pimehakanis.*

monopoly *kwayask kespayihtahk esehcikewin.*

monotone *peyakwayak ketatamohk.*

monitor *kîkway ka wapahtehewemakahk.*

monument A memorial structure, *nakataskewasinîy.*

moonshine *ka pakahtahk etakamascikan.*

moor *ka mecimahpitamihk osih.*

mop *kisepekihtakinkakan.*

morass A marsh or bog, *wakinakaniskaw.*

morbid Mentally unhealthy, *namoyakwayask isâyâwin.*

morgue *onipowak eta ka kanawiyimihtwaw* (Northern).

morning-glory *meyo wapansowin.*

morocco A goatskin leather, *mayatihkwapihkan.*

mortality The condition of being mortal, *nipowin.*

mortgage A conditional conveyance of property, *kiskinawatastawin.*

mother country *askîy eta kohtaskanesihk.*

motherland *kistaskanesowin.*

mother tongue *kisci pikiskwewin awîyak otaskehk ohci.*

motive *ka iyihikohk kîkway.*

motor *askihkos kasepwepayihciket;* the Cree word means "an imitation pail", *askehkokanis.*

motorboat The Cree word means "artifical rowing", *sehkepimiskawin; sehke ka pimpayik osih; pimiy osih; pimiy osi.*

motor car The Cree name means "artifical running", *sehkepimpayes.*

motor cycle The Cree name means "the galloping machine", *kotiskaweses.*

motorhome *pimpiciwikamik; pimpiciw tâpânâsk.*

motor hotel Or inn, *ka pesewkamik opapampicowak ohci.*

mountaineer *awîyak ka amacowet wacehk.*

mountain range *ka nahnawayostekwaw waceya.*

mousetrap *apakoses wanehekanis.*

mouthpiece *pokokîkway metonihk ka apatahk;* a biting apparatus, *tahkwahcikan.*

mover *opicihewew.*

movie *cikastepayihcikan.*

movie projector *cikastepayicikan.*

mucilage A kind of paste, *pasakwahikan.*

muffin A small round bread, *pahkwesikanis.*

muffler A warm scarf, *kîsowahpison (Plains);* a car muffler, *yawehtakohcikan (Northern);* a muffler pipe, *sehkepimayis okohtaskwayihkân (Plains).*

mug *minihkwacikan;* a big mug, *misiminihkwacikan.*

mulatto *apehtaw moneyaw.*

mumps *paki kwayawewin.*

municipal The government property of a city, *otenawotipeyicikewina.*

municipality *ka paminsomakahk ôcenas.*

murderer *onipahtakow.*

muscle-bound *ka maskaw sehcikasohk.*

muscleman *omaskawsêwiyinow.*

muslin A thin material, *papakekin.*

museum *wapahtehiwewikamik.*

musket A gun, *paskisikan.*

mustard A mustard plaster, *akopisowin.*

mutant *ekâ ka naspetakehk.*

mutate *ka pîtos isihcikehk.*

mutual fund *ka mamawepameniht sônîyâw.*

muzzle A device to prevent an animal from biting, *kipotonehpicikan.*

myriad *mecetasiwak.*

myrrh An aromatic resin from certain plants, *wehkimasikan.*

myth A legendary fable or story, *âtayohkewin.*

mythic The legend of, *âtayohkan; wesakecahk.*

mythical *ka nihtâ âtayohkehk.*

mythological *âtayohkewna ka pimitsahamihk.*

N

nameless *ekâ kowehyowenihk.*

namesake *awîyak owehyowenihk ohci;* someone with the same name, *nikwemiy.*

nanny *mosiskwew awâsisa kapaminat.*

napkin *kasetonehwakan.*

narcissus *nepehkanis;* a spring flower, *meyoskamewapikwanes.*

narcotic *maskihki ka nipeskakohk.*

narrate Giving an account of, *wehcikewin.*

narrative *kîkway ka atôtamihk.*

narrow-minded *ka kepaci mâmitoneyihcekan.*

nation *mamawâyâwin; peyakosihtwawin (Northern).*

national *ka mamawintohk.*

nationality *tantowahk ayisinow; wahkotowin.*

nationally *ka ispehtaskewik.*

national park *ka kanaweyihtamihk askîy.*

nationality Race of people, *tantowayisiyinow.*

nation-wide *kespehtayakaskak askîy.*

native-born *kistaskanesowin.*

nativity The birth of Christ, *manitonehtawikiwin.*

natural gas *itamaskamik pimiy kohtinamihk ka ponkakehk.*

natural history *mecim ohci acimowin.*

naturalize Admit to citizenship, *meskocesâyâwin.*

near-miss *etataw ka patahamihk.*

near-sighted *kisowak ka isi nahapih.*

neckband *meksitapiskakanis; tapiskan.*

neckline *ka iskwamok mekwayaw.*

necktie *mistekimaw tapiskakanis.*

neckwear *tapiskakana.*

necromancer *okiskowehikew.*

necromancy *kiskowehikewin.*

nectar *mensapoy ka osehcikakehk.*

negotiation *kwayaskosehcikewin.*

neighbor or **neighbour** Someone who lives close by, *awîyak kisowak kawekit;* a next door neighbor, *wetakemakan.*

neighborhood or **neighbourhood** *kahkisowak wikowin.*

neighborly or **neighbourly** *ka meyo wecihwehk; meyowetapimakan;* being a kindly person, *meyohtwawin (Northern).*

nerveless *ekâ ka sohkiyimohk.*

nervous breakdown *mâmitoneyihcikan ka wanihtahk.*

network *ka mamawepikiskwatohk.*

neuter *ayihkwewatim.*

neutral *apihtawayihk ka ayâhk; namoyakispewatew.*

neutrality *papeyakwâyâwin.*

neutralize *kîkway ka peyakohtahk.*

never do well S/he does a worthless job, *kitimakinakocikew.*

nevertheless *âtaweya maka.*

newlywed *anohcpoko wikihtowin.*

new moon *ôskipîsim.*

newsboy *acimimasinahikaneweyines.*

newscast *acimowin kanatohtamihk.*

newsletter *acimomasinahikan.*

newsman *ôtacimow.*

newspaper *acimomasinahikan.*

newsprint *acimowin ka masinahamihk.*

newsroom *eta ka wehcikatek acimowin.*

newsstand *eta ka asowatekwaw masinahikana.*

newsworthy *takahki acimowin.*

next-door *ayahtôkamik.*

next of kin *wahkomakanak.*

nick-of-time Just at the right time, *nahiyikohk.*

nickel *pîwâpisk ekâ wehkac ka meseyapiskak;* five cents, *niyanan pîwâpiskos.*

nickel-plate *wasihkopîwâpisk.*

nickname *kwanta kiskinowac wehowin.*

niggard *sasaksêwiyinow.*

nightgown *nîpawasakay.*

night light *nîpawasaskotenkan.*

night school *nîpakiskinohamakewin.*

nightshirt *nîpaw pakowayan.*

night watch *ka kanaw tipiskwehk.*

night watchman *okaniwetipiskwew (Northern); okanawitipiskiw (Plains).*

nobility *ka kihcayahk meyohtwawnihk (Northern).*

noble *kihcâyâwin meyotehewnihk.*

nocturnal Active at night, *tipiskahkamikisowin.*

nocturnally *tipiskaw isihcikewin.*

nocturne *nîpa kitohcekewin.*

node A hard swelling, *pakipayowin.*

nodule *ka piskopayihk nânitâw.*

noisemaker *kîkway ka kisêwek.*

nomad *awîyak ka papampicit.*

nomadic *ekâ peyakwanohk kakeh ayâhk.*

nominal *ekâ kehcina ka akihtek kîkway.*

nominally *kwanta mamases.*

nominate *awîyak ka pehtokahiht isihcikewinihk;* appoint to an office, *nawasoniwewin.*

nomination *pehtokahewewin.*

nominative *ka pehtokepayihtahk.*

nominee *ayseno ka pehtokahiht; nawasoniwew;* a person appointed to an office, *nawasonaw.*

nonacceptance *âtawiyimowewin.*

nonaggression *sakotehewin.*

nonappearance *ekâ ka pesakewehk.*

nonattendance *ekâ ka pewecihewehk.*

noncommittal *ekâ ka papekiskwehk.*

noncompliance *ekâ ka wecehewehk nânitâw.*

nonconformist *awîyak ekâ kîkway katapwetahk.*

nonconformity *ekâ nânitâw ka isitapwewokiyihtamihk.*

noncooperation *ekâ ka oweciwakanihk.*

nondelivery *ekâ kawe papamohcikehk.*

nonessential *ekâ kîkway ka apatahk.*

nonexistence *kîkway ekâ ka ihtâmakahk.*

nonfiction *tâpwe ka ispayik kîkway.*

nonintervention *ekâ ka nakinamihk.*

nonjuror *ekâ kakih weyasowewihk.*

nonliving *ekâ ka pimatsimakahk kîkway.*

nonmetal *ekâ ka pîwâpiskowik kîkway.*

nonmoral *ekâ ka tawa isâyâwin.*

nonoperating *ekâ ka apatahk kîkway.*

nonpayment *ekâ ka tipahikehk.*

nonperformance *kwanta âyâwin.*

nonproductive *ekâ kosehcikemakahk.*

nonprofit *ekâ ka sônîyâhkemakahk.*

nonresidence *ekâ nânitâw wikowin.*

nonresident *ekâ ekotah ohci awîyak.*

nonresistance *ekâ kîkway naskwawin.*

nonresistant *ekâ ka naskwahk.*

nonrestrictive *ekâ ka nakinkatek kîkway.*

nonscheduled *ekâ kakwayace isihcikehk.*

nonsensical *nânatohk ka isimohconikehk.*

nonstop *namakîkway nakewin; sapohtewin.*

nonsupport *namakîkway pamihewewin.*

nontreaty *ekâ ka tipahamowakanowihk.*

nonunion *ekâ ka mamawintohk atoskewnihk.*

nonviolence *ekâ kîkway kisiwasowin.*

nonvoter *ekâ opimipahtaw.*

nonwhite *namakîkway moneyawiwin.*

nonwoven *ekâ ka apihkatek.*

noodle *mecimapohkakan.*

nook An out of the way corner, *wehkwehcakas.*

noon hour *nesosaptepahikan.*

normality *kwayask kwesâyâwin.*

normalize *kwayask kohewewin.*

northernmost *kihci kewetinohk.*

northland *kewetinohk askîy.*

nosegay *ka asamokih nîpikansa.*

nostalgia *kaskiyihtamowin.*

nostalgic A sentimental person, *kakaskiyihtaskihk;* it is sentimental or nostalgic, *kewateyitakwan.*

notability *kiskeyihtakosowin.*

notable *kîkway ka kiskeyihtakwahk*; an important person, *kihcihkawiyinow*.

notably *kiskeyihtakosowenihk*.

notarize *weyasowewnihk ka astahk*.

notary *mosci weyasowewin*; a special person appointed to attest deeds, *kihciweyasowew*.

notation *kîkway kakiskinwasinahamihk*.

note *ka itsahamatohk masinahikanis*; a written record to assist the memory, *masinahikanis*.

noted S/he is well-known, *kiskeyitakosow*.

notice A written statement giving information or warning, *kiskeyitakokewin*.

notification *kiskeyitamohiwewin*.

notwithstanding *tânsitoke sôskwac*; in spite of, *acipoko*; although, *ahpô cî mîna*.

nought *metoni namakîkway*.

noun *kîkway ka mamiskotamihk*.

novelette A little story, *acimowinis*.

novelist *otacimow*; a writer of small novels, *acimomasinahikewenow*.

nowadays *anohc kakisikak*.

noxious *ka nihtâ mayetotakohk kîkway*.

nuance *apisis pecoses*.

nubile *oskinekiskwewin*.

nudism *mostapekasêwnihk ka wecihewehk*.

nudist *omostapekasêw*.

nugget *osâw sônîyâw kamiskaht*.

null *ekâ kîkway ka ispehteyihtakwahk*.

nullify *isihcikewin ka pekonamihk*.

nullity *ekâ kîkway kespehteyihtamihk*.

numerator *otakihcikew*.

numerical *ka oyakihtamihk kîkway*.

numerically *oyakihcikewnihk*.

nurse A medicine woman, *maskihkewiskwew*.

nursemaid *maskihkewiskew ka nesohkamakot iskwew*.

nursery *awâsisis ka nakateyimihtwaw eta* (Northern); a children's nursery, *awâsisêwikamik*.

nurseryman *nâpew ka nesohkamatiket awâsisisa itah ka nakateyimiht*; one whose business is growing plants and trees, *ahtaskicekewenow*.

nursery school *ka kiskinohamahtwaw awâsisisak eta* (Northern).

nutcracker *pâkân pastatahikan*.

nutmeat *pehcayihk ka mecihk pâkânihk*.

nutrient *kîkway ka meyoskakohk*.

nutrition *meyoskakowin*; the act of nourishment or food, *meyo asahkewin*.

nutritionist *awîyak ka paminahk meyometisowin*.

nutritious *kîkway ka mewasihk tamecihk*.

nymph *manicos ekâ ceskwa ka kesohpikit*; a beautiful young woman, *kakatawasisit iskwew*.

O

oarlock *eta ka tapsihkwaw asipoyewakanak*.

oarsman Persons who pull the oars, *pimisikaweniwak*; *nâpew ka asipoyet*.

oasis A watering hole in the desert, *mohkicowanipek*.

oat *mistatim omecowin*; a feed for horses, *mistatimomeciwin*.

oath *kihci pekiskwewin*; s/he makes an oath, *kihci pekiskwew*; a solemn statement with God as your witness, *kihcipekiskwewin*.

oatmeal *kekisepaw mecowin*; a morning meal, *kekisepamecowin*.

obituary *ekâ ka pematsit awîyak masinahikanihk kastahk*; announcing the death of a person, *nakataskewin*.

oblique *ekâ ka kwayaskwak*.

oblique angle *nawâc poko ka iyipestek*.

obscene *ka weyakweskihk*; offensive to modest sensibilities, *wanatisiwin*.

obscenity *mosci pesikwatsowin*.

obsolescence *poni apatisowin*.

obsolescent *ka ponapatahk kîkway*.

obsolete Gone out of use, *ponapatan*; *kîkway ka ponpayik*.

obstetrics *ka nakatiyimiht iskwew ka ayawawasot*.

occident Towards the west, *pahkisimotahkisi*.

occupancy *nânitâw ka pehtokepicihk*.

occupant One who resides in a place, *owekow*; *awîyak ka pehtokepicit*.

occupation *kîkway ka atoskatamihk*; *atoskewin*; *itapatisiwin*; working for a living, *atoskewin*.

occupational *ka nihtâ ispayik atoskewin*.

oceanic *kihcikamehk ohci kîkway*.

ochre or **ocher** *pastew asiskîy ka pîwâpiskopayik*; *wâpatonisk* (Plains).

o'clock Time, *tipahikan*.

octopus A sea animal with eight arms, *ayinanewopiton*.

ocular *oskesikohkana*.

oculist *miskesik maskihkewiyinow*.

oddball *ka ayiwâkepayit awîyak*.

off-and-on *kahkehtwam*.

off-balance *pacipayowin*.

offbeat *ka pîtoswepinkehk kitocikewinihk*.

offcast *pîtos isâyâwin*; rejected, *âtaweyicika*.

off-color or **off-colour** *ka pîtos nakwahk*.

offhand *sîsîkoc kîkway ka tôtamihk*.

office *masinahikew kamikos*; a room for transacting business, *masinahikewikamik*.

officer *onekanew*; a boss, *okimâw*.

official *kihcina sepwepayihcikewin*; properly authorized, *kihcihtwewin*.

officially *kihcina ka yohtenamihk kîkway*.

521

officiate *kîkway metawewin ka nakateyihtamihk.*

offish *wanesâyâwin.*

off-key *ka pîtoswepinkehk.*

off-screen *ekâ ka cikastepayihtahk.*

off-season *ka mekwa kepahamihk kîkway.*

offset *ka patotesicikehk.*

offshore *nimitaw;* a distance from shore, *sipweyahokow.*

offside *or* off-side *kwantite.*

offspring *eta ka ohcehk; nihtâwikihakan.*

off-track *patotesikanahk.*

ogre *wihtiko ka acimiht atayohkewnihk.*

oilcloth A table cloth, *aspimetis wakan; anaskewin.*

oiler *otominkew.*

oil driller *omonahipimewinow.*

oil field *monahikewin pimiy ohci.*

oil man *opimiwenow; opimiwinow.*

oil paint *sopekahikan ka sopekahohtwaw masinpayowenak (Northern).*

oil sand *iyikaw katomak.*

oilskin *pimiwekin.*

oil tanker *misinapihkwan ka awatat pimiy.*

oil well *monahipimewin.*

ointment *tominikan.*

old-fashioned *kayâs ka pimitisahamihk.*

old hat *kayâsastotin.*

old-line *kasyâsitwewin.*

old-time *kayâs kîkway.*

old-timer *kayâs ohci peyakwanohk kayâhk.*

oleo margarine Artifical butter, *tohtosapopimihkan.*

olives A yellowish green fruit, *pimemina.*

omission *kîkway ekâ metoni ka kesehtahk.*

omlette Beaten eggs cooked as pancakes, *wawitehkasikan.*

omnipotence *ayamihew maskawsêwin.*

omnipotent *ayamihawinihk ka isi maskawsehk.*

omnipresence *misiwi ka ayâhk.*

omnipresent *manito misiwi ka wecihiwet.*

omniscience *manito iyinesowin.*

omniscient *ka keyaw kîkway ka kiskeyihtamihk.*

omnivorous *otahaskehk ka ohtacihohk.*

oncoming *ka ahkampapayik kîkway.*

oneness *nistweyakehowin.*

onrush *ka nekan keyasohk.*

onset *maciwepinikewin.*

onshore *kapawin.*

on-site *mecim ekota.*

onslaught *ahkam nipahtakewin.*

opal An expensive stone, *asinikamistakisot.*

opaque *kîkway ekâ ka saponokwahk.*

open air *wayawetemihk.*

open-end *kîkway ka yohteyak.*

open-eyed *ekâ ka pasakwapihk.*

open-handed *awîyak ka napakcicestaht.*

open-hearted *awîyak ka kisêwatisit.*

open house *meyoti kanatohkemohk.*

open-mouthed *awîyak ekâ ka mana pekiskwet.*

opera *metawewin nayestaw ka nikamohk;* a drama done by singing, *nikamowin.*

operation Having an operation, *manisokasowin.*

operator One who runs things, *paminikew; opimipayihcikew.*

operative *kîkway kanihtapimipayik.*

optic *kîkway miskesikwah ohci.*

optical *nahapowin ohci kîkway.*

optician *awîyak oskesikohkana katawaket;* an eye doctor, *miskesiko maskihkeweyinow.*

orb *kîkway ka wawîyak.*

orbit *kîkway ka wasakakotek.*

orchard *nepehkana kohpikihtahk;* a grove of fruit trees, *menisahtikwak.*

orchestra *ka mamawekitohcikehk;* a group of players on various instruments, *kitohcikewak.*

orchestrate *ka ketohcekewnihkehk.*

orchestration *ketohcekewinihkewin.*

ore A piece of metal, *pîwâpisk.*

orderly A male hospital attendant, *atoskewiyakan ahkosêw kamikohk.*

ordinance *kwayask ahiwewin.*

organdy A piece of stiffened material, *papakekin.*

organic *tânsi ka isihcikasot ayisinow.*

organization *mamawintowin.*

Orient *osekipacwaw askehk ohci;* an area of Asian countries, *sekipacwawaskîy.*

oriole An American black and orange colored bird, *wasîpîscan; osaw pîwâyisis.*

orphanage A home for orphan children, *kewacikamik.*

orthodontist *mepetah ohci maskihkewiyinow.*

orthodox *peyakwayak poko ka isimewasik.*

oscillate *kahkekwask kesiwaskawehk.*

oscillation *kahkekwask isi waskawewin.*

oscillator *kîkway kahkekwask kespayik.*

osprey *emisikitit pîwâyis kinosêwa.*

ossify *kîkway oskana ka osehcikakehk.*

ostrich *apsisistikwan.*

ought *kîkway taki ispayik.*

outbid *maskahcihewewin.*

outbreak *ka sekotahkamkahk kîkway; asoskamatowin.*

outbuild *wayawetemihk kîkway kosehtahk.*

outbuilding *wayawewikamkos.*

outcome The outcome of something, *tânsi kesipayik; tânsi ka isi kesipayik.*

outcrop *ekâ metoni ka ayahamihk.*

outdated *nestokayâs kîkway; kayâsosecikewin.*

outdid *awîyak kaki paskeyaht.*

outdistance *wâhyaw ka nekanehk.*

outdo *ayiwâk ka tôtamihk.*

outer *wayawetimayihk; wayawetimiyihk.*

outermost *mamaweyâs wayawetimayihk.*

outerspace *tipiskâw anohk.*

outflow *ka wayawecowahk.*

outgo *ekâ peyakwanohk kakeh ayâhk.*

outgoing *ka papamohteskihk.*

outgrow *nakacekehcikewin.*

outguess *ka mosci tapeyihtamihk.*

outing Out walking or out driving, *papamotew; papampayow.*

outlandish *sôskwac namoya katawa;* it looks odd, *mahtawinakwan.*

outlast *kîkway kapaskeyatamihk.*

outlaw *awîyak ka nihtâ mayeniket; papamamos;* a habitual criminal, *omamayinikew.*

outlay *kwanta ayiwâk mestinkewin.*

outlet *eta ka wayawecowahk sîpî;* a means of escape or exit, *wayawetamon.*

outline A drawing showing only the shape, *masinipekahikewin.*

outlive *ka ayiwâkes pematisihk.*

outlook *tânsi kesekanawapahtamihk pematsowin.*

outlying *wayawetimayihk ohci kîkway;* remote from the centre, *wasakam.*

outmanoeuvre or **outmaneuver** *ka aspihiht awîyak.*

outmoded *kayâs ka kewepnamihk kîkway.*

out-of-bounds *kahkwanitite.*

out-of-date *ka ponikipiskamihk; kayâsosicikewin.*

out-of-the-way *ka ponikipiskamihk.*

out-of-town *ohpimiy ka etohtehk.*

outpace *ka nakacipahiht awîyak.*

outpatient *otahkosow wekihk kohpamihiht.*

output *taneyikohk ka kesehtahk kîkway;* the amount produced, *kesehcikewin.*

outrank *ayiwâkes kespehtapihk.*

outreach *kapapam wapamihtwaw ayisenowak (Northern).*

outride *kapapam tehtapihk; paskiyawew; meyaskawew.*

outright *sôskwac semak kahkeyaw; semak*

outset *eta koh macepayik.*

outshine *kihkayasêwek.*

outsize *ayiwâk kespehcak.*

outskirts *eskwastek ôcenas.*

outspoken *ekâ ka mana pekiskwehk; macitonew.*

outspread *wâhyaw keskwastek.*

outstanding *metoni kwayask ka tôtamihk.*

outstay *ayiwâkes awîyak ka ayat.*

outstretched *ka misakami tasonamihk kîkway.*

outstrip *ka ceyahiwehk.*

outward *wayawetimihk isih;* seen from the outside, *wayawetimayihk.*

outwear *ayiwâk kîkway ka mewasik.*

outweigh *ayiwâk ka kosikwahk.*

outwit *ayiwâk iyinesowin; ka kayeyisemat.*

outwork *ayiwâk ka nohtesimiht; nihtâ atoskewin;* s/he outworked her/his, *paskiyawew.*

outworn *kîkway ka mestiskamihk.*

ovation The clapping of hands, *pakam cicehamawin.*

oven *nawâcew kotawanapisk;* a chamber in a stove for baking or roasting, *kaskamotihkasikan.*

ovenware *nawâcewiyakana.*

overalls *latweltas (Northern, French Cree); misêwetasak;* a pair of over pants, *ahkwetawetas.*

overactive *wawîyak ka kayawatsowin.*

overawe *ka osâm meyowapahkehk.*

overbalance *ayiwâk napati isih.*

overbear *kosam watehiht awîyak.*

overbearing *osâm watehiwewin;* being very arrogant, *mâmihteyimowin.*

overbid *ka ayiwâk tepwatamihk.*

overblown *ka kawasit mistik.*

overcame *ka sakohtwahk.*

overcharge *ayiwâk ketakihcikehk.*

overcloud *ka kasketaskwak.*

overcome *ka sakohikohk kîkway; sakohtaw; ahkoseskakow.*

overdevelop *ka pasci osehcikehk.*

overdose *wawîyak mistahi kotinamihk maskihkeya.*

overdraft *ka ayiwâk ociptiht sônîyâw.*

overdraw *mestinam;* asking over your due, *ayiwâknatôtamowin.*

overdrive *ayiwâk ka sohkepayihk.*

overdue *ka ayiwâk asinahikehk; meyaskamopayow;* it is overdue, *meyaskamopayow.*

overexposure *ka ayiwâk wapahtehiwehk kîkway.*

overhang *ka pastakocikehk.*

overhaul *ahtisihew.*

overhauling *kwayask nanapacicikewin.*

overhead *ispimihk ka pimakotek kîkway;* drawing over your limit, *mamawimestinikewin.*

overhead projector *mahkipayihcikan*

overkill *wawîyak mistahi nipahcikewin.*

overlaid *ka pastascikehk.*

overnight bag *ka tikoniwat.*

overpass *pastohteskanaw.*

overpower The act of overpowering, *sakohtwawin (Northern).*

overrule *namoya tâpwehtam;* overruling on something, *sakocimowewin.*

overshadow Darken as by casting a shadow on, *akow cakasteskawew.*

overshoe A rubber overshoe, *ahkwetaweskisin.*

523

oversubscribe *ka ayiwâk atawehk*.

oversubscription *ayiwâk atawewin*.

overtax *ayiwâk tepahikewin*.

overthrew *ka pasci pimosinehk*.

overthrow *pekonam oyasiwewin*; defeat, force out by power, *sakociskawew*.

overthrown *pasci pimosinewin*.

overtime *ka ayiwâk atoskehk*.

overture *kwayaskomowewin*.

overturn *kakwes kastahk*.

overwork S/he is played out, *nohtesin*.

owing A bunch of bills, *masinahikewina*.

oxford A short cut shoe, *keskaskisin*.

P

pacific *okihcikame pahkisemotahk*; the Pacific Ocean, *kihcikame*.

pacifier *ococosemihkans*.

pacifist *awîyak ekâ nôtinitowin ka mewiyihtahk*; opposition to trouble, *naheyitamowin*.

pack train *ka kwahtapekahototwaw onayahcikewak* (*Northern*).

pact *koweciwakanpayihohk*; a total agreement, *mamawitipeyihtamowin*.

padlock *kaskihtakahikan*.

pagan *awîyak ekâ kotâpwehtamowenit*.

paganism *ekâ kîkway ka tâpwehtamihk*.

page A page of a book, *paskekinikan*; one page in a book, *peyak paskinikan*.

pageant A happy spectacle, *mocikeyitamowin*.

painkiller *wesakahpinew nipahcikan*.

painstaking Very carefully, *asweyihtamowin*.

paint A spreading material, *sopihikan*.

paintbrush A big paintbrush, i.e.: for painting a house, *sopikahikakan*; a paintbrush for picture painting, *masinipehikanahtik*; *sopikahikanacikos*.

painting A piece of art, *masinipehikanis*; *sopikahikanis*; painting a picture, *masinpayowin kasopikahamihk*; the act of painting, *sopikahikewin*.

pajamas A pair of sleeping clothes, *nipâwayiwinisa*.

pallet *mistikonipewin*.

palomino *wâposâwâstim*; a golden colored horse, *osâwâstim*.

palsy *nipopayowin*; a shaking disease, *nanamaspinewin*.

pamphlet A small book, *masinahikanis*.

pancake A flap jack, *kweskiwepinikan* (*Northern*); *kwiskipayicikan*; hot cakes, *astapisikanisak*.

pandemonium *ka misiwanatahkamikahk*.

pane A window pane, *wasinamawinapisk*; *wapamonapisk*.

panel A group answering questions, *onaskwew osimowewak*; *ka kehtwam amohtahk napakihtak*.

panelling or **paneling** *kehtwam amohcikana*.

panhandle *ka mosci natôtamahk*.

panic-stricken *awîyak ka sasopayit*.

pansy *nepehkanis*.

pantaloon A special pair of pants, *mitasak*.

panther A large wild cat, *pwaciminos*.

pantomime *weyâsinkewin*.

pantry *ohpayihcikanikamik*; a food storage room, *mecowin ascikewikamikos*.

pantyhose *iskwew tasak ka kinokatewesitwaw* (*Northern*); *sâpwâstewasika mitâs*.

paper Writing paper, *masinahekanekin*; *masinahekanekan*.

paper bag or **paper box** *masinahekanekinwat*.

paper birch *peyakwan masinahekanekin waskway*.

paper money *masinahekanekin sônîyâw*.

paperwork *mistahe ka masinahekehk masinahekanihk*.

par *mwehci pahpeyakwan*.

parable *ka keskihkemowin*; a fictitious story pointing out a moral, *atayohkan*.

parachute *pakicewakan*.

parade *ka wecehewehk wapahtehewewnihk*; walking in a parade, *mamawipimohtewin*.

paradox *ka aymahk takehtâpwehtamihk*.

paraffin *mosci wasaskotenkansa kosecikakehk*.

paragraph *peyah piski tasinahikewin*.

parallel It runs parallel, i.e.: trails, *tipiskoc*; all the very same, *tahtapiskoc*.

paramount *metoni nîkân apowin*.

paraphernalia *kîkway ka tipeyawehohk*.

paraphrase *pahpîtos pekiskwewin*.

paraplegic *kistapowin ekâ kake pemohtehk*.

parasol *akawastehon*.

parcel *kaskahpecikewnis*; a package, *kaskahpicikan*.

parcel post *kîkway ka itsahamatohk*.

parchment *ahpin kosehtahk pahpekin*; a dried piece of animal hide, *ahpinekin*.

park *ka kanaweyihcikatek askîy*; the ground set apart for public use, *kapesowin*.

parka *kesowasakay*.

parkland *ka naweyihcikatew askîy*.

park ranger *okanaweyihcikew*.

parkway *katawinamihk askîy kawe nakateyihtakwahk*.

parlay *kwayask ka pekiskwatitohk*.

parliament *kihci okimanahk*; the legislative assembly, *okimanahk*.

parliamentarian *awîyak ka nakacitat kihci okimanahk*.

parliamentary *kihci okimanahk isihcikewin*.

524

parlor *or* **parlour** *kehokewikamik; apew kamikos.*

parody *kwanta ayisinakewin;* a humorous imitation of an artist, *katapasinahamihk.*

parole *kihci pekiskwehiwewin pamayes awîyak ka pakitiniht;* a conditional release from prison, *nomipakitinowewin.*

parrot A tropical bird capable of imitating speech, *ayistohtakewpîwâysis.*

parsley *ohpikecikana; kistikanis;* a herb with aromatic leaves, *wehimak ohpikecikana.*

parsnip *wâpisk oskatask;* a white carrot, *wâpiski oskatask;* ginger or parsnip, *manito oskatask.*

particle *apisis kîkway;* just a little, *apisis.*

part-time *aspehtaw.*

party line *ka mamawapiskamok pewâpiskos.*

passbook *ka sapohtewakehk masinahikan.*

passenger A traveler in a vehicle, *oposow.*

passkey *ka ayâhk apihkokahikan.*

passport *masinahikan ka sapohtewakehk.*

password *asawi wehtamatowin;* a secret word, *kemocipekiskwewin.*

paste An adhesive substance, *pasakwahikan.*

pastel *wawesehcikan miscikos ahohci.*

pasteurization *ka kanâcicikemakahk tohtosapoy.*

pasteurize *ka kanâtakamihtahk tohtosapoy.*

pastime *ka tipipayihtahk kesikaw.*

pastry *pahkwesikansak kosehihtwaw (Northern).*

patchwork *kîkway ka mesahamihk.*

pate *awîyak kapaskostekiwanet.*

patency *kîkway ka moscak.*

patent *masinahekasowin;* a temporary monopoly to an inventor, *ocehcikan.*

pathology *nânatohk ahkosowin kakakwi kiskeyihtamihk.*

patio *wayawetemihk kakihtwam anaskehk;* a shaded sitting place, *wayawetimakawastepowin.*

patriarch *mawaci kihtiyinow;* a venerable old man, *kisiyinewokimâw.*

patriarchal *metoni kihtehayowin.*

patriarchy *kakihtemâmitoneyihcikanihk.*

patricide *awîyak kanipahat tepeyaw opapawa.*

patrimony *asaw namatowin.*

patriot *awîyak mistahi ka sakihtat otaskîy.*

patriotism *ka kewetôtamihk askîy;* defending your country, *kispewew askewin.*

patrol *kanaweyihcikewin;* the act of taking care of things, *nakateyihcikewin.*

patrolmen A person who patrols, *onakatohkewak.*

patron *awîyak owehyowin kamekit;* an influential supporter, *natamâkew.*

patronage *okihcitwawsow owehyowin ka apacitawiht (Northern).*

patroness *iskwew okihcitwawsow (Northern).*

patronize *ka nesohkamatamihk kîkway;* giving support or custom to, *nesohkamâkewin.*

patty *pahkwesikanis; kesisikan.*

paunch *nipew ka mistatayet.*

pauper *awîyak asahtowin kohtacihot;* a destitute person, *kitimakis.*

pauperism *sôskwac ka pomehk.*

pave *ka asinikahcikehk;* the paving of a road or yard, *ka asiniwihtahk.*

pavement Paving a street or road, *asiniwanaskewin; ka asinikahtek meskanaw.*

pavilion *emisak mamawapew kamik;* a dance hall, *nemihitowikamik.*

paving *meskanaw kahkam asinikahtamihk.*

pawn *kiskinowatascikewin; kiskinawatastahk;* to pawn something, *kiskinawatascikewin.*

pawnbroker *awîyak ka kiskinowatatawet;* a pawn buyer, *okiskinawacatawew.*

pawnshop *kiskenowat atawikamik;* a place for pawning things, *kiskinawacatawewikamik.*

pay When someone receives money for work, *awîyak ka tipahamaht;* the act of paying the way for someone, *tipahamâkestamâkewin;* s/he pays her/his way for her/him, *tipahamâkestamawew;* someone who pays, *tipahamâkew;* s/he pays for it, *tipaham;* s/he has been paid, *tipahamâkosow;* the act of receiving payment or being paid, *tipahamâkosowin;* s/he pays her/his wages, *tipahamâwew;* s/he pays, *tipâhikew;* the act of paying, *tipahikewin;* s/he paid it for her/him, *tipahwew;* your pay, *tipahike.*

payment *tipahikewin; tipahamâkewin.*

payable *tipahikewin;* it comes time to pay, *ocecipayontipahikewin.*

payday *tipahikew kisikaw.*

payee *awîyak ka tipahamaht.*

payload *ka misi posihtasohk.*

paymaster *awîyak tipahikewin kapaminahk.*

pay-off *kesitipahamatowin.*

peacemaker *omeyopayihcikew.*

peace offering *kîkway ka mekihk meyo wihcetowin ohci.*

peacetime *ka mekwamoywasik.*

peach A soft fruit, *yoskimin.*

peacock A bird with beautiful feathers, *katawasêw pîwâyis.*

peanut A small peanut, *pâkânis.*

pear *misimenis;* a fruit with lots of juice, *ahkostimomenis.*

pearl *asinis ka nânatohkonakosit.*

pearly *naspic ka meywasik kîkway.*

peasant *opapampecow;* a hard up working man, *kitimakatoskeweyinow.*

peasantry *papampicowin.*

525

peat *kisastaw kaskitehkan*.

pecan A type of nut, *pâkân*.

pedal *makoskacikan*.

pedantic *ka kepatinkeskowin*.

pedantry *awîyak kakakepatinket*.

peddle *ka papam acawakesihk kekwasa*.

pedestal *kîkway ka nehpemastek kawapahtehiwehk*.

pedestrian *awîyak ka mostohtet*; a person who walks, *ayisiniw*.

pedigree *tepeyawewocewin*; a genealogical record, *tepeyaw wahkohtowin*.

pedlar A person who sells, *ocacawes*.

peephole *kimôtâpowin*.

pekinese A tiny dog, *atimosis*.

pelican *cahcakow*.

pell-mell *kiyekaw*; in great confusion, *waneyihtamowin*.

penal *tipahikehewewin*; inflicting punishment, *weyasowacikewin*.

penalize *ka tipahikehewehk*; s/he is made to pay, *tipahikehaw*.

penalty *tipahikehetowin*; a punitive punishment, *tipahikewin*.

pencil A large pencil, *masinahikanâhtik*; a small pencil, *masinahikanâhtikos*; *masinahikanâhcikos*; a pencil sharpener, *masinahikanitik kenipocikan (Northern)*; *ikinkipotayan masinahikanacikos (Plains)*.

pendant *paskwepeson ka wawesêwakehk*; a hanging ornament, *kiskinawacihcikan*.

pendulum *kîkway ka wepsopayik kahkikwask etakotek*.

penicillin A powerful bacteria killing substance, *nipahcikew maskihkîy*.

penitentiary *ka misak kipahotokamik*; a prison for criminals, *kihci kipahotokamik*.

penknife *pihkihkomanis*.

penniless *metoni ka pekopayihk*.

penny One penny, *peyak pîwâpiskos*; *osawapisk*.

pension *kesiyinew asahtowin*; a payment for past services, *tipahikewin*.

pensioner *awîyak ka kisiyinew asamiht*; old age pensioner, *kihtetipahamatowin*.

percale A cotton fabric for jackets, *miskotakayekin*.

percentage *pahki poko*.

perchance It could be or maybe, *ahpohetokwe*.

percolate *papeyahtik kosamihk*.

percolator *askihkos peyahtik kosot*; a coffee maker, *pihkahtewapoyihkakanis*.

percussion *kîkwaya ka kisêwehtahk*.

percussion instrument *kitohcikan ka kisêwek*.

perennial A plant that grows year after year, *tahtwaskekahpikihk*.

perforate *ka sahsapo tahkahtamihk*.

perforation *sahsapotahkahcikewin*.

perforator *sahsapotahkahcikan*.

perforce *yahkiskakewin*.

perfume A pleasant smelling odor, *wehkimakwahon*; *wehkimakohon*; s/he puts on perfume, *wehkimakohow*; the act of putting on perfume, *wehkimakohowin*.

perfumery A perfume making house, *wehkimakohonikamik*.

perishable *kîkway ka nihtamisiwanatahk*.

periwinkle A trailing evergreen flower, *ka papamikihk wapikwane*.

perjury *weyasowewnihk kakeyaskihk*.

permanent wave *mokotowehkasamawin*.

permeability *kîkway ka swepayik*.

permeable *kîkway ka swepayihtahk*.

permeate *misiwi ka pecemakasikehk*.

permeation *misiwi ka sapohtemakahk kîkway*.

permutation *poko isi ka isi nahawascikehk*.

perpetuity *ekâ wehkac ka ponipayik*.

personification *powamowin*.

personnel *mamawi otatoskewak*; employees of a particular employer, *mamawikamasinahiketwaw (Northern)*.

perspective *tânsi ka isi oyehtamihk kîkway*.

pesticide *manicosak ka nipahcikakehk*.

pestilence *ka sohkipayih ahkosowin*.

pestilent *awîyak mistahi ka pakwatekosit*.

pestle A kind of crusher, *sikwahikan*.

pet *ka kitemakeyimiht pisiskîs*.

petite *iskwew ka apsesit*.

petition *masinahikan ka mamawi osehtahk*; a formal request, *ka kwecekemowin*.

petitionary *mamawi natôtamawin*.

petrify *kîkway ka asinewpayik*; *sekihew*; turning into stone, *asiniwpayowin*.

petroleum Oil from the ground, *askewipimiy*.

petticoat A woman's undercoat, *pehtawesakan*.

petty cash *apisis sônîyâs*.

petty larceny *apiscikekwas ka kemotihk*.

pew *ayamehekamkotehtapowin*; seats in a church, *ayamihewikamik tehtapowina*.

phantasm *cepaykawapamiht*; an illness like seeing a ghost, *amatsowin*.

phantom *awîyak ka sekihtasot*; *cepiykawapamiht*.

pharmacology *maskihkeya ka kiskenohamakosihk*.

pharmacy *maskihkiw'kamik*; a medicine store, *maskihkewatawkamik*.

pheasant *ahkiskow*.

phase *kîkway ka wapahtehewehk*.

philanthropist *omeyo tôtakew*.

philanthropy *meyo tôtakewin*.

philosopher *metoni otiyinesow.*

philosophic *ka iyinesihk.*

philosophical *iyinisêwâyâwin.*

philosophy *iyinisowin ka masihtahk.*

phone *pîwâpiskos;* the act of calling one another on the phone, *sewepitamatowin.*

phonograph *kitohcikan kantohtamihk;* an old cranking gramophone, *peminikew kitohcikan.*

photo *masinpayowin;* a snapshot, *masinpayiwin.*

photocopier *kamasinakepayik aspasinahikan.*

photocopy *kehtwam masinatahikewin.*

photogenic *ka wahkew masinpayik kîkway.*

photograph *masinpayowin.*

photographer *omasinpayihcikew.*

photography *masinpayihcikewin.*

phrasing *pahpiskihtasinahikewin.*

physic A laxative, *saposikan.*

physical education *ka kiskinohamakehk sohkatsowin.*

physical training *tapitawi ka sesawehk.*

physician A doctor, *maskihkiwiyinow.*

physique The structure of the body, *ihtâkîyawehk.*

pianist A music maker, *okitohcikew.*

piccolo A small high pitched flute, *kweskosêw pocacikanis.*

pickaxe An axe for digging roots, *monahicepihkakan.*

pickerel A pickeral, *kinosêw okâw.*

picket fence *mistikowasakankan.*

pickle A food preserved in vinegar, *sewakohcikan.*

pickpocket *ayisiyinow ka nihtâ kimotit; kimotisk.*

pick-up A small hauling vehicle, *awacikew câpânâskos.*

picnic *papametsowin;* the act of preparing a picnic lunch, *nemawinihkewin.*

pictograph *naspasinahikewin.*

pictographic *ka naspasinahikehk.*

pictures Photographs, *masinipayiwina.*

picturesque *peyakwan masinipayowin kesinakwahk askîy.*

picture tube Or movie projector, *cikastepayihcikan.*

piddling *kwanta âyâwin.*

pie A double crusted pie, *wewekihkasikan;* a single crusted pie, *napatehkasikan;* something cooked from the inside, i.e.: a meat pie, *pehtohkasikan.*

piebald *wapihkwewatim.*

piecemeal *ahapsis ohci.*

pie crust *kaspihkasikan.*

pier A bridge for launching boats, *kapawin asokan.*

pigeon *mehmew; omemew.*

pigeonhole *nahascikewin kiskinohamatokamkohk.*

pigeontoed *ka pehtokehamehk.*

piggish *metoni ka wehteko atsihk.*

piggy bank *peyak pîwâpiskosak ka nahahihtwaw (Northern).*

pig-headed *kosam maskawistekwanehk.*

pigment *kîkway ka kiyikawestahk sopekahikanihk.*

pigmy *apisciyines.*

pigpen *kohkos waskahikan.*

pigsty *kohkos asowacekan.*

pigtail *mestakaya ka apihkatamihk.*

pill *misiwepayihcikan;* a small medicine tablet for swallowing, *misiwepayecikan.*

pillar A support column, i.e.: a pillar, *setwaskwahikan.*

pillow *aspiskwesimon.*

pilot An airplane pilot, *opimeyaw (Northern); opimihaw (Plains);* the person who holds the helm or rudder in a boat, *otahkwaham.*

pilot fish *kinosêw okihcikamehk ohci.*

pilot study *ka nîkânastahk kiskinohamâkewin.*

pinafore A child's apron, *aspastakanis.*

pinball machine *awâsis metawewin.*

pincers *âpacicikan ka tahkwahcikemakahk;* a pair of pliers, *makwacikan.*

pinchers *sakahikana kocipicikakehk.*

pink It is pink in color, *okinewapikonewow.*

pinnacle A church spire pointed straight up, *kacepiwaskitek.*

pinochle A shuffling card game, *itenikew metawewin.*

pinpoint *metoni kwayaskweyihcikewin.*

pint About two cups of water, *nânitâw neso menihkwacikanis iyikohk nipîy;* one pint, *peyakwâpisk;* the liquid measure for two cups full, *nesominihkwacikana.*

pioneer *awîyak koskiyohtenahk askîy; nistam ka takosihk;* one who goes ahead, *onîkânew.*

piper *otosip wakanihkew.*

piping *kîkway kosehcikakehk osipwakanak.*

piquant *ka wesakahk kîkway.*

piracy *ka kîmôc otinamihk kîkway.*

pirate *ohcitaw ka kîmôtiskihk.*

pistol A small fire arm, *paskisikanis.*

pitch dark *kaskitipiskuw.*

pitcher *awîyak ka pimosinet pakahacowansa;* a baseball pitcher, *opimosinew.*

pitcher plant *askihkosihk kohpikihcikesihk.*

pitchfork *cestahaskosowakan.*

pitfall *askamatowin.*

placard *masinahikan ka nehpemastahk.*

plagiarism *ka kîmôtihk masinahikewin.*

plagiarize *awîyak omâmitoneyihcikan ka âpacitawiht.*

plague *ahkosowin ka sohkipayik; mamawaspinewin.*

plain-spoken *ka kihkapekiskwehk.*

527

plaintive *kaskeyitamowin.*

plane An airplane, *pimehakan;* a hand tool to smooth wood surfaces, *mohkocikan;* s/he carves or planes it, *mohkotew.*

planer A machine to smooth lumber in a mill, *mohkocikan;* a planer mill or woodworking workshop, *mohkocikewikamik;* a planer man, *mohkocikewiyinow.*

planet *acakosak iteh kayatwaw (Northern); kotak askîy; wahiyaw askîy; wahyow askîy.*

planetary *waskoh ohci kîkway.*

plank Or wooden board, *napakihtak; kînohtâkaw;* it is sheet-like, plank, flat, *napakihtâkisow; napakihtakaw.*

planking *napakihtakohkacikewin.*

planner *otoyisihcekew.*

plantain A large leafed weed, *mahkipakiw macikwanas.*

planter *kistikakan;* a plant holder, *kistikew âpacicikan.*

plaster cast *ka asinikahtamihk mispiton.*

plastering *kasinikahtamihk waskahikan.*

plastic *ka saponokwahk masihikanekin; sapwastewekin (Northern); sapostiwikin (Plains).*

plasticine *oyiskowakinikan (Northern); wiskowakinikan (Plains); kawiskowakinikan.*

platform A raised flooring, *ispimihk anaskewin.*

platter A serving dish, *kapateskwewyakan.*

playback *kakehtwam metawehk.*

playground *metawewinihk;* an outside playground, *wayawetim metawewinihk.*

playhouse *metawewikamkos.*

playing card *pakesanak.*

playmate *awîyak ka wecemetawemiht; wecewakanisa.*

playoff *iskwayâc mawenehotowin.*

plaything *metawakan.*

playtime *ka macimetawehk.*

plaza *misi atawikamik ôtenahk;* an inside open place, *pehtokewin.*

plea *natôtamawin; naskwestamowin.*

plead *ka kesemowin;* the act of pleading for something, *natôtamawin.*

pleadings *ka kesemotôtakewna.*

pleat *kîkway ka tipikwatamihk.*

pledge *kîkway ka meskoc mekihk; asotamâkewin.*

pleurisy A swelling of the lungs, *ohpanpakipayiwin.*

pliers One set of pliers or metal pinchers, *makwahcikanapisk;* wire cutters or metal choppers, *keskapiskisikakan;* a gripping tool, *makwahcikan.*

plot *askîs ka waskahekanihkatamihk.*

plough *or* **plow** Something used to break ground, i.e.: a plow, *pekopicikan;* s/he plows the ground or s/he

is ripping things up, *pekopicikew;* the act of plowing the land or ripping things up, *pekopicikewin;* a soil cutter, *pekopicikan.*

ploughman *or* **plowman** *opekopcikew;* a soil cutter operator, *pekopicikewenow.*

ploughshare *or* **plowshare** *asiskew manisikan.*

plover A snipe, *sesesow; sîsîsow.*

plug A stopper, *kipahikan.*

plug-in *waskotepayow ka sakicitahk.*

plumb bob *kwayask tipapekinkan.*

plumber *awîyak nipîy kâ nakacihtat;* a worker on water and sewer pipes, *nipîkatoskatahk.*

plumbing *nipîkastahk waskahikanihk.*

plunder Rob or take by force, *maskahtwewin.*

plural *ayiwâk peyak.*

pluralism *mihcetwayak kesehcikehk.*

plywood *waskahikan ka wekinkakehk.*

pnuemonia *ohpanahpinewin;* an inflamation of the lungs, *pakihpanepayowin.*

poach *kakemoc nocicikehk.*

pocketbook *sônîyâwat.*

pocket knife A pocket knife, *pihkihkomanis;* a small knife, *mohkomanis.*

pocket money *pekinsônîyâs.*

poem *nikamon ka masinahamihk;* a composition in verse, *masinahikewinisa.*

poet One who writes poems, *masinahikewenow; awîyak ka masinahahk nikamona.*

poetess *iskwew ka nihtâw asinahiket.*

poetic *nihtâwasinahikewin.*

poetry *pikiskwewin ka aymihtahk.*

pointer A hunting dog, *macewatim.*

point of view *tânsi kitiyihtamihk.*

poise Mental stability, *kwayas mâmitoneyihcikan.*

poison ivy *ka piscipomakahkwaw nepeya; piciposkakîs.*

poker *kantwahkwehk;* the act of playing poker, *nitwahkwewin.*

poky A slow person, *yekicikaw.*

polar *kici kewetinohk.*

police Or law officer, *simâkanis (Northern).*

police court *weyasowewkamik.*

police dog *simâkanatim.*

police force *simâkansak.*

policeman *simâkanis;* a member of the police force, *simâkaneyinow.*

police station *simâkanisêwikamik (Northern); simâkanisikamik (Plains).*

policewoman *simâkaniskwew.*

policing *simâkansowiwin.*

policy *tânsi kesehcikewnehk;* a course of conduct based on principle, *kwayaskotisahikewin.*

polish *opetatowewihkan*; to shine something,
wasehkwahikewin.
politic *isihcikewin ka pimpayihtahk*.
political Pertaining to governmental affairs,
oyasiwewinihk isi.
politician *otiyinesêw iyinow*; *opimpataw kimaw*.
politics *iyinesowena*; *esipimpayitâhk isîhcikewin*.
polka A type of dance, *nemehitowin*.
poll *wehowena kotinamihk pimpahtawnihk*.
pollen *wapikwanewin*.
pollute *iyipatakamihcikewin*.
pollution *piscipohtawin*; *ka iyipatakamihcikehk*.
polo A game played on horseback, *tehtâpew
metawewin*.
polygamy Having many wives, *mihcetoskwewewin*.
pompadour *sekahowin*.
pone *mahtamin pahkwesikan*.
pongee A soft silk fabric, *senipânekin*.
pontoon An airplane pontoon, *pimeyakanosi*.
pooch *acimosis*.
poodle A small dog, *atimosis*.
pool *tahkahcikewin ka metawehk*; the act of making
a swimming pool, *pakasimonihkewin*.
poolroom *tahkahcikewikamik*.
poorhouse *kitemakikamik*; a hobo's home,
kitimakikamik.
poor law *kitemak weyasowewin*.
poor-spirited *ka macitwawisayâhk (Northern)*.
pop *menihkwewnis*; *pastipayow*; *siwapoy*.
popcorn *potawehkasikansak*; *pastaminak*.
poppy *nôtinitowapikwanes*.
popsicle *ka ahkwatehtahk nipoy*.
populace *mehcet ayisiyinowak*.
popularity Having a good name, *meyowehowin*.
population *ka mamawakimihtwaw ayisiyinowak
(Northern)*; *ohpikehitowin*.
populous *ka samyatitwaw ayisiyinowak (Northern)*.
porcelain A fine white translucent china,
mekiseyakan.
porch A covered approach to a doorway,
pehtokwekapawiwin.
porcupine A small animal with sharp spines for
protection, *kakwa*.
pornography *pisikwatciwapahtehiwewin*.
porous *ka pahposkwasakayesihk*.
port A coast city where ships lands and unload,
misinapihkwanikapawin.
portage A place for carrying canoes over land,
kaskewewin.
porter One who carries and loads baggage for people,
oposihtamâkew; a porter,
okanowowiskwatemiwew.

portrait *masinpayowin*; the picture of a person,
masinpayiwin.
portrayal Or presentations, *ayimota kîkway*; *ayimota
kîkway ikiyosihtayin*.
positive Being very sure, *kihcinahow*.
possessor A person who possesses, *tipiyicikew*.
post *wasakankanahtikos*; *peciwepiniset
waskwahikan*; a barbwire fence post,
pîwâpiskowasakanikanahtik.
postage *masinahikan tatipahamihk*.
postage stamp *oscikwanis*.
postal *isihcikewin masinahikanikamkohk ohci*.
post box *eta ka posiwepinamihk masinahikana*.
postdate *ka ahtastahk kesikaw*.
posted *ka posiwepinamihk*.
poster *masinahikan ka akohtakahamihk*.
posthumous Something awarded after a death,
kasispowocikan.
postman *awîyak masinahikana ka pemohtatat*; a
mailman, *masinahikanewenow*.
postmark *tanima kesikaw ka masinatahamihk*.
postmaster *masinahikana ka paminahk nâpew*; a
mailman or postmaster, *masinahikanewiyinow*.
postmistress *masinahikana ka paminahk iskwew*.
post office *masinahikanikamik*; *masinahikewikamik
(Northern)*; *masinakiwikamik (Plains)*; a place for
mailing letters, *masinahamatowikamik*.
postpaid *ka nîkân tepahikehk*; paying in advance,
nîkântipahikewin.
postpone Defer until later, *ahtascikewin*.
postulate *mosci tapeyihtamowin*.
posture *tânsi awîyak kesikapawit*.
posy *ka asahpetekwaw nipîhkansa*.
potable *kîkway take menihkwehk*.
potato chip *lapatak kaspihkasikansa (Northern,
French Cree)*; *askipwâw kâspihkaskanisa (Plains)*.
pothole *ka watowahcak*.
pothook *akotaskihkwan*.
pottery *askihkwak eta kosehihtwaw (Northern)*;
dishes molded from clay and baked,
asiskewoyakana.
poultice A soft, warm mass applied to a sore spot,
akopisowin.
pound One pound, *peyak kosikwan*.
poverty *metoni kitimaksowin*; being poor,
kitimakisiwin.
powder *kâpîkinipayik*; baking powder, *opihkasikan*.
powerboat *ka sohkikotek osih*.
powerhouse *waskotepayewikamik*.
practicality *awîyak ka nihtâtotahk kîkway*.
practical joke *sohki naniweyacihewewin*.
practical joker *awîyak ka nihtâ sohkeniweyatsit*.

practioner A good professional doctor, *maskekewenow*.

pragmatic *awîyak ka kiskenohamasot*.

pragmatical *kiskenohamasowin*.

pragmatism *kiskenohamâkewin*.

pragmatist *okiskinohamâkew*.

preamble *ka nakayâskamohtahewehk*.

precedence *nîkan payihowin*.

precedent *kîkway ka nîkânastahk*.

precept *kiskinowasomiwewin*.

preceptor *okiskinowasomiwew*.

precinct *ka piskihtastahk askîs kotak kîkway ohci*.

precipitant *kîkway kosehcikemâkahk nipîy*.

precipitate *kîkway ka osehcikepayik*.

precognition *neyak ka kiskeyihtamihk*.

predecessor *awîyak ka meskotapit*; one who preceded another in the same position, *aniskoskawewokimâwa*.

predestinate *ka yahti ka keseyihtamihk*.

predicate *ka wehtamihk kîkway*.

predication *kwayask wehcikewin*.

pre-existence *kayahti âyâwin*.

pre-existent *kayahti pematisowin*.

preface *nîkân ka masinahamihk kîkway*; an introduction to a book or speech, *matasinahikewin*.

prefiguration *nâkân oyehtamowin*.

prefix *nîkân ascekewin*; letters or syllables that go before and qualify another, *pekiskwewinis*.

prehistoric Preceding recorded history, *kayâs ispayiwin*.

prejudge *ayemiwewin*.

prejudice *pemamiyihcikewin*.

prejudiced *awîyak ka pemamiyimiht*.

prelude *ka nâkân sehcikehk*.

premarital *pamayis kihciwekihtohk*.

premeditate *ka nîkân oyehtamihk*.

premeditation Thinking ahead of time, *nîkân oyehtamowin*; a reflection, premeditation, *oyetamowin*.

premier *onîkânapow*; the chief minister of a province, *kihci okimâw*.

premise *eta ka wekihk*; owning real estate such as a building or land, *katipeyihtamihk*.

premium *tahto pîsim tepahikewin*; anything given as an inducement, *tahkockamekihk*.

prepay An advance payment, *nîkântipahikewin*.

preposition *awîyak kesehcikatiht*.

prerequisite *kwayaci nitaweyihcikewin*.

prerogative *awîyak tipiyaw omâmitoneyihcikan*.

prescribe *ka tepahamihk masinahikana*; *itwewin*; advise the use of medicine, *wehtamâkewin*.

prescriptive *ka tawa kesemekihk maskihki*.

prescribe *ka tepahamihk masinahikana*; *itwewin*.

prescript *kwayatasinahikewin*.

prescription *masinahikanis ka mekihk maskihkeya ohci*.

presence of mind *ka mekwa mâmitoneyihtamihk*.

presentation *kîkway mekowin*; presentations or reports, *mamiskota kîkway*.

preservative *kîkway ka manacitahk*.

preside *ka nekanehk mamawapowenihk*; presiding as chairperson of a meeting, *apestamowin*.

presidency *kihci nîkân apowin*.

president *okimâw kihci mohkomaninahk*.

press Smooth or flattened by pressure, *makwahikanimasinatahikewin*.

pressure cooker *sasow kaskihkasikakan*; *kaskamôtihkasikan*.

presto *keskaw*.

prewar Just before war, *pâmayes askanotitohk*.

price *koyakihtek kîkway*; *takehtew*.

priceless *ekâ kîkway ketakihtek*; *namoya tawecinehamihk*.

price tag *ka masinahikacesik tânsi ketakihtek*.

prime minister *nâpew ka paminahk kitaskenaw*.

primer An instrument to promote ignition, *macipayihcikan*.

priming *nîkân isihcikewin*.

primitive *kayâs pimacisowin*.

prince *mistekimaw okosisa*; the son of a ruler, *kihci okimasis*; *kicowiyasowew*; *kicowiyasowiw*.

princess The daughter of the ruler, *kihci okimaskwesis*; *mistekimaw otanisa*.

principal *ka nîkânet kiskenohamatokamkohk*; the head of a school, *kiskinohamakew nîkânapow*.

principle *awîyak omeyowehowin*.

print *ka mosci masinahikehk*.

printer *omasinahikew*; a machine that prints, *masinahikewenow*.

prison *kipahotokami*.

privy A private ownership, *tipiyawetipehtamowin*.

probability *maskoc tâpwi*.

probation *kocehaw*; a period of test or trial, *kocehiwewin*.

probational *masinahikepaketinowewin*.

probationer *omasinahikepaketinowew*.

probation officer *omayinikewa kakiteyimat* (Northern); *omayinikiwa kakitimat* (Plains).

proceeding *sipwepayowin*.

proceeds Money taken in, *sônîyâhkewin*.

procession *mamawipimohtewin*; a parade, *mamawohtewin*; a funeral procession, *askôcikewin*.

processional *askôkewin*.

proclamation *wehtamowewin*; an announcement, *wehtamakewin*.

procrastinate *ekâ kakeh keseyihtamihk*.

procurator *onesohkamâkew weyasowewnihk.*

prodigal *ka mestinikeskihk;* a lavish or wasteful person, *opapamacihow.*

prodigality *ka kepaci mestinikewin.*

prodigious *tamamaskatiht awîyak.*

prodigy *awîyak nânatohk kesinahet.*

producer *awîyak ka mamekit kîkway.*

production The act of making things, *osecikewin.*

profanatory *ka weyahkwewesâyâhk.*

profane *ekâ kwayask kesâyâhk; oyahkwewin;* profane language, *weyahkwewin.*

profanity *weyahkewin.*

profession *kîkway ka nakacitat awîyak;* a vocation in a branch of learning, *kiskeyihtamowin.*

professional *onakacitaw.*

professionalism *nakacitawin.*

professionally *nakacitawnihk.*

professor A teacher of high rank, *kiskinohamakew.*

profit *sônîyâhkewin.*

profitable *kîkway ka sônîyâhkakehk.*

project A public works development especially in housing, *ka miyamawi osehtahk.*

projector *cikastepayihcikan; cikastipayihcikakan.*

promenade A stroll for pleasure, *mocki pimohtewin.*

promiscuity *pisikwacimâmitoneyihcikewin.*

promiscuous *pisikwatisiwin.*

promissory S/he makes a promissary note, *kiskinowatasinahikew.*

promote Raise to a higher rank, *yahkotahewewin.*

promoter *osipwepayihcikew.*

promotion *sipwepayihcikewin.*

pronoun A word used to represent a noun, *pekiskwewin.*

pronouncement *kakihka pekiskwehk.*

propaganda *mayi peskiskwewin ka pamohtatahk.*

propellant *sipwepayihcikakan.*

propeller *pimeyakan sipwepayihcikan;* a device with revolving blades to drive forward, *sipwepayihcikan.*

propensity *mecim ohci isâyâwin.*

property *ka tipiyawehohk kîkway; tipiyawewisiwin.*

proponent *awîyak ka wecihiwet isehcikewnihk.*

proportion The relation of one thing to another in respect to size, *koyehtamihk kîkway.*

proposition Making a proposal to something, *isihcikatowin.*

proprietary *peyakwan ka tipiyawehohk.*

proprietor An owner, *tipiyicikew.*

propriety *tipiyawehowin.*

prosaic *wawîyak papeyahtikowisowin.*

proscribe *awîyak ka pomemiht.*

proscription *pomehewewin.*

proscriptive *kîkway ka ponihtahk.*

prose *ka wehcasik pekiskwewin.*

prosecute *ka weyasowatiht awîyak; tipahikehew; mawinewhew;* institute legal proceedings against, *sehkitisahikew.*

prosecutor A lawyer, *owiyasiwew; owiyasowiw.*

prospector *nocisônîyâwew.*

proverb *tâpwewin;* a form of speech, *itwewin.*

province *misisitipahaskan;* a large land reserve, *tipahaskan.*

provincial *misitipahaskanihk ohci.*

proxy *ka nîpawestamaht awîyak;* authority to act for another, *natamatowin.*

prune The black fruit, *kakaskitestwaw (Northern).*

psychic *otoywascikew.*

ptarmigan A white grouse, *wâpipihew.*

pubescent *ka maci opewahk.*

public Pertaining to the people at large, *ayisininahk.*

publication The act of publishing, *masinahikewin; ka masinahamihk.*

publicist *omasinahikew.*

publicity *masinahikanihk kapihk.*

publicize *masinahikanihk kastahk.*

publish *acimomasinahikanihk kastahk.*

publisher *omasinahikewiyinow.*

puck A hockey puck, *soniskwâtahikewinihk; papâmiwepahikanis.*

pudding *sewimecowin.*

pugilist A boxer, *opakamahotow.*

pullet *pakahakwanis.*

pulley *ocipicikakan.*

pullman A railroad car's sleeping quarters, *iskotewtâpânâsk nipawikamikos.*

pullover *waskicipcikan.*

pulp *masinahikanekin kosehcikakehk; sikwahikewin;* wooden chips, *mistikosikwatahikana.*

pumice *kanacicikakan.*

pump *kapâpicikâtek nipîy (Plains);* a machine for pulling liquids up a pipe, *pecipicikan.*

punctual *mweci ekota.*

punctuate *ka otamihtasohk.*

punctuation *otamihtasowin.*

punish *ka kitimahiht awîyak; tipahikehaw; nocihaw.*

punishable *kitimahiwewnihk.*

punishment *kitimahiwewin.*

pupil *kiskinohamakaniskesik.*

puppet *acimohkanis; awasihkan.*

puppetry *acimohkanisak ka pekiskwehihtwaw (Northern).*

puppy love *oskihsakihitowin.*

purchase *kîkway ka atawehk; atawew.*

purple *sepihkomehkwaw.*

purport *kîkway ketwemakahk.*

531

purse Or wallet, *sônîyâwiwat (Northern).*

pursuance *ka nawaswatamihk kîkway.*

pursuant *nawaswacikewin.*

push-up *sesawewin.*

putdown *nehtasta.*

put-on *tahkohtasta.*

putty *akoskowahcikan; kipahikan.*

puzzle *wawaneyihtamowin; katapihtahk; masinipayiwin; katapastak.*

pyre *nahinokewahtik.*

python *piscipokinepihk.*

Q

quadrant *kanewayakehtahk kîkway peyak kotinamihk.*

quadruple Four times, *newaw; newaw ayiwâk.*

quagmire *ka tostokahcak.*

quaint Pleasingly odd or unusual, *mamaskatikohkasowin; kayâsikîkway ka meyonakwahk.*

qualification *nahiskamohiwewin.*

qualified Fit and competent, *nahewin; awîyak ka nahiskahk isihcikewin.*

qualifier *awîyak ka nahiskamohiwet.*

qualify *ka nahiskamihk.*

quandary *wanâyâwin.*

quantity How many, *tantahto; tanimayiko;* of several quantities, weight, content, length, *nânantôk.*

quarantine Be in an isolation room, *piskihtaskenahiwewin; ekatamamaweyatik; piskihtaskinewin.*

quarry *ka macetotaht awîyak.*

quart Liquid measure of four cups, *newominihkwacikan; apihtaw tipahopan.*

quarter Twenty-five cents, *peyak sônîyâs;* an animal quarter, *paskesowin.*

quarterly *tahto nistopîsim;* four times a year, *newawpeyakaskîy.*

quarter section *ka newayakihtahk askîy peyak kotinamihk.*

quartet A group of four singers, *newonikamowak.*

quaver A shaking and trembling of a singing voice, *namihtakosowin.*

queen *kihcokimaskwew; kicokimaskew;* the wife of a king, *kihci okimaskwew;* the playing card, *okimaskew pehikan.*

queenly *kihcokimaskwewâyâwin.*

queen mother *omâmâwa kihcokimaskwew (French Northern); kihcokimâskwew okâwiya (Plains).*

quilt A warm bed cover, *kesowakohp; natohkwatêw akohp.*

quilting *natohkwasowena.*

quinine A medicine bark from a certain tree, *maskihkewayakesk; maskeki.*

quintessence *mawaci itah kamewasik kîkway.*

quirk *waneyihtam isâyâwin.*

quiz Asking questions, *kawecihkemowin; ka kwecikemowin.*

quorum The number of members who must be present, *tepipayowin.*

quota A share assigned to one of a group, *pahkipako; taniyekohk ka mekihk.*

quotable *meyopekiskwewin.*

quotation Repetition of words previously spoken, *kahkehtwamimowin; ka masinahikatek awîyak opikiskwewin.*

R

rabbi A Jewish clever person or teacher, *sotawenow kiskinohamâkew.*

rabies *atim wakosowin; ahkosowin; asoskamatowin.*

racer *okakwenakato; kotskawewiyinow;* a racing car and its driver, *okotaskasowew.*

race track *kociskawew meskanahk.*

racial *tantowak aysiyinow.*

racialism *pakwatowin.*

racism *aysiyinowak kapakwatihtwaw (Northern).*

radar *kawehcikemakahk (Northern); kawicihkimakahk (Plains); ispihtakociniwin; tipapiskocihkan.*

radial *tantakohmacipayik kîkway.*

radiator *kesowihkasikan.*

radical *awîyak kakakwi kweskinwet.*

radicalism *kakwi kweskinwewin.*

radio *kanotohtamihk; kapikiskwimakahk.*

radish *mihkotsehkanis; wapikoskatask.*

raffish *kihkac isâyâwin.*

rafter *apahkwanahtik.*

ragweed *maskihkewahtik.*

raid *ka sîsîkoc moskestakehk.*

rail *pîwâpisk ka meskanahkakehk;* a fence pole, *apasoy.*

railing *wasakankanahtik.*

railroad *pîwâpiskomeskanaw.*

raincoat *kîmowanasakay.*

rainwear *kîmowan ayowinsa.*

raisin *sominis.*

rake *asipicikan; kaskipicikan.*

rally *awîyak ka menot; astepayow;* a quick recovery, *astepayowin.*

ramrod *kitistapiskahikan paskisikan ohci; pehtasowin.*

ranch *eta kohpikihihtwaw pesiskowak (Northern);* a large farm for raising livestock, *kanawemostosêwin.*

randy *macesâyâwin.*

ranger *kanaweyicikew.*

rangy *awîyak ka kinosit.*

rank *tanta ka aksohk.*

ransom *tipahikestamâkewin; tipahikewin;*

rarely *metoni namoya kahkiyipa.*

rascal *mâcatis.*

rate *oyakihcikewin.*

rateable *ka oyakihtamihk kîkway.*

ratification *kwayaskopayihcikewin.*

ratify It is confirmed, *masinahikatew.*

rating *oyakihcikewin; itakihcikewin.*

ratio *kwayask oyakihcikewin.*

ration *ka ohtinamâkehk; asahtowin.*

rat root *wacaskomicisowin.*

rayon *senipânekin.*

raze *masakohkahtew.*

reactionary *kîkway ka tôtamomakahk.*

reader *otayamihcikew; masinahikan ka ayamihtahk.*

readership *otayamihcikewak.*

realism *kakwe kihcinahowin.*

realistic *mweci tahtâpwi kîkway;* things as they are, *mweci ekosi.*

ream *mahkisihtawin.*

reamer *âpacecikan.*

reaper *awîyak kanihta mawasakonket.*

rearm *kehtwam nemaskwewin.*

reasoning *kwayask mâmitoneyihcikan.*

rebellion *mayeyihcikewin.*

rebate *tepahikewin ka aseptamâkehk.*

rebirth *kehtwam nihtâwkowin.*

rebut *kîkway ka anwehtamihk.*

rebuttal *anwehtamowin.*

recant *awîyak ka acimso.*

recantation *acimsowin.*

recapitulate *kakehtwam wehtamihk.*

recapitulation *kahkehtwam isihcikewin.*

receipt *ka mwestas mekihk masinahikanis.*

receivable *kîkway ka masinahikew otinamihk; ocicipayow;* an account due from another, *tipahikewin.*

receiver *okahtinikow, ka otihtikot.*

receivership *kîkway ka masaskonewehk.*

receptacle *kîkway ka kahtinkimakahk;* a barrel or a dish, *mahkahk oyakan.*

reception *pehtokahiwewin;* a greeting or welcome, *wehkomowewin.*

receptionist *opehtokahiwew.*

recipe *kestepo masinahikanis; isihtawin.*

reciprocate *ka meskoc meyototakehk.*

reciprocity *meskoc meyototakewin.*

recital *kahkehtwam pekiskwewin.*

recitation *kaka kehtwam pekiskwehk;* recite with me, *ayistohtawin; kisonohtawin.*

reconcile *pekiskwatitowak.*

reconciliatory *kîkway ka meyowecehtahikohk.*

reconciliation *kawe meyowecetowin; kawipekiskwatitowak.*

reconstruction *pîtosehcikewin.*

reconstructive *ka nihtâ pîtosehcikehk.*

record *tapasinaham.*

recorder A registering instrument, *tapasinahikan.*

recruit *awîyak ka mosahkiniht; kamasinahiket.*

rectangle *nistwayak ka isi cepwak kîkway; kakinwak ehasawiyak* (Northern); *ayisawiyahk* (Plains).

redeem S/he pays for it, *tipaham.*

redirect *menotisahewewin.*

redouble *kakâ kehtwam sehtahk.*

red pepper *mehkopeskomin.*

redraft *kehtwam asinahikewin.*

red tape *kwantayiwâk masinahikewin.*

redundance *kwahci tonamowin.*

redundancy *ka nihtâ kwahcitonamohk.*

redundant *awîyak kakwa citonamoskit.*

reel A device for winding fishing line, *kwaskwepicikew tipipicikan.*

refer *ka miskawasihiht awîyak.*

referee *onakateyihcikew;* a hockey referee, *soniskwâtahikew opamomiwew.*

reference *miskawasihiwewin.*

refill *kakehtwam isakaskinahtahk.*

refinery A refiner's factory, *meyosehcikewikamik.*

reflector *cakastenkan.*

reformatory A reforming school, *kiskinohamatokamik.*

reformer *omenosehcikewiyinow.*

refresher *meyomahcihowakan.*

refreshment *mecisowin;* a refreshing rest, *ayiwepowin.*

refrigerate *ka tahkascikehk;* s/he puts it in the cooler, *tahkastaw.*

refrigeration *tahkascikewin.*

refrigerator *tahkascikukun;* a cooling system, *tahkascikan; takascikan.*

refuel *kakehtwam sakaskinahiht askihkos.*

refuge *nakisk ka pesêwikamik; tipinawasimowin.*

refugee One who flees for safety, *otapasêw.*

refund *kawi tipahikewin; asenikewin* (Plains).

refurbish *ahci sehcikewin.*

regenerate *kakehtwam ohpikihtahk kîkway;* make over completely, *kehtwam isihcikewin.*

regeneration *kehtwam ohpikihetowin.*

regenerative *kakehtwam ohpikihcikemakahk.*

533

regent *omeskotapestamâkew;* one who governs when the ruler cannot, *meskotapestamâkew.*

regimen *koyinamâkehk isi metsowin.*

regiment *nôtinitowenihk ka wecihiwehk.*

region *wasakam eta askehk; kitaskenaw.*

register *masinahikanihk kapihk; kanowasinahikewin;* a registrar, *masinahotowin.*

registration *masinahowewin.*

regulation *nahaw isihcikewin; peyakwanisi; ka ispayik.*

rehabilitate *ka kwayaskwahiwehk.*

rehabilitation *kwayaskwahiwewin.*

rehearsal The act of practicing, *sesawewin;* a singing rehearsal, *kotatamowin.*

rehearse *kasesawehk.*

reimburse *sônîyâw katap mekihk; tipahamowew.*

reincarnate *kakehtwam nihtâwkihk.*

reincarnation *kehtwam nihtâwkowin.*

reins *menos kwepicikana.*

reinstate S/he is reinstated, *kawi otinaw.*

remand *kahtastahk weyasowewin.*

Remembrance Day *kiskisokesikaw; kiskisitotaw kîsikâw (Plains).*

remittance *kewetisahamâkewin.*

remodel *ka pîtos nakohtahk kîkway.*

renaissance *kawi ka moskinamihk kîkway.*

render S/he pays for something, *tipaham.*

rendezvous *nakiskatowin.*

renegade *okakayesow; ponayamihaw.*

renege *ka kayesimetawewin.*

renovate *ka nânapacitahk waskahikan;* restore to freshness or new condition, *nânapacitaw.*

renovation *nânapacicikewin.*

rent *wikowin ka tepahamihk;* the act of renting, *nitahtamowin.*

rental The rate paid for rent, *tipahikehiwewin.*

reorder *kehtwam natocikewin.*

reorganization *kehtwam nahawascikewin.*

reorganize *ka kehtwam nahawascikehk; ahcimamawapowak.*

repaid *kehtwam tepahamatowin.*

repairman *onânapacicikew.*

reparation *nânapacicikewin.*

repatriate *ka kewetotamihk askîy.*

repay *tepahikewin;* s/he repaid it, *kawitipaham.*

repayable *kîkway kawi ka tepahamihk.*

repeal *ka nâkînamakehk kîkway.*

repellent *maskihki ka yekatetsahekemakahk.*

repertory *masinahikan koyastahk.*

replica *naspisihcikan;* an exact copy, *tapasinahikewin.*

replication *naspasinahikan.*

reporter *otacimow.*

repository *eta ka nahasicikehk.*

repossession *kawi otinkewin.*

represent S/he is representing them, *nokosestamawew.*

representation *meskocestamâkewin;* the act of representing, *pekiskwestamâkewin.*

representative *pekiskwestamâkew; opimpayihcikestamâkew.*

reprieve S/he was spared for a time, *pakitinawimoniy.*

reprint *ka ahtasnahamihk.*

reprobate *opastahow.*

reproduction *ahkami ohpikehitowin.*

reptile A snake, *kinepik; osikiyâs.*

republic A country, *askîy.*

repurchase *kehtwam atawewin.*

requisition *natôtamawin;* the act of demanding, *natocikewin.*

requital *tepahikipayihcikewin.*

resale *kehtwam atawakewin.*

research *natonikewin; nitawikiskeyihcikewin.*

researcher *onitawahikew.*

reservation *manacitamâkewin; nehiyaw askîy.*

reservoir A large water well, *misimonahipan.*

resettlement *kakehtwam kwayas kosehcikehk.*

residential *ka tawak askîy wikowin ohci.*

residue *aywakipayihcikan;* what is left over, *iskwacikan.*

resign Quitting, *poyowin;* s/he resigns, *pakitinisow;* the act of resigning oneself, *pakitinisowin;* s/he lets it go, *pakiteyihtam.*

resignation *pakiteyimisowin.*

resigned *kakeh poyohk; poyo; pakitinam.*

resin *kitohcikan piko.*

resoluble *maskisina take mesahamihk.*

resonance *kesewepayihcikewin.*

resonate *kesewepayihcikatek.*

resonator *kesewepayihcikakan.*

restaurant *mecisowikamik* (Northern); *mecisokamik (Plains).*

restoration *menosehicikewin.*

restorative *natawihiwewin.*

restriction *keskinamâkewin.*

retrospection *otâhk ka nawapahcikewin.*

retrospective *tânsi ka kehispayik kayâs.*

resultant *tânsi isi ponipayowin.*

resurge *kakehtwam pasehkohk.*

resurgent *kehtwam pasekowin.*

resuscitate *awîyak ka pemacihiht;* the act of bringing back to life by breathing, *ohtacikewin.*

resuscitation S/he gives her/him mouth-to-mouth resuscitation, *otamew.*

resuscitator *otahcikan.*

retainer *ka tepahamaht opekiskwestamâkew*; that which holds in as a retaining wall, *miciminikew*.

retaliate To return a fight, *naskwawin*.

retardant *otahkipicikakan*.

retinue *ayisiyinowak ka askoketwaw (Northern)*; a body of followers or attendants, *opimitisahikewak*.

retirement *poni atoskewin*.

retraction *asepicikewin*.

retractor *asepicikakan*.

retriever *macewatim*; a duck retriever, *natahisîpîyatim*.

return trip *kakwayinohtehk*.

reunification *kawi wecehtowin*.

reunify *kawi wecehtohewewin*.

reunion *kawi ka wecehtohk*.

revamp *ayiwâk meyosehcikewin*.

revenue *sônîyâhkewin*; income from personal property, *kespinacikewin*.

reviewer *otahcikanawapahcikew*.

revisionism *meskoc isihcikewin*.

revisionist *omeskoc isihcikew*.

revivalist *awîyak ka pemacihiwet*.

revoke *keskinamâkewin*; *kaseham*; annul by taking back, *maskahcihiwewin*.

revolt *mawineskakewin*; an uprising against authority, *kisoweyitamowin*.

revolution *mawineskacikewin*; a revolutionary war, *nôtinitowin*.

revolutionist *omawineskacikew*.

revolutionize *mawineskakewin ka sehkiskamihk*.

reward *tipahamâkosiwin*.

rewire *ka meskotastahk pîwâpiskos waskahikanihk*.

rewrite *kehtwamasinahikewin*; s/he rewrites it, *acimasinaham*.

rhapsodic *awîyak ka nihtâ kwahcimot*.

rhapsodical *ka kwahcesâyâwin*.

rhapsodist *awîyak ka nihtâ pekiskwet*.

rhapsodize *kakwahci mamihtocikewin*.

rhapsody *kakwahci mamihcimowin*.

rhetoric *ka nihtâ pikiskwehk*.

rhetorician *opikiskwestamâkew*.

rheumatic fever *anskokanana ka wesakeyihtamihk*.

rheumatism *oskanahpinewin*.

rheumatoid arthritis *miskana ka mayikihkwaw oskanahpinewin ohci*.

rhubarb Rhubbarb leaves, *sewipakwa*; one stalk of rhubarb, *sewipak*.

rhyme *piyakwan ketihtakwahkwaw pikiskwewna*.

ribbing *naniweyacimowewin*.

ridgepole *wawkanahtik waskahikanihk*.

right angle *kihtiniskehk ka itamok*.

right face *kihtinskehk kesi kweskipayihohk*.

right-minded *kwayask mâmitoneyihcikan ka apacihtahk*.

right wing *kihciniskehk isi metahtahkwan*.

ringleader *nîkânew*.

ringworm *ka wasaka moskipayit masakay*; *omîmîmowin (Plains)*.

rink *soniskwâtahekewin*.

riot *ka misi mayahkamikahk*; a big brawl, *wayahkamikan*.

ritual *isihcikewin*.

ritualism *ka kiskinohamakosihk isihcikewina ohci*.

ritually *isihcikewinihk ohci*.

rival Standing in competition with, *ka kwepaskiyakew*.

rivet *napwahpiskahikan*; a metal pin used to fasten pieces together, *sehtapiskatahikan*.

roadbed *koyahcahekehk meskanaw ohci*.

roadblock *ka kipahamihk meskanaw*.

roadhouse *metsokamik sone meskanahk*.

road salt *siwihtakanapoy*.

roadworthy *poko eta ka pimpayet otâpânâsk*.

roaster *nawacewinapisk*.

rocker *wewepisotehtapowin*.

rocket *ispahki pimocikan*.

rodeo *mohkawkanewastimwewnihk*; riding broncos, *katehtapihk*; *emokawikanewastimwek*; *imokawikanihiwastimiwik*.

role *ometawew kawehtamaht tânsi tatôtahk*.

roller coaster *posowin ka wasakakotek*.

roller skate *cicipipayesak ka soniskwâtahikakehk*.

rolling pin *tihtipinikan*; *napakinikan*.

rompers *awâsis asiyanak*; a small child's overalls, *awâsisicasis*.

roof *apahkwan waskahikanihk*.

roofer *otapahkwew*.

roofing *apahkwanekin*.

roofless *ekâ ka apahkwatek waskahikan*.

rooftop *tahkoc waskahikanihk*.

room *piskihcikipahikan*.

roomer *kapesêwenow*.

roomful *kasakaskinewekihk*.

roost *pewayisisak otohowiniwaw*.

rootworm *wacapis manicos*.

rosette A decoration, *wawesecikan*; *wawesêwakanis*.

rose water *wehkimâkwahon*.

rosin *kitohcikapikis*; a violin rosin, *kitohcikanpikow*.

roster A list of names, *wehowina*.

rouge *mihkohkwakanihon*; a red coloring for the face, *mehkokwehowin*.

roughage *kekisepawimecowin*; animal roughage, *asamastimiwewin*.

rough-and-ready *asweyihcekewin*.

rough-and-tumble *pokoyisih kesimawineskamihk*.

535

roughhouse *kisowemetawewin; kisometawewin.*
roughshod *mahmasis kapîwâpiskwahoht mistatim.*
round-shouldered *ka waweyi tihtimanehk.*
round trip *kawayinohtehk.*
roundup *ka akimihtwaw pisiskowak (Northern);* a round up of cattle, *mawasakotisahikewin.*
route *meskanaw kosehtahk; pimoteskanaw.*
row boat *ka asepoyehkosih.*
royal *kihciyihtakosowin.*
rubber *ahkwetaweskisin;* a rubber overshoe, *ahkwetaweskisin;* rubber boots, *pakopewaskisina; pakopiwaskisina; pikiwaskisina.*
rubble *ka sikwatahoht asinîy.*
ruff In a card game, to play a trump, *nikwahkwewin.*
ruffian *ahkwatis.*
rug *aspitahkoskewin.*
ruler One who governs people, *otipeyicikew;* a small measuring stick, *tipahikanacikos.*
rummage Buying at a rummage sale, *wehcinehikewin; oyâpicikewin.*
rumpus room *awâsis metawewikamik.*
runaround *ka wasakapahtahk.*
run-down *netaciwepahtaw.*
runner *opimpahtaw; pimpatawenow.*
running board *tehtahkoskewin.*
running shoes *pimpatowaskisina.*
run-off *ka sekawicowahk nipîy.*
runway An airplane runway, *tohowin.*
rural *peyakwayak mamawâyâwin;* out in the country, *patosayihk.*
Russians *apotasakiyak.*
rye *iskwesisihkan; kistikan.*

S

sabbatical *ka ayemihekesekawayak.*
sabotage *ka kîmôcipekonkehk.*
sable *kaskitew wapiscanis.*
sabre *tahkahtowakan.*
saddlery *aspapowenihkewnihk.*
sadism *ka meweyihtamihk kitimahewewin.*
sadist *okitimahiwew.*
sadistic *kanihtâ kitimahewehk.*
sail A sail on a boat, *yâhkâstimowin;* s/he sails by, *pimasow;* the act of sailing, *pimasowin;* s/he makes her/him sail, *yâhkâstimew;* material for the sail, *yâhkâstimonekin;* s/he sails, *yâhkâstimow.*
sailboat A sail boat, *yâhkâstimon;* the pole on a sail boat, *yâhkâstimonâhtik.*
sailor *oyakastimow.*
salad *askipakomecowin.*
salamander *osikiyasis.*

salary *koyastahk tepahekewin;* earning a salary, *kespinacikewin.*
saleable or salable It is saleable, *atawakaniwan; meyo atawakewin.*
salesman A sales person, *otâtawew.*
salience *semakipayowin.*
salient *ka semakamok.*
saline *sewihtakan kosehcikakehk.*
salinity *sewihtakanowin.*
salon *eta ka tepawehkasamahk.*
saloon *minihkwewikamik.*
sampler *koteyihcikan.*
sanctuary *pewayak eta ka kanaweyimihtwaw (Northern);* a holy convent or mission, *ayamihewikamik.*
sandal *maskisinihkan.*
sandpaper *ka soskopocikakehk masinahikanekin;* a wood smoother, *soskohtakahikan.*
sandpiper *sesesis.*
sandstone *kenpocikew asinîy;* a stone made of sand, *yekawasinîy.*
sandwich *nemaw nihkewinis; nesonikan;* food taken along on a trip, *nemawinihkewin.*
sanitation The act of being clean, *kanâtisiwin; kanâcihcikewin.*
sanity *kanâtsowin; meyopimatan; meyomâmitoneyicikewin.*
sardine *kinosesis.*
sash *wasenamawin tapihcikan;* a window frame, *wasenamawinahtik.*
satchel *masinahikaniwat.*
satellite *wiyâkanihkân.*
satin *senipânekin.*
satire The act of ridicule in writing, *ayimiwewin.*
satirist *otayimiwew.*
sauce *aspahcikewin.*
saucer *aspascikanis; wawiyewiyakanis (Northern); wawiyakanis (Plains); napakiyakanis (Plains).*
sauna *moneyaw matotsan.*
sausage *ocakisesa.*
savagery *pikwaciyinehkewin.*
savings *mawacicikewina.*
sawdust *pewpocikana.*
sawhorse A wood cutting tool, *keskipocimihtakan.*
sawmill *tâskipocikewin;* a board making machine, *tâskipocikan;* a sawmill shack, *tâskipocikewikamik.*
say-so *itwewin.*
scaffolding *akotitahkoskewin ka osehtahk;* a tool for climbing, *kecekosêwin.*
scale *tipâpeskocikan.*
scalp Scalping someone, *paskwatihpepicikewin.*

536

scandal *ka mayahkamikahk; macâyimomitowin;* a disgraceful act, *mayâhkamikisowin.*

scandalize *mayisihcikewin; koskweyihtamowin.*

scandalous *awîyak ka mayisihcikeskit;* it is considered very disgraceful, *koskweyihtakwan.*

scarcity *nawâc poko ka nohtepayik.*

scarecrow *ayisiyinihkan.*

scarlet fever A red skin disease, *mihkwasêwin; mihkwas pinewin.*

scavenger *omosahkahcikew;* a person that goes through garbage, *mosahkacikis.*

scenery *askîy ka wapahtamihk; katinokwak.*

scenery *askîy ka wapahtamihk; katinokwak.*

schedule *pimpayetawin;* the act of making a scheduled arrival, *kiskimowin.*

schism *ka kakwepekonamihk ayamihawin.*

scholar *otiyinesewiyinow;* a student, *kiskinohamowikan.*

scholarly *metoni yinisowin.*

scholarship Being smart or intelligent, *iyinisowin; ka wapahtehiwehk iyinesowin.*

scholastically *kiskinohamâkewnihk isih.*

school A school house, *kiskinohamâtowikamik (Northern); kiskinahamatokamik (Plains).*

school attendance *kiskinohamakosêwin.*

school bus *kiskinohamatotâpânâsk.*

schooling Going to school, *ka kiskinohamâkosihk;* the act of going to school and learning, *kiskinohamâkosowin;* the act of teaching, *kiskinohamâkewin.*

schooner *misiyahkastimon.*

science *iyinesowin ka kiskinohamâkosihk.*

scientist *ayinisêwenow.*

scion A descendant from way back, *aniskaciwahkohtowin.*

scissor A pair of scissors, *paskwahamatowin.*

scone *eyoskihkasot sewpahkewsikan.*

score *pihtokwewepahikewin.*

scoreboard *cawiwin ka akihtamihk.*

scrabble *metawewin pekiskwewinsa kosehtahk.*

scrapbook *masinahikan ka kanaweyihtamihk masinahikewinsa.*

scratch paper *ka wepinkatek masinahikanekin.*

scrawl Careless writing, *mayasinahikewin.*

screen A steel net, *pîwâpiskosakimewayan.*

screwball *owanewiyinow.*

scribbler *masinahikew asinahikanis;* a book, *masinahikan.*

scrim A curtain cloth, *akopicikewekin.*

scrimmage The act of testing one another, *koteyimitowin.*

scrimpy Just enough, *eyitataw.*

script *ka yaskakeh isi masinahikehk;* start writing a script, *matayakmasinahikewin.*

scroll *kayâs ohci masinahikewin ka kanaweyihtamihk;* a roll of decorating paper, *kiskinawacihcikan.*

scruple *ekâ ka nahayâhk.*

sculpt *ayisinehkan kosehiht.*

sculptor A wood carver, *otoyihkocikew.*

sculptress *iskwew ayisinehkana kosehat.*

sculpture *oyihkocikewin.*

sculptured *awîyak ka naspisihiht.*

scurvy *ahkosowin misiwi ka pahpakipayihk; saposowin.*

scythe A grass cutting tool or an instrument for cutting hay, i.e.: a scythe, *manaskosowakan; manaskosiwakan; mansikan;* s/he cuts hay with a scythe, *manaskosiwew;* the act of cutting hay with a scythe, *manaskosiwêwin.*

sea horse An ocean animal, *kicikamepisiskiw.*

seam *pihkikwasowin; pimikwacikan;* sewing a seam on clothes, *pihkikwacikan.*

seaman *kihcikamewenow.*

seamer *pihkikwacikakan.*

seamstress *iskwew okaskwasow;* a dress maker, *miskotakekew.*

seaplane *nipîwpimehakan.*

searchlight *wasaskotenikan ka asawapahcikakehk;* a light for searching, *natonikewaskotenikan.*

search warrant *natonikew masinahikan; simakanis onatonikewasinahikan.*

season *ka atikweskayak; askiw meskwacipayowina; askiwihtâwina; mameskotaskiwin.*

seasonable It is seasonable, *mahmeyokesikaw.*

seasonal Every year, *tahtwaskîy.*

seasoning *kiyikawenikan;* a food mixture, *kiyikawehkasikan.*

seaweed *asisîy.*

secede *ka sîsîkocipoyohk kihci isihcikewnihk.*

secession *ka mekwaweyasowehk.*

second-class *mwecinesow kiskinohamâkewin.*

second nature *kehtwam isâyâwin.*

second-rate *ekâ tâpwl ka mewaslk.*

second wind *kakehtwam atahtamihk (Northern).*

secretarial *masinahikesesowewin.*

secretary *omasinahikeses;* a writer, *masinahikeses; masinahekeses;* s/he is a secretary, *omasinahikesesiwow.*

secret society *okemotatsowak.*

sect *peyakwayi otayamihawak.*

sectarianism *pîtos ayamihawin.*

section *piskihc; pahki.*

sectional *ka piskihcak; papiskicayaw;* it is in sections, *pahpiskihcayaw.*

537

sectionalism *ka piskihteyimohk.*

sectionalize *ka piskihteyihtamohewehk.*

sector *ka pahpiskihtaskatamihk askîy.*

secular *ekâ ka isihkamihk ayamihawin.*

secularism *sehki ka papimatisihk.*

security *nakateyicikewin.*

sedan *sehkepimpayes.*

sedation *ka kamwacihewehk.*

sedative *ka kamwacihekohk maskihki.*

sediment *kakotawpayik.*

sedimentation *mawasakopayihcikewin.*

sedition *kisowi apehowin.*

seditionary *ka kisowi apehohk.*

seedbed *eta ka kiscikisihk.*

seeder *kiscikakanis.*

seedling *oskimiscikos; ahtaskicikewin.*

seedlings *ahtaskicikewina.*

seeing-eye dog *atim ka kiskinohtahiwet.*

seepage *osih ka ocistihk; pehti kweciwan;* water seeping in, *pehtipew.*

see-saw *cahkaskwahotowin.*

segregation *piskihtiyimowewin.*

segregationist *opiskihtahiwew.*

segregative *ka piskihtiyimowayahk.*

seizure *sîsîkoc mayâyâwin; epahkisihk; ocipitikow.*

selection *nawasonikewin.*

self-abasement *peweyimsowin.*

self-abhorrence *pakwateyimsowin.*

self-absorption *takahkeyimsowin.*

self-acting *ka peyak kweyimsohk.*

self-addressed *ka kwayat tasinahamihk weyowin.*

self-assertion *kakeh cinahot akiyimsohk.*

self-assertive *kihcinahot akiyimsowin.*

self-assurance *kihcinahot akiyimsowin.*

self-command *meyo paminsowin.*

self-communion *acimsowin.*

self-conceit *mistan nakiyimowin.*

self-conscious *nepewisewâyâwin.*

self-contained *nihtâ nakinsowin.*

self-contradiction *keyaskehisowin.*

self-contradictory *ka keyaskehisomakahk.*

self-criticism *ekâ ka tâpwehtasohk.*

self-deceptive *ka nihtâ kiyaskimisohk.*

self-denial *aniwehtasowin.*

self-denying *ka aniwehtasohk.*

self-deprecation *âyimihisowin;* s/he is self-deprecating, *âyimihisow.*

self-educated *ka kiskinohamasohk.*

self-esteem *ka takahkeyimsohk.*

self-evident *kîkway ka wapahtehisowin.*

self-examination *kanawapamesowin.*

self-expression *tânsi kesipikisk westamasohk.*

self-filling *ka atamihisohk.*

self-governing *pimpayihisowin.*

self-government *ka paminisotwaw ayisiyinowak (Northern).*

self-help *nesohkamasowin.*

self-important *mistiyimsowin.*

self-indulgence *otinamasowin.*

self-love *sakihisowin.*

self-made *ka osehtamasohk.*

self-moving *ahcipicihisowin.*

self-ordained *tânsi ka isihisohk.*

self-pity *kitimakeyimisowin.*

self-possessed *papeyahtik ka ayâhk; kamwatisow.*

self-possession *papeyahtik mâmitoneyihcikan.*

self-preservation *nakatiyimsowin.*

self-regulating *ka oyinsohk.*

self-reliance *mamisetotasowin; kihcinahowin;* the act of self-reliance, *mamisêwakeyimesowin.*

self-respect *mamihcihisowin;* the act of one's own self-respect, *kihceyimisowin.*

self-restraint *soki miciminsowin.*

self-righteous *kwayaskwesâyâwin.*

self-sacrificing *pakiteyihcikewin.*

self-satisfaction *atamihisowin.*

self-service *ka paminisohk.*

self-sufficiency *tepipayowin.*

self-sufficient S/he does not need help and s/he helps herself/himself, *pimacihisow.*

self-support *pimacihisowin.*

self-sustaining *peyakopaminisowin.*

self-taught *kiskinohamasowin.*

self-will *ka mâmitoneyihtamasohk.*

self-willed *mâmitoneyihtamasowin.*

self-winding *ka mosci wasakanamihk.*

sell *atawaki.*

seller *ocacawes.*

sell-out *mestatawakewin.*

semen *nâpew awâsihkewapiy.*

semester *apihtaw ka pahkwenamihk.*

semi-annual *nikotwasik pîsim;* twice a year, *neswawpeyakaskîy.*

semi-annually *tahto nikotwasik pîsim kespayik.*

semicivilized *ka nomikiskinohamakosihk.*

semicolon *ka piskihtastahk pekiskwewin.*

semiconscious *pawini ka kiskeyihtamihk.*

semimonthly *neswaw peyak pîsim.*

seminal *paskisikew napoy ka otinamihk.*

seminar *ka mamawapik kiskinohamâkewnihk.*

seminarian *okiskinohamâkosow.*

seminary *eta ka kiskinohamâkosihk.*

semi-official *ekâ kihcina isihcikewin.*

semiprecious *ekâ tâpwi mistahi ketiyihtakwahk.*

semiweekly *neswaw peyak ayamihekisekaw.*

semiyearly *neswaw peyak askîy.*

senator A leader in the senate, *anekanapow*.

senile *mocokihkawin*.

senility *ka mohcokihkahk*.

senior citizen *kihtiyinow*.

senior citizen lodge *kiseniwikamik; kisiniwikamik*.

seniority *ayiwâkes kayâs kohtatosket awîyak*.

sensationalism *ka meyowapahtehiwehk*.

sensualism *mosihtawin*.

sensuality *ka wahkew meyomosihtahk*.

sentence *pekiskwewin ka masinahamihk;* putting
  words together, *mamawipekiskwewina*.

sentience *ka nihtâ moyisihk*.

sentient *moyicikewin*.

sentimental *ka kitimâkinakehk*.

separate school *piskihc kiskinohamatokamik*.

separatism *ka paskepayihohk*.

sepulchre *or* **sepulcher** *asiniw kihkwahaskan;* a
  burying shed, *nahinokewkamikos*.

sequel *tânsi ka isi kesipayik acimowin*.

serenade A love song, *sakihitonikamon*.

serf A very poor working man, *kitimak atoskewenow*.

serge A twilled worsted fabric for a jacket,
  miskotakayekin.

sergeant A highly placed cop, *kihcisimâkanis*.

servant A person put to work and doing service for
  someone, *atoskewiyakan*.

service Supplying service, *pamestamâkewin*.

serviceability *kiyapic ka apacitâhk*.

serviceable *kiyapic ka apatâhk;* it is of good use,
  apatan.

service berry *misaskwatomin*.

serviette A mouth wipe, *kasetonewin*.

session *ka mekwaweyasowehk;* a meeting session,
  mamawapowin.

sessional *ka mekwapekiskwehk*.

setback *kotahkipisowehk;* it went backwards,
  otahkepayow.

set-off *ka saskahamihk pahkisawan; sipwehtew*.

settlement *kwayasko sehcikewin; kistapinan;* a
  permanent living settlement, *kisciwikowin*.

settler *otôtinaskew;* a person settled in one place,
  okistapow.

set-to *nôtinikewin*.

sewage *wepinkewina;* thrown away waste,
  wepinkewin.

sewer A sewage pipe, *wepinkew okohtaskwayihkan*.

sewerage *wepinkewinihk*.

sewing machine *kaskikwaswâkan*.

sex appeal *kâkâwâtitohk*.

sexton *okanacicikew ayamehekamkohk*.

shackle *aysiyinew nânapwahpisona;* a hobble,
  napwahpicikan.

shaft *akaskohkan;* a big round piece of steel,
  misinôtim pewapisk.

shaker *pahpawiwepinikan;* a salt container,
  sewintakaniwatis.

shale *asinîy ka pahpahkwepayit*.

shampoo A hairwash liquid, *kisepekistikwanewapoy*.

shamrock Lucky leaves, *papewewpakosa*.

shank *mihcikwanihk ohci capasis miskat; miskat*.

shanty *mahmases kosehtahk waskahikanis;
  napakikamikos*.

shape-up *kwayask ka isâyâhk*.

sharp-eyed *ka nahapihk*.

shay *yahkicâpânâskos*.

sheaf *ka tahkopsot kistikan;* a bundle of wheat,
  pakwesikanihkan tahkopicikan.

sheathing A covering or outer layer, *pehtawenikan*.

shed *ascikewikamkos*.

sheepish S/he looks embarrassed, *nipewinakosow*.

sheet A bed sheet, *anaskanekin*.

sheeting *anaskanekin*.

sheet iron *piwâpisk apahkwan*.

shellac A varnish, *pasakoskowipekanikan*.

shepherd A person who keeps sheep,
  mayatikanawiyicikew.

sherbert A frozen milk, *ahkwacitohtow*.

sheriff *simakanis*.

shiner *wasihkwahikes;* black eye, *apihtapowin*.

shingle *apahkwanihtakwa*.

shingles *apahkwewahtikosa*.

shipment *itsahamâkewin;* loaded freight,
  positasowin.

shipping *sepwetsahikewin; sipwetsahikewin*.

shirt-sleeve *pakowayan ka keskanakweyak*.

shoal A bunch of fish together in a group,
  mecetkinosêwak piskwapiskwaw.

shoeblack *mistikwaskisin wasihkwahikan*.

shoehorn *maskisin poscipcikan*.

shoelace *maskisinyapes; cestanihkwanan*.

shoemaker *omistekwaskisinihkew; maskisinihkew*.

shoeshine *wasihkwa askisinewin*.

shoestring *cestanihkwanan*.

shoe tree *maskisin akocikan*.

shop *atawikamik*.

shopkeeper *atawikamkowiyinow*.

shoplifter *kimotis*.

shopper *opapamatawew*.

shortbread *sewpahkewisikan ka nanihkosehiht*.

shortcake *sewmecowenis kosehtahk*.

shortcoming *ka nohtepayihtahk isâyâwin*.

shortening Lard, *pimiy; pimiy ka kesisikakehk*.

shorthand *pîtos masinahekewin; cimicecew;* fast
  writing, *kisiskamasinahikewin*.

short-handed *ka nohtepayihk otatoskiwak*.

539

short-lived *aciyawes poko.*

short-range *metoni kisowak.*

short-sighted *kisowak nahapowin; namoya nahapow;* s/he can barely see, *namoyanahapow.*

short story *keskaw acimowin.*

short-tempered *wahkew yawesowin.*

short-term *namoya kinwes.*

short-winded *ka wahkewatahtamihk.*

shotgun A gun that fires a small shot, *niskasinewihtak; kotokohtak; paskisikan.*

shotput *asinîy kapimosinihk.*

shoulder strap *nayahcikanyape.*

shovel A steel paddle used for digging soil, *pîwâpiskwapoy.*

showdown *iskwayac ka mawinehotohk.*

showmanship *ka nihtâ wapahtehiwehk.*

shrinkage *otek ka pawacikewin.*

shuck *ka poyakinamihk kiscikansa.*

shut-down *ponihcikewin.*

shut-eye *ka nipahk.*

shut-in *kipahikasowin.*

shutter A thing that shuts, *kipohtenikan.*

shuttle *kahkekwask ka pimpayihk.*

sickle *manaskosowakanis;* a short handled scythe, *manisikanis.*

sideboard A cupboard for dishes, *oyakanikamikos.*

side channel *pimickohpehtokecowahk.*

side effect *mâyipicikewin.*

side-kick *weciwakansemowin.*

sideline *mostapahkewin.*

side road *pimitehkeskanaw; paskeskanaweskanaw.*

side step *iyikatetahkoskewin; iyikatipayihow.*

side-swipe *kitihkahôtowin;* s/he side-swipes her/him, *kitihkahwew.*

sidetrack *paskepayiwin.*

sidewalk *kosehtahk pemohtewin.*

sideway *pemipayow.*

side-wheel *otihtipipayew pimic ka akikamot.*

siding *paskepayowin.*

siege *ka yaskohci ahkosihk.*

sierra A row of mountain peaks, *waceya.*

sieve *sapokawihcikan;* a strainer, *sekopatinikan.*

sightseeing *ka papam wapahcikehk.*

sightseer *opapam wapahcikew.*

signalize *kwayask ka kiskinwahikehk.*

signature *awîyak owehyowin; wehowinkamasinamihk.*

sign language *meciciya ka pekiskwakehk.*

signpost *kiskinowacicikanahtik.*

silhouette *ka masinihcikehk.*

silk Or ribbon cloth, *senipânekin.*

silken cord *senipaneyapiy.*

silky *peyakwan senipânekin.*

sill *ka simakamok napakihtak wasenamawnihk.*

silt *ka mawasakwapotek asiskîy ahpô yekaw.*

silver A coin or change in silver, *pekinsônîyâs;* a piece of silver money, *sônîyâs.*

silvery *ka wasihkwak pîwâpisk.*

simplehearted *ka meyohtwahk.*

simple-minded *ka iyinisêwayahk.*

single file *ka askotohk.*

single-handed *ka peyakohkamatohk; peyakowecesowin;* all by oneself, *peyakohkamatowin.*

single-minded *ka peyako mâmitoneyihtamihk.*

sinus *wesakastanewin.*

siphon The siphoning of gas, *otahtamonikan.*

siren *otâpânâskohk tepwepicikan;* a loud whistle or bell, *sewepicikan.*

sirloin *nawacew wîyâs;* tender meat, *yoskiwîyâs.*

sitting duck *nehpemapowin.*

sixtyfold *nikotwasomitanawaw.*

skate An iceskate, *soniskwâtahikan;* s/he skates, *soniskwâtaham;* s/he is skating, *soniskwâtahikew;* skating, *kasoniskwâtahamihk (Northern);* *mawiniwihtohk soniskwâtamihk (Plains).*

skater *osoniskwâtahikew.*

skating arena *soniskwâtahikewikamik.*

skein *peyakwahpitew sestak; sestak;* a bundle of yarn, *peyakwahpites sestak.*

skeleton Skeleton bones, *cepayoskana.*

skewer A steel rod used in roasting meat, *nawâcewinapisk.*

ski *sôskwacowakan;* a pair of gliding runners, *sôskopemohtakana.*

skiff A flat boat, *napakosi.*

ski jump *sôskwacowew mawinehotowin.*

skillet A roasting pan, *nawacewoyakan.*

skin-tight *sehcipayow.*

skipper *otâhkwaham.*

skit *waweyasinkewinis.*

sky-high *ispimeskamik.*

skylight *apahkwanihk wasinamawin; wasinamawinis; apahkwan wasinamawinis.*

skyline *keskonakwahk wasko.*

skyscraper *kwahtapekikamik.*

skyward *ispimehk isi.*

slapshot *sohki pimocikewepahikewin; pasastewpahikewin.*

slapstick *ka sohkitahekakehk mistik.*

slate *ka masinahikehk asinihk;* a rock you can write on, *masinahikanapisk.*

slave A person who is property of another, *awahkan.*

slaver *otawahkew.*

slavery *awahkewin.*

slave trade *ka atawakehk awahkanak.*

slaw A chopped up cabbage, *otehipak pinisawacikewin*.

sledge *misipakamakan; misi otâpânâsk; pipontâpânâskos pakamahakan*.

sledge hammer *misipakamakan*.

sleepwalker *ka keskwehkwasihk; keskwekwasow*.

sleepwalking *keskwehkwasowenihk ka papamohtehk*.

sleigh A winter vehicle, *pipontâpânâsk*.

sleighing *pipontâpâsowin*.

sleight of hand *miciciya ka nahewakehk*.

sleuth *ka wansehot semakanis*.

slicker A raincoat, *kimowanasakay*.

slinger *owepahaskwew*.

slingshot *wepinaskwan*.

slip-on *maskisina ka posciptamihk*.

slipper A low cut shoe, *keskaskisin*.

slip-up *pacowepinikewin*.

sloe-eyed *ka taseskacapihk*.

slogan *pikiskwewin kapacitahk kaweh atawakehk kîkway; a type of speech, *itwewin*.

sloop *awacikew câpânâskos*.

slot *sônîyâs eta ka posiwepiniht; watis*.

sloth *ka kihtimihk*.

slothful *kihtimowin*.

slow cooker *iyikicikâwihkasikan*.

slow-motion *peyahtik waskawewin*.

slow-witted *ka kepatsowin*.

sluice *ka iskipehamihk; a channel for carrying off surplus water, *sipweciwanihkewin*.

sluice-box *iskipehikan*.

slum In the poor part of the city, *kitimakanohk*.

small-minded *awâsis mâmitoneyihcikan*.

smallpox *ka mihkwasehk; a scabby disease, *omikewin*.

small talk *kwanta kwahcipikiskwewin*.

small-time *namoya kihcina kîkway*.

small-town *apiscôcenas*.

smart aleck *or* **smart alec** *omamaskatikonkew*.

smash-up *sikosinowin*.

smelling salts *kapaswatamihk sewihtakan*.

smelt A type of small fish, *kinosesis*.

smelter *tihkisikewikamik*.

smith *pîwâpiskwiyines*.

smock A top coat, *waskitasakay*.

smoke drift *ka petapahtek*.

smoke fish *namestek*.

smokehouse *kaskapasekewikamik*.

smoke screen *ka wanapasawehk*.

smooth-spoken *ka nihtâwehk*.

smooth-tongued *ka nihtâwitonamohk*.

smokestack *okohtaskwayihkan*.

smut A grain disease, *kistikanahkosiwin*.

snack *ka askawahcikehk; a meal on the run, *naskwehcikewin*.

snack bar *metsokamikos*.

snake pit *kinepikwak wekowaw*.

snakeroot *kinepikocepihk*.

snapshot *masinipayowin*.

snare wire *tapakwaneyapey*.

sneaker *onatciyoscikew*.

snobbery *misteyimisowin*.

snobbish *ka misteyimisohk*.

snooker *tahkahcikewin*.

snoop A spy, *okemotatisow*.

snow blindness *ka paskapaheket konak*.

snow boot *kespakwaw piponaskisina*.

snow-capped *ka wasakonastek wace*.

snowman *ayisinihkan konak kosehcikakehk*.

snowmobile *pipon capânâskos; sôskipayis*.

snowbird *wâpahkwacoweses*.

snowplough *or* **snowplow** A snow cleaner, *wepahakonakan*.

snowslide *ka akwanakonepayik meskanaw*.

sober-minded *ka astepew mâmitoneyihtamihk*.

soccer A football game, *kwaskwentawan metawewin (Northern); kwaskwitowan kataskowiht (Plains); pakatowan katakiskawiht*.

society *mamawehitowin*.

socket *âpahikan; pehtamohtakan; a socket wrench, *pehtamohcikew âpahikan*.

soda *minihkwenis ka wehkasik; a water mixer for drinking, *kiyikawakamihcikan*.

sodbuster *asiskîy ka sikwatahamihk*.

sofa *yoskapowin; a small bed, *nipewinis*.

soft drink *nânotohk isi sewiminihkwewinisa*.

soft-headed *meyohtwawin (Northern)*.

soft-hearted *meyotehewin*.

soft-spoken *ka meyopekiskwewinehk*.

softwood *yoskahtik*.

solar The sun shining solar system, *pîsim wastinohk*.

solder To join with solder, *akohkasikan*.

soldier *simakansihkan nôtinitowenihk; an army soldier, *simakanisihkan*.

solicitation *natôtamawin*.

solicitor *onatôtamestamâkew*.

solitaire *tenikew metawewin*.

solidify *maskawipay wihcikewin*.

solo Singing alone, *peyakônikamowin*.

soloist *opeyakônikamow*.

solubility *miskotisahekewin*.

soluble *tahkipayow; it is dissolved, *tihkipayow*.

solution An explanation of things, *nahipayihcikewin*.

solvency *nihtâ tipahikewin*.

songbird *nikamopîwâyisis*.

song sparrow *waskahikan pîwâyisis ka nikamot*.

541

songster *onihtanikamo*; *nikamosk*; a person who likes singing, *onikamosk*.

soot Stovepipe ashes, *kohtaskwayikanipihko*.

soothsaying *niyak wehtamâkewin*.

soporiferous *nayestaw kawe nepahk*.

soprano *nikamowin*.

sorceress *iskwew ka powamit*.

sorcery *powamowin*; doing something mysterious, *mahtawitôtamowin*.

sot A habitual drunk, *keskwepewenow*.

soundproof *ka kaskamocak waskahikan*.

souvenir *kiskowehikan*.

sovereign *kihcitipeyicikew*.

spacer *tawascikakan*.

spade *piwapiskwapoy*; a digging utensil, *monahikakan*.

spar The pole on a sail boat, *yahkastimowinahtik*.

sparrow A house bird, *waskahikan pîwâyisis*.

spearmint *pikes ka misemiht*.

species *tanta ka ohtaskanesihk*; *itiwa*; all different kinds, *pahpîtositiwa*.

specification *kihcina oyascikewin*.

specimen *wapahtehiwewin*.

spectacle *wapahcekewin*.

spectacled *koskesikohkahk*.

spectacles *miskesikokana*.

spectator A watcher, *okitapacikew*.

speculate *pakwanawatawewin*.

speed-up *nawâc kisiskapayowin*.

spell The reading of words, *ka ayamihtahk pekiskwewina*.

spellbinder *omamaskasihtakosow*.

spellbound *ka mamaskasihtakehk*.

speller *kiskinwahikew masinahikan*.

spice *kekawenikan*; adding herbs to something, *kiyikawehkasikan*.

spiel *ka nihtâ pikiskwehk*.

spike *sakahikan*.

spinach *kistekan ohci nepeya ka mecihk*; soft leafs to eat, *yoskipakwa*.

spindle A spinning rod, *tihtipicikan*.

spinner *kwaskwepicikan emihkwanis*.

spinoff *sipwepayihcikewin*.

split-second *mweci tanima cipahekanis*.

spokesman S/he talks for people, *pekiskwestamâkew*.

spokesperson Someone who speaks for other, i.e.: a spokesperson or a lawyer, *opekiskwestamâkew (Northern)*.

sponge *sopahcikakan*.

sponger *ka sopahcikakehk*.

sponsor *nemihitowinikew*.

sponsorship *nîpawestamâkewin*.

sports day *metawew kesikaw*.

sportsmanship *ka meyo metawewiyinewihk*.

spot check *meskanahk ka nakiniwehk*.

springboard *pakasimow kwaskwepayihowin*.

spring fever *kasekwanasipinehk*.

spruce budworm *manicos sihtihk ka ayat*.

spruce hen *oskahtakopihew*.

spur *paskepayowin*.

spy *okemotapahkew*; a spying person, *okemotapahkew*.

squab A baby pigeon, *omemesis*.

squad A group of soldiers, *simakanisihkanak*.

squadron A group of pilots, *opimehawak*.

square It is square, *ayisaweyaw*.

squatter *otôtinaskew*.

squire *onakatiyimowew*.

stabilizer *sohkisihcikakan*.

stable *mistatimokamik*.

stadium *misimetawewikamik*.

staff *otatoskewak*; people on the job, *masinahikehakanak*.

stag beetle *napakimanicos*.

stage *metawewanaskewin*.

stager *otanaskihtakohkew metawewna ohci*.

stair Steps, *amacowewnahtik*; steps for going up, *amaciwewin*.

staircase *tahkoskewna kosehtahk amacowewinihk*.

stairway *kihcekosêwinahtik*; a climbing stairway, *amaciwenahtik*.

stamp A postage stamp, *masnahikanihk oscikwanis*; s/he stamps her/his boots, i.e.: to remove snow or dirt, *pahpawistesimow*; putting a stamp on a letter, *okimawostikwan*; *tipahikewin*.

stampede *nakayahastimiwewin*; *mohkawkanehastimiwewin*.

stanchion *setwaskwahikanahtik*.

standard of living *tânsi isi pîmatisiwin*.

stand-by *kwayatapowin*.

stand-in *omeskocestamâkew*.

standing room *sakaskinekapawiwin*.

stand-off *askamacikewin*.

standpoint *kihci mamiskocikewin*; standing at a point for view, *itapowin*.

standstill *ka koskwawacikapawihk*; *keyamikapawow*.

stand-up *ka simacikapawihk*.

staple *pîwâpisko sakahikanis*; a tool for fastening something, *sakamohcikan*.

stapler *pîwâpisko sakahikakan*.

stardom *metoni nîkâneyihtakosowin*.

starter *mâcipayihcikakan*.

starting point *mâcipayowin*.

state *tânsi ka itamahcihohk*; *itwe*.

statesman *kihcimohkomaninahk ohci okimâw*.

542

statesmanship *kihci mohkomanowiwin.*

statement *itwewin.*

stateswoman *okimaskwew kihci mohkomaninahk ohci.*

static *kiceskwew.*

station *nakewin;* a stopping place, *kipecewin.*

stationery Writing material, *masinahikewina.*

statism *kihci mohkomanowiwin.*

statistic *wehyowin masinahikanihk kastahk.*

statistics *masinahikanihk ka apihk;* keeping track of things, *akihcikewina; wîhona kâkitamihk.*

statuary *ayisinihkanak kosehihtwaw (Northern).*

statue An image of a person, *ayisiyinehkan.*

statuette *apisisit ayisinehkan.*

status The act of relative standing, *wahkohtowin.*

status quo *isihcikewin tanta ka ayamakahk.*

statute *weyasowewin koyascikatek.*

stave A piece from a wooden barrel, *mahkahkwahtik.*

steak *nawâcewîyâs.*

steam bath *moneyaw matotsan.*

steamboat *iskotewosi.*

steam boiler *ohtewapoy ka maskawisemakahk.*

steamer *iskotewosi;* a steam ship, *ka skapahtewosi.*

steel *pîwâpisk.*

steel cable *pîwâpiskopeminahkwan.*

steelhead *mistahi namekosak.*

steeplechase An obstacle horse race, *nayitawikociskawewin.*

stein *misi minihkwacikan.*

stele *kehkwahaskanihk kacimatahk mistik.*

stellar *kîkway peyakwan acâhkos.*

stellate *peyakwan acâhkos ka isinakwahk.*

stemmer *onakinowew.*

stemwinding *metoni nîkânewin.*

stencil *wewekinikakan;* a form of branding, *masinaskisikewin.*

stenography *masinatahikewin.*

step-down *nici tahkoskewin.*

step-in *pehtoki tahkoskewin.*

stepladder *kihcikosêwinahtik.*

stepper *onesosimow.*

stepping stone *ahasaw tahkoskewin.*

step-up *ispimihk isi tahkoskewin.*

sternum *maskanikan.*

stew *pakahcikewin.*

steward A person that helps people, *opamihiwew; nâpew ka nakatiyimowet posowenihk.*

stewardess *iskwew ka nakatiyimowet pimehakanihk.*

stewardship *nakatiyimowewin.*

stewpan *mecimapoyakan.*

sticker *sakicihcikan.*

stickhandle *meciminikanahtik.*

stickle *kwetate isâyâwin.*

stickpin *kiskinowacihon.*

stick-up *sônîyâw ka kimotihk.*

stiff-necked *ka setaw kwayawehk.*

stigma *misiwanacipayowin.*

stigmatism *kwatakihewewin.*

stilt *ka pemohtewakehk mistikwa.*

stimulant *maskihki kôtinamihk;* something that makes a stronger heart, *maskawitehenikan.*

stipend *aspehtaw kîkway ka tipahamihk.*

stock A herd of cattle, *pisiskowak.*

stockade *ka kipowasakanamihk wikowina.*

stockstill *metoni ka ayiwastihk.*

stocktaking *masihikanihk kastahk atawakana.*

stockyard *pisiskow wasakanikan;* a cattle fence, *pisiskowasakanikan.*

stone-blind *metoni ekâ kîkway ka wapihk; paskapowin.*

stoneboat *awacikew câpânâskos.*

stone-broke *ahpô ekâ peyak pîwâpiskos kosônîyâmihk.*

stonecutter *asiniw mansikakan.*

stone-deaf *metoni ekâ ka pehtamihk.*

stone's throw *asinîy kesko pemosinehk.*

stooge *omihsihkemow.*

stook *kistikan cimacikewin.*

stool *cehcapowenis; tehtapowinis.*

stool pigeon *omisihkemow; omisimiwew.*

stoplight *wasaskotew nakinikakan.*

stopoff *nomih nakewin.*

stop order *natsahikewna ka nakinamihk.*

stopover *nayewâc ate kapesowin.*

stopper *onakinikew;* a plug, *kipahikan.*

stop-watch *pîsimohkanis ka nakinikakehk.*

storage Safekeeping, *astacikowin.*

store *atâwewkamik (Northern);* storing away, *nahascikewin; atawikamik (Northern); atowikamik (Plains).*

storehouse *ascikewikamik.*

storekeeper *atawikamikowiyinow.*

store manager *ocacawes (Northern); atowikamikowinow (Plains).*

storeroom *ascikewikamikos.*

storey *ka ispimihtakowik waskahikan.*

stork A long legged bird, *ocahk; pîwâyis akamaskehk ohci.*

storage *astahcikowin; astacikowin.*

storm cellar *watihkan sepa waskahikanihk.*

storm centre or storm center *eta kohmacipayik mayikesikaw.*

stout-hearted *sohkitehewin.*

stowage *nahasicikewin.*

stowaway *ka kîmôciposit napihkwanihk.*

543

straight-arm *kwayaskopiton.*

straightaway *metoni kwayask itiyisih.*

straightway *kakwayaskwak meskanaw;* straight ahead, *kwayask nîkân.*

strait-laced *naspic meyo isâyâwin.*

strangulate *ka nakinamihk mihko.*

strangulation *nepahikipihkitonenikewin.*

strategic *katawa ka isihcikehk.*

strategical *kwayaskowepinikewin.*

strategics *kwayaskosehcikewna.*

stratification *kahkehtwam sehcikewin.*

stratify *kaka kehtiwamastahk.*

straw-hat *maskosêwastotin.*

straw man *ayisinihkan kosehiht pawatahikewna ohci.*

streamer *masinahikanekin ka wawesehcikakehk;* a decoration, *kiskanawacecikan.*

streamlet *sîpîsowayis;* a little trickling stream, *sîpîsisihkan.*

streamline *pewapis komeskanaw.*

street *ôtenawimeskanaw.*

stretcher *onkataskwahekakan ayisinow ohci;* a stretcher for pelts, *sepahikan;* s/he stretches them on a stretcher, *sepahwew.*

striation *nânatohk wasinasowin.*

stridden *pehtahamewin.*

strike-bound *ka wehnakinkatek atoskewin.*

strikeout *nistwaw ka patahoht pakahacowanis* (Northern).

striker *opakamahikew.*

stripling *oskayisiyinow;* a young fellow, *oskinekes.*

stripped-down *ketayowinsêwin.*

stroller *awâsiscâpânâskos.*

strong-arm *maskaw pîtonewin.*

strongbox *sônîyâw mistekowat kamaskawisehcikatek.*

stronghold *maskawisêwin ka ayâhk.*

strongman *maskawisêwin ka nokohtat awîyak.*

strong-minded *ka maskawak mâmitoneyihcikan.*

structural *osehcikewinihk.*

structure *kîkway ka osehtahk; manokewin.*

stubble *ka kisimanisoht kistikan; sekawaskose;* a clean cut grain or hay field, *sekawakosowewin.*

stucco *ka asinihkahtek waskahikan wayawetimayihk ohci;* putting stucco on the wall, *asiniwinikacikewin.*

stuck-up *mistahi kitiyimsohk.*

studio *sopekahikewikamikos.*

stuffing *sakaskinahcikan pîwâyis ka nawâcehk; sepahikewin.*

stylize *pîtos ka isimeyosehcikehk.*

subconscious *pakwanaw kiskiyihcikewin.*

subculture *pîtos isihtwawinihk kawecihewehk* (Northern).

subdivide *pahpiskihc tipahaskewin.*

subdivision *ka pahpiskihc tipahaskatamihk.*

subfamily *neswayak kohtaskanesihk.*

subgroup *piskihc mamawintowin.*

subheading *ka piskiht tasinahikatek.*

subjection *mamiskocikewin.*

subjective *ka nakayamamis kotamihk.*

subliminal *metoni kihcitwaweyihcikewin* (Northern).

submarine An underwater boat, *kosapewosi.*

submersion *itampek âyâwin.*

subnormal *astam ekohkes nawâc.*

suborder *ekâ kihcina eta ka wecihiwehk.*

subordinate *ka macetwat onekanapo.*

subordination *macetwawâyâwin* (Northern).

subscribe *acimomasinahikan ka tipahamihk;* consent to receiving a magazine or paper, *natisaham.*

subscription A book or paper for reading, *masinahikan; ka natisahamihk masinahikan.*

subserve *ka mîyo apatisihk.*

subservience *mîyo apatsowin.*

subsidize *ka nometipahamihk.*

subsidy *nometipahikewin.*

subsist *metoni ketisk pimatsowin.*

subsistence *tânsi kesi pimacehisohk.*

substance *kosehcikakehk kîkway.*

substandard *mamasesihkewin.*

substructural *ka tehtastek ita waskahikan.*

substructure *piwapisk komeskanaw ka oyastahk.*

subtile *pîtoseyihkasowin.*

subtenancy *kakehtwam awehowehk wikowin.*

subterfuge *wayesipaskeyakewin.*

suburb *eskwayak ôtenaw;* in a town, *ôtenahk.*

subversion *mayepayihiwewin.*

subvert *mayiwehowin ka mekihk.*

subway *kotawipayew meskanaw.*

succession *kahkehtwam; meskotapestamâkewin.*

successor *meskotapestakew.*

suchlike *mweci ekotowa.*

sucrose *sesepaskwat kosehcikakehk.*

sudden death *nanakahetowin ka pekonamihk; sisikotahpinewin.*

sue Making a petition against someone in law, *sehkitsahikewin.*

suede *apihkan.*

sufferance *ekâ meyote kotinowehk.*

suffix *otâhk ohci ka takwastahk.*

suffocate *ka kipwatamopayihk; kipotamow.*

suffocation *kipwata mopayowin.*

suffrage *ka pimpahtatôtamihk nekanewin.*

suffuse *tahkoc sopekahikewin.*

544

suffusion *tahkoc kasopekahamihk.*
sugar *sewinikan; sesipaskwat.*
sugar cane *sesipaskwatwahtik.*
suicide *nipahisowin; nipahisow.*
suit *peyakayowinis.*
suitcase *asowacikan;* a traveling bag, *pamohtew maskimot.*
sulferstone *osawiskwaw.*
sulphur *or* **sulfur** A chemical used in medicine, *kotawakan; kâkwahkotek (Plains).*
summer cottage *nîpinikamkos.*
summer house *nîpin waskahikan.*
summer resort *nîpin ka pesêwikamik.*
summoner *onatohkemow.*
summons An order to appear in court, *weyasowewasinahikan.*
sun-baked *pîsim kakes siket.*
sun bath *astamastesinowin.*
sunbonnet *pîsim ascocinis.*
sunburn *kosamihkasohk pîsim ohci.*
sundog *ka nemiskotawehtet pîsim.*
sun-dried *pîsimohk ka pasikehk.*
sundry *pîsimopasikewin.*
sunflower *pîsimonepehkan.*
sun-glasses *pîsim oskesikohkana.*
sunspot *ka masinasot pîsim.*
sunstroke *ka nestotehehkasohk.*
sunsuit *nîpinayowinsa.*
suntan *ka pihkahtekasohk.*
superabundance *wawîyak weyotsowin.*
superabundant *wawîyak mistahi kîkway.*
superdominant *wawîyak okimâwakiyimowin.*
supereminent *metoni mistapowin.*
superficial *waskitasakay;* it sits on top, *tahkohtastew.*
superficiality *namoya kihcina isihcikewin.*
superficially *kwanta pakwanaw.*
superfine *metoni ka mewasik.*
superfluity *ayiwâk isâyâwin.*
superfluous *ayiwâk tôtamowin.*
superheater *naspic ka meyosit awasiwakan.*
super-highway The main road, *kihchmeskanaw.*
superhuman *metoni ka takahki iyinekehk.*
superintend *pimpayihcikewin.*
superintendence *ka pimpayihcikehk.*
superintendency *ka nîkânapestamihk.*
superintendent *onekanapow.*
superlatively *ayiwakeyihcikewinihk.*
superman *metoni ka maskawisit awîyak;* a super person, *kihciyinow.*
supermarket *misi atawikamik.*
superposition *tahkohtasicikewin.*
superscribe *kakehtwam asinahamihk.*

supersede *ka meskotasicikehk.*
superstition *kwanta tâpwehtamowin.*
supervision *nakatiyimowewin.*
supervisor *onakatiyimowew.*
supervisory *tânsi ka isi nakatiyimowehk.*
suppository *maskihkiya miciskihk ohci.*
supremacy *mistiyimowin;* state of being in high power, *nîkânihtakosowin.*
surgeon *maskekewenow kamanisowet.*
surgery *manisikasowin;* the act of surgery, *manisowewin.*
surname Someone's last name, *owehowin; otasipikasowin; otasipiwihowin.*
surpass S/he does better than her/him, *paskiyawew.*
surplice *wâpiskasakay.*
surplus *ayiwâkipayiwin.*
surrogate *meskotahiwewin.*
survey *ka tipahaskehk; tipahaskatam;* making a survey of land, *tipahaskewin.*
surveyor *otipahaskew.*
suspenders A pair of suspenders, *pîmakamepisona.*
suspension bridge *asokan ka miciminisomakahk.*
suture *ka sihpokiwatihk masakay.*
swab *kisepekihtakinikakan.*
swabber *okisepekihtakinikew.*
swain *oskinekes.*
swampland *ka maskekwahcak.*
swarm *kohpweskahtwaw âmôwak (Northern).*
swash buckler A scared bully, *sakotehesk.*
swathe *manisikewin.*
swayback *kahkekwask kespayik.*
sweatband *pasiskwehpeson.*
sweat bath S/he is having a sweat bath, *matotisow.*
sweater *kesowasakas.*
sweet potato *sewilapatakwa (Northern, French Cree).*
sweatshirt *keskipakowayan.*
sweeper A person who sweeps, *owepahikew.*
sweepstake *ka misi otahowehk sonîyâw.*
sweetner A sweetening agent, *sewinikan.*
sweetmeats *ka sewakwaw wîyâsa.*
sweet talk *meyopekiskwewin.*
sweet tooth *kawehkistamihk sewayi.*
swift-footed *ka tastap pemohtehk.*
switch *meskotonikewin; pasastehikan.*
switchback *meskanaw ka wahwakamok.*
switchblade *mohkoman tasipicikan.*
switchboard *ka mahmes kotamohtahk pîwapiskosa.*
switchgear *meskocipicikakana.*
switchman *omeskocipicikew iyinow.*
switchover *meskotamohcikewin.*
switchyard *pîwapiskomeskanaw ka mahmeskocipitamihk.*
swivel *pîmikanapisk.*

545

swivel chair *tehtapowin ka wasakapayik*.
swizzle stick *itihikakan*.
sycamore A kind of special tree, *metosahtik*.
syllabic Syllabic writing, *nehiyawasinahikewin (Northern)*; *nihiyawasinahikewin (Northern)*; it is written in syllabics, *nehiyawasinahikatew*; syllabic writing, *cahkipehikana*.
syllable *ka akayasew asinahikatek nehiyawewin*; the forming of words, *pekiskwewinisa*.
sylvan *metoni patosayihk kayak*.
symbol *kiskinawacicikan*.
symbolic *kiskesohikowin*.
symbolism *ka nihtâ kiskisohiwehk*.
symbolist *okiskisohiwew*.
symbolize *kiskisohiwewin*.
symptom *tânsi ka itamahcihohk*; *pisiskapahtam*; the signs of a certain disease, *nistawinakwan*.
synagogue *sotaweniwotayamihewikamik*.
syndicate *omamawinitowak*.
syringe *pehtapawacikakan*; something to pump liquid into the body, *pehtapawacikan*.
system *tânsi ka isi wepenikehk*; *isi cikewin*; *paminikewin*.
systematic *katawa isi wepinikewin*.
systematically *katawa isi wepinikewnihk*.
systematize *katawa ketascikehk*.
systemic *katawa ketastek*.
systemize *katawa ketastahk*.

546

T

tab *sônîyâw ka masinahikehk*; keeping tab, *nakateyicikewin*.
table land A flat piece of land, *tahtawawaskîy*.
tabby *noseminôs*; a cat, *minôs*.
tablespoon *mehkwan*; *ka misitit emihkwanis*.
tablet *ka masinahamihk masinahikanekin*; medicine you swallow whole, *misiwepayicikana*.
tableware *nânatohk isi oyakana*.
tabulate *katawa ka itascikehk*.
tabulation *ka oyakihcikehk*.
tacit *ekâ kake cinahohk*.
tacitly *kwanta mamases pekiskwewin*.
tack *sakahikanis ka akosakahikakehk*; a small nail, *sakahikanis*.
tackle *ispakepicikan*.
tactical *manatisewâyâwin*.
tactics *tânsi ka isiwepenikehk*.
tag *awâsis metawewin*; a small tag, *kiskinowatasinahikanis*.
tail lamp *otâhk ohci wasaskotenkan*.
tail light *otâhk wasaskotenkanis*.

tailor *otayowinisihkew*; one who makes clothes, *ayowinsihkew*.
tailoring *ayowinisihkewin*.
tail wind *ka namowanak*.
take-off *ohpahowin*.
talebearer *omisihkemow*.
talebearing *ka misihkemoskihk*.
taleteller *otatayohkew*.
talisman *ka naspesehiht ayisiyinow tapiskoc emamahtawisit*.
talking-to *ka kisowepekiskwatiht awîyak*.
tall story Or tale, *kiyaskew acimowin*.
tamale *meciwin*.
tambourine *kitohcikan*.
tamp Press, *sehtatahikewin*.
tamper *ayapinikewin*.
tampon *akopsowin mihko ohci*.
tandem *ka aniskosimiht otâpânâsk*; a vehicle pulling a load behind, *sakapekinkan*.
tangerine A small orange, *osawâsis*.
tangy *sokemakosowin*.
tank *nôtinikew*; *tâpânâsk*; a container, *asowacikan*.
tankard *minihkwewaskihk*.
tanker *osihkawatat pimîy*; *nôtinikew osih*.
tankful *ka sakaskinet otâpânâsk*.
tank truck *otâpânâskipimîy ka awatat*.
tannic A type of dye, *atsikan*.
tap dance *nesosimowin*.
tape A measuring tape, *tipapekinikan*.
tape-recorder *ka pehtokepayihtahk kitohcikewin*.
tape recording *pehtokepayihcikan*.
tapestry *pehcayihk ohci wawesehcikana*.
tapioca *sewikestepowin kosehtahk*.
tar Black pitch, *kaskitepikow*.
tariff *akihtamâkewin*.
tar sand *iyikaw ka pekewik*.
tart It tastes sour, *ahkospakwan*.
tartan A woolen or worsted cloth with various colored stripes, *pekisekin*.
tassel A pendant or fringe of threads, *kosawepicikan*.
tat Knotted thread with shuttle to make lace, *apehkewin*.
tattoo *ka petowehekehk mistikwaskihk ohci*; *ka masinaskisikasohk*; an inscription on the skin, *masinaskisikasowin*.
taupe A grayish brown color, *wepinakwan*.
tavern *minihkwewikamik*.
tawny Dark brown in color, *kaskitewosawisow*.
tax *sônîyâw ka akihtamâkehk atoskewinihk*; an enforced contribution to public funds, *okimâwtipahikehiwewin*.
taxability *sônîyâw akihtamâkewin*.

taxation *tipahikehewewin;* the act of paying tax, *ka tipahikehk.*

taxi *pimohtahiwewin ka tipahamihk;* a car for public hire, *oposihiwew.*

taxicab *sehkepimpayes; otâpânâsk ka pimohtahiwet.*

taxidermy The art of stuffing animal skin, *sepaskwacikewin.*

taxonomy *kwayaskweyihcikewin.*

taxpayer *otipahikew kahkiyaw kîkway ohci.*

tax rate *okimanahk koyastahk tipahikewin.*

tea cosy or **tea cozy** *ka weyakihkakamik lete (French Cree).*

teacup *minihkwacikan; letewyakanis (Northern, French Cree).*

teacupful *peyak minihkwacikanis îyikohk.*

teamwork Working as a team, *mamawi atoskewin.*

tear bomb *apisasik pahkisawanis.*

tea set *peyakwayisa lete ohci (French Cree).*

teaspoon *apiscimihkwanis.*

tea towel *ka seyakanakan.*

technical *nihtaw sehcekewin.*

technicolor or **technicolour** *nânatohkopehikewin.*

technique *tânsi ka isinanehk;* knowing how, *ka kiskeyihtamihk.*

teddy bear *metawakan maskohkanis;* a stuffed toy bear, *maskohkan.*

teen-age *ka oskayowihk.*

teenager *awîyak ka oskayowit;* a young teenaged girl after puberty, *oskinikiskwesis;* a young teenaged boy after puberty, *oskinikes.*

teens Young people, *oskayisak.*

teetertotter *cahcahkaskwahotowin.*

teething *awâsis ka maci sakapitet.*

teetotal *ekâ ka isihkamihk minihkwewin.*

telecast *acimowin ka cikastepayihtahk;* what is seen on television, *kawapahtamihkosapacikanihk.*

telegram *wehtamatowin.*

telegraph *wehtamatowin ka sipwetisahamihk piwâpiskosihk;* sending a telegram, *piwâpiskosipiwetisahikan.*

telephone *piwâpiskos;* talking through the phone to one another, *seweptamatowin.*

telephoto lens *ka masinpayihcikehk.*

telescope *kanawapakan wahyaw ohci;* an instrument to make objects look closer, *kanawapahcikan.*

teletype *ka sipwetisahamihk pikiskwewin ka masinahikepayik.*

televise *kosapacikewacimowin.*

television *cikastepayihcikan; kosapacikan; kanawapacikan; moniyaw kosapahcikan.*

teller One who counts money at a bank, *otakihcikew.*

temple *kayâs mawemoscekewkamik.*

tenancy *eta ka wekihk.*

tenant *onitahtamow.*

tenantry *peyakwanohk ka ahkamiwawekihk.*

tenderfoot S/he is tender footed, *kaketisow.*

tenderloin *otastisewak.*

tenement *mamawi wikowin.*

tenement house *waskahikan eta ka mamawiwekihk.*

tenet *tapeyihtamowin.*

tenor A singing voice of high range, *wacewew nikamowin.*

tenpin *metawewin ka kawatahamihk miscikosa;* a bowling game, *metawewin.*

ten-strike *mitatahtwaw ka sewesihk pesimohkan (Northern).*

tent *pakwayanikamik.*

termite *manicosak kesopwenohk ohci;* an ant worm, *ayikos; mohtew.*

tern *nisto akihtasona ka otahowewakehk;* a seagull, *kiyask.*

terrace The balcony on a house, *nawesehcikan.*

terrapin A sea turtle, *miskinahk.*

terrier A small dog, *acimosis;* a hairy faced dog, *cimstâw wihkew atim (Plains).*

territorial *pahpiskihtaskewin.*

territorially *pahpiskihtaskanesowenihk.*

territory A separate piece of land, *kapiskihtaskiwik;* aboriginal land or territory, *nehiyawaskîy;* a piece of land, *askîy.*

547

terrorism *sekihtasowin.*

terroristic *ka nihtâ sekihiwehk.*

testate *ka kesehtahk kihcipekiskwewin.*

testify *awîyak kapîkiskwehiht; pîkiskwew;* giving testimony in court, *pîkiskwewin.*

testimonial *pîkiskwehiwewin.*

testimony *acimsowin; itacimowin;* a statement made under oath, *kihcipîkiskwewin.*

tête à tête A friendly talk, *meyopîkiskwewin; acimostatowin.*

textbook *masinahikewasinahikanis;* a book used for instruction, *kocew masinahikan.*

textile *ayowinsikîkwaya;* a durable piece of cloth, *maskawekin.*

textually *masinahikasowenihk isi.*

textural *masinahikanihk kîkway kastek.*

thatch Putting a roof on, *apahkwewin.*

theatre or **theater** *cikastepayihcikew kamikohk;* a picture show hall, *cikastepayew.*

theatric *masinipayihcikewin.*

theatricality *masinipayihcikew isâyâwin.*

theme *kosehtahk nikamowenis wehowin;* a discussion, *itwewin.*

thence *mena ekospe.*

thenceforth *oteh ati nîkân.*

thenceforward *tahki ayiwâk nîkân.*

theological *ayamihew kiskenohamâkosowin.*

theology *ayamihawin ka kiskenohamâkosihk;* the study of religion, *ayamihaw kiskeyihtamowin.*

theoretical *ekâ kakihcinahohk.*

theoretically *ekâ kihcinahowenihk.*

theoretician *awîyak kantaw kihcinahot.*

theorist *onatotisahekiw.*

theorize *kakwi tapeyimowewin.*

theory *kakwi tapeyihcikewin.*

thereabouts *ekota nânitâw; nânitâw ekota.*

thereafter *mwestas iyikohk; mwestas.*

thereat *ekota anta.*

thereby *tasepwa; kisiwak.*

therefrom *ekota ohci.*

therein *ekota pehcayihk.*

thereinto *eta ka pehtokepayihk.*

thereof *ekota ohci.*

thereon *ekota tahkoc; ekota astew.*

thereto *ekota atihmwestas.*

thereunder *sepa ohci.*

thereunto *nîkân ohci.*

thereupon *macika mwestas; ekota.*

thermometer A measure of temperature, *kisintipahikewin.*

thick-headed *kispakistikwanewin.*

thick-skinned *kispakasakayewin.*

thick-witted *ka kepatsowin.*

thimble *kaskwasonâpisk.*

thimble berry *miskisikomin.*

thimbleful *kaskwasonâpisk esakaskinet.*

thine Another word for you, yours, thou, *keya.*

thin-skinned *ka papakasakayesihk.*

third-class *mwehci nisto ka aksohk.*

third degree *mwehci nisto ka akihtek.*

third party *mwehci nisto ka aksotwaw (Northern).*

thither Towards that place, *ekote.*

thorax *meyaw;* the breast part of the body, *meyaw maskanihk.*

thoroughfare *meskanaw;* a main road, *kihcimeskanaw.*

thoroughgoing *ayâhkwateyihtamowin.*

thrasher *kistikan pawahikan;* a thrashing machine operator, *opawahikew.*

threadbare Very raggy and shabby, *sikwacipayow; ka mestiskamihk ayowinsa.*

three-ply *nistwaw ka ahkwehtawamok.*

thresher *ka pawahikemakahk;* a threshing machine, *pawahikan.*

threshold *aspitahkoskewin;* a doorsill, *iskwahtemahtik.*

throne *kihcokimaw apowin;* the king's seat, *kihci okimâwotapiwin.*

throng *kakwayakahkamik ayisiyinowak.*

throttle *pîwâpiskomeskanaw ka pimpayihcikakehk;* a valve regulating the fuel to a motor, *yohtepicikan.*

throughout *sapwayihk isko;* all over the place, *misiwete.*

through street *ka sapopayik meskanaw.*

throwaway *ka iyikate pimosinehk.*

throwback *otâhk ka isiwepinamihk.*

thug *nipahtakew;* a geniune cut throat, *onipahtakew.*

thumbscrew *ka mosci peminamihk sakahikanis.*

thumbtack *ka makonasihk sakahikanis.*

thyself *keyamaka; keyatipiyawe.*

tiara An ornament worn on the head by women, *kihci astotin.*

ticket *posewasinahikanis;* a bus or train ticket, *posewasinahikan.*

tick-tack-toe *mecawewinis.*

tidal *okihcikami ka iskipipayik.*

tiddlywinks *metawewinis oyakansa eyâpacihtahk.*

tide *nipîy iskipew; nipîy ihkipayow iskipewin;* the tide is up, *iskipepayow.*

tie-in *neswapisowin.*

tier *otâhkopecikew; peyakow pimascikewin.*

tie-up *nomih nakewin.*

tiff *ka kisowayasihk.*

tiger *pekwaciminôs.*

tigerish *peyakwan pikwaciminôs.*

tiger lily *yoskihtepakwa.*

tight-fisted *ayimisowin; sasakisêwin.*

tight-lipped *kasowewin.*

tights *sehcipayew mîtas.*

tight squeeze *sehcisenowin.*

tightwad *sasakisêwin.*

tile *napakihcakosa ka anaskehk;* a thin plate of clay used as building material, *asiniwosehcikana.*

tiling *anaskewna.*

till *sônîyâwocipicikan.*

tillage Cultivation of land, *pekopicikewin.*

tiller *tahkwahikan.*

timberland *ka mistikoskak.*

timber limit *eta ka otinahtikwehk.*

timber line *eta ka iskwaskweyak.*

timber raft *mistikomihtot.*

time exposure *masinipayihcikewin.*

time-honoured *kayâs manacicikan.*

timekeeper *omasinahikeses.*

time of day *tantato tipahikan.*

timepiece *pîsimohkanis;* a clock, *pîsimohkan.*

timer *kanaw tipahikakan.*

timesaving A shortcut, *taskamohtewin.*

timetable *ka masinahamihk tânsi ka wehtôtamihk.*

time zone *ka meskocipayik tepahikan.*

timing *askihkos kwayask ka pahkisot otâpânâskohk.*

timothy *ka asamastimiwehk maskoseya kohpikihtahk*; a grass grown for hay, *maskoseya*.

tincture A solution of medicinial substance in alcohol, *minihkwew maskihki*.

tinderbox *cakihkasikanis ka saskahikakehk*.

tine The prong of a fork, *mepitihkan*.

tin foil *wewekinikakan*.

tinker *pewapiskwiyines*.

tinsel *wawesehcikakan sihtihk*; a Christmas decoration, *nepayamihawawesicikan*.

tinsmith *pewapiskweyines*.

tip *sônîyâw kamekihk*.

tipple *nawâcpoko kaminihkweskihk*.

tire A wheel, *tihtipayew*; car wheels, *sehkepimpayes tihtipayesak*.

tissue *ka pakasik masinahikanekin*; the top of the skin, *waskitasakay*.

tissue paper *kase ohswakan*; *kimisahon*.

tit for tat *meskotomatowin*.

title *wehowin ka mekihk*; *otapowin*.

titled *wehowin ka astâhk acimowenihk*.

title page *wehowin kastâhk masinahikanihk*.

tittle-tattle *kwanta ayemiwewin*.

toadstool *mayokwatay omecowin*.

to-and-fro *kahkekwask*.

toast *ka kaspihkasot pahkwesikan*; a toasted slice of bread, *kaspihkasikan*.

toaster *pihkasikakan*.

tobacconist *ocitemawinihkew*.

toboggan *napakitâpânâsk (Northern)*; *napakâhtik (Northern)*; s/he loads her/his toboggan, *otâpânihkatew*; s/he prepares a proper load for her/his toboggan, *otâpânihkew*; a flat sleigh, *napakitapan*.

toddler *ka oskipimohcesit awâsis*.

toe hold or **toehold** *wanaskosicansa ka nepawakehk*.

toffee *iyoskak maskihkes*.

toggle *sakahpitastimiwakan*.

toilsome *ka kakayawatsihk*.

token A sign or symbol about something, *kiskinawacihowin*.

toleration *nepawestakewin*.

toll *ayimihewkakohk ka sewepicikehk*; a tax collected for a particular service, *tipahikewin*.

tollgate A bridge toll tax, *asokwan tipahikewin*; *ka tipahamihk iskwahtem*.

toll road *ka tipahikehk meskanaw tapacitahk*.

tom *nâpewehowin*.

tomb *kehkwahaskan*; *kihkwahaskan*.

tomboy *ka napisisihkasot iskwesis*; an athletic, boyish girl, *nâpewatisow iskwew*.

tomcat *napeminôs*.

tomfool *omohcokasosk*.

tomfoolery *mohcohkasoskowin*.

ton *peyak posihtason*; one ton, *peyak otapan*.

tonality *ka meyohtakwanihtahk*.

tonally *meyohtamowenihk*.

tone *tânsi ketasteyak kitohcikan*; *itihtakwan*.

toneless *ekâ ka meyohtakosihk*.

tongs An implement for grasping something, *makwahcikan*.

tongue-in-cheek *ka kweskeyihtamihk*.

tongue-lash *ka kehkamiht awîyak*.

tongue-tie *ekâ kake waskawinamihk miteyane*.

tongue-tied *ekâ kwayask ka pîkiskwehk*; s/he is tongue-tied, *sakamoteyanew*.

tongue twister *ka kiniwapekihtahk pîkiskwewin*.

tonic *maskihki ka minihkwehk*; *maskeki*; a medicine lotion that improves body tone, *maskekewehkimakwahon*.

tonnage *posihtasona*.

tonsillectomy *iyihkosak kotinihtwaw (Northern)*.

tonsillitis *iyihkosak ka wesakeyimihtwaw (Northern)*.

tonsure *ka paskwayakatihpesawasohk*.

toolmaker *awîyak âpacicikana kosehtat*.

toothbrush *kisepekapitewakan*.

toothpaste *mepit ka nacicikan*.

toothpick *sekwapitehon*; *tastawapitehikan*; s/he uses a toothpick, *sekwapitehow*.

tootle *ka ketohcikew nikamohk*.

top brass *onekanewak*.

topcoat *kesowasakay*.

top drawer *tahkoc asowacikewin*.

top-flight *metoni ka nîkâneyihtakosit*.

topic *ka pîkiskwatamihk*.

topknot A tuft of hair on top the head, *wawesewahamawin*.

top-level *metoni tahkoc ohci*.

topmost *metoni tipispimihk*; the highest, *mamawiyasispimihk*.

top-notch *metoni ka nîkân akihtamihk*.

topographer *awîyak askew asinahikana ka osehtat*.

topsail *tahkoc ohci yahkastimon*.

top-secret *metoni ka nîkâneyihtakwuhk kîmôc isihcikewin*.

topside *tahkoc ohci kîkway*.

topsoil *tahkoc ohci askîy*.

toque A woolen hat, *sestakwastotin (Northern)*; a stretchy hat, *sîpihkiskâwascocinis (Northern)*.

torpedo An underwater bomb, *itapekpakisikan*.

torpid *maskwa ka nahapit*.

torpidity *kiniwes peyakwinohk ka apihk*.

torrential *metoni kasekipestak*.

torrentially *nosamacipayowin*.

torsion *mosci menopicikan otâpânâskohk*.

549

toss-up *ka ispahkiwepinkehk.*

totalitarian *awîyak metoni ka oynat aysiyinowa.*

totalitarianism *metoni koyinihtwaw aysiyinowak (Northern).*

toucan A tropical bird with a huge beak, *mahkikot.*

touch-and-go *metoni kahketisk.*

tour A trip to several places in succession, *papamohtewin.*

tourism *papamiwapahcikewin.*

tourist *opapamiwapahcikew.*

tournament *papami mawinehikewin;* having a competition, *mawinehotowin.*

tourney *papami metawewin.*

tourniquet A tight bandage to stop bleeding, *pîmastenikan.*

towel A drying cloth, *pahkohkwehon.*

tower man *otasawapow.*

towline *ocipicikanyape.*

town *ôtenas (Northern); ôcinas (Plains);* a smaller town, *ôcenasis (Northern); ôcenâsis (Northern);* s/he makes it a town, *ôtenawihtaw;* the act of living in a town or being an urbanite, *ôtenawiwin.*

town hall *ôcenasihk mamawapewikamik.*

town house *ôcenas waskahikan.*

town meeting *ôcenasihk mamawapowin.*

townsfolk *ôtenawiyinowak.*

townsite *mamawi waskahikanihkewin.*

townsman *ôcenasihk ohci nâpew.*

townspeople *ôcenasihk ohci aysiyinowak.*

towrope *pemenahkwan kocipcikakehk.*

toxic *piscipowin ka otatahtamihk.*

track and field *eta ka pimpahtahk.*

track meet *kotaskatitowin.*

tract A tract of land, *askîy.*

tractability *nihtâ wayesihkemowin.*

traction *ka micimonamihk.*

tractor *askihkokanis; ka atoskakehk otâpânâsk.*

trade *meskotonkewin; meskotona; meskoton.*

trade agreement *ka meskoc isihcikatitohk.*

trade-in *meskotonkan otâpânâsk.*

trademark *tânsi ka isi nistaweyihtakwahk kîkway;* making a mark with a branding iron, *masinaskisikewin.*

trade name *isihcikew wehowin ka âpacitahk.*

trader *otisehcikewiyinow.*

tradesman *nâpew ka isihcikeskit;* a buyer and seller, *otatawew.*

tradespeople *otisehcikewiyinowak.*

trade union *isihcikew mamawintowin.*

tradeswind *kesoyotin.*

trading post *sakahk atawikamkos.*

trading stamp *atawew masinatahikan.*

traffic *eta otâpânâskwak ka pimpayitwaw (Northern);* the coming and going of vehicles, *pimpayiwin.*

traffic circle *wasakapayowin.*

trailblazer *okiskinowaci meskanahkew.*

trailer *wikowin ka papamitapehk; waskahikanihkanis (Northern); wasaykanihkanis (Plains);* a house that is pulled around, *kotapehk waskahikan.*

train Or locomotive, *pîwâpiskomeskanaw (Northern); iskotewitapan (Northern);* being trained for something, *awîyak kasesawet;* a steam locomotive, *iskotewtâpânâsk.*

trainer One who trains others, *yospisihiwew; okiskinohamâkew.*

training *sesawewin.*

trainload *pîwâpiskomeskanaw ka sakaskinek.*

trainman *pîwâpiskomeskanaw nâpew.*

tramp *pakosetask.*

trampoline *kwaskwepayihowin kosehtahk.*

tramway *ôtenahk pîwâpiskomeskanaw.*

trance *nipawin.*

tranquil It is very quiet, *kamwatan.*

tranquillize *or* **tranquilize** *kamwacihewewin.*

tranquillizer *or* **tranquilizer** *ka kamwacihekohk maskihki.*

transact *ka isihcikatitohk;* making a deal or transaction, *isihcikewin.*

transaction *isihcikatitowin.*

trans Atlantic Across the ocean, *akamikihecikamehk.*

transcend *ayiwâk ka tôtamihk.*

transcendence *ayiwâk ehtôtamowin.*

transcendent *kwanta ayiwâk ka tôtahk awîyak.*

transcendental *ayiwâk mamaskatekonikewin.*

transcontinental The land across the ocean, *akamaskehk.*

transcribe Making a written copy of, *masinahikewin.*

transcript *awîyak omasinahikewin;* a written copy, *tapasinahikan.*

transduce *asawipayihtamâkewin.*

transfer Placing something from one place to another, *ahtascikewin;* the spiritual power is transfered to others, *mamatawihiwewin;* move from one place to another, *meskotahiwewin.*

transferability *ahcipayihcikewin.*

transferable *kîkway ka ahtastâhk.*

transference *ahtahiwewin.*

transfiguration *pîtos nakosowin.*

transfigure *awîyak ka pîtosespayit.*

transfix *micimimipayowin.*

transform *pîtos kesehiwehk;* make it look different, *kweskinakohtaw.*

transformation *pîtos isihiwewin.*

transformer *wasaskotepayew ka pîtos wepahikemakahk.*

transfuse *asawpayihcikewin.*

transfusion *mihko ka asawpayihtahk;* the giving of blood, *mehkomekiwin.*

transience *ka papamâyâhk.*

transiency *papamâyâwin.*

transient *awîyak ka papamâyat;* one who stays briefly or who is always on the go, *papamâcihosk.*

transit *ahtohtewin;* passage from one place to another, *posowin.*

transition *ahtotewin; ahtohtahiwewin.*

transitory *ka nohti ahtohtehk.*

translate *ka itwestamakehk; itwestamâwatam;* s/he speaks for them, *pekiswestamâwew.*

translation *meskotasinahikewin; itwestamâkewin.*

translator *otitwestamâkew.*

transmigrate *ahcipecowin.*

transmigration *ka ahcipicihk.*

transmission *ahciwepahikan.*

transmitter The sending part of a radio or telephone, *sipwetisahikakan.*

transmutation *meskotsehcikewin.*

transom *piwapisk ka akomohtahk wasinamawinihk;* a hinged window above a door, *wasinamawinis.*

transparency *masinisicikan; masinisicikanis.*

transpire *ka nokosihk.*

transplant *ka ahci pakitinkehk;* s/he transplants something, *ahtaskicikew.*

transplantation *ahci pakitinkewin.*

transport *pimohtataw;* a transport truck, *otawatasow.*

transportation *awatasowin; pimohtewin.*

transpose *ka meskotascikehk.*

transposition *meskoc wepinkewin.*

transverse Something lying across something else, *pimitastew.*

transvestism *nâpew ka iskwewisehot.*

transvestite *nâpew ka iskwewayat apôh iskwew ka nâpewayat.*

trap door A small door, *iskwatemis; anaskanihtakohk ka iskwatemowîk; iskwatemis.*

trapeze Swinging all kinds of ways, *nânatôkisiwepisowin.*

trapping license *nohcihcikewasinahikan.*

trappings *mistatimoyape wawesehcikana.*

trashy *ekâ nânitâw ka tapatsihk.*

trauma *ka wesakaspinatisohk.*

traumatic *wesakaspinatisowin.*

travail Having a painful childbirth, *ayimihowapamawasowin.*

travesty *pewenakohcikewin.*

tray *napakeyakan;* a tray for picking up dishes, *mawasakoyakanakan.*

treadle *ka makosikamihk kaskwasiwakan;* a lever operated by the foot, *mamakoskacikan.*

treason *kîmôtatisowin; mayahkamikisiwin.*

treasure An accumulation of money, *weyotisiwin.*

treasurer *sônîyâwikanaweyicikew.*

treasury *eta ka kanaweyimiht sônîyâw.*

treatise *masinahikanihk kastahk isihcikewin.*

treaty *nehiyaw otinkewin; okimâw asotamakewin.*

treaty day *tipahamatokesikaw.*

treaty Indian *tipahamowakan; tipahamohwakan.*

treaty money *tipahamato sônîyâw.*

treaty rights *nehiyaw otinkewin.*

treble Something done three times, *nistwaw.*

tree farming *sihcisak kohpikihihtwaw (Northern).*

tree frog *mayokwatas mistikohk kawekit.*

trellis A framework of cross bars used for climbing, *amaciwe ahtawewin.*

trench *watihkewin; monahikan;* a shelter in a war, *kasowin.*

trend *peyakwayak ka iteyimohk;* a trend to go in a particular direction, *sapweyihtamowin.*

trendy *kahnihtâ ayisinakehk.*

tresses A braid of hair, *sekipatwansa.*

trestle *asokanihkewin;* a bridge supported by a framework, *asokewinis.*

trial *weyasowatitowin.*

trial jury *weyasowewin ka mamawi natohtahkwaw.*

tribunal A court of justice, *weyasowewin.*

tribute A gift as a mark of respect, *okihtawihiwewin.*

tricolour *nistwayaketasinastek.*

tricycle *ka nistokatet ocâpânâskos;* a three wheeled bike, *nistokatew tihtipiwepiskacikan.*

trimming *kwayaskosawacikewin.*

trinket *metawakanis;* a trifling ornament or keepsake, *wawesehcikan.*

trio *nisto ayisiyinowak; nistiwak;* there are three of them, *nistowak.*

triple *nistiwaw ohci kîkway;* three of a kind, *nistiwayi.*

tripod A stand having three legs, *tastawikeskicikan.*

trivet *ka nistokatimakahk cecapowenis.*

trivot A three legged stool, *nistokatew apowin.*

trite It has gone stale or hackneyed, *mestapahtew.*

trolley A street car, *ôtenaw posowin.*

troop *ka mamawiyatwaw nâpewak (Northern);* an assembly of people, *ka mecetihk.*

trooper *semakansihkan.*

trophied *manacicikewin.*

trophy A prize or medal from the war, *kesipinamasowin.*

trouble-shooter *okwayaskiwascikew.*

551

trouble-shooting *kwayaskopayihcikewin.*
troupe *ayisiyinowak ka papami wapahtehiwetwaw nânatohk isi metawewna* (Northern).
trouper *nânatohk isi metawewiyinow.*
troth *asotamatowin.*
trotter *pimpatawatim.*
troubadour *onikamow.*
troupe *ometawestamakewak.*
trousers *mitâs.*
trousseau *wekihtowasakay.*
truant One who is absent without reason, *opamacihosk.*
truce *kawe meyowecehtowin; ponahkamikisiwin.*
truck *âwatâswâkan;* a hauling vehicle, *âwacikewtâpânâsk;* a water truck, *okwapikewtâpânâsk;* a garbage truck, *wepinokiwotâpân* (Northern); *wipinokiwotâpânâsk* (Plains).
truculence *maci isâyâwin.*
true-blue *metoni kwayask isâyâwin.*
trump A trump card, *keskisikan.*
trumpet A blowing instrument, *potacikan.*
trumpeter A person who blows the trumpet, *opotacikeweyinow.*
trunk *misimistekowat; miyaw;* tree, *mistik;* a large container or box, *mistikowat.*
trunk line *awatasow meskanaw.*
truss A belt worn for support of a hernia, *sehtahpison.*
trustee One who is entrusted to manage property, *masinahikehakan.*
trust fund *ka nahastamâkehk sônîyâw.*
trustworthy *awîyak ka sohki mamisihk.*
tryst *okocew.*
t-shirt *ka keskanakweyak pakowayan.*
tube A long hollow cyclinder used to siphon liquid, *oyahcikakan.*
tuber A potato-like vegetable, *lapatakohkan* (Northern, French Cree).
tuberculosis *ohpanahpinewin;* s/he has tuberculosis, *ohpanahpinew.*
tubing *apihkanayi ka sepekipayik.*
tubular *pehcipotacikewin.*
tuck Cover up snugly with blankets, *kesowa kwanahowin.*
tuft A small bunch of hair tied at one end, *piskwahpitew mescakasa.*
tugboat *osih kotapemakahk.*
tuition *kiskinoham totipahikewin.*
tumble-down *ka nehcacowe tihtipipayihk.*
tumbler *otihtepew;* a glass cup, *moteyapiskominihkwacikan.*
tumbleweed *macikwanasa ka tihtipastakwaw.*
tumour *piskopayiwin.*

tune *kitohcikan ka oyastehamihk.*
tuneful *ka meweyihtamihk kitohcikewin;* it sounds melodious, *nikamowihtakwan.*
tune-up *oyastehikewin.*
tunic A soldier's jacket, *simakan asakay.*
tunnel *sapopayipahcahikewin; saposkamikohkan.*
turban A wrap around the head, *wekistikwanepison.*
turf *maskosehsa kohpikihtahk.*
turnabout *sîsîkoc kweskipayihowin.*
turnip *otsekan.*
turnout *tânsi ka isinahipayihk.*
turntable *sehki ka wasakakotek kitohcikan.*
turpentine An oily substance used in making paint, *sopekahikanihkakan.*
turquoise A bluish color, *sepehkonakwan.*
tutor *onesohkamâkew kiskinohamatokamkohk;* a teacher helper, *kiskinohamakew.*
tutorship *kiskinohamatow nesohkamakewin.*
twang The sharp sound of a violin string when tightened, *ka cewehtawahk.*
tweed *ayowinsa ka natohkwasinastekwaw;* a warm soft fabric, *kesowekin.*
tweezers A small two pronged gripping tool, *ocipicikanis.*
twelvefold *nîsosâpwaw.*
twelvemonth *nîsosâp pîsim.*
twentyfold *nîstanawaw.*
twine *maskosêw peminahkwanis;* strong thread, *maskawasapap.*
twister *owahwakipayihow.*
twit *naniweyacihtowin.*
two-faced *ka nîsohkwakanehk.*
two-fisted *nîswayak kohpakamahikehk.*
twofold *nîswaw;* it is double or times two, *nîswamon.*
two-handed *nîswayak kesenahehk.*
twopence Two cents, *nîspîwâpiskos.*
two-ply *nîswaw ka pimastek.*
twosome *ka nîsihk.*
two-time *nîskwayak ka sakihiwehk.*
two-way *nîskwayak ka itapatahk.*
tympanum The vibrating device of an eardrum, *ka pehtamihkoci mihtawakay.*
type *ka masinatahikehk.*
typewrite *masinatahikewin.*
typewriter A machine for writing, *masinatahikan.*
typewriting *masinatahikan ka masinahikakehk.*
typewritten *masinatahikanik ka masinahamihk.*
typhoid *mistahi ka kisisohk;* the poisoning disease of the intestines, *piscipowaspinewin.*
typhoon *misikestinipayow.*
typical *tânsi kesihtwahk;* just like, *mweci.*
typically *tânsi isi twawinihk.*

552

typify *kiskinowatapowin;* represent by a type of symbol, *isihtwawin.*

typist *omasinatahikew.*

tyrannical *ka kostanakew isâyâhk.*

tyranny *kostanakeyimowin.*

tyrant A despot or absolute ruler, *otaspihiwew.*

U

ukelele An instrument, *kitohcikan.*

ulcer *ka kawatihtahk omiki;* an infected sore, *omikewintahkacihk.*

ulcerate *ka kawatimisohk.*

ulceration *kawatimisowin.*

ulterior *tahki ayiwâk wahyaw.*

ultimatum *tanta ka kisipipayik.*

umbrella *kimowanapahkwasonis;* a portable shelter from rain or sun, *akawastehon.*

umpire An arbiter or referee, *ometaweweyasowew.*

unaccountable *ekâ ka akihtamihk.*

unaccountably *ekâ akihcikewinihk.*

unanimous *peyakwayak isi wehkowin;* all being of one mind, *peyakwantehtamowin.*

unanimously *kwayask paskeyakewin.*

unarm *masaskonowewin.*

unarmed *namoya nemaskwew.*

unbalanced *keskwewayaw; ekâ kwayask isâyâwin; keskwew.*

unbeknownst *ekâ ka kiskemowehk.*

unbiassed *or* **unbiased** *ka kwayask wesayâhk.*

unbusinesslike *mamases isihcikewin.*

uncharitable *ekâ kakisêwatsihk.*

uncivil *nawâc poko pikwacisâyâwin.*

uncivilized *ka pikwaceyinewihk.*

unconditional *ekâ ka nakacitahk.*

unconditionally *ekâ nakacitawinihk.*

unconventional *sôskwac pokwesi kesehcikehk.*

uncultivated Uncultivated land, *pikwacask.*

underbred *nohtaw ohpikihiwewin.*

undercarriage *sîpâ otâpânâskohk.*

undercharge *nohtaw akihtamâkewin.*

underdeveloped *eka metoni ka kesehtahk.*

underestimate *peweyihcikewin.*

underlay *sîpâ kohsetosikamihk.*

underline *sîpâ kohkiskinawatasinahamihk;* s/he underlines it, *kiskinawatasinaham.*

underlying *sîpâ ohci kake twamastahk.*

undermost *mitonicapasis.*

underpay *nohti tipahikewin.*

underprivileged *ka nohtipayihk meyopayowin.*

underrate *nohtaw akihcikewin;* s/he is underrated, *astamipitaw.*

underscore *nohtipayihtamâkewin.*

undersell It sells for less, *astamâkehtew.*

undersigned *masinahikanihk wehowin ka masinahamihk.*

undersong *sîpâ ohci nikamowin.*

understatement *nohtaw mamiskocikewin.*

undervalue *nohtaw kespehteyihtakwahk.*

unemployed S/he does not work, *namoya atoskew; awîyak ekâ ka atosket.*

unemployment *ekâ ka atoskehk.*

ungovernable *ekâ kake paminowehk.*

unhand S/he lets it go, *pakitinam.*

unheard-of *ekâ wehkac ka pehtamihk.*

uniform *ayowinsa kakikiskamihk tohnistaw nakosihk kîkway kosehtahk;* all the same, *papeyakwan.*

union *mamawinitowin;* making one, *mamawihtowin.*

unionize *ka mamawesehcikehk.*

universe *misiwe askîy;* in the whole universe, *misiwetehesikamik.*

unity State of being united, *wecewakanihtowin.*

unjust *ekâ kwayask isihcikewin; kayesow.*

unlawful *awîyak ka pikonahk weyasowewin;* not right with the law, *namoya kwayask weyasowewin.*

unlawfully *ka pikonamihk weyasowewin.*

unprincipled *ekâ kwayask kohpikihawasohk.*

unprintable *namoya takehmasinahikatek.*

unprofessional *ekâ ka nakaciwepinkehk.*

unprofitable *ekâ ka sônîyâhkakehk.*

unqualified S/he cannot do it as s/he is not qualified, *namoyakaskihtaw; ekâ osam ka nakacitahk; namoyanawasonaw.*

unrest *makekay ayiwepowin; mikoskatisowin;* s/he is uneasy, *mamoyakwayaskwatisow.*

unseat S/he lost her/his seat in office, *wayaweskawaw.*

unsociable *ekâ ka otôtemihkehk.*

unsung *ekâ ka nikamosicikatek.*

unto *iskohanoc ka kesikak;* even unto, *paskac.*

untoward *nayihtawipayowin.*

untried *ekâ kakocitahk.*

untrod *ka poni pimpahtawayasihk.*

unwritten *ekâ ka masinahikatek;* it is not written, *namoyamasinahikatew.*

unwritten law *ekâ masinahikanihk kastek weyasowewin.*

upbound *ispimihk itiyimowin.*

upcountry *patosayihk askehk.*

update *kwayask kesikaw ka astahk.*

upheld *kwayask ka kehispayihcikehk.*

upholster *ka wewekinamihk tehtapowin.*

upkeep *ka nakateyihtamihk kîkway.*

uppermost *mawaci ispimihk.*

553

upside *tahkoc ohci*.

upstairs *ispimihtakohk*.

upstart A person who has risen fast and assumes an arrogant behavior, *mamaskatikohkosow*.

uptake *ka amacowekotek okohtaskwayihkanihk*.

uptight *nanihkipayowin*.

up-to-date *metoni anohc isko*; up until today, *isko anohc*.

up-to-the-minute *metoni isko tanima cipahikanis*.

uptown *metoni apihtaw ôcenasihk*.

urban *ôtenahk ohci*; belonging to a city, *ôtenaw pimacihowin*.

urchin *ka naniweyatsiskit nâpesis*.

urn A very large teapot, *misiletewaskihk (Northern, French Cree)*.

usher Someone who escorts people, *kiskinohtahiwew*.

utensil *âpacicikan*.

utilities A quality of being useful or the ability to satisfy human wants, *meyow apatisowin*.

utmost *metoni sohki ka kocehk*; *kihci*.

uttermost *metoni sohkahâc*; *kihcikespinatamâsowin*.

V

554

vacancy There is an opening, *tawaw*; *ka tawak wikowin*.

vacant It is empty, *mosawiyaw*.

vacate S/he has left it, *nakatam*; *ka nakacipicestamihk*.

vacation *ka papamiwapahtamihk askîy*; a period of release from work, *nomiponatoskewin*.

vacationist *opapamiwapahcikew*.

vaccinate Immunization from disease, *cestahowewin*.

vaccination *cestahikasowin*.

vaccine A vaccine against a disease, *maskihkekanipahcikemakahk*; *maskihki omikewin ohci*.

vacuum A machine that sucks in dirt, *otahcikewin*; *asiskiyotahcikâkan (Plains)*.

vacuum cleaner *ka nacicikan*.

vagabond A hobo person, *papamacihos*.

vagrancy *ka papamaticihohk*.

vagrant One without reputable means of support, *onotehkatew*; *opapamaticihow*.

valence *akopicikan*.

valentine Valentine's Day, *kihcikesikokesikam*; *wicimosokesikaw (Northern)*; *otikesikaw*; *mitewikîsikaw (Plains)*; *sâkihitowikîsikâw (Plains)*.

valerian A herb with medicinal value, *maskihkewahtik*.

valet A working person, *atoskewenow*.

valid *ka kwayaskwastek*.

validate *ka kwayaskwastahk*.

validity *kwayaskwascikewin*.

valise *asiwacikan*; *asowacikewin*.

valuation Estimated worth, *tânsi etaketehk*.

valve A shut off lever, *kipipicikan*; *yohtepicikanis*.

vampire *omihkowahcikew*.

van A large covered truck or vehicle, *akwanahikasotâpânâsk*; *misiwetâpânâsk*.

vandal One who willfully destroys beauty, *omisiwanacicikew*.

vandalism *nânatoh ka papamitahkamikisihk*.

vandalize *mistahi ka papamipekonikehk*.

vane A device that tells which way the wind blows, *kawehcikemakahtanitehohtihk*; *oyapacikakan otepahaskewak ohci*.

vanguard *simakanisak nîkânewin*.

vanilla *kiyikawenikan sewipahkwesikanihk*.

vantage point *eta ka nîkânapihk*.

variant An altered form of something, *pîtosihtowin*.

variegate Marked with different colors, *pahpîtosipekaham*.

varnish Material that produces a glossy surface, *wasihkwahikan*; *mistik ka wasihkwahikatek*.

vascular Blood veins, *mihkwayapiya*.

vase A flower pot, *wapikwanewascikan*; *asowacikan nepehkana ohci*; a vase made of birch bark, *kâkwaywat*.

vat A wooden barrel, *mahkahk*.

vault *kwaskweyaskwahosowin*; *ka kwaskwey âskwahosohk*.

veal *moscososwîyâs*; *oskimostosisowîyâs*.

vehicle Any kind of transportation, *otâpânâsk*; s/he has a vehicle, *ototâpânâskow*.

velocity The rate of speed, *kisepayowin*.

velour A type of velvet material, *sôskwekinihkan*.

velvet *sôskwekin*.

velvety It is soft like velvet, *yôskaw*.

vend S/he sells it, *atawakew*.

vendetta *kinwes kisesitakewin*.

vendor A person that sells, *atâwakewenow*.

veneer A thin layer of wood material applied as outer coating, *pehtawenikan*.

ventilator *tahkeyawehikan*.

verandah *nistampehtokwewin*; *wayawetimihk apowin kosehtahk*.

verb *pîkiskwewin ka wehtamomakahk tânsi ka tôtamihk*.

verbal *ka nihtâ pîkiskwehk*; relating or consisting of words, *pîkiskwewin*.

verbena *wehkimakow wapikwani*.

verdant *askîtakwaw*.

verdict The decision of a jury after a hearing, *kesasowewin*; *keseyihtamowin*.

verification *kwayask kwascikewin*.

verify *kihcinahow*; to confirm the truth or accuracy of, *kihcinahowin*.

verily In the truth of, *tâpwewinihk*.

veritably *tâpwepayowenihk*.

vermilion *pakaskimihkwaw*.

verse *piskitasinahikan*; *peyak misakami masinahikewin*.

version A passage translated from one language to another, *itatamowin*.

versus Fighting for one's own rights, *naskwawin*.

vertebra A jointed bone in the spinal column or backbone, *aniskwawikanan*.

vertebrate Having a spinal column, *mawikanowow*.

vertex The highest point of a hill, *tahkohtamatin*.

vestibule A porch on a house, *nistampehtokwewin*.

veteran Someone with a long experience in some activity, *onakacihtaw*.

veterinarian *maskihkewiyinow pisiskowak ohci*.

veterinary *maskihkewikamik pisiskowak ohci*; an animal doctor, *pisiskiw maskekewenow*.

via *ekoteyisi*.

viaducts A high bridge, *ispimikasokan*.

vial *mohte apiskos*.

vicarious *miskocestamâkewin*.

vice A habitual disposition to choose evil, *macesehcikewin*; *ohcitaw ka matcesâyâhk*.

viceroy A person appointed by someone to rule in her/his place, *omescestamâkew*.

vicious circle *mâcayowenihk ka wecehewehk*.

Victoria Day *kicokimaskwew kesikaw*.

viewpoint *tânsi kesi mâmitoneyihtamihk*; *ekota ohci ketapihk*.

vigilante *otasweyihcikew*.

villa *weyotisêwikamik*.

village *ôtenas*; *apiscôcenas*.

vinegar A sour liquid, *sewapoy*; *mecowenihk ka kikastahk nepewayi*.

violate The act of breaking the law, *weyasowewipekanikewin*; *ka pekonamihk weyasowewin*.

violation *macitotamowin*; violating the law, *mâyitôtamowin*.

viper *piscipokinepik*.

virginia creeper A vine that grows and crawls up the wall, *amaciweyacawes*.

virulent A poisonous disease, *piscipow payewahkosowin*.

virus A contagious disease caused by a virus, *asoskamatow ahkosowin*; *asoskamipayow*.

viscount A British high distinguished person, *akayasew keci okimâw*.

vise *or* **vice** A gripping tool, *setastehikan*; *makwahikan*.

visitation *kihokatowin*.

visualization *kihkanamowin*.

VLT A video lottery terminal, *sônîyâw kâsîwepayit*; *sônîyâhkakan*.

vocabulary The range of language, *pîkiskwewin*; *tânsi kesipîkiskwehk*.

vocal cords *eta kesêwewin kohcemakahk*.

vogue A prevalent or popular fashion, *isihowin*.

volcanize To treat with sulphur for strengthening, *maskawisihcikewin*.

Volkswagon *micihcikepayîs*.

volleyball *pakatowân kapakamahot (Plains)*; *kwaskwitowan kapakamahoht (Northern)*.

volume *masinahikan*.

voluntary Acting or doing freely, *nisohkamâkewin*.

volunteer A volunteer helper, *onesohkamâkew*; *meyote onesohkamâkew*; *nisohkamâkew*.

vote The giving of names, *wehowina kamekihk*; *wehowin kastahk ahpô ka pimpahtahk*.

voucher *neso kamâkewin*.

vowel A voiced sound, *itehtakosowin*; *nehiyawewinihk ka apatâhk*.

555

W

wad *sepaskiwacekan*; in a muzzle-loader, *kipahapwan*.

wafer A thin, crisp pancake, *papakihkasikanis*.

waffle *kaspihkasikanis*.

wage *tipahamâkewin*; making money, *kespinacikewin*.

wager A betting game, *astwatowin*.

wainscoting The sheathing panels on the wall of a house, *pehtawenikewina*.

waiter A person employed to serve food or drinks, *pamihiwew*.

waive To agree to forgo or prefer not to insist on, *pakiteyihtamowin*.

walk-way *pimohtewinihk*.

wall *misiwi kipihtakahikan*; something that separates rooms, *piskihcikipatahikan*; an interior wall, *nakihtakaw*; corner of a house, *wehkwehtakaw*; the end of a building, *kapiy iskwastik waskahikan*.

wallet Or purse, *sônîyâwiwat (Northern)*; *sônîyâwiwacis (Northern)*.

walleyed pike *or* **walleyed perch** *asawesisak*; *okâw*.

wallow *pisiskowak ka tihtipetwaw (Northern)*.

waltz A dance, *nîmihitowin*.

wand A magic rod or stick, *mamahtawahcikos*.

war cry *opakamitonehamâw*.

ward *oskayis ka kanaweyimiht*; a minor under the care of a legal guardian, *okanaweyimakan*.

warden An official having special duties, *simakanisihkan*; *okanaweyihcikew*.

ware Goods for sale, *atâwewina*.

warehouse *ascikiwikamik*.

warm-hearted *ka kisewatisihk*.

warrant *weyasowewinihk ka ahiwehk*.

warren *eta ka kanaweyimihtwaw pisiskesak* (Northern).

warship A battleship, *nôtinikewosi*.

washcloth *ka sîhkwakanis*.

washer A washing machine, *kisipekinikakan*.

washroom *kisipekinkewkamik*; *wayawiwikamik*.

wastebasket *wepinikew asowacikan*.

wastepaper *masinahikanekin ka wepinamihk*.

watch *kanâwapahcikiwin*; a wristwatch or pocket watch, *pîsimohkanis*.

watchman *kanâweyicikew*; night watchman, *kanâwitipiskwew*.

water beetle *amiskoses*.

watercolor or **watercolour** Water painting colors, *nipesopekayikan*.

waterproofed *namoya ohcistin*; material that sheds water, *namoya sâpwapawew*.

watertight *osih ekâ ka ohcistihk*; it does not leak, *namoya ohticistin*.

waterway *pimiciwan*; a traffic route by water, *sapostikweyaw*.

wattles *misihew okwayaw*.

wax A floor shine, *wasihkohtakahikan*.

waylay *askamacikewin*; to catch someone on her/his way somewhere, *askamawew*.

wayward Willfully turning away from what is right, *nayihtawisow*.

weak-kneed *ka neyamakwaw mihcikwana*.

weak-minded *mâmitoneyihcikan ekâ ka maskawak*.

weather-bound *ka kitistinahokohk*.

weed *macikwanas*; a bad weed, *macaskosiy*; it is weedy water, *asêwakamow*.

weld S/he welds something, *akohkaswew*; the act of welding, *akohkasikewin*.

welder *otakohkasikew* (Northern); *ocakokasikis* (Plains).

welfare Government help, *okimanahk ohci nesohkamatowin*; a welfare worker or feeder of people, *otasahkew* (Archaic Cree); a welfare or social worker or a helper of people, *owîcihtâsow*; help for people, *nesohkamâkewin*.

well *monahipan*.

well-being *meyopew*; s/he is in good shape, *meyo ayaw*.

well-bred *kwayask ohpikihiwewin*; s/he is well brought up, *meyow ohpikow*.

well-connected *meyonohk ka ohcehk*.

well-disposed *kisewatsowin*.

well-favored or **well-favoured** *iskwew ka meyonakosit*.

well-marked *kwayask ka kiskinowacicikatek*.

well-meaning *kwayask mâmitoneyihtamowin*.

well-ordered *kwayask ka natocikehk*.

well-placed *kwayask ascikewin*.

well-preserved *kwayask nahascikewin*.

well-spoken *kwayask pekiskwewin*.

whale *mistamek*; the king of the ocean fish, *kihcikame okimas*.

whale bone *okimasoskan*.

whatsoever *tânsipoko*.

wheelbarrow A small vehicle for hauling stuff, *awacikew câpânâskos*; *pîwâpiskow tihtipayis*.

wheel chair *tihtipipayew tihtapowin*.

whensoever *poko ispe sôskwac*.

whereabouts *tante nânitâw*.

whereas Maybe, *ahpô*.

whereat Where, *tanta*.

whereby *macika*.

wherefore *tanehkimaka*.

wherein *ekota ohci*.

whereof *eyok ohci*; *awena ci*.

whereto *tante poko*; whereto now, *tante ekwa*.

whereupon *ekosi sôskwac*.

whiplash *ka wesakipayik mikwâyâw*.

whippoorwill *wasepesican*; *kihcimohkemam pîwâyisis*.

whirligig *metawakan*.

whirlpool *apamociwan*.

whist *tenikewin*.

white wash White wash for a house, *wâpihtakahikan*; the white wash on a house or fence, *wâpiskahikewin*.

whole-hearted *espehcotehit awîyak*.

wholesale To buy by the case, *miswi atâwewin*.

wholesome *metoni meyomahcihowin*; *maskawisostakan*; good wholesome food, *meyos kakowin*.

whomsoever *awena sôskwac*.

whooping cough *ka sohki payik ostostôtamowin*; an infectious bacterial disease, *naspitatamopayiwin*.

whorl *setak ka osehcikake*.

whosoever *awena sôskwac*; *pakotana*; anyone who could be, *pakotana*.

wide-awake *metoni ka waspawi ayâhk*.

wide-eyed *mahkacapipayowin*.

wide-open *ka misakameyohtekotek*.

wigwag *kahkekwask isikwakohtowin*.

556

wild flower *or* **wild-flower** *pikwac nepehkanis*.
wildlife *pikwace pimatisowin*.
willow ptarmigan *îyîntow pehew*.
winch *ispahkepicikan*.
window *wasenamawin*.
window pane *wasenamawinapisk*; a cloth used in place of glass for a window pane, *wasenamawinekin*.
window sill *wasenamawnihk tehtascikewin*.
winsome *ka meweyihtakosit awîyak*.
winterer *awîyak ka nihtâ ponisit*.
winterkill *ka nipahaskatihkwaw nepehkansa*.
winter solstice *ka meskocipayih kesikaw*.
wire *pîwâpiskos*; wire for baling hay, *maskosêw tahkopecikan*; a wire to tie things, *tahkopicikanapisk*.
withdraw *ka kawehotinkehk*; *ponetaw*; *asenam*; quitting something, *poyowin*.
withdrawal *kawi otinkewin*.
withdrawn *kake kawi otinkehk*.
withstand S/he can handle it, *nîpawestam*.
witless *ka nôhtepayik iyinesowin*.
witness A person who testifies to a certain observation, *sehtoskakew*.
witticism *naniweyacimitowin*.
woebegone *mistahikaskeyihtamowin*.
wording *ka masinahamihk tânsi kesipikiskwehk*.
workbook *atoskew asinahikan*.
workday *atoskew kesikaw*.
workman *atoskewenow*.
workmanship *nokohtawin*.
workout *sesawewin*.
worldliness *mistiyimowin*.
worldwide *kespehtaskewik*.
worsted A soft material, *pesiwekin*.
worth-while *mistahi kespehteyihtakwahk*.
would-be *ka akawatamihk isâyâwin*.
wrangler *opaminastimiwew*.
wrapper S/he is a wrapper, *wewekinikew*.
wrapping *masinahikanekin*; wrapping paper or anthing used for wrapping, *wekinikan*.

wreath *asapicikewin*
wreckage *pekwatahikasow*.
wrench *âpahikan*.
wringer A hand operated wringer, *senikakan*.
writ *weyasowewin ka masinahamihk*.
writer An author, *omasinahikew*; s/he is an excellent writer, *nihtâwasinahikew*; a person who writes, *masinahikewenow*.
wrongdoing *naspâc ka tôtamihk*.
wrought *oyatahikewin*.
wrought-up *metoni ka papasipayihk*

X

xerox *kwayakopayihcikan*; *âsopayihcikan*.

Y

yachting *papamasiwak*.
yea *îhi*.
yeast *ohpayihcikanis*.
yellow perch *osâwes*.
yew A type of tree from the evergreen family, *mîtosatik*; *mîtos*.
yodel A yodeling song, *nikamowin*.
yonder On the other side, *awasayihk*.

557

Z

zebra A type of wild horse, *pakwacimisitatim*; *masinasowatim*.
zero *metoni nama kîkway*; nothing, *namakîkway*.
zinc A type of paint that prevents steel from rust, *sopekahikan*.
zipper A zipper fastener on clothes, *kipopicikan*; *sihpohpicikan*.
zoo A place where animal are kept for show, *pakwacipisiskewikamik*; zoo animals, *pisiskow kanawimâkanak*; *kanawîmâkanak*.
zone *piskiht tipahaskan*.

Appendices

A Legal Oath

nehiyawewin/Cree

ki kihcinisk ohci saminah manitomasinahikan.
oma kaweh kihci pekiskweyan kihci
   weyasowewinihk,
tapwêwin ci eweh apacihtayin?
kimanitominaw ayisk ki natohtak.
ascih kanesohkamak tapwêwin kita apacihtawat.

English/akayasemowin

Touch the Bible with your right hand.
Now that you are under oath
   in the court of law,
are you going to use the truth?
Because our God is listening to you.
And he will help you tell the truth.

There are no legal equivalents in Cree for the terms of "guilty" and "non-guilty". For a plea of "guilty", a Cree speaker would say **niyakatotaman,** which translates to "I am responsible for doing it." For a plea of "not-guilty" a Cree speaker would say **namoyaniya katotaman**, which translates to "I am not responsible and I did not do it."

Months

nehiyawewin/akayasemowin
Cree/English

kisepîsim (NI) January; the elder moon or month *(Northern)*; the cold moon or month *(Plains)*.

mikisowipîsim (NI) February; the eagle moon or month; the bald eagle moon or month *(Plains)*.

niskipîsim (NA) March; the goose moon or month.

ayikîpîsim (NI) April; the frog moon or month *(Plains)*.

ayîkiwipîsim (NI) April; the frog moon or month.

apiniyâwepîsim (NA) May; the egg laying moon or month.

opiniyâwewipîsim (NA) May; the egg laying moon or month. *(Plains)*.

sâkipakâwipîsim (NA) May; the leaf budding moon or month. *(Northern)*.

opâskahopîsim (NA) June; the egg-hatching moon or month *(Plains)*.

opâskâwehopîsim (NA) June; the egg hatching moon or month *(Northern)*.

opâskâwewowipîsim (NA) June; the egg hatching moon or month *(Northern)*.

opaskowipîsim (NA) July; the moulting moon or month.

ohpahopîsim (NA) August; the flying moon or month *(Plains)*.

ohpahowipîsim (NA) August; the flying moon or month *(Northern)*.

onôcihitowipîsim (NA) September; the mating moon or month.

kaskatinowipîsim (NI) October; the freeze-up moon or month.

iyikopiwipîsim (NI) November; the frosty moon or month.

manito kîsikan pîsim (NI) December; God's moon.

pawacakinasîs (NA) December; the tree cleaning moon or month *(Northern)*.

pawahcakinasîs (NA) December; drift clearing moon or month *(Plains)*.

English/Cree
akayasemowin/nehiyawewin

January The elder moon or month *(Northern)*; the cold moon or month *(Plains)*, **kisepîsim** (NI).

February The eagle moon or month; the bald eagle moon or month *(Plains)*, **mikisowipîsim** (NI).

March The goose moon or month, **niskipîsim** (NA).

April The frog moon or month, **ayîkiwipîsim** (NI); **ayikîpîsim** (NI) *(Plains)*.

May The egg laying moon or month, **opiniyâwewipîsim** (NA) *(Plains)*; the leaf budding moon or month, **sâkipakâwipîsim** (NA) *(Northern)*. *Var.* **apiniyâwepîsim** (NA).

June The egg hatching moon or month, **opâskahopîsim** (NA) *(Plains)*; **opâskâwehopîsim** (NA) *(Northern)*; **opâskâwewowipîsim** (NA) *(Northern)*.

July The moulting moon or month, **opaskowipîsim** (NA).

August The flying moon or month, **ohpahopîsim** (NA) *(Plains)*; **ohpahowipîsim** (NA) *(Northern)*.

September The mating moon or month, **onôcihitowipîsim** (NA).

October The freeze-up moon or month, **kaskatinowipîsim** (NI).

November The frosty moon or month, **iyikopiwipîsim** (NI).

December The tree cleaning moon or month, **pawahcakinasîs** (NA) *(Northern)*; drift cleaning moon or month, **pawahcakinasîs** (NA) *(Plains)*; God's moon or month, **manitow kîsikan pîsim** (NI).

563

APPENDIX C

Numbers

nehiyawewin/akayasemowin
Cree/English

peyak (IPC) One.
nîso (IPC) Two.
nisto (IPC) Three.
newo (IPC) Four.
nîyânan (IPC) Five.
nikotwâsik (IPC) Six.
tepakohp (IPC) Seven.
ayinânew (IPC) Eight.
kîkâmitâtaht (IPC) Nine. *(Northern). Alt.* **kekâymitâht**
   (Plains).
mitâtaht (IPC) Ten.
peyakosâp (IPC) Eleven. *Var.* **metataht peyakosâp**.
nîsosâp (IPC) Twelve. *Var.* **mitâtaht mîna nîso**.
nistosâp (IPC) Thirteen.
newohsâp (IPC) Fourteen.
nîyânanosâp (IPC) Fifteen.
nikotwâsosâp (IPC) Sixteen.
tepakohposâp (IPC) Seventeen.
ayînânewosâp (IPC) Eighteen.
kîkâmitâtahtosâp (IPC) Nineteen.
nîstanaw (IPC) Twenty.
nistomitanaw (IPC) Thirty.
nemitanaw (IPC) Forty.
nîyânanomitanaw (IPC) Fifty.
nikotwâsomitanaw (IPC) Sixty.
tepakohpimitanaw (IPC) Seventy.
ayinânewomitanaw (IPC) Eighty.
kîkâmitâtahtomitanaw (IPC) Ninety.
mitâtahtomitanaw (IPC) One hundred.
nîswâw mitâtahtomitanaw (IPC) Two hundred.
nistwâw mitâtahtomitanaw (IPC) Three hundred.
ncwâw mitâtahtomitanaw (IPC) Four hundred.
nîyânanwâw mitâtahtomitanaw (IPC) Five hundred.
nikotwâsikwâw mitâtahtomitanaw (IPC) Six hundred.
tepakohpwâw mitâtahtomitanaw (IPC) Seven hundred.
ayinânewâw mitâtahtomitanaw (IPC) Eight hundred.
kîkâmitâtahtwâw mitâtahtomitanaw (IPC) Nine
   hundred.
peyakwâw kihci mitâtahtomitanaw (IPC) Thousand;
   one thousand.
peyakosâpwâw mitâtahtomitanaw (IPC) Eleven
   hundred.
nîswâw kihci mitâtahtomitanaw (IPC) Two thousand.

nistwâw kihci mitâtahtomitanaw (IPC) Three
   thousand.
mitâtahtwâw kihci mitâtahtomitanaw (IPC) Ten
   thousand.
mitâtahtomitanawâw kihci mitâtahtomitanaw (IPC)
   One-hundred thousand.
peyakwaw kisipakihtasowin (IPC) Million; one million.
nîswâw kisipakihtasowin (IPC) Two million.

peyakwâw (IPC). Once; one time; first time.
nîswâw (IPC) Two times; second time.
nistwâw (IPC) Three times; third time.
newâw (IPC) Four times; fourth time.
nîyânanwâw (IPC) Five times; fifth time.
nikotwâsikwâw (IPC) Six times; sixth time.
tepakohpwâw (IPC) Seven times; seventh time.
ayinânewâw (IPC) Eight times; eighth time.
kîkâmitâtahtwâw (IPC) Nine times; ninth time.
mitâtahtwâw (IPC) Ten times; tenth time.
peyakosâpwâw (IPC) Eleven times; eleventh time.
nîsosâpwâw (IPC) Twelve times; twelfth time.
nistosâpwâw (IPC) Thirteen times; thirteenth time.
newosâpwâw (IPC) Fourteen times; fourteenth time.
nîyânanosâpwâw (IPC) Fifteen times; fifteenth time.
nikotwâsosâpwaw (IPC) Sixteen times; sixteenth time.
tepakohposâpwâw (IPC) Seventeen times; seventeenth
   time.
ayînânewosâpwâw (IPC) Eighteen times; eighteenth
   time.
kîkâmitâtahtosâpâw (IPC) Nineteen times; nineteenth
   time.
nîstanowâw (IPC) Twenty times; twentieth time.
nistomitanawâw (IPC) Thirty times; thirtieth time.
nemitanawâw (IPC) Forty times; fortieth time.
nîyânanomitanawâw (IPC) Fifty times; fiftieth time.
nikotwâsomitanawâw (IPC) Sixty times; sixtieth time.
tepakohpimitanawâw (IPC) Seventy times; seventieth
   time.
ayinânewomitanawâw (IPC) Eighty times; eightieth
   time.
kîkâmitâtahtomitanawâw (IPC) Ninety times;
   ninetieth time.
mitâtahtomitanawâw (IPC) A hundred times;
   hundredth time.

565

English/Cree
akayasemowin/nehiyawewin

one *peyak* (IPC); *piyak* (IPC) *(Northern)*; one each or one by one, *pahpeyak* (IPC); one time, *peyakwâw* (IPC); of one kind, *peyakwayihk*; each in its own place, *pahpeyakwayak*; in one place, the same area, *peyakwayak*; s/he is number one or first, *peyakow* (VAI).

two *nîso* (IPC); two each, *nahnîsow* (IPC); two times, *nîswâw* (IPC); two of a kind, *nîsôskân*; two different kinds, *nîswayi*; in two places or two directions, *nîswayak*; two in each place, *nahnîswayak*; s/he is number two or second, *nîsow* (VAI).

three *nisto* (IPC); three each, *nahnisto* (IPC); three times, *nistwâw* (IPC); three of a kind *nistwayi*; of three different kinds, *nahnistwayi*; in three places or three directions, *nistawayak*; in three different directions, *nahnistawayak*; in three different ways, *nistwayakisi*; s/he is number three or third, *nistow* (VAI).

four *newo* (IPC); four each, *nahnewo* (IPC); four times, *newâw* (IPC); four of a kind, *newayih*; four different kinds, *nahnewayih*; in four places or four directions, *newayak*; in four different places, *nahnewayak*; s/he is number four or fourth, *newiw* (VAI).

five *nîyânan* (IPC); five each, *nahnîyânan* (IPC); five times, *nîyânanwâw* (IPC); five of a kind, *nîyânanwayih*; five different kinds, *nahnîyânanwayih*; in five places or five directions, *nîyânwayak*; in five different places, *nahnîyânwayak*; s/he is number five or fifth, *nîyânanowiw* (VAI).

six *nikotwâsik* (IPC); six each, *nahnikotwâsikwâw* (IPC); six times, *nikotowâsikwâw* (IPC); six of a kind, *nikotwâsikwayih*; six different kinds, *nahnikotwâsikwayih*; in six places or six directions, *nikotwâsikwayak*; in six different places, *nahnikotwâsikwayak*; s/he is number six or sixth, *nikotwâsikowiw* (VAI).

seven *tepakohp* (IPC); seven each, *tahtepakohpwâw* (IPC); seven times, *tepakohpwâw* (IPC); seven of a kind, *tepakohpwayih*; seven different kinds, *tahtepakohpwayih*; in seven places or seven directions, *tepakohpwayak*; in seven different places, *tahtepakohpwayak*; s/he is number seven or seventh, *tepakopowow* (VAI).

eight *ayinânew* (IPC); eight each, *ahayinânew*; eight times, *ayinânewâw* (IPC); eight of a kind, *ayinânewayih*; eight different kinds, *ahayinânewayih*; in eight places or eight directions, *ayinânewayak*; in eight different places,

ahayinânewayak; s/he is number eight or eighth, *ayinânewiw* (VAI).

nine *kîkâmitâtaht* (IPC), *kekâymitâht* (IPC) *(Plains)*; nine each, *kahkîkâmitatahtwâw* (IPC); nine times, *kîkâmitatahtwâw* (IPC); nine of a kind, *kîkâmitâtahtwayih*; nine different kinds, *kahkîkâmitâtahtwayih*; in nine places or nine directions, *kîkâmitâtahtwayak*; in nine different places, *kahkîkâmitâtahtwayak*; s/he is number nine or ninth, *kîkâmitâtahtowiw* (VAI).

ten *mitâtaht* (IPC); ten each, *mamitâtaht* (IPC); ten times, *mitâtahtwâw* (IPC); ten of a kind, *mitâtahtwayih*; ten different kinds, *mamitâtahtwayih*; in ten places or ten directions, *mitâtahtwayak*; in ten different places, *mamitâtahtwayak*; s/he is number ten or tenth, *mitâtahtowiw* (VAI); it is in tenth place or there is ten of it, *mitâtahtowan*.

eleven *peyakosâp* (IPC); *mitâtaht peyakosâp* (IPC); eleven times, *peyakosâpwâw* (IPC); there are eleven of them, *peyakosâpowiwak*.

twelve *nîsosâp* (IPC); twelve times, *nîsosâpwâw* (IPC).

thirteen *nistosâp* (IPC); thirteen times, *nistosâpwâw* (IPC).

fourteen *newohsâp* (IPC); fourteen times, *newosâpwâw* (IPC).

fifteen *nîyânanosâp* (IPC); *neyânanosâp* (IPC); fifteen times, *nîyânanosâpwâw* (IPC).

sixteen *nikotwâsosâp* (IPC); sixteen times, *nikotwâsosâpwâw* (IPC).

seventeen *tepakohposâp* (IPC); seventeen times, *tepakohposâpwâw* (IPC).

eighteen *ayenânewosâp* (IPC); eighteen times, *ayinânewosâpwâw* (IPC).

nineteen *kîkâmitâtahtosâp* (IPC); nineteen times, *kîkâmitahtatosâpâw* (IPC).

twenty *nîstanaw* (IPC); twenty times, *nîstanowâw* (IPC).

twenty-five *nîstanaw nîyânanosâp* (IPC).

thirty *nistomitanaw* (IPC); thirty times, *nistomitanawâw* (IPC).

forty *nemitanaw* (IPC); forty times, *nemitanawâw* (IPC).

fifty *nîyânanomitanaw* (IPC); fifty times, *nîyânanomitanawâw* (IPC); s/he is number fifty or fiftieth, *nîyânanomitanowiw* (VAI).

sixty *nikotwâsomitanaw* (IPC); sixty times, *nikowâsomitanawâw* (IPC).

seventy *tepakohpimitanaw* (IPC); seventy times, *tepakohpimitanawâw* (IPC).

eighty *ayinânemitanaw* (IPC); eighty times, *ayinânemitanawâw* (IPC).

ninety *kîkâmitâtahtomitanaw* (IPC); ninety times, *kîkâmitâtahtomitanawâw* (IPC).

hundred One hundred, *mitâtahtomitanaw* (IPC); a hundred times, *mitâtahtomitanawâw* (IPC); several hundred, *mihcetomitanaw* (IPC); it is number one hundred or one hundredth, *mitâtahtomitanawiw* (VII).

two hundred *nîswâw mitâtahtomitanaw* (IPC).

three hundred *nistwâw mitâtahtomitanaw* (IPC).

four hundred *newâw mitâtahtomitanaw* (IPC).

five hundred *nîyânanwâw mitâtahtomitanaw* (IPC).

six hundred *nikotwâsikwâw mitâtahtomitanaw* (IPC).

seven hundred *tepakohpwâw mitâtahtomitanaw* (IPC).

eight hundred *ayinânewâw mitâtahtomitanaw* (IPC).

nine hundred *kîkâmitâtahtwâw mitâtahtomitanaw* (IPC).

thousand One thousand, *peyakwâw kihci mitâtahtomitanaw* (IPC).

eleven hundred *peyakosâpwâw mitâtahtomitanaw* (IPC).

two thousand *nîswâw kihci mitâtahtomitanaw* (IPC).

three thousand *nistwâw kihci mitâtahtomitanaw* (IPC).

ten thousand *mitâtahtwâw kihci mitâtahtomitanaw* (IPC).

one-hundred thousand *mitâtahtomitanowâw kihci mitâtahtomitanaw* (IPC).

million One million, *peyakwaw kisipakihtasowin* (IPC).

two million *nîswâw kisipakihtasowin* (IPC).

first *mwecipeyakwâw* (IPC); first time, once, *peyakwâw* (IPC); first of the month, *peyak akimâw pîsim*.

second *mwecinîso* (IPC); second time, *nîswâw* (IPC); second of the month, *nîso akimâw pîsim*.

third *mwecinistwâw* (IPC); third time, *nistwâw* (IPC); third of the month, *nisto akimâw pîsim*.

fourth *mwecinewo* (IPC); fourth time, *newâw* (IPC); fourth of the month, *newâw akimâw pîsim*.

fifth *mwecinîyânan* (IPC); fifth time, *nîyânanwâw* (IPC); fifth of the month, *nîyânan akimâw pîsim*.

sixth *mwecinikotwâsik* (IPC); sixth time, *nikotwâsikwâw* (IPC); sixth of the month, *nikotwâsik akimâw pîsim*.

seventh *mwecitepakohp* (IPC); seventh time, *tepakohpwâw* (IPC); seventh of the month, *tepakohp akimâw pîsim*.

eighth *mweciayinânew* (IPC); eighth time, *ayinânewâw* (IPC); eighth of the month, *ayinânew akimâw pîsim*.

ninth *mwecikîkâmitâtaht* (IPC); ninth time, *kîkâmitâtahtwâw* (IPC); ninth of the month, *kîkâmitâtaht akimâw pîsim*.

tenth *mwecimitâtaht* (IPC); tenth time, *mitâtahtwâw* (IPC); tenth of the month, *mitâtaht akimâw pîsim*.

eleventh *mwecipeyakosâp* (IPC); eleventh time, *peyakosâpwâw* (IPC); eleventh of the month, *peyakosâp akimâw pîsim*.

twelfth *mwecinîsosâp* (IPC); twelfth time, *nîsosâpwâw* (IPC); twelfth of the month, *nîsosâp akimâw pîsim*.

thirteenth *mwecinitosâp* (IPC); thirteenth time, *nitosâpwâw* (IPC); thirteenth of the month, *nistosâp akimâw pîsim*.

fourteenth *mwecinewosâp* (IPC); fourteenth time, *newosâpwâw* (IPC); fourteenth of the month, *newosâp akimâw pîsim*.

fifteenth *mwecinîyânanosâp* (IPC); *mwecineyânanosâp* (IPC); fifteenth time, *nîyânanosâpwâw* (IPC); fifteenth of the month, *nîyânanosâp akimâw pîsim*.

sixteenth *mwecinikotwâsosâp* (IPC); sixteenth time, *nikotwâsosâpwâw* (IPC); sixteenth of the month, *nikotwâsosâp akimâw pîsim*.

seventeenth *mwecitepakohposâp* (IPC); seventeenth time, *tepakohposâpwâw* (IPC); seventeenth of the month, *tepakohposâp akimâw pîsim*.

eighteenth *mweciayinânewosâp* (IPC); eighteenth time, *ayinânewosâpwâw* (IPC); eighteenth of the month, *ayinânewosâp akimâw pîsim*.

nineteenth *mwecikîkâmitahtatosâp* (IPC); nineteenth time, *kîkâmitahtatosâpâw* (IPC); nineteenth of the month, *kîkâmitahtatosâp akimâw pîsim*.

twentieth *mwecinîstanaw* (IPC); twentieth time, *nîstanawâw* (IPC); twentieth of the month, *nîstanaw akimâw pîsim*.

thirtieth *mwecinistomitanaw* (IPC); thirtieth time, *nistomitanawâw* (IPC); thirtieth of the month, *nistomitanaw akimâw pîsim*.

fortieth *mwecinemitanaw* (IPC); fortieth time, *nemitanawâw* (IPC).

fiftieth *mwecinîyânanomitanaw* (IPC); fiftieth time, *nîyânanomitanawâw* (IPC).

sixtieth *mwecinikotwâsomitanaw* (IPC); sixtieth time, *nikowâsomitanawâw* (IPC).

seventieth *mwecitepakohpomitanaw* (IPC); seventieth time, *tepakohpomitanawâw* (IPC).

eightieth *mweciayinânemitanaw* (IPC); eightieth time, *ayinânemitanawâw* (IPC).

nintieth *mwecikîkâmitâtahtomitanaw* (IPC); nintieth time, *kîkâmitâtahtomitanawâw* (IPC).

hundreth, One hundreth, *mwecimitâtahtomitanaw* (IPC); hundreth time, *mitâtahtomitanawâw* (IPC).

567

thousandth One thousandth, *mwecipeyakwâw kihci mitâtahtomitanaw* (IPC); thousandth time, *peyakwâw kihci mitâtahtomitanawâw* (IPC).

APPENDIX D

Kinship Terms

Cree/English
nehiyawewin/akayasemowin

kesikos *pl.* **kesikosak** (NA) Your aunt. *Var.* **kimamasis**; **kisikos** *(Plains).*

kiciwam *pl.* **kiciwamak** (NA) Your cousin.

kikawes *pl.* **kikawesak** (NA) Your godmother. *Var.* **kikawîs** *(Plains).*

kikawîs *pl.* **kikawîsak** (NA) Your godmother. *(Plains).* *Var.* **kikawes**.

kikosisihkawin *pl.* **kikosisihkawinak** (NA) Your godson.

kimamasis *pl.* **kimamasisak** (NA) Your aunt. *Var.* **kesikos**; **kisikos** *(Plains).*

kimosôm *pl.* **kimosômak** (NA) Your grandfather. *Var.* **kimosômiwaw**.

kimosômiwaw *pl.* **kimosômiwawak** (NA) Your grandfather. *Var.* **kimosôm**.

kinîkihikonawak (NA) Our parents.

kisikos *pl.* **kisikosak** (NA) Your aunt. *(Plains).* *Var.* **kimamasis**; **kesikos**.

kisis *pl.* **kisisak** (NA) Your uncle. *Var.* **kocawîs**.

kitânsihkawin *pl.* **kitânsihkawinak** (NA) Your goddaughter.

kocawîs *pl.* **kocawîsak** (NA) Your uncle. *Var.* **kisis**.

kohcawes *pl.* **kohcawesak** (NA) Your godfather. *Var.* **kikohtawîs** *(Plains).*

kohcawîs *pl.* **kohcawîsak** (NA) Your godfather. *(Plains).* *Var.* **kohcawes**.

kohkom *pl.* **kohkomak** (NA) Your grandmother. *Var.* **kohkomwâw**.

kohkomwâw *pl.* **kohkomwâwak** (NA) Your grandmother. *Var.* **kohkom**.

kokôm *pl.* **kokômak** (NA) Your grandma.

kôcwamihtolik (NI) Being male cousins.

nahâhkis *pl.* **nahâhkisak** (NDA) A son-in-law.

nahâkaniskwem *pl.* **nahâkaniskwemak** (NDA) A daughter-in-law.

nicahkos (NA) Women say "my brother's wife".

nicicim *pl.* **nicicimak** (NA) My grandson or my granddaughter (diminutive). *Var.* **nôsisim**.

niciwâm *pl.* **niciwâmak** (NA) Brothers say "my brother"; my first cousin (male), *var.* **nistes**, **nimis**, **nîtim**.

niciwâmihkawin *pl.* **niciwâmihkawinak** (NA) My stepbrother; my adopted brother.

nicosim *pl.* **nicosimak** (NA) My nephew; my stepson.

nikawihkawin *pl.* **nikawihkawinak** (NA) My godmother.

nikâwîs *pl.* **nikâwîsak** (NA) My stepmother or my aunt.

nikâwiy (NA) My mother. *Var.* **nimâmâ**.

nikosihsikawin *pl.* **nikosihsikawinak** (NA) My godson.

nikosis *pl.* **nikosisak** (NA) My son; men say "my brother's son", *var.* **nitôsim**.

nimâmâ (NA) My mother. *Var.* **nikâwiy**.

nimâmâsis *pl.* **nimâmâsisak** (NA) My mother's sister or my maternal aunt.

nimis *pl.* **nimisak** (NA) My older sister; my first cousin, *var.* **nistes**, **niciwam**, **nîtim**.

nimisihkawin *pl.* **nimisihkawinak** (NA) My stepsister.

nimosôm *pl.* **nimosômak** (NA) My grandfather; my grandpa; my grand uncle.

nimosôm nitânskotapân *pl.* **nimosômak nitânskotapânak** (NA) My great-grandfather.

nimosôminân *pl.* **nimosôminânak** (NA) Our grandfather.

ninahâhkisîm *pl.* **ninahâhkisîmak** (NA) My daughter-in-law or my son-in-law. *(Plains).* *Var.* **ninahâkaniskwem**.

ninahâkaniskwem *pl.* **ninahâkaniskwemak** (NA) My daughter-in-law. *Alt.* **ninahâhkisîm** *(Plains).*

ninâpem (NA) My husband.

ninîkihikwak (NA) My parents.

nipâpâ (NA) My father. *Var.* **nohtâwiy**.

nipâpâsis *pl.* **nipâpâsisak** (NA) My father's brother or my paternal uncle. *Var.* **nôhkomis**, **nôhcâwîs**.

nisikos *pl.* **nisikosak** (NA) My father's sister or my paternal aunt; my mother-in-law.

nisis *pl.* **nisisak** (NA) My mother's brother or my maternal uncle; my father-in-law.

nisîmis *pl.* **nisîmisak** (NA) My younger brother or my sister.

nistamôkosisân *pl.* **nistamokosisânak** (NA) My first-born son.

nistamôsân *pl.* **nistamôsânak** (NA) My first-born child.

nistamôsâniwiw *pl.* **nistamôsâniwiwak** (VAI) S/he is the first-born child.

nistes *pl.* **nistesak** (NA) My older brother; my first cousin, *var.* **nimis**, **niciwam**, **nîtim**.

nistim *pl.* **nistimwak** (NA) My daughter-in-law or my sister's daughter; men say "my sister's daughter"; women say "my brother's daughter".

nitawemâw *pl.* **nitawemâwak** (NA) Brothers say "my sister".

nitânis *pl.* **nitânisak** (NA) My daughter.

nitânisihkawin *pl.* **nitânisihkawinak** (NA) My niece; my stepdaughter; my goddaughter.

nitânskotapân *pl.* **nitânskotapânak** (NA) My great-grandchild, *var.* **nôsisim**; my great-grandparent.

nitikwatim *pl.* **nitikwatimak** (NA) Men say "my sister's son"; women say "my brother's son".

nitisaniskwew *pl.* **nitisaniskwewak** (NA) Sisters say "my sister".

nitosis *pl.* **nitosisak** (NA) My aunt; my mother-in-law.

nitôsim *pl.* **nitôsimak** (NA) My nephew; men say "my brother's son", *var.* **nikosis**; women say "my sister's son"; my stepson.

nitôsimiskwem *pl.* **nitôsimiskwemak** (NA) My stepdaughter; my adopted daughter; men say "my brother's daughter"; women say "my sister's daughter".

nîcakos *pl.* **nîcakosak** (NA) Second cousin, what a woman calls a woman.

nîcimos *pl.* **nîcimosak** (NA) Second cousin, what a man calls a woman or what a woman calls a man. *Var.* **nîtim**.

nîcisân *pl.* **nîcisânak** (NA) My sibling; my sister or my brother. *Var.* **nîtisân**.

nîscas *pl.* **nîscasak** (NA) Second cousin, a man calls a man on the maternal side of the family.

nîstâw *pl.* **nîstâwak** (NA) My brother-in-law; men say "my sister's husband".

nîtim *pl.* **nîtimak** (NA) My sister-in-law; women say "my sister's husband"; men say "my brother's wife"; my first cousin, *var.* **nistes, nimis, niciwam**; second cousin, what a man calls a woman or what a woman calls a man, *var.* **nîcimos**.

nîtisân *pl.* **nîtisânak** (NA) My brother or my sister; sisters say "my brother". *Var.* for my brother, **nîcisân**.

nîwa (NA) My wife. *Var.* **nîwah**.

nîwah (NA) My wife. *Var.* **nîwa**.

niwîkimâkan (NA) My marriage partner; someone you live with, i.e.: my spouse.

nohkôm *pl.* **nohkômak** (NA) My grandmother; my grandma; my granny or my grannie; my great-aunt.

nohkôm nitânskotapân *pl.* **nitânskotapânak** (NA) My great-grandmother.

nohkomnan *pl.* **nohkomnanak** (NA) Our grandmother.

nohtawehkawin (NA) My godfather.

nohtâwiy (NA) My father. *Var.* **nipâpâ**.

nôhcâwîs *pl.* **nôhcâwîsak** (NA) My father's brother or my paternal uncle. *Var.* **nôhkomis, nipâpâsis**.

nôhkômis *pl.* **nôhkômisak** (NA) My father's brother or my paternal uncle, *var.* **nipâpâsis, nôhcâwîs**; my stepfather *(Northern)*.

nôsisim *pl.* **nôsisimak** (NA) My grandchild; my granddaughter or my grandson, *var.* **nicicim** (diminutive); my grandnephew or my grandniece; my great-granddaughter; my great-grandchild, *var.* **nitânskotapân**.

nôsisim iskwesis *pl.* **nôsisimak iskwesisak** (NA) My granddaughter.

nôsisim nitânskotâpan *pl.* **nitânskotapânak** (NA) My great-grandson.

nôsism napesis *pl.* **nôsismak napesisak** (NA) My grandson.

ocakosimâw *pl.* **ocakosimâwak** (NA) Sister-in-law. **ocakosiwâwa** (ob.).

ociwama *pl.* **ociwamiwâwa** (ob.) (NA) His stepbrother or his adopted brother.

ociwâmihtowak (VAI) They are cousins.

ociwâmihtowin *pl.* **ociwamihtowina** (NI) Being cousins; a cousin relationship.

ociwâmimâw *pl.* **ociwâmimâwak** (VAI) He is a cousin.

ociwâmiskwemâw *pl.* **ociwâmiskwemâwak** (VAI) She is a cousin.

ohkoma (ob.) (NA) Her or his grandmother.

ohkomimâw *pl.* **ohkomimâwak** (NA) A grandmother.

ohkomisimâw *pl.* **ohkomisimâwak** (NA) A stepfather. *(Northern)*. *Alt.* **ohtâwihkawin** *(Plains)*.

ohkomiwâwa (ob.) (NA) Their grandmother.

ohpikihâwasiw *pl.* **ohpikihâwasiwak** (VAI) S/he raises children.

ohtâwihkawew *pl.* **ohtâwihkawewak** (VTA) He becomes her/his father.

ohtâwihkawin *pl.* **ohtâwihkawinak** (NA) A godfather *(Northern)*; a stepfather *(Plains)*; *alt.* **ohkomisimâw** *(Northern)*.

ohtâwiskâkew *pl.* **ohtâwiskâkewak** (VAI) He is a father of people.

ohtâwiskakam *pl.* **ohtâwiskakamak** (VAI) He is a father to it.

ohtâwiskawew *pl.* **ohtâwiskawewak** (VAI) He is her/his surrogate father.

ohtâwîmâw *pl.* **ohtâwîmâwak** (NA) A father. *Var.* **opâpâmâw**.

okawisa *pl.* **okawisiwâwa** (ob.) (NA) Their stepmother.

okâwiw *pl.* **okâwiwak** (VAI) S/he has a mother. *(Plains)*. *Alt.* **omâmâw** *(Northern)*.

okâwîm *pl.* **okâwîmak** (VAI) She has a mother. *Var.* **omâmâw**.

okâwîmâw *pl.* **okâwîmâwak** (NA) A mother (generic).

okâwîmew *pl.* **okâwîmewak** (VTA) S/he has her as a mother. *Var.* **omâmâmew**.

okâwîmiwew *pl.* **okâwîmiwewak** (VAI) S/he has someone as a mother.

okosimâw *pl.* **okosimâwak** (NA) A son.

okosisihkâw (VTA) S/he adopts him as a son. *(Plains).* *Alt.* **okosisimew** *(Northern);* s/he sponsors her/him as godson.

okosisimew (VTA) S/he adopt him as a son. *(Northern).* *Alt.* **okosisihkâw** *(Plains).*

okosisimiwew (VTA) S/he adopts others as sons.

okômâw *pl.* **okômâwak** (NA) A great-grandmother. *Var.* **otânskotapew.**

omâmâmew *pl.* **omâmâmewak** (VTA) S/he has her as a mother. *Var.* **okâwîmew.**

omâmâw *pl.* **omâmâwak** (VAI) S/he has a mother. *(Northern).* *Alt.* **okâwiw** *(Plains).*

omâmâwaw *pl.* **omâmâwawak** (NA) A mother. *Var.* **okâwîmâw.**

omisahkomew *pl.* **omisahkomewak** (VAI) S/he has her as an older sister. *(Plains).* *Alt.* **omisimiw** *(Northern).*

omisimâw *pl.* **omisimâwak** (NA) The eldest sister.

omisimâwiw *pl.* **omisimâwiwak** (VAI) She is the eldest sister.

omisimiw *pl.* **omisimiwak** (VAI) S/he has her as an older sister. *(Northern).* *Alt.* **omisahkomew** *(Plains).*

omosôma (ob.) (NA) Her or his grandfather.

omosômâw *pl.* **omosômâwak** (NA) A great-grandfather; a great-uncle. *Var.* **otânskotapew.**

omosômimâw *pl.* **omosômimâwak** (NA) A grandfather; a grandpa.

omosômiwâwa (ob.) (NA) Their grandfather.

onahâhkisîmâw *pl.* **onahâhkisîmâwak** (NA) A son-in-law.

onâpemiw *pl.* **onâpemiwak** (VAI) She has a husband.

onekihikiw *pl.* **onekihikiwak** (VAI) S/he has parents.

onekihikomâw *pl.* **onekihikomâwak** (NA) A parent. *(Northern).* *Alt.* **onîkihikomâw** *(Plains);* a great-grandparent. *Var.* **otânskotapew.**

onekihikomâwiwin *pl.* **onekihikomâwiwina** (NI) Being a parent; parenthood.

onekihikow *pl.* **onekihikowak** (VAI) S/he has parents.

onıkıhıkomaw *pl.* **onıkıhıkomawak** (NA) A parent. *(Plains).* *Alt.* **onekihikomâw** (NA) *(Northern).*

opâpâmâw *pl.* **opâpâmâwak** (NA) A father. *Var.* **ohtâwîmâw.**

osikosimâw *pl.* **osikosimâwak** (NA) A mother-in-law; a paternal aunt.

osikosiw *pl.* **osikosiwak** (VAI) S/he has a mother-in-law.

osisimâw *pl.* **osisimâwak** (NA) A father-in-law.

osisimâwiw *pl.* **osisimâwiwak** (VAI) He is a father-in-law.

osisiw *pl.* **osisiwak** (VAI) S/he has a father-in-law.

osîmimâw *pl.* **osîmimâwak** (NA) A younger sibling; younger brother or younger sister.

osîmimâwiw *pl.* **osîmimâwiwak** (VAI) S/he is the youngest sibling of the family.

oskiskwewiw *pl.* **oskiskwewiwak** (NA) A new wife.

ostesimâw *pl.* **ostesimâwak** (NA) The eldest brother.

ostesimâwiw *pl.* **ostesimâwiwak** (VAI) He is the eldest brother.

ostimâw *pl.* **ostimâwak** (NA) A daughter-in-law.

ostimimâw *pl.* **ostimimâwak** (NA) A niece or a daughter-in-law.

otânisihkâw *pl.* **otânisihkâwak** (VTA) S/he has her as a daughter. *(Plains).* S/he has her as a god daughter. *(Northern).* *Alt.* **otânisimew** *(Northern).*

otânisihkâwew *pl.* **otânisihkâwewak** (VTA) S/he has her for a daughter. *(Plains).* *Alt.* **otânisimew** *(Northern).*

otânisihkâwin *pl.* **otânisihkâwinak** (NA) A stepdaughter or adopted daughter. *Var.* **otôsimiskwew.**

otânisimâw *pl.* **otânisimâwak** (NA) A daughter.

otânisimew *pl.* **otânisimewak** (VTA) S/he has her as a daughter. *(Northern).* *Alt.* **otânisihkâw** *(Plains).*

otânisiw *pl.* **otânisiwak** (VAI) S/he has a daughter.

otânskotapan *pl.* **otânskotapanak** (NA) Great-grandchild; great-granddaughter; great-grandson; great-nephew; great-niece; great-grandfather, *var.* **omosômâw;** great-grandmother, *var.* **okômâw;** great-grandparent, *var.* **onekihikomâw;** great-uncle, *var.* **omosômâw;** great-aunt.

otikwatimâw *pl.* **otikwatimâwak** (NA) A nephew. *Alt.* **tehkwatim** (slang).

otôsimiskwew *pl.* **otôsimiskwewak** (NA) A stepdaughter or adopted daughter. *Var.* **otânisihkâwin.**

owîkimâkanimew (VTA) S/he has her/him as a spouse.

owîkimâkaniw (VAI) S/he has a spouse.

owîkitiw *pl.* **owîkitiwak** (NA) A spouse; a married partner. *Var.* **wikimâkan.**

tipiyaw nîcisân (NA) A full sibling; my brother or sister; a full brother or sister.

wahkomâkan *pl.* **wahkomâkanak** (NA) A cousin.

wewow *pl.* **wewowak** (VAI) He has a wife.

wicisânitowin (NI) Having siblings. *(Plains).* *Alt.* **wîtisânitowin** *(Northern).*

wikihto wahkohtowin (NA) An in-law.

wikimâkan *pl.* **wikimâkanak** (NA) A spouse or a married partner. *Var.* **owîkitiw.**

wikimâkanimew (VAI) S/he is a spouse to her/him.

wîtisânitowin (NI) Having siblings. *(Northern).* *Alt.* **wicisanitowin** *(Plains).*

571

English/Cree
akayasemowin/nehiyawewin

aunt My aunt (or my mother-in-law), *nitosis* (NA); my father's sister or paternal aunt, *nisikos* (NA); my mother's sister or maternal aunt, *nimamasis* (NA); your aunt, *kesikos* (NA); *kisikos* (NA) *(Plains)*; *kimamasis* (NA); someone's parent's sister, *awîyak osikosa* (NA); *awîyak omamasisa* (NA); *awîyak otôsisa* (NA); someone's father's sister, *awîyak osokisa* (NA); someone's mother's sister, *awîyak okawîsa* (NA).

brother The eldest brother, *ostesimâw* (NA); younger brother (or sister), *osîmimâw* (NA); my brother (or sister), *nîtisân* (NA); *nîcisân* (NA); my older brother, *nistes* (NA); my younger brother (or sister), *nisîmis* (NA); sisters say my brother, *nîtisân* (NA); brothers say my brother, *niciwam* (NA); someone's male sibling, *awîyak nâpew wîtisana* (NA); he is the eldest brother, *ostesimâwiw* (VAI); s/he has him as a brother, *nâpew owîtisânimew* (VAI).

brother-in-law My brother-in-law, *nîstâw* (NDA); men say my sister's husband, *nîstâw* (NA); women say my sister's husband, *nîtim* (NA); someone's brother-in-law, *awîyak wîstâwa* (NA); *awîyak wîtîmwa* (NA).

cousin *wahkomâkan* (NA); my first cousin, *nistes* (NA); *nimis* (NA); *niciwam* (NA); *nîtim* (NA); second cousin, a man calls a man, *nîscas* (NA); second cousin, a man calls a woman, *nîcimos* (NA); *nîtim* (NA); second cousin, a woman calls a man, *nîcimos* (NA); *nîtim* (NA); second cousin, a woman calls a woman, *nîcakos* (NA); your cousin, *kiciwam* (NA); he is a cousin, *ociwâmimâw* (VAI); she is a cousin, *ociwâmiskwemâw* (VAI); they are cousins, *ociwâmihtowak* (VAI); being cousins, *kôciwamihtohk* (NI); being cousins or a cousin relationship, *ociwâmihtowin* (NI).

daughter *otânisimâw* (NA); my daughter, *nitânis* (NA); someone's daughter, *awîyak otânsa* (NA); s/he has her for a daughter, *otânisihkâwew* (VTA) *(Plains)*; *otânisimew* (VTA) *(Northern)*; s/he has a daughter, *otânisiw* (VAI).

daughter-in-law *ostimâw* (NA); my daughter-in-law (or sister's daughter), *nistim* (NA); my daughter-in-law, *ninahâkaniskwem* (NDA); my daughter-in-law (or son-in law), *ninahâhkisîm* (NA) *(Plains)*; a daughter-in-law (generic), *nahâkaniskwem* (NDA)

father *ohtâwîmâw* (NA); *opâpâmâw* (NA); my father, *nohtâwiy* (NA); *nipâpâ* (NA); someone's father, *awîyak ohtâwîmâh* (NA); *awîyak opâpâmâh* (NA); he is her/his surrogate father, *ohtâwiskawew* (VAI); he becomes her/his father, *ohtâwihkawew* (VAI).

father-in-law *osisimâw* (NA); my father-in-law (or uncle), *nisis* (NA); someone's father-in-law, *awîyak osisisa* (NA); he is a father-in-law, *osisimâwiw* (VAI); s/he has a father-in-law, *osisiw* (VAI).

goddaughter My goddaughter, *nitânisihkawin* (NA); your goddaughter, *kitânsihkawin* (NA).

godfather My godfather, *nohtawehkawin* (NA); your godfather, *kohcawes* (NA); *kohcawîs* (NA) *(Plains)*.

godmother My godmother, *nikawihkawin* (NA); your godmother, *kikawes* (NA); *kikawîs* (NA) *(Plains)*.

godson My godson, *nikosihsikawin* (NA); your godson, *kikosisihkawin* (NA).

grand uncle My grand uncle, *nimosôm* (NA).

grandchild My grandchild, *nôsisim* (NA); having a grandchild, *kosisimihk*.

grandchildren My grandchildren, *nôsisimak* (NA); having lots of grandchildren, *mihcet kosisimihk*.

granddaughter My granddaughter (or grandson), *nôsisim* (NA); my granddaughter, *nôsisim iskwesis* (NA); having a granddaughter (or grandson), *iskwew kosisisimihk*.

grandfather *omosômimâw* (NA); my grandfather, *nimosôm* (NA); our grandfather, *nimosôminan* (NA); his or her grandfather, *omosôma* (NA); their grandfather, *omosômiwawa* (NA); your grandfather, *kimosôm* (NA); *kimosômiwaw* (NA).

grandma My grandma, *nohkôm* (NA); your grandma, *kokôm* (NA).

grandmother *ohkomimâw* (NA); my grandmother, *nohkôm* (NA); our grandmother, *nohkomnan* (NA); his or her grandmother, *ohkoma* (NA); their grandmother, *ohkomwâwa* (NA); your grandmother, *kohkom* (NA); *kohkomwâw* (NA).

grandnephew My grandnephew, *nôsisim* (NA).

grandniece My grandniece, *nôsisim* (NA).

grandpa *omosômimâw* (NA); my grandpa, *nimosôm* (NA).

grandson My grandson (or granddaughter), *nôsisim* (NA); *nicicim* (diminutive) (NA); my grandson, *nôsism napesis* (NA); having a grandson (or granddaughter), *iskwew kosisisimihk*.

granny *or* **grannie** My granny or grannie, *nohkôm* (NA).

great-aunt *otânskotapân* (NA); my great-aunt, *nohkôm* (NA).

great-grandchild *otânskotapân* (NA); my great-grandchild, *nôsisim* (NA); *nitânskotapân* (NA).

great-granddaughter *otânskotapan* (NA); my great-granddaughter, *nôsisim* (NA).

great-grandfather *otânskotapew* (NA); *omosômâw* (NA); my great-grandfather, *nimosôm nitânskotapân* (NA);

great-grandmother *otânskotapew* (NA); *okômâw* (NA); my great-grandmother, *nohkôm nitânskotapân* (NA).

great-grandparent *otânskotapew* (NA); *onekihikomâw* (NA); my great-grandparent, *nitânskotapânak* (NA).

great-grandson *otânskotapân* (NA); my great-grandson, *nôsisim nitânskotapân* (NA).

great-nephew *otânskotapân* (NA).

great-niece *otânskotapân* (NA).

great-uncle *otânskotapew* (NA); *omosômâw* (NA).

husband My husband, *ninâpem* (NA); my marriage partner, *niwîkimâkan* (NA); someone's husband, *awîyak onâpema* (NA); she has a husband, *onâpemiw* (VAI).

in-law *wikihto wahkohtowin* (NA).

mother-in-law Or paternal aunt, *osikosimâw* (NA); my mother-in-law (or aunt), *nisikos* (NA); s/he has a mother-in-law, *osikosiw* (VAI).

mother *okâwîmâw* (NA); *omâmâwaw* (NA); my mother, *nikâwiy* (NA); *nimâmâ* (NA); someone's mother, *awîyak okâwîmâh* (NA); *awîyak omâmâwah* (NA); she has a mother, *okâwîm* (VAI); *omâmâw* (VAI); s/he has her as a mother, *okâwîmew* (VTA); *omâmâmew* (VTA).

nephew *otikwatimâw* (NA); *nitehkwatim* (NA) (slang); my nephew (or my stepson), *nicosim* (NA); men say my brother's son, *nitôsim* (NA); *nikosis* (NA); women say my brother's son, *nitikwatim* (NA); men say my sister's son, *nitikwatim* (NA); women say my sister's son, *nitôsim* (NA); someone's nephew, *awîyak otihkwatimah* (NA).

niece *ostimimâw* (NA); my niece (or stepdaughter), *nitânisihkawin* (NA); men say my brother's daughter, *nitôsimiskwem* (NA); women say my brother's daughter, *nistim* (NA); men say my sister's daughter, *nistim* (NA); women say my sister's daughter, *nitôsimiskwem* (NA); someone's niece, *awîyak ostima* (NA).

parent *onekihikomâw* (NA) (Northern); *nîkihikomâw* (NA) (Plains); my parents, *ninîkihikwak* (NA); someone's parents, *awîyak onekihikwa* (NA); s/he has parents, *onekihikiw* (VAI).

sibling Younger brother or sister, *osîmimâw* (NA); my younger brother or sister, *nisîmis* (NA); my sisters and brothers, *nîcisânak* (NA); a full sibling or a full brother or sister, *tipiyaw*, i.e.: *tipiyaw nîcisân* (NA); having siblings, *wîtisânitowin* (NI) (Northern); *wicisanitowin* (NI) (Plains); s/he is the youngest sibling in the family, *osîmimâwiw* (VAI).

sister The eldest sister, *omisimâw* (NA); younger sister (or brother), *osîmimâw* (NA); my sister (or brother), *nîtisân* (NA); my older sister, *nimis* (NA); my younger sister (or brother), *nisîmis* (NA); sisters say my sister, *nitisaniskwew* (NA); brothers say my sister, *nitawemâw* (NA); someone's female sibling, *awîyak iskwewa wetcisâna* (NA); she is the eldest sister, *omisimawiw* (VAI); s/he has her as an older sister, *omisimiw* (VAI) (Northern), *omisahkomew* (VAI) (Plains).

sister-in-law *ocakosimâw* (NA); my sister-in-law, *nîtim* (NDA); women say my brother's wife, *nicahkos* (NA); men say my brother's wife, *nîtim* (NA); their sister-in-law, *ocakosiwawa* (NA); someone's sister-in-law, *awîyak ocakosa* (NA); *awîyak nâpiw wîtimwa* (NA).

son *okosimâw* (NA); my son, *nikosis* (NA); my first-born son, *nistamôkosisân* (NA); someone's son, *awîyak okosisa* (NA); someone looked upon as a son, *mikosisimâw* (NA).

son-in-law *onahâhkisîmâw* (NA); my son-in-law, *nahâhkis* (NDA); my son-in-law (or daughter-in-law) *ninahâkaniskwem* (NA).

spouse A married partner, *owîkitiw* (NA); *wikimâkan* (NA); my marriage partner or someone you live with, i.e.: my spouse, *niwîkimâkan* (NA); someone's marriage partner, *awîyak owîkimâkana* (NA); s/he has her/him as a spouse, *owîkimâkanimew* (VTA); s/he has a spouse, *owîkimâkaniw* (VAI); s/he is a spouse to her/him, *wikimâkanimew* (VAI).

step-parent *ohpime ohci konikihikohk*.

stepbrother My stepbrother or adopted brother, *niciwamihkawin* (NA); his stepbrother or adopted brother, *ociwama* (NA); someone's stepbrother or adopted brother, *awîyak ociwamihkawina* (NA).

stepchild *awâsis ohpime kopâpât ahpô komâmât*.

stepdaughter Or adopted daughter *otôsimiskwew* (NA); *otânisihkâwin* (NA); my stepdaughter or adopted daughter, *nitôsimiskwem* (NA); my stepdaughter (or niece), *nitânisihkâwin* (NA).

stepfather *ohkomisimâw* (NA) (Northern); *ohtâwihkawin* (NA) (Plains); my stepfather, *nôhkômis* (NA) (Northern); someone's stepfather, *awîyak ohkomisa* (NA) (Northern); *awîyak ohtâwihkawina* (NA) (Plains; *awîyak opâpâsah* (NA).

stepmother Their stepmother, *okawisa* (ob.) (NA); my stepmother, *nikâwîs* (NA); someone's stepmother, *awîyak omâmâsisah* (NA).

stepsister *ohpime ohci komsihk*; my stepsister, *nimisihkawin* (NA).

stepson *ohpime ohci kokosihk*; my stepson (or my nephew), *nitôsim* (NA).

uncle My father's brother or paternal uncle, *nôhkômis* (NA); *nipâpâsis* (NA); *nôhcâwîs* (NA); my mother's brother or maternal uncle (or father-in-law), *nisis* (NA); your uncle, *kocawîs* (NA); *kisis* (NA); someone's father's brother, *awîyak ohkomisa* (NA); *awîyak opâpâsisa* (NA); *awîyak ohcawisa* (NA); someone's mother's brother, *osisa* (NA).

573

wife My wife, **_nîwah_** (NA); my marriage partner,
  niwîkimâkan (NA); someone's wife, **_awîyak wewa_**
  (NA); he has a wife, **_wewow_** (VAI).

Selected Bibliography

Ahenakew, Freda. *Cree Language Structures: A Cree Approach*. Winnipeg: Pemmican Publications, 1987.

———. (ed.). *Kiskinahamawâkan-Âcimowinsa/Student Stories*. Winnipeg: Alqonquin & Iroquoian Languages, 1986.

"American Languages," *The Church Missionary Intelligencer* (1854): 67–72.

Anderson, Anne. *Cree Language*. Edmonton: 1970.

———. *Cree Tenses*. Edmonton: 1972.

———. *Cree Vocabulary*. Edmonton: 1970.

———. *Cree, What They Do Book*. Edmonton: 1970.

———. *Introduction to Vowel Sounds and Drawings*. Edmonton: 1970.

———. *Learning Cree*. Edmonton: 1971.

———. *Let's Learn Cree—Namoya Ayiman*. Edmonton: 1970.

———. *Little Hunter Book—Machesis*. Edmonton: 1972.

———. *Neheyawewin—Cree Phrases*. Edmonton: 1970.

———. *Owasis*. Edmonton: 1972.

———. *Plains Cree Dialect Dictionary in the Y dialect*. Edmonton: 1971.

———. *Read and Write—Ayamichikewin Mena Musinahikewin*. Edmonton: 1972.

———. *Wapi*. Edmonton: 1972.

Anthony, Robert J. "A Preliminary Report on the Swampy Cree of Shamattawwa, Manitoba," *Linguistic Circle of Manitoba and North Dakota*, Proceedings, Vol. 12, pp. 24–28, 1972.

Baker, W. "Bibliography of the Algonquin Languages by J.C. Pilling," *American Anthropologist* 4 (1983): 101–4.

Balter, Leon Guillaume. *Courtes Instructions on Langue Crises*. Edmonton: La Survivance, 1940.

Bampos, William Carpenter. *Cree Primer*. London: Gilbert and Rivington, n.d.

Becker, Dolores M. "Written American Indian Languages," *On Smoke Signals* 6, no. 5–6 (1952).

Bloomfield, Leonard. "Algonquian," in *Linguistic Structures of North America*. Osgood: 1946.

Bloomfield, Leonard. "The Plains Cree Language," *International Congress of Americanists*, Proceedings 22.2, pp. 427–31. Rome: 1928,

Bowery, Thomas. *A Dictionary of the Hudson's Bay Language*. London: British Museum Library, 1701.

Cardinal-Collins, Mary. *Nihiyaw Pikiskwiw Masinahikan: Cree Vocabulary Booklet*. Peace River: Northland School Division No. 61, 1994.

Chamberlain, A.F. "Algonkian Words in American English," *Journal of American Folklore* 15 (1902): 240–67.

Clarke, Sandra and Marguerite MacKenzie, "Cree/Montagnais/Naskapi Reference Bibliography," *Algonquian and Iroquoian Linguistics* 20, no. 4 (1995): 39–56.

Conversational Cree. Saskatoon: Indian and Northern Curriculum Resource Centre, University of Saskatchewan.

"Cree Shorthand System," *Guting Magazine*, Vol. 66 (July 1915): 466–67.

Dictionary Catalogue of the Edward R. Azer Collection of American Indians in the Newberry Library. Boston: G.K. Hall and Company, 1961.

A Dictionary of the Cree Language, as Spoken by the Indians of the Hudson's Bay Company's Territories, Edwin Arthur Watkins, comp. London: Society for the Promotion of Christian Knowledge, 1865.

A Dictionary of the Cree Languages as Spoken by the Indians in the Provinces of Quebec, Ontario, Manitoba, Saskatchewan and Alberta, Richard Faries, ed., Edwin Arthur Watkins, comp. Toronto: Church of England in Canada, 1938.

Ellis, C. Douglas. "Meet Cree—A Practical Guide to the Language," *Canadian Journal of Linguistics* 23, no. 1–2: 194–97.

———. "A Note of Okima-hka-n," *Anthropological Linguistics* 2, no. 3 (1960): 1.

———. "The So-Called Interrogative Order in Cree," *International Journal of American Linguistics* 27, no. 2, (1961): 119–24.

———. *Spoken Cree: West Coast of James Bay*. Toronto: Anglican Book Centre, 1962.

———. *Spoken Cree: West Coast of James Bay*, revised edition. Edmonton: Pica Pica Press (University of Alberta Press), 1983.

———. "Tagmemic Analysis of a Restricted Cree Text," *Journal of the Canadian Linguistic Association* 6 (1960): 35–59.

Example of the Syllabic Printing of the Cree Language at the Moose Factory in 1856. Moose Factory: 1856.

First Reading Book, James Hunter, trans. London: 1858.

Fisher, William, comp. *News Travel Among the Indians of North America, Being a Compilation Taken from the Communications Already Published of Captain Lewis and Clark to the President of the United States and Partly from Other Authors who Travelled Among the Various Tribes of Indians — with a Dictionary of the Indian Tongue.* Philadelphia: James Sharan, J. Maxwell, Printer, 1812.

Giliareveskii, R.S. and V.S. Grivnin. *Opredelitel'iazykiv mira po pis'mennostiam.* Moskva: Izd-vo Navka, 1965.

Glass, Ervin Bird. *Primer and Language Lessons in English and Cree*, Rev. John McDougall, trans. Toronto: W. Briggs, 1890.

Glass, Ervin Bird. "The Cree Language," *Royal Canadian Institute Proceedings*, Vol. 1, 1898, pp. 104–6.

Hines, Harry Ernest. *A Cree Grammar Being a Simplified Approach to the Study of the Language of the Cree Indians of Canada.* Saskatoon: Mission Society of the Church of England in Canada, Modern Press, 1948.

———. *Cree Grammar.* Toronto: 1948.

Horden, John. *A Grammar of the Cree Language, as Spoken by the Cree Indians of North America.* London: Society for the Promotion of Christian Knowledge, 1881.

———. *Language of the Cree Indians of North-west America.* London: Society for the Promoting Christian Knowledge, 1902.

Howse, Joseph. *A Grammar of the Cree Language.* London, 1844.

———. *A Grammar of the Cree Language, with which is Combined an Analysis of the Chippeway Dialect.* London: Trubner and Company, 1865.

Hunter, Emily, Betty Karpinski and Jean Mulder. *Introductory Cree: Part I.* Edmonton: School of Native Studies, University of Alberta, 1993.

Hunter, Emily and Betty Karpinski. *Introductory Cree: Part II.* Edmonton: School of Native Studies, University of Alberta, 1993.

Hunter, James. *A Lecture in the Grammatical Construction of the Cree Language*, London: 1875.

Indian Child's Book: A Primer in English and Cree Languages.

Introduction to the Cree Language. Saskatoon: Indian and Northern Curriculum Resource Centre, University of Saskatchewan.

Jacker, Edward. "The Red Man Gauged by His Speech," *American Catholic Quarterly Review* 2 (1877).

Joseph, B. "Locatives and Obviation in Cree," *International Journal of American Linguistics* 46, no. 3 (168–69), 1980.

Lacombe, A. *Dictionnaire de la Langue des Cris.* Montreal: Beauchemin et Valois, 1874.

Lacombe, Albert. *Petit Manuel pour Apprendre a Lire la Langue Crise.* Montreal: Beauchemin, 1986.

Leach, Bro. Frederick, O.M.I. *60 Years with Indians and Letters on Lake Winnipeg.* Winnipeg: 1971 (?).

Le Calvex, Victor. *Lecons de Cris.* Legoff, Alberta: Unpublished paper, 1964.

Lees, Herbert W., comp. *Lo the Poor Indian: Being a Short Vocabulary of Useful Words and Phrases in the Cree Tongue.* 1910.

Leguerrier, Jules. "Allons-nous Abandonner la Langue Indienne?" *Kerygma* 1, no. 2 (1967): 51–55.

Li, Fang-Kuei. "A Type of Non-Formation in Athabaskan and Eyak," *International Journal of American Linguistics* 22, no. 1 (January): 45–48.

Logan, Robert A. *A Cree-English Dictionary and Remarks on the Cree Language.* Duluth: Robert A. Logan, 1964.

———. *The Cree Language as It Appears to Me.* Lake Charlotte, N.S.: Loganda Limited, 1958.

———. *The Cree Language, Its Basic Structure and Cree Language Notes.* Saskatoon: University of Saskatchewan, Indian and Northern Curriculum Resources Centre.

———. *Cree Language Notes.* Lake Charlotte, N.S.: Loganda Limited, 1958.

———. *Cree Language Structures.* Private printing, 1964.

———. *Cree Language Structure and the Introduction to Cree-English Dictionary.* Lake Charlotte, N.S.: Loganda Limited, 1964.

Longacre, Robert E. "Quality and Quantity in Cree Vowels," *Journal of the Canadian Linguistic Association* 3 (1957): 66–70.

MacKenzie, Marguerite. "The Eastern (Mistassini) Cree Verb: Derivational Morphology," *Dissertation Abstracts*, MA Thesis, McGill University, 1972.

MacLean, John. *Brief Sketch of the Life and Work of Rev. James Evans (inventor of Cree syllabics).* Winnipeg: John MacLean, 1925.

———. *James Evans: Inventor of the Syllabic System of the Cree Language.* Toronto: William Briggs, 1890.

MacLean, L.V. "Indian Teens Agree, take Cree and See," *Senior Scholastic* (Teacher edition), Vol. 99 (December 1971), pp. 8–9.

Martin, P. "Length of Cree Vowels," *Canadian Journal of Linguistics* 23, no. 1–2 (1978): 84–106.

Michelson, Truman. "Linguistic Classification of Cree and Montagnais-Naskapi Dialects," *Bureau of American Ethnology*, Bulletin No. CXXIII, 1939, pp. 67–95.

———. "The Linguistic Classification of Rupert's House and East Main Cree," *American Anthropologist* 26 (1924): 295.

———. "The Linguistic Classification of the Tete de Boule," *American Anthropologis* 35 (1933): 396.

———. "Plains Cree Kinship Terms," *American Anthropologist* 40 (July 1938): 531.

———. "Preliminary Reports on the Linguistic Classification of Algonquian Tribes," *Bureau of American Ethnology*, Annual Report No. 28, 1906–1907, pp. 221–290b.

———. "Proto-Algonquian Archetype of Fire," *Language* 9: 270–72; *Language* 11: 149.

———. "Report on a Linguistic Expedition to James and Hudson Bays," *Language* 12 (April 1936): 135–36.

Minde, Emma. *kwayask ê-kî-pê kiskinowâpahtihicik/ Their Example Showed Me the Way: A Cree Woman's Life Shaped by Two Cultures.* Edited and translated by Freda Ahenakew and H.C. Wolfart. Edmonton: University of Alberta Press, 1997.

Oxendale, Joan. "Reflections of a Structure of Cree in the Spoken English of Bilingual Crees," *Western Canadian Journal of Anthropology* 1 (1969): 65–70.

Peep of Day in the Language of the Cree Indians Living on the Eastern Shore of Hudson Bay, Reverend W.G. Walton, trans. London: Society for Promoting Christian Knowledge, 1920.

Pentland, David. *A Historical Overview of Cree Dialects—Papers of the Ninth Algonquin Conference*, W. Cowan, ed. Ottawa: Carleton University Press, 1978.

Piiyesiisak Mena Pisiskiwak: Birds and Animals — A Cree First Reader. Edmonton: Alberta Education, 1969.

Pilling, J.C., comp. *Bibliography of the Algonquian Languages.* Washington: 1891.

Pilling, James Constantine. "Bibliography of the Algonquian Languages," *Bureau of American Ethnology*, Bulletin No. 13, 1891.

A Proposed Standard Roman Orthography for Cree. Ottawa: Department of Indian Affairs and Northern Development, 1970.

Smithurst, John. *English-Cree Ojibway Word Book.* Rossville: Mission Press, 1848.

Soveran, Marilylle. *From Cree to English, Part 1: the Sound System.* Saskatoon: University of Saskatchewan, College of Education, 1970.

Speck, F.G. "Some Comparative Traits of the Maskogian Languages," *American Anthropologist* (1907): 470–83.

Stobie, Margaret. "Background of the Dialect Called Bungi," *Historical and Scientific Society of Manitoba Papers*, Series 2, no. 24 (1967–68): 65–75.

"Syllabic Systems—Moose Factory," *The Church Missionary Intelligencer* (1853): 63–72.

Syllabic Type of the Cree Language. Rupert's Land: Norway House, 1841.

Tait, Joyce. *Introduction to the Cree Language.* Saskatoon: Department of Indian and Northern Education, University of Saskatchewan.

Todd, Eveleyn M. "Ojibwa Syllabic Writing and Its Implications for a Standard Ojibwa Alphabet," *Anthropological Linguistics* 14, no. 9 (December, 1972): 357–60.

Vaillancourt, Louis. "L'origine des Caracteree Syllabiques," *Anthropologica* 5 (1957): 125–29.

Watkins, E.A. *A Dictionary of the Cree Language*, Richard Faires, ed. Toronto: Anglican Church of Canada, 1938.

Weze, Johanna. "Anne Anderson Saves a Language," *Heritage* 4, no. 5 (Sept-Oct. 1976): 2–4.

Wolfart, H. Christoph. "Boundary Maintenance in Algonquian: A Linguistic Study of Island Lake Manitoba," *American Anthropologist* 75 (October 1973): 1305–23.

———. "The Current State of Cree Language Studies," *Western Canadian Journal of Anthropology* 3, no. 4 (1973): 37–55.

———. *Plains Cree: A Grammatical Study*, Transactions of the American Philosophical Society 63, No. 5 (1973): 1–90.

Wolfart, H. Christoph and Janet Carroll. *Meet Cree: A Practical Guide to the Cree Language.* Edmonton: University of Alberta Press, 1973.

———. *Meet Cree: A Guide to the Cree Language.* Second edition. Edmonton: University of Alberta Press, 1981.

577

578